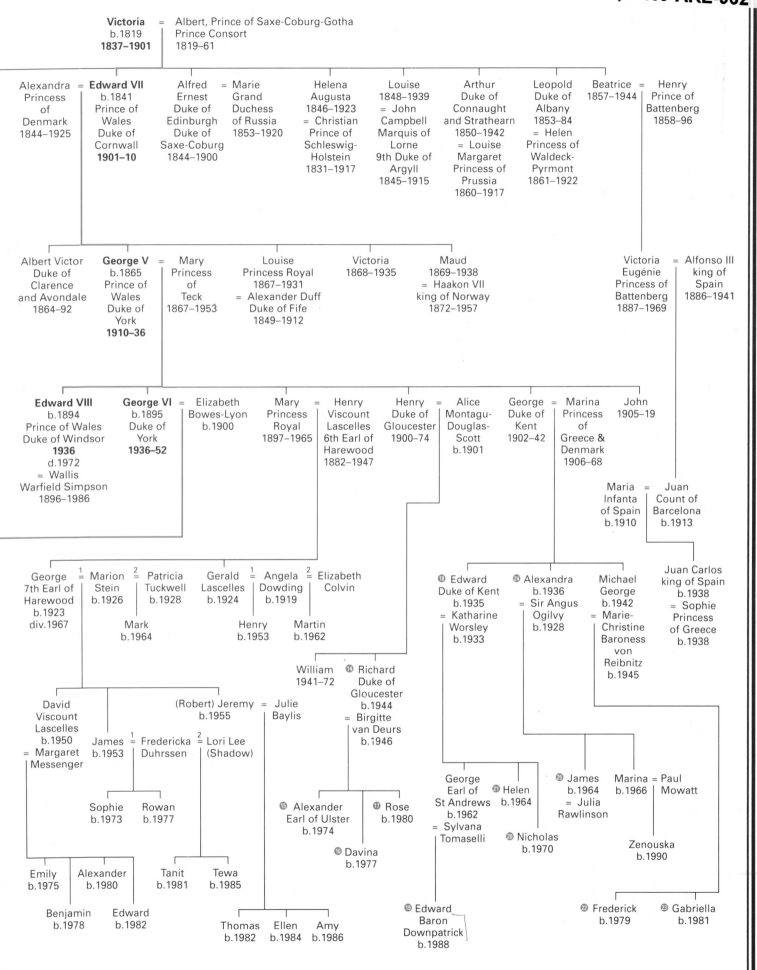

Chronicle
of the
Royal Family

CHRONICLE
Communications Ltd

Acknowledgements

The principal contributors to this book are credited on page three, with the agencies which supplied photographs identified in the pages 621-24. A book of this kind is inevitably a team operation, and there are others to whom we would like to acknowledge our gratitude.

The content of this book has been chosen to complement a larger and more ambitious volume, *Chronicle of Britain and Ireland*, which is currently in preparation. For the early years of the period covered by this book the overlap is greater than will be the case in the era of constitutional monarchs. We were therefore grateful to draw upon the research initiated by Jerome Burne, when he was editing the book on British and Irish history. As ever, we subjected photographic agencies to a barrage of detailed requests; we would like to thank them all for the speed and diligence with which they responded to these requests.

In general terms we would like to thank all at the Mary Evans Picture Library, Photographers International, Popperfoto and Topham. In addition, we would like to thank Fiona Purvis at ET Archive, Anna Calvert at the Hulton Picture Company, Shruti Patel at the National Portrait Gallery, Peter Newark at Peter Newark's Pictures and Simon Cobley at Weidenfeld Archives. The assistance of the people and institutions who are responsible for the royal collections was also greatly appreciated.

The artwork was coordinated by our art editor Chris Jackson, who also edited certain sections of the book in terms of text. The artists whom we used are credited at the front of this book, but we also owe a corporate debt to the Right Setting Company; this company was responsible for the typesetting which appears not only in the artwork but also in the many family trees which we hope help to explain the often complex relationships within the royal houses of England, Scotland and, indeed, Europe.

As a company we are part of a group which publishes Chronicle books in the English and French languages. Our English-speaking colleagues in the Australian and Canadian companies provided coverage of royal links with their countries, while the staff in Paris coordinated the production of the book, liaising with typesetters, colour separation houses and our estimable printers, Brepols, in Belgium. We are grateful to all our colleagues for this cooperation.

I began by saying that this is a team operation. So it is, but the responsibility for what appears rests with us. We have tried, by employing expert consultants to check the text, to ensure that the book is accurate. But even experts can make mistakes or – more likely – disagree. Picture captions supplied by agencies can be inaccurate. If, in word or picture, mistakes have evaded the scrutiny of experts, we apologise – but ask to be told so that they can be corrected for future editions. **DM**

Notes about consultants

Dr Jeremy Black, Senior Lecturer in History, University of Durham
Dr Keith Brown, Lecturer in History, University of Stirling
Dr David Crouch, Senior Lecturer in History, North Riding College, Scarborough
Dr David Englander, Lecturer in European Humanities, Open University
Brian Hoey, consultant editor, *Majesty* magazine
Dr Clive Holmes, Tutor in History, Lady Margaret Hall, Oxford
Dr Rosemary Horrox, Lecturer in History, University of Cambridge
Professor David Loades, Department of History, University College of Wales, Bangor
Simon Loseby, Junior Research Fellow, St Anne's College, Oxford
Philip Waller, Tutor in Modern History, Merton College, Oxford

---

Details of illustration inside front cover: members of the royal family after Trooping the Colour, 1989. Photograph on page 5: the Queen, Queen Mother, Prince of Wales and Prince William after the christening of Prince William, 1982.

First published in 1991 by Chronicle Communications Ltd.,
154 Clerkenwell Road, London EC1R 5AD
Tel.: 071-410-9090 – Fax: 071-410-9091

ISBN 0582-09006-7 in United Kingdom and Ireland and ISBN 1-872031-20-X in Canada

Typesetting: Imprimerie Louis-Jean, Gap (France)
Colour process work: Christian Bocquez
Printing and binding: Brepols, Turnhout, Belgium

Editor: Derrik Mercer

Picture Editors	Ruth Darby, Susanna Harrison
Assistant Editors	Peter Bently, David Gould, Henrietta Heald, Chris Jackson
Associate Editors	Elizabeth Abbott, Montreal John Ross, Melbourne
Consultants	Dr Jeremy Black, Dr Keith Brown, Dr David Crouch, Dr David Englander, Brian Hoey, Dr Clive Holmes, Dr Rosemary Horrox, Professor David Loades, Simon Loseby, Philip Waller – *see note on consultants, opposite page*
Writers	Bruce Arnold, Frank Barber, Ray Boston, Patrick Brogan, Christopher Dobson, Jonathan Green, Charles Langley, Peter Lewis, Rupert Morris, Andrew Morton, Charles Phillips, Denis Pitts, Nigel Thomas, Richard Trench, Barry White
Chronologies	Bronwen Lewis
Research	Joan Thomas (Manager), Marion Dain, Gillian Mercer, David Rendall
Index/style	Laura Hicks
Artwork	Colin Salmon, Mike Saunders
Production Director	Catherine Balouet
Editorial production	Nathalie Palomba (manager), Chris Allman, Emmanuelle Berenger, Barbara Levinson
Computer systems	Martine Colliot, Dominique Klutz

Publisher: Jacques Legrand

Contents

How to use this book

This book follows the formula which has proved so successful in predecessors such as *Chronicle of the 20th Century* by reporting the events of the past as though they had just happened. It has again been produced by bringing together the disparate talents of leading historians and journalists: the historians and other experts have helped us to select the content and then checked it for accuracy after the text had been written by journalists.

The result is a hybrid between history and journalism which we hope provides an entertaining and accessible account of the past without sacrificing authority. *Chronicle of the Royal Family* is a book of reportage rather than analysis and does not purport to offer a contemporary account of what was known at the time of the events which it reports. The reports draw upon diaries and other documents which often became available to scholars years later. Illustrations, too, are rarely contemporary to the events until the invention of photography in the nineteenth century. Where illustrations are drawn from different periods, we have sought to indicate the date, although information supplied by picture agencies is often cursory and occasionally contradictory.

We have sought to give due prominence to the separate events of Scottish and Welsh royalty in the centuries before the United Kingdom. However, the chronologies which divide the book at regular intervals reflect the dates of reigns of English rather than Scottish monarchs. From 1603 a panel summarises key facts about sovereigns.

Capital letters. The use of capital letters has been minimised. They appear in full titles and in cases where there has only ever been one person with a particular name – the Queen Mother, Prince Regent and Prince Consort. Also, in accordance with convention, the present Queen has a capital letter, while her predecessors such as Victoria are lower-case "queens".

Names. For countries and individuals, we have aimed to use whatever name or title was correct at the time of the event being reported. For other placenames, the modern versions are used so that readers are able to locate places more easily.

Units of measurement. Imperial measurements are used in the first instance, generally with metric conversions. Metres are abbreviated to "m", kilometres to "km" and hectares to "ha".

Chronologies and cross-references. The chronology summaries of events do not aim to cover all the most important events of an era since these are reported in greater detail in the pages between the chronologies, where news reports are arranged according to their importance or newsworthiness. The chronology summaries include less important events and also those leading up to the main events reported elsewhere plus their consequences. These chains of developments can be followed through a system of cross-references which complements the index and which works by pointing to the next link in the chain. Arrows indicating the next link appear at the end of reports; they point only forward in time, not backwards, and work like this:

* if a cross-referenced event occurs in the same year, the day and the month will be given without the year if both are known – for example (→11/9) – or with month and year if the precise day is unknown – for example (→9/1856).

* if the cross-referenced event occurs in a later year, the cross-reference will follow the principles above with years from 1000 abbreviated to the final two digits (→11/9/56) unless only the year is known (→1856) or at the beginning of a century (→1602).

Where an arrow appears by itself in the chronology, it indicates that an event summarised there is reported in greater detail in one of the pages that follow. Only one cross-reference appears for any article and the index should be used to find earlier entries on a subject or individual.

DM, London, July 1991

Kings of the Britons fall to conquerors from Rome

The earliest British rulers whose names we know lived in the southeast of England in the first century before Christ. At this time there were no such entities as England, Scotland and Wales: from Land's End to the highlands Britain was a patchwork of tribal groupings.

These groups had names such as the Trinovantes (based in roughly Essex), the Catuvellauni (roughly Hertfordshire) and the Atrebates (roughly Hampshire, Surrey and Sussex). Except in the far north of Scotland, they were linked by a more or less common Celtic language, the ancestor of Welsh, Cornish and Breton. By the year 55BC

the Roman leader Julius Caesar had overrun Gaul and turned next to Britain. His first raid, in autumn 55BC, had mixed results, but the next, in 54BC, was a success. During the second raid the Britons chose as their leader King Cassivellaunus, probably of the Catuvellauni, who was the most powerful British ruler; but Caesar had the upper hand, and returned to Gaul with hostages, financial guarantees and pledges of alliance. Britain was left in peace – for a time.

Resisting Roman control did not mean rejecting Roman splendours, which greatly impressed British rulers such as Cunobelin (c.AD10-

41), Shakespeare's Cymbeline. An ally of Rome, he called himself *rex* (Latin for king) and ruled a great "empire" which had grown from the kingdom of the Catuvellauni, north of the Thames, to take in the whole south-eastern corner of England. His capital was at Colchester, in the lands of the conquered Trinovantes tribe.

Meanwhile, the Romans kept thoughts of invasion alive. Emperor Augustus (27BC-AD14) received two kings, Tincommius (c.20BC-c.10AD) of the Atrebates and Dubnovellaunus (probably) of the Trinovantes, who wanted help against the Catuvellauni. Emperor

Gaius, better known as Caligula, even embarked on an invasion plan in 40, but lost heart at Boulogne.

Caligula was assassinated in 41 and replaced by his uncle, Claudius. Cunobelin also died that year and was succeeded by his two sons, Caratacus and Togodumnus. In 42 they expelled Tincommius's son King Verica of the Atrebates, who fled to Rome for help. Claudius, anxious to prove himself as emperor, decided that the time was ripe to add Britain to his empire, and in the summer of 43 a force of 40,000 troops landed in three waves on the south-east coast. Four centuries of Roman rule were about to begin.

Resistance leaders defy Roman armies

Southern England, 43-60

The Britons were stunned by the massive scale of the Roman invasion, but were not going to give up without a fight. Togodumnus was killed, but after the Roman victory his brother Caratacus continued to harry the invaders in the west until he was defeated in Wales in 51 and betrayed by Queen Cartimandua, the pro-Roman ruler of the Brigantes tribe based in Yorkshire. Caratacus was paraded through Rome in chains, but his dignified appeal for mercy so impressed Emperor Claudius that he was allowed to live in Rome as a free man.

Another pro-Roman ruler was King Prasutagus of the Iceni tribe, based in Norfolk, who died in 60 leaving half his estate to the emperor. But Roman officials tried to seize all his wealth, their troops flogging his widow Boudica [Boadicea is a 16th-century misspelling] and raping their daughters in the process. The Iceni revolted, and Queen Boudica's revenge on the Romans was breathtaking. Thousands were butchered before she faced the Romans at Mancetter in Warwickshire for a showdown.

Despite being outnumbered ten to one, the 10,000-strong Roman army won the day by its superior discipline. Tens of thousands of Britons died in the battle and its bloody aftermath. Defeated, Boudica is said to have taken poison.

Queen Boudica, or Boadicea, as imagined by a late-17th-century artist.

Four centuries of Roman domination

The key rulers of Roman Britain between 60 and 410 were:

Agricola: governor 77-84. Crushed Wales and south of Scotland.

Hadrian: emperor 117-38. Gave orders for the building of the great frontier wall named after him.

Antoninus Pius: emperor 138-61. Ordered another wall to be built – as the Forth/Clyde frontier.

Septimius Severus: emperor 193-211. Crushed revolts; reorganised Britain from York, where he died.

Marcus Postumus; Tetricus: breakaway emperors of Britain, Gaul and Spain, 260-74.

Carausius; Allectus: breakaway emperors of Britain, 286-96.

Constantine I (the Great): emperor 306-37. Proclaimed emperor at York; made Christianity official.

Valentinian I: emperor 364-75. In 367 Britain was attacked on all sides by Saxons, Picts and Scots.

Magnus Maximus: breakaway emperor of Britain, 383-88.

Honorius: western emperor, 395-423. Told Britons in 410: "Defend yourselves".

The kingdoms that the Romans left behind them

Barbarian invaders pose new challenges

British Isles, 400-800

Four centuries of imperial rule left their mark, and the decision in 410 of Emperor Honorius to tell Britain to defend itself did not mean an end to Roman Britain. In fact, the withdrawal was aimed at providing troops to fight the Germans and other "barbarians" who were eventually to overrun the western empire, and it was seen as temporary.

Despite great economic decline and depopulation, Roman-style life clung on in cities such as Bath, Carlisle and York, where Roman buildings were still standing centuries later. The countryside, especially in the south of England, was still dominated by the great villa estates. But who was then in charge? Was there a power struggle among the Latin-speaking Romano-British aristocrats who had been left to run the government? Whatever happened, by about 430 one strong ruler had emerged called Vortigern, which means "great king".

Vortigern faced the task of organising Britain's defences against barbarian raiders, who included not only Germans in the east, but also, and more immediately, Picts in the north and Irish in the west. He adopted an old Roman custom of recruiting from among the Germans themselves (mainly Angles, Saxons and Jutes) to boost his forces, in return for permission to settle in the east. This policy backfired in 449 when troops under – legend has it – Hengest ("The Stallion") and Horsa ("The Horse") revolted in Kent and began to carve out territory of their own.

Thus began the long struggle between British and Germanic kings which became the stuff of British legend for centuries. Many Britons, whom the Anglo-Saxons called Welsh ("foreigners"), must simply have been assimilated, but certainly the Britons' language and what remained of their Roman way of life were wiped out wherever the great tidal wave of migrants from northern Germany settled.

Despite British victories such as the battle of the still-unlocated Mount Badon in c.500, the Germans pushed westwards and northwards until by 600 the areas of British control were restricted to Wales, Dumnonia (Devon, Cornwall and parts of Somerset), Strathclyde and Cumbria. Meanwhile, many Britons from the south-west crossed the Channel to what was later called Brittany after them.

King Arthur: the man and the mythology

A mediaeval view of King Arthur.

England, 500-600

Many of the kings who fought the Anglo-Saxons are shrouded in obscurity, but the haziest of all has become one of the greatest figures in western literature and legend: King Arthur. The Arthurian stories are so well known that it is often forgotten that Guinevere, Merlin, Camelot, Excalibur and the Round Table were made up centuries later, starting with Geoffrey of Monmouth in c.1150 [*see page 44*].

As for the real Arthur, the earliest sources are the *History of the Britons* (c.830), by a Welshman called Nennius, and the *Annals of Wales* (c.960). The *Annals* claim that Arthur fought at Badon [*see story left*] in c.500 and that he died at "Camlann" in c.539. Nennius lists 12 Arthurian battles, including Badon but not Camlann. Badon almost certainly did take place, because another Briton, Gildas, wrote of it in c.540 as recent history. One snag: he did not mention Arthur. Some of the other battles point to the north (Camlann could be Birdoswald in Cumbria, *Camboglanna* in Roman times). Another snag: if Arthur was operating here in 500 then he was not fighting Anglo-Saxons; they had not got this far.

But trying to trace Arthur may be missing the point. By the time of Nennius and the *Annals*, Arthur was already a legend whose very obscurity allowed him to be laden with tales of greatness. As the British frontier retreated so his name became an ever prouder symbol of British resistance to the Saxon foe.

Vortigern the Briton meets Hengest and Horsa: a 19th-century engraving.

Notable British kings after the Romans

The most significant rulers of Britons between 450-850 were:

Ambrosius Aurelianus: British leader c.490-500, possibly victor at Mount Badon [*see above*].

Constantine: king of Dumnonia. Blamed c.540 for British decline by Gildas, who called him "adulterer and sacrilegious murderer". (Other notable kings of this time who were castigated by Gildas were **Vorteporix**, king of Dyfed and alleged rapist of his daughter, and **Cuneglasus**, king of mid-Wales and said to be a violent maniac and adulterer.)

Condidan; Conmail; Farinmail: kings slain at Battle of Dyrham,

Gloucestershire, 577, which cut off south-western England from Wales.

Urien: king of Rheged (Cumbria); murdered, 590.

Cadwallon: king of Gwynedd. Laid waste Northumbria, 633; killed, 634.

Owen: king of Strathclyde. Defeated and slew Scots king, 642.

Teudubr: king of Strathclyde. Defeated king of the Picts near Glasgow in 750 (→870).

Merfyn: king of Gwynedd, nicknamed "the Freckled"; succeeded by Rhodri in 844 (→872).

Angles and Saxons forge powerful new kingdoms

England, 500-867

The German migrants who swamped eastern Britain after the Romans left were made up of three principal groups: Angles, probably from the area still called Angeln in north Germany; Saxons from further south; and Jutes, who although traditionally associated with Jutland in Denmark seem more likely to have come from the lower Rhine.

On the whole the Angles ended up in East Anglia and north of the Humber, the Jutes in Kent and the Saxons in the south. They were linked by their language (Anglo-Saxon or Old English), their worship of Germanic gods and their Germanic society. They forged countless petty states based on kinship ties and headed by warrior kings or chieftains. By 600 four main kingdoms had coalesced, usually by conquest: Northumbria ("Land north of the Humber"), Wessex ("Land of the West Saxons"), East Anglia ("Land of the East Angles"), Kent (from a pre-Roman name for coastal peoples), Mercia ("People of the Marches"). Smaller kingdom included Essex ("East Saxons") and Sussex ("South Saxons").

A romanticised view of an early Anglo-Saxon king, Edwin of Northumbria (ruled 616-33), being baptised in 627; by Ford Madox Brown (1821-93).

Kent: the cradle of the English church

The legendary figures of Hengest and Horsa, the leaders of the Jutes in Kent, led the first revolt against the Britons in 449, and an independent Kentish kingdom lasted until its effective annexation by the fearsome King Offa of Mercia (757-96). The most famous Kentish king was Æthelbert (possibly 560-616), who was responsible for the founding of the English church. In 597, perhaps influenced by his Frankish queen, who was a Christian, he gave the Roman Augustine permission to set up a mission at Canterbury. Augustine, the first archbishop of Canterbury and later a saint, made so many converts that in c.600 Æthelbert himself abandoned his pagan gods to become the first Christian Anglo-Saxon king.

Northumbria: the crucible of culture

At its zenith the Anglian kingdom of Northumbria stretched from the Humber to the Forth, but it actually began as two kingdoms, Bernicia in the north and Deira in the south, which were united by 616. Northumbria reached its heyday under the kings Edwin (616-33), who was acknowledged as overlord by the kings south of the Humber, Oswy (642-70), Egfrith (670-85) and Aldfrith (685-705). It became Britain's cultural power house; monasteries like Lindisfarne and Jarrow, scholars like Bede and bishops like Cuthbert and Wilfrid were famous across Europe. The sack of Lindisfarne by the Vikings in 793 heralded the end of this glorious age, and the kingdom fell to the Danes in 867.

East Anglia: the splendours of kingship

Sutton Hoo helmet: reconstruction.

East Anglia was one of the earliest Anglo-Saxon kingdoms and was in its prime in the early seventh century, although it remained a power until conquered by the Vikings in 869. In 731 the Northumbrian scholar Bede wrote of seven kings who in their day had been mightier than any other. He called each of them *Bretwalda* [wide-ruler or Britain-ruler], and the fourth was Rædwald, the king of East Anglia.

Rædwald died in c.625 and was probably honoured or buried in the Sutton Hoo ship, although no trace of a corpse was found. The ship, discovered in 1939, revealed for the first time the splendours of Anglo-Saxon royalty; it contained riches of breathtaking craftsmanship, including the remains of a royal helmet, and imported luxuries from Egypt and Constantinople.

Kings pave the way for English unity

Mercia: Offa rules mighty Midlands

The people of central England seem to have been Angles in origin, but called themselves the *Mierce*, People of the Marches, which in Latinised form gives the name of their kingdom: Mercia. The Mercian heartland was the upper Trent valley, around which a strong kingdom had arisen by the late 500s.

A few decades later Mercia had become a force to be reckoned with under such kings as Penda (633-55) and Wulfhere (657-70). Wulfhere pushed his power to the Thames, but Mercia reached its zenith during the long reigns of Æthelbald (716-57) and Offa (757-96). Æthelbald, who boastfully styled himself "king of Britain", annexed Middlesex and London from Essex, controlled much of Wessex and made forays deep into Wales. He was assassinated in 757, and a power struggle ensued from which Offa emerged victorious. Offa's genius,

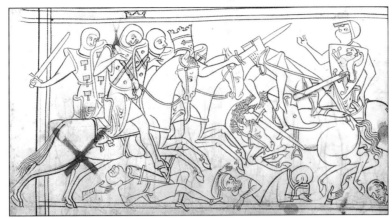

King Offa of Mercia (centre) in battle, as seen by a mediaeval artist.

energy and savage ruthlessness came closer to forging a single English kingdom than any ruler before Athelstan 150 years later; by 775 his overlordship ran from the Humber to the Channel, including Kent, Sussex, East Anglia and most of Wessex, and he occasionally called himself "king of the English". Offa's fame was such that he could negotiate trade deals on equal terms with Emperor Charlemagne, who called him "brother". His greatest monument, though, was the huge rampart which he ordered to be built between his kingdom and the Welsh. "Offa's dyke" – still visible for much of its 150 miles (240km) – ranks with Hadrian's wall as a feat of engineering and organisation.

Mercia was a potent force for decades after Offa's death, but in 874 it submitted to the Vikings. It was left to the kings of Wessex to keep alive the idea of English unity.

Wessex: kings of the West Saxons square up to Viking threat

Most royal dynasties of England proudly claimed that their earliest ancestor was the pagan war god Woden. This sense that they belonged to one ancient family may have made it an unconscious ambition of Anglo-Saxon kings to forge a single kingdom; certainly they admired the feats of those overlords whom they called *Bretwalda*.

The West Saxons, whose kings were to realise this ambition, produced the second Bretwalda, Ceawlin (560-93). Ceawlin's predecessors, Cerdic (c.490-534) and Cynric (534-60), began to push westwards from the Wessex heartland of the middle Thames. Ceawlin, Cynric's son, went even further and in 577 defeated and killed three British kings at Dyrham in Gloucestershire to drive a great Saxon wedge through British territory.

Wessex was under the overlordship of Northumbria and Mercia in turn from 626-70, but it recovered under King Ine (688-726). It was then subject to the Mercian kings Æthelbald and Offa, but with the accession of Egbert (802-839) Wessex never looked back. Egbert annexed Kent, Sussex and Surrey and turned the tables on Mercia, defeating one king in 825 and briefly expelling another four years later. His next target was Northumbria, which acknowledged his overlordship as Bretwalda.

But by now all the English kings faced a new threat: Vikings, who had been carrying out brutal plundering raids since the 790s. Egbert was defeated by a Danish army in 836, and although he beat them in turn in 838 the shock must have been considerable to other, less powerful, kings. The Vikings hung like a cloud over the reigns of Egbert's son Æthelwulf (839-58) and Æthelwulf's sons Athelstan (king in Kent, 839-c.851), Æthelbald (858-60), Æthelbert (860-65) and Æthelred (865-71). The stage was thus set for the arrival of Æthelwulf's fifth and youngest son, whose fame was to resound through history like no English king's before him. His name was Alfred.

Æthelwulf of Wessex: a later view.

Migrant Irish tribe forges united Scottish kingdom

The rise to dominance of the Scots in the land now named after them was no foregone conclusion. In Roman times the region beyond Hadrian's wall was peopled by two main Celtic groups: Britons, a continuation of the British tribes further south, and other tribes – of which the most powerful were the Caledoni – known as Picts whose territory stretched roughly from Fife to the Pentland Firth.

The Picts are in many ways a mystery, and the word, from the Latin *Picti*, simply means "painted people", a Roman nickname from their war-paint. There is evidence to suggest two linguistic traditions: one Celtic, related to British and thus to modern Welsh, Breton and Cornish, the other unrelated to any known tongue. They were illiterate, and apart from some beautiful artefacts that testify to a sophisticated culture they have left few traces.

Both Picts and Scots were Celtic peoples with similar cultures, but the Picts probably ceased to exist as a separate cultural entity by c.1000, 150 years or so after being finally subjected to the Scots in 847 under King Kenneth mac Alpin (840-58), who is regarded as the first king of Scotland. Other kings had been overlords of both peoples, but Kenneth's claim is justified in that it marked the end of a long struggle between the two nations.

The Scots were relative latecomers to Scotland. Originally from Ulster, they were the most successful of a number of Irish

Pictish warriors, a stone carving from Birsay in the Orkney Islands.

tribes which began to settle in western areas of Britain in the later decades of Roman rule. They established a kingdom in Argyll which was known as Scotia or Dal Riata, their tribal name, from where they began to spread inland.

King Aedan mac Gabrahain (574-608) pushed Scots influence northwards and southwards before meeting a potent new force in the south-east: the English as represented by the Anglian kingdom of Northumbria. To counter this threat Aedan put together a coalition of Scots, Irish and Strathclyde, the British kingdom of what is now south-western Scotland and Cumbria, with its capital at Dumbarton ("Fortress of the Britons"). In 603 this alliance was crushed by

Æthelfrith in Liddesdale.

Despite the English presence the Scots consolidated their gains under Aedan's son Eochaid (608-29) but were beset with calamity in the reign of Eochaid's son, Domhnall Brecc. He managed to lose the ancestral Dal Riata lands in Ulster and died leading the Scots to a massive defeat by King Owen of Strathclyde in 642. The Scots and the Picts turned to Northumbria's King Oswy (642-70), Æthelfrith's son, for protection. As a result of Northumbrian influence two of Oswy's nephews, Talorgen (653-57) and Drest (657-71), whose mother was a Pictish princess, were successively kings of the Picts. Drest was expelled by the Picts in 671 in favour of another outsider,

Bridei II (671-93), the brother of Owen of Strathclyde. Oswy's successor, Egfrith (670-85), keen to retain Northumbrian influence in Pictland, defeated the Picts in 672.

Bridei avenged this defeat in 685 by butchering Egfrith and his army near Forfar. Northumbria got its own back on one of Bridei's successors, Nechtan (708-24), in 711, and a Pictish civil war followed the latter's abdication in 724. But the Picts were not to be crushed. Oengus I (729-61) emerged as king and in 736 captured the Scots' fortress of Dunadd to become overlord of both Picts and Scots. He allied with Northumbria against Strathclyde whose king, Teudubr (c.750), was a thorn in the side of his neighbours.

By the time of King Oengus II of Picts and Scots (820-834), the Vikings were making their violent presence felt. They killed Oengus's successor Eoganan (834-39), and in 840 their Scots ally Kenneth mac Alpin (Kenneth I) wrested Dal Riata from Pictish control.

Seven years of war followed, at the end of which Kenneth had brought Pictland under his control within a united kingdom called Alba. Like Alfred the Great, to whom he is compared, he reorganised Alba to meet the Viking threat, moving the centres of his realm from the vulnerable west to Scone, Forteviot and Dunkeld near Perth. His gains were consolidated in the short reign (858-63) of his brother, King Donald I.

A much later artist's impression of King Aedan mac Gabrahain.

Notable Scottish and Pictish monarchs

Bridei I mac Maelchon: king of Picts (died 585).

Aedan mac Gabrahain: king of Scots 574-608.

Eochaid I: king of Scots 608-29.

Talorgen I: king of Picts 653-57.

Drest: king of Picts 657-71.

Bridei II: king of Picts 671-93.

Nechtan: king of Picts 708-24.

Oengus I: king of Picts 729-36, of Picts and Scots 736-61.

Constantine mac Feargus: king of Picts 789-811, of Picts and Scots 811-20.

Oengus II: king of Picts and Scots 820-834.

Kenneth I mac Alpin: king of Scots 840-47, of Scots and Picts 847-58.

Donald I mac Alpin: king of Scots and Picts 858-63.

King Kenneth I: a later engraving of the "Scottish Alfred".

THE BRITISH ISLES IN THE LATE
NINTH CENTURY

Land under
— Celtic control
— Anglo-Saxon control
— Danish control
Areas of Norwegian
settlement

ORKNEY
ISLANDS

HEBRIDES

Atlantic Ocean

MORAY

SCOTLAND

Dunottar

Scone

St Andrews

Dollar

Dumbarton

Edinburgh

LOTHIAN

Lindisfarne

Bamburgh

Tweed

BERNICIA

STRATHCLYDE

ENGLISH
NORTHUMBRIA

Derry

ULSTER

GALLOWAY

Tyne

AIRGIALLA

DEIRA

North Sea

BREIFNE

Tees

ISLE
OF
MAN

CONNACHT

DANISH
NORTHUMBRIA
(KINGDOM
OF YORK)

Ouse

MEATH

Tara

York

Irish Sea

Dublin

ANGLESEY

Humber

Bangor

Chester

Lincoln

Limerick

GWYNEDD

LEINSTER

Offa's
Dyke

Derby

Nottingham

POWYS

MUNSTER

Repton

DANISH
MERCIA

Wexford

ENGLISH
MERCIA

Leicester

Waterford

Cork

Wye

GUTHRUM'S
KINGDOM

SEISYLLWG

Worcester

St David's

DYFED

Northampton

Cambridge

MORGANNWG

Gloucester

Colchester

Thames

Lea

Ashdown

Bath

Reading

London

Edington

Basing

Canterbury

Wedmore

Winchester

WESSEX

KENT

Athelney

Exeter

WEST
WALES

ISLE OF WIGHT

English Channel

11

Æthelred I 865–871	Constantine I 863–c.877
Alfred 871–899	Aed c.877–878
	Giric ⎫ 878–
	Eochaid ⎬ 889
	Donald II 889–900

Wessex, autumn 865. Æthelbert dies; his brother Æthelred becomes king of Wessex (→871).

East Anglia, 866. A "great army" of Danes lands and takes control of the region.

Northumbria, 866. King Osbert of Northumbria is deposed by his rival, Ella (→21/3/867).

York, 21 March 867. King Ella, recently deposed by the invading Danes, joins forces with his rival Osbert against them and attacks their base; both die in a heavy defeat. Ivar, the king of the Danes, instals Egbert as king (→872/3).

Nottingham, 868. King Burgred of Mercia, Æthelred of Wessex's brother-in-law, buys peace from the Danes.

Hoxne, Suffolk, 869. Ivar of the Danes executes King Edmund of East Anglia (→870).

Dumbarton, 870. Ivar and Olaf the White sack the capital of the kingdom of Strathclyde.

Reading, Berkshire, 871. The Wessex king, Æthelred, and his brother Alfred unsuccessfully attack the Danish base.→

Dorset, 23 April 871. Æthelred dies; Alfred succeeds (→871).

Northumbria, 872/873. A popular revolt ousts Egbert, the Danes' puppet king.

York, 873. The new Danish leader, Halfdan, regains Danish control of Northumbria (→875).

Derbyshire, autumn 874. King Burgred of Mercia flees; the Danes make Ceolwulf puppet (→8/877).

Dollar, Central, 875. Halfdan of Northumbria defeats Constan-

tine, the king of the Scots and the Picts (→877).

Dorset, autumn 876. Alfred makes peace with Guthrum, the king of the Danes in southern England, who split from Half-dan, the Danish leader in the north, last year (→878).

Gloucester, August 877. Guthrum forces King Ceolwulf to divide Mercia (→5/878).

Wales, 877. The Danes expel King Rhodri of Gwynedd, who flees to Ireland (→878).

Wales, 881. King Anarawd ap Rhodri of Gwynedd defeats Æthelred, who is now the ruler of Mercia (→c.890).

Mercia, 883. Æthelred accepts Alfred's overlordship.

Kent and East Anglia, 885. After retaking Rochester from a new wave of Danish invaders, Alfred moves north, attacking Danish settlements (→886).

London, 886. Alfred seizes the city from the Danes and gives it to Æthelred, the Lord of Mercia, who is to marry Alfred's daughter, Æthelflæd.→

Dundurn, Tayside, 889. Donald, the son of King Constantine, defeats and kills Giric, who killed his uncle, Aed, in 878. He becomes King Donald II and then expels Eochaid, the native ruler of Strathclyde (→900).

Hadleigh, Suffolk, 890. King Guthrum of the Danes dies.

Wessex, 893. Asser, the Welsh-born bishop of Sherborne, completes a life of Alfred (→895).

Wessex, 26 October 899. Alfred dies; in accordance with his will his son Edward succeeds.→

English king turns tables on Danish army

Ashdown, Berkshire, spring 871
Four days after being defeated in battle at Reading, the West Saxons, led by King Æthelred and his 22-year-old younger brother Alfred, have driven the Danish invaders from the battlefield. Many thousands of Danes, including a king and five earls, were slaughtered.

The Danes were established on the Ridgeway above the famous white horse cut through the turf into the chalk centuries ago. Æthelred prepared for battle by praying and hearing Mass; he stayed in his tent for so long that Alfred lost patience and led the charge alone, storming uphill with his troops "like a wild boar", as one observer

put it. By the time that Æthelred joined in the Danes were beginning to crumble and were soon in full flight to their redoubt at Reading.

The battle is unlikely to prove decisive, however, as the Danes are a formidable force. They first came to England among the hit-and-run Viking raiders seeking plunder; recently they began to settle, and one after another the English kingdoms of Mercia, Northumbria and East Anglia have succumbed, some of their kings suffering the "blood eagle" sacrifice, in which the lungs are cut from the body. Only Wessex remains free, led by Æthelred and Alfred, the surviving sons of King Æthelwulf (→23/4/871).

Royal troops: it was once thought that Alfred's men cut the Ridgeway horse.

Constantine's rule boosted by murder

Scotland, 871
King Artgal, the refugee ruler of Strathclyde, has been murdered on the orders of Constantine, king of the Scots and the Picts since 863. His death consolidates Constantine's authority over the region and confirms him as the dominant ruler in the north. Artgal, who was Constantine's brother-in-law, fled to Scotland last year to escape the ravages of Viking invaders in his more southerly kingdom of Strathclyde [see map, page 11]. The invaders forced the surrender of Dumbarton Rock, the fortress capital of Strathclyde, after a four-month siege, taking much booty and many slaves (→875).

Rhodri of Gwynedd gains Welsh power

Wales, summer 872
Rhodri ap Merfyn, the king of Gwynedd, now holds sway over more of Wales than any previous Welsh ruler following his marriage to Angharad, the sister of King Gwgon ap Meurig of Ceredigion, who died recently. Rhodri's overlordship extends over the three largest Welsh kingdoms of Gwynedd in the north, Powys in the centre and Seisyllwg in the south. Rhodri, whom some are calling *Mawr* [the Great], inherited Gwynedd from his father in 844 and Powys through his mother's side in 855. His sway now extends to almost every part of Wales except the far south (→877).

Alfred becomes king and buys peace

Wessex, winter 871

After a year of nine major engagements and countless skirmishes with Danish forces, King Alfred of Wessex has finally bought off the battle-hardened Danes, at least for the time being. The invaders set their mark on his reign as soon as it began in April – they scattered his army while he was attending the funeral of his brother, King Æthelred, at Wimborne – but now the new king has at last gained some respite from conflict.

The young king, who has still to celebrate his 23rd birthday, grew up in a hard and dangerous world, increasingly menaced by rapacious Danish Vikings. But his was a close-knit pious Christian family with a vision of the wider world beyond the horizons of Wessex. Taken to Rome at the age of four by his father King Æthelwulf, the infant Alfred was received by the pope.

From an early age Alfred has suffered from bouts of ill-health. One suggestion is that his affliction is chronic haemorrhoids, but there is speculation that he may be an epileptic, or the victim of a venereal disease contracted before his marriage three years ago to the Mercian princess Ealhswith (→ 876).

A Christian king: Alfred is shown as a hero in this statue at Winchester.

Scots king is slain in a bloody battle against the Vikings

Inverdovat, Tayside, 877

Constantine, king of the Scots and the Picts for the past 14 years, has been killed in a battle with the Danes at Inverdovat. His enemies were remnants of the army of Halfdan, the ruler of the Danish kingdom of York. Halfdan himself died fighting in Ireland this year, and his men were on their way back to York when they encountered and defeated the Scottish king.

Constantine's father, Kenneth mac Alpin, had united the Scots and the Picts. Kenneth died in 858 and was succeeded by his brother, Donald. On Donald's death in 863 his nephew Constantine became king and spent much of his reign beating off Viking assaults or attempting to extend his authority southwards. Among his victims was Artgal, the king of Strathclyde, whom he had murdered in 871. But sometimes he bought peace with his enemies by paying tribute.

The Scots king's death was foreshadowed two years ago, when Halfdan, after ravaging Strathclyde, destroyed an army under Constantine at Dollar. His brother, Aed, succeeds him (→ 889).

Fugitive king gets a flea in his ear for burning cakes in hideout

Alfred is berated for burning the cakes: a 16th-century engraving.

Athelney, Somerset, Easter 878

To his small band of loyal retainers Alfred is still the king of Wessex, but with his armies scattered by the Danish host he has retreated into the marshlands of Somerset, where, according to one rumour, he has found refuge in a cowherd's hut.

One day, the story goes, he was sitting by the kitchen fire restringing his bow when the cowherd's wife, unaware that she was addressing her king, furiously berated him for forgetting to turn the cakes which she had asked him to watch and allowing them to burn. The tale may be a colourful invention, but it reflects the sorry situation of Alfred's current fortunes and his distracted state of mind. Yet the king refuses to admit defeat; he is said to be planning to emerge from his hideout soon in a bid to regain his kingdom (→ 5/878).

Great Welsh ruler dies, sword in hand

Prestatyn, Clwyd, 878

Rhodri the Great, the king of Gwynedd and overlord of most of Wales, is dead, cut down by English troops in battle at Prestatyn. His brother Gwriad tried desperately to save him but also fell under the blows of English swords.

King Ceolwulf of Mercia may have led the attack. If so he would be the latest of a series of invaders, mainly English and Danish, to attack Rhodri. The Danes have proved the greater threat; they forced Rhodri into exile in Ireland last year, and Ceolwulf, who has thwarted his comeback, is himself a puppet of Guthrum, the king of the Danes in southern England. It will now be up to Anarawd, Rhodri's son and successor, to avenge his father's death (→ 881).

King Alfred is victorious

Somerset, May 878

Alfred has scored a decisive victory over the hitherto all-conquering Danish invaders, and the strict peace terms which he has imposed include the withdrawal of all enemy forces from Wessex after King Guthrum's baptism as a Christian.

Guthrum, with 30 of his retainers, was received by Alfred for 12 days at Aller, near Athelney. He raised the barbarian leader from the holy font and accepted him as his adoptive son before bestowing on him, in a gesture of magnanimity in victory, many fine gifts.

Alfred recognises that, since the Danes intend to stay as settlers in eastern England, they must be shown friendship as well as firmness. The transformation in Alfred's fortunes came about during the six weeks which he spent hiding in the Somerset marshlands; from there he mounted a succession of guerrilla raids on Danish outposts. When he judged that the enemy had been sufficiently weakened, he assembled supporters from Somerset, Hampshire and Wiltshire and fell upon the main Danish forces at Edington, on the northern edge of Salisbury Plain, driving them back to their base camp at Chippenham, 15 miles (24 kilometres) distant.

Men, horses and cattle were slaughtered wholesale as the remnants of the pagan horde sought the sanctuary of their camp. They held out for 14 days before hunger and cold forced them to beg for peace, with a humiliating pledge to turn over to Alfred as many hostages as he desired (→ 880).

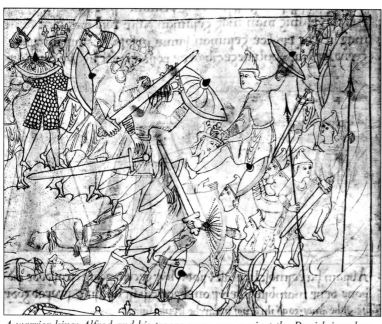

A warrior king: Alfred and his troops wage war against the Danish invaders.

Welsh kings accept English overlordship

Wales, c.890

The most powerful king in Wales has formally placed himself under the supremacy of the traditional enemy, the English. The move follows the decision of King Anarawd of Gwynedd, the eldest son and successor of Rhodri the Great, to seek the protection of King Alfred in the face of the continuing Danish threat to his territory.

Although Anarawd has had some success in countering the threat to his frontiers – he defeated King Æthelred of Mercia, a Danish puppet, last year – it seemed sensible to win the backing of the most powerful independent English kingdom against a common enemy. The deal was sealed during a recent ceremonial visit to the king of Wessex's court at Winchester, the first ever paid by a Welsh ruler to an English king. Anarawd was received with all royal formalities and generously treated by his host.

England is divided between Wessex and the Vikings as Norsemen settle in east

The Norsemen's presence: a ninth-century grave-marker from Lindisfarne.

England, 880

The withdrawal from Wessex of King Guthrum's Danish forces after their crushing defeat by Alfred two years ago marks the effective partitioning of England between English and Danish rulers.

Under the terms of the treaty finalised at Wedmore in Somerset shortly after his baptism, Guthrum promised to leave Wessex in peace, but he had no intention of returning to his continental homeland. Leaving Wessex, he established himself in East Anglia, with bases at Cambridge and Thetford. He has shared out the land among his troops and they are settling down as farmers.

The other two English kingdoms, Mercia and Northumbria, have also lost their independence to the Danes. The Danelaw prevails north and east of Watling Street, the old Roman road that runs from London to Chester, and Danish traders are flourishing, with villages rapidly growing into prosperous towns where both local produce and goods imported from Europe are on sale (→ 885).

Alfred replans his kingdom's chief cities

London, c.886

Alfred has advanced into Danish territory and captured the Mercian city of London. He has entrusted it to Æthelred, the Lord of Mercia and his future son-in-law, who has the task of repairing the old city walls and setting out new streets to encourage settlers and foster trade.

Another city to receive Alfred's attentions is Winchester, where his father, Æthelwulf, is buried. Alfred's plans include the reconstruction of the old minster – the church of the royal family – the rebuilding of his palace and the creation of new streets on a grid pattern. He also intends to establish a system of *burhs*, or fortified centres, to safeguard them from the Danes (→ 892).

Alfred in London: a later view.

King boosts naval and military defences

Isle of Wight, 896

Alfred has taken on the Danes where they have always been supreme – at sea. Deploying nine swift 60-oar warships of his own design, Alfred's naval forces have all but wiped out a Danish coastal raiding party of six vessels in a bloody clash off the Isle of Wight.

The battle, which was fought partly on the beaches, left 62 English and 120 Danes dead. One Danish crew escaped back to base in East Anglia; two crews were captured and taken to Winchester, where Alfred has had them hanged.

In 20 years Alfred has completely overhauled Wessex's de-fences. The militia is now divided into halves, one of which remains at home while the other takes up arms; in a long campaign the forces can be rotated without disrupting farm work. Alfred has also organised fixed defences by building some 30 *burhs* [fortified centres] along the frontiers and in the interior of Wessex. Some are based on old Roman towns while others are on the king's estates or in open and vulnerable areas. The strategy, to use the burhs as static defences with the militia as a highly mobile force, has proved itself over the last three years, seeing off a new Danish invasion force (→ 26/10/899).

King Alfred's longships defeat the Danish threat, by Colin Gill (1927).

Wessex mourns king who made it great

Winchester, 26 October 899

King Alfred died today at the age of 50 after nearly three decades on the throne. When he became king in his early twenties few would have gambled on the survival of his homeland, already threatened by the marauding Danes, who had previously crushed the other English kingdoms. Today, as news of his death spreads across the land, he is mourned as the king who not only preserved his beloved Wessex from the enemy but also spread wisdom and learning among his people; to the scribes of the *Anglo-Saxon Chronicle*, one of his projects, he is seen as the hero of the English.

Alfred is to be buried in the old minster at Winchester, a city which he rebuilt as a setting for religious ceremonies and acts of state. Five miles (eight kilometres) of new road were surfaced by 8,000 tonnes of cobbles; there are also a royal palace and a mint, and a new monastery and a nunnery are planned. Alfred's biographer, Bishop Asser of Sherborne, says of the late king that he was the "unshakeable pillar of the western people, a man replete with justice, vigorous in warfare, learned in speech, above all instructed in divine learning".

Alfred's marriage in 868 to the Mercian princess Ealhswith was commemorated by the issue of special coins. Of their children, many died in infancy, but three daughters and two sons survived. Edward, the elder son, will succeed his father as king of Wessex (→ 902).

Alfred, illiterate until his teens, throws his energies into a revival of learning

Winchester, c.892

Like most noble and royal children Alfred was brought up to excel in hunting and the art of war, and he was a teenager before he took his first steps in reading English. He soon gained a great respect for learning, which intensified when he became king.

About five years ago he was seized with the desire to read a Latin passage himself and turn it into English. Thus, at the age of 38, he undertook to teach himself Latin, the international language of western Christendom, and was soon producing his own translations. "I began in the midst of the other various and manifold cares of this kingdom to turn into English the Latin *Pastoralis* [by Pope Gregory the Great]", he wrote later. He sent a copy of his translation to every bishop in his kingdom, along with a beautifully made *æstel*, a bookmark or pointer.

He insists that the clergy should be proficient in Latin and English, and, determined that certain books "most necessary for all men to know" should be made into English, has opened a school to teach reading. At Winchester he has gathered around him an entourage of learned men, and together they talk about the Christian faith, affairs of state and the decay of learning and scholarship under the impact of the Danish invasions.

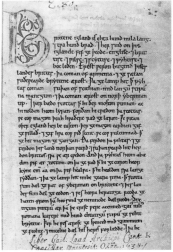

The "Anglo-Saxon Chronicle", a work sponsored by King Alfred.

In addition Alfred has sponsored a monumental *Anglo-Saxon Chronicle*. Backdated to Julius Caesar's raid of 55BC, it will be a continuous record of annual events. He also keeps a book of quotations and reflections copied for him by his biographer and devoted admirer Bishop Asser of Sherborne.

Alfred is renowned in Europe as a pious statesman and scholar in the mould of Charlemagne of the Franks. Alfred's stepmother was Frankish, and he is in regular contact with Frankish and Flemish intellectuals and churchmen. He sends alms to Rome, which he visited as a child, and corresponds with Pope John VIII (→ 893).

The head of a pointer or bookmark, inscribed "Alfred had me made".

Edward the Elder
899–924
Ælfweard
924
Athelstan
924–939

Constantine II
900–943

Northumbria, 902. Æthelwold, who failed to depose his cousin, King Edward of Wessex, in 899, sails south with the Danes to try once more to seize the throne.

Dyfed, 904. Hywel ap Cadell, the grandson of King Rhodri the Great, becomes king (→ c.930).

Tiddingford, Bucks, 906. King Edward makes a truce with the Danes (→ 5/8/910).

Staffordshire, 5 August 910. Edward defeats the Danes at Tettenhall and advances on East Anglia (→ 917).

Mercia, 12 June 918. Æthelflæd, Lady [ruler] of the Mercians since the death in 911 of her husband Æthelred, dies. She took Derby and Leicester from the Danes.→

Mercia, December 918. Edward secures direct control of Mercia from his niece, Ælfwynn, ruler since her mother Æthelflæd's death (→ 17/7/924).

Northumberland, 918. King Constantine II of Scots fights an inconclusive battle at Corbridge with Rægnald, the Danish king of York, who defeated him there in 914 (→ 943).

France, 919. Edward's daughter Eadgifu marries King Charles of the West Franks.

Cheshire, 17 July 924. Edward, who retook East Anglia and Mercia from the Danes, dies; his son Ælfweard succeeds (→ 1/8/924).

Oxford, 1 August 924. King Ælfweard dies. His illegitimate half-brother Athelstan succeeds (→ 12/7/927).

England/France 926. King Athelstan's half-sisters Edith and Eadhild marry Sihtric, the Danish king of York, and Hugh, the Count of Paris, respectively.

Gloucester, 27 October 939. Athelstan, the first ruler of all England, dies. Edmund, his 18-year-old half-brother, succeeds him.→

Constantine is king after mystic Scone rite

Scone, Tayside, 900
Constantine II, the grandson of Kenneth mac Alpin – the man who brought together the Picts and the Scots – has been enthroned in a solemn public ritual as king of Alba, as the united kingdom is now known. He succeeds his cousin, Donald II, in whose reign the ancient British kingdom of Strathclyde also came under Scottish domination.

Like previous ceremonies, the enthronement took place on Moot Hill at Scone, probably in a barrow or chambered cairn. Seated on a mysterious "stone of destiny", Constantine was invested simply with a sceptre and robe – there is no Scottish crown. Following precedent, the king was then symbolically married to the land and the people, and his ancient genealogy was recited. After this, members of the nobility who were present

King Constantine's tomb (detail).

demonstrated their fealty to the new ruler. It is possible that the proceedings involved ancient practices such as sacrifice or ritual bathing (→ 918).

King Edward is secure as rebel is killed

East Anglia, 902
King Alfred's son, Edward, has emerged triumphant as king of Wessex after the death of his cousin and rival, Æthelwold, in battle with Edward's Kentish allies. When Edward succeeded in October 899, Æthelwold seized the royal palace at Wimborne in Dorset after kidnapping a nun for his gratification.

He then sought refuge with the Danes, begging them to help him overthrow his cousin. In response to Danish attacks Edward launched a punitive strike into the Danelaw. The Kentish forces were defeated in a battle at Holme, but not before they had killed both Æthelwold and his ally, the Danish king of East Anglia (→ 906).

Edward reconquers Danish territories

Midlands and East Anglia, 917
In a year of dazzling victories, King Edward has crushed a succession of Danish armies, regaining the east Midlands and Essex and forcing the East Anglian Danes to submit. Unlike his father King Alfred, who was mainly concerned with the defence of the borders of Wessex, Edward has pursued an actively aggressive policy against Danish-held territory.

Aided by his formidable sister, Æthelflæd, the Lady [ruler] of the Mercians, Edward has repeatedly defeated Danish forces and consolidated his gains by building a series of *burhs*, or fortified centres. These, and his ability to raise fresh armies (at least three this year), owe much to his father's military reforms. The English reconquest of the Danelaw does not seem far away (→ 12/918).

A silver penny of King Edward.

Edward annexes the lands of his sister, Mercia's mighty ruler

At the head of her army: a romanticised view of Lady Æthelflæd.

Staffordshire, 12 June 918
Edward's sister and comrade-in-arms, Æthelflæd, the Lady of the Mercians, has died at Tamworth in the hour of her greatest triumph, when she was about to receive the submission of the Northumbrian Danish kingdom of York.

When Æthelred of Mercia, who ruled under Wessex's overlordship, died in 911, his widow Æthelflæd took command of Mercian forces to drive the Danes back towards the Humber. She and her brother were a formidable combination, and her death leaves Edward the greatest power in the land. Although Æthelflæd's young daughter Ælfwynn succeeds her, the absorption of Mercia into Edward's kingdom is surely one step nearer (→ 12/918).

Athelstan is the first king to rule all of England

North yields to the power of Athelstan

Cumbria, 12 July 927

King Athelstan has overcome the Danish kingdom of York and now holds sway over the whole of England. At a ceremony today at Eamont Bridge, near Penrith, the overlordship of King Alfred's grandson was acknowledged by the chief rulers of the north: King Constantine II of Scots, the king of Strathclyde and the lord of the English enclave of Bamburgh. They also promised to wipe out all pagan practices. Athelstan, who is 33, grew up in the household of his aunt Æthelflæd, the ruler of the Mercians. Three years ago he succeeded his father Edward as king of united Mercia and Wessex (→ c.930).

Welsh pay tribute

Hereford, c.930

Hywel, the ruler of the south Welsh kingdom of Dyfed, known as *Dda* [the Good] from his piety, is among a group of five Welsh kings who have acknowledged the overlordship of King Athelstan at Hereford. It was agreed that they should pay tribute of gold, silver, cattle, hunting dogs and hawks as token of their submission. They also agreed to accept the river Wye as part of the Anglo-Welsh frontier (→ 942).

Athelstan and St Cuthbert on a manuscript commissioned by the king in 934.

Coalition is routed by Athelstan's men

Northern England, autumn 937

In a day-long battle on the field of Brunanburh, somewhere between the Solway and the Mersey, King Athelstan has routed a formidable coalition led by Olaf, the king of the Dublin Norse, King Owen of Strathclyde and his overlord, King Constantine II of Scots – the latter two in defiance of pledges of loyalty to Athelstan. The beaten kings fled in disarray. The *Anglo-Saxon Chronicle* is exultant over the victory: "King Athelstan, lord of warriors, ring-giver of men, with his royal brother Edmund, won undying glory with the edges of swords ... the Scots and the host from the ships fell doomed" (→ 27/10/939).

King backs reforms

Hampshire, c.930

King Athelstan and his counsellors have been meeting at Grately in Hampshire to draw up legislation governing the treatment of thieves, the punishment of witchcraft, the responsibilities of lords for their dependants, control of the coinage and the regulation of trade. The king has insisted on banning Sunday trading, and has also ruled that a perjurer must be buried in unconsecrated ground (→ 934).

Monarch dies at the peak of his fame

Gloucester, 27 October 939

King Athelstan died today in the bedchamber of his palace at Gloucester. He was just 44, but in his 14-year reign he had brought most of England under his rule and acquired an international fame unsurpassed by any previous English monarch.

Athelstan was active right up to his death; just a few months ago he dispatched an English fleet to Flanders to help his nephew, Louis of France. It was the first time that the English had intervened militarily on the continent. Athelstan, handsome and slender with flaxen hair, is renowned for conquering the Danelaw, but he also accepted the submission of five Welsh kings and crushed the Britons of Cornwall. He enjoyed the adulation of poets and clerics, and in his charters he was "King of the English, raised to the throne ... by the hand of the Almighty".

The king kept close ties with European royalty through the marriages of his half-sisters. Kings' sons were tutored at his court, such as Haakon of Norway, whose father King Harald gave Athelstan a splendid ship.

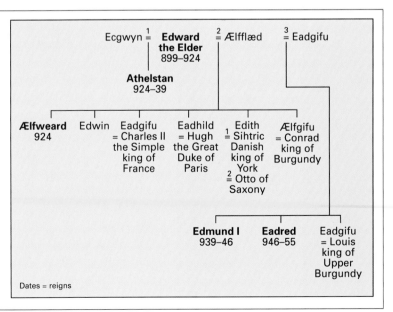

Edmund I
939–946
Eadred
946–955
Eadwig
955–959

Constantine II
900–943
Malcolm I
943–954
Indulf
954–962

York, 939. Olaf Guthfrithson, the king of Dublin, seizes York after Athelstan's death (→ 941).

Northumbria, 941. Olaf Guthfrithson dies; his cousin Olaf Sihtricson succeeds him at Dublin and York (→ 943).

Mercia, 942. Edmund regains lands seized by the Danes.

St Andrews, Fife, 943. King Constantine II retires to become a monk; Malcolm, the son of Donald II, succeeds.→

Mercia, 943. The Scandinavian kings Olaf Sihtricson of York and his rival Rægnald II submit to Edmund and are baptised (→ 944).

York, 944. Edmund retakes the city to depose Olaf (→ 945).

Cumbria, 945. Edmund recognises Malcolm of Scots' overlordship of Strathclyde and Cumbria (→ 26/5/946).

Surrey, 16 August 946. Edmund's brother Eadred is crowned at Kingston (→ 947).

West Yorkshire, 947. Northumbria bows to Eadred (→ 948).

North Yorkshire, 948. Eadred burns Ripon minster and expels Eric Bloodaxe, a Norse invader who has won support north of the Humber (→ 955).

Northumberland, 949. King Malcolm of Scots invades in support of Olaf Sihtricson, who has regained York (→ 952).

Wales, 950. King Hywel the Good of Dyfed dies.

St Andrews, Fife, 952. The former King Constantine II dies.

York, 952. Olaf is deposed by the Northumbrians, who accept Eric Bloodaxe as their king once more (→ 954).

Fife, 954. Malcolm of Scots is killed; Indulf, the son of Constantine II, succeeds him.

Somerset, 23 November 955. Eadred dies and is succeeded by his nephew Eadwig.→

Wessex, 1 October 959. Eadwig dies; England is reunited as Edgar succeeds.

New king is forced to give up conquests

Leicester, 940

King Edmund, 18 years old and less than a year into his reign, has presided over a severe blow to the prestige of the royal line of King Alfred and the repartitioning of England. In a peace treaty brokered by the archbishops of York and Canterbury he has been forced to concede the land between Watling Street and the Humber to Olaf Guthfrithson, the king of the Dublin Norse. At a stroke, he has given away many of the conquests of his half-brother Athelstan.

After his defeat at Brunanburh in 937, Olaf waited until the death of Athelstan last October before invading once more across the Irish Sea with his Norsemen. He probably judged that the young King Edmund would prove no match for him. Edmund was no push-over, however, and hoped to bring Olaf to a decisive battle at Leicester. But he found to his dismay that the

A later portrait of King Edmund.

Northumbrians had backed Olaf, and that Olaf's supporter, Earl Orm, was poised to take over the "Five Boroughs" of the Danes: Leicester, Nottingham, Derby, Stamford and Lincoln (→ 942).

Edmund is brutally murdered by robbers

King Edmund is stabbed by the outlaw Leofa: an 18th-century engraving.

Gloucestershire, 26 May 946

King Edmund's renowned bravery and gallantry have cost him his life. The king was foully murdered at Pucklebury today when he rode to help his steward, who was being attacked by Leofa, a banished thief.

After losing much of the north of his kingdom to Olaf Guthfrithson in 940, Edmund won it back two years later, and in 943 both Olaf Sihtricson, Guthfrithson's successor, and his rival Rægnald II submitted to Edmund and were bap-

tised. When they continued to give trouble, Edmund saw them off. He attacked Strathclyde, which had allied with the Danes, and recognised King Malcolm of Scots as its overlord in an anti-Danish deal to secure his northern frontier.

Edmund was a notable patron of the church, and among the rising talents he spotted was Dunstan, whom he made abbot of Glastonbury. Edmund's two sons are too young to rule, so his brother Eadred will succeed (→ 16/8/946).

Hywel plans united kingdom in Wales

North Wales, 942

King Hywel of Dyfed seems to have ended anarchy in Wales once and for all. By seizing control of the kingdoms of Gwynedd and Powys from the rightful heirs after their predecessors had been killed in action against the "Saxons", King Hywel has almost restored the Welsh overlordship to what it was when his grandfather, Rhodri the Great, was alive.

Hywel's move amounts to a fairly naked act of aggression against his more northerly neighbours. But he has already set about consolidating his gains into a viable unified kingdom and is planning to call a conference to institute legal reforms for the whole of his domains. His efforts will be helped by the fact that war with the "Saxons" is unlikely; Hywel is on excellent terms with the English court (→ 950).

Scots king retires to become a monk

St Andrews, Fife, 943

Constantine II's tumultuous 43 years as king of Scots have ended with his retirement to a monastery at St Andrews. The move reflects an abiding interest in the church – in 906 he forged the union of the Pictish and Scottish churches under Cellach, the bishop of St Andrews – but his life was otherwise far from contemplative.

During his reign Constantine defended and consolidated the Scots kingdom and increased Scottish influence over the British kingdom of Strathclyde and the English region of Lothian. He used both force and diplomacy to defuse the Scandinavian threat. In recent years, however, the victories of Athelstan and – despite early setbacks – of Edmund have threatened to expose the Scots to a powerful English presence in Northumbria. Constantine never really recovered from the humiliation at Brunanburh in 937, when the Scots and their allies were routed by Athelstan's army.

Constantine is succeeded by his second cousin Malcolm, who has begun his reign with the capture and subjugation of Moray (→ 952).

Viking king thrown out

Stainmore, Yorkshire, 954

Eric Bloodaxe, the Norwegian king of York, has fallen in a grim last stand against his enemies on a bleak Pennine moor. His death and the reconquest of the Scandinavian kingdom of Northumbria centred on York remove the last important opposition to King Eadred.

Eric was one of the dying breed of old-style pagan Viking warriors and pursued a chequered, blood-stained career. The son of King Harald Fairhair of Norway, he came to the throne about ten years ago and immediately set about earning his gory nickname with acts of brutality that included killing at least one brother. The Norwegians soon had enough of his savagery and in 946 placed his brother Haakon, a peaceable man who had been raised as a Christian at King Athelstan's court, on the throne.

Eric headed for Britain, terrorising the Scottish islands before taking up the kingship of York at the invitation of Northumbria's Danish nobles. In 948 Eadred moved against Eric but met a heavy setback at Castleford. However, Northumbria was by now fed up with his brutality and kicked him out. He went back to the Western Isles for two years while Olaf Sihtricson of Dublin ruled York.

Northumbria recalled Eric in 952, and he ruled for two more years before being ejected again and betrayed to his enemies at Stainmore. The Northumbrians seem at last prepared to accept the rule of the royal line of Wessex.

Eadred, from a C14th manuscript.

A Viking warrior, on an C8th stone.

Fifteen-year-old boy comes to the throne

Frome, Somerset, 23 Nov 955

King Eadred has died after a nine-year reign. The king, who had been ill for some time, leaves behind a united kingdom, a fabulous fortune, but no obvious heir to succeed him. However, with no clear enemy threat to the kingdom, the sons of his brother King Edmund, who were infants at their own father's death, are now judged grown up enough to rule with the help and advice of the *Witan*, the king's "council of the wise". The elder of the two boys, Eadwig, who is 15 and known as "All-Fair" because of his striking good looks, will become king.

Although honoured for his campaigns to unite the English and remove the Scandinavian threat in the north, Eadred will be remembered less fondly by the people of Thetford in East Anglia. In 952 he massacred many of them for the killing of an abbot (→1/956).

Boy king in coronation day sex scandal

Kingston Upon Thames, Jan 956

King Eadwig has launched his reign with a sordid sex scandal on the very day of his coronation. It has left his bishops and chief advisers dumbfounded with shock and dismay, and already things do not bode well for England's 15-year-old monarch.

Eyebrows were raised during the coronation feast when Eadwig seemed to become bored with the celebration and slipped away – taking with him Ælfgifu, a young woman whom he is known to favour, and her mother. Both are said to harbour hopes of marrying the young king. The assembled nobles and churchmen grew steadily more uneasy until it was decided that Abbot Dunstan, the distinguished monastic reformer and protegé of the late King Eadred, should go with the bishop of Lichfield to remind the king of his duties.

When the two clerics entered the king's chamber they encountered

Dunstan pulls Eadwig off Ælfgifu.

all three truants on a sofa, their clothes dishevelled, and the crown of England lying unregarded on the floor. Rumour has it that the boy king felt the back of Dunstan's hand before being unceremoniously dragged back to the feast (→2/957).

Eadred provides for the royal household

Winchester, 955

Although he is only about 30, King Eadred is ill and has turned his thoughts to what will happen after his death. His most obvious bequest to the two nephews who are his heirs – he is unmarried – is a united kingdom, but he has also left a fabulous treasure with an estimated worth of several thousands of pounds.

In his will Eadred specifies that £1,600 should be kept aside to pay off an invading heathen army; he is obviously not convinced that the Scandinavian threat is over. The money, which is also for the relief of famine, has been left to the people of England and will be held in trust by prominent churchmen.

The king has also made specific bequests to members of his household, such as the *discthegns*, or stewards, who are responsible for the royal table, the *birele*, or royal butlers, and the *hræglethegns*, or keepers of the royal wardrobe. They will each receive 80 mancuses (one mancus is made up of 30 silver pennies). Thirty mancuses each also go to the king's *stigweards*, or dispensers (→23/11/955).

Half of England revolts against the king

Mercia and Northumbria, Dec 957

Disillusion with King Eadwig has finally found concrete expression. The nobles of Mercia, like those of Northumbria, have renounced his rule. But in a clear sign that their objections are to the present wearer of the crown rather than the Wessex royal line, they have chosen his younger brother Edgar in his place. Edgar is just 14 years old.

The move comes a year after the long-standing quarrel between Eadwig and the church came to a head when the king forced Abbot Dunstan, who caught him with two women at the coronation feast, to leave the country. In retaliation Archbishop Odo of Canterbury has forced Eadwig to separate from his wife Ælfgifu, the younger of the women involved in the original incident, on the grounds that they are too closely related.

Although it might seem that once again the unity of the kingdom is threatened, it is noticeable that these actions come at a time of no serious outside threat. If there were one, the national interest might override any pious objections to the king's private morals (→1/10/959).

Edgar
959–975
Edward the Martyr
975–978

Indulf 954–962
Dub 962–c.967
Culen
c.967–971
Kenneth II
971–995

Wessex, 959. King Edgar has married Æthelflæd, the daughter of Ordmær, a senior royal official (→ 21/10/960).

Canterbury, 21 October 960. Edgar launches a series of church reforms with Dunstan, whom he has made archbishop of Canterbury (→ 962).

Strathclyde, 962. Danes fleeing from York kill King Indulf of Scots; Dub, the sub-king of Strathclyde, succeeds (→ 966).

Wessex, 962. Queen Æthelflæd dies in childbirth, leaving a son, Edward (→ 962/3).

Wilton, Wiltshire, 962/963. A daughter, Edith, is born to Edgar and Wulfthryth, a former lay sister (→ 964).

Wessex, 964. Edgar puts aside Wulfthryth to wed Ælfthryth, the widow of a royal official (→ 966).

Forres, Grampian, 966. The body of King Dub of Scots is found under a bridge; it is thought that his assassins acted for Culen, the new king (→ 971).

Winchester, Hampshire, 966. Queen Ælfthryth bears a son, Edmund. There is great celebration to overcome the rumours of the impropriety of Edgar's marriage (→ c.967).

Wessex, c.967. Queen Ælfthryth has another son, Æthelred (→ 971).

Wessex, 971. Edmund, Edgar's five-year-old son, dies.

Wessex, 8 July 975. Edgar dies aged 31; he will be buried at Glastonbury. A dispute arises between the rival supporters of his two young sons, Edward and Æthelred.→

Surrey, 976. Edward, the elder legitimate son of King Edgar by his first wife Æthelflæd, is crowned king, against the will of his stepmother, Ælfthryth, the mother of his half-brother Æthelred (→ 18/3/978).

Corfe, Dorset, 18 March 978. King Edward is murdered; his stepmother Ælfthryth is linked to the plot.→

New broom Edgar reunites the kingdom

Edgar enthroned between Bishop Dunstan (r) and Bishop Æthelwold (l).

Wessex, winter 959
With a sigh of relief the ancestral kingdom of the West Saxons has greeted the death of the licentious 19-year-old King Eadwig by joining the rest of the English in acknowledging his pious younger brother Edgar as their king. The widespread hope now is for a period of peace and prosperity.

One of Edgar's first tasks will be to heal the rift with the church made by his elder brother, and he has already made it known that Dunstan, the leading church re-former, forced to live abroad until Eadwig's death, will return to the bishopric of Worcester. It is rumoured that Edgar will appoint him to Canterbury, and other clerics, such as Æthelwold and Oswald, are also tipped for promotion.

Edgar has also indicated that the great nobles of the realm, such as Ælfhere of Mercia and another Æthelwold, of East Anglia, will remain the linchpins of his government. The theme of the reign is established: continuity and the rule of law under the king.

Fourth Scots king in a row meets with a bloody, violent end

Lothian, 971
King Culen of Scots has been assassinated in Lothian by Riderch, the sub-king of Strathclyde, in revenge for Culen's rape of his daughter and murder of his brother during a Scottish campaign to reassert control over Strathclyde. He is the fourth Scots king in a row to die violently.

The cycle of blood-letting began in 954, when King Malcolm was killed in the Mearns [*Grampian*] by the people of Moray, whom he had forcibly subjugated on coming to power in 943. Under the *tanistry* system – a recipe for violence in which the succession, in theory, alternates between two branches descended from King Kenneth mac Alpin – Malcolm was succeeded by his cousin Indulf. As *tanist*, or recognised heir, Indulf had previously been installed by Malcolm as sub-king of Strathclyde; when he became king of Scots, these titles passed to Malcolm's own son, Dub.

Dub succeeded to the throne in 962 after Indulf was killed by Danes. His reign was short and shaky; in 966 his body was found covered in turf in a ditch at Kinross. He had been kidnapped the previous night by men thought to have been acting for his tanist, Culen, "the Whelp", Indulf's son. The alleged usurper has now suffered a similar bloody fate (→ 995).

King Edgar's reforming zeal stamps his mark on the kingdom

Winchester, 973
The 29-year-old King Edgar has now presided over 14 years of tranquillity, in which time he has been untiring in his efforts to forge a unified English kingdom by the pen rather than the sword.

In the early 960s, with the aid of three highly talented men, Dunstan, Oswald and Æthelwold, all of whom he made bishops, he rooted out abuses in the church; the great ecclesiastical and monastic revival which has followed is reflected in the art pouring from centres like Winchester. He has also enforced a system whereby a tenth or "tithe" of produce goes to the church. Under Edgar the boundaries of the shires have taken on firmer shape as each "hundred" [shire subdivision] has been organised with its own lawcourt, achieving greater uniformity of administration. He has regulated weights and measures and this year recalled the coinage to be melted down and reissued with a new design. Moneyers must buy new dies from the government, so Edgar is both tightening central control of money supply and earning extra income for the treasury.

With all his reforms, however, Edgar respects the traditions of Mercia, Northumbria and the Danelaw. He says he rules for "all the nation, whether Englishmen, Danes or Britons" (→ 11/5/973).

Art made for Bishop Æthelwold.

Edgar celebrates peak of his prestige

Coronation held in ancient Roman city

Bath, 11 May 973
Finally, 14 years into his reign, Edgar has been crowned king of England. But it was no ordinary coronation that took place in Bath abbey today, Whit Sunday, before a glittering crowd of priests and nobles. In this ceremony, the brainchild of Archbishop Dunstan, the climax came not when the crown was placed on Edgar's head but when he was anointed, in a deliberate echo of a priest's ordination.

It is no coincidence either that Edgar waited until his 30th year, the minimum age for priesthood, before going ahead with such a ritual, nor that it was staged amid the imperial ruins of this ancient Roman city. Only a king as confident in his grip on the throne as Edgar, and of his maturity and dignity, would have gone along with the archbishop's scheme to enhance the majesty of kingship. The message is clear: the king derives his authority from God, and this sets him apart from and above all other men as their natural ruler.

As he watched the proceedings today Dunstan must have felt satisfaction at such a clear demonstration of the new links between an ascendant church and an unchallenged monarch (→973).

A Victorian impression of Edgar being rowed by eight kings on the river Dee.

Eight kings row Edgar's ship at Chester

Chester, summer 973
After being anointed king in the eyes of God, Edgar has sailed with his fleet to a grand summit of the royal rulers of Britain. In a striking ceremony no fewer than eight kings recognised Edgar in his palace before taking the oars of his ship and rowing him across the Dee to the church of St John the Baptist. King Edgar steered the boat, which was accompanied by a flotilla of small vessels containing his nobles. The gesture is a sign of the prestige which Edgar enjoys among his Celtic neighbours. The monarchs at the oars of Edgar's ship included King Kenneth II of Scots – who in return for recognising Edgar has been acknowledged as ruler of Lothian – with his son King Malcolm of Strathclyde, King Maccus of Man and the Western Isles, and King Iago of Gwynedd (→8/7/975).

Unease grows over succession dispute between royal sons

Glastonbury, mid-July 975
King Edgar has been laid to rest in Glastonbury abbey after his sudden death on 8 July at the age of only 31. Already there are fears that with him England has also buried the peace and prosperity which he brought to the land.

Edgar leaves two young sons, Edward, aged 13, and Æthelred, aged about eight, whose claims are already being vigorously upheld by rival factions. The group supporting Æthelred, led by his mother Queen Ælfthryth, is alleged to be anti-monastic and jealous of the power of Archbishop Dunstan. He, together with the majority of the nobles, backs Edward, Edgar's son by his first marriage; the queen's plans may be foiled (→976).

King's hunters reap handsome rewards

A fowler, on a manuscript of c.1000.

Wessex, c.975
Hunting is among the favourite pastimes of every king, and the jobs of royal hunter or fowler are highly prized. The hunter uses hounds to flush out his prey, such as deer and boar, which he brings down with nets or a spear. To catch birds the fowler has trained hawks, nets, nooses and birdlime, a glue used to trap small birds. All catches go to the king, who pays his men with their food and clothing and gifts such as a horse or a ring.

Æthelred comes to the throne amid mystery over royal murder

Corfe, Dorset, 18 March 978
Two years of increasing disorder and confusion have been brought to a tragic end by the treacherous murder of the young King Edward. Edward, who was 15, was not much loved by some for his violent rages; but kings are regarded as ordained by God and his brutal murder, on a visit to his stepmother Queen Ælfthryth, has shocked everyone. He rode into her courtyard and was accepting the respects of his half-brother Æthelred's retainers when he was stabbed to death. Æthelred, now king, is 11 and probably cannot be blamed, but there are mutterings that Ælfthryth, his mother, has blood on her hands.

Edward is treacherously stabbed, as seen by an early 19th-century artist.

Æthelred II
978–1016
Edmund II
1016

Kenneth II
971–995
Constantine III
995–997
Kenneth III 997–1005
Malcolm II 1005–1034

Kingston, Surrey, 4 May 979.
King Æthelred II is crowned
(→ 985).

South coast, 980. Danes ravage
England for the first time for
years, raiding along the coast.

Wessex, 985. Æthelred marries
Ælfgifu, the daughter of the
chief royal official of
Northumbria (→ 991).

Wessex, 990. The dowager
Queen Ælfthryth, exiled from
the court since 895, is restored.

Tayside, 997. Constantine III
of Scots, who succeeded
Kenneth II in 995, is killed;
Kenneth III, the son of the
late King Dub, succeeds
(→ 1005).

Norfolk, 1004. King Sweyn of
Denmark invades to avenge a
massacre of Danish settlers,
including his sister (→ 1011).

Islip, Oxfordshire, c.1005.
Emma, Æthelred's second
wife, has a son, Edward.

Monzievaird, Tayside, 1005.
Malcolm, the son of Kenneth
II, kills Kenneth III and his
son, Giric, in battle; he
becomes King Malcolm II
(→ 1008).

England, 1011. Æthelred sues
King Sweyn for peace (→ 1013).

England, 1014. Cnut, king of
England and Denmark since
the recent death of his father
Sweyn, is driven out on
Æthelred's return from exile.→

Mercia, summer 1015.
Edmund, Æthelred's son by
his first wife, dubbed
"Ironside" from his bravery,
marries Ealdgith (→ 1016).

North Midlands, 1015.
Edmund, in revolt against his
father, rallies support against
Cnut.

London, 23 April 1016.
Edmund is hailed as king on
the death of his increasingly
ineffective father, who has been
ill for some time (→ 30/11/16).

London, 30 November 1016.
Edmund dies; Wessex accepts
Cnut as king of all England
(→ 2/1016).

Æthelred pays to keep Danes away

South-eastern England, 991
King Æthelred and his councillors
have decided to pay protection
money to the Danes. They see it as
the only way to fend off the ever increasing raids that are threatening
to bring the country to its knees.

The decision follows a number of
serious defeats, culminating this
year in the disastrous battle at
Maldon, where Brihtnoth, the chief
royal official of Essex, attempted to
trap a Danish raiding fleet of 93
ships led by Olaf Tryggvason, the
heir to the crown of Norway.

Brihtnoth caught the fleet while
it was beached on Northey Island,
just outside Maldon, but in the fight
that followed he was killed and his
army shattered. Still, the English
drew comfort from the fact that
they had stood up to the Danes for
the first time for many years. Now
Æthelred has undermined any deterrent effect of Brihtnoth's attack
by taking the advice of Archbishop
Sigeric of Canterbury in drawing
up a treaty which includes paying
£22,000 in gold and silver to
Tryggvason to go away. This tribute, known as *Danegeld*, is a vast
sum, and many fear that it will only
encourage more raiders looking for
easy pickings (→ 1002).

King Æthelred (r) beside his father Edgar and predecessor Alfred: c.1250.

Scandinavian hero: illustration from a life of the warrior Olaf Tryggvason.

Bizarre trap kills Scots King Kenneth

The Mearns, Grampian, 995
King Kenneth II of Scots is dead –
rumoured to be the victim of an
outlandish revenge hatched by
Finvela, a noblewoman whose son
was killed by the king. She is said
to have lured Kenneth into her
home promising to unmask traitors. In one room was a statue connected to several hidden crossbows,
which were set to fire bolts from
every side when a golden apple on
the statue was lifted. After a great
feast, at which wine flowed freely,
Finvela took her drunken guest into
the fatal room and offered him the
apple as a gesture of peace. As he
lifted it a hail of bolts struck him
down. Kenneth's efforts to secure
the throne for his son Malcolm
seem to have failed with the accession of his distant relative, Constantine III (→ 997).

Orkney's Norse ruler weds Scots princess

A decorated hilt of a Viking sword.

Scotland, 1008
Malcolm II of Scots has married his
daughter Donada to Sigurd the
Stout, the Norse Earl of Orkney
and effective ruler of Caithness,
Sutherland and the Western Isles.
The marriage may prove more effective than military might in subduing this independently-minded
part of Malcolm's kingdom, ruled
by the Norse for many decades.

Vikings first settled in Orkney
and Shetland over a century ago,
when Scots and Picts were fighting
for control of the Scottish heartland. The Norse who came to dominate the northern isles were just as
powerful as the mainland kings further south, and they extended their
domain to cover a large part of northern Scotland. Traditionally they
have suffered little interference
from the kings of Norway and Scotland, although their lands are formally subject to them (→ 1016).

Æthelred takes a Norman for queen

Wessex, summer 1002
King Æthelred II has married for the second time. His new bride is Emma, known to the English as Ælfgifu, the daughter of Duke Richard II of Normandy. The marriage will strengthen ties between the two countries, which formed alliances in 991 and again last year in the face of a growing Danish threat. Normandy, founded by Vikings, has long been a stopping-off point for Scandinavian raiders. Æthelred's policy of paying the Danes to go away has – as he was warned it would 11 years ago when he first began it – only served to encourage them. This year he has had to pay £24,000 in silver (→ c.1005).

A later mediaeval manuscript illustration of King Sweyn invading England.

Æthelred returns to reclaim throne

Southern England, 1014
King Æthelred has been restored to his throne. His return follows the sudden death of King Sweyn of Denmark on 3 February, just a few weeks after he had ousted Æthelred and taken over the kingdom.

The Danish fleet elected Sweyn's son Cnut as king, but Æthelred raised an army and forced him out. On his nobles' insistence, though, Æthelred made a gesture of trust, and in the first pact between an English king and his people he promised to be a better ruler and bring in reforms. However, his habits of paying off the Danes and provoking them by brutal acts have already re-emerged (→ 23/4/16).

Queen Emma in a later manuscript.

'Evil counsel' Æthelred flees his kingdom

Normandy, 1013
After reigning for 34 years King Æthelred II has lost his crown to King Sweyn of Denmark and fled to his wife's Norman homeland. It is the culmination of years of Danish attacks and growing disarray in the kingdom.

Æthelred never seemed to recover from the stigma of becoming king through the murder of his elder half-brother King Edward. Many regarded it as an appalling sacrilege against one ordained by God, and although Æthelred himself was too young to be implicated, his mother was. This may help to explain his weak leadership and the deep mistrust between him and his nobles. The situation was made worse by poor decision-making and an unwillingness to listen to advice that has led to his nickname of "*Unraed*" – "evil counsel" or "no counsel" – a pun on his name, which means "noble counsel".

His decision to buy off Danish raiders only encouraged more raids, while his planned massacre of all the Danes in England on St Brice's day, 13 November 1002, backfired by provoking attacks and alienating the Danish immigrant community of the Danelaw. Nevertheless, Æthelred kept his crown – until now – and managed to carry out far-reaching reforms of the law and create an efficient tax system. In less traumatic times he might have achieved far more (→ 1014).

England split in two by rival monarchs

Alney, Gloucestershire, 1016
After a series of battles which have left both sides exhausted, King Edmund Ironside and King Cnut of Denmark have agreed to divide England between them. When Æthelred II died in April rival factions of the nobility backed Edmund and Cnut, the son of the late King Sweyn of Denmark. The kings fought in Wessex, burnt London and clashed again at Ashingdon in Essex, where Cnut won a decisive victory. But the Danes are too weak to exploit their advantage, and so Cnut will rule north of the Thames, including London, while Edmund rules Wessex (→ 23/4/16).

Royal rule attacked

York, 1014
In a savage sermon on the dire state of the kingdom, Wulfstan, the archbishop of York, has warned that the present troubles of the English are their own fault. The Danish takeover, the weakness of the country and the ineffectiveness of its response are God's punishments for the moral corruption of the people, says Wulfstan, nicknamed "the Wolf". He stresses that "great is the necessity to keep God's laws", especially for kings. "The end of the world is nigh," he warns.

Danish king rules England after brief reign of Edmund Ironside

Edmund Ironside (l) and Cnut do battle, as imagined by a later artist.

London, December 1016
Following the sudden death of King Edmund Ironside, Wessex has submitted to the rule of King Cnut. Edmund, who was renowned for his bravery, was born in around 990, the third son of Æthelred II and his first wife Ælfflæd. He rebelled against his father in 1015, possibly because his stepmother planned to secure the throne for her own son, Edward, and won considerable support in the north. He returned to his father when Cnut began to pose a serious threat.

Cnut
1016–1035
Harold I
1035–1040
Harthacnut
1040–1042

Malcolm II
1005–1034
Duncan I
1034–1040
Macbeth
1040–1057

England, 1017. To secure his throne, Cnut murders Eadwig, Æthelred II's son; two of Æthelred's other sons flee to their uncle, Duke Richard II of Normandy.→

Denmark, 1019. Cnut becomes king on the death of his brother, Harald.→

England, 1019. Queen Emma has a son, Harthacnut (→ 12/11/35).

Denmark, 1023. Cnut makes peace with Thorkell, the ruler of East Anglia whom he exiled in 1021; Thorkell will rule Denmark in Cnut's absence (→ 1026).

Denmark, 1026. Cnut's fleet is defeated at the Holy River by Scandinavian rivals (→ 1027).

Borders, 1027. Malcolm II of Scots makes peace with Cnut after a series of raids (→ 1034).

Rome, 1027. Cnut arrives on a state visit.

Scandinavia, 1028. Harthacnut becomes king of Denmark while Cnut takes control of Norway (→ 12/11/35).

Normandy, 1035. William, the illegitimate son of Duke Robert of Normandy and great-nephew of Queen Emma, succeeds as duke (→ 1051).

Dorset, 12 November 1035. Cnut dies at Shaftesbury. It is uncertain whether his heir, Harthacnut, will be able to leave Denmark to claim the English throne (→ 1037).

Ely, 1036. Alfred, Æthelred's son, returns from Normandy but is taken and blinded. He dies of his wounds.

Flanders, 1037. Emma, the widow of Cnut, flees after failing to oust Harold, the son of Cnut by Ælfgifu, who has made himself king (→ 17/3/40).

Durham, 1039. King Duncan of Scots is defeated in a raid which seriously undermines his authority at home (→ 1040).

London, 17 March 1040. King Harold "Harefoot" dies; his half-brother, Harthacnut, claims the throne (→ 8/6/42).

Cnut imposes mastery on the English

Cnut orders purge to secure position

London, December 1017
King Cnut has acted swiftly to deal with any opposition. He has had Eadwig, the brother of the late King Edmund Ironside, assassinated, and would undoubtedly have had Edmund's baby sons Edward and Edmund killed too had they not been taken to Hungary, where his agents cannot reach them.

Frustrated, Cnut turned on the man who advised him to carry out the murders. This was Eadric Streona, the Earl of Mercia, a devious character who had repeatedly betrayed every king he had ever served. For example, he defected from Ironside's army at the moment that it was going into battle, giving Cnut victory. But Cnut is tougher than his predecessors and knew better than to trust Eadric. He has had him killed, together with three other nobles (→ 1019).

King Cnut: a C13th stained glass.

King marries widow of his predecessor

London, 1017
One of Cnut's first acts upon gaining the crown of England has been to seek the hand of Emma, the widow of the late King Æthelred II. It is a shrewd move, since it associates him directly with the family of the late king and will preserve England's alliance with Emma's brother, Duke Richard II of Normandy and stop him intervening on behalf of his nephews, Æthelred's sons Edward and Alfred, who have fled to his court.

Emma is about 32 and her new husband 22. He has two sons by an existing partner, Ælfgifu, but Emma has insisted as part of the marriage terms that only her own children by Cnut will succeed. Nonetheless, although Emma is his official wife, it seems that Cnut has no intention of abandoning Ælfgifu altogether (→ 1019).

King Cnut becomes ruler of a great Anglo-Scandinavian empire

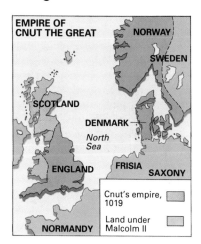

EMPIRE OF CNUT THE GREAT

NORWAY
SWEDEN
SCOTLAND
DENMARK
North Sea
ENGLAND
FRISIA
SAXONY
NORMANDY

Cnut's empire, 1019
Land under Malcolm II

England, 1019
The kingship of Cnut has been a revelation to the English. Enormous benefits have flowed from his accession, and no one could have guessed that such a young man – he is still only 24 – could rule so wisely, or prove so tough.

For the first 12 months after his takeover on the death of King Edmund Ironside in 1016, Cnut treated England as a conquered land. He divided the country into four military districts and murdered likely rivals and various malcontents. But once stability was

restored, he dismissed most of his fleet – a huge drain on national resources – agreed a return to the much-admired legal code of King Edgar and announced plans for a joint Anglo-Danish state, to marry the wealth of England to the armed might of Denmark.

His brother, King Harald of Denmark, died this year, and to forestall trouble Cnut, as his rightful heir, led a large fleet to Denmark and made himself king there. He believes that England is set for a period of peace and prosperity as part of this empire (→ 1023).

King Malcolm of Scots takes over Lothian and Strathclyde

Carham, Northumberland, 1016
King Malcolm II of Scots has pulled off a remarkable double success in his latest campaign to extend and consolidate his southern border. He has secured firm control of Lothian and Strathclyde, following the crushing defeat of his old enemy Earl Uhtred of Northumbria at Carham on the river Tweed. Mal-

colm's huge Scottish army was bolstered by the support of Owen the Bald, the king of Strathclyde, who died in the battle. Following the battle – in which the men of Northumbria suffered very heavy losses – Malcolm's overlordship of Lothian, the most northerly part of Northumbria, seems more or less secure, with the river Tweed as the

border between England and Scotland.

At the same time, the death of King Owen has allowed Malcolm to impose direct Scottish rule on the British kingdom of Strathclyde, long semi-independent under Scots overlordship. Malcolm will rule there through his grandson, Duncan (→ 1027).

Uncertainty grips Britain as dynasties rise and fall

Malcolm bequeaths Scotland to grandson

Scotland, 1034

King Malcolm II of Scotland, hailed by his countrymen as "the honour of all the west of Europe", has died of wounds after a conflict in Moray. He was over 80, and had ruled Scotland for 28 years. He will be chiefly remembered for securing control of Strathclyde and Lothian, and for establishing a cohesive Scottish kingdom. In accordance with his wishes, his grandson Duncan, the 33-year-old son of his eldest daughter, Bethoc, has been proclaimed king of a larger inheritance than any of his predecessors had.

The accession of Duncan marks an important break with the discredited system of *tanistry*, which has traditionally regulated the Scottish succession. Under this system the succession was shared between two branches of the dynasty of Kenneth mac Alpin, and passed from one branch to the other, from uncle to nephew, or from cousin to cousin, with each king naming his *tanist*, or successor. Its chief effect, however, was to ensure a constant state of feud between the two royal families. Malcolm was determined to keep the throne in his own family. To this end, he killed the male descendants of his cousin and predecessor, Kenneth III.

A later engraving of King Malcolm.

An imaginative portrait of Duncan.

Macbeth kills Duncan and seizes throne

Grampian, 1040

Macbeth, the Earl of Moray, has seized the throne of Scotland after killing the 39-year-old King Duncan in battle at Pitgaveny, near Elgin. Macbeth himself has no rightful claim to the throne, but his wife, Gruoch, is a granddaughter of Kenneth III, who was murdered by Malcolm II, Duncan's grandfather. This new killing reopens the bloody feud that ravaged the mac Alpin dynasty about 40 years ago.

During Duncan's six-year reign doubts were raised over his ability as a war leader, and he is thought to have provoked Macbeth by interfering in the affairs of Moray. Duncan's sons, Malcolm and Donald, have fled into exile in Northumbria and Ireland (→ 1045).

King in Scotland: Macbeth.

Cnut's death causes breakup of empire

London, 1037

With the death of Cnut his empire of England, Denmark and Norway has begun to fall apart. Cnut died young, aged only about 40, but it is clear that he intended England and Denmark to pass to Harthacnut, his only legitimate son by Emma of Normandy, Æthelred II's widow.

But Harthacnut is in Denmark, menaced by King Magnus of Norway and unable to leave, and his half-brother Harold, Cnut's son by his mistress Ælfgifu, has taken over. At first it was intended that he should be no more than regent, but his powerful mother rallied the great magnates behind Harold and he has now been declared king. Despite this, there is every reason to believe that his mother will be the real power in the land (→ 17/3/40).

Welsh king crushes English on Severn

Shropshire, February 1039

Gruffudd ap Llywelyn, the new king of Gwynedd and Powys, has made his mark by surprising a large English force encamped on the banks of the river Severn and inflicting a crushing defeat upon it. The clash, which happened at Rhyd y Groes, a ford near Welshpool, has sent a clear signal to Gruffudd's neighbours that Gwynedd is again a power to be reckoned with.

The English, led by Gruffudd's old enemy Edwin, the brother of Earl Leofric of Mercia, were caught off guard by the Welsh attack. Edwin fell in the battle, with many other Mercian nobles and troops. The rout was so devastating that Gruffudd need not fear a counter-attack, and the English can expect further surprise raids (→ 1055).

Danish line ends when king drops dead

English coins showing Harthacnut (r), and Harold, who usurped his throne.

London, 8 June 1042

After a reign of less than two years Harthacnut, the son of Cnut, has dropped dead while drinking heavily at a retainer's wedding. He was about 23, and will not be greatly missed, as his brutal actions since coming to England have alienated many of his old supporters.

When Cnut died Harthacnut was tied down in Denmark, and the throne was usurped by his half-brother Harold. Harthacnut later planned to invade England, but Harold's death allowed him to succeed in peace. He spent most of his short reign drinking and roistering, but he had a benign streak, recalling his half-brother Edward, the surviving son of Æthelred II, from exile and taking him into his household. Edward's brother Alfred had returned under Harold but had died after being cruelly blinded.

Edward is almost certain to be elected king by the *Witan* [royal council], marking a return to the Wessex dynasty. But Edward, who is about 37, is half-Norman by birth and all Norman by training, having spent the last 25 years of his life in Normandy.

Edward
the Confessor
1042–1066

Macbeth
1040–1057
Lulach
1057–1058
Malcolm III
1058–1093

Winchester, 3 April 1043. Edward is crowned king (→16/11/43).

Westminster, 1044. Edward pardons his mother, Queen Emma, and reinstates her confidant Bishop Stigand; she will have no political role (→6/3/52).

Dyfed, 1044. Gruffudd ap Rhydderch succeeds as ruler of Deheubarth (→1047).

Bath, 23 January 1045. Edward marries Edith, the daughter of Earl Godwin (→1047).

Tayside, 1045. Macbeth, who killed King Duncan in 1040, secures his throne with the murder of Crinan, Duncan's father and the abbot of Dunkeld (→1050).

Dyfed, 1047. Despite Gruffudd ap Llywelyn's use of English help, Gruffudd ap Rhydderch succeeds in throwing off north Welsh domination.

Herefordshire, 1047. Edward banishes Earl Sweyn, the son of Earl Godwin, for impropriety, and promotes his own nephew, Ralph de Mantes, to an earldom, a position hitherto held only by Anglo-Danish nobles (→1051).

Norway, 25 October 1047. King Magnus of Norway dies, and with him a Norwegian invasion threat to England. His uncle Harald *Hardrada* [the Ruthless] succeeds him (→1/1066).

Rome, 1050. Macbeth is on a pilgrimage, handing out money "like seed" to the poor, according to one report (→27/7/54).

Southern England, 1051. Earl Godwin leads a revolt against Norman influence; it fails, and he is banished with his family apart from his daughter, Queen Edith (→10/1052).

England, October 1051. Edward begins divorce proceedings against his wife, Edith, after the exile of her father, Earl Godwin of Wessex (→10/1052).

London, winter 1051. William, the Duke of Normandy, visits the English court; it is rumoured that King Edward intends to make him his heir.

Winchester, 6 March 1052. Emma, the queen mother, dies.

Winchester, 15 April 1053. Godwin, who forced a settlement on Edward last year, dies; his son Harold becomes Earl of Wessex and main royal adviser (→1064).

Northumbria, 1055. Tostig, the brother of Earl Harold, is the first southerner to become Earl of Northumbria (→28/10/65).

London, 1057. Edward, the son of Edmund Ironside, returns from exile but dies soon after.

Wales, 1058. Gruffudd ap Llywelyn allies with Magnus, the son of Norways's King Harald, to attack England (→7/1063).

Northumbria, 1061. King Malcolm III of Scots raids lands governed by his old ally, Earl Tostig of Northumbria (→1069).

Wales, July 1063. Campaigns by Earl Tostig and his brother Earl Harold put Gruffudd ap Llywelyn to flight (→5/8/63).

Westminster, 28 Dec 1065. Queen Edith consecrates the new abbey church; Edward is too ill to attend (→5/1/66).

London, 5 January 1066. King Edward dies, having reportedly designated Earl Harold of Wessex as his successor (→6/1/66).

King Edward dispossesses his mother

Edward is crowned on Easter Day, from a mid-13th-century manuscript.

Winchester, 16 November 1043
King Edward, who was crowned at Easter, dropped in on his mother, Queen Emma, today with three of his mightiest lords. But this was no courtesy call. The king stripped her of all her lands and possessions and announced that he was sacking her chief confidant, Bishop Stigand.

Rumours are afoot that Emma has backed King Magnus of Norway, who claims the English throne. Her Scandinavian links are certainly strong; she is a great-granddaughter of the Viking Rollo, the ancestor of the dukes of Normandy, and in 1017 she married King Cnut a year after the death of her first husband, King Æthelred II, Edward's father. As a result Edward spent 25 years in exile, and although Cnut and Emma's son Harthacnut invited him back two years ago, the years of exile seem to have destroyed the family bonds between Edward and Emma (→1044).

Nobles thwart king's pro-Norman policy

Westminster, October 1052
King Edward has been forced into a humiliating climbdown following a bitter row over his appointment of Normans to top jobs in England. Edward, half-Norman himself and mostly brought up in Normandy, upset many nobles last year by making a Norman, Robert of Jumièges, archbishop of Canterbury.

The matter simmered for months until, in September, the arrogant behaviour of a Norman count's retinue sparked a bloody riot at Dover. Edward, the count's host, ordered Godwin, the most powerful lord in the kingdom, to teach Dover a lesson; he refused and after a rebellion was expelled from England with all his family except his daughter Edith, Edward's wife. She was sent to a nunnery. Godwin returned in June and, joining forces with his son Harold, has staged a spectacular comeback. Godwin, who says his row is not with Edward himself, has been reinstated, along with the queen, while Archbishop Robert and other influential Frenchmen have fled (→1059).

Royal power struggle hits Scotland

Defeated Macbeth cedes half kingdom

Scone, Tayside, 27 July 1054
King Macbeth of Scots has had to give up half his kingdom after suffering defeat in a bitter clash at Dunsinane, near Scone. His vanquisher was Siward, the Earl of Northumbria, who led a combined English, Scandinavian and Scottish force. After the battle, Macbeth, supported by Normans who had fled from England after Earl Godwin's rebellion in 1052, managed to escape to the north, leaving Siward to establish his nephew Malcolm *Canmore* [Bighead] in control of Lothian and Strathclyde.

Malcolm is the son of King Duncan, who died in battle with Macbeth in 1040. For the past 14 years he has been living in exile in England with his maternal relatives, the Siwards, as a protegé of King Edward, awaiting his chance to regain the throne. Macbeth has beaten off several challenges to his rule, and in 1050 he felt secure enough to embark on a pilgrimage to Rome, where he is said to have scattered alms "like seed" to the poor. He has also been a generous benefactor to the religious community on St Serf's Island in Loch Leven. Now, however, the tide of fortune appears to be against him (→ 15/8/57).

A anonymous picture (1901) of a production of Shakespeare's "Macbeth".

Reign of Macbeth ends amid bloodshed

Grampian, 15 August 1057
Only three years after his ignominious defeat by Siward, the Earl of Northumbria, at the battle of Dunsinane, King Macbeth of Scots has died of wounds received in a skirmish with his rival, Malcolm. The two men came into violent conflict at Lumphanan, about 20 miles (32km) west of Aberdeen.

Malcolm, the son of the late King Duncan, established control of the southern regions of the kingdom, Strathclyde and Lothian, after Macbeth's defeat in 1054. However,

another obstacle now stands in his path to the throne of Scotland: Lulach, the 25-year-old son of Macbeth's wife, Gruoch, and her first husband, Gillacomean, Macbeth's predecessor as Earl of Moray. As Macbeth's stepson, his supporters in the north have proclaimed him king at Scone.

However, after spending 14 years in exile following his father's death, Malcolm is not to be thwarted in his ambition. He has no intention whatsoever of allowing Lulach to rule in peace (→ 17/3/58).

Wales is once more united under rule of Gwynedd's king

Wales, 1055
Wales is united under a single king following the defeat and death of Gruffudd ap Rhydderch, the ruler of the southern kingdom of Deheubarth, by Gruffudd ap Llywelyn, the king of Gwynedd. The defeat of Gruffudd of Deheubarth brings to a close many years of rivalry and generally destructive military duelling between the rulers of the north and the south, punctuated by raids across the border into England. With one supreme overlord to unite the several Welsh kingdoms, the Welsh may be able to harass their English neighbours even more.

Gruffudd of Gwynedd has won Welsh unity by a combination of boldness and resourcefulness, especially for one daring attack on the English. In 1047 he enlisted the help of Earl Sweyn, the eldest son of Earl Godwin of Wessex, who died in 1052. Sweyn and Gruffudd entered south Wales and crushed Gruffudd ap Rhydderch's followers as soon as they were sighted. They then ambushed the Deheubarth royal household, killing 140 of them before they could reach their main force. But Gruffudd ap Rhydderch narrowly escaped to be a thorn in the side of both the English and his Welsh rivals for another eight years (→ 1058).

Council puts limits on the king's power

Westminster, 1052
The recent crisis sparked by the Norman influence at King Edward's court [*see opposite*] highlights the key role in state affairs of the king's royal council, the *Witena gemot* or *Witan*, literally the council of the wise. When Earl Godwin rebelled he had to face the Witan to answer the king's charges, and after his defiant return from exile the Witan heard his defence and agreed to his reinstatement.

The Witan has existed in some form for around four centuries and comprises a cross-section of the powerful interest groups in the realm. The king usually pre-

sides, and the body may include the queen, the royal sons, *ealdormen* [regional governors], *thanes* [royal followers], bishops and abbots. Some Witans have even included Danish lords and Celtic princes.

Custom requires that kings consult the Witan on important matters of state, and it plays a major part in kingmaking. In a sense England has an elected monarchy, because it is hard for a king to wield power without the Witan's approval, and its voice can be vital in succession disputes; it offered the crown to Cnut in 1016 and to Edward himself ten years ago.

King Edward consults his nobles: from the Bayeux Tapestry, c.1077.

Scots strife ends as Malcolm succeeds

Grampian, 17 March 1058
Malcolm Canmore has finally achieved his desire of becoming king of Scotland. His last hurdle to the throne was cleared today when Macbeth's stepson, King Lulach, died in an ambush at Essie in Strathbogie. Lulach was enthroned just a few months ago, after his step-father was killed by Malcolm in a clash at Lumphanan, to the west of Aberdeen.

As Malcolm III, the new king has now regained the throne of which his father, Duncan, was violently deprived by Macbeth 18 years ago. He has been the effective ruler of Strathclyde and Lothian since 1054, when Macbeth was defeated at the battle of Dunsinane; now, with the dispatch of Lulach, Scotland is reunited under a single king (→ 1061).

King Malcolm: a later portrait.

Gruffudd is killed

Wales, 5 August 1063
King Gruffudd ap Llywelyn, the man who united Wales and proved a thorn in the side of England, has been killed by his own men. Gruffudd, a fugitive since this summer's campaign of the English under Earl Harold and his brother Tostig, had hoped to escape to Ireland to raise forces for a comeback. No one is sure who was behind Gruffudd's assassins, although his head and the prow of his ship have been sent to Earl Harold. What is certain is that Wales is divided and weakened.

Edward orders abbey as last resting place

Edward holding Westminster abbey, which he founded: a C20th banner.

Westminster, 1059
King Edward is now an elderly man of 54 and has decided that the abbey of St Peter at Westminster, two miles upstream from London, will be his last resting place. Work has already begun on a great new church in the grandest continental style, where he will be buried.

The abbey, a rather poor monastery on a marshy island, might at first sight seem an odd place for a royal burial, although King Harold "Harefoot" was buried there in 1040 (his corpse was later dumped in a bog on the orders of his successor Harthacnut.) Edward's father, King Æthelred, was buried in St Paul's in London, and his mother, Queen Emma, who died in 1052, lies at Winchester with her second husband, King Cnut.

But Edward, like his wife Queen Edith, is a pious man and especially reveres St Peter, Westminster's patron saint. Indeed, his piety is such that he is said to live a celibate life, which has raised the question of who will succeed him. A nephew, also called Edward, who was exiled by King Cnut when still a baby, was tracked down in Hungary and returned to England in 1057, only to die within weeks. The king has vowed to bring up Edward's young son, Edgar, as his own. It is on this infant that the future of Alfred's line now hangs (→ 28/10/65).

Harold moves to quell northern uprising

Oxford, 28 October 1065
Concern for King Edward's failing health is growing in the wake of a rebellion by Northumbria against its earl, Tostig, the brother of Queen Edith and Earl Harold of Wessex. Harold himself met rebel leaders today at Oxford and on the king's behalf agreed to their demand that his brother be outlawed.

The uprising began on 3 October when Northumbrian rebels marched on York, butchered Tostig's men and pillaged arms and gold. They declared Morcar, the brother of Earl Edwin of Mercia, their new earl and headed south to face the king. As in 1052, when Tostig's father Godwin rebelled, Edward gave in rather than risk a civil war.

Harold tried to save Tostig, but his brother has fled to Flanders suspecting him of provoking the revolt to clear his own path to the throne. But the general view at court is that Tostig brought his fate on himself through his own brutal misrule. Harold now has to win over Edwin and Morcar if he is to stand a chance of success (→ 28/12).

Mystery surrounds Norman oath claim

Normandy, 1064
The key question of who will succeed Edward, now a sick man of almost 60, as king of England has been complicated further by claims that Earl Harold Godwinson, the powerful brother of Queen Edith, who is strongly tipped as a candidate, has sworn allegiance to Duke William of Normandy and promised to help him to the throne.

Harold's pledge to William apparently came after he and his party, who were heading for the continent on royal business, were driven ashore in Normandy. A local count, Guy of Ponthieu, seized the Englishmen, but as Guy was a vassal of William, the duke soon obtained Harold's release and took him to his court, where the Englishmen were lavishly entertained. Harold even joined William on a campaign against Duke Conan of Brittany, performing heroic deeds such as rescuing some of William's troops from quicksand.

The episode remains shrouded in mystery. What was Harold's original mission? Was his oath to William made at the express wish of King Edward, who is known to have Norman sympathies and is a cousin of the duke? Most importantly, will the ambitious Harold, the mightiest magnate in England, keep his promise (→ 1/1066).

A model ruler: King David, from a psalter made at the royal city of Winchester, c.1060.

Succession crisis looms as Harold succeeds Edward

Westminster, 6 January 1066
A wintry chill hung over the new abbey church of Westminster today as the most powerful men in the land assembled to bury and to crown their king. Yesterday King Edward finally succumbed after months of illness; today the magnates of England hastily consecrated Earl Harold of Wessex as his successor. It is a decision which is bound to have powerful repercussions. The king's death had been expected for weeks. The strain of facing the Northumbrian uprising last autumn took a heavy toll, and Edward fell ill – probably with a stroke – soon afterwards.

By 28 December he was too weak to witness the consecration of his new abbey at Westminster, the greatest monument to his piety; a week later he was buried there. Because the king and the queen had no children – allegedly because of Edward's celibacy – one issue dominated the later years of his reign: who would follow him. Edward's nobles have wasted no time in making up their minds, and the official version is that their choice, Harold, received Edward's blessing at the dying king's bedside.

From their point of view the election of Harold makes sense; there are rumours that King Harald of Norway and Duke William of Normandy will press claims to the throne and that Tostig, Harold's exiled brother, might return in force with the support of his ally King Malcolm of Scots. If these fears prove justified England will need strong leadership, and Edward's great-nephew Edgar, who is still a youth, has been passed over in favour of Harold, who will be a tough nut to crack (→ 11/10/63).

The nobles' choice: Harold Godwinson

January 1066
Earl Harold Godwinson of Wessex, or King Harold II as he has become, is a popular choice as king for the nobles of the realm. Although he has no direct claim by blood, his family has long been close to the throne and Edith, King Edward's widow, is Harold's sister.

Harold was born in around 1022, the son of the formidable Godwin, whom he succeeded as Earl of Wessex – the most powerful man after the king – in 1053. Gytha, his mother, is a Scandinavian princess related by marriage to King Cnut.

Godwin's sons were rapidly promoted under King Edward, who made Harold Earl of East Anglia in 1044. He went into brief exile after Godwin's rebellion of 1051, but was restored on his father's comeback the next year. Renowned for his intelligence and bravery, Harold made his mark as a general in his

Ready for battle: King Harold.

campaign in Wales three years ago. This is probably a key factor in the widespread support for his succession; despite the stronger dynastic claims of Edgar the Atheling, Harold is best able to defend the kingdom from possible attack.

The Norman champion: Duke William

January 1066
Duke William of Normandy was born in 1028, the bastard son of the fearsome Duke Robert "the Devil" and Herleve, the daughter of a prosperous tanner from Falaise. Duke Robert, who died in 1035, was the nephew of Queen Emma, King Edward's mother; William's claim is rooted in this blood tie.

William became duke in 1035, when Duke Robert died on his way back from a crusade. He had persuaded his barons to accept his bastard as his heir before he went away, but his death unleashed years of turmoil throughout Normandy; not until 1054 was William secure.

William insists that King Edward, who had spent years of exile in his mother's homeland and had many Norman advisers, made him his heir early in 1051. This was confirmed when the duke visited England later that year, and in 1064,

The ambitious Duke William.

when Earl Harold swore an oath to help him to the throne. Even if Edward made Harold his heir on his deathbed, William says, Harold was bound by his oath. On past form, the Norman will not let matters rest as they stand (→ 18/6).

The boy contender: Edgar the Atheling

January 1066
Edgar the Atheling, or royal prince, has the strongest claim to the throne by blood but, because he is only about 14, probably the least chance of winning it. He was born when his father Edward, the son of King Edmund Ironside, was living in Hungary, after the family had fled from King Cnut. In 1057 a mission from King Edward traced Edgar's father and persuaded him to come back to England as the king's heir. Edward died soon after, and Edgar and his two sisters were brought up at court (→ 10/1066).

How the main claimants are related

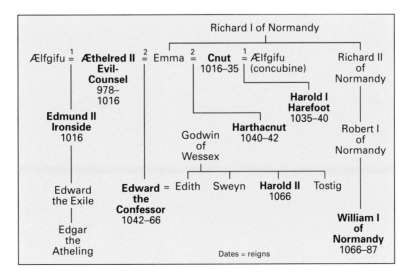

| | Richard I of Normandy | | |

Ælfgifu ¹= **Æthelred II Evil-Counsel 978–1016** ²= Emma ²= **Cnut 1016–35** ¹= Ælfgifu (concubine) / Richard II of Normandy

Edmund II Ironside 1016

Harold I Harefoot 1035–40

Godwin of Wessex / **Harthacnut 1040–42** / Robert I of Normandy

Edward the Exile / **Edward the Confessor 1042–66** = Edith / Sweyn / **Harold II 1066** / Tostig

Edgar the Atheling

William I of Normandy 1066–87

Dates = reigns

Norway's claimant: 'Ruthless' Harald

January 1066
Born in 1016, King Harald *Hardrada* [the Ruthless] has ruled Norway since 1047. His predecessor and nephew, King Magnus, agreed with King Harthacnut (then of Denmark, later of England) that if either died without issue the other would succeed. Harthacnut died childless in 1042; Magnus failed to establish his claim, but Harald is now poised to revive it (→ 8/1066).

Overleaf: Preparing to invade, shown on the Bayeux Tapestry.

PORTANT:ARMAS: ADNAV

TRAHVN

CVMVIN

Harold II
1066
William I
1066–1087

Malcolm III
1058–1093

London, January. Harold marries Ealdgyth, the widow of Gruffudd ap Llywelyn of Wales and sister of Earls Edwin of Mercia and Morcar of Northumbria.

Humberside, May. Earls Edwin and Morcar defeat Tostig, the exiled brother of Harold, who has been harrying the coasts; he takes refuge with Malcolm III of Scots (→ 20/9).

Caen, Normandy, 18 June. William offers his daughter Cecily as a nun to secure God's blessing for his invasion of England.

Rome, summer. A Norman mission persuades the pope to proclaim Duke William as the lawful claimant to the English throne by his relationship to Queen Emma and because of Harold's oath of 1064.

Orkney, August. King Harald *Hardrada* of Norway stops en route to his planned invasion of England (→ 20/9).

London, 8 September. Harold's fleet is damaged transferring here from the Isle of Wight (→ 20/9).

St Valery, Normandy, 12 September. William moves his invasion fleet to the mouth of the river Somme (→ 14/10).

Fulford, 20 September. Tostig and Harald Hardrada defeat Earls Edwin and Morcar (→ 24/9).

Tadcaster, 24 September. Harold and his army, after four days' march, prepare to fight Harald Hardrada (→ 25/9).

East Sussex, 13 October. Worn out by their march south, Harold's men arrive outside Hastings (→ 14/10).

London, October. After the death of Harold, Earls Edwin and Morcar choose Edgar the Atheling [royal prince], aged 14, as his successor (→ 1068).

Berkhamsted, December. The nobles join the lead of Edgar the Atheling and submit to William.

Rivals square up for royal showdown

Troops mobilised as tension grows

England, August 1066

Tension has steadily mounted since King Harold's coronation as he and his rivals have launched vigorous efforts in readiness for the widely-expected battle for the crown.

One of Harold's first acts after his accession was to marry Ealdgyth, the sister of the powerful Earls Edwin of Mercia and Morcar of Northumbria. Edwin and Morcar led last year's revolt against Harold's brother Earl Tostig, and proved the value of their support by seeing off an attempted comeback by Tostig in May. He is now in Scotland and is in contact with King Harald of Norway, who is reported to be planning to invade England in the near future.

King Harold's other main rival, the Duke of Normandy, is also preparing to mount an invasion. Since the spring William has been assembling an army and a fleet and has launched a diplomatic offensive, making an important coup by securing the support of the pope. The pope has sent him a special banner in confirmation of his blessing. Harold is taking William's threat seriously. He has stationed troops along the south coast and assumed personal command of a large fleet off the Isle of Wight.

Hectic combat: a C13th illustration of the Battle of Stamford Bridge.

Hardrada is routed at Stamford Bridge

York, 25 September 1066

King Harold's supporters are jubilant tonight after the crushing defeat and death of one of his rivals, King Harald *Hardrada* of Norway, at Stamford Bridge, 7 miles (11km) east of York on the river Derwent.

Harald's massive invasion fleet landed on the Northumbrian coast early this month and joined up with Tostig, King Harold's rebel brother. The combined force then sailed down the coast, harrying and pillaging as it went. The few English ships in the area withdrew up the Ouse and inland to Tadcaster; Harald anchored his own fleet nearby to bar their escape and marched on York, 10 miles from his base.

Five days ago the Norwegians met stiff resistance from Earl Edwin of Mercia and his brother, Earl Morcar of Northumbria, at Gate Fulford, just south of York.

Harald won the day, occupied York and withdrew to Stamford Bridge to draft terms to impose on the defeated earls. No final agreement was signed. As soon as King Harold had learnt of the invasion he had set out on a lightning advance from the south; today he marched through York and took his rival by surprise. The rout was total. Both Harald and Tostig fell in a slaughter so great that the survivors are heading home in just 24 of their original 300 ships (→ 2/10).

Harold heads south as Duke William lands unopposed in Sussex

Duke William and his men land in Sussex: an 18th-century engraving.

York, 2 October 1066

Today, barely a week after his resounding victory at Stamford Bridge, news has reached King Harold at York that Duke William of Normandy, his remaining rival for the throne, has landed in Sussex with a great invasion fleet. Harold is heading south without delay.

For days strong northerlies have kept the duke's fleet holed up in the mouth of the Somme, but on 27 September the wind changed and William set sail. He met no opposition: King Harold's Channel fleet had been moved to London. Thus on Thursday 28 September, at nine in the morning, William dropped anchor in Pevensey Bay (→ 13/10).

William wins after a long, hard battle at Hastings

The Battle of Hastings, as depicted in the Bayeux Tapestry; it is not certain that the knight struck in the eye beneath the name Harold (r) is the king.

Harold is slain in battle at Hastings

East Sussex, 14 October 1066

King Harold is dead, fallen in a day of savage fighting against Duke William of Normandy on a hillside just north of Hastings. The battered remnants of Harold's army have dispersed into the dusk, leaving William the master of the battlefield.

The king's army of about 7,000 marched the 250 miles from York to Sussex via London in an amazing 11 days. But the men were then exhausted, and Harold chose not to wait for his full force, despite the threat of a select, disciplined foe which, unlike the English, had archers and cavalry. Even so, when the battle began the English had the advantage of the high ground and seemed set for victory. But the duke rallied his men, and, although the English fought grimly, they crumbled when Harold fell, apparently to a random arrow (→ 12/1066).

Last claimant leads submission of English nobles to William

An imaginative view of Duke William killing Harold at the Battle of Hastings.

Hertfordshire, December 1066

Duke William's triumph is complete. The English have bowed to the inevitable and formally offered him the throne left vacant by the death of Harold at Hastings.

After Hastings the English nobles in London had turned to the remaining legitimate claimant to the throne, Edgar the Atheling [royal prince], the grandson of King Edmund Ironside, a boy of barely 15. At the same time the duke, in a bid to force London to submit, embarked on a broad path of destruction through Sussex, Kent – where he was held up for a month by a bout of dysentery – and westwards around London to Hertfordshire. As the duke progressed, Edgar's party lost heart until at Berkhamsted, some 20 miles north-west of London, Edgar himself led a delegation to William to offer him the crown. Norman rule has begun (→ 25/12).

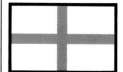

William I
1066–1087

Malcolm III
1058–1093

Westminster, 25 Dec 1066. Duke William of Normandy is crowned king of England.→

London, March 1067. King William begins a victory tour of Normandy; he leaves as regents William fitz Osbern, the newly-appointed Earl of Hereford, and his half-brother, Bishop Odo (→11/5/68).

Exeter and York, Spring 1068. William quashes revolts in the south-west and north.

Scotland, Spring 1068. Edgar the Atheling [royal prince], his mother and his sisters, Margaret and Christina, flee to Scotland (→18/7/74).

Westminster, 11 May 1068. Queen Matilda is crowned by Aldred, the archbishop of York.→

Yorkshire, September 1068. Matilda gives birth to her ninth child, a son, Henry (→2/11/83).

Scotland, 1069. King Malcolm III of Scots, recently widowed, marries Margaret, the sister of Edgar the Atheling (→87).

Abernethy, 15 August 1072. Malcolm III submits to William; his son, Duncan, is taken hostage, and Edgar the Atheling has to go to Flanders (→1072).

Wales, 1072. Maredudd of Deheubarth is killed by the Norman-backed Caradog ap Gruffudd, the ruler of Gwent (→1081).

Edinburgh, 8 July 1074. Edgar the Atheling returns to the Scottish court from exile.

Scotland, 1074. Malcolm III begins to refortify the castle at Edinburgh (→9/1079).

Winchester, 1074. William's second son, Richard, dies of injuries from a riding accident.

Normandy, Spring 1077. William makes peace with Fulk IV of Anjou and King Philip of France after having been defeated in Brittany last year (→1078).

London, 1078. William begins the building of the White Tower (→1/1079).

Normandy, January 1079. William is defeated at Gerberoi by his rebellious eldest son, Robert Curthose (→1080).

Northern England, Sept 1079. Malcolm III breaks the truce of 1072 and devastates the north.→

Falkirk, Autumn 1080. After a reconciliation of father and son, early this year, Robert Curthose heads north to negotiate a peace deal with Malcolm III (→1083).

Mynydd Carn, Dyfed, 1081. Gruffudd ap Cynan of Gwynedd and Rhys ap Tewdwr of Deheubarth defeat Caradog ap Gruffudd of Gwent and his Norman allies, but Gruffudd is captured and imprisoned by Normans soon after the battle.

Normandy, 2 November 1083. Queen Matilda dies at Caen.

Normandy, Autumn 1083. Robert Curthose again rebels against his father, King William (→12/9/87).

Denmark, 1086. Cnut, the king of Denmark, who had planned to invade England, is murdered.

Normandy, 9 September 1087. William dies; his third son, William Rufus, will be king, leaving Normandy to his eldest son, Robert (→12/9).

Conqueror is crowned

Westminster, Christmas Day 1066
William the Bastard, the Duke of Normandy and conqueror of England, was crowned today in Westminster abbey. The archbishop of York officiated at the coronation of the third king to sit on the English throne in less than a year.

The ceremony was designed to stress continuity rather than conquest. However, after swearing to govern justly, William introduced a change to the traditional ceremony which nearly led to disaster. All those present were asked in English and French whether they acknowledged William as their rightful king. The Norman guards outside thought that the shouts of acclaim were the start of a revolt, and in a panic burnt down all the houses around the church. When the uproar subsided the ceremony continued smoothly until William – visibly shaken by the confusion – was finally crowned and enthroned.

William's wife Matilda is still in Normandy and missed today's ceremony. The new king intends to give her a coronation of her own.

William leaves Westminster abbey after his trouble-marred coronation.

William: fierce warrior and family man

Westminster, 11 May 1068
King William's consort, Matilda, was crowned queen of England in the abbey today, 18 months after his own coronation. Unlike previous queens she was acclaimed as queen ordained by God.

The marriage between William and Matilda is a byword for fidelity. Kings are expected to have mistresses; William has none. They are oddly matched, he being nearly six feet tall and she only just over four feet. When he was 18, she rejected his proposals, saying that she would marry no bastard. According to popular belief, he rode straight to her palace – she is the granddaughter of a king of France – forced his way in and dragged her round the room by her hair. This won her heart. Three years later the pope banned them from marrying, apparently because they were distant cousins. Thanks to Lanfranc, the distinguished abbot of Bec in Normandy, the ban was lifted, and the couple married in about 1050.

William's affection for Matilda is his one tender streak. He made her his regent in Normandy, and she is the only person who has defied him with impunity. He is an illiterate, ruthless soldier of Viking blood, prone to fearful rages – witness the revenge he once took on the defenders of Alençon, whose hands and feet he cut off because they had mocked his bastardy. He is known for his cruelty and avarice, yet also for his shrewdness and sobriety and his devout Christianity – but not always to the point of bowing to papal authority (→9/1068).

Duke William is crowned king.

Royal Norman broom sweeps through English life

English to lose top government jobs

England, 1070

The Normanisation of English life is proceeding apace, and English holders of office in church and state are now few and far between. The officers of the royal household, the steward and butler, the constable and the chancellor, have all been replaced by Normans. King William has been lavish in rewarding the Norman counts who came over with his army, on the principle that all land belongs to the king.

The old English nobility, the Siwards of Northumbria, Edwin of Mercia and the Godwins of Wessex have been dispossessed and their earldoms given to Normans. William made his half-brother, Odo of Bayeux, Earl of Kent and his crony William fitz Osbern Earl of Hereford. Many "honours" – lands centred on castles – were given to tenants-in-chief obliged to provide the king with many armed knights to serve him. The earls on the Welsh and Scottish borders are to maintain the security of the realm. The sheriffs of the English shires have been replaced by Normans who thereby become rich.

Meanwhile the bishops and abbots of the church are gradually being replaced by Normans. Soon Wulfstan of Worcester may be the only English-born bishop left.

The new king has reformed English public life: a C13th portrait of William.

William stamps out 'resistance' rebels

Isle of Ely, April 1071

The Norman conquest of England seems to be complete. Another flicker of resistance died out here when King William first besieged the rebels and then received their submission – but failed to capture their leader, Hereward the Wake. He disappeared into the swampy maze of the Fens with a few of his noble friends after his Danish support faded away last year.

The four and a half years since the Battle of Hastings have seen frequent risings against Norman rule all over the kingdom, all of which have been put down with exemplary ruthlessness by William. There have been risings in Kent, Devon and Cornwall, the Welsh Marches, the Midlands and Northumbria. In Durham a Norman earl, Robert de Comines, was trapped with 900 men and burnt alive.

Danish forces, under Cnut's nephew, King Sweyn, helped the rebels take York, but withdrew when William appeared with his army. He retaliated by systematically devastating the land north of the Humber. Every town, village and house between York and Durham is said to have been destroyed and all crops, herds and flocks burnt. In the resulting famine, thousands perished (→ 1077).

William's abbot to be new archbishop

Winchester, April 1070

King William has shown that he intends to make his authority over the church in England supreme, as it is in Normandy, by deposing the English archbishop of Canterbury, Stigand, with the connivance of the pope, at his Easter council here. The new archbishop is set to be Lanfranc, an Italian whom William made abbot of St Stephen's in Caen, partly out of gratitude for his obtaining papal consent for William's marriage to Matilda. He is trusted by William to impose Norman ways upon the English church.

A great warrior: King William.

English prince to be expelled as price of Anglo-Scottish peace

Tayside, 1072

A deal struck at Abernethy, southeast of Perth, has staved off a potentially bloody encounter between the Scots and English. King William of England had invaded Scotland by the eastern route with naval support.

Deciding not to engage William's better-equipped Norman cavalry, Malcolm III, the Scottish king, made a show of drawing the invaders into the highlands north of the Tay river. However, at Abernethy, in the shadow of an ancient Pictish tower, the two kings got down to talks and reached a compromise to avoid bloodshed. William agreed to withdraw on three conditions. He insisted that Malcolm hand over his son Duncan as a hostage, make a face-saving show of submission, and expel from Scotland the English fugitive Edgar the Atheling [royal prince], the grandson of King Edmund Ironside. Malcolm reluctantly agreed to the terms.

The Scots had been expecting an English invasion for the past two years, in retaliation for King Malcolm's attack on Northumbria in 1070 and his marriage to Margaret, Edgar's sister, who sought sanctuary in Scotland with her mother, brother and sister in the wake of the Norman conquest (→ 1077).

King Malcolm leads brutal revenge raid

Northumbria, 8 September 1079
King Malcolm III of Scots has taken advantage of King William's absence in Normandy to launch a devastating raid into the north of England. He is now heading back into Scottish territory after three weeks of unopposed ravaging of the lands between the rivers Tweed and Tees.

The raid is in flagrant breach of the agreement struck between the two kings seven years ago at Abernethy on the Tay. This deal followed William's own attack on the Scots king, who was forced to recognise the Norman succession as a result. Malcolm is evidently intent on seeking revenge for his humiliation in 1072; he is taking advantage of William's own humiliating defeat in January at Gerberoi in Normandy, at the hands of his rebellious son Robert Curthose.

Little was spared by Malcolm's marauding troops. One place had a lucky escape, though. As the Scots advanced on Hexham a thick fog descended, saving the abbey from a terrible fate (→ 1090).

William creates 'New Forest' for hunting

Hunting grounds: William has created the "New Forest" as a deer preserve.

Hampshire, 1074
King William's passion for deer-hunting has led him to decree that a large area of southern Hampshire is to be set aside as a deer preserve, with savage penalties against poaching. It is called the "New Forest" and consists of 75,000 acres of empty wooded country to which he has added 20,000 more of cultivated land from which 2,000 inhabitants have been evicted. More than 20 villages and many more hamlets have ceased to exist. The forest laws that the king has brought into force are draconian: to kill a stag means death. Even to shoot arrows at one means losing one's hands, while merely disturbing the game can be punished by being blinded.

Many English rulers, such as King Edward, have been keen hunters, but the enclosure of so much land for his private pleasure is seen as yet another example of William's greed. "He loves the tall stags as if he were their father," writes the author of the *Anglo-Saxon Chronicle* – more than he does his subjects, he implies (→ 1077).

Conqueror honours widow of Edward

Westminster, 20 December 1075
Queen Edith, the widow of King Edward and sister of King Harold, defeated at Hastings, was buried today beside her husband in Westminster abbey as a mark of respect by King William. It is another instance of his desire to convince the people of the legitimacy of his claim to be Edward's chosen successor.

The abbey was Edward's great legacy to his people. It was consecrated exactly ten years ago, but he was too ill to attend the ceremony and died a few days later. He was buried before the high altar. His wife Edith, at his insistence, had lived a celibate life with him. Soon after the battle of Hastings she surrendered Winchester and the royal treasury to William, under threat of a siege. She has since lived in honourable retirement under William's protection.

Besides honouring Edith's claim to lie beside her husband, King William uses the abbey to show the continuity of his kingship. He was crowned there, as was his wife Matilda two years later.

Great tapestry commemorates Conquest

Queen Matilda and her ladies sew the Bayeux Tapestry: a Victorian painting.

Bayeux, Normandy, 14 July 1077
Odo, the bishop of Bayeux, ordered a 240-foot-long tapestry for his cathedral's dedication today. It tells in Latin the life story of William, his half-brother, who was present at the ceremony. Its climax depicts his victory over Harold at Hastings.

It is also a most effective piece of propaganda. In days when few men can read this picture-story is their only source of knowledge of recent history. One of the key episodes shows how the future King Harold, as Earl of Wessex, visited the court of Duke William and allegedly swore an oath of allegiance to him as the future king on two chests of holy relics – an oath that he never kept, but which was central to William's claim to the throne. Others depict William sailing to England and Harold, apparently, being fatally injured in the eye (→ 9/1088).

Pious Margaret encourages church reform

Scotland, 1087
Margaret of Scotland's confessor, Turgot – a Benedictine monk at Dunfermline priory – has been appointed prior of Durham. The queen, who has wrought great changes in the Scottish church, will miss his spiritual guidance. She has worked hard for reform of abuses which shocked her on her arrival here 20 years ago, urging the Scottish church to conform to Roman ways and opening up Scotland to English and continental influences.

Turgot himself describes the queen as a very godly and pious woman, rigorous in her religious observances. She and her husband, King Malcolm, founded the priory at Dunfermline, and she has shown great generosity to the church elsewhere in Fife. She is renowned throughout the kingdom for her concern for the needy. The sister of Edgar the Atheling, Margaret has taken steps to counter complaints about the English influence at church and court (→ 17/11/93).

A godly woman: Queen Margaret.

A royal son's road to courtly manhood

The king bestows a knighthood.

Westminster, Whit Sunday 1086

King William was at Westminster today to knight his son Henry, the youngest of his ten children and the only one born in England. The ceremony marks the formal end of the 17-year-old youth's childhood. Henry has probably had an upbringing typical of a king's son. A *paedagogus*, or tutor, usually a knight, will have taught his royal charge how to dress, speak and behave at court, table and prayer, as well as how to ride, hunt and fight in battle. Chaplains, musicians and tutors of reading teach more intellectual skills; literacy is increasingly seen as an important royal accomplishment (→ 10/1087).

William dies after falling from his horse

Normandy, 12 September 1087

King William was buried at Caen today in a gruesome ceremony at his abbey of St Stephen. He died at Rouen of injuries he received while leading the sack of Mantes in France. Among the burning ruins, his horse stumbled and threw him. He never recovered. During his dying weeks he confessed to the sins on his conscience: "I was bred to arms from my childhood and am stained with the rivers of blood that I have shed." Of his conquests in England he said: "I am prey to cruel fears and anxieties when I reflect with what barbarities they were accompanied." His body, now grossly fat, was too large for its stone sarcophagus and burst its bonds in a funeral hurriedly concluded by the choking mourners.

William is laid to rest at Caen.

Domains split between Conqueror's sons

Caen, 12 September 1087

Four days ago, on his deathbed, King William reluctantly separated his domains into two. Normandy passes to his eldest son, Robert Curthose, who has often revolted and is at present with William's enemy, Philip of France. William had warned that Robert is unfit to rule but was persuaded by his nobles to allow a normal inheritance.

To his second son, William, he gave his crown, sword and sceptre and a sealed letter to Archbishop Lanfranc, who is acting as regent, and ordered him to leave for England immediately. To his third son, Henry, he gave £5,000 in silver – a princely sum – but no land.

To his conquered people William leaves decidedly mixed memories. In the words of one writer he was "kind to those good men who loved God" but "stern beyond measure" to opponents. His new castles were "a sore burden to the poor", and he levied stiff taxes "most unjustly" because "he was sunk in greed". But although "the rich complained and the poor lamented," says the writer, William "was too relentless to care though all might hate him".

Royal fortresses remind conquered who is in charge

Newcastle upon Tyne, 1080

Robert Curthose, the eldest son of King William, has ordered the building of a great royal castle near the mouth of the river Tyne. The fortress will serve as a base for expeditions against marauding Scots and is the most northerly of the many castles built since 1066 to awe the kingdom into submission.

William's very first castle in England was actually built before the Conquest. This went up at Hastings a few days after his landing, while he was preparing for battle. Like the castle erected within the old Roman walls of London shortly after his coronation, it consisted of a simple earth mound, or motte, on top of which was a sturdy wooden tower. At London the mound was surrounded by a bailey (an area enclosed by a tall wooden rampart), and most castles follow this pattern.

The grandest and most formidable castles are built with towers of stone. This will be the case with the new castle on the Tyne and with the replacement for William's first tower at London, which was begun two years ago. The walls of this imposing building, designed by Bishop Gundulf of Rochester, will be over ten feet thick.

The White Tower at the Tower of London: building was begun in 1078 on William's orders.

'Domesday' survey reveals more royal landholdings than ever

A page from the "Domesday book".

Winchester, 1087

King William's comprehensive survey of the ownership and worth of his kingdom, which he called "The Description of All England" and to which his subjects have given the name of "Domesday" because it reminded them of the Last Judgement, has been completed in less than a year. The survey shows that the king personally holds a fifth of the land – more than any of his predecessors – and other Normans about half of the rest.

At his Great Council and Midwinter Feast at the end of 1085, the king consulted with his councillors about "how the land was peopled and with what sort of men", according to the *Anglo-Saxon Chronicle*. Because of the threat of a Danish invasion, he intended to levy a countrywide land tax.

Four commissioners were sent to every shire to discover how the land was divided in King Edward's time, who owns it now, and how many men and cattle it supports. Not a yard of land "nor so much as an ox nor a cow nor a swine" was omitted, runs the *Chronicle*. The parchment rolls cover all of England, except the most northerly counties; much of Yorkshire is listed as "waste", indicating the legacy of the repression in the 1070s.

William II
1087–1100

Malcolm III
1058–1093
Donald III
1093–1097
Duncan II 1094
Edgar 1097–1107

Westminster, 26 Sept 1087. William Rufus is crowned King William II of England (→ 15/7/88).

Normandy, October 1087. Henry, William's younger brother, buys land and the title of count from his brother, Duke Robert of Normandy (→ 6/8/1100).

England, 15 July 1088. William refuses to cede lands belonging to his mother, Queen Matilda, to his younger brother, Henry (→ 2/1091).

Kent, September 1088. Bishop Odo, after the siege of Rochester, is exiled for life by William, his nephew.

Rouen, 3 November 1090. Duke Robert and Count Henry stop a revolt, inspired by William, to claim the duchy.

Northumbria, 1090. Malcolm of Scotland invades, urged on by Edgar the Atheling (→ 11/1093).

England, 6 March 1093. Anselm, the abbot of Bec, finally accepts the archbishopric of Canterbury (→ 23/2/94).

Fife, 17 November 1093. Queen Margaret of Scotland dies on hearing of the murder of her husband and son.

Stonehaven, 11 Nov 1094. Donald III retakes the throne on the murder of his nephew, Duncan II, invested as king in May when Donald was deposed (→ 7/1095).

Wales, 1094. Cadwgan ap Bleddyn and Gruffudd ap Cynan, the princes of Powys and Gwynedd, initiate a Welsh revolt (→ 1116).

Winchester, 1096. Duke Robert resigns his lands in Normandy to William and joins the crusade. William raises taxes to finance the extension of Norman control (→ 15/7/99).

Scotland, 1099. Donald III, deposed and blinded on the orders of King Edgar, his nephew, dies (→ 8/1/07).

King's reign gets off to stormy start

Normandy tensions fuel royal rivalry

Rouen, Normandy, February 1091
William Rufus, the king of England, and his brother Duke Robert Curthose of Normandy made peace here today to end three years of sporadic warfare. It began with a rising to put Robert on the English throne, led by Bishop Odo, the uncle whom William Rufus had reinstated as Earl of Kent.

At Easter 1088 the conspirators rose against William, expecting Duke Robert to land with an army in the south-east. Odo and the rebels captured several towns and castles, including Rochester, Pevensey and Tonbridge. But the vanguard of the Norman fleet was sunk and Robert never arrived. Odo surrendered and was exiled.

William retaliated in 1090 by invading Normandy, part of which Robert had sold to Henry, their younger brother. When William besieged Robert in Rouen a rich merchant named Conant opened the gates to William, but at the same moment Henry arrived with relief forces and won the ensuing street battle. He then summoned Conant to the top of the castle tower and personally executed him by pushing him over the edge. But the elder brothers' new treaty disinherits Henry. He has now been driven out of Normandy (→ 1096).

The new king: William II, drawn by the C13th illustrator Matthew Paris.

Archbishop attacks long hair and decadence at Rufus's court

Hastings, 23 February 1094
A long-running quarrel between King William and Archbishop Anselm of Canterbury reached a new peak here today, where the king is preparing to sail for Normandy. In a sermon for Lent the archbishop attacked the king's courtiers for immorality, effeminacy and the practice of sodomy. He complained of their dandyism, mincing gait in curly-tipped shoes and long, girlish hair, combed and held in headbands. These fashions contrast with the short hair and plain garb of the Conqueror's time.

The king stubbornly refused to appoint an archbishop for four years after the death of Lanfranc, until he fell ill last year and thought he was going to die. Then he summoned Anselm, the abbot of Bec in Normandy, who was in England, to his bedside. Despite the pleas of king and clergy, Anselm refused until the crozier was forced into his hand. When the king recovered he could not get rid of Anselm, who insisted on the king giving back all the church's lands at Canterbury.

Anselm is an unworldly intellectual, with a habit of rebuking sinners, including the king. William, shorter than his father but equally fat, and dubbed "Rufus" (Latin for red) because of his choleric complexion, is a creature of impulse; Anselm has compared him to a young bull. He cracks blasphemous jokes and likes to swear "by the Holy Face of Lucca" (a famous icon). Inarticulate in public, he is reduced to blustering incoherence by his foul temper, but with friends and cronies (he is unmarried) he is jovial and generous. Rufus is wily, but has a streak of vain gullibilty. When brought a pair of new shoes that cost three shillings, he swore and demanded a dearer pair. The next pair were cheaper, but he was told the opposite, prompting the remark: "Now *these* are more fitted to our majesty" (→ 8/11/97).

King Malcolm dies with son in ambush

Northumbria, November 1093

King Malcolm III of Scots has been killed by a man who claimed to be his "sworn brother", in an ambush close to the river Aln. The trap was laid by Robert of Mowbray, the Earl of Northumberland, whose nephew, Arkil Morel, delivered the mortal wound. Malcolm's eldest son Edward was fatally pierced by a lance during the encounter, leaving the Scottish succession in doubt. At the time of the attack, Malcolm was engaged in his fifth attack on England, following a fruitless attempt to negotiate with William II at Gloucester last year over the English king's recent advances into Scottish territory.

Malcolm III came to the throne of Scotland in 1058, after his successful dispatch of Macbeth and his stepson, Lulach. His close ties with the English royal family – through his wife, Margaret – and his determination to hold on to territory in Cumbria and Northumbria repeatedly brought him into conflict with the new Norman dynasty in England. His policies ended in failure; he died with the status of a client vassal, and with William firmly in control of the disputed territory. The death of the king and his heir has plunged Scotland into uncertainty and a grief-stricken Queen Margaret into despair.

Rufus killed by accident – or was he?

Killed in a hunting accident: a later engraving of King William's death.

Winchester, 3 August 1100

The king of England, William Rufus, was killed yesterday in a mysterious hunting accident in the New Forest created by his father, William I. His body was brought here today on a charcoal-burner's cart and buried beneath the cathedral tower. His brother Henry, who was out hunting with him, rode here ahead of the body, seized the royal treasury and, after a council at which he was hurriedly elected king, rode on to London to secure the crown before the imminent return of the rightful heir, Robert, from his Crusade.

All that is known of the death is that William was struck in the chest by an arrow shot, it appears, by one of his companions, Walter Tirel. The king died immediately. Tirel rode off and made for France. Strangely, he was not pursued. People in general believe that the king's death was the judgement of God for his wicked way of life and his exiling of the saintly Archbishop Anselm. Rumours of plots to seize the throne abound.

Half-English Edgar is new Scots king

Tayside, October 1097

Edgar, a son of Malcolm III and his English wife, Margaret, is the new Scots king. He has secured the throne by defeating Donald Bane at Rescobie with an army paid for by William II and led by Edgar the Atheling, his maternal uncle. His victory ends a very disturbed period in Scotland in which the throne has been contested between three sons of Malcolm III and Malcolm's brother, Donald Bane.

When Malcolm died in 1093 the surprise successor was his 60-year-old brother Donald, returned from a long exile. The next year, however, Donald was overthrown by Duncan, Malcolm's son by his first wife, who had spent 21 years as a hostage in England. Duncan's coup was backed by William Rufus, but before 1094 had ended Duncan was himself murdered by his half-brother Edmund, a son of Queen Margaret. Edmund had acted in concert with his uncle Donald, and the two men then divided the rule of Scotland between them.

In 1095 William of England, claiming to act as overlord of Scotland, gave the crown to Malcolm's son Edgar, and he has now backed this move with force. Donald has been taken prisoner, and Edmund is said to be planning to retire to an English monastery (→ 1099).

King breaks with archbishop after feud

Anselm, the reforming archbishop.

Dover, 8 November 1097

Archbishop Anselm sailed from here today on his way to Rome to see the pope and, he hopes, be relieved of his archbishopric. He has not been allowed to reform the moral abuses of the kingdom, and neither he nor King William can endure the other's company. Their four-year quarrel came to a head last month when Anselm again demanded the calling of a council to reform such abuses as sodomy and long hair. He also demanded permission to go to consult the pope. William said that if Anselm went he would seize all the property of the archbishopric, and gave him 14 days to leave the kingdom. It looks as if Rufus has finally broken with his reluctant prelate (→ 9/10/1100).

Royal crusader brother enters Jerusalem

Jerusalem, 15 July 1099

Robert Curthose, the Duke of Normandy and brother of William Rufus, entered Jerusalem today at the head of the crusade which set out three years ago at the bidding of Pope Urban II. William lent his brother 10,000 marks and took over Normandy as a pledge for repayment. Robert's incompetence as a ruler is well-known. William has secured Normandy and taken Maine, regaining all his father's lands – no small achievement. He is planning the conquest of all western France. However it now seems likely that Robert will soon be back in England and that William's activities may lead to trouble between William I's ever-suspicious trio of sons once more (→ 2/8/01).

Robert Curthose: an effigy (c.1106).

Henry I	Edgar
1100–1135	1097–1107
	Alexander I
	1107–1124
	David I
	1124–1153

Westminster, 6 August 1100. Robert Curthose, the Duke of Normandy and William the Conqueror's eldest son, is again denied the throne as Henry is crowned in the abbey (→11/11).

Westminster, 9 October 1100. The saintly Archbishop Anselm of Canterbury returns.

Alton, Hants, 2 August 1101. Henry and Robert Curthose make a treaty under which the duke renounces his claim to England for a big subsidy (→1104).

England, 1102. Cross-Channel links improve with the marriage of Mary, the sister of King Edgar of Scots and sister-in-law of Henry, to Eustace, the Count of Boulogne.

Winchester, spring 1103. Queen Matilda gives birth to a son, William, following the birth of a daughter, also Matilda, last year (→1/5/18).

Normandy, 1103. Sybil de Conversano, the wife of Robert Curthose, dies after the birth of a son, William *Clito* [prince]. She fell ill when a midwife told her to bind her breasts tightly to stop the copious flow of milk.

Normandy, 1104. Henry accuses Robert Curthose of breaking the 1101 treaty and forces him to hand over the lands of Evreux (→4/1105).

Normandy, April 1105. Relations between the royal brothers worsen; Henry invades and claims Caen and Bayeux from Robert Curthose (→10/1106).

Normandy, October 1106. War breaks out as Henry beseiges Robert at Lisieux (→8/1107).

France, March 1109. Louis VI of France orders Henry to give up Gisors and do homage; he refuses and war erupts (→1115).

Normandy, 1115. Henry forces the Normans to swear allegiance to his son William (→20/11/19).

Powys, 1116. Henry's ally, Owain ap Cadwgan of Powys, dies fighting his rival Gruffudd ap Cynan of Gwynedd (→1137).

Westminster, 1 May 1118. Queen Matilda dies.

Normandy, June 1119. Henry's son William marries Matilda, the daughter of Count Fulk V of Anjou; her dowry is the province of Maine.

Windsor, 29 January 1121. Henry marries Adeliza of Louvain, hoping for a new male heir after his son William's death (→1/1/27).

Windsor, 1 January 1127. Henry persuades his barons to accept his daughter Matilda, the widow of Holy Roman Emperor Henry V, as heir to the English throne (→5/1127).

Normandy, May 1127. Empress Matilda is betrothed to Count Geoffrey of Anjou, dubbed "Plantagenet" from his emblem, the broom plant, in Latin *planta genista*. She is 24, her bridegroom 14 (→5/3/33).

Grampian, 1130. King David of Scots breaks up the Moray earldom held by King Macbeth's descendants, which has long been a centre for rebellion against Scots kings (→1/12/35).

Le Mans, France, 5 March 1133. Empress Matilda gives birth to a son, to be called Henry Plantagenet (→1/12/35).

Rouen, Normandy, 1 Dec 1135. Henry dies of food poisoning.→

Norman and English royal families united

Queen Matilda: a later engraving.

London, 11 November 1100
The dynasties of Alfred the Great and William the Conqueror were united today at the high altar of Westminster abbey, when King Henry of England married Edith, the sister of King Edgar of Scots and great-granddaughter of King Edmund Ironside. The royal wedding is quite a coup for the youngest son of the Conqueror; it gives him an ally in King Edgar and, more crucially, removes any doubts about the legitimacy of the Norman succession. Edith will take the Norman name Matilda, borne by Henry's mother.

Henry acted swiftly after the death of his brother William Rufus in a hunting accident in the New Forest – swiftly enough to forestall the claims of his eldest brother, Duke Robert Curthose of Normandy, who was on his way back from the crusade, and swiftly enough to provoke rumours that he knew about the "accident" in advance. On 3 August, a day after William's death, he seized the royal treasury in Winchester, and two days later he was crowned at Westminster. He promised to rule better than his brother, imprisoned William's oppressive minister, Bishop Ranulf Flambard, and invited back the exiled Archbishop Anselm.

Henry's marriage strengthens his hold on the crown, but does not secure it. Robert is a distinguished soldier who led assaults on Jerusalem and Antioch and was offered the crown of Jerusalem by his fellow crusaders. He regards England as his rightful inheritance.

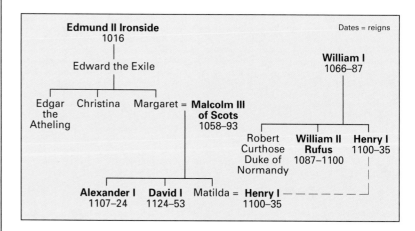

Gentle King Edgar of Scots dies childless

Edinburgh, 8 January 1107
Edgar, king of Scotland since 1097, has died at Edinburgh castle at the age of 33. He was unmarried, and the throne now passes to his younger brother Alexander.

In contrast to most of his royal predecessors, Edgar won a reputation as a kind and gentle king. Although he abandoned Iona and ceded the Western Isles to King Magnus of Norway, he was a firm ruler. He was a great patron of the church, and his godly and even-tempered character is thought to owe much to the influence of his mother, Queen Margaret. When she died in 1093, just a few days after his father Malcolm III and his brother Edward – reputedly of a broken heart – he carried her body to its burial in Dunfermline.

Henry tightens reins of royal power

Rival brother held and pope pacified

London, August 1107

After seven years of conflict, King Henry's throne is finally secure. His brother and rival, Duke Robert Curthose of Normandy, is a prisoner in Devizes castle, and his conflict with the church over his right to appoint bishops has been resolved in his favour. For years Robert was a willing tool of barons who sought Henry's overthrow until Henry's decisive defeat of Robert at Tinchebrai in Normandy last September. Equally importantly, Henry has sealed a treaty with Archbishop Anselm of Canterbury under which bishops must do homage to Henry for the estates that go with their office. The deal ends the feuding which began under William Rufus and has gained Henry the support of the pope (→ 3/2/34).

Exchequer fills up the king's coffers

Winchester, c.1110

Twice a year, at Easter and Michaelmas, England's sheriffs – the chief royal officers of the shires – pour into Winchester to present the taxes that they have collected for the king's treasury. They face a daunting session before the "Exchequer", recently set up to make the collecting of taxes more efficient – Europe's first centralised instrument of bureaucracy since Roman times.

As the sheriffs nervously wait their turn, all eyes are fixed on a table, ten feet by five, resembling a huge chess- or chequerboard, in Latin *scaccarius*, whence the nickname "exchequer". At one end sit all the king's chief ministers; at the other, alone or with a clerk, stands the sheriff whose accounts are undergoing the *auditum*, or hearing. The exchequer acts like a giant abacus, divided vertically into units of £10,000, £1,000 and so on down to pence, and horizontally into sums due and sums received. All can see at a glance how much has been paid; sheriffs who fall short risk losing their jobs.

King Henry: after years of bitter conflict, his throne is now secure.

Pope arranges peace with Louis of France

Gisors, France, 20 November 1119

Two decades of warfare over the duchy of Normandy have been brought to an end through the arbitration of Pope Calixtus II. In a meeting with King Henry at Gisors the pope has negotiated a peace with Louis VI of France under which Louis recognises Henry's son, William, as heir of Normandy.

The deal follows Henry's crushing defeat of the French king at Brémule on 20 August and is the latest in a series of diplomatic triumphs, to be added to his alliances with Anjou, Flanders and, through the marriage of his daughter Matilda, the Holy Roman Empire. It also ends years of wrangling over Normandy, which did not stop with the defeat and imprisonment of Robert Curthose, the Duke of Normandy and Henry's elder brother, in 1105. Soon after, Henry was at war with Louis over the ownership of Gisors, on the border of Normandy, and in 1111 Louis recognised William *Clito*, Robert's young heir, as Duke of Normandy. Hostilities ended in 1114 but broke out again in 1116, with Normandy pillaged by the armies of France, Flanders and Anjou. Henry's rout of Louis's army at Brémule paved the way for Pope Calixtus's diplomatic intervention (→ 29/1/21).

Insane priest kills son of heir to the Scottish throne

Huntingdon, 1114

Malcolm, the infant son of Earl David of Huntingdon, the brother and heir of King Alexander of Scots, has been brutally murdered by a deranged Scandinavian priest. Earl David had taken the man into his household out of pity, after he had been blinded and had his hands and feet chopped off for sacrificing a colleague on the altar of a church in his native Norway. The priest repaid the earl by attacking his son and ripping open his abdomen with two fingers of his iron artificial hand. A grief-stricken David has ordered him to be tied to wild horses and pulled apart (→ 23/4/24).

Malcolm's uncle, King Alexander.

Daughter of a king is now an empress

Germany, 7 January 1114

Princes, dukes and archbishops were among the hundreds of dignitaries present today at the royal wedding of the year. Minstrels, jugglers and dancers were on hand to entertain the guests as Matilda, the daughter of King Henry of England, was married to Holy Roman Emperor Henry V. The bridegroom is in his early thirties; his wife, now Empress Matilda, is barely 12. Matilda, who has learnt German, left England on her betrothal in 1110. Until now she has been thought too young to marry (→ 1/11/27).

Heir is among royals dead in shipwreck

Normandy, 25 November 1120
Three of King Henry's children, including William, the heir to the throne, and 300 courtiers were among those who drowned today when the royal boat, the *White Ship*, foundered on a rock in the English Channel off Barfleur. For hours before the ship's departure courtiers and crew feasted and caroused, and by the time she put to sea the pilot was drunk. Just outside Barfleur the ship's hull struck a rock and was ripped open; William was hurriedly placed in the ship's only boat, but it soon sank under the weight of struggling passengers. Only one survivor has been picked up, a butcher from Rouen.

Henry himself almost sailed on the ill-fated ship, but instead travelled ahead. He and his court were returning to England after his recent successes in France; today's tragedy undoes much of his work at a stroke, because now there is no male heir for England and Normandy. Henry is likely to be devastated at the news.

Henry: mourning his lost children.

Henry's menagerie is England's first zoo

Woodstock, Oxfordshire, c.1120
King Henry is gathering together some of the most extraordinary creatures ever seen in England at Woodstock, his hunting lodge near Oxford in the great forest of Wychwood. He is the first king to create such a huge menagerie of animals.

Woodstock was a royal manor before the Conquest, but Henry enclosed it as hunting grounds and built the lodge in the early years of his reign. Among the animals that now roam here are lions, leopards, lynxes and camels, many of them brought by returning crusaders anxious to curry favour with the king. Earl Paul of Orkney, for instance, has furnished the royal menagerie with numerous bizarre creatures. One of the strangest and most fascinating of all is an African porcupine, donated by a knight, William de Montpellier.

Lions are among the animals resident in King Henry's zoo at Woodstock.

Third brother takes crown of Scotland

Stirling, 23 April 1124
King Alexander of Scots has died at the age of 47. He became king when his brother Edgar died 14 years ago and, since he leaves no legitimate son, is succeeded in turn by the youngest brother, David, until now Earl of Huntingdon.

People will remember Alexander particularly for his interest in the church. He worked hard to stamp out lingering paganism and also to keep the Scottish church from being dominated by the archbishops of York and Canterbury. For all his piety Alexander was a man who appreciated the good things in life; his court boasted such exotic items as Arab horses and Turkish arms. Unfortunately his queen, Sibylla, was generally considered unattractive and flighty.

The new king, David, is a popular figure and no stranger to the arts of government. He shares Alexander's lively concern with the church and is also likely to keep up the good relations established by him with England. David has a number of English connections. He has been married for 11 years to Maud, the daughter of the late Earl Waltheof of Northumbria, and also knows the English court well, having lived there in the 1090s as an exile. Furthermore he is, like his two brothers before him, related to King Henry through their sister, Henry's Queen Matilda, who died six years ago (→9/2/36).

Royal jester founds hospital in London

A later portrait of Rahere.

London, 1123
Rahere, King Henry's former jester and now a canon at St Paul's, has founded a hospital and priory just outside the walls of the City at Smithfield. The hospital will be served by a master, eight brothers and four Augustinian nuns, "to wait upon the sick with diligence and care in all gentleness".

Like so many in King Henry's court, Rahere saw the sinking of the *White Ship* as an omen of divine judgement, and he made a pilgrimage to Rome. He contracted malaria, and on his way home he had a vision of St Bartholomew who instructed him to found the priory and hospital. Rahere has named them both after the saint.

Murder and marriage simplify succession

Bouvines, Flanders, August 1128
William, the Count of Flanders and a nephew of King Henry, has been betrayed by his mistress and murdered. His death removes one of the chief claimants to the thrones of England and Normandy, for William, dubbed *Clito* [prince], was the only legitimate son of the king's eldest brother Duke Robert Curthose of Normandy, who was deposed and imprisoned by Henry in 1107.

William Clito intrigued for years against King Henry, and when Henry's son, also called William, went down with the *White Ship* in 1120, he became the strongest male claimant to the throne. To forestall his claim Henry remarried in 1121; this marriage proved unfruitful, so last year he declared his daughter Matilda, the widow of Holy Roman Emperor Henry V, his heir.

Henry's barons swore to accept the empress as heir, but they are less than keen on the youth whom Henry made her marry in June, Geoffrey Plantagenet, the Count of Anjou, who, at 15, is ten years her junior. At the prospect of this ambitious count of non-royal blood becoming king, support is growing for a new contender, the wealthy Stephen of Blois, the Count of Boulogne and son of the king's sister Adela (→20/12/35).

Gluttony kills the king

Rouen, Normandy, 1 Dec 1135
King Henry has died of food poisoning caused by gorging himself on lampreys, against the advice of his physician, while on a hunting expedition in the Forest of Lyons. Only one child, his illegitimate son Robert, the Earl of Gloucester, was at his deathbed.

The only son of the Conqueror to be born in England (at Selby in 1068), he was excluded from the succession in 1091 following the wars between his brothers King William Rufus and Duke Robert of Normandy (in which he took Robert's side). But when William was killed in 1100 he seized the treasury in Winchester, had himself elected by the *Witan* [royal council], and was crowned at Westminster. Henry patched up Rufus's row with the church, reformed the judiciary, overhauled the tax-collecting system and established a civil bureaucracy. But much of his treasury was wasted on wars in France and Normandy, and he could be as ruthless as his two predecessors, sharing their notorious rages.

Henry had 24 children, all but three of them illegitimate. He was devastated by the sinking of the *White Ship* in 1120, in which his sole legitimate son, William, was drowned; afterwards he became obsessed with the succession crisis, ending up at war with his daughter Matilda and son-in-law Geoffrey of Anjou, his designated heirs.

The man who was never king dies at 80

Robert Curthose: a brilliant soldier who was outwitted in peacetime.

Cardiff, 3 February 1134
Robert, the eldest son of William the Conqueror and former Duke of Normandy, has died at the age of 80. Nicknamed "Curthose" [short trousers] from his stubby legs, he spent his last 28 years a prisoner of his youngest brother, King Henry.

Heir to the duchy of Normandy after William I's death, he was a stocky, black-haired, genial man whose brilliant soldiering was not matched by political skill. An inveterate plotter, he was soon at war with his brother William Rufus, typically winning the battles but losing the peace. He distinguished himself in the First Crusade, and returning to Normandy heard that Rufus was dead and that Henry was king of England.

Incensed at being passed over yet again, he invaded England in 1101 but was tricked by Henry into recognising him as king. But Robert continue to plot and Henry invaded Normandy, taking Robert prisoner at Tinchebrai in 1106. He lived the rest of his life in honourable captivity, at Devizes and Cardiff.

Short hair and piety stage a return at Henry's court after lax morals of Rufus

Male costume of about this time.

Mid-C12th fashion for women.

Canterbury, 4 May 1130
King Henry and King David of Scots were at the home of the English church today to attend the consecration of the newly-rebuilt choir of Canterbury cathedral. The ceremony was typical of Henry's patronage of the church, which is in contrast to the cynical attitude of his brother, William Rufus.

Henry has made a point of keeping the church on his side. The morals of Henry's court, too, are more to the liking of his bishops than those at Rufus's court, where long hair and beards and extravagant dress were the fashion. On an expedition to Normandy in 1105 Henry and his courtiers heard a sermon by Bishop Serlo of Sées, who said that long hair, "in woman's fashion", was for those "bristling with sins". Men with long beards were "like he-goats, whose filthy vices are shamefully imitated by the degradation of fornicators and sodomites".

On hearing this, King Henry gladly consented to having his hair and beard cut by the bishop himself. Henry's courtiers, fearful of provoking the king's infamous family foul temper, dutifully queued up behind him.

A carved liturgical comb, made at St Albans at about this time.

Stephen
1135–1154

David I
1124–1153
Malcolm IV
1153–1165

Normandy, 20 December 1135.
The English throne is claimed by King Henry's nephew Stephen, the younger brother of Count Theobald of Blois (→ 22/12).

Durham, 5 February 1136.
King David of Scots and King Stephen seal a peace treaty (→ 5/1137).

Normandy, May 1137. King Louis VI of France recognises Stephen as king of England (→ 5/1140).

Lisieux, June 1137. Earl Robert of Gloucester gives his support to Empress Matilda (→ 4/1138).

Gwynedd, 1137. Gruffudd ap Cynan, aged 82, dies; his two sons, Owain and Cadwaladr, divide his kingdom.

Northumberland, April 1138. King David gives support to his niece, Empress Matilda (→ 22/8).

Bath, May 1140. The bishop of Winchester, Henry of Blois, arranges peace talks between Empress Matilda and Stephen (→ 25/12/41).

England, January 1148. After the death of Earl Robert of Gloucester, Empress Matilda resigns all claims to the throne to her son, Henry Plantagenet (→ 10/9/67).

England, 3 May 1152. Stephen is shattered by the death of his wife, Queen Matilda.

Bordeaux, 18 May 1152. Henry Plantagenet, Count of Anjou since his father's death last year, marries Eleanor of Aquitaine, the former wife of King Louis VII of France (→ 19/12/54).

Carlisle, 24 May 1153. Only a year after the sudden death of his son and heir, Earl Henry, King David of Scots dies. His 12-year-old son Malcolm succeeds.

Winchester, 6 November 1153. Henry Plantagenet and Stephen make peace; Henry is to be Stephen's heir (→ 25/10/54).

Stephen crowned after lightning coup

Henry's daughter is left out in the cold

London, 22 December 1135
Stephen of Blois, who sailed from Boulogne to seize the reins of power in England the moment he heard of the death of his uncle, King Henry, was today crowned king by the archbishop of Canterbury. The reluctant archbishop was persuaded to legitimise Stephen's accession despite the oath sworn to Henry by Stephen and other notables recognising his daughter, Empress Matilda, as heir to the throne. Matilda, the widow of Holy Roman Emperor Henry V and now married to Geoffrey of Anjou, is a formidable woman who will fight for her inheritance (→ 5/2/36).

Scots king beaten

Yorkshire, 22 August 1138
King David of Scots lost to an English force today on Cowton Moor near Northallerton. The clash has been dubbed the "Battle of the Standard" since the English displayed the banners of St Peter of York and other northern saints. David was advancing south in pursuit of his claim to Northumberland, but he has now retreated to Carlisle, his pride dented. Fortunately for him he has not been pursued by the English (→ 22/5/49).

England's new king, Stephen of Blois: a 13th-century portrait.

Welsh writer's royal history starts off a craze for King Arthur

King Arthur and the sword Excalibur, from a later manuscript.

London, 1151
Geoffrey of Monmouth, an Anglo-Welsh scholar whose *History of the Kings of Britain* has aroused such interest in the Arthurian romance that King Arthur has become a cult figure in Britain, has been appointed bishop of St Asaph.

His great work, published three years ago, drew on ancient legends of the Dark Ages which he wove together with the accounts of the chroniclers of those troubled times. He also claims to have based his narrative on an ancient book which he refuses to produce. His critics accuse him of a liberal use of fiction, but this has not detracted from the success of his work which caused an immediate sensation among educated people with its vividly written account of a time of chivalry when, according to the author, Britain was among the great European powers.

His tales of heroism, wizardry, violence, adultery and betrayal are the first definitive, and flattering, account of the island of Britain's misty history. Such is the power and scope of Geoffrey's account that no future historian will be able to ignore it. The book's publication at a time of political turmoil was also timely, for it preaches the value of unified rule.

Year of turmoil ends with king recrowned

Canterbury, 25 December 1141

King Stephen was recrowned by the archbishop of Canterbury here today after an astonishing year which saw him defeated, captured and deposed and then victorious, free and restored to power.

In February, while he was besieging the rebellious Earl "Moustaches" Ranulf of Chester in Lincoln castle, he was overwhelmed by the superior forces of Empress Matilda led by her half-brother Robert of Gloucester. Refusing to flee, Stephen fought until his battle-axe and sword were broken and he was felled by a stone and captured.

He was held in chains in Robert of Gloucester's castle while Matilda, unprepared for this sudden change in fortune, made her way cautiously towards London. She first made a deal with Stephen's brother, the bishop of Winchester, but it was not until the middle of June that the Londoners allowed her to enter the capital.

She then displayed an intolerable arrogance and wilfulness, spurning her advisers and demanding a large sum of money from the Londoners. While she was preparing for her coronation the Londoners rose against her, forcing her to flee.

Stephen's supporters defeated her army outside Winchester and captured Robert of Gloucester. It was the end of her short reign; Stephen and Robert were exchanged in November, and now Stephen is king again. But the civil war is not over (→6/11/53).

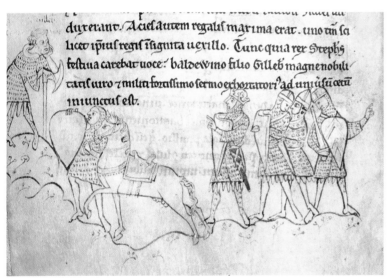

An illustration from a manuscript account of the siege of Lincoln in 1141.

David rules largest ever Scots kingdom as he wins Northumberland down to the Tees

A formidable ruler: King David of Scotland beside his grandson Malcolm.

Carlisle, 22 May 1149

King David of Scotland has won a major diplomatic victory today at a meeting with his great-nephew Henry Plantagenet. Henry, the son of Empress Matilda, travelled here to be knighted by David. He has promised David in return that he will recognise Scottish control of Cumberland and Northumberland from the Tyne to the Tees, including Newcastle.

David can now bask in the glory of having extended his kingdom's borders further south than they have ever been. But this is only one of his many achievements. Over the last 25 years he has in effect modernised Scotland. The Norman-style feudal system has been introduced, whereby the king owns all land and parcels it out in return for service. Scottish royal government now has an Anglo-Norman flavour with a new post of chancellor and the writing of charters like those of the English kings.

A pious man with strong views on moral questions, David has also done much for the church. He has welcomed Cistercians, Augustinians and other monastic orders to Scotland and appointed Anglo-Norman bishops to dioceses that he has helped to establish. The king's popularity also rests on his reputation for fairness. It is said that he once gave up a day's hunting in order to hear the petition of a humble subject (→24/5/53).

Queen and empress: the two Matildas

Queen Matilda (above, with Stephen, on a coin) and Empress Matilda (right, from a manuscript) are both formidable women, respectively the king's chief supporter and opponent.

Stephen's death ends strife-torn reign

Faversham, 25 October 1154

King Stephen was buried today alongside his wife and son in the choir of the Cluniac abbey that he founded here. He was a brave knight and could act decisively, but he was feckless and lacked the judgement England needed from its king in turbulent times.

His reign was bedevilled by his protracted civil war with Empress Matilda who refused to relinquish her – legitimate – claim to the throne. Only in the last year, after agreeing that Matilda's son Henry Plantagenet would succeed him, did he know any peace. One of Stephen's greatest mistakes was to alienate the church, especially his powerful brother Bishop Henry of Winchester. He could, however, always count on the loyalty of his beloved queen, also Matilda, who held his cause together when he was captured. Her death and that of his son Eustace made him lose heart, while the empress dropped out of the fight after the death of her half-brother and champion Robert of Gloucester.

Henry, the son of the empress from her second marriage to Geoffrey of Anjou, is not hurrying to take the throne. There is no danger of a disputed succession and England is tired of civil war.

Henry II
1154–1189

Malcolm IV
1153–1165
William I
1165–1214

Westminster, 19 Dec 1154.
Henry Plantagenet, aged 21, is
crowned Henry II (→ 7/1155).

England, January 1155. Thomas
Becket is the new chancellor
(→ 23/6/62).

London, 28 February 1155.
Henry's wife, Eleanor of Aquitaine, gives birth to a second son,
called Henry after his father
(→ 24/12/67).

Reading, April 1156. William,
Henry II's eldest son, dies
(→ 2/11/60).

Normandy, 2 November 1160.
Henry arranges the marriage of
his son Henry to Margaret, the
daughter of Louis VII of France
(→ 14/6/70).

Powys, 1160. Madog ap Maredudd, the ruler of Powys, dies,
leaving Henry no Welsh ally.

Dumfries and Galloway, 1160.
King Malcolm IV subdues Galloway, dividing it among the
sons of its captive lord, Fergus
(→ 12/1165).

Canterbury, Kent, 23 June 1162.
Thomas Becket, Henry II's chancellor, is the new archbishop
(→ 12/1164).

Scotland, December 1165.
Malcolm IV dies; his brother
William succeeds.→

Wales, 1165. Gwynedd and Deheubarth defeat Henry (→ 1177).

England, 1166. Henry establishes the first trial by jury.

Normandy, 10 September 1167.
Empress Matilda dies at Rouen.

Oxford, 24 December 1167.
Queen Eleanor, aged 45, gives
birth to John, her eighth child
(→ 23/3/73).

England/France, 1167. Henry
II and Louis VII make peace
(→ 29/12/70).

England, 1 December 1170.
Thomas Becket, finally recon-
ciled with Henry, returns to
England (→ 29/12).

Ireland, October 1171. Henry
arrives and receives homage
from the Anglo-Norman in-
vaders of Leinster.

France, 11 June 1172. Henry's
second son Richard, aged 14, is
invested as Duke of Aquitaine
(→ 1173/4).

Normandy, 1173/1174. Henry's
sons Henry the Young King,
Richard and Geoffrey rebel
against him (→ 28/5/75).

Canterbury, Kent, 28 May 1175.
Henry and his sons, who are
now reconciled, make a pilgrimage to Becket's shrine
(→ 6/10).

Sicily, 13 February 1177. Joan,
Henry's daughter, marries
the king of Sicily.

Oxford, 1177. The Welsh
princes swear fealty to Henry
(→ 1188).

Limoges, France, 11 June 1183.
Henry, the Young King, dies of
dysentery (→ 1185).

Ireland, 1185. John, Henry's
youngest son, becomes Lord of
Ireland (→ 1188).

Oxfordshire, 5 September 1186.
King William of Scots marries
Ermengarde, a cousin of Henry.

France, 1188. Henry is at war
with his son Richard and Philip
II of France (→ 6/7/89).

Chinon, France, 6 July 1189.
Henry dies.→

Henry sets about consolidating his rule after a smooth transfer of royal power

King Henry II enthroned, from a later manuscript of Plantagenet kings.

Westminster, July 1155
To the relief and gratitude of a population weary of civil war under his
predecessor Stephen, King Henry
II is rapidly proving himself a powerful and charismatic monarch. He
has already dealt with baronial
opposition, and there is now no one
to pose a serious challenge to his
authority.

Henry Plantagenet, powerfully
built, with red hair and a fiery temper to match, claimed his throne
last December after the death of
King Stephen, who recognised him
as his heir a few months before his
death. Henry had already proved
his courage and leadership on behalf of his mother, Empress Matilda, in campaigns against Stephen
and his son Eustace. King Henry
wants to expunge the memory of
Stephen's turbulent and lawless
reign and establish himself as the
natural successor of his grandfather
Henry I. The king has broken the
last remaining links with Stephen's
reign by granting no favours to
Bishop Henry of Blois, Stephen's
once influential brother. He has
appointed Richard de Lucy and
Robert of Leicester as his justiciars,
responsible for the royal administration and for safeguarding England when he is attending to his
extensive French dominions.

Henry's new chancellor is
Thomas Becket, who is the favourite clerk of Theobald, the archbishop of Canterbury (→ 4/1156).

Scots king bullied into ceding towns

Chester, 1157
The 16-year-old king of Scotland, Malcolm IV, has resigned control of Cumberland and Northumberland, including the towns of Carlisle, Bamburgh and Newcastle. It is a bitter blow for the Scots who only eight years ago were riding high following his grandfather King David's acquisition of these territories. Ironically, the man who conceded Scottish control in the north of England is the same one who is putting an end to it. Henry Plantagenet knuckled under to David, but now, as Henry II of England, he has successfully pressured Malcolm into abandoning his grandfather's gains.

The situation is very different now, of course. Back in 1149 Henry was himself a young man, barely 16 years old and on the make. King David was an experienced soldier and a useful future ally. Now it is Henry who is the older and more powerful partner in Anglo-Scottish affairs.

In recompense, King Malcolm has been granted the English earldom of Huntingdon, for which he has had to do homage to Henry. But Malcolm has been careful to avoid any suggestion that this is a general act of homage to the English king, which would be tantamount to declaring King Henry the overlord of Scotland (→ 1160).

Young King Henry is crowned (l) and acknowledged by his father (r).

Coronation gives England a second king

Westminster, 14 June 1170
Henry, the 15-year-old eldest son of King Henry II, was today anointed England's Young King, following the French practice of crowning the heir to the throne in the king's lifetime to ensure a peaceful succession. Roger, the archbishop of York, performed the ceremony in Westminster abbey.

The Young King's coronation came after repeated efforts were made last year to reconcile his father with King Louis VII of France, to fix the limits of their dominions and to end various rebellions. It was hoped also that a treaty might enable Archbishop Thomas Becket, who fled abroad after a fierce row with the king, to return to England with royal blessing. For Henry's part, the coronation gives expression to his plans to divide the kingdom between his sons. Young King Henry is to receive England, Normandy and Anjou. Richard is to receive his mother's inheritance of Aquitaine, and Geoffrey is to be Duke of Brittany, as a vassal of the younger Henry. Relations with France are to be cemented by the marriage of Richard to Louis's daughter Alice.

Ironically, today's coronation could spell trouble. Louis VII will surely be offended that his daughter Margaret, the Young King's wife, was not crowned with him and that the ceremony was not performed by the archbishop of Canterbury. It looks as if the old king will have to meet the exiled Becket (→ 1180).

King gives blessing to Irish expedition

France, 23 August 1170
From his sick-bed, King Henry has sanctioned the assembling of an expeditionary force to Ireland to counter the success of Richard "Strongbow" de Clare, the Earl of Pembroke, who has crossed the Irish Sea with a band of knights. Henry has had designs upon Ireland since 1155, when the English Pope Adrian IV granted him overlordship. Three years ago King Dermot of Leinster approached him for help against his opponents; Richard went, but now appears to be forging a power base of his own. Dermot has promised him his daughter's hand in marriage.

Pope Adrian IV, who granted Henry the overlordship of Ireland in 1155.

Royal saint's body is moved to shrine

Westminster, 13 October 1163
The bones of King Edward, who died nearly a century ago, were moved today to a shrine in Westminster abbey. The ceremony was conducted by Thomas Becket, the archbishop of Canterbury, and King Henry was among the men who bore the coffin. Edward, whom people are calling "the Confessor" for his piety and the miracles which he has allegedly wrought since his death, was canonised two years ago by the pope. But today's ceremony has not obscured growing tension between King Henry and Archbishop Becket over the limits of state authority.

Archbishop flees after clash with king

Becket: a C12/13th stained glass.

Pontigny, France, December 1164
An obscure Cistercian monastery is currently home to Thomas Becket, the archbishop of Canterbury, who has fled in disguise from the wrath of his former friend King Henry. The exiled archbishop has been promised the protection of the pope and the king of France.

Becket's flight from England came after he rejected Henry's Constitutions of Clarendon, which demanded that all clerics submit to the crown. Becket, as proud and charismatic as the king himself, insisted that the state's jurisdiction does not cover the church. A fierce row blew up and Becket decided to flee. Henry has confiscated all his possessions (→ 1/12/70).

Too much fasting kills King Malcolm

Borders, 9 December 1165
King Malcolm IV died today, aged only 23. His premature death is being put down to excessive fasting, a sign of his religious zeal. Malcolm became king when barely 12 years old on the death of his grandfather David (both David's sons predeceased their father).

A capable administrator, Malcolm grew up to be also a great patron of the church, encouraging the monastic orders in particular. The ascetic life appealed to him; he took a vow of chastity and was known as "the Maiden". It is rumoured, however, that he has left one bastard son.

▷

King's men kill Becket

Thomas Becket is savagely murdered at Canterbury: from a text of 1180.

Canterbury, 29 December 1170

Four knights, purporting to act on behalf of King Henry, today murdered Thomas Becket, the archbishop of Canterbury, before the cathedral altar. As he faced their drawn swords, the archbishop declared: "I am ready to die for my Lord, that in my blood the church may obtain liberty and peace."

This bloody and infamous act brings a shocking conclusion to a power struggle between Becket and his king which resurfaced when the archbishop returned from exile in France four weeks ago. Far from

mending fences with King Henry, Becket processed through crowded streets and proclaimed disciplinary measures against those bishops who had usurped his authority.

Faced with his archbishop's renewed defiance, the king is said to have cried in exasperation: "Will no one rid me of this turbulent priest?" Sir Reginald FitzUrse and three other knights took him at his word. They made their way to Canterbury to confront Becket in the cathedral and, after fierce arguments, butchered him in front of several witnesses (→ 12/7/74).

Barefoot and shirtless king does penance

Canterbury, 12 July 1174

Humble and barefoot like a pilgrim, King Henry has done penance at the tomb of his old adversary Thomas Becket, the archbishop of Canterbury murdered three and a half years ago by knights claiming to act on their king's behalf.

Thomas Becket was canonised only 15 months after his murder, and although the papal legates absolved Henry of direct responsi-

bility for the crime, the domestic and international outrage led him to promise to make a public gesture of repentance. Today he kept his promise, walking to the cathedral before prostrating himself at the martyr's tomb, weeping and begging forgiveness. The king then endured a severe flogging at the hands of the monks before promising money to light the martyr's tomb in perpetuity.

Formidable queen backs revolt of sons

Chinon, France, 23 March 1173

Queen Eleanor of Aquitaine has been captured by soldiers loyal to her husband, King Henry. She was attempting to escape, disguised as a man, to join her rebellious sons now sheltering at the French court.

The rebellion flared up when the eldest son, the 18-year-old Young King Henry – crowned three years ago as his father's heir apparent – grew impatient at having the trappings of kingship without the power. He also resented being told by his father to share some of his lands with his landless youngest brother John, aged seven. Eleanor, estranged from her husband in recent years, encouraged the younger Henry's rebellion, which was joined not long after by her and Henry's middle sons Richard and Geoffrey, aged 15 and 14 respectively.

This second major crisis in Henry's reign, only three years after the murder of Thomas Becket, is essentially the work of Eleanor, a highly intelligent politician who has been marginalised by her husband. A keen patron of the arts, she is the daughter of the Count of

A later engraving of Queen Eleanor.

Poitou and heiress to the duchy of Aquitaine. A great (and sexually active) beauty in her youth, she married the pious Louis VII of France and bore two children, but the couple were incompatible and divorced by mutual consent. She married the 18-year-old Henry, 11 years her junior, in 1152, but has now been supplanted in his affections by his mistress, Rosamund Clifford (→ 1/4/1204).

Irish and Scots submit to overlord Henry

Henry confronts the Irish clergy.

Windsor, 6 October 1175

King Henry has been recognised as the dominant force in the British Isles and throughout much of France, following treaties with the Irish, the Scots and his rebellious sons Henry, Richard and Geoffrey. The Treaty of Windsor, signed today with King Rory of Connacht,

confirms Henry as overlord of Ireland. The Treaty of Falaise of last December dealt a similar blow, at least in theory, to Scottish independence, for in it the captive King William of Scots submitted to Henry. William's humiliating capture had taken place at Alnwick in Northumberland, when the allies of King Henry in the north of England defeated the Scots.

The rebellion of his sons, fostered by Queen Eleanor and capitalised upon by King Louis VII of France, was brought to an end at Montlouis a year ago, after Henry had lifted a siege at Rouen and put Louis's forces to flight. He was magnanimous with his recalcitrant offspring, however. Young King Henry was required to accept his youngest brother John's claims in England, Normandy and Anjou, but in return was given two castles in Normandy and £15,000. Richard was given two residences and half the revenues of Poitou, while Geoffrey received half the revenues of Brittany (→ 1177).

Young King trounces tournament rivals

Lagny, France, 1180
Young King Henry and a team of English knights have beaten all comers at a grand tournament near the French royal capital. The brilliant spectacle marks the coronation of King Philip of France.

England's Young King is a great enthusiast for the increasingly popular pastime of jousting, which in the last century or so has grown into something like a sport for dashing young royal and aristocratic knights on both sides of the Channel. The first jousts seem to have been training sessions in the new technique of using a lance couched under the right arm, rather than wielding it overarm or underarm. This technique, which developed in north-western France, means that the knight can put far more power behind a heavier lance and is far less likely to lose it.

Although more refinements are creeping in, tournaments tend to be rumbustious free-for-alls which resemble real battles. Deaths are not uncommon, and the church has generally slammed jousting as a needless danger to life and limb. King Henry II officially discourages tournaments in his lands, which means that the Young King has to seek his pleasure elsewhere, mainly in France (→ 11/6/83).

Two knights duelling: tournaments often end in bloodshed or death.

'Fair Rosamund', the king's true love

Godstow, Oxfordshire, 1176
King Henry is grief stricken at the death of his true love – Rosamund Clifford, the mistress with whom he has lived openly since his estrangement from Queen Eleanor three years ago. Henry has paid for her to be buried before the high altar at Godstow nunnery, near Oxford. Rosamund was the best-loved of Henry's mistresses but not the first. He has two bastard sons, Geoffrey and William, from premarital affairs and another, Morgan, born to a Welsh noblewoman called Nest. Morgan is being brought up by Nest and her husband, a Marcher knight.

"Fair Rosamund": a later view.

Heartbroken Henry dies

In remembrance: King Henry's carved tomb at Fontevrault abbey, France.

Fontevrault, France, July 1189
King Henry II of England lies in state at the abbey here, the achievements of his 34-year reign overshadowed by the ignominy of his end – betrayed by his sons, his empire in ruins, obliged to surrender to his greatest enemy, King Philip of France. When his rebellious son and heir, Richard, came to attend his father's corpse, blood oozed from its nostrils. Those present were horrified – corpses are said to bleed in the presence of their murderers.

A few days ago the dying king was propped up on his horse to go and meet the French king, who had just taken Tours. He agreed to pay homage to Philip for all his lands in France, and to grant England and the Plantagenet lands to Richard. Then he was handed a list of the allies ranged against him. Top of the list was John, his youngest, favourite and hitherto loyal son. It was the final blow for Henry and he would hear no more. Two days later his last words were "Shame, shame on a vanquished king!".

Henry II was a man of awesome power and a terrible temper, destined to rule an empire which no one man could control. By his very dominance he eventually alienated those closest to him – first Thomas Becket, then his queen, then his own sons. He conquered all his enemies in the British Isles, but Queen Eleanor, imprisoned since 1173, remained a focus for the rebellions in France which finally undid him.

The legal legacy of Henry Plantagenet

England, 1189
The reign of King Henry II will be remembered for great advances in the law. Landowners and tenants are protected against unwarranted seizure of land, and the truth of evidence is increasingly judged not by ordeal of fire, water or battle but by the opinion of a 12-man jury.

Henry was a man of learning, passionately interested in the law. His first major problem was the habit of *disseisin*, the forcible seizure of another's land, which gave rise to countless disputes. Henry made disseisin illegal unless previously sanctioned by a court, and later introduced the law of *novel disseisin*, in which a royal justice, acting on the evidence of local people, determined who had the stronger claim.

The administration of criminal law caused Henry and Becket to fall out when the king insisted that not even the clergy should be immune from prosecution. Despite the church's objections, the 1164 Constitutions of Clarendon were confirmed two years later in the Assize of Clarendon, which authorised sheriffs and county justices to pursue criminals anywhere in the country and take evidence from juries of community leaders.

The Assize of Northampton in 1176 increased the punishments and reinforced the authority of the king's justices, who tour the country.

**Richard I
1189–1199**

**William I
1165–1214**

Westminster, 3 Sept 1189.
Richard is crowned king of England.→

Canterbury, 5 December 1189.
Richard cancels the Treaty of Falaise in return for £10,000 from King William of Scots, ending 15 years of English overlordship (→ 24/8/98).

Westminster, December 1189.
William Longchamps becomes chancellor and governs in King Richard's absence (→ 8/10/91).

Sicily, 6 October 1190. En route for the Holy Land, Richard ravages the island to secure the dowry of his sister, Joan, who was married to the late king of Sicily (→ 4/1191).

Sicily, April 1191. Richard, revises plans for government and sends Queen Eleanor, his mother, and Archbishop Walter of Rouen to England (→ 12/5).

Cyprus, 12 May 1191. Richard marries Berengaria, the daughter of Sancho VI of Navarre, despite his betrothal to Alice, the sister of King Philip of France. Berengaria is crowned queen of England (→ 9/8/92).

London, 8 October 1191. William Longchamps is deposed in Richard's absence and John, Richard's younger brother, takes power (→ 7/1193).

Holy Land, 9 August 1192. Richard fails to reach Jerusalem but forces Saladin to allow Christians to make pilgrimages unharmed.→

Vienna, 20 December 1192. Richard, en route for England, is captured by the Duke of Austria (→ 23/3/93).

England, July 1193. John flees to France on the news of Richard's return (→ 7/1195).

Normandy, July 1195. Richard begins to regain lost lands (→ 6/4/99).

Wales, 28 April 1197. Lord Rhys, the powerful ruler of Deheubarth, dies.

Mob murder of Jews mars coronation

Westminster, 3 September 1189
Duke Richard of Aquitaine, the son of the late King Henry II and Eleanor of Aquitaine, was crowned king of England at Westminster abbey today. Richard is popular for his dashing knightly qualities, although the chivalrous new king is said to be more interested in wooing men than women. He is especially close to King Philip of France.

The coronation, attended by all the nobles of the country, and followed by a magnificent banquet at the palace of Westminster, went well, but it was marred by the massacre of a delegation of Jewish leaders from the City of London, who went to the palace to pay their respects to the new king.

The king is furious, partly because the Jews had ignored a decree banning them from the coronation festivities and partly because they are regarded as "his" property. He also fears for their wealth, on which he depends to finance the forthcoming crusade.

Richard hopes to leave soon for the Holy Land, and his reluctance to stay for long in his new country is typical of his life to date. He owes little allegiance to England. Born in Oxford in 1157, he was brought up

A new and popular king: Richard is crowned at Westminster abbey.

in France, where his mother Eleanor, who had separated from her husband soon after the birth of Richard's brother John in 1167, had set up court at Poitiers. Here he

learnt the knightly arts, and he showed them off in 1179 when, in a campaign to subdue the rebel barons of Aquitaine, he took the fortress of Taillebourg (→ 5/12/89).

Storming Richard leads western coalition to Middle East victory

Crusaders' conflict: a French manuscript view of an army like King Richard's.

Jerusalem, 9 August 1192
The Third Crusade, which began in 1190 when King Richard and Philip of France joined forces to drive the Moslem leader Saladin from the Holy Land, is over. The Christian army has halted, just 12 miles (19km) from Jerusalem, and under the Treaty of Jaffa the king has agreed to three years' peace.

The capture of Acre and Arsuf, and the conquest of much of the coastal plain, have ensured Richard's fame. But the failure to take Jerusalem is a disappointment, as is Richard's quarrel with his ally, and probable lover, Philip. Richard was betrothed to Philip's sister Alice, but married Berengaria, a princess of Navarre whom he met in Sicily, soon after occupying Cyprus en route for Palestine. Philip was furious and returned home in disgust; he is now believed to be plotting against Richard (→ 20/12/92).

'Lionheart' faces challenges at home and abroad

Richard is held to ransom in Germany

Speyer, Germany, 23 March 1193
Richard, a prisoner of his old enemy the Duke of Austria, whom he once insulted, was handed over today to a new captor, Holy Roman Emperor Henry VI. His freedom, it has been announced, will cost 100,000 marks. Richard has agreed to the imperial terms, which include supplying ships and troops and paying homage to Henry, but until the cash arrives he must remain locked up.

Richard was captured on his way home from the Holy Land. Hearing that his brother John and Philip of France were plotting to keep him from returning to England, he disguised himself and attempted to skirt France by sailing up the Adriatic towards Germany. The plan failed. He was shipwrecked, and arriving in Vienna in December 1192 he was recognised and imprisoned.

The pope was one of many influential figures to condemn the treatment given to so honoured a crusader, but England's king was politically too important a figure for the emperor to toss aside such an opportunity. On the one hand the emperor has a great bargaining tool, and on the other he needs the money that Richard could bring in, to finance his plans for the conquest of Sicily (→ 17/4/94).

King Richard, in disguise, is captured and taken to the Holy Roman Emperor.

Returned to restore order: King Richard sits in state before his barons.

The wandering king is crowned again

Winchester, 17 April 1194
Richard, who was first crowned king in 1189, was crowned again today by the new archbishop of Canterbury, Hubert Walter. The ceremony was not strictly a coronation, but rather a "crown-wearing" during which the king, before the great nobles and clergy of the realm, was reaffirmed as England's sovereign lord.

The king's imprisonment abroad is over after the payment of the ransom, the plots of his brother John and King Philip of France have been defeated, and the real monarch, backed by the church, is firmly on his throne. Richard, ever gallant in victory, has forgiven his errant brother. He is also indebted to his mother Eleanor, still a powerful force at the age of 72, who made sure that while Richard languished in jail, John's attempts to hand over his French possessions to Philip were utterly foiled.

Another victor is Walter, now not only archbishop but also papal legate and Richard's justiciar or chief minister. Walter is a true man of the world, an able minister and distinguished lawyer, in whose businesslike person are combined the great offices of both church and state. Richard, a brilliant soldier, now has an equally competent administrator (→ 7/1195).

Heir finally born to William of Scotland

Lothian, 24 August 1198
King William the Lion has an heir at last, following the birth at Haddington today of a son, Alexander. The 55-year-old king has been anxious to have a legitimate son – he has several illegitimate ones – as it is now accepted that the Scottish throne passes from father to son. The older system, with the throne alternating between two branches of the royal house, either from cousin to cousin or from uncle to nephew, was a recipe for feuding and is now discredited (→ 7/9/09).

Lone French crossbowman kills England's swashbuckling king

The tomb of Richard and his queen, Berengaria, at Fontevrault in Normandy.

Limousin, France, 6 April 1199
King Richard is dead. He was hit in the shoulder by a crossbow bolt during the siege of the unimportant castle of Chalus six days ago; the wound, although not serious, became gangrenous. It is an ironically paltry end for the feared and fearless warrior known as "the Lionheart". Typically, for a king who spent only six months in his kingdom in ten years, he died abroad, repairing his French possessions, which had been ravaged during his imprisonment, and plotting revenge on Philip of France. He is succeeded by his brother John.

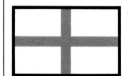

John
1199–1216

William IV
1165–1214
Alexander II
1214–1249

Bad omen marks the start of John's reign as he drops his insignia during ceremony

Westminster, 27 May 1199.
John is crowned king by Hubert Walter, the archbishop of Canterbury.→

France, 24 August 1200. After divorcing his first wife, Isabella of Gloucester, on the grounds of consanguinity, John marries Isabella of Angoulême, aged 12 (→29/9).

Westminster, 29 Sept 1200. Isabella of Angouleme is crowned as queen (→1/10/07).

Aquitaine, France, March 1201. Hugh de Lusignan, originally betrothed to Queen Isabella, rebels against John (→8/1202).

France, August 1202. Unrest continues between John and the de Lusignan family, joined by Arthur, John's nephew and the heir to the duchy of Brittany (→4/1204).

France, 1 April 1204. Queen Eleanor dies, aged 82.

France, April 1204. Suspicion falls on John after the murder of his nephew, Arthur (→1206).

Canterbury, Kent, 13 July 1205. Archbishop Hubert Walter, the chief minister of both King Richard and King John, dies (→12/1206).

Gwynedd, 1205. Llywelyn is recognised as ruler by John and marries Joan, the king's illegitimate daughter (→8/1211).

Canterbury, December 1206. Following the death of Hubert Walter, John refuses to accept the papal nominee, Stephen Langton, as the new archbishop of Canterbury (→1207).

Winchester, 1 October 1207. Queen Isabella gives birth to a son, Henry (→5/1/09).

England, 1207. John introduces an income tax which is highly unpopular; opposition to his rule grows (→7/9/09).

Rome, 24 March 1208. The pope issues an interdict on England, effectively banning all church functions except baptism and confession for people who are dying (→12/1209).

Winchester, 5 January 1209. Queen Isabella has a second son, to be called Richard.

Northumberland, 7 Sept 1209. John and King William of Scots make a deal at Norham following the latter's latest incursion across the border. John is to arrange marriages for William's two daughters (→4/12/14).

Wales, August 1211. John forces the Welsh prince, Llywelyn of Gwynedd, to swear that his lands will revert to the crown of England should he die without a legitimate heir (→1215).

Northampton, April 1215. The barons prepare to rebel against King John after his failure to meet their demands (→17/5).

London, 17 May 1215. The barons seize the city, besieging King John in the Tower of London (→27/7).

England, December 1215. The pope decrees that John need not adhere to *Magna Carta*, and civil war breaks out.

Kent, December 1215. John flees from baronial rule in London and besieges Rochester after securing Dover (→18/10/16).

Wales, 1215. Llywelyn of Gwynedd ousts Gwenwynwyn of Powys, a Welsh ally of King John, regaining much land from English control (→1216).

King John enthroned, from a later series of portraits by Matthew Paris.

Westminster, 27 May 1199
King John was crowned today, a month after he was invested Duke of Normandy in Rouen, and seven weeks after the death of his brother Richard. There was a bad omen at the Rouen ceremony: John dropped his ducal banner while chatting with his friends. The king's wife, Isabella, did not attend the coronation. He intends to divorce her.

John is 32, the youngest of Henry II's eight children and his fifth son. Henry originally gave great possessions to his three surviving brothers and nothing to John, who thus acquired the nickname "Lackland." John's three brothers have all died, and John has inherited everything, although Anjou and Touraine have declared for his nephew, Arthur of Brittany. His mother, Queen Eleanor, holds her own duchy, Aquitaine, for him.

John lacks King Richard's heroic reputation; he was sent to Ireland in 1185 and the expedition was a fiasco. He was his father's favourite son, but broke his heart when he joined Richard in the last revolt against him. John plotted against Richard when he went on crusade and was captured in Germany, and had to sue Richard for forgiveness.

However, John has some administrative acumen and has kept on his brother's chief minister, Hubert Walter. Walter has begun a system of keeping permanent records of government business (→24/8/1200).

John loses French lands

London, Summer 1206

Chinon and Loches, the king's last castles in central France, have fallen to the French. The king has now lost all of Normandy except the Channel Islands, as well as Anjou, Poitou, Maine and Touraine. All that remains is Aquitaine.

The war was provoked by John's feud with the de Lusignan family. He married Isabella of Angouleme, who was betrothed to one of them, and then tried to confiscate their lands. They appealed to King Philip of France. John refused to recognise Philip's authority, so Philip declared Normandy forfeit and gave John's other French lands to his nephew, Arthur of Brittany. King John showed some military ability at the start of the war. He defeated and captured Arthur and the de Lusignans at Mirebeau in July 1202, but then alienated his own supporters by his suspicions and treacheries. He was believed to have murdered Arthur, and the Bretons rose in revolt. They overran Anjou and Touraine while Philip attacked Normandy, laying siege to Château Gaillard on the Seine, the key to the duchy.

The barons in Normandy and Anjou abandoned John. He marched from Normandy into Anjou late in 1203 but was turned back and went to England. On 6 March 1204 Philip stormed Château Gaillard. Caen fell in May and Rouen on 24 June; Normandy was lost (→ 24/10).

JOHN'S TERRITORIAL LOSSES, 1199-1216

FLANDERS

Rouen

Caen

English Channel

NORMANDY

Paris

ILE DE FRANCE

CHAMPAGNE

HOLY ROMAN EMPIRE

BRITTANY

BLOIS

MAINE

ANJOU

TOURAINE

Loches

Chinon

to Duke Arthur, John's nephew; under French control by 1205

POITOU

BURGUNDY

Mirebeau

Lusignan

Atlantic Ocean

AQUITAINE

SAINTONGE

Bordeaux

PERIGORD

LANGUEDOC

GASCONY

CASTILE

NAVARRE

TOULOUSE

Mediterranean Sea

English possessions in France

— lost by John during his reign

— still held by John at end of reign

Pope orders the king's excommunication

The excommunicated king: John and his son, by JS Cotman (1782-1842).

Westminster, November 1209

Pope Innocent III has taken the drastic step of excommunicating King John after years of bitter feuding between the king, who is rumoured to be an agnostic, and Rome. The dispute began when Archbishop Hubert Walter died in 1205. The monks at Canterbury elected their prior to succeed him, and the king obliged them to reverse the election and chose his own candidate. Both sides appealed to the pope, who declared both elections invalid and instructed the monks to elect the eminent English divine Cardinal Stephen Langton.

John rejected the pope's ruling and brought a papal interdict upon England in 1207. Since then, on Rome's order, priests have carried out no functions apart from baptisms and confessions of the dying – there are no weddings or funerals. In other words, the church is on strike.

John responded to the interdict by confiscating all church property and forcing abbeys and churches to buy it back. It was a very profitable transaction for him; however, his obstinacy has alienated the church when he needs its support to recover his French lands and crush incipient rebellion. The excommunication is the latest stage in the pope's campaign against the king and has deeply shocked most of John's subjects, as it means that their king is offically shunned by the church and may even be deposed by the pope (→ 20/7/13).

John's three lions herald royal power

London, 1199

King John has adopted a new personal device: three gold lions on a red shield. It is a development of a coat of arms used by Henry II and Richard the Lionheart, which bore two lions.

Heraldic devices of one sort or another have been in use for some time. They are in one sense practical, a means of identifying friends and foes in battle when soldiers' faces are obscured by their helmets and visors. Increasingly, however, heraldry has been used to denote noble birth. A lord's coat of arms is his unique property, and woe betide anyone who mistreats it; to insult it is to insult the owner. It is also a sign of authority. John will, for example, be setting his new coat of arms on the royal seal.

King William of Scots is said to be impressed by this symbol and is showing interest in having something similar for the royal arms of Scotland. Instead of three lions *passant*, or striding, William prefers a single lion *rampant*, rearing up.

Heraldic symbols identify knights, as in this 14th-century manuscript.

King shows barons in Ireland who is boss

King John's agent oppressing the people: now it is Ireland's turn.

Dublin, 1210

King John has secured control of Ireland from rebellious barons who were undermining his authority there. In two months he marched from Waterford to Dublin and then into Ulster, defeating opposition everywhere. He is now Lord of Ireland in fact as well as in name.

John's father, Henry II, crossed to Ireland in 1171 to bring to heel the English barons whom he had allowed to go there as mercenaries. His authority remained weak, so in 1185 he sent his youngest son, John, to reassert control as "Lord of Ireland". That expedition was a disaster, and John returned in disgrace.

His main purpose in Ireland this year was to defeat William de Briouze and his relatives, the de Lacys. De Briouze was a great magnate in France and Wales, and the king, without any justification, became suspicious of him and seized most of his lands. John then ordered his arrest, and he fled to Ireland, where the king pursued him and captured his castles. Matilda de Briouze fled to Hugh de Lacy in Ulster, while de Briouze himself escaped to France.

John followed Matilda to Ulster, capturing Carlingford and Dundrum. Hugh de Lacy and Matilda sailed to Scotland, and Lacy's last fortresses, Carrickfergus and Antrim, surrendered. All the Irish lords paid homage to the king at Dublin, where he has ordered a new castle to be built (→ 20/7/13).

King John becomes vassal of the pope

Winchester, 20 July 1213

King John was reconciled with the church today in a solemn ceremony at which the archbishop of Canterbury, Stephen Langton, absolved him of his excommunication. The king abandoned his opposition to Langton last year, and made England and Ireland feudal fiefs of Rome in May this year.

His dramatic reversal saved him from an almost unheard-of sentence of deposition by the pope and also means that the papal interdict of 1207 will be lifted. John's change of heart came as a baronial rebellion was brewing against him and the king of France was preparing an invasion. The pope, as the king's feudal overlord, will now support him in everything and will force the bishops to follow (→ 27/4/14).

Scotland's longest reigning monarch dies

Scotland, 4 December 1214

William the Lion, the king of Scots, has died at the age of 71. His reign of almost 49 years – the longest in Scotland's history – has been a turbulent one, but William became undisputed master of a kingdom stretching from the river Tweed to the Pentland Firth.

However, William dies having failed in his dream of recovering Northumberland for the Scots. His brother Malcolm IV signed the land away to Henry II in 1157, and William's attempt to recover it ended in humiliation. In 1174 he rose against Henry, only to be captured and brought to his enemy with his legs chained together under his horse's belly. It was a bitter disgrace.

For 15 years Scotland's barons were obliged to owe their primary allegiance to the king of England – the price that Henry exacted for William's rashness. In 1189, however, Richard the Lionheart sold William back his overlordship of Scotland for 10,000 marks.

Elsewhere William's fortunes ran more smoothly. He stamped his authority on rebels in Galloway, Ross and Orkney, where Norse earls had coveted the Scottish throne. William's blinding and castrating of one of their number

William: an 18th-century portrait.

proved a powerful deterrent to further rebellion.

Throughout his reign William adopted more and more of the modern methods of government first introduced by King David. He founded burghs and widened the network of sheriffs and justices. He won a great success when the pope declared that the Scottish church was free of any foreign – in other words, English – archbishop.

William, who will be remembered as a strong and popular king, is to be buried at the Tironensian abbey in Arbroath that he himself founded. He is succeeded by Alexander, his 16-year-old son.

Defeat of John's allies dashes hopes of regaining French lands

Flanders, 27 July 1214

King Philip of France has defeated King John's allies, including Holy Roman Emperor Otto and the Earl of Salisbury, in battle at Bouvines. The defeat spells the end of John's hopes of recovering Normandy and his other French possessions, and it also probably means that Otto will lose to his rival Frederick von Hohenstaufen in their contest for the German throne.

Otto is John's nephew, and the king arranged for him and his Flemish allies to attack Normandy from the north-east while he himself attacked from Poitou in the south. The king sailed with a large army to La Rochelle in Aquitaine and invaded his ancestral lands in Poitou and Anjou; to begin with he scored some success. He captured Angers, his grandfather's capital, and tried a reconciliation with the

Defeat for John's allies: the Battle of Bouvines, by EJH Vernet (1789-1863).

de Lusignans of Poitou by offering to marry his daughter to Hugh de Lusignan's son. But then the barons refused to fight for him against the French king's son, Louis, and he retreated to La Rochelle. William Longsword, the Earl of Salisbury, led an army to Flanders, where he joined the Count of Boulogne and the emperor and invaded France. King Philip marched north to face them and won a great victory. The emperor and the earl barely escaped (→ 4/1215).

Barons force 'Magna Carta' on king

Llywelyn is Welsh overlord after ruler of Powys is exiled

Runnymede, 27 July, 1215

King John has given way to his barons and grudgingly accepted a charter of liberties which they presented to him here by the Thames west of London. It includes grievances that he has vowed to redress and sets up a council of barons to enforce his compliance.

Many barons, particularly in the north and the south-east, have been plotting revolt for years. They complained about the king's officials and a long history of royal abuses. Some of them accused the king of seducing their wives. When John tried to raise further taxes, it was the last straw. Some barons renounced their oaths to the king and formed an "army of God" to fight him. They seized London.

Others were loyal, but most demanded reform; Archbishop Langton and other bishops mediated and helped draft the Great Charter (*Magna Carta* in Latin). It reforms royal abuses and protects barons' properties and privileges as well as the church, citizens of London and other towns, and the Welsh. In one passage, the document declares: "No free man may be arrested or imprisoned, outlawed or exiled, or in any way brought to ruin, nor shall we go against him nor send others in pursuit of him save by the legal judgement of his peers or by the law of the land" (→ 12/1215).

King John seals the Charter of Liberties: a 19th-century painting.

Luckless 'Lackland' dies after losing crown jewels in the Wash

King John's tomb, Worcester cathedral, carved in Purbeck marble in 1232.

Newark, 18 October 1216

King John died here today of dysentery, six days after losing his baggage train in quicksands as he crossed the rivers at the head of the Wash. The crown jewels and John's treasure were lost, a symbolic end to a reign beset by disasters. The king will be buried at Worcester. Despite his administrative and legal reforms, and his success in Ireland, John got on badly with his barons. He was finally deserted by most of them when he renounced the Great Charter of Liberties (*Magna Carta*) that he had accepted last year. Louis, the son of the French king, came to their aid in a bid to depose him; John's death comes as Louis and the rebels hold London and much of the country.

Wales, 1216

After suffering many years of savage attacks and repeated attempts to challenge his hegemony over all the rulers in Wales, Llywelyn ab Iorwerth, the prince of Gwynedd, has finally defeated Gwenwynwyn, the lord of Powys. He has forced him into solitary exile in England and annexed all his lands.

Matters came to a head recently when Llywelyn was informed of the details of a secret visit by Gwenwynwyn to the court of King John in England to discuss a joint expedition against Gwynedd. King John being his father-in-law, Llywelyn was incensed by this double-dealing. He openly discussed the matter with his wife Joan, the bastard daughter of King John, and publicly concluded that Gwenwynwyn was chiefly to blame.

This was not strictly true, however, since it had been King John who had made most of the financial and military preparations and had issued the original invitation to conspire against his son-in-law. Nonetheless, Llywelyn had Gwenwynwyn tried in his absence for treachery. He then summoned a host of Welsh lords and marched south into Powys.

Returning hurriedly from England, where he was at the time, Gwenwynwyn was seriously hurt in a vain attempt to regain his kingdom. He was forced to flee back to England, taking refuge in Cheshire where he now lies mortally sick from his wounds (→ 1223).

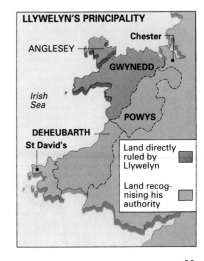

LLYWELYN'S PRINCIPALITY

Chester

ANGLESEY

GWYNEDD

Irish Sea

POWYS

DEHEUBARTH

St David's

Land directly ruled by Llywelyn

Land recognising his authority

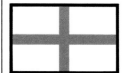

Henry III 1216-1272	Alexander II 1214–1249 Alexander III 1249–1286

Devizes, 19 October 1216.
Henry, John's nine-year-old son, is proclaimed king (→ 26/10).

England, 12 November 1216.
The regent, William Marshal, and the papal legate, Cardinal Guala, reissue a slightly revised *Magna Carta* (→ 11/1217).

London, 12 September 1217.
The Treaty of Lambeth brings peace between France, the barons and the supporters of Henry (→ 17/5/20).

Westminster, 17 May 1220. The archbishop of Canterbury re-crowns Henry (→ 1/1227).

Rome, 1221. The pope refuses to grant King Alexander II of Scots the right to be crowned and anointed, following intense English lobbying (→ 19/6).

South Wales, 1223. Llywelyn of Gwynedd is defeated by William Marshal, the Earl of Pembroke (→ 11/4/40).

Westminster, February 1225.
Henry invests his brother Richard with the title of Earl of Cornwall (→ 4/1/57).

Gwynedd, 1230. Llywelyn of Gwynedd hangs William de Briouze, the lord of Brecon, after discovering him in the chamber of his wife Joan (→ 11/4/40).

Scotland, June 1237. King Alexander II recognises Robert Bruce as his heir to the Scottish throne (→ 9/1237).

England, 1238. The Earl of Leicester, Simon de Montfort, marries Eleanor, the sister of Henry III (→ 8/1252).

Gwynedd, 11 April 1240. Llywelyn ab Iorwerth, the ruler of Gwynedd, dies (→ 15/5).

Newcastle, 14 August 1244.
Henry and Alexander II of Scots renew a truce (→ 8/7/49).

Gwynedd, 25 February 1246.
Dafydd ap Llywelyn, the Prince of Wales, dies.

Gascony, France, August 1252.
Simon de Montfort, the king's lieutenant since 1248, resigns because of his unpopularity (→ 4/1263).

Spain, October 1254. Edward, the eldest son of Henry, marries Eleanor of Castile (→ 19/8/70).

Paris, 1259. Henry signs a treaty in which he gives up his claims to French lands (→ 25/1/64).

England, April 1263. Simon de Montfort joins the rebel barons against the king (→ 4/2/64).

England, 2 May 1264. King Henry annuls the Provisions of Oxford (→ 14/5).

Kenilworth, 24 August 1266.
Parliament meets, and Henry is compelled to offer rebels who surrender a favourable deal (→ 29/7/67).

Montgomery, 29 July 1267.
Llywelyn ap Gruffudd, the ruler of Gwynedd, seals a treaty with Henry (→ 12/8/77).

Tunis, 19 August 1270. Henry's son Edward joins his uncle, King Louis IX of France, on a crusade.

England, February 1271. Henry falls seriously ill (→ 16/11/72).

Hertfordshire, 2 April 1272.
King Richard of Germany dies after suffering a stroke.

Westminster, 16 Nov 1272.
Henry III dies; his son, Edward, succeeds him.→

Nine-year-old king comes to the throne

The nine-year-old King Henry is presented to the barons: a later engraving.

Gloucester, 26 October 1216
At a simple, makeshift ceremony in the abbey church here today, nine-year-old Henry was crowned king of England. Such was the haste in which the coronation was organised that the queen's bracelet was substituted for the crown – which was lost in the Wash by King John with the rest of the royal regalia.

With the French and the rebel barons in control of much of the south-east of England, and Welsh princes already attacking in the west, it was essential that a successor should occupy the English throne at once. Even as the late king was being buried at Worcester, a knight was riding pell mell to Devizes castle where he found young Henry at play. At some risk, the boy was brought through rebel-controlled countryside to the royal castle here where a team of seamstresses put together some improvised coronation robes.

In a service of dubious legality, Henry was crowned by Peter des Roches, the bishop of Winchester – the archbishop of Canterbury is in Rome – and took the customary coronation oaths. He inherits a country with no organised government and no money (→ 12/9/17).

Young king's regent is a chivalrous hero

A tomb effigy of William Marshal.

London, November 1217
It was King John's dying wish that the Earl of Pembroke, William Marshal, perhaps the most powerful and chivalrous of his knights, should care for the boy king Henry. William was reluctant to take on what must have appeared a hopeless cause until he saw the helpless child, "sole hope of the torn kingdom". He shares the regency with the statesman Hubert de Burgh.

William's career is a remarkable story of romance and chivalry befitting a Norman nobleman. He was trained as a squire, ransomed as a knight by Eleanor of Aquitaine and fought both for and against Henry II. His seal appeared this month with that of the papal legate on the newly-reissued *Magna Carta*.

Scots king marries King Henry's sister

York, 19 June 1221

King Alexander II of Scots celebrates today a marriage designed to keep his southern border quiet. His bride is Joan, the sister of King Henry III and daughter of King John, with both of whom the Scottish king has had rough times.

Six years ago Alexander sided with barons in northern England in rebellion against John. A year later John got his own back by ravaging Lothian in a bid to "hunt the red foxcub from his lairs" (Alexander has red hair).

At Christmas 1217 Alexander decided that diplomacy was the better course and did homage to Henry for his English lands. Today's marriage is to be seen as another attempt to improve relations with his southern neighbour (→ 6/1237).

Foreigners at court purged after revolt

Gloucester, 28 May 1234

In a remarkable volte-face, Henry has made it up with his former chief minister, Hubert de Burgh, disgraced two years ago on the advice of Peter des Roches, the French-born bishop of Winchester. The king is purging his court of foreign influence; Peter des Rivaux, his treasurer, has been fired, and des Roches must not dabble in secular matters. Other French advisers have been banished.

A year ago Richard Marshal, the third Earl of Pembroke and son of Henry's former regent, grew so incensed at the growing influence of French advisers on the king that he led a successful rebellion in Wales and Ireland in which he himself perished last month. Edmund Rich, the archbishop of Canterbury, led the barons in persuading the king to take over the administration of the country and appoint new advisers. The imprisonment in fetters of de Burgh has been declared illegal, a significant legal victory under the terms of *Magna Carta*.

It was the shock of Richard Marshal's death that brought the king and de Burgh together here today. Peace should now be restored in Ireland and the west.

Henry takes on full mantle of power

The young king has taken on full authority as King Henry III of England.

London, January 1227

Eleven years after his unorthodox coronation, Henry, still only 20 years old, has assumed full control of the government of England. When he was crowned half his kingdom was in the hands of French-backed rebels, and few believed that Henry would survive. Much has happened since, however.

In 1217, English forces led by William Marshal, the Earl of Pembroke and Henry's regent, succeeded in driving French and rebel occupying forces from the crucial stronghold of Lincoln – the elderly regent himself leading a relatively small force against greatly superior odds in what many saw as a "holy war". Even more important, an English fleet succeeded in outmanoeuvring a French naval force off Sandwich in Kent and ensuring that the French garrison in London was without supplies. The Treaty of Lambeth then established a peace with the rebel barons.

The Earl of Pembroke has, sadly, been unable to witness his protegé's assumption of power. He died two years ago at the age of 75 after years of loyal service to no fewer than four monarchs (→ 28/5/34).

Henry marries his queen amid splendour

King Henry's bride, Eleanor.

Canterbury, 14 January 1236

Nineteen-year-old Eleanor, the second of the four beautiful daughters of the Count of Provence, was married in great splendour in the cathedral here today today to King Henry III. The bride had travelled the length of France for the ceremony and will be crowned in Westminster abbey in 16 days' time.

Henry has spared no expense in renovating the palace of Westminster for his bride. Plumbing has been installed, glass has been fitted in the windows, and Henry is making sure that Eleanor will not miss the warmth of Provence by building huge fireplaces in the palace. The king had originally negotiated for the hand of the Countess of Ponthieu, but changed his mind when he was told of the four beauties of Provence. There was some haggling over the dowry, but the indications are that this will soon become a love match (→ 17/6/39).

Anglo-Scots border is fixed by kings

York, September 1237

King Alexander II of Scots and King Henry III have met to fix the border between their two countries. The Anglo-Scottish frontier will now run from just south of Gretna in the west to just north of Berwick in the east. The status of Northumberland in particular has been hotly disputed by both kings in the past. Alexander has renounced his claim to it in return for other lands and income in England (→ 14/8/44).

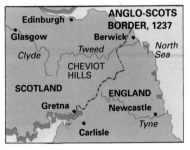

Dafydd is premier prince of Wales

Gloucester, 15 May 1240

Dafydd, the younger son of Llywelyn the Great of Gwynedd and his wife Joan, the illegitimate daughter of King John, was today created paramount prince in Wales by his uncle, King Henry III of England. The grand ceremony, which was held at Gloucester, confirms Dafydd as the heir to his father's great position in Wales, sidestepping the claims of his elder half-brother Gruffudd.

A princely *talaith*, or coronet, was placed on Dafydd's head by King Henry himself at the ceremony, which formed part of a royal council meeting in Gloucester. Dafydd was knighted, offered up homage for Gwynedd and, wearing the talaith, received the homage of the great Welsh magnates.

The bestowal of this princely honour is of the greatest significance for Dafydd and the future of Wales as a whole. It confers on its bearer the undisputed right to rule and is second only to the honour of kingship itself. Henry is clearly intent on good relations with his neighbour and nephew, although Dafydd's title to certain highly-prized and disputed lands gained by his father were ignored at today's ceremony.

The legal rights of Llywelyn the Great's elder son, Gruffudd, born to his first partner before his marriage to Joan, were also skated over during today's proceedings.

The death of Llywelyn, Dafydd's father: by Matthew Paris (d.1259).

But the legal conflict between the two brothers remains unsettled and will be very difficult to decide amicably when Gruffudd, who is currently imprisoned at Criccieth together with his son Owain, is eventually released. However, Dafydd's position is strong, since Llywelyn declared him his successor before assembled Welsh lords two years ago, at which time he first received their homage (→25/2/46).

King Henry and his brother clash over their sister's new match

Kingston, Surrey, February 1238

Fierce rivalry between King Henry's brother Earl Richard of Cornwall and their new brother-in-law, Simon de Montfort, the Earl of Leicester, has brought England to the brink of civil war. Henry has fled to the Tower while barons led by Richard meet here to draw up a set of demands. Eleanor is the 23-year-old widow of the second Earl of Pembroke, the son of William Marshal. With Henry's blessing, she married de Montfort last month; Richard was furious, both because of de Montfort's growing influence and because Eleanor had taken a vow of chastity on her husband's death (→8/1252).

King's refuge: a model of the Tower of London in the 12th century.

Henry tightens his hold over Ireland

Ireland, 1243

Henry's determination to establish his supremacy over the population of Ireland took a new form today when the king dispatched commissioners charged with the task of extending English holdings in the island. The commission follows other moves by the king in the last ten years to tighten English control, which have included setting up a separate chancery for Ireland and requisitioning all the money in the Irish treasury.

Henry's justiciar for Ireland, Maurice FitzGerald, has successfully campaigned against the Irish in recent years. He crushed opposition in Connacht and in 1238 went on to campaign in Ulster, exploiting existing internecine strife among its people.

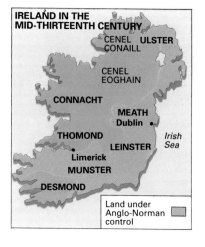

IRELAND IN THE MID-THIRTEENTH CENTURY

CENEL CONAILL · ULSTER · CENEL EOGHAIN · CONNACHT · MEATH · Dublin · THOMOND · LEINSTER · Irish Sea · Limerick · MUNSTER · DESMOND

Land under Anglo-Norman control

Pious Henry gives son a saint's name

London, 1239

Henry's firstborn son has been named Edward after Henry's favourite saint – King Edward the Confessor. The choice of an old English name for the boy is significant, especially with growing resentment at what many see as undue influence by Henry's French queen, Eleanor. Edward should be the first king with an English name since King Edward himself (Harold is a Scandinavian name). Henry's veneration for his saintly predecessor is taking the form of a rebuilding of Westminster abbey church, which Edward founded (→10/1254).

Alexander succumbs to fever on campaign

An engraving of Alexander's seal.

Strathclyde, 8 July 1249

King Alexander II of Scots has fallen sick with a fever and died on Kerrera island, opposite Oban. He was on his way to the Western Isles to oust their Norwegian earls and impose his own rule when death overtook him. Alexander was king for 34 of his 50 years, and it is to his credit that Scotland has enjoyed peace for much of that time. His own nobles respected him, as did King Henry III of England, whose sister he married and with whom he settled the long-running dispute over the Anglo-Scottish border.

But although nicknamed "the Peaceful", Alexander could be an implacable adversary when occasion demanded. In 1221 he punished Caithness rebels, who had killed the local bishop, by ordering a hand and a foot of each rebel to be cut off. Shrewd and vigorous on campaign, Alexander stamped his authority on rebels in the northwest and in Galloway. He modernised justice in Scotland by collecting and codifying laws. He is to be buried at Melrose, and is succeeded as king by his eight-year-old son Alexander [*see report below*].

Ten-year-old Scots monarch is married

York, 26 December 1251

A ten-year-old king married an eleven-year-old princess in the abbey here today and foiled an attempt by her father to trick him out of his kingdom.

King Alexander III of Scots was knighted with other young nobles yesterday on the eve of his wedding to King Henry III's daughter Margaret. The wedding took place at first light to avoid public clamour and Margaret brought a 5,000 marks dowry with her. At the wedding reception, Henry angered the Scots guests by trying to persuade the boy king to do homage to him for all of Scotland. Clearly well schooled, Alexander said that he had come to marry and "not to answer about so difficult a matter".

However, Henry appears to have acquired the right to demand the resignation of his son-in-law's officials and replace them with men that he can trust (→ 26/2/75).

A page from an illustrated apocalypse book made c.1270 for King Henry.

Henry builds a house in the Tower for his elephant, the first ever seen in England

A home for an elephant: an illustration from a late 12th-century bestiary.

London, 1256

Citizens watched in awe today as an elephant lumbered its way from Tilbury docks to the Tower of London. The great beast is a present from King Louis IX of France to King Henry III and will reside in the menagerie which Henry has had built in the Tower.

The elephant was brought from Dover to the docks by water and will live in a specially built house, 40ft long by 20ft wide (12 by six metres). Hundreds are flocking to see it and other animals in the royal collection. Henry's great-great-grandfather, Henry I, was the first king to have a menagerie. In his park at Woodstock, in Oxfordshire, he kept lions, leopards and camels. Richard the Lionheart brought a crocodile home with him from the Crusades, but it slipped into the Thames, never to be seen again.

English royal is chosen to rule Germany

London, 4 January 1257

With the death of King Frederick II of Germany, the ambitious Earl Richard of Cornwall, Henry III's younger brother, has been elected king of Germany. A deeply pious prince whose loyalty to the king has never been doubted but often sorely tested, Richard is one of the most thoughtful of today's noblemen.

Apart from being the king's brother, Richard is well connected by his marriages. His first was to Isabella, a daughter of the great William Marshal, the former regent. The relationship stood him in good stead in disputes with his brother. His second marriage in 1243 to Sanchia, the sister of the queens of France and England, put him in a strong position in Europe and has helped keep good relations between Henry and King Louis of France.

The earl is pious, certainly, but he is also a brilliant businessman, financing a reform of the coinage in 1247 in exchange for a half share in the profits (→ 2/4/1272).

Henry's patronage promotes golden age of arts, architecture and scholarship

Westminster, 1269

Henry III is an exceptionally pious king, hearing mass several times a day, and a man of sensitivity and taste who has sponsored a great boom in the arts and learning.

His greatest memorial will undoubtedly be the rebuilding of Westminster abbey church at his own expense as a home for the shrine of its royal founder, St Edward the Confessor. The shrine was consecrated this year. The abbey rebuilding aims to further the mystique of kingship and show that Henry rivals King Louis of France as a patron of the church. He chose a French cathedral plan and an architect known as Master Henry of Reyns, obviously familiar with the newly-completed cathedral of Rheims where French kings are crowned. There are influences of the royal *Sainte Chapelle* which Louis began in Paris three years before work began on the abbey in 1245. But the result is a combination of English and French Gothic on an exalted scale, with the highest vaulted roof in England.

The shrine for the bones of the Confessor, of gold and precious stones, is set on a base of mosaic in coloured marble, commissioned from an Italian, Pietro Oderisi, and cost £5000. It was inaugurated this year. So far Henry has spent not far short of £50,000 on the abbey. He has also spent over £100,000 on his

A late C13th portrait, probably of Henry, in Westminster abbey.

castles, including £15,000 for new apartments and a chapel at Windsor.

At his palace of Westminster Henry has ordered fine wall-paintings for his bedchamber and replaced horn in the windows by glass. Mural painting flourishes, as does the "court school" of more realistic sculpture in tomb effigies in Westminster abbey and elsewhere. Such wonders as the west front of Wells cathedral, a gallery of portraits in stone, show the healthy state of English sculpture.

Learning has been boosted under Henry with the establishment of England's first university at Oxford. Three permanent colleges – University, Balliol and Merton – have been set up under the auspices of a chancellor, Bishop Robert Grosseteste.

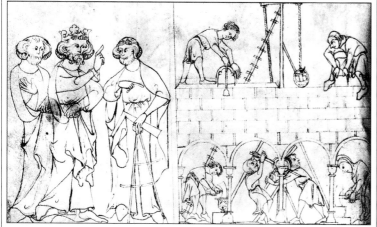
King Henry supervises masons at work rebuilding Westminster abbey.

Aggrieved nobles force pledge from king

Oxford, June 1258

With England facing the most serious constitutional crisis since *Magna Carta*, King Henry and his eldest son Edward are being forced to hand over a large share of government to the country's peers. The king and prince must also swear an oath on the Bible that their French relatives, the de Lusignans, will be expelled from England.

Under the provisions of the agreement made here, the king has nominated 12 members of the new council, with the peers electing a further 12. The Great Seal of the kingdom is in the hands of the confederates, who include the Earls of Gloucester and Norfolk and the king's brother-in-law, Simon de Montfort, the Earl of Leicester, one of the prime movers of the coup.

The king has agreed that no taxes will be levied on the clergy or the laity to pursue plans against Sicily. A new justiciar, or chief legal official, Hugh Bigod, has been appointed and is already hearing pleas at the Tower of London, and three parliaments will be held annually. The chancellor and treasurer will be subject to the control of the council; and the whole administration is now firmly under the control of both the barons and the king.

Much has happened since 12 April when the confederates decided to act together when parliament reopened. Henry has yet to call on the French (→ 1259).

Henry comes to an agreement with his nobles, as imagined by a later artist.

Norwegian king is routed by Scots

Strathclyde, 2 October 1263

In a ferociously-fought battle at Largs on the west coast a thousand Norwegians led by their king, Haakon, have been defeated by a Scottish army. Haakon had been trying to salvage ships beached by storms at Largs when the Scots attacked. The ships were from a fleet which Haakon had assembled to intimidate the Scots into accepting his lordship of the islands from Man to Shetland. His claim still stands, but after today's disaster it now looks highly precarious.

King Louis throws out barons' claims

Amiens, France, 25 January 1264

King Henry III has been freed from his obligations under the Provisions of Oxford of 1258 at a *mise*, or arbitration tribunal, here headed by King Louis IX, his brother-in-law. Louis was chosen by the king and his baronial adversaries to adjudicate on the king's oaths to observe the Provisions. Both sides have agreed that they will abide by Louis's arbitration, but his decision to declare the Provisions null and void will not be well received in England (→ 4/2).

Henry faces a civil war

Gloucester, 4 February 1264

As civil war draws closer, bridges across the river Severn were being destroyed today to prevent attacks from across the border by armies under by the two sons of Simon de Montfort, who is leading the opposition to King Henry.

The king's brother, Richard of Cornwall, is dashing west to pave the way for the return of the king and his son Edward from France. Battle lines are being drawn up all over the country. The north is hostile to Earl Simon, and so are many magnates, but he has considerable support from lesser landowners and reformers who include Oxford students and nobles like the Earls of Gloucester and Norfolk (→ 2/5).

War erupts: Henry is captured at Lewes

SEAL OF SIMON DE MONTFORT.

An engraving of the seal of Simon de Montfort, the king's enemy.

Lewes, East Sussex, 14 May 1264

Henry III and his son Edward are prisoners of Simon de Montfort, the Earl of Leicester, tonight after a fiercely fought battle in which they were outwitted by dissident barons. Victory has given de Montfort unprecedented power.

Edward made the grave mistake of charging a brilliantly decorated litter which he assumed was carrying de Montfort. It was empty, and Edward's charge took him out of the field of battle, giving Earl Simon the opportunity to outflank the king's army with his armoured cavalry (→ 4/8/65).

King supreme as rebel dies at Evesham

Evesham, 4 August 1265

The body of Simon de Montfort, the soldier-reformer, lies dismembered and horribly mutilated on a battlefield here tonight after he and his army were overrun by the forces of King Henry's son Edward. His head has been sent to the wife of his arch-enemy, Roger Mortimer. Thus perished the most powerful man in England for the past three months – beaten because those he had led had begun to mistrust him. Earl Simon's men had fought valiantly, but his Welsh archers fled when they were blinded by a fierce rain squall. Simon formed a ring of knights around the king whom they held captive, but their slaughter was inevitable. The king escaped.

De Montfort had brought both the king and his son with him to the west country where he was seeking to consolidate his victory at Lewes in May. With the connivance of loyal knights, Edward escaped while out riding and joined up with loyalist allies (→ 24/8/66).

Simon de Montfort, hacked to pieces by royalists at the Battle of Evesham.

Henry is laid to rest after 56-year reign

London, 16 November 1272

King Henry III died peacefully today after the longest reign in English history. He had been in failing health for some years. Henry will be buried in the rebuilt abbey church at Westminster, an architectural masterpiece to which he devoted the latter years of his life – leaving day-to-day government to his son Edward, now king.

It is for the abbey and the construction of Salisbury cathedral that Henry is most likely to be remembered. As a king he did not command respect and was an odd mixture of petulance and piety. His piety was shown during his several visits to France when he infuriated his brother-in-law, King Louis IX, by demanding that every priest he saw on the road should say a mass for him; his great obsession in life was to see the bones of his favourite saint, King Edward the Confessor, buried in a shrine in the newly-completed abbey. This ambition was achieved three years ago when Henry and his brother, Earl Richard of Cornwall, and their sons carried the Confessor's remains to the high altar.

Henry was notoriously mean. On Edward's birth, messengers were dispatched to tell the news to the country's nobles. Henry returned presents that he regarded as unsatisfactory and made his anger clear. According to the St Albans historian Matthew Paris, a nobleman said at the time: "God gave us this child, but the king sells him to us."

King Henry III: a gilt-bronze effigy in Westminster abbey, which he rebuilt.

Henry III: good, bad or indifferent king?

London, 1272

Henry was not a great king by any constitutional standard, although his legacy to the nation of Westminster abbey and other fine buildings ensures that he will always have a singular place in history.

He came to the throne at a time of great change. The ink on *Magna Carta* was hardly dry, and French troops occupied much of southern England. He was fortunate in the two regents who governed during his minority. William Marshal secured a great victory for the king at Lincoln, and Hubert de Burgh was equally effective in destroying the French fleet off Dover. Henry's petulance began to show when he dismissed de Burgh and surrounded himself with foreign advisers, but it was his misgovernment and clear contempt for the spirit of Magna Carta that led to the rebellion led by Simon de Montfort, his brother-in-law.

His lack of trustworthiness was shown when he repudiated the Provisions of Oxford – which limited royal power – despite his solemn oaths. But for all his faults, Henry was a pious and sensitive man who presided over a period of great intellectual and artistic achievement.

Edward I 1272–1307	Alexander III 1249–1286 Margaret 1286–1290 INTERREGNUM 1290–1292 John 1292–1296 INTERREGNUM 1296–1306 Robert I 1306–1329

Westminster, 19 August 1274. King Edward is crowned.→

Scotland, 26 February 1275. Margaret, the wife of King Alexander III, dies (→28/10/78).

Westminster, April 1275. King Edward calls the first parliament of his reign (→1285).

Wales, 29 August 1277. Edward invades to force Llywelyn ap Gruffudd of Gwynedd to pay homage, which he has persistently refused (→13/10/78).

Worcester, 13 October 1278. Llywelyn ap Gruffudd, who defeated Edward last year, marries Eleanor de Montfort, Edward's cousin (→11/12/82).

Norway, July 1281. Margaret, the daughter of Alexander III, king of Scots, marries King Eric II of Norway (→9/4/83).

Scotland, 15 November 1282. Alexander, the only son and heir of Alexander III, marries Margaret, the eldest daughter of the Count of Flanders.

Wales, 11 December 1282. Llywelyn ap Gruffudd of Gwynedd dies in battle against King Edward (→25/11/83).

Norway, 9 April 1283. Queen Margaret of Norway, the daughter of Alexander III, dies in childbirth; her daughter is also named Margaret (→25/2/84).

Tayside, 5 February 1284. Margaret, the "Maid of Norway", the granddaughter of Alexander III, is recognised as his new heir following the death of his son Alexander last month (→14/10/85).

Caernarfon, 24 April 1284. Queen Eleanor has her fourth son, Edward (→17/12/90).

Scotland, 14 October 1285. Alexander III marries Yolande, the daughter of Robert, the Count of Dreux (→20/3/86).

Deheubarth, September 1287. Rhys ap Maredudd of Drwslyn rebels against the rule of King Edward (→4/1292).

Strathclyde, 1287. Robert Bruce, a claimant to the throne, rebels against the succession of the four-year-old "Maid of Norway" (→17/11/92).

France, 19 May 1294. Anglo-French relations break down after Margaret, the sister of Philip IV, spurns Edward's offer of marriage (→6/1294).

England, June 1294. King John Balliol of Scots declares he will fight for Edward against Philip IV of France (→3/1296).

Newcastle, March 1296. The Scots ally with France and invade England; John Balliol refuses to meet Edward.→

Central, 11 September 1297. The Scots rebel against English rule; led by William Wallace they deliver a stunning defeat to the English at the Battle of Stirling Bridge (→22/7/98).

Falkirk, 22 July 1298. Edward crushes William Wallace and his rebel army (→23/8/1305).

Canterbury, 10 September 1299. Edward marries Margaret of France as part of a peace deal between the two countries.→

France, January 1302. John Balliol, the former king of Scots, is freed from his imprisonment (→4/1313).

Cumbria, 7 July 1307. Edward dies of dysentery en route for Scotland.→

Edward comes to throne while on crusade

Sicily, 17 November 1272
At the age of 33 Lord Edward, the eldest son of Henry III, is to be England's new king. Barons proclaimed him king within hours of his father's death yesterday; the Earl of Gloucester led the way, publicly swearing allegiance to King Edward. Other barons and churchmen followed to begin the reign without dissent and, indeed, without Edward's knowledge; he is in Sicily with Charles of Anjou on his way home from the crusades.

Edward's reputation, already high after his role in the Battle of Evesham, has been enhanced by his part in the crusade for which he left England in 1270. He relieved Acre, captured Nazareth and fought off an assassination attempt in June this year. As crusades go, his success was modest, but tales of princely valour are spreading (→19/8/74).

Edward returns to spectacular coronation

A magnificent occasion: King Edward is crowned in Westminster abbey.

Westminster, 19 August 1274
Nearly two years after he was proclaimed king, and just one day after he returned to his capital after four years overseas, Edward was today crowned in sumptuous splendour in Westminster abbey. Vast crowds had cheered the king's return, and celebrations continued today. Wine flowed freely in the city of London while the king and Queen Eleanor enjoyed a spectacular coronation banquet in Westminster Hall. Preparations for the feast have been going on for six months, the organisers taking full advantage of Edward's delayed coronation.

The tables groaned under oxen, chickens, sheep, salmon, boars and gamefowl. New kitchens were built; the palace was redecorated; thrones were cast in stone. A silk canopy covered the carpeted path from palace to abbey (→4/1275).

Welsh rebellion is brutally put down

Aberconwy, 25 November 1283
Dafydd, the Prince of Gwynedd and would-be Prince of Wales, was executed today, and with him is extinguished another brief flowering of a united and independent Wales. Edward has quashed the Welsh uprising which had already claimed the life of Dafydd's brother, Llywelyn ap Gruffudd.

Since 1256 Llywelyn had had greater authority over Wales than any of his predecessors. Even England's Henry III had recognised his power by reaching deals over land and titles. But Llywelyn angered Edward, Henry's successor, by failing to pay homage, and in 1276 Edward declared the Welsh prince a rebel and sent forces into Wales. By 1277 Llywelyn was compelled to accept a peace settlement which reduced his rule to a mountainous fiefdom in Snowdonia.

Now even this independence has gone. Llywelyn's brother, Dafydd, lit the fuse when in March last year he led an attack on Hawarden in Clwyd. Initial Welsh success encouraged Llywelyn to return to the fray but stiffened Edward's resolve to conquer Wales once and for all. On 11 December Llywelyn was killed near Builth. Edward moved deeper into Wales until in June Dafydd, now with only a handful of men, was betrayed. Today possibly the last Welsh prince was the first man to be hanged, drawn and quartered as an example to other potential "traitors" to Edward (→ 9/1287).

The mighty fallen: a romanticised view of the death of Prince Llywelyn.

Brothers-in-law avert new Scottish crisis

Westminster, 28 October 1278
The threat of a serious diplomatic breach between the kings of England and Scotland was averted today when King Alexander III of Scots paid homage to his brother-in-law Edward for his lands in England. But tension was heightened when the bishop of Norwich, who was present, suggested that Alexander should acknowledge that he held Scotland, too, with Edward's consent.

Alexander brushed aside the bishop's suggestion. "To homage for my kingdom of Scotland no one has right except God alone," he said. "Nor do I hold it except of

God alone." Edward did not press the matter, but it is clear that the English have simply reserved their position. For the time being the good personal relations between the two monarchs prevent enmity between their kingdoms.

These relations are close in a literal sense: in 1251, at the age of ten, Alexander married Margaret, Edward's 11-year-old sister. She and her husband were honoured guests at Edward's coronation in 1274, and even after her death three years ago the two families have remained in friendly contact, with the two royal brothers-in-law content to preserve peace (→ 7/1281).

Tot is queen after a clifftop tragedy

Fife, 20 March 1286
King Alexander III of Scots died last night when he was thrown from his horse in stormy, misty weather as he was returning from Edinburgh to Dunfermline palace. Devastated courtiers found his body this morning. The king was 45 and had reigned for 36 years.

Unless Alexander's widow, Queen Yolande, is pregnant, his heir is Margaret, the two-year-old daughter of the king of Norway, his sole surviving grandchild. All three of Alexander's children predeceased him.

Edward tackles law and order in the kingdom

Westminster, 1285
Two "statutes" of legal changes have this year confirmed King Edward's reputation as a great law reformer. One, agreed at Winchester, deals with criminal law, whilst the second, at Westminster, covers land ownership. Both statutes reflect Edward's desire to make the law clearer and more effective.

The far-reaching changes over which Edward has presided do not challenge the basic nature of society, let alone countenance any dilution of the royal prerogative. If anything, the king's power has been strengthened by the various statutes which have been agreed by councils and parliaments.

The king's European connections may have made him aware of the interest in new forms of law at universities such as Bologna, but Edward's aim has been to improve and codify existing English law rather than to introduce new concepts. His principal aide has been his chancellor, Robert Burnell. The first evidence of the new mood at court came with what is now known as the First Statute of Westminster. This was agreed by the parliament of 1275 and followed an inquiry by local commissioners which produced the "Hundred Rolls" report. This statute had 51 sections and, in effect, tidied up inconsistent practices unearthed by the Hundred Rolls inquiry.

This was followed in 1278 by an attempt to define the rights of barons. In 1279 the Statute of Mortmain dealt with gifts of land by the church. This year's Statute of Winchester appoints justices of the peace and strengthens the laws to preserve public order (following the king's moves last year against crime and prostitution in London). And now the Second Statute of Westminster establishes hereditary ownership of land; it is potentially the most significant reform yet (→ 1295).

King and queen in thunderbolt drama

Gascony, France, 1287

King Edward and Queen Eleanor came close to death this year when lightning struck the room where they were, killing two people. The royal couple escaped unhurt, but there are some who see the incident as an omen of trouble to come in Edward's French lands.

Edward returned to Gascony, in south-western France, last year. The value he places on his French inheritance was demonstrated in 1273 when, returning from the crusades, he chose to visit Gascony as Duke of Aquitaine before arriving in England to be crowned.

He returned to his duchy in the autumn of last year, intent on a major reorganisation of government and the law. Overshadowing these internal changes, however, is the possibility of a challenge from Edward's cousin, the French king, Philip IV, who came to the throne two years ago. The English king holds Gascony as a fiefdom from France under a 1259 treaty. Philip III accepted this but his son resents the English presence (→ 17/12/90).

Edward expels all Jews from English soil

The Jews are expelled by royal decree (taken from a later manuscript).

Westminster, 18 July 1290

All Jews are to be expelled from England, according to a royal edict issued today. Years of controversy about usury – the Jews' practice of charging interest on money lent, which Christians cannot do under canon law – will culminate in the expulsion of around 3,000 people. Last year Edward banished Jews from his lands in Gascony.

The king's move will be highly popular. Knights sanctioned a new tax to boost royal coffers on condition that the Jews were expelled. In 1275 the first parliament of Edward's reign had banned usury and ordered Jews to live by trade and to wear yellow strips of cloth. They were given 15 years to comply with the law, but some usury continued with interest payments disguised.

Prejudice also played a part in today's decision; the king is renowned as a crusader and regards Jews as anti-Christian. But royal safe-conduct passes will protect Jews as they travel to the ports.

Child queen will never sit on throne

Kirkwall, 26 September 1290

The seven-year-old Queen Margaret of Scots has died as she travelled from her native Norway to her kingdom. Her death throws the succession wide open.

The "Maid of Norway" never even set foot on Scottish soil. She had lived in Norway where her mother, the daughter of Alexander III, died in childbirth. Alexander's two sons also died young, leaving Margaret as the sole heir in 1286. Since then her future had been the topic of fierce controversy within Scotland as six guardians took control of the kingdom in her name. She also figured in treaties with King Edward under which she was to marry the English king's son.

But a rough crossing from Norway proved too much for the frail child, and she was dead by the time her ship reached the Orkneys. The rivalries within Scotland now seem certain to surface - especially between the two powerful Anglo-Scots baronial families of Bruce and Balliol - and with them the prospect of English intervention.

King Edward orders monuments to commemorate his queen

Westminster, 17 December 1290

A grieving King Edward today laid to rest his beloved wife, Queen Eleanor of Castile, who died at Harby in Nottinghamshire on 28 November. She was 54 years old, and Edward plans to commemorate her life by erecting elaborate memorial crosses at each of the 12 places where her funeral cortege stopped overnight on its long journey to Westminster abbey.

Thus ends an arranged marriage which turned out to be one of genuine affection. Eleanor was only nine when she married her 15-year-old prince. She grew up to become a striking dark-haired woman who loyally followed her husband in his travels. She went with him on his journeys to the Holy Land, Wales and Gascony.

Eleanor and Edward had 15 children, 11 daughters and four sons; the last child, a girl, was born and died this year. Seven daughters and one son, Edward, the heir to the throne, survive. Neither the

Eleanor: laid to rest in the abbey.

A cross in Eleanor's memory.

king nor Eleanor seemed overly preoccupied with their family, frequently leaving them behind when they travelled abroad. Four children were born on their travels, including two in Palestine.

The queen herself acquired a mixed reputation in her adopted country. She was a cultured woman, hiring scribes to write books and fond of tapestries with which she liked to decorate her rooms in the palace. But she could also be a tough landlady, imposing heavy taxes on her tenants and eager to increase her property.

Gruesome end for Welsh royal line

York, April 1292

King Edward drove another nail into the coffin of Welsh independence this month with the grisly death of Rhys ap Maredudd, the Lord of Drwslyn and the last important member of the royal house of Deheubarth, the former kingdom of south Wales. Rhys was hanged, drawn and quartered for leading a revolt in 1287.

Ironically, the root of the revolt was Rhys's loyalty to King Edward in the Welsh wars a decade ago. Edward promised him land as a reward, including his ancient family seat of Dynefwr, but legal wrangles over Rhys's estates followed and in June 1287 Rhys seized Dynefwr and other castles by force. Edmund of Cornwall, the king's lieutenant, led the counter-attack, and by the following January the rising was over. Rhys escaped and lived a fugitive life in the Welsh hills until his betrayal this year.

Scots feel the weight of Edward's fist

New king of Scots is English vassal

Berwick, 17 November 1292
John Balliol was today named as the new king of Scots, ending two years in which the Scottish throne stood vacant. Yet John is not the only victor; England's King Edward has exploited the interregnum to advance his claim to be Scotland's overlord. Next month, after being crowned on the ancient "Stone of Destiny" at Scone, King John has promised to do homage to Edward, acknowledging the English king as his superior.

The death in 1290 of the "Maid of Norway" left two strong claimants: John Balliol and Robert Bruce, both descended from daughters of King David (1124-53). Edward offered himself as mediator, presiding over 13 rival claims at Norham near Berwick.

Balliol won, as he is descended from David's eldest daughter whereas Bruce is descended from the second daughter. He is 42 years old, the son of an English baron and relatively unknown in his new kingdom. Edward's aim to make the new king his vassal gives King John an uneasy inheritance (→ 6/1294).

John Balliol, as the new king of Scotland, pays homage to King Edward as his "overlord"; Edward has eased John's passage to the throne.

Edward calls a new parliament to put stamp on his rule

Westminster, 1295
The largest parliament yet to meet in England was held this year at Westminster, and, as usual, the king's need for money was the principal factor in summoning the assembly. What makes this year's parliament unusual is that it was more representative than ever before, with two knights chosen by the courts of each shire and two citizens from each city or borough.

These elected representatives from the community joined the other two estates – the barons and clergy – in what some are calling a "model parliament". In the past, Edward's parliaments have been fairly informal affairs. They would meet wherever the king happened to be, and the composition would vary from year to year.

After the turmoil in his father's reign, when Simon de Montfort led attempts to assert parliament's power, Edward has sought to retain the support of the people for his rule, particularly when he needs to raise money, as he does this year for his French wars. His call to parliament that "what touches all should be approved by all" signals an important precedent.

Balliol is defiant as Edward threatens

Berwick, March 1296
Scotland's embattled King John has defied a demand by King Edward that he bow to England's power over Scotland. War is now inevitable, and the English king is mustering a powerful army at Newcastle Upon Tyne. John had acknowledged the overlordship of Edward when he was chosen to be king in 1292, but relations soured when Edward sought to impose the right of English courts to hear appeals from Scotland. Last year Edward summoned John to Westminster. He went (which upset the Scots) but refused to answer questions (which upset the English). A treaty with France followed, but the Scots will face the English army without their new allies (→ 10/7).

Scots king abdicates after bitter defeat

King John is now powerless.

Tayside, 10 July 1296
King John has been stripped of his crown and forced to surrender the Scottish kingdom to the forces of England's King Edward. In a ceremony designed to humiliate John and to mock Scottish independence hopes, the king of Scots signed a paper admitting his crimes against his English overlord. He was then publicly and symbolically stripped of his crown, sceptre, sword, rings and even the fur from his robes.

John's rebellion was quickly and bloodily crushed. After he failed to pay homage to Edward in March, the English king sacked Berwick, massacring 7,000. Then at Dunbar John's forces were routed, and the Scottish castles began to surrender. John will be exiled in England, along with the insignia of his once-independent kingdom (→ 1/1302).

Edward puts down uprising in Wales

Conwy, June 1295
King Edward has crushed a revolt which began last autumn with attacks on English castles throughout Wales. High taxes appear to have been the cause of the uprising, which is the second since Edward defeated Llywelyn, the last independent Prince of Wales, in 1282 and took control two years later.

During the winter the English king assembled a large army which covered much of the principality, from Caernarfon to Glamorgan. A key battle was at Maes Moydog, north-west of Montgomery, in March when Madog ap Llywelyn, one of the leaders, was defeated. He escaped, but the struggle was lost, enabling Edward to turn his campaign into a victory procession.

▷

Awesome Edward brings Scots and Welsh to heel

King orders a grisly end for Scots hero

London, 23 August 1305
William Wallace, the Scottish rebel who resisted and eluded King Edward for eight years, was today executed for treason, with his head and limbs severed for public display. To many Scots he was a hero: the man who had defeated an English army at Stirling in 1297, and who had championed Scottish independence by defying English rule. To Edward and the English he was an outlaw: a man who reputedly killed anyone who spoke English, even children or nuns. Wallace was subjected to a peremptory trial at Westminster yesterday, after which he was dragged to the grisly death which King Edward hopes will deter other potential rebels against his rule.

William Wallace: a later portrait.

Marriage seals peace with French king

Canterbury, 10 September 1299
King Edward today married for the second time. His wife is Margaret, the sister of King Philip IV of France, and it is a marriage which has been arranged to help end years of tension between the two kingdoms. These have included disputes over Edward's fiefdom in Gascony, French support for the Scots, and a war over French territorial claims in Flanders. A truce was agreed after papal intervention. This has now been sealed by today's wedding, but many complex issues remain to be resolved.

English king creates son Prince of Wales

Lincoln, 7 February 1301
King Edward today bestowed on his son and heir Edward the vacant title of Prince of Wales, making him the first English royal officially to be called a prince. The young Edward is being presented to the people of Wales as a prince born in the principality – he was born at Caernarfon on 25 April 1284. That was also the year when the English king ended Welsh independence by the Statute of Rhuddlan.

Whether Welsh pride will be assuaged by today's announcement is doubtful. There have been two revolts against English rule since 1284 – each swiftly suppressed by King Edward – and the newly-created prince has had no known connections with Wales since his birth. Even his place of birth cannot be represented as having been a deliberate royal choice; at the time an elder brother, Alphonso, was still alive. Nonetheless Prince Edward, who also becomes Earl of Chester, is to be dispatched to Wales later this year to receive the homage of the people.

The prince has begun to play an active role in his father's military campaigns in Scotland, leading a

Prince Edward is Prince of Wales.

successful assault on Caerlaverock castle in Galloway last year. Here he won the praise of a poet who described him as strong in battle and "well-proportioned and handsome". Edward's relationship with the tough, strict king does not appear to be close, and his mother died when he was six. He is said to find solace in very close and emotional male friendships (→ 7/7/07).

New throne adds insult to injury for Scots

The coronation chair: for Edward.

Westminster, 1300
In a move calculated to infuriate Scottish national feeling, King Edward has ordered the construction of an elaborate new coronation chair to house the ancient "Stone of Destiny" on which kings of Scots have been enthroned for centuries at Scone. Edward, who seized the stone as war booty, intends the chair to be used for the coronations of future English monarchs, symbolising Scotland's subservient role.

English dominance was demonstrated again this year in Galloway with Caerlaverock castle falling to Edward in July, and a Scottish defeat on the river Cree. In October Edward bowed to the pope's plea for peace and granted the Scots a truce, but nobody doubts that he will use force again if the Scots challenge his authority.

Bruce brings hopes of end to English yoke

Tayside, 27 March 1306
Robert Bruce today raised the flag of Scottish independence when he was proclaimed king in a ceremony at Scone. The enthronement was performed by Isabel, the Countess of Buchan, who claimed the right of the Macduffs to set the king on his throne, in this case a makeshift replacement for the "Stone of Destiny" seized by King Edward.

Robert moved quickly to assert his claim after a quarrel last month in which he and his supporters killed John Comyn, an ally of Scotland's exiled ex-king, John Balliol. Bruce, the Earl of Carrick, has switched sides more than once between his countrymen and his overlord, Edward. His defiance now will surely prompt ruthless retaliation by a king who is not to be crossed with impunity (→ 25/12/07).

Robert Bruce, Scotland's new king.

Scotland cheers as 'Hammer' Edward dies of dysentery

Cumbria, 7 July 1307

King Edward is dead. He died not in battle but of dysentery in the arms of his servants at Burgh by Sands, north-west of Carlisle, as he prepared for yet another Scottish campaign. He was 68 years old and will be succeeded by his son who, at 23, now becomes Edward II.

The news will delight followers of Robert Bruce, whose family and friends suffered savage reprisals after Robert was proclaimed king of Scots last year. Edward moved north to combat the renewed Scots challenge, but poor health slowed his progress. Already buoyed by successful skirmishes in Ayrshire, Robert will be boosted further by the death of the man known as "the Hammer of the Scots" (→8/7).

'Longshanks': the bold, brutal king

Westminster, 24 July 1307

More than two weeks after his death, officialdom today finally came to terms with the passing of King Edward I when his seal was used on state documents for the last time. Edward had ruled for 33 years, succeeding with a reputation forged in battles at home and crusades in the Holy Land. He was an imposing figure, standing six feet (1.8 metres) tall, hence one nickname, "Longshanks". Age turned his black hair white but did nothing to mellow the ferocity with which he enforced his authority. Although devoted to his first queen, Eleanor, he was a remote and even harsh father, for instance banishing his son's friend – or rather, it is rumoured, lover – Piers Gaveston.

It was a reign of remarkable achievements. He conquered the Welsh and subdued the Scots. He encouraged a series of legal and administrative reforms which transformed the criminal and civil law. He called more frequent and more representative parliaments. Abroad he was less successful, fighting a costly French war which leaves an uneasy peace in Europe as well as fresh trouble in Scotland.

Edward leaves a string of massive castles in Wales to prevent further rebellions against the authority of England's rulers

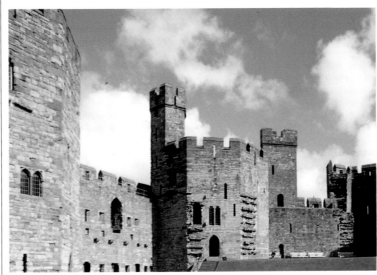

The spacious palace-fortress at Caernarfon, built by King Edward in 1284.

The lavish spread and stern aspect of the castle at Conwy, in Gwynedd.

The forbidding Beaumaris castle on Anglesey, Gwynedd, built in 1294/5.

Wales, 1307

One of King Edward's greatest legacies is the network of massive fortresses which have gone up on his orders throughout Wales. It is the greatest castle-building programme ever seen in the principality, although the Welsh can hardly be pleased with the new structures which are designed to ensure that independence, crushed with the death of Prince Llywelyn in 1282, never rears its head again.

The £80,000 programme began in 1277 when Edward marched into north Wales with the objective of confining Llywelyn within the mountains of Gwynedd. He recruited a force of nearly 3,000 workers, masons, carpenters and diggers from all over England. They threw up castles at Flint, Rhuddlan, Aberystwyth and Builth, all completed within four years.

Edward had seen the latest developments in castle-building in France, and he persuaded a master mason from Savoy, James of St George, to enter his service to bring the new techniques to Wales. Master James provided Flint castle with its great round tower commanding the shore and linked it with a new fortified town on the French pattern. Rhuddlan was on the concentric plan, with outer and inner curtain walls protecting the central ward with towering twin gatehouses. It guarded another fortified town.

After the revolt of 1282 came a new spurt of castle-building on an even more ambitious scale. This produced Caernarfon, a palace-fortress built as the seat of government, the birthplace of the first English Prince of Wales, Edward, in 1284. Buttressing the town wall, it contains a great hall and seven great towers, yet it can be garrisoned, like all Edward's new castles in Wales, by just 30 men. Other new castles are at Ruthin, Caergwrle, Conwy, Beaumaris and Harlech, which has the most impressive site of all, perched high above Tremadog Bay.

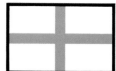

Edward II
1307–1327

Robert I
1306–1329

England, 8 July 1307. Edward of Caernarfon accedes to the English throne (→6/8).

Grampian, 25 December 1307. King Robert of Scotland ends his campaign with the defeat of Earl John Comyn of Buchan (→15/9/08).

Westminster, 25 February 1308. Edward is crowned king of England (→25/6).

Bristol, 25 June 1308. Edward sends his exiled favourite, Piers Gaveston, the newly-appointed Earl of Cornwall, to Ireland as lieutenant (→27/6/09).

Strathclyde, 15 September 1308. After the victory of his brother, Edward, at Galloway, King Robert defeats Alexander Mac-Dougal in the Brander Pass (→16/3/09).

Fife, 16 March 1309. Robert holds his first parliament and firmly states the Bruce claim to the Scottish throne (→24/2/10).

Chester, 27 June 1309. Despite strong opposition, Gaveston returns from Ireland and is greeted by King Edward (→7/1309).

Stamford, July 1309. Edward agrees to the demands of the barons (→27/9/11).

Powys, 1309. Llywelyn ap Owain, the last descendant of the princes of Deheubarth, dies.

Tayside, 24 February 1310. King Robert gains the support of the Scottish clergy for his sovereignty (→24/6/14).

France, April 1313. John Balliol, the deposed Scottish king, dies in exile.

Westminster, 14 October 1314. Following the assassination of Gaveston two years ago, Edward and his barons are formally reconciled (→8/1316).

Paisley, 2 March 1316. King Robert's only daughter, Marjorie, who married Walter "the Stewart" last year, dies in a riding accident (→3/12/18).

Eltham Palace, 15 August 1316. Queen Isabella gives birth to a second son, John.

York, August 1316. Earl Thomas of Lancaster, the chief councillor, has a violent quarrel with King Edward over Scotland (→6/1317).

Yorkshire, June 1317. The route to Scotland is barred by the Earl of Lancaster's army (→9/8/18).

Scone, 3 December 1318. The Scottish parliament declares Robert's heir to be Walter the Stewart (→25/12/19).

Berwick, 25 December 1319. Edward signs a truce with Robert of Scots and pays homage to Philip V of France for his French lands (→19/8/21).

Tower of London, August 1323. Roger Mortimer, imprisoned for opposing Edward's favourites, the Despensers, manages to escape (→21/9/25).

Fife, 5 March 1324. David, King Robert's son, is born (→1/2/27).

France, 25 August 1326. Queen Isabella arranges the betrothal of her son, Edward, to Philippa, the daughter of Count William III of Hainault; she uses the dowry money to mount an invasion of England (→2/10).

London, 24 January 1327. King Edward abdicates his throne in favour of his 14-year-old son, Edward.→

Edward II comes to the throne: his first act is to bring his lover back from exile

Edward II: the new king has proved himself an able warrior against the Scots.

Dumfries, 6 August 1307

One month after he became king, Edward II today shocked English barons by proclaiming his friend Piers Gaveston the new Earl of Cornwall. This is a title which, with its large landholdings, has traditionally gone to members of the royal family, so Edward's elevation of Gaveston provides a controversial start to his reign.

Gaveston had been banished from England earlier this year by King Edward I, who brusquely rejected his son's efforts to win favours for Gaveston. "You base-born whoreson," the king is said to have replied, tearing at his son's hair. "Do you want to give lands away now, you who have never gained any?" However, Gaveston has now returned and today received the title and riches previously denied to him.

Suspicion of Gaveston, with whom the new king is said to have a homosexual relationship, has marred Edward's inheritance. At 23 he has otherwise proved himself on the battlefields of Scotland and as regent during his father's absences from court. The only surviving son of Edward I, the new monarch has the outward trappings of kingship, being tall, strong, handsome and brave. It is his judgement which is now questioned by barons who resent the pivotal role that he apparently plans to allow his friend, Piers Gaveston, to fulfil (→25/1/08).

Gaveston storm mars royal wedding

King Edward II's envoys are received at the French court in 1299 (C14th).

Isabella: from a text of 1326.

Boulogne, 25 January 1308
Edward II was today married to Isabella of France, the daughter of the French king. It was a marriage arranged in 1299 when the new queen was only four years old. Since then her groom has become king, and she will travel to England next month for his coronation. Yet even the sumptuous royal wedding failed to dispel the rumblings of discontent which have accompanied Edward's first months on the throne. And, again, it is Piers Gaveston, the king's close friend, who is at the centre of the storm.

Before leaving for France Edward appointed Gaveston regent, further alienating the barons who already resent the power of the king's favourite. It was the third time in six months that Edward had demonstrated his determination to honour his friend. First came the title of Earl of Cornwall (formerly a royal preserve) with its rich estates. Then came a marriage in which Gaveston was matched with the king's niece, Margaret de Clare. Now Gaveston is regent, to symbolise his role as the second most powerful figure in the land.

Many English lords fear the influence of Gaveston over a young king who faces formidable challenges to his rule from King Robert of Scotland. Now 25 years old, Gaveston joined the court in 1297 when his father, a Gascon knight, joined Edward I in his Flanders campaign. Piers Gaveston soon attracted notice for his ebullient personality and martial skills, nowhere more so than in the regard of the impressionable English heir.

Edward has long made no secret of his affection for Gaveston, but it is not this of which the barons disapprove. They are angered by the favouritism which now enables Gaveston to flaunt his power as the king's principal aide, exercising royal patronage and excluding them from the innermost counsels. A challenge to Gaveston seems inevitable when parliament reassembles later this year (→ 25/2).

Royal power curbed as king bows to the demands of barons

London, 27 September 1311
King Edward was today compelled to bow to the demands of England's leading barons, which strengthen the power of parliament and call for the expulsion of the royal favourite, Piers Gaveston. This follows an 18-month inquiry by a committee of barons and churchmen known as the Lords Ordainers, angered by what they regard as the king's wilful exercise of power.

Today they published a list of 51 ordinances which greatly curb the royal prerogative, not only embracing general principles but also singling out specific individuals for punishment. Royal officials will be more accountable to parliament, whose consent is needed for kings to wage war. Financial reforms will require customs dues and other royal revenues to be paid directly to an independent exchequer. The king will delay implementation wherever possible. But one edict brooks no compromise: Piers Gaveston must be exiled, and stripped of his title, by 1 November or the king faces civil war (→ 19/6/12).

Son born to Edward and Queen Isabella

London, 13 November 1312
England has a new heir. A son was born today to Queen Isabella, and he is to be named Edward after his father. The news has lifted some of the gloom which has hung over the court since a distraught king heard the news last June that his long-time favourite, Piers Gaveston, had been murdered on the orders of some of England's leading barons.

The birth is also likely to enhance the closer relationship which has developed between king and queen since the death of Gaveston. The marriage had been arranged to serve diplomatic ends, but the king has been grateful for his wife's support during the last months. His spirits have also been lifted by support from some nobles critical of the manner of Gaveston's death, when promises of safe conduct were so bloodily broken (→ 15/8/16).

Lords give up hope of agreement with king and lynch Gaveston

Warwickshire, 19 June 1312
Piers Gaveston, the royal favourite who pushed the barons to the brink of civil war, was killed today on the orders of four leading barons, including the Earls of Warwick and Lancaster. Three times he has been banished, first by Edward I and then twice, under pressure, by Edward II; three times he has returned. This year, as the barons planned military action against the king, they kidnapped Gaveston and marched him barefoot to Warwick castle. Today he was taken two miles to Blacklow Hill where he was beheaded (→ 14/10/14).

Trouble brewing: a later engraving of Edward strolling with Gaveston.

Robert Bruce crushes the English at Bannock burn

A graphic portrayal of the Scottish victory in the battle at Bannock burn.

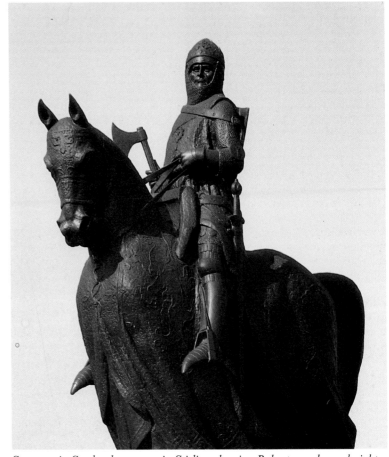

Supreme in Scotland: a statue in Stirling showing Robert as a brave knight.

Edward flees battleground for his life

Stirling, 24 June 1314
England's King Edward is tonight fleeing for his life after seeing his forces routed at the hands of King Robert of Scotland. Edward had sought sanctuary at Stirling castle, only to be told that it would be surrendered to the victorious Scots. Now the English king, who had fought bravely and was forced by his knights to leave the battlefield, is being escorted south to Dunbar.

Edward had led an army of 2,500 knights and 15,000 infantry towards Stirling where the castle was being besieged by Robert. It was one of only five strongholds to remain in English hands, and by far the most important. The Scots were outnumbered, but they were united under Robert's leadership. "Fight for the honour of your nation," the Scottish king told his men.

The battle lasted two days, with the English forces compressed into a small, marshy area between the river Forth and a small stream known as the Bannock burn. Yesterday it was the Scottish cavalry which surprised the English; today it was the *schiltrons* – battalions of spearmen – which led the assault. The English knights, fearing Edward's capture as much as his death, forced him to flee, causing panic among their forces as news spread of the king's flight. Thousands were slaughtered (→ 14/10).

Robert's family and friends hunted down

Stirling, 24 June 1314
Vengeance is sweet for King Robert tonight as he stands on the brink of entering Stirling castle. Now it is an English king on the run for his life, after years when Robert's own family and supporters have been hunted down, butchered or imprisoned by the English. Dozens have died, among them Robert's brothers and brother-in-law. His wife, Queen Elizabeth, was placed under house arrest, his sisters imprisoned or confined to nunneries. Edward I saw savagery as a deterrent, with prominent supporters of the Scottish king such as Simon Fraser being hanged, drawn and quartered, with parts of his body left on public display.

Victory boosts King Robert's reputation

Stirling, 24 June 1314
King Robert tonight stands supreme in Scotland, his authority unquestioned after putting the English king to flight. Past indecision, as when he made truces with England's Edward I, is forgotten. Internal rivalry, as when he battled against the supporters of the exiled John Balliol, will be vanquished.

Ironically, the hero of all Scotland was not born north of the border, but near Chelmsford, in Essex, in 1274. He is the grandson of the Robert Bruce whose claim to the throne in 1292 was rejected in favour of John Balliol's. It was 1304 before Robert Bruce, the Earl of Carrick as he had become, emerged finally on the side of Scottish nationalism when he secured church backing for his claim to the throne by the Bond of Cambuskenneth agreement. Two years later, he was king [*see report, page 66*].

The manner of his accession left enemies, notably in the Comyn family, but the death of Edward I and the weakness of the new English king helped Robert to secure some morale-boosting victories over the English which enhanced his authority at home. He even took the battle into England, raiding as far south as Durham to take some revenge for the brutal treatment suffered by his supporters [*see story left*] during his early years in power (→ 2/3/16).

Earl and king agree an uneasy truce

Nottingham, 9 August 1318

The two most powerful men in England – the king and the Earl of Lancaster – met on a bridge over the river Soar today and exchanged a kiss of peace. A few hours earlier, Lancaster signed a treaty at Leake with leading courtiers – although this treaty is to his disadvantage. The treaty ends several years of acute hostility. Edward remained furious at Lancaster's refusal to support him at Bannockburn and did not offer any help when Lancaster himself mounted an expedition against the Scots.

Then marital disharmony in Lancaster's household brought England to the brink of civil war. Alice, Lancaster's wife, was abducted by one of the Earl of Surrey's knights, Richard de St Martin, who claimed to be her lover. Surrey, spoiling for a fight, backed his man; with the two earls at war, Edward marched north to aid Surrey. The Earl of Pembroke, a king's man, negotiated today's treaty after successfully restraining Edward from an all-out campaign (→ 25/12/19).

Rebel earl defeated by a vengeful king

Boroughbridge, 17 March 1322

With the surrender here today of his arch-enemy, Earl Thomas of Lancaster, King Edward has finally regained complete control of his kingdom. Lancaster's army was soundly beaten by armies led by the king from the south and by Sir Andrew Harclay, the steward of Carlisle, whose men held the line of the river Ure.

Victory at Boroughbridge ends months of campaigning by the king in the south and west of England. Most of his successes were bloodless, and his army was in excellent condition when he headed north at the beginning of the year.

Lancaster was completely outmanoeuvred and forced to retreat. He had expected help from the Scots, but none was forthcoming. Confronted by Harclay's well-disciplined forces, many of his men fled. There will be no mercy for Lancaster after his part in the death of Piers Gaveston (→ 30/5/23).

In conflict with King Edward: a later view of Earl Thomas of Lancaster.

Scots declare their hatred of England

Tayside, 6 April 1320

The case for Scottish nationalism was set out in black and white today. The Declaration of Arbroath makes clear Scotland's thirst to shake off English domination and to strive for liberty – "which no honest man will lose but with his life".

King Robert is the moving force behind the declaration, which is to be sent to Pope John XXII. Not surprisingly Robert is praised for seeing off the English, but at the same time the declaration states baldly that if he should ever try to grant England power over Scotland, then the people would replace him. In other words, the nation comes first, not the king.

It is hoped that Pope John will get the message: Scotland will fight for its independence, no matter what (→ 30/5/23).

Despensers exiled

London, 19 August 1321

With rebel armies controlling much of this capital city, the king submitted to parliament's will today and agreed to the banishment of the hated Despensers, father and son. Having seized lands in the west, a powerful alliance of Marcher earls and other leading magnates under the Earl of Lancaster has arrested the king's close friends. Edward's relationship with Hugh, the younger Despenser, is said to be very close (→ 17/3/22).

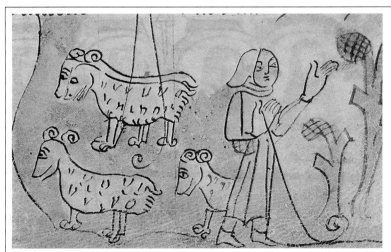

Boom time: English shepherds are happy because their wool is selling well.

Wool trade brings enormous wealth

London, June 1321

Despite constant internecine wars, Britain is enjoying a remarkable economic boom. And by encouraging the growth of a wealthy merchant class from which it can borrow money, the monarchy also stands to benefit.

This is the age of wool, and England is the most prolific producer in Europe, with wool exports a main pillar of the English economy. Hugh Despenser, the king's unpopular chamberlain, masterminded recent changes to the "staple" system – under which wool and sheep-hides were legally compelled to go through foreign ports – to allow exports to go through home ports, with adequate security assured for foreign merchants.

It has been agreed that the export of these staples should be shared between nine English, three Irish and two Welsh ports, rather than through one major port such as London, although the London merchants favoured a single wool-port system.

Robert of Scotland forces King Edward to sue for peace

Yorkshire, 30 May 1323

At long last King Edward has made a truce with the Scots. In the game of cat-and-mouse raids across the border it has usually been Edward's lot to play the mouse, but now enough is enough.

Today's truce with King Robert of Scotland, signed at Bishopthorpe, ends a series of humiliating setbacks for the English. Apart from spectacular defeats such as that at Bannockburn nine years ago, there have been a number of Scots raids into Yorkshire and Cumbria, leaving a trail of destruction. In recent years Berwick has been besieged and then occupied, while Preston and Lancaster were burnt only ten months ago.

Edward has attempted to call a truce before but has not been able to make it stick. The failure of his Scottish campaign last autumn has evidently persuaded him to try again. In October, after all, he barely escaped capture by Robert when the Scottish army invaded Yorkshire and tried to snatch Edward at his headquarters in Rievaulx abbey. Its interception by the Earl of Richmond gave Edward just enough time to take to his heels.

Edward has agreed to a 13-year truce. He has also promised not to obstruct Robert's attempts to reverse the excommunication imposed on him in 1318 for refusing to negotiate a peace (→ 8/1323).

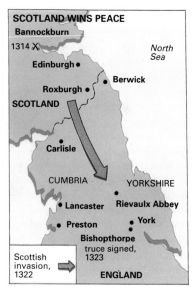

SCOTLAND WINS PEACE
Bannockburn
1314 X
Edinburgh •
North Sea
Roxburgh •
Berwick
SCOTLAND
Carlisle
CUMBRIA
YORKSHIRE
Lancaster •
Rievaulx Abbey •
Preston •
York •
Bishopthorpe
truce signed, 1323
Scottish invasion, 1322
ENGLAND

Isabella is estranged from her husband

Queen Isabella arrives in Paris: from Jean Froissart's "Chronicles" (C14th).

London, 21 September 1325

A bishop returned from France in disguise to break the news to the king that his wife, Isabella, was living openly in France as the mistress of Roger Mortimer, the rebel Earl of March. The queen blames Edward's close, possibly homosexual, relationship with Hugh, the younger Despenser. "Someone has come between my husband and myself trying to break this bond," she said, refusing to return to England.

Despenser and his father were allowed home from exile – during which the son had pursued a successful career as a pirate along the south coast – after Edward's victory at Boroughbridge. The younger man is playing a major role in reforming Edward's finances.

Unknown to Edward or the Despensers, Isabella has been plotting the downfall of both the latter for several months and has formed powerful alliances in England.

The queen, it is said, was prepared to accept her husband's love for Piers Gaveston, even to accept the sight of him wearing her jewels and treating her with contempt. But she has matured into a formidable woman, and she is no longer concealing her fury. Court gossips are already calling her the "She-wolf of France" (→ 25/8/26).

Roger and Isabella: a formidable team

Paris, 1326

Isabella was 12 when she married King Edward; he was 24 and for the past four years had been deeply involved with Piers Gaveston. Despite his continuing attachment to Gaveston the marriage worked well, and there was nothing in Isabella's demeanour in those early days to suggest the fieriness for which she was to become famous.

It was Edward's closeness to the younger Despenser after the killing of Gaveston that stirred a murderous fury in Isabella. Currently in Paris with her son, Edward, who is doing homage to the French king for English possessions in France, she has found a kindred spirit in the militant and acquisitive Roger Mortimer, whose own hatred of the Despensers is boundless.

The very openness of the affair between queen and commoner indicates the level of contempt that she has for her husband. Mortimer has a grudge against the king, who imprisoned him in the Tower in 1322 after defeating him at Shrewsbury. Now the two of them are raising an army to attack Edward, and are proposing to marry the young Edward to the daughter of the Count of Hainault to pay for it.

King, dominated by favourites, is target for hatred

London, 1327

No one can doubt the depth of the king's feelings for Piers Gaveston and Hugh Despenser, but the exact nature of their relationships is less certain. One chronicler is sure that Gaveston and the king were more than just friends, writing: "Anon, he had home his love, Piers of Gaveston." The king and Gaveston spent Christmas together in 1309, said one report, "in long-wished-for sessions of daily and intimate conversation". Whatever the truth, the gossip flows non-stop.

The Earl of Pembroke has urged the king to control his passion for Hugh Despenser. "He perishes on the rocks that loves another more than himself," he warned. Yet Edward has given the queen four children and is known to have sired at least one bastard, called Adam. Affection between men is regarded as natural in today's militaristic society, and the king's evident bisexuality is not in itself offensive to the hard-living aristocracy.

Gaveston's simpering, jewel-encrusted presence on the arm of the preening, exhibitionist king may simply have made too repulsive a spectacle at court. Despenser's policies as chamberlain have made him very unpopular, but it is his rumoured sexual domination of the king that has made him the object of such extreme loathing.

Courtly friendship: a king and his favourite decorate a C13th tile.

Queen and her lover throw Edward off the throne

Queen returns from exile with an army

Queen Isabella lands in Suffolk.

Orwell, Suffolk, 2 October 1326
Queen Isabella's long-awaited invasion fleet anchored in the Orwell river at first light this morning, and already her mercenaries are swarming ashore. She has been joined by several barons who have demanded that the king appear before them. But Edward, with Hugh Despenser, is fleeing to Wales to organise a hasty defence.

The public mood is strongly pro-Isabella. Such is the hatred of Despenser that the royal fleet at Portsmouth has mutinied. Isabella has sworn to wear only widow's weeds until she has seen the head of Hugh Despenser. And so, dressed in black, the "She-Wolf of France" has come ashore (→ 15/10).

Londoners throw weight behind Isabella

Popular with the people: Queen Isabella and her troops arrive in Bristol.

London, 15 October 1326
Fierce rioting broke out in London today as news of the king's flight to the west reached the city. A mob set on the king's staunch ally Walter Stapledon, the bishop of Exeter, and cut off his head with a knife before dispatching a messenger to take it to Isabella, who is encamped with her army at Gloucester.

Troops entered the Tower, setting its prisoners free under an amnesty announced by the queen. The result is an unprecedented outbreak of murder and rape, with former members of the king's party facing vicious treatment. Hundreds have been stripped of all their possessions and hounded from their city homes. The mob had been whipped to a frenzy by Adam Orleton, the rabble-rousing bishop of Hereford, a prime mover in Queen Isabella's party (→ 24/11).

King's favourite dies a gruesome death

Isabella looks on as (in the background) Hugh Despenser is brutally killed.

Hereford, 24 November 1326
Queen Isabella enjoyed a splendid banquet here today and then left the table to watch – and no doubt enjoy – the horrific end of Hugh Despenser whose death she has craved for so long.

Despenser arrived here on horseback, mocked by trumpets and cymbals in every village. After a short trial, the king's closest friend was tied to a tall ladder in order that all could see and a fire lit in front of him. First his genitals were cut off – because "he was held to be guilty of unnatural practices with the king", after which he was disembowelled and forced to watch his entrails being burnt before him.

Only then was his head cut off and sent to London, and the rest of his body quartered and dispatched to the four quarters of the kingdom. Despenser's father, the Earl of Winchester, suffered a similar fate at Bristol last month. Isabella's vengeance is almost complete. Her husband is her prisoner; her eldest son has already been made guardian of the realm; she and Mortimer have the Great Seal of England and can make decrees. All that remains to be settled now is the fate of King Edward II (→ 24/1/27).

Edward II has no choice but to abdicate

Kenilworth Castle, 24 Jan 1327
Under intense pressure, and without any allies, King Edward II has broken down and agreed to abdicate in favour of his son. He was forced to renounce the throne after threats to set up a king who was not of the royal blood line. The king, dressed in black, received a deputation led by Bishop Adam Orleton of Hereford. Warned of the consequences of refusal, he burst into tears and fainted, only to be brutally revived by Orleton before signing the instrument of abdication (→ 1/2).

Edward II: the king who abdicated.

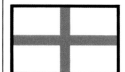

| Edward III
1327–1377 | Robert I
1306–1329
David II
1329–1371 |

Westminster, 1 February 1327. Edward III, aged 14, is crowned king of England.→

Norham, 1 February 1327. The Scots, led by King Robert, attack Norham castle (→26/10).

Gloucestershire, April 1327. Isabella imprisons Edward II in Berkeley castle (→22/9).

Cullen, 26 October 1327. Elizabeth, the wife of King Robert of Scots, dies (→17/7/28).

Gloucester, 21 December 1327. Edward II's murdered body is buried in the abbey (→1350).

York, 24 January 1328. Edward marries Philippa, the daughter of Count William of Hainault (→15/6/30).

Lothian, 17 July 1328. David, the four-year-old heir to the Scots throne, marries Joan, Edward's seven-year-old sister; Edward is not present at the wedding as he disagrees with the terms of the Edinburgh treaty (→7/6/29).

Woodstock, 15 June 1330. Queen Philippa gives birth to Edward, the heir to the English throne (→3/1340).

London, 29 November 1330. Roger Mortimer, imprisoned by Edward, who feared that he might try to seize power again, is executed; he is hanged, drawn and quartered.

Tayside, 24 September 1332. Edward Balliol, the son of the deposed King John, is crowned king after his defeat of Donald of Mar, the guardian of Scotland (→12/6/34).

Boulogne, France, 14 May 1334. David II of Scots arrives to begin life in exile (→1340).

Perth, 18 August 1335. After constant attacks from England, many leading Scots accept Edward Balliol as their king (→2/6/41).

Perth, 13 September 1336. The earldom of Cornwall is left vacant following the death of John, the younger brother of King Edward III (→16/3/37).

France, October 1339. Edward pledges the English crown to the archbishop of Trier to finance war with France (→24/7/40).

Ghent, Flanders, March 1340. Queen Philippa gives birth to a son, John of Gaunt [*Ghent*], her sixth child (→4/1362).

Flanders, 1340. The exiled King David joins Philip VI of France against Edward (→2/6/41).

Scotland, 2 June 1341. On the expulsion of Edward Balliol, David II returns to reclaim his throne (→17/10/46).

Brittany, September 1342. King Edward allies with Duke John de Montfort of Brittany against France (→5/7/46).

Windsor, 27 November 1344. Edward's round house, built to house a round table, a replica of the legendary King Arthur's table, is completed (→24/6/48).

Scotland, October 1346. Robert Stewart is appointed as king's lieutenant on the capture of David II (→27/3/52).

Westminster, March 1348. Parliament grants Edward taxation rights on condition that he does not hold David II of Scots to ransom (→6/4/54).

France, 1350. Philip VI of France dies; he is succeeded by his eldest son, John.

Sadistic assassin murders King Edward

Gloucester, 22 September 1327
After months of humiliation and near starvation, the former Edward II was brutally murdered in his cell in Berkeley castle today. His fate was sealed when a plot to rescue him was discovered.

A wave of popular sympathy has been growing for Edward, helped along by an equal wave of revulsion for Queen Isabella and Mortimer who are proving to be as evil as Hugh Despenser. But it was not enough to save the king, whose humiliations are thought to have included being crowned with hay and shaved in ditchwater as he was dragged around the countryside.

Only the most sadistic of minds could have plotted his murder. It was essential that his corpse should not be marked. A metal funnel was thrust into his body and a red-hot plumber's soldering iron plunged into his bowels. Although his assassin tried to stifle his yells, the screams are said to have been heard throughout the castle (→21/12).

Tall teenager is crowned King Edward III

The king anointed: Edward III is crowned with full church ceremony.

Westminster, 1 February 1327
With his father still alive but held prisoner at Kenilworth, young Edward, the 14-year-old grandson of the first King Edward, has been crowned king of England in the abbey by Walter Reynolds, the archbishop of Canterbury.

Edward is tall and well-built and wore the heavy crown with no sign of discomfort. He looked every inch a king, but whether he will be allowed to be one is another question. He owes his accession to the unpopularity of his father and the plots of his mother, Queen Isabella, and her lover Roger Mortimer. Between the regency council, dominated by Henry of Lancaster, and a court in the thrall of the queen and Mortimer, there is little leeway for a young man whose chief function has been to legitimise the deposition of his father (→4/1327).

Death of Bruce brings David to the throne

Strathclyde, 7 June 1329

All Scotland is in mourning following the announcement of the death of King Robert Bruce. Seriously ill with leprosy for the last two years, he has died at his residence at Cardross on the Firth of Clyde.

Robert recently made a pilgrimage to the shrine of St Ninian at Whithorn in Galloway in search of a divine cure. None was found, but at least the excommunication pronounced against him by the pope in 1318 was lifted last year. All the same, as spiritual insurance, Robert announced on his deathbed that he will go on crusade – albeit posthumously. Sir James Douglas, who had served "the Bruce" for over two decades, promised to take the king's heart with him to the Holy Land.

Already Robert's life is the stuff of legend. One of the best-known tales about him concerns the way that he drew inspiration for his struggle against Edward I by watching a spider trying eight times to complete its web before succeeding. There are many, however, who have less romantic memories of the late king. To the Comyns, Macdowells and Macdougals he was a determined fighter who ruthlessly crushed their opposition to him. People in the north of England knew him only as an enemy who terrorised them for over a decade.

To most Scots, though, Robert is the man who saved them from bondage to England and bolstered their national pride. Above all else

A view of King David in later life.

his name will always be associated with the great victory over the English at Bannockburn in 1314. Bannockburn gave the Scots the upper hand in the long struggle with England which culminated in a peace treaty signed at Edinburgh last year. This treaty will probably come to be seen as Robert's greatest diplomatic triumph. In it King Edward admitted defeat, recognised King Robert and renounced for ever feudal superiority over him.

Robert leaves this life at peace with his southern neighbour. To cement that peace he had his son David, now aged five, married last year to Joan, Edward's seven-year-old sister. David now succeeds his father (→ 14/5/34).

Edward III takes control

Regime topples as Mortimer is jailed

Nottingham Castle, 19 Oct 1330

Boldness has paid off for King Edward. Last night he staged what amounted to a coup in his own kingdom and was rewarded with total success. With a handful of trusted supporters, Edward arranged to be guided into the castle at Nottingham through a secret underground passage. Edward himself led the raiding party with his sword drawn. They reached the bedchamber of Queen Isabella, his mother, without being detected, and there found her preparing for the night.

There, too, was Roger Mortimer, the Earl of March, whose manoeuvrings have brought near civil war to England and made Edward's crown seem hollow. The earl was seized, and Edward's men then secured the castle from within so that no news leaked out until morning.

Now Mortimer and several of his henchmen are on their way to the Tower, while the queen has been sent into obscurity at Castle Rising in Norfolk. Henry of Lancaster must have backed the plot, which was brought forward after Mortimer engineered the execution of the king's uncle, the Earl of Kent, but the triumph is Edward's. Eighteen next month, he is secure on his throne at last (→ 29/11).

ANCESTRY OF EDWARD III	
Harold II 1066	
Gytha 1125	= Vladimir Monomakh Grand Duke of Kiev
Mstislav–Harold Grand Duke of Kiev 1132	
Euphrosyne 1161	= Geza II king of Hungary
Bela III king of Hungary 1196	
Andrew II king of Hungary 1235	
Yolande 1251	= James I king of Aragon
Isabella 1271	= Philip III king of France
Philip IV king of France 1314	
Isabella 1357	= **Edward II** king of England
Edward III 1377	
Dates = deaths	

Dynasty: how King Edward traces his lineage of royal blood.

Edward seeks peace treaty with France

King Edward pays homage to Philip.

France, 30 April 1331

Terms have been agreed for a lasting peace with Philip of France at a clandestine meeting between the two kings at Pont St Maxence. Edward travelled diguised as a merchant, and, in exchange for a reaffirmation of his homage to the French king as liege lord over Edward's lands in Aquitaine, he has been promised that the boundary disputes between the buchy and lands directly subject to Philip will be settled by law, not war. The treaty is a poor one for Edward, but if it holds it will leave him free to turn his attentions to the north and the Scots (→ 7/10/37).

Queen Isabella seized by soldiers at Nottingham, as imagined by a later artist. ▷

How Edward Balliol has undone Robert Bruce's good work

Newcastle, 12 June 1334
King Edward Balliol of Scotland has paid homage to Edward III, recognising the English king as his overlord for the second time since coming to the throne two years ago. At a meeting with Edward today Balliol handed over to him most of the south of Scotland and allowed the English to regain control of Berwick. What he has done is overturned the achievements of King Robert, who died five years ago and who did so much to keep his country free from English domination.

Balliol's concessions are by way of repaying Edward for helping him

King Edward: in control of Berwick.

depose the boy king David II. Two years ago Balliol, whose father John was himself deposed by Edward I in 1296, returned to Scotland after eight years' exile in England to claim the throne. With military help from Edward he defeated the Scottish army on Dupplin Moor and went on to be enthroned at Scone.

Only three months later, in December 1332, Balliol was driven out of Scotland by men loyal to the deposed king. Yet in March 1333 he was back, laying siege to Berwick in the name of his overlord, Edward III. On 19 July they together crushed the Scots army at Halidon Hill. With Balliol in power and King David fled to France, the future looks bleak for Scottish independence (→ 18/8/35).

Edward stakes claim to French crown

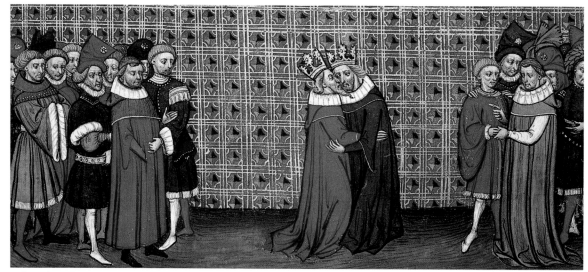

Edward III does homage to King Philip for his French domains, shortly before staking his claim to the throne of France.

Westminster, 7 October 1337
War between England and France now appears inevitable. Relations between Philip of France and Edward have been deteriorating all year, and today Edward has put his seal to a document in which he revives the claim to the French throne that he abandoned, reluctantly, to Philip of Valois when Charles IV died without a male heir in 1328. The bishop of Lincoln has been entrusted to take the sealed document to Paris in a direct challenge to the French king. It is a powerful and uncompromising reply to Philip's attempt to confiscate the duchy of Gascony in August. Both now lay claim to France, and only a war will settle the issue.

The pope is still campaigning hard for peace, since a conflict between two such powerful Christian kings would ruin his plans to mount another crusade. Edward has for some time been building alliances in the Rhineland and the Low Countries. Duke John of Brabant has joined the English cause for a reputed £60,000, and so too has Emperor Ludwig of Bavaria. His price is reported to have been 300,000 florins (→ 10/1339).

More earls and new dukedoms mean more powerful monarchy

Westminster, 16 March 1337
For the first time in England there is a position in society which ranks between the king and his earls, until now the traditional leaders of the aristocracy. Edward has made his son Duke of Cornwall, following the death of the earl without an heir last September. The creation of England's first duchy, which borrows from the French practice, could well be a useful way of differentiating those who can boast royal blood from the rest of the nobility.

King Edward has also taken the opportunity to inject fresh blood into the ranks of the English aristocracy by creating a further seven earldoms for those swashbuckling young men who match his own appetite for chivalry, war and hard living. Chief among them is his old companion William Montagu, his greatest aide during the seizure of Mortimer in 1330. He becomes Earl of Salisbury. Other revived earldoms, like those of Hunting-

The king with his warrior eldest son, Edward, the Prince of Wales.

don, Northampton and Gloucester, give the king a core of nobles that he can rely on inside the country and as trusted lieutenants in war.

But thanks to his restrained treatment of the supporters of Mortimer, whose horrible execution on the common gallows at Tyburn taught its own lesson of the virtues of loyalty, Edward has already united his powerful subjects behind the crown (→ 12/5/43).

England beats France in battle at Sluys

Sluys, Flanders, 24 July 1340
Thousands of Frenchman have died in a bloody sea battle here which has ended in total victory for Edward and the destruction of virtually the entire French fleet. The two forces came upon each other in the mouth of the Zwin, where the much larger French fleet was bunched in three lines, the ships chained together in an attempt to block the English fleet's access to the approaches to Bruges.

With typical daring, King Edward decided to attack as soon as the tide and the wind were in his favour. He arranged his ships so that a vessel of archers alternated with one full of men-at-arms, and charged into the cumbersome French squadrons. Although the battle took place at sea, the actual combat was exactly the same as a land battle – except that there was nowhere for the losers to go to escape the slaughter, which explains the enormous casualties.

While the English bowmen kept the air thick with arrows, men with spears, axes and swords grappled hand to hand. Sailors hurled stones and quicklime down into the mêlée from the masts.

The fighting was so fierce that it went on throughout the night, illuminated by the glare of burning ships. By morning it was clear that just 30 of some 200 French ships had escaped, and that many soldiers on both sides had been dragged under the water by their heavy armour and drowned (→ 1341).

The Battle of Sluys, as shown in Jean Froissart's "Chronicles" (14th century).

Taxation is granted only after king meets Commons' demands for greater influence

One victim of war is the royal purse.

Westminster, 1341
The continued need for money to finance the war has forced King Edward to call parliaments with unprecedented frequency in order to raise taxes. An unlooked-for result has been to increase the power of parliament, particularly of the House of Commons. Now the Commons have begun to meet separately from the Lords. They are making demands which they insist are met. In 1339 they agreed to new taxes only on condition that some old ones were abolished, and only after consulting the communities which they represent.

Last year they went much further. Previously the king had been able to levy some taxes without parliamentary consent; now he had to agree that no new taxes would be imposed without the assent of the Commons in parliament. He is also being asked to provide proof that the money is being well spent by producing an audit of the tax accounts for parliament to inspect.

This year it is being insisted that, from now on, the king's ministers and judges shall swear before parliament to observe *Magna Carta* and the law of the land. More than that, the king's ministers will in future have to appear before parliament to answer questions about any complaints that may be made against them. Some nobles fear that, if this goes on, the Commons will end up running the country (→ 9/1342).

Edward presides over sophisticated court

London, 1342
King Edward has created a new type of royal court: more than just a military camp or an administrative centre, it is also a place of artistry, play-acting and dancing. This is partly thanks to the queen, whose feminine touch has introduced more women to the royal household. She particularly enjoys the company of writers, poets and musicians. The king plays as hard as he works: he enjoys masques, feasts and dancing into the night.

Jousting reflects king's love of chivalry

England, 1340
Nothing shows the appeal of King Edward, and the character of his court, so much as the current fashion for jousting. These formal displays of knightly qualities perfectly dramatise the value that this warrior-king places on chivalric virtues.

The tournaments of massed battle have given way to elegantly matched contests between single fighters or small evenly numbered groups, and elaborate ceremonial and costumes have become an important part of the show. But although the pageantry is often whimsical, with knights dressed up as cardinals or even as the Seven Deadly Sins, the fighting is serious enough and deaths are common.

The most extreme examples are the jousts of war, in which real battles are fought according to the rules of chivalry, with heralds to organise events and even award prizes to those thought to have acquitted themselves with most honour.

A knight's rank: Sir Geoffrey Luttrell, from an English psalter c.1340.

Edward is crowned Prince of Wales in ritual ceremony

King Edward with his eldest son.

Westminster, 12 May 1343

In a deeply moving ceremony, the king's eldest son, Edward, today was crowned Prince of Wales following the rituals used to invest Dafydd ap Llywelyn as Prince of Wales nearly 100 years ago.

This continues the tradition begun by the first King Edward of giving the English heir the title by which Llywelyn ap Gruffudd was first acknowledged as the supreme Prince of Wales by the other Welsh princes in 1267. In the hushed presence of parliament, a gold coronet was placed on the 12-year-old boy's head and a silver sceptre in his hand.

In March 1333 young Edward was officially created Earl of Chester, the usual title for a king's eldest son, and the revenue attached to that honour is much more significant for the prince's household, still part of his mother's court, than the lands in Wales that come to him now.

This does not mean, however, that his new title is just a meaningless traditional honour given to the heir to the English throne. Edward is now the overlord of the Welsh principality and has the right to collect the usual dues and to raise troops among the Welsh footmen, archers and spearmen who form the backbone of the English army on the continent (→ 13/7/46).

David taken by English

Durham, 17 October 1346

It has not been a good day for King David of Scots. He started it in confident mood, pressing home the invasion of England planned to assist his French ally, Philip VI. He ended it with an arrow in his face, his army routed and its generals dead or, like himself, captured.

The 22-year-old king had marched his army south as far as Neville's Cross, near Durham, where the Scots found themselves up against an English force led by Archbishop William la Zouche of York. As arrows rained down on them the Scots attacked, but without success. Soldiers advancing in the first wave found themselves stumbling about in dykes that criss-crossed the wet and foggy battlefield. King David's own men had no better luck, while a third battalion, commanded by Robert the Stewart, disgraced itself by fleeing without striking a single blow.

The Scottish army began to crumble and David, hit in the face by an arrow, joined the rout. When an English soldier, John Coupland, tried to stop him, a hand-to-hand fight ensued. Despite his wound David put up a spirited fight and knocked two of Coupland's teeth out before he was eventually overpowered. David had gambled on asserting his independence from the

A later portrait of King David II.

English while Edward III was preoccupied with campaigning in France. But the gamble has been costly, with heavy losses on the Scots side in today's battle. Among the dead are John Randolph, the Earl of Moray, as well as the marshal, constable and chamberlain of Scotland.

So ends David's attempt to consolidate his hold on his kingdom, only five years after returning from exile in France where he had fled to escape the clutches of Edward Balliol. The one comfort for the Scots is that King Edward is too involved with the siege of Calais to exploit his victory to the full (→ 27/3/52).

King David fighting bravely at Neville's Cross, near Durham (C15th).

Huge fleet waits to set sail for France

Portsmouth, 5 July 1346

King Edward has gathered the greatest invasion fleet ever seen in England to take a great army across the Channel to France. At least 1,000 ships are lying ready in Portsmouth and Plymouth, waiting for the wind to change and set for France.

While the king has a few ships of his own, most of the invasion fleet consists of merchant ships that have been requisitioned and temporarily converted for war. The sailors' wages are being paid by the crown at the rate of 3d a day, with 6d a day for the masters.

The ships are called "cogs" and have had temporary fighting platforms, called castles, built both fore and aft. They are no match for the French fighting galleys, but by keeping his destination a secret even from his ships' captains, Edward hopes to avoid any confrontation with the French fleet on the way over [*see story below*].

Prince of Wales knighted by king

Normandy, 13 July 1346

King Edward landed at St Vaast-la-Hogue yesterday to begin a huge raid on France designed to bring the French to battle and defeat them. This marks a significant shift in policy, for all military effort so far has been directed towards Gascony and Aquitaine. English troops, even now under siege in the castle of Aiguillon, in Gascony, will get no relief. Godfrey of Harcourt has convinced Edward that Normandy is a better and richer target.

Edward's first act on landing was to knight his 16-year-old son Edward, the Prince of Wales. The honour marks the start of his active military career; he will be given the nominal command of one wing of the army, but the real commanders are Edward and the Earls of Warwick, Arundel and Northampton.

After disembarking, Edward plans to send the fleet along the coast to burn the undefended ports while he strikes inland looking for plunder. The port of St Vaast will be burnt as he leaves (→ 4/8/47).

French burghers surrender to English king

An heroic victory: English archers in the thick of battle at Crécy.

Calais, France, 4 August 1347
Calais is now an English possession. Nearly a year since the English first laid siege to this fortified town on the Normandy coast, the chief citizens today rode out to offer King Edward the keys to the town. They had roped themselves together as a sign of abject submission and surrendered after King Philip of France failed to come to their relief. It is believed that the king wanted to hang them all, but the queen stepped in to save their lives. The burghers of Calais will now be taken to an English jail.

Today's surrender is the result of a long campaign that reached a bloody climax at Crécy on 26 August last year. There, the French king was wounded and the flower of the French aristocracy and upwards of 10,000 men were killed for English losses of just 40 dead.

King Edward personally directed his army of about 8,500 men, a good half of them archers, from a windmill overlooking the field of battle. The French knights charged at dusk, and the archers replied with their longbows. Almost every arrow found its mark, and in the dark few French came close enough to see the men who killed them.

At Crécy the 16-year-old Prince of Wales won his battle spurs, killing many men including the king of Bohemia, whose emblem of three feathers and motto of "*Ich Dien*" ["I serve"] he has taken (→ 3/48).

Edward founds the Order of the Garter

Windsor, 24 June 1348
The first official ceremony of the new Order of the Garter – inspired by the chivalry of King Arthur – was held today. It was part of the celebrations held to mark the purification of Queen Philippa after the birth of William, her sixth son.

King Edward has always had a strong attachment to the ideals expressed in the tales of King Arthur and his "Knights of the Round Table" and has often tried to recreate the atmosphere of Camelot. In 1344 he held his own Round Table tournament at Windsor, at which he took an oath to establish an order of Arthurian knights, but it was not until after the fall of Calais last year that the opportunity presented itself. Then, at a ball to celebrate the capture of the city, the garter of one of the court ladies came undone and fell to the floor as she was dancing.

Some say that she was Edward's mistress, the Countess of Salisbury, others that it was the beautiful Joan of Kent, but whoever she was the king acted immediately. To spare her embarrassment he picked up the powder-blue garter and tied it to his own knee with the words "*honi soit qui mal y pense*" – "evil be to him who evil thinks". This courtly response has become the motto of the 26 knights who are the founding members of the new Order of the Garter.

Splendid shrine to Edward II finished

Edward II's tomb at Gloucester.

Gloucester, 1350
The shrine that King Edward has had built at Gloucester abbey to the memory of his murdered father, Edward II, has become a major place of pilgrimage. Immediately after the murder in 1327, Edward's body was buried in Gloucester abbey with considerable state and in the presence of Queen Isabella, although she must have had foreknowledge of the murder and may have helped to plan it.

Edward III, then aged 14, was also present, and if he did not then know the truth about his father's murder he certainly learnt about it later. When he seized power three years after his father's death he built him a splendid tomb, surmounted by a gossamer stone canopy, beneath which reclines a graceful alabaster effigy of the murdered king.

Edward made only a half-hearted attempt to promote his father as a national saint-king, but the cult quickly became popular. The pilgrims brought so much wealth to Gloucester that the abbey could be rebuilt with the addition of the largest stained-glass windows in England. Nearly 100 feet (30 metres) tall, they are said to resemble more a wall of glass than a window.

Black Death, blind to rank or privilege, claims king's daughter

Bordeaux, 2 September 1348
The deadly plague known as the Black Death has struck at the heart of the royal family and killed the young Princess Joan, King Edward's second daughter. Joan was in Bordeaux on her way to be betrothed to the eldest son of King Pedro of Castile.

Edward was greatly affected, and in a letter to the bridegroom he announces her death with "sighs and sobs and a heavy heart", remembering with tenderness that his daughter was a child "in whom all the gifts of nature met, and whom also, because of the elegance of her manners, we sincerely loved beyond all our other children".

The Black Death has laid its cold hand on King Edward's daughter Joan.

Edward III
1327–1377

David II
1329–1371
Robert II
1371–1390

Scotland, 27 March 1352. King David II of Scots is allowed home on parole to agree terms for his release from captivity (→17/1/57).

Flanders, 6 April 1354. A draft treaty is drawn up; Edward will keep sovereignty over much of France on condition that he abandons formal claims to the throne (→3/11/55).

South-west France, 3 Nov 1355. Following the collapse of last year's Anglo-French treaty, Edward, the Prince of Wales, invades (→19/9/56).

Berwick, 20 Jan 1356. Edward Balliol hands the crown of Scotland to Edward III (→1363).

Scotland, 17 January 1357. The Scots negotiate for the release of King David II (→7/10/57).

Norfolk, 22 August 1358. Queen Isabella, the widow of Edward II, dies.

Brétigny, 8 May 1360. An Anglo-French peace treaty is drafted (→9/1360).

England, April 1362. John of Gaunt, the fourth son of Edward III, who married Blanche of Lancaster three years ago, inherits the title of Duke of Lancaster (→4/4/66).

Hertford, 7 September 1362. Joan, the wife of David II and a sister of Edward III, dies (→1363).

Scotland, 1363. King David overcomes a rebellion by noblemen (→4/3/64).

Scotland, 4 March 1364. Robert the Stewart is named as heir to the Scottish throne should King David die without an heir of his own (→1369).

Angoulême, 27 January 1365. Joan of Kent gives birth to Edward, the son and heir of the Prince of Wales (→6/1/67).

Lincolnshire, 4 April 1366. Blanche of Lancaster gives birth to a son, to be named Henry Bolingbroke (→10/1/67).

Gascony, 6 January 1367. A second son is born to the Prince of Wales; he is named Richard of Bordeaux (→1/1371).

Gascony, 10 January 1367. Edward, the Prince of Wales, and John of Gaunt leave for Castile (→9/1371).

Ireland, 13 August 1368. Lionel, the Duke of Clarence, dies.

England, 14 August 1369. Queen Philippa dies aged 52.

England, 12 September 1369. Blanche of Lancaster dies suddenly of the plague.

Scotland, 1369. King David II divorces his wife, Margaret Drummond; despite two marriages, the Scottish king has no children (→26/3/71).

Aquitaine, January 1371. Edward, the Prince of Wales's son, dies aged six (→8/6/76).

Castile, 1372. John of Gaunt, who last year married Constance, the daughter of the former king of Castile, assumes the title of king (→11/1385).

Westminster, May 1376. Parliament wins the right to investigate abuses and impeaches Alice Perrers, the king's mistress.

Windsor, 23 April 1377. Edward invests his heir, Richard of Bordeaux, and his cousin, Henry Bolingbroke, as knights of the Garter (→21/6).

French king captured in battle at Poitiers

The English victory at Poitiers, from Jean Froissart's "Chronicles" (C14th).

Poitiers, 19 September 1356
The French have today suffered an even greater defeat than at Crécy. Edward, the Prince of Wales, has destroyed an enormous army, and King John II of France has been captured and is being held to ransom [*see story below*].

The campaign began when the prince left Bordeaux on 6 July with about 8,000 men, most of them archers, and went on a long and profitable raid as far south as Bourges. On the way back he found himself cornered at Poitiers by King John and an army of 50,000 French.

Undismayed, the prince deployed his men in a strong defensive position among narrow lanes where the French cavalry could not manoeuvre. King John then decided to attack on foot, with disastrous consequences. The English longbowmen's arrows tore the French apart, and 13 counts, one archbishop, 66 barons and innumerable common soldiers all perished (→5/1360).

Gold ransom wins French king's freedom

A later view of John's surrender.

Calais, France, September 1360
The treaty to free King John II of France, held captive at Windsor castle for four years, has at last been settled, although not without considerable difficulty.

After long haggling, the French have agreed to ransom their king for three million gold pieces. They have also agreed to award full sovereignty over Gascony, Poitou, Calais and other lands in northern France to King Edward. In return, Edward has dropped his claim to the French throne.

But the treaty has to be implemented by 1 November next year. This is an impossibly tight schedule and suggests that neither side expects the terms to be kept.

King David is set free

Berwick, 7 October 1357

King Edward has signed a treaty granting David II of Scots permission to return home, ending his 11 years of captivity in England. Freedom comes at a huge price, however – 100,000 marks, to be precise. The Scots are to pay this to Edward over the next ten years. They also have to hand over 23 hostages as a guarantee for what is in fact a ransom.

The money is, furthermore, a pledge of the ten-year truce that is to exist from now on between the two countries. It may also take some of the sting out of Edward's failed ambition to beat the Scots into accepting his authority.

Since David's capture in 1346 at Neville's Cross, Scotland has known little peace. The usual cross-border raids have worn grimly on, with now the Scots, now the English gaining the upper hand. Edward's raids have achieved nothing beyond plunder and destruction, and his installation of Edward Balliol as puppet king of Scotland meant nothing while David still

Edward and David: now at peace.

commanded the allegiance of the Scots. It was time to negotiate.

Defeated militarily, Edward still has his eye on a diplomatic victory. As David has no legitimate heir as yet, Edward wants him to consider accepting one of his own sons as heir to Scotland's throne (→ 7/9/62).

Hailstones destroy English army in France

Chartres, France, May 1360

An English raid deep into France has been a disaster – not because of the French, who are militarily impotent after a string of English victories, but because of extraordinarily bad weather.

The French king, John II, has been a captive of the English for three years, but the French have proved unusually slow to raise the four million gold florins that Edward III is demanding as a ransom. To hurry them Edward led his army once more into French territory with the idea of either forcing them to pay the ransom or crowning himself king of France.

Battle-shy of the fearsome English archers, the French made no attempt to stop him, and Edward proceeded to Rheims, the city where French kings are traditionally crowned. However, the city was too well fortified, and so he marched on to Paris, which also proved too strong to besiege.

As they returned to Chartres a storm broke with hailstones so big

King Edward lays siege to Rheims.

that it killed most of the horses and immobilised the army. Rather than take any more risks, Edward has decided to reduce his ransom demands in the hope of signing a speedy treaty to consolidate his territorial gains (→ 8/5).

Prince with black armour is renowned for battlefield triumphs and bad debts

Hero of the battlefield: a later engraving of the Prince of Wales.

Canterbury, 4 July 1360

Edward, the Prince of Wales, is staying here as a guest of the archbishop together with the captured French King John, whom he is escorting to Dover. He hopes that his share of John's expected four million gold florins will be enough to clear his debts, for he shares his mother's tendency to extravagance.

His extraordinary success as a military commander is overshadowed by a cloud of crippling debt. His critics say that he spends ludicrous amounts on presents for his friends: ruby-and-sapphire brooches and gold cups for men, massive belt clasps encrusted with jewels for women. His gambling also gets out of hand, but a prince must live like a prince and most of his expenditure goes on maintaining his household. He must feed and water a retinue of knights, hor-

ses, dogs, falcons and over 100 servants. As is expected of him, he stages tournaments and dresses himself, his family and his courtiers in precious finery. Finally, he is building a magnificent new palace at Kennington, south of Westminster.

Easily distinguished on the battlefield by his burnished black armour, the prince first showed his outstanding military skills at Crécy. But it was at the Battle of Poitiers [*see story opposite*], that he made his reputation, conducting a skilled defence before ordering his archers to open fire. In the final stages of the battle he led his knights in hand-to-hand fighting.

Like his father, he is a powerful man of action rather than an administrator or an intellectual. His role as king-in-waiting is to serve as the king's right-hand man in battle (→ 10/10/61).

Prince weds cousin in secret ceremony

England, 10 October 1361

Edward, the Prince of Wales, has surprised everyone by secretly marrying his cousin, the beautiful Countess Joan of Kent – known as "the fair maid of Kent".

Today's marriage is remarkable in several ways. First of all, it is extraordinary that the prince has reached the age of 30 before marrying, for this is an age where nobles marry young and the children of kings are frequently pledged, or even married, before they reach their teens. His father, King Edward, had been expected to arrange a dynastic marriage for him which would have linked the English crown to a continental royal house

The prince's bride: Joan of Kent.

and helped secure the English claim to the throne of France.

Political considerations apart, the marriage is still surprising because of Joan's chequered past. It is rumoured that the stunning countess was one of the king's mistresses before she married Sir Thomas Holland in 1339. A year later she married William, the Earl of Salisbury, and stayed with him until 1349, when their union was annulled and the validity of the Holland marriage was confirmed.

Any, or all, of these reasons may be behind the decision of the prince and his recently-widowed bride to marry in secret and present the world with a *fait accompli*. Two things are certain: the match is a love match, and it is now too late for anyone to intervene (→ 19/7/62).

Scots king in pay of English is dead

England, 1363

Edward Balliol, the son of Scotland's deposed King John, has died – and with him dies a lifelong ambition to secure for himself the Scottish crown.

In September 1332 – 36 years after the removal of his father – Balliol was enthroned as King Edward of Scotland, following his defeat (with English backing) of David II's forces at Dupplin Moor. But three months later he was driven out of his kingdom and proceeded to lay siege to Berwick in the name of Edward III of England, whom he had acknowledged as his overlord.

In 1334 Balliol regained superficial control of most of Scotland and ceded much of the Scottish borders to England. But major English advances in Scotland over the next few years were reversed, and by the time that David II returned from exile in France in 1341 most of Scotland had been freed from English or Balliol occupation.

The English king renewed his attacks, taking King David prisoner after a Scottish defeat at Neville's Cross in 1346, but Balliol failed to re-establish his position, and David was allowed to return to Scotland again in 1352. Four years later Balliol finally resigned his Scottish crown to Edward III of England in return for a rich pension.

Prince scores decisive victory in Castile

The Prince of Wales leads the English to victory at Najera, in Spain.

Castile, 3 April 1367

When Pedro the Cruel, the king of Castile, was overthrown by his half-brother Henry the Bastard, he called on Edward, the Prince of Wales, for help under the terms of a 1362 treaty in which England had promised to aid Pedro against his French-backed rival. The result was two years of planning, travelling and campaigning, leading up to today's decisive victory for the prince at Najera.

Prince Edward's brother, John of Gaunt, opened the attack on Henry with an infantry assault under covering arrow fire. When the prince moved in with a flanking cavalry attack, Henry's front-line horsemen fled, forcing him to bring up his reserves to try to defend his beleaguered infantry. A furious battle ensued, but Henry's forces failed to engage the English effectively and eventually collapsed and fled to Najera. Edward pursued them and swiftly gained control of the town, taking captive those men he did not slaughter. The triumph is yet another feather in his cap.

Marriage gives John of Gaunt a claim to a throne in Spain

A later portrait of John of Gaunt.

Bordeaux, September 1371

As the fourth son of Edward III, John of Gaunt could not expect to succeed to the English crown, but he has long hankered after the throne of Castile. His chance came when Constance, the 17-year-old daughter of England's ally Pedro the Cruel, sought refuge in Aquitaine after her father was stabbed to death by his half-brother, Henry, two years ago.

Constance, pretty and pious, met the 31-year-old Gaunt soon after his first wife, Duchess Blanche of Lancaster, died of the plague. Catherine longed to return to Castile as the rightful queen, and the ambitious Gaunt saw that as her husband he could be crowned with her in the cathedral of Burgos. Today they were married, and he has already assumed the title of "King of Castile and Leon".

Privately, though, the English are scandalised by Gaunt's continuing relationship with Katherine Swynford, the governess of his children by his first marriage. He rides through the streets with the woman, his hand affectionately resting on her horse's bridle and touching her, even in the presence of Constance. And this year she bore him a son, John. It seems that Gaunt has married Constance for political reasons, but his heart belongs to Katherine (→ 1372).

Royal court clings tightly to extravagant fashions

The poet Chaucer at King Edward's court, by Ford Madox Brown (1821-93).

A C20th view of the flamboyant dress favoured by noblemen at this time.

London, 1363

So anxious are the upwardly-mobile lower orders to imitate the royal court's extravagant dress that parliament has passed a law defining what clothes are permitted to each class. Many nobles feel that commoners are getting above themselves as a result of higher standards of living in the wake of the plague. This new law is one way to reassert the established hierarchy.

Many people – and not only conservatives and churchmen – are shocked by the clothes worn by King Edward's courtiers. Men's garments cling so tightly that they leave nothing to the imagination. Belts and girdles threaded with gold and studded with jewels hang promiscuously from the hips. Men wear their sheath-tight hose in a multitude of contrasting colours matched by shoes with long pointed toes (known as "Crackowes" after the Polish city where the fashion is supposed to have originated). Women wear sleeves so long they trail onto the ground and pick up the dirt.

Common people attempting to dress like this will now be committing a criminal offence. Ermine and pearls are prohibited to everyone except the royal family and the highest nobles. Cloth of gold and silver are permitted only to peers and to knights with incomes of more than 400 marks a year. Lesser knights may not wear fabric costing more than six marks per yard.

"Tradesmen, artificers, and men in office called yeomen shall wear no cloth in their apparel exceeding the price of 40 shillings the whole cloth; neither shall they embellish their garments with precious stones, cloth of silk or of silver; nor shall they wear any gold or silver upon their girdles, knives, rings, garters, ribands, chains, bracelets or seals," says the statute.

Sophisticated leisure: a later view of life at the royal court in about 1380.

Robert II crowned king

House of Stewart is new Scots dynasty

Scone, Tayside, 26 March 1371
Robert, the nephew of David II – who died suddenly last year – has been crowned Robert II at Scone. At 55, he is eight years older than his predecessor. The new king is the son of Walter Stewart, the sixth hereditary steward of Scotland, and Marjorie Bruce, the eldest daughter of Robert I, who died giving birth to him in 1316.

The Stewart accession involves not just a new king but a whole new dynasty. In contrast to David II, who died childless, Robert has five surviving sons and seven daughters (as well as several illegitimate children). His eldest son, John, the Earl of Carrick, has been recognised as his heir, although Robert did not marry John's mother, Elizabeth Mure, until after his birth. Their marriage subsequently made their several children legitimate in the eyes of the church.

The Stewarts did not come to the throne by chance. Walter Stewart was the head of one of the oldest and richest families in Scotland, and was deliberately selected by Robert Bruce as a suitable husband for his daughter. Marjorie's son was regarded as her father's heir until Robert Bruce himself produced a son, David, in 1324. After David's birth, Robert Stewart was confirmed as his heir presumptive, but he has had to wait 45 years

King Robert II with his queen.

before succeeding to the crown. David became king of Scotland when he was only five years old, and Robert Stewart has spent many of the intervening years engaged in war with the English and governing the country during David's minority and absences.

The late king spent seven years exiled in France and 11 years in captivity in England, from which he was freed in 1357. After his release, David proved himself an able king, tough in his dealings with Edward III of England and his own magnates. But relations between nephew and uncle were not easy: Robert was imprisoned for offending David's second wife, Margaret, and David was reluctant to accept him as his successor (→ 3/1384).

Alice Perrers, the 'Lady of the Sun', uses the king's bed to gain riches and power

Windsor, 1375
One of the richest and most powerful women in Edward III's entourage is the former lady-in-waiting to the late Queen Philippa. While the queen was still living, Alice Perrers was already sharing the king's bed and receiving the first of many gifts – two tuns of wine.

The acquisitive Alice persuaded the king to give her his late wife's jewels; he also bestowed on her the manor of Wendover and an annuity of £100 a year. In spite of her marriage to Sir William de Windsor, the deputy of Ireland, she appeared in public at the Smithfield fair as Edward's "Lady of the Sun" and presided over a tournament. She soon began to busy herself with the lawsuits being heard in the king's court at Westminster Hall, where she sits on the marble bench, the royal seat. Such is her influence over Edward that she is allowed to join in the hearings to secure sentences in favour of her friends.

Court gossip claims that Alice is the daughter of a tiler from Essex, but it seems more likely that she comes from a family of minor gentry. Her greed and lack of shame have scandalised public opinion, and leading figures in parliament intend to petition the king to banish her and confiscate her great wealth. They also want to rid the court of Edward's other favourites who, they contend, are increasingly controlling access to the king.

"The Lady of the Sun" presided over a tournament such as this in London.

English fleet trapped by stormy weather

Winchelsea, August 1372
Dismayed by news of the destruction of his English fleet off La Rochelle, Edward ordered a new naval force to be assembled at Sandwich. He would set sail at once with his sons, the Prince of Wales and John of Gaunt.

The La Rochelle fleet had been part of the king's plans for a double offensive against France: a naval expedition in the south and a landing in northern France. But Edward has long neglected his navy, and the French now have Castilian galleys to fight for them. Off La Rochelle two months ago the English armed merchantmen were no match for the galleys; they were burnt and sunk by a storm of flaming arrows and stone cannonballs.

Edward's new fleet has also been an abject failure. When the king set sail aboard his flagship, the *Grace de Dieu*, the weather was unseasonably stormy and worsened as the days passed. The fleet never got beyond Winchelsea, and after struggling for a fortnight a despondent Edward was obliged to abandon the expedition (→ 5/1376).

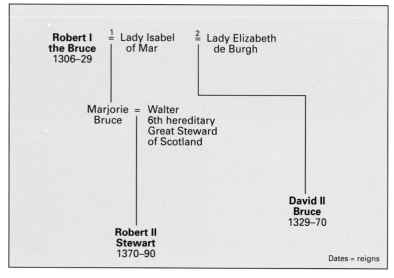

Robert I the Bruce 1306–29 ═1 Lady Isabel of Mar ═2 Lady Elizabeth de Burgh

Marjorie Bruce = Walter 6th hereditary Great Steward of Scotland

David II Bruce 1329–70

Robert II Stewart 1370–90

Dates = reigns

Prince of Wales is dead

Nine-year-old Richard is heir to throne

Westminster, 20 November 1376

An exhausted Richard, the nine-year-old son of the late Prince of Wales, was carried out of Westminster abbey today after collapsing as he was being invested with the ring and gold rod of the Prince of Wales. The long ceremonial, following a period of fasting, had taken its toll of the boy who will soon succeed his ageing and increasingly senile grandfather, Edward III [*see report below*].

Richard became heir to the throne when the Prince of Wales died six months ago. All the splendours of royalty will be his. He has been given a state barge, with 12 oarsmen in striped livery to row him down the Thames. At Kennington palace his retinue will consist only of high-born boys, though his mother, Joan, "the Fair Maid of Kent", is determined to retain her influence. A power struggle over the direction of state affairs seems certain. His senior uncle, John of Gaunt, is extremely unpopular, and any claim by him to act as regent will probably be resisted. This is likely to mean some less formal arrangement involving Richard's other uncles, Edmund of Langley and Thomas of Woodstock.

Edmund has so far had an undistinguished career, apparently preferring a quiet life to high politics. By contrast, Thomas, the younger brother, already seems a force to be reckoned with and may seize the chance to make his mark. Much will depend upon the strength of character revealed by Richard as he matures (→ 16/7/77).

The Prince of Wales: a reproduction of his tomb in Canterbury cathedral.

Canterbury, 8 June 1376

Edward, the Prince of Wales, once the most feared military leader in Europe, died today, at the age of 46, after a long, lingering illness. Some say that he contracted dysentery during the 1367 campaign to restore Pedro the Cruel to the throne of Castile. On his return to France the next year, he was already suffering from what chroniclers called "a great and grievous sickness".

Castile was a military triumph but a political disaster at home. Pedro failed to pay his share of the costs of the expedition, and Edward was obliged to impose heavy taxes on his Gascon subjects, including the widely-disliked hearth tax.

Heavy taxation provoked the people of Limoges to rise against the prince. When the citizens refused to surrender, he ordered the city to be razed to its foundations. To direct this act of vandalism and terror, he had to be taken to the battleground in a carriage drawn by horses. A few months later he was obliged reluctantly to recognise that he would never fight another battle, and he returned to England. On the day of his departure his elder son, Edward of Angoulême, died of the plague; he was six.

The Prince of Wales first went into battle at the age of 16, beside his father, Edward III, at Crécy; at 26 he inflicted a crushing defeat on the French at Poitiers, taking the king prisoner. But his French victories came to nothing. Four years ago he was forced to renounce his titles in Aquitaine, and thereafter he witnessed the loss of almost all the Plantagenet lands in southern France.

The man who lived for fighting, hunting and tourneying spent his last years in a bed covered in blue silk patterned with roses. He is to be buried in Canterbury cathedral. His tomb will carry the words *Houmout* [High Courage] and *Ich dien* [I serve].

Perrers steals from dead king's corpse

Sheen, 21 June 1377

Just two people were present when Edward III died today, at the age of 65, in his palace at Sheen: a priest, who administered the last rites, and Alice Perrers, the senile king's mistress, who waited until the priest had departed and then robbed the corpse of its jewellery, pulling the rings from the fingers.

Alice – "that wanton baggage", as malicious court gossip speaks of her – was impeached and banished from court by a House of Commons outraged by both her influence over the king and her extravagance. But she returned in triumph to join the amorous king at his palace of Sheen on the Thames west of London. It is said that Alice infected the king with gonorrhoea, although this has never been proved.

However, Edward's senility was widely blamed on over-indulgence with his mistress. Though some speak of Alice as simply a high-spirited woman with a fancy for the good life, others claim that she gained her influence over the king by witchcraft "with the aid of certain friars and waxen images, incantations, potions and Moses rings of memory and oblivion".

Despite the scandal of his affair with Alice Perrers, Edward was liked and respected by his people for much of his reign. For 40 years he was married to the plump and

The late king: Edward III.

homely Philippa of Hainault; she bore him 12 children, seven sons and five daughters, one of whom died of the plague. He was generally on good terms with the nobility, who enjoyed his glittering tournaments and were impressed by his creation of the Order of the Garter, whose members became "partners of the king in peace and war".

But the revival of French power overshadowed Edward's earlier victories, and the decline of England's continental empire was blamed on Alice for seducing the king away from affairs of state and the glory of war (→ 20/11).

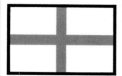

Richard II
1377–1399

Robert II
1371–1390
Robert III
1390–1406

Westminster, 16 July 1377. Richard of Bordeaux, aged ten, is crowned, but effective power will rest with his council until the new king comes of age.→

London, 13 March 1381. The Earl of Arundel, Richard Fitzalan, and Michael de la Pole are chosen as advisers to the king (→15/6).

Essex, March 1381. Henry Bolingbroke, a cousin of King Richard, marries Mary de Bohun, the co-heiress to the earldoms of Essex and Hereford (→16/9/87).

Edinburgh, March 1384. Anglo-Scottish hostilities begin, following the expiry of the 14-year truce (→6/8/85).

Borders, 6 Aug 1385. Richard marks the beginning of his new military campaign in Scotland by giving the dukedoms of York and Gloucester to his two younger uncles, Edmund of Langley and Thomas of Woodstock (→10/1386).

Wallingford, 8 August 1835. Princess Joan, the mother of King Richard, dies.

London, November 1385. King Richard makes a loan to John of Gaunt in support for his Castilian claims.

London, October 1386. Parliament, led by the Duke of Gloucester, impeaches the chancellor, Michael de la Pole, the Earl of Suffolk (→4/1387).

Wales, April 1387. Richard and Robert de Vere, the newly-appointed Duke of Ireland, plot to raise troops against the Duke of Gloucester (→9/1387).

Monmouth, 16 September 1387. Mary de Bohun gives birth to

Henry, the first-surviving son of Henry Bolingbroke, the Earl of Hereford (→16/9/98).

Waltham Cross, 14 Nov 1387. The Lords Appellant, led by the Duke of Gloucester, accuse King Richard's advisers of treason (→20/12).

London, 26 December 1387. Richard is threatened with deposition unless he answers last month's charges by leading barons of treason (→3/6/88).

Surrey, 9 April 1395. Richard, grief-stricken at the death of his queen, destroys Sheen palace.

Lincoln, 13 Jan 1396. Following the death of Constance, his second wife, John of Gaunt marries his mistress, Katherine Swynford (→3/2/99).

Paris, 9 March 1396. An Anglo-French truce is signed with the betrothal of Richard to Isabella, the daughter of France's King Charles VI (→7/1/97).

Scotland, 27 January 1399. David, the Duke of Rothesay and eldest son of Robert III, is appointed as lieutenant; he replaces his uncle, the Duke of Albany, who had abused his power (→21/8/1400).

London, 3 February 1399. John of Gaunt, the Duke of Lancaster, dies (→18/3).

England, 18 March 1399. Richard, who last year exiled Bolingbroke for ten years, makes the exile lifelong (→13/7/99).

Doncaster, 13 July 1399. Bolingbroke joins Northumberland against Richard (→20/8).

Westminster, 30 August 1399. Richard surrenders his crown to Henry Bolingbroke.→

Boy Richard is crowned

The boy king, Richard II, is crowned with full ceremony at Westminster.

Westminster, 16 July 1377

Richard II was crowned king today in splendid ceremony. Yesterday the ten-year-old king rode through London from the Tower to Westminster, and the City laid on a magnificent pageant for him.

Today he was led in procession to the abbey by his uncle John of Gaunt. He swore his coronation oath, and the archbishop of Canterbury anointed him with holy oil, set the crown upon his head and the ring upon his finger and put the sceptre into his hands. He was enthroned in the coronation chair, and all the nobles paid homage. The boy king was so tired that he had to be carried back to the palace. These are bad times for England. Most of Edward III's and the

Prince of Wales's conquests in France have been lost, and the French are raiding the south coast. There is great tension between serfs and their lords, between parliament and the council. Even the council itself, which will govern during the king's minority, is hopelessly split.

Richard himself was born in Bordeaux when his father, the Prince of Wales, was ruling Aquitaine. He had a lonely childhood in a household where his two half-brothers and two half-sisters, the children of his mother's earlier marriages, were already grown up. He is a handsome boy, but he seems to be more a scholar and lover of the arts than the warrior that his father was. Yet what England needs is a strong ruler (→13/3/81).

Young king defies rioters in poll-tax showdown

London, 15 June 1381

The king faced down the rebels at Smithfield today, saving himself and his court from massacre. The mayor of London had just killed Wat Tyler, the rebel leader, and the peasants were about to attack when the 14-year old king rode over to them, crying: "Sirs, would you kill your king? I am your king, I am your captain and your leader."

The rebels hold London and the south-east. They have murdered the archbishop of Canterbury and other royal officers, burnt and looted much of the city and sacked the Savoy palace, John of Gaunt's house.

The rebellion began as a protest against the poll tax of one shilling for every adult in the country, but soon expanded to include demands for an end to serfdom, reform of the church and a purge of the king's councillors. The rebels cry: "King Richard and the true Commons."

Rebels from Essex and Kent converged on London, burning castles and killing officials and lawyers. On 13 June they entered the City of London and surrounded the Tower, where the king and his councillors were sheltering. On the next day the king went to negotiate with the rebels at Mile End, promising them everything that they demanded. While he was away rebels broke into the Tower and murdered the

The poll-tax revolt: Richard looks on as Wat Tyler, the rebel leader, is stabbed (l) by the mayor, William Walworth.

archbishop. The king's cousin, Henry Bolingbroke, was almost killed. Today the king heard Mass at Westminster. On his way back to London he was waylaid by the rebel army at Smithfield. Wat Tyler rode up to him and made further demands in a rude and menacing manner. The mayor, William Walworth, then stabbed Tyler. The rebels cried that their chief was murdered, and the king and his followers would have been killed but for his bravery. It now seems that the rebels may disperse (→ 20/1/82).

King's troublesome uncle, John of Gaunt, bids for Spanish prize

Plymouth, April 1386

The king's uncle, John of Gaunt, the Duke of Lancaster, regarded as the most powerful man in England, has sailed for Spain with a large army. He hopes to win the crown of Castile in his wife Constance's name. His departure will be a relief to the king and many other nobles. The duke is suspected of coveting the English crown for himself. He has not rebelled against the king, but his vast possessions in the north and west of England give him an ideal base from which to do so.

The duke is a bad soldier and a mediocre administrator. England has been in chaos for many years while he has been the king's chief adviser. Now his rivals will have their turn (→ 13/1/96).

On his travels: John of Gaunt is royally entertained by Portugal's King John.

Teenage king takes a Bohemian bride

Westminster, 20 January 1382

The king was married in the abbey here today to Anne of Bohemia. She is the daughter of the late Holy Roman Emperor Charles IV and sister of the imperial claimant Wenceslaus. The marriage will strengthen the anti-French alliance. The king and queen are both 15. Anne is plain, but gentle and loving. The king, who has led a lonely and restricted life, appears much in love with her and looks to her for support and advice. The king's mother, Joan, the Princess of Wales, advised Anne to ask the king to pardon the rebels captured after the Peasants' Revolt. He granted the request, which was a very popular move.

▷

Richard and barons battle for power

Royal favourite is catalyst for revolt

London, September 1387

Richard II, who is now 20, is chafing under what he sees as the undue dominance of his uncle, the Duke of Gloucester, and his aristocratic allies. Richard, who reacts badly to any hint of contradiction or restraint, wishes to wield complete power in the realm.

The king's party is led by his favourite, Robert de Vere, whom he has made Marquis of Dublin and Duke of Ireland. He is the most detested man in the kingdom because of his ambition, corruption, and vainglory.

The king can refuse him nothing. It is said that if de Vere said black was white, Richard would not contradict him. De Vere married the king's cousin, Philippa, and has now deserted her to live with his mistress, one of the queen's Bohemian ladies. The king has not opposed this scandal.

The Duke of Gloucester is outraged at the insult to his niece, but is more interested in his own power. His chief allies are the Earls of Arundel, Warwick, Derby (the Duke of Lancaster's son) and Nottingham. Parliament supports the lords against the king and has impeached some of the king's men.

The king and de Vere are reported to be preparing an attack on their enemies. De Vere has raised an army in the west, which will march to London to defend the king (→ 14/11).

King Richard II rides into London, by James Northcote (1746-1831).

De Vere is humiliated at Radcot Bridge

Oxford, 20 December 1387

Robert de Vere, the Duke of Ireland, was defeated at Radcot Bridge near here today by Henry Bolingbroke, the king's cousin, and the Dukes of Gloucester and York, his uncles. De Vere abandoned his army and fled, losing his horse and armour in his flight.

The king is isolated in Westminster. Last month the rebel lords gathered their forces at Waltham Cross, in Hertfordshire, and sent an "appeal" to the king accusing de Vere, the Earl of Suffolk, Robert Tresilian and Nicholas Bembre of treason. They said that "it is in the interests of the state that any traitors who cluster around you deserve to be thrown out and punished, since it is better for some men to die than for the whole nation to perish".

The king rejected the appeal and called on de Vere for help. His complete defeat puts the king at the mercy of the "Lords Appellant", as they are now called because of the appeal from Waltham Cross. They have arrested those of the king's friends who have not fled abroad. The lords now propose to dismiss all the king's loyal friends and pack the court with their supporters. The king has agreed to call a parliament next February to try his friends, whom the Lords Appellant accuse of treason (→ 26/12).

Parliament shows no mercy as lords punish royal favourites

Westminster, 3 June 1388

King Richard II solemnly repeated his coronation oath in the abbey today, under the watchful eyes of the Lords Appellant who challenged his rule last year. The king is no more than a cipher now. His friends and favourites have been killed or exiled, and the lords exercise all the power in the land.

The parliament that convened on 3 February has won the name "the merciless parliament". The king presided, in the White Hall at Westminster. When the five Lords Appellant entered arm-in-arm they bowed deeply to the king, but there was no doubt who held the power.

The Duke of Gloucester is the leader of the appellants. The others are the Duke of York and the Earls of Derby, Arundel and Nottingham. First they impeached Sir Nicholas Bembre, the former mayor of London. He was executed. Then Sir Simon Burley, formerly the king's tutor, was tried and condemned, despite the protests of the

Duke of York and the Earl of Derby. Queen Anne knelt at Gloucester's feet to beg for him, but in vain.

The king's other friends were condemned *in absentia*. Robert de Vere and the Earl of Suffolk are in exile, but Sir Robert Tresilian, the former chief justice, was found hiding in London. He fled to the abbey but was dragged out and executed. Finally, parliament imposed the coronation oath on the king. Gloucester is all-powerful, but the king is set on revenge (→ 21/9/97).

First cookery book in English offers food fit for a king

Westminster, 1390

The secrets of the royal table have been revealed in a cook-book by the king's chef. It is called *The Forme of Cury* and is the first book to be written in English about cooking. It describes exotic dishes and methods of presenting familiar ones to make them interesting and palatable. Vinegar and spices are used to give a popular "sweet and sour" taste. French wines are essential, especially from Bordeaux, but the king also eats oysters cooked in Greek wine. Kings, like their subjects, have to regulate their diets according to the season. Fish from the sea must be salted or smoked, as there is no means of keeping it fresh.

The court moves constantly around the country, between the king's many palaces, so that game may be hunted for the table. Great nobles do the same thing. The main dishes fit for a king are meat and fish, pastries and sweetmeats. But chefs go to great lengths to surprise diners – offering gilded "apples" which turn out to be meat balls, for instance.

The great novelty is sugar, which is used with almonds and spices to make moulded desserts called "subtleties." One royal banquet ended with a confection shaped like a tiger led by St George.

English cooking: a C14th psalter.

Ailing Robert to be king

King Robert III with his wife Annabel Drummond: from a later manuscript.

Scone, Tayside, 14 August 1390
The new king of Scotland is John, the Earl of Carrick and eldest son of Robert II who died in April at the age of 74. The name John is considered unlucky for a king, however, and Carrick has insisted on being crowned as Robert III.

Carrick took over the daily government of the country in 1384, after his ageing father had admitted his own weakness. But four years later Carrick was so badly kicked by a horse that he was thought unfit to rule; his younger brother, the ambitious and forceful Earl of Fife – another Robert – assumed control. With the accession of Carrick – an invalid and depressive 53-year-old – Fife is expected to be confirmed as governor of the realm.

Robert III is the second Stewart monarch to occupy the Scottish throne, and his family now dominates the upper ranks of the Scottish nobility. His father had five sur-viving sons and seven daughters, and they have established their prominence in a single generation through marriage and substantial grants of land and titles. Relations between the sons, however, have been fraught with rivalry. The third son, Alexander, the lord of Bade-noch in central Inverness-shire, has quarrelled with most of his brothers; he has acquired the nickname "Wolf of Badenoch" through his feuding and lawlessness – which may have prompted his father's fall from effective power in 1384.

Ironically, that same year saw the greatest achievement of Robert II's reign: the liberation of Scotland from English occupation, when the Scots overran the English-held territories in the south. From 1385 the Scots started raiding England and two years ago won a major victory at Otterburn, but the English have refused to recognise Scottish independence (→27/1/99).

Richard marks his coming of age with first royal portrait painted from life

King Richard has given Westminster abbey a splendid portrait of himself to mark his coming of age. It is the first known contemporarily painted portrait of an English monarch. Likenesses of earlier kings have appeared on coins and also, after their deaths, as effigies on their tombs. Some monarchs have been painted before, but not always while they were alive and more often to convey a particular view. An example of this, albeit in a different medium, is the portrayal of William the Conqueror (and his predecessor King Harold) in the Bayeux Tapestry. Artists have under-standably sought to show their patrons in a similarly flattering light. What makes this painting of Richard by Andre Beauneveu of Valenciennes distinctive is that it is essentially a straight portrait of an individual.

Richard combines arms and charm to bring Irish to heel

Ireland, 15 May 1395

Richard sailed today from Waterford after leading an army of 4,000 knights and 30,000 archers in a successful eight-month campaign to quash the island's state of anarchy, which brought administrative costs of £20,000 a year and no income to offset it. But by a statesmanlike combination of pacification and appeasement, Richard has brought the Irish to heel, culminating in a triumphant ceremony in Dublin when 80 Irish chiefs paid homage to the "Lord of Ireland" – a title dating back to Henry II.

Richard's troops found Ireland a strange country, full of ruthless enemies reputed to slit the throats of the English and to cut their hearts out in order to eat them. The king led a vicious campaign, burning the lands of the unruly MacMurroughs and then making them swear on the cross of Dublin "to be our faithful and loyal subjects". His reward was another rebellion, which was put down by his cousin, the Earl of Rutland.

Richard knighted four Irish kings and taught them to wear breeches, use stirrups and eat at separate tables from their servants. He wanted to stay longer to secure a lasting peace, but he was urgently called back to England to deal with the revolt in Gascony (→9/3/96).

Richard becomes a dictatorial tyrant

King devastated by death of his queen

Westminster, 3 August 1394

Queen Anne of Bohemia, who died on 7 June aged 28, was buried here today. The king has ordered a magnificent tomb for himself and his wife, with effigies of each of them. The king is devastated by the loss. The queen was his closest and most loyal friend and gave him the self-confidence that he lacked. The Earl of Arundel arrived late for the funeral and the king, in a moment of blind Plantagenet rage, knocked him down with his sceptre. He has ordered Sheen palace, where Anne died, to be demolished (→9/4/95).

The death of Richard's queen, Anne.

Richard confronts the Duke of Gloucester: Froissart's "Chronicles" (C14th).

Rebel barons die as king takes revenge

Westminster, 21 September 1397

The Earl of Arundel was beheaded on Tower Hill today after he, the Duke of Gloucester, the Earl of Warwick and the archbishop of Canterbury had been impeached by parliament. It is the king's revenge on the "Lords Appellant".

Richard has been waiting for this day for nine years. He has never forgiven those who humiliated him and killed and exiled his friends during the "merciless parliament". The peers were accused of plotting against the king, as they had in 1387. Warwick begged for his life and was imprisoned, and the archbishop was exiled. Henry Bolingbroke and Thomas Mowbray, the Earl of Nottingham, have made their peace with the king. He may be going to deal with them later.

The king's uncle, the Duke of Gloucester, was arrested at his castle at Pleshy by the king himself. The king arrived while Gloucester was in bed, ordered him to dress and carried him off to the Tower. He was then sent to Calais and murdered (→16/9/98).

King marries child to seal peace treaty

Westminster, 7 January 1397

Isabella of France, the eldest daughter of Charles VI, was crowned queen of England today. Richard married her in Calais in November, just over two years after the death of his first queen, Anne of Bohemia. Isabella is seven years old.

The marriage is unpopular because of her age and nationality. The king chose her in the hope of assuring a permanent peace with France. He also considered marrying Catherine, Isabella's younger sister, to Henry Bolingbroke, the Duke of Lancaster's eldest son, whose wife died two years ago. Bolingbroke's son, Henry of Monmouth, who is only nine, might be a more suitable match. King Richard went to France twice to meet King Charles and discuss the marriage and the proposed truce between the two countries. The meetings were conducted with great splendour, with each king rivalling the other in magnificence. Those expeditions, the wedding and the coronation cost £200,000.

The Duke of Lancaster accompanied the king, along with his son, Henry Bolingbroke, and his new wife, Katherine Swynford. She had been his mistress and has borne him several children; recently legitimised by King Richard, they have been given the family name of Beaufort (→28/7/1401).

A painting of the 1390s [known later as the Wilton Diptych] shows Richard and his patron saints in heaven, where angels wear the king's livery – equating the king's court with heaven as a statement of divine right.

Richard ousted by Bolingbroke coup

Bolingbroke exiled after Gosforth duel

Coventry, 16 September 1398

The king dramatically interrupted a duel at Gosforth today between the Earl of Hereford and the Duke of Norfolk. Henry Bolingbroke of Hereford had accused Thomas Mowbray of Norfolk of treasonable words; Mowbray had denied them. Under the laws of chivalry the duel would determine who was right, but Richard declared them both guilty and banished Mowbray for life and Bolingbroke for ten years. They were the two survivors of the lords who clashed with the king in 1388 (→ 18/3/99).

Henry's army lands

Chester, 20 August 1399

Henry Bolingbroke, the Duke of Lancaster, is on the brink of usurping the crown barely seven weeks after he landed at Ravenspur on 4 July with a band of just 300 men. He had been banished by King Richard last year and at first maintained that he had returned only to reclaim his title. But he quickly gathered support, his army swelling to thousands as it moved through the Midlands to Bristol and Chester [*see map*]. He has sent envoys to Richard, who is sheltering in Conwy castle after returning from Ireland to find his troops scattered and his reign imperilled (→ 30/9).

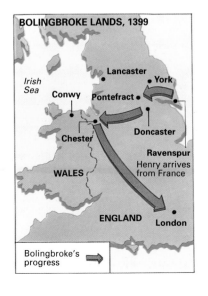

BOLINGBROKE LANDS, 1399

Irish Sea
Lancaster
York
Conwy
Pontefract
Chester
Doncaster
Ravenspur
Henry arrives from France
WALES
ENGLAND
London

Bolingbroke's progress

The alleged abdication: Richard shown giving up his crown to Duke Henry.

Richard abdicates: Henry seizes power

London, 30 September 1399

King Richard II was deposed in parliament today. His cousin, Henry of Lancaster, claims that he formally abdicated, giving his crown and sceptre to Henry.

Richard has such faith in the sacred and absolute nature of kingship that he could not easily be persuaded to abdicate. He has been lodged in the Tower since he was brought back from Wales, where he was arrested after his return from Ireland. He was led through London riding on a pony and was mocked by the Londoners. Four of his last loyalists were arrested in the Tower, in the king's sight, dragged on their backs behind two horses to Cheapside and beheaded on a fishmonger's slab. Their heads were set up on London Bridge.

Henry went to see Richard, who demanded: "Why do you keep me so closely guarded by your men-at-arms? Do you acknowledge me as your lord and king?" The duke replied that Richard was his lord and king but that the council had ordered him to be imprisoned until parliament met. Henry ensured that parliament would do his bidding. He reported that Richard had abdicated; Richard was declared deposed, and Henry was then acclaimed as king.

King who failed to win his subjects over

Westminster, 1399

Richard II was never understood by his subjects, and in the end he proved unfit to be king. His belief that compromise showed weakness led him to alienate powerful noblemen, rather than using them as supporters. Instead, he preferred the company of men politically dependent upon him.

Part of the problem was that he had no model of kingship. He had known his grandfather, Edward III, only after that king's decline into senility. His own father, the Prince of Wales, died when his son was only nine, leaving him to measure himself against the ghost of the greatest hero of the age; he always found himself wanting.

Richard had good traits. He was loyal to his friends and capable of bravery, as he showed during the Peasants' Revolt. But he had a violent temper and could be devious and deceitful.

Maverick dies after founding dynasties throughout Europe

London, 18 March 1399

John of Gaunt, the Duke of Lancaster, was buried in St Paul's cathedral today next to his first wife. He died last month at the age of 59. He was the king's uncle and the greatest nobleman in England.

His son, Henry Bolingbroke, is in exile in France, and King Richard has seized all his inheritance. The king visited Gaunt on his deathbed, and the duke raged at him for the attack on his son.

His other children include the queens of Spain and Portugal and the Beauforts, the children of his mistress, Katherine Swynford, who were legitimised when he married her after his second wife died.

John of Gaunt played a major role in the wars with France, although he was eclipsed by his elder brother, the Prince of Wales, and conducted campaigns in Scotland and Spain. He was out of England during the Peasants' Revolt, of which he was a prime target. He was also absent in the crisis over the "Lords Appellant", when his links to both sides could have defused the tension. He was always loyal to Richard, though often suspected of coveting the throne.

A later engraving of Gaunt's tomb.

Henry IV
1399–1413

Robert III
1390–1406
James I
1406–1437

Westminster, 13 October 1399.
Henry Bolingbroke, who was declared king of England by parliament last month, is crowned as Henry IV (→15/10).

Westminster, 15 October 1399.
King Henry IV invests his son, also called Henry, as Prince of Wales (→23/10).

Westminster, 23 October 1399.
Henry decides on the former King Richard's fate: life imprisonment (→21/8/1400).

Edinburgh, 21 August 1400.
Henry assaults the castle unsuccessfully after the Scottish king, Robert III, refuses to pay homage (→10/1400).

Wales, 16 September 1400.
Owain Glyndwr, the lord of Glyndyfrydwy, claims the title Prince of Wales (→15/10).

Borders, October 1400. Anglo-Scots peace talks fail when Robert III of Scots questions Henry's right to the English throne (→5/1402).

Blackheath, 25 December 1400.
Henry entertains the Byzantine emperor, Manuel II, on his state visit to western Europe.

Conwy, 31 May 1401. Owain Glyndwr, the self-proclaimed native Prince of Wales, is exiled by Henry (→10/1402).

Dover, 28 July 1401. Isabella, the widow of Richard II, returns to France.

Southern Wales, October 1402.
Owain Glyndwr seizes control (→14/7/04).

Winchester, 7 February 1403.
King Henry marries Joan of Navarre, the dowager Duchess of Brittany; she is his second wife (→1420).

Wales, May 1403. Prince Henry, aged 16, the English Prince of Wales and heir to King Henry IV, begins a campaign of military raids (→21/7).

Shrewsbury, 21 July 1403.
Henry Percy (nicknamed "Hotspur"), the son of the Earl of Northumberland, dies fighting Prince Henry.→

York, 11 August 1403. The Earl of Northumberland submits to Henry (→23/5/05).

Wales/France, 14 July 1404.
The French ally with Owain Glyndwr, the Welsh leader, against Henry (→15/8/04).

Hereford, 23 May 1405. Henry abandons his plans to invade Wales on receiving news of a revolt by the Earl of Northumberland (→28/2/06).

Aberdaron, 28 February 1406.
Owain Glyndwr and his allies Edmund Mortimer and Henry Percy, the Earl of Northumberland, agree to partition England if they win (→19/2/08).

North-east coast, March 1406.
Prince James, the heir to the Scottish throne, is caught by the English at Flamborough Head while fleeing to safety (→4/04).

Westminster, March 1410. Archbishop Arundel, the chancellor, resigns; Prince Henry and his allies, the Beauforts, gain influence during the king's illness.

London, 17 June 1412. Prince Henry publicly declares that he is not planning to overthrow his father, despite the suggestions that Henry IV should abdicate in his favour (→9/1412).

Westminster, 20 March 1413.
Henry IV dies; his son, Henry, will succeed him.→

Henry Bolingbroke, warrior and usurper, claims the English throne for himself

The new king: a portrait of Henry IV, from Chichester Cathedral, Sussex.

Westminster, 30 September 1399
Richard II has been deposed, and Henry Bolingbroke has been acclaimed as king of England in his stead. Archbishop Arundel, on behalf of the Lords Spiritual and Temporal and the Commons, led Bolingbroke to the throne.

The man who will become Henry IV claimed the throne by descent from Henry III, but his right of succession is complex. Henry Bolingbroke is the son of Edward III's *fourth* son, John of Gaunt, by Blanche of Lancaster. He is Richard's male heir because his claim through John of Gaunt is in the male line. If the crown can descend through a woman (as it has before), the heir is the young Edmund Mortimer, the Earl of March, the great-grandson of Lionel, the Duke of Clarence, who was the *second* son of Edward III.

Bolingbroke claims that his Lancastrian ancestor Edmund was in fact the elder brother of Edward I, but few give credence to this. More to the point is the fact that Bolingbroke is a brave soldier, an educated man unjustly deprived of his lands by the deposed king, apparently capable of uniting the country behind him, whereas Mortimer is only a child. Nonetheless, it was the support of powerful barons for Henry which toppled Richard, and they will try to ensure that King Henry IV rules by consent of parliament (→13/10).

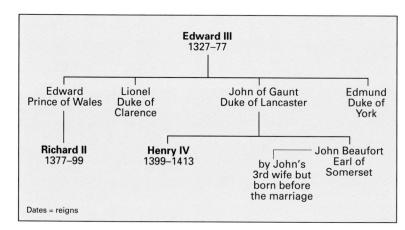

Henry IV is crowned

A new royal line: King Henry IV is crowned with all possible majesty.

Westminster, 13 October 1399

Henry Bolingbroke was today crowned as King Henry IV by Thomas Arundel, the archbishop of Canterbury. It is the feast of the translation of St Edward, and the coronation has been accompanied by several auspicious rituals.

Yesterday, in his first act of pageantry, the new king knighted 50 nobles, including his four sons, who walked before him to the throne. The eldest, Henry of Monmouth, carried the sword of Lancaster, the "sword of mercy" which King Henry had worn himself at Richard's coronation. The king was accompanied to the throne by the mayor and aldermen of London, and the fountains ran with red wine in his honour.

Perhaps the most important part of the ritual was the unction. King Henry was anointed with a holy oil said to have been discovered in France by Thomas Becket, the most venerated of all English saints.

Henry halts Glyndwr rebellion in Wales

Wales, 15 October 1400

The king's anger with the Welsh for supporting the anti-English rebellion led by Owain Glyndwr last month knows no bounds. He feels personally insulted by the actions of this self-styled Prince of Wales and is determined to hold the Welsh nation responsible for this and any future uprising. He also considers that he has been given unacceptable excuses for the irregular payment of feudal dues, worth more than £60,000 to him.

In a speech to his generals, marking the successful conclusion of a personally-led punitive raid into Wales and the re-assertion of his rule there, King Henry announced his intention of introducing penal legislation against the Welsh. Henceforth, he said, no Welshman will be allowed to carry arms for any purpose whatsoever. And, as of now, Welshmen will be excluded absolutely from acquiring land in England, or in English towns in Wales, and from being burgesses.

"Entire Englishmen", he said, would be protected from conviction at the suit of any kind of Welshman "entire or otherwise" (ie both parents being Welsh or only one). And no Welshman would ever again be knighted as in the days of Edward III, he concluded angrily. The storm which caused all this grave

A later view of Owain Glyndwr.

damage to Anglo-Welsh relations broke on 16 September when Glyndwr was proclaimed Prince of Wales in his lordship of Glyndyfrydwy, near Llangollen.

Glyndwr then launched a raid against the leading English boroughs of north-eastern Wales. His intention could have been simply to register a private protest at the greed of English landlords. But he seems also to have had a loftier purpose in mind involving the overlordship of Wales (→31/5/01).

Former King Richard dies: rumour says he was murdered

Pontefract, 14 February 1400

The deposed King Richard II has died in his prison at Pontefract castle. It is said that he was hacked to death on the orders of his usurper, King Henry IV. Richard's death comes as no surprise in the light of the several plots against King Henry which have been foiled in the past few months. His continued existence was bound to be a threat to the new king.

The most colourful account tells of the former king being set upon by eight assassins with axes. Richard is said to have killed four of them before being felled by Sir Peter Exton. There are further rumours of covert payments to servants. Richard's body is to be displayed publicly, which may give credence to the official story – that he starved himself to death.

The former King Richard's funeral: from Froissart's "Chronicles" (C14th).

Albany accused of killing Scots heir

Lothian, May 1402

A public inquiry into the death of King Robert III's eldest son has concluded that David, the Duke of Rothesay, "departed this life by divine providence". However, suspicion remains that his uncle, Robert, the Duke of Albany (formerly the Earl of Fife), was implicated.

Rothesay had served as lieutenant to the invalid Robert III for three years, after ousting Albany from the guardianship. When his appointment expired he was arrested for corruption and extortion, on Albany's advice, and taken to Albany's castle, where he died on 26 March. The official cause was dysentery, but Rothesay's friends have accused his jailers of starving him to death (→3/1406).

▷

Henry forced to fight desperate war on two fronts

Close combat: the Battle of Shrewsbury, after a picture by John Rous (1485).

GLYNDWR REBELS AGAINST HENRY IV

Principality of Wales

Marcher lordships

Castles under
— Welsh attack
— English attack

Irish Sea

ANGLESEY

Conwy Rhuddlan Flint

Bangor Denbigh Ruthin Chester

CAERNARFON COUNTY PALATINE OF CHESTER

MERIONETH

Harlech Dolgellau

POWYS

Machynlleth Shrewsbury

Aberystwyth SHROPSHIRE

CARDIGAN MARCH OF WALES

CARMARTHEN HEREFORD

Haverfordwest Carmarthen Brecon Gloucester

Abergavenny Usk

Milford Haven Tenby GLAMORGAN

COUNTY PALATINE OF PEMBROKE Cardiff

Percy rebellion challenged at Shrewsbury

Shrewsbury, 21 July 1403
King Henry has today survived the most serious crisis of his reign so far with a battlefield win over a rebel army raised by a family which had done much to put him on the throne. The Percies, led by the Earl of Northumberland, who feels that Henry has failed to give his clan the preferment it deserves, staged a rebellion purportedly in support of the claim to the throne of Edmund Mortimer, the Earl of March. Owain Glyndwr, their most lethal ally, did not arrive to help them today.

The rebel force, led by Northumberland's son Henry Percy (known as "Hotspur"), arrived here to challenge Prince Henry to a battle only to find the royal standard already flying; King Henry had just arrived, having marched west after hearing news of the growing revolt.

Today's desperate fight began at around midday with a tremendous slaughter of the king's men by Hotspur's crack team of Cheshire archers. Prince Henry was hit in the face, and two knights who had donned the king's surcoat as decoys

were killed. The king was staring defeat in the face when suddenly Hotspur was cut down; the enemy scattered in confusion, and the royal forces killed about 1,600 and wounded 3,000 of the 5,000-strong Percy army. Hotspur's uncle, Thomas, the Earl of Worcester, has been taken prisoner. The king has nipped the revolt in the bud and prevented the dangerous alliance of Percy and Glyndwr (→11/8).

Glyndwr scores massive success in Wales

Wales, 5 August 1404
Lewis Byford, the bishop of Bangor and King Henry's most important Welsh cleric, has joined the Welsh national movement led by Owain Glyndwr. This defection, announced today, reinforces the claim of Glyndwr to assume the pretensions of a national prince instead of those of a mere guerrilla leader.

The announcement, made before what purported to be a Welsh

national parliament gathered in Machynlleth, came from the bishop himself as he stood by Glyndwr's side in the assembly hall. Urged on by Glyndwr, who was enjoying the occasion hugely, the bishop then revealed to the gathering how he had been persuaded to lead an embassy in secret from Dolgellau in Gwynedd to the French court in Paris on 10 May, requesting an alliance and practical help against the English. It had involved, he said, "a long and restful sea voyage from Milford Haven".

Welshmen hope that this university-trained former papal courtier will continue to be responsible for the polished image which Glyndwr's cause currently presents to the world outside Wales. It is common knowledge that he was able to secure the valuable French alliance in May by pointing eloquently to the uninterrupted success of Glyndwr's army, which this year has reduced English control over Wales to a few isolated castles and small boroughs such as Abergavenny and Coety [*Glamorgan*] (→29/08/05).

A later view of Owain Glyndwr's national parliament at Machynlleth.

Scottish king dies after hearing that his son has been captured by English pirates

A later engraving shows Henry IV handing Prince James into his tutors' care.

Bute, Strathclyde, 4 April 1406
King Robert III of Scots has died at Rothesay castle on the isle of Bute, aged 69. The king had been an invalid for the past 18 years and was living in semi-retirement. His death followed hard on the news that his only surviving son, 11-year-old James, had been taken prisoner by the English.

James – who now becomes king in exile – was captured by English pirates while aboard ship on his way to France. His elder brother, the Duke of Rothesay, died in suspicious circumstances four years ago, and their father decided to send James to France for his own safety. Handed over to King Henry IV of England, the boy has now been imprisoned in the Tower of London. The governorship of Scotland remains in the hands of his uncle, the Duke of Albany.

The late king, who apparently lost the will to live after hearing of his son's fate, once said that he would be content to be buried in a midden with the epitaph "Here lies the worst of kings and the most wretched of men in the whole realm" (→ 1412).

King Henry bedbound by strange illness

Westminster, December 1408
King Henry is gravely ill. For the past two years he has been partially confined to bed with what some people believe to be leprosy. Now he has suffered a stroke. The first signs of illness came in 1406 when the king was exhausted after putting down several rebellions and campaigning against the Scots and Welsh. As pustules began to erupt on his face, he screamed that he was on fire. It is seen by some as God's punishment for the execution of the rebellious archbishop of York, Richard Scrope, in 1405.

Master Malvern, the court physician, has been unable to make any impression on the disfiguring disease, which may be venereal in origin, or tubercular gangrene, or a kind of embolism. Pietro di Alcobasse and Davido di Nigarello, two Jewish specialists from Italy, have been summoned, but they have been unable to find a cure.

Although the mystery illness lets up from time to time, the recurrent attacks affect the king's mind as well as his body, making it impossible for him to govern. When Henry is thus incapacitated, the government of the realm is chiefly conducted by his chief confidant, Archbishop Arundel.

However, the influence of the king's son, Prince Henry, is increasing, and it seems possible that he may soon take over the throne from his ailing father (→ 3/1410).

The royal bird: an enamelled gold version of Henry IV's swan badge.

Welsh rebel evades battle with Henry

Worcester, 29 August 1405
A dispirited force of more than 10,000 well-armed French soldiers under the command of Owain Glyndwr, the self-styled Prince of Wales, preferred to evade battle with King Henry today when its allies from northern England failed to arrive. The size of the army was proof of the value of the French alliance, but, by all accounts, the French expedition into England was not well attuned to either Glyndwr's tactics or his resources.

After camping for several weeks on Woodbury Hill, some eight miles (12.5km) short of Worcester, the soldiers heard that support for Glyndwr was crumbling in northern England. Their retreat began early today (→ 28/2/06).

Percy executed after defeat in battle ends bid to topple king

Henry Percy is dead; here, in earlier days, he stands by King Richard II.

Bramham Moor, 19 February 1408
Henry Percy, the Earl of Northumberland, has been executed after the defeat of his rebel army at the hands of the sheriff of Yorkshire. The death of Percy removes the last substantial internal threat to King Henry IV and his heirs.

The Earl of Northumberland has been a thorn in the king's side ever since the Percy rebellion of 1403 was crushed at Shrewsbury. He was then believed to have signed a compact with Owain Glyndwr and Edmund Mortimer, the Earl of March, to partition the realm after unseating King Henry. After the capture and execution of his fellow conspirators Archbishop Scrope and Thomas Mowbray in 1405, Percy became a fugitive in Wales, Scotland and France until this final – and fatal – expedition.

Henry bids to ease family tensions

Guilt-stricken king makes humble will

Westminster, 21 January 1409

King Henry has made a will, in which he declares: "I, Henry, sinful wretch, ask my lords and true people forgiveness if I have misentreated them in any wise." The caveat is typical of a man who has been racked by guilt since he came to the throne, and who wants nothing more than a stable kingdom and a sure succession.

The very act of usurpation, although Henry had popular support, has made his kingship illegitimate in many eyes. And although he has shown himself a merciful king, he made an exception in the case of the rebel Archbishop Scrope, executed in 1405 after being promised clemency – an act that has tormented him as much as the fate he ordained for Richard II.

Now that effective opposition to King Henry has been eliminated, the main effort of this pious and conscientious man is spent on achieving moral dominion over his people. But that is handicapped by his own ill health.

He spends hours in a library he built for himself at Eltham Palace, studying questions of morality. His will is astonishingly humble. He has commanded that his body be buried not at Westminster, where his predecessors lie, but at Canterbury. He has given no instructions for his tomb.

Prince Henry, here shown paying homage to France's King Charles VII.

Uneasy truce reconciles king and prince

London, September 1412

Prince Henry and his father have been reconciled for the second time this year. In Coventry, in June, the prince publicly scotched rumours that he was planning a coup, and now he has come home from Calais to rebut accusations that he stole the garrison's pay. Yet despite this truce, family tension remains high between father and heir. Since 1409 Prince Henry has found himself in increasing conflict with his father. Having won respect for his military prowess he has come to dominate the king's council, while abroad, in Aquitaine, he has pursued an alliance with the Duke of Burgundy, although the king favours his rival, the Duke of Orleans (→ 20/3/13).

Usurper to leave new dynasty securing the English throne

England, 1412

The reign of King Henry IV began with his usurping the throne. It will end with his family secure, it seems, as a new dynasty, with no fewer than six surviving children by his late wife Mary Bohun. Of these the eldest is Henry, the Prince of Wales, who is impatient to step into his father's shoes.

Thomas, the Duke of Clarence, is second in line to the throne (if Edmund Mortimer, the Earl of March, is excluded).

Born in 1388, Thomas is a proud and impetuous youth, recently married to Margaret, the widow of the king's half-brother John Beaufort, the Earl of Somerset. Thomas was sent to France by his father to support the Duke of Orleans [*see report opposite.*]

John is a year younger than Thomas and was created constable of England in 1403. Last year he was made joint ambassador to Scotland. A competent soldier, he enjoys a good relationship with Prince Henry. Humphrey was born in 1390 while his father was in Prussia. He was knighted in 1399 and fought at the Battle of Shrewsbury in 1403. Educated at Oxford, he is now constable of the castle at Marlborough and keeper of two royal forests.

Blanche is the elder of the two princesses; now aged 20, she married Ludwig, the Count palatine of the Rhine, in 1402. Philippa, aged 18, is also living abroad; she married King Eric IX of Denmark in 1406.

Lollard spurns plea by prince and dies a martyr's death

A Lollard is put to a grisly death.

Smithfield, 5 March 1410

Prince Henry offered a last-minute reprieve to a heretic today, but his attempt at mercy was spurned. John Badby, a humble smith and an adherent of the Lollards, cried out in pain as he began to burn at the stake, and the prince ordered the flaming timbers to be pulled away; but Badby refused to recant, and the sentence was carried out.

The execution of Badby was carried out under the 1401 statute *De heretico comburendo* [On the burning of heretics], which King Henry passed in response to the church's demands. Although sheriffs had been authorised to arrest unlicensed preachers since 1382, the tide of heresy had not been stemmed, and the church felt increasingly threatened. The king had an interest, too, for some preachers had been inciting revolt by insisting that Richard II was still alive.

The Lollards, however, were a new threat. They gained their inspiration from John Wyclif, who wrote radical theological tracts, rejecting transubstantiation and other tenets of the established church, until his death in 1384. The name derives from a Middle Dutch word meaning "a mumbler". Lollards were so called because they often prayed aloud.

Although Wyclif's ideas took root in Oxford, where he taught, they are now strongest in the large towns of the midlands and south – notably in Leicester, Coventry, and Bristol.

King puts brake on Beaufort advances

Westminster, 5 January 1412

Archbishop Arundel has been re-appointed as the king's chancellor, replacing Thomas Beaufort. King Henry is reasserting his authority over his son, Prince Henry, and putting the brakes on the advance of the Beaufort family.

Since the suppression of the Percy rebellions and the rise to prominence of Prince Henry, the Beauforts have become the most powerful family in the land. Their mother, Katherine Swynford, was governess in John of Gaunt's household and gave birth to three sons and one daughter before graduating from Gaunt's mistress to his wife.

John Beaufort, the Marquis of Somerset, was the eldest son and died in 1410. Henry Beaufort, the next brother, is a brilliant lawyer who became bishop of Lincoln, then bishop of Winchester in 1404; he has made a fortune out of his church revenues and lives a secular life, with a mistress. Thomas Beaufort, the third brother, served alongside Prince Henry in the campaigns in Wales where he was reputedly a fine, dependable soldier. Their sister, Joan, has married the Earl of Westmorland. While Prince Henry retained control of the king's council, the Beauforts rode high – too high, the king now thinks.

Henry IV dies in 'Jerusalem chamber'

At rest: the tomb effigy for King Henry IV in Canterbury cathedral.

Westminster, 20 March 1413

Henry IV, the usurper king, is dead. His last years overshadowed by his debilitating disease, King Henry fainted as he made an offering before the shrine of Edward the Confessor, the patron saint of King Richard II. He was carried into the the so-called "Jerusalem Chamber" in the abbot's house for the last rites. This was appropriate, because it had been prophesied that the king would die in Jerusalem, and he was planning a crusade there.

On his deathbed, King Henry was invited to repent of the execution of Archbishop Scrope in 1405, and the usurpation of the crown. He pointed out that the pope had absolved him of guilt for Scrope's death, and there was little he could do about the usurpation since his sons would not let go of the crown.

As King Henry appeared to slip into unconsciousness, his eldest son took the crown from the deathbed. The dying king reclaimed the crown and asked his son what right he thought he had to it, since he himself had none. Prince Henry replied: "As you have kept it by the sword, so will I keep it while my life lasts."

Although wars and rebellions filled much of the reign of Henry IV, his realm was never so united as at his death (→9/4).

Lord of the Isles submits to the power of the Duke of Albany

Highland, Summer 1412

Donald, the rebellious Lord of the Isles, has been forced to submit to Scotland's governor, the Duke of Albany, after Albany sent three armies into the highlands.

Donald's humiliation follows his defeat last year at Harlaw, near Aberdeen, by Albany's nephew Alexander Stewart, the Earl of Mar. Donald had been trying since 1402 to gain control of the earldom of Ross but had met repeated opposition from Albany, who has custody of Euphemia Leslie, the heiress of Ross. Last summer, however, Donald overran the earldom and captured Inverness; he came up against the Earl of Mar's forces while marching on Aberdeen.

Donald's defeat and submission consolidate Albany's hold on the

troublesome highlands, where five earldoms and several lordships are already under his control.

Albany has been the dominant force in Scotland for much of the last 25 years, since his elder brother – who became King Robert III in 1390 – was badly kicked by a horse. The king's eldest son, David, died in mysterious circumstances in 1402 at Albany's castle of Falkland. Robert III himself died four years later, shortly after hearing that his only surviving son, James, had been taken prisoner by English pirates and put in the Tower of London by King Henry IV of England. On his brother's death, Albany was confirmed as governor of Scotland – a position he has held ever since, while James remains captive in the Tower (→28/2/16).

Albany: Scotland's governor.

Clarence campaigns to regain Aquitaine

Bordeaux, France, 10 August 1412

Thomas, the Duke of Clarence, has arrived here to reclaim the lands of Aquitaine on behalf of his father, King Henry IV. He has left a trail of death and destruction on his way from Normandy. Reversing the Burgundian alliance fostered by his brother, Prince Henry, Clarence came to the aid of the Orleanists with 800 men-at-arms and 300 archers. By the time that he had looted and burnt his way to Blois, his allies wanted to be rid of him and were obliged to pay jewellery and money worth £35,000. Clarence's forces continued their destructive progress southwards, allegedly kidnapping children for sale as servants (→22/3/21).

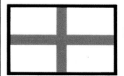

Henry V
1413–1422

James I
1406–1437

Henry V is crowned king

The handsome young king: an anonymous portrait of Henry painted c.1520.

Westminster, 9 April 1413.
Henry, the Prince of Wales, is crowned king of England.→

Leicester, April 1414. Henry presides over the first parliament of his reign (→6/7/15).

Westminster, 24 July 1415. Henry makes his will (→5/8).

Wales, July 1415. Owain Glyndwr, the once-powerful ruler, dies; his son, Maredudd, succeeds (→1421).

Southampton, 5 August 1415. Richard, the Earl of Cambridge, is executed following the discovery of a plot to overthrow Henry and replace him by his cousin, Edmund Mortimer, the Earl of March (→18/1/25).

Normandy, 14 August 1415. Henry lands to claim the crown of France (→17/9).

Harfleur, France, 17 Sept 1415. Henry and his army are hit by a dysentery epidemic (→22/9).

Harfleur, 6 October 1415. Having taken the city, Henry begins the long march towards Calais, the nearest English-occupied town (→25/10).

Dover, 16 November 1415. Henry, battered but victorious, returns to England (→23/11).

London, 28 February 1416. Murdoch Stewart, the eldest son of Robert, the Duke of Albany and governor of Scotland, is ransomed by Henry, having been captured in 1402.

Harfleur, 15 August 1416. John, the Duke of Bedford and brother of Henry V, lifts the siege and regains control of the Channel.

Caen, France, 4 Sept 1417. The city falls to Henry, who arrived last month; only the castle still remains under the control of French forces (→30/7/18).

Rouen, France, 30 July 1418. Henry and his army lay siege to the city (→19/1/19).

Northern France, 25 Dec 1419. Anglo-French peace talks fail after the murder of Duke John of Burgundy; Henry and Philip II, the new duke, ally against France (→21/5/20).

France/England, 21 May 1420. Henry signs the Treaty of Troyes and arranges his marriage to Catherine, the daughter of Charles VI of France (→2/6).

Paris, 1 December 1420. Henry enters the city with Charles VI of France and Duke Philip II of Burgundy (→1/2/21).

Dover, 1 February 1421. Henry and Catherine return from France (→23/2).

Westminster, 23 February 1421. Catherine is crowned as queen of England (→6/12/21).

Westminster, 23 April 1421. Henry invests the captive King James of Scots as a knight of the Garter (→4/9/23).

Calais, 1 June 1421. Henry returns to France on the news of the death of his brother and heir to the throne, Thomas, the Duke of Clarence (→5/1422).

Wales, 1421. Maredudd, the son of Owain Glyndwr, finally accepts the pardon first offered to him in 1417 and brings peace to Wales.

France, 31 August 1422. Henry dies in the dysentery epidemic after the surrender of Meaux; his baby son, Prince Henry, will succeed him.→

Westminster, 9 April 1413
The Prince of Wales was crowned king today, Passion Sunday, in the middle of a blizzard. He looked solemn and gloomy and did not touch the food at the coronation banquet. He was aware that many of the nobles in the abbey considered him a usurper like his father; the Earl of March has a better title to the throne, and it is popularly believed that the deposed King Richard is still alive in Scotland.

The new king is 25, athletic – it is said that he can outrun deer – and considered handsome with his long nose and military haircut. The wild riots of his youth are celebrated – such as the tavern brawl in Eastcheap with his younger brothers which brought the mayor and sheriffs out in the small hours. One of his diversions was to ambush and rob officers of his own household in disguise, and he shockingly boxed the lord chief justice on the ear. But all agree that on his father's death he has suddenly "become a new man", confessed his past sins and banished his old drinking companions, who are not allowed within ten miles (16km) of him.

As Prince of Wales he proved himself as a soldier in the campaigns against Owain Glyndwr and the Welsh rebels. At 19 he besieged and took Aberystwyth and Harlech castles. His quarrels with his father caused his dismissal from the king's council, but he is a great reader, especially of works of Christian piety (→4/1414).

Warrior king battles fiercely to win French crown

Henry claims the throne of France

Winchester, 6 July 1415

King Henry today declared war on France after the final breakdown of negotiations over his claim to the French throne. The claim, through his great-grandfather Edward III whose mother was the daughter of King Philip IV, rests on not recognising the "Salic Law" debarring succession through women.

France's king, Charles VI, is intermittently mad, and there is civil war between the Armagnacs and the Burgundians. Earlier this year Henry was offered most of Aquitaine and the Limousin, plus the king's daughter Catherine with a dowry, but he demanded all western France or vowed that he would take it. He has spent two years preparing for war. The French said that as Henry was young they would send him "little balls to play with until he should have grown to a man's strength" (→ 14/8).

The battle of Agincourt, as shown in a 15th-century French manuscript.

Harfleur surrenders after month's siege

Harfleur, 22 September 1415

After a month's siege the port of Harfleur surrendered to the English army today. The garrison commanders and 66 hostages came out of the town wearing nothing but shirts, with halters round their necks, to kneel down for several hours before being admitted to the presence of King Henry, clad in cloth of gold and seated on a throne in a silk pavilion. He rebuked them for having witheld "our town of Harfleur, against God and justice".

The garrison is starving, and the walls and bastions were breached by the huge English siege cannon hurling gun-stones as big as mill-stones. The rich bourgeois have been taken hostage for ransom, but 2,000 poorer citizens are being expelled and their houses offered to English settlers. But Henry's army has been reduced by a third through dysentery (6/10).

English triumph in battle at Agincourt

Agincourt, 25 October 1415

Terrible slaughter was inflicted on the French by King Henry's much smaller English army here today through a combination of continuous rain, bad French tactics and the skill of English archers. It was a battle that Henry did not seek. His 6,000 men, short of rations and weakened by dysentery, met a French force of perhaps 20,000 blocking the road to Calais.

On sodden ground, hemmed in between two woods, the French in heavy armour could not get up again once they fell. After the cavalry had been beaten off by the archers, the men-at-arms, too closely packed to use their weapons, advanced on boggy ground. As they began to fall, ranks piled on top of each other and suffocated or were butchered where they lay. Nearly 10,000 perished, including the prisoners who were put to death at Henry's order. English losses were at most 500 (→ 16/11).

The Duke of Orleans, taken at Agincourt, shown (r) in the Tower of London.

Henry returns, the all-conquering king

London, 23 November 1415

King Henry made a triumphant return to London today from France. Despite the king's edict that there should be no celebrations because the victory was God's, he was welcomed by City leaders and greeted at London Bridge by giant effigies on the bridge tower holding out huge keys to him with the slogan "A Giant full grim of sight to teach the Frenchmen courtesy". As he rode through the city, crowds sang to him: "Welcome, Henry V, king of England and France."

With Henry clad in purple on his horse, his retinue could only just pass through the crowds. Lords and ladies decked in gold and scarlet filled the windows. There can be no more question of his right to rule. The carol written to celebrate the victory began:

"Our King went forth to Normandy
With grace and might of chivalry
God for him wrought marvellously
Deo Gratias."

Henry battles on to capture Rouen

Rouen, France, 19 January 1419
Rouen, the capital of the duchy of Normandy, surrendered its keys to King Henry today as he sat in gold state robes in a local monastery before riding through the city on a black charger to hear Mass at the cathedral. The people of Rouen who lined the streets to watch him were emaciated by over six months of siege, during which they were reduced to eating dogs, mice and rats and dockroots. They begged for food, which was sent in, but the dead are still lying in the streets.

Henry's siege, like all his conquest of Normandy, succeeded by the deliberate use of terror. He sent Irish troopers to raid the surrounding countryside, committing atrocities, even killing babies. He hanged his prisoners on gibbets in view of the city walls. When 12,000 non-combatant citizens – old men, women and children – were turned out of the city, he had them herded into the ditch around the walls and left to die of hunger and exposure. "Fellows, who put them there?" he demanded of the French envoys.

He insists on his right to Rouen, "which is mine inheritance". Once again Henry has proved that terror and hunger will breach the stoutest defences. Last year he took Caen by assault after a terrifying bombardment with iron balls filled with flaming tow. He then had 2,000 of the civilian inhabitants massacred by the troops in the market place. Everyone from the age of 12 was cut to pieces. By such means Henry has made a Norman Conquest in reverse, for the uchy's other towns are surrendering fast and the king is installing English settlers in the Norman nobility's estates. Many Normans have emigrated to escape the brutal occupation (→ 25/12).

The English lay siege to Rouen before King Henry V seizes the town.

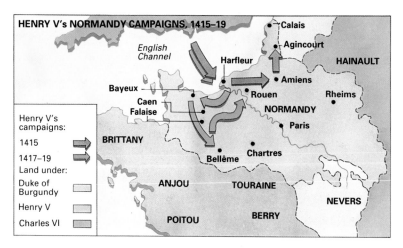

King jails his own stepmother for evil plot to murder him

Leeds Castle, Kent, 1420
King Henry has imprisoned his own stepmother, Queen Joan of Navarre, in this moated castle following her arrest last October on the charge of "compassing the king's death by sorcery and necromancy" – spells involving the spirits of the dead. Joan's father, King Charles, had a reputation as a sorcerer, and one of Joan's sons fought for the French at Agincourt.

But the dowager queen, who married Henry's father in 1402 when Henry was 15, has always been liked by her stepsons and has no imaginable motive for trying to kill Henry. Her confessor, Friar John Randolph, who accused her, was personally interrogated by the king and himself sent to the Tower.

No trial has been set down, and Joan is being confined with every luxury and a large staff of retainers. But her state dowry of £6,000 a year has been made forfeit; this may have been the motive for her arrest, since Henry is chronically in debt.

Queen Joan: a cast of her effigy.

Emperor Sigismund backs England in the war against France

Canterbury, 24 May 1416
King Henry demonstrated his prowess as a commander in battle at Agincourt last year. Now he has shown his skill as a diplomat by winning the Holy Roman Emperor to his side over his claim to the French throne. A treaty was signed here pledging their mutual support. Emperor Sigismund, who is the king of Bohemia, has been in England since May Day, when he sailed into Dover from France accompanied by 1,500 knights. He was met by the king's brother, Prince Humphrey, the Duke of Gloucester, who rode into the sea with a large welcoming party with drawn swords, demanding that the emperor forswear any claim to sovereignty before they let him land. He was then treated with lavish hospitality by the king who rode with him through London to Westminster, where he was given the royal palace for his stay. The king dubbed him a knight of the Garter. In return he gave the order the heart of St George, which he had brought with him (→ 4/9/17).

Shakespeare's 'Prince Hal' creates historic myth

Henry V was one of the most successful kings that England had ever known. His reputation for winning battles, which was what counted in an age of near-continuous warfare, was second to none. His personal valour was obvious from the age of 16 when he was wounded in the face by an arrow at Shrewsbury in the 1403 battle there against Hotspur's forces. At Agincourt he inspired a small, exhausted and sick army whose morale was at rock bottom by sheer personal courage and his stubborn faith that God was on his side; his battle cry was not "God for Harry" but "Jesus, Mary and St George!" He seemed invincible.

Having restored England's prestige and had the good fortune to die at 34, before the dual kingdom of England and France proved untenable, he was immediately converted into a symbol of national pride: the swashbuckling youth who became a leader of men. English chroniclers of the next 100 years exalted him (while the French ones deplored his brutality). There were several plays about Henry V before Shakespeare wrote his in 1599, one called the *Famous Victories of Henry V*. Shakespeare gave the heroic view of him imperishable form. The Victorians saw him as the chivalrous Christian knight. British morale was boosted in the Second World War by Laurence Olivier's film, which omitted all the darker passages in the text. They were restored by Kenneth Branagh in his film of 1989 which was realistic about the butchery of Agincourt.

The other side of Henry was his ruthlessness in pursuing his "rights" to France by starving, massacring, executing and dispossessing the French. Despite his extreme piety (he heard Mass three times a day) he declared: "War without fire is like sausages without mustard." He sanctioned the persecution of the Lollards, one of whom was his friend Sir John Oldcastle (often but wrongly supposed to be the model for Falstaff).

Though courteous and venerated, Henry was not a beloved king, nor was he romantic. His face in victory was invariably stern. "I am the scourge of God," he said.

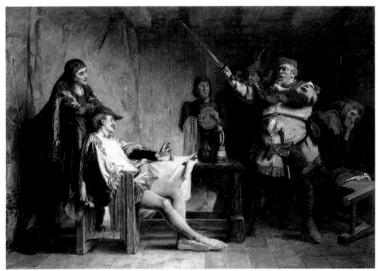

The Victorian view: this painting by Laslett John Pott shows Prince Hal in his swashbuckling tavern days, with Shakespeare's Sir John Falstaff.

Wartime propaganda: Laurence Olivier rallied national morale with a 1944 version of "Henry V" showing heroic English exploits in France.

More realistically into the breach: Kenneth Branagh starred as a 1989 version of Henry, restoring the butchery which Olivier had omitted.

Henry's heirs are promised French crown

Royal wedding: Henry marries Catherine, the daughter of the French king.

Troyes, France, 2 June 1420

King Henry married Catherine, the daughter of the French king, here in the Champagne region of France today. The wedding sets the seal on the greatest triumph of Henry's reign: the treaty signed here 12 days ago which means that he will be the next king of France.

The treaty recognises Henry as heir to his new father-in-law, King Charles VI, and the French king's regent during his now more or less constant periods of insanity. The treaty was agreed with Queen Isabel, acting for King Charles, and Duke Philip of Burgundy, the lead-

er of one of the two main factions which have grappled for power in France during the king's infirmity. Philip was won over to Henry's cause by the treacherous murder last year of his father, Duke John, during talks with his rival, the *Dauphin*, Charles VI's son.

The wedding was attended by a host of nobility and royalty, including King James of Scots, Henry's honoured prisoner of many years. The honeymoon will be short, however. Much of central and southern France is in the hands of the Dauphin; Henry must tackle him to secure his inheritance (→1/12).

A later engraving of the execution of the Lollard Sir John Oldcastle, whose friendship with King Henry did not save him from a heretic's death.

Scottish governor Albany dies, aged 80

Stirling, 3 September 1420

Robert, the Duke of Albany and governor of Scotland, has died at Stirling castle. The second son of Robert II – the first Stewart king of Scotland – Albany had effectively governed the country since 1388. He was more than 80 years of age at the time of his death.

Power first came to Albany when his father was still on the Scottish throne. In 1384, acknowledging his own ineffectiveness, the ageing Robert II transferred responsibility for daily government to his eldest son, the Earl of Carrick. But four years later Carrick was incapacitated by a kick from a horse, and control passed to his brother, the future Duke of Albany. Carrick – who remained an invalid for the rest of his life – was enthroned as Robert III in 1390.

The only serious challenge to Albany's authority since that time came from his nephew David, the Duke of Rothesay, who replaced him as the king's lieutenant for

three years from 1399. At the end of his term of office, Rothesay – on Albany's instigation – was arrested on corruption charges and taken to Albany's castle of Falkland, where he died two months later, reputedly of starvation.

Rothesay's younger brother, James, was taken prisoner by the English shortly before their father's death in 1406. He has remained a a prisoner of the English – a king in exile – ever since. James has accused Albany of not working hard enough for his release, contrasting this with the duke's efforts to secure the freedom of his own son, Murdoch – who was ransomed by the English in 1416.

As a ruler, Albany avoided open clashes with most of Scotland's higher nobility. Widespread corruption, the tolerance of private violence and the incessant ambitions of the Stewart family inspired little criticism of the late governor. He is likely to be succeeded in this office by Murdoch (→23/4/21).

King James of Scotland: he is still imprisoned in the Tower of London.

Clarence, heir to King Henry, dies

A tomb effigy of Clarence.

Baugé, France, 22 March 1421
King Henry has been dealt a double blow by the death in battle today of his brother the Duke of Clarence, the heir to the throne. The duke, left in charge of Normandy while the king is in England, had advanced into Anjou in search of forces loyal to Henry's rival, the *Dauphin*. Hearing of a French army at Baugé, near Angers, he decided to attack. This was a rash move: the French army was 5,000-strong and based at the top of a slope, whereas Clarence had only 1,500 men to hand and, crucially, no archers. The French struck first, and in the ensuing fracas the duke and many of the best English soldiers died or were captured.

Clarence's death changes the English succession – John, the Duke of Bedford, is next in line – and the defeat has also damaged Henry's military prestige (→ 1/6).

Son and new heir born to Catherine

Windsor, 6 December 1421
A wave of relief is sweeping the English court following the birth today of a son to Queen Catherine and King Henry. The arrival of the baby prince, who will also be called Henry, will bring a direct line of succession from the king, whereas until now it would have passed to his eldest surviving brother.

The news will come as a fillip to the king and his army, currently enduring the frost, snow and rain of an unusually bitter winter to besiege the town of Meaux, 25 miles north-east of Paris. Meaux looks set to be the latest stronghold of his rival, the *Dauphin*, to fall since Henry's return to France in June. Coming after a successful English spring campaign, Henry's offensive has largely restored the damage done to his prestige by Clarence's defeat and death at Baugé.

The birth of Prince Henry.

Dysentery kills Henry V

A likeness of Henry V, from a late 15th-century manuscript.

Vincennes, Paris, 31 August 1422
King Henry V will never wear the crown of France which he devoted so many years to winning. Between two and three o'clock this morning the victor of Agincourt, wasted and feeble after months of illness, succumbed to dysentery, the dreaded "bloody flux" which is the curse of Europe's armies. He was not yet 35.

Henry became ill shortly after the siege of Meaux, near Paris, which finally capitulated in early May [*see below, left*]. It was the latest of the warrior king's victories against those trying to keep him from what he saw as his rightful inheritance, the French throne, to which Henry devoted nearly all of his nine-year reign, right up to his death. Other kings have been as single-minded as the stern and rather humourless Henry, but few have combined his grim fanaticism with such brilliant generalship and astute diplomatic skills. His stunning win at Agincourt, the conquest of Normandy and – his greatest triumph of all – the Treaty of Troyes, recognising him as the heir of the king of France, staggered even his enemies.

Henry was as unflinchingly merciless in punishing disobedience as he was scrupulous in seeing justice done. He cared deeply for his men's wellbeing and shared their hardships. For the eight-month-old infant who is now king, Henry V will be a hard act to follow.

Henry's guns bring walls tumbling down

Meaux, France, May 1422
King Henry's capture of the stronghold of Meaux this month highlights his fascination with artillery as a part of modern warfare, which began before he became king. On his accession he ordered new stocks of cannon for his planned French expedition. These weapons, with colourful names such as bombards, serpentines, veuglaires, culverins and ribaudequins, are built from iron rods which are soldered together and, a recent improvement, bound by iron rings to lessen the risk of their blowing up.

They have to be dragged around by whatever means gunners can find, which with their inaccuracy and short range makes them of limited use on the battlefield. But when the target is large and static, like a town, they can be very useful. The great holes made by Henry's cannon in the walls of Meaux are proof of that (→ 31/8).

Baby king makes for uncertain future

Paris, 31 August 1422
As he lay dying, Henry V made hasty plans for the future. On his deathbed he said that one of his brothers, Humphrey, the Duke of Gloucester, was to be made regent of England, with the other brother, John, the Duke of Bedford, as regent of France.

Henry also wants Thomas Beaufort to be the guardian of the infant Henry VI, but this instruction is likely to be resisted by Gloucester as a weakness within the council of regency which will have to govern England until the baby king comes of age. Other details in the arrangements made by the dying Henry are also likely to be challenged.

The most unenviable task is here in France, however, where the infant Henry is due to become king on the death of King Charles VI under the Treaty of Troyes. And Charles is not expected to outlive King Henry for very long.

1422–1441

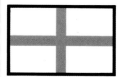

Henry VI
1422–1461

James I
1406–1437
James II
1437–1460

England, 1 September 1422.
Henry of Windsor, aged nine months, accedes to the throne; his uncles, John, the Duke of Bedford, and Humphrey, the Duke of Gloucester, are expected to become regents in France and England (→ 21/10).

France, April 1423. Anglo-French links improve with the marriage of the king's uncle John, the Duke of Bedford, to Anne, the sister of Duke Philip II of Burgundy (→ 18/12/33).

London, 4 September 1423.
Terms are finally agreed for the ransom and release of King James of Scots after 18 years of imprisonment (→ 5/4/24).

Scotland, 25 December 1424.
Joan, the daughter of John Beaufort, the Earl of Somerset, who married King James of Scots in February, gives birth to a daughter, Margaret (→ 7/1428).

Ireland, 18 January 1425. Edmund Mortimer, the Earl of March, dies of plague; his heir is his nephew, Richard, the Duke of York (→ 5/1436).

France/Scotland, July 1428. A marriage is arranged between Louis, the son of the *Dauphin*, and Margaret, the daughter of James of Scots (→ 16/10/30).

England, 1428. The Earl of Warwick becomes tutor to Henry (→ 11/1432).

Westminster, 1428. Parliament passes a law aimed at Queen Catherine which declares that dowager queens may remarry only with the permission of the monarch (→ 2/1/37).

France, 17 July 1429. Charles, the *Dauphin*, is crowned as king, defying the terms of the Treaty of Troyes (→ 30/5/31).

Lothian, 16 October 1430. Joan of Scots gives birth to twins, Alexander and James; the elder, Alexander, dies shortly after birth (→ 25/6/36).

Westminster, 18 Dec 1433. The Duke of Bedford, the regent of France, who returned earlier this year to raise money for Norman defences, remains in England as head of the government (→ 6/6/34).

Westminster, 6 June 1434. After arguing openly with his brother, Humphrey, the Duke of Gloucester, over the defence of Normandy, the Duke of Bedford returns to France (→ 15/9/35).

Normandy, May 1436. Richard, the Duke of York, who has just been appointed regent, consolidates the English position in France (→ 7/1447).

France, 25 June 1436. Louis, the *Dauphin*, aged 13, marries Princess Margaret, the 11-year-old daughter of King James of Scots (→ 21/2/37).

Edinburgh, 25 March 1437. While the murderers of James I are put to death in Perth, his seven-year-old son, King James II, is crowned in Holyrood abbey (→ 15/7/45).

London, 1438. Owain ap Maredudd ap Twdwr, the former Welsh squire who was the secret husband of the late dowager Queen Catherine, escapes from Newgate prison and flees to Wales.

Hertfordshire, 30 August 1439. Henry VI refuses to abandon his claims to France (→ 8/1443).

Westminster, 15 Dec 1440. Henry knights his half-brothers, Jasper and Edmund Twdwr, Owain and Catherine's sons.

Baby is king twice over

Richard Beauchamp, the Earl of Warwick, holding King Henry (late C15th).

Windsor, 21 October 1422
A ten-month-old baby is king of both England and France. Henry of Windsor, the only child of King Henry V and Catherine of Valois, became Henry VI when his father died suddenly on 31 August. With the death today of his grandfather, Charles VI of France, the infant is monarch of two kingdoms.

When Henry was born every bell in London rang out to greet the royal birth, and in France, where the king was besieging Meaux, his troops rejoiced. Now, king of both countries long before anyone had been expected, Henry, if only from his mother's lap, must try to fulfil his dual role. It may not be easy. Just six weeks ago his father had been in the prime of life, and plans for the division of power after his death were made in a hurry. People are worried. An infant king will not be able to hold the power-greedy nobility in check (→ 6/12).

Bedford and Gloucester to be protectors

London, 6 December 1422
The king is one year old today, but he is monarch in name alone. His twin kingdoms are in the hands of two regents: his royal uncles the Dukes of Bedford and Gloucester. This was ordered by his late father and proclaimed yesterday at the first parliament of the new reign.

John of Bedford, already Henry's military commander in France, for which he now has the responsibility, is his principal protector and guardian. Humphrey of Gloucester, Henry V's youngest brother, is to rule England, although only in Bedford's absence, and will be the boy's protector there.

Although, as the elder, Bedford might have been expected to rule England, and he has made his seniority clear, it has been revealed that on his deathbed Henry charged him with keeping France secure. This has become his primary duty as regards his infant nephew (→ 5/11/25).

Scottish king returns from 18-year exile

Borders, 5 April 1424

King James of Scotland today returned to the country which he last saw 18 years ago, as a boy of 12. In 1406, shortly before the death of his father, Robert III, James was taken captive by English pirates while on his way to France and put in the Tower by Henry IV of England. He has remained a king in exile ever since. Terms for James's release were sealed last year in London; the Scottish king agreed to pay a ransom of £40,000 in instalments, guaranteed by hostages.

During his captivity James learnt a great deal about England's system of government and gained military experience with Henry V in France. In 1423 he fell in love with Joan Beaufort, a relative of the English king, and married her two months before regaining his freedom. Joan is said to have been the inspiration for the *Kingis Quair* [*King's Book*], a complex and passionate collection of poems written by the king while in exile.

In James's absence Scotland has been governed by his uncle, the popular but devious Duke of Albany – who did little to secure the king's release. Albany's son Mur-

Joan Beaufort: a later view.

doch succeeded his octogenarian father in 1420, but his rule has proved a disaster for the country, and the Scots have been agitating for their king's return. Two of James's first tasks will be to confront Murdoch and to crack down on lawlessness (→ 25/12).

Henry V buried after long procession

Westminster, 7 November 1422

The last of Henry V's many great processions came to an end today when his body was laid to rest in Westminster abbey, seven weeks after leaving Vincennes on 14 September. Thousands of people turned out on both sides of the Channel to watch the magnificent royal cortège, and hundreds of masses were

said for the soul of the warrior-king. The funeral arrangements included the grisly task of preparing the rapidly decaying corpse for its long journey. As is common in such cases, the entrails were removed and the body dismembered and boiled to separate flesh from bone. The remains were then placed in a lead coffin with many spices.

The effigy of King Henry which adorns his tomb in Westminster abbey.

Gloucester and Beaufort squabble over control of boy king's minority council

London, 5 November 1425

The four-year-old boy king rode in state through London today, seated next to his guardian, the Duke of Gloucester, but the cheering crowds and the splendour of the procession cannot mask a growing reality: the increasingly hostile relations between Gloucester and Henry Beaufort, the bishop of Winchester, chancellor of England and, through their common ancestor John of Gaunt, also Henry's uncle.

Their rivalry began when Henry reached the throne, and, as both men sought to use their positions to further their own ambitions, it has intensified. Gloucester believes himself continually slighted, and is frustrated by Beaufort's efforts to control the council of regency. Beaufort's refusal to allow him

lodgings in the Tower is highly galling. So he has accused his rival of usurping the authority of the council, attacking the protector and insulting the Ciy of London. Nor has the chancellor's alleged favouring of foreign merchants over Englishmen boosted his popularity.

Affairs reached their peak a week ago when Beaufort assembled a force of men, so Gloucester claims, to seize the king at Eltham and take over the government. The coup was only foiled when the City, rallied by its mayor, declared itself loyal to the protector and drove the attackers back from London Bridge. Today, the victor at least for the time being, Gloucester paraded the king, riding at his side and leaving no one in doubt as to who rules. And Beaufort has fled (→ 23/4).

A stone effigy of Henry Beaufort.

A later portrait of Duke Humphrey.

Royal duke ditches plan for love duel

London, 23 April 1425

Like knights of old, two noblemen – the Dukes of Burgundy and Gloucester – were ready to fight a duel over a fair lady, Jacqueline of Holland, but the contest has been abandoned. Humphrey, the Duke of Gloucester, has been persuaded to scrap his romantic but misguided plan. The aim was to settle disputed control of Jacqueline's lands in Holland, but Gloucester has accepted that his rival is more useful as an ally than an enemy.

Stewarts purged by a vengeful James

Stirling, 25 May 1425

King James has carried out a successful purge of the Stewart family and executed Murdoch, the Duke of Albany, and two of his kinsmen outside Stirling castle. Ever since the king's return to Scotland last year – after 18 years of exile – he has sought revenge against Murdoch, who succeeded his father as governor of Scotland in 1420. James has long believed that father and son left him languishing as a prisoner in England (→ 1430).

Joan drives out English

The maiden warrior: the view of Joan in a contemporary German tapestry.

The heroine: a later statue of Joan.

France, 1 July 1429

A 17-year-old peasant girl who claims that she is inspired by divine "voices" has taken up the banner of French resistance, and England's military might is reeling under her army's blows. The girl, Joan of Arc appeared at the French court earlier this year. She promised the *Dauphin* that she would drive the English out of France. Now, after a string of victories, it appears that, whatever the truth behind her claims, this deeply religious girl who leads her troops dressed in a full suit of armour has revolutionised France's will to fight.

Joan began her amazing campaign by raising the siege of Orleans. She arrived at the town on 3 May and five days later drove the Earl of Suffolk and his men from their lines outside the town. On 12 June she went further, defeating Suffolk at Jargeau and capturing him. On 18 June she routed Lord Talbot and Sir John Fastolf at Patay. The Duke of Bedford has withdrawn his men into Normandy.

The way to Paris is open, but there is a growing determination to hold the city. The council has ordered the Duke of Beaufort, who has assembled an army for a crusade, to reinforce France. The Dauphin intends to have himself crowned. Now Henry is to have his own coronation in Paris to reinforce English claims that he is the legitimate king of France (→ 17/7).

Henry VI is crowned king of England

Westminster, 5 November 1429

Henry of Windsor, king of both England and France from the age of ten months, was crowned today, one month short of his eighth birthday, at Westminster abbey. Symbolically, he was carried into the abbey by his tutor, the Earl of Warwick, but he strode out on his feet, flanked by two bishops and with Warwick carrying his train.

A coronation is a splendid sight, but it is a drawn-out, gruelling occasion capable of exhausting many an adult, let alone an eight-year-old boy. But Henry never faltered, taking it all in his stride. He dealt with last night's ritual washing and the creation of 32 knights of the Bath, today's procession from the Tower to Westminster Hall and thence to the abbey and the ceremony there, and finally the gargan-tuan banquet in which, as tradition demands, the royal champion appears to defend his right.

The young king looked both sad and wise as he went through the long crowning, holding the elaborate regalia, each piece with its own meaning, allowing himself to be stripped and then dressed afresh several times, prostrating himself before the altar and, at the climax, being anointed with holy oil by the archbishop of Canterbury.

The sacred oil, poured from a flask shaped like an eagle, was allegedly given to St Thomas Becket by the Holy Virgin. It is the first time that a king has been anointed with this oil alone. Previously two ordinary oils were used instead, but they have been abandoned. Only a liquid that, like the king it anoints, is blessed in heaven is used now.

The seven-year-old Henry is crowned king of England at Westminster.

James brings English ideas to Scotland

Scotland, 1430

Football and after-hours drinking have been banned as part of a package of new laws passed this year by the Scottish parliament. The Scots have been instructed to wear clothes appropriate to their social status, and unemployed people who fail to seek work have been threatened with imprisonment.

The new legislation is the latest attempt by King James to enforce strong government in Scotland after decades of lawlessness. Severe punishments, including execution, are meted out to transgressors.

Influenced by his 18 years' exile in England, the king uses parliament to implement his reforms. Since his return in 1424 he has strengthened the role of the lesser nobility in parliament – perhaps in imitation of the English House of Commons – and begun a total revision of royal finances. He has had to drop plans for direct taxation, however, because of widespread opposition (→ 21/2/37).

Joan is burnt at stake

With great pageants and celebrations, Henry VI is crowned king of France

The "poor maid": Joan is tied to the stake at which she will be burnt.

Paris, 16 December 1431

Two years after he was crowned king of England, Henry VI has become king of France. The ceremony of his second coronation took place today in *Notre Dame*.

The king arrived in Paris two weeks ago and was immediately plunged into a round of celebrations, presentations, processions and similar tributes, each more splendid than the last. It would seem that the whole of Paris, from highest to most lowly, has determined to pay individual homage. Despite being in France, the king was crowned by the bishop of Winchester, and the service was taken from the English, and thus simpler, rite. One other feature was completely English: the recognition, a great shout from throughout the cathedral acknowledging Henry's kingship, not heard in France for 150 years. A coronation feast was held in the banqueting hall, and here, too, the English rather than the French took charge, a decision that was generally judged to be a great mistake.

Rouen, France, 30 May 1431

A virgin saviour to some, a witch to others, Joan of Arc, who described herself as a "poor maid, knowing nothing of writing and fighting", and who changed the course of the war between France and England, is dead. She was executed today, burnt at the stake after being convicted of heresy and witchcraft.

Between the early days of 1429, when she appeared, talking of her "voices", and persuaded the *Dauphin* to let her lead his army, and the year's end, Joan, the victor in a string of battles, seemed invincible.

On her way to raise the British siege of Compiègne in May last year, Joan was captured by John of Luxembourg, an ally of the pro-English Duke of Burgundy. He sold her to his allies for £80,000; she remained in jail until her trial.

Politics, not justice, dominated her trial. It was vital for England to see her condemned, and her captors have spared no efforts. Charged with heresy and witchcraft, with special emphasis laid on her wearing of men's clothing, Joan fought back courageously, defending herself against every attack, never wavering from her faith.

But even Joan, so brave in battle, grew weak under the constant pressure and the undisguised bias of her judges. When even the priest to whom she had confessed was revealed as an English agent, she gave in. She rejected her "voices", put on female clothes and accepted her sentence: life imprisonment.

It was a brief weakening. She had expected to be kept in a church prison, but when this was denied she withdrew her confession and put on men's clothes once more. Recalled to court as a relapsed heretic she was given a new sentence: death. She died quickly, but once her clothes had been burnt away the fire was raked back and her naked body – unmistakeably female – was revealed. Then the fire burnt up again and the Maid of Orleans was reduced to ashes (→ 10/12).

A second coronation: a later view of Henry VI being crowned king of France.

Maturing king shows a precocious desire to flex royal muscles

Royal authority: Henry's seal.

Windsor, November 1432

The king is almost 11 years old, and the Earl of Warwick, his tutor, has paid tribute to his increasing maturity and the "conceit and knowledge of his high and royal authority".

While this may well be true, it also reveals that Warwick has had problems in controlling his royal charge. Henry is becoming increasingly independent, and Warwick has been forced to ask the council of regency for increased powers. These he has received, so that he can screen the king from "unsuitable" influences. He is also to be present at any royal audiences. But Henry can still flex his muscles.

The perennial struggle between Gloucester and Beaufort flared up during the king's absence for his French coronation. A number of household officials were dismissed. Most were pro-Beaufort; certainly their replacements favoured his rival. Some fear that Henry had a hand in this "palace revolution".

Scottish king murdered: six-year-old takes over

James tries to escape: a later view.

Perth, Tayside, 21 February 1437
King James of Scots has been hacked to death by members of his own family. The 43-year-old monarch was staying at Blackfriars priory in Perth when the assassins broke in and attacked him. Their entry was made possible by James's chamberlain and cousin, Sir Robert Stewart, who laid planks over the ditch surrounding the priory and unlocked the doors. Stewart – the grandson of the elderly Earl of Atholl, who is next in line to the throne after James's son – sought revenge on behalf of his father, whom James had allowed to die as a hostage in England.

The seven killers were led by Sir Robert Graham, whose father also died as a hostage in England.

Graham had earlier been arrested for opposing James's request for a tax in the last parliament and for making a speech accusing the king of tyrannical behaviour.

When James heard his attackers approaching, he loosened the floorboards in his chamber with a poker and let himself down into a vault below. Graham and his men burst into the room, injuring Queen Joan as she and her ladies tried to bar the door. The portly king could not escape through the sewer which ran through the vault as the entrance was too narrow. Cornered by the assassins, he was repeatedly and fatally stabbed.

All the men responsible have now escaped to the highlands. There are many reasons why they

might have wanted James dead. Among them is his abuse of the tax raised to pay the ransom agreed before his release from England in 1424. The king defaulted on the ransom payments, instead spending the money privately.

In addition, his harsh treatment of the nobility and his avaricious policies had contributed to his growing unpopularity. Matters were not improved by a military disaster in the borders last year. In a campaign fraught with divisions between the king and the nobility, James had ignominiously to abandon a siege of Roxburgh on the arrival of a relief force.

The king is succeeded by his sole surviving son, James, who is only six years old (→ 25/3).

Duke of Bedford, great conciliator of family quarrels, is dead

Rouen, France, 15 September 1435
John of Lancaster, the Duke of Bedford, died here today after failing to prevent England's ally, the Duke of Burgundy, from negotiating a treaty with Charles VII of France that effectively recognises what the Duke of Bedford strove for 15 years to forestall, the military supremacy of France. His death comes just a few days before the treaty is to be signed. He will be buried in Rouen cathedral.

A younger brother of Henry V, he was made governor of Berwick-Upon-Tweed and warden of the east Marches by his father, Henry IV. His brother made him Duke of Bedford in 1414, and during the war with France he became the lieutenant of the kingdom.

When his brother died in 1422, and his nephew, Henry VI, became

a king in swaddling clothes, Bedford became regent of France, from where he did what he could to reconcile the factions around the king, one led by his own brother, Humphrey, the Duke of Gloucester, the other by their uncle, Henry Beaufort, the bishop of Winchester.

In the wars with France, Bedford proved a general worthy of his brother, defeating the French at Verneuil in 1424. But the ineffectiveness of his nephew's council, its inability to provide him with political or material support, the change in French fortunes since the appearance of Joan, the Maid of Orleans, and the defection of his ally the Duke of Burgundy forced him to come to Rouen where he failed humiliatingly to prevent the alliance so disastrous to English interests in France (→ 28/7).

Duke John (l) with St George.

France agrees new pact with Burgundy

Arras, France, 21 September 1435
Henry's ambitions for his lands in France were dealt a heavy blow today when his former ally, Duke Philip of Burgundy, signed a peace treaty with Charles VII of France. This comes two weeks after the English delegation walked out of the negotiations. They had refused to drop Henry's claim to French lands on the grounds that he is too young to decide (→ 25/6/36).

A gold cup (c.1380) given to Henry by the Duke of Bedford.

Council allows Henry to take a much greater role in government

Canterbury, 28 July 1436
Since Bedford's death [*see above*] the king is wielding more influence than ever, and one sign of his growing participation in government is that he is putting his own signature to important documents. Today he signed a warrant granting part of the late Duke of Bedford's lands to his great-uncle, Cardinal Beaufort, with a self-assured "Henry". The

council now lets Henry attend all its meetings and keeps him informed of all matters of state, but it has had to struggle to contain his impatience. At the end of 1434 the king took the privy seal from its usual place in Westminster and started to issue government documents without supervision. The entire council rushed to the king, at Cirencester, to deliver a respectful

rebuke: while they could not stop Henry from ruling without them – and were working to transfer full powers – he was still not ready to rule; anyone who told him otherwise was not acting in his, or the country's, best interests. Having made it clear that he wants power for himself, the 14-year-old king gracefully promised to submit to the council's will (→ 14/11/37).

Teenage king to exercise full powers

London, 14 November 1437

King Henry VI took over the full powers of kingship today. The 16-year-old monarch will no longer defer to his quarrelsome council. A king at eight months old, following the death of his father, Henry V, he spent his childhood in the household of his mother, Queen Catherine. At eight years old he was placed in the care of Richard Beauchamp, the Earl of Warwick, who was to teach him "literature, language and other manner of cunning, to chastise him when he doth amiss and to remove persons not behoveful nor expedient".

Although Henry has shown himself eager to take control, and the country is anxious for an effective king again, people who know Henry are expressing some uneasiness. The young king likes to be seen to be generous and finds it difficult to say "no" to petitioners.

On balance, the country is ready for a change. The 16 years of Henry's minority produced little good government. In England the king's council has been ineffective, and power has been divided between two rivals: Humphrey, the Duke of Gloucester, the king's uncle, and Henry Beaufort, the bishop of Winchester, the king's great-uncle. In France the regent, the Duke of Bedford, Henry's other uncle, who died two years ago, had been steadily losing territory

King Henry has now taken on full royal powers; a C16th portrait.

against revived French ambitions. English arms have not won a major victory in France since 1424.

In 1429, aged only seven years old, Henry was crowned king in London; two years later he was crowned in Paris. His pious and rather naïve character may not equip him to live up to his awesomely responsible position (→ 15/12/40).

Queen mother dies after her marriage secret comes out

London, 2 January 1437

The dowager queen, Catherine de Valois, the widow of Henry V, has died at Bermondsey abbey at 35 years of age. Her death comes only a few months after her retirement to the nunnery at Bermondsey, following the disclosure of her secret marriage to Owain Twdwr, an obscure Welsh squire who belonged to her son's entourage.

The daughter of Charles VI of France, she was neglected by her mother as a child. On 2 June 1420 she was married to Henry V, and just over a year later she gave birth to the future Henry VI. When her husband died in 1422 she followed his funeral cortège from Vincennes to London, then settled in Baynard's castle, granted by parliament as her permanent home.

Still a young woman, she was courted by Edmund Beaufort, and it was to prevent that politically sensitive marriage that in 1428 parliament passed an act prohibiting dowager queens from marrying without council approval. Two years later she secretly married Owain, by whom she had three sons and a daughter.

When knowledge of the marriage became public last summer Catherine went to Bermondsey and Twdwr was sent to Newgate prison as a sign of royal displeasure. It is unlikely, however, that he will remain there for long.

Henry, fond of learning, founds colleges at Cambridge and Eton

The charter for King's College, Cambridge, founded by Henry VI.

Cambridge, 2 April 1441

King Henry has endowed a new college at Cambridge, to be called the Royal College of St Nicholas. It will have a rector and 12 scholars, and its foundation stone was laid by the king himself today. The college will stand beside the divinity school, separated from the river Cam by a meadow. Henry's establishment of St Nicholas's comes only seven months after he established a school of 25 scholars at Eton, within sight of his castle at Windsor, and suggests that he has been much influenced by the ideas of the educationalist William of Wykeham, which have been put into practice at Winchester and Oxford.

The queen mother: Catherine.

Henry VI
1422–1461

James II
1437–1460
James III
1460–1488

England, 7 July 1441. Eleanor of Cobham, the wife of King Henry's uncle, the Duke of Gloucester, is arrested for trying to cause the death of the king by magic (→22/5/44).

Tours, France, 22 May 1444. William de la Pole, the Earl of Suffolk, arranges the marriage of Henry to Margaret of Anjou (→13/11).

England, 13 November 1444. The Marquis of Suffolk, as the earl has now become, sails for France to finalise the Anglo-French truce and collect Margaret of Anjou (→22/4/45).

Westminster, 30 May 1445. Margaret of Anjou is crowned queen (→22/12).

Lothian, 15 July 1445. Queen Joan, the mother of King James II of Scots, dies (→1/4/49).

London, 22 December 1445. Henry, under the influence of his wife, Margaret, agrees to surrender Maine to her father, René of Anjou (→5/7/50).

Bury St Edmunds, 18 Feb 1447. Henry, dominated by Suffolk, arrests the Duke of Gloucester, Suffolk's rival (→6/11/49).

Ireland, July 1447. Richard, the Duke of York, becomes Lieutenant of Ireland (→10/3/52).

Flanders, 1 April 1449. Relations between France and Scotland improve with the betrothal of James II of Scots and Mary of Guelders (→5/1452).

Westminster, 17 March 1450. Henry exiles the Duke (formerly Marquis) of Suffolk, allowing him to flee his enemies (→2/5).

London, 10 March 1452. The Duke of York, who confronted

Henry with his army, submits to the king and takes an oath of loyalty (→27/3/54).

St Andrews, May 1452. Queen Mary of Scots gives birth to a son, James, who is the heir to James II (→23/2/61).

Westminster, 23 Nov 1452. Henry bestows the earldoms of Richmond and Pembroke on his two half-brothers, Jasper and Edmund Twdwr (→12/63).

France, 17 July 1453. The English defeat at Castillon means the loss of Gascony. Only Calais remains in English hands.

England, 13 October 1453. Margaret of Anjou gives birth to Edward, King Henry's son and heir (→25/10/62).

Westminster, 15 March 1454. Prince Edward is proclaimed Prince of Wales (→8/63).

England, December 1454. With Henry now recovered from a serious bout of illness, the Duke of York ceases to be protector of England and loses much of his influence (→22/5/55).

Coventry, 20 November 1459. The Duke of York is proclaimed a traitor by a parliament strongly influenced by Queen Margaret (→7/1460).

Borders, 10 August 1460. James III of Scots, aged eight, is crowned king after the sudden death of his father (→23/2/61).

Dumfries/Galloway, Dec 1460. Queen Margaret flees from the Duke of York's troops, seeking refuge and aid in Scotland (→30/12).

England, 4 March 1461. Henry is deposed by Edward, the Earl of March; he flees to Scotland.→

King sends Somerset to wage French war

Siege warfare: a C15th illumination demonstrates the latest weapons.

Cherbourg, France, August 1443
John Beaufort, the Duke of Somerset, has at last landed here with a powerful army after much procrastination following his orders from King Henry to "use most cruel and mortal war ... to fight his adversary and get the victory of him".

The expedition follows the failure of Henry's attempt to make peace with Charles VII by releasing the Duke of Orleans, held in England for 25 years following Agincourt. It is not, as originally planned, to go to the aid of Gascony or Normandy, both hard-pressed by

the French, but to attempt to conquer the land in between.

The whole affair reeks of Henry's notorious vacillation. Gascony and Normandy are crying out for help. Somerset is a sick man. His appointment has enraged Richard, the Duke of York, Henry's lieutenant in France, who has been told by the king that "the manner and conduct of the war" must be changed.

It is typical of this ill-thought-out venture that no provision has been made for feeding or housing Somerset's 8,000 men. They will have to live off the land (→22/5/44).

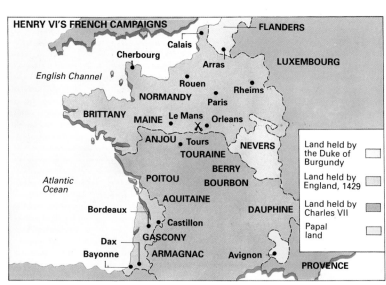

King Henry marries Margaret of Anjou

The marriage of King Henry to Margaret of Anjou: a later engraving.

Hampshire, 22 April 1445
King Henry married Margaret of Anjou at the abbey of Titchfield today, the Vigil of St George. The new queen, only 15, was laid low by seasickness on her voyage from Cherbourg, and the king had to wait for a week while she recovered at Southampton. It is said that he visited her, dressed as a squire supposedly delivering a letter from the king, and was captivated by her.

She comes without a dowry except for her beauty and intelligence, for her family, while rich in titles, has little money. Her father is René of Anjou, the titular king of Sicily and brother of the French queen. Henry does not care that Margaret is poor. Not only has he fallen in love with his bride; the marriage has also brought him what he most desires, a truce with Charles VII.

Margaret is to make her state entry into London on 28 May and will be crowned in Westminster abbey two days later. Henry, soliciting loans to pay for the celebrations, says that the whole kingdom will have cause to thank God for this queen "of a high and noble birth, greatly endowed with gifts of

grace and nature". Charles, the king of France, is also looking for benefits from the marriage. He has already won solid political and military advantages from the marriage settlement which he negotiated at Tours with the Earl of Suffolk and sees the strong-willed Margaret as a persuasive representative at the court of King Henry (→ 30/5).

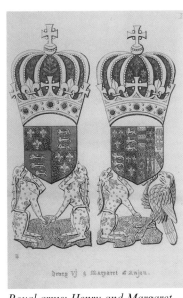

Royal arms: Henry and Margaret.

Duke of Suffolk has maritime execution

Dover, 2 May 1450
The Duke of Suffolk, one of the most powerful men in the kingdom for the last ten years, has been murdered at sea; tonight his headless body lies on the beach at Dover.

Suffolk had been reviled for neglecting the defences of Normandy, whose strongholds are falling one after the other into the hands of Charles of France. After a riot in London and armed demonstrations in Kent the Commons charged Suffolk with treasonable dealings with the French and shut him in the Tower of London.

There was no question of hism being guilty of treason, but the people needed a scapegoat for the shame of the defeats in Normandy, and he would undoubtedly have been found guilty if he had faced trial. Henry, perhaps realising that he was as guilty as his favourite, sent him into exile instead.

Suffolk set sail for Burgundy from Ipswich on 30 April after spending six weeks putting his affairs in order, but early today his ships were intercepted by a small fleet off Dover, and he was forced on board the *Nicholas of the Tower*, the flagship of the fleet, amid cries of "Welcome, traitor".

He was put into a small boat and beheaded on the gunwale with several blows from a rusty sword; his body was then dumped at Dover. His death is seen as an act of justice against both him and the king.

Commons resist king's unpopular policies

Westminster, 6 November 1449
The House of Commons, summoned to provide money for the defence of beleaguered Normandy, met in truculent mood today. At their previous meeting, dissolved on 16 July, the Commons had adamantly refused to make any effective grants unless the king resumed similar grants from his own exchequer.

They are hardly likely to be any more accommodating now. Humiliating military disasters in France are matched by an economic crisis at home. Exports of cloth and wool are falling alarmingly. French pirates are raiding coastal towns in the south-east, and Henry cannot keep

the Channel open for trade. There is much grumbling among the ordinary people. Much of it centres on the queen, who is disliked because she is high-handed and French. Henry is said to be a natural fool and unfit to govern.

The keeper of Guildford prison has been accused of saying that he wished the king hanged and the queen drowned, adding that nothing had gone right since Margaret arrived in England. The Commons are careful not to attack the king personally. They are directing their anger at the Duke of Suffolk and his coterie, on whom they blame the nation's miseries (→ 17/3/50).

Rebels dispatched by confident queen

Queen Margaret: a later view.

London, 5 July, 1450
Queen Margaret, who stood fast at Greenwich while the king fled in the face of the Kentish rebellion led by Jack Cade, has brought an end to the disorders by offering pardons to the rebels after a fierce all-night battle at London Bridge. The queen's resolute behaviour has been in marked contrast to that of her weak husband, who has been compared to a sheep by one critic. Still only 20, the imperious Margaret shows the belligerence of a warrior. Her bravery is, however, offset by what critics charge is a lack of political judgement and a capacity for vindictiveness (→ 13/10/53).

Power of Douglas family crushed in Scotland by James

Dumfries & Galloway, May 1455

The power of the mighty Douglas family – which has been troubling James II for much of his reign – has finally been broken in its defeat at Arkinholm on the Esk river. Archibald Douglas, the Earl of Moray, has been killed and his head presented to the king. His brother, Hugh Douglas, the Earl of Ormond, has been taken prisoner and executed.

The defeat is the culmination of a major military onslaught against the Douglas family launched two months ago by King James. In recent years the ambitions of the Douglasses, who commanded a large empire in the south-west of Scotland, had provoked three civil wars, and their relations with the king had been peppered by notorious incidents.

In 1440 – when the king was only nine – William, the teenage sixth Earl of Douglas, and his younger brother were beheaded at Edinburgh castle. The boys had been invited to dine with the king and were killed at the instigation of James's chancellor, William Crichton. Three years ago the eighth Earl of Douglas was stabbed to death by the king himself at Stirling castle. James has been systematically destroying the Douglas castles in the south-west, and all the leading members of the family are now dead or in exile (→ 3/8/60).

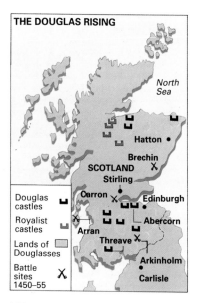

THE DOUGLAS RISING

North Sea

Hatton

Brechin

SCOTLAND

Stirling

Carron

Edinburgh

Abercorn

Arran

Threave

Arkinholm

Carlisle

Douglas castles

Royalist castles

Lands of Douglasses

Battle sites 1450–55 ✕

The king loses his mind

Duke of York is to step in as regent

Westminster, 27 March 1454

Richard, the Duke of York, was today appointed protector and defender of the kingdom of England. He is to hold this post while Henry remains in the catatonic state into which he lapsed last summer. The king is quite incapable of ruling. He cannot even comprehend that he has at last fathered a son. His illness, which has been kept secret until now, is thought to be hereditary, passed on from his grandfather, Charles VI of France. Nothing that the doctors do evokes any response. He has no control over his mind and little over his body. He smiles sweetly but says, and does, nothing (→ 12/4/54).

Protector: Duke Richard of York.

York leads rebel army to defeat the king

Hue and cry: a later view of the battle in the streets of St Albans.

St Albans, 22 May 1455

King Henry is tonight a puppet in the hands of the Duke of York following a battle lasting under an hour in the streets of St Albans in which the Yorkist forces defeated Henry's Lancastrian army. York's hated rival, the Duke of Somerset, was cut down after being trapped in the Castle inn, and the king himself was slightly wounded in the neck by an arrow. He took refuge in the house of a tanner where York found him and, swearing allegiance, took him to the safety of the abbey. They will ride to London together in the morning.

This clash became inevitable once Henry recovered his wits in January and the ambitious York had to relinquish his protectorate. Henry released Somerset from the Tower where he had been imprisoned at York's behest. The battle lines were then drawn. Who would own the king? (→ 20/11/59).

Gun accident kills James II – Scots are ruled by minor

Borders, 3 August 1460

King James II has been killed in a gun accident during his second siege of Roxburgh castle. James, who came to the throne at the age of six, was only 29 when he died. The king – an artillery enthusiast who spent huge sums on improving army firepower – was standing next to a gun when it exploded. His death is a severe blow to the Scottish nation, which is once again left with a minor, the eight-year-old James III, on the throne.

James II's reign was marked by civil war and factionalism which culminated in a long-running and bloody struggle with the powerful Douglas family, whose ambitions were finally thwarted five years ago at the Battle of Arkinholm. The late king continued his father's efforts to stamp out lawlessness in Scotland, but he was a hot-tempered man with a love of war. The best-known example of his impetuosity was his murder, in 1452, of William, the eighth Earl of Douglas, at Stirling castle. He fostered political instability in the country by continuing his father's tradition of attacking noblemen in order to increase royal revenue.

Over the last three years James had turned his attention away from domestic conflict to wage war on the English border, where he had gained military superiority by the time he died. In England, therefore, the news of his death is likely to be greeted with relief (→ 10/8).

A later portrait of King James II.

England torn apart by the 'Wars of the Roses'

London, July 1460
The fortunes of the civil war between the Yorkist and Lancastrian branches of the royal house of Plantagenet – whose symbols are respectively the white and the red rose – have swung once again towards the Yorkists. Following the defeat of the Lancastrian army by the Earl of Warwick at Northamp-ton, the hapless King Henry – whose madness and marriage to the hated Margaret of Anjou helped to fuel the conflict – has fallen into the hands of the Yorkist nobles, just as he did at St Albans in the opening battle of this intermittent war.

Richard of York, in Ireland since his defeat at Ludlow last year, is now expected to return. His follow-ers are poised to take control of London. A parliament has been summoned to meet on 8 October at which his condemnation by the parliament held at Coventry under the influence of the queen will be repealed as the work of seditious and covetous persons. It is difficult to see how York can make this success permanent. Earlier attempts to con-trol Henry have been short-lived and followed by reprisals – a vicious circle which he must break.

A solution would be to claim the throne for himself as descended from the Mortimers, with Edward III as an ancestor. So far he has resisted this – whatever he plans, he stresses his loyalty to Henry and just attacks his advisers (→12/10).

Yorkists enter the heart of London

Westminster, 12 October 1460
The Yorkists are in London in the full panoply of their power. It is now quite plain that Richard, the Duke of York, is about to claim the throne for himself. He has broken the seals on the king's apartments and installed himself, while the king stays in the queen's rooms. Even more significantly, Richard has adopted the full coat of royal arms, an extravagant sign of his claim to be the rightful king and his intention of usurping the throne.

His arrival at parliament today as the Commons were choosing their speaker was heralded by trumpets, and a naked sword was carried before him. There was consternation among the Lords when he approached the vacant throne as if to occupy it. He may find that he has overreached himself: among his noble supporters there are those who still regard their vow of allegiance to Henry as sacred (→25/10).

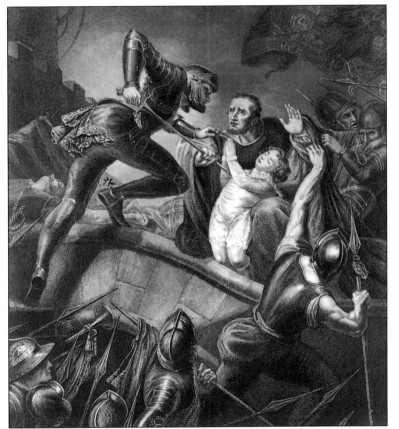
Edmund, the Earl of Rutland, is killed at Wakefield by Lord Clifford.

York and heir are killed at Wakefield

Wakefield, 30 December 1460
Two months ago Richard, the Duke of York, forced King Henry to name him as heir to the throne. Tonight his head, cruelly adorned with a paper crown, grins down from the city gate of York. He, his son Edmund, the Earl of Rutland, and many other Yorkist nobles were killed today at Wakefield. Richard had gone north to deal with a Lancastrian army; he left the safety of Sandal castle when many of his men were out foraging and threw away his life.

The king has played no part in these events. After renouncing his son's right of accession he has retreated into contemplation. York's death, however, will certainly spur the queen into action. She is in Scotland with her son arranging a military treaty, and it now seems likely that she will march south, gathering her forces, and take control of her husband once more (→4/3/61).

Lords promise York the English throne

Westminster, 25 October 1460
The Duke of York is to be the next king of England. In the face of his demands to be recognised as king the peers have proposed a compromise under which King Henry will remain on the throne but will disinherit his son of favour of York. The settlement, which is bound to be opposed by the queen, gives to the duke all the lands belonging to the heir to the throne. It leaves the duke impatient but all-powerful, and the king stripped of everything but the crown (→12/1460).

King Henry VI, defeated and taken prisoner, as imagined by a later artist.

Edward stakes new claim to be king

London, 4 March 1461
Edward of York, the 19-year-old younger son of the slain duke, who entered London last week at the head of the Yorkist army, today proclaimed himself King Edward IV. In a carefully stage-managed ceremony, he proceeded from St Paul's to Westminster where he donned the royal robes before crossing to the abbey and taking possession of the coronation regalia. He was then enthroned in the coronation chair, and the nobles paid homage to him (→29/3).

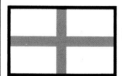

Edward IV
1461–1470

James III
1460–1488

Westminster, 28 June 1461.
Edward of York is crowned king of England.→

Westminster, 4 November 1461.
Edward IV's first parliament meets; it legitimises his claim to the throne and bestows the dukedoms of Clarence and Gloucester on his brothers George and Richard (→11/1462).

Bamburgh, 25 October 1462.
Margaret of Anjou, the wife of the deposed Henry VI, who fled to France and the safety of her cousin, Louis XI, returns to England (→4/11).

Scotland, 4 November 1462.
Margaret of Anjou and Henry VI flee to Berwick (→8/1463).

Northumberland, July 1463.
The young James III abandons his attempt to capture Norham castle, being forced to retreat by the Earl of Warwick (→9/7/66).

Northumberland, August 1463.
Margaret of Anjou and the Prince of Wales sail for France (→3/5/71).

Wales, December 1463. Henry, the Duke of Somerset, rejoins the Lancastrian cause, uniting with Jasper Twdwr, Henry VI's half-brother, against the forces of Edward (→6/1468).

Northamptonshire, 1 May 1464.
Edward secretly marries Elizabeth Woodville (→28/9).

York, 11 June 1464. King Edward seals a truce with the Scots, overturning previous ties with Lancastrians (→7/1465).

Westminster, 26 May 1465.
Elizabeth Woodville is crowned queen (→11/2/66).

Northern England, July 1465.
Henry VI, a fugitive since last year's Anglo-Scots truce, is captured (→6/10/70).

Westminster, 11 February 1466.
Queen Elizabeth gives birth to her first child, a daughter, Elizabeth of York (→2/11/70).

Wales, June 1468. Jasper Twdwr sacks Denbigh (→2/1471).

Denmark, 8 Sept 1468. Christian of Denmark agrees to marry his daughter, Margaret, to James III; the Danish king meets Margaret's dowry by mortgaging Orkney to the Scottish crown (→11/1469).

Yorkshire, April 1469. A revolt breaks out led by an ally of the Earl of Warwick, Sir John Conyers of Hornby, also known as "Robin of Redesdale" (→10/7).

Newark, 10 July 1469. Edward moves northwards to face the forces led by Clarence, Warwick and Conyers (→10/9).

York, 10 September 1469.
Edward, who was captured by George Neville after the battle at Edgecote, is given his freedom (→10/1469).

Dartmouth, April 1470. After failing to raise a rebellion in Lincolnshire, Clarence and Warwick flee into exile (→22/7).

France, 22 July 1470. To cement his new alliance with Warwick, Edward, the Prince of Wales, the son of the imprisoned Henry VI, marries Warwick's daughter Anne Neville (→13/9).

Ripon, 16 August 1470. Edward and his troops move north to deal with unrest (→13/9).

Dartmouth, 13 September 1470.
Clarence and Warwick land. They plan to restore Henry VI to the English throne (→21/10).

Battle at Towton seals Edward of York's declaration of himself as king of England

Edward IV: he has secured his position as king by winning at Towton.

Towton, 29 March 1461
Edward of York, the well-built warrior who proclaimed himself King Edward IV earlier this month, today captured his prize after a savage battle here, three miles (4.8km) from Tadcaster. He desperately needed this victory to demonstrate the justice of his cause and win more support. Now, with the hapless Henry VI, Prince Edward and Margaret of Anjou in desperate flight to Scotland, he can return to London confident that he can be properly crowned.

Henry played no part in today's battle, refusing to take the field because it is Palm Sunday and his piety would not allow him to fight on such a holy day. The Lancastrian forces were led by the Duke of Somerset, and most of the surviving nobles of England took part. A blizzard driven by a bitter wind blinded the numerically superior Lancastrians as the Yorkist infantry attacked beneath a shower of arrows.

Edward, battleaxe in hand, hammered at his enemies in the vicious hand-to-hand fighting which raged for several hours. The issue was in doubt until the Duke of Norfolk, arriving late, drove into the Lancastrian flank under cover of the snowstorm. Somerset's men wavered, then broke and fled. The day and the crown of England belonged to Edward (→28/6).

The crowning of Edward IV founds new dynasty

Westminster, 28 June 1461

Edward, all doubts about his fitness to rule banished by his victory at Towton, was crowned king of England today. The tall 18-year-old king made a fine figure in the coronation robes and was crowned with due pomp and ceremony to the acclamation of the Londoners. Despite promising to end the factionalism that has torn England apart,

he is not absolutely secure. Margaret of Anjou waits in Scotland, ready to do battle to restore Henry VI to the throne and to secure the succession for their son, Edward.

The new king promises to be the complete opposite to the saintly Henry with his bouts of madness and fatal indecision. Edward is an affable, approachable man, who nevertheless manages to carry a

great deal of authority. Not particularly pious, he already has a reputation as a womaniser. He likes rich food and fine wines and, unlike the ascetic Henry, he preens in sumptuous clothing.

The Yorks have always been great landowners, martial noblemen with their own army. They are powerful men, close to the throne, who assume that it is their right and

duty to play a major role in governing the affairs of the nation.

Their claim to the throne descends from Edward III through both male and female lines and is as legitimate as that of the Lancastrians. Yet it is doubtful whether Edward's slain father, Richard, would have asserted it if Henry had allowed him the vote in government which he thought his due (→4/11).

Secure on his throne: the imposing warrior-king Edward IV at court.

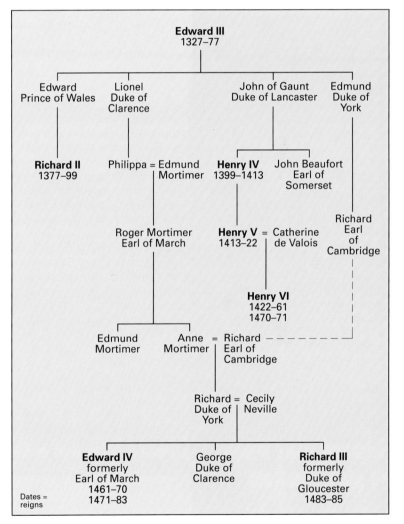

Scottish child king brings unstable rule

Lothian, 23 February 1461

Scotland's parliament today gave custody of the eight-year-old King James III to his mother, Mary of Guelders. The Scottish leaders are anxious to ensure that the succession of a boy king, following the death of his father in an accidental explosion last year, does not lead to unrest in the kingdom. Rumblings of disorder have been reported in

the highlands, but Mary, the queen dowager, is determined to take control until James reaches maturity. A niece of Philip of Burgundy, she is a capable, forceful, cultured woman with a reputation for devout prayer. She may need all her reputed strength since not all Scottish noble families are likely to welcome their affairs being dictated by a foreign-born queen (→7/1463).

Scotland backs Lancastrian supporters

Borders, November 1462

King Edward is backing raids on the Scottish borders in retaliation for moves by the Scots to back his Lancastrian rivals for the English throne. Talks have been held with both Lancastrians and Yorkists by the advisers to Scotland's ten-year-old King James. So far the Lancastrians have won the diplomatic battle for Scottish support, with the

queen dowager, Mary of Guelders, playing a leading role on behalf of her son. In return, the exiled Lancastrians last year handed over the disputed border town of Berwick-Upon-Tweed to the Scots. A truce with England was agreed at Carlisle in June, but its fragility has been exposed by this month's English raids led by an exiled Scot, the Earl of Douglas (→11/6/64).

Smart dress is for the top people only

Westminster, 1463

Parliament has passed a "sumptuary law" strictly regulating the type of clothes that may be worn according to the class to which the wearer belongs. People have been getting above themselves, and it has become difficult to tell a peasant from a squire, a squire from a knight. Under the new law only lords may wear gold, purple or sable; knights may dress in satin, velvet and silk; squires, in nothing finer than damask; commoners are strictly regulated, being forbidden to wear scarlet or foreign cloth.

Furs are a sensitive guide to class barriers. Ermine, marten and vair, the belly skin of the squirrel, are reserved for royalty and courtiers. The lesser nobility and middle classes may flaunt in beaver, otter, hare and fox. Commoners must make do with sheepskin or goatskin.

Nowhere is the difference in rank by clothes more apparent than on the fine figure of the king himself. He employs expert tailors who make him fur-lined gowns with full cut sleeves. Few of his court have the stature to carry off such fashions; even fewer would dare to try.

Edward supports the new law not only because it sets him apart but also because it will cut the import of foreign fabrics in favour of English wool and so increase his revenues. Unsurprisingly, members of parliament from "wool" constituencies were all in favour of it.

Edward uses trade to play markets

London, 1467

King Edward's expertise is not limited to the battlefield and the negotiating table; he has become a keen trader who uses royal wealth to play the markets. With excellent contacts in London's merchant community, he is exporting wool, tin and cloth. It is one step towards Edward's goal of rescuing the crown from the financial chaos which he inherited from Henry VI. The king enjoys the company of merchants and has given London a new charter with extra privileges in return for their support.

King Edward marries beneath his station

This later view of King Edward's wedding depicts it as a public event.

Westminster, 28 September 1464

The king acknowledged today that he has secretly married Elizabeth Woodville, a widow, whose husband, Sir John Grey, was killed fighting for the Lancastrians at St Albans three years ago. This revelation has shocked the court, not so much because she is five years older than Edward and has two sons, but because she is regarded as being too far beneath him in the social scale to be queen.

This is somewhat unfair, for her mother, Jacquetta of Luxembourg, had been the youthful wife of John, the Duke of Bedford. However, when the duke died Jacquetta married his steward, Sir Richard Woodville, thereby incurring the anger of the aristocracy, and she was fined £1,000 for marrying beneath her. It is said that Edward met Elizabeth while resting at a castle when hunting and was immediately captivated by her. She rejected his advances, even when he held a dagger to her throat, and told him that a wedding ring was the price of her favours. So he succumbed.

Edward recognised the dangers of such an alliance, so they were married in great secrecy on May Day, and only now, because of the pressure that Warwick has put on the king to make a political foreign marriage, has the king revealed that he is married. Here lies the danger: the "kingmaker" is the most powerful man in the kingdom and he will not appreciate being thwarted in this way (→ 26/5/65).

Boyd family seizes James III of Scots

Linlithgow, 9 July 1466

The teenage king of Scotland, James III, was kidnapped today by Sir Alexander Boyd, a nobleman. He has taken James to Edinburgh where he is keeper of the castle. The king was abducted when hunting with Sir Alexander, and it is not yet clear who outside the Boyd family was involved in the plot.

James, who is now aged 14, became king in 1460 when his father, James II, was killed in an accidental explosion at Roxburgh castle. His mother, Mary of Guelders, was given custody of the king by the Scottish parliament and took a leading role in the court, assisted by Bishop Kennedy of St Andrews. But the initially firm direction of James's reign has since weakened.

Mary herself died in 1463, her reputation for piety tarnished somewhat by her taking a lover, Adam Hepburn. Her death weakened the pro-Lancastrian forces with whom she had sought to ally Scotland against the Yorkist Edward IV in England. A truce with England was signed at York in 1464, but hopes of stability were dashed by the death on 24 May 1465 of Bishop Kennedy, the head of Scotland's government.

The resulting power vacuum has led to today's kidnapping of a king who, despite joining a border raid in 1463, has shown few signs of emulating the military reputation of his warrior father (→8/9/68).

Edward falls out with Warwick, England's most powerful noble

Richard Neville: Earl of Warwick.

Coventry, 25 December 1467

The king is spending an uneasy Christmas keeping his eye on his brother, the Duke of Clarence, whom he suspects of plotting with the Earl of Warwick. Relations between Edward and Warwick, the "kingmaker", are strained because of the favours that the king is showering on his queen's family, the Woodvilles. She has five brothers and seven sisters, and Edward is raising them to high rank and marrying them into money.

Warwick is particularly enraged by the marriage of his own aunt, the elderly dowager Duchess of Norfolk, to the 20-year-old John Woodville. The queen's seven sisters have cornered the most eligible heirs, while Edward has refused permission for Warwick's daughters to marry his brothers, George of Clarence and Richard of Gloucester.

The formation of a Woodville-dominated clique surrounding the king is another source of trouble. Warwick says that they are easing him out of his rightful place at the king's side, which he feels that he has earned by playing such a large part in bringing the Yorkists to power. There are, moreover, differences of policy over foreign alliances, Warwick favouring France and Edward, Burgundy (→3/7/68).

Royal marriage alliance with Burgundy

Bridegroom: Charles the Bold.

The English princess: Margaret.

Damme, Holland, 3 July 1468

Margaret of York, King Edward's sister, married Charles the Bold, the Duke of Burgundy, here today. The ceremony was quiet, but the bride later made an extravagant state entry into Bruges. She was seated in a litter hung with cloth of gold over crimson velvet and carried by twelve of the duke's knights.

More than 1,800 people travelled from England with Margaret in 14 ships, and Edward has set aside £2,450 6s 8d for his sister's expenses. He also sent two of his jesters to entertain the wedding party. Tonight the guests are celebrating at a noble banquet in the palace, while the citizens of Bruges are celebrating with free wine in the streets. The marriage unites England and its traditional ally, Burgundy, against France. It is a personal success for Edward, who sees it as the way to guarantee protection for England's commercial interests in Flanders and Brabant and hopes for Burgundy's help in recovering England's lost lands in France.

He has failed, however, to tie a double knot with Burgundy by marrying his brother, Clarence, to Mary, Charles's daughter by his previous marriage. This is partly because the Earl of Warwick is scheming for Clarence to marry his own daughter, Isabel. Warwick is also opposed to the alliance with Burgundy. He believes that it would be wiser for England to ally itself with Louis XI of France, the strongman of Europe (→4/1469).

A court fool, from a C15th text.

Imperial ambitions backed in Scotland

Lothian, November 1469

The Scottish parliament has declared that the king has "full jurisdiction and free empire within his realm". The vote means that James III, now come of age, can rule unfettered by papal authority. This autonomy will be useful for a king whose marriage to Margaret of Norway this year shows that he harbours expansionist ambitions. Parliament has also backed a royal move to bring treason charges against the Boyd family, which kidnapped James three years ago. The Boyds now face death (→17/3/73).

Captive king is set free

Westminster, October 1469

The king, accompanied by his nobles, has made a ceremonial entry into London and reoccupied his throne after the astonishing events of this summer when the Earl of Warwick conspired with the king's brother, the Duke of Clarence, to overthrow him.

The plot included a revolt in Yorkshire by the so-called Robin of Redesdale who was, in fact, Sir John Conyers, a close supporter of Warwick. The rebels issued a manifesto accusing the king of excluding the lords of his blood from the council chamber and relying on the advice of greedy favourites, especially the queen's family, the Woodvilles. This accurately represents Warwick's complaints against the king.

Edward at first took little notice of the rebellion, but when he eventually moved against it his army was defeated at Edgecote and he was imprisoned by Warwick. His father-in-law, Earl Rivers, and others were executed on Warwick's orders. But Warwick, whose daughter, Isabel Neville, had married Clarence at Calais during the rebellion, soon realised that he would not be able to reassert his old influence over the king and was forced to set Edward free (→4/1470).

Rebel lords force Edward to flee into exile

Edward leads his troops into battle; but now he has been forced to flee.

King's Lynn, 2 October 1470

King Edward set sail from here today with a small group of faithful men-at-arms, fleeing to exile in Burgundy after being betrayed by the Marquis of Montagu, the brother of the Earl of Warwick. Edward's troubles started when he moved north to deal with revolts inspired by Warwick. This gave the exiled "kingmaker", who had made his peace with Margaret of Anjou on bended knee, the chance to land with his ally Clarence on the exposed south coast.

Edward soon scattered the rebels but delayed overlong to impose his will on the north. He was confident that he could deal with Warwick, for he had no great opinion of the earl's military skills and knew that he himself could put a more powerful army into the field. He halted at Doncaster to allow Montagu and his men to join him, put his soldiers into quarters and sat down to a pleasant dinner.

Then news came that Montagu, only a mile away, had pledged his loyalty to Warwick and Henry VI. With his men dispersed, there was little that Edward could do except flee for his life. He sailed with his enemies hard behind him (→6/10).

Henry VI
1470–1471

James III
1460–1488

London, 6 October 1470. The Earl of Warwick and the Duke of Clarence enter the city and reinstate Henry VI.→

Holland, 11 October 1470. Edward arrives at The Hague (→26/11).

Westminster, 2 Nov 1470. Queen Elizabeth, who took sanctuary when Edward fled to Holland, gives birth to her first son, Edward (→17/8/73).

Westminster, 26 Nov 1470. Parliament disinherits King Edward IV (→1/1471).

Burgundy, January 1471. Edward seeks the help of his brother-in-law, Charles, the Duke of Burgundy (→15/3).

England, February 1471. The Twdwrs are among the main beneficiaries of Henry VI's return; Henry Twdwr, a nephew of the king's half-brother, claims the earldom of Richmond (→9/1471).

Humberside, 15 March 1471. Edward lands in England and heads for York, supported by the Earl of Northumberland (→3/4).

Warwick, 3 April 1471. Edward is reconciled with his brother, the Duke of Clarence (→5/4).

Warwick, 5 April 1471. Edward marches on London to reclaim the crown (→14/4).

Gloucester, 3 May 1471. After his success at Barnet, Edward goes in search of Margaret of Anjou and her allies (→5/5).

Tewkesbury, 5 May 1471. Margaret of Anjou's army is defeated in battle after pausing by the river Severn (→7/5).

London, 18 May 1471. Richard, the Duke of Gloucester and brother of Edward, assumes the position of great chamberlain, a role previously taken by the late Richard Neville, the Earl of Warwick (→17/2/72).

London, 21 May 1471. A battle-weary but victorious King Edward enters the city to reclaim his crown.→

Henry leaves Tower to be king again

Tower of London, 6 October 1470
Warwick and Clarence entered London today to find the capital given over to rioting and looting following the flight of the king. In the prevailing anarchy they went directly to the Tower and swore allegiance to an understandably bewildered Henry VI. They then released him and reinstalled him on the throne.

Henry is described as being "not so worshipfully arrayed, nor so cleanly kept" as befitted a prince. He may have been neglected by his jailers, but he now thanks God for setting him free. He now awaits the arrival of Margaret of Anjou. While Warwick and Margaret have sealed their alliance by marrying the Prince of Wales to Warwick's daughter, Anne, the old hatreds still simmer. Warwick wants to keep the power that he feels is his due. Clarence will seek a reward for opposing his brother, but it is unlikely that he could be accepted in a Lancastrian court (→11/10).

The prisoner set free: a bewildered Henry VI is recrowned as king of England.

Henry's brief return to throne ends on the battlefield at Barnet

Edward's victory: Warwick's troops are crushed in the battle at Barnet.

Hertfordshire, 14 April 1471
King Edward settled his quarrel with Warwick at Barnet, north of London, this Easter Sunday in a three-hour battle which ended with Warwick and his brother Montagu lying dead on the battlefield and their army defeated. It was, however, a close-run thing; when the two armies took up positions in the darkness they overlapped one another, and when the fighting started Warwick's strong right wing shattered Edward's left. Because the visibility was so bad this reverse had no effect on Edward's men.

Edward fought valiantly, and soon his stronger right wing crushed its opposition and Warwick's centre caved in. The Lancastrians broke and ran – and were slaughtered. Tonight the bodies of Warwick and Montagu are on display outside St Paul's cathedral, while Edward, who took Henry VI to Barnet with him, has returned in triumph to the capital. Henry is safely back in the Tower of London and Edward, reconciled with his brother, Clarence, is once more king of England (→3/5).

Edward trounces supporters of imprisoned rival

Margaret seized in Tewkesbury battle

Tewkesbury, 7 May 1471

King Edward has crowned his dazzling progress since his return from exile in Burgundy by outmanoeuvring and utterly defeating the army of Margaret of Anjou here two days ago. The formidable but unhappy queen had returned from exile in France just a few hours after her ally, Warwick, had been defeated and killed at Barnet three weeks ago. Today, after her army paused by the banks of the Severn, she was captured by Edward's troops.

She has lost everything. Her beloved son, the Prince of Wales, was killed as he tried to flee from the battlefield. Her most loyal supporters – including the Duke of Somerset and his brother, John Beaufort – were killed or swiftly beheaded after being tried before the Duke of Gloucester. Her husband, Henry VI, is again in the Tower.

All hope for the House of Lancaster has been destroyed, and this remarkable woman has finally admitted defeat after maintaining the struggle on behalf of her poor mad husband and their son for nearly 20 years. Brought up in a family renowned for its strong-willed women, she gave her strength to Henry, and when he recovered from his first bout of madness she became the power behind the throne.

It was she who raised the Lancastrians when Richard, the Duke of York, made his grab for the throne, and she who defied his son. Her supporters have not found her easy to work with for she is headstrong and vindictive, but tonight she is a broken woman (→18/5).

A later engraving of the death of the Prince of Wales at Tewkesbury.

Margaret of Anjou is seized after the battle: a romanticised painting.

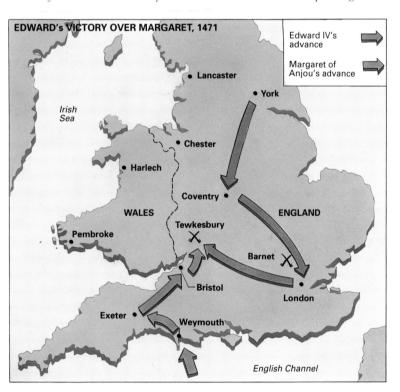

EDWARD's VICTORY OVER MARGARET, 1471

Edward IV's advance

Margaret of Anjou's advance

Lancaster

York

Irish Sea

Chester

Harlech

Coventry

WALES

Tewkesbury

ENGLAND

Pembroke

Barnet

Bristol

London

Exeter

Weymouth

English Channel

Henry VI meets his end in the Tower

St Paul's, London, 24 May 1471

King Henry VI lies in state here, his face uncovered to the people who pass reverently by. When he was brought here his body is said to have bled on the pavement. Some have taken this as a sign of his saintliness; others say that it is a sure sign that he was murdered. He died in the Tower three days ago, a few hours after Edward returned in triumph to London with the captured Margaret of Anjou.

It is claimed by Edward's men that Henry died "of pure displeasure and melancholy" when he was told of the disaster at Tewkesbury, but there is little doubt among the ordinary people that he was murdered on Edward's orders and that the man who carried out those orders at dead of night was Richard of Gloucester, Edward's loyal and increasingly powerful brother.

Henry's fate was sealed when his son, Edward, the Prince of Wales, was cut down at Tewkesbury. He would probably have been killed in the 1460s had Edward not been alive to take his place as claimant. With him dead and Margaret captured, Henry was the last possible rallying-point for the Lancastrians. So he had to die.

It is typical of the tragic life of this well-meaning but inept ruler that his wife's last glimpse of him was from her own cell in the Tower as his body was carried away. In death, he is being treated with more honour than he was in life. He has been wrapped in some 28 yards of Holland linen and is guarded by soldiers from Calais (→8/1484).

Bastard of Fauconberg mounts resistance

London, 18 May 1471

The last flame of Lancastrian resistance has been snuffed out. The Bastard of Fauconberg, the illegitimate son of William Neville, Lord Fauconberg, a cousin of Warwick, has given up his attempt to capture London and withdrawn his motley army of seamen, soldiers from Calais and Kentish rebels. With Edward preoccupied at Tewkesbury, Fauconberg might well have succeeded, but the mayor and citizens, with the garrison of the Tower under Earl Rivers, held London Bridge while artillery duelled across the river. Despite repeated assaults he could not break into the city and, with Edward on his way, his army faded away (→21/5).

King again, Edward IV returns to London

London, 21 May 1471

Edward IV re-entered the city today in a triumphal procession which has sealed his recovery of the English crown. Londoners, whose resistance to the Bastard of Fauconberg's assault [*see report, left*] bore witness to their staunch loyalty to the king, lined the streets to welcome him. He was preceded by his standard bearers, the massed ranks of troops and all his leading commanders in a show of strength that puzzled many observers – for, as they remarked, the enemy has been vanquished. But the king does not consider his campaign over until he has taught the people of Kent a lesson, and that is where he and his army are heading (→8/1473).

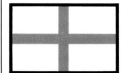

Edward IV
1471–1483

James III
1460–1488

Brittany, September 1471. Jasper Twdwr, the half-brother of the late Henry VI, and his nephew, Henry, the Earl of Richmond, who fled from the rule of Edward IV, find safety in exile with Duke Francis II of Brittany (→ 27/10/85).

Sheen, Surrey, 17 Feb 1472. The royal brothers, Richard and George, argue bitterly over Richard's wish to marry Anne Neville, the daughter of the late "kingmaker", the Earl of Warwick; George has married Anne's sister Isabel (→ 12/7).

Scotland, 17 March 1473. Queen Margaret of Denmark, the wife of James III of Scots, gives birth to a son, James (→ 26/10/74).

Shrewsbury, 17 August 1473. Queen Elizabeth gives birth to her sixth child and second son, Richard (→ 15/1/78).

Calais, France, June 1475. King Edward, who allied with Charles, the Duke of Burgundy, in preparation for war with France, moves his army across the Channel (→ 12/8).

Rouen, France, 22 Jan 1476. Margaret of Anjou, released from her Windsor prison last year, signs an agreement renouncing all claims to the English throne (→ 25/8/82).

Fotheringay, 1476. The three royal brothers attend a formal reburial ceremony for their father, Richard, the Duke of York (→ 19/1/78).

Westminster, 19 January 1478. George, the Duke of Clarence, is put on trial before parliament for treason (→ 18/2).

England, March 1478. Edward's third son, George of Windsor, aged one, dies of the plague.

Edinburgh, April 1479. Alexander, the Duke of Albany, who was imprisoned by his brother, James III, escapes; he garrisons Dunbar against the king before fleeing to France (→ 31/12).

Borders, April 1480. Anglo-Scottish hostilities break out as relations between James and Edward worsen (→ 12/5).

Fotheringay, 10 June 1482. Proclaiming himself king, Alexander, the Duke of Albany, agrees to do homage to Edward IV, break the French alliance and hand over Berwick in return for military aid against James of Scotland (→ 7/1482).

Lothian, July 1482. Richard of Gloucester and Alexander of Albany march against Edinburgh (→ 22/7).

France, 25 August 1482. Margaret of Anjou, the widow of Henry VI who was exiled after her defeat at Tewkesbury, dies aged 53.

Lothian, 29 September 1482. James III is freed by his uncles, Atholl and Buchan, on the condition that he makes peace with his brother, Alexander of Albany (→ 11/12).

Lothian, 11 December 1482. James III ignores a government suggestion to make Alexander lieutenant-general (→ 3/1/83).

Scotland, 3 January 1483. James foils another coup planned by his brother, Alexander of Albany (→ 22/7/84).

England, 25 March 1483. Edward falls seriously ill (→ 9/4).

Windsor, 9 April 1483. Edward IV dies, aged 41; his son, Prince Edward, aged 12, now succeeds him.→

Duke of Gloucester marries Anne Neville after a bitter wrangle in royal family

Anne Neville, Gloucester's bride.

Westminster, 12 July 1472

A bitter row between King Edward IV's two brothers looks set to intensify today after Richard, the Duke of Gloucester, married his second cousin Anne Neville, the teenage widow of Henry VI's son Prince Edward who is also the daughter of the Earl of Warwick, killed last year at the Battle of Barnet.

Following last year's defeat of the Lancastrians, Richard, aged 19, the king's youngest brother, received many of Warwick's honours and lands and requested the hand of Anne, whom he had known since childhood. King Edward consented, but his brother George, the Duke of Clarence, had other ideas. He is married to Anne's elder sister Isabel and wanted all Warwick's inheritance to go to her – in other words, himself – without Richard having a claim. Clarence declared himself Anne's guardian and went to great pains to keep Anne from Richard, even hiding her in a friend's house as a scullery-maid.

Richard would not give in. He found Anne sanctuary in a church and then appealed to the king; it took till this spring to fix a settlement. For Anne's hand Richard has had to give up much of Warwick's estate to Clarence, who has shown that he has no one's interest at heart but his own (→ 1476).

King gets ready for campaign in France

London, 1473

The royal coffers are filling fast as the king builds up to a campaign against France. Edward is determined to make Louis XI, the king of France, pay for his support of Henry VI in the recent débâcle which temporarily deposed him. More importantly, the king hopes that war with England's traditional enemy – with the aim of gaining the French throne for himself – will underpin his rule, which has been badly shaken by recent events.

While cultivating an international alliance against France, Edward has been busy raising the estimated £150,000 cost of the proposed campaign from parliament. The usual tithes and fifteenths have been joined by two new taxes. First, property owners have to pay ten per cent of their net worth. Secondly, a voluntary tax under which the wealthy give what they can is proving surprisingly lucrative.

A later picture of Margaret of Denmark, who married King James III of Scotland in 1469.

Edward IV seeks to impose will on Wales

Ludlow, August 1473

At a meeting of the governing council in the Marches, King Edward declared that it was time to sweep away ancient enmities and begin life anew in Wales. He called for a friendlier period of coexistence, to be started immediately in order to bring peace and prosperity to all the peoples of the border shires, from Cardiff to Chester. Wales has been divided and lawless for much too long, he said, particularly those shires of the principality in the west and north-west.

The king is also determined to reduce the power of the Marcher lordships in south and east Wales. They must be made more mindful of their fealty and service to the crown. Henceforth, he announced, the council would not be confined to advising the Prince of Wales and running his estates but would take on the supervision of justice throughout Wales, the Marches and the English border shires. To this end, Ludlow will be firmly established as the financial centre of the prince's dominions, in a bid to ensure that he and the king of England will be able to live on their own resources, without recourse to Parliament for funds.

During his address, King Edward, who is also the Earl of March and the biggest landowner in Wales, was surrounded by a strong bodyguard of Welshmen from the Marches (→ 26/10/74).

The seat of Edward IV's council in the Marches: Ludlow castle (Shropshire).

England and Burgundy to invade France

Bruges, Flanders, 25 July 1474

King Edward and his brother-in-law Duke Charles the Bold of Burgundy are to mount a joint attack on King Louis XI of France, according to a treaty sealed today at Bruges in the Burgundian Netherlands. The treaty is Edward's first step towards getting his own back on the French king for supporting the Lancastrian cause.

Edward began to plan his French war two years ago by allying with the Duke of Brittany, but this came to nothing when the duke made peace with France. Talks with Burgundy proved more fruitful; today's treaty will give the duke a large chunk of French territory when Edward is king of France. Edward has largely neutralised Scotland by securing the betrothal of his daughter Cecily to James, the son of King James III [*see story, left*]. He also won financial support from Parliament and has used his charm and authority to raise another £20,000. Indeed, such is his charm that it is rumoured that at least one wealthy widow doubled her "gift" to the king when he kissed her in thanks (→ 6/1475).

James scores notable diplomatic success

An astute and able diplomat: the peace-loving King James III of Scotland.

Edinburgh, 26 October 1474

Forty-five years of peace could be on the way for the kingdom of Scotland and its southern neighbour, according to a treaty signed today in the Scottish capital. The deal, under which an Anglo-Scots truce will last until October 1519, represents something of a triumph for the aesthete King James III, whose interests in government do not extend much beyond the minting of fine coins and the delicate, refined world of diplomacy.

The fixing of such a long truce is more a formality than a guarantee of peace, however, as the winds of Anglo-Scottish relations are nothing if not changeable. Of more real significance is the betrothal of James's seven-month old-son and heir, James, the Duke of Rothesay, to Cecily, the four-year-old daughter of King Edward IV. Edward is planning a war with France and is anxious to keep the Scots king, a traditional ally of the French, neutral; King James, who dislikes war, has astutely taken advantage of this opportunity to secure the marriage alliance with the English which has long been his goal.

Edward will pay Cecily's dowry in yearly instalments until the couple are old enough to be married. Under another clause, both kings agree not to harbour each other's rebels (→ 31/12/79).

Edward's trellis-talk seals French pact

Edward's lukewarm ally: Charles of Burgundy is advised by his courtiers.

Northern France, 12 August 1475
Barely a month after launching his French war, King Edward IV today came face to face with King Louis XI – to make peace. Regally clad in golden robes and bejewelled black velvet cap, Edward met Louis on a specially-built bridge over the Somme at Picquigny. For security reasons the kings talked through a trellis; Edward spoke "fairly good French", said an eyewitness.

The pursuit of the French crown maintains its hold on English monarchs. Elaborate war preparations were made – some reports put the English invasion force at 11,000 – and in a symbolic gesture the troops camped overnight at Agincourt, the scene of an earlier triumph. Yet Edward was open to a peaceful outcome, not least because he was furious over the lukewarm attitude of his ally, Charles the Bold of Burgundy. And Edward has not done badly out of the peace; Louis has promised him £15,000 to quit France and £10,000 a year for life. One of Edward's daughters will marry Louis's heir, and Margaret of Anjou, Henry VI's widow, will be allowed to live in France if she gives up all claims to Edward's throne (→ 23/12/82).

Strife over, royal building can start again

Windsor, 1477
Over £1,000 a year is being poured into the king's great rebuilding project here. Edward is remodelling Henry III's old St George's chapel in order to turn it into a celebration of the Yorkist monarchy, with his own tomb as its architectural focus.

Henry Janyns, whose father designed Eton college and Merton college, Oxford, is the architect of the new chapel. Visitors to Windsor are already marvelling at the delicate columns and slender piers starting to rise up on the building site, not least because works on this scale have not been seen for many years. The feuding and instability of the civil war kept the monarchy fully occupied with politics and warfare; military necessity swallowed up financial reserves which might have gone towards royal building schemes. The new St George's chapel perhaps signals the start of a more peaceful era.

Richard, youngest son of the king, gets married; he is four, his bride just five

Westminster, 15 January 1478
A glittering royal wedding took place today in St Stephen's chapel in the palace of Westminster, where Richard, Duke of York, the younger son of King Edward and Queen Elizabeth, married Anne Mowbray, heiress of the late John Mowbray, the Duke of Norfolk. Richard is just four, and his wife five years old. Anne is heir to the enormous and fabulously wealthy estates of the Mowbray family; should she die, Richard would come into a glittering inheritance.

The royal wedding: a C19th view.

Today's marriage is the result of long negotiations between the king and Elizabeth, the widowed Duchess of Norfolk. King Edward has given his infant son all the honours of the late Duke – including the earldom of Nottingham – "for the maintenance of his high estate".

This morning, the bride-to-be processed through the royal apartments to St Stephen's, which was splendidly festooned for the occasion with blue and gold hangings. All eyes were on the king and queen and their children, including the bridegroom, who awaited the bride beneath a gorgeous cloth of gold canopy alongside Anne's mother, the dowager Duchess of Norfolk.

A priest declared that the pope had given permission for the union – the couple are cousins once removed – and then the wedding began. When it was over the groom's uncle, the Duke of Gloucester, showered gold coins among the ordinary citizens waiting outside for a glimpse of the royal couple, and the newly-weds went on to a grand state banquet in their honour. One small cloud hovers over the festivities: Clarence, the groom's other uncle, is to stand trial for treason (→ 16/6/83).

William Caxton is presented to the king with his "Dictes and Sayings of the Philosophers" (1477), the first dated book printed in English.

Clarence dies in Tower for 'treason'

London, 18 February 1478
Last month, while the celebrations for his son's wedding were still in full swing, King Edward attended a more sombre royal occasion: the opening, before parliament, of the treason trial of his brother George, the Duke of Clarence. Today Clarence, found guilty on all counts, died in the Tower; rumour has it that he was drowned in a butt of Malmsey wine to avoid making a public spectacle of his execution.

For Edward the trial of his 28-year-old brother was a sorry affair but one which Clarence brought on himself through his incorrigible ambition and deviousness. The wonder is that Edward, although by nature forgiving, was so tolerant for so long. Clarence first turned traitor in 1467, when, as heir presumptive to the then sonless king, he conspired with the Earl of Warwick against Edward. When Edward returned from exile in 1471, Clarence switched back to his brother, only to throw away Edward's favour by quarrelling with Gloucester.

But Clarence was not to be warned. Last year, following the death of his wife Isabel in December 1476, he sought to marry Mary of Burgundy. She had just become ruler of the duchy on her brother Charles's death. But Edward refused to back this marriage for fear that if Clarence became Duke of Burgundy he

A later engraving of Clarence's alleged drowning in a butt of wine.

would invade England. Relations between the brothers were now strained, and Clarence was rarely at court; when he was, he pointedly ate and drank nothing, as if to imply that he might be poisoned.

In June last year one of Clarence's household was among those hanged for trying to predict when Edward and his sons would die – in other words, when Clarence

would become king. Had Clarence laid low all might have been well, but instead he burst into a royal council meeting at Windsor to harangue the king's stunned advisers with a defence of two of the guilty men. Edward could take no more. He ordered Clarence before him, told him furiously that he had "violated the laws of the realm" and sent him to the Tower (→ 3/1478).

King James murders one of his brothers and exiles another

Scene of strife in the royal family: a map of Scotland c.1479/80.

Edinburgh, 31 December 1479
Trouble is brewing for King James of Scots following his treatment of his two brothers, Alexander, the Duke of Albany, and John, the Earl of Mar. Alexander fled the country in April, and news has just emerged that John has bled to death after apparently being stabbed, on the king's orders, while in captivity in Edinburgh castle.

The two brothers were arrested this year on suspicion of plotting against James. It seems likely that the charges were justified, because Scottish nobles have been growing more and more disillusioned with James's style of government, or rather lack of it. James is a great patron of the arts and a keen diplomat, but he is simply not interested

in the unglamorous daily grind of running a country. Albany and Mar are far more conventional and became popular because they seemed more capable of giving the sort of kingship that the nobles are used to. Most kings enjoy the trappings of monarchy and are fond of patronising the arts; the trouble with James is that he likes little else.

His extravagant spending at a time of economic hardship and his fondness for listening to artists and intellectuals rather than his barons have done little to endear him to those who expect a king to be made of sterner stuff. Scots kings need to be strong to keep rebellion in check; whether James's move against his brothers will pacify the realm remains to be seen (→ 4/1480).

Edward IV is a king with an eye for the ladies

Westminster, 1479
King Edward is a big man – six foot four – with a big appetite for the pleasures of life. At 37 his taste for fine food seems insatiable (he is getting fat and sometimes makes himself sick during banquets so he can continue gorging), and his sexual desires also show no sign of abating.

Edward's lust ignores social background and marital status, and he is not beyond using the threat of physical violence to try to win a woman. He is said to have held a knife to the throat of Elizabeth Woodville, then a nobleman's widow with two children, whose secret marriage to Edward in 1464 caused a rumpus at court when disclosed. But she called Edward's bluff and refused to be cowed; he only won her heart when he treated her with more respect.

The king is said to have jested that he has three mistresses, "one the merriest, the other the wiliest, the third the holiest harlot in all the realm". The "merriest" royal mistress is Mrs Elizabeth Shore, the wife of a London grocer, who is renowned for her wit and vitality as well as her more physical charms. Another mistress, Elizabeth Lucy, has given the king an illegitimate son, Arthur Plantagenet, one of his surprisingly small brood of two or three bastards.

Elizabeth Shore: wife of a London grocer, mistress to the king.

Duke of Gloucester rules firmly in north

York's white rose in stained glass.

London, 12 May 1480

The king has appointed his younger brother, Richard, the Duke of Gloucester, as his lieutenant in northern England, making him responsible for policing the sensitive border with Scotland. The 26-year-old duke's new title authorises him to call out all the king's lieges in the Marches and adjoining counties and consolidates his strong power base in the north.

His rise to prominence in the area began shortly after King Edward's restoration, and the death of Warwick, nine years ago. The king gave Richard many of Warwick's old offices, making him great chamberlain of England (although this reverted to his brother George, the Duke of Clarence, between 1472 and 1478), chief steward of the duchy of Lancaster and keeper of the royal forests in the north. Since then Richard has swapped many of his properties in the south for lands and lordships at Scarborough, Skipton, Richmond and other places, and gained the entire Neville inheritance in the north by act of parliament. His marriage to Warwick's daughter Anne Neville [*see page 120*] confirmed his arrival in the closed, self-contained ranks of the northern aristocracy.

Richard has proved himself to be able and ruthless – for example, in conniving at the execution of Clarence, his only rival outside the Woodville family – both qualities which he will need in his new post. Since the signing of an Anglo-Burgundian alliance earlier this year, the king of France has pressurised Scotland's King James into mounting skirmishes along the border in order to tie down English forces and stop them being deployed on the continent.

Richard must coordinate a response. Edward is thought to be contemplating a full-scale invasion of Scotland in the next year or so, but action is needed now to maintain security along England's northern border (→ 10/6/82).

Barons seize Scots king

Scotland's King James with his son.

Lauder, 22 July 1482

James III, Scotland's unpopular king, has been unseated by his own nobles under the leadership of his uncle, the Earl of Atholl, and is now on his way to live under house arrest at Edinburgh castle, where it is felt that he will be able to do less harm. James's diplomatic efforts to make peace with England have done nothing to endear him to the Scottish aristocracy. The king is blamed for mismanaging the economy (which has seen a series of inflationary price rises) and for failing to dispense fair justice.

Despite James's efforts, tension on the border with England has been rising ever since Richard of Gloucester took control of Edward IV's forces in the north of England. News that the Duke of Albany, exiled since 1479, was claiming the throne as Alexander IV and marching on Edinburgh at the head of a 20,000-strong army forced James to muster a defending force in the Scottish border region. Asked for their support, the nobles refused unless the king acted to restore the currency (which he had debased with copper farthings) and to purge his favourites from the court.

The king would not accept any conditions, and the noblemen lynched six of the detested royal favourites, including the musician William Rogers and Robert Cochrane, an architect and artist, held responsible for the new copper coins spurned as "Cochrane's plaks" and "the blak pennyis".

The road to Edinburgh is now open to Albany and Gloucester; but the nobles have at last vented their spleen over this pious, art-loving king with whom they cannot identify, and now they have him in their grasp (→ 29/9).

King shows taste for expensive clothes

The seat of power: King Edward in discussion with his councillors.

London, 1480

King Edward is spending a fortune on clothing of exquisite beauty and luxury. At this, the most fashion-conscious court in Europe, the king has excelled himself with a range of clothes designed to make that sure his courtiers know who is in charge.

He is showing this above all by his love of expensive furs, including multi-layered cloaks made of the finest vair (squirrel), marten and ermine. Rich materials are also favoured, in particular cloths of gold or velvet of every description: "green satyn lined with gold", "crymsen velvet", "motley velvet", "chekkerd velvet", "velvet russet" and "green chaungeable velvet", to quote from a recent catalogue. Among the new gowns that drape the royal shoulders is one of purple with ermine trimmings, lined with satin and gold.

Piers Curtis, the keeper of the great wardrobe, strives to obtain the best materials and tailoring, with money no object. A few years ago one royal tailor, George Lovekyn, was charging 20 shillings for long velvet gowns and 13s 4d for jackets and doublets. In an average month, the king might order four new gowns, three pairs of doublets and five jackets. Meanwhile the top wage for a skilled craftsman is just 6d a day.

Margaret of Anjou, queen who plunged England into civil war, dies in France

Saumur, 25 August 1482

Margaret of Anjou, the queen whom many blame for the fall of the house of Lancaster, has died aged 53. She spent her last years in obscurity, living off a pension provided by Louis XI in return for giving up her French inheritance.

As a 15-year-old girl she married Henry VI, bringing her confident and determined character to bear on an easily-influenced king. Soon this foreign queen constantly intervening in English politics raised hackles at court, reminding nobles of that previous interfering French queen, Isabella, whose brief rule is remembered with horror.

Margaret helped her uncle, King Charles VII of France, to persuade Henry to give up his French possessions, but remained childless for eight long years – seen as a serious dereliction of her duty to the English crown. Then, when Henry VI became mentally unstable, she dragged the crown into the factionalism which was to end with his bloody deposition.

In 1453, her close friendship with the Duke of Somerset roused the fury of Richard of York. From 1456 to 1461 she made more enemies by running the monarchy with all the energy that the king lacked. She masterminded Lancastrian strategy during the conflict of

Queen Margaret receives a gift.

the 1460s, making military deals with the Scots and the French, constantly trying to regain the throne for her captive husband; she succeeded, for a while, in 1471. After her final defeat at Tewkesbury she was kept under house arrest at Wallingford. Seven years ago, her cousin, Louis XI of France, paid King Edward £10,000 for her release. She finally agreed to renounce her title and all her rights in England, and was set free.

Tentative peace with France is shattered

Arras, France, 23 December 1482

King Edward's foreign policy lies in shreds tonight following the French king's decision to renege on the marriage alliance agreed at Picquigny in 1475 [*see page 122*]. Louis has made peace with Maximilian, the Duke of Burgundy, and the *Dauphin's* hand in marriage is to go to the infant Margaret of Burgundy instead of to Princess Elizabeth. Margaret's dowry will be a vast area of Burgundy, sufficient to give Louis effective control of the country. Burgundy and Artois are to acknowledge French authority.

Edward's annoyance at being duped has been fuelled by his realisation that the enormous pension (£10,000 a year for life) paid by Louis as a bribe to stop English

campaigning on the continent will dry up, with serious effects on the royal finances. The pension and the prospect of the marriage had helped him to resist Maximilian's appeals for help against French attacks; now he has lost them both and his valuable ally as well. Moreover, the prized English stronghold of Calais will be under more pressure than ever because the surrounding district of Artois will come into French hands.

Edward's foreign policy has veered between appeasing and attacking the expansionist policies of France. Today's incident has proved that there can be no friendship with the French, and observers expect Edward to start preparing for war once again (→ 25/3/83).

Sudden illness kills king

Windsor, 9 April 1483

The king is dead after being struck down by a mystery illness two weeks ago. His sudden death has come as a great shock. The fear is that, without Edward's controlling influence, the order which he reimposed on England after the instability of Henry VI's reign will fall apart.

The shadow of the civil war seemed to fall over the king as he lay dying. Edward, who rode a wave of internecine enmities to the throne, begged two of his feuding nobles to live in peace with each other. "For the love that you have ever borne to me, for the love that I have ever borne to you, for the love that the Lord bears to us all, from this time forth ... each of you love the other," he entreated. The Marquis of Dorset and Lord Hastings held hands and wept as they

promised to fulfil his wishes. The doctors cannot agree on what struck Edward down so suddenly at the age of 40.

Some say that he was burnt out by a life of hard fighting, heavy eating and sexual indulgence. He certainly allowed his magnificent physique to go badly out of condition in the last year or so. Others claim that it was a stroke; the deathly paralysis of his final days meant that some people thought that he was dead three days ago, and a Requiem Mass was mistakenly said for him in York. Louis XI's breach of promise last year when he signed a treaty with Burgundy is said to have caused Edward to have an apoplectic fit; poison and malaria have also been mooted. But the illness is thought most likely to have been pneumonia, caught after a fishing trip on the river Thames.

King Edward IV and Queen Elizabeth: a stained-glass window, c.1482.

Uncertain succession is doubtful future

London, 9 April 1483

The sudden death of the king has left unresolved and growing tensions at court and no clear authority to control them. Edward IV's own dying wishes are unclear, but the royal council is pressing ahead with plans for the coronation of Edward V early next month, so making a formal minority government unnecessary.

Fears are already being expressed in some circles that this will give too much power to the family of

Edward IV's queen – the Woodvilles – who have been closely associated with the prince. Their history of aggressive opportunism does not bode well for future political harmony. Some of the Woodvilles' critics, among them William, Lord Hastings, are thought to favour a delayed coronation and the appointment of a protector during the king's minority. The obvious candidate for such a role would be the king's uncle, Richard, the Duke of Gloucester.

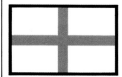

Edward V
1483
Richard III
1483–1485

James III
1460–1488

Ludlow, 24 April 1483. Edward V and his uncle, Anthony Woodville, Earl Rivers, begin their journey to London (→ 30/4).

Westminster, 2 May 1483. Queen Elizabeth seeks sanctuary after hearing of the arrest of her brother and seizure of her son, the king (→ 1/3/84).

Northampton, 3 May 1483. Gloucester sends Earl Rivers, under guard, to Pontefract castle (→ 6/5).

London, 6 May 1483. The coronation of Edward V is rescheduled for 22 June; Gloucester becomes protector (→ 13/6).

London, 13 June 1483. William, Lord Hastings, is executed for plotting against the Duke of Gloucester (→ 16/6).

Tower of London, 16 June 1483. At the Duke of Gloucester's request, Richard, the Duke of York, Edward's younger brother, joins Edward in the royal apartments (→ 26/6).

London, 22 June 1483. Claims are made that Edward IV was betrothed to Lady Eleanor Butler before his marriage to Elizabeth Woodville, making his sons illegitimate.

Westminster, 6 July 1483. The Duke of Gloucester is crowned King Richard III (→ 8/1483).

York, 8 September 1483. Richard invests his son, Edward, as Prince of Wales (→ 9/4/84).

Brecon, 18 October 1483. Henry Stafford, the Duke of Buckingham and a former ally of Richard, plots to overthrow him; in the belief that the princes have died in the Tower, he plans to make Henry Twdwr (Tudor) king (→ 23/10).

Westminster, 23 October 1483. Richard offers a free pardon to all rebels who surrender and a reward for the capture of the Duke of Buckingham (→ 2/11).

Plymouth, 8 November 1483. On hearing news of the execution of the Duke of Buckingham, Henry Tudor decides to turn back (→ 4/1485).

Westminster, 1 March 1484. Elizabeth Woodville leaves sanctuary with her daughters.

London, 2 March 1484. King Richard founds the College of Arms (→ 7/1484).

Yorkshire, 9 April 1484. The Prince of Wales, aged 11, dies.

D'fries/Galloway, 22 July 1484. The Duke of Albany's rebellion against his brother, James III, fizzles out after an unsuccessful attack on Lochmaben castle.

North Yorkshire, July 1484. Richard creates the council of the North, headed by his nephew, John de la Pole, the Earl of Lincoln, to maintain royal authority in the north of the country (→ 11/3/85).

Calais, 11 March 1485. Richard appoints his bastard son, John of Gloucester, as captain of Calais.

London, 16 March 1485. Queen Anne dies.→

English Channel, April 1485. Richard's fleet prepares for an invasion by Henry Tudor (→ 7/8).

Milford Haven, 7 August 1485. Henry Tudor lands and starts to gather support (→ 22/8).

Leicestershire, 22 August 1485. Richard dies in battle at Bosworth Field; Henry Tudor now claims the throne.→

Edward V is declared king, a 12-year-old boy fought over by his jealous relatives

Ludlow Castle, 24 April 1483
The death of Edward IV at 40 has left the succession of his 12-year-old son as Edward V in some doubt. His mother, the unpopular and grasping Queen Elizabeth, immediately asked her elder brother, Anthony Woodville, Earl Rivers, who for several years has been the prince's governor, to take him to London with an armed escort of 2,000 men to be crowned as soon as possible. They set out from the earl's home here today.

The heir to the throne is a lively adolescent, good-looking like his father, with a precocious charm and intelligence. His upbringing has been dominated by his mother and her family, the Woodvilles, who are mistrusted by most other noble families in the Yorkist ranks.

In his will Edward IV is thought to have nominated his brother Richard, the Duke of Gloucester, as protector and guardian of the young king, but he is in Yorkshire and neither the queen nor any of her family have informed him of his position. Instead, she and the Marquis of Dorset (her son by her first husband) have taken the royal

The boy king Edward V.

treasure from the Tower and to the palace at Westminster. They plan to hold a coronation on 4 May before Gloucester can gain authority over the king. But Duke Richard is now en route for London from Yorkshire. He plans to secure his position by meeting Edward at Northampton and accompanying him to the capital (→ 30/4).

Richard takes king away from escort

Northampton, 30 April 1483
A dramatic reversal of fortune has removed the young King Edward from the hands of his Woodville uncle, Earl Rivers, and put him in the charge of his Plantagenet uncle, Richard of Gloucester. Rivers was invited to dinner here last night by the Dukes of Gloucester and Buckingham, who had arrived with armed escorts to help to conduct the king to London. During the night the earl was locked into his room at the inn and arrested at dawn. Then the two dukes rode to Stony Stratford, greeted the king and arrested his half-brother, the Marquis of Dorset, and his retainer, Sir Thomas Vaughan, claiming that they were conspiring against Gloucester, and sent his 2,000 armed troops home. On hearing this news, the queen has sought sanctuary in Westminster abbey (→ 3/5).

Anxious duke who has seized Edward

London, 1483
Richard, the Duke of Gloucester, who has taken charge of his nephew, the young King Edward, is 30 and has had more ups and downs than most men even in today's troubled times. By the age of eight he had been sent abroad for his safety, and his father and a brother had been killed in battle. At nine he was Duke of Gloucester, and his eldest brother Edward was king. The seesaws of power in the civil war sent him fleeing abroad again, but at 18 he led the Yorkist victors at Tewkesbury, proving his valour.

Unlike his well-built brother, Richard is short and slight, with uneven shoulders. He is reserved, even secretive, with an anxious, tight-lipped look. He was brought up in the north by Warwick, known as "the kingmaker", and married his daughter Anne Neville.

Nobles ask Duke of Gloucester to take the throne

London, 26 June 1483
An assembly of lords who had come to London for the coronation of the boy king, Edward V, today requested the lord protector, Richard, the Duke of Gloucester, to assume the throne himself. Led by the Duke of Buckingham, they arrived at his house, Baynard's castle, with the mayor and aldermen of London. After hesitation, Richard accepted the proposal and rode with the lords to Westminster Hall where he took his seat upon the marble king's bench. He is to be crowned on 6 July.

Two weeks ago preparations were in full spate for the coronation of King Edward, who is in the royal apartments at the Tower. There, at a council on 13 June, Gloucester accused the queen and Elizabeth Shore (the late king's mistress) of practising sorcery on his person, and Lord Hastings (Elizabeth Shore's new protector) of plotting to kill him. Hastings, loyal to King Edward, was beheaded on the spot. But it is hard to think that the queen and the late king's mistress could plot anything together.

After this the archbishop of Canterbury was sent to plead with the queen to release her younger son, the Duke of York, who is in sanctuary in the abbey with her, to attend his brother's coronation. The abbey was surrounded by armed men, and the nine-year-old duke joined his brother in the Tower. Yesterday Earl Rivers and Sir Richard Grey (the queen's brother and son) were beheaded at Pontefract castle.

Meanwhile Richard is putting out a doctored version of a public sermon preached by Ralph Shaw, the mayor of London's brother, which claims that the king and Elizabeth Woodville were not validly married and that their children are illegitimate; Gloucester is therefore the rightful king. Few people seem to believe it (→6/7).

Edward under escort: a later view.

Silence from princes in Tower raises fears that they are dead

London, August 1483
It is being openly said in London that the two princes confined in the Tower have been done away with, though no man knows their fate for certain. When Richard was crowned king last month, the two boys were removed from the royal apartments to the Garden Tower, its arch leading to the constable's garden in which they were seen playing with bows and arrows.

Their servants and doctor were later withdrawn. The doctor says that Prince Edward believed that he was going to die and made daily confession. He is reported to have said: "I would my uncle would let me have my life though I lose my kingdom."

The princes were believed to have been moved to the White Tower, where many upper rooms are used to house prisoners. No one has seen them at any of the windows. Nothing has been heard of or from them since King Richard rode from the Tower to Westminster to be crowned.

Rumours of the princes' death began to spread after Richard crushed a conspiracy aimed at rescuing them from the Tower. Earlier deposed kings never survived long after proof that they remained as threats to their successors. One rumour now current is that a Sir James Tyrell, acting for King Richard, ordered two men to smother them in their beds and bury them in the Tower grounds (→18/10).

Missing boys: "The Princes in the Tower", by Sir John Millais (1826-96).

Rebellion crushed by confident king

Salisbury, 2 November 1483
Henry, the Duke of Buckingham, who aided Richard of Gloucester all through the coup which brought him the crown, was beheaded here today after leading an unsuccessful rebellion against him. The king refused to see the man who had betrayed his friendship. Buckingham had written to Henry Tudor, who is in Brittany, inviting him to join his revolt when it began on 18 October. Henry was already being urged by his mother, Margaret Beaufort, and the queen, Elizabeth Woodville, to return and march against Richard. But his ships were dispersed by storms, and Buckingham's Welsh troops deserted him. Other risings crumbled.

Tudor is to marry Edward's daughter

Rennes, Brittany, 25 Dec 1483
Henry Tudor solemnly promised at a Christmas ceremony in the cathedral here today to marry Elizabeth of York if he becomes king of England. All those present – about 500 exiles who had fled to Brittany when their rebellion under the Duke of Buckingham failed so ignominiously – swore homage to him as if he were already king. Elizabeth is still in sanctuary with her mother in Westminster abbey (→18/1/86).

Enigmatic king whose martial interests are combined with a zest for learning

King Richard is an enigma to his subjects. At the time when he brought his nephew Edward V to London and showed him to the crowds as their king he was a popular figure, a good general, with a record as a valiant fighter. Even his seizure of the crown might yet be accepted, had the princes remained visible. No one wanted another weak minority reign like Henry VI's, and the Woodville family commands little support, as Buckingham's failed rebellion shows.

But the presumed death of the young princes, with the king held responsible for their murder, is steadily undermining his credibility, however enlightened his rule. Although north of the Trent he is still a popular king, his gifts of lands and titles to his friends from the north are resented in the south. He is accused of promoting a northern take-over of the south, even though the bills that he has submitted to parliament have promised to improve justice for all.

The popular picture of Richard as a cruel and cynical usurper is contradicted by his interest in religion and scholarship. He gives lavishly to churches and colleges at Cambridge and in the north. His love of books and music are reflected in the scholars and fine singers that he has gathered at his court, where courtly dances are the rage, as they are throughout Europe.

A tough but cultured man: a 16th-century portrait of King Richard.

Queen Anne dies, leaving king heirless

Westminster, March 1485

The death of Queen Anne after a long consumptive illness has started extraordinary rumours that the king may have procured her death in order to marry Elizabeth of York, who is his niece. There are two reasons which might compel him to such a course: since the death of his only son Edward a few months ago, he has no heir – and the queen, though only 30, had had no more children; and Elizabeth is declared to be the prospective bride of Henry Tudor and would greatly reinforce his claim to the throne.

There is so much suspicion of Richard's plans at court that he has been obliged to call his supporters together and assert that such an idea as marriage to Elizabeth has never entered his mind. He was told to his face by his closest friends, Sir Richard Ratcliffe and William Catesby, that if he did not publicly renounce such an incestuous intention, the whole of the north, where his greatest support lies, would rise against him and accuse him of the death of Queen Anne, whose lands first set up his position (→4/1485).

Queen Anne: a contemporary view.

Henry VI's body is moved to Windsor

Windsor, August 1484

The body of Henry VI, which was obscurely interred in Chertsey abbey after his sudden and mysterious death in the Tower in 1471, was today transferred to a splendid tomb in the choir of St George's chapel, Windsor, across the aisle from the tomb of his rival Edward IV. This was done at the orders of King Richard, who has also made generous gifts to continue the building of King's college, Cambridge, which Henry founded.

In this he is following public professions of concern for the memory of the king ousted by his brother Edward. Many of his subjects regard Henry VI as a saint, and there are legends of the miracles that have been worked at his tomb. While Edward IV had been keen to criticise the king from whom he had seized the throne, Richard III wants to promote the institution of monarchy of which he claims to be the great upholder.

James and Edward make wedding pact

Nottingham, 21 September 1484

Another attempt to end the intermittent fighting between England and Scotland was made today with the signing of a three-year truce. The idea of a marriage alliance was also revived – having foundered in the 1470s – with an agreement for James III's eldest son, the Duke of Rothesay, to marry Richard III's niece, Anne de la Pole. The pact follows the English decision in 1482 to back a rising led by James's exiled brother, the Duke of Albany.

Berwick fell to the English, and this defeat enabled Scottish nobles, long disenchanted with James's rule, to attack unpopular royal favourites and imprison the king at Edinburgh. Yet internal divisions among his enemies eventually enabled James to rebuff the challenge. Albany went into exile again, and by then the English were more concerned with their own troubles. Today's pact removes one threat to Richard (→7/8/85).

Henry Tudor slays Richard III at Bosworth Field

Succession is decided at point of sword

Market Bosworth, 22 August 1485
King Richard slept badly last night on the eve of his battle with Henry Tudor, although he had the advantage in numbers, battle experience and command of the high ground at Bosworth Field, near here. The king told his intimates that he had had bad dreams and looked "pale and death-like" according to witnesses. In the end he lost the battle through his own rashness when his army still had superiority. As soon as his troops saw that their king was killed they surrendered.

Richard had declared that this day's battle would decide his and England's future and insisted that he would fight wearing his crown. From the top of the hill he could watch Henry Tudor advance with his troops across the marshy plain and could observe Sir William Stanley's troops to the south keeping separate from both sides. Stanley, whose nephew was being held hostage by Richard, was still waiting to see which side he would fight for.

Henry's vanguard battled up the lower slopes under the Earl of Oxford, while Henry waited in the rear. The king's vanguard, under the Duke of Norfolk, fell upon them with pike and axe near the foot of the hill. Neither Richard's main force nor his rearguard joined

in; the Earl of Northumberland led a trickle of desertions from the king's camp which turned into a flood. The fighting was fierce and the casualties heavy, including the Duke of Norfolk. Seeing Henry's distant standard amid only a small body of troops, Richard decided to stake all on a single charge. In a last, desperate attack, he led a party of horsemen around the front in order to launch himself at his enemy for single combat – if he could kill him, he had won. He nearly brought it off.

The momentum of his charge carried him into the thick of the Tudor pretender's bodyguard, where he laid low several knights including Henry's standard bearer. Richard's horse was killed under him. He had the offer of another one on which to escape but refused it and fought on on foot. But at this point Sir William Stanley led his men in a charge to support Henry and cut Richard off, scattering most of his men. Fighting valiantly in the midst of the enemy Richard was cut down alone. The battle was over. His naked body was displayed across a horse's back to the troops and then taken to Leicester. His crown, which was found under a bush, was put on Henry's head by Stanley. England had a new king.

A later view of King Richard (l) wearing his crown in combat at Bosworth.

New king's claim to the English throne

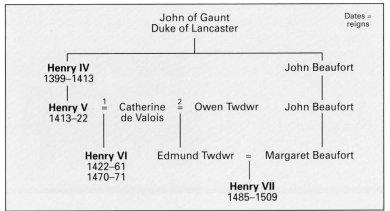

Henry's claim to the throne rests on his Lancastrian ancestry through his mother, Margaret Beaufort, the granddaughter of John of Gaunt and his mistress Katherine Swynford. The main Lancastrian line disappeared with the murder of Henry VI. He has another royal connection: Henry V's widow, Catherine de Valois, was, by her second marriage, his grandmother.

How Henry's campaign gathered support

Market Bosworth, 22 August 1485
After 12 years spent in exile and obscurity, Henry Tudor's route to confrontation with King Richard has been a long and anxious one. Only last year it looked as though he would be arrested by his host, the Duke of Brittany, and handed over to his enemy. But Henry escaped across the border to France, where he was promised money and troops to fit out an expedition. He sailed from Harfleur for Milford Haven on 1 August.

With him sailed a few hundred disaffected Yorkists, who had fled in peril of their lives from Richard, and some 2,000 unruly Norman troops lent by the king of France. In his march through Wales few

men rallied to him at first. Morale was low until an elderly seer and sage, Dafydd Llwyd, predicted a great victory for Henry. He pushed on across the Welsh mountains to Shrewsbury, picking up support as he went.

Then his army was swelled by the arrival of Rhys ap Thomas, one of the most powerful men in Wales, who had previously proclaimed his loyalty to King Richard. He brought with him up to 2,000 troops, thus doubling at a stroke the size of Henry's army. Considerably encouraged, Henry moved on to Stafford where he was met by Sir William Stanley, whose intervention on Henry's side decided today's battle.

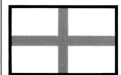

Henry VII
1485–1509

James III
1460–1488
James IV
1488–1513

Henry Tudor is crowned

Leicester, 22 August 1485.
Henry Tudor secures the throne to become King Henry VII of England (→ 23/8).

London, 23 August 1485. Edward, the Earl of Warwick, the son of George, the Duke of Clarence, the only remaining Yorkist heir to the throne, is put in the Tower of London by Henry, removing any rival (→ 17/2/87).

South Wales, 25 August 1485. Rhys ap Thomas, one of Henry's main allies, is appointed as chamberlain of south Wales, giving Henry almost total control in that area.

Westminster, 27 October 1485. King Henry bestows the title Duke of Bedford upon his uncle, Jasper Tudor (→ 30/10).

Westminster, 30 October 1485. Henry Tudor is crowned King Henry VII of England.→

London, 1485. King Henry forms the Yeomen of the Guard.

Stirling, July 1486. Queen Margaret of Scots dies.

Winchester, 19 September 1486. Elizabeth gives birth to Arthur, Henry's first son (→ 25/11/87).

London, 17 February 1487. On hearing rumours of a pretender who claims to be Edward, the Earl of Warwick, the Yorkist heir to the throne, Henry parades the real earl through the streets (→ 4/6).

Lancashire, 4 June 1487. The pretender Lambert Simnel, who was crowned in Dublin as Edward VI last month, lands at Furness (→ 16/6).

Westminster, 25 Nov 1487. Elizabeth of York, Henry VII's wife, is crowned queen (→ 18/3/96).

Dumbarton, December 1489. James IV captures Dumbarton castle, thus bringing to an end the three-month-long rebellion which had threatened his insecure regime (→ 5/1493).

Cork, November 1491. Another pretender to the throne makes his appearance; Perkin Warbeck claims to be Richard, the Duke of York, the younger of the two princes believed to have been murdered in the Tower of London by supporters of King Richard III (→ 1492).

Bermondsey, 8 July 1492. The dowager Queen Elizabeth, the widow of Edward IV, dies.

Europe, 1492. Perkin Warbeck, the pretender to the throne, is accepted by Margaret of Burgundy, the sister of Edward IV, the French and the Scots as Richard, the Duke of York, and therefore the rightful king.→

Highland, May 1493. King James IV forfeits the lordship of the Isles (→ 27/11/95).

London, December 1493. After Maximilian, the Holy Roman Emperor, recognises Perkin Warbeck as the king of England, Henry puts an embargo on trade with Antwerp and the Low Countries (→ 3/7/95).

London, 16 February 1495. Sir William Stanley, whose intervention at Bosworth swung the battle in Henry's favour, is executed for treason.

Kent, 3 July 1495. With help from Emperor Maximilian's son, Philip of Burgundy, Perkin attempts unsuccessfully to invade at Deal (→ 27/11).

England, 1495. Cecily Neville, the mother of Edward IV and Richard III, dies.

Henry VII: an early 16th-century portrait, from the Flemish school.

Westminster, 30 October 1485
Two months after the crown of England fell from a dying king and rolled under a bush, it has been placed formally on the new king's head. Today's glittering ceremony of coronation and anointing followed traditional lines but was notable for the magnificence of the costumes and trappings of the royal household. It shows just how far Henry Tudor has come since August when he landed near Milford Haven to claim his throne.

Then he was too poor to dress in the style of a king and was virtually unknown in England, which is hardly surprising since he spent his childhood in Wales and the last 14 years in exile in France. Although accepted as the heir of the house of Lancaster, his claim might have seemed weak, descending through the female line from John of Gaunt. Yet he has worked hard and decisively since Bosworth to secure the crown that proved so insecure for Richard III. At 28, the new king is tall and dark with blue eyes. He is also proving to be clever.

His promise to marry Elizabeth of York, the sister of the deposed King Edward V, is meant to unite the warring factions of the Red and White Roses, and he has shown restraint in dealing with many who took the Yorkist side. Yet by officially dating his reign from the day before the battle he retains the power to treat anyone who fought against him as a traitor, with all the dire punishment that brings.

The heir to the House of York, 15-year-old Edward, the Earl of Warwick, has already been taken to the Tower of London. In the days before the coronation Henry has rewarded his supporters, including his uncle Jasper Tudor, who was created Duke of Bedford three days ago, and the Earl of Oxford, Henry's chief military captain, whose estates and honours have been restored (→ 18/1/86).

Pope gives his approval to the new king

London, March 1486

With the belated arrival of Pope Innocent's confirmation of the dispensation which permitted Henry's marriage to Elizabeth on 18 January, the king has secured another coup in his various, complex manoeuvres to base his reign on firm legal foundations.

The pope's ratification of the match, which was needed because as cousins they are too closely related according to strict church law, is dated 2 March. However, it also contains a threat of excommunication against anyone who should rebel against Henry or his heirs. And heirs are what he needs if he is to finally resolve the competing claims which fuelled the Wars of the Roses and start a healthy dynasty to rule England.

The king's first parliament, which met at the beginning of November last year, had already granted that the "inheritance of the Crowns of the realms of England and France ... remain and abide in the most Soveraigne Lord King Harry VII ... perpetually with the grace of God". It also restored the estates of those dispossessed by Richard, including Henry's mother Margaret Beaufort.

With the blessing of the pope, the support of parliament and the reality of a victorious battle behind him, Henry can now afford to ignore those who argue that legitimacy can only descend through the senior male line.

What he cannot ignore are the ambitions of those who might hope to benefit from his fall, and he has also been busy reassuring the lesser supporters of Richard while dispossessing his 28 leading followers of their land and honours (→ 19/9/86).

Church support: King Henry with the monks of Westminster abbey.

James's exiled brother dies after joust

Paris, 7 August 1485

The Duke of Albany, the exiled brother of Scotland's King James, died today after being wounded in a joust with the Duke of Orleans. Albany had been living in France since his forces were defeated at Lochmaben in Galloway last year.

Albany was born Alexander, the second son of James II, and he had been at loggerheads with his brother since 1479. The king had then ordered his arrest, fearing plots against his increasingly unpopular rule. Albany managed to escape, returning in 1482 as "Alexander IV" at the head of an English-backed army. He won the military contest but was outmanoeuvred by his brother, who appeared ready to enlist him as his principal aide.

But by 1483 Albany was in exile again, returning in 1484 to find only defeat and the prospect of a perpetual exile, ended by today's death in France.

King crushes Yorkist military expedition and, with it, Simnel's claim to the throne

Lambert Simnel defeated: a later engraving of the Battle of Stoke.

Stoke, 16 June 1487

Early rumours that Henry has been defeated by the Yorkist army here are false. Today the king routed the force, which had assembled in Ireland to press Lambert Simnel's claim to the throne. Many men were killed, including their leader John de la Pole, the Earl of Lincoln, and Sir Thomas Fitzgerald, the leader of the Irish contingent. Simnel, the pretender in whose name the Yorkist faction rose up, has been captured [*see next page*].

The king's vanguard first attacked de la Pole's 2,000-odd German mercenaries, who put up a stiff resistance. The issue was in doubt until more men loyal to King Henry joined the fighting. The Irish contingent fought hard, but its members had no armour.

When the Yorkists broke, 4,000 of them were butchered in a narrow gully leading to the river, which ran red with blood. Henry may have won a decisive victory on the battlefield today, but the seeds of a Yorkist defeat were already sown when Lincoln attempted to raise support for the White Rose in its traditional heartland and was met with apathy. The city of York closed its gates against the rebel army.

Henry's marriage boosts hopes of peace

Westminster, 18 January 1486

Today England is celebrating not only the union of a king and his queen but also the union of the Red and White Roses, which should mean the end of the civil war. Henry's marriage to Elizabeth of York, the daughter of Edward IV, brings the hope of peace between the rival dynasties. Archbishop Thomas Bourchier presided over today's ceremony, which was celebrated with a style to match the hopes it carries. Elizabeth is tall, like her husband, but fair instead of dark and an acknowledged beauty. The couple met for the first time last year (→ 3/1486).

The king's bride: Elizabeth of York.

Yorkist pretender sent to kitchens, not the gallows

Stoke, 16 June 1487

Although he could be hanged for treason, Henry has decided to spare Lambert Simnel, the young man whose claim to be the Earl of Warwick was the excuse for the recent Yorkist rebellion. Henry has always insisted that he has the real Warwick in the Tower, and now that he has captured Simnel he is resolved to keep him alive as an example to others. Powerless after today's battle [*see page 131*], Simnel no longer poses any danger to the king, who intends to employ him as a menial in the royal kitchens. Richard Simons, the priest who coached him, will be jailed (→ 11/1491).

The king's sentence: a later view.

King Henry signs two vital treaties

Medina del Campo, 17 March 1489

Two treaties have been signed within six weeks which show how much more time King Henry feels able to give to foreign affairs now that he is securely on the throne. That at Redon on 14 February repays Brittany, where Henry was in exile, by guaranteeing military assistance against France, while today's agreement with Ferdinand of Spain for the marriage of Prince Arthur to Catherine of Aragon establishes the Tudor line in the front rank of European monarchies (→ 1492).

James dies after Sauchieburn battle

Stirling, 15 June 1488

James III of Scotland has been defeated and killed after a battle at Sauchieburn, near Stirling, with rebels fighting under the nominal command of his son James, the Duke of Rothesay, who has been proclaimed king. A few days after the fighting, which took place on 11 June, his father's body was found; he had been stabbed to the heart.

The nobles who fought the king were expressing a variety of complaints. They said that James debased the coinage, neglected to ensure that justice was dispensed and put his court favourites – notably one Robert Cochrane – before the nobles' legitimate interests. Above all he pursued policies friendly to the English, failing to respond to his French allies' demand that he attack England, making a treaty with Scotland's old foe and even trying to arrange a marriage alliance with the English crown.

This year the bishop of Glasgow and the Earls of Angus and Argyll decided that it was time for action. Four months ago they seized the heir to the throne and won his support by persuading him that his father was favouring his younger brother. They demanded the removal of the royal favourites and the withdrawal of the hated copper coinage. Negotiations failed, and they challenged the king to fight.

Today's battle comes after a number of minor skirmishes. The new king – James IV – is said to be both shocked and angry at his father's death, and his supporters are keen to stress that the battle orders forbade any violence against the king. They say that his death was an accident, but supporters of James III are sure he was killed deliberately. The disappearance of James III's enormous gold hoard has caused almost as much heartbreak among the victorious rebels.

James has been proclaimed King James IV in the wake of Sauchieburn.

Arthur is created Prince of Wales, but policy stays the same

Henry VII's eldest son, Arthur.

Ludlow, 29 November 1489

Prince Arthur, the first-born son of Henry VII, was created Prince of Wales today in a public ceremony in the great hall of Ludlow castle. The three-year-old prince, named Arthur after the semi-legendary British hero whose image remains a potent symbol of kingship, was not very well behaved during the ceremony. He insisted that his mother, Elizabeth of York, carried him everywhere. But the moment when the boy was crowned, amid fanfares of trumpets and frenzies of drumming, was most impressive, producing heartfelt emotion from the mainly Welsh audience. Tudor spokesmen are keen to promulgate the idea that a new era for the Welsh is about to begin.

Henry, with his Welsh roots, was himself hailed as the heir to the bardic tradition, the son of prophecy, a Welsh avenger of Welsh defeats, the new king of the Britons, and the first of a Welsh dynasty to bring order out of chaos while restoring self-respect to the Welsh. But in fact the king intends simply to follow Yorkist policy in Wales: rule by a council of his appointees, under the nominal leadership of the prince (→ 19/5/99).

Henry joins archduke to invade France

France, 1492
England is once again at war with France, although neither side seems quite sure of how it has come about or has committed itself to its full-scale prosecution. After spending most of last year assembling a war chest by collecting the "voluntary" gift of benevolences, Henry has crossed the Channel himself and is now besieging Boulogne.

Ostensibly the issue remains Brittany, the duchy long coveted by France where Henry spent the years before his accession. The Treaty of Redon [see opposite] obliged Henry to help the Bretons against France, a promise that he reluctantly made good in 1489, although without conclusive results.

Archduke Maximilian, pursuing conquest by other means, then married Anne of Brittany by proxy in 1490 and was enraged last year when Charles VIII of France took the region and then, having had the marriage annulled on the grounds of non-consummation, married the duchess on 6 December.

Henry has joined Maximilian partly in order to avenge earlier English losses and partly to secure his position on the Brittany coastline. But another motive is that the Treaty of Medina del Campo, with its promise of a fruitful alliance with Spain through Arthur's marriage to Ferdinand's daughter Catherine, appears to commit England to a war against France.

But now messages from the archduke, talking variously of his dysentery and his poverty, are making

Maximilian: a stained glass.

it abundantly clear that he has no intention of fighting. Spain, too, despite its interests in the south of France, is keeping away.

Henry is now left with salvaging his pride and rescuing what credibility is left in the English kings' traditional claims to the throne of France (repeated when Henry became king) by a plain show of force and determination (→ 3/11).

Treaty of Etaples ends French support for new Yorkist pretender, Perkin Warbeck

Etaples, France, 3 Nov 1492
Henry's expedition to France with an army has ended surprisingly well for the king, without bloodshed. The treaty signed here today brings peace, the promise of substantial reparations to defray the cost of the English intervention (the figure of 745,000 gold crowns has been given), and Charles's promise not to support any pretenders to Henry's throne.

King Charles made the first overtures for a settlement even before Henry landed and sent distinguished ambassadors to begin negotiations outside Calais.

For Charles, too, this is a satisfactory result. His eye is firmly fixed on Italy and the coming campaign against Ferdinand in Naples, and he has no desire for distractions from English invaders, or from those Bretons dissatisfied enough with French rule to use the excuse for a rebellion.

But for Perkin Warbeck, known to his supporters as the Duke of York and King Richard IV of Eng-

Regal authority: Charles VII.

land, the treaty is a severe blow. Charles has been supporting his claim to Henry's crown, and Warbeck is at this moment being maintained by Charles in some style at the castle in Amboise. Unless the pretender can escape from France quickly, the agreement states that Charles must hand him over to King Henry (→ 12/1493).

Scots greet Warbeck as 'Prince Richard'

Warbeck: welcomed in Scotland.

Stirling, 27 November 1495
James IV of Scotland has welcomed Perkin Warbeck, the pretender to the throne of England, with full royal honours. King James believes that the plausible young man from Flanders is truly the long-lost Duke of York and addresses him as "Prince Richard". The two men,

both in their early twenties, have developed an easy friendship and rapport which is underpinned by their compatible political ambitions and the strategic value which each has to the other.

Since he came to the throne, King James has been an implacable opponent of Henry VII. Relations deteriorated in 1491 when Henry sponsored an attempt to kidnap James; since then, the Scottish king has reopened the Auld Alliance with France and negotiated new alliances with Irish chiefs and with Holy Roman Emperor Maximilian. Henry, meanwhile, has been busy arming Scottish rebels.

In a gesture calculated to raise Henry's hackles, James will provide Warbeck with a personal allowance of £1,200 sterling a year, a courtly retinue such as befits a king in exile and the hand of the king's cousin, Lady Catherine Gordon, in marriage. In return, the pretender has promised to restore Berwick, captured by Richard III 13 years ago, to the Scots (→ 17/9/96).

Handsome pretender is king's problem

Scotland, November 1495
Whether or not Perkin Warbeck, who has just arrived here [see report, right], really is Edward IV's youngest son, he follows that other claimant to royal blood, Lambert Simnel, in being extremely good-looking.

Reports say that when he arrived in Cork in 1491 it was his appearance allied to his gorgeous clothes which first attracted attention, and that he was mistaken for both the Earl of Warwick and King Richard's illegitimate son John before he

staked his claim to be Prince Richard, the Duke of York.

His persistence in being a focus for opposition to Henry, in France, in Ireland, with Holy Roman Emperor Maximilian in the plot of 1493, and now with James IV in Scotland, has made him one of the king's greatest problems. James is said to be personally convinced of the young man's claims. But others say that poor judgement and the signs of cowardice that he has shown are a truer measure of the nobility of his lineage.

Henry VII
1485–1509

James IV
1488–1513

Richmond, Sy, 18 March 1496. Queen Elizabeth gives birth to her fifth child, a daughter called Mary (→ 22/2/99).

Scotland, June 1496. The Scottish Parliament passes an act to relieve the pressure of appeals on the royal courts and improve the quality of local justice.

England, 17 September 1496. Perkin Warbeck invades England with the help of James IV, whose cousin Catherine Gordon he has married (→ 26/9).

Borders, 26 Sept 1496. James IV retreats, ignoring Warbeck's ambitious plans for deposing Henry (→ 6/7/1497).

Strathclyde, 6 July 1497. Perkin Warbeck flees to Ireland after a failed uprising (→ 7/7).

Bodmin, 7 September 1497. Warbeck proclaims himself King Richard IV and attempts to rally support (→ 10/1497).

Borders, 30 September 1497. James IV forces Henry VII to agree to a seven-year truce at Ayton (→ 24/1/02).

London, 9 June 1498. After escaping from custody, Perkin Warbeck is recaptured and imprisoned in the Tower of London (→ 24/11/99).

Greenwich, 22 February 1499. Queen Elizabeth gives birth to Prince Edmund; he is her sixth child (→ 19/6/1500).

England/Spain, 19 May 1499. Prince Arthur is married by proxy to Catherine, the youngest daughter of King Ferdinand II of Aragon and Queen Isabella of Castile (→ 2/10/01).

Highland, 22 April 1500. The Earl of Argyll, Archibald Campbell, is granted vice-regal powers over the lordship of the Isles in an attempt to increase royal control.

Hatfield, 19 June 1500. Henry and Elizabeth's youngest son, Edmund, dies; he was 16 months old (→ 2/4/02).

Plymouth, 2 October 1501. Catherine of Aragon arrives to marry Prince Arthur, the heir to the throne (→ 14/11).

London, 1501. Henry chooses Baynard's castle in the city, built by William I, as his principal town residence; he starts a major rebuilding programme.→

Ludlow, 2 April 1502. Prince Arthur dies unexpectedly and Henry, his younger brother, becomes heir to the throne.→

London, 11 February 1503. Queen Elizabeth and her newborn daughter Catherine die of an infection caught during childbirth (→ 27/6/05).

London, 18 February 1503. Henry invests his son, Prince Henry, as Prince of Wales and Earl of Chester (→ 23/6).

St Andrews, April 1504. King James's seven-year-old illegitimate son, Alexander, is nominated as the archbishop of St Andrews (→ 1507).

London, 24 March 1506. Philip, the Duke of Burgundy, hands Edmund de la Pole, the exiled Earl of Suffolk and one of the leaders of the Perkin Warbeck uprisings, over to the English; he is to be imprisoned by King Henry (→ 17/12/08).

Richmond, 21 April 1509. King Henry, aged 52, dies at Richmond palace; his son, Henry, succeeds him.

West Country rises against 'unfair' taxes

Blackheath, London, 17 June 1497
Forces loyal to King Henry today crushed an uprising which began in Cornwall and had spread eastwards gathering support as the rebels moved towards the capital. Until today they had met little opposition, with the king apparently distracted by a threat from Scotland. But at Blackheath forces led by Lord Daubeney struck back, killing an estimated 2,000 rebels and arresting the alleged leaders of the Cornish revolt.

The protests had been sparked by calls for higher taxes voted by parliament in January. These were to enable the king to resist the threatened invasions by James IV of Scotland and the Yorkist pretender to the throne, Perkin Warbeck. It does not seem that the Cornishmen were moved primarily by hostility to the king, let alone by support for the claims of Warbeck. Nevertheless the rebellion swiftly gathered momentum, moving from the rebels' home county via Wells, Salisbury and Winchester before heading to a confrontation near London.

It was said that the Cornishmen planned to enter London itself and seize the Tower where, they wrongly believed, the king was hiding; but he was just waiting to attack when they were tired and far from home. It is not yet clear whether today's crushing victory for the king will deter Warbeck from his plans to seek support in Cornwall.

Henry backs exploration of 'new world'

A later painting of John Cabot leaving Bristol on his voyages.

Bristol, 10 August 1497
John Cabot has returned from his voyages in search of a "new world" to report to his patron, the king. Cabot told Henry that the royal flag had been planted on a land far across the Atlantic Ocean. A delighted king gave Cabot a present of £10, and there is talk of an annual pension to encourage further voyages by the Bristol-based explorer.

Henry gave his blessing to Cabot on 5 March last year, when he issued letters patent authorising Cabot to undertake an expedition to discover and annex lands "unknown to all Christians". In other words, Henry did not want to antagonise the Spanish, but he is anxious that England is not left behind if there are new empires to be built. All lands discovered were to be occupied in the king's name, with one-third of any profits going to the royal coffers.

Cabot, an Italian by birth and citizenship, left Bristol with 17 men in the *Matthew* last May and made landfall on 24 June, exactly where it is not known. He returned four days ago to tell his story to the king and to plan fresh adventures.

New palace started after Sheen destroyed

A 19th-century view of Sheen palace, which has been destroyed by fire.

Sheen, Surrey, December 1497

King Henry had only just arrived at Sheen palace, where he had planned to celebrate the Christmas festivities, when disaster struck. The fire that destroyed the huge palace started in the king's own quarters at 9pm, and by the following morning Sheen palace was no more. Henry has already ordered a new and even finer palace to be built at nearby Richmond, and has offered substantial rewards of up to £20 for finding the crown jewels in the burnt-out building.

The original manor house of Sheen was given to Isabella, the murderous wife of Edward II. When she died in 1358 her son, Edward III, spent a fortune creating Sheen as one of his finest palaces and was the first to live, and die, here.

Subsequent kings were equally attached to Sheen. Richard II came here with his much-loved queen, Anne of Bohemia, as often as he could. Anne died here in 1394, and Richard in his grief decreed that the palace should be "utterly destroyed". Henry V then had two manor houses pulled down and bricks and white stone brought from Calais and Caen to rebuild the palace as a "delightful mansion, becoming to the royal dignity" (→ 1501).

A later painting of the visit to King Henry's court in 1499 by the Dutch scholar Erasmus. He visited the king and his children in the company of Thomas More, and was impressed by the intelligence of Prince Henry.

Perkin Warbeck seized

Beaulieu, October 1497

Perkin Warbeck, the man who claimed to be "Richard IV", has been captured by forces loyal to Henry VII. For six years he has pursued his claim to the throne, purporting to be Prince Richard, the Duke of York, who is thought to have been murdered with his brother, Edward V, in the Tower in 1483. But now he has confessed that the claim was false and asked the king for forgiveness.

The downfall of the Yorkist pretender was as abrupt as it was complete. He had left Scotland in July after spending some time there as a rallying-point for opposition to Henry. James IV had begun to show signs of impatience with his guest, however, so Warbeck headed for Ireland and Cornwall. Rebuffed in Ireland, he set off with two small ships to Cornwall, the scene of an anti-Henry revolt earlier this year.

He landed at Whitesand Bay, near Land's End, on 7 September and several thousand people did indeed rally to his banner. But he failed to gain support from the key cities of Exeter and Taunton. By then the king's forces were closing in on Warbeck's dwindling army, forcing their leader to flee. Now he has been captured at Beaulieu, and his claim to be "Richard IV" looks like what Henry always claimed it was – a sham (→ 9/6/98).

Warbeck executed for plots against king

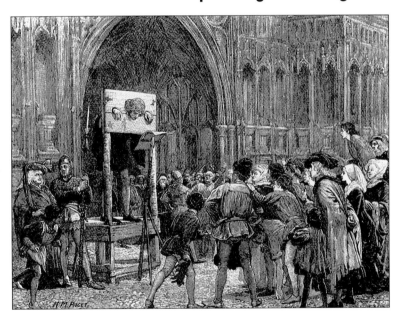

Publicly shamed: the pretender Perkin Warbeck in the pillory (a later view).

London, 24 November 1499

Perkin Warbeck was hanged today, some eight years after he first claimed to be England's rightful king – "Richard IV". Executed alongside him was the Earl of Warwick, both men convicted of trying to escape custody while being held for plotting against the king.

Warbeck had surrendered to Henry's forces in 1497 after an abortive, and short-lived, attempt to rally support in Cornwall against the king. He confessed then that he was not Richard, the Duke of York, thought to have been killed in the Tower in 1483. Warbeck's position was then so weak – previous Scottish support had been withdrawn – that Henry decided to impose no punishment upon the Yorkist pretender. But Warbeck tried to flee Henry's court and was arrested in June last year – and this time there was to be no reprieve.

A public confession and two stints in the stocks preceded his incarceration in the Tower of London. There it was alleged that he became involved in a plot against the king with the Earl of Warwick. On 16 November the two men went on trial and were found guilty; today they paid with their lives.

▷

Prince Arthur weds Catherine of Aragon

London, 14 November 1501
They were first betrothed in 1488 when Prince Arthur was only 18 months old. The heir to the English throne was to marry Princess Catherine of Aragon, the daughter of Spain's King Ferdinand. Today, with sumptuous splendour at St Paul's cathedral, the wedding for so long desired by King Henry finally occurred. It links Henry's dynasty with one of the most powerful royal houses in Europe.

Henry had repeatedly used the prospect of marriage to Arthur, his eldest son, as a diplomatic tool. It first arose in 1488, was confirmed in the 1489 Treaty of Medina del Campo and reconfirmed by yet another treaty in January 1500. In November last year the couple were married by proxy, but today the ceremony was completed. Elaborate preparations had been made for the arrival of the 17-year-old princess from Spain. Six spectacular pageants were staged in London when she arrived in the capital two days ago from Southampton. Civic leaders and lords headed the welcome to the woman who one day would be their queen. Today the crowds cheered Catherine and Arthur, now aged 15, on their wedding day.

Games and tournaments are being organised as Henry strives to show that he can more than match the pageantry which until now has been more common in Europe than in England. Arthur, named after one of England's greatest kings, carries his father's and the nation's hopes for the future (→ 2/4/02).

A diplomatic marriage: Prince Arthur and Princess Catherine at court.

Anglo-Scottish marriage alliance agreed

London, 24 January 1502
Diplomatic representatives of the Scottish and English kings have met to sign a treaty of perpetual peace which, with luck, will end their almost traditional pastime of cross-border raids. In order to cement today's treaty a marriage deal has also been arranged between James IV of Scots and Margaret Tudor, Henry VII's eldest daughter. The wedding is planned to take place next year in Edinburgh.

It was high time for a diplomatic settlement. James and his southern neighbour Henry have not, after all, been on exactly friendly terms in recent years. In 1491 Henry made a secret deal with the Earl of Buchan to kidnap James and deliver him to the English court. The plot was soon thwarted.

James did not have to wait long to return the compliment. When Perkin Warbeck, the self-styled "Prince Richard of England" and pretender to the English crown, turned up in Scotland in 1495 James did not hesitate to lend him support. James crossed the border with an army in the following year and, despite some setbacks, showed the English that he deserved his reputation at home for courage and leadership. In September 1497 he arranged a truce with Henry at Ayton which laid the foundation for the present treaty (→ 8/8/03).

New royal palace at Richmond completed as king moves into Baynard's castle

A later engraving of the splendid palace at Richmond, built by King Henry.

Richmond, Surrey, 1501
The great palace on the banks of the Thames is complete and ready for royal occupation. The building – which Henry VII says will impress the world with the power and genius of the Tudors – is to be called Richmond because the king and his father were Earls of Richmond in Yorkshire. He will retain Baynard's castle, near the city of London – which he has recently refurbished – as his town residence.

The vast new palace has been built near the site of Sheen palace, which burnt down in 1497. The king describes it as "this earthly and second paradise of our realm of England". The palace faces the river to the south and is approached through two gateways with "strong gates of double timber and heart of ash struck full of nails wrought and thick and crossed with bars of iron". It has towers in each corner, and the entrance to the private quarters has a four-centred perpendicular arch, 18 feet (5.4 metres) high, sculpted with Henry's arms and the red dragon of the Tudors.

Richmond has several courtyards. The main one is 60 yards long and 26 yards wide, surrounded by buildings for the gentlemen of the bedchamber. The middle court contains a fountain of "purest water". Perhaps the finest feature is the 100-foot-long great hall, its timber roof lined with lead and decorated with hanging pennants. The walls are lined with pictures of warrior-kings, Henry included.

King Henry's new residence at Baynard's castle: an 18th-century view.

Court stunned by death of Prince Arthur

Ludlow, 2 April 1502

Prince Arthur, the heir to the throne, is dead at 16, a victim of consumption. He leaves a widow, Catherine of Aragon, herself only 18, to whom he was married just five months ago, a wedding that was designed to cement his father's desire for an alliance with Spain. The princess is not pregnant.

Arthur, who was born in Winchester in 1486, represented more than just a son and heir. Henry believes firmly in his descent from the ancient British kings. Not for nothing was the prince named for the legendary hero King Arthur.

The king and queen, naturally, are devastated, and the whole court is in mourning. Arthur leaves a younger brother, Henry, the Duke of York, who will replace him as heir, but the loss of their first-born is one that cannot be replaced. And for all their position and power, they have shown themselves as overcome with sorrow as would be any of their subjects (→ 11/2/03).

James weds Tudor bride

The marriage procession of James IV and his English queen, Margaret Tudor.

Death of prince is a loss to the nation

London, 2 April 1502

As Prince Arthur embarks upon his final journey from Ludlow, where he died, to London, where he will be buried, many are reflecting sadly on the king who might have been.

From his birth onwards the Prince of Wales was guided carefully towards the role that everyone expected would one day be his. He was trained in the latest humanist and literary scholarship – which included the philosophy of Erasmus – by the poet, classicist and chronicler Bernard André.

He was also well versed in the realities of power. His own council, under Jasper Tudor, began administering Wales once Arthur had been invested as its prince in 1489, and 12 years later he moved to Ludlow where he began to direct its operations himself.

A later view of Prince Arthur.

Edinburgh, 8 August 1503

A magnificent wedding between James IV and Margaret Tudor, the daughter of Henry VII of England, is being celebrated at Holyrood palace. A dazzling round of banquets, pageants and tournaments fuelled with enormous quantities of wine will keep guests entertained for the next five days. The court poet William Dunbar has marked this union of the Stewarts and the Tudors more soberly, with a new work entitled *The Thistle and the Rose* [*see below*] published as early

this morning King James brought his future queen here – a rather plain 14-year-old whom he met only four days ago at Dalkeith.

Their arrival has put all of Edinburgh in holiday mood, yet there is a serious side to the festivities. The marriage aims to cement last year's peace treaty between Scotland and England. It also presents the intriguing possibility of there one day being a Stewart on the English throne, as Princess Margaret is second in line in the English succession (→ 4/1504).

Prince Henry to marry Arthur's widow

Richmond, Surrey, 23 June 1503

Prince Henry, who on his brother Arthur's death last year took over his position as heir to the throne, is now to take on another of his responsibilities: his wife. By a treaty signed today with Spain's ambassador, Henry is betrothed to Catherine of Aragon. Their wedding will take place when the prince is 14.

The pope will have to give special permission for the marriage, since marrying one's brother's widow is considered, by some, to be prohibited by canon law. Apart from any religious considerations, the betrothal has important political implications. It will maintain the vital alliance with Spain. Within weeks

of Arthur's death Catherine's parents, Ferdinand and Isabella of Spain, demanded the return of her dowry, the handing over of the revenues fom Cornwall, Chester and Wales that had been given to her, as Princess of Wales, by the king, and her own return home. The king wanted none of this.

At the same time, however, the Spanish monarchs also instructed their ambassador to begin negotiating a marriage between Catherine and Henry. This, both sides understood, would help to solve the outstanding financial problems. A draft treaty was agreed on 24 September 1502; today's signatures make it formal (→ 24/6/09).

Poet marks union of 'Thistle & Rose'

Edinburgh, 1503

Dame Nature has assembled every beast, bird and flower in order to assign them their responsibilities. Giving a crown of rubies to the Thistle (James IV) she tells him to be like a flower "of virtue and of odour sweet" , shunning the "nettle vile and full of vice". Above all he is to hold no other flower in such esteem as Margaret Tudor, "the fresh Rose of colour red and white" [original dialect version on the left]:

For gife thow dois, hurt is thyne honesty,
Conciddering that no flour is so perfyt,
So full of vertew, plesans, and delyt,
So full of blisfull angellik bewty,
Imperiall birth, honour and dignite.

For if you do, hurt is your honesty,
Considering that no flower is so perfect,
So full of virtue, pleasure and delight,
So full of blissful angelic beauty,
Imperial birth, honour and dignity.

Arts and science shine under patronage of Scotland's charismatic young king

Scotland, 1507

The Scottish court is becoming one of the brightest beacons of European culture, with both the arts and the sciences flourishing as never before. The credit for this belongs to Scotland's young and charismatic king, James IV. Generous and intelligent, James has surrounded himself with artists, musicians, poets and craftsmen, with new palaces built at Falkland and Holyrood.

A royal chapel has been founded at Stirling castle, and in 1495 James founded King's college at Aberdeen, the first university in all of Britain to boast a chair of medicine, the science which most fascinates the king. He has founded a college of surgeons in Edinburgh and is something of an amateur dentist; he once tried pulling teeth from an unfortunate subject.

School is now compulsory for the sons of Scottish gentry and freeholders. James is no mean scholar himself, being a vora-

Falkland: built by James IV.

cious reader – the poets Robert Henryson and William Dunbar are favourites – and able to speak seven languages. A royal charter established Scotland's first printing press in Edinburgh. Alchemy interests him, too, and he employs an Italian, John Damien, to research both this and man-powered flight.

Holyrood: a modern view of the palace built by James in Edinburgh.

King takes a shine to Joan of Naples

London, 27 June 1505

Two years after his beloved wife Elizabeth died in childbirth, robbing him of both wife and heir within ten months, the king is seeking a new consort. He has turned to Spain and the newly-widowed Joan of Naples, the cousin of his daughter-in-law Catherine of Aragon. To find out if she is a suitable mate he has dispatched two envoys to Valencia, where they have interviewed her. Henry's instructions ran to 24 questions, concentrating on her finances and her physical charms. The latter appear acceptable, but the former, it seems, are less appealing (→ 1/2/06).

Duke of Burgundy visits Henry's court

Windsor, 1 February 1506

Two kings, the one firmly set on his throne, the other hoping to take what he claims is his, met today when King Henry played host to Philip of Habsburg, who hopes to become king of Castile if he is able to press his claim against that of King Ferdinand of Aragon. Sailing from Burgundy to Spain, Philip was blown ashore at Weymouth. The king lodged him at Windsor and joined him for dinner. Now Philip hopes to gain Henry's support for his claims, which are based on those of his wife, Joanna, the eldest daughter of Ferdinand and his wife Isabella of Castile (→ 24/3).

Prince given a good all-round education

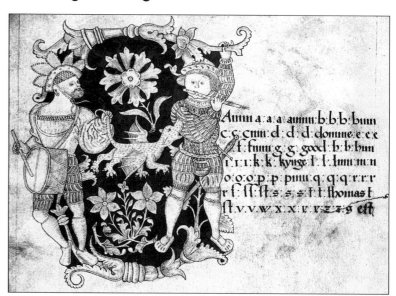

A prince's education: a page from a 16th-century textbook on calligraphy.

London, June 1508

An enthusiastic devotee of all sports, Prince Henry has turned to a new one: jousting. Riding against his teacher, Richard Grey, he rode so well that he broke Grey's arm.

Jousting is but one of the "noble arts" in which the young prince has been trained. Blessed with a strong body and a taste for all sorts of athletic pursuits, Henry enjoys hunting and hawking, shoots accurately and both swims and runs well.

And, as befits one who is destined to be king, the intellectual side of his education has not been entirely ignored. Like his late brother Arthur, he has enjoyed the best

available tuition in the classics from the poet John Skelton, a spiky if learned figure. As his first tutor Skelton taught him the basics of knowledge and in 1501 wrote the *Speculum Principis*, a handbook of kingship.

Yet Henry knows little of practical power. Despite all the great offices that he was given almost from the day of his birth, his father has deliberately kept him from gaining any real experience, even after the death of his elder brother left him as heir to the throne. Whether this is because Henry dislikes his son, or because he doubts his ability to rule, must remain in question.

Habsburg alliance to be sealed by the marriage of Mary

Richmond, Surrey, 17 Dec 1508
Almost three years since the king showed his support for the Habsburg claims on Spain by signing the Treaty of Windsor with Philip of Burgundy in February 1506, he has underlined his allegiance by betrothing his daughter Mary to Archduke Charles, Philip's son, the grandson of both Ferdinand of Aragon and Holy Roman Emperor Maximilian.

The betrothal is the latest in a series of foreign policy manoeuvrings in which the king, well aware of England's comparative weakness when set against Europe's great powers, has tried to increase its influence by strategic alliances. His entanglements with the Habsburgs are further increased by the fact that England has now lent them some 342,000 crowns [£85,500].

Negotiations for the betrothal have been under way since late 1506, when Maximillian himself suggested it. There had also been plans for Henry to marry Margaret of Savoy, Philip's sister, but she was uninterested. She was satisfied, however, to back the betrothal.

The immediate cause of the arrangement was the treaty secured between Ferdinand and Louis XII of France. Henry needs his own security, and with France allied to Ferdinand he saw that his best policy lay in opting for Ferdinand's Habsburg rivals (→ 7/8/14).

A view of London c.1493 from the German manuscript history the "Nuremberg Chronicle".

Henry VII dies with dynasty secure

A later engraving of King Henry.

Richmond, Surrey, 21 April 1509
Henry VII, the victor of Bosworth and the first king for a century to bring peace to a country long ravaged by civil war, is dead. He had reigned for more than 23 years and was 52 years old.

The king's health had been failing for some time, and when in 1507 he had fallen seriously ill of a "quinsy" it was feared that he had but days to live. In fact he lived two more years, but the tuberculosis from which he suffered undermined his rapidly failing health. By late March a new bout left him "utterly without hope of recovery", and after a final struggle lasting 27 hours he slipped into oblivion. His death has heralded a wave of complaints

and disenchantment with his reign which had been carefully suppressed while he was alive – for Henry had never balanced his obvious statecraft with the common touch that guarantees popularity.

Yet Henry was an astute, capable ruler. Above all, he was a working monarch who came to a throne racked by decades of dissension and left it secure in the hands of a new dynasty with his son, Henry, now becoming king. He set himself three goals: restoring the royal authority, improving the nation's finances and government, and giving England a place in Europe. Through clever management, a certain ruthlessness and a flair for diplomacy he achieved all three (→ 11/5).

Henry and the arts: European culture finds a welcome at court

Richmond, Surrey, 21 April 1509
The late king may well go down in history for his setting up of a stable government but, like many of his peers, Henry showed himself as much a patron of the arts as he was a diplomat and administrator.

Brought up in Europe, Henry had always been well aware of cultural developments there. Such major figures as the humanists Erasmus and Polydore Vergil have been welcomed to these shores. At the same time Henry encouraged the growth of the church, becoming the first king in 70 years to found new religious houses – another reflection of movements abroad.

His cultural achievements reach their peak in the chapel which he has had added to Westminster abbey. Here his own remains will lie, no doubt surrounded by a fittingly magnificent monument.

King Henry is presented with a book by its author, Antoine Verrat, c.1494.

Henry and diplomacy: forging alliances to boost power at home

Richmond, Surrey, 21 April 1509
In a Europe dominated by such arch-intriguers as Ferdinand and Isabella of Spain and great powers who include Holy Roman Emperor Maximilian and Charles VIII and Louis XII of France, King Henry proved himself to be quite their equal, scheming and plotting with the best of them and giving England a role that it had long lost in the

continental power struggle. Unlike his rivals, Henry had to accept that his was an essentially weak country which lacked the territorial clout of the European monarchies.

His own rule was, initially at least, far from secure, and there was little money to be spent on foreign adventuring. What mattered most to Henry was maintaining his own power at home. Even his foreign

policy was devoted to that. Through a series of judicious treaties – for both trade and marital alliances – Henry managed to keep England both uninvolved and yet far from isolated. He abandoned its old claims on European lands, preferring to make England an ally whose support would benefit every side – and would be well paid for.

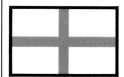

Henry VIII
1509–1547

James IV
1488–1513
James V
1513–1542

Westminster, 24 June 1509.
Henry VIII and his bride, Catherine of Aragon, the widow of his brother, Prince Arthur, are crowned king and queen.→

England, November 1509. King Henry appoints Thomas Wolsey, the king's chaplain, as his royal almoner (→7/8/14).

London, 31 January 1510. Queen Catherine gives birth to a stillborn daughter (→1/1/11).

Scotland, 1510. Prince Arthur dies, leaving James IV without a male heir (→12/10/11).

Richmond, Surrey, 1 Jan 1511. Queen Catherine gives birth to Henry, the Duke of Cornwall, the son and heir of Henry VIII (→22/2).

Scotland, March 1512. James IV renews his French alliance after his excommunication by the pope for refusing to join the Holy League against France (→10/4/12).

Scotland, 10 April 1512. Queen Margaret gives birth to James, a new heir to the Scottish throne (→9/9/13).

London, April 1512. Henry declares war on France and sends an army to Gascony (→4/5/13).

London, 4 May 1513. Edmund de la Pole, the imprisoned Earl of Suffolk and Yorkist heir, is executed on King Henry's orders (→13/6).

Calais, 30 June 1513. Henry and his invasion force of 35,000 men land (→23/9).

Ulster, August 1513. The Scottish fleet, equipped with French galleys, bombards Carrickfergus castle en route for Normandy to aid Louis XII of France (→9/9).

Richmond, November 1513. Queen Catherine, desperate to provide an heir to the throne, tragically gives birth to a stillborn son, Henry (→12/1514).

Scotland, 6 August 1514. Queen Margaret, the widow of James IV and regent of Scotland, causes a stir by her marriage to Archibald Douglas, the Earl of Angus (→12/7/15).

London, 7 August 1514. An Anglo-French truce arranged by Thomas Wolsey, the chief adviser to Henry VIII, includes the marriage of Mary Tudor, Henry's sister, to Louis XII (→9/10).

Richmond, December 1514. Queen Catherine gives birth in the royal palace to another stillborn son (→20/2/16).

York, 1514. Henry appoints Thomas Wolsey to the archbishopric of York (→10/9/15).

Paris, February 1515. Mary Tudor, the widow of Louis XII of France, secretly marries Charles Brandon, the Duke of Suffolk (→25/6/33).

Scotland, 12 July 1515. John, the Duke of Albany and a cousin of the infant James V, is accepted as governor and regent of Scotland in the place of Queen Margaret, the child king's mother (→26/8/17).

Richmond, 10 November 1518. Queen Catherine gives birth to a stillborn daughter.

London, 1519. Henry orders the suppression of all brothels.

Edinburgh, 30 April 1520. Archibald Douglas, the Earl of Angus and husband of Queen Margaret, seizes the city of Edinburgh (→19/11/21).

Henry VIII is new king

A portrait of the young king: Henry VIII, by Joos van Cleve (d.1540).

London, 24 April 1509
King Henry VIII has succeeded peacefully to the throne on the death of his father. He has already seized the reins of power, and has arrested the late king's detested ministers, the tax collectors Richard Empson and Edmund Dudley. Their sudden fall is hugely popular. Clearly the new king, who is not yet 18, intends to be his own master and be a very different king from his father.

Henry VII was quiet, parsimonious and authoritarian. Henry VIII will be equally autocratic, but he delights in the splendours of monarchy and his court will be as youthful, as gay and as dazzling as he is. The new king is an active sportsman but is also highly educated and cultured. He writes and plays music, speaks good French as well as Latin and delights in the new arts from Italy. He is six feet three inches tall, red-headed, strong and imposing, with a small, cruel mouth and suspicious eyes in a wide, florid face. Physically he resembles his maternal grandfather, Edward IV. It remains to be seen if he is equally dissolute and ruthless.

Henry VII died on 21 April at Richmond Palace, but the death was not announced until yesterday when the new king was proclaimed king by the heralds throughout the realm. He is the first uncontested, adult king to succeed since Henry V, a century ago, and England rejoices that the times of civil wars and disputed successions are over.

The king has two sisters, one of them married to James IV of Scotland. His elder brother, Arthur, died in 1502, five months after his marriage to Catherine of Aragon. She has remained in England ever since. The late king intended to marry her to Prince Henry. The new king's matrimonial intentions are not known (→11/6).

Henry VII is buried in own chapel in Westminster abbey

Westminster, 11 May 1509

King Henry VII was buried today next to his wife, Elizabeth of York, in a vault under the chapel which he built in the abbey. The ceremony was very splendid and began on 9 May when the late king's body was brought from Richmond to London. The funeral procession, including over 600 men carrying candles, the king's choir, bishops, priests and monks, was led by Sir Edward Howard on a charger with the late king's banner.

Yesterday the body was brought to the abbey where it lay in state until the funeral today. The choir sang *Libera Me* as the body was lowered into the vault, and the lord treasurer, the lord steward, the lord chamberlain and the treasurer and comptroller of the king's household all broke their staves of office and threw them into the vault. Then garter king of arms cried out in a loud voice: *"Vive le Roy Henri le huitième, roy d'Angleterre et de France, et sieur d'Irelande."*

Henry VII originally built the chapel at Westminster to house the tomb of Henry VI, whom he hoped would be canonised by the pope, and to serve as a necropolis for the Tudors. The chapel is still being built, and Henry VI has been left at Windsor. The roof will have elaborate fan vaulting, and the chapel will be decorated with modern sculpture; the new king intends to find an Italian master to build the tombs of his parents (→1515).

Henry marries his brother's widow

Catherine, royal bride twice over.

Greenwich, 11 June 1509

King Henry VIII married his brother Arthur's widow, Catherine of Aragon, in the church of the Franciscans at Greenwich today. The king is just 18 years old and the princess is five years older. The marriage has been much discussed since Prince Arthur's death in 1502, and the king has said that he decided to marry Catherine to fulfil his late father's dying wishes.

Princess Catherine, who will be crowned queen together with the king later this month, is the daughter of King Ferdinand of Aragon and the late Queen Isabella of Castile. Her nephew, Charles, will become the most powerful prince in Christendom: king of Spain, Duke of Burgundy and heir to the Holy Roman Emperor. An alliance with Spain will allow Henry VIII to face the hereditary enemy, France, if they should ever go to war again.

Catherine is exceedingly devout but is also highly educated, with a thorough grounding in the humanities. She speaks and writes excellent Latin and French as well as Spanish. Her English, however, leaves something to be desired. She is very intelligent and determined, and is also considered beautiful. The king is clearly in love with her and trusts her completely (→24/6).

Jousts and feasts celebrate coronation of new king and queen

Westminster, 24 June 1509

King Henry and Queen Catherine were crowned together today, in a most magnificent ceremony followed by the most splendid festivities that England has ever seen. The coronation followed ancient ritual, with the archbishop of Canterbury anointing and crowning the king and queen, and the assembled peers, prelates and commons of England shouting their assent when the heralds asked if they would take this most noble prince as their king.

After the ceremony there was a banquet in Westminster Hall, and the king's champion rode into the hall to challenge anyone who contested the king's right to the throne. Nobody did. Then began the ceremonial celebratory jousts, which will last for a week (→31/1/10).

Ceremonially crowned: a later 16th-century view of Henry's coronation.

Emperor gives superb armour to the king

London, 1511

The Holy Roman Emperor, Maximilian, has sent the king a magnificent suit of armour in recognition of his prowess at the joust. The king has held many tournaments since his accession, and the emperor had evidently heard of the king's enthusiasm for the sport. It is a suit of the finest German work, far beyond anything that can be made in England; the king has decided to establish a royal armoury in Southwark to remedy this defect.

A later engraving of the armour.

James launches world's biggest warship

Lothian, 12 October 1511

Colourful celebrations have marked the launch of the *Michael*, King James's latest addition to the already powerful Scottish fleet. Crowds gathered at Newhaven to watch as £30,000 worth of naval hardware slipped into the waves for the first time.

The *Michael* has taken five years to build at almost crippling expense. Vast amounts of timber, much of it imported from Norway, were used in the construction. The ship is almost 180 feet (54 metres) long, carries 27 cannons of varying sizes and 300 smaller guns and requires a crew of 470 men. She is expected to be very effective.

There is no other ship like the *Michael* in the world, and she serves as a potent symbol of the king's desire to enhance Scotland's international prestige. Rather ominously, however, she may soon be needed for active service. The threat of war is looming on the continent, with the English spoiling for a fight with James's close ally, Louis XII of France (→3/1512).

Henry leads his soldiers into France

Heir to throne dies aged seven weeks

Richmond, 22 February 1511
A great calamity has befallen the king and all England. Prince Henry, the heir to the throne, has died aged seven weeks. The celebrations marking the little prince's birth have been abruptly cancelled. This was the queen's second child; she had a stillborn daughter a year ago. When the prince was born, the king ordered a splendid tournament at Westminster and took part in the jousting himself while the queen watched. The fountains ran with wine; there were public banquets and all manner of rejoicing. The death is the first shadow on the reign of King Henry (→ 11/1513).

A later engraving of the great English victory at the "Battle of the Spurs".

Truce confirmed by a marriage alliance

Abbeville, France, 9 October 1514
An astonishing reversal in European alliances was sealed here today as Princess Mary, Henry VIII's younger sister, was married to King Louis XII of France. For two years England has been allied with Spain and Austria against France, and Mary was promised to Charles, the heir to Spain and the Holy Roman Empire. Now, suddenly, England is allied with the hereditary enemy. This is the first marriage between the French and English dynasties

Massive battleship launched by king

A later view of the "Great Harry".

Greenwich, 13 June 1514
The greatest battleship in the world, the *Henri Grace a Dieu*, popularly known as the "Great Harry", was christened here today by King Henry VIII. The whole court attended the magnificent ceremonies that marked the occasion. The Great Harry has five tiers of guns and five masts and was laid down two years ago. The king, like his father, has lavished much treasure on the navy. Henry VII encouraged exploration, including voyages to the New World. Henry VIII is not interested in such adventures but will use the navy for European wars and to protect the coasts and shipping lanes (→ 30/6).

English forces win 'Battle of the Spurs'

Tournai, France, 23 Sept 1513
Tournai surrendered to the allies today, and King Henry VIII plans a triumphant entry tomorrow. The war with France has gone well so far, at least in the north, with the capture of the fortress of Thérouanne a month ago and the defeat of the French cavalry at the "Battle of the Spurs" on August 16. There is no more time this year for further campaigning, however, and Tournai is not much to show for such a vast expedition.

The king hopes to emulate the exploits of Henry V and reconquer France. Like every king since Edward III, he calls himself king of France. He spent three years forming an alliance, with the support of Pope Julius II, and went to war even though Ferdinand of Spain had abandoned the alliance and

Holy Roman Emperor Maximilian had not provided the promised large army. Ferdinand undertook to invade southern France while Henry and Maximilian attacked from the north, but then made a separate peace with Louis XII. Undeterred, Henry landed at Calais with a large army on 30 June and marched 40 miles to Thérouanne, where Maximilian joined him.

The "Battle of the Spurs" won its name because the French cavalry fled without fighting, losing six standards and several important prisoners. When Thérouanne surrendered the king handed it over to the emperor, who razed it to the ground. This salutary example persuaded Tournai, a much more important town, to surrender when the king and the emperor arrived before its walls (→ 7/8/14).

Louis XII is married to Mary.

since Henry V married Catherine de Valois 100 years ago.

The war against France was unsuccessful despite some minor conquests last year. Ferdinand of Spain, the king's father-in-law, and Emperor Maximilian deserted the alliance. The new pope worked for peace with France. So did Thomas Wolsey, who argued that the costs of wars were enormous and the benefits slight.

The king accepted these arguments partly because he felt betrayed by Ferdinand and was determined on revenge. The new queen of France is 17. Louis is 52, toothless, sick and childless. If Mary does not provide a son, the crown will go to his cousin, Francis of Angoulême (→ 2/1515).

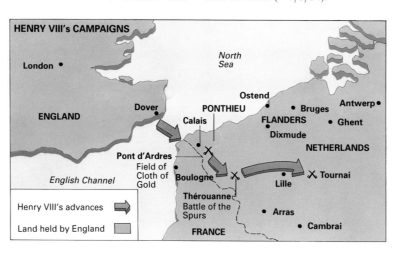

HENRY VIII's CAMPAIGNS

- London
- North Sea
- ENGLAND
- Dover
- Ostend
- PONTHIEU
- Bruges
- Antwerp
- Calais
- FLANDERS
- Ghent
- Dixmude
- NETHERLANDS
- Pont d'Ardres
- Field of Cloth of Gold
- English Channel
- Boulogne
- Tournai
- Lille
- Thérouanne Battle of the Spurs
- Arras
- FRANCE
- Cambrai
- Henry VIII's advances
- Land held by England

Scotland in chaos after king's death

The English rout the Scots at the Battle of Flodden Field: a later view.

Baby crowned, but Margaret in charge

Stirling, 21 September 1513

Scotland's new king has been crowned at Stirling castle. He is James V, a baby of 17 months, the only son of James IV, killed at Flodden just 12 days ago. The ceremony held in the Chapel Royal was a sombre occasion. The shock of Flodden has yet to sink in, not helped by the fact that James IV has not even been allowed Christian burial: the pope excommunicated him a year ago. Power in Scotland lies for now with a council of regency and the infant king's mother, Queen Margaret, a sister of Henry VIII of England (→6/8/14).

James IV is killed in battle at Flodden

Northumberland, 9 Sept 1513

King James has been killed along with most of his army at Flodden in Northumberland. The Scots king had crossed the border a fortnight ago in support of Louis XII of France, himself under attack from the English. This move has proved a tragic mistake, ending in what amounts to sheer massacre. As many as 10,000 Scots may have been killed, including James's illegitimate son Alexander, two abbots, nine earls and over a dozen lords. It was a defeat that should

never have happened. James's men were drawn up in a strong defensive position while the English, under the 70-year-old Earl of Surrey, were tired after their long forced march north.

But James, a courageous leader, charged down at the English when they tried to outmanoeuvre him. This left the Scots to slither about in the mud as the English used their short spears to deadly effect. James hacked his way to within feet of the Earl of Surrey before he too was cut down (→21/9).

James IV of Scotland has died.

Craftsmen put finishing touches to abbey's showpiece chapel

Westminster, 1515

Craftsmen working under the Florentine sculptor Pietro Torrigiano are completing the decoration of what is sure to be reckoned a masterpiece of church architecture: Henry VII's chapel in Westminster abbey. The late king had intended the new chapel for Henry VI, but instead he lies there himself alongside his queen, Elizabeth of York.

Henry VIII has seen the project to fruition, bringing the glories of the European artistic revival to England. Torrigiano is well qualified to do just that, being a man who was trained alongside Michelangelo –

whose nose he once broke. For the tomb of Henry and Elizabeth he has, for example, taken the Gothic convention of recumbent effigies on a rectangular chest and introduced typically Italian decoration such as the child angels at each corner. His combination of black and white marble with gilt bronze is, meanwhile, a complete innovation.

No previous king can have had a more magnificent resting-place. With its heraldic panels and graceful sculptures the chapel is intended to stand as a monument not only to the late king but also to the Tudor dynasty which his son is determined to establish.

Henry VII's chapel at Westminster.

Top royal adviser becomes a cardinal

The king's minister: Wolsey.

London, 10 September 1515

Thomas Wolsey, the archbishop of York, has been made cardinal by the pope. He is now unquestionably the king's chief minister. He is immensely industrious and self-assured, with sound judgement and a sharp eye for detail. He has worked with the king since his accession, first as almoner. In that capacity he stood in for the king in day-to-day administration while Henry hunted and jousted. Now he is so powerful that he is often called a second king. Wolsey is the son of an Ipswich grazier; he became a priest and rose through the church. He is the most splendid of prelates and has immense projects for palaces for himself and for the king (→12/7/21).

King rejects clerical demands on justice

London, November 1515

King Henry VIII has insisted that the clergy in England must obey English law unless they can appeal to a Roman canon based on divine law. In future, if English clergy want to appeal to Rome against an English court they must first obtain the king's permission. This curb on papal power follows a furore over a murder case. The king boasted: "By the ordnance and sufferance of God we, king of England, and the kings of England in times past, have never had any superior but God alone" (→12/7/21).

Baby princess to be christened Mary

Greenwich, 20 February 1516
King Henry VIII and Catherine of Aragon have at last produced a child who looks capable of surviving into adulthood. At an extravagant ceremony here the two-day-old princess was christened Mary. Today's christening comes nearly seven years after the newly-crowned king married the beautiful Catherine, the widow of his brother Arthur.

This glamorous royal couple have always seemed very much in love, but their efforts to have children have repeatedly failed. Their first child, a girl, was stillborn in 1510, then a second, the Duke of Cornwall, was born a year later and christened Henry amid much feasting, celebration and jousting. All seemed well; but the infant Henry died within two months. In 1513 another son was born but died within hours, and a year later the queen's third boy child was stillborn.

King Henry has pursued a flamboyant lifestyle, only breaking off from his favourite pursuits of sport and hunting to mount a campaign in France. He would be even more overjoyed to be christening a son as heir to the Tudor dynasty established by Henry VII (→ 10/11/18).

At the king's pleasure: an 18th-century engraving of Will Somers, Henry VIII's renowned and much-loved court jester.

Henry VIII misses out on emperorship

Frankfurt, 28 June 1519
Charles, the king of Spain, has been elected Holy Roman Emperor in succession to his Habsburg grandfather, Maximilian. King Henry of England entered the contest belatedly, with oblique encouragement from the pope, but his campaign was mismanaged, and he has now been emphatically put in his place.

Henry's ambitious attempt to succeed to the greatest office in Europe can be traced back to 1513 when Holy Roman Emperor Maximilian first suggested to the young English king that he might make him his heir in return for money and a division of European spoils. At the time Henry was engaged in campaigns in France and showed little interest. Three years later he rejected a similar scheme.

English foreign policy had changed after 1514, however, as the exchequer struggled to meet the cost of the French conflict. As King Francis, who had succeeded to the French throne in 1515, vied with England for influence with Spain and the emperor, Henry and Cardinal Wolsey began to explore ways of achieving influence through diplomacy. The Treaty of London in 1518, signed by France, Spain, England, the Holy Roman Empire and the papacy, was their triumph, providing that if any of the signatories were attacked the others would come to its protection.

Within a few months of Emperor Maximilian's death on 12 January this year, Henry began to consider himself as a potential emperor. Pope Leo was ostensibly supporting Francis, but he was concerned at the power that either Francis or his

The new emperor, Charles V.

A later portrait of King Francis.

main rival, Charles of Spain, might wield. Encouraged by a letter from the pope, Henry sent his ambassador, Richard Pace, to sound out the electors. But Pace persuaded few to vote for the English king. Wolsey must now start a new diplomatic effort to try to maintain his country's influence (→ 25/6/20).

Mistress gives king a healthy baby boy

London, 1519
King Henry VIII has fathered a son. Elizabeth Blount, his mistress for the past two years, gave birth recently to Henry Fitzroy. Although the bastard child is scarcely a plausible heir to the throne, his birth has reassured the king of his ability to produce male issue.

Yet this very fact is now likely to place increasing strain on his marriage to Catherine of Aragon, who has so far failed to produce a son for Henry. Five years his senior, she fears that she will soon be past the child-bearing age. There have already been problems between the king and queen, not only on account of Henry's infidelities but also because Catherine's father, King Ferdinand of Spain, betrayed the alliance with England against France (→ 18/6/25).

Race riots hit city

London, 2 May 1517
Violence erupted in the English capital yesterday when a mob of apprentices and young workmen began to attack the houses and workshops of Flemings and other foreigners living in the city. The attacks, alleged to have been incited by a Dominican friar, started in the parish of St Martin's, where several shops were plundered. The mayor of London sent immediately for the assistance of Lord Thomas Howard, the lord high admiral. When he arrived with several other lords and, more importantly, a large body of troops, the rioters were soon suppressed.

Scotland forges new marriage alliance with French royal family

France, 26 August 1517
The Scots and their old allies the French have signed a new treaty at Rouen. It promises to James V, Scotland's five-year-old king, at some point in the future, a bride from among the daughters of the French royal family. The treaty is the brainchild of John, the Duke of Albany, who was appointed governor of Scotland just two years ago. Since then John has had custody of the young king, in effect becoming his regent. Queen Margaret, the king's mother, was forced to give up being his guardian after she married the young Archibald Douglas, the sixth Earl of Angus, in 1514.

As this was barely a year after her husband James IV had been killed in the slaughter of Flodden, Margaret has hardly endeared herself to her people. She is also regarded with mistrust since she is the sister of Henry VIII of England and, not surprisingly, appears keen to increase his influence in Scottish affairs.

The Duke of Albany has his own ambitions, meanwhile. A grandson of James III, he is in fact the heir to the Scottish throne, although he is really more French than Scottish – he has lived all his life in France and speaks no English. Nonetheless he is welcome among Scots caught in the grip of anti-English sentiment following the catastrophic defeat at Flodden (→ 30/4/20).

Henry makes ostentatious peace with French rival

Summit is cloaked by 'cloth of gold'

Calais, 25 June 1520

The kings of England and France have concluded a meeting which has lasted for nearly three weeks in which each has tried to outdo the other in magnificence. The "Field of Cloth of Gold", as the ostentatious display of wealth has become known, was the brainchild of Henry VIII and Cardinal Wolsey, his chancellor. For the moment at least, the two kings seem to have set aside their traditional rivalry and sworn peace.

The election of Charles V of Spain as Holy Roman Emperor last year threatened to unravel the 1518 Treaty of London. But through Wolsey's mediation, the new emperor was persuaded to visit England last month, when he had a cordial, if inconclusive, meeting with the king. Henry's subsequent meeting with King Francis of France has required elaborate preparation to avoid noses being put out of joint.

The "Field of Cloth of Gold" has provided both kings with the chance to display their culture and good taste by showing off all their fine fabrics, furnishings and hangings. Jousts and sporting competitions have been followed by banquets believed to be the most sumptuous ever to have been staged in Europe. Despite all the extravagance this occasion has been useful, if only in proving that England and France need not be permanently at war with each other (→ 25/8/21).

King Henry aboard the "Great Harry", bound for talks with Francis of France at the "Field of Cloth of Gold".

Royal magnificence: the "Field of Cloth of Gold", near Calais, where King Henry and King Francis met.

A formal and courtly procession: King Henry and his councillors.

Henry backs moves to purge court fops

Westminster, May 1519

King Henry's court has been the subject of a purge. Leaders of the council took exception to the growing influence of young members of the king's privy chamber. With Henry's consent, several of the more foppish courtiers were removed from their posts and replaced by more venerable knights like Sir Richard Weston and Sir William King-ston. Sir John Pechey, Nicholas Carew and Francis Bryan were among the most prominent of the king's soulmates to be re-deployed to Calais, Ricebanke and elsewhere. They had mostly come from the French court and made fun of the staid ways of the English gentry. They were not suitable company for a king, the council insisted – and Henry agreed.

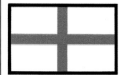

Henry VIII
1509–1547

James V
1513–1542

Scotland, 19 November 1521. The regent John, the Duke of Albany, has the support of the French as the new heir presumptive (→ 13/6/22).

France, 13 June 1522. King Francis ratifies the Treaty of Rouen with Scotland (→ 25/10).

Scotland, 16 November 1524. The Duke of Albany's regency is ended on his failure to return from France; this follows a coup in July in which Queen Margaret regained power (→ 3/26).

Europe, June 1525. Emperor Charles V repudiates the terms of the Treaty of Bruges.

Scotland, March 1526. Queen Margaret, now divorced from Archibald, the Earl of Angus, marries Henry Stewart, the Lord of Methven (→ 18/10/41).

England/France, 31 May 1526. After the French defeat in 1525, marriage negotiations reopen for Princess Mary to marry Henry, the Duke of Orleans, the second son of King Francis of France (→ 7/1527).

Lothian, 4 September 1526. Archibald, the Earl of Angus, who refused to release James V, has successfully defeated the Earl of Lennox and killed him in his bid to rescue the young Scottish king (→ 27/5/28).

England, May 1527. Henry makes known to Cardinal Wolsey his desire to divorce Queen Catherine (→ 22/6).

England, July 1527. Marriage plans for Princess Mary are abandoned due to uncertainty about her status after a divorce.

Stirling, 27 May 1528. King James V of Scots makes his escape from Archibald, the Earl

of Angus, and flees to Stirling castle (→ 6/7).

Greenwich, 25 October 1529. King Henry appoints Sir Thomas More as his new lord chancellor (→ 30/10).

London, 21 January 1530. Thomas Boleyn, the father of Anne, plans to visit Rome to ask the pope to agree to the king's divorce (→ 9/1530).

Windsor, 14 July 1531. Henry gives up all pretence of treating Catherine as his queen; he departs for Woodstock with Anne Boleyn, leaving Catherine behind (→ 25/1/32).

Rome, 25 January 1532. Henry is threatened by the pope with excommunication (→ 16/5/32).

Scotland, May 1532. James V receives news that Holy Roman Emperor Charles V has created him a "Knight of the Golden Fleece" (→ 1/2/37).

England, 1 September 1532. Henry bestows the title of Marchioness of Pembroke on Anne Boleyn (→ 25/1/33).

London, 25 January 1533. Henry secretly marries his pregnant mistress, Anne Boleyn (→ 1/6/33).

Suffolk, 25 June 1533. Henry's sister, Mary Tudor, the wife of Charles, the Duke of Suffolk, dies (→ 10/1537).

Greenwich, 7 September 1533. The newly-crowned Queen Anne gives birth to a daughter, Elizabeth (→ 30/3/34).

Hatfield, 17 December 1533. Princess Mary, now classed as illegitimate, is to live with her young stepsister under a form of house arrest (→ 7/1536).

Henry VIII has treacherous duke executed

Tower Hill, 17 May 1521
Edward Stafford, the Duke of Buckingham, was beheaded today for high treason. Buckingham was a proud aristocrat and landowner who was descended from Thomas of Woodstock, the youngest son of Edward III, and related by marriage to the powerful Percy, Pole and Howard families. His execution proves that royal authority cannot be challenged by even the mightiest nobleman.

Once a close companion of the king, Buckingham had estates all over England and Wales and entertained lavishly. But he was foolhardy. From his surveyor, Charles Knyvet, Cardinal Wolsey, the chancellor, learned of a meeting in 1514 between the duke and a prior called Nicholas Hopkins who had prophesied Buckingham's accession to the throne. Knyvet gave evidence that the duke had on another occasion declared his intention of killing the king. Other servants gave evidence against him.

The unsuspecting duke came to London in response to a royal

Edward, the Duke of Buckingham.

summons last month and was arrested on his way down the Thames. Four days ago he was tried by his peers at Westminster, found guilty and sentenced to death by the lord steward, the Duke of Norfolk.

Scottish governor seeks French backing

John, the Duke of Albany.

Strathclyde, 25 October 1522
John, the Duke of Albany and governor of Scotland, has set sail from Dumbarton on his way to France. Once there he will ask for military aid against the English. This is the latest move in the long-running power game between Albany's pro-French faction and the pro-English one led by Queen Margaret and the

Douglasses. So far the duke has had the upper hand, but he has still to unite the country behind him. Back in July he mustered a large army with the intention of invading England – but nothing happened. French promises of military aid were not fulfilled and, to Albany's great embarrassment, the Scottish nobility refused to cross the border.

This was not cowardice but caution. For the Scots, an invasion of England means massive expense and great military risk. No one has forgotten the massacre of Flodden nine years ago. And, in any case, why should the Scots pay with their blood to further the aims of the king of France?

Last month Scotland and England signed yet another truce, so the border should remain quiet for the meantime. Yet the pro-English party has not given up. Archibald Douglas, the Earl of Angus, and Queen Margaret separated some time ago, after they fled to England, but Douglas and his pro-English allies are still a force to be reckoned with (→ 16/11/24).

Alliance is forged to fight the French

Bruges, 25 August 1521

Cardinal Wolsey and Holy Roman Emperor Charles V have negotiated a complicated and secret treaty preparing for war against France. Wolsey and his king have tried to maintain friendly relations with France despite King Francis's aggression against the empire. Indeed, Wolsey is now on his way back to Calais ostensibly to resume a peace conference with the French.

The Treaty of Bruges is to be endorsed by a marriage between Charles and Henry VIII's daughter Princess Mary. The treaty gives the emperor the support that he wants but postpones any direct English involvement in a European war for at least 22 months (→6/1525).

Tax failure dooms king's war plans

Westminster, summer 1525

King Henry has won the gratitude of his people by cancelling the so-called "Amicable Loan", raised by Wolsey to help pay for the war against France. The Duke of Suffolk was defeated in his winter campaign of 1523 to capture Paris, and the real glory went to England's ally, Holy Roman Emperor Charles V. He defeated and captured the French king, Francis, at Pavia in February of this year, thereby completely upstaging Henry's efforts. Henry's failure to raise fresh funds through the Amicable Loan seems certain to end the war effort.

King Francis, by Titian (d.1576).

King and Wolsey attack Luther's theology

King Henry and Cardinal Wolsey, by Sir John Gilbert (1817-1897).

England, 12 July 1521

King Henry VIII has published a detailed rebuttal of Lutheran heresies under the title *Assertio Septem Sacramentorum*. The king's book is dedicated to Pope Leo, who is understood to be discussing with his cardinals the possibility of conferring a new title on Henry to match those boasted by the kings of Spain and France.

Publication of the *Assertio* is the latest volley in Henry's and Wolsey's campaign against Lutheranism [*see panel below*]. Two months

ago there was a solemn ceremony outside St Paul's cathedral: John Fisher preached against heresy, followed by the public burning of some of Luther's works. Wolsey sat amongst the distinguished audience clutching a manuscript copy of the king's book.

Henry's work, aided by scholars, is a conventional defence of the sacraments, the authority of the pope and the indissolubility of marriage, and a condemnation of schisms such as Lutheranism within the church (→5/1527).

How Lutheranism challenged the church

Europe, 1525

The teachings of Martin Luther are gaining increasing currency in England. Luther emerged as a public critic of the church in 1517 when he posted a list of 95 theses on a church door at Wittenberg in Germany. These criticised the church for its use of indulgences and argued that

priests should not stand between men and the teachings of the Bible. This challenge to the authority of the established church was followed by a denial of transubstantiation – the doctrine that, at the moment of consecration by the priest, the bread and wine of the Mass become the body and blood of Christ.

Illegitimate son is given a dukedom

England, 18 June 1525

Henry Fitzroy, the six-year-old bastard son of King Henry by his former mistress Elizabeth Blount, has been created the first Duke of Richmond. The title echoes that of the boy's grandfather, Henry Tudor, who was the second Earl of Richmond until he became Henry VII after the Battle of Bosworth.

Fitzroy's ennoblement is a clear attempt by the king to make him a plausible heir, as otherwise the throne will pass to Henry's only daughter, Mary. As she may soon marry Emperor Charles V, under the terms of the Treaty of Bruges, this could make England a mere outpost of the Holy Roman Empire (→22/7/36).

Henry Fitzroy: a later engraving.

Princess Mary gets control of Marches

Greenwich, July 1525

Mary Tudor, the only daughter of Henry VIII and heir to the throne, is to leave her mother's quarters in Greenwich palace and proceed to Ludlow castle, the centre of royal authority in the Marches, to become the first Princess of Wales.

She has been given her own household and a personal bodyguard. But, even though she is only nine years old, she is to be deprived of her mother's company until the current dispute between Henry and Queen Catherine has been settled. The princess, acting for the king, will seek full and personal control over the whole of Wales (→31/5/26).

Marriage is over, Henry tells queen

London, 22 June 1527

After sharing his bed with her for 18 years, Henry VIII today told Catherine of Aragon that they have never been truly man and wife. He plans to ask the pope to revoke the dispensation which permitted their marriage; she was the wife of Henry's elder brother, Arthur, and was widowed at the age of 17.

Henry married her two months after he succeeded to the throne. She bore six children, five of whom were stillborn or soon died. The surviving child, Princess Mary, is now eleven years old. These pregnancy disasters persuaded Henry that he had committed a sin by marrying Catherine, and he has taken to quoting the book of Leviticus, which says: "If a man shall take his brother's wife, it is an impurity; he hath uncovered his brother's nakedness; they shall be childless." But Catherine's supporters are ready to hit back with a quotation from Deuteronomy: "When brethren dwell together, and one of them dieth without children ... his brother shall take the wife and raise up seed for his brother."

Catherine is said to have shown herself "very stiff and obstinate" about the matter. She said that, in spite of her marriage to Arthur, she was still a virgin when she married Henry, so the question of an incestuous union, as Henry had expressed it, did not arise. She also insists that she will not agree to a course of action that would make Mary a bastard and remove her from the direct line of succession.

Whether Henry ever loved Catherine or merely wished to avoid returning the dowry that his brother had received from Ferdinand and Isabella hardly matters now. He desperately wants a son and heir, and he is infatuated with the 26-year-old Anne Boleyn (→3/8).

A portrait of Princess Mary later in life, with King Henry and the jester Will Somers, by the court artist Hans Holbein.

King bewitched by the beauty of his mistress, Anne Boleyn

London, 3 August 1527

The latest gossip at court, that Anne Boleyn is a witch, has done nothing to cool the king's ardour for the raven-haired beauty whose vivacity and polished manners were acquired during a spell with the French royal family. When she returned to England she quickly attracted Henry's attention, and he at once transferred his affections from her sister, Mary, his mistress.

Anne, however, has no intention of repeating her sister's mistake. She readily accepts the torrent of expensive jewellery that the king is pouring out – today's gift is an emerald ring – but she intends to keep him at arm's length until he is free to marry. As for her father, Sir Thomas Boleyn, he is beside himself at the thought of having a queen for a daughter.

The talk of her being a witch began when it was noticed that, despite her great beauty – the almond-shaped mouth and eyes and the slender neck – she has a disfigured hand with a rudimentary sixth finger. In the past she had managed to conceal this, but now that she is the focus of attention at court this birth defect can no longer remain hidden (→16/7/29).

The king's new love: Anne Boleyn.

James reaches the age of sixteen and asserts full control

Lothian, 6 July 1528

James V has at last been able to make himself king in deed and not just in name. He has entered Edinburgh at the head of an army of his supporters and put to flight Archibald Douglas, the earl of Angus. Douglas was supposed to be the 16-year-old king's regent, but for the last three years he has in fact held him captive. Now the tables are turned, and it is the Douglasses and their allies who face imprisonment.

The misery of the young king's childhood now seems to be past. He was brought up virtually without friends, his father dead and his mother remarried to a man whom he detested – the same Douglas whom he ousted today. First his mother was his guardian, then the Duke of Albany, until his hated stepfather took him four years ago.

In 1524 the Duke of Albany lost his title of governor of Scotland when a palace coup brought to power the pro-English faction under Queen Margaret. Four earls, including Douglas, were to take turns at looking after James, but Douglas refused to give him up at the appointed time. By now divorced from Margaret, he was in the pay of her brother, Henry VIII of England. James was caught up in other people's power games, but in May this year he managed to escape from Douglas – and is now in control of his own destiny (→5/1532).

Sweating sickness puts court to flight

London, May 1528

The king and his court have fled from London this spring after an outbreak of a disease known as the "sweating sickness". The disease strikes with appalling speed, with its victims usually dying within five or six hours of experiencing the first symptoms. One of the casualties was Sir Francis Paynes, a member of the court. Normal life in the city has been brought to a halt as the disease has spread. Parliament has been adjourned and the law courts have been suspended.

Wolsey, fallen from favour, is stripped of all his powers

London, 30 October 1529

Thomas, Cardinal Wolsey, was at Henry's side from the first days of the king's reign. He became lord chancellor and a member of the privy council and acquired several wealthy bishoprics; he was the most powerful man in England after the king and, indeed, was known as *alter rex*, the other king. Now he has been stripped of his positions of power and packed off to York to do the job of archbishop.

As papal legate with a direct line to the pope Wolsey seemed well placed to persuade Clement VII to annul Henry's marriage to Catherine of Aragon. But Rome is in turmoil after the Habsburg Charles V sacked the city, and since Charles is Catherine's nephew there was never a chance of his succeeding. Henry lost patience; Wolsey has been found gound guilty of usurping the powers of the sovereign.

Wolsey, the son of an Ipswich butcher and grazier, delighted in playing the autocrat – he compelled bishops to tie his shoes and dukes to hold his wash-basin – and his fall is gratifying, not least to Anne Boleyn and her scheming family. Those who have seen Wolsey in recent days say that he is a broken man and, at the age of 55, has lost the will to live (→1530).

Royal clash with church draws closer

Queen Catherine and the cardinals, by the Victorian artist Sir John Gilbert.

Cardinal stalls verdict of powerless court

Blackfriars, 16 July 1529

The king has been frustrated once again in his bid to rid himself of his wife, Catherine of Aragon. The legatine court, appointed by the pope to hear Henry's appeal for annulment and sitting at Blackfriars, has been under pressure from Henry to reach a quick decision. But the pope's representative, Lorenzo, Cardinal Campeggio, has secret orders from Rome to stall the proceedings, and today, at last, he succeeded in getting an adjourn-ment until October. At this, the Duke of Suffolk banged the table and cried: "There never was a cardinal that did good for England."

Catherine has been demanding that Pope Clement VII should give orders for the case to be heard in Rome – a demand backed by her nephew, the Habsburg Charles V. Under these pressures Clement, in near despair, has retreated to his sick-bed, where he has signed the order revoking the powers of the Blackfriars court (→30/10/29).

Scholar engaged to argue for divorce

Waltham, Essex, September 1530

A chance encounter in a lodging-house has brought Henry an ingenious idea for getting round the pope's unwillingness to annul the royal marriage. This summer the sweating sickness drove Thomas Cranmer, a lecturer in divinity at Cambridge, to seek refuge here in the Essex countryside; the king happened to be visiting nearby, and his lord high almoner, Edward Fox, was staying in the same house as Cranmer.

Conversation turned on the royal marriage problems, and Cranmer suggested that if the universities and specialists in canon law should decide that Henry's marriage to his brother's widow was illegal then the ordinary ecclesiastical courts could declare the marriage null and

Thomas Cranmer: a later portrait.

void and there would be no cause to appeal to Rome.

An excited Fox went off to tell the king, who sent for Cranmer and ordered him to drop everything and prepare a treatise supporting his arguments with quotations from the scriptures. Cranmer will live with Anne Boleyn's father, now the Earl of Wiltshire, while working on the treatise. The king has also made him one of his chaplains and appointed him archdeacon of Taunton. It is already being said that Cranmer will soon be made archbishop of Canterbury (→11/2/31).

King takes over Wolsey's palatial residence at Hampton Court

The king's new residence: Hampton Court palace, begun by Wolsey in 1515.

Hampton Court, 1530

The king is moving house. He is taking over the magnificent 1,800-room Hampton Court palace built by Cardinal Wolsey beside the Thames 15 years ago. The palace, with its roofline of turrets, pinnacles and curlicued chimney stacks, is set amid a huge garden with painted dragons and unicorns. There, the cardinal entertained in style to impress foreign visitors.

When he began to lose favour at court, he made the grand gesture of deeding the palace to Henry. In vain. Shorn of all his once great power, he died a few weeks ago at Leicester as he was being taken to the Tower. Henry is now busy renovating the palace.

King and clergy thrash out fudged deal on leadership

London, 11 February 1531

The king's attempt to browbeat the English clergy into repudiating papal authority and accepting him as head of both church and state has ended, for the time being, with a fudged compromise and a play on words. Thwarted by the pope, who refuses to annul his marriage to Catherine of Aragon, Henry VIII is persuaded that he can settle the matter at home by bringing the clergy to heel.

When the convocations of York and Canterbury met he stunned the assembled bishops by announcing that they and their fellow clerics were all guilty of *praemunire* – usurping the royal authority by accepting the jurisdiction of Rome in religious matters. However, he would pardon them if they paid a fine of £100,000 and acknowledged him as "Protector and only Supreme Head of the Church and Clergy of England".

After lengthy discussions, the clerics submitted with the caution that the king was supreme head of the Church only "as far as the law of Christ allows". Henry went on to claim that the "cure of souls" belonged to him; the clerics shuffled the words around, and the king was left merely "caring" for those whose souls were the responsibility of the clergy (→ 28/11/34).

Henry's mistress is crowned queen

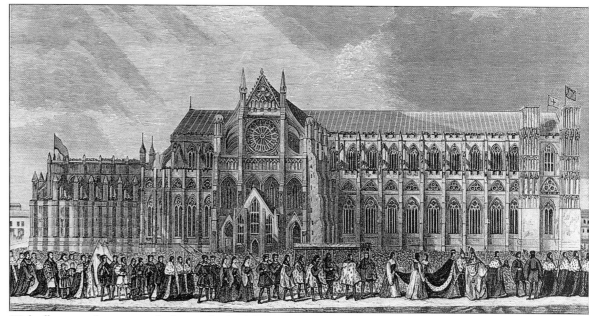

With all state and ceremony: the long and splendid coronation procession for Queen Anne (a later engraving).

Westminster, 1 June 1533

The king had been determined to turn this Whit Sunday coronation of Anne Boleyn into such a spectacle of royal magnificence as would prove irresistible to the citizens of London. She paraded through the City with a richly apparelled company of lords, knights and gentlemen, and the Lord Mayor presented her with purse of cloth of gold containing 1,000 gold marks. But the crowds were noticeably subdued, and Anne's advanced state of pregnancy, which was all too evident, did nothing to help. It

has been a race against time. At the turn of the year, when Anne told Henry that she was pregnant, he was still married to Catherine of Aragon. His increasingly frantic appeals to the pope brought the cynical advice from Clement VII, a Medici, that Henry should forget about marrying Anne and keep her on as his mistress.

Henry's chance came when the see of Canterbury became vacant and he appointed as archbishop Thomas Cranmer, the cleric who had first suggested to the king that he had no need of the pope's dis-

pensation to end his marriage to Catherine. Cranmer was appointed on 23 January this year, and the next day Henry and Anne were secretly married. An act of parliament ending appeals to Rome was passed in April; the marriage was made public just three days ago.

In Westminster abbey Cranmer anointed Anne and placed the crown on her head. The banquet afterwards proved a considerable ordeal; two ladies-in-waiting sat under the table with chamber-pots to accommodate her frequent need to relieve herself (→ 8/1533).

Protestant princes want to be friends

Schmalkalden, Saxony, 1531

A small town in Germany has become the rallying-point for protests against the excesses of the Catholic Church: the Schmalkaldic League, launched by Philip of Hesse and John Constant of Saxony and joined by leaders from free German cities, is now seeking England as an ally in the fight to defend the reforms of Martin Luther against the threat from the Catholic Holy Roman Emperor Charles. Despite his quarrel with Rome over his marriage problems, Henry VIII, who still thinks of himself as a Catholic, is unlikely to join the league.

Thomas More resigns as royal chancellor

Sir Thomas More: a later portrait.

London, 16 May 1532

For Sir Thomas More it was the last straw. Yesterday the convocations of Canterbury and York surrendered to pressure from the king and parliament and accepted that Henry VIII, rather than the pope, has final authority over the English church. Today, after a night of struggle with his conscience, More handed the king the Great Seal of his office and retired to private life. He has expressed his own doubts about the claim that papal supremacy is divinely ordained, but he is firmly opposed to Henry's manipulation of the church in order to divorce Catherine of Aragon and marry Anne Boleyn (→ 13/4/34).

Catherine is placed under house arrest

Buckden, Cambs, July 1533

A high-powered delegation led by Lord Mountjoy called on Catherine of Aragon to surrender her title of queen and agree to become Princess Dowager. Henry's new wife, Anne Boleyn, was crowned queen last month, so there are now two queens of England. Catherine firmly rejected Mountjoy's proposition and, on the king's orders, she was placed under house arrest at Buckden in Cambridgeshire, with ten ladies-in-waiting, a physician, an apothecary and a chaplain. Her plea to be allowed to see her daughter Mary has been rejected (→ 7/1/36).

Henry severs links with Rome to take over church

London, August 1533

The king's break with Rome has become an accomplished fact with Henry's defiant rejection of an ultimatum from Pope Clement VII. Only a few weeks ago Clement had given formal confirmation to the appointment of Thomas Cranmer as archbishop of Canterbury. Now Cranmer has repudiated papal authority and given the king something that he has been pursuing and the pope has been refusing for more than five years: the annulment of the marriage to Catherine.

When news of Cranmer's perfidy reached Rome, Clement was outraged; he told Henry that he would be excommunicated if he refused to take back his discarded queen.

Henry has responded with a series of punitive measures. He has activated an act of parliament, the "Restraint in Annates", which cuts off all church payments to Rome. Another blow is the "Restraint in Appeals", which gives the king "whole and entire" authority to reject judgements, interdicts and excommunications from Rome. Although there is little sign of popular opposition to Henry's defiance of Rome, he is anxious both to give his rule legitimacy and to counter claims such as that from the so-called "Nun of Kent", famous for her prophetic utterances, who has said that with his marriage to Anne Boleyn Henry ceases to be king in the eyes of God (→ 7/9).

Royal divorce made official by statute

Westminster, 30 March 1534

Nine months after Henry VIII announced his marriage to Anne Boleyn and six months after she gave birth to a daughter, Elizabeth, parliament has finally given legal endorsement to the marriage. The Act of Succession rules that all leading figures of church and state must take an oath of allegiance to Anne and accept Elizabeth, and any other children Anne may have, as heirs to the throne. The act makes it high treason to slander the marriage.

The act also annuls Henry's marriage to Catherine of Aragon and bastardises her daughter Mary. A judgement on these issues was made last year by the church at the instigation of Thomas Cranmer, the archbishop of Canterbury. Now the civil act provides a legal framework for rooting out dissidents loyal to Catherine. Two men certain to be taken to the Tower are Sir Thomas More, who resigned as lord chancellor over the Boleyn affair, and John Fisher, Catherine's confessor.

More, the author of *Utopia*, the picture of an ideal state, is widely respected in England, but it is the fate of Fisher that is of greater import. By striking at a leading churchman, Henry has delivered a public affront to Rome; it seems certain that this will make the pope issue the bull prepared in secret for Henry's excommunication.

The man behind Henry's drive for supremacy is Thomas Cromwell, the brewer's son who travelled widely in Europe before joining the staff of Cardinal Wolsey; when he replaced Wolsey as royal counsellor he urged Henry to cut all links with Rome and assume supreme power over his church (→ 22/6/35).

King Henry VIII, who has rejected the authority of the pope in Rome.

King to be head of the English church

Westminster, 28 November 1534

It began with Henry VIII, a loyal Catholic, seeking help from Rome to rid himself of a wife who had failed to produce a son and heir. It has erupted in revolution with consequences which, in the words of the apostle Paul, we can as yet only see through a glass darkly, but which seem certain to change the course of history.

In two marathon sessions, parliament has enacted measures which recognise the king as "the only supreme head in earth of the Church of England" and give him wide-ranging powers to control "all honours, dignities, privileges, immunities, profits and commodities" in a rich and powerful church that now owes no scrap of allegiance to the pope. Indeed, the law of heresy has been changed to allow attacks on papal authority. Common-law safeguards, such as the two-witness rule and hearings in open court, are to be enforced in ecclesiastical trials. The road to reformation, espoused by Anne Boleyn and her family, is wide open.

None of this could have been foreseen when Clement VII, instead of doing as other popes had done and obliging a friendly monarch, began vacillating because Catherine of Aragon stubbornly refused to allow her marriage to be broken up and her daughter Mary declared illegitimate; she also had the support of her nephew, Holy Roman Emperor Charles, who, having occupied Rome, had the pope under his thumb. Catherine lost, but Mary is only 18; should she ever approach the throne, England's return to Rome would extinguish her alleged illegitimacy.

1535–1547

Henry VIII
1509–1547

James V
1513–1542
Mary, Queen
of Scots
1542–1567

London, 22 June 1535. Cardinal John Fisher, arrested by Henry for his refusal to accept the Act of Succession, is executed.

London, summer 1535. Queen Anne is reported to be pregnant again (→29/1/36).

Hampton Court, 1536. Henry adds a great hall to the palace.

Kimbolton, 7 January 1536. Catherine of Aragon, the divorced wife of Henry, dies.

Greenwich, 29 January 1536. Anne gives birth prematurely to a stillborn son (→30/4).

England, 10 February 1536. Henry, desperate for an heir, turns his attention towards Jane Seymour, one of the queen's ladies-in-waiting (→30/5).

London, 30 April 1536. Queen Anne is arrested on charges of adultery and incest (→19/5).

Westminster, July 1536. The princesses Mary and Elizabeth are declared to be illegitimate following Henry's third marriage, to Jane Seymour, the sister of Edward Seymour.→

London, 22 July 1536. Henry Fitzroy, the Duke of Richmond and illegitimate son of Henry, dies of consumption.

Scotland/France, 1 Jan 1537. King James V marries Madeleine, the daughter of Francis of France (→7/7).

Leicester, October 1537. Lady Jane Grey, a granddaughter of the Duke of Suffolk and Mary Tudor and a claimant to the throne, is born (→5/1553).

London, 12 November 1537. Jane Seymour, who died last month, is buried.

Fife, 10 June 1538. Mary of Guise, who married James V by proxy on 4 May, arrives to join her husband (→6/1/40).

Surrey, 1538. Henry begins to build a lavish palace, to be called Nonsuch, near Cheam (→1545).

Hampton Court, 6 Oct 1539. Henry, under protest, agrees to marry Anne, the sister of the Duke of Cleves (→6/1/40).

Scotland, 22 May 1540. Queen Mary gives birth to her first son, James (→8/12/42).

Lambeth, June 1540. After his disastrous fourth marriage, to Anne of Cleves, Henry has a new mistress, Catherine Howard, the niece of the Duke of Norfolk (→28/7).

Westminster, 9 July 1540. Thomas Cromwell is arrested on a charge of treason (→28/7).

Scotland, 18 October 1541. Margaret Tudor, the mother of James V of Scots, dies.

Middlesex, 14 November 1541. Queen Catherine Howard, the king's fifth wife, is arrested on a charge of adultery (→10/12).

Scotland, 8 December 1542. Queen Mary gives birth to a daughter, Mary (→14/12).

England/Scotland, 1 July 1543. The Treaty of Greenwich is agreed; Mary Queen of Scots will marry Prince Edward, in this way uniting the two royal houses (→6/1544).

London, 1545. Henry establishes the "Master of Revels" to censor theatrical performances.

Westminster, 28 January 1547. Henry VIII dies; his son, Prince Edward, succeeds him (→31/1).

Anne Boleyn is executed

London, 19 May 1536
The queen of England has been executed today for treason, adultery and incest. Dressed in black, yet witty to the end, Anne Boleyn told the 2,000 nobles, notables and guards assembled on Tower Green: "The king has been good to me. He promoted me from a simple maid to a marchioness. Then he raised me to be a queen. Now he will raise me to be a martyr." Then the executioner, brought over from France at her own request, seized the two-handed sword that had been hidden beneath a pile of straw and severed her head with a single stroke.

It is nearly three years since she left the Tower to be crowned queen in Westminster abbey. Three months later she gave birth to a girl, Elizabeth, but she failed to produce a male heir. When she gave birth to a stillborn son last January, Henry turned his attentions to one of her ladies-in-waiting, Jane Seymour.

Conservative courtiers, quick to seize an opportunity to damage the Protestant and (in their eyes) unlawful queen, spoke of Anne indulging in witchcraft to prevent

Anne Boleyn executed: a later view.

Henry from siring a male heir, and of the stillborn baby as a punishment from God for an incestuous affair with her brother, Lord Rochford. Others whispered to the king the names of her alleged lovers.

On 2 May she was taken to the Tower where, after a hearing by a court presided over by her uncle, the Duke of Norfolk, Queen Anne and her alleged lovers were sentenced to death.

Cromwell takes over as top royal aide

London, April 1534
Thomas Cromwell, the man who promised to make Henry the richest king to reign in England, has been appointed principal secretary and chancellor of the exchequer. He is now the most powerful man in England after the king.

Born 49 years ago, the son of an innkeeper, he studied the law and spent eight years on the continent, serving as a mercenary in the Italian wars. By 1514 he was being employed by Wolsey, who arranged for his election to parliament in 1523, and he was Wolsey's chief agent in the dissolution of some minor religious houses in 1525.

Wolsey's fall meant Cromwell's rise, and he was quick to tell the king what he wanted to know, that he could divorce Queen Catherine and declare himself head of the church. He further endeared himself to Henry by his masterful handling of parliament and his ability to increase the income of the crown and establish a sound bureaucracy,

THOMAS CROMWELL.

The king's man: Thomas Cromwell.

matters which the king finds tedious when he is content.

Discontented, however, the king is liable to visit his wrath on his ministers, and none is more likely to feel that wrath than the man who has concentrated so much power in his own hands (→9/7/40).

Jane Seymour is Henry's new queen

Queen Jane, by Holbein (d.1543).

London, 30 May 1536

King Henry VIII married his third queen, Jane Seymour, today at a quiet ceremony in the queen's closet at Whitehall palace. He had proposed to her the day after the previous queen, Anne, had been executed for treason, adultery and incest earlier this month.

Jane had been lady-in-waiting to both Queen Catherine and Queen Anne. The king first noticed her last summer when her father, Sir John Seymour, was entertaining him at his house, Wolf Hall, in Wiltshire. In January, during Anne's confinement, Henry sent Jane "dishonourable proposals", accompanied by a purse full of sovereigns. Jane, quietly ambitious and encouraged by the king's chief minister, Thomas Cromwell, to seek a crown, had no intention of becoming a short-lived mistress and sent back his letters and gifts unopened. By the spring Henry was bored by Anne, who had been unable to produce a living male heir, and obsessed with Jane. He has always had a preference for women with childlike faces. Jane, though 27, has the face of a 13-year-old.

The marriage is a blow to both the conservative Catholics, who supported Queen Catherine, and the Protestant hard-liners, who saw Queen Anne as their champion. It is a victory for Thomas Cromwell and the cause of dynastic expediency. With both Henry's previous wives dead – Queen Catherine died last January – the king and court are now praying for a legitimate male heir (→ 7/1536).

Mary and Elizabeth made illegitimate

London, July 1536

Princesses Mary and Elizabeth have been declared illegitimate by a second Act of Succession. Princess Mary, already bastardised by parliament's first Act of Succession (which named Princess Elizabeth as heir to the throne), is now joined by her half-sister, who is also declared illegitimate.

England's new heir will be the offspring of King Henry's third marriage, to the present queen, Jane. In the event of the queen failing to produce a male heir, the king will have the extraordinary constitutional right of nominating a successor of his choosing. It is thought that the king, when he conceived the act, planned to name his 17-year-old illegitimate son, the Duke of Richmond, as his heir, but the duke is now dying of consumption and has only weeks to live.

All hopes rest on the king successfully impregnating Queen Jane, and on her then producing a boy. Should she fail, or should Henry die without naming a successor, civil war is likely, with the Catholics and the conservatives supporting the claims of Mary, and the radicals and the Protestants supporting those of Elizabeth (→ 15/1/40).

Queen Jane dies after producing a son

Hampton Court, 24 October 1537

Queen Jane died here today, just 12 days after producing the long-awaited male heir, Prince Edward. King Henry's third queen, and almost as popular amongst the people as his first, Jane will be buried in St George's chapel at Windsor.

The king was not with her when she gave birth to Prince Edward. The plague had driven him to Esher. When he heard the news, he rode exuberantly to Hampton Court, ordered banquets and proclaimed celebrations throughout the land.

Although the king's principal minister, Thomas Cromwell, puts the queen's death down to eating "things that her fancy called for", the chances are that she died of postnatal fever. Today the king's emotions see-saw between profound sorrow at losing Jane and deep relief at having finally produced a male heir.

Jane was 27 years old when she became queen in May 1536. She was a daughter of Sir John Seymour, the warden of Savernake Forest near Marlborough in Wiltshire, and had been a lady-in-waiting to Queen Catherine and Queen Anne. Patient and discreet, outwardly modest, she had the knack of appearing to be all things to all people. She did much to

The longed-for heir: Edward, the son of Henry and Jane Seymour.

reconcile the king with his daughter Mary, though those who know her suggest this was motivated as much by the desire to offset the claims of her future children's rival, Elizabeth, as by disinterested benevolence.

She allied herself with neither conservatives nor radicals, while both groups saw her as their ally. She humoured the ever-demanding king. And she was popular with Londoners, who will always remember her gamely riding across the frozen Thames last January with the king (→ 12/11).

Monastery closures spark 'pilgrimage of grace' protests

An allegorical print showing King Henry, helped by Thomas Cranmer, trampling Pope Clement underfoot.

Doncaster, November 1536

Forty thousand men are on the march in Yorkshire this month as protests grow over the king's moves to close down the monasteries and seize their wealth. The protesters claim that they are not rebelling against Henry. They call their campaign, which started a month ago in Lincolnshire, a "pilgrimage of grace". But it is unlikely that the king will view with much sympathy their demands for the reunion of the English church with Rome, the restoration of Princess Mary as the rightful heir and the dismissal of Thomas Cromwell (→ 9/12/38).

James's frail queen dies at age of 16

Lothian, 7 July 1537

The Scottish court is in mourning following the death today of Queen Madeleine, a mere two months after her arrival in Scotland. A daughter of the French King Francis, she had been married to James V for just seven months. Although only 16 years old, Madeleine had a history of poor health. James chose her for his bride, invoking the Treaty of Rouen which entitled him to a daughter of the king of France, when he found out that his first choice, Marie of Vendôme, was a hunchback. James may have lost his young queen, but at least he keeps the huge dowry – 100,000 *livres* of it (→ 10/6/38).

Henry executes his treacherous cousin

London, 9 December 1538
Henry Courtenay, the Marquis of Exeter, and Lord Montagu, the head of the ancient Pole family, were executed for treason on Tower Green this morning. Courtenay was a grandson of Edward IV and a cousin of the king. Lord Montagu was the elder brother of Cardinal Reginald Pole. They were charged with treason and with conspiring with the exiled cardinal to persuade Holy Roman Emperor Charles V, a nephew of the late Queen Catherine, to take military action to enforce the bull of deposition just issued by the papacy.

The two noblemen represented the old religion and the old social order and were seen by conservatives as the leaders of Catholic reaction in the west country. Their deaths – together with the executions of the leaders of the Pilgrimage of Grace, Lords Darcy and Hussey and Sir Robert Constable, all scions of the great feudal families of the north – have effectively destroyed the conservative opposition. This is a triumph for the king's minister, Thomas Cromwell, who is in any case anxious to bypass the old feudal political structures, of which these men were representatives, and create a more modern centralised bureaucracy (→ 8/5/39).

Continental rulers threaten to invade

London, 8 May 1539
As England prepares for invasion by France and Germany, King Henry reviewed the London Trained Bands at St James's today. The thousands of militiamen assembled in Whitechapel and marched past the Tower and through the City to Westminster.

Since 12 January, when King Francis and Emperor Charles concluded their pact at Toledo, settling their differences in preparation for war against heretical England, parapets have been dug, blockhouses built and militias mustered. What effect these shopkeepers in harness will have on the mercenaries of the Holy Roman Empire is, however, open to question (→ 6/10).

Henry weds fourth wife

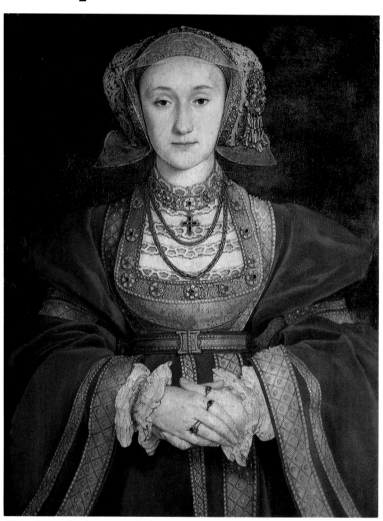

Henry's new bride, Anne of Cleves, by Hans Holbein the younger (d. 1543).

London, 6 January 1540
King Henry married his fourth wife, Princess Anne of Cleves, at a quiet ceremony at Greenwich palace today. The marriage was postponed for 48 hours while Henry tried unsuccessfully to find an escape from it. "My Lord, if it were not to satisfy the world and my realm, I would not do that I must do this day for none earthly thing," he told his minister, Thomas Cromwell, the mastermind of the match.

For three years Henry has been searching Europe for a bride. First he wooed Mary, the daughter of the Duke of Guise, who listened politely when Henry's ambassador explained that "he was big in person and had need of a big wife" and then married King James of Scotland. Then he turned his attentions to Christina, the niece of Emperor Charles V and widow of the Duke of Milan. After fruitless negotia-

tions he concentrated his hopes on two of Mary of Guise's sisters, Louise and Renée, then on two other French noblewomen, Marie of Vendôme and Anne of Lorraine. But when he suggested that all four should come to Calais so he could inspect them, King Francis replied that this was not a horse sale.

Last year Cromwell turned to Germany for a royal bride. His choice was Anne of Cleves – a marriage that would bind the princes of the anti-imperial Schmalkaldic League to Henry against Charles V. He instructed his ambassador, Christopher Mont, to do all in his power to secure the match from the Duke of Cleves. But the duke was strangely reticent about letting Mont inspect her, and when Mont complained the duke asked sarcastically if he would prefer to see her naked. Tonight Henry must face her naked (→ 6/1540).

Holbein is official portrait painter to King Henry

London, 30 August 1539
Hans Holbein has been Henry's court painter for two years now, and his career has become inseparable from the king's search for a new wife. Born in Augsburg 40 years ago, he first made his name in Basel in Switzerland. But religious conflicts drove him to England where, with a recommendation from Erasmus to Thomas More, he established himself as the most fashionable painter of his day.

The last two years of Holbein's career have been spent painting a series of prospective royal brides. Last year he travelled to Flanders to paint the Duchess of Milan, Le Havre to paint Louise of Guise, Joinville, where Louise's sister Renée eluded him, and Nancy to paint Anne of Lorraine. This week he returned from Cleves where he painted a most flattering miniature of Princess Anne.

Hans Holbein's masterly portrait of Christina of Denmark.

Rumours link Mary Tudor with Duke Philip of Bavaria

England's princess: Mary Tudor.

Rome, 15 January 1540
There is consternation all over Catholic Europe following the rumour from England of Princess Mary's betrothal to Duke Philip of Bavaria. The French ambassador to England, Charles de Marillac, claims that the wedding will take place "within ten to fifteen days". The imperial envoy, Eustace Chapuys, reports that the story is untrue. What *is* known is that the Lutheran duke was in England over Christmas, negotiated preliminary marriage terms with the king and then ambushed Mary in the garden of the abbot of Westminster on Boxing Day and stole a kiss (→ 1544).

Henry VIII falls for Catherine Howard

Marriage to Anne comes to an end

London, 28 July 1540
Henry VIII has taken a fifth wife, Catherine Howard, a niece of the Duke of Norfolk. The marriage comes just 18 days after his divorce from Queen Anne of Cleves and marks the ascendancy of the conservative cause led by Norfolk and the demise of the radical faction of Thomas Cromwell, who was executed this morning [*see report below left*].

Catherine had caught the king's attention when she was a maid of honour to Queen Anne of Cleves. Henry became obsessed by her and, encouraged by the Council to provide "some more store of fruit of succession", he divorced Queen Anne on the grounds that a previous marriage contract between her and the son of the Duke of Lorraine had been signed 12 years ago, and that his own marriage had not been consummated.

The king, who is 49 years old, appears revived by the match and declares himself to be utterly in love. Catherine, who is an experienced and buxom 19-year-old, may be less satisfied.

Henry is elated at his escape from the "Flanders mare" into the arms of Catherine. Encouraged by Cromwell to marry Anne for reasons of state, he disliked her from the moment that he first set eyes on her at

King Henry's fifth wife, Catherine Howard, by Hans Holbein (d.1543).

Rochester, where he had dashed in disguise to catch a glimpse of his bride before officially receiving her at Greenwich palace.

King Henry's divorce from Queen Anne was handled most amicably by the couple. Two weeks before the case opened Queen Anne went to Richmond palace at Henry's suggestion, "purposing it to be more for her health, open air and pleasure". The queen happily agreed to the divorce, when the chancellor led a deputation to her to secure her consent, and confirmed that the marriage had never been consumated. In spite of the efforts of her brother, the Duke of Cleves, to persuade her to go back to Germany, Queen Anne has elected to stay in England and has settled for two houses and an income of £500 per year for the rest of her life (→ 14/11/41).

James uses play to get message across

Lothian, 6 January 1540
Sir David Lindsay's new play *Ane Satyre of the Thrie Estaitis*, portraying immoral clergy, has amused King James. After tonight's performance in Linlithgow palace James lectured the archbishop of Glasgow and other bishops on their loose living. Yet James, unlike his uncle Henry VIII of England, is no radical reformer. Indeed, the pope allows the high taxes that James levies on the church as the price for his continued recognition of papal supremacy (→ 28/11/42).

Abbey riches fund regius professorships

Henry pictured at his books.

Cambridge, 1540
King Henry VIII has endowed five new regius professorships here, in Greek, Hebrew, law, divinity and medicine. It will cost the king nothing, though, since they will be financed from the revenues of Westminster abbey. Henry has little interest in higher education and did it much harm by dissolving the monasteries. He promised John Fisher £2,800 for St John's college but only produced £1,200. Student numbers are half what they were two years ago, and many of the best scholars have gone to Italy, where the universities are flourishing.

Cromwell executed for treason, heresy

London, 28 July 1540
Thomas Cromwell, the Earl of Essex, was executed on Tower Hill this morning. The axe was blunt, and he died in great agony. Cromwell rose to become the king's chief minister by virtue of his efficiency and sense of expediency, and he was ruthless in pursuit of his master's interest. But the king's irritation at Cromwell's marriage arrangements for him, and the persistent opposition of the conservative faction led by the Duke of Norfolk, ensured his downfall.

▷

Catherine Howard's infidelity revealed

Queen Catherine: under guard.

Tyburn, London, 10 Dec 1541

The axe fell today on Thomas Culpeper and Francis Dereham, the two lovers of Queen Catherine Howard. Culpeper stood beside the gallows and, after a speech in which he begged the people to pray for him, his head was struck off. Dereham was half-hanged, then disembowelled before being beheaded and quartered.

Queen Catherine and Lady Rochford, the matron of her household, who arranged her meetings with Culpeper, are under armed guard at Syon House. King Henry is so distressed that he cannot bear to learn the details himself and has appointed a commission to hear the queen's case (→ 13/2/42).

King James dies after rout by English

Defeat at Solway Moss cripples king

Cumbria, 24 November 1542

In a military disaster reminiscent of Flodden, a Scottish army took to the field today at Solway Moss, west of Carlisle, only to be routed by an English force one-third of its strength. Standards, valuable equipment and a large number of nobles have been captured. For the second time within living memory Scotland has been left to come to terms with overwhelming defeat at the hands of the English.

James V has been openly at war with Henry VIII of England since the summer and until now had been enjoying some success. A large English raiding party intercepted at Haddon Rig was smashed while the Duke of Norfolk's men blundered around the border for a week without firing a shot.

After the Haddon Rig victory James thought the time ripe to invade England, so while he left Edinburgh for Lochmaben another force under Oliver Sinclair moved south over the border. Sinclair led a divided army, however; some of his men resented being led by the king's favourite, while the Protestants among them thought it no coincidence that they were to fight where casualties would be heaviest. James, meanwhile, seems mentally crippled by this humiliation, and the future of the whole campaign now looks in doubt (→ 14/12).

A 16th-century portrait of King James V with his wife Mary of Guise.

Doomed king dies a broken man

Fife, 14 December 1542

Scotland has a child monarch yet again following the unexpected death of James V at Falkland palace today. Unwell since a hunting accident five years ago, James had recently suffered a series of bitter disappointments and personal tragedies which left him a broken man.

Although he leaves a daughter, Mary, born less than a week ago, he lost both his young sons in April last year. Three weeks ago his campaign against Henry VIII of England foundered in humiliation, through military incompetence, while his nobles bickered acrimoniously among themselves. Showing signs of nervous collapse, James retired to Falkland five days ago. Although only 30 years old, he seemed to have lost the will to live.

Few will mourn James. The nobility found him harsh and authoritarian. Churchmen reeled under the taxes that he levied on them, their only consolation being that he did not turn Protestant. The common people admired his zeal for justice, but James was also avaricious, spending fortunes on his castles at Stirling, Falkland and Holyrood – which may remain his greatest legacy to Scotland.

Henry imposes will on Irish chieftains

Dublin, June 1541

An Irish parliament has conferred on Henry the title "King of Ireland", making it clear that his right to Ireland does not depend upon a papal grant. The Irish chiefs responded by expressing their "liberal consents". The new title confirms that Henry intends to rule the Irish more directly, strengthening his hold on the island to prevent possible intervention by an enemy. The king is already the head of the Church of Ireland.

Mary, a baby just six days old, is the first ever Queen of Scots

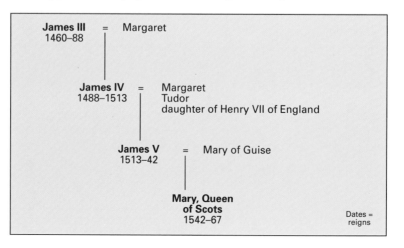

James III 1460–88	= Margaret
James IV 1488–1513	= Margaret Tudor daughter of Henry VII of England
James V 1513–42	= Mary of Guise
Mary, Queen of Scots 1542–67	

Dates = reigns

Fife, 14 December 1542

Scotland's first queen has come to the throne. The six-day-old child, Mary, inherits the kingdom of Scotland as the only surviving legitimate child of the late King James [*see reports above*]. Already the jockeying for power during her anticipated long minority has begun. The Earl of Arran claims the hereditary right to govern as regent; Cardinal Beaton, on the other hand, claims that the king's will lays down that *he* shall be regent with the help of a committee. It is not an auspicious start (→ 3/1543).

Henry and emperor make an alliance to invade France

Westminster, 11 February 1543

King Henry has concluded a treaty with Charles V, the Holy Roman Emperor, to attack France. This treaty has been worked on for two years and has only been signed after a great deal of difficulty – not the least of which was caused by Henry's breach with the pope, which has put Charles in a politically embarrassing position.

The Holy Roman Emperor, defender of the papacy, may find it hard to explain why he has joined forces with Henry, the schismatic who denies papal rights, to attack that most Catholic of monarchs, the king of France. Although the English retort, that papal rights did not stop Charles from burning Rome in 1527, did not impress the emperor, he has signed (→ 7/1545).

King Henry's ally: Charles V.

Scottish parliament approves new Bible

Scotland, March 1543

James, the Earl of Arran, who has secured the position of regent during the infancy of Mary Queen of Scots, has persuaded parliament to authorise the reading of the Bible in the vernacular. In January he announced that he did not recognise the pope, but this does not mean that he is following in the steps of England's king. It is more to do with his animosity towards Cardinal Beaton, who challenged his right to be regent (→ 1/7).

Queen executed for brazen adultery

Tower Green, 13 February 1542

Queen Catherine Howard and the matron of her household, Lady Rochford, were beheaded here this morning. Queen Catherine was the second niece of the Duke of Norfolk to be married to the king, and the second to be beheaded. The first was Anne Boleyn, whose brother was Lady Rochford's husband. Both queens were executed for committing adultery, which is a treasonable offence for the king's consort. King Henry has been badly hurt by the whole Howard episode [*see report opposite*], and, although Catherine's guilt was undeniable, he has refused to have anything to do with the inevitable prosecution, saying that he could not bear to hear the "wicked facts of the case".

He shocked courtiers by calling for a sword to kill Catherine himself, a request which they refused, and spent Christmas morosely moving from palace to palace. Some wonder if he may not be losing his mind under the strain of his grief at Catherine's betrayal.

Among the other victims of the scandal have been various members of the Howard dynasty, arrested for failing to report Catherine's brazen adultery with Thomas Culpeper and Francis Dereham. However, the head of the Howards, the Duke of Norfolk, has survived the purge. Neither he nor Henry attended the execution.

Catherine Parr, a twice-married widow, becomes sixth queen

Hampton Court, 12 July 1543

King Henry has married again – for the sixth time. His bride this time is Catherine Parr, the 31-year-old daughter of a Northamptonshire knight, who has been married and widowed twice already. Her second husband was Lord Latimer, who died earlier this year. She then seemed certain to marry Thomas Seymour, the brother of Lord Hertford and a man generally viewed as dangerous, unreliable and lecherous. But Seymour has been pushed aside by the king, and the marriage took place quietly here today with Bishop Stephen Gardiner of Winchester officiating.

Her infatuation with the dark Seymour apart, Catherine appears to be an intelligent, impressive and wholly likeable woman. She is no conservative, but a moderate who has received reformers such as Miles Coverdale into her home. A mature woman of sound education, Catherine is in stark contrast to the dizziness of Anne Boleyn and Catherine Howard or the dullness of Anne of Cleves. The new queen is also much taken with the humanism of Erasmus, and she is certain to form her own circle and wield considerable influence within the court (→ 7/1547).

The sensible new queen: an ideal companion for the king in his old age?

The six women who married Henry VIII – and those who died

Catherine of Aragon
Married: 11 June 1509, aged 23
Divorced: March 1534
Anne Boleyn
Married: 25 Jan 1533, aged 32
Beheaded: 19 May 1536

Jane Seymour
Married: 30 May 1536, aged 31
Died: 24 October 1537
Anne of Cleves
Married: 6 Jan 1540, aged 24
Divorced: 9 July 1540

Catherine Howard
Married: 28 July 1540, aged 20
Beheaded: 13 February 1542
Catherine Parr
Married: 12 July 1543, aged 31
Prospects: uncertain

Henry starts 'rough wooing' when plan for marriage is off

Scotland, June 1544

King Henry VIII has embarked on a campaign of wanton destruction in Scotland which has acquired the nickname of "rough wooing". His move was prompted by the failure of plans to arrange a marriage between his heir, Prince Edward, and Mary, the infant Queen of Scots. The betrothal was agreed last year under the Treaty of Greenwich, but the prospect of English domination has made the governor, the Earl of Arran, have second thoughts.

An English army led by Edward Seymour, the Earl of Hertford, disembarked at Leith in May with no resistance. It joined up with another force that had crossed the border and proceeded to burn much of Edinburgh. The English then went on the rampage across the country, plundering scores of villages and destroying or burning monasteries, abbeys and five market towns (→ 11/9/47).

Loss of flagship mars navy triumph

South Coast, July 1545

The naval war with the French has begun disastrously with the sinking of the *Mary Rose*, the best ship in England, which capsized in the Solent on 20 July as she was putting out to meet the enemy. Yet, despite this, the fleet has triumphed, and the Channel is back under English control, although not without a stiff fight.

Francis, the king of France, has been anxious to retake Boulogne after its capture by Henry VIII last year. He gathered an army of 50,000, laid siege to Boulogne and sent a fleet of more than 200 ships into the Channel to attack the English coast and prevent Henry from reinforcing Boulogne.

The *Mary Rose* was an old ship, having been launched in 1511, when she had been of revolutionary design. Rebuilt in 1536, she was regarded as one of the most seaworthy ships in the navy. But when she sailed this month she was carrying a very heavy armament, being designed as a floating gun platform,

England's pride: the warship "Mary Rose", now lost in the Solent.

and her lower gun deck was close – perhaps dangerously so – to the water line.

As the *Mary Rose* left Portsmouth, King Henry rode out to Spithead to watch her progress. A stiff wind was blowing, but it was nothing out of the ordinary, when suddenly, before the king's eyes, the

great ship began to list violently. She rolled over, and within a minute the pride of the English fleet had sunk, and of the 700 men on board only 40 were saved. No one is sure why she took in water and sank, but it is said that she sailed out of Portsmouth harbour with her gun ports open.

Outstanding tutors school royal children in learning as warfare

London, 1544

Some outstanding tutors have been brought in by the king to further the education of the royal children, the princesses Mary and Elizabeth and the young prince Edward, now aged seven. Their education has not been neglected, but it now moves into a higher gear with the arrival of the noted Cambridge humanist Anthony Cooke, John Cheke, the regius professor of Greek at Cambridge, and the learned clergyman Richard Cox. All the tutors are of the Protestant and Erasmian persuasion that Queen Catherine Parr wants instilled into her husband's successors.

Cox, Edward's main tutor, tries to make lessons relevant, and when Henry invaded France he urged his pupils to see learning as "conquering the captains of ignorance" as the king conquers the French. Latin and Greek verbs are seen as fortresses to be besieged and taken. The method works well, and all the young royals – Elizabeth in particular – have become proficient in languages (→ 25/12/50).

A royal childhood: Princess Elizabeth at the ages of three, five and six years.

Surrey executed as Howard family falls

Tower of London, December 1546

Henry Howard, the Earl of Surrey and son of the great Thomas Howard, the Duke of Norfolk, has been executed for treason. His death comes amid a welter of plots and counterplots that surround the king, whose health is deteriorating alarmingly. The duke has also been arrested and is being questioned about a secret cipher that he has used and about his attitude to the pope and his loyalty to the king as head of the church.

Henry Howard's demise was brought about largely by arrogance and boastfulness. He made too much of being a descendant of Edward III and said that after Henry's death his father ought to rule the country. He was also said to have planned to overthrow Henry and seize the young Prince Edward. But the final straw that brought him to the block was his quartering of his arms with those of Edward the Confessor. This was high treason, and he has paid the full price.

'Good King Harry' dies after long, eventful reign

A friend in his old age: a later engraving of Catherine Parr with Henry.

News of king's death is kept from public

London, 31 January 1547
King Henry VIII died three days ago. His death came in the early hours of 28 January after a long illness caused by his obesity and a bad sore on his leg. The news had been kept secret while the Earl of Hertford secured the leadership of the regency council, which will rule the country during the minority of Edward VI. Parliament was left in session, and Edward, aged nine, was taken to the Tower while Hertford seized the secret jewel-houses of the late king. All this was unconstitutional, but Hertford has become so powerful that there is no stopping him. There is also the problem of the Duke of Norfolk, who would have been executed on the morning of 28 January if the king had not died in the night. He is to remain alive in the Tower.

Henry with his son and heir Edward.

Dying king alters will to benefit Hertford

London, 31 January 1547
In his last days Henry VIII revised his will several times, the last being on 30 December last year. This will was not signed but was stamped by his secretary, a system authorised and used by the king for some time. When it was read to parliament today it contained two provisions that give Thomas Seymour, the Earl of Hertford, enormous power. First the regency council, which Hertford leads as high chamberlain, may take "any action" necessary for the government of the kingdom. Then there is the "unfulfilled gifts" clause, empowering the council to award gifts that Henry would have made had he lived. This places vast patronage in the hands of Hertford, allowing him to shower gifts, titles and money on his supporters should he bid to take over the country, as some believe that he may.

Reign started quietly yet ended in tumult

London, 1547
Looking back on Henry VIII's reign it seems that for the first 20 years almost nothing happened, but in the last 17 years and eight months the action was so furious that even his most devoted servants found it hard to keep up. He saw off rebellion, excommunication, five wives, the threat of foreign invasion, the king of France, the Holy Roman Emperor and the pope – and still managed to die in bed. It was a remarkable performance.

He destroyed religious houses, pensioned off their inmates and wrested control of the church from the pope, but more than anything Henry brought a divided country to heel. His towering authority enabled him to weld together a country largely divided on religious, local and dynastic lines and create a recognisable English nation.

New palace of Nonsuch is nearly finished

A red-rose window from Nonsuch.

Surrey, 1545
Most of the workmen have gone, and only a few remain to put the finishing touches to Henry's great palace of Nonsuch, set in 2,000 acres of Surrey parkland. The village of Cuddington, near Cheam and Ewell, was demolished to make way for the palace, and the finest craftsmen were imported from Italy and France. The frontage is 200 feet long, with 75-foot towers; the gardens hold fountains, a maze and 200 pear trees. The cost of it all is £24,000 and it took seven years to build. Henry visited the site twice to complain about the pace of work.

New colleges for Oxford and Cambridge

Oxford, 1546
King Henry's dissolution of the monasteries has brought considerable gains to the university towns of Oxford and Cambridge by providing the money for new colleges. Before he fell, Cardinal Wolsey himself closed 30 monasteries and used the money to found Cardinal's college, the name of which was changed this year to Christ Church. At Cambridge, money from the dissolution founded Magdalene college in 1542, and Henry himself founded Trinity college, endowing it with the revenues of 26 suppressed religious houses.

Christ Church: a drawing of 1566.

1547–1553

Edward VI
1547–1553

Mary, Queen
of Scots
1542–1567

Boy king Edward VI seems unlikely heir to the turbulent throne of his late father

The boy king, Edward VI: a later portrait, after Hans Holbein (d.1543).

Westminster, 19 February 1547. Edward, aged ten, is crowned king of England.→

Inchmahome, 11 Sept 1547. After a massive Scottish defeat in battle at Pinkie, near Musselburgh, Mary Queen of Scots, aged five, flees to the island for safety (→7/7/48).

Lothian, 7 July 1548. A Franco-Scottish treaty confirms that Mary Queen of Scots will marry the *Dauphin* [heir to the crown] of France (→7/8).

Gloucester, 7 Sept 1548. Catherine Parr, Henry VIII's widow, who last year married Thomas Seymour, dies eight days after her daughter's birth (→1548).

London, 1548. Persistent rumours of a romantic affair between the young Princess Elizabeth and Thomas Seymour are spreading (→20/3/49).

Westminster, 15 January 1549. The House of Lords passes the Act of Uniformity, making the Catholic Mass illegal and introducing a new Book of Common Prayer (→6/1549).

Devon, June 1549. Rioters rebel against the introduction of the new Prayer Book (→7/1549).

Scotland, July 1549. The English force under Edward Seymour, the Duke of Somerset and lord protector of Edward VI, is forced to withdraw to reinforce the royal army dealing with the rebels against the Prayer Book in southern England (→1/8).

Norwich, 1 August 1549. The royal army is defeated in a clash with rioters protesting against field enclosures (→18/8).

Devon, 18 August 1549. The royal troops suppress the rebels,

and thus succeed in raising the siege of Exeter (→27/8).

Norwich, 27 August 1549. John Dudley, the Earl of Warwick, defeats the anti-enclosure rioters in East Anglia (→1549).

Westminster, 21 February 1550. Following his arrest last October of Edward Seymour, the Duke of Somerset, John Dudley, the Earl of Warwick, further asserts his power by arresting the lord chamberlain, the Earl of Arundel (→11/10/51).

London, 25 December 1550. Edward rebukes his elder sister, Mary, for her adherence to the Catholic faith (→24/1/51).

France, 19 July 1551. A marriage is agreed between Edward and the daughter of King Henry II of France.

London, 11 October 1551. John Dudley, the Earl of Warwick, is made Duke of Northumberland, becoming the country's most powerful noble (→22/1/52).

Westminster, 14 April 1552. A second Act of Uniformity, introducing a more radical Book of Common Prayer, is approved by parliament.→

Westminster, 31 March 1553. Despite Edward's obvious ill health, parliament is dissolved without having decided who should be his successor (→21/6).

England, May 1553. Lady Jane Grey, a possible successor to the Edward IV's throne, marries Lord Guildford Dudley, the son of John Dudley, the Duke of Northumberland (→6/7).

Greenwich, 6 July 1553. The king, suffering from pulmonary tuberculosis, dies aged 15; Lady Jane Grey will succeed him.→

London, 28 January 1547
A small pale-faced boy and his half-sister wept for hours today when they learnt of the death of their father, Henry VIII. Nine-year-old Edward is an unlikely heir to Henry's throne. As a young man, Henry was rumbustious, athletic and outgoing; his son is small, introverted and precocious. Henry was overjoyed at the birth of a son – although his joy was clouded by the death of Edward's mother, Jane Seymour, 12 days later – but became increasingly obsessed by the boy's well-being.

Edward has been brought up mainly by nurses and knew no family life until his stepmother, Catherine Parr, brought Henry's children together for Christmas four years ago. Catherine insisted that the boy should have the best tutors in the land. By the time of today's accession to the throne he was fully conversant with Greek, Latin and French and had made a deep study of the religious reformation which is sweeping northern Europe.

Unhappily for the boy, he has been largely deprived of the company of others of his age. His outlook is serious and mature, and he enjoys the solitary pleasures of playing the lute and studying the stars. Edward VI's maternal uncle Edward Seymour, the Earl of Hertford, will be protector of the realm during the king's minority [*see story opposite*] (→31/1).

Pageantry hails crowning of boy king

The splendid coronation procession for King Edward: seen passing from the Tower (l) to Charing Cross (r).

London, 19 February 1547

For a few vivid, noisy and often hilarious hours, London became a city of magic and pageant yesterday as little King Edward was brought in procession from the Tower of London to Westminster abbey on the eve of his coronation. Today's service was as solemn and splendid as befits the crown, but the procession was an excuse for London to burst into life with a thousand different diversions for the nine-year-old king.

Edward left the Tower dressed in white velvet and cloth of silver, riding on a white horse under a crimson canopy held by four outriders. He led a procession of lords, the mayor, aldermen, heralds, trumpeters and minstrels through a city clearly determined to put on a colourful show for the sovereign.

At St Paul's, Edward was delighted by an Aragonese high-wire artist and stopped his procession to demand more. As he rode through a triumphal arch at Cheapside, an "angel" was let down to hand him a purse with £1,000. Children sang an anthem to the king at Cornhill where wine flowed from the fountains. The little king marvelled at a giant at London Bridge and at a whole series of pageants acted out along the route to the abbey. In Fleet Street three children represented truth, faith and justice;

Temple Bar was a mass of bunting.

The procession followed a pattern established at the crowning of Richard II, but the speed of Edward's coronation following King Henry's death three weeks ago had caught the organisers unawares and much of the ceremonial had to be hastily improvised.

Today's coronation was a deeply moving affair. The abbey's walls were hung with Arras tapestries, the aisles laid with rushes. Trumpets sounded as the three crowns were placed in succession on the king's head and a ring of gold was placed on his wedding-ring finger. The boy king stayed unsmiling and deadly serious throughout.

Somerset is made protector of young king

London, 31 January 1547

As Edward was brought to the security of the Tower of London to be prepared for his coronation, his uncle – his mother Jane Seymour's brother Edward – advanced himself from the earldom of Hertford to the dukedom of Somerset and declared himself to be the protector of the kingdom. Somerset and Sir William Paget agreed to make this move even as the late king lay dying. Henry had sought government by a regency council, and the two men withheld news of the king's death until the council had agreed Paget's dubious nomination of Somerset as protector [*see page 159*]. Both men are suspected of Protestant sympathies (→ 19/2).

Edward Seymour: Duke of Somerset and protector (a later engraving).

Henry's widow has remarried in secret

London, July 1547

England's lord high admiral, Thomas Seymour, has been married in secret to Catherine Parr, Henry VIII's widow, it was learnt today. Catherine is said to be delighted, but Seymour's amorous antics have caused many eyebrows to be raised in Edward VI's court. Since Henry's death the ambitious and charismatic Seymour is known to have paid court to Princess Mary, and it is rumoured that he has tried to bed Elizabeth as well. Despite this, Catherine is clearly much in love and has written to her beloved: "God is a marvellous man" (→ 7/9/48).

Earl of Arran loses in battle at Pinkie

Pinkie, 10 September 1547

Edward Seymour, the Duke of Somerset, has inflicted heavy casualties on the Scots at a battle at this village near Musselburgh. At first it looked as if the Scots, under the Earl of Arran, were going to win the day, but English discipline and tactics proved superior in the end. Seymour is relieved that his hitherto lacklustre Scottish policy – which led to the loss of St Andrews castle this summer – has resulted in a face-saving victory today. But he will probably be unable to follow it up effectively, while Arran is now likely to turn to the French for military aid (→ 11/9).

Mary, Queen of Scots, exiled with relatives in France

Dumbarton, 7 August 1548

Mary, the five-year-old Queen of Scots, set sail today en route for France. Her departure follows the crushing defeat of the Scots last year at Pinkie, near Musselburgh [*see above*], by an English army under the command of Edward Seymour, the former Earl of Hertford, who is now Duke of Somerset and lord protector. Somerset's campaign is an extension of the offensive launched four years ago by the late English king, Henry VIII.

Immediately after the battle Mary was removed from Stirling castle and sent to the island of Inchmahome, on the lake of Menteith, while Somerset continued to rage about the lowlands. He now occupies much of eastern Scotland, and it was thought best for the young queen's safety that she no longer remained in the country. In France she will be put in the care of her mother's relatives, the powerful Guise family.

In June this year 6,000 French troops arrived to support the Scots, and last month a Franco-Scottish treaty was signed betrothing Mary to the French *Dauphin*, Francis. Under the treaty, Henry II of France promises to guarantee the customary liberties and laws of the Scottish people (→ 24/4/58).

Treasonable frolics lead to execution of the king's uncle

London, 20 March 1549

Extraordinary stories of buttock-slapping frolics in a royal bedroom cost Thomas Seymour, the king's flamboyant uncle, his head today. Seymour, whose brother Edward is lord protector, had been charged with high treason. Apart from hoarding military supplies and forming a private army at his estate at Sudeley in Gloucestershire, he was found guilty of attempting to manipulate the succession by seeking to marry Princess Elizabeth.

Seymour was a close friend of the late King Henry; his sister, Jane, was the king's third wife and Edward VI's mother. His clandestine marriage to Henry's widow, Catherine Parr, shocked the court, and stories leaking from Catherine's Chelsea house were to prove his fatal undoing.

Servants, including Kat Ashley, Princess Elizabeth's governess, told – under "interrogation" – of a love triangle that developed between Seymour, Catherine and Elizabeth. One one occasion, Catherine – who has since died in childbirth – discovered her husband and the flame-haired Elizabeth in a close embrace, and Kat Ashley told of an occasion when Seymour slit Elizabeth's mourning dress into a hundred pieces with his dagger.

It was even suggested that Elizabeth had secretly given birth to Seymour's baby, although there is no proof of this.

Executed: Lord Thomas Seymour.

England erupts with popular protests

The Norwich revolt: a later view.

Norwich, 1549

A remarkable peasants' uprising that began bloodlessly on Mousehold Hill near here this spring ended in a massacre by German mercenaries that claimed the lives of at least 3,500 men and women. The rebellion began when about 16,000 peasants, many of them dispossessed by their landlords' enclosures, gathered in a camp of turf huts roofed with boughs. Under a large oak tree their leader, Robert Ket, a tannery owner, acted as the judge in a continuous trial of the local gentry who were charged with robbing the poor.

The landowners were not physically hurt, their punishment simply being the restoration of their lands to the public, with their sheep and cattle being slaughtered in order to feed the rebels. With the rebellions spreading to the Midlands and Yorkshire, government intervention was inevitable, and John Dudley, the Earl of Warwick, was given command of the troops. Aware of the size of the revolt and its own limitations, the government offered a free pardon to the peasants; but trouble was certain in Norfolk when a cheeky urchin used "words as unseemly as his gesture was filthy". He was shot down with an arquebus, and a massacre followed.

Catholics in the west country have risen against the new Book of Common Prayer, and the protector, Somerset, is being criticised for his religious reforms and his apparent sympathy for the peasants. He has found little support from his peers or the privy council (→ 13/10).

Religious changes have to be imposed in the teeth of opposition

London, 1549

With five of England's leading bishops in prison and civil war raging in the west and north, the religious reforms introduced by Henry VIII are not proving universally acceptable by any means. The protector, the Duke of Somerset, has the task of imposing change – part of it being the abolition of "abused images", including stained glass, carvings and paintings.

Archbishop Cranmer's Prayer Book required an act of parliament – the Act of Uniformity – to ensure that clergy throughout the kingdom adopted the reformed religion under pain of severe penalties.

A nostalgia for the "old" religion remains, but public resentment is directed much more at wealthy landowners who have profited from Henry VII's dissolution of the monasteries (→ 14/4/52).

"The pope stoned by the four evangelists", by the Italian artist da Treviso.

Treaty of Boulogne brings Anglo-French peace agreement

Boulogne, France, January 1550

The long dispute between England and France over the territory of Boulogne has been resolved. England has occupied the city since 1544, but last August King Henry II of France moved his army to the weakly-defended city to try to win it back. The attack failed because the French were unable to control the sea, so that the English navy was able to get reinforcements into Boulogne. Constant bombardment and direct assault failed.

John Dudley, the Earl of Warwick, realised that England could not afford a prolonged campaign in France. He negotiated a treaty under which England conceded Boulogne for 400,000 crowns in two instalments. The English have also agreed to withdraw entirely from Scotland, which is effectively recognised as a French sphere of influence. It is expected that an Anglo-Scottish treaty will be signed in the near future (→ 19/7/51).

Warwick ousts Somerset as protector

Making his move for power: a later engraving of the Earl of Warwick.

London, 13 October 1549
Edward Seymour, the Duke of Somerset and lord protector of England, is a prisoner in the Tower of London tonight after being deposed by his arch-rival, the Earl of Warwick. Somerset's poor handling of the rebellions in the south-west and East Anglia has done much to damage his credibility.

The aristocracy, represented by Warwick, alleged that he was too sympathetic to the peasants whose land was being enclosed and too soft with them when they rebelled. But it did not help Somerset's cause with the common people that he, who claimed to be a reformer, had accumulated large estates in the west country and practised the enclosures that he preached against.

Just as much as Warwick, he stood to benefit personally from enclosure and the mass unemployment that it created.

Somerset's introduction of the Protestant Prayer Book brought about opposition of another kind. The west was still largely Catholic and showed its resentment in rebellion. Warwick was quick to take advantage of the lord protector's weakness – which was added to by his own brother's attempt to unseat him. After Warwick used his army to put down the Norfolk rebellion in August, he began his move to unseat Somerset. The protector appealed fruitlessly to all quarters, including the king, for help, but it was the king's vice-chamberlain who arrested him (→ 21/2/50).

Relations between Mary Tudor and King Edward worsen as religious divide grows

Norfolk, 24 January 1551
A bitter religious battle between the king and his half-sister, Mary, has brought the threat of invasion from Mary's cousin, Charles V, the Holy Roman Emperor. Edward has demanded an end to the illegal Masses said in Mary's household. When his half-sister called on him at Westminster, he recorded in his journal: "She was called with my council into a chamber where it was declared how long I had suffered her Mass, in hope of her reconciliation.

"She answered that her soul was God's and her faith she would not change, nor hide her opinion with dissembled doings. It was said I did not constrain her faith but willed her only as a subject to obey." The confrontation between the 13-

year-old and 34-year-old half-siblings was fruitless. Edward is as determined a Protestant as Mary is a passionate Catholic. He has given Mary opportunities to escape, but she has refused. The emperor's threat was delivered by his ambassador, but the king's council continued its pressure on Mary.

Thomas Cranmer, the archbishop of Canterbury, joined with Nicholas Ridley, the bishop of London, to announce that "to give licence to sin was sin" and that all haste must be used to stop the illegal Masses. Mary's chaplains have been arrested, but the princess remains defiant. She will obey the king in all things, she says – except her faith. She will carry on practising what she believes in (→ 21/6/53).

In council: King Edward VI and his statesmen, by John Pettie (1839-93).

Elizabeth unmoved by wedding moves

London, March 1551
Anxious to find friends abroad, the Earl of Warwick has made a number of simultaneous offers of Princess Elizabeth in marriage. The eldest son of the Danish king, the second son of the Duke of Saxony and the brother of the Duke of Ferrara are among those believed to have been approached. What will happen if they all accept has not been resolved. Elizabeth is understood to be disinclined to marry (→ 21/6/53).

Duke convicted as king looks other way

London, 22 January 1552
King Edward today wrote in his diary: "The Duke of Somerset had his hed cut off on Tower Hill between 8 and 9 a cloke in the morning." The execution eliminates a serious threat of opposition to the the new protector, John Dudley, the Duke of Northumberland, who is determined to impose a more rigid puritanism on England. Somerset's conviction on trumped-up charges of treason and felony was secured with fabricated evidence while his enemies diverted the

king's attention from his uncle's trial. Northumberland used the Christmas festivities to keep the king occupied. A lord of misrule was appointed and an office of revels set up to devise all manner of entertainments for Edward – including masques of apes and cats, pageants and a mock tournament on hobby-horses – while the show trial progressed.

Londoners backed the old protector, and a rumour that Somerset had been cleared led to noisy demonstrations in his favour.

Scottish churchmen discuss reforms

Fife, 1549
The council of the Scottish church has met at St Andrews at the invitation of the archbishop, John Hamilton. Church reform is high on the agenda, in particular the meaning of the Mass and the pope's authority. The teachings of Calvin and Luther have made a powerful impact on church life in England, but Hamilton is no firebrand. Any reforms proposed are therefore likely to be moderate.

Commissioners are to strip churches

London, 12 December 1552

For most of this year, commissioners under the Great Seal have been working in every county, making inventories of the plate and vestments of parish churches, now made redundant by the new Prayer Book of Thomas Cranmer, the archbishop of Canterbury. The new liturgy – which replaces the previous revision of 1549 – introduces an uncompromising Protestantism and has disposed of many Catholic-tinged ceremonies which have lingered on despite Henry VIII's reforms. The previous version had been a provisional reform, carefully engineered to remain consistent with Catholicism. But now, with altars already ordered to be removed and chantries demolished, the rich robes and valuable old plate which were used in the Catholic Mass must go.

Today a general commission has been issued to the Duke of Northumberland and nine others, to enquire how much of this has been sold and how much ought to come to the crown. The income is badly needed. A general plunder of parish churches is feared (→ 14/9/53).

Church adopts new radical prayer book

London, 14 April 1552

Stringent new measures against what the puritan young king describes as the "hounds of hell" – the crypto-Catholic priests – were introduced today in the form of a new prayer book which pushes England's form of worship into severe Protestantism. Vestments are banned, so are prayers for the dead, and, for the first time, laymen face severe punishment for attending any other form of worship.

Radical clergymen led by Bishop John Hooper have taken to sitting at the sacraments and now, in what is known as the "black rubric", the book declares that kneeling does not mean worship. Such is the ignorance and confusion in today's religious scene that Hooper reported that half the clergy in his diocese could not even repeat the Ten Commandments (→ 12/12).

Edward's persistent illnesses cause grave concern at court

London, December 1552

Edward has still not recovered from the illnesses – diagnosed as smallpox and measles – that he contracted in the summer, and now the coldest winter in living memory is taking its toll. Edward is coughing "livid black sputum" and is thought to be suffering from pulmonary tuberculosis.

Word of the king's illness has brought deep gloom to the country, which is undergoing a major economic crisis. Inflation rages, and an alarming flood of debased coinage has lowered the value of a shilling to sixpence. The royal debt is a quarter of a million pounds; there is no money to pay the army, even though the French are plotting to seize Calais and scheming to invade Ireland.

The domestic scene is equally grim. The Duke of Northumberland is virtual dictator of the country, but he dares not try to raise income from taxes, such is his unpopularity. Enclosure of land has created mass unemployment, and the streets of London and other cities are littered with people forced to sleep out of doors in bitter cold.

Northumberland long ago lost any support from the Catholic community, and now he faces a moral revolt from the Protestants. Bishop Ridley has preached: "Christ is hungry, naked and cold in the streets of London." St Bartholomew's and St Thomas's hospitals have been re-endowed and other provisions made for the poor. The king knows little of this. His hair is falling out. He gets weaker every day. It is rumoured that he has been poisoned, or that he is suffering from congenital syphilis caught from his father (→ 31/3/53).

A portrait of Edward in healthier times, from Chichester Cathedral, Sussex.

King issues blue coats and yellow stockings to lucky orphans

Educational patron: a later painting of King Edward granting a petition.

London, 1553

In an attempt to reduce the ever-growing number of orphans on the teeming streets of London, Edward VI has founded a new school in premises once used by the Grey Friars in Newgate Street. More than 700 boys will learn the arts of spinning and weaving and will be dressed in distinctive uniforms with blue coats and yellow stockings. They will also be taught how to read and write.

England has always lagged behind Europe in education – two-thirds of the nation is said to be illiterate – and the young king is determined to change the situation. Edward has founded what are known as "grammar schools" in several towns and cities; but, unfortunately, the present harsh economic situation is causing many students in universities and schools to "drop out" of the education offered to them.

Religious factions battle for control of succession

Protestants want Lady Jane to succeed

London, 21 June 1553
England is certain to be plunged into a major crisis with the imminent death from tuberculosis of the boy king Edward VI. As the king lies dying in Greenwich palace, the powerful Duke of Northumberland – knowing that his own head is in grave danger should the Catholic Princess Mary become queen – is making one last desperate bid to maintain his position.

Northumberland's first move was to marry his son, Guildford Dudley, to Lady Jane Grey, who is descended from Henry VIII's sister Mary and thus has a place in the line of succession, albeit a vague and tenuous one.

The strictly Protestant king is determined that a Catholic shall not inherit the throne and with Northumberland's aid has drawn up a "device" – a form of will – that bars both Mary and Elizabeth from the line of succession. Henry's will decreed that his two daughters should succeed if Edward died childless [*see below*]. The curious device names the male heirs of the almost unknown Lady Jane Grey as inheritors of the crown, she being

the first beneficiary. Lady Jane is 16, the daughter of the Duke of Suffolk whose wife Frances is the late Mary's elder daughter. Northumberland has carefully ensured that Frances – who would have been the first choice under his scheme – is not eligible.

Lady Jane is naturally enough a staunch Protestant and well taught in Greek, Latin and Hebrew. Her mentor, Northumberland, is confident that she will have the backing of the French who would be worried if Mary, a close relative of Holy Roman Emperor Charles V, should win the throne.

The device found little favour with the king's council when it met today, although councillors gave their assent subject to parliament's agreement. The judges were wholly against the document when they were called before the king, but gave way when he insisted. Thomas Cranmer, the archbishop of Canterbury, was among the last to put his name to the document and did so only because the judges had agreed.

A *coup d'état* is in hand, and Edward's Protestant government is prepared for bloodshed (→ 6/7).

Wanted to found a Protestant dynasty: the learned Lady Jane Grey.

Will bars Princesses Mary and Elizabeth

London, 21 June 1553
Town criers were ordered to stand on every street corner in London today and proclaim that Mary and Elizabeth, the daughters of the late Henry VIII, are bastards. The orders were issued by the Duke of Northumberland following the council's reluctant agreement to the "device" which declares Lady Jane Grey to be the future queen.

The boy king's will is intended to supplant the will of Henry VIII which fixes the succession first on Mary and then on Elizabeth. This will was ratified by parliament, and the whole country from the council downwards had pledged itself to accept the line of succession as laid down by Henry.

Northumberland's last-minute scheming – the device was drawn up by a dying king – is not likely to succeed. Lady Jane is unknown

Princess Elizabeth: by a later artist.

and has no following. Princess Mary has shown great dignity and religious courage, and the Catholic faith which she holds still has many adherents in England (→ 15/7).

Edward: never in touch with his country

London, 6 July 1553
Edward VI, who died today, had been bequeathed a most difficult legacy by his father, Henry VIII. While Henry had been ambivalent about the reformation that he himself created, from an early age Edward made it clear that he had no doubts about his Protestant faith and was always eager to attach Britain to the Lutheran revolution.

The great mistake that this unsmiling, precocious monarch and his ambitious backers made was to overestimate English interest in religious affairs. The country was generally content with the old Catholic faith and showed its resentment at the imposition of the new Prayer Book by riot and rebellion in the west country.

Largely screened from the outside world by his intense need to study and by frequent bouts of ill

health, the king was never fully aware of the misery being inflicted on his realm by rural enclosure, benefiting the wealthy and hurting the poor, and its encouragement by both Warwick and his own uncle, the supposedly liberal Somerset.

The weight of responsibility imposed upon this frail youngster was astonishing. He was forced to agree to the execution of his favourite uncle, Thomas Seymour. The fact that it was his other uncle, Somerset, who made him agree clearly caused the young king much bitterness which he showed in his lack of concern at Somerset's beheading.

Edward's latter years were guided largely by the ambitious Duke of Northumberland who helped him to draw up the will which is certain to have a major impact on the English royal scene during the coming days and weeks (→ 10/7).

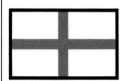

Mary I
1553–1558

Mary, Queen
of Scots
1542–1567

Mary claims the crown

England's queen: an anonymous French portrait of Mary Tudor.

London, 10 July 1553. The council, in accordance with the will of Edward VI, proclaims Lady Jane Grey queen. She is the granddaughter of Henry VIII's sister Mary (→15/7).

Suffolk, 15 July 1553. Mary Tudor, the half-sister of King Edward VI, proclaims herself queen (→19/7).

London, 19 July 1553. The council declares Mary Tudor queen; Lady Jane Grey is arrested for treason and confined in the Tower (→3/8).

Westminster, 9 August 1553. Queen Mary, a devout Catholic, allows a simple Protestant funeral for Edward VI (→1/10).

London, 22 August 1553. John Dudley, the Duke of Northumberland, is executed in the Tower for treason.

London, 1 October 1553. Mary is crowned as the first queen regnant of England (→16/11).

London, 16 November 1553. Mary makes known her decision to marry Philip of Spain, the Catholic son of Holy Roman Emperor Charles V (→6/3/54).

Westminster, 5 December 1553. Mary closes parliament after validating her parents' marriage, repealing all Edward VI's religious changes and reconciling the council to her choice of husband (→28/11/54).

Whitehall, 1553. Mary ceases to use her title of "Supreme Head of the Church", looking to the pope as head.

Kent, January 1554. A plot to frustrate Mary's marriage to Philip is discovered. One of its leaders, Sir Thomas Wyatt, raises a rebellion (→11/4).

London, 9 February 1554. Princess Elizabeth is imprisoned under suspicion of involvement in the recent uprisings (→22/5).

London, 6 March 1554. Mary is officially betrothed to Philip of Spain (→25/7).

Scotland, 12 April 1554. Mary of Guise, the dowager queen, is elected regent (→5/1556).

London, March 1555. John Bradford, called by his supporters the "proto-martyr", is burnt for heresy after claiming that Mary was trying to divert the succession from Elizabeth.

Oxford, 16 October 1555. On Mary's orders, the bishops Nicholas Ridley and Hugh Latimer are burnt at the stake as heretics (→21/3/56).

Canterbury, 22 March 1556. Cardinal Reginald Pole is the new archbishop; he replaces Thomas Cranmer (→6/1557).

Europe, September 1556. Queen Mary's relationship with Rome deteriorates when King Philip II of Spain, her husband, is provoked into a war with Pope Paul IV (→6/1557).

London, 31 March 1557. Princess Elizabeth declines an offer of marriage from Duke Emmanuel Philibert of Savoy (→6/7).

London, June 1557. Following Sir Thomas Stafford's raid on Scarborough, England declares war on France (→7/1/58).

Chelsea, 17 July 1557. Anne of Cleves, the fourth wife of Henry VIII, dies.

St James's, 17 November 1558. Mary dies of dropsy, aged 42; her sister, Elizabeth, will succeed her as queen.→

London, 3 August 1553
Thousands lined the streets of London to cheer Mary Tudor, Henry VIII's elder daughter, who has arrived here at the head of an ever-growing army of supporters to occupy the throne of England as the country's first "queen regnant". Lady Jane Grey, the 16-year-old Norfolk aristocrat who was proclaimed queen nine days ago, has been outmanoeuvred and occupies a cell in the Tower of London.

Events have moved at an incredible speed since Edward VI died on 6 July. The Duke of Northumberland wasted no time in proclaiming Jane queen. The ambitious Northumberland had wanted Jane to declare her husband – his son, Guildford – king, but she courageously refused. Northumberland had not allowed for public opinion, however. He had become a much hated figure in the country, and Londoners resented the way in which he kept the boy king's death secret while he mustered his forces. Only one leading cleric – Nicholas Ridley – spoke out for Jane Grey.

As Northumberland marched towards Suffolk, where Mary had installed herself in Framlingham castle, his army began to desert in large numbers. Mary's support continued to grow, with more and more defections to her cause from both gentry and commoners. Her enemies had underestimated the English public's respect for the queen's piety and its concern for a lawful succession (→22/8).

England thrown into turmoil by religious strife

Leading churchmen taken into custody

London, 14 September 1553

Queen Mary has wasted no time in demonstrating her determination to eradicate Protestantism from the English scene. Since her accession in July her agents have been rounding up leading churchmen and imprisoning them in the Tower on charges of heresy.

Today saw the arrest of Thomas Cranmer, the archbishop of Canterbury and author of the controversial Prayer Books of 1549 and 1552 – even though he had opposed Edward VI's "device" which left the throne to Lady Jane Grey.

Others in custody include Bishop John Hooper and the elderly Hugh Latimer. Nicholas Ridley, the bishop of London, was among the first to be arrested, for the sermon in which he attacked Mary's claim on the grounds of her bastardy. He faces almost certain death for treason; his backer, Northumberland, has already been beheaded.

Mary's half-sister, Elizabeth, is under suspicion. She is known to admire Archbishop Cranmer and his work, so she now faces a crash course in conversion at Mary's insistence. She has been given a rosary of red and white coral and is being tested on the catechism by an ardent Mary, who continues to distrust her (→ 16/10/55).

Londoners look on as Sir Thomas Wyatt, the leader of the rising, is executed.

Mary crushes uprising by Kentish rebels

London, 11 April 1554

Sir Thomas Wyatt was executed at the Tower today for leading a revolt by men from Kent against Queen Mary's rule. The aftermath of the rebellion, which broke out three months ago, saw savage royal reprisals, with scores of bodies hanging from gibbets throughout London. Among the victims were Lady Jane Grey and her husband, even though they took no part in the uprising [*see report below*].

A passionate appeal by the queen to the people of London almost certainly saved her crown as the 7,000 rebels prepared to attack the City of London. Mary rode to the Guildhall and vowed that the coronation ring would never leave her finger. "I love you as the mother loves a child," she told the cheering mob.

Opposed to Mary's forthcoming marriage to Philip of Spain, the rebels massed at Southwark on 3 February, but it was four days later that they advanced north of the river Thames – to confront a resolute defence. There was skirmishing at Ludgate and in Hyde Park, but eventually Wyatt was captured and brought to Whitehall.

Mary seals union with Philip of Spain

Winchester, 25 July 1554

Five days after arriving in England, Philip II of Spain has married Mary of England in a magnificent ceremony at Winchester cathedral. At their first meeting yesterday, Mary was apparently impressed with her future husband – who is 11 years her junior – and today, before the marriage service, Philip was proclaimed king of England.

Mary is 38 and desperate for an heir who will sustain her Catholic principles; Philip, a widower, is set to become the most powerful ruler in Europe. The marriage will be of great advantage to Spain against its traditional enemy, France.

In England, however, there has been great opposition to the match. The queen's council – including Stephen Gardiner, whose opinion counts for much with Mary – believes that Philip, the heir to Charles V's huge empire, will treat England as little more than a distant colony. The Commons have petitioned in vain for Mary to marry an Englishman.

The public is also opposed; anti-Spanish ballads and broadsheets are circulating in London. Opponents are eager to point out that Mary herself is half-Spanish. Her mother was Catherine of Aragon, Henry VIII's first wife (→ 26/8/55).

Archbishop Cranmer is arrested.

Lady Jane Grey and husband executed

London, 12 February 1554

A few hours before her execution, 16-year-old Lady Jane Grey bade farewell to her equally youthful husband, Lord Guildford Dudley, from her cell window and watched as his head and carcass were brought back to the Tower chapel in a cart. Prayer book in hand, she prayed all the way to Tower Green and, before she declared her innocence, loosened her gown and blindfolded herself. "What shall I do?" she asked. A bystander helped her find the block. "Pray dispatch me quickly," she pleaded.

Princess Elizabeth freed from Tower

London, 22 May 1554

After two months of confinement in a damp, dank room in the Tower of London, Princess Elizabeth is today on her way to the royal palace at Woodstock with an escort of 100 guardsmen. The princess was suspected of complicity in the Wyatt rebellion of last February, and her life has hung on the silk thread of her sister's mercy ever since. She has denied receiving a letter from Sir Thomas Wyatt, and lengthy torture has failed to extract confessions from her alleged co-conspirators (→ 31/10/55).

A royal match: Philip and Mary.

Mary sees England reconciled to Rome

Reginald Pole, the papal legate.

London, 28 November 1554
Queen Mary's cherished ambition to restore England to the Roman faith came closer to fulfilment today when parliament petitioned for reconciliation with the Holy See. In two days' time Cardinal Reginald Pole, the papal legate, will pronounce a solemn absolution. Pole, a member of the House of York, has lived abroad for 25 years, disenchanted with Henry VIII's religious policies; Henry had Pole's brother and aged mother executed. The cardinal played a major part in the talks on reconciliation.

Today's petition does not mean the return of seized monastic property to the church; the present holders can remain in occupation. It does portend persecution of Protestant heretics, however – although gentle persuasion will be tried first.

Elizabeth returns to her own house

Hatfield, 31 October 1555
Princess Elizabeth's appearance on the London streets nearly caused a popular riot this month. So loud were the clapping and cheering that the princess – keen to avoid public attention – turned her horse and fell into place behind her household officers until the party reached the open countryside. Elizabeth is now back in her house at Hatfield, maintaining a small staff and keeping a low public profile (→ 31/3/57).

Court admits queen's phantom pregnancy

Hampton Court, August 1555
The queen of England sits on a cushion in this royal palace clutching her tear-stained missal in one hand and her deflated belly in the other. The midwives and physicians have given up all hope that Mary is about to deliver an heir to the throne; the queen has endured a "phantom" pregnancy while Protestants suffer the horrors of her repression. Eight more men and women were burnt to death during the first two weeks of this month, and many think that Mary was convinced that she must burn every heretic before she gave birth.

Below in the palace, her husband, Philip, is growing impatient; he is concerned about his vast Spanish possessions, and, apart from that, he is clearly disenchanted with Mary, whom he finds repugnant and smelly.

Philip speaks no English and has found little pleasure at Mary's court – except in the company of her half-sister, Elizabeth, who can converse with him in Italian and French. Elizabeth – next in line to the throne – was brought to Hampton Court in case Mary died in childbirth. She is thought to be less of a threat if kept here.

Mary's "pregnancy" was a time of joy; bonfires were lit when false tidings of a birth leaked out – only to be doused when the truth was known. Meanwhile, the bonfires of death continue to blaze (→ 26/8).

Queen's husband is number one in Europe

Holy Roman Emperor Charles V: the father of Mary's husband, Philip.

Greenwich, 26 August 1555
Mary said goodbye to Philip today as he set out to see his new possessions in the Netherlands. The gift of the Netherlands – made to Philip by his father, Emperor Charles V – makes Mary's husband the most powerful man in Europe. The 28-year-old Philip was given Naples last year, and Charles has indicated that he will soon retire and leave the Holy Roman Empire to his own brother, Ferdinand.

The departure of Philip, England's first king-consort – Mary regards him as her co-regent in the Spanish style – is heartbreaking to his queen. Mary is deeply in love with the swarthy Spaniard, in whose presence she is said to be schoolgirlish and giggly; he is less so with her and has shocked courtiers by his callous treatment of his wife and his flirtations with the attractive Princess Elizabeth.

Mary's health is poor; Elizabeth is strong and lithe, and many surmise that Philip may envisage a marriage with his wife's sister. Having gained a foothold in England, Philip is clearly determined to keep it. This may not suit the English, however; Philip is even more bigoted a Catholic than his wife and is suspected of an even greater zest for burning heretics (→ 10/9/56).

Mary loses valued religious adviser

Stephen Gardiner: trusted adviser.

Winchester, November 1555
With the death of her chancellor, Stephen Gardiner, the queen has been deprived of her trusted adviser at a time when she can ill afford to lose wise counsel. Gardiner was one of the most experienced churchmen in the country and a key figure in Mary's counter-reformation.

A former secretary to Henry VIII, he was a protégé of Cardinal Wolsey and a leading player in the drama of Henry's divorce from Catherine of Aragon, Mary's mother. He defended the supremacy of the king over the church, and Henry made him bishop of Winchester. Edward VI deprived him of his see and sent him to the Tower. It was Mary who freed him.

Gardiner was a devout Catholic, keen and ruthless against heretics, although, surprisingly, there were no burnings in his see (→ 3/1556).

Gentry arrested for plot to oust queen

England, March 1556
Several leading members of the gentry have been taken into custody following the discovery of a plot to depose Queen Mary in favour of her sister, Elizabeth. Driven principally by hatred of the Spanish connection, the conspirators, led by Henry Dudley, intended to invade England with an army of mercenaries and exiles from France. An additional plan to rob the exchequer led to their undoing (→ 10/9).

Cranmer joins ranks of royal victims

Oxford, 21 March 1556

Thomas Cranmer, the archbishop of Canterbury and founding father of the English Protestant church, has become the latest victim of Queen Mary's heresy acts. The 67-year-old primate – renowned as the principal author of the 1552 Prayer Book – was tied to a stake in an Oxford street today and burnt alive.

Cranmer, who had witnessed the burnings of two of his colleagues, Bishops Ridley and Latimer, from his prison cell last October, had appeared to recant his Protestant beliefs in a set of "submissions" which recognised papal authority. He was sentenced to the flames and recanted once again, this time in the most abject terms. The court could have made much of this and pardoned him – with great advantage in terms of propaganda – but instead ordered him to the stake.

Cranmer was taken to St Mary's church to hear his own funeral sermon and make a final public confession. To the fury of his prosecutors, he withdrew his recantation, and when the first faggots were lit he held his writing hand in the flames and said: "This hand hath offended." Cranmer was the most important religious reformer to pay the cruel price for defying Mary and the pope. Public burnings have become almost commonplace in England, but if the aim is to deter heretics it is failing. Public sympathy is growing for the Protestant victims, whose deaths are often hastened by bags of gunpowder being thrown into the flames (→ 22/3).

Archbishop Cranmer is burnt at the stake, defiant of persecution at the end.

A public execution: Bishops Ridley and Latimer are burnt as heretics.

Queen Mary beseeches emperor to persuade Philip to return

London, 10 September 1556

Appeals by Mary for her husband to return to England have met with a stony response, and now a desperate queen has begged her father-in-law, Charles V, the Holy Roman Emperor, to influence Philip to return. With her reign shaken almost daily by reports of conspiracies, real and unreal, Mary is becoming daily more exposed and insecure. Already this year ten people, including their leader, Henry Dudley, have been executed for plotting to divert the succession to Princess Elizabeth. Philip is in the Netherlands, clearly in no mood to return, despite Mary's assurance that they might still conceive an heir.

The marriage has apparently become a one-sided affair. The queen looks for Philip's comfort and support, while he remains preoccupied with the affairs of his own country, and his courtiers are clearly unwilling to return to the chill rigours of the English court.

In one anguished letter to the emperor, Mary begs her cousin "...to remember the unspeakable sadness which I experience because of the absence of the king". In her most recent correspondence, Mary's pleas are less emotional and more concerned with national security. England needed Philip's firm hand, she wrote, even though she had not defined her husband's role while he was in the country.

It may be that the queen has left it too late. Charles V is an old and sick man who plans to leave his kingdoms to Philip and his empire to his brother Ferdinand and retire to a monastery (→ 6/7/57).

Scottish protests mount at growing French influence

Edinburgh, May 1556

Smouldering resentment at the arrogant rule of the regent, Mary of Guise, continues to threaten serious uprisings in Scotland. Mary's constant demand for money is one factor. Her latest proposal is for a perpetual tax to pay for the large contingent of French soldiers in the country. Her commissioners are demanding returns of every acre, with the names of freeholders and tenants.

The treasurer has reported that the tax can only be collected with "danger, grudge or murmour of the pepill", and religious leaders are outraged by a series of new demands.

Taxation is not the only factor to anger Scotsmen. The presence of so many French soldiers at garrisons like Broughty, Dunbar and Inchkeith is causing continual friction – especially with delays in paying the troops' wages. And few Scots can accept a law which makes it illegal to "speak evil against the queen's grace and of Frenchmen".

The French are so concerned at the obvious Scottish hostility that they are hurrying through the proposed marriage of Mary Queen of Scots to the French *Dauphin*. The move will have a marked effect on Scottish independence, they hope (→ 1/9/58).

Mary of Guise: James V's widow, currently regent in Scotland.

Philip strives to manipulate succession to stop English crown going to French

London, 6 July 1557

After months of pleading by his lovelorn queen, King Philip has returned to London in a new attempt to resolve the English succession crisis. At the age of 41, Mary is convinced she can still bear Philip's child; but, despite Mary's delirium at seeing her husband once more, there is nothing romantic about his stay at the English court.

His first task is to persuade England to join Spain in war against France; the second, to persuade Princess Elizabeth to marry Duke Emmanuel Philibert of Savoy. He believes that this would save the English crown from falling into French hands via the Stewart line.

Elizabeth is resisting any such move. She has recently turned down a proposal from Prince Erik of Sweden, stressing that, even if she were offered "the greatest prince of all Europe", she is not

A princely suitor: Erik of Sweden.

inclined to marry at the moment. Philip has threatened to force Elizabeth to return to Europe with him. Mary's hatred for her half-sister has continued to grow, and she is implacably opposed to the idea.

French capture Calais

Calais, 7 January 1558

White flags flew today over the walled city of Calais – an English possession for more than 200 years – as English troops gave up the fight against far superior French forces. No one had expected the Duke of Guise to attack during this bitter winter, even though the garrison of Calais was down to 600 men against a potential invading force of at least 27,000.

The English commander, Lord Wentworth, was appealing for reinforcements when the French swept in with their artillery, fighting off the English fleet from the fort. Had reinforcements succeeded in reaching the harbour, the result might

well have been victory for the English, but the advantage was with the French, and remains so as a storm is reported to have damaged ships carrying more reinforcements hurrying from Kent. The garrison at Guisnes is preparing to put up a tough fight.

The loss of Calais is a bitter blow to England; but more ironic is the rift between its passionately Catholic queen and the pope, who has dismissed his legate, Cardinal Pole. The pope has been forced into a reconciliation with Philip of Spain after being deserted by the French – and resents the part played by the English in making him dependent on Spain (→ 20/9/62).

Calais: the city has been taken by French troops under the Duke of Guise.

Catholic queen involved in row with Rome

London, June 1557

After four years of struggling to return her country to Catholicism, Queen Mary finds herself at odds with the pope in Rome. The new pope, Paul IV, is pursuing a vendetta against the English legate, Cardinal Reginald Pole, who was himself a favoured candidate for the papacy. Pole has been ordered to Rome – to face possible charges of heresy. Mary has refused to

allow her closest adviser to leave the country and has refused permission for the pope's messenger to enter England. The pope's vicious reaction has been to appoint a new legate in the form of William Peto, a Franciscan friar, once Catherine of Aragon's confessor, now senile and wholly incompetent. An embittered Mary insists that her dispute is with the pope and not with the Holy See.

John Knox blasts the 'monstrous regiment' of women rulers

Edinburgh, October 1557

The long-standing quarrel between the Calvinist preachers and the Scottish regency has taken a dangerous turn with the publication by the fiery preacher John Knox, from his exile in Geneva, of a tract entitled *First blast of the trumpet against the monstrous regiment* [meaning "rule"] *of women*, a blistering attack on the Scottish regent, Mary of Guise, and Queen Mary of England. "It is more than a monster in nature," writes Knox, "that a woman should reign and bear empire above man." He will not be easily forgiven (→ 12/11/72).

The first blast of the trumpet: blown by the Calvinists Knox and Goodman.

Mary believes she is pregnant again

London, 30 March 1558

Again convinced that she is bearing an heir to the throne, Mary today made her will in case she dies in childbirth. Under its terms, only the queen's own children can succeed to the English crown. The guardianship and regency of the realm is bequeathed to her husband, Philip. The king, who is away in the Netherlands, has expressed satisfaction at the news of his 42-year-old wife's "pregnancy"; elsewhere it has been received with undisguised scepticism (→ 17/11).

Queen of Scots marries French Dauphin

The young Scots queen, who has lived in exile since she was six years old.

Paris, 24 April 1558

In a glittering ceremony in Notre Dame cathedral, the beautiful 15-year-old Mary Queen of Scots was married today to the French *Dauphin* (heir) – cementing an alliance which England has dreaded.

Rarely has the French court put on such a show. The bride's procession was headed by Swiss Guards to the sound of tambourines and fifes; followed by more musicians in yellow and red, with trumpets, flageolets and violins. The brilliant costumes of 100 gentlemen-in-waiting were outshone only by those of the princes of the blood, who were followed by bishops bearing rich bejewelled crosses and the princes of the church in equal finery.

The only factor to mar the occasion was the appearance of the young *Dauphin*, who is singularly ugly and given to a constantly run-

ning nose. His presence was virtually ignored, however, when the bride entered the cathedral in a lily-white robe of sumptuous silk – defying tradition, for white is the colour of mourning in the French court – her train carried by two young girls. Her golden crown glistened with rubies, pearls and sapphires, surrounding one great diamond reputed to be worth over 500,000 crowns.

This was the first of three days of celebration with much feasting and merriment. Those in the crowd were not left out: with a shout of "*largesse!*" the Duke of Guise hurled a mass of gold coins to them. At the wedding feast, Mary complained of the weight of the crown. Some more thoughtful witnesses may have read more into the symbolism of the burden weighing on the young queen's neck (→11/11).

First English queen dies

London, 17 November 1558

It seems likely that, even on her deathbed, Mary Tudor, who died early today, was secretly hoping again that she was not ill but pregnant. For the past four and a half years the first queen regnant of England had lived with two obsessions. The first was bearing an heir to the throne; the second was ensuring that her half-sister, Elizabeth, did not succeed to that throne.

The court is in mourning for a queen whose life always seemed doomed to be tragic. Born to be the most devout of Catholics, she was forced to witness the humiliation of her own mother, Catherine of Aragon, at the hands of her father, Henry VIII – whose second wife, the hated Anne Boleyn, produced Elizabeth, the Protestant who, Mary knew, was certain to wear her crown. Elizabeth's palace has been *en fête* for several weeks, ever since the constant threat of Mary's fury diminished as the queen's life began to run out.

For much of the past four years, the streets of London, Oxford and other main cities have reeked with the odour of burning heretics and of decaying corpses of rebels swinging from gibbets, their heads decorating London Bridge and other vantage-points. Mary grew more ruthless as her reign advanced. Already the mob is calling this tragic

woman "Bloody Mary", and there is little doubt that hundreds have died, often horribly, to further her interests. However, her passion for her husband, Philip – who treated her so badly – was genuine and deep, and her devotion to Catholicism was based on love and a determination that England should return to the "old religion" that she cherished even though a pope turned against her.

She was deeply affected by the loss of Calais to France earlier this year, saying shortly before her final illness: "When I am dead and opened, you will find Calais lying in my heart" (→14/12).

The late queen: a devout Catholic.

Protestant riots break out in Edinburgh

Edinburgh, 1 September 1558

Scottish resentment at French religious persecution – spearheaded by the regent, Mary of Guise – exploded into serious rioting in the streets of the capital today. Tension has been mounting steadily since April when Walter Myln, an 80-year-old Protestant parish priest from Lunan, near Montrose, was burnt at the stake at St Andrews.

Preachers of the Protestant faith are now openly defying the Catholic government. In July, for instance, several of them refused to obey a summons and celebrated their independence by destroying a statue of St Giles. Today's riot broke out when a substitute statue was carried in procession through the streets of Edinburgh. The Guise

regime is particularly concerned about the formation of what is known as the "First Band", or covenant, of the Protestant congregation in Scotland. It was established in December last year by five high-ranking Scots – including three earls – known as the "Lords of the Congregation".

The language of the covenant is typical of the fiercely iconoclastic Scots faith. The five men swore "to forsake and renounce the congregation of Satan with all the abomination and idolatry thereof" and promised to maintain, set forward and establish the most precious word of God and his congregation. Above all, the lords are concerned that France intends to make Scotland a French province (→26/3/59).

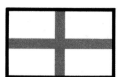

Elizabeth I
1558–1603

Mary, Queen
of Scots
1542–1567
James VI
1567–1603

Elizabeth is enthroned

Scotland, 11 November 1558. The Scottish Parliament agrees to offer the French *Dauphin* the crown matrimonial, which would make him king of Scotland even if Mary Queen of Scots dies first (→10/7/59).

England, 17 November 1558. Queen Elizabeth, aged 25, accedes to the throne (→10/1/59).

Hatfield, 17 November 1558. Elizabeth appoints Sir William Cecil as her chief secretary of state (→25/2/71).

Westminster, 14 Dec 1558. Queen Mary is buried.

England, 10 January 1559. King Philip of Spain, the husband of the late Queen Mary, proposes marriage to Elizabeth (→15/1).

London, 15 January 1559. Elizabeth is crowned queen.→

Scotland, 26 March 1559. Mary of Guise, regent for Mary Queen of Scots, affirms her opposition to Protestantism (→21/10).

London, 5 June 1559. Elizabeth rejects a plan to marry her to one of the sons of the Holy Roman Emperor, Charles or Ferdinand.

Edinburgh, 21 October 1559. Mary of Guise is suspended as regent of Scotland by the Protestant Lords of the Congregation (→11/6/60).

Edinburgh, 11 June 1560. Mary of Guise dies of dropsy.

Edinburgh, 6 July 1560. English and French troops withdraw on the signing of the Treaty of Edinburgh (→24/8).

France, 5 December 1560. Francis II of France, the 16-year-old husband of Mary Queen of Scots, dies (→19/8/61).

Scotland, 15 July 1562. Elizabeth cancels a meeting with Mary Queen of Scots because of Mary's continued attacks on French Protestants (→22/2/63).

London, 20 September 1562. Elizabeth signs a treaty giving aid to the French Protestants; in return, the English are to hold Le Havre as a pledge for the recovery of Calais (→8/1563).

Canterbury, February 1563. The Convocation of Canterbury approves the 39 articles of the Church of England, reduced from the 42 of Edward VI's reign (→3/1566).

France, 11 April 1564. The Treaty of Troyes ends the Anglo-French war, confirming England's loss of Calais.

London, December 1564. Rumours circulate about the possible marriage of Mary Queen of Scots to Robert Dudley, the Earl of Leicester (→29/7/65).

London, August 1565. Lady Mary Grey, a great-niece of Henry VIII, is found out in her secret marriage to Thomas Keyes, a serjeant porter at court.

Scotland, 12 April 1567. James, the Earl of Bothwell, is acquitted of the murder of Henry, Lord Darnley (→20/6).

Scotland, 20 June 1567. Letters implicating Mary Queen Scots in the murder of Henry, Lord Darnley, are found (→2/7).

Rome, 2 July 1567. The pope ends all contact with Mary Queen of Scots (→15/5/68).

Solway Firth, 15 May 1568. Mary Queen of Scots, defeated by rebels at Langside, flees across the border into England(→16/5).

A magnificent presence: an anonymous portrait of the new queen, Elizabeth.

Westminster, 15 January 1559
Elizabeth, the daughter of Henry VIII and Anne Boleyn, and half-sister of the late Queen Mary, was crowned at Westminster abbey today after two days of public display which suggest that she has already won the affection of her people. At the coronation service the 25-year-old queen made her most emphatic mark by refusing to be present while Bishop Oglethorpe elevated the host – a Roman Catholic ritual that she hates. Her gesture gave heart to all those persecuted under Mary who now wish to see the return of Protestantism.

Yesterday's coronation procession was notable for the informality with which the young queen made contact with her subjects. They thronged the streets of London from the Tower of London to Whitehall, saluting her with five separate pageants. Dressed in a robe of cloth of gold and wearing the crown of a princess, she stopped her procession from time to time to accept floral gifts and spontaneous tributes from even the humblest. It was a clever propaganda exercise, emphasising reconciliation and harmony in contrast to the discord and suffering of Mary's reign.

At today's ceremony, the queen did nothing to discourage her keenest admirers, who cut off pieces of the blue carpet after she had walked on it. Organs, fifes, drums and bells accompanied her to the abbey, and she shouted greetings to the crowd as she went to the traditional banquet afterwards. Despite English misgivings about another female monarch, it has been an auspicious start to her reign (→10/2).

Queen 'content to remain a virgin'

Westminster, 10 February 1559
Queen Elizabeth – clearly the most desirable match in Europe – has sought to quell speculation about her possible marriage by assuring the House of Commons that she is content to remain a virgin. Her declaration is unlikely to reduce the enormous interest shown in her by ambassadors from various European courts, led by the Count of Feria, the Spanish envoy. Feria apparently believes that Elizabeth's marriage is within the gift of her brother-in-law, Philip II of Spain – who himself proposed to her last month. Potential suitors also include several English aristocrats.

A few days ago the Commons carried a motion that the queen – who thoroughly enjoys being the centre of so much attention – should be requested to marry as soon as possible for the sake of the succession. They were not prepared for her response.

She had no present intention of marrying, Elizabeth told parliament, but she assured them that if she changed her mind she would choose a husband as committed as herself to the security and prosperity of the realm. "And in the end," she concluded, "this shall be for me sufficient, that a marble stone shall declare that a queen, having reigned such a time, lived and died a virgin" (→ 5/6).

Gossip links queen to mysterious death

Oxfordshire, 8 September 1560
Amy Robsart, the wife of Lord Robert Dudley, one of Queen Elizabeth's most favoured courtiers, has been found dead at the foot of the stairs at her home, Cumnor Place, outside Oxford. She appears to have fallen downstairs and broken her neck, but the court is alive with rumours that she was murdered in order to enable Dudley to marry the queen. Today's shocking news comes after months in which the young queen's familiarity with the handsome Dudley – to whom she has given lands and all kinds of privileges – has been a source of concern to her senior advisers. Dudley, the son of the late Duke of Northumberland, is particularly distrusted by William Cecil, the queen's secretary (→ 28/9/64).

A later view of Amy Robsart's death.

Scots outlaw Mass and break with pope

Edinburgh, 24 August 1560
The religious reformation in Scotland is complete. The Scots Parliament has abrogated papal authority and proclaimed the performance of the Catholic Mass to be a capital offence. This revolution was carried through in the face of widespread opposition; its success depended on clever propaganda by Protestants, who presented the fight against the regent, Mary of Guise – who died in June – as a war of national liberation against French occupation.

John Knox and his Protestant followers ignited a revolt in Perth last year, since when many leading noblemen and lairds have publicly declared support. The Scots are determined to avoid becoming a French satellite and have had covert backing from their old enemy, England. Today's proclamation comes a month after the Treaty of Edinburgh, which recognised Elizabeth's right to the English throne and provided for the removal of French troops from Scotland.

Parliament passes Act of Supremacy

Westminster, 29 April 1559
Despite the opposition of Catholic bishops, parliament has passed Acts of Supremacy and Uniformity, naming Queen Elizabeth as supreme governor of the church. The acts – which formally re-establish Protestantism in England – provide for Communion in both kinds and the repeal of the heresy laws; they restate Henry VIII's formula for consecrating bishops.

The new acts effectively restore the Prayer Book of 1552 while leaving ornaments and dress to the discretion of the queen. The Communion sentences deny transubstantiation, but allow communicants to "feed on him in thy heart by faith" (→ 2/1563).

France seals peace

Cateau-Cambrésis, 3 April 1559
France and England have at last made peace in a treaty signed here today, and the town of Calais returns to French control, although this depends on a payment of half a million crowns eight years hence. But this is an uneasy peace. Since Mary Queen of Scots married the French *Dauphin*, her coat of arms has included the arms of England. The threat of a Franco-Scottish alliance against England is all too obvious (→ 20/9/62).

Queen Elizabeth in parliament.

Mary of Scots' husband proclaimed king of France and Scotland

France, 10 July 1559
Francis, the 15-year-old husband of Mary Queen of Scots, has been proclaimed King Francis II of France in succession to his father, Henry II, who died from a wound received in a tournament. The young man has already been recognised as king of Scots.

Francis II is a weakling, and the effective government of France will be in the hands of Queen Mary's powerful uncles, the Cardinal of Lorraine and the Duke of Guise. Mary – who has lived in France since being removed from Scotland for her own safety ten years ago – is only 16 years old. Her mother, Mary of Guise, is regent of Scotland (→ 5/12/60).

A royal tragedy: the tournament at which Henry II received a fatal wound.

Lady Jane's sister put in Tower after marrying in secret

Tower of London, November 1560
Lady Catherine Grey, a potential successor to the throne of England, has been imprisoned with her alleged husband, Edward Seymour, the Earl of Hertford. The couple are said to have married in secret, and 19-year-old Lady Catherine is pregnant. Queen Elizabeth is furious, and Lady Catherine's future looks doubtful in view of a 1536 law which makes it a treasonable offence for a person of royal blood to marry without the permission of the sovereign.

The beautiful Lady Catherine is a great-granddaughter of Henry VII, and next in line to the throne under Henry VIII's will. Her sister Jane was proclaimed queen in 1553 on the death of Edward VI, before being confined to the Tower and later executed on the orders of Queen Mary. Catherine seems to have no more luck or judgement than her late sister.

Lady Catherine's first husband was Henry Herbert, the son of the Earl of Pembroke, who secured a divorce after Lady Jane's execution. When she became attached to Edward Seymour, Catherine seems to have been too frightened to ask the queen's permission to marry. It is a touchy subject for a queen whose own marriage plans are the subject of continual rumour-mongering.

Mary Queen of Scots returns home

Leith, 19 August 1561
On a damp and misty morning, the cannon from her galleys announced the return of Mary Queen of Scots to the shores of her homeland after a 12-year absence in France. Holyrood palace in Edinburgh is being prepared for royal occupation, and people are converging from afar to see the tall, chestnut-haired 18-year-old widow of the king of France who has come to claim her throne following the sudden death of her husband last December.

Mary's arrival was preceded by awkward negotiations between herself and her cousin Elizabeth. Mary had refused to ratify the Treaty of Edinburgh recognising Elizabeth as queen of England, and Elizabeth, in turn, refused Mary safe conduct through England. Eventually she relented, but by the time her offer of a safe conduct reached its destination, Mary had set sail for Scotland.

Rivalry between the two cousins is finely balanced. While the queen of Scots might make a more tempting match for a European monarch than the elusive Elizabeth, Mary's Catholicism can only cause problems in Scotland, where the Protestant reformation was carried through last year (→ 15/7/62).

Mary: come to claim her throne.

Gift of silk stockings enthrals Elizabeth

Royal splendour: a later portrait of Elizabeth, by Nicholas Hilliard.

Westminster, 1561
Queen Elizabeth is so pleased with her new silk stockings – a gift from one of her servants – that she has vowed to wear none other. The stockings are the latest regular item in the increasingly elaborate royal wardrobe. The queen is fastidious about her personal appearance, and spends several hours every morning preparing herself with the aid of the ladies of the bedchamber. The queen's ladies and maids-of-honour dress in black and white so that she, in her jewels and finery, stands out all the more. She favours low-cut dresses, often embroidered with silver and pearls. She uses marjoram as a scent, and lotion to whiten her face.

Gaelic lord reneges on deal with queen

Ulster, 1562
Shane O'Neill, a Gaelic lord, has claimed the kingship of Ulster in repudiation of an understanding reached with Queen Elizabeth. O'Neill's rebellion is an acute embarrassment to Thomas Radcliffe, the Earl of Sussex, the English governor of Ireland.

English rule in Ireland is confined within a coastal strip known as the Pale, with Dublin at its centre. The rest is Gaelic. Reluctant to embark on a full-scale conquest, Queen Elizabeth allowed O'Neill to be recognised as captain of Tyrone, provided that he yielded to her overlordship (→ 7/1579).

Fears for queen's life lift as she fights to overcome smallpox

Hampton Court, October 1562
Queen Elizabeth is gravely ill with smallpox. Dr Burcot, the skilled German physician, has returned to administer medicine, with the result that red spots have begun to appear on the queen's hands. The irascible doctor, on hearing the patient moan, cried: "God's pestilence! Which is better? To have the pox in the hand or in the face, or in the heart and kill the whole body."

His implication is that the worst is over, but the queen's most trusted advisers remain at her bedside. When Dr Burcot originally diagnosed smallpox the queen refused to believe him and sent him packing. Within a few days she was in a high fever and periodically lapsing into unconsciousness; her doctors, fearing for her life, sent for her councillors. She demanded that they appoint Lord Robert Dudley protector of the realm, at a salary of £20,000 a year, and swore to God that, though she loved him, there was no impropriety in their relationship. She was making other provisions for her death when Dr Burcot was persuaded to return, allegedly at the point of a knife. Following an Arabic remedy advocated by the physician John of Gaddesden, the patient has been wrapped in red cloth (→ 10/4/63).

A coin marks Elizabeth's recovery.

Poet obsessed with queen is beheaded

St Andrews, 22 February 1563
Pierre de Châtelard, a handsome French courtier and poet, was beheaded here today after making repeated improper advances towards Mary Queen of Scots. The queen was pleased at first by his verses, but ordered him to leave the court after he was found hiding under her bed. He foolishly followed her here and broke into her rooms. When the Earl of Moray, Mary's half-brother, was disturbed by her cries for help, he arrested the Frenchman, who was tried and condemned to death (→ 12/1564).

Elizabeth denies taking celibacy vows as parliament grows anxious over succession

All-knowing: the eyes and ears indicate that nothing escapes the queen.

Westminster, 10 April 1563

In response to anxious petitions from peers and MPs about the succession, Elizabeth, who is now 29, has assured parliament that she has taken no vows of celibacy.

The Commons referred to the alarm caused by her recent bout of smallpox and asked her to ensure that, in the event of her untimely death, her people would not face the horrors of anarchy as rival claimants fought for her throne. The Lords were more direct in their request that she should marry. Today the queen promised to heed parliament's wishes, saying that, while she might think a single life

best for a private woman, she was striving to think that it was not suitable for a monarch. She insisted that they should trust her.

Elizabeth's chief adviser, Sir William Cecil, is pursuing plans for a match with the Austrian Archduke Charles. Meanwhile, the queen's household complains about the favouritism shown to Lord Robert Dudley. He has apartments next to hers in all her principal residences, hosts parties for her and takes charge of her travel arrangements. While there has been gossip about their possible marriage, socially and domestically Dudley already fills the role of consort (→ 28/9/64).

Prejudice increases against woman ruler

England, August 1563

Severe humiliation at the loss of Le Havre to the French has rekindled English prejudice against their woman ruler. Weakened by plague, the English garrison at Le Havre, led by Robert Dudley's brother, the Earl of Warwick, surrendered on 29 July after months of siege.

The English presence in the town arose from a hard bargain driven by Elizabeth with the Prince of Condé, the Huguenot leader. In exchange for English help in their war against the French Catholics, the Huguenots agreed last year to surrender Le Havre and allow Elizabeth to keep it until France restored Calais to England. In return, Elizabeth paid the Huguenots a subsidy and sent an army to occupy Le Havre.

When the French civil war ended earlier this year, the Catholics and Huguenots united in a common front against the English. Determined to regain Calais, Elizabeth decided to fight on. Had it not been

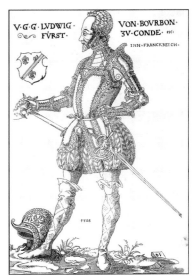

Prince of Condé: Huguenot leader.

for the plague, the venture might well have ended in victory. As it is, Calais now seems irretrievable, and the fiasco has been blamed on the queen's lack of judgement as a woman (→ 11/4/64).

Unauthorised portraits of queen banned

England, 1563

A draft proclamation has been prepared to ban the production of debased portraits of Queen Elizabeth. There is great public demand for portraits of the sovereign, but the queen has been unwilling to sit for many painters – with the result that very few official portraits have been released, and unauthorised versions are being hawked on the

streets. The queen is not generally considered a great beauty, but fine-featured, with a regal manner and delicate hands. Her desire is to suppress representations that detract from her good image as a woman and a queen. The proclamation is understood to provide for an official portrait, from which authorised copies might then be taken and disseminated (→ 1596).

Elizabeth invests in John Hawkins's slave-trading expedition

A favourite pastime: the queen is handed a knife by one of her huntsmen as the royal hunting party closes in on the kill.

Plymouth, 1564

Queen Elizabeth has invested in a potentially lucrative new expedition to the West Indies, providing its leader, John Hawkins, with a 600-ton warship which saw service in Henry VIII's navy. Hawkins returned from his first, illegal voyage to the West Indies in September last year, laden with hides, ginger, sugar, pearls and other valuables. These goods had been acquired in return for negroes captured in Africa and sold as slaves in the Spanish Main and American settlements. There is great enthusiasm in England for Hawkins's activities, which have infuriated the Spanish.

Hawkins, the son of a Plymouth merchant seaman and son-in-law of Elizabeth's treasurer of the navy, led 100 men in three ships via the Canary Isles to the coast of Guinea. There they captured 300 negroes and took them across the ocean to Hispaniola. Stopping at three ports there, he sold goods from England, as well as his entire cargo of negroes. So profitable was this trade that Hawkins had too much to carry in his three ships, so he sent another two vessels, piled with hides and other commodities, on to Spain, where the merchandise – which he had been hoping to sell there – was confiscated.

John Hawkins: trader in slaves.

Mary of Scots marries Lord Darnley

Edinburgh, 29 July 1565

Holyrood palace was the scene today of the second marriage of the 22-year-old Queen Mary of Scots. Her husband, who becomes king of Scots, is the 19-year-old Henry Stuart, Lord Darnley; his mother, Margaret, and Mary's father, James V, were half-siblings, children of Margaret Tudor from her first two marriages. Not only are Mary and Henry cousins, therefore, but also, as great-grandchildren of Henry VII of England, they each have a claim to the English throne.

Not surprisingly, their cousin Queen Elizabeth disapproves of the match, seeing it as a move by Mary towards seizing the English crown. But Mary has been utterly infatuated with Darnley since they met in February, and her passion has both deafened her to warnings of the marriage's political consequences and blinded her to Darnley's faults. For, although handsome, elegant and accomplished, he is also weakwilled, spoilt and vain.

As Mary's love has grown he has become insufferably proud, insulting courtiers who cannot answer back. He is a Catholic, which does not help. As Thomas Randolph, an English diplomat in Edinburgh, said recently: "It is greatly to be feared that he can have no long life among these people" (→ 20/6/67).

The bride and bridegroom: Mary Queen of Scots with Lord Darnley.

Growth of 'puritan' Cambridge radicals alarms Elizabeth

Westminster, 9 December 1565

Queen Elizabeth was briefed today by her chief minister, Sir William Cecil, on a disturbing outbreak by an outspoken and at times almost violent dissenting religious movement at Cambridge university.

The adherents of the new movement, which is centred on Cecil's old college, St John's, are strongly influenced by the radical Protestantism of Calvin and reject anything which, in their eyes, smacks of Rome or the pope, the Antichrist himself. Nicknamed "puritans", or purists, they are not against the reformed Church of England itself, but think that it has not gone far enough in areas such as liturgy (still too much like the Mass) and vestments ("popish trumpery"). A survey ordered by the queen in 1561 revealed a vast variety of practice in these areas even among senior churchmen.

"Puritans" are loyal to Elizabeth as the chief agent of the reformed church, but some of the more extreme are beginning to criticise her for not wiping out all "popery". But she has no intention of being told what to do. She has ordered Cecil "to use all severity expedient" to end the trouble (→ 3/1566).

Robert Dudley created Earl of Leicester and given new estates

Courtly entertainment: Queen Elizabeth dancing with the Earl of Leicester.

London, 28 September 1564

Today, amid great grandeur at St James's palace, Elizabeth made her long-standing favourite Robert Dudley one of the foremost nobles in the kingdom. Dudley, a son of John, the Duke of Northumberland, becomes Earl of Leicester – a title traditionally given only to a son of the monarch – and picks up a long list of new estates, including Kenilworth castle in Warwickshire.

The ceremony is meant as a prelude to Dudley's betrothal to Mary of Scots – Elizabeth is keen for Mary to marry someone in whom she herself has perfect trust – but there are fears that he may be disliked in Scotland. Another possible contender for Mary's hand is the dashing Lord Darnley, a cousin of both queens [see report above left].

Modelling themselves on the queen, fashionable young women are wearing whalebone corsets and ruffs stiffened by a newly discovered process: starching.

Violent unrest rocks Scottish throne

Rebellion against Mary's rule flops

Borders, 6 October 1565

The leaders of a rebellion against Mary Queen of Scots have today fled across the border into England. This latest challenge to Mary was led by her half-brother James, the Earl of Moray, who was joined by other nobles alienated by Mary's Catholic marriage to Lord Darnley and by Darnley's insufferable behaviour. But Moray failed to raise enough support, and aid promised by Queen Elizabeth never arrived. Mary's men hunted Moray from one town to the next – already some are calling it "the Chaseabout Raid" – and her triumph deals a serious blow to pro-English and Protestant factions (→ 9/3/66).

David Riccio, Queen Mary's secretary and favourite, meets a brutal end.

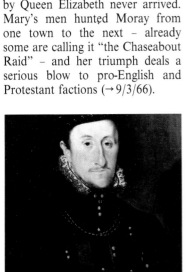
Failed rebel: the Earl of Moray.

Queen's secretary murdered at Holyrood

Edinburgh, 9 March 1566

Mary of Scots is captive in her own palace of Holyrood tonight after a bloody coup involving her husband, Darnley. The coup began when armed men, led by the sick Lord Ruthven, burst into the queen's apartments as she was eating dinner with friends, including her Italian private secretary, David Riccio.

The queen – who is six months pregnant – was roughly handled, but not hurt. Riccio, however, screaming "Save me, my lady, save me!" in French, was dragged to an outer chamber, where he was butchered by over 50 dagger blows. Close by, a friar was also killed.

Darnley, convinced that Mary and Riccio were lovers, also wants Mary to make him king in his own right rather than king-consort. But Ruthven is a Protestant; this and the friar's murder hint at an anti-Catholic motive. There are even rumours that Darnley is a front man for the Earl of Moray and other exiled Protestants (→ 19/6).

Mary gives birth to James, Scottish heir, at Edinburgh castle

Edinburgh, 19 June 1566

Three months after foiling a coup attempt in which her Italian secretary was murdered, Mary Queen of Scots has given birth to a son, James, after a long and difficult labour in the royal apartments of Edinburgh castle.

Mary chose to give birth to her baby in the safety of the castle rather than in Holyrood palace, which was proved by the coup bid on 9 March to be highly vulnerable. Mary's husband, Darnley, the king-consort, had been a prime mover in the plot, but Mary convinced him that his fellow con-

spirators would turn on him. They escaped down a privy staircase and through servants' quarters, and made for Dunbar. From there Mary led an army which reoccupied the capital on 18 March. The plotters had fled.

James's birth is a major event, for the baby – a great-great-grandson of Henry VII of England – is heir not only to the throne of Scotland but also, while Queen Elizabeth is childless, to that of England as well. With an heir, Mary's own claim to the English crown is stronger; her relations with Elizabeth seem unlikely to improve (→ 10/2/67).

Queen Mary with her baby son.

Preachers sent to prison for wearing the wrong clothes

London, March 1566

Elizabeth has ordered the suppression of dissent within the Church of England over the clothes worn by priests during services, or "the livery of Antichrist" as the more radical clergy call them. Churchmen who disobey the queen face a spell in jail. In what is becoming known as "the Vestiarian Controversy", the radical purists or "puritans" see the vestments prescribed by the church as unnecessary "dregs of popery", like wedding rings and church organs. Matthew Parker, the archbishop of Canterbury, has issued a *Book of Advertisement* on the queen's orders, laying down rules for services. But a large minority of clergymen insist that they will not conform (→ 12/1566).

Archbishop Parker of Canterbury.

Elizabeth rebukes MPs over religion

Westminster, December 1566

Queen Elizabeth has closed her second parliament after a sometimes stormy session. She showed that she would not allow parliamentary interference in the religious settlement by rejecting calls by her chief minister, Cecil, and the bishops for the 39 Articles of Religion to be made statutory. She also refused to be browbeaten into a commitment to marriage. "I am your anointed queen," she told MPs haughtily. "I will never be by violence constrained to do anything."

Embattled Queen of Scots struggles to keep crown

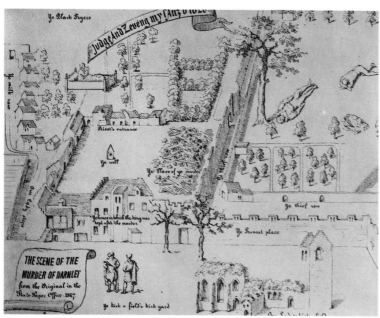

King-consort murdered: a detailed plan of the scene of Lord Darnley's death.

Mary is led into Edinburgh after the defeat of her forces by rebel nobles.

Darnley killed in massive bomb explosion

Edinburgh, 10 February 1567

At two o'clock this morning the Scottish capital was rocked by a massive explosion which destroyed Kirk o'Field house, the lodgings of Lord Darnley, Mary's 21-year-old husband and king-consort.

But Darnley did not die in the blast. His body, naked except for a nightgown, was found with that of his valet in an adjoining orchard;

both had been strangled. It seems that Darnley, sensing danger, had fled from the house – straight into the hands of the assassins preparing to blow him up. Whether Queen Mary, who saw Darnley last night, was involved is unclear; their marriage had failed, and she is close to a prime suspect, the Earl of Bothwell. Yet there were signs of a reconciliation in recent days (→ 15/5).

Bloodless defeat imperils Mary's reign

Lothian, 15 June 1567

The reign of Queen Mary appears all but over following the almost bloodless defeat of her forces today at Carberry Hill, outside Edinburgh. Tonight she is in the hands of rebel nobles who had always opposed her marriage to Bothwell.

The battle which had seemed likely to take place at Carberry ended up as a stalemate between a

defiant Mary and Bothwell, and their opponents, led by Sir William Kirkcaldy. They assured the queen that the crown itself was not being attacked, and she agreed to go with them while Bothwell retreated to Dunbar to await developments. He was wise to do so because, far from being treated like a queen, Mary is tonight under guard like a common criminal (→ 17/6).

Mary marries third husband after 'rape'

Edinburgh, 15 May 1567

Mary Queen of Scots married her third husband today in a hastily arranged Protestant ceremony at the palace of Holyrood. It is just three months since the murder of her second husband, Darnley, by plotters believed to have included her new bridegroom: James Hepburn, the Earl of Bothwell.

Weak and depressed from a recent illness, Mary was returning from Stirling to Edinburgh on 24 April when Bothwell and an armed band intercepted her. Bothwell – rumoured to have been the queen's lover while Darnley was still alive – told her that she was in danger and took her to Dunbar castle; there he cajoled her into promising to marry him and, to make sure

Bothwell: Mary's third husband.

that she would, "persuaded" her into his bed. Scottish nobles are aghast at the ambitious Protestant Bothwell's rise and are planning armed resistance against him and the discredited queen (→ 15/6).

'Whore' is imprisoned in island fortress

Lochleven Castle, 17 June 1567

A grim island fortress in Loch Leven, from which she used to go hunting in the Kinross countryside, is tonight the prison of Scotland's fallen queen. With just the clothes she stands up in, Mary has been brought to the home of Sir William Douglas while the nobles who arrested her fan flames of resentment against her and plan her fate.

As she was led from Carberry Hill to Edinburgh two days ago she was shocked by cries of "Burn the whore!" People are calling her an adulteress who plotted with her married lover, Bothwell, to murder her husband, Darnley, the king-consort. Her captors, up to their necks in Darnley's blood, are happy to let such stories flourish (→ 20/6).

Mary and Bothwell represented as a mermaid [prostitute] and a hare.

Mary abdicates throne of Scotland

Lochleven Castle, 24 July 1567
Scotland has a new monarch: King James VI, the 13-month-old son of Mary Queen of Scots, who abdicated her crown today. It is six years since she returned to her kingdom, and six weeks since the 24-year-old queen was taken into captivity by her rebellious lords.

However, the abdication was carried out under duress. Mary, alone apart from a few trusted servants and her captors on a remote island in Loch Leven, had miscarried twins and was bedridden after losing a lot of blood. One of the rebels, Lord Lindsay, came to her as she lay there and demanded that she sign papers of abdication. She was petrified for her life, but regarded the request as outrageous and refused, demanding in turn to be heard by the Scottish parliament. Lindsay said that if she failed to sign they would simply have to cut her throat. She signed (→ 29/7).

Mary Queen of Scots is forced to give up her throne under threat of death.

Infant son crowned king of Scotland

Stirling, 29 July 1567
The rebellious nobles who forced Mary Queen of Scots to resign her crown five days ago have wasted little time in putting her abdication into effect. Today her 13-month-old son was taken from his current home of Stirling castle to a kirk by the castle gates, where he was crowned King James VI of Scots.

Two of the aristocrats who now effectively control the government of Scotland, the Earls of Morton and Home, swore the oaths of kingship on behalf of the infant James, who is the first Scottish monarch to be crowned in accordance with Protestant rites.

During the ceremony – which was attended by only five earls and eight other lords – documents which Queen Mary had signed were read out. These confirmed her abdication and the setting up of a regency council for James under her bastard half-brother James Stewart, the Earl of Moray. At Lochleven castle, Mary's captors are taunting their prisoner with a day of noisy celebrations for the new king (→ 12/7/70).

Fugitive queen seeks English sanctuary

Cumbria, 16 May 1568
Following the defeat of her army three days ago at Langside by the regent Moray's forces, the former Queen Mary of Scots today crossed the Solway Firth to Workington and the relative safety of England. The flight comes two weeks after her dramatic escape from captivity in Lochleven castle on 2 May.

Sir William Douglas, the laird of Lochleven, is an enemy of Mary. Not so his brother George, who was attracted to the queen. With Willie Douglas, a servant of the laird, George devised a May Day pageant to divert Mary's captors, during which Willie holed the laird's boats. While the laird was at supper Mary went to her chamber, ostensibly to pray, but instead disguised herself. Willie stole the laird's keys, and at a signal Mary walked out of the gates to a waiting boat. George was waiting for them on the mainland. Mary was free (→ 20/12/69).

Mary embarks on a hazardous journey after escaping from Lochleven castle.

Elizabeth's soldiers crush rebellion by northern Catholics

Northumberland, 20 Dec 1569
The biggest anti-Protestant uprising yet to hit Queen Elizabeth's reign has disintegrated, its armies dissolving into the rugged northern countryside and its leaders, the Catholic Earls of Westmorland and Northumberland, being chased across the Scottish border by loyal troops under the Earl of Sussex.

Trouble had been brewing in the strongly Catholic north for months, and the plotters had aimed to remove Elizabeth's non-Catholic "ill-disposed advisers" or even to replace the queen with Mary of Scots. The rebels seized Durham last month and marched to within 50 miles (80 kilometres) of Tutbury, where Mary was being held. But she was simply taken further south and the rebels, deprived of their goal, began to collapse (→ 2/1570).

Spanish treasure seized by Elizabeth

Southern England, January 1569
Decades of warm relations between London and Madrid are close to collapse following Queen Elizabeth's confiscation of a treasure-laden Spanish fleet which had sought refuge in English ports.

The fleet of five ships was on its way to the Spanish Netherlands with £85,000 – a loan from Genoese bankers to King Philip II – to pay the huge army recently sent there under the Duke of Alva. However, bad weather drove the ships into Plymouth and Southampton, and Elizabeth, who was short of money, decided to impound the Spanish vessels and take over the Genoese loan herself.

Spanish reaction has been predictably outraged, although Elizabeth acted within her rights as a sovereign. Madrid has seized English ships and goods in the Netherlands; the queen has responded in kind. At a stroke Elizabeth has almost made enemies of England's old friends, the Habsburgs. With a Spanish army of 35,000 just across the Channel, the strain in relations could prove very costly.

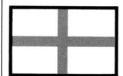

Elizabeth I
1558–1603

James VI
1567–1603

Scotland, February 1570. Queen Elizabeth blocks all attempts by Mary Queen of Scots, who is confined under house arrest, to make contact with her son, James VI (→ 15/10/86).

Scotland, 12 July 1570. The Earl of Lennox, Matthew Stuart, the father of the murdered Lord Darnley, is appointed regent for his three-year-old grandson, King James VI (→ 4/9/71).

London, 3 August 1570. Sir William Cecil, the chief secretary of state, persuades Elizabeth to free Thomas Howard, the Duke of Norfolk, into house arrest; he was convicted of treason for his part in the northern rebellion (→ 3/9/71).

England/France, Sept 1570. Elizabeth, despite the distress of Cecil, considers a marriage alliance with Henry, the Duke of Anjou, a Catholic and the heir to the French throne (→ 6/1572).

London, 3 September 1571. The Duke of Norfolk, Thomas Howard, is rearrested and charged after the discovery last month of a plot to assassinate Elizabeth and replace her with Mary Queen of Scots (→ 2/6/72).

Stirling, 4 September 1571. The regent of Scotland, Matthew Stuart, the Earl of Lennox, is shot dead during a raid on the castle (→ 28/10/72).

England, 1 March 1572. Elizabeth expels the Dutch refugees known as the "Sea Beggars" for piracy. They seize the port of Brill, in the Netherlands.

Plymouth, Devon, 24 May 1572. Francis Drake sets off on a voyage across the Atlantic, intent on avenging his mistreatment by the Spanish on previous expeditions (→ 9/8/73).

England/France, June 1572. As negotiations to marry Elizabeth to Duke Henry of Anjou collapse, Catherine de' Medici, the duke's mother, suggests a younger son, Francis, the Duke of Alençon, as a suitor (→ 6/1578).

Edinburgh, 24 November 1572. John Knox, the scourge of the Catholic Church and harsh critic of Mary Queen of Scots, dies.

London, October 1575. Queen Elizabeth and her favourite Robert Dudley, the Earl of Leicester, both have their portraits painted by the Italian Federico Zuccaro (→ 1579).

Worcester, 23 September 1577. Attempting to reduce the growth of puritanism, Elizabeth, who earlier this year made John Aylmer bishop of London, appoints John Whitgift as bishop of Worcester (→ 11/11).

Whitehall, 11 November 1577. Sir Christopher Hatton joins the privy council as part of Elizabeth's fight against puritans.

Edinburgh, March 1578. James VI, aged 12, assumes his role as head of the government, following a coup against the regent, Morton (→ 30/9/79).

France/England, June 1578. Marriage negotiations begin again between Elizabeth and Francis, the recently promoted Duke of Anjou, after his brother Henry's accession to the French throne (→ 3/11/79).

Ecuador, 28 February 1579. Francis Drake, on his ship the *Golden Hind*, captures the Spanish vessel *Cacafuego*.

Edinburgh, 30 September 1579. King James VI makes his first elaborate state entry into the city (→ 22/8/82).

Elizabeth is excommunicated by the pope

Pope Pius hands down the bull excommunicating Queen Elizabeth.

London, 8 August 1570
John Felton, a rich Catholic living in Southwark, has been executed today for nailing the papal bull excommunicating Queen Elizabeth to the door of the bishop of London. The bull – which deprives Elizabeth of her title to the kingdom of England and frees her subjects from their allegiance to her – was not at first taken particularly seriously by the government, but Felton's action was a direct challenge to authority and had to be acted upon.

A member of an old Norfolk family, Felton was married to a former maid-of-honour to Queen Mary Tudor. He obtained his copy of the bull from the Spanish ambassador and, between two and three o'clock on the morning of 15 May, fixed it to the door of the bishop's palace in St Paul's churchyard.

Felton's house was surrounded by a large force led by the mayor and the lord chief justice, and he quickly gave himself up and admitted responsiblity. Tortured on the rack, he would not give any information about his accomplices. Instead he refused to acknowledge Elizabeth as queen and said that he would die for papal supremacy – which he has done.

Scottish regent is shot by hired assassin

Moray is killed: detail from a window in St Giles's church, Edinburgh.

Linlithgow, 23 January 1570
The Scottish regent, James Stewart, the Earl of Moray, has been shot dead by an assassin who gunned him down in the main street of Linlithgow today. At first it was said that the regent had fallen victim to the vengeance of a poor man whose wife he had driven out to die in the snow, but this now appears to be untrue.

While the facts have yet to be established fully, it seems likely that Moray was killed by an assassin hired by his deadly rivals, the Hamilton clansmen. Moray was ambitious, and many suspected that he, as a half-brother of Queen Mary, would use his position as regent to seize the throne for himself. Now it looks as though his enemies decided to strike first (→ 12/7).

Queen thanks Cecil by giving peerage

England, 25 February 1571

William Cecil, Elizabeth's shrewd secretary of state, has been made Baron Burghley in recognition of his great gifts. The "inner circle" surrounding the queen consists mainly of peers; its most important members are Burghley, Leicester, Sussex, Bedford and Sir Francis Walsingham. Of these Leicester is the most militant. His ambition is to lead an English army to support the Protestant Dutch against their Catholic Spanish rulers. Walsingham is the most single-minded, a "political puritan" dedicated to the Protestant cause; Burghley is the most cautious (→1587).

A portrait of Cecil riding a donkey.

Renewed Catholic uprising put down

Yorkshire, February 1570

The queen is delighted at the news that the northern Catholic rebellion against her rule, which began in November with the tearing up of the bible in Durham cathedral, has finally been laid to rest. The uprising ended with a small but bloody battle on 19 February in which Lord Hunsdon decisively defeated the last of the rebels, Leonard Dacres. Dacres has fled across the border to Scotland to join the other northern leaders. The punishment of their peasant followers has been in progress since December, when the government retook large areas of the north. Hundreds have already been hanged, and more will follow (→ 29/5/71).

England allies with France against Spain

Blois, France, 19 April 1572

England and France have sealed a treaty here today from which the English appear to have secured the most advantage. Although under its terms Queen Elizabeth finds herself in the unusual position of being allied with Catholic France against the Protestant Netherlands, it has three great bonuses for her. It ends England's diplomatic isolation; it blocks French interference in Elizabeth's dealings with Mary Queen of Scots, and it creates a defensive pact against Spain.

The treaty has come about partly as a result of the failure of negotiations to marry Elizabeth to the Duke of Alençon, the fourth son of the French regent, Catherine de' Medici. Alençon is a spotty youth, whose lack of good looks has been made worse by smallpox, which has left his face, particularly his nose, deeply pitted and scarred.

Elizabeth is 20 years older than Alençon, and she has decided that to marry a gawky boy would provoke a scandal – in her own words, an "absurdity that in the general opinion of the world might grow". Catherine de' Medici's plans to marry Elizabeth to Alençon's elder brother Henry, the Duke of Anjou, foundered last year. Nevertheless, both Elizabeth and Catherine needed an alliance and, as marriage was out, the treaty sufficed (→ 6/1572).

French ducal suitors: Anjou ...

... and Francis of Alençon.

Catholic threat prompts tough new laws

Catholics are being sternly treated.

London, 29 May 1571

Three acts of parliament have been passed to counter what is seen as a growing Catholic menace. It is now high treason to say that Elizabeth is not the lawful queen, or to publish, write or say that the queen is a heretic, schismatic, tyrant, usurper or an infidel. This places even the most loyal of Catholics in a dilemma as, from their point of view, she is both a heretic and a schismatic (in that she has promoted separation from the Catholic Church). A second act makes it treasonable to bring into the country papal bulls; also banned are crosses, religious pictures and beads from Rome. A third orders Catholics who have fled abroad to return within six months or forfeit all that they possess (→ 18/3/81).

Norfolk executed after Ridolfi plot

London, 2 June 1572

The Duke of Norfolk was beheaded this morning at Tower Hill for his part in the Ridolfi plot. The conspiracy aimed to remove Queen Elizabeth from the English throne and elevate Mary Queen of Scots to rule both Scotland and England. The duke's role would have been to raise general rebellion against Elizabeth and to marry Mary.

The duke had previously been arrested in 1569 for dabbling in Mary's affairs, but was released after promising Elizabeth that he would not do so again. Ridolfi was a Florentine banker living in London and also a secret agent of the pope. His plot was simple: the Spaniards would invade, Norfolk would lead a simultaneous rebellion, Elizabeth would be kidnapped or killed, and with Mary on the throne England would return to the Catholic fold.

Queen Mary and the pope were captivated by the plan and Norfolk approved, but the Spanish commander, the Duke of Alva, dismissed it as military nonsense. Before it could be put to the test the plot was discovered, and after a short delay Norfolk was identified as one of the leaders. He was tried before his fellow peers and sentenced to death.

Regents put life on the line in Scotland

Scotland, 28 October 1572

Being regent of Scotland is beginning to look like one of Europe's riskiest jobs. Two have been murdered and a third has died in only two years. The outlook for their successor is not much brighter, as the country continues to be divided by rival factions which support or oppose the exiled Queen Mary.

The anti-Mary Earl of Lennox was appointed after the murder of the Earl of Moray in July 1570, but was murdered by pro-Mary forces 14 months later. Lennox was succeeded by the Earl of Mar, who died after 13 months and has now been replaced by the most determined of Mary's enemies, the earl of Morton (→ 28/5/73).

Gifts of jewellery bring new glitter to royal treasury

The queen's Phoenix Jewel.

Westminster, 1573

The vast cost of running the royal household, now approaching several hundred pounds a week, is partly offset by the large amount of jewellery, gold and silver that the queen receives almost daily as presents. Her collection is now reckoned to be the most valuable in Europe.

Elizabeth has numerous bracelets, necklaces, brooches, rings and bejewelled watches. There are long lists of presents of gold: gold buttons, cups, bowls, toothpicks and, an especial favourite, a gold warming-pan which she uses frequently. Pearls are the fashion, and the queen has no shortage; she posed for a portrait wearing a gown sewn with 319 of them. Gifts reckoned to be inferior in value or workmanship are sold to offset the household costs.

Elizabeth's fine Barber Jewel.

Edinburgh castle is captured by regent

Edinburgh, 28 May 1573

After eleven days of bombardment Edinburgh castle has fallen to the regent, James Douglas, the Earl of Morton. It is a great victory for the reforming and strongly Anglophile party that surrounds the seven-year-old King James VI, and it may yet prove to be the final defeat for those who still support his mother, the exiled Mary Queen of Scots, imprisoned in England.

Defections from the queen's party had allowed the regent to re-occupy the town of Edinburgh in the autumn, but a strong garrison still held out in the castle and refused all calls to surrender. Faced with this obduracy the regent sent for English help, and in April an army crossed the border and siege guns were sent by sea to Leith. After 11 days of bombardment by the heavy cannon, the garrison surrendered to the combined Scots and English army, and its leaders will be tried for their lives (→ 7/1581).

Diplomatic queen plays double game

Westminster, 7 May 1574

On the face of it, the murder of French Protestants in the St Bartholomew's day massacre two years ago should have soured relations between England and France beyond redemption. In fact, nothing much has happened because Elizabeth and France need each other too much in the face of expansionist Spain. Instead, the queen has been forced into a double game of showing moral outrage while doing little.

She allowed munitions to be sent to the Huguenots while at the same time standing as godmother to the Catholic French King Charles IX's daughter and agreeing to consider a marriage with his brother Francis, the Duke of Alençon. But when strong elements in the privy council wanted armed intervention to help the Protestant Dutch she refused. Following the death of Charles, she has today renewed the defensive Treaty of Blois with his successor, Henry III, while at the same time sending money to help the French Protestants.

Drake completes spectacular expedition

Plymouth, 9 August 1573

Captain Francis Drake has returned to this port today from South America, after a voyage of more than 15 months. He has lost his brother and one of his two ships, but to the delight of a queen keen to challenge Spain he has returned with an enormous treasure captured from the Spaniards, and a story of adventure the like of which has not been heard before.

Captain Drake left here with two small ships, the *Pasha* and the *Swan*, on 24 May 1572 and set off for the Spanish holdings in South America intent on remaking his fortune, a great deal of which had been lost in an expedition with Captain John Hawkins four years before.

After capturing and destroying many Spanish ships, Drake attacked Nombre de Dios and burnt Porto Bello, but he lost the *Swan* and his brother Joseph died. Then, on 3 February this year, he landed on Panama and with 30 natives began to march westwards. As they reached the highest point of the dividing ridge, the natives pointed out a tree from which it was possible to see the oceans on either side of the isthmus. Drake climbed to the top and became the first Englishman to set eyes on this new ocean [*the Pacific*]. He led his men on into Panama in search of plunder, but missed a rich caravan be-

An heroic explorer: Francis Drake has a weathered face in this portrait.

cause of the untimely intervention of a drunk. After burning Vera Cruz Drake returned to his ship, but after taking fresh supplies he set off with his men once again in search of treasure.

This time they had better luck and intercepted three caravans, numbering 190 mules, each carrying 300 pounds of silver: a total of nearly 30 tons. Unable to carry so much, they took away what they could and buried the rest, but unfortunately the Spaniards found it. After this it was home, and even though they had left so much behind, they still returned to England with the most spectacular haul of treasure yet seen (→ 28/2/79).

'Sacred Songs' honour royal patronage

London, 1575

Queen Elizabeth's keen patronage of artistic talent has been amply demonstrated this year by her grant of a licence to print and sell music to the two greatest musicians in the kingdom, Thomas Tallis and William Byrd. To mark the occasion they have composed and published a set of beautiful vocal works, *Cantiones Sacrae* [Sacred Songs].

Both musicians are Gentlemen of the Chapel Royal, the monarch's personal musical body. Tallis, who is 70, is revered throughout Europe for works such as the amazing *Spem in alium*, written for eight choirs at once, and was one of the first to write music for the Anglican Church. His pupil Byrd, aged 32, is at the other end of his career, but his genius is already acknowledged.

Tallis (top) and William Byrd.

Parker, a reluctant archbishop, is dead

Lambeth Palace, 17 May 1575
The archbishop of Canterbury, Matthew Parker, who had held office for 15 years, died here today. Known in puritan quarters as "the pope of Lambeth" because of his tolerant views towards Roman Catholics, he was plucked from obscurity by Queen Elizabeth herself because she found his moderate views on religion largely, if not entirely, in tune with her own.

Parker had advanced no further than being dean of Lincoln when he was approached with the archbishopric, a position he was most reluctant to accept. Persuaded by Queen Elizabeth, he took the post, and the two worked well together, apart from occasional spats over the archbishop's wife and the "papist" candles and crucifixes in the queen's private chapel.

Elizabeth did not wholly approve of married clergy and wholly disapproved of married bishops and archbishops. She firmly refused to acknowledge Mrs Parker, or to address her by her title, and sometimes spoke so bitterly of her that the archbishop "was in horror to hear her".

Archbishop Parker: a statue at Corpus Christi college, Cambridge.

The superb entertainments laid on at Kenilworth in honour of the queen.

Lavish revels greet queen at Kenilworth

Warwickshire, 27 July 1575
Eighteen days of some of the most lavish revels ever held ended today with the departure of Queen Elizabeth and her court from Kenilworth castle to continue their "summer progress" through the country. The queen was so well entertained by Robert Dudley, the Earl of Leicester, at his newly-restored castle that courtiers now declare they have never seen anything like it.

On arrival the queen was greeted in the park by local maid dressed as a prophetess, who welcomed her and prophesied long life. The castle gates were found to be guarded by a scholar of Oxford university who, in the guise of Hercules, welcomed her in verse before handing over the castle keys. Once inside Elizabeth was surrounded by King Arthur's knights, a lady rose from the castle lake, and gifts from the gods were showered upon her.

The days were spent in hunting and dancing, the evenings in feasting and pageants. Leicester, who at one time had been considered a candidate for Elizabeth's hand, was so concerned for the queen's comfort that, when she mentioned that she could not see the castle gardens from her room, he had a garden built silently beneath her window during the night. When Elizabeth awoke and looked out, the garden was complete (→ 10/1575).

Leicester: he is a matchless host.

Eccentric puritan MP lambasts the queen

Westminster, 15 March 1576
Parliament was dissolved today after a short session disturbed only by the antics of Peter Wentworth, the aggressively puritan MP for Barnstaple. His attack on Queen Elizabeth, all the bishops of England and sundry other targets was so outrageous that his speech was interrupted and he was thrown out of the chamber. He made the mistake of returning later to submit himself to the judgement of the House which, finding him just as outrageous as before, imprisoned him in the Tower for a month. But the queen has forgiven him, and he has been released (→ 23/9/77).

Elizabeth says No to plea from Dutch

Netherlands, 1576
Queen Elizabeth has turned down an offer from the Protestant Dutch provinces to become their sovereign. All the Dutch provinces are now in revolt against Spanish rule, and the king of Spain has sent Don John of Austria, the legendary victor of the sea battle of Lepanto against the Turks, to quell the revolt. However, all sides – English, Dutch and Spanish – are aware that Don John's real intention is not just to put down the revolt, but afterwards to use his troops to invade England, oust Elizabeth, marry Mary Queen of Scots and rule a united kingdom of England and Scotland himself.

The Dutch answer is to form a united Protestant front and army, with Elizabeth at the head. The queen is not keen on the scheme, as she would have to finance it. She has already lent the rebels £20,000 and guaranteed them loans of £100,000 – half the English state income for the year. To go further and risk losing both crown and money in a war is too big a risk for her to take, and so she has declined the Dutch offer (→ 1/1578).

Queen challenged by new archbishop

Lambeth Palace, 20 December 1576
The future of the new archbishop of Canterbury, Edmund Grindal, looks bleak. After only a few months in office he has clashed with Queen Elizabeth over the suppression of "prophesyings". Despite their name, these are nothing more than exercises where the clergy practise their preaching skills and ability to use scripture before gatherings of lay people.

Quite why the queen wants them supressed is not clear, particularly as the bishops think they are useful. But she has ordered Grindal to have them stopped. In a 6,000-word riposte Grindal has compared himself to the fourth century bishop of Milan who lectured the Roman Emperor Theodosius on his duty. The queen has not yet replied, but even Grindal's friends think that he has gone too far (→ 5/1577).

Archbishop is held under house arrest

Lambeth, May 1577

Despite his defiant message that he would rather "offend an earthly Majesty than the heavenly Majesty of God" Archbishop Grindal has quickly learnt that earthly consequences are both more certain and quicker. He has in effect lost his office. Elizabeth has forbidden him to exercise his authority as archbishop and placed him under virtual house arrest.

Edmund Grindal's mistake was to consult his conscience when asked to forbid "prophesyings", those meetings at which clergy practise preaching and the exposition of scripture, which have become a focus for those who wish to "purify" the church. Elizabeth ranks obedience above theology in the priestly virtues.

Archbishop Grindal: out of favour.

'Summer progress' has political aim

Queen Elizabeth seen here on one of the annual "progresses" that have become an important feature of her reign.

Norwich, 22 August 1578

Glittering ceremonial and inventive entertainments have signalled the arrival of Queen Elizabeth here, but they cannot disguise the hard-headed purposes behind this year's stately "summer progress" through East Anglia. The pageantry, with young men decked out as kings of ancient Britain, fulfilled the twin aims of honouring the sovereign and displaying local wealth. But today's play-acting had a more serious message.

Twenty-three prominent Catholic gentlemen were summoned before the council and asked to conform with the English Church established by the Acts of Uniformity and Supremacy. All but one refused, and the 22 were led off to prison. The queen then knighted several leading Protestants and a few Catholics who had professed to conform and given her hospitality. Whether they are sincere or not she shows, as usual, no inclination to "open windows into men's souls". She has also reinstated puritan preachers suspended by Bishop Freke, thus reminding all parties that their quarrels are subordinate to their duty to their queen.

England signs treaty with Dutch rebels

Gembloux, January 1578

Despite the alliance agreed just before Christmas between Elizabeth and the Protestant Dutch rebels, an English military expedition to the Low Countries now seems most unlikely. The Protestant army has just suffered a decisive defeat here at the hands of Don John, the Spanish governor of the southern provinces. This news can only confirm the queen's doubts about the wisdom of giving the Earl of Leicester his head and supporting a war against the Spanish with both men and money.

Elizabeth has already been negotiating in both directions in an attempt to get Philip of Spain's acceptance of a settlement in the Low Countries which recognises both religious sides (→ 10/8/85).

Former husband of queen dies insane

Dragsholm, Denmark, 4 April 1578

Chained to a pillar, and quite mad, the human wreck that was once James, the Earl of Bothwell, died here today. It was a terrible end, even if he had murdered a queen's husband and carried her away so that he could marry her himself.

Since he and Mary Queen of Scots were defeated at Carberry Hill in 1567 he had been arrested and held in first Norway and then Denmark, where he was denounced by a discarded mistress, Anne Thorssen. At first he was treated with respect, but when it became clear that Mary's cause was hopeless his conditions worsened. Rigorous imprisonment enfeebled his once powerful body, and fear of execution unhinged his mind.

Although Mary has been a constant source of rumour during her imprisonment, little notice has been taken of Bothwell. But that could change if there is any truth in the stories here that he has left a confession which exonerates Mary of any complicity in the murder of her husband, Lord Darnley, in 1567.

Top astronomer called in to advise on significance of comet

Cambridge, November 1577

Tall, thin, with a long white beard, the astronomer called in by the queen to explain the meaning of the strange comet which appeared in the skies recently looks every inch the popular image of a great magician. But John Dee owes his reputation as one of England's greatest scientists to more than his looks and to more, too, than his monarch's patronage.

However, he has been Elizabeth's favourite counsellor on heavenly matters since his astrological calculations were used to choose the precise day of her coronation over

18 years ago. His learning – his personal library here in Cambridge is one of the wonders of the age, and he is a close friend of Geraldus Mercator, the Flemish maker of globes – has helped to educate and inspire the new generation of English maritime adventurers.

He is a committed believer in the idea of a "north-west passage" to Asia. Only last year he was one of those behind Martin Frobisher's expedition which appears to have discovered its eastern entrance in the icy waters of the north Atlantic, as well as bringing back specimens of gold-bearing rock.

John Dee: a learned astronomer.

Irish rebel against 'heretic' English queen

English forces muster to put down the revolt against Elizabeth in Ireland.

Ireland, July 1579
This largely Catholic island is once more in revolt against the English crown. James Fitzmaurice Fitzgerald, an Irishman who had been in exile since an abortive revolt in south-western Ireland ten years ago, has landed at Smerwick, on the Dingle peninsula in County Kerry. With him is Nicholas Sanders, an exiled Englishman recently made papal legate. They are jointly in charge of a small military force preaching a crusade against England's "heretic" queen. The expedition has received covert aid from the pope and Philip II of Spain. Munster and Leinster have taken up arms in sympathy, and revolt is stirring in Ulster and Connacht.

English rule in Ireland has been precarious throughout Queen Elizabeth's reign. The replacement of the Earl of Sussex by Sir Henry Sidney in 1565 did nothing to improve civil order, despite Sidney's determination to conquer the "barbarian" Irish and rule by means of regional councils. Shane O'Neill's rebellion ended in 1567, but the arrival of English adventurers claiming to be heirs of Norman settlers prompted further rebellions.

Following Fitzmaurice's first revolt in 1569, defiance by his cousin, the Earl of Desmond, ended when Derrinlaur was taken in 1574 and its defenders were executed. Anti-English feeling mounted, with Pius V's bull fuelling Catholic anger. Harsh English tactics have also rallied Irish opposition (→ 10/11/80).

Leicester's secret wedding angers queen, as she weighs match with French Catholic

Greenwich, summer 1579
Overcome with rage, Elizabeth has threatened to send the Earl of Leicester to the Tower after finding out that he has married in secret. His bride is Lettice Knollys, the widowed Countess of Essex, whose name has been linked with Leicester's in the past. The fact – already well known at court – was revealed to Elizabeth by a French envoy who is in England to renew talks about a match between the queen and Francis, the former Duke of Alençon. Plans are afoot for a visit here by Francis, who took the title Duke of Anjou from his brother when the latter became Henry III [*see report below*].

Leicester's bride: Lettice Knollys.

Royal marriage critic has hand cut off

London, 3 November 1579
Popular feeling against the much-mooted marriage between Elizabeth and Francis, the brother of the French King Henry III, was dramatically demonstrated here today by the stubborn bravery of John Stubbe, a puritan gentleman from Norfolk who has been shown to be the author of a widely-circulated pamphlet against the match.

Stubbe and his printer were sentenced to have their right hands cut off, and the sentence has just been carried out before a large crowd.

Although Stubbe refused to take back any of his objections to the marriage of his queen to a French Catholic, he regretted having "disquieted or troubled her". But more remarkably, when the blow was struck, he lifted his hat with his remaining hand and shouted "God save the Queen" before fainting away.

The incident follows the visit to England by the prospective French suitor, during which he and the queen appeared to establish a close understanding (→ 2/11/81).

King James falls under influence of affectionate French cousin

Impressionable: the young James.

Scotland, September 1579
Young King James, still only 13 and torn between the squabbling power-brokers of the Scottish nobility like a prize of great value and no feelings, has conceived a great passion for a cousin of his visiting from France and is said to be quite transformed by the relationship.

Esmé Stuart, the Sieur d'Aubigny, is a distant cousin of the king's and a Catholic, but so strong has the attachment between the pair grown that the Frenchman is talking of converting to Protestantism, while his royal kinsman is said to be planning to make Esmé the Duke of Lennox. Esmé Stuart is a dramatically handsome man, with a sophistication and wit to match the manners of the French court, and it is easy to see why he has made such an impression on a lonely boy who has grown up apart from his mother, Mary Queen of Scots.

However, there are many at court who object to the friendship. Apart from powerful men who see their own influence diluted, like the former regent, Morton, and those who fear a Catholic connection, there are mutterings that Esmé, abetted by his friend Captain James Stewart, has corrupted the young king to further his own ambitions. Whatever the truth of this, James is basking in the first genuine affection to have come his way (→ 1/1581).

On the high seas: Francis Drake, in the "Golden Hind", captures the Spanish fighting ship "Cacafuego" off the coast of Ecuador in March 1579.

Elizabeth I
1558–1603

James VI
1567–1603

Southampton, 26 Sept 1580. Francis Drake returns with his ship, the *Golden Hind*, laden with treasure after circumnavigating the world (→4/4/81).

Ireland, 10 November 1580. An English force led by Lord Grey de Wilton, Elizabeth's deputy in Ireland, massacres an Irish rebel garrison at Smerwick, in Munster (→11/11/83).

Edinburgh, January 1581. Esmé Stuart, the Duke of Lennox and the king's cousin, is forced to subscribe to the "negative confession" denouncing Rome and the pope (→22/8/82).

London, 2 November 1581. Francis, the Duke of Anjou and heir to the French throne, arrives on another visit in pursuit of a marriage with Queen Elizabeth (→2/1582).

St Andrews, 27 June 1583. King James escapes after ten months in captivity following last August's Ruthven raid (→9/6/84).

Canterbury, 23 September 1583. John Whitgift, formerly bishop of Worcester, is consecrated archbishop of Canterbury; he replaces Archbishop Grindal, who died in 1580 out of favour with Elizabeth.

London, November 1583. After torture, a Catholic conspirator, Francis Throckmorton, reveals a plot to depose Elizabeth and place Mary Queen of Scots on the throne (→28/2/85).

London, 1583. Sir Edmund Tilney, the Master of the Revels, forms the "Queen's Players", a theatre group.

France, 10 June 1584. Francis, the Duke of Anjou, the former suitor to Elizabeth, dies; the heir presumptive to the French throne is now Henry of Navarre, a Protestant (→10/1589).

Northamptonshire, 15 Oct 1586. Mary Queen of Scots, who is accused of complicity in the recent Babington plot to assassinate Elizabeth, is put on trial at Fotheringhay (→1/2/87).

London, 1 February 1587. Following weeks of pressure from the privy council, Elizabeth at last agrees to sign the death warrant of Mary Queen of Scots issued after her trial (→8/2).

Scotland, 31 March 1587. King James VI says that he will not break the Anglo-Scots alliance to avenge the death of his mother (→6/1588).

England, 24 December 1587. Robert Dudley, the Earl of Leicester, who resigned his commission, returns to England in disgrace; his replacement, Lord Willoughby of Eresby, is under strict royal instructions not to interfere in Dutch politics.→

Ostend, 27 February 1588. A last attempt is made at Anglo-Spanish talks to prevent the sailing of the Armada (→5/1588).

Plymouth, May 1588. The fleet prepares for the onslaught of the Spanish Armada (→28/7).

Dumfries/Galloway, June 1588. King James crushes a Catholic rebellion (→22/12/89).

Calais, 28 July 1588. After the breakdown of Anglo-Spanish peace talks yesterday the English send in fireships, causing chaos and confusion (→3/8).

Oxfordshire, 4 September 1588. Robert Dudley, the Earl of Leicester and former favourite of Elizabeth, dies suddenly at his home in Cornbury.

Elizabeth ends betrothal to French heir

Sandwich, February 1582
The issue of Elizabeth's marriage to the French heir, Francis, the Duke of Anjou, has finally been settled. It will not take place. She has seen him off for the Netherlands with three warships, £10,000 of England's money and his pride intact, but without the queen's hand.

While their prolonged courtship was mostly a matter of statecraft, and the result is certainly satisfactory for England and a great relief to its Protestant population, there was also real affection between the pair. The duke is a short, odd-looking fellow whom Elizabeth called her "frog", while she enjoyed playing along with his extravagantly romantic courtship.

When she finally announced to her ministers that the marriage plans were dead, she is reported to have wept openly in front of them. Not perhaps for the loss of a great love but because she realised that at 48 her last chance of children was gone along with him (→10/6/84).

Drake knighted after sailing round world

Deptford, 4 April 1581
On the deck of his ship the *Golden Hind*, and to the delight of everybody in England except the Spanish ambassador, Queen Elizabeth today knighted Francis Drake in honour of his great voyage around the world, the second circumnavigation and the first by an Englishman.

After the capture of the Spanish treasure ship *Cacafuego* off the Pacific coast in March 1579 had ensured the financial success of the voyage – the queen was a major shareholder – Drake made his way home across the Pacific and around the Cape of Good Hope. He has now clearly shown the vulnerability of the rich Spanish possessions in the Americas (→7/7/87).

A gift from Drake to his queen.

Queen takes tough line against Catholics

Elizabeth: the queen at prayer.

Westminster, 18 March 1581
Missionaries from abroad have provoked Elizabeth into her harshest measures yet against Catholics. Parliament, which left to itself would have preferred even stronger measures, has passed a new Statute of Recusancy which raises the fines for failure to attend church to an enormous £20 a month. In 1559 the price was just 12 pence. To say or hear Mass can now bring a year in prison, while to convert or be converted to Rome will be treated as treason. The seminarists trained by William Allen in France, together with Jesuits like Edmund Campion, represent the most idealistic strain of Catholicism, but Elizabeth will now treat them as enemies of the state.

King James kidnapped while out hunting

Perth, 22 August 1582

Scotland's young king has been taken prisoner by a group of Protestant nobles determined to break the power of James's dearest friend, and ambitious favourite, Esmé Stuart, the Duke of Lennox [*see report below*]. The king was kidnapped while hunting today near the Earl of Gowrie's castle at Ruthven. Once at the castle James was told that he would not be allowed to leave until he had issued a proclamation condemning Lennox. The conspiracy was led by the Earls of Gowrie, Mar and Angus, together with Lord Lindsay.

When he saw there was nothing he could do, and that he must lose his friend, the 16-year-old king burst into tears. But his jailer, the Master of Glamis, was unmoved, merely saying: "Better that bairns should weep than bearded men." Although jealousy of Lennox, and

King James's friend: Lennox.

of his influence over James, lies at the root of most Scottish plots these days, the immediate cause was the French-born duke's rumoured involvement in a plan to convert James to Catholicism by force and invade England (→ 27/6/83).

Pro-English regent executed for murder

Scotland, July 1581

The former Scottish regent, the Earl of Morton, has been executed after being found guilty of complicity in the murder of Henry, Lord Darnley, the king's father, in 1567. Morton's accuser was James Stewart, a close associate of the Frenchman Esmé Stuart, the Duke of Lennox, who is suspected of opposing

Morton's staunch Protestantism and policy of friendship with England. Morton held the post of regent until 1578 and was not unpopular during that time. His demise will increase the alarm among Scottish nobles over the undisputed hold which Lennox now has over the impressionable 15-year-old James.

Irish rebellion crushed

Munster, 11 November 1583

The capture and death of the Earl of Desmond bring to an end the Irish rebellion started four years ago by Desmond's cousin, James Fitzmaurice Fitzgerald, and met with unprecedented ferocity by far superior English forces. The lands held by Desmond are now forfeit to the English crown.

The chief author of the slaughter of thousands was Lord Grey de Wilton, appointed Elizabeth's lord deputy in 1580. An English army of 6,500 men, commanded by Nicholas Malby and William Pelham, easily defeated the rebels and their Italian and Spanish reinforcements. But Grey wanted more. He saw the

revolt as part of a widespread Catholic plot which it was his political and religious duty to crush. The English soldiers responded with a will, massacring one entire garrison after it had surrendered. The 1580 harvest was burnt, and cattle were slaughtered; widespread famine was the inevitable result.

Some Irishmen who wavered in their loyalties to Elizabeth's England did not live long to regret their actions. Suspected rebels in the Pale area of Ireland were hanged, drawn and quartered. Before dying, they were pressed to recant their Catholic faith. Ireland has never seen such slaughter and devastation (→ 12/5/96).

Slaughtered in a hovel: a romanticised view of the Earl of Desmond's death.

The four classes of Elizabethan England

England, 1583

In a new study the statesman Sir Thomas Smith has provided a revealing anatomy of Elizabethan England in which he divides the nation into four classes: gentlemen, citizens, yeomen and manual workers. He sees the gentlemen as the class which runs the country. Whether or not a monarch seen as the pivotal power in Europe [*see left*] would agree must be doubtful; but who are the "gentlemen"?

The English gentleman is defined in Sir Thomas's book *De Republica Anglorum*: "Whosoever studieth the laws of the realm, who studieth in the universities, who professeth liberal

sciences and who can live idly ... without manual labour and ... will bear the countenance of a gentleman, he shall be called master and taken for a gentleman." The category of gentleman thus includes both the titled nobility and the relatively humble landowners and knights of the shire. Although his "citizens" include merchants whose wealth outstrips that of the grandest duke, politics remains the business of gentlemen only. His yeomen, as the farming backbone of Tudor England, are given due importance, but the rest have "no voice nor authority ... and no account is made of them but only to be ruled".

Elizabeth represented as the supreme power in Europe: the cow she is leading is the Netherlands; Spain's Philip II sits on its back, while the Duke of Alba milks the beast; "William the Silent" steadies its horns.

The paradox of James: uncouth, lazy but a poet

Edinburgh, 9 June 1584

Today is the 18th birthday of James VI, who has been king of Scotland since he was a year old. All the most dramatic events of his life occurred before he was conscious of them: his father's murder, his mother's marriage to the murderer and her deposition by the Scottish nobles. Since then he has not set eyes on her and has been brought up almost entirely by men, notably his tutor, the well-known scholar George Buchanan.

From the age of 12 James has been nominally king in person, although he ruled through favourites, Esmé Stuart, the Duke of Lennox, and James Stewart, the Earl of Arran. Their unpopularity led to his kidnapping by William Ruthven, the Earl of Gowrie, when he was 16. Lennox was banished, Arran jailed. James escaped from Castle Ruthven last year, reappointed Arran and had Gowrie executed.

Although a Protestant, James is religiously and politically conservative. He is also highly educated in theology and languages. Physically inelegant, with spindly legs, he dresses in slovenly style. His speech is uncouth, with much profanity and bawdiness. His attachment to his favourites is indiscreet, and he is lazy about state business, preferring to go hunting, his chief passion. Yet he is also a patron of poets and writes poetry himself.

James: he has been king for 17 years; today he has come of age.

Spanish envoy expelled

The ambassador is thrown out of England for complicity in a Catholic plot.

Westminster, 15 January 1584

War with Spain looked closer as the Spanish ambassador, Bernadino de Mendoza, was hauled before the privy council today and told that the queen knew all about his dealings with Mary Queen of Scots, the disaffected Catholics and the invasion planned by the Duke of Guise to put the Scottish queen on the throne of England. Elizabeth was therefore graciously pleased to allow him 15 days to leave England.

Mendoza protested that he knew nothing of these charges, but Sir Francis Walsingham, speaking Italian, told him that he was lucky to

escape so easily. Walsingham had discovered the plot through the arrest and torture of Sir Francis Throckmorton, who confessed that he was acting as a go-between for Mendoza, Mary and the invasion forces, financed by the king of Spain and the pope. All that remained, he said, was to organise a Catholic rising in England and the point of invasion, which the Duke of Guise wanted to be Arundel. Other invasions were planned in Scotland and Ireland. Till now Walsingham had wrongly suspected the French ambassador of plotting the "great treason" (→ 28/2/85).

Law passed to bar Mary of Scots from English succession

Westminster, 28 February 1585

The atmosphere of crisis inspired by two plots to assassinate the queen led to a bill for her safety being passed by parliament today. It enacted the Bond of Association, to which thousands subscribed last year and swore that they would defend the queen's life and pursue by all means of revenge "all persons of what estate so ever that shall attempt the harm of her majesty's royal person to the uttermost extermination of them". They swore that no pretended successor to the throne "by whom or for whom any such detestable act shall be attempted or committed" would be tolerated. In other words, if the queen's life were taken Mary Queen of Scots should be killed.

Parliament excluded James VI of Scotland from these provisions. The question of who would succeed if Elizabeth were murdered is on everyone's mind. Burghley drafted a bill to appoint a great council of 30 to take over, but the queen will not have it. Another act requires all those who have entered the Catholic priesthood since 1559 to leave the realm within 40 days and makes it treason for them to return.

Newly-knighted Raleigh names discovery after 'virgin queen'

London, 6 January 1585

Walter Raleigh, a Devon man who is known equally as a warrior, adventurer and scholar, was knighted today by Queen Elizabeth, whose favourite he is. She also made him lord warden of the Stannaries and vice-admiral of Devon and Cornwall and heaped estates upon him. Raleigh asked to name a new territory that his expedition discovered last year after her.

The queen was pleased to name it Virginia but will not allow him to lead his fleets because she misses his company at court. Last year his ships brought back two Indians, and pipes for smoking tobacco, which is understood to preserve the health of the Indians by opening the pores and passages of the body. Sir Walter has done much to spread the healthful habit (→ 7/8/92).

Soldier and scholar: Walter Raleigh shown here waging war for the queen.

Dutch rebels enlist queen's backing

Surrey, 10 August 1585

Queen Elizabeth committed herself to assisting the Dutch rebels in their struggle with Spain by a treaty signed at Nonsuch palace, near Richmond, today. Since the shooting of their leader, William of Orange [*see below*], their cause has come close to defeat. The Prince of Parma has captured one city after another, culminating in the fall of Antwerp. Elizabeth was offered the title of sovereign, but agreed only to be protector of the Netherlands.

She has promised to keep an army of 7,000 there and maintain it at her own expense, appointing a nobleman, the Earl of Leicester, to command them and to act as political adviser to the States General. Flushing and Brill are to be garrisoned by English troops. In fact,

if not in letter, England is at war with Spain. The queen's reason for taking this risky initiative is her conviction that if the Dutch revolt should end in disaster, Philip of Spain will next launch "the Enterprise of England", as his plan to invade is called. He has already seized all English shipping in Spanish ports, on the pretext that he needs it for a fleet assembling at Lisbon.

English merchants, who have hitherto been opposed to a war which would destroy their trade with Spain, now have nothing to lose by it. Indeed, men expected this Spanish fleet to sail against England. The queen's problem is money. The Netherlands army will cost half her annual revenue of £200,000 (→ 3/1586).

Leicester: commanding the army.

Assassination puts pressure on queen

William of Orange is shot dead.

Delft, 10 July 1584

The assassination of William of Orange, the leader of the Dutch revolt against their Spanish overlords, today brought Queen Elizabeth nearer to intervening in the war of the Dutch against the Spanish. William, known as "the Silent" because of his secrecy, was shot dead by a French agent of Philip II, against whom he had raised the banner of the seven United Provinces of the Netherlands which, like him, are Protestant.

Philip of Spain plans war with England

Madrid, March 1586

King Philip of Spain, once king-consort of Mary's England, has finally decided to invade the England of Elizabeth, whose hand he once sought in marriage. She is in his eyes an illegitimate heretic, whose claim to the throne is inferior to his own. Elizabeth's support of the Dutch rebels in the Netherlands has provoked him, but the impudence of Sir Francis Drake has proved the last straw.

Drake sailed last September with 22 ships and 2,000 men to attack West Indian harbours and intercept the Caribbean treasure fleet. He had the queen's backing – she contributed £10,000 to the cost. From Plymouth he landed first at Vigo, which he occupied for ten days while he continued to fit out and supply his fleet on Spanish soil – a huge loss of face for Philip. From there he sailed on to sack Santo Domingo, Habana and Cartagena, the capital of the Spanish Main.

Philip has written to the new pope, Sixtus V, who supports the idea of recapturing England for the Catholic faith, calling on him for his blessing and financial help. The invasion will cost at least three million ducats, he warned him. The plans for the invasion have been drawn up by the Marquess of Santa Cruz, the captain general of the

Ocean Sea, and require immense resources of men and material.

The 600 ships of the Armada will include 25 Spanish galleons from Cadiz and Lisbon, 20 galleons from Portugal, which Philip annexed five years ago, 105 merchantmen from the Mediterranean, and over four hundred support vessels. These are to carry an invasion force of 55,000 troops with orders not to engage in sea battle but to defend themselves and land intact (→ 10/1586).

Philip: planning to invade England.

Royal favourite is ousted by English-backed agreement

Stirling, 2 November 1585

King James VI of Scotland surrendered at Stirling today to his rebel lords, released by Queen Elizabeth from their exile in England. His favourite, the chancellor, the Earl of Arran, has fled. Arran was unpopular in Scotland; he had passed the "Black Acts" denouncing Presbyterianism and confirming the king's authority.

Negotiations between James and Elizabeth reached agreement last May when the queen's emissary, Sir Edward Wotton, took James a present of horses from the queen and an offer of £4,000 annually to support a defensive treaty. James was delighted, although he well understood that such a treaty implied that his mother, Mary Stewart, would be kept in captivity and not, as she hoped, "associated" with him as monarch.

When Mary heard that her son had agreed to exclude her from the settlement she became hysterical and cursed his ingratitude. But James has more to gain from friendship with Elizabeth (→ 5/7/86).

Chivalrous courtier mourned by queen

Netherlands, 17 October 1586

The death of Sir Philip Sidney here, 26 days after being shot in the thigh at the Battle of Zutphen, near Arnhem, has plunged Elizabeth's court into mourning. He was admired as the most attractive and chivalrous of courtiers and the Earl of Leicester, his commander, writes: "Never did I hear of any man that did abide the dressing and setting of his bones better than he did."

After being shot in a charge against the Spanish cavalry (he had left off his leg armour because a friend of his had none) he rode for a mile to the camp, "not ceasing to speak of Her Majesty, being glad if his hurt and death might honour her". When he was to be given a drink of water, he ordered it to be given to a dying foot soldier instead with the words: "Thy necessity is yet greater than mine." He was 31. ▷

Anglo-Scots treaty ends Mary's hopes

Holyrood, Edinburgh, 5 July 1586

James VI of Scotland has formally scuppered a plan to share the throne with his mother, Mary, who abdicated in 1567. His repudiation of the proposal came in a treaty signed today with Elizabeth of England, in which each monarch agreed to aid the other if either of their countries were attacked by a third power. James – who has long sought such an alliance between Scotland and England, in order to secure his succession to the English throne – also accepted an annual English pension of £4,000.

The king has not seen his mother since he was a baby. Mary – a prisoner in England for the past 18 years – had hoped to win freedom through an "association" with her son in the crown of Scotland, but James wrote to her last year arguing that he could not join in a treaty with her while she remained captive. He has clearly decided that the support of the English queen is more important to him than the fate of his mother (→ 31/3/87).

Babington conspirators meet hideous fate

Anthony Babington and his accomplices meet to consider their plans.

London, 20 September 1586

Anthony Babington and six of his conspirators were hideously executed today on a scaffold erected in a field at Holborn. Found guilty of a plot to assassinate Queen Elizabeth, the traitors were taken down from the gallows before death and brutally mutilated.

Babington, a rich young man from Derbyshire and a fervent Catholic, was an acquaintance of Mary of Scots, and the plot origin-ally came to light in letters between him and the dethroned queen. Held captive since taking refuge in England in 1568, Mary was promised freedom by Babington, who won her approval for his plans. But spies working for Sir Francis Walsing-ham, Elizabeth's secretary of state, intercepted their correspondence, the plotters were apprehended, and Babington confessed in the Tower. The future looks bleak indeed for the former Queen of Scots.

Graceful dancer is new lord chancellor

London, April 1587

Sir Christopher Hatton has been named as the new lord chancellor. The queen's promotion of her gifted and loyal favourite – who has a limited knowledge of the law and is believed not to have wanted the job – has raised a few eyebrows.

Hatton first attracted the queen's attention more than 20 years ago with his graceful dancing, and they became devoted to one another. He rose to become vice-chamberlain of the royal household and one of Eliz-abeth's recognised spokesmen in the House of Commons, where he sat for his native Northampton-shire. Over the years the queen has lavished favours on him, calling him her "Mutton", her "Belwether" and her "Lids" (the Earl of Leic-ester being her "Eyes").

Promoted: Sir Christopher Hatton.

Elizabeth's rich protégé completes building of Burghley House

A 20th-century view of William Cecil's magnificent Burghley House.

Interior grandeur at Burghley.

Stamford, Lincolnshire, 1587

William Cecil, Baron Burghley, Elizabeth's lord high treasurer since 1572, has finished building a magnificent house near Stamford – the product of more than 30 years' work. Its creation has been made possible by Cecil's ever-increasing rise to power and pros-perity under the queen's patronage. Built of tough local stone, Burgh-ley House, as it is known, was begun in 1555, incorporating some monastic remains bought by Cecil's father, and the east and south sides were completed by 1565. There was then a ten-year interval while Cecil built Theobalds, his Hertfordshire mansion – which has often been used for entertaining the queen – for his younger son, Robert.

A further period of work on Burghley in the mid-1570s saw the construction of the west front with its spectacular turreted gatehouse. The final phase was the building of the north front.

Built around a courtyard with towers at each corner, Burghley House recalls a mediaeval castle and combines French, English and Flemish architectural influences; one finishing touch, added two years ago, is an obelisk supported by heraldic beasts that crowns the clock-tower (→ 4/8/98).

Spanish invasion rumours confirmed

England, October 1586

Fears that Spain is planning a huge invasion of England are mounting, fuelled by the sailor Sir John Haw-kins, just back from a cruise recon-noitring the coasts of Spain and Portugal. On the cruise Hawkins took prisoners who claimed that naval preparations were under way. The poor relationship between Eng-land and Spain has been worsened by English plunder of Spanish treasure (→ 7/7/87).

Mary Queen of Scots is executed

Fotheringhay, 8 February 1587

The tragic life of Mary Queen of Scots ended at about ten o'clock this morning with her execution in the great hall of Fotheringhay castle in Northamptonshire. She was 44 years old and in the 19th year of her English captivity.

Mary's death comes four months after she was found guilty of complicity in the Babington plot to assassinate Queen Elizabeth. It was the final chapter in a turbulent history which had seen Mary as the focus of numerous plots to oust Elizabeth from the English throne and replace her with the Catholic Scottish queen. Mary had been kept prisoner since fleeing to England after her abdication of the Scottish crown in July 1567.

Mary met death with dignity, protesting her devotion to the Catholic faith. Before some 300 spectators she calmly approached the scaffold wearing a white lace-edged veil and black outer garments. These were removed to reveal a dark red petticoat and bodice; and so – dressed entirely in red, the colour of blood, and the Catholic Church's colour of martyrdom – the Queen of Scots died. Before the axe fell, Mary forgave her executioners, saying: "I hope you shall make an end of all my troubles" (→ 10/1612).

The death of a Catholic monarch: Mary Queen of Scots is executed.

Mary's rosary and prayer book.

A posthumous portrait of the queen.

Elizabeth grief-stricken at Mary's death

London, February 1587

Queen Elizabeth is grief-stricken and hysterical at the news of Queen Mary's execution. Sir William Davison, her secretary of state, who saw to the dispatch of the death warrant, has been tried in the star chamber and locked up in the Tower during the queen's pleasure.

Elizabeth herself signed the death warrant on 1 February – after much prevarication. Ever since Mary was found guilty of involvement in the Babington plot last October, Elizabeth had sought a means other than execution of dealing with her cousin. While ambassadors from France and Scotland vigorously interceded on Mary's behalf, the English queen made repeated excuses to parliament for her delay in reaching a decision. Dreading to appear before

her own people and in the eyes of Europe as a woman who would sacrifice a fellow queen for her own safety, she even suggested assassination as a better way of disposing of Mary. When she finally realised that there was no way out, she signed the warrant and asked to hear no more of it. After the execution, she insisted that she had never meant to send it and accused Davison of improper behaviour. He appears to have been used as a scapegoat in order to save England's recently forged league with Scotland.

Accounts of James's reaction to the death of a mother of whom he has no direct memory are more ambiguous. Some say that he showed sadness, retiring to bed without any supper, while others report that he remarked gleefully to those about him: "I am now sole king."

The troubled life of Queen Mary

14 December 1542: six days old, succeeds to the throne.
24 April 1558: marries Francis, the French *Dauphin*, in Paris.
19 August 1561: widowed last year at 17, returns to Scotland after 13-year absence in France.
29 July 1565: marries Darnley.
9 March 1566: murder of David Riccio, her secretary.
10 February 1567: Darnley killed and his house blown up.
15 May 1567: marries Bothwell.
24 July 1567: abdicates.
15 May 1568: after escape from Lochleven, and Langside defeat, seeks sanctuary in England.
14 October 1586: found guilty of complicity in assassination plot.
8 February 1587: executed.

Drake raids Cadiz 'to singe the king of Spain's beard'

Plymouth, 7 July 1587

Sir Francis Drake returned here today claiming to have delayed the planned Spanish invasion of England by "singeing the king of Spain's beard". He set sail three months ago and arrived off Cadiz on 29 April – unaware that, since his departure, the queen had rescinded her orders for the harrying of all Spanish shipping and stores.

The English entered Cadiz harbour and destroyed thousands of tons of shipping and a large quantity of food and other provisions meant for the Armada (as the Spanish invasion fleet is known). Drake then seized Cape St Vincent, blockaded the Armada's supply route, and later caused panic in Spain and Portugal by leaving for the Azores on a decoy mission. But, despite his successes, Spain still boasts a formidable navy, and the English are under no illusion that the invasion threat has evaporated (→ 27/2/88).

Queen fumes over earl's Dutch failure

England, December 1587

The Earl of Leicester has returned to England in disgrace after causing havoc in the Netherlands and incurring the queen's fury. Leicester, who backs a coalition with the Protestant United Provinces in the Netherlands, had been delighted by Elizabeth's treaty of alliance with the Provinces two years ago. He arrived in Flushing in December 1585 to conduct a defensive strategy on behalf of the Provinces, which are in rebellion against Spanish rule in the Netherlands.

But two months later he infuriated Elizabeth by becoming the governor-general of the Provinces without consulting her (politically provocative in relations with Spain). He further angered the queen – a stickler for prudent money management – by allowing a great deal of corruption. He finally resigned his command in September after a failure of statesmanship which had brought the Provinces to the brink of civil war (→ 4/9/88).

Spain's mighty Armada suffers humiliating defeat

The Spanish Armada is driven to desperate flight: an unsigned painting of the English victory later attributed to the court artist Nicholas Hilliard.

Armada is smashed by English fireships

Channel, 3 August 1588

Spain has suffered the most humiliating defeat in its naval history. The ragged and scattered remnants of the once-mighty Armada which was to win the English crown are now sailing north along the east coast of England, seeking to escape into the Atlantic round the Orkneys and Shetlands. The Spanish were overwhelmed by the power of the English fireships and battered by raging south-westerly winds. Their retreat was confirmed today when the Duke of Medina Sidonia, the Armada's commander, held a council of war and issued instructions for the homeward voyage.

The great Armada of 130 ships carrying almost 17,000 soldiers sailed from Lisbon on 30 May, resolved to halt English interference in the Spanish Netherlands and to win freedom of worship for English Catholics. Hostility had built up over many years, during which time Spanish colonies and ships had been at the mercy of raids by Francis Drake, John Hawkins and other English adventurers. Finally, with the death of Mary Queen of Scots – the likely successor to the English throne in the event of a

Spanish victory – Philip of Spain had come to believe that the English crown was his for the taking.

Delayed by storms, the Armada was first sighted off the Lizard on 19 July. Medina Sidonia's intention was to sail up the Channel to the Flemish coast and escort 16,000 more troops under the command of the Duke of Parma, Philip's regent in the Netherlands, across to England. Hilltop beacons spread the news of the fleet's approach across southern England. Drake and the English commander, Lord Howard of Effingham, set sail from Plymouth and engaged the enemy in a number of indecisive actions, but by 27 July the Armada was anchored off Calais.

The English, standing ready with fireships stacked with wood, pitch and explosives, went in at midnight. The raging forest of fire caused panic and confusion in the Spanish fleet, which was scattered by high winds and unable to regroup. By the time the final action was completed off Gravelines two days later, the Spanish had lost 11 ships and more than 2,000 men. The English lost less than 50 men and not a single ship (→ 24/11).

How the course of the struggle developed

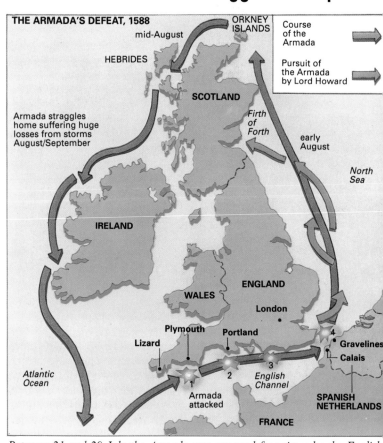

Between 21 and 29 July the Armada was engaged four times by the English. (1) off Eddystone; (2) off Portland; (3) off the Isle of Wight; and (4) off Gravelines – before fleeing up the east coast with Lord Howard in pursuit.

With 'the heart and stomach of a king', Elizabeth instils courage in her troops

Tilbury, Essex, 8 August 1588
Not knowing that the immediate danger was past, the queen today addressed her troops at Tilbury:

'Let tyrants fear ... I have always so behaved myself that, under God, I have placed my chiefest strength and safeguard in the loyal hearts and good will of my subjects, and therefore I am come amongst you as you see at this time, not for my recreation and disport, but being resolved, in the midst and heat of the battle, to live or die amongst you all, to lay down for my God, and for my kingdom, and for my people, my honour and my blood, even in the dust. I know I have the body of a weak and feeble woman, but I have the heart and stomach of a king, and of a king of England too, and think foul scorn that Parma or Spain or any Prince of Europe should dare invade the borders of my realm, to which, rather than any dishonour shall grow by me, I myself will take up arms, I myself will be your general, judge and rewarder of every one of your virtues ... By your valour in the field, we shall shortly have a famous victory over these enemies of my God, of my kingdom and of my people.'

The triumphant Queen Elizabeth in George Gower's "Armada portrait".

King James marries Anne of Denmark

King James VI with Queen Anne.

Oslo, 22 December 1589
James VI of Scotland left Oslo by sledge today for the long journey to Copenhagen, where he has been invited to visit his new family-in-law. The trip comes in the wake of a month of festivities following his marriage here to the 14-year-old Princess Anne, the younger daughter of Frederick II of Denmark. The Scottish king, now aged 23, is delighted with his Scandinavian bride, whom he met for the first time only a few days before they were married.

The couple's marriage was celebrated by proxy in Copenhagen on 20 August – after James had dropped his request for a large dowry – and several days later Anne set sail for Scotland. But her ship was forced to turn back in heavy storms and berthed at Oslo. News of her fate did not reach James until October, whereupon – in what appears to have been a determined show of independence – he embarked to fetch her home in person. The 15-year-old Duke of Lennox and the unstable Earl of Bothwell were left in charge of the Scottish government.

James arrived safely in Norway, and the match was finally sealed on 23 November in the hall of the old bishop's palace in Oslo (→1/5/90).

Elizabeth backs French Huguenot king

England, October 1589
Determined not to allow France to fall into pro-Spanish hands, Queen Elizabeth has sent a small army and £35,000 to France in support of Henry of Navarre, the Huguenot leader. Navarre was named as successor to the French throne by Henry III, who was assassinated in July by a fanatical monk – in retribution for Henry's own murder of the Duke of Guise. When the penniless Navarre succeeded as Henry IV, Philip II of Spain decided to intervene openly against the Protestant king, intensifying the French civil war. Spain's resolution to provide full military support for the Catholic League has forced Elizabeth to end her diplomatic isolation and draw upon England's hard-pressed coffers (→3/1591).

Bad fortune haunts Armada remnants

London, 24 November 1588
Elizabeth today held a grand service in St Paul's to celebrate the defeat of the Armada. By contrast, the Spanish council earlier this month voted to back Philip's plan to continue the war against England. This decision was taken despite the terrible fate that befell the surviving Armada ships on their way home around Scotland and Ireland: 51 failed to return home, wrecked by severe Atlantic gales and the rocky coastlines. More than 11,000 men perished at sea.

Drake's Portuguese foray ends in fiasco

Plymouth, July 1589
Ten thousand men have died on an expedition to Portugal, headed by Sir Francis Drake and Sir John Norris, which achieved nothing. The queen had provided £49,000 for the venture, whose aim was to destroy the Armada's surviving ships. However, Drake and Norris unsuccessfully attacked Lisbon and then, ignoring the queen's orders, made for the Azores to try to capture the Spanish treasure-fleet – but gales drove them back to England empty-handed (→29/1/96).

A religious killing: Henry III of France is assassinated by a monk.

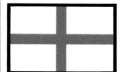

Elizabeth I
1558–1603

James VI
1567–1603

Scotland, 1 May 1590. King James VI of Scotland returns with his new wife, Anne of Denmark, after their honeymoon in Denmark (→ 7/2/92).

Dieppe, March 1591. English troops, sent by Elizabeth, arrive to support Henry IV of France against Spain (→ 7/1593).

Dieppe, 3 August 1591. Robert Devereux, the Earl of Essex, the stepson of Elizabeth's great favourite the late Earl of Leicester, is given his first major command (→ 2/1593).

Edinburgh, December 1591. The Earl of Bothwell, Francis Hepburn, who escaped from Edinburgh castle last June, fails in his attempt to capture King James (→ 24/7/93).

France, July 1593. Henry IV becomes a Catholic and promises to expel all foreign troops.

Stirling, 19 February 1594. Queen Anne of Scots gives birth to James's first son and heir, Prince Henry (→ 19/11/1600).

Whitehall, 26 March 1594. Elizabeth argues with the Earl of Essex over his attempt to put Francis Bacon into the office of solicitor-general (→ 17/11/95).

Scotland, 9 January 1596. James VI establishes a new government composed of eight officials – the Octavians – who had successfully reformed Queen Anne's household finances (→ 1597).

Whitehall, July 1596. Robert Cecil, the son of Lord Burghley, takes up the duties of chief secretary to Queen Elizabeth, a position that he has held unofficially for years (→ 3/1601).

England, 1596. The privy council, on the orders of Elizabeth,

seizes all paintings in which she appears old, frail or looking ill (→ 1/1603).

Whitehall, December 1597. The Earl of Essex, who retired from court in October, is made earl marshal by Queen Elizabeth (→ 10/1598).

Spain, September 1598. Philip II of Spain dies; he is succeeded by his son, Philip III.

London, October 1598. The Earl of Essex, who argued this year with Elizabeth and Cecil over the appointment of his uncle, Sir William Knollys, as lord deputy of Ireland, makes his peace with the queen (→ 5/4/99).

Dublin, 5 April 1599. The Earl of Essex begins his new post as lord lieutenant of Ireland by defending Tyrone and trying to save his career (→ 29/9).

Westminster, May 1599. Sir Thomas Sackville, an opponent of the Earl of Essex and a supporter of Robert Cecil, is appointed lord treasurer.

Surrey, 29 September 1599. Having deserted his post in Ireland, the Earl of Essex bursts in on the queen in her chamber at Nonsuch palace before she is dressed. →

Dunfermline, 19 Nov 1600. Queen Anne of Scots gives birth to her second son, Prince Charles (→ 2/3/1619).

London, 8 February 1601. Freed from house arrest, the Earl of Essex, the queen's fallen favourite, launches an abortive coup (→ 25/2).

Richmond, 24 March 1603. Elizabeth dies aged 69; her successor will be King James VI of Scotland. →

Raleigh sent to Tower for an illicit liaison

London, 7 August 1592
Swashbuckling Sir Walter Raleigh, a former royal favourite, has spent a month in the Tower after seducing Bess Throckmorton, one of the queen's maids-of-honour, who became pregnant. The affair was a personal affront to Elizabeth, who has a royal responsibility for the morals – and marriages – of her maids-of-honour. On one occasion she imprisoned a man for kissing one of the young ladies.

Raleigh could have languished in the Tower indefinitely had it not been for the orgy of plunder by English sailors when the captured Spanish treasure ship *Madre de Dios* came into Dartmouth. The jewels and other valuables aboard the ship were worth about £800,000. Most of this haul – the richest ever – vanished into the pockets of the English sailors, who ran riot when the Earl of Cumberland and others tried to retrieve the booty. Sir John

Out of favour: Sir Walter Raleigh.

Hawkins appealed to the court for Raleigh to be released and brought to Dartmouth. He was given a rousing welcome by the sailors, but much of the treasure remains missing. However, Raleigh has now married Bess (→ 26/10/97).

Queen's spymaster dies deep in debt

Elizabeth, with Walsingham (r).

London, 6 April 1590
The queen's devoted spymaster, Sir Francis Walsingham, who is said to have had over 50 agents planted in European courts, died today deeply in debt. He was particularly successful in "turning" Catholic spies to work for the Protestant cause; by such means he frustrated many plots against Elizabeth. He was ambassador to France at the time of the St Bartholomew massacre, and his Paris home became a sanctuary for Huguenots.

James is linked to death of Scots earl

Edinburgh, 7 February 1592
The court of James VI is in a state of feverish excitement after the murder today of James Stewart, the Earl of Moray, a popular member of the Protestant kirk and the son-in-law of the regent Moray, who was killed in 1570. His killer, the Catholic Earl of Huntly, is a favourite of the king, and the royal link has led to speculation that James had a hand in the plot. Moray was staying in his castle on the Firth of Forth. He had been outlawed for fostering revolt but was now hoping to make peace with James.

Huntly, whose support was vital to the king as a counterweight to the Anglophile Protestant party, had a long-standing blood feud with Moray. Yesterday he left the king at Holyrood and, crossing the Forth, set fire to his enemy's castle. Moray fled but was spotted among the rocks on the shore. Huntly caught up with him and felled him with a savage blow. The king's role remains obscure; though he hated Moray, murder in cold blood seems out of character. Yet he appears ready to protect Huntly from the consequences of his act (→ 24/7/93).

Scots Catholics are linked to claims of Spanish conspiracy

Scotland, 1 January 1593

A bizarre plot to promote a Spanish invasion of Scotland has been exposed by the discovery of a number of sheets of blank paper, each signed at the bottom by a Catholic nobleman, one of them the Earl of Huntly, the notorious murderer of the Protestant Earl of Moray. The papers were found in the possession of a Scottish Catholic, George Ker, who was arrested as he was about to sail for Spain.

Under torture, Ker confessed. A Scottish Jesuit living in Spain, Father William Crichton, believed that King Philip would invade Scotland if he received promises of support from Scottish Catholics. Huntly and the others joined in the plot, giving Ker blank papers so that the details could be filled in.

Presbyterian ministers are demanding tough action against the Catholic community. Some ministers claim that James is involved; Ker had a paper written by the king reviewing the possibility of invading England. James rejected the idea, saying that he would wait for Elizabeth's death, when he would inherit the English crown "without the stroke of a sword".

Earl of Essex admitted to queen's council

London, February 1593

The chivalrous, impulsive and imperious Earl of Essex, a long-time favourite of Elizabeth despite his frequently capricious behaviour, has been admitted to the queen's council at the age of 27. He owes the distinction to a skilful exploitation of Elizabeth's passion for secret intelligence, which she reckons gives strength to her diplomatic forays into Europe.

Essex had been courted by the two Bacon brothers, Francis and Anthony, who saw the young earl as a means of securing remunerative court appointments. Together they created a new intelligence network in Europe which enabled Essex to challenge the queen's chief adviser, Lord Burghley, as a source of information.

Essex, enjoying the perquisites of power, is pocketing substantial gifts

Robert Devereux: Earl of Essex.

from hangers-on who count on him to push their cause at court. But Elizabeth is firmly resisting the bid to get Francis Bacon the attorney-general's job (→ 26/3/94).

New poem celebrates the 'Faerie Queen'

London, 1596

All six books of the most admired poem of the day, *The Faerie Queen* have appeared in print this year, although its author, Edmund Spenser, calls it still unfinished. He wrote most of his mystical romance of the age of chivalry – in which there are many references to con-

temporary history, such as the struggle between Elizabeth and her sister Mary – in Ireland, where he settled in 1586. Sir Walter Raleigh brought him back to court in 1589 to lay the first three books at the feet of the queen. Elizabeth, he wrote, "to mine oaten pipe inclined her ear" – and gave him a pension.

Elizabeth dismisses parliament in row over war taxation

Westminster, 10 April 1593

The queen has dismissed parliament after a dispute with MPs over taxation for war and repeated attempts by a puritan MP to raise the question of the succession – something that Elizabeth finds almost too painful to discuss, since she is unmarried and without issue.

Peter Wentworth, a lawyer, has been obsessed with the succession question for 30 years. He was imprisoned two years ago for writing a pamphlet urging the queen to fix the succession. He got himself re-elected, and when the Commons met in February he alarmed his fel-

The queen in the House of Lords.

low MPs by raising the question yet again. Last month he was questioned by the privy council and then sent to the Tower with three other MPs. Another puritan MP who attacked the court of high commission, the government's agency for repression of puritans, has also been arrested.

When the demand for further taxation for war came up, the Commons resisted and the Lords were brought in to put pressure on the lower house. By a majority of over a hundred, MPs still refused the taxes. After a good deal of arm-twisting behind the scenes, the MPs finally gave way, still protesting at having to prostrate themselves "at her majesty's feet".

Noble accused of witchcraft stages palace coup at Holyrood

Edinburgh, 24 July 1593

As King James was dressing this morning in Holyrood palace a commotion broke out in the next room. Rushing in he found the Earl of Bothwell on his knees with a drawn sword lying before him. This bizarre scene told the king that Bothwell had seized the palace but would not harm the royal person.

Two years ago Bothwell was accused of consorting with witches and sorcerers, and the king suspected him of supernatural powers. Today, crying "Treason!", James told Bothwell that he might kill him but would never have his soul, witchcraft notwithstanding. Soon James calmed down, and Bothwell agreed to stay away from court. The king told a crowd of loyal citizens who had assembled outside the palace that all was well (→ 19/2/94).

Scottish witchcraft: the Devil preaching to an attentive gathering of witches.

Cadiz put to the torch

Lord Howard: expedition sponsor.

Cadiz, 5 July 1596

This Spanish port on the Atlantic coast, the wealthiest in western Europe, is today a smoking ruin after two weeks of looting and burning by English and Dutch forces. The narrow streets are choked with smashed furniture and wine caskets and trampled olives, almonds and raisins. The Earl of Essex ordered that churches and convents were to be left untouched, but most of them have been burnt. Women and chil-

dren have been deported to Port St Mary, a small town some seven miles (11km) distant.

The expedition, financed jointly by Elizabeth, Essex and Lord Howard of Effingham, should have been a triumph for the English and their Dutch allies. Some 10,000 men and 150 ships were assembled. Philip's forces at Cadiz were taken by surprise, and the attackers' casualties were relatively light. Two Spanish galleons were destroyed and two captured. But the Spanish denied the attackers some 12 million ducats of goods by scuttling the outgoing Indies fleet.

Essex wanted to retain Cadiz as a base for operations against the Spanish and for an attack on Lisbon, but his fellow commanders and other ranks were determined to get back home with their plunder. Philip's main fleet at Lisbon was left untouched, and the incoming treasure fleet from the Spanish Main was not intercepted.

The expedition barely repaid the investment and exposed the underlying flaw in the English strategy. Lacking the resources to establish a sizeable professional navy, Elizabeth relies on operations jointly financed by the state and wealthy individuals. Inevitably, these become privateering raids in pursuit of booty; military considerations get low priority.

Irish rebel leader given royal pardon

English troops in Ireland: they have suffered losses in conflict with O'Neill.

Westminster, 12 May 1596

Queen Elizabeth today issued a royal pardon for Hugh O'Neill, the Earl of Tyrone, a former ally of the English who was proclaimed a traitor a year ago. Tyrone has played a subtle political game over the past year or so, cooperating with the English occupiers in Ireland until he felt that he had the breadth of support to challenge certain aspects of English rule. The queen prefers not to embark on another major conflict in a land which has been posing problems throughout her reign.

O'Neill – who is both a Gaelic lord and an English earl – had eloped with and married Mabel, the sister of Sir Henry Bagenal, the marshal of Ireland, shortly before

the two men joined in an uneasy alliance against the Catholic Hugh Maguire. In spite of submitting to Sir William Russell, the new lord deputy, in 1594, O'Neill began to distance himself from the English rulers of Ireland. By late last year he had been created Earl of Tyrone and was in command of 1,000 pikemen, 4,000 musketeers and 1,000 cavalry.

Tyrone then tried to expel English officials from the Ulster provinces and began to build up his army, inflicting losses on the English in a skirmish at Clontibret. As the O'Donnells of Tyrconnell rose in revolt, Tyrone was proclaimed a traitor, and Sir John Norris was summoned with 1,600 veterans from Brittany (→ 14/8/98).

Royal doctor killed for anti-queen plot

London, February 1594

The queen's principal physician, the Jewish Dr Roderigo Lopez, has been castrated, disembowelled and quartered in front of a screaming crowd inflamed by anti-Semitic hysteria. Lopez was supposed to have plotted to poison Elizabeth in collaboration with Spanish agents. The queen refused to believe the charge, and the only evidence produced pointed to a Spanish plot against Don Antonio, the pretender to the Portuguese throne, and did not implicate Lopez. But the Earl of Essex, determined to involve the doctor, triumphantly produced confessions forced from supposed collaborators by torture.

Earl of Essex exploits accession day tilt for self-glorification

Jousting is a popular sport on Elizabeth's accession day anniversaries.

London, 17 November 1595

The court entertainments for the 37th anniversary of Elizabeth's accession to the English throne have been marked by a bizarre bid by the Earl of Essex to enhance the queen's opinion of him. Essex portrayed himself in the tiltyard, or contest arena, as being wooed by a hermit, a soldier and a secretary, who beg him to choose between lives of contemplation, experience and fame. A blind Red Indian appears, and his sight is restored at the touch of the queen's hand. The Indian dedicates himself to the queen's service, as does Essex. Elizabeth, having sat through this fol-de-rol, remarked that had she known what to expect she would not have attended (→ 5/7/96).

Royal hero, Drake, dies of dysentery

Panama, 29 January 1596

Somewhere off the Panama coast, the sailor who for more than 20 years had been a symbol of Queen Elizabeth's expansionist England and the scourge of Spain was today buried at sea. Sir Francis Drake, in his mid-50s, succumbed to a virulent form of dysentery. In 1577, after raiding Spain's colonial outposts in South America from the *Golden Hind*, he returned to England with treasure for his queen and champion valued at £1,125,000. He played a key role in the defeat of the Spanish Armada in 1588. His last voyage was a failure.

Drake: hero of many exploits.

Elizabeth blames Essex for voyage's flop

London, 26 October 1597

Quarrels between two royal favourites, the Earl of Essex and Sir Walter Raleigh, have dogged an ambitious expedition backed by the queen to capture the Spanish treasure fleet returning from South America. Essex had lobbied hard to be appointed as the expedition's commander, but he has now returned to confront an angry queen who blames him for its failure.

The "islands expedition", as it was known, had been hit by a fierce gale which left the English ships in no fit state to attack the Spanish fleet when they arrived off the naval base of Ferrol. They turned therefore to the Azores where Sir Walter Raleigh, the second-in-command, took the Spanish by surprise, capturing a town before Essex arrived. An enraged Essex threatened to court-martial Raleigh and execute him, but while the two leaders were falling out the Spanish treasure fleet slipped past them and into its home port (→ 12/1597).

Essex: the great adventurer.

Second Armada is broken up by storms

Madrid, October 1596

Yet another attempt by Philip II of Spain to teach the English a lesson has come to naught. Dismayed and humiliated by Elizabeth's buccaneers, who have undermined the Spanish economy by seizing over a thousand of his treasure ships, Philip dispatched another Armada, as large as that of 1588. The English have no cause for concern, however; this huge fleet had scarcely left Spanish waters when it ran into a storm off Finisterre and was scattered. Faced with the need to rebuild his navy for the third time in a decade, and with the royal treasury empty, Philip is preparing to declare his country bankrupt for the third time (→ 9/1598).

King's essay fuels flurry of witch-hunting hysteria in Scotland

Edinburgh, 1597

Public hysteria about witchcraft has been further fuelled this year in Scotland by the publication of an essay, *Demonologie*, written by the king himself. The last winter saw an orgy of speculation about the supernatural with stories of witches meeting to worship the Devil apparently widely believed. Suspected witches are now regularly dragged before local magistrates.

James became fascinated by tales of supernatural powers in 1591 when the Earl of Bothwell's plot to kill the king was linked to sorcery. In his essay James says that if witches hold their breath, they can fly; they can raise storms, cause insanity, impotence and urgent sexual desire. The king admits to some doubts but these seem unlikely to quell public speculation (→ 9/1598).

Witch-hunting: an alleged sorceress, Agnes Samson, before King James.

Royal plays head theatrical boom of queen's reign

Bankside, London, 1598

Plans are afoot to build an ambitious new theatre by the Thames on Bankside. Called the Globe, it will be the home of the Lord Chamberlain's Men, a company founded by James Burbage, an actor who built the first public theatre in Shoreditch in 1576. Burbage, his son Richard, William Shakespeare and others will jointly own the Globe, which will join the Rose and the Swan theatres in an area noted for prostitution and bear-baiting.

Shakespeare, described as "honey-tongued", has already written 16 plays, some of which have been given at court. Last year *The History of Henry the Fourth, with the Humorous Conceits of Sir John Falstaff* was so enjoyed by the queen that she asked for a play that shows Sir John in love. *The Merry Wives of Windsor* was the result.

Since the theatres reopened after the plague of a few years ago, they have prospered. Christopher Marlowe's *Dr Faustus* and *Edward II*, Robert Greene's *Friar Bacon and Friar Bungay* and Ben Jonson's *Everyman In His Humour* show the richness of current talent. Jonson, who went to prison for an earlier satire, is thought by some to rival Shakespeare's genius.

A popular stage: the interior of the Swan theatre on Bankside.

James argues for kings' divine right

Edinburgh, September 1598

James VI has published a treatise on the divine right of kings and their absolute power over their subjects. This lofty view of monarchy is a striking contrast to the restless violence of modern Scotland. The book is called *The Trew Law of Free Monarchies: Or the Reciprock and Mutuall Dutie Betwixt a Free King and his Naturall Subjects*. It is lucid, vivid and forceful. The king is an intellectual as well as a practical monarch and intends to leave his mark by precept as well as by practice. The king claims that his authority derives from scripture: "Kings are called gods by the pro-

James VI: lofty view of monarchy.

phetical King David because they sit upon God his throne in earth and have the count of their administration to give unto him."

Their duties are to administer justice, to establish and enforce good laws, and to procure the peace. The people's duty is to obey the king. "Only God could make a king, and God alone could unmake him," James writes.

The king asserts that he owns the whole kingdom and, as the overlord of the whole land, so is he "master over every person that inhabiteth the same, having power over the life and death of every one of them". Many in Scotland do not accept these doctrines; one minister of the kirk called James "God's silly vassal" to his face. The English, who believe in the rights of parliaments, may also object (→ 5/8/1600).

Queen grieves over loss of Burghley

A great statesman: William Cecil.

London, 4 August 1598

Lord Burghley died at his house on the Strand today. The queen visited him on his deathbed and herself fed him with a spoon – an unprecedented sign of royal favour. He has been her chief minister since her accession, and his son Sir Robert Cecil is now her principal secretary.

Sir William Cecil, later Lord Burghley, was a leading figure in the government of Edward VI. He played no role under Queen Mary, but was summoned by Elizabeth when she became queen. He counselled her well as princes sought her hand and she rejected them, and maintained the peace while preparing for the war with Spain.

Essex charged after Irish campaign fails

London, 29 November 1599

The Earl of Essex was charged in the star chamber today with maladministration and abandoning his command in Ireland against the express orders of the queen. His fate was sealed in September, when he precipitately deserted his post and returned to London. Learning that Elizabeth was at Nonsuch palace, near Ewell in Surrey, he rode straight there, arriving early on 29 September, and – covered in mud – burst into her chamber before she was dressed. No man alive had seen her in her nightgown, with her hair loose and without any makeup. She received him kindly and allowed him to kiss her hand but later took offence at this behaviour.

Lord Essex went to Ireland last March with 16,000 men and 1,300 horses. He had bitterly criticised the generals in Ireland for failing to crush the Earl of Tyrone's rebellion and was given everything that he asked for. When he reached Dublin, he marched the army around Ireland instead of following orders and attacking Tyrone in Ulster.

He finally led a small force against Tyrone – only to agree a truce with him. Essex met the rebel at a river and had a long private talk with him. Spies suggest that they discussed taking an army back to England to seize the throne. The expedition was a total failure, and Essex came back to England in a desperate attempt to justify himself to the queen.

After he had left her chamber at Nonsuch, Elizabeth put on her wig and finery. She received him again, coolly, and then summoned her council, which decided to place him under house arrest while his conduct was examined (→ 5/6/1600).

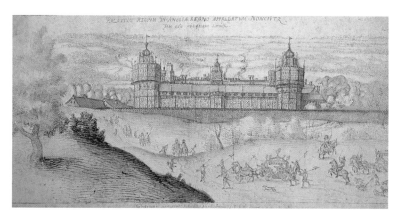

Nonsuch palace, where Essex burst in and took the queen by surprise.

Earl of Tyrone wins major victory over English forces in Ulster

Blackwater fort, Ulster: its English defenders have been forced to surrender.

Armagh, 14 August 1598

The main English army in Ireland has been routed at Yellow Ford by forces led by Hugh O'Neill, the Earl of Tyrone. The English commander, Sir Henry Bagenal – O'Neill's brother-in-law – was killed with 830 of his troops. Over four hundred were wounded, and 300 Irish have deserted to Tyrone. Blackwater fort has surrendered. It is the worst setback to English rule in Ireland in living memory.

Tyrone, who has the support of the influential O'Donnell clan and control of Connacht, is seen as Ireland's leader. He is demanding liberty of conscience, withdrawal of garrisons and control over government officials (→ 3/1603).

James narrowly avoids assassination

Perth, 5 August 1600

The Earl of Gowrie and his brother, the Master of Ruthven, were killed today in their own house in a struggle with the king and his guards. King James claims that they planned to murder him. The Gowries were the king's enemies. Their father was executed for treason, and their grandfather was a member of the gang who killed David Riccio, Queen Mary's favourite, in Holyrood palace in 1566.

The king says that young Ruthven, who was 19, came to him while he was out hunting and said that a stranger had arrived at his house in Perth with a pot of gold. He asked the king what should be done with it. The king says he rode over to the Gowries' house to examine the matter, with 16 men.

After dinner, says the king, Ruthven led him off to see the gold. He took James into a tower, locking every door behind him. There was no gold but a man in armour holding a dagger. Ruthven seized the dagger and said that the king must die for murdering his father. James tried to reason with the young man, who then rushed away to speak to

Mayhem: an imaginative view of the Gowries' attempt to kill King James.

his brother. When Ruthven returned to the tower and repeated that the king must die, the king succeeded in opening a window and calling for help. He grappled with Ruthven while his men ran to his rescue and in the confusion killed Ruthven and Gowrie. Few people believe this

story. Some think that the king went to Perth to kill the Ruthvens; others that the king and Ruthven, being alone together, began quarrelling, the king called "Treason!" and his guards then killed the brothers. King James afterwards invented the lie to explain matters.

Financial crisis forces Elizabeth to sell royal family treasures

England, 1600

The spiralling costs of war with Spain and its detrimental effect on trade have brought Queen Elizabeth's government to the brink of financial crisis. Commenting on the huge gap between income and expenditure, the queen's chief adviser, the diminutive Sir Robert Cecil, said: "My hair stands upright to think of it." The queen has been compelled to sell crown lands – and even some of her family jewels and heirlooms, including her father Henry VIII's great seal, bracelets and gold chains – in order to pay England's debts.

In contrast to the halcyon days of the 1570s and 1580s, when the queen's favourites made great fortunes, many of her courtiers are also feeling the pinch. There has been an explosion of corruption at court, centred on the system of "monopolies". Already challenged twice by parliament, these monopolies – designed to reward in-

Elizabeth and her courtiers: a sculpted frieze from Hatfield House (Herts).

dividuals or raise money for the crown – are royal grants giving the sole right to make or sell certain commodities. The profusion of monopolies – they have come to include everyday articles such as soap, salt and starch – and the abuses practised by their holders have transformed the system into a national scandal.

The disastrous inflation caused by the sale of monopolies is being blamed on Queen Elizabeth, who is accused of meanness and of playing off her courtiers against one another for her own amusement. The dispute has fuelled general dissatisfaction with the ageing queen's government and speculation about the possibility of her death.

Star chamber trial replaced by private hearing for Essex

Westminster, 5 June 1600

The Earl of Essex was brought before a special committee of the privy council today and threw himself upon the queen's mercy. "The tears in my heart", he said, "have quenched all the sparkles of pride that were in me." Sir Edward Coke, the attorney-general, laid out Essex's crimes with his usual thoroughness, but the council decided that Essex should remain under house arrest until Elizabeth ordered his release.

The queen – who agreed in February that Essex should be tried at this private hearing rather than by the star chamber – still hopes to make use of him. Her advisers, led by Robert Cecil and Walter Raleigh, believe that he will resume plotting if he is set free. Essex has been seriously ill since he was arrested last September and held at York House, but he has now recovered and been allowed to return to his own house, though still under guard. He told the queen: "God is witness how faithfully I vow to dedicate the rest of my life to your majesty, without admitting any other worldly care." Cecil fears the violence of the earl's followers, and also that, if he can get near the queen again, he will recover his old influence over her (→ 25/2/1601).

The London base of the young East India Company; the queen gave its founders a charter to trade in the rich markets of the East Indies late in 1599.

Essex beheaded after admitting treason

London, 25 February 1601
The Earl of Essex was beheaded in the Tower today. All the arrogance of his last days was gone. When condemned earlier this month, he had said: "I think it fitting that my poor quarters, which have done her majesty true service in divers parts of the world, should now at the last be sacrificed and disposed of at her majesty's pleasure." Today he told Elizabeth's chief minister, Robert Cecil: "I must confess to you that I am the greatest, the most vilest, and the most unthankful traitor that ever has been in the land."

Essex had plotted to gain Cecil's post by force. Following his arrest 17 months ago – after a disastrous campaign in Ireland – he lost all his offices, but was not formally tried. Freed from house arrest last August, he was ruined two months later when he lost his monopoly of imports of sweet wines. On 7 February he paid Shakespeare's men 40 shillings to play *Richard II* – on deposing kings; the next day, with

All support lost, Essex surrenders.

200 troops, he attacked London. Ludgate was locked against him, and the City did not rise. He tried to storm the gate but was repulsed. Deserted by all, he fled to his house on the Strand and surrendered.

Cecil sends secret messages to James

London, March 1601
Sir Robert Cecil has begun a secret correspondence with the king of Scotland to prepare his succession to Queen Elizabeth, who is now 67. He has told the king that he must expect nothing from him that could cause the slightest harm to the queen. He insists on complete secrecy and has begged the king to be patient, to be guided by him and to do nothing rash.

The king has replied that he will meet all Cecil's conditions, and that Cecil may count on the king's gratitude in the future. "My dearest and trusty Cecil," he wrote, "My pen is not able to express how happy I think myself for having chanced upon so worthy, so wise, and so provident a friend" (→22/5/07).

Forward-looking: Sir Robert Cecil.

'Golden speech' of queen soothes MPs

Whitehall, 19 December 1601
With anger mounting in the Commons over the abuse of monopolies, the queen today received a deputation of MPs and defused the row with what was called a "golden speech": "Though God hath raised me high, yet this I account the glory of my crown, that I have reigned with your loves. This makes me that I do not so much rejoice that God hath made me to be a queen, as to be a queen over so thankful a people and to be the means under God to conserve you in safety and to preserve you from danger."

Announcing the end of monopolies, she said she had been unaware that they caused her subjects misery. "That my grants shall be made grievances to my people, and oppressions be privileged under colour of our patents, our princely dignity shall not suffer," she went on.

The MPs accepted her claim that "I never was any greedy, scraping grasper, nor a strict, fast-holding prince, nor yet a waster; my heart was never set upon any worldly goods, but only for my subjects' good ... It is not my desire to live or reign longer than my life and reign shall be for your good. And though you have had, and may have, many a mightier and wiser prince sitting in this seat, yet you never had, nor shall have, any that will love you better." Then she dismissed the deputation, first allowing every one of them to kiss her hand in farewell.

Parliament creates Elizabethan poor law

Westminster, November 1601
Parliament has completed work on the Poor Law, codifying previous acts. Sturdy beggars and others of the out-of-work poor are to be returned to their native parishes, and every parish is to provide a poorhouse and to feed the destitute. Returning soldiers who refuse to work are to be executed. A poor

rate is to be levied throughout the country to pay for these provisions.

The great increase in population, the recurrent famines and the break-up of the feudal system have greatly increased the numbers of the poor. They are a menace to society, and queen and parliament were determined to bring them under control.

Queen shocked by her truthful reflection

Richmond Palace, January 1603
The queen is seriously ill. She sits on cushions on the floor, staring at the ground, refusing all medicine, refusing to eat. She ordered her servants to bring her a true mirror for the first time for 20 years, looked at her own face and saw that she is an old, sick woman. She railed at her servants and courtiers, who have always called her beautiful and young, honoured her with the name of "Gloriana" and promised that she was immune to the ravages of time. They lied to her, and she allowed them to lie, and now she is faced with the truth. The doctors cannot say what ails her (→24/3).

Elizabeth: an old woman now.

Irish rebel leader finally submits to crown

Ireland, March 1603
Hugh O'Neill, the Earl of Tyrone, has at last abandoned his guerrilla war against the English and formally submitted to the crown in return for a royal pardon. The truce was engineered by the English commander Charles Blount, Lord Mountjoy, whose military force finally overwhelmed the Irish rebels. Generous terms have been provided for Tyrone – he remains chief lord of Ulster under the crown – but his defeat may well mark the end of Gaelic power in Ireland.

It has taken four years for Mountjoy to complete the conquest so ineffectually begun in 1599 by

the Earl of Essex. Tyrone was safely encamped on the Cork coast when Mountjoy arrived. The English general Sir George Carew soon expelled Tyrone from Cork and set about subduing Munster, while Mountjoy brutally settled the Pale.

English rule looked fragile in September 1601 when 3,400 crack Spanish troops arrived to back the rebellion. They landed at Kinsale, while Tyrone and O'Donnell advanced from the north. But Mountjoy emerged the victor from a final battle fought near Kinsale on Christmas Eve; the rebels and the Spaniards surrendered. It has been a clearing-up operation since then.

Curtain falls on the extraordinary Elizabethan age

Richmond Palace, 24 March 1603
Queen Elizabeth has died, aged 69. In her last hours the council came to her to ask who would inherit her crown. She told the councillors that it would be no rascal and explained that a king should succeed her: "And who should that be but our cousin of Scotland?" she said. "I pray you trouble me no more, I'll have none but him." Later, when she was beyond speech, they asked

her again for a sign, and she raised herself in her bed and joined her fingers above her head, in the form of a crown, to show that she wished James to inherit the kingdom.

The archbishop of Canterbury, John Whitgift, came to pray with her. He told her what she was and where she was going, saying that, although she had long been a great queen upon earth, yet shortly she would have to yield an account of

her stewardship to the king of kings. He stayed praying with her for a long time and then left her with her ladies. At last, between two and three o'clock this morning, she died peacefully.

She was the last and greatest of the Tudors, the most famous monarch to rule England since Henry V and the most beloved. She defended the realm against Spain, sent Drake around the world, and saw a bril-

liant flowering of drama, poetry, painting and music. During her reign England was more at peace at home and abroad than ever before. The Elizabethan age is now over, and horsemen have galloped north to bring the news to James VI of Scotland, who will now be proclaimed King James of England. The peaceful union of the crowns may be Elizabeth's finest legacy (→4/1603).

Peace at home was greatest triumph

England, 24 March 1603
Elizabeth's greatest achievement at home in her long and glorious reign was to maintain the peace. France, Scotland and the Netherlands were torn apart by religious wars, the Inquisition stoked its fires in Spain, but the queen kept to the moderate path set by her father. She would not persecute the Catholics, as long as they were loyal, and although she was a Protestant queen, praised and cherished by Protestants all over Europe, she would not impose a strict puritanism on England.

As a result, the Catholics kept the peace, except for the northern rebellion in 1569, and the doctrines of the Church of England spread steadily. The queen was the most popular monarch that England has known. She cemented her popularity by embarking on "progresses" around the country every year. She would spend many weeks travelling, dragging her unhappy court with her, showing herself to her people, winning hearts everywhere. She rode on horseback, or in an open litter. She was still "progressing" in her late sixties, after ordering her "old" courtiers to stay behind.

Throughout her reign, politics were dominated by the question of the succession and what to do with Mary Queen of Scots. Approving her execution was the most painful act of Elizabeth's life. But, behind these great questions, the steady reform of government, started under Henry VII, continued. The mediaeval monarchy that the Tudors inherited has been revolutionised under their rule (→26/3).

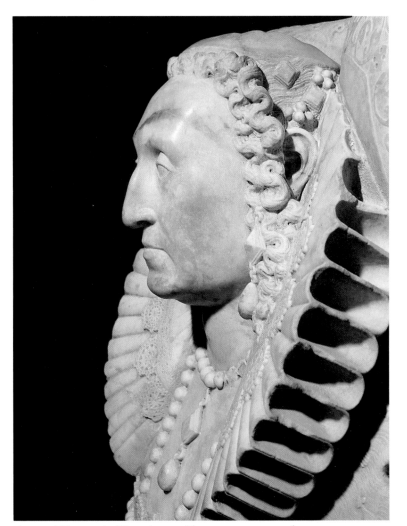

A carved likeness in Westminster abbey commemorates the great queen.

The queen is dead: a solemn but splendid funeral procession for Elizabeth.

England becomes a major world force

London, 24 March 1603
When Elizabeth came to the throne, England was a minor power on the margin of Europe and had just lost its last toehold on the continent: Calais. England is now a force in the world. Elizabeth's ships have circled the globe and explored all the coasts of the New World. Though left far behind by Spain and Portugal, England is now pursuing its own quest for a foreign empire. Elizabeth has fought a long and successful war against Spain and inflicted Philip II's greatest defeat upon him. For many years she was the leading Protestant monarch in Europe, held in reverence by Huguenots, Scandinavians and Germans.

The queen's policies were not always successful. Sir Walter Raleigh's colonies in Virginia have failed, and Ireland remains troublesome. Her military expeditions on the continent were unremarkable; she did not recover Calais. However, she established a lasting peace with Scotland, in alliance with the Protestant party there, and her policy's success may be measured by the union of the crowns.

None of the queen's marriage proposals was concluded. Among her many suitors were King Philip's son, Don Carlos, the Duke of Anjou and his brother, the Archduke of Austria and a Danish prince. Playing one off against the others in a diplomatic carousel helped to keep the peace for over 20 years, which was always the main object of her policy. She saw that the wealth of England was in trade and gave it every encouragement.

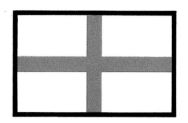

James VI of Scots 1567–1625 and I of England 1603–1625

Edinburgh, 26 March 1603. King James VI of Scots learns of his accession to the throne of England (→ 7/4).

London, April 1603. Queen Elizabeth is buried in Westminster abbey after an elaborate funeral procession through the City.

Borders, 7 April 1603. King James is given a warm welcome as he crosses the Berwick border into England (→ 7/5).

London, September 1603. A Spanish embassy negotiates peace talks with James after two decades of war (→ 8/1604).

London, 1603. King James takes William Shakespeare's theatrical company under his protection as the "King's Men" (→ 1613).

Westminster, 22 March 1604. King James opens his first parliament and outlines his policy for an Anglo-Scots union under the name of "Great Britain" (→ 11/1604).

Westminster, July 1604. King James demonstrates his anti-Catholic stance by passing an act against recusants (Catholics who refuse to attend Church of England services) (→ 25/12).

England/Scotland, Nov 1604. After the fixing of the exchange rate last April, it is decided that a common currency will now be introduced and customs tariffs abolished between the two countries (→ 7/1605).

Canterbury, 25 December 1604. Richard Bancroft, the newly-appointed archbishop of Canterbury, who replaced John Whitgift, begins to expel clergy who refuse to conform (→ 11/1610).

London, July 1605. King James is furious to discover that 19 of his ministers have called a general assembly in Scotland without royal permission; he calls for an investigation (→ 12/4/06).

England, 1605. James introduces a Scots sport, played with stick and ball, known as "golf".

England, February 1606. The archbishop of Canterbury continues his campaign against non-conformists (→ 11/1610).

Britain, 12 April 1606. King James orders the first union flag, which will combine the crosses of St Andrew and St George, to be adopted by both English and Scottish shipping (→ 7/1606).

London, 3 May 1606. The Jesuit Henry Garnet, the remaining conspirator in the gunpowder plot, is executed.

Perth, July 1606. King James summons the "Red Parliament" – all the nobles and officials wear red cloaks – which grants the first major tax to the king (→ 2/1607).

Westminster, 1606. The courts uphold "impositions" – new and potentially lucrative duties on imports; the king is able to exploit England's international trade, one of the products of peace with Spain.

England, spring 1607. Robert Carr, the youngest and attractive son of the Fernihurst family, who caught the eye of King James at a recent jousting tournament, is fast becoming the new favourite at court (→ 9/5/09).

Virginia, spring 1607. British settlers arrive. They name natural features – the James river; Capes Henry and Charles – in honour of the Stuart dynasty; their settlement is called Jamestown (→ 9/1620).

Hertfordshire, 22 May 1607. Robert Cecil gives his country mansion, Theobalds, to King James; Cecil now plans to rebuild Hatfield House, the former residence of Queen Elizabeth, for himself (→ 5/1612).

Britain, 1608. Dual nationality is to be given to all Scots and Englishmen born after James's accession to the throne.

Edinburgh, 10 March 1609. Lord Balmerino, James's Scottish secretary, is sentenced to death following a confession of forging James's signature on a letter to the pope.

London, 9 July 1610. James imprisons Arabella Stuart, his cousin and possible heir to the throne, in the Tower on his discovery that she has married William Seymour, the Earl of Hertford (→ 6/1611).

Canterbury, November 1610. Archbishop Richard Bancroft dies; he is replaced by George Abbott, a fiercely anti-Catholic controversialist.

Westminster, February 1611. James dissolves his first parliament, which has sat intermittently since 1604. He is angered by the MPs' refusal to pay serious attention to his financial needs.

England, March 1611. Robert Carr is given the title Viscount Rochester (→ 11/1613).

Britain, 1611. James, in an effort to raise money, creates the title of baronet, which will be sold for the sum of £1095.

Britain/Europe, May 1612. Negotiations are completed for the marriage of Elizabeth, James's eldest daughter, to Frederick, the Elector Palatine (→ 14/12/13).

London, October 1612. The body of Mary Queen of Scots is exhumed from Peterborough cathedral on the orders of James and reburied in the Henry VII Chapel in Westminster abbey.

London, 15 September 1613. Sir Thomas Overbury, a friend of Viscount Rochester, dies in the Tower (→ 12/10/15).

England, November 1613. King James gives the earldom of Somerset to Robert Carr, Viscount Rochester (→ 12/1613).

London, 1613. William Shakespeare completes his latest play *Henry VIII*. It ends with the christening of Princess Elizabeth, who is predicted to bring "a thousand thousand blessings" on her people (→ 23/4/16).

The life and times of King James VI/I

Name: James VI of Scotland and James I of England.
Birth: 19 June 1566.
Accession: 24 July 1567 (Scotland); 24 March 1603 (England).
Coronation: 29 July 1567 (Scotland); 25 July 1603 (England).
Predecessors: mother (Scotland) and cousin (England).
Hair: light brown.
Eyes: blue.

Marriage: Anne of Denmark, 23 November 1589, Oslo.
Children: Henry, Elizabeth, Charles and four others.
Favourite home: Theobalds.
Likes: hunting, young men.
Dislikes: tobacco, all things military.
Greatest problem: his mother.
Greatest success: keeping peace.
Death: 27 March 1625.

Opposite: King James VI of Scotland and I of England.

James unites the crowns of England and Scotland

New king finishes triumphal journey

London, 7 May 1603

James VI's triumphal journey from Edinburgh reached its climax today when he led his retinue into London, which, once he has been crowned king of England, will be his new capital.

This has been a dazzling progress, growing ever more splendid as it proceeded south. Nobles, courtiers and local dignitaries in every town have vied in the magnificence of the welcome that they have offered to the new king, while he, in turn, has lavished honours with unparalleled generosity. He leaves 300 new knights in his wake.

At the same time, he has been able to confer with several influential men, notably Sir Robert Cecil, a pillar of Elizabeth's court, who travelled up from London to York and – in brief moments between the numerous banquets, presentations and sundry amusements – has given sage advice to the king.

Among those seeking attention was a group of Protestant divines, who presented the king with a "millenary petition" outlining a programme for church reform. James is sympathetic to their suggestions, but Archbishop Whitgift is appalled by such radicalism (→ 25/7/03).

Scots regret 'loss' of their monarch

Scotland, May 1603

England may be rejoicing at the accession of its new king, but the Scots, who have enjoyed James's rule since 1567, are feeling deprived. Many wept as he left Edinburgh on 5 April, and his solemn farewell, delivered at St Giles's church two days earlier, was a brave attempt at consolation by the departing king. He vowed to visit them every three years and urged them not to mourn his leaving. Their interests, he said, would remain at the forefront of his heart. Yet the Scots know that James is taking with him the pomp and power that once were theirs.

Pressed close from every side: King James makes his entry into London.

The triumphal arch erected for King James at Fenchurch Street, London.

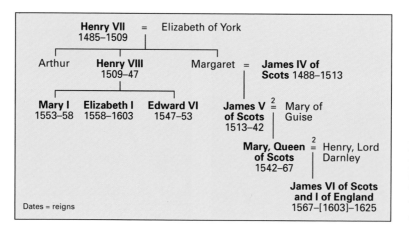

No-frills monarch enjoys coronation

Westminster, 25 July 1603

James VI of Scotland was crowned king of England today, uniting the two kingdoms and setting the Stuart dynasty on two British thrones. The ceremony lacked something of the traditional splendour thanks to an outbreak of the plague, but King James and Queen Anne delighted their new subjects as they rode in procession to the abbey.

The one problem is that the king, used to a quieter way of life, has begun to find the tumultuous reception that has greeted his every step since he left Scotland all too much. He relishes his power, but would prefer a little more privacy. As he put it, in the no frills manner to which the court is becoming accustomed: "God's wounds, I will pull down my breeches and they shall also see my arse" (→ 9/1603).

Conspirators freed while on scaffold

London, 10 December 1603

In a hair's-breadth escape, a number of condemned men have been spared execution just seconds before the axe fell. Lord Cobham, an associate of Sir Walter Raleigh – and like him arrested on 17 July on suspicion of plotting to depose James in favour of the king's cousin Arabella Stuart – was due to die today at the Tower of London together with several other alleged conspirators, although without Sir Walter, whose execution was scheduled for a later date.

Cobham, alongside some of the others, had actually mounted the scaffold and readied himself for death. Instead, even as the executioner raised his axe, a messenger arrived brandishing a royal warrant ordering the execution to be halted. It was with great relief that the men left the scaffold, undoubtedly impressed by this calculated demonstration of royal power. Now they will remain in jail, as will Raleigh, whose sentence has also been commuted (→ 3/1616).

King backs bishops and warns Puritans

Hampton Court, January 1604
The Church of England is to have a new translation of the Bible, as suggested by John Reynolds of Oxford university and endorsed by the king. This was among several reforms agreed at the Hampton Court conference, called to determine the church's direction under its new sovereign. The conference was headed by Archbishop Whitgift, backed by eight other bishops, and attended by four moderate puritans, led by Dr Reynolds.

The king made some concessions to the puritans, but stressed his opposition to their gaining power at the expense of the bishops. "I know what would become of my supremacy," he retorted. "No bishop, no king." He insisted on conformity to his will as head of the church, warning dissidents that he would "harry them out of the land" (→ 1611).

King James adopts a new British title

London, 20 October 1604
The king, whose twin titles reflect his special role as ruler of both England and Scotland, has enshrined his position in a new one: "King of Great Britain". The new title was proclaimed today, although the Commons, from whom James had hoped to win approval, refuse to accept the new "single" kingdom. The king has defied them, claiming that his new title embraces "the whole circuit of the island".

As one member put it, to cross the rose with the thistle might well produce a monster. "England" was a name under which the nation had long prospered; the plan to subsume it under "Great Britain" had little support. It was agreed that the new name might be used after an act of union – but even then laws passed for one country should not automatically govern the other.

Gunpowder plot is foiled

Fawkes – deputed to plant the gunpowder – is brought before the king.

London, 5 November 1605
That king and parliament may sleep safely in their beds tonight is no thanks to a group of Catholic plotters who tried to blow up the palace of Westminster today. Their plan to explode barrels of gunpowder during the opening of the new session was foiled before the gang could touch off the charges.

The plot was devised by Robert Catesby, a devout Catholic set on avenging what he saw as the persecution of his co-religionists. With him, and arrested even as he prepared to light the fuse, was one Guy Fawkes. Catesby had two plans: to blow up parliament, and to trigger a Catholic uprising in the Midlands. Fawkes was deputed to plant the gunpowder, placing iron bars on top of the barrels to cause maximum destruction. Catesby, meanwhile, had arranged a hunting party in Warwickshire, to which he invited Catholic gentry earmarked to help the gang to seize power.

But the plotters were betrayed when one, Francis Tresham, sent a warning to his Catholic brother-in-law, Lord Mounteagle – who, as a lord, would be among the potential victims; he in turn told the government. Fawkes is now in custody, and it is expected that Catesby will be taken too (→ 1/2/06).

Royal diplomacy ends the war with Spain

Peace agreed: the English delegates, led by Robert Cecil, are on the right.

London, August 1604
Spain, England's bitter enemy for nearly 50 years, is now its ally, thanks to a treaty signed this month in London by James and the Spanish king, Philip III. The treaty, which was agreed against the advice of those counsellors who saw a weakened Spain as ripe for one final blow, and despite the efforts of King Henry IV of France and of the Dutch – equally implacable enemies of the Spanish – is a tribute to royal diplomacy.

It frees England from the costs of war and opens Spain to English traders, but, for all their angry complaints, it has not weakened England's alliance with the Dutch. The fact is that Spain needs peace more than England and has accepted all of James's terms (→ 1606).

MPs confront king on royal privilege

London, 19 March 1604
The king rules by divine right, but the people's representatives in the House of Commons, have their own views on the privileges that come with that divinity. That was shown today when James clashed with MPs over the case of Francis Goodwin, whose election to a seat in Buckinghamshire had been overturned by the chancery court on the pretext of his being an outlaw.

To the Commons that summary act, and Goodwin's replacement by Sir John Fortescue, both smack of royal meddling – even if the king claims that all their privileges are subject to his authority. To them there is no argument: disputed elections are parliamentary affairs, and theirs alone to resolve.

The king's profound dislike of smoking is reflected in the anonymous publication in 1604 of his "Counterblast to Tobacco", in which he ridicules the argument that tobacco is beneficial.

Debauchery marks visit by Danish king

Hertfordshire, July 1606

"The entertainment went forward and most of the presenters went backward, or fell down, wine did so occupy their upper chambers," wrote the wit Sir John Harington on the meeting between James and his brother-in-law, Christian IV of Denmark. The two kings were staying at Theobalds, the Hertfordshire home of Lord Salisbury.

According to Harington, the court is not usually known for its drinking, but – spurred on by the uninhibited royal guest – lords, ladies and monarchs indulged in what can only be described as an orgy of excess, quite in keeping with the masque of *Solomon and Sheba* which was being performed.

Christian himself collapsed early in the proceedings, a victim of too much drink and a coating of jellies, cakes, spices and sundry sweetmeats which had been poured over him when the girl playing Sheba, equally inebriated, had tumbled at his feet, dropping her sickly "gifts".

Other revellers fared no better. Those playing "Hope" and "Faith" were found vomiting in an antechamber; "Victory" expired after trying in vain to present James with a symbolic sword. "Peace" forgot

Danish reveller: Christian IV.

herself completely, laying about all and sundry with the olive branches that formed part of her costume. James himself has a strong head for liquor and appears unmoved by declining standards at court.

Scots attacked as 'beggars and traitors' as debate rages on union of kingdoms

London, February 1607

Whatever King James may feel about the possible union of his two kingdoms, neither the House of Commons nor the Scottish Parliament is keen on the project. This month has seen discussion of the union in both assemblies, and the debates have been notable for their bitterness.

Sir Christopher Piggott, describing the whole Scottish people as "beggars, rebels and traitors", said that there was not a single Scottish king who had not been murdered by his own people. It was, he added, as reasonable to propose such a union as it would be to suggest that a prisoner at the bar was the equal of the judge on the bench.

A day later Mr Fuller took another tack, claiming that – were the Scots, as proposed, to become naturalised Englishmen – England would be like a rich pasture facing invasion by a herd of famished cattle. There was neither room nor wealth enough in England to accommodate hordes of immigrants.

The Scots are equally negative, if more subtle. They have voted to repeal any anti-English legislation

The royal heraldry of Scotland.

and accept the union if England reciprocates. Since the Commons have been so hostile, such a compromise seems impossible, and the idea of union must be dead.

The king, of course, is livid and humiliated. His furious protests over Piggott's speech have induced the Commons to send the outspoken MP to the Tower (→ 1608).

Scottish theologian is jailed by James

London, 30 November 1606

The king has maintained remarkably equable relations with both the Anglican and the Presbyterian churches, but now one cleric has gone too far. Dr Andrew Melville, a Scottish divine whose beliefs are uncompromisingly anti-papist, has made his opinions felt once too often; he has been arrested and jailed on the king's orders.

Accused of publishing verses that satirised Archbishop Richard Bancroft (and indeed his royal master), Melville was summoned to London, where he today faced the privy council. He would not bow to his accusers, choosing instead to launch into an impassioned lecture during which he grabbed Bancroft's sleeve, denouncing his episcopal vestments as "popish rags". He was removed to jail and awaits the king's pleasure.

Gunpowder traitors meet horrible fate

London, 1 February 1606

Guy Fawkes – the most notorious survivor of the gunpowder gang whose plot to kill the king and parliament was foiled last year – was hanged, drawn and quartered today, five days after his trial before Sir Edward Coke. The leading plotter, Robert Catesby, is already dead, shot resisting the king's men at Holbeche House in Staffordshire.

Fawkes – found standing amid his own powder-filled barrels in the cellars beneath the palace of Westminster – was among the last to die. Another group of plotters was dealt with in similar fashion yesterday. So extreme were the tortures which Fawkes had suffered before he confessed that he had to be carried up the steps of the scaffold.

Now there is only one plotter left: Garnet, the head of the English Jesuits. He is in hiding, but few doubt that he will be found and brought to punishment (→ 3/5/06).

A grisly end: Guy Fawkes and the other gunpowder plotters are executed.

James backs Ulster resettlement plans

Ulster, December 1608

King James has approved plans for the plantation, or resettlement, of Ulster chiefly by English immigrants. The king has given particular encouragement to Englishmen who have served the crown in either a civil or a military capacity. Known as servitors, these men are to have responsibility for preserving order among the natives and introducing more settlers on their estates. Plantations are to be established in six of the Ulster counties, in Wexford, Leitrim and Longford, in Tipperary and the royal counties.

The move has been prompted by the recent Irish rebellion and the belief that the continued existence of Catholic landowners in Ireland is a threat to English security. The ultimate goal is thought to be the expropriation of all property held by such landowners.

James is embroiled in bitter legal row

London, 2 February 1609

In a display far more human than regally divine, the king openly lost his temper today during a venomous dispute with Sir Edward Coke, the chief justice. The cause was Coke's attempt to set a boundary between common law and church law, and his claim that, while the former was the law of the land, the latter was a foreign imposition.

So enraged was the king that he appeared ready to hit Coke, who prudently gave up his arguments, fell to the floor and grovelled there, begging for mercy. Rather than go any further with what had become an impossible situation, James postponed the debate.

It will, however, have to be continued. Backed by Archbishop Bancroft, the ecclesiastical lawyers have no intention of losing their lucrative positions within the legal system. Against them, the common lawyers wish to exert their right of "prohibitions", under which they can prevent the church courts from

The king's opponent: Edward Coke.

determining the legality of their own acts. It could mean the end of their powers. The king wishes to mediate, but he will have to control his emotions better if such efforts are to work (→ 16/11/17).

Excessive favouritism provokes disquiet

London, 9 May 1609

Not satisfied with promoting Robert Carr to his innermost councils and showering him with gifts, both of money and of possessions, the king today gave his young favourite a new toy: the manor of Sherborne, the last remaining property of the disgraced Sir Walter Raleigh.

This latest display is bound to give new ammunition to those, both Scots and Englishmen, who dislike the king's taste for favourites. While many at court detest what they see as James's unnatural affection for Carr, it is his profligate generosity that worries them more.

The exchequer is being robbed to enrich these men. Some £68,000 has been dispensed in gifts and pensions since James succeeded to the English throne, and there appears to be no limit to his indulgence of those who please him (→ 3/1611).

MPs and king clash on customs duties

London, March 1610

The collection of royal finances, a persistent problem, is causing new difficulties as James's expenditure continues to rise. This month has seen a series of angry debates in the Commons, with many MPs arguing that the king must give up certain privileges, which they claim are at best only half-legal. James believes that it is part of his royal prerogative to levy special taxes on imports, known as "impositions". Parliament says otherwise (→ 10/1610).

Royal budget plans fail to win support

London, October 1610

The "Great Contract" engineered by Lord Salisbury to boost royal income has collapsed amid recriminations on all sides. Salisbury had proposed that the king should surrender his unpopular revenue-producing royal prerogatives in return for a firm annual grant of taxation. Five months ago it seemed as if the plan would be accepted, but recently both king and Commons raised their terms to unacceptable levels, and now all is chaos (→ 1611).

Henry is Prince of Wales

London, 6 January 1610

Prince Henry, the heir to the throne, was instituted as Prince of Wales today. The prince, who was born in Stirling castle almost 16 years ago, is expected to be the second Stuart to succeed to the twin thrones of England and Scotland.

As he has grown older and begun to establish his own court, it has appeared to many observers that in many respects the prince has qualities that his father lacks. An athletic young man, and an enthusiast for the martial arts, he is proficient at many sports, notably tilting at the ring. He has also shown a distinct interest in naval matters.

As opposed to the favourites who flutter around the king, Henry has shown himself a serious young man, with an independent outlook. He has little time for the favourites and has risked incurring his father's well-known anger by his open attacks on the current "favourite son", the effeminate, arrogant and ultimately stupid Robert Carr. Indeed, Henry has made it clear that he despises what he has criticised as the unseemly manners at court.

For himself he prefers the company of learned men and indulges in a variety of intellectual pursuits. He is a patron of scientists, and

Henry: he is now Prince of Wales.

numbers Sir Walter Raleigh, the dashing explorer and discoverer of that same "tobacco" that his father loathes, among his intimates.

Raleigh has gone so far as to add a eulogy of the prince to the end of the first part of his *History of the World* and has remarked that only a father such as King James could "keep such a bird in a cage". Others, including Henry himself, talk of a figure from the age of chivalry; he has even been compared to Henry V (→ 11/1612).

Masques become all the rage at court

The design for Henry's costume.

London, 6 January 1610

Today's investiture of Prince Henry as Prince of Wales was notable not just for its pomp but also for the elaborate masque that accompanied it. Written by Ben Jonson and produced by Inigo Jones, it featured Henry himself in the leading role, as Moeliades – an anagram of *Miles a Deo*, or soldier of God.

Such masques – elaborately costumed dramas with songs and dances – have become an important hallmark of Jacobean court life, combining entertainment and symbolism. When the king appears as a pagan god, and his wife as a classical queen, this is not just dressing up but a statement of the way in which James sees himself and the whole institution of kingship.

King's cousin flees imprisonment, but is soon recaptured

Dover, June 1611

Lady Arabella Stuart, a cousin of the king and a theoretical successor, has been captured in the English Channel. Lady Arabella had secretly married William Seymour, another royal cousin, against the wishes of King James who feared that they or their offspring might challenge his own right to the English throne. They were imprisoned but escaped, proclaiming that theirs was a love match, not a political challenge. They missed each other at the Essex coast, so planned to meet in Europe. Seymour reached Ostend, but Arabella was overtaken a few miles off Calais.

Captured: Lady Arabella Stuart.

Nation mourns death of royal heir

Prince Henry: now he is dead.

London, November 1612

The Prince of Wales is dead. The heir to the English and Scottish thrones died on 6 November at the age of only 18, prompting a remarkable outpouring of public and private grief. "Our rising sun is set ere scarce he had shone and all our glory lies buried," wrote the Earl of Dorset to a fellow nobleman. The royal family, and especially the queen, have been shattered by Prince Henry's death.

He had begun to look ill last month, but until the final days of October had maintained his regular public appearances. So athletic and handsome was the young prince, however, that at first nobody took his fever too seriously. After all, Henry had come to personify the ideals of a Protestant knight: courageous in spirit, learned in culture.

It was the arrival of Dr Theodore de Mayerne on 27 October which first signalled concern. Teams of doctors joined the battle to save the prince, but to no avail. On the evening of 6 November he died, probably of typhoid fever.

Henry combined a serious religious spirit with an extrovert flair for public life. He took an active part in promoting the fashion for "masques" and emerged as a noted patron of the arts. He loved military life, too, relishing opportunities to hone his equestrian skills and fascinated by new developments in ships. The new heir, Charles, will find his elder brother's reputation hard to live up to.

James's 'authorised' Bible is published

England, 1611

A new translation of the Bible has been published to meet the king's desire that the words should be easily understood by the people of England and Scotland. The result is a work bearing the stamp of royal approval as "authorised" by King James. It is dedicated to him "not only as our king and sovereign, but to the principal mover and author of the work". James first suggested a new translation in 1601 when he was king of Scotland. The idea was revived and accepted at the Hampton Court conference of 1604. James supervised the 47 scholars and bishops who then worked on the translation, which relies mostly on words of Anglo-Saxon rather than Latin origin.

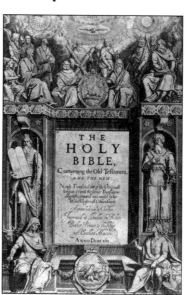
The frontispiece to the new Bible.

Salisbury, king's chief minister, dies

Marlborough, Wiltshire, May 1612

The Earl of Salisbury, who as Robert Cecil was chief minister to both Queen Elizabeth and King James, has died. It was Cecil who prepared the way for James's accession, writing secretly to the Scottish king in the final years of Elizabeth's reign. He had become Elizabeth's secretary of state in 1596, following in his father's footsteps: born in 1563, he was the second son of Lord Burghley. He was equally loyal to James, labouring hard to improve the royal finances, but had recently found himself relegated in favour of Viscount Rochester.

A great statesman: Robert Cecil.

James reorganises the central administration of government

London, May 1612

King James has decided that he will rule without a secretary of state to replace the Earl of Salisbury, who has just died [*see report right*]. Salisbury's industrious competence has served the king well both at home and abroad, but James is anxious to demonstrate that he can run the affairs of state by himself.

This decision will be a blow to Francis Bacon, an able solicitor-general who had seen Salisbury's death as his opportunity for promotion. In terms of ability he has strong claims, but he has never been a royal favourite in the sense in which Sir Robert Carr (now Viscount Rochester) has become one recently. Even Salisbury had been taking second place to Rochester, a striking if arrogant Scot from the borders, in the last months of his life. It seems likely that Rochester encouraged the king's belief that it is the monarch, and not his courtiers, who should be seen to take charge. Whether or not this new-found royal confidence will survive the daily rigours of administration is uncertain. James is undoubtedly a man of vision (as he showed by commissioning the authorised translation of the Bible) but although in his mid-forties he has yet to demonstrate a capacity for sustained hard work. The king's need for money, despite the efforts of Salisbury, is the major problem.

James's daughter marries German ruler

Westminster, 14 February 1613

Today, St Valentine's day, the king's only surviving daughter, Princess Elizabeth, was married to Frederick, the Elector Palatine of the Rhine and Protestant claimant to the crown of Bohemia. The couple, who are both 16, were married in Westminster abbey amidst lavish ceremonies and great popular enthusiasm. A mock battle is being staged on the Thames at a cost of no less than £9,000.

Elizabeth wore a dress of silver and was attended by bridesmaids dressed in white to symbolise her maidenhood. Her long hair was topped by a bejewelled coronet which the king values at "a million crowns". The beauty of the bride contrasted sharply with the drab and melancholy appearance of the king himself, still grieving over the death of his elder son, Henry, last November. Henry's effigy, in fact, was visible in the abbey today.

Yet this was a marriage which King James had long favoured. He saw the alliance with a Protestant prince in Europe not only as a

A royal bride: Princess Elizabeth.

means of demonstrating his own true faith but also as a counter to his attempts to improve relations with Catholic Spain. Elizabeth herself has a lively personality which has made her more popular than any of the king's surviving children. The king, too, regards "Bessy" as his favourite. Inauspiciously, however, James forgot to dub Frederick when he made him a knight of the Garter before today's wedding.

New Spanish envoy wields royal influence

London, March 1613

Just a few weeks after his arrival in London as Spain's new envoy, Count Sarmiento of Gondomar, has demonstrated a powerful influence over James in his intercession with the king on behalf of Donna Luisa de Carvajal.

A Spaniard who spent eight years in England forcefully promoting the cause of Catholicism, Donna Luisa was recently arrested on the orders of George Abbot, the archbishop of Canterbury, after rumours that her house in the Barbican was a nunnery in disguise. Sarmiento immediately protested to James, who said that he would free her only on condition that she left England forthwith. The ambassador threatened that, if Donna Luisa were expelled, he would leave England with her. The king saw to it that the captive woman was released unconditionally the same evening.

Sarmiento is a perfect diplomat, wily, dignified and determined. The quick-witted ambassador seems to know exactly how to amuse and

Sarmiento, the Spanish envoy.

flatter the king, and he is using his influential position to promote a possible marriage between Prince Charles, the heir to the throne, and the Spanish *Infanta*.

James, meanwhile, is keen to enhance his own image as a peacemaker. He believes that it is possible to achieve peace by encouraging friendly relations with Spain while pursuing alliances with Protestant states (→ 1614).

King's favourite marries Frances Howard after scandalous divorce case splits court

London, December 1613

Lady Frances Howard has married Sir Robert Carr, the royal favourite and recently-created Earl of Somerset, in a ceremony of great magnificence paid for by the king. The marriage took place after a divorce saga which pitted king against archbishop and scandalised society.

Lady Frances was only 13 when she married the 14-year-old Earl of Essex in 1606. The bride, from the influential Howard family, was the youngest daughter of the Earl of Suffolk. Playwright Ben Jonson wrote a masque for the occasion, but there was little joy in the union. The earl travelled abroad while his wife developed great beauty and acquired many lovers, including,

briefly, the late Prince Henry. When Essex returned, Lady Frances at first refused to live with him and then denied him access to her bed. Aided by her mother and a quack doctor, she gave drugs to her unsuspecting husband. After these bleak years, both partners wanted a divorce. But Lady Frances fought for an annulment on the grounds that her husband was impotent with all women, not just with her. Essex predictably denied this.

A commission which heard the tawdry tale, spiced by allegations of witchcraft, was almost evenly split. But, in the face of protests from the archbishop of Canterbury, King James exerted great influence to secure the annulment (→ 2/1615).

Partners in a court scandal: Sir Robert Carr and Lady Frances Howard.

James diverted by passion for the chase

Theobalds, Hertfordshire, 1613

While supposedly entertaining the Duke of Saxe-Weimar at his country retreat of Theobalds, James has, as usual, spent most of his time in the hunting field. Hunting is one of the king's great passions, which – to the exasperation of his advisers – often diverts him from the more mundane business of government.

In contrast to his normal timidity, the king shows great daring on horseback, but there are violent and bloody aspects to the sport which disgust some of his subjects. After

pursuing his hounds at a wild gallop across the countryside to the scene of a kill, the king habitually dismounts, cuts the dead stag's throat and opens its belly. He thrusts his hands and feet into the stag's entrails, sating the dogs with its blood and daubing the faces of his courtiers in recognition of their sportsmanship.

The king's temper depends upon the success or otherwise of a day's sport – happy and elated after achieving a kill, sad and downcast if the quarry has eluded him.

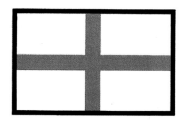

James VI of Scots 1567–1625 and I of England 1603–1625

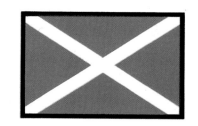

London, July 1614. King James appoints Thomas Howard, the Earl of Suffolk, as the new lord treasurer; James's favourite Robert Carr, the Earl of Somerset, succeeds Suffolk in the office of lord chamberlain (→ 7/1618).

London, August 1614. King James meets George Villiers, an attractive 22-year-old courtier, for the first time (→ 4/1615).

Britain/Spain, 1614. King James begins negotiations for a marriage alliance between his son Charles and *Infanta* Anna, the catholic daughter of King Philip III of Spain, in an attempt to bring peace to Europe (→ 11/1616).

Edinburgh, 6 February 1615. Patrick Stuart, the Earl of Orkney and a cousin to James, is executed on the king's orders for his involvement in a rebellion to overthrow James and his government.

London, February 1615. James writes to the Earl of Somerset – who, because of his boorish behaviour and attitude towards James, has recently fallen from favour – attempting to regain their old friendship (→ 7/1615).

England, July 1615. James and the Earl of Somerset reconcile their differences (→ 12/10).

London, September 1615. Lady Arabella Stuart, the cousin of James, who has been imprisoned in the Tower of London since her marriage in 1610 to William Seymour, the Earl of Hertford, dies aged 40.

England, 1615. James appoints the poet John Donne as his chaplain.

London, January 1616. George Villiers, the king's new favourite at court, is given the title of master of the horse (→ 4/1616).

London, March 1616. Sir Walter Raleigh is released, on the orders of James, after 13 years' imprisonment in the Tower of London (→ 29/10/18).

Warwickshire, 23 April 1616. William Shakespeare, the celebrated playwright and poet, dies at Stratford-upon-Avon.

London, April 1616. James makes George Villiers a knight of the Garter (→ 8/1616).

Westminster, June 1616. Sir Francis Bacon is appointed to the privy council (→ 1618).

London, August 1616. George Villiers becomes a member of the peerage: James makes him both Viscount Villiers and Baron Whaddon (→ 1/1/18).

London, November 1616. Prince Charles, aged 16, the eldest surviving son of James and heir to the throne, is invested as the Prince of Wales.

Scotland, 10 December 1616. The Scottish Parliament passes an education act in which the crown gives its backing to the church's demand for a school in every parish.

Britain/Spain, 1616. Negotiations continue for a marriage between the Prince of Wales and *Infanta* Anna, despite the religious problems of a possible Catholic succession to the English throne (→ 3/1622).

Scotland, 13 May 1617. King James, desperately lacking in finances, returns to his homeland for the first time since he inherited the throne in 1603 (→ 4/8/17).

Scotland, November 1617. The general assembly of the Scottish Church, meeting at St Andrews, rejects the controversial Five Articles of Perth which James

wishes it to adopt, on the grounds that both king and church are too Anglicised (→ 1/8/18).

London, 1 Jan 1618. Continuing his astonishing rise to power, George Villiers – who was made an earl last year – becomes the Marquis of Buckingham (→ 7/1618).

Tayside, 1 August 1618. The general assembly of the Church of Scotland, brow-beaten by the king, finally passes the Five Articles of Perth (→ 4/8/21).

Britain/Spain, Autumn 1618. The Anglo-Spanish marriage talks are temporarily suspended following James's refusal of the Spanish terms.

London, January 1619. The Marquis of Buckingham is promoted by James to lord high admiral.

Hampton Court, 2 March 1619. Queen Anne, aged 45, dies; James, with his dreadful horror of illness and death, is not present in her last hours.→

Plymouth, September 1620. The Pilgrim Fathers, a group of puritans, set sail in the *Mayflower* to make a new life in the New World (→ 12/1620).

England, 1620. Like his father Prince Charles is totally mesmerised by George Villiers, the Marquis of Buckingham, and falls under his influence (→ 7/2/23).

Westminster, 26 March 1621. Parliament revives the ancient procedure of impeachment.

The Netherlands, April 1621. Frederick V, the Elector Palatine of the Rhine, and his wife, Elizabeth, the eldest daughter of King James, who fled into exile with her husband seek refuge in the Netherlands (→ 13/6/23).

London, 16 June 1621. Sir Francis Bacon, the lord high chancellor, who has been held in the Tower of London on suspicion of accepting bribes, is released.

Scotland, 10 September 1621. The laird of Menstrie, Sir William Alexander, is given by James a piece of land in the New World, between New England and Newfoundland; it will be known as Nova Scotia.

Dover, 7 February 1623. Prince Charles and the Marquis of Buckingham, his close friend, set out incognito on their expedition to Spain to bring back Charles's bride, *Infanta* Anna (→ 5/10/23).

Germany, 13 June 1623. The Elector Palatine, Frederick V, the son-in-law of King James, is dethroned while in exile in the Netherlands.

London, 6 October 1623. The Prince of Wales and Buckingham – now created a duke – return from their unsuccessful Spanish expedition and begin to pressure James to renew hostilities with King Philip III of Spain (→ 3/1624).

New World, June 1624. King James takes over Virginia as the first royal colony in the New World.

Britain/France, November 1624. An Anglo-French marriage treaty is arranged between Prince Charles and Princess Henrietta Maria, the youngest daughter of Henry IV of France.→

Hertfordshire, 5 March 1625. James falls ill after a hunt in Theobalds Park (→ 27/3).

Hertfordshire, 27 March 1625. James, suffering from a stroke and kidney failure, dies aged 69; his son, Charles, aged 24, will succeed him.→

Royal decrees slap a ban on duelling

London, February 1614

Duelling has been banned by royal proclamation. From now on, anyone who kills an adversary in a duel is answerable before the courts of law and may eventually face the death penalty. The order follows the killing of Lord Kinloss, the son of one of King James's most trusted advisers, in a squalid duel fought against Sir Edward Sackville, the brother of the Earl of Dorset, knee-deep in water in a meadow near Antwerp.

This is the king's second proclamation against duelling. Last October he issued one against deliberate provocations aimed at forcing a duel. At the same time he told his attorney-general, Sir Francis Bacon, that in prosecuting duellists he was not to distinguish between "a coronet and a hat band". King James is determined to stamp out what he sees as a vicious and wasteful practice, with its false code of honour. The sword of justice, he says, must smite the duellist's rapier.

James mediates in international row

Xanten, Germany, August 1614

King James's intervention in the affairs of the Lower Rhine is gaining dividends – a rare event in English foreign policy. He has brought together the claimants to the disputed territory of Cleves-Jülich and their respective allies, and arranged for the withdrawal of foreign troops from the duchy.

In 1609 John William, the Catholic Duke of Cleves-Jülich, died, and the duchy was disputed between two Protestants, John Sigismund of Brandenburg and Wolfgang Wilhelm of Neuburg. Holy Roman Emperor Rudolf occupied it pending a settlement, and a coalition of French, Dutch, English and German Protestants evicted him. Then Wolfgang Wilhelm became a Catholic and gained Spanish help, and the rivals were at war again.

King James is pleased with his diplomacy, but it is hard to see how he can actually force the warring parties to honour the treaty.

King dissolves the 'addled parliament'

The king's stern authority: now James has dissolved parliament.

London, 7 June 1614

The king has dismissed parliament with the comment: "I am surprised that my ancestors should have permitted such an institution to come into existence." It had been called on the advice of the attorney-general, Sir Francis Bacon, who argued: "Until your Majesty have tuned your instrument you will have no harmony." But its two-month sitting only widened the gap between the House of Stuart and the House of Commons. Dissolved without having passed a single measure, it has been derisively described as the "addled parliament". James's main reasons for calling parliament were financial.

Extravagances, such as selling £10,000 of crown lands to provide a wedding gift for Robert Carr, the Earl of Somerset, have left the treasury empty. MPs had no intention of voting him funds, however, until they had dealt with their grievances: James's pro-Spanish foreign policy, his tolerance of the pro-Catholic sympathies of the Howard family at court, and his attempts to influence the elections. The result was impasse and dissolution.

King's friends arrested on murder charge

Sir Thomas Overbury at his desk.

London, 12 October 1615

The king's former favourite, the Earl of Somerset, and his wife, Lady Frances Howard, have been arrested for murder. The arrest follows the revelation of Sir Gervase Helwys, the lieutenant of the Tower, that two years ago Sir Thomas Overbury, a former friend of Somerset, was poisoned.

Overbury had been opposed to Lady Frances's scandalous divorce from the Earl of Essex and to Somerset's wish to marry her, fearing the dominance of the pro-Catholic Howards at court. The question on everyone's lips is: was the king a party to the murder? (→7/1616).

Villiers given royal job and knighthood

London, April 1615

The king's new favourite, George Villiers, has been made a gentleman of the bedchamber and given a knighthood. The king is enslaved by him, constantly petting him and calling him "my Steenie", and looks with disdain at his former idol, Robert Carr, the Earl of Somerset, who is now tainted by scandalous rumours involving divorce and even murder.

The king and his new friend are an unlikely couple. The 22-year-old Villiers is exquisitely propor-

Villiers: "Steenie" to the king.

tioned, with chestnut hair and blue eyes. The 47-year-old king is corpulent and weak-kneed, feasting on his lover with bulbous eyes while his fingers, according to one courtier, are constantly "fiddling about his codpiece".

George's mother, the ambitious Mary Beaumont, is responsible for her son's rise to power and influence. The widow of an impoverished squire, she scrimped, seduced and saved to send George to Paris, to perfect his skills in dancing, duelling and lovemaking. It proved a sound investment; from the time that James first set eyes on Villiers at Apethorpe House last August he has grown in the king's favour to become his most intimate counsellor (→1/1616).

Murder scandal tarnishes image of James

London, July 1616

In an affair highly damaging to the king, the Earl of Somerset and his wife, Lady Frances Howard, have been sentenced to death for murder. Lady Frances had pleaded guilty to the murder of Sir Thomas Overbury in the Tower in September 1613 with poison administered by an apothecary's boy, and her charm and sober demeanour almost won her a reprieve. Somerset, a close friend of the king, insisted on his innocence but was found guilty after 12 hours of interrogation.

Overbury, like many at court, had been opposed to Somerset's marriage to Lady Frances – who had recently divorced the Earl of Essex amid great scandal – and to the benefits that the union would bring to the pro-Catholic Howard faction. According to the evidence, the nymphomaniacal Lady Frances instigated the plot, while Somerset, like Adam in the Garden of Eden, was led astray by his wife. Constant

Robert Carr, the Earl of Somerset.

rumours that the king was party to the conspiracy forced James to allow the murder investigation to go on without interference. But so much affection does the king retain for Somerset that it is inconceivable that he will permit the death sentences to be carried out.

Chief justice sacked after royal challenge

London, 16 November 1617

Sir Edward Coke, the chief justice, has been dismissed by the king. Since last June, when Coke refused in front of his fellow judges to be intimidated by the royal prerogative, James has been determined to rid himself of this turbulent lawyer.

Coke is England's most outstanding jurist, and served at different times as solicitor-general, attorney-general and speaker of the House of Commons in the reign of Queen Elizabeth. He has constantly resisted the royal prerogative and defended the independence of the bench. Constitutionalists are outraged at this interference in the courts, and James has lost much of his moral authority.

King returns to Scotland

Berwick, 4 August 1617

King James is back in England after completing a three-month tour of Scotland. It is his first visit to his original inheritance since becoming king of England 14 years ago, and his most extravagant "royal progress" yet.

The visit, which coincided with the opening of the stag-hunting season, produced some first-rate hunts and debaucheries in the Grampian mountains. It did little, however, to win over the alienated Scots, who feel that their king is ignoring their interests and that they are being ruled by the English.

In spite of the fawning on James by the Scottish nobility, and the masques and banquets put on in his honour, there was outspoken hostility to what the Scottish clergy suspect are "popish rites" which were performed in the Chapel Royal at Holyrood palace, and a deep discontent among Presbyterians at James's pro-Catholic policies.

The clergy are not alone in their unprecedented criticism of their monarch. On a secular level, Scots from all social backgrounds fear that *their* king has become Anglicised, and that Scotland has lost its independence from England.

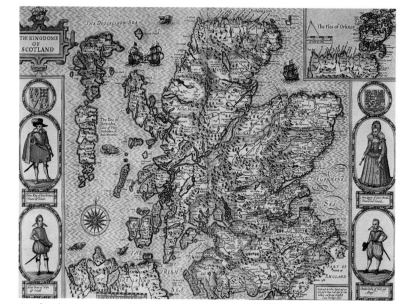

Scotland: a map from John Speed's "Theatre of Great Britain", 1610.

Inigo Jones completes splendid house for queen at Greenwich

Greenwich, 1616

Inigo Jones, the king's surveyor, has presented his plan for the queen's new palace here at Greenwich. The old palace was a favourite of the Tudors, and it was here that Queen Elizabeth signed the death warrant of the king's mother, Mary Queen of Scots. It was settled on Queen Anne in 1605.

The design is classical, much influenced by the Italian architect Andrea Palladio and unlike anything seen in England. Courtiers applaud it, but outside court circles it is suggested that Jones is merely indulging in one of the extravagant and sycophantic court masques for which he is famous.

Classical architecture: a 20th-century view of the Queen's House, Greenwich.

Indian princess is presented at court

London, January 1616

An Indian princess, Pocahontas, has been presented at court and has sat with the king watching a masque by Ben Jonson. King James finds her fascinating; he has spoken of founding a college in Virginia for Indian pupils and urged the bishops to raise funds. Ten years ago she saved the life of the English explorer Captain John Smith and preserved the English colony of Jamestown, in Virginia, from Indian attack. Since then she has embraced Christianity and married an Englishman, John Rolfe, who has brought her to London.

Hard-up king faces financial reforms

London, 1618

Government finances are to be put on a firmer and more economical footing by Sir Lionel Cranfield, the new lord treasurer. Sir Lionel is well qualified. He rose from humble beginnings to become one of the country's wealthiest financiers.

The king is virtually bankrupt, owing almost £1 million. Wasteful royal progresses, expensive gifts to worthless favourites, and the corruption of officials such as the Earl of Salisbury and the Earl of Suffolk – who built their sumptuous mansions, Hatfield House and Audley End, with public funds – have emptied the treasury.

Though Cranfield is somewhat lacking in sophistication and social graces – and much mocked by the court – his aggressive manner and financial skills promise success in what the Earl of Salisbury significantly failed to achieve: a drastic reduction in the king's expenditure.

His appointment follows the dismissal of the Earl of Suffolk from the treasury on charges of corruption [*see report right*]. Suffolk, a member of the powerful Howard family, had to go; apart from his incompetence, the enthusiasm with which his wife accepted gifts was thought to give a bad example to others (→ 5/1624).

Buckingham's rise eclipses Howard family

Thomas Howard: Earl of Suffolk.

London, July 1618

The Earl of Suffolk has been dismissed as lord treasurer. Together with his wife, he has been found by the king's new financial adviser, Sir Lionel Cranfield, to have embezzled tens of thousands of pounds.

Considering his notorious inefficiency, it is assumed that his wife was the mastermind of the fraud.

The dismissal marks the final eclipse of the house of Howard, to which Suffolk belongs, and the total ascendancy of Buckingham's faction at court. On New Year's Day, the king – who calls Buckingham "Steenie" and is constantly stroking his face and hair – promoted him to the rank of marquis and made his avaricious and scheming mother a countess.

The marquis has risen from a lowly post in the royal household to become the richest nobleman in the land and has made many enemies on the way. At a recent dinner celebration he toasted his family, the Villiers, and announced: "I desire to advance [my family] above all others; of myself I have no doubt, for I live to that end" (→ 1/1619).

Sir Francis Bacon becomes lord chancellor

London, 1618

Sir Francis Bacon, the Elizabethan parliamentarian who became the "king's man", has been appointed lord chancellor and raised to the peerage as Lord Verulam. Bacon's qualification is that he always puts loyalty to monarch before loyalty to friends. He prosecuted his friend Essex for treason, his friend Somerset for murder and his friend Raleigh for piracy.

Queen Elizabeth admired his intellectual brilliance – he went up to Trinity college, Cambridge, at the age of 12 – but she distrusted his lack of principles. King James finds his philosophical mind and advocate's integrity a perfect instrument of state (→ 5/1621).

James opens his 'Book of Sports'

King James's "Works" (1616).

London, 1618

James has struck a blow against the puritans by writing and publishing a *Book of Sports* which sets out the recreations that the king considers lawful on Sundays. The puritans claim that the Sabbath is a day of not only no work but also no play. This caused angry complaints in Lancashire, where the magistrates suppressed Sunday amusements. James now intends to have his own favourable ruling read from pulpits throughout the country, licensing "dancing, archery, leaping, vaulting, having of May games, Whitsunales and Morris dances" (after church), but not bull- or bear-baiting, or bowling.

Walter Raleigh executed for his alleged part in plot of 1603

A later engraving of Sir Walter Raleigh in court before his imprisonment.

London, 29 October 1618

Sir Walter Raleigh has been executed at Whitehall. As he stood on the scaffold he inspected the axe. "This is sharp medicine; but it is a sure cure for all diseases," he said.

He was a favourite of Elizabeth, but his legendary exploits in the New World against Spain were his undoing. Stripped of his offices by James, he was sentenced to death in 1603, but this was commuted to life imprisonment in the Tower. There he wrote his *History of the World*, suppressed by James as "too saucy in censuring the acts of kings". In April 1617 James, short of money, released him to search for gold on the Orinoco river in South America. He returned without any, was sent back to prison and, on Spanish insistence, executed.

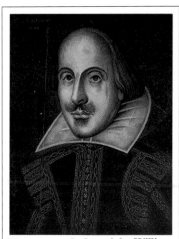

The poet and playwright William Shakespeare, who died in 1616.

Dropsy kills Queen Anne

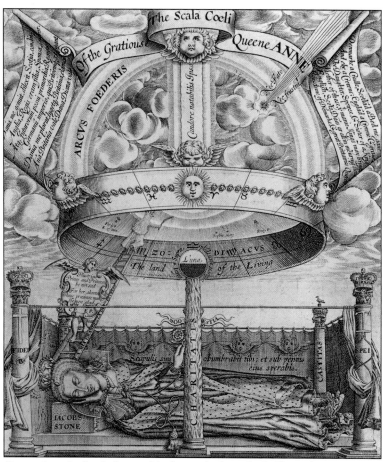

Queen Anne in death: her soul is shown climbing the ladder to heaven.

Greenwich, 2 March 1619
Queen Anne died of dropsy at her home, Denmark House, here today after several years of ill-health. Born in 1574, she was the second daughter of King Frederick II of Denmark and married King James in 1589, when he was king of Scotland, but 14 years before he became the first king of Great Britain.

She was a high-spirited, good-looking but rather silly woman, who loved expensive court masques and had little in common with her grubby but learned husband; they ceased living together 13 years ago. One reason for their estrangement was her conversion to Catholicism and the way in which she became dominated by the priests whom she kept around her late in her life.

They did, however, produce seven children (only two of whom survive her), and when Anne fell into her last illness James visited her twice a week. He was not with her when she died because he is ill himself at Newmarket. He has, moreover, a morbid fear of being in the presence of death.

Puritan pilgrims settle in the New World

Cape Cod, Mass., December 1620
The *Mayflower*, with her cargo of strict puritans from the east coast of England and less strict "Strangers" from the west coast, has arrived in the New World after a two-and-a-half-month journey across the Atlantic. The puritans – sober, industrious people who originally fled to the Netherlands to escape religious repression – decided to seek a new life free of the troubles of Europe. They sent a delegation to London and obtained the backing of the Virginia Company and a licence from King James. He was won over when they told him that they would live by fishing. "Tis an honest trade," he said. "It was the apostles' own calling" (→ 6/1624).

Royal diplomacy is in shreds as Frederick of Bohemia, James's son-in-law, flees

Prague, November 1620
James's son-in-law, Frederick, the newly-crowned king of Bohemia, has been defeated by the forces of Ferdinand II, the Holy Roman Emperor, at the White Mountain outside Prague and is fleeing for his life from the Austrian cavalry. His reign was so short that he is being called "the Winter King".

Frederick's adventure in Bohemia has thrown the whole of Europe into turmoil. Safely ensconced as the Elector Palatine of the Rhine when he married Elizabeth, the daughter of James and Anne of Denmark, he rashly accepted the invitation of the rebellious Protestants of Bohemia to be their king in place of the Catholic Ferdinand. In 1618 they underlined their dislike for the old regime by throwing its leading officials from the windows of the royal palace.

Frederick's acceptance of the crown as the champion of the Protestants could not be tolerated by the Catholic powers. Now he is in danger of losing not only the crown of Bohemia, which he has hardly had time to wear, but also his hereditary rule of the Palatinate itself,

Frederick shown with his family.

which is under attack from the Habsburgs and the Spanish.

This affair is desperately embarrassing for James, who sees himself as the peacemaker of Europe and is trying to arrange a politically beneficial marriage between his son, Charles, and the *Infanta* of Spain. He rages against Frederick's stupidity but cannot bring himself to abandon his daughter, and he faces difficulties with an anti-Spanish House of Commons (→ 4/1621).

Lord chancellor fined and sent to Tower

Westminster, May 1621
Francis Bacon, the lord chancellor, has been found guilty of corruption by the House of Lords. He has been sentenced to a fine of £40,000 and to imprisonment in the Tower during the king's pleasure; he has been barred from state employment, from sitting in parliament and from coming within 12 miles of the court. Bacon, created Lord Verulam by the king, did not deny the charges and in his confession said that he was "heartily and penitently sorry". A brilliant career as a statesman has thus ended in shame.

Bacon is a complex character. Queen Elizabeth distrusted him, and the manner in which he surrounds himself with young male servants gives rise to suspicions of homosexuality. His decision to act for the prosecution at the trial of the Earl of Essex, his former friend, also brought him criticism. There is little doubt of his guilt, but it is

Publicly shamed: Francis Bacon.

likely that King James, who admires him, will remit all or part of the sentence. Bacon will, however, now be able to concentrate on his other interests of philosophy and literature (→ 16/6).

King destroys parliamentary papers

Westminster, 30 December 1621

The king dissolved parliament today while its members were at home on holiday and, demanding to see the House of Commons' journal, ripped out the pages in which the members had recorded their "protestation" asserting their parliamentary privileges.

This dangerous situation arose when James summoned parliament to reassemble on 20 November. His purpose was to raise money to help defend his son-in-law's Palatinate territories against the Spanish, but the Commons insisted on discussing his conduct of foreign affairs.

They could not understand why they should supply money to defend the Palatinate while James was attempting to make an alliance with the invader. Speaker after speaker condemned Spain and Catholicism and, while they granted one meagre subsidy to help the Palatinate through the winter, they also drew up a petition demanding war with Spain, a Protestant bride for Prince Charles and the strict application of the anti-Catholic laws. James, growling "God give me patience",

MPs under threat: King James has clashed with parliament once again.

reacted angrily, telling the Commons that they had no right to meddle with his government nor with the deep mysteries of state, nor "deal with our dearest son's match with the daughter of Spain, nor touch the honour of that king".

After a frigid meeting between the king and 12 of their members, the Commons reacted with equal spirit, drawing up their protestation

declaring that their privileges are their ancient and undoubted birthright and that every member enjoyed freedom of speech and freedom from arrest. This has proved too much for James. Urged on by his favourite, Buckingham, and the cunning Spanish ambassador, Count Gondomar, he has today by this action destroyed his relationship with parliament.

King pushes plans to marry his son to Spanish Infanta

Westminster, March 1622

John Digby, the Earl of Bristol, has returned to his post as ambassador to the court of Spain with the task of completing the negotiations for the marriage of the Prince of Wales to the *Infanta* of Spain, the sister of King Philip IV. No man is more committed to this union than Digby, for it was he who proposed such an alliance in 1608 beween the Infanta and the late Prince Henry.

The negotiations lapsed on the death of Henry in 1612, but were revived with Charles as the prospective groom the following year when Gondomar became Spain's ambassador to London and Digby returned to Madrid. They have dragged on since then in the face of severe political and religious obstacles.

Prince Charles: wedding plans.

There is bitter opposition among the English to their future king marrying a woman who is not only a Catholic but also a Spaniard.

In Madrid the negotiations are seen more cynically, rather as a way of preventing an Anglo-French alliance than of making an Anglo-Spanish one. Digby, who has "laboured so long and suffered so much" to bring about the marriage, does not seem to understand the political game. He believes everything that the Spaniards tell him.

James, although aware of the dangers, is determined that the marriage will go ahead. He sees it as the means of binding the most powerful nation in Europe to Britain's side (→ 7/2/23).

Scots vote to back king's line on religion

Scotland, 4 August 1621

The Five Articles of Perth were passed into law today after a passionate debate in the Scottish parliament. The vote was close, 85 to 59, and when the Marquis of Hamilton rose to touch the bills with the sceptre to signify their passage, there was a flash of lightning, the skies darkened and rain poured down. The presbyterian party has been quick to claim that this is a sign of God's wrath at "popery".

The offending articles provide for the observation of Christmas, Good Friday, New Year and other holidays which the Scots regard as Catholic festivals. Private baptism and Communion are to be recognised, and episcopal blessing and examination of children are to be encouraged. Most offensive of all to the presbyterians is the directive to kneel during Communion which, to them, implies a "papist" worship of the sacraments.

The closeness of the vote, despite heavy pressure and bribery by the

A pious king: James (centre, in box) is shown at a sermon at St Paul's.

crown, is indicative of the widespread popular anger against the articles and has shocked the king's representatives. Having been voted over £1 million Scots, the largest tax ever provided by a Scottish parliament, the king might be wise to allow the articles to gather dust in the statute book.

Gentry ordered to return to the shires

London, 1622

King James has issued a proclamation ordering the nobility and gentry to quit the frivolities of London and return to their duties on their estates. The pursuit of fashion angers him, and he sometimes shouts abuse at the overdressed. This order follows his instruction to clergymen to preach "against the insolency of our women and their wearing broad-brimmed hats, pointed doublets, their hair cut short and trinkets of the moment".

The king blames the women for forcing their husbands and fathers to live in London because "the new fashion is nowhere to be had but in London" and, while he threatens the men with the star chamber, he tells their ladies in verse: "... depart in peace and look not back,/ remember Lot's wife ere you suffer wrack/ of fame and fortune, which you may redeem/ and in the country live in good esteem ..."

Prince Charles backs war with Spain

Secret royal trip ends in disillusion

Portsmouth, 5 October 1623
Prince Charles and the Duke of Buckingham arrived here today safe but disillusioned after their adventure in Spain. King James's "sweet boys" set out in disguise last February to woo the *Infanta*, calling each other John and Thomas Smith and wearing false beards that slipped round their faces. They paid an incognito visit to the French court and then rode from Paris to Madrid in 12 days. At first all went well for Charles. He fell in love with the Infanta at first sight, but she told her brother that she would rather be a nun than marry a heretic. So Philip played the prince along, demanding concessions that dimmed Charles's ardour until he gave up, a decision welcomed by most of England (→ 6/10).

Buckingham, Charles's companion.

King James greets his son Charles after the prince's trip to Spain.

Parliament resolves to open hostilities

Westminster, March 1624
The new parliament, asked by the ageing and sick King James for its "good and sound advice" on the nation's foreign affairs, has replied that the negotiations for the proposed marriage between Prince Charles and the *Infanta* of Spain should be broken off and that Britain should join the Protestant countries of northern Europe in their defence of the Palatinate against the Catholic powers.

The anti-Catholic Commons are eager for war with Spain and, for once, they are in alliance with Charles and Buckingham who, furious at the way they were bamboozled by the Spaniards during their adventure in Madrid, have been converted to a policy of war rather than wedding with Spain.

However, despite the general eagerness for war, the Commons have granted only £300,000 to fight it. Their idea is that an old-fashioned piratical naval war should be waged which would not only pay for itself but make a profit. The king has different ideas. If he has to go to war, he wants to engage in campaigns in Europe which will see the restoration of the Palatinate to his son-in-law.

Moreover, although his two "sweet boys", Charles and Buckingham, persuaded him, against his better judgement, to ask the Commons for their advice, he remains reluctant to take it. His instinct and long experience argue for peace, and so far he has neither severed diplomatic relations with Spain nor officially declared war (→ 11/1624).

East India Company workers massacred by Dutch in New Guinea

London, May 1624
News has just arrived of an appalling massacre of English traders by the Dutch at Amboyna in the East Indies. Relations between the two communities have always been strained, and the English were not permitted to establish their factory inside the Dutch fortifications.

It appears that in February last year the Dutch, fearing an English attack, seized a number of the traders and tortured them until they confessed. They then be-

headed ten of them against all the rules of the Anglo-Dutch pact.

This story is causing great indignation in London, and the king is deeply affected. In ordinary times there is little doubt that the case against the Dutch would be vigorously pursued but, preoccupied by the impending war with Spain, the Commons are in no mood for trouble with one of Spain's enemies. The king has made dire threats to the Dutch ambassador, but there is little that he can do.

The cruel torture at Amboyna.

Treasurer accused of bribery is fired after impeachment

Westminster, May 1624
The lord treasurer, Lionel Cranfield, impeached by the Commons, has been dismissed after being found guilty of "bribery, extortion, oppression, wrong and deceits". The real reasons for his downfall, however, may be found elsewhere – in his opposition on financial grounds to war with Spain and in the enmity of Buckingham, who had looked to him for financial gain but had been disappointed.

Cranfield, a London merchant, was made Earl of Middlesex by the king for his brave but unavailing attempts to make sense of James's feckless financing. "The more I look into the king's finances," he wrote, "the greater cause I have to be troubled".

The king is said to be furious at Cranfield's dismissal and to have told Buckingham: "You are a fool and will shortly repent this folly." James then rounded on Charles and told him that "he would live to have his bellyful of parliaments". It is a sign of his waning power, however, that he could not save Cranfield.

King backs moves against prostitutes

London, 1624
Prostitution is now so rife that James has enlarged and reissued his 1622 ordinance, "Touching upon Disorderly Houses", attacking certain areas in the capital "pestered with divers immodest lascivious and shameless women ... common whores ... in divers howses for base and filthy lucre's sake."

Every part of the City is now infected, according to the king, and the reissuing of the ordinance has been followed by raids on several brothels. The court itself is tainted by scandal, for the abortionist and astrologer "Dr" John Lambe, found guilty of raping a girl of seven, has been freed on the intervention of the Duke of Buckingham. Lamb's services were much needed at court to end unwanted pregnancies. He has, however, been lynched by a mob in Cripplegate.

Treaty agreed for prince's betrothal to French princess

London, November 1624

Prince Charles has been betrothed to the 15-year-old French princess Henrietta Maria, the sister of King Louis XIII. So the heir to the throne of Great Britain, who first met his prospective bride while on his way to Madrid to woo the *Infanta* of Spain, has exchanged one Catholic princess for another.

There is no doubt that the people would have preferred him to marry a Protestant, but the king takes the view that if he cannot have a marriage alliance with Spain he must have one with France. Buckingham is even keener on a French marriage than he was on a Spanish one, and the union is favoured by Marie de' Medici, the princess's mother.

Henrietta Maria later in life.

Nevertheless, despite this powerful support, the talks have not gone smoothly. The king had promised the Commons that no future marriage treaty would include the concessions to English Catholics that he had agreed to with the Spaniards, but the French insisted on a treaty no less favourable to their English co-religionists than that accepted in the Spanish negotiations.

James, mindful of his promise to the Commons, was ready to abandon the enterprise, but Buckingham insisted; the king yielded and in a private letter agreed to the French terms. The treaty as published seems harmless enough, but the secret promises are certain to cause much trouble for Charles if not for his senile father.

'The wisest fool in Christendom' dies

Uneasy legacy of a king of contrasts

Hertfordshire, 27 March 1625

King James – dubbed "the wisest fool in Christendom" by Henry IV of France – died today at Theobalds, his favourite home. Crippled by arthritis, he caught a fever and then suffered a stroke which caused him to lose control of his body. It was not a kingly death, but James, despite having been a king almost all his life, was never regal.

Physically unpleasing, with an over-large tongue which made him slobber over his food, he was slovenly in dress and bawdy in speech. He was also lazy, keener on hunting than on attending to affairs of state, and his favouritism for effeminate males was notorious. Yet he was a man of much learning, a linguist and a prolific writer.

The remarkable thing was that he was able to rule at all. His father was murdered; his mother married the murderer and was later executed. He became James VI of Scots at the age of one and was in time an effective ruler. So there was some truth in his claim on riding south to take the English throne at 36 that he was "an old, experienced king, needing no lessons".

He did not change this view throughout his reign, and his supporters can point to a number of solid achievements to prove his point. He delighted in his image as a peacemaker, which was indeed largely justified; peace at home and abroad was maintained until his last days. Harmonious union with Scotland and a generally accepted national church are further monuments to his shrewdness.

Against these achievements must be listed his judicial murder of Sir Walter Raleigh to appease Spain, his indulgent mismanagement of the country's finances at a time of economic depression, his reliance on inefficient favourites and, especially, his inability to understand and work with the House of Commons. It is the distrust which he has established between the crown and the Commons which will undoubtedly be the greatest burden for his son and successor, Charles.

The first king of England and Scotland soon after his union of the crowns.

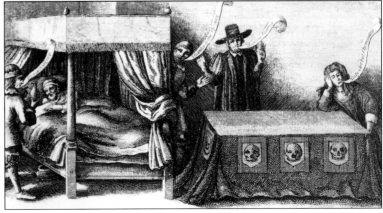

The king's deathbed: an engraving of James's last hours at Theobalds.

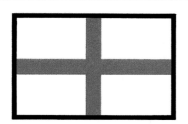

Charles I
1625–1649

London, 27 March 1625. Charles, the Prince of Wales, aged 24, succeeds to the throne on the death of James.→

England/France, 1 May 1625. Charles marries by proxy his 15-year-old bride, Henrietta Maria, the youngest daughter of Henry IV of France and Queen Marie de' Medici (→ 6/1625).

Westminster, 7 May 1625. The funeral of James takes place after a magnificent procession through the city; the occasion is marred by the refusal of the archbishop of St Andrews to take part, following the orders of King Charles to wear English vestments.

Dover, June 1625. Princess Henrietta Maria arrives from France for her official wedding ceremony to Charles

Westminster, 11 July 1625. King Charles's first parliamentary session opens with an attack by John Pym on the Arminians, a clerical group which emphasises the doctrines of the early church and is suspected by Calvinists of reintroducing the tenets of Roman Catholicism (→ 1/8).

Oxford, 1 August 1625. Parliament is moved here from London after an epidemic of bubonic plague is reported to be spreading through the capital (→ 8/1625).

Oxford, August 1625. King Charles brings his first parliamentary session to an abrupt halt after continual attacks on not only Arminianism, which the crown favours, but also the expensive and unsuccessful continental war being waged by George Villiers, the Duke of Buckingham (→ 26/3/26).

Scotland, 12 October 1625. Charles issues a Bill of Revocation which upsets Scottish landowners; it will allow him to revoke all land grants made since 1540 in a bid to increase revenue to the crown and boost church resources (→ 10/1625).

Cadiz, Spain, 16 November 1625. After a disastrous campaign to seize the port of Cadiz the defeated British fleet returns home under its leader, Charles's favourite the Duke of Buckingham (→ 15/6/26).

London, 19 November 1625. Charles celebrates his 25th birthday.

London, 1625. Charles appoints Daniel Mytens as his official court painter (→ 3/3/31).

Scotland, January 1626. A deputation of Scottish noblemen fails to persuade Charles to give up his Bill of Revocation (→ 23/3).

London, 11 February 1626. George Villiers, the Duke of Buckingham and favourite of Charles, gives his support to the Arminian cause in a religious debate at York House.

Scotland, 23 March 1626. King Charles's unpopularity in Scotland grows when he breaks up the system of government employed by his father and purges the privy council (→ 2/1627).

Westminster, June 1626. Parliament complains to King Charles over what it says is his unauthorised collection of tonnage and poundage (→ 15/6/26).

London, September 1626. King Charles announces his intention of collecting a forced loan in order to finance his continuing war with Spain (→ 8/11/27).

Scotland, February 1627. King Charles establishes a tithe commission on property; the revenue will increase clerical salaries and his own income and will allow landowners to buy out their feudal superiors.

Britain/France, 8 Nov 1627. Britain is at war with France; troops led by George Villiers, the Duke of Buckingham attempt to relieve the French Huguenots who have been besieged in the Atlantic port of La Rochelle.→

London, November 1627. King Charles appoints William Laud, the bishop of Bath and Wells, to become a member of the privy council (→ 1627).

Westminster, 7 June 1628. King Charles agrees grudgingly to the "Petition of Right" proposed by parliament, which was summoned in March.→

Portsmouth, 23 August 1628. King Charles is devastated on hearing of the assassination of his great favourite, George Villiers, the Duke of Buckingham.→

La Rochelle, France, Oct 1628. Following a disastrous campaign and defeat for the British, the city falls to the forces of King Louis XIII of France (→ 24/4/29).

London, 1628. King Charles appoints the bishop of Bath and Wells, William Laud, who is widely thought to be an Arminian supporter, as the new bishop of London (→ 4/1630).

London, 17 January 1629. King Charles suppresses the publication of an anti-puritan pamphlet, *Appello Caesarem*, by Richard Montagu, the bishop of Chichester, to avoid strong parliamentary opposition (→ 2/3/29).

Westminster, 10 March 1629. After imprisoning Sir John Eliot and his supporters in the Tower on a charge of treason, King Charles dissolves parliament, resolving to rule alone.→

Britain/France, 24 April 1629. The Treaty of Susa ends the Anglo-French war (→ 5/11/30).

Greenwich, 13 May 1629. The first-born son and heir of King Charles and Queen Henrietta Maria, Charles James, the Duke of Cornwall, dies soon after his premature birth today at Greenwich palace (→ 29/5/30).

Oxford, April 1630. Bishop Laud of London is made chancellor of the university (→ 1631).

Britain/Spain, November 1630. The signing of the Treaty of Madrid brings an end to the Anglo-Spanish war.→

The life and times of King Charles I

Name: Charles Stuart.
Birth: Dunfermline palace, 19 November 1600.
Accession: 27 March 1625.
Coronation: 2 Feb 1626 (England); 18 June 1633 (Scotland).
Predecessor: father.
Hair: chestnut brown.
Eyes: grey-blue.
Height: 5 feet 4 inches.
Marriage: Henrietta Maria, 13 June 1625, Canterbury.
Children: Charles, James and seven others.
Favourite homes: Theobalds, Whitehall, Oatlands.
Likes: his family, the arts.
Greatest problem: attitude to role of parliament.
Greatest success: patronage of the arts.
Beheaded: 30 January 1649.

Opposite: a fine sculpted bust of the young king, Charles.

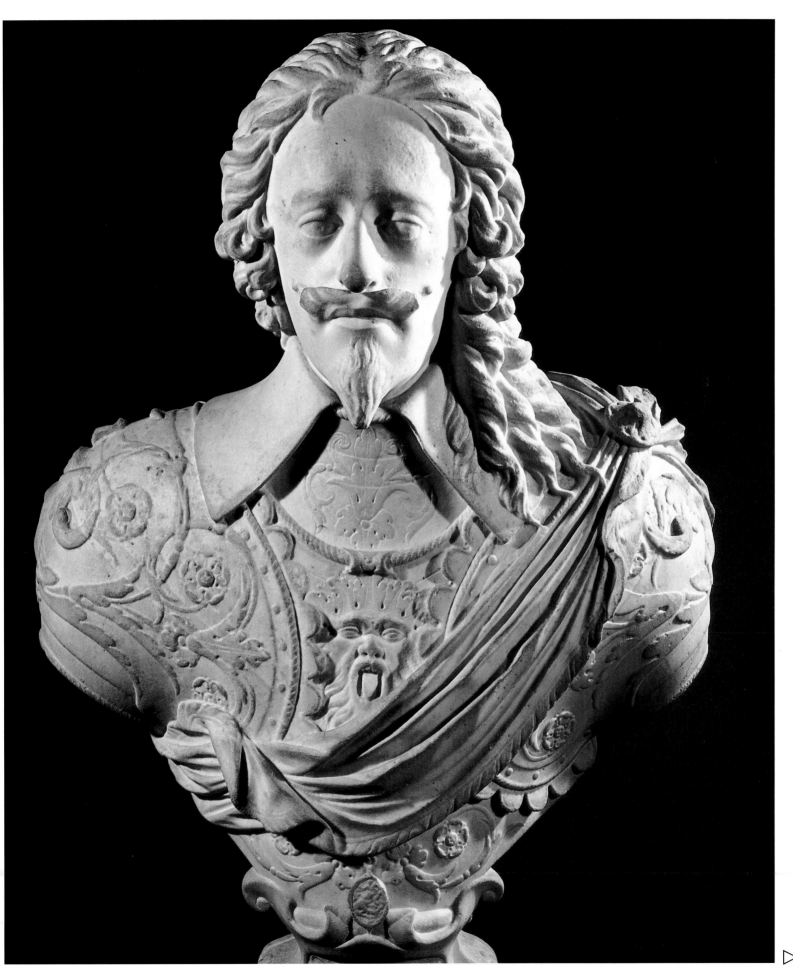

Thoughtful but haughty Charles is the new king

Artistic monarch to end old informality

Westminster, 27 March 1625

King James's death has brought to the throne his 24-year-old second son Charles, a serious-minded, dignified and pious figure. A frail and sickly child, Charles grew up in the shadow of his elder brother, Henry, who died of typhoid in 1612. He is shy and has a slight speech defect; but in recent years he has grown in strength and confidence, and with his elegant beard and moustache he certainly looks the part of a monarch.

The new king spent his early childhood in Scotland and was not well enough to move to London with his parents on James's accession in 1603. He was brought up largely by his guardian Lady Elizabeth Carey, but when he was 12 his father transferred him to the care of four male governors. Apart from a shared love of masques, he had a lukewarm relationship with his mother, who insisted on his taking her place at Henry's funeral – which affected Charles deeply.

There were initial quarrels between Prince Charles and the Duke of Buckingham, his father's favourite, but for the past seven years the two have worked closely together, and Buckingham is sure to be as strong an influence under King Charles as he was under James. The king is also very attached to his sister Elizabeth, who is married to Frederick, the Elector Palatine, and determined to help them to recover the Palatinate from Catholic forces.

King Charles's court is likely to be more splendid and more formal than his father's, reflecting both his love of music and art and his fastidious belief in not only the divine right of kings but also the importance of spectacle and dignity in the maintenance of authority. Though modest in personal dealings, the new king insists on people standing in his presence, and dinner is an elaborate ritual. Since he turned against Spain, Charles has been popular, but there are men in parliament suspicious of both his high-church preferences and his sometimes haughty manner (→ 1/5).

The Duke of Buckingham stands in for the king at his proxy marriage to Henrietta Maria in Paris.

The new king welcomes French princess to England as his bride

Dover, June 1625

King Charles today officially met his prospective bride, Henrietta Maria, the 15-year-old daughter of Henry IV of France, for the first time. They have already been married by proxy in Paris, and Charles appears delighted by his young queen whose warmth and wit promise to add style and vivacity to court life. The couple are to be married at Canterbury this month.

Henrietta Maria is a Catholic, though, so fears of popery have meant that the marriage is not universally welcomed in Britain. Yet the marriage will undoubtedly be more popular than the union with Spain which had been favoured by the new king's father. Philip IV of Spain made such exorbitant demands, however, and Charles was such an incompetent suitor, that

the project was abandoned. Negotiations began soon afterwards for a marriage between Prince Charles and Henrietta Maria, conducted chiefly by Cardinal Richelieu. The French princess was born in the Louvre and is nine years younger than her husband. She has large, flashing eyes and prominent teeth,

but she is not as short as Charles had expected.

Indeed, the king was surprised to see that she came up to his shoulder. He looked down to see if she was wearing high heels. "Sire," she said, "I stand upon my own feet. This high I am and am neither higher nor lower" (→ 2/2/26).

Queen stays away as the king is crowned

Westminster, 2 February 1626

King Charles, dressed in white to symbolise his "marriage" to the people, was today crowned in a ceremony marred by the refusal of his Catholic queen to attend. Her place in the abbey stayed empty, despite pleas that she should overcome her objections to the coronation being performed by a Protes-

tant bishop. Furious but undaunted, the king went ahead, giving a prominent role to his favourite, the Duke of Buckingham who, as lord high constable, presented the regalia to the monarch. But some saw the king's stumble as he arrived and the initially ragged shouts of "God Save King Charles" as bad omens for the new reign (→ 1627).

Scots infuriated by royal move to take back land grants

Scotland, October 1625

Landowners here are in a state of alarm over an Act of Revocation by which King Charles plans to take back all grants of land made by the crown since 1540. The edict also rescinds all dispositions of church property, much of which has passed into the hands of Scottish lords. Since England and Scotland were united under James there has been scarcely a whiff of trouble, but this move has fuelled fierce resentment.

The revocation has been rushed through as, under Scottish law, any changes to grants of royal property had to be enacted before the king's 25th birthday next month. Yet this was meant to cover only land grants made during a king's own minority. In July Charles offered to compensate holders of church property if

The royal arms of Scotland.

they surrendered their lands, but this did not end the outcry over the apparent threat to property. Even members of the Scottish privy council – recently purged to make it more compliant – are protesting.

Although he was born here, the king has taken little interest since and does not seem to understand his Scottish subjects. He takes the view that the reformed church should be entitled to all the old ecclesiastical revenues. Yet even Scottish churchmen who stand to gain from the revocation are amazed at the king's determination to sweep tradition aside and undermine old loyalties (→ 2/1627).

King asserts power over parliament

Tension rises over lost royal jewels

Westminster, 26 March 1626

The second parliament of King Charles's reign is sinking into accusations and recriminations. A collection of royal jewellery, said to date back to Henry VIII's dissolution of the monasteries, has disappeared, and Sir John Eliot, the leader of the Commons, claims that it has been pawned abroad. The house is also refusing to grant the king any more money until the Duke of Buckingham is removed, implying that he is corrupt.

Relations between the king and the commons have been tense since his first parliament last year was dissolved, having only granted the king tonnage and poundage rights for one year. King Charles has since disqualified the two most prominent members of the House of Commons, Sir Edward Coke and Thomas Wentworth, by appointing them as sheriffs. But Sir John Eliot is even more antagonistic, while the king is anything but emollient.

Today Charles delivered a veiled warning in an address to both houses. He said: "I think it is more honour for a king to be invaded and almost destroyed by a foreign enemy, than to be despised by his own subjects. Remember that parliaments are altogether in my own power for calling, sitting and dissolution; therefore as I find the fruits of them good or evil, they are to continue or not to be" (→ 6/1626).

The royal jewels, once worn by Queen Elizabeth, are missing.

Under fire: George Villiers, the Duke of Buckingham, with his family.

Parliament dissolved to save Buckingham

Westminster, 15 June 1626

King Charles has dissolved parliament a second time. The object is to save the Duke of Buckingham from impeachment and death at the hands of the House of Commons. Sir John Eliot and Sir Dudley Digges were imprisoned in the Tower last month for comparing Buckingham to Sejanus, an adviser to Rome's tyrannical Tiberius. Both have since been released, but the Commons remain determined to unseat Buckingham.

Nor are relations any better between the crown and the Lords. The upper house was angered by the king's attempt to prevent the pro-Spanish Earl of Arundel from attending debates, since when an even more emotive row has arisen with John Digby, the Earl of Bristol, who was King James's highly-respected ambassador to Spain.

Prince Charles and Buckingham had always tried to blame Bristol for the failure of their attempt to create a Spanish alliance by marriage to the *Infanta*. King Charles has now accused the former ambassador of trying to convert him to popery in Madrid. Bristol has demanded a trial and is claiming that Buckingham is too frightened to let him sit. Each accuses the other of treason.

Favourite blamed for Spanish disaster

Westminster, 15 June 1626

Although parliament's quarrels with the Duke of Buckingham go back well into King James's reign, it is the humiliating failure of his recent foreign initiatives which has caused the greatest offence. It was bad enough when English conscripts under the German Mansfeld failed to get further than Flushing in an ill-judged attempt to recover the Palatinate; since then, an English expedition has resulted in an even worse fiasco at Cadiz. Memories of Elizabethan glory and plunder may have persuaded Buckingham to plan an expedition to capture Cadiz, but he failed to secure the funds that he needed, and it was an indisciplined, poorly-led and ill-equipped fleet which was repulsed with ease by the Spanish.

As news comes home of disease, drunkenness and desertion among the English crews, Buckingham's reputation as a military man looks threadbare to say the least. Only King Charles seems determined to resist demands for his favourite to be dismissed (→ 9/1626).

▷

Buckingham attracts more fire for failed campaign to help Huguenots in France

Ships of Buckingham's fleet: he failed in his assault on La Rochelle.

France, 8 November 1627

Two expeditions to relieve the besieged French Huguenots in the fortress of La Rochelle, on the coast south of Brittany, have ended in failure. Although the Duke of Buckingham took personal command and is reported to have led his troops with courage, the 8,000 men with whom he made the first assault were not equal to the task. A further attack under the Earl of Denbigh did no better.

King Charles has demanded that France recognise him as the official protector of the Huguenots. He has rejected the chance to resolve an Anglo-French shipping dispute along lines suggested by Cardinal Richelieu. He has effectively willed war with France, at the same time as England is at war with Spain and with the German Catholics. To fund this expensive foreign policy he has had to introduce the unpopular "forced loan" while parliament remains dissolved.

Disputes over money meant that the fleet which should have supported Buckingham's raid never arrived. The French army from the mainland attacked as his force tried to re-embark, and the English suffered heavy losses (→ 23/8/28).

Fears grow of secret Catholicism at court

Westminster, 1627

The gulf between King Charles and his Protestant subjects has been widened by rumours that the king is tacitly encouraging Catholic practices within his court. Memories of the persecutions of Queen Mary's reign have survived generations, and fears of a renewed "popish" influence were increased by the king's marriage to the Catholic Henrietta Maria. Now concern centres on the influence of his favourite bishop, William Laud.

In 1625 parliament took exception to the writings of Richard Montague, which appeared to belittle the European reformed churches and be unduly sympathetic to Rome. King Charles responded by making Montague a royal chaplain. Now his chief adviser on church matters is Laud, the bishop of Bath and Wells, who believes that the Church of England is the only true Catholic Church, preserved from Roman blasphemies by its mediaeval isolation.

The most contentious feature of Laud's approach is that he seems to reject Calvinist theories of predestination and embrace the Arminian doctrine of free will. Whether it is a difference of emphasis or something more fundamental, it means major differences in the conduct of services. Laud takes the emphasis away from the sermon and puts it on Communion at a high altar; vestments and ceremonial are restored. The Laudian emphasis is on faith rather than understanding, and to sensitive Protestants it smacks of popery (→ 1628).

Religious paranoia: Protestants destroying symbols of the Catholic faith.

Charles and Henrietta: stormy partners

London, 1627

All is not well with the king's marriage. Religious differences have caused many of the problems, and, so far at least, there have been few signs of the spirit of compromise which it was hoped would follow the marriage. King Charles was greatly angered by his French queen's refusal to be crowned according to Protestant rites or even to attend his own coronation [*see report page 220*]. But the queen's intransigence has been matched by his own refusal to fulfil promises of greater freedom for his Catholic subjects.

Tension at court has been exacerbated, however, by other differences. Henrietta Maria is still only 17, and the couple seem to have little in common. She clearly resents her husband's closeness to the Duke of Buckingham. The deteriorating marriage could yet affect Anglo-French relations. Last year, irritated by what he saw as the arrogance of his wife's courtiers, Charles sent her entourage back to France (→ 13/5/29).

The royal couple: a later portrait by the court painter Anthony van Dyck.

King and Commons clash over civil rights

Westminster, 7 June 1628

Londoners are rejoicing tonight at the news that King Charles has approved a "petition of right" which some are hailing as a landmark in civil liberties. The petition enshrines crucial rights for the crown's subjects over the four contentious issues of billeting, martial law, arbitrary taxation and arbitrary imprisonment. For the best part of a week the king has appeared unwilling to sign, but now his decision might mark a turning-point in the troubled relationship between monarch and parliament.

Billeting has been the prime cause of distress among the populace as ill-disciplined young soldiers abuse their hosts, frequently forming armed bands to rape, pillage and murder anyone in their way. Martial law, imposed to deal with these unruly elements, did no favours to countryfolk, whose grievances got short shrift from the military authorities. Under the new act, "no man is forced to take soldiers, but inns and they to be paid for them". Military courts have no power over civilians.

The law now says that "no man hereafter be compelled to make or yield any gift, loan, benevolence, tax or such like charge, without common consent by act of parliament". As for those imprisoned for refusing to pay the "forced loan", it is promised that "no free man be imprisoned or detained without any cause showed, or without being charged with anything to which they might make answer according to the law" (→ 17/1/29).

The House of Commons: Charles has approved the MPs' petition of right.

Charles reverses pro-Catholic Irish policy

Ireland, 1629

Considerable anger and fear from Protestant settlers here has forced King Charles to reverse his previous policy of giving "graces", or concessions, to Roman Catholics and to issue a new proclamation against Catholic religious houses. The king had conceded a number of graces – such as the suspension of fines on landowners for non-attendance at Protestant services – to conciliate Irish opinion and ensure the flow of revenues for war against France and Spain. Charles had even promised Irish landowners that they would be freed of the threat of further English settlers. His policy of restraining the Dublin government from enforcing penal statutes against Catholics may have won him Catholic friends but lays him open to criticisms from the Protestants (→ 1/1632).

Hated duke is murdered

Murdered at the Greyhound inn: a 19th-century view of Buckingham's death.

Portsmouth, 23 August 1628

The Duke of Buckingham was stabbed to death at the Greyhound inn here today by a lone assassin, John Felton, while on his way to make a further attempt to recover La Rochelle. Felton, who is said to be an embittered survivor of Buckingham's last abortive campaign, was being toasted in southern towns last night for having rid the country of its most hated courtier.

On the face of it, the removal of Buckingham might make it easier for King Charles and parliament to resolve their differences. But the king is a proud and stubborn man, and he has already made clear his contempt for the Commons' remonstrance of 11 June in which they pleaded again for the duke's dismissal. The king is certain to be deeply wounded by the open rejoicing at his friend's death.

George Villiers, the Duke of Buckingham, was a handsome and talented man flawed by vanity and lack of judgement. He was responsible for many policy errors in the reign so far.

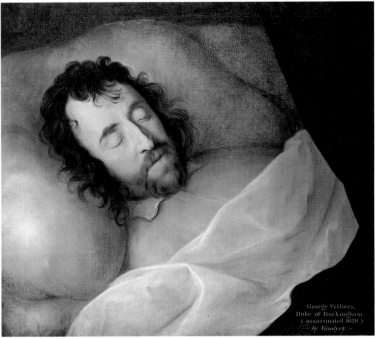

The king's friend lost: the death of Buckingham, by van Dyck (d.1641).

Defiant parliament clashes with king

Radical MPs hold speaker by force

Westminster, 2 March 1629

Parliament today challenged royal authority more dramatically than ever before. Sir John Finch, the speaker of the House of Commons, was forcibly held down in his seat, and the chamber was locked to exclude the king's messenger, Black Rod, while radical MPs voted through measures underlining their own powers and challenging the prerogatives of the king.

As he did on 28 February, the king had ordered the speaker to leave his chair if anyone attempted to speak, thereby adjourning the session before any kind of debate might begin. But before he could do so Denzil Holles and Benjamin Valentine seized his arms and thrust him back down. He broke away, only to be seized again. "God's wounds," said Holles, "you shall sit till we please to rise!" Another MP locked the doors, pocketing the key while Black Rod hammered outside, having been sent by the king to dissolve the house.

Amidst great excitement, Sir John Eliot then rose to put forward three motions dealing with the central arguments between king and Commons: two condemned any attempt to raise taxes without parliamentary approval, while a third attacked efforts to modify Protestant orthodoxy by favouring the Arminians (→ 10/3).

A violent struggle: the speaker is held down in the Commons (a later view).

Denzil Holles, who helped to hold the speaker down in his chair.

Sir John Eliot, who proposed the resolutions which enraged Charles.

Charles dissolves parliament and blames 'vipers' in Commons

Westminster, 10 March 1629

In an extraordinary display of royal power, the king today went to the House of Lords and dissolved parliament, declaring that henceforth he would rule alone. The move follows the defiance of MPs last week when the speaker, Sir John Finch was forcibly held in his seat to stop him adjourning the session.

The king said: "I never came upon so unpleasant an occasion. The reason is to declare to you, and all the world, that it was merely the undutiful and seditious carriage in the lower house that has caused the dissolution ... I know that there are many there as dutiful subjects as any in the world, it being but some vipers amongst them that did cast this mist of undutifulness over most of their eyes."

Charles went on to warn these "vipers" that they must look for their punishment, and he told the Lords that they could "justly expect from me that favour and protection that a good king owes to his loving and faithful nobility". The king seems untroubled by talk of a constitutional crisis, although how he will raise money is unclear. The conflict between king and Commons came to a head last week, but it has far deeper roots.

In recent years England's disastrous involvement in the European war, the king's affection for the Arminian clergy, and the levy of a forced loan (and the jailing of people who refused to pay) have all infuriated the Commons. The king has been enraged by parliament's opposition to war taxes, its attempted impeachment of the Duke of Buckingham and, above all, the Petition of Right guaranteeing parliamentary privilege (→ 27/11/32).

Informal household of King James laid to rest by his son

London, 1630

King Charles has begun to make significant changes to the ways in which the royal household is organised. The moves may perturb some accustomed to the free-and-easy style of his father's court, but they will delight those who feel that a king should be seen to be as regal in private life as he is on the public stage. And Queen Henrietta Maria, now much closer to Charles, is playing an increasingly influential role.

Gone are the unbuttoned days of King James, when informality and extravagance ruled, and his favourites vied with each other in drunken excess and disorder. King Charles has set a new tone, demanding of others the same standard of dignity, respect and regularity upon which he prides himself. The father may have opted for intimacy in his relationships, but for the son the keynote is distance.

Charles, like his father, sees himself as divinely appointed, but unlike James he is determined to match his beliefs with the way in which he conducts his own life. Every aspect reflects the new philosophy, and there is no doubt that the king is making a deliberate rebuttal of the old ways that as Prince of Wales he was unable to escape.

Helping to reorganise the royal household: Henrietta Maria.

Happier marriage gives birth to heir

Whitehall, 29 May 1630

Barely a year since his namesake lived but a single day, a new Prince Charles has been born to the king and queen: England once more has an heir to the throne. The country rejoices, but none more so than the royal parents themselves, for whom the birth brings not just a child but a symbol of the way in which their own relationship has gained a far happier aspect.

Charles and Henrietta Maria, the daughter of Henry IV of France, were married in June 1625. It was not at first a happy alliance. She was a lively young girl of 15; at 24 Charles was a solemn prig whose affections were focused on his friend the Duke of Buckingham. So estranged were the couple – particularly over her Catholicism – that she did not even attend his coronation, and they appeared loveless victims of a political marriage.

Yet in 1628, when Buckingham was murdered, everything changed. The king was distraught at losing his intimate friend; he turned instinctively to his wife and found himself well rewarded for this be-

A royal heir: Queen Henrietta Maria has given birth to Prince Charles.

lated appreciation of her importance in his life. No one could have been more understanding, considerate and loving. If Henrietta had been a homesick child when she arrived in England, she had matured, showing self-confidence and

sophistication. The king has responded in kind, although, if anything, she is the stronger figure.

A year ago the royal couple mourned their first son. Now, with a thriving baby, they can forget that sorrow and rejoice (→4/11/31).

Local government reformed by introduction of 'Book of Orders'

Westminster, November 1630

In an attempt to set up much-needed reforms in local government the privy council today issued a "Book of Orders", a detailed list of instructions issued to justices of the peace and other municipal authorities, setting out the way in which their duties, especially as regards poor relief, are to be carried out. The privy councillors themselves will become commissioners, with responsibility for overseeing the efficiency of the local offcials.

Books of Orders have been issued before – under Elizabeth – but none has laid out so precisely just how each level of local officialdom will work. The intention is to counter the increasing discontent that has been emerging in the countryside among those who have suffered the effects of the last two years' bad harvests.

To do this the officials are duty-bound to carry out not just vital poor relief but also "other public services for God, the king and the

A court of wards and liveries: local government is to be reformed.

commonwealth". How efficient the book will prove to be remains to be seen, but for the first time there exists a proper framework – with each level reporting its findings and

requirements to the one above – in which to make some real efforts to improve the situation. It may only be crisis management, but few of the hungry will criticise that.

Treaty of Madrid brings peace to England and Spain

Madrid, 5 November 1630

Peace has been established between England and Spain and is guaranteed with today's signing of the Treaty of Madrid. However, it is very much an agreement of convenience. While England's intervention in the European war can hardly be seen as a success, at least this peace should help the national finances – the drain on which has been at the heart of the clashes between the king and his parliament.

Indeed, once Charles had decided to abandon parliament and start ruling by himself, it was vital that the country be extricated from so disastrous a foreign policy. The king might claim the prerogatives of divine right, but without parliament he could not raise taxes.

Making friends with France was relatively simple, and the 1629 Treaty of Susa, following the fall of La Rochelle, cemented that relationship. Spain, however, offered greater problems. Charles was unwilling to negotiate other than with the States General and was determined to persuade Spain to help in the recovery of the Palatinate. Despite this the treaty has been signed; it is very similar to an early Anglo-Spanish treaty, that of London, signed in 1604 (→ 1634).

Royal official flees across the Atlantic

Suffolk, April 1630

John Winthrop, a Suffolk gentleman who of recent years has held a position in the royal bureaucracy, has been so dismayed by what he sees as the king's promotion of Arminianism that he and a number of religious associates have set sail for the new world. Winthrop says that he believes that evil times are coming for England and that the godly must "fly to the wilderness" to escape. He and other puritans (as some of the fiercely Protestant believers are known) set sail in the *Arbella* for Massachusetts where other English pilgrims have already established colonies on the other side of the Atlantic Ocean.

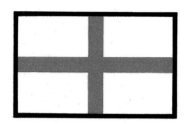

Charles I
1625–1649

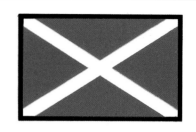

London, 4 November 1631. Queen Henrietta Maria gives birth to a daughter, Mary; she is also to be known as the Princess Royal and is the first royal princess to bear this title (→ 14/10/33).

London, 1631. King Charles and William Laud, the bishop of London, campaign to raise money for the renovation of St Paul's cathedral (→ 8/1633).

London, January 1632. Thomas Wentworth is appointed as the new lord deputy of Ireland by King Charles (→ 7/1633).

Nova Scotia, July 1632. The colony is ceded to France, ending the plans of Sir William Alexander, the Scottish secretary, to build a Scots colony in North America.

London, 1632. The Dutch painter Anthony van Dyck is appointed by King Charles as his official court painter (→ 10/5/34).

Europe, 1632. Elizabeth of Bohemia, the widow of the exiled Frederick V, the Elector Palatine, and sister of Charles, refuses his offer of a home in England, being dissatisfied with his efforts to support her son, Prince Rupert, in his attempts to reclaim his kingdom.

Edinburgh, 18 June 1633. King Charles is crowned king of Scotland in a ceremony which offends many Scots because of the Anglican and English ceremonial rites.→

Edinburgh, 28 June 1633. King Charles has brought his first Scottish parliament to an end after only 11 days; his reputation has been damaged by his authoritarianism (→ 11/10/33).

Ireland, July 1633. Thomas Wentworth, recently appointed lord deputy, arrives to take up his position (→ 22/9/39).

Canterbury, Kent, August 1633. William Laud, the bishop of London, succeeds as the new archbishop of Canterbury after the death, earlier this month, of Archbishop Abbot (→ 8/1636).

Edinburgh, 11 October 1633. Charles designates the city as a new bishopric (→ 12/1634).

London, 14 October 1633. Queen Henrietta Maria gives birth to her third son; James (→ 12/1634).

London, May 1634. William Prynne, the puritan pamphleteer, who was imprisoned last year for his publication *Histriomastix*, which condemned court entertainments, is found guilty of libel by the star chamber; he is fined £5,000 and pilloried and his ears are cut off (→ 30/6/37).

Scotland, December 1634. Fears have arisen in Scotland of clerical dominance in the privy council with the appointment of the archbishop of St Andrews as chancellor; ten of Scotland's 14 bishops now serve as privy councillors (→ 3/1635).

England/Spain, 1634. King Charles, seeking a Spanish alliance, begins negotiations with Spain to try to achieve a partition of the United Provinces (→ 5/1635).

France/Spain, May 1635. War is formally declared.

London, 29 December 1635. Queen Henrietta Maria gives birth to a second daughter, Princess Elizabeth (→ 17/3/37).

London, 1635. In the absence of parliamentary taxation, Charles increases customs duties with orders which determine new rates of payments (→ 6/1635).

England, 1635. Charles grants a charter for a new company to trade in the Indian Ocean; this infringes the monopoly of the English East India Company.

London, 1635. Peter Paul Rubens finishes *The Apotheosis of James I* which adorns the ceiling of the great banqueting House in Whitehall (→ 1639).

Scotland, January 1636. King Charles, despite strong opposition, orders that the heavily Anglicised book of canons must be used in all Scottish churches (→ 7/1636).

Dumfries/Galloway, July 1636. Samuel Rutherford, the minister for Anworth, is banished to Aberdeen for his book condemning Arminianism, a form of Protestantism favoured by the crown and court (→ 23/7/67).

Oxford, August 1636. William Laud, the archbishop of Canterbury and chancellor of the university, hosts a lavish festival in honour of Charles (→ 18/12/40).

Surrey, 17 Mar 1637. Henrietta Maria gives birth at Richmond to her third daughter and sixth child, Princess Anne (→ 17/7).

London, 17 July 1637. Giovanni Bernini, an Italian sculptor and painter, sends a bust of Charles, the likeness taken from a van Dyck painting, to Henrietta Maria as a gift (→ 1640).

Edinburgh, 18 October 1637. After a second major riot in the city yesterday, a supplication is delivered asking for the removal of all ten bishops from the privy council (→ 28/2/38).

Deptford, London, 1637. King Charles and his court attend the launch of the *Sovereign of the Seas*; it is postponed due to low tides.

Scotland, June 1638. The Marquis of Hamilton, acting as the king's commissioner, negotiates with the Covenanters (→ 10/9).

London, 10 Sept 1638. Charles, after consultation with the Marquis of Hamilton, concedes the suspension of the Prayer Book, the book of canons, the Five Articles of Perth and the court of high commission; he agrees to a king's covenant, including parts of the National Covenant (→ 21/11).

Scotland, 21 November 1638. The general assembly of the Church of Scotland meets for the first time for 20 years in Glasgow; it is dominated by Presbyterians and Covenanters (→ 25/12).

Westminster, 1638. Charles proclaims his son, Charles, as Prince of Wales.

London, 27 March 1639. Charles heads north to raise an army in York to fight the Scottish Covenanters (→ 14/5).

Aberdeen, 14 May 1639. A royalist army drive the Covenanters out of the city (→ 18/6).

Aberdeen, 19 June 1639. The Marquis of Montrose recaptures the city (→ 12/8).

Whitehall Palace, 29 June 1639. Queen Henrietta Maria gives birth to her seventh child, a fourth daughter, Catherine, who dies soon after (→ 8/7/40).

Edinburgh, 12 August 1639. The decisions made at the Glasgow assembly are ratified and bishops are condemned as contrary to the law of God; the assembly orders that subscribing to the National Covenant be mandatory (→ 22/9).

Westminster, December 1639. King Charles, on the advice of Thomas Wentworth, summons parliament for the first time since 1629 (→ 13/4/40).

Diplomatic Spanish artist is knighted

London, 3 March 1631
The court of King Charles is becoming renowned for the king's patronage of the arts. Great works of the past are being added to the royal collection, while leading contemporary artists such as van Dyck and Rubens have been given commissions by the king. Today Charles signified his enthusiasm for the work of Peter Paul Rubens, a Spanish diplomat as well as an artist, by giving him a knighthood.

The art is more likely to win approval than the diplomacy since

Rubens: self-portrait with friend.

most Englishmen, especially those in parliament, retain a deep suspicion of anything which might smack of favouritism towards Catholic Spain. Concerning the art, though, there is no dissension. Among the works which Rubens has undertaken for the English court is the ceiling of the Banqueting House in Whitehall which has been designed by Inigo Jones.

Charles takes a close interest in both encouraging new artists and acquiring masterpieces of the past. He has greatly extended the royal collection by adding works by Flemish, Spanish and Italian painters. He aims to give his court as fine a collection of Renaissance paintings as any royal house in Europe. Works by Titian and Mantegna are among those which have been acquired, plus some notable cartoons by Raphael (→ 1632).

Sir John Eliot dies a martyr in Tower

London, 27 November 1632
Sir John Eliot, one of parliament's champions in its battle against the king's favourite, the Duke of Buckingham, died today in the Tower. He had been imprisoned twice during the rows over Buckingham before being sentenced a third time in 1629 when he infuriated Charles by his leading role in the disruption at the end of the 1629 parliament.

This year Charles has exacted his revenge, spurning Sir John's plea to be allowed a move to the country for health reasons. A fiery orator, Sir John refused to buy his freedom by acknowledging any guilt for his role in the 1629 confrontation [*see report on page 224*]. His refusal to yield, despite declining health, has led to his now being hailed as a martyr for parliamentary rights.

Yet Sir John regarded himself as a monarchist. He wrote a book while held in the Tower, *The Monarchy of Man*, which balances an idealised view of the Commons with a staunch belief in monarchy as the best form of government. But he argued that a king had to rule for the benefit of all his citizens, not just for his private gain, and he criticised Charles for failing to understand the grievances of his people.

Charles orders gentry to leave London

Judges' robes: early 17th century.

London, 20 June 1632
The king has ordered members of the gentry to return to their estates in the country. To Charles this reflects a somewhat nostalgic vision of the harmonious social order which he wishes to foster – a society where landowners fulfil their magisterial duties and attend to the tenants and the poor of their estates.

However, many landowners are suspicious, resenting what they see as further "interference" of central government in their affairs, and today's order will increase their hostility to the privy council's attempts to rule without parliament. It was in 1629 that Charles dismissed parliament. Several parliamentary leaders were imprisoned; others, such as Wentworth, were recruited into royal service. But the key to rule without parliament was soon realised to be the ability to raise revenue. The king has therefore been endeavouring to obtain money by resurrecting moribund royal rights.

Last year, for instance, judges upheld the king's right to fine those of his subjects with lands worth more than £40 a year who failed to seek a knighthood at his coronation. This law had not been enforced for a century, and its unpopularity has made some landowners see the order that they must return to their estates and enforce these laws as yet another fiscal ploy.

Yet Charles does not appear to see the order in this way. His vision of the social order elevates hierarchy and deference, whether between parliament and monarch or landowner and tenant. Landowners who act as JPs were given specific duties under the "Book of Orders" issued two years ago, but the king also believes that the wealthy have paternalistic obligations such as hospitality to the people in their areas of the country.

Doctor who discovered blood circulation is new royal physician

The king's physician: Charles with William Harvey, by R Hannah (d.1909).

London, 1632
King Charles has chosen William Harvey, regarded by many as the leading doctor of his generation, to be his personal physician. Harvey has been associated with the court since 1618 when he was first appointed to a similar position by Charles's father, James. Four years ago he achieved Europe-wide renown with the publication of his book *De Motu Cordis*, in which he propounds the theory that blood circulates around the body.

Harvey, who was born in 1578, studied at Cambridge and at Padua in Italy before returning to practise medicine at St Bartholomew's hospital in London. His theory of blood circulation was based on the dissection and vivisection of animals. His royal appointment shows the king's desire to be in the vanguard of scientific discovery.

Scots crown their native son as new king

King Charles: finding Scotland.

Edinburgh, 18 June 1633
King Charles was crowned king of Scots in the palace of Holyrood here today, but it was not a ceremony that brought satisfaction to his Scottish subjects.

To begin with they feel slighted that he has waited eight years since ascending the throne to visit the land of his birth, which he left as a sickly and backward child of three who could neither walk nor speak. Secondly, the coronation service was performed with much Angli-

can ceremony and ostentatious ritual. To Presbyterian ears it might as well have been a Roman Catholic rite. On top of that the over-taxed citizens of Edinburgh are by no means pleased with the privilege of paying for the coronation and also for a new parliament building that the king has ordered to be built.

Scotland is already indignant at the king's fiscal policy which has seen taxation rise and the number of taxes increase. Much of this was used to pay for foreign military expeditions about which the Scots have never been consulted. Most of all, the nobles resent Charles's Bill of Revocation of 1625 which took back land granted since 1540. Although Charles did not in the end confiscate these lands – taken mainly from the church at the Reformation – he made ownership conditional on paying an annual rent (such as tithes) to the church.

The Presbyterians are also increasingly critical because of the king's clear intention of imposing an Anglican form of worship uniformly in Scotland. Even Episcopalians are unhappy over the king's determination to replace the Calvinist Prayer Book with one modelled on the more Arminian English version. He also insists on the king's prerogative as head of the church acting through the bishops, in Scotland as in England (→ 28/6).

Royal descendant falls from favour

Edinburgh, 7 May 1633
The Earl of Menteith has been demoted for having said – or let it be said – that he has a better title to the throne of Scotland than King Charles. He is a descendant of King Robert II's son by his second marriage, Prince David. The king made him lord president of the privy council until he claimed the earldom of Strathearn, a title of Prince David's. His offices were taken from him in March, and he is now being tried by the College of Justice as to whether he has claimed that he should be king. Charles, who is due to be crowned in Scotland next month, gave him leave today to retire to his estates until he comes to Scotland to clear it up (→ 18/6).

Charles revives old laws to tax forests

Whitehall, October 1635
King Charles's search for ways of raising revenue without parliament has led him to revive old laws and fines which had long been forgotten to try to cover an annual deficit of £20,000. Ancient forest laws are now being revived, for instance, along with the forest courts. Any landowner within their jurisdiction is held to have encroached on royal forest land and is fined. It is being held that forest law applies to large areas which are no longer forest – most of Essex, for example. These moves will further anger landowners, many of whom were hit by fines on people owning land of a certain value if they had failed to apply for a knighthood.

Puritans attack king's 'Book of Sports' as tempers flare over laws for the Sabbath

Sabbath relaxations such as dancing are forbidden among Puritans.

Westminster, October 1633
The old disputes about how Sunday should be observed – with or without games and recreations – have become bitter again because King Charles has reissued his father's edict known as the *Declaration* or *Book of Sports*. He has gone further than James by insisting that it is to be read in every parish church – a course from which James was wisely dissuaded because of the offence that it would cause to puritans.

The puritans, who regard sport as a profanation of the Sabbath, have attempted to suppress Sunday games in Somerset. The Episcopalians, who welcome Sunday sports, argue that if people are deprived of them they will meet in alehouses and talk dissent. Some puritans

have taken things into their own hands, running into the streets or into private houses to prevent games or music from being played, even breaking the instruments and belabouring the musicians. They also pull down maypoles on village greens. Many say that no meat may be cooked on Sunday, nor wine be sold, nor dishes washed.

King James argued that the puritan Sabbath hindered the conversion of Catholics, who would conclude that "no honest mirth or recreation is lawful or tolerable in our religion". He also thought that Sunday exercise for the common people "may make their bodies more able for war, when we have occasion to use them". Dancing and leaping served higher purposes (→ 12/1634).

Puritans gather to burn the offending "Book of Sports" later in the 1630s.

Papal legate visits the queen, fuelling fears of 'popery'

Whitehall, December 1634

The arrival of a papal legate, Gregorio Panzani, to see Queen Henrietta Maria has fuelled fears amongst Protestants that the king's devotion to the queen will influence him towards popery. The queen already shows open favour to Catholics, even Jesuits, while priests celebrate Mass daily in the palace.

Even Archbishop Laud has warned the king of the danger of there being undue influence from "the queen's party", and this has been further exacerbated by her eager reception of the pope's agent. She now intends to appoint her own agent to reside at the papal court in the Vatican, and it is feared that there will be further conversions to Rome among her English courtiers.

As part of the marriage treaty with his French-born queen the king undertook to relieve the penalties imposed on English Catholics. Despite his adoration of her, he has not yet done so (→ 30/6/37).

Scottish lord found guilty of treason

Edinburgh, March 1635

King Charles's intolerance of any sign of opposition to his policies, even couched in humble terms, was confirmed here by the sentencing to death of John Elphinstone, Lord Balmerino. The charge was the extraordinary one of "treasonable leasing-making" or the spreading of rumour.

The opposition of some Scottish nobles to the king's religious and fiscal policies led to some of them drawing up a petition to the king. This complained of the innovations in the church, the use of bishops to manipulate the Scottish Parliament and the high taxes being levied in Scotland. A copy of the paper, which was first drawn up in 1633, was found in the hands of Lord Balmerino.

The king has further provoked aggrieved Scottish nobles by appointing Archbishop Spottiswoode as lord chancellor in Scotland, instead of a layman (→ 1/1636).

Masques offer a right royal show

Costume designs by Inigo Jones for the masque "The Fortunate Isles".

Inigo Jones: masque designer.

"Oceania": another Jones design.

William Prynne, the puritan author punished for attacking masques.

London, 10 May 1634

Throughout his reign the king has loved masques, elaborately-staged entertainments in which the courtiers themselves are the stars. Here, amid the splendour of sets and costumes designed by Inigo Jones, Charles can admire the kind of ordered society which is so elusive in the real world outside. In masques, at least, the king and his court are always revered and always triumphant. Not everyone shares his tastes, however, and today a puritan pamphleteer, William Prynne, lost his second ear after criticising court entertainments.

Prynne's other ear was cut off three days ago after he was condemned by the court of star chamber for libel. He was also imprisoned for life, expelled from Lincoln's Inn, stripped of his Oxford degree and fined £5,000. All this because of a book, *Histriomastix: A Scourge of Stage Players*, which condemns the stage and all its works as the work of the devil, inciting drunkenness and lust. He calls women actors "whores", and this is thought to refer to the queen, who happens to be appearing in a masque at court, called *The Shepherd's Pastoral*.

As many as 16 masques are performed in a single season. The queen and the courtiers dance in them, representing gods, nymphs and mermaids, while stage machinery creates perspectives of hills, ocean or clouds behind a proscenium arch invented by the ingenious Mr Jones. He and the poet Ben Jonson collaborated on more than 30 masques from King James's time until 1631.

After that other poets took over, such as James Shirley whose *Triumph of Peace* was lavishly staged before the king by members of the Inns of Court in February to show their disagreement with their fellow lawyer Prynne. Masques are written primarily to flatter their patrons, and this year Thomas Carew's *Coelum Britannicum* is an apotheosis of Charles as a god-like source of earthly harmony.

Inland counties face a 'ship money' tax

Westminster, June 1635

A furore is brewing over King Charles's latest method of raising money in the absence of parliament, which he has not called for six years. He has decided to impose the tax called "ship money", levied to pay for warships, on inland counties as well as maritime ones.

Ship money itself is nothing new. It is generally accepted that the English ports and coastal towns have an obligation to provide vessels for the fleet, especially in times of national emergency when ship money is traditionally levied. Last year, following this tradition, Charles issued a writ to oblige the ports to pay the tax. London, for example, was asked to supply warships for delivery to Portsmouth on the grounds that pirates were threatening merchant shipping.

Most ports accepted the measure (only London petitioned against it), but the king is going to find his attempt to extend the tax inland less than plain sailing.

Unlike Charles's other money-spinning schemes, such as his revival of defunct but unrepealed legislation such as the forest laws, the extension of ship money is new and has far deeper implications. He is taxing the whole country partly for a "national emergency" – piracy – that has always been a threat and is unlikely to go away, suggesting that ship money, which will now pay for virtually the entire navy, is also here to stay. The implied precedent it sets is also worrying to many people: does the king have the right to impose as many taxes as he wants, as often as he wants? (→ 6/1638).

"Ship money": King Charles's decision to impose this tax is causing trouble.

Scots riot in Edinburgh over introduction of new 'papist' Book of Common Prayer

Members of an Edinburgh congregation riot against the new Prayer Book.

Edinburgh, 23 July 1637

A popular riot broke out in St Giles's cathedral in Edinburgh today and rapidly spilt into the streets. The cause of the riot is the introduction, at King Charles's insistence, of a new Book of Common Prayer for Scotland.

The foisting of the Prayer Book on the kirk by the king's royal prerogative has deeply upset Scots, who are unconvinced by the strenuous efforts of the bishops to remove any hint of "popery" or Anglicanism from the book. However, by announcing months in advance that the new book would be used for the first time today, the king played straight into the hands of its opponents, chiefly the Presbyterians in the church and dissenting nobles, including the Earl of Rothes.

They prepared their protest well. Today, as the bishop of Edinburgh addressed the congregation, a woman cried out: "The Mass is entered among us!" Other women picked up their stools and hurled them at the bishop. This triggered an outburst of protest at the government in the Scottish capital. Apart from the crown's religious policy, its economic policies and high taxation have provoked widespread discontent, while Scottish nobles are alienated by attacks on their interests and their exclusion from central decision-making (→ 18/10).

Land enclosures to come under royal fire

Westminster, summer 1635

King Charles faces trouble over yet another controversial revenue-raising idea that he and his ministers have devised. This time he risks alienating one of the country's most powerful interest groups, the large landowners, who are having to face stiff fines under the new measure.

The scheme involves the resuscitation of ancient acts of enclosure. In May a royal commission of depopulation was set up with the task of discovering those landlords whose enclosure of common land, or whose preference for pastoral rather than arable farming, had

resulted in peasants being dispossessed, with a consequent reduction in the population of a village. The royal commissioners are charged with imposing fines, sometimes as great as £4,000, on such landowners, who also face having to rebuild farms long since demolished.

Many landowners are still smarting from the revival of ancient forest laws, whereby they were fined for encroaching on land once defined as forest – such as all but a tiny part of Essex. The latest impost will fuel the growing resentment of the king's personal rule (→ 10/1635).

Cash shortage annoys extravagant king

London, 1635

With no parliament sitting, and therefore no new subsidies made to the crown, since 1629, King Charles is in debt to the tune of some £1.5 million. Those who see his fabulous art collection or hear of the generous gifts that he makes to his friends might be surprised to learn that his personal extravagance is only partly responsible; simply living as befits a king is enormously expensive.

For a start, there are 19 royal residences which have to be kept up and staffed. It costs over £30,000 a year to keep Queen Henrietta

Maria, the French king's sister, in the style to which she is accustomed. Charles's expensive hobbies increase his debts yet further. His love of art leads him not just to commission works by Rubens and van Dyck but also to scour the continent for masterpieces.

Until recently the king financed it all with the help of bankers such as Philip Burlamachi, to whom over £500,000 is owed; but Burlamachi's financial empire crashed two years ago, partly because of the king's bad debts. The king now relies on heavy customs duties for most of his income (→ 10/1635).

Court punishes puritans

Charles styles himself 'happiest king'

London, 30 June 1637

Three puritan opponents of King Charles's religious policies were pilloried and mutilated today after the royal court of star chamber found them guilty of publishing libellous pamphlets aimed at bishops.

The three are William Prynne, Henry Burton and John Bastwick. Prynne, a lawyer, and Bastwick, a physician, have been in trouble for their views before, suffering heavy fines, imprisonment and expulsion from their professions. Prynne also had had his ears cut off in an unusually severe sentence that showed the government's determination to stamp on opposition to the policies instituted by Archbishop Laud.

The men's recent target has been the bishops and so-called Arminianism, which emphasises the God-given authority of bishops. Prynne, in one pamphlet written while he was imprisoned, tells the king that the bishops want his crown. Burton lays into excessive church ritual, blaming it by implication on the bishops, whom Bastwick calls a "limb of Antichrist".

The men were fined £5,000 each and condemned to life imprisonment, after first being pilloried and having their ears cut off. The star chamber court, at which Archbishop Laud presided, decreed that the ear-less Prynne be branded on the face with the letters SL, "Seditious Libeller", although Prynne says that they stand for *Stigmata Laudis* [scars of Laud]. Three years ago few people cared about Prynne, but today the crowds at the pillory were on his side.

The royal family: King Charles's three eldest children, by van Dyck.

Westminster, July 1637

For all his political tribulations King Charles recently told his young nephews that he was "the happiest king in Christendom". Indeed, one royal-watcher has noted that the king appears to be in "the full flower of robust vigour".

In his domestic life Charles has never been happier. His marriage to his French queen, Henrietta Maria, the sister of King Louis XIII, is of a sort rare among royalty: a political alliance which is also a genuine love match. She is at her husband's side virtually always, apart from when he is in council or out hunting, and her lively wit and radiant personality complement Charles's serene and slightly melancholy exterior. The couple are devoted to their children and to those of their friends, and the queen bore a sixth child, Anne, in March. Charles's cool manner belies a warm and sensitive heart. Both he and his wife are lovers of the arts, the queen being especially fond of masques, elaborate stage spectacles with music. Charles is also keen on the stage, Shakespeare being among his favourite dramatists.

Paintings and sculpture, too, are a royal passion, and great names such as Rubens and van Dyck are enthusiatically patronised. Last year van Dyck painted a particularly splendid portrait of Charles on horseback, as well as a triple portrait of the king to send to the great sculptor Bernini in Rome. The bust which Bernini made from the painting arrived this month, and it has so delighted the queen that she is going to send him a magnificent diamond in reward.

Archbishop Laud shown dining on the severed ears of his puritan opponents.

Two big religious factions emerge

England, 1637

As the religious controversy within the church deepens, two opposing camps have emerged. The puritans believe that anything not in the Bible – such as church rituals and the episcopal hierarchy – is at best suspect. They are not necessarily against bishops, but believe that they hold office only from the state, not from God. Arminians, called after the Dutch theologian Arminius, reject puritans' Calvinist extremism and, controversially, believe that bishops are in direct line from the apostles.

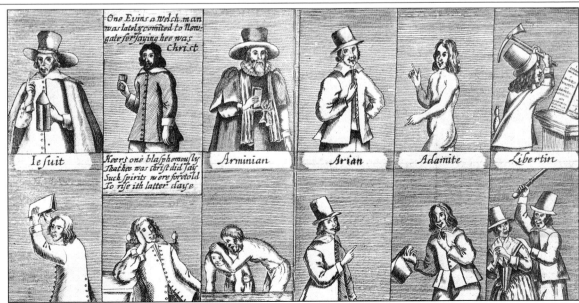
Across the whole religious spectrum: the varieties of belief as laid out in a mid-17th-century pamphlet.

Scots nobles defy king

The people signing the National Covenant in Edinburgh: a later view.

Edinburgh, 28 February 1638

Crowds gathered outside the Greyfriars kirk today as nobles and lairds joined ministers in pledging their support for a "national covenant" to uphold the purity of their Calvinism in the face of attempts by the king to impose Anglo-Catholic doctrine and ritual on them. Ministers and burgesses are expected to sign the covenant tomorrow.

In enforcing his religious ideas Charles has gone much further than his father, James, who reintroduced bishops, kneeling at Communion and other controversial measures. Matters came to a head last year when Charles ordered that a prayer book almost identical to the English one must be used in Scotland. Widespread disorders followed, and there was talk of armed rebellion.

In London, an uncomprehending king that believed a firm hand would settle things. He orderd a proclamation censuring those who had dared to protest against the Prayer Book; but if they submitted completely he would overlook their conduct. However this, far from appeasing the Scots, fuelled their anger and led directly to the new National Covenant, which one observer in the Greyfriars kirk described as a celebration of "the great marriage-day of this nation with God" (→ 6/1638).

King wins pyrrhic victory for ship money

London, June 1638

The king has secured a court judgement endorsing his right to collect the controversial "ship money" tax. The courts have also found against John Hampden, a wealthy landlord from the Chilterns who refused to pay the tax. But even the king's attorney-general, John Bankes, says that the victory could be damaging.

For the past nine years Charles has been ruling without parliament and raising money without parliamentary approval. He revived the ancient and almost forgotten ship money tax levied on seaport towns to pay for a navy. Still short of funds, the king extended the tax to inland counties. Hampden then claimed that the tax was illegal.

He hired a friend and long-time student of constitutional law, Oliver St John, who presented two arguments. First, if the king claimed the right to tax his people at will, then the very foundations of property rights were destroyed. His second argument took up an earlier court ruling that, at a time of national peril, the king could raise taxes without parliamentary approval – but there had been no mention of a national emergency when the ship money writ had been issued. As for the later claim that pirates represented a threat, St John pointed out that pirates had always threatened English shipping. Why had they suddenly to be dealt with

Hampden: an 18th-century view.

as an emergency? St John and a colleague spoke for eight days. The solicitor-general was on his feet for four days and Bankes for three.

The court's verdict was for the king, but only by a narrow 7-5 majority. While only one of the judges denounced the tax as absolutely illegal, four others accepted St John's claim that the way in which the tax was levied undercut the king's contention that it was an emergency measure. Some of the judges who found for the king used a rhetoric so inflated that it seemed to leave the subject no property rights against the king. The judgements have thus inflamed public opinion and provoked deep resentment against the king.

Mother-in-law stirs new fears of popery

London, September 1638

Fear of popery is never far below the surface in a Protestant England whose king is married to a Catholic, and a French one at that. Old suspicions have now been aroused by the unexpected arrival in London of Charles's scheming mother-in-law, the Italian-born Marie de' Medici. Accompanied by 600 attendants, she has already set up a centre of popish worship. Unease has not been diminished by her haughty attitude and profligate lifestyle, particularly as she now depends on funds provided by Charles and his queen. After intriguing against her son, Louis XIII, Marie was forced to flee from France. She is plotting a return to power.

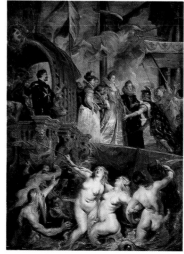

Marie de' Medici in Marseilles, by Peter Paul Rubens (d.1640).

War looks likely as Scots tension rises

London, 25 December 1638

At court all talk is of war to bring the rebellious Scots to heel. The Christmas festivities have been curtailed, and the king is insisting that only the use of force can now restore royal authority in Scotland.

Last month he called a general assembly of the Church of Scotland in Glasgow. Charles offered what he saw as major concessions in the hope that the Covenant would be repudiated. He promised to introduce the Prayer Book in a fair and legal manner, for instance, and offered to limit the authority of Scottish bishops. But far from welcoming the king's overtures, the church increased its demands, voting to abolish the book of canons and the episcopacy, excommunicating all the bishops in Scotland and ordaining that the Covenant be taken by all Scots.

Charles now believes that there is no alternative to war. He says that it is no longer a dispute over prayer books but over his right to be king. Landowners in northern England have been told that they must contribute to an army, and Charles has commissioned a report on the feasibility of blockading the Scottish coast. Money, it seems, is not an obstacle to a Scottish war. And the Scots are also preparing for battle. Nobles and lairds have begun to raise armies, and a dowager duchess is said to have bought up all the gunpowder in Edinburgh (→27/3).

King admits defeat in war of religion against the Scots

Berwick, 18 June 1639

A peace treaty was signed here to-day between Charles and the Scottish Covenanters who fought to protect the Calvinist purity of their kirk from the malign influence of bishops. The treaty is presented as a compromise – both armies will disband – but in fact the so-called Bishops' War was a defeat for the king. He will visit Scotland for a meeting of parliament and a general assembly, both of which will be dominated by Covenanters.

The war was already lost when Charles arrived at York last March to lead his troops. Covenanters had captured Edinburgh castle and the king's main arsenal at Dalkeith. The only important royalist on the Scottish side of the border, the Earl of Douglas, had fled. The arms that Charles had ordered from Holland were largely useless, and his troops were disgruntled and already deserting (→ 19/6).

Ruthless 'turncoat' recalled by Charles

London, 22 September 1639

Thomas Wentworth, for the last six years lord deputy in Ireland, has returned to London in response to an urgent message last month from the king: "Come when you will, ye shall be welcome to your assured friend, Charles R."

Wentworth's task is to crush the Scottish revolt against the king's attempt to force the kirk to conform to the English episcopal system. He brings with him a reputation for arrogance, ruthlessness and efficiency. He reorganised the Irish administration and increased revenues so that no subsidy was needed from England. But he made many enemies.

It was much the same story earlier, when he was the king's lord president of the north, in his native Yorkshire, where he humiliated local magnates. The lawyer son of a wealthy landowner, he began his career as a critic of royal policy; when he changed sides he was denounced as an apostate (→ 12/1639).

King Charles assembles one of Europe's finest art collections

Whitehall, 1639

Abraham van der Doort, the Dutch expert appointed as the first surveyor of the king's pictures, has almost completed his inventory of Charles's collection of European art. Nearly all of the masters are represented in it, including Titian, Raphael, Rembrandt and Caravaggio, known for his realistic depiction of religious subjects, notably *Death of the Virgin*. Rubens painted the ceiling of the Whitehall Banqueting House.

Charles sent ambassadors all over Europe for works of art. He pressured relatives, friends and people who hoped for royal favours into making gifts. His largest and most controversial acquisition came from the House of Gonzaga, whose members had ruled Mantua for centuries. When the main branch of the family ended, Charles acquired the bulk of its collection, causing great resentment in Italy. The collection included *Triumphs of Caesar* by Mantegna, who had painted the frescoes in the ducal palace at Mantua.

Even before he became king, Charles was collecting under the tutelage of his friend George Villiers, the Duke of Buckingham. In 1623, when the duke and Charles secretly visited Spain in an ultimately fruitless attempt to negotiate a marriage to the *Infanta*, the two men, posing as Mr Smith and Mr Brown, acquired several Titians, a Correggio and the famous Raphael cartoons.

A discerning patron of the arts: three views of King Charles.

Endymion Porter and Anthony van Dyck: a self-portrait by the artist.

The Banqueting House ceiling.

A work by Raphael: Charles was a keen collector of the Italian artist.

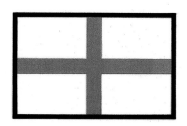

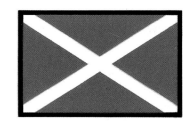

C h a r l e s I
1625–1649

London, January 1640. Thomas Wentworth, formerly lord deputy in Ireland, is created Earl of Strafford (→ 12/1640).

Westminster, 13 April 1640. Charles summons the first parliament since 1629 (→ 5/5).

Ireland, June 1640. The Irish Parliament advances £150,000 to Charles to finance the second Bishops' War (→ 1/11/41).

Surrey, 8 July 1640. The queen gives birth to her eighth child, Henry; he is to be the Duke of Gloucester (→ 5/11/40).

North of England, 21 Aug 1640. The Earl of Strafford takes over as commander-in-chief of the English army (→ 28/8).

Northumberland, 28 Aug 1640. The Scots defeat the English army at Newburn (→ 30/8).

Newcastle, 30 August 1640. The advancing Scots army captures the city (→ 1/10).

Westminster, October 1640. Charles recalls parliament to raise the money needed to keep the Treaty of Ripon, signed earlier this month (→ 12/1640).

Richmond, Surrey, 5 Nov 1640. Anne, Charles's three-year-old daughter, dies (→ 2/5/41).

Westminster, 18 Dec 1640. Archbishop Laud of Canterbury is impeached.

Westminster, 10 April 1641. The impeachment proceedings against Thomas Wentworth, the Earl of Strafford, collapse (→ 21/4).

Westminster, 21 April 1641. The Commons pass a bill of attainder, seeking to make the Earl of Strafford's goods forfeit and to disinherit his heirs (→ 23/4).

London, 23 April 1641. Charles writes to Strafford and explains that he is unable to provide any help to him (→ 12/5/41).

Westminster, 5 May 1641. After a possible plot to destroy parliament, all males are made to take the protestation oath, opposing popery and maintaining Protestant unity.

London, 8 June 1641. Parliament accuses Charles and Henrietta Maria of plotting with disaffected elements in the English army with a view to staging a coup and overthrowing parliament (→ 17/7).

Westminster, 5 July 1641. The concessions that parliament has been able to extract from King Charles now include the abolition of the court of star chamber, which the king had used against Prynne and other opponents of his regime in the 1630s.

London, 10 August 1641. King Charles signs the Treaty of London, which recognises the demands of the Scottish Covenanters (→ 14/8).

Scotland, 14 August 1641. Charles tries to persuade the Covenanters to give him support in his struggle against parliament (→ 12/10).

Scotland, 17 November 1641. King Charles leaves for London, having consolidated the Covenanters' power but done little to advance his own cause.

Westminster, December 1641. Parliamentary leaders demand control of the militia (→ 5/3/42).

London, 31 January 1642. Opponents of the king's party stage a demonstration in the City at Moorfields against the power of the bishops (→ 13/2).

Westminster, 13 February 1642. The Bishops' Exclusion Act, preventing all clergy from holding

secular offices, receives the royal assent.

Westminster, 5 March 1642. The Militia Ordinance is passed, this will enable parliament to raise troops without requiring royal consent (→ 11/8).

Beverley, 23 April 1642. After failing to seize Hull, Charles returns to his base here (→ 3/6).

Ulster, April 1642. Scottish troops arrive to crush rebels after a deal is struck with the king and the English Parliament.

Westminster, 11 August 1642. The Commons continue to stand firm against Charles, despite his offer of pardon to the rebels led by Robert Devereux, the Earl of Essex (→ 9/9).

London, 9 September 1642. Parliamentary troops (sometimes known as "roundheads") led by the Earl of Essex head for the Midlands and the north (→ 23/10).

Britain, September 1642. King Charles sends for his nephew Prince Rupert, the son of the late Frederick V, the Elector Palatine, to join him to fight the parliamentarians (→ 23/10).

Banbury, October 1642. After a victory at Powick Bridge last month, Charles takes the town.

Oxford, 29 October 1642. The roundheads retreat to Warwick as the royalists ("cavaliers") take over the city (→ 4/11).

Reading, 4 November 1642. The town has become a royalist stronghold (→ 13/11).

Westminster, November 1642. Parliament asks the Scots for their support against Charles (→ 1/1643).

Cleveland, 16 January 1643. The royalists, after a defeat at

Guisborough, are forced to make their retreat (→ 28/1).

Cheshire, 28 January 1643. Roundheads under Sir William Brereton seize control of the town of Nantwich (→ 25/4).

Scotland, January 1643. In a bid to secure peace in England, Scottish nobles sympathetic to the cause of King Charles sign the "Cross Petition" (→ 25/9).

Reading, 25 April 1643. The royalist stronghold is captured by troops led by Robert Devereux, the Earl of Essex (→ 13/5).

Grantham, 13 May 1643. Oliver Cromwell defeats the royalist forces.

Westminster, 23 May 1643. Parliament votes unanimously to impeach Queen Henrietta Maria for selling the royal jewels in Europe to raise money for the cavaliers (→ 14/7).

Oxford, 14 July 1643. Queen Henrietta Maria arrives from York with a convoy of arms and money, having evaded the parliamentary forces (→ 16/6/44).

Bristol, 26 July 1643. The royalists, led by Prince Rupert, capture the city (→ 8/1643).

Westminster, August 1643. A crowd of women, demanding peace and supporting the king, forces its way into Whitehall palace (→ 11/10).

London, 8 December 1643. John Pym, the architect of the revolution and leader of the parliamentarian government, dies of cancer.

Oxford, 16 December 1643. Charles arrests his old ally, the Duke of Hamilton, who is accused of double-dealing with the Covenanters while negotiating for the king.

Charles dissolves hostile parliament

Westminster, 5 May 1640

The first parliament for 11 years was dissolved today by an angry and frustrated Charles after three weeks of defiance by MPs under the capable leadership of John Pym, the member for Tavistock and a long-time opponent of the king's abuse of power. The decision to hold elections for a new parliament was made by Charles on the advice of Thomas Wentworth, the Earl of Strafford, who, as lord deputy in Ireland, had coaxed and cowed the Irish Parliament into doing as he wished; he believed that he could do the same at Westminster.

The opposition, however, is well-organised and determined. Pym, as secretary of the Providence Company – founded to foster settlements in the New World – has had the backing of the company's directors, mostly Puritans and men of influence. They provided a coherent counterweight to the "court" party which relied on royalist lords getting their families and dependants into the Commons.

The former lord chief justice, John Finch, undertook the task of addressing the Commons on behalf of the king. In 1629 he had been held down in his chair by angry MPs [*see page 224*]; now his speech praising Charles and his "virtuous" Catholic wife, and denouncing the "wicked" Calvinist Scots was brushed aside as MPs proceeded to air their grievances.

Pym spoke for almost two hours, pointing to the injury done to com-

The king in parliament: but now Charles has angrily dismissed the MPs.

merce and colonial expansion by the king's illegal and arbitrary taxation. The next week he objected to voting funds for the king, and when the Earl of Strafford pressured the Lords into voting the funds, Pym denounced the action as a breach of Commons privilege. For Charles,

the last straw came yesterday when MPs resolved that Pym should petition the king to come to terms with the Scots and avoid a second Bishops' War. Rather than be confronted by this challenge he abruptly dissolved the parliament that he could not bend to his will (→ 24/9).

Lords appeased to sidestep Commons

York, 24 September 1640

The king has surprised his critics, who believed that he had summoned the great council of peers in a bid to win the peers' support against the parliamentarians. Yet when they met, Charles permitted criticism and agreed to their demand for a new parliament. But the king has not changed his policies; he is just seeking to gain time in the hope that he can divide his opponents. He is even considering using the archaic institution as an alternative to parliament (→ 10/1640).

Parliament sends Strafford, king's closest adviser, to the Tower

John Pym: the Commons' leader.

Westminster, December 1640

The second parliament this year has assembled in an atmosphere of deep suspicion of the king and his advisers. Alarming stories have been circulating of popish plots encouraged by Charles's Catholic wife, Henrietta Maria; the king's adviser, the Earl of Strafford, is said to be ready to accuse opposition MPs of treason by conspiring with the Scots to bring their armies into England.

The Tower garrison is to be replaced by one more firmly loyal to the king – evidently in anticipation of the arrival of arrested MPs.

The Commons, greatly alarmed, agreed to John Pym's proposal that the doors should be locked. MPs went on to appoint a committee to prepare charges against Strafford.

A suggestion that a full investigation should be made before deciding to charge Strafford brought a fierce response from Pym: Strafford had to be arrested or he would urge the king to dissolve parliament again. When Pym went to the Lords with the writ, Strafford was defiant, but he has few friends among the peers. He was impeached, relieved of his sword and sent to the Tower (→ 10/4/41).

Scottish war again ends in humiliating defeat for English

Ripon, 1 October 1640

King Charles's second war against the Scots in two years has collapsed in humiliating defeat. The armistice signed here today allows the Scots to occupy six counties of northern England; they will be paid £850 a day until a peace treaty is agreed. The terms of the treaty, to be worked out by Scottish and English negotiators in London, will be referred to the new parliament that the king has been obliged to summon.

Throughout the summer Charles was issuing orders for raising a new army and desperately seeking funds to pay for it. Spain, France and even the pope were touted in vain; he tried to hijack the bullion deposited in the mint by London merchants. He was driven to wringing contributions from court officials and privy councillors.

The country gentry, responsible for raising the local levies, were uncooperative, and the troops themselves were disorderly and ready to desert. The Scots, for their part, were keen, well-trained and well-armed, with guns from Holland.

When Charles reached York to place himself at the head of his forces, the Scots had already crossed into England and reached the Tyne. They seized Newcastle and swept on to Gateshead, scattering the demoralised English. As one observer put it: "Never so many ran from so few" (→ 10/1640).

Charles pins hopes on marriage of Mary

'Black Tom' is executed

London, 12 May 1641

Thomas Wentworth, the Earl of Strafford, or "Black Tom the Tyrant" to his enemies, has been executed. An enormous crowd had gathered to watch. The king – who had specifically guaranteed the earl's safety, yet was forced to sign the Bill of Attainder which sent him to the scaffold – is shattered and regards the execution as a rape of his honour.

The parliamentary leaders John Pym, John Hampden and Lord Sale and Sele, who had already led the opposition in both houses against the royal prerogative, saw Strafford as the most competent of the king's ministers and were determined to destroy him. First they tried impeaching him for "cumulative treason". Pym opened the case in Westminster Hall on 23 March, arguing that Strafford planned to use the army in Ireland to impose Charles's vision of an absolute monarchy on England.

Strafford defended himself with fortitude and forbearance, but when it became obvious that he would win his case, Pym dropped

"Black Tom": Lord Strafford.

the impeachment for a bill of attainder, an ancient piece of legislation much used in mediaeval times to punish subjects without the need for a trial. On 8 May, in a tense atmosphere heightened by rumours of a royalist coup, the bill passed its third reading. Two days later, with his palace surrounded by the London mob, Charles signed it – heartbroken.

A royal alliance: Charles's daughter, Mary, and the Dutch Prince William.

Whitehall Palace, 2 May 1641

King Charles and Queen Henrietta Maria are celebrating today's marriage between their elder daughter Mary and Prince William of the House of Orange, the son of Frederick Henry, the *stadhouder* [viceroy] of the United Provinces. The marriage, which parliamentarians see as an attempt by the king and queen to buy foreign support in their struggle against parliament, points to the increasing isolation of the monarch at home and abroad.

The negotiations which led up to today's nuptials also show the dominance that the queen has gained over government policy since the death of the Duke of Buckingham. In the last two years Henrietta Maria – a Catholic – has raised money from English Catholics, appealed to the pope for military aid against the Scots, encouraged the Earl of Strafford to bid for a Spanish alliance, contacted Cardinal Richelieu and proposed an alliance

with her native France, and conspired with army officers in York to release Strafford from the Tower.

So far she has met with little success. The Scots still occupy Northumberland, a Spanish alliance has become politically impossible, Richelieu (who has no intention of helping a friend of Spain) is ignoring her, and the news of the conspiracy to release Strafford has inflamed moderate opinion.

In the Netherlands the stadhouder is said to be happy to link his family with a long-established royal house – which will help to legitimise his rule – but unlikely to give Charles any military aid. The Dutch have a tradition of absolute toleration and of hospitality to refugees regardless of their politics or religion, and the stadhouder will no doubt furnish his young son and daughter-in-law with a house in which they will live in a less volatile political setting than that currently prevailing in Britain (→ 8/6).

The crowd presses close to see the execution of the widely-hated Strafford.

Queen and jewels must stay in England

London, 17 July 1641

In what King Charles considers one of its most provocative decisions yet, parliament has refused to allow Henrietta Maria to leave the country. The queen has pleaded sickness and claims that she must go to a spa for her health.

Members of parliament are fully aware of rumours that she has been instigating secret diplomacy with Spain, France and the Netherlands

and has been in touch with the pope for military assistance against the Scottish Covenanters. They have no intention of letting the deeply unpopular Catholic queen go abroad. Parliamentary leaders also feared that she intended to take the crown jewels with her and sell them to finance an invasion which would establish Charles as an absolute monarch and Catholicism as the state form of religion (→ 23/2/42).

Royalist plot mars Charles's Scottish trip

Onward Christian soldiers? A later view of the armed might of the Covenanters.

Edinburgh, 12 October 1641
The king has denied any knowledge of a royalist plot, nicknamed "the incident", to kidnap the Covenanter leaders, the Marquises of Argyll and Hamilton and the Earl of Lanark. But the presence of scores of armed royalists who accompanied the king as he made his denial before the Scottish parliament has wrecked any possibility that his protestations will be believed.

When Charles arrived in Scotland in August he looked set to gain strong support. Many resented the intolerance of the Covenanters, and opposition to them was crystallising around the Earl of Montrose and 17 fellow noblemen who had signed the "Cumbernauld Bond" to protest at the "particular and indirect practising of a few".

But Charles remained aloof from the Bond, and his latest concession – of the key principle that state appointments in Scotland need parliamentary confirmation – has been interpreted here as a sign of weakness rather than of moderation. He is losing power (→ 17/11).

Catholic revolt is new worry for king

London, 1 November 1641
News has just reached London that Ulster's Catholics have risen in revolt. Rumours that tens of thousands of Protestants have been slaughtered are spreading through London. The Irish, who see their religion, their culture and their land threatened by the continual arrivals of Scottish immigrants, have directed their anger against the Protestant settlers.

Many of the revolt's leaders, including Phelim O'Neill and Rory M'Guire, fearing that a puritan parliament in England would only increase the repression against Irish Catholics, are claiming to be fighting on behalf of King Charles and in defence of his rights. Other leaders, like the Earl of Antrim and Lord Dillon, have been in close attendance on the king.

The crisis could not have come at a worse time for Charles. An army of Scottish Presbyterians is still encamped in Northumberland and calling for the abolition of "popish" rituals in the Church of England. Strafford's execution last May only encouraged Charles's critics to press for further attacks on the royal prerogative.

The troubles in Ulster find King Charles, who is still absent in Scotland, with his hands tied. If he shows any lack of resolution against the Irish rebels he will be accused by his parliamentary critics of being a party to their revolt, and of conspiring to reintroduce Roman Catholicism throughout Ireland. But if he tries to raise an army to suppress it, they will say that he is conspiring to use that army to suppress Protestant liberties (→ 8/11).

Parliament gives narrow majority to royal attack

London, 22 November 1641
By a majority of just 11, the House of Commons today passed the "Grand Remonstrance": a stinging attack on royal power and the episcopacy. The work of a parliamentary committee over 11 months, it is an appeal to the nation consisting of a long list of the king's errors, a statement of reforms achieved by parliament, and a catalogue of grievances in need of redress.

That parliament would issue a manifesto against the reigning monarch would have been inconceivable 50 years ago. But

A pamphlet backs royal rights.

the inability of the Stuarts to live within their means, the growing confidence of a Protestant-minded group in parliament and the stubbornness of the king have turned the inconceivable into a political reality.

The king has never been more isolated. He has lost popular support in the capital and increasingly relies for advice on men who tell him only what he wants to hear. Whitehall palace has become an armed camp, with hundreds of "cavaliers", as royalist troops are now being nicknamed, sleeping in the corridors (→ 12/1641).

Parliament given power to approve choice of king's councillors

London, 8 November 1641
The House of Commons has passed its most revolutionary proposal yet. Faced with a Catholic rebellion in Ireland that might turn into an invasion of England, yet unable to trust the king to command the army that must be raised to suppress it, the Commons have announced that the appointments of key officers of state must be approved by parliament. Additional instructions to the parliamentary joint committee in Edinburgh further state that if the king does not accept this proposal then parliament will take steps to crush the rebellion itself.

So close are the votes in the House of Commons between the two sides that three days ago a less radical resolution, which proposed that unless Charles accepted officers approved by parliament MPs would not assist him in the reconquest of Ireland, failed to obtain a majority. Should the new proposal be passed by the Lords, there is bound to be a confrontation between king and parliament.

Given Charles's vision of kingship, and the influence that his wife has over him, it would be impossible for him to accept the proposal and remain, in his own eyes, a king worth the title (→ 22/11).

Charles squares up for showdown with parliament

King fails in move to arrest rebel MPs

London, 11 January 1642
The king has fled and London is in the hands of parliament. Just a week after Charles confidently entered the House of Commons to arrest John Pym, John Hampden, Arthur Haslerig, Denzil Holles and William Strode, the MPs have returned to Westminster in triumph.

A single, crazy blunder has ended with the collapse of royal power in London. On 3 January the king, infuriated that the Commons were about to impeach the queen, decided to indict the five MPs for treason. The next day Charles burst into the Commons chamber at the head of a troop of cavalry and announced that he had come to arrest the five. The Commons were stunned at this outrage: no king had ever entered their chamber before. Charles walked up to the speaker. He told the MPs that parliamentary privilege did not apply to traitors. He demanded the five, but they had been forewarned, and were already on their way to the safety of the City by barge.

"All the birds have flown," he remarked, and strode out with the MPs' sharp cry of "Privilege! Privilege!" ringing in his ears. The

An unwelcoming reception: King Charles in the House of Commons.

next day he went to the Guildhall to demand the five. But he was greeted by a mob shouting "liberty of parliament" and a motley array of armed shopkeepers and Thames watermen, all pledged to defend parliament. He turned back.

Parliament and the Londoners formed a joint committee of public safety. Mariners and lightermen flocked into the barricaded city, vowing to fight and die for the Protestant cause; Philip Skippon, an experienced veteran of the Dutch

wars, was appointed commander of a new parliamentary army, known as the London-trained bands.

Last night King Charles finally realised that he had lost London. Taking his wife and three eldest children with him, he fled to a totally unprepared Hampton Court palace, the royal family sleeping together in one bed to keep warm.

This morning Pym led his colleagues back to Westminster as heroes. Few kings have received such a welcome (→ 23/2).

The queen flees to seek European aid

Dover, 23 February 1642
The queen and Princess Mary left England today, sailing for the Low Countries on the warship *Lion*. King Charles was devastated to see his wife and daughter leave, and on parting with them he burst into tears. He galloped his horse along the clifftop, keeping the ship in view until she disappeared over the horizon.

Henrietta Maria's task is to secure financial help from the Prince of Orange and from France and military help from the king of Denmark for King Charles's cause, but it is hard to believe that she will get very much. The Dutch Estates are openly supporting the radicals' cause, Cardinal Richelieu of France favours a parliamentary victory and the Danish king is busy with wars in Germany.

But the royal women, at least, will be safe and Princess Mary, who is married to the son of the *stadhouder* [viceroy] of the United Provinces, is looking forward to joining her husband. Henrietta Maria has taken the crown jewels with her and could, in the last resort, pawn them to aid her husband's cause (→ 2/1643).

Both sides prepare for armed struggle

York, 3 June 1642
The king rode out to Heyworth Moor today to receive a "demonstration of loyalty" from the royalist gentry of Yorkshire – in effect a review of troops. In the southeast, meanwhile, parliamentary supporters are equally busy drilling. Three weeks ago parliamentary leaders reviewed their force of Londoners in Finsbury Fields.

On both sides of the political divide there have been jostles to secure forts, magazines, and war supplies destined for Ireland. These are still the work of minorities – on both sides. The majority remain uncommitted and still prefer pragmatic neutrality (→ 7/7).

City of Hull declares for parliament by refusing royalists entry

A closed city: Sir John Hotham (above) refuses to open Hull's gates.

Hull, 7 July 1642
The king has failed to take the strategically important town of Hull after two attempts. The fort's magazines, packed with arms and ammunition for the Scottish wars, would have maintained a royalist army in the field for a year.

Sir John Hotham, Hull's governor, was undecided in his loyalty, like most of the country, but sympathised with parliament. On 23 April, during a surprise visit to Hull by the king's son, James, the Duke of York, the royalists, using the prince as their "Trojan horse", failed to take the town. This week, after Lord George Digby misjudged Hotham, who he thought would open the town's gates, they failed again (→ 11/8).

Constitutional struggle turns into armed conflict

Nottingham: royal standard is raised

Nottingham, 13 September 1642
The king has unfurled his standard and called his subjects to arms. The day was wet and gloomy, and the royal proclamation had been so altered by Charles at the last moment that his herald could hardly read it out. It was greeted by Nottingham's 5,000-strong population with neither enthusiasm nor hostility but simply indifference.

This attitude is understandable. It is harvest time, the king's studied moderation is seen as a sign of weakness and his first military effort, to dislodge parliamentary sympathisers from Coventry last week, was hesitant and unsuccessful.

The parliamentary camp appears more organised. Last July parliament formed a committee of safety and appointed the Earl of Essex, the God-fearing son of the flamboyant Elizabethan, to command its untrained army (→9/1642).

A call to arms: King Charles's standard is raised at Nottingham.

Edgehill: opening clash is a draw

Banbury, 23 October 1642
The first major clash between the rival armies ended this evening at Edgehill, on the road to London. Both sides claim victory.

It began unexpectedly. The Earl of Essex, whose army was manoeuvring to divert the king from an attack on London, was on his way to church when he was told that Charles's army was drawn up on a ridge three miles away. He found his enemy in conventional formation, with infantry in the centre and cavalry on the flanks, and positioned his regiments in the same way.

Battle began in the afternoon. Prince Rupert's cavalry swept the parliamentary horse off the field, but in its enthusiasm disappeared from the battlefield in pursuit. Seeing the royalist infantry unprotected Essex sent in his remaining troops, wrecking the royalist centre and even temporarily taking the royal standard, before the two armies withdrew exhausted (→29/10).

Chaos reigns at the Battle of Edgehill: a view by a Victorian artist.

Royal commander: Prince Rupert.

Essex: the parliamentary leader.

Turnham Green: a defeat for Charles

London, 13 November 1642
The king has abandoned his assault on London. His 12,000-strong army, confronted by a parliamentary army twice its size at Turnham Green, six miles (9.6km) west of St Paul's, has withdrawn to Reading.

Since the Battle of Edgehill [*see left*], Charles's army has been meandering towards London, but the Earl of Essex's parliamentarian army beat Charles to it. Six thousand volunteers joined Essex's ranks, and the citizens built barricades from Mayfair to Clerkenwell.

The initial assault swept away Denzil Holles's redcoated regiment at Brentford two days ago; but though the royalists took Brentford they were unable to regain the momentum of their assault. Today they resumed their march on the capital, only to be stopped at Turnham Green and then ignominiously withdraw (→31/12).

Soldiers of fortune lead both armies

London, 31 December 1642
After three months of civil war the royalist army, which has no single commander, continues to be dominated by one man, Prince Rupert. In contrast, the parliamentary army, commanded by one man, the Earl of Essex, is dominated by subordinates: Sir William Waller, Sir Thomas Fairfax, Philip Skippon. One and a half centuries without war have had their effect on England. The only men on either side capable of leading troops into battle are former soldiers of fortune.

Prince Rupert, Charles's 23-year-old nephew and a veteran of the German wars, is the royalists' most aggressive commander. His rivals, Waller, Fairfax and Skippon, are also veterans of the German and Dutch wars. They lack the dash and boldness of Rupert and avoid taking risks. Yet Fairfax in the north, with only a semi-trained force, has shown an astonishing grasp of strategy.

▷

Britain split asunder as the civil war intensifies

Charles's 'cavaliers' claim first victories

Royalist victory: a later view of the Battle of Hopton Heath in Cornwall.

Devizes, Wiltshire, 13 July 1643
The royalist army added another victory to its many successes this year by inflicting a crushing defeat on the parliamentarians at Roundway Down near here today. Virtually the whole of south-western England has now been delivered into the king's hands, and his nephew Prince Rupert can prosecute his siege of Bristol without fear of attack by the parliamentary army.

The "cavaliers", as the royalists are known after their swagger and finery, have also prevailed in Yorkshire where the Marquis of Newcastle has taken the whole of the county except for Hull, the only parliamentary stronghold left in the north. The unwarlike but brave marquis is now turning his attention to the eastern counties.

The only real success for parliament's forces so far this year has been the capture of Reading, needlessly surrendered when the muskets of the king's relieving force could be heard. The Earl of Essex, commanding the parliamentary forces, has become so disillusioned that he has suggested reopening peace talks with the king (→ 26/7).

'Roundheads' fight back successfully

Lincolnshire, 11 October 1643
Colonel Cromwell's disciplined "roundheads" – nicknamed after the close-cropped apprentices who backed parliament in the London scuffles of 1641 – defeated the Marquis of Newcastle's cavalry at Winceby today and confirmed that the tide of war has swung to the parliamentarians. Newcastle's men, never keen to fight far from home, are in retreat to the north, and Hull is now safely held.

All three of the king's lines of advance on London are now blocked. In the south-west the victorious Cornish pikemen, unwilling to advance too far while the roundheads hold Plymouth behind them, have stopped at Devizes. Plymouth, like Hull, has declared its loyalty to parliament. The king's advance down the centre of the country was similarly halted by the resistance of Gloucester. The king himself mounted the siege on 10 August, and it was felt that it was only a matter of time before the town, held by a puritan minority, would fall and Charles could resume his march on London.

The danger was well recognised by parliament. Every shop in London was closed and the trained bands of militia were called out to relieve Gloucester. The king sent Prince Rupert's men to stop them crossing the Cotswolds but they marched on, and when they came within sight of Gloucester the besiegers melted away. The two armies clashed again at Newbury, and after a cruel day's fighting Charles, sick at heart at the deaths of so many of his friends, left the field to the roundheads (→ 16/12).

Staging a comeback: the leaders of the resurgent parliamentary forces.

Queen brings arms from Low Countries

Bridlington, February 1643
Queen Henrietta Maria arrived here today from the Low Countries with a ship carrying a cargo of weapons for her husband. The queen, who defied her astrologer's warnings of a dangerous conjunction of planets, slipped through the parliamentarian blockade under the escort of the Dutch admiral, Tromp, but the patrol ships chased her ship into the bay and bombarded the house where she is staying. Urged to take cover, she refused until she had rescued her terrified lap-dog.

Tromp has now put an end to this bombardment by threatening to fire on the patrol boats, which are only armed colliers. The weapons brought by the queen – mainly cannon and gunpowder – are sorely needed by the king, whose arms are trapped in the roundhead stronghold of Hull (→ 23/5).

Parliamentarians and Scots join forces

Westminster, 25 September 1643
John Pym, who although seriously ill remains the heart and brains of the parliamentary cause, today led his colleagues in signing the "Solemn League and Covenant" with the Scots. Under its terms the English bind themselves to maintain the church in Scotland as it is now established and to reform religion in England "according to the example of the best reformed churches". In return for this promise and a generous subsidy the Scots are to provide an army to fight the cavaliers.

It is, in fact, a military pact disguised as a religious manifesto, a recognition by puritans on both sides of the border that they must stand together. Distrust remains, for the English feel that it gives the Scots too much influence over the English church; the Scots think that they have not enough (→ 8/12).

CIVIL WAR AND UNREST IN THE BRITISH ISLES, 1642–1648

Legend:
- Areas loyal to Parliament (Roundheads) throughout the Civil War
- Areas won by Parliament from the Monarchy (Cavaliers) by the end of the war
- Areas loyal to the Monarchy throughout the Civil War
- ✗ Battle sites and dates 1643

Atlantic Ocean

North Sea

Scots Covenanters fight for Charles I

✗ 1645 Auldearn

Alford 1645 ✗ ✗ 1644 Aberdeen

SCOTLAND

● Montrose

✗ 1645 Inverlochy

✗ 1644 Tippermuir ✗ 1644 Dundee

Glasgow ● ✗ 1645 Kilsyth ● Edinburgh

● Dalkeith

● Berwick

✗ 1645 Philiphaugh

● Derry

ULSTER

Catholic landowners rise up against Protestant settlers, 1641

● Belfast

● Newcastle

Carlisle ● ● Gateshead

ISLE OF MAN

CONNACHT

IRELAND

Irish Sea

● Ripon

✗ York ● ● Bridlington

Galway ●

Drogheda ●

✗ 1644 Marston Moor

✗ 1642 Hull

Dublin ●

LEINSTER

Liverpool ●

● Manchester

Chester ● ENGLAND

Gainsborough ●

Limerick ●

● Kilkenny

Harlech ●

✗ 1644 Nantwich

Newark ●

✗ 1643 Winceby

1643

MUNSTER

● Shrewsbury

Nottingham ●

Wexford ●

WALES

● Ashby de la Zouch ● Leicester

Cork ●

Cardigan ●

Hereford ●

Worcester ●

✗ 1645 Naseby

● Newmarket

✗ Powick Bridge 1643

✗ Banbury

Gloucester ●

Edgehill ✗ 1642 ✗ 1644 Cropredy Bridge

Pembroke

Woodstock ●

● Oxford St Alban's

Bristol ●

Uxbridge ● Brentford ✗ ● London

✗ 1643 Roundway Down

✗ Reading 1642 Turnham Green

1643,1644 Newbury

Dover ●

✗ 1644 Cheriton

Lyme Regis ●

Exeter ●

● Poole

Newport

● Plymouth

Corfe Castle

ISLE OF WIGHT

✗ 1644 Lostwithiel

Carisbrook Castle

English Channel

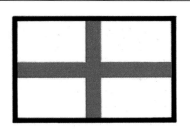

C h a r l e s   I
1625–1649

Cheshire, 28 January 1644. Royalist troops are defeated in a battle at Nantwich by Sir Thomas Fairfax (→ 4/1645).

Oxford, January 1644. King Charles summons a royalist parliament (→ 1/2).

Scotland/England, Jan 1644. The parliamentarians and the Scots Covenanters form a committee to coordinate the war effort (→ 19/1).

Borders, 19 January 1644. A Covenanter army of 21,000 men invades England in support of parliament (→ 2/7).

Oxford, 1 February 1644. King Charles appoints the Earl of Montrose, James Graham, as the king's lieutenant-general in Scotland (→ 4/1644).

Newark, 21 March 1644. Prince Rupert, Charles's nephew, relieves the town (→ 29/3).

Hampshire, 29 March 1644. Royalist forces retreat after a defeat at Cheriton (→ 21/4).

York, 21 April 1644. The roundhead forces, having defeated the royalists at Selby, lay siege to the city (→ 11/6).

Dumfries, April 1644. The royalist forces led by the Earl of Montrose retreat (→ 13/9).

Liverpool, 11 June 1644. Prince Rupert, who captured Stockport and Bolton last month, lays siege to the city (→ 2/7).

Exeter, 16 June 1644. During the siege by the Earl of Essex, Queen Henrietta Maria gives birth to a daughter, Henrietta Anne (→ 14/7).

Marston Moor, 2 July 1644. The Scots presence around York forces a confrontation in which the royalists are outnumbered.→

South Coast, 14 July 1644. Queen Henrietta Maria flees across to France with her baby, seeking refuge with her sister-in-law, Anne of Austria, the queen regent of France (→ 30/6/46).

Aberdeen, 13 September 1644. Forces led by James Graham, now the Marquis of Montrose, sack the city (→ 2/2/45).

Newcastle, 19 October 1644. The Covenanters seize the city.

Scotland, 11 February 1645. The Scottish parliament declares James Graham, the Marquis of Montrose, to be a traitor (→ 9/5).

Westminster, April 1645. Sir Thomas Fairfax is appointed as the first commander-in-chief of the new parliamentarian army (→ 14/6).

Grampian, 9 May 1645. Montrose leads his army to a royalist victory at Auldearn (→ 15/8).

Leicester, 31 May 1645. Prince Rupert sacks the city.

Kilsyth, 15 August 1645. The Marquis of Montrose stands ready to reclaim all Scotland for the King Charles following his sixth victory in a year (→ 9/1646).

Cheshire, 24 September 1645. After his defeat by roundheads at Rowton Heath, King Charles is unable to link up with his Scottish supporters (→ 28/10).

Chester, 3 February 1646. The roundheads seize the city from the royalists (→ 5/5).

Newark, 5 May 1646. King Charles surrenders to the Scots after escaping from Oxford last month in disguise (→ 7/1646).

Westminster, June 1646. Parliament forbids the use of the Prayer Book (→ 5/9).

Newcastle, July 1646. Charles refuses to meet the terms of the "Propositions of Newcastle" which have been presented to him by parliament (→ 20/12).

Westminster, 5 September 1646. Parliament votes unanimously to abolish the offices of bishop and archbishop (→ 5/1647).

Westminster, May 1647. Parliament orders the army to be disbanded (→ 26/7).

Westminster, 26 July 1647. A royalist mob invades parliament and forces through a resolution to invite King Charles back to London (→ 3/1/48).

Hampton Court, July 1647. Oliver Cromwell opens negotiations with Charles (→ 1/11).

Hampton Court, 11 Nov 1647. Charles escapes from house arrest and seeks freedom on the Isle of Wight (→ 26/12).

Westminster, 3 January 1648. On the discovery of King Charles's secret deal with the Scots, parliament passes a vote of "no addresses", thereby ending all negotiations (→ 15/11).

Pembroke, March 1648. The governor of Pembroke castle declares for Charles (→ 11/7).

London, 21 April 1648. James, the Duke of York, Charles's middle son, escapes from house arrest, fleeing to safety in the Netherlands.

England/Scotland, 8 July 1648. The Duke of Hamilton marches his army south into England, intending to restore King Charles to the throne (→ 20/8).

Pembroke, 11 July 1648. John Poyer, the governor of Pembroke castle, surrenders to Oliver Cromwell's army.

Uttoxeter, 25 August 1648. After his defeat at Preston, the Duke of Hamilton is forced to surrender to Cromwell's army (→ 4/10).

Edinburgh, 4 October 1648. The radical Covenanters are reinstated in power after a coup and the arrival of Cromwell's army in support (→ 5/2/49).

Westminster, 15 Nov 1648. Parliament votes to allow Charles to return to London (→ 2/12).

London, 5 December 1648. All those who voted for negotiations with Charles are expelled from parliament (→ 7/12).

Windsor, 17 December 1648. Charles is moved under guard from Hurst castle, in Hampshire, to Windsor (→ 26/12).

Westminster, 2 January 1649. A high court is appointed to try Charles for treason (→ 4/1).

Westminster, 4 January 1649. The Commons assume supreme control of the nation (→ 27/1).

Whitehall, 30 January 1649. Charles is executed (→ 4/2).

The Hague, 4 February 1649. Charles, the Prince of Wales, learns of his father's execution from his chaplain (→ 5/2).

Rotterdam, 9 April 1649. Lucy Walter, Charles's mistress, gives birth to a son, James (→ 1658).

Westminster, 19 May 1649. Parliament, after abolishing the House of Lords and the monarchy, declares Britain to be a commonwealth (→ 2/1/50).

Jersey, September 1649. Charles, accepted as king by the island, moves his exiled court here and with his uncle, Prince William II of Orange, plans to claim his throne.

Charles loses the north after battle in Yorkshire

A triumph for the parliamentarians, a tragedy for the royalists: this romanticised view of the battle at Marston Moor is by James Ward (1769-1859).

Marston Moor, 2 July 1644

The parliamentary armies, reinforced by the Scots and inspired by Cromwell's crack cavalry force, have won a crushing victory over the royalists here today. The triumph has vindicated the wisdom of the Solemn League and Covenant [*see page 240*] which brought the English parliament powerful military assistance in the north. Prince Rupert's cavaliers have been swept from the field, and Cromwell is claiming: "God made them as stubble to our swords." Having dealt with the cavalry, Cromwell's men turned on the foot. Many fled, but Newcastle's men held their positions in a series of enclosures and died where they stood.

They had vowed that they would dye their white coats with the blood of their enemies, but it is their own blood that stains their coats as they lie on the battlefield tonight. Much of the blame falls on the reckless Prince Rupert, who insisted on taking the field against the numerically superior roundhead army.

Rupert had been sent north by the king to relieve York where the Marquis of Newcastle was being besieged. He accomplished this task by brilliantly outmanoeuvring the besiegers, who then withdrew to Marston Moor. Newcastle argued that as the north was now safe Rupert should rejoin the king, but the prince insisted that his orders meant that he must give battle to the king's enemies.

The result has been the worst defeat yet suffered by the royalists.

Royalists fight back in the south-west

Lostwithiel, 2 September 1644

King Charles, undaunted by the disaster at Marston Moor, continues to strike back at his enemies in the south-west of England. He has today forced the surrender here of the parliamentary forces under the Earl of Essex. Two thousand roundhead horsemen did manage to break through the cavalier lines, but 6,000 men surrendered along with 5,000 muskets and pistols and 42 artillery pieces with their ammunition. However, the roundhead cavalry escaped, and Essex has fled by boat to Plymouth where he must explain his actions to his parliamentary masters (→ 27/10).

The whole of the north is now open to the combined parliamentary and Scottish forces. In one afternoon's fighting everything that Rupert gained has been lost and Newcastle's powerful army has been destroyed. The effects will be far-reaching. York, so bravely defended and brilliantly relieved, must now fall like a ripe plum to the parliamentarians and their Covenanter allies. The royal threat from the north-east has been wiped out, and the recruiting grounds and resources of the north will now be denied to the royalists.

The only comfort for the king is that Rupert was able to extricate his horsemen from the slaughter, but General Oliver Cromwell's well-disciplined and zealously religious soldiers have destroyed their aura of invincibility (→ 2/9).

King forced to retreat after disastrous campaign

The royalists and Cromwell's "New Model Army" line up at Naseby.

Charles is defeated in battle at Naseby

Naseby, Northants, 14 June 1645
A Scottish nobleman saved the king's life today when he seized the reins of Charles's horse to steer it from danger. But the sudden move was misunderstood: despite a successful series of charges the royalists took flight, and Prince Rupert had to fight hard to protect the king who has retreated to Leicester.

The defeat at Naseby is a major blow for Charles, who has lost most of his footsoldiers, cavalry and artillery in this set-piece battle. Yet the campaign had opened well for him. On 30 May Prince Rupert surrounded Leicester and stormed and sacked the town after it refused to surrender. Hundreds of royalist troops defected with their plunder.

Parliament was determined to stamp out the growing royalist activity in the Midlands. Its 22,000-strong "New Model Army", set up this February to combine the forces of Essex, Waller and Manchester with the renowned "Eastern Association" force, has proved its mettle. Its lieutenant-general is one Oliver Cromwell (→ 7/1645).

Letters found which discredit Charles

London, July 1645
Letters found in the king's cabinet, captured at the Battle of Naseby, are proving dangerously incriminating to the royalist cause. They prove beyond doubt that the king has been secretly intriguing to land an Irish army in England and to abolish laws against English Roman Catholics.

Worse still, the king is seen to have been prepared to introduce the soldiers of the Duke of Lorraine into his army, and one letter makes it clear that – despite his public protestations to the contrary – Charles has never regarded parliament as a lawful authority.

The letters have caused a major public outcry. Both houses of parliament listened in shocked silence as they were read out; Londoners rushed to buy printed versions as they appeared on the streets. Anyone doubting the authenticity was invited to view the originals.

The evidence is unassailable. One of the letters was written as late as 8 June. One London pamphleteer has written: "The key of the king's cabinet as it hath unlocked the mystery of former treaties so I hope it will lock up our minds from thoughts of future" (→ 14/9).

Rupert surrenders Bristol to Fairfax

Victorious: Sir Thomas Fairfax.

Bristol, 14 September 1645
A furious king sacked his nephew from all his offices today and ordered him to seek his fortune in another country. Prince Rupert's crime was to surrender Bristol after a fierce battle. The most desperate fighting took place at Prior's fort where parliamentarians slaughtered most of the defenders. Rupert had no chance. After firing the city in three places he accepted terms dictated by the New Model Army's captain-general, Sir Thomas Fairfax, eager to save lives (→ 27/4/46).

Royalists shock the Scots Covenanters

Inverlochy, 2 February 1645
As the wintry sun sets over the mountains, 1,500 men of the Campbell clan lie dead in the shadow of Inverlochy castle. James Graham, the Marquis of Montrose, has scored a sensational victory over the forces of the Covenant. Montrose wrote to the king at Uxbridge in Middlesex, where peace negotiations inspired by the Scots have almost stalled, urging him not to make peace after so many victories had been gained in Scotland. Montrose and his Highland bands have been so successful that many now believe that a major royalist revival has begun in Scotland (→ 11/2).

Nobles do their best to fend off parliamentary money-raisers

King Charles with one of his loyal supporters, Sir Edward Walker.

Hertfordshire, 1645
Life is not all a bed of roses for the wealthy Countess of Sussex in these wartime days. "I am loath to eat off pewter," she has confided. "But truly I have put up [hidden] most of my plate and say it is sold." She and other English nobles can expect regular visits from commissioners charged with raising weekly sums to pay for the war. Evasion is commonplace, needless to say, especially by the king's supporters. The wealthy Marquis of Worcester gave local commissioners a warm welcome, but then he made a servant turn on a noisy hydraulic machine before shouting: "The lions are all got loose!" The commission withdrew at speed.

Prince of Wales is safe with mother

France, 30 June 1646
The Prince of Wales has arrived in this Catholic country and settled at St Germain with his mother. For the past summer he has enjoyed a season of sailing and social pleasure in Jersey, eating off gold and silver platters in Elizabeth castle and attending levées. Now, only 15 years old, he is at the centre of a complex – and unlikely – plot to unite French, Irish and English Catholics and royalists (→ 4/2/49).

Montrose retreats after heavy defeat

Scotland, September 1646
James Graham, the Marquis of Montrose, has retreated to the highlands following his disastrous defeat near Selkirk this month. A Covenanter army led by David Leslie attacked the Irish mercenaries who make up the bulk of Montrose's infantry at their camp at Philiphaugh; Montrose and his cavalry, quartered a mile away, arrived too late to rescue them from a humiliating surrender. The defeat spells the end of Charles's hopes in Scotland. It has been a long decline since August of last year, when Montrose's triumph at Kilsyth made all Scotland seem vulnerable. Now he will probably flee (→ 20/12).

Raglan castle falls to the roundheads

Raglan, Gwent, 19 August 1646
To the beat of drums and the proud blasts of trumpets, the garrison of this castle marched out in surrender today. Heavy artillery has pounded the great building for the past two months and, despite an heroic defence, the Marquis of Worcester was forced to fly the white flag and watch from the great window in the hall as General Fairfax and his officers entered.

The king stayed here for a few weeks after the defeat of the royalist army at Naseby and relaxed by playing bowls against the local champion on a courtyard overlooking the village of Raglan.

Charles escapes 'disguised as a servant'

Oxford under siege: but King Charles has now escaped, in disguise.

Oxford, 27 April 1646
Disguised as a servant, his hair and beard closely trimmed, the king made his escape from Oxford today and headed for London. As Charles rode over Magdalen Bridge in apparent attendance on two gentlemen, the governor called out: "Farewell, Harry!" London is not the eventual destination, however; Charles is in fact planning to meet Montrose and his Scottish army at Newark in the east Midlands.

With Fairfax's army advancing from the west, the siege of Oxford is imminent. During his stay here – and it has been his secure headquarters since 1642 – Charles has tried to negotiate with the army, but Cromwell has instructed Fairfax not to listen to any overtures for peace. An appeal to Colonel Rainsborough, the commander of the force attacking Woodstock, ten miles (16 km) north-west of Oxford, to take the king under his protection has not been answered.

Charles has placed his hopes on the Scots, who he hopes are prepared to drop their demands for his conversion to Presbyterianism. One report speaks of 2,000 cavalrymen prepared to meet the king at Gainsborough. The king reached the outskirts of London tonight before he turned north (→ 5/5).

Scots lose patience with royal 'guest'

Edinburgh, 20 December 1646
The Scottish parliament has told its "guest", the king of England, that it will hand him over to the English unless he agrees to impose the Covenant and confirm the Presbyterian national church. The Scots have lost patience with the king's equivocation between themselves and the English parliament.

Charles has been delaying a response to the "Propositions of Newcastle" – put to him by the English last June – in the hope that he might get a better deal from the Scots. After his escape from Oxford he made his way through the parliamentary lines to the Scottish camp at Newark. Charles expected to find himself an honoured guest, as the possession of the king was regarded as a trump card in the diplomatic game being played out between England and its northern neighbour. Instead, he found himself a prisoner.

Apart from the major demands on the national religion, the Scottish Parliament is seeking control of the armed forces for the next 20 years and the king's consent to the punishment of all his leading supporters. The king had hoped to exploit differences between the Scots and the English to his own advantage. He had not allowed for the possibility of a settlement between the two sides (→ 1/1647).

Radical agitators demand far-reaching and irreversible reforms

A broadsheet illustrating the cruelties inflicted by the royalist army.

London, November 1646
A pamphlet called *London's Liberty in Chains* is currently causing a stir around the capital. The tract, by John Lilburne, a leading member of the "Levellers" faction, is a devastating attack on parliament's achievements so far. Lilburne says that things are little better than they were before and, together with his fellow pamphleteers Richard Overton and William Walwyn, advocates a programme of reform which includes manhood suffrage, the formation of a republic, the abolition of the House of Lords and total religious freedom. The extent to which these radical ideas are winning supporters in London is starting to worry parliament.

▷

Scots hand the king back to parliament

Delivered to the parliamentarians: Charles is handed over at Newcastle.

Cromwell backs the army in new clash

Newmarket, 4 June 1647
Oliver Cromwell, the lieutenant-general of the New Model Army and MP for Cambridge, has arrived for Sir Thomas Fairfax's general rendezvous of the army, having left London hurriedly to avoid being arrested by Presbyterian extremists in the Commons. After months during which Cromwell was unsure whether to back the king, the army, parliament or the Scots in the complex negotiations on the future British constitution, news of the king's arrest [*see report below*] seems to have made up his mind. One of the most formidable figures in the confused British political scene has thrown in his lot with the army.

The military's relations with parliament have reached a new nadir. Fewer than one in ten soldiers have volunteered for service in Ireland because the conditions are so poor. Parliament has treated a petition from the men as mutiny and voted in April to disband the army with no more than six weeks' pay.

Army regiments have elected agents, known as "agitators", to represent their grievances on pay and disbandment. Fairfax has created a general council in which agitators, officers and generals debate grievances collectively. But there is a worrying tide of radical puritanism, influenced by the Levellers [*see previous page*] in the ranks (→14/6).

General demands reform of Commons

Ireton: challenging parliament.

St Albans, 14 June 1647
A new civil war – this time between parliament and the army – is threatening to engulf England as the New Model Army, refusing to disband, advances on London and parliament. General Henry Ireton has drafted a manifesto here that makes it clear that the army is not a "mere mercenary army" but a political force with a political programme. Ireton insists that the army was "called forth and conjured by the several declarations of parliament to the defence of our own and the people's just rights and liberties".

Parliament has tried to raise a counter-force from disbanded soldiers, with little success. Bound together by common grievances, the troops are united behind Fairfax and Cromwell. Ireton's document demands that parliament purges itself of members unworthy of their trust and fixes a date for its dissolution. It also wants seats to be redistributed, to make the Commons more representative, and elections to be held every three years.

The king, now held by the army and often in discussion with its leaders, must assent to these reforms before his own position can be properly established "so far as may consist with the right and freedom of the subject". Whether he will remains to be seen (→7/1647).

Newcastle, January 1647
The king of England was returned to the English parliament tonight following the latter's agreement to cover the cost of the Scottish army in the war. The Scots handed "Charles Stuart" over to commissioners dispatched to the north from London. As soon as the weather improves, Charles will be taken to a parliamentary "safe house" at Holmby, in Northamptonshire, where he will rest while parliament decides how to proceed.

The king has adamantly refused to accept the concept of Presbyterianism as the official form of worship for England and Scotland despite the pleadings of his queen

and two trusted courtiers, Digby and Ashburnham. Had he done so, he might have won the support of the Scottish kirk and thus divided parliamentary opinion.

Charles might have made his refusal clear last June had he not preferred to vacillate while parliament became weaker and more divided by the day. But he has now lost the secure protection of the Scots and helped to bring in a new factor. With the return of relative peace, parliamentary soldiers who had been kept busy fighting have now had time to think. Radical ideas abound, and many soldiers regard the English Parliament as being too soft on the king (→3/6).

King Charles is seized by roundhead soldiers at Holmby House

Holmby, Northants, 3 June 1647
King Charles has been taken away from the certainties of house arrest here into an altogether more uncertain future. He has spent the last few months relaxing under parliamentary supervision, whiling away the hours by reading, playing chess and bowls with his jailers and going riding. That peace was shattered in the early hours of this morning when one Joyce, a cornet in Colonel Whalley's regiment, arrived at Holmby House at the head of a troop of horse, saying that he had come to fetch the king. Charles made ready to depart at dawn. He hopes to have better luck dealing with the army than he had with parliament and the Scots (→4/6).

Joyce's soldiers take King Charles from his bedroom at Holmby House.

King signs a secret deal with the Scots

Isle of Wight, 26 December 1647

A secret treaty between King Charles and the Scots was tonight wrapped in lead and buried in the garden of Carisbrooke castle, where Charles has been imprisoned. The "Engagement", as the document is known, was negotiated by three Scottish commissioners who have been allowed access to Charles by the sympathetic governor.

Under the terms of the treaty, the Scots are to raise another army to restore the king, who has promised to establish a Presbyterian church in England for three years. Charles has been careful to retain his personal freedom of worship while agreeing to suppress the independent sects – like the Anabaptists – which pose a radical challenge to Presbyterian and Episcopalian Churches alike.

This year has seen the army, parliament and the Scots all discussing terms with Charles, and today the Scots have won. The parliamentarians, who have treated him well so far, will not be pleased (→ 3/1/48).

Cromwell crushes royalists at Preston

Preston, 20 August 1648

Exhausted, and caked with mud after two days of fierce fighting in heavy rain, hundreds of Scottish and English infantry and cavalrymen surrendered today to Oliver Cromwell. It is a roundhead victory which has crushed all hopes of a royalist comeback.

In May the Earl of Norwich led a 10,000-strong royalist force which captured several coastal towns and forts in Kent and tried to march on London, but which faded away when faced by Fairfax's well-disciplined campaign. Currently under siege at Colchester, Norwich's men are not expected to last long once they hear of the defeat at Preston.

The Marquis of Hamilton led the most serious challenge to Cromwell's new order with an Anglo-Scottish force of over 20,000 men, but Cromwell and his lieutenant, Major-General John Lambert, dealt with it confidently (→ 25/8).

Army takes control of king and Commons

A broadsheet showing Charles under house arrest on the Isle of Wight.

London, 2 December 1648

Affairs have taken a sudden turn for the worse for King Charles. Frustrated by the indecision of the Commons, the army reoccupied the capital today. Yesterday soldiers seized the king and took him under close guard from the Isle of Wight across the Solent to Hurst castle. It is probably his first step on the road to Westminster and his trial.

Events have moved swiftly since 20 November, when General Henry Ireton – a civil war veteran who is also Cromwell's son-in-law – presented parliament with the *Remonstrance of the Army*, a manifesto demanding that the king be put on trial for treason, his crime being to start the war which tore the nation apart. The Commons, clinging to the hope of a negotiated settlement with Charles, dithered before finally rejecting the Remonstrance. Ireton wants to dissolve parliament altogether, but the army's general council has instructed him merely to purge it of all but the radical minority who will back the impeachment of the king.

Oliver Cromwell is meanwhile occupied in the north of England. As both an MP and the leader of the army, he is trying to keep aloof from the tumultuous events which look set to culminate in the use of force against the elected members of parliament (→ 5/12).

Parliament reduced to obedient 'rump'

"Pride's Purge": MPs are ejected.

Westminster, 7 December 1648

For the second day running, Colonel Thomas Pride has stationed himself at the door of the House of Commons with a troop of musketeers. Acting on the instructions of General Ireton, he has excluded or ejected from the chamber about 140 members. A remnant or "rump" of some 60 reliable independents remains. The incident, already known as "Pride's Purge", leaves a lower house which will comply with the next step in the army's programme by providing a legal framework in which to try King Charles and abolish the monarchy (→ 17/12).

Could fate be the key to the rapid rise of Cromwell?

Westminster, 26 December 1648

Oliver Cromwell has always believed in submitting to fate, and today was no exception. Until now he has argued against putting the king on trial, but today in parliament, where he is the MP for Cambridge, he saw which way the tide was flowing: "Since the providence of God hath cast this upon us, I cannot but submit to providence," he declared, putting his weight behind the move to try King Charles for treason.

It is, perhaps, a surprising attitude for a man who has been one of the main catalysts in the Civil War. Always a radical, and puritan by belief, he came into his own in 1642 when he helped to propel the nation into armed resistance to the king's army. A series of triumphs in 1643 with his own "Ironside" regiment made his military reputation. Two years later he was made lieutenant-general of the New Model Army, which he helped to create. His military brilliance, combined with vigorous and intelligent speech-making in parliament, has made Cromwell, at 49 years old, the main contender for the leadership of a kingless nation (→ 2/1/49).

Man of the moment: Cromwell.

Charles is beheaded after conviction for treason

The king accused: Charles on trial in Westminster Hall, by Wm Fisk (d.1872).

Parliament condemns the king to death

London, 27 January 1649
Charles Stuart was found guilty of treason today and sentenced to death. Efforts are under way to collect signatures on his death warrant – not an easy task, as the possibly lethal consequences are measured. Fifty-nine men, mostly soldiers led by Oliver Cromwell and Henry Ireton, have signed the warrant. One notably absent signature is that of General Sir Thomas Fairfax, who played such a major part in the king's defeat. Fairfax has made only one appearance at the trial, although Lady Fairfax made a dramatic protest against it.

Eight days ago the king was brought to London at short notice and housed at St James's palace. On the following day he was carried to Whitehall in a sedan chair, its blinds drawn, with a strong escort of infantry. He was lodged in a room adjoining the Banqueting House, and then all privacy, for either his prayers or his needs to obey nature, was denied to him.

The tribunal heard evidence that the king had permitted or encouraged the ill-treatment of prisoners and that he had plotted for a resumption of the war during his captivity. Charles, refusing to recognise the legality of a court trying a king for an offence against his own crown, declined to plead. "It is the freedom and the liberty of the people of England" that were on trial, he proclaimed. "... pretend what you will, I stand more for their liberties." The king's defence was so moving that one judge burst into tears. But it was not enough to save him from the guilty verdict and death sentence today (→ 30/1).

King Charles is brought to the scaffold, by Ernest Croft (d.1911).

Dignified last moments on the scaffold

Whitehall, 30 January 1649
A great howl went up from the crowd huddled outside Whitehall palace today as Charles, the British king, was beheaded for treason.

It was a bitterly cold morning and the king put on two shirts lest, he said, he might be seen to shiver on the scaffold. He gave directions for the disposal of his bible, his gold watch and other personal effects among his children, two of whom, Princess Elizabeth and Henry, the Duke of Gloucester, aged 13 and eight, bade him farewell yesterday; then the king knelt to receive the sacrament of Communion.

Between nine and ten o'clock a knock on the door warned the king that it was time for him to walk from St James's palace across the park to Whitehall where his executioners were waiting.

Then there was an interminable delay when it was pointed out to Cromwell that the law demanded that the Prince of Wales must be proclaimed king as soon his father was dead. The king was ushered into an ante-room to wait while parliament rushed through three readings of a bill that made such a proclamation illegal.

At two o'clock the king came out of the Banqueting House "with the same unconcernedness and motion that he usually had ... on a masque night". The crowd was noisy, and few heard Charles's last words which he read from a small piece of paper. He proclaimed his Christian faith, emphasised his loyalty to the Church of England and forgave "even those in particular that have been the chief causers of my death".

The block was unusually low, and the king was forced to lie rather than kneel for his execution. He stretched out his hands – a prearranged signal – and his head was severed in one blow. It was when the executioner's assistant held the head up to the crowd that a great shout went up. It was a howl more of horror at the act of regicide than of grief at the king's death (→ 8/2).

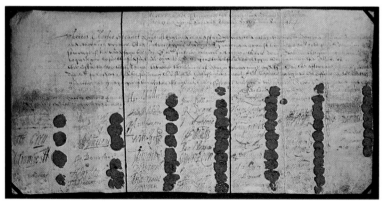

The king condemned: the warrant which will send Charles to his death.

Scots declare that young Prince Charles is king – if he becomes Presbyterian

Scotland, 5 February 1649
The Scottish Parliament today showed its disgust at the execution of King Charles by declaring his son to be the lawful successor to the throne. The English judges have offended Scots loyalties by killing a Scottish king without any reference to the Scottish nation.

Parliament is composed of three estates, the nobles and representatives of the gentry and of the towns, who elect a committee of estates which wields executive power. A general assembly of ministers and elders is elected by local presbyteries of the kirk.

At present the most powerful Scotsman is Archibald Campbell, the Marquis of Argyll, who has held on to high office throughout his country's last few chequered years and is the virtual dictator of Scotland. The red-haired, squint-eyed Campbell is from the kirk party – the one with the most representation in parliament – and is at the forefront in the fight to reform the Church of England; King Charles II would be a valuable tool to achieve this.

The kirk party has every reason to back an alliance with the new king, Charles II: it would confirm its power, even though it is generally detested by the more traditional Scots leaders. Argyll's party has insisted that the king subscribes to

Charles, the exiled Prince of Wales.

the Solemn League and Covenant of 1643 [*see page 240*] and promises to establish Presbyterianism in both England and Scotland. The kirk party also expects Charles to dismiss exiled Scottish royalists from his court and drop anyone to whom it has taken exception.

Commissioners from both parliament and the general assembly have visited Charles in exile at The Hague to set out the terms. Argyll sent his agent ahead to assure the king of his personal loyalty and plead with the king to join the alliance. It looks as though Charles might be tempted.

Parliament attacks book written by king

London, 16 March 1649
Now the king's death has become a matter for propagandists from both royalists and their enemies. A book supppposedly written by the king – *Eikon Basilike, the Pourtraiture of His Sacred Majestie in his Solitude and Sufferings* – is in constant demand and has reached its 50th reprint. Every effort is being made to suppress the book, but translations are appearing throughout Europe. The English council of state has been forced to employ John Milton, the poet and author, as a counter propagandist. His book, with the lengthy title *The Tenure of Kings and Magistrates; proving it is lawfull, and hath been held so through all ages, for Any, Who hath the power to Account a Tyrant or Wicked King, and after Due Conviction to Depose and Put Him to Death*, much of it written as an observer at Charles's trial, has so far sold two editions only.

An anti-royalist tract represents King Charles glorying in his vanity.

Monarch and Lords abolished by vote

London, 17 March 1649
Sweeping moves to abolish the monarchy and the House of Lords are contained in an act passed by parliament today declaring England to be a "commonwealth and free state" and defining parliament itself as the "supreme authority of this nation." Parliament was united on this, but deep divisions are beginning to show now that the king has been executed. In an attempt to stop the mutinous tide sweeping an army still furious at being sent to Ireland, Cromwell has sent leading Levellers – whose propaganda has fuelled the discontent – to the Tower of London (→ 19/5).

The late king's body is secretly buried in the chapel at Windsor

A secret funeral: a Victorian view of Charles's burial at Windsor.

Whitehall, 8 February 1649
The head and carcass of Charles Stuart were loaded onto a cart here tonight and taken in the greatest secrecy to Windsor castle. The king's embalmed remains will be entombed in St George's chapel, the traditional resting-place of the crowned heads of England. The scenes that followed the execution – hundreds fought to dip cloths in the king's blood – have led to fears that the king might be more potent dead than alive. There will be no state funeral, and public mourning will be banned. Before the king was moved, a lone man, his face hidden in his cloak, was seen to approach the body and say "Cruel necessity". It was Oliver Cromwell.

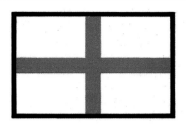

COMMONWEALTH
1649–1653
PROTECTORATE
1653–1660

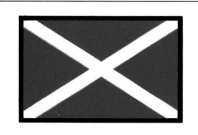

Low Countries, 16 March 1650. Charles and his council meet the Covenanters at Breda to negotiate his return (→ 17/4).

Breda, 17 April 1650. After much compromise, Charles agrees that he will endorse the Covenant, confirm all acts of parliament and recognise the authority of the Scottish Parliament (→ 27/4).

Highland, 27 April 1650. James Graham, the Marquis of Montrose, leads a royalist expedition against the Covenanters but is defeated at Carbisdale (→ 21/5).

Edinburgh, 21 May 1650. The Marquis of Montrose is hanged for treason after his defeat at Carbisdale last month.

London, 4 June 1650. Oliver Cromwell returns as a hero after subduing the Irish (→ 26/6).

Garmouth, 24 June 1650. Charles lands in Scotland to claim his throne (→ 22/7).

Scottish Borders, 22 July 1650. Oliver Cromwell, the newly-appointed army chief, crosses the river Tweed with his forces to invade Scotland (→ 3/9).

Scotland, 3 September 1650. Charles, unable to fulfil the promises that he made, writes to William II of Orange and lays plans for his flight (→ 5/10).

Isle of Wight, 8 September 1650. Elizabeth, Charles's 14-year-old sister, dies in Carisbrooke castle.

Tayside, 5 October 1650. King Charles is recaptured by the Covenanters at Glen Clova, following his escape during a botched royalist coup (→ 1/1/51).

The Hague, 4 November 1650. Mary, the Princess Royal, gives birth to the first son and heir of the late Prince William II of Orange; he is called William (→ 7/9/53).

Edinburgh, 24 Dec 1650. The castle surrenders to Oliver Cromwell's forces (→ 20/7).

Tayside, 1 January 1651. Charles II is crowned king of Scotland at Scone.→

Inverkeithing, 20 July 1651. Royalist troops are defeated by Oliver Cromwell (→ 2/8).

Perth, 2 August 1651. Having seized the town, Oliver Cromwell pursues fleeing Scottish royalists across the border into northern England (→ 3/9).

Lancashire, August 1651. King Charles and his supporters join forces with Charles Stanley, the Earl of Derby and prepare to face the parliamentarians (→ 3/9).

Worcester, 3 September 1651. Charles's ragged Scottish army is crushed by Oliver Cromwell's forces (→ 14/10).

West Sussex, 16 October 1651. King Charles flees into exile after his disastrous defeat last month at Worcester (→ 5/1652).

Westminster, 24 December 1651. The English Parliament makes public its intention of incorporating the kingdom of Scotland into that of England (→ 24/2/52).

Westminster, 24 February 1652. Parliament pardons all royalists by passing the Act of Oblivion.

Paris, May 1652. The French king, Louis XIV, awards the exiled Charles Stuart a pension of £450 a month (→ 6/1653).

Inveraray, 12 August 1652. Archibald Campbell, the Marquis of Argyll submits to the English occupying forces, marking the completion of the English conquest of Scotland.

France, 1652/53. It is rumoured that Elizabeth Killigrew, the wife of an Anglo-Irish courtier, is Charles's new mistress.

Germany, 7 September 1653. Homeless and poverty-stricken, Charles visits the spa town of Aachen with his sister Princess Mary of Orange (→ 11/1653).

England, November 1653. Royalist sympathisers form the "Sealed Knot", an organisation which is determined to put Charles Stuart back on the throne (→ 3/1655).

London, 16 Dec 1653. Cromwell becomes the Lord Protector.→

Dalkeith, Scotland, 22 April 1654. General George Monck arrives as the new commander-in-chief of the English occupying army (→ 19/7).

Westminster, April 1654. Relations between Britain and the United Provinces improve with the signing of a treaty (→ 12/9).

Highlands, 19 July 1654. The royalist rising in Scotland suffers a major setback with the defeat of General Middleton.

Westminster, 12 September 1654. Oliver Cromwell, the Lord Protector, demands that parliament must promise not to change the constitution (→ 12/1654).

Westminster, December 1654. Oliver Cromwell tries to stop parliament restricting religious toleration (→ 9/1655).

Wiltshire, March 1655. Major-General John Desborough crushes a royalist uprising led by John Penruddock.

Dublin, 9 July 1655. Oliver Cromwell's younger son, Henry, arrives to take up his position as commander-in-chief (→ 1657).

Edinburgh, September 1655. A council of state is appointed by Oliver Cromwell to control Scotland (→ 14/5/60).

Cologne, March 1656. Charles, despite his austere style of living, is in debt for £3,200 (→ 2/4).

Westminster, 26 June 1656. As the rising cost of war with Spain mounts, Oliver Cromwell calls a new parliament (→ 8/5/57).

Bruges, Low Countries, 1656. Charles creates his own regiment of guards (→ 6/1657).

Westminster, 26 June 1657. Oliver Cromwell is inaugurated as Lord Protector for the second time.

Spain, June 1657. Charles's regiment goes into service under the Spanish flag (→ 14/6/58).

Ireland, 1657. Henry Cromwell is given the title lord deputy of Ireland.

Flanders, 14 June 1658. The Cromwellian army allies with the French against the Spanish (→ 3/9).

England, 23 November 1658. A funeral procession takes place for the late Oliver Cromwell, who was buried two weeks ago (→ 16/5/59).

Westminster, 24 May 1659. Richard Cromwell, who has succeeded his father Oliver as lord protector, resigns after the army revolts and insists on recalling the members of the rump parliament. Britain is a commonwealth once again (→ 13/10).

Westminster, 13 October 1659. Major-General John Lambert attempts to mount a coup to overthrow the recalled rump parliament (→ 6/2/60).

Cromwell takes control

Oliver Cromwell is now commander-in-chief of the Commonwealth forces.

London, 26 June 1650

The news that King Charles II has landed in Scotland and reached an agreement with the Covenanters has made a military clash inevitable, and Oliver Cromwell is to lead the English attack. Sir Thomas Fairfax, the commander-in-chief of the army, has just resigned his commission rather than attack Presbyterians. Since the execution of King Charles I – with which he did not agree – Fairfax has become increasingly withdrawn.

Perhaps it was the realisation that he was unable to stop the execution of the king which brought home to Fairfax that, despite his title, it was his theoretical subordinate Oliver Cromwell who really wielded the power. Even so, Cromwell has been remarkably reluctant to take charge. Having just returned from a particularly bloody campaign in Ireland, during which the defenders of Wexford and Drogheda were massacred, Cromwell was not keen to go to war again so

soon, even though he was convinced that the Scots would invade in an attempt to put Charles II on the throne.

Cromwell thought that it was vital to attack first, but – understandably, being just back from Ireland – felt that he had done enough for the moment and it was up to someone else to march north and foil the Scots. The obvious candidate to lead the army was its commander-in-chief, but Fairfax refused to do so on principle.

In an argument that went on for most of last night, Cromwell tried to persuade him to go, pointing out that if there had to be a war it was better to fight in Scotland than in England. But Fairfax remained unmoved and replied that "probabilities are not sufficient ground to make war upon a neighbouring nation". Faced with Sir Thomas's refusal, Cromwell has today taken up the appointmen of commander-in-chief of all the forces of the Commonwealth (→ 22/7).

All men must swear allegiance to state

Westminster, 2 January 1650

Britain is no longer a monarchy, and the rump parliament today ordered every man aged 18 or over to swear an oath of loyalty to the new Commonwealth "without a king and House of Lords". The Engagement, as the new oath is called, is intended to protect the fragile new constitution from attacks from royalists on the one hand and ultra-radical "Levellers" on the other.

The Commonwealth is run by a 41-member council of state which acts on the resolutions of the rump parliament – the MPs left after Pride's Purge had removed any supporters of the king [*see page 247*]. Supreme power over the nation no longer rests in the monarchy, even as a figurehead, but in the House of Commons (→ 24/12/51).

Cromwell snatches victory over Scots

Dunbar, 3 September 1650

Oliver Cromwell, now commander-in-chief of all the forces of the Commonwealth, has inflicted a total defeat on the Scottish army here today. His victory is all the more to be admired since his demoralised army had been chased all the way from Edinburgh by the Scots under their veteran general David Leslie.

Cromwell found himself in retreat, trapped with his back against the sea at Dunbar by Leslie's much larger army. His skill as a tactician snatched victory from the jaws of defeat: a dawn strike quickly overwhelmed Leslie's infantry in the centre of his battle line, whereupon Cromwell led a flanking movement that wiped out the Scottish horse. Ten thousand Scots have been captured and 3,000 killed (→ 24/12).

Golfing new king is crowned in Scotland

Charles is crowned king (right), and (left) prepares for battle.

Scone, 1 January 1651

King Charles II was crowned king of England, Scotland, Ireland and France (the latter title merely traditional) today at a ceremony which reflected the austere preferences of the Covenanters. The king wore a rich robe and sat beneath a canopy of crimson velvet, but pomp was kept to a minimum; the crown and sceptre were handed to him by Covenanter lords, and the anointing with oil was left out on the grounds that it was mere superstition. The

ceremony was dominated by a long and tedious sermon by the moderator of the general assembly, who took as his theme the collapse of monarchy – a subject hardly likely to endear him to the new king. Next, the names of over a hundred of Charles's predecessors were recited. When it was all over Charles II retired to a long overdue feast that included partridges and 22 salmon. The new king then worked it off by playing a round of golf, the Scottish national game (→ 8/1651).

Capture of Dundee smashes Scottish royalist uprising

Dundee, 1 September 1651

The last Scottish resistance to Cromwell ended today when parliamentary forces under General Monck stormed Dundee and in a bloody fight routed the defenders. It was the end of a long struggle by the Scots which had been going on for two years, and they fought every inch of the way.

Despite their demoralising defeat at Dunbar last year, resistance continued to spark and flare all over the country. Edinburgh castle refused to surrender until 24 December, after the Covenanter army had been crushed. The coronation of Charles II [*see previous page*] shortly afterwards acted as rallying call, and from then on the quarrel between English and Scots stopped being doctrinal and became a national struggle. Scotland gathered the last of its strength for an invasion of England that would put Charles on the throne – an expedition that is now approaching Worcester. Almost all of the remaining Scottish fighting men who stayed behind perished or were captured in the battle for Dundee.

Cromwell has already made it clear how he intends to deal with the Scots for their support of the king. Last month, while in Scotland, he had the entire standing committees of parliament and the general assembly – the only remnants of an independent Scottish government – arrested (→ 12/8/52).

Parliamentary hero: George Monck, who destroyed Scottish resistance.

Charles flees after military disaster

Tree hides fugitive king at Worcester

Shoreham, W Sussex, 14 Oct 1651

Charles II has set sail for France after spending six weeks on the run in the most dangerous circumstances. Hunted by parliamentary troops, he had a £1,000 price on his head, and as he is a big man – over six feet tall – with distinctive black hair and a dark complexion, he is not easy to hide.

The king became a fugitive after Cromwell had inflicted a crushing defeat on his army at Worcester. In early August, as Cromwell occupied Perth, Charles had seized his chance to lead a 14,000-strong force of Scots and royalists over the border into England. But he had fallen into a trap. General Monck occupied Stirling to prevent any retreat, and Cromwell shadowed the king as he made his way towards London to reclaim the throne.

Charles failed to gather the support that he had hoped for in the north, and as the armies headed south Cromwell's force hovered over the royalists' left flank. If and when the king turned east towards London, a terrible slaughter would be inflicted. Charles headed west instead, and battle was joined at Worcester on 3 September. Cromwell routed his army and cut off his escape route to Wales; the king fled the town in a desperate cavalry charge down the high street.

King Charles then disguised himself, blacking his face and donning a worn suit. After finding that the ferry across the river Severn was guarded, he turned back, intending to hide in woods around Boscobel House. There Charles met William Carlis, another Worcester fugitive and a Catholic, who warned him that the woods were being searched by Cromwell's men. The two men hid in the branches of a lone oak tree in an open field, correctly reasoning that it was too isolated to attract attention. Disguised as the servant of Jane Lane, the sister of one of his colonels, the king made the hazardous trek southward. After great tribulations, he is at last sailing across the Channel in a coal-brig called *Surprise* (→ 16/10).

Mr Iane Lane and King:

the Kings escape in the sea Adventure

King Charles makes a daring escape after his defeat at Worcester.

Mystery illness hits exiled king in France

Paris, June 1653

King Charles II has recently become seriously ill with a fever whose cause cannot be diagnosed. Weighed down by the troubles of his exile, his lack of money, the uncertainty of his future and the piteous pleas of his dwindling and increasingly impecunious band of courtiers for financial help which he cannot give, it is perhaps not surprising that he has finally been brought down by illness.

The French government has granted Charles a pension of almost £6,000 a year, paid in monthly instalments. This sounds generous enough, but unfortunately the French are extremely lax about paying it, and often the money does not appear for months on end. To bridge the gap Charles is forced to borrow, and the pension, when it *does* turn up, has to be used to pay off his existing debts – after which he is forced to borrow still more.

In an attempt to raise cash, Charles has taken to issuing privateering warrants to French captains, allowing them to prey on English shipping. Charles is entitled to a share of the profits of this piracy, but the French are so adept at avoiding payment that, of warrants totalling £3,300, the king's agent received just £24. The agent then pocketed the £24, saying that it was part payment for £70 that he had lent the king. In such circumstances it is understandable that King Charles has been laid low. He has been bled five times for his fever, but he remains sick and withdrawn (→ 7/9).

Cromwell is installed as Lord Protector

Whitehall, 16 December 1653
Oliver Cromwell was installed today as Lord Protector of England, Scotland and Ireland. In future he will be addressed as "His Highness the Lord Protector" and will sign documents as Oliver P. In fact, only two days ago he was being petitioned to become king by Major-General John Lambert and other officers, but refused. According to reports, it was Cromwell himself who balked at the idea of being made king because he felt that it had two disadvantages.

The first was that the title would have angered an army still obsessed at all levels by republicanism. The second was that Cromwell felt that "Lord Protector", a title used before during the minority of monarchs, would convey the idea of a more temporary hold on power and be more acceptable to all strata of society than the idea of permanence implicit in the title of king.

The protectorate itself was established by the council of army officers as part of the Instrument of Government, which became law today. This statute sets up a new constitution, vesting authority in the Lord Protector and a 460-member House of Commons, and ensuring religious toleration for all except Catholics (→ 10/7/54).

The 'Barebones' parliament is dissolved

This Dutch print shows Cromwell dissolving the "Barebones" parliament.

Westminster, 12 December 1653
In a move that has surprised everyone, including Oliver Cromwell, the "Barebones" parliament has voted to dissolve itself and place all its powers in Cromwell's hands. This is the result of a coup organised by Major-General John Lambert, who wants Cromwell to adopt a constitution drawn up by himself and several officers. Known as the Instrument of Government, it is the first written constitution in English history [*see above*].

The Barebones parliament, called after one of its more colourful figures, the Anabaptist extremist Praisegod Barebones, was not elected but nominated after Cromwell dissolved the rump parliament earlier this year. Hoping to get a compliant legislature, Cromwell and the army leaders wrote to the churches in each county asking for nominations. They then selected those whom they thought would be politically reliable.

The plan backfired because many of the nominees were religious zealots. Their desire to impose godliness did not make up for their lack of experience in public affairs, and they proved capable of agreeing on almost nothing. Finally, encouraged by Lambert, the moderates rose early one morning and voted themselves out of power before the zealots were awake (→ 16/12).

Lawyers and generals are aristocrats of the British republic's new ruling class

Peace at last: an idyllic scene of the rural English life of this time.

England, 1656
Cromwell might not be popular, but people are mainly ready to accept his government because it guarantees peace after a period of traumatic social upheaval and war. There is certainly no great desire to restore the monarchy, waiting, in the form of Charles II, on the continent, although there are plenty of plotting royalists and Scotland has been in a state of rebellion since 1653.

Cromwell's government has not in fact resulted in anything that could be called fundamental social changes. There have been changes; plenty of land has been sold by royalists to fund the fines and extra taxes that they have to pay, but it has not been sold to the poor – who cannot afford it – but to those members of the gentry who support parliament. Those gentry have almost exactly the same social outlook as the previous owners.

More progress has been made towards some sort of social change by the confiscation and disposal of the estates of the crown, the church and conspicuous cavalier leaders. These were mostly sold to solid supporters of the regime, which has formed a new, synthetic ruling class of lawyers, generals and officials – men of varied social status who have risen in the service of parliament or the army and are now able to run their districts on the regime's behalf.

The greatest achievement of Cromwell has been the organisation of religious life. Only a minimum of state control over religion is being exercised, although bodies of "ejectors" (able to expel ministers unfit to hold office) and "triers" (to approve the appointment of ministers) have been set up. In practice they do not exercise their powers very often. What concerns most people are the campaigns to suppress alehouses, gambling and sports, particularly on Sundays. This gives the regime a kill-joy image.

A leading republican poet and pamphleteer: John Milton.

Royalist plotter is executed for trying to kill Cromwell

Colonel John Gerard: executed.

London, 10 July 1654

Royalist plotters whose scheme to ambush and kill the Lord Protector on the road to Hampton Court was discovered by Cromwell's efficient secret service have paid the price. The former cavalier colonel John Gerard, who was to have led a posse of 30 men to seize the Protector, was executed today. One other conspirator has been sentenced to death, and three face the perils of transportation to the New World. Gerard died bravely, speaking in defence of his royalist beliefs to the very end. A French envoy, Baron de Baas, has also been ordered to leave England for his involvement in the plot (→ 12/9).

Charles makes an alliance with Spain

Brussels, 2 April 1656

Charles Stuart, the eldest son of the executed king and himself proclaimed as Charles II in Scotland, has just concluded a treaty with the Spanish. This promises that if the royalists in England should manage to secure a port, Spain will provide 6,000 soldiers to spearhead an attempt to win back the kingdom. In return, Charles has promised to cede some of England's possessions in the West Indies, lend Spain 12 warships to recapture Portugal and, in a secret clause, protect the rights of English Catholics (→ 1656).

Cromwell rejects offer of the crown

Whitehall, 8 May 1657

After three months of agonising, Oliver Cromwell has refused the crown of England which had been offered to him by the Commons for the second time. Although this decision matches his high-minded principles – and even his enemies acknowledge that these are sincerely held – the talk is that it was a very close-run thing.

Having had experience of ruling as Protector, Cromwell (and his advisers) could see that the title of king had its attraction: a title known to the law, its rights and duties established by tradition. In return for accepting some limitation of his powers, Cromwell would gain the legal defences that secured the monarchy and the popular loyalty attached to the title. He seemed to be on the brink of accepting. But while the issue was in the balance,

three leading commanders of the roundhead army – John Lambert, Charles Fleetwood and John Desborough – approached Cromwell in St James's park and warned that if he took the crown they would all resign their positions.

Yet it is said that Cromwell was even more deeply moved by the humble petitions of lesser officers who had fought alongside him, from Edgehill to Worcester, against the old monarchy. The sectarian churches also swayed him with a series of remonstrances begging him not to be "a captain to lead us back to Egypt".

Cromwell has now told parliament: "I would not seek to set up that that providence hath destroyed and laid in the dust, and I would not build Jericho again." And so he has opted for constitutional uncertainty in the future (→ 26/6).

Cromwell is shown here as king.

Oliver Cromwell dies and leaves a power vacuum to be filled

Whitehall, 3 September 1658

This afternoon Oliver Cromwell succumbed to the illness from which he had been suffering for the past six months. He was 59 years old. For several days he had been pitifully weak, but he had continued to express his certainty of the grace of salvation. In his last hours he was heard to cry out: "Truly, God is good." So great is the uncertainty left by his death, the sense that England does not know what to do without him, that many were convinced that God would not let him die even as he entered what was clearly a fatal decline.

Cromwell had not been at full strength since the summer when he was overcome by the death of his daughter, Bettie, from a painful wasting illness. His grief and the hours that he spent watching by her bed were a reminder that, though he rose to the greatness of a supreme ruler, he was always also a man. For some time he had conducted much state business in the more relaxing environment of Hampton Court.

Just as Cromwell put his trust in divine providence, even when it was clear to mortal minds where that was leading, the politicians have had to trust in the Protector even

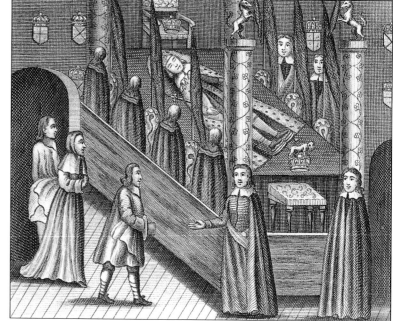

Oliver Cromwell lies in state in London, from a contemporary broadsheet.

when his purposes seemed equally obscure. Such as the awe in which they held him that it was only yesterday that the council summoned the courage to ask him to nominate his own successor, as had been his right since last year. But by then he was too weak to speak. However, when the name of his son Richard was put to the dying man, witnesses

say that they detected a nod of affirmation. Just as the ceremonies of Cromwell's investiture after he had refused the crown matched the splendour of any imaginable coronation, his lying-in-state in Somerset House will rival the most royal obsequies and, in a last great irony, there are plans to place a crown on the dead commoner's head (→ 10/9).

Protector's court is muted version of royal power

Whitehall, 1658

He may not have had the title of king, but the absolute ruler of England could hardly avoid having a court. Oliver Cromwell chose to make his in Whitehall, the palace of the last king of England. Tapestries, pictures and furnishings – even a red velvet chamber pot from Greenwich – for the Lord Protector's home were fetched from royal buildings throughout the country. Cromwell also used Hampton Court, where he lead a simple domestic life in keeping with puritan preferences. The Protector's wife, Elizabeth, acknowledged this by serving plain food such as sausages and puddings at table.

While no one would have expected Cromwell's court to be a whirlwind of sensual pleasures, there were music, dancing and the drinking of port. In fact the Protector enjoyed drinking wine and had a positive weakness for tobacco.

Since the closing of London's theatres, public performance is now most often found in private venues such as Holland House, although opera is tolerated and musicians are prospering. Cromwell's religious tolerance extended to most forms of private behaviour, but he never forgot that the show and panoply of a court were symbols of where real power and authority lie.

The Protector's wife, Elizabeth Cromwell, by S Cooper (d.1672).

Exiled king's lover Lucy Walter dies

Lucy Walter, Charles's ex-mistress.

Paris, 1658

Poor Lucy Walter has died here in misery. One of the great beauties of Europe ended her days repenting of her life and confessing its details to Bishop Cosin. She was about 28 years old and died of a disease probably contracted from one of her many lovers. "Mrs Barlow", as she liked to be called, was the greatest love so far of the many who have caught the heart of Charles Stuart, the would-be king of England. Over nine years ago they had a son, James, whom Charles has acknowledged and is publicly fond of.

Although Charles ended the romance, the rumour that the couple were secretly married at the height of their passion refuses to go away. If it could be proved, the legitimate son of the claimant to the throne would cut an important political figure (→ 2/6/80).

Cromwell's son, Richard, is new Protector

London, 10 September 1658

The Lord Protector is dead; long live the Lord Protector? These words do not carry the solution to England's constitutional problems. A week ago Oliver Cromwell died, on the double anniversary of the Battles of Dunbar and Worcester, but that sense of continuity has not survived the succession of his son Richard, despite the prompt implementation by the council of his death-bed nomination.

The new Cromwell was preferred over his more dynamic brother Henry precisely to avoid the creation of another dictatorial ruler. But as Richard tries to emphasise his constitutional position, as set down in the "Humble Petition", and to show himself the best defender of both the army and the powers of parliament it is becoming clear that this is a balancing trick that only a man who dominates both can pull off.

Richard has done no important jobs either in the army or in civilian life, but his instincts are to seek a

The Lord Protector's son, Richard.

broader support for his rule among the gentry. A parliament is to be elected in January to recognise his protectorate. However, the revived republican agitation in the middle and lower ranks of the army does not augur well for its new commander-in-chief (→ 23/11).

Richard, not suited for high office, quits

London, 16 May 1659

Cromwell the second has today been effectively deposed, although such is the constitutional confusion in England that it has happened on the nod, without any formal declaration. The army leaders have announced the recall of the rump parliament of 1648 dismissed by Oliver Cromwell in 1653 and have conceded that this is the only legitimate government in the country. This

means that everything done in the name of the Protectorate was done without proper authority, and the new protector's title is meaningless.

Only a handful of soldiers answered Richard Cromwell's call to an assembly in Whitehall last month, while many thousands collected at St James's, so any plan that he might have had of arresting dissident ringleaders became quite impossible (→ 24/5).

Britain, the Commonwealth once again, drifts without a ruler

Westminster, August 1659

Furious parliamentary activity cannot hide the fact that the government of England has all the appearance of a headless monster. The recalled members of 1653 have rejected the claim of the members of the 1648 rump parliament to retake their seats, and so the republican Commonwealth of England would seem to be firmly in control once more. But increasing demands for new and fair elections (a dissolution has been tentatively promised for next May) have exposed the

dilemma. Neither the army nor the rump knows exactly what it want, but both suspect that what England would choose on a free vote might be the return of the king.

A half-hearted purge of army and civil service of any Cromwellian influence has revealed just how personal a thing the Protectorate was. Richard Cromwell was not so much deposed as exposed as irrelevant. The army leadership saw its own best future in a weak protectorate, only to discover that the thing was an impossibility. The

army is trying to win the acceptance of the rump that it is its equal partner in government, while parliament still insists on its sovereignty. The only thing which keeps the two together is the threat to both of a royalist insurrection.

However, Major-General John Lambert has shown recently that the army is still in firm military control with his decisive defeat, at Winnington Bridge, of the Cheshire rebellion which clearly failed to provoke a general rising in support of the king (→ 10/9).

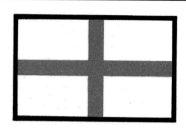

C h a r l e s   I I
1660–1685

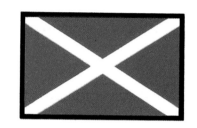

Westminster, 2 May 1660. Parliament recalls the 29-year-old Charles Stuart to England from his exile in Europe (→ 14/5).

Edinburgh, 14 May 1660. Charles, proclaimed king by the English earlier this month, is proclaimed king by the Scots (→ 29/5).

London, 29 May 1660. Charles enters the City in an elaborate procession which includes, it is rumoured, his new mistress, Barbara Palmer, the wife of the royalist Roger Palmer (→ 25/2/61).

Edinburgh, 23 August 1660. The government of Scotland returns to Scottish hands, thus ending nine years of English military occupation (→ 28/3/61).

Whitehall, 24 Dec 1660. Mary, the Princess Royal, the wife of the late Prince William II of Orange and the sister of King Charles, dies.

Westminster, 29 Dec 1660. The convention parliament, which invited Charles to return even though it contained many MPs sympathetic to puritan opinion, is dissolved (→ 8/5/61).

London, 25 February 1661. The court is full of rumours that the king is the father of his mistress Barbara Palmer's first child, a daughter named Anne (→ 8/11).

Scotland, 28 March 1661. The first parliament since 1651 passes the Act Recissory, under which Charles is to regain all power and any legislation passed by the Covenanters is revoked (→ 28/5).

Paris, 31 March 1661. Henrietta Anne, Charles's younger sister, marries Philippe, the Duke of Orleans and son of Louis XIII of France (→ 22/5/70).

Westminster, 23 April 1661. Charles is crowned king.→

Whitehall, 5 May 1661. Charles, the Duke of Cambridge, the Duke and Duchess of York's son, dies aged seven months (→ 30/4/62).

Westminster, 8 May 1661. The first parliament elected since the restoration of Charles II meets; consisting mainly of royalists, it has been nicknamed the "cavalier" parliament (→ 4/1664).

London, 8 November 1661. Charles creates Roger Palmer, the husband of the king's mistress Barbara, Earl of Castlemaine (→ 1662).

London, 14 November 1661. King Charles persuades James Sharp, a leade of the Presbyterians, to become archbishop of St Andrews to help to implement the king's policy of restoring episcopacy in Scotland (→ 27/5/62).

London, 30 April 1662. James and Anne, the Duke and Duchess of York, have their second child, a daughter, Mary (→ 12/7/63).

Edinburgh, 27 May 1662. The Scottish Parliament restores the episcopacy, thus threatening an increase in the persecution of Presbyterians (→ 23/9/63).

London, spring 1662. Barbara Palmer, the Countess of Castlemaine, the king's mistress, gives birth to a son, Charles.

England, 26 December 1662. Charles announces that he will allow some religious toleration within the church (→ 1/1663).

London, January 1663. King Charles is much taken by the beauty of the 15-year-old Frances Stewart, who has recently arrived at court (→ 3/1667).

London, 12 July 1663. The Duke and Duchess of York have their third child, James, the Duke of Cambridge (→ 6/2/65).

Scotland, 23 September 1663. The Scottish Parliament votes to allow Charles to levy a Scots army for use in Britain (→ 11/1666).

London, September 1664. King Charles recognises Lady Castlemaine's daughter Charlotte as his own, giving her the surname of Fitzroy (→ 12/1665).

London, 6 February 1665. Anne, the Duchess of York, gives birth to a daughter, Anne (→ 4/7/66).

France, June 1665. Queen Henrietta Maria, the mother of Charles II, returns to her native land and settles at Colombe, near Paris (→ 31/8/69).

Oxford, October 1665. Parliament moves here to avoid the plague in London.

Oxford, December 1665. Lady Castlemaine gives birth to a third son, Henry Fitzroy (→ 1682).

France, January 1666. Louis XIV declares war on England (→ 22/5/70).

London, 4 July 1666. Anne, the Duchess of York, gives birth to her fifth child, Charles, the Duke of Kendal (→ 14/9/67).

London, 6 September 1666. The great fire which started three days ago is still raging (→ 1676).

Kent, March 1667. Charles is livid after the court beauty Frances Stewart elopes with the Duke of Richmond.

London, 14 September 1667. Anne, the Duchess of York, gives birth to her sixth child, Edgar, the Duke of Cambridge; two of her young sons, James and Charles, died earlier this year (→ 15/11/69).

Paris, 31 August 1669. Queen Henrietta Maria dies at Colombe.

London, 15 November 1669. Henrietta, who was born on 13 January, and Edgar, the two youngest children of the Duke and Duchess of York, die (→ 20/8/70).

Edinburgh, 16 November 1669. The Act of Supremacy brings the Scottish church under the direct control of the king (→ 24/1/78).

London, 8 May 1670. Nell Gwynn, King Charles's actress mistress, bears him a son, who is named Charles Beauclerk (→ 1687).

Paris, 30 June 1670. Henrietta Anne, the youngest sister of Charles II and wife of Philippe, the Duke of Orleans, dies.

The life and times of King Charles II

Name: Charles Stuart.
Birth: 29 May 1630.
Accession: 30 January 1649.
Coronation: 1 Jan 1651 (Scotland), 23 April 1661 (England).
Restoration: 29 May 1660.
Hair: black.
Eyes: dark brown.
Height: 6 feet 2 inches (188cm).
Marriage: Catherine of Braganza, 21 May 1662.

Children: At least nine, all illegitimate.
Favourite homes: Whitehall, Windsor.
Likes: women, theatre, science and architecture.
Greatest problems: religious strife, lack of money.
Greatest success: retaining the throne.
Death: 6 February 1685.

Opposite: a delicately-carved marble bust of King Charles II.

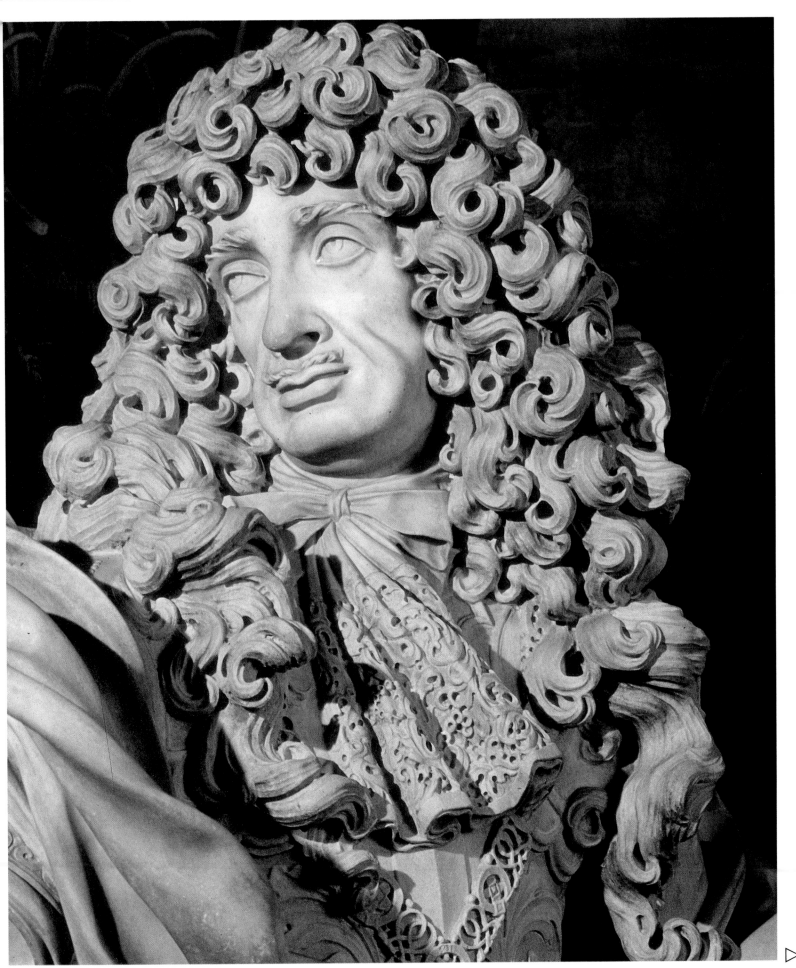

Britain prepares for restoration of the monarchy

Army general calls for new parliament

London, 6 February 1660

General Monck, whose army is the only effective source of power in the leaderless British kingdoms, has added his voice to calls for a new parliament. His call came only days after his soldiers had destroyed the gates of the City of London on the orders of parliament in an effort to frighten the citizens into paying taxes. Now Monck has been welcomed into the city and has issued an ultimatum to MPs showing his exasperation with the rump of a parliament first summoned in 1640.

These members, who survived the purge of 1648 which preceded the execution of the king, were recalled last year by the army as Richard Cromwell's protectorate crumbled away, but they have failed to provide decisive leadership or solve the question of how the kingdoms should be governed. They have also refused to permit the return of the purged members, which Londoners had demanded as a condition of paying taxes.

Monck – who last year said that "I ever shall reverence the parliament's resolutions in civil things" – has now demanded that the rump parliament dissolve itself. As he marched his army down from Scotland at the beginning of the year he was met with petitions calling for new elections and an end to "arbitrary government". However, he also firmly declared his opposition to the rule of any one man, including a king.

By withdrawing his soldiers from parliament itself, he makes it possible for the excluded members to retake their seats. But he has taken the precaution of getting their agreement, in writing, that once back in the House of Commons they will determine the high command of the army (it will undoubtedly be Monck), raise money for the soldiers' back pay and then call fresh elections. The return to a traditionally constituted parliament leaves open the possibility of the return of other former institutions of government, such as the House of Lords – and a king (→4/4).

George Monck: a portrait of the general by Sir Peter Lely (d.1680).

Charles Stuart with supporters: now he looks set to return to the throne.

Charles makes the declaration at Breda, guaranteeing freedom of conscience.

Charles Stuart and his royal ancestors

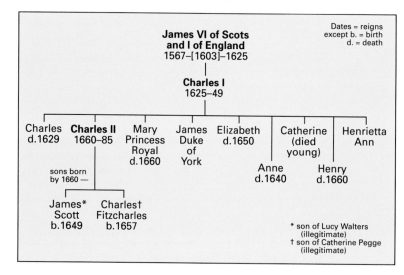

Charles pledges to 'heal the wounds'

Low Countries, 4 April 1660

Liberty of conscience under a king – that promise made today at Breda should be enough to see Charles Stuart back on the throne, especially when combined with his commitment to pay off the arrears owed to General Monck's army. In a declaration made public here today Charles has offered to heal the wounds of the past 20 years with a settlement to be based on moderation and reconciliation. It contains four main headings:

First, there will be a free and general pardon; after two decades of strife the fear of revenge and the paying of old scores has become a serious barrier to any lasting peace.

Second, there will be liberty of "tender consciences" – nobody will be "called in question for differences of opinion in matters of religion". This should guarantee that the sectarian congregations and, more importantly, their allies among the under-officers of the army, will not oppose the restoration of the king.

Third, the army will be paid, and soldiers will be accepted into the king's service on the same terms and conditions as they had enjoyed before.

Fourth, all the land questions raised by forced sales and confiscations will be settled by parliament. This will undoubtedly produce endless disputes, but simply to restore property that might have changed hands several times to the owners (or heirs) of 20 years ago would be unworkable.

For all these conditions Charles says that he will accept any amendments properly put forward by parliament, thereby involving it in an inevitably imperfect restoration settlement. Charles is also holding separate talks with the Scots. He supports the restoration of Scottish independence, and talks are focusing upon a religious settlement. Presbyterians hope to retain power in the church, while the aristocrats foresee a restoration of their lost power with the anticipated return of the king (→2/5).

Huge welcome for restored Charles II

Whitehall, 29 May 1660

London's newest citizen forced his way into the world early today to greet the king. Such was the excitement as Charles Stuart arrived in the capital to claim his throne that the landlord's wife at the King's Head, an ironically-named tavern, went into premature labour. The king paused to greet his new subject before moving on down the Strand to Whitehall.

Onlookers estimate that 20,000 people lined the streets, waving swords and shouting, as the bells of the City were rung to welcome Charles back into his kingdom. The lord mayor and his aldermen had put on their official finery, and the nobility dressed up for the occasion in rich and colourful robes.

The contrast in style with the puritan severity of preceding years could hardly be greater, but a sign that the differences are more than clothes deep also comes from the news that the thanksgiving service in Westminster abbey has been cancelled. Charles is said to prefer to spend his first evening as England's king privately, with his mistress Barbara Palmer.

The triumphant return began when the king landed at Dover four days ago. General Monck met him there and handed him his sword, sheathed, as a sign of loyalty. The mayor then presented Charles with a magnificently-bound English bible which the king promised to value "above all things in the world", perhaps as a sign to his new subjects not to heed rumours of his Catholic sympathies.

The royal party then moved slowly through Canterbury and Rochester, greeted in each town by cheering crowds, to arrive in the capital today. It is Charles's 30th birthday (→ 25/10).

The king returned: Charles makes a triumphant entry into London.

Charles dancing with his sister Mary on the eve of his restoration.

Smallpox kills the king's brother, the Duke of Gloucester

London, 13 September 1660

Smallpox has suddenly killed the king's young brother, Henry, the Duke of Gloucester. He was ill with what was thought to be a mild attack of the disease, but he suddenly worsened last night and died today. He was only 20 and was the king's favourite brother, noted for his sweet nature and intelligence. Henry was more popular than his elder brother, the Duke of York, outside the court as well as in it as his uncompromising Protestantism was seen as a counter-weight to the openly Catholic leanings of Charles's heir, James.

Duke is father of child, claims Anne

Whitehall, October 1660

Anne Hyde, the daughter of the king's lord chancellor, has given birth to a son and – to the consternation of the palace, not to mention of James himself – has named the king's brother as the father. She also claims that she and James were secretly married at the beginning of September. This is being denied, but Charles has taken the precaution of making her father Edward Hyde a peer to avoid the possible ignominy of his brother and heir being married to a commoner (→ 5/5/61).

Anne Hyde, by Peter Lely (d.1680).

King meets Presbyterian leaders for religious toleration talks

London, 25 October 1660

After a meeting organised with leading Presbyterians at Worcester House, the home of Lord Hyde, the lord chancellor, Charles has come up with proposals for a tolerant religious settlement. The broad outlines aim to satisfy nonconformists by setting up Presbyterian councils to keep a check on the powers of bishops and by establishing a national synod in which all Protestant factions would meet to discuss questions of liturgy.

The move will give great encouragement to those who would like to see the building of a broad-based, tolerant and comprehensive church in England. However, all-party agreement is still a long way off. The convention parliament has sat in grand committee once a week since July to settle the religious question and has failed to come up with a solution which would be acceptable to both Anglicans and nonconformists (→ 29/12).

King marks restoration with splendid coronation

An ostentatious spectacle: a simplified view of King Charles's splendid procession from the Tower of London to Westminster, by Dirck Stoop (c.1614-83).

London, 23 April 1661
Last night the king moved in state to the Tower of London by barge along the Thames. Today – St George's day – he rode through the streets of the city to Westminster abbey to be crowned. The procession set off from Tower Hill at eight this morning, but crowds had been packing the abbey and makeshift scaffolding along the way since before dawn.

The sheer ostentation of the spectacle was clearly intended to impress. Historical records had been studied to inspire royal pageantry of lavish and symbolic splendour. Even the Yeomen of the Guard and the pages were in wonderful costumes, while the king himself was dressed in crimson velvet, ermine and cloth of gold. Even his high-heeled sandals were gilded, and the saddle of his splendid horse was embroidered with pearls and gold. When all the bills are in the celebrations will have cost around £30,000.

A series of tableaux along the way spelled out a simple message: the years of anarchy and drabness are over. The crown is back, and a new "golden age" is begun. To emphasise continuity one of the two new crowns commissioned will be known as St Edward's crown. Tonight the celebrations end with a great feast in Westminster Hall where, 12 years ago, Charles's father was tried for his life (→ 8/5).

Scots Restoration sealed by Argyll death

Edinburgh, 28 May 1661
The head of Archibald Campbell, the Earl of Argyll, looks out from a spike at the tolbooth here following the earl's beheading earlier today. Argyll, the chief of Clan Campbell, was found guilty of treason: letters between him and Cromwell showed that he had co-operated with the parliamentary regime.

It is an ignominious end for a man who was at one time the effective ruler of Scotland, leading the Covenanters who overthrew the government of Charles I here. In 1649, appalled by the king's execution, he switched sides and presided over the coronation of Charles II as king of Scotland in 1651. It is ironic that the man he crowned decided to destroy him, but Argyll was much too powerful, and his execution goes hand-in-hand with the Restoration.

In March the Scottish Parliament passed the Act Recissory, which abolished all legislation pass-

Argyll: a casualty of the Restoration.

ed since 1633 when the last parliament under crown control met. The king regains his old influence over parliament, with the unrestrained power to choose his own privy councillors and officers of state. The clock has been turned back 28 years, making the Scottish Restoration in many ways more complete than the English one (→ 14/11).

Royal Society crowns new enlightenment

London, August 1662
As if to prove that Restoration England has a place for those who seek enlightenment as well as for those who seek pleasure and entertainment, King Charles II has granted a charter to a group of scientists who follow Francis Bacon as "merchants of the light of understanding". The Royal Society is intended to bring together the leading men of learning who believe that the workings of the material world should be subjected to dispassionate examination.

The king's imprimatur formalises a cooperation between the various strands of scientific enquiry, such as those of the biologists of Cambridge university and the physicists of Oxford, which began two years ago when John Wilkins chaired a series of weekly meetings at Gresham college. It is also likely to accelerate the fashionable amateur interest in science among the land-owning classes. The king himself is understood to be building his own

Charles, the patron, is celebrated.

laboratory in Whitehall palace. In a similar quest for enlightenment, groups of philosophers and theologians are to meet to discuss questions of theology. This move will encourage those who would like to see the building of a broad-based, tolerant and comprehensive church in England. All-party agreement, however, is still a long way off.

Royal bride retains her Catholic faith

London, 22 May 1662

Twice today, if rumours are to be believed, King Charles has gone to the altar to get married. Each ceremony was, however, with the same woman, the 23-year-old daughter of the king of Portugal, Catherine of Braganza. The first, private wedding was according to her Catholic faith; the second was conducted publicly by the bishop of London. Catherine will remain a Catholic, but will bring up any children as Protestants.

The new queen is tiny and neat-looking, with an olive skin. She appears reserved and rather pious, and her severe retinue of cowled monks is in grim contrast to the king's extravagant court, but she seems to adore her husband, as much for the romantic story of his exile and restoration as for the flowery courtship conducted in Spain on his behalf by Sir Richard Fanshawe. With typical gallantry, and perhaps as typical sincerity, the king has declared his firm intention of being a good husband.

The marriage creates an important alliance with Portugal which puts England on the same side as France against Spain and will set the tone for its future European policies. The Spanish are furious about the king's marriage. They have been trying to marry one of their princesses to Charles since his restoration, and in spiteful disappointment the Spanish ambassador has said that he hopes the match proves barren.

Of more interest to the Earl of Clarendon – as the lord chancellor, Lord Hyde, became last year – is the considerable dowry which Catherine brings with her. This includes the possessions of Tangier and Bombay, as well as £360,000 in sugar, timber and cash.

Catherine arrived at Portsmouth on 13 May after a rough voyage. She refused a glass of ale and asked instead for a cup of tea (→ 1663).

Britain's petite and pious new queen.

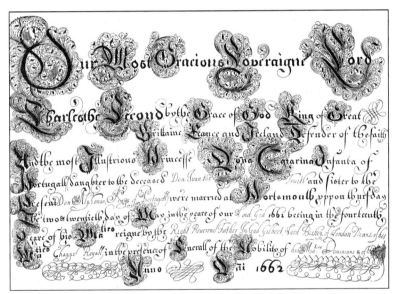

A facsimile of the marriage certificate of Charles and Catherine of Braganza.

King finds marriage no reason to give up taking mistresses

Hampton Court, 1663

Any hopes which Queen Catherine had that Charles would change his ways after their marriage have been swiftly disappointed. He included the name of Lady Castlemaine, his mistress, on the list of ladies of the bedchamber, despite the queen's protests. Lady Castlemaine bore Charles a son last year. Although the king sat for hours comforting his wife during her recent illness, he still visits Lady Castlemaine every evening. But Barbara, too, may soon have a rival. The king is much attracted by a 15-year-old beauty, Frances Stewart, who joined the court this year as a maid to the queen. Unfortunately for Charles, Frances appears to be as virtuous as she is beautiful (→ 9/1664).

Lady Castlemaine: longtime lover.

Frances Stewart: new court belle.

King to urge softer parliamentary line against dissenters

England, January 1663

The king has released a "declaration of indulgence" which he hopes will lessen anger over the way the Act of Uniformity is leading to hundreds of clergy, teachers and scholars losing their livings. The tolerant spirit of the Declaration of Breda which paved the way for the Restoration looks increasingly hollow as the new parliament shows itself to be exclusively Anglican and bent on revenge. So far nearly a thousand clergymen have decided that they would rather live with their consciences than with their jobs.

The king's declaration of indulgence offers no guaranteed respite; it simply declares his intention to ask parliament, at its next session, to allow individual dispensations from the Act of Uniformity and to revive the process of removing laws against Catholics. Some nonconformists are to be released from jail, but it is by no means certain that parliament will heed the king's call for tolerance (→ 2/1668).

King backs return of London theatres

Drury Lane, London, 7 May 1663

Live theatre is back in London as the first of the two theatres granted patents by King Charles last year is ready to open. The dramatist and theatre manager Thomas Killigrew will open at the Theatre Royal in Brydges Street near Covent Garden tonight with a revival of *The Humorous Lieutenant*, written by Francis Beaumont and John Fletcher. The cast is headed by Charles Hart and Michael Mohun.

Killigrew has won the race to reopen the first theatre since the puritans shut down all London's stages. With Sir William Davenant, who has the patent for the Duke's House theatre, Killigrew, who maintains the roguish traditions of theatre in life as well as on stage, has a monopoly of London drama. The King's Men company, based at the Globe on Bankside during the reigns of James and Elizabeth, will now be based in Drury Lane.

Second daughter born to king's brother James and his 'buttered bun' Anne Hyde

Whitehall, 6 February 1665

A second daughter born today to the Duchess of York is to be christened Anne after her mother. The elder daughter, Mary, was born three years ago. Anne Hyde, whose father, Lord Clarendon, is now lord chancellor, met James, the Duke of York, when the royal family was in exile in Europe and short of money. The prospect of a restoration of the monarchy and a return to England seemed remote, and James, then in his late twenties, was reconciled to remaining a commander of soldiers of fortune in the armies of France and Spain.

Anne, big-bosomed and blue-eyed, captivated James, but she was a strong-willed woman and held out until he signed a cast-iron marriage contract. Then, within months, everything changed. Anne discovered that she was pregnant and James's brother, Charles, became king. Since Charles was childless, James was now heir to the throne. Everybody told him to rid himself of Anne, but she would have none of it. They were married in secret and their first child, a boy, was born six weeks later, only to be carried off by smallpox in 1661.

James has no appetite for gambling or strong drink. His favourite pastime is hunting, and his preference is for stags and women. He is said to be "the most unguarded ogler of his time", with a special

James, the Duke of York.

fancy for women considered ugly by other men. He fell for one of Anne's ladies-in-waiting after she was thrown from her horse. Coming upon Arabella Churchill, tall, pale-faced, all skin and bone, lying in a hedge with her clothes in disarray, he cried out in amazement "that limbs of such exquisite beauty could belong to a face like Miss Churchill's".

Despite his philandering, James has remained fond of Anne – "the buttered bun", as the poet Andrew Marvell has called her – and with her constant nagging she has retained a strong influence over her husband (→4/7/66).

Royal family quits London to flee plague

London, July 1665

King Charles and his court have abandoned the capital and fled to Oxford in an attempt to avoid the ravages of the plague which is now afflicting London. Parliament has been prorogued, and the exchequer has moved to Nonsuch palace, near Ewell in Surrey. Yet the plague was so virulent following last month's heatwave that even the royal flight failed to stop death touching the court, despite its belief in a monarch's ability to heal the "king's evil" by laying hands on victims.

After leaving London the wife of one of the court grooms suddenly began to display the familiar and feared symptoms of purple and black blotches on the body and swellings in her groin and armpit. Her death was hushed up, and Charles plans to stay in Oxford until the plague relents.

Since the beginning of the century there have been only four years without some plague deaths. This year, in the hot rainless summer, the scourge has devastated London. Plague carts rumble through the streets collecting naked bodies to be thrown into hastily dug pits. From Holborn to Cripplegate, fires are burning day and night in the hope of dispersing the "poisoned air".

The coming of the plague is said to have been presaged by the passing of a comet over London. Many believe that the pestilence is God's punishment for the sins of the people. If this is true, God is partic-

Charles healing the "king's evil".

ularly angry with the poor in their crowded tenements, for they are dying in large numbers. Clowns, puppet shows, rope-dancers and other entertainments have been banned.

The lord mayor, Sir William Lawrence, one of the very few public figures to remain in London, has ordered the destruction of all cats and dogs. In the first few weeks, some 40,000 dogs were put down and probably five times as many cats. Rats and mice are also being destroyed. The plague has played havoc with England's foreign trade. There is no port in Europe that will admit an English ship, and exports are at a standstill (→10/1655).

Parliament to give ground to the king

Westminster, April 1664

The Triennial Act, passed more than 20 years ago during the struggle against Charles I, is to be repealed and replaced by another identically-named act which will strengthen the position of the king. The 1641 act laid down that there must be no interval of more than three years between parliaments and set out rules for summoning MPs if the king failed to do so. The new act repeats the three-year rule but, to avoid any anti-monarchical flavour, leaves it to the king to call parliament without providing any means of enforcement (→10/1665).

King rolls up sleeves to lead battle against London's great fire

The city blazes: Londoners desperately try to save their possessions.

London, 4 September 1666

King Charles today joined the citizens of London in the front line of the battle to stop the spread of a fire which has now been raging through the capital for three days. All day the king helped desperate efforts to control the fire. Ankle-deep in water, his clothes soaking and his face blackened, the king toiled as the fire-fighters worked to demolish buildings in the hope of establishing "fire-breaks". He also sent officials with food to help the poor and money to aid the rescue efforts. But the fire, which started in a bakery near London Bridge, is still spreading and is now threatening Whitehall palace (→6/9).

English hit back in war with Dutch

North Sea, 8 August 1666
English seamen have fought back to inflict heavy losses on the Dutch as they retreated to the safety of port at Vlieland. The Dutch lost 20 ships and 7,000 men in this latest, bloody battle which gives England command of the Channel once again. It is also revenge for the English fleet – commanded by Prince Rupert of the Rhine, the grandson of James, the first Stuart king of England – for its humiliating defeat at the hands of the Dutch in June.

Then, in four days of fighting, the English lost 8,000 men (including two admirals) and 20 ships against Dutch losses of 2,000 men and seven ships. It was a serious blow to national pride.

Hostilities between the two countries began almost two years ago, when an English squadron raided Dutch settlements in West Africa and New Amsterdam on the Hudson river in North America, but war was not officially declared until March last year. The conflict is essentially a struggle for command of the sea and the lucrative maritime trade world-wide and for the transporting of slaves from West Africa to the Americas.

The two sides are fairly evenly matched. England began the war with some 160 ships with 5,000 guns and 25,000 men; the Dutch had rather fewer and smaller warships but, surprisingly, they carried more guns and men. The heavier

Last month's battle which the Dutch won: now England has had its revenge.

English ships are steadier in rough weather, but the flat-bottomed Dutch ones manoeuvre better.

At first the war seemed to go well for the English. In June last year the Duke of York, in command off Lowestoft, gained what Samuel Pepys of the navy board described as "a greater victory never known in the world"; 16 Dutch ships were sunk and nine captured. But disaster followed two months later when the great Dutch admiral Michael Adriaanszoon de Ruyter was conveying home a rich merchant fleet from the east and sailing round

Scotland. In return for a share of the booty, the Danes agreed to allow the English to use the harbour of Bergen in Norway; misunderstandings led to Danish guns being turned on the English, who lost 400 men killed and wounded. The Dutch fleet escaped.

At the start of the war, MPs agreed to a grant of £2.5 million to be spent over three years; just one year later, parliament was asked for a further £1.25 million, and even that is running out. Another £1.8 million is being demanded, and stalemate looms (→ 31/7/67).

King advises hated councillor to flee to safety in exile

Clarendon: a sacrificial victim?

Westminster, 27 November 1667
Lord Clarendon, who played a key role in the restoration of the monarchy, has been sacrificed by King Charles in a bid to appease the government's many critics. Clarendon served the king loyally, in exile and after the Restoration, but he was blamed, unfairly, for the disastrous Dutch war, and his narrow Anglicanism has become unpopular. His disapproval of the king's many mistresses has irritated the king, who has told him to flee the country if he is to save himself from a charge of treason.

Churchmen fail in Scottish rebellion

Edinburgh, November 1666
Royal rule in Scotland has been boosted by the failure of a revolt by some three thousand rebels from south-western Scotland. They arrived at the gates of Edinburgh to find that the city would not support them. The rebels were suspected to have links with the Dutch but, despite the unpopularity of the Dutch wars, the rebellion has flopped. The protest drew its strength from ministers who lost parishes for refusing to accept the return of bishops. But not even dedicated Presbyterians among the nobility have backed their brief revolt.

England gains 'New York' in peace treaty

Low Countries, 31 July 1667
A peace treaty ending the two-and-a-half year war with the Dutch was signed at Breda today, and the English have gained New Amsterdam, the North American port which is to be renamed New York after Charles II's brother. Both parties came to the negotiating table exhausted and ready for peace. Despite their huge financial resources the Dutch were running out of funds, while the English had been devastated by the plague and the Great Fire of London.

The decisive move came when the Dutch, seizing the opportunity offered by the English decision to save money by keeping its battle

fleet in port, sent their ships into the Thames estuary, broke the boom guarding Chatham harbour, burnt four warships and towed away the Duke of York's flagship, the *Royal Charles*.

The port of New York gives the English command of the lucrative fur trade route from the Great Lakes to Manhattan Island and the Hudson river. The Surinam settlement on the north coast of South America has been surrendered to the Dutch, and their conquests of Portuguese possessions in the far east have been recognised. The Breda treaty could bring to a close a long period of colonial and economic rivalry (→ 27/11).

King Charles II, by Godfrey Kneller. The king has started a fashion among gentlemen for wearing full-length wigs.

King treads warily around religious sensibilities

The Quakers are forced to meet in secret and behind locked doors.

Scottish Presbyterians meeting in the open, but under guard: a later view.

Westminster, February 1668

The king has received a stinging rebuff from the House of Commons after he opened the new session of parliament with an appeal for religious toleration. MPs responded by refusing to make the customary vote of thanks for the royal address and promptly went to work on a bill to renew the 1664 act banning conventicles – secret or unauthorised assemblies for worship.

Appeals for toleration from King Charles are viewed with deep suspicion by MPs and the public alike. Not only is the king's apparent fair-mindedness believed to mask a secret sympathy for the Roman Church (after all, he is married to the Catholic Catherine of Braganza) but also memories of the sectarianism of the 1650s are still strong.

Charles returned to England to be proclaimed king after he had publicly promised liberty of conscience and agreed to leave a full religious settlement to MPs. His first parliament, elected in 1661, was overwhelmingly Anglican; it passed the Act of Uniformity, which restored bishops to their cathedrals and made use of the Book of Common Prayer

compulsory. This drove many moderate Presbyterian ministers from the church. They have now been lumped together with the other, more radical sects such as the Baptists and the Quakers and have been ostracised as "nonconformists".

Little more than two years after being crowned, Charles provoked a political explosion by issuing a declaration of indulgence to enable nonconformists and Catholics to worship outside the Act of Uniformity. He quickly backed down when outraged MPs demanded the deportation of Jesuits and Catholic priests from the country.

Charles's true religious beliefs remain a matter for conjecture. He is rumoured to be in contact with his sister, Henrietta Anne, the Duchess of Orleans, to arrange an alliance with France and his own conversion to Catholicism. Yet he is said to be wary of the attraction to the Catholic faith of his brother James, the Duke of York. Perhaps the truth is that he is happy to allow freedom of religious belief as long as it does not conflict with his own authority or create difficulties for him with parliament.

Behold our Church (like Esther here doth tender Her Supplications to the Faiths Defender: In vain Rome Plots, whilst Charles ý Scepter Sways May Sled and Gibbet end all Traitors Days.

The church asks Charles to protect it from the "machinations of Rome".

Prince William of Orange comes of age

Amsterdam, 14 November 1668
Prince William of Orange, who is 18 today, celebrated his coming of age by taking over the administration of his estates and having himself declared "First Noble of Zeeland". The prince, whose English mother, Mary, was the eldest daughter of Charles I, should have succeeded his father as *stadhouder* [viceroy] of the United Provinces. For although the title is not hereditary, the House of Orange has held it for generations and regards it as its own property. But when William's father died of smallpox in the year of his son's birth, the republican leader Johann de Witt took a long-awaited opportunity to halt the slide towards an Orange monarchy. De Witt became head of state with the title of Grand Pensionary, and William was declared "a child of state" under his tutelage and protection.

The young prince still fully intends to become stadhouder before long, an ambition encouraged by King Charles II who sees an active Orange movement as a useful source of trouble for de Witt and the Dutch merchants whose mas-

Prince William as a boy.

tery of maritime trade is being challenged by England. Charles, in fact, looks on William as an Englishman and a Stuart who would readily fall in with English policies if he came to power. For the present, though, the Dutch have other preoccupations. Louis XIV of France has invaded the Spanish Netherlands and is threatening the small Calvinist Dutch republic (→ 11/1670).

Duchess admits to Catholic conversion

London, 20 August 1670
In a move which is certain to provoke controversy, Anne, the Duchess of York, today admitted that she has been converted to Catholicism. For some time there has been gossip in court circles that the Duchess and her husband, James, were secretly taking the same path towards Rome. In fact James was converted almost two years ago but was forbidden by his brother, Charles II, to declare it publicly.

It seems certain that Anne joined the Roman communion before her husband and, as the dominant, even domineering, partner in the marriage, she took James with her. Both of them spent many years on the continent during the puritan Protectorate in England, and they acquired many Catholic friends. With his new faith, James is now filled with remorse over his past sins, and Nell Gwynn calls him "Dismal Jimmy" (→ 9/2/71).

William is shocked by king's hobbies

London, November 1670
On a four-month visit to England as guest of Charles II, the upright and abstemious Prince William of Orange has been greatly put out by his uncle's hard-drinking, hard-riding ways. William had expected Charles to start repaying a long-standing debt owed to the Dutch; Charles, who is secretly allied to the French, hoped to use the prince and his supporters as a tool to weaken the republican regime in the United Provinces. Both seem to have fallen short of expectations.

Although William enjoyed great popular acclaim during his visit, the endless round of London banquets and Newmarket horse-races bored him; nor was he impressed by the honorary degrees awarded him by Oxford and Cambridge. The king did on one occasion manage to get the Dutchman drunk; he was later found climbing into one of the maids' bedrooms (→ 10/1677).

Treaty has a public and a private face

Dover, 22 May 1670
When Charles II arrived in Dover a few days ago he put it about that he was there to meet his sister, Henrietta Anne, the Duchess of Orleans, arriving from France on a purely social call. In fact, she brought with her a treaty for her brother to sign in secret, and he did so today. Under the terms of the treaty Charles has promised Louis XIV he will declare himself a Catholic and return England to Rome at a time of his own choosing. Louis is to give Charles a lot of money and to join him in attacking the thorn in both their sides – the Dutch.

These secret clauses in the Dover treaty provide for a French subsidy of £225,000 a year when England goes to war with the Dutch. A further £150,000 will be paid when Charles becomes a Catholic, and 6,000 French troops will be provided to put down the expected disorders in England. The king's motives in taking such risks with English public opinion if his Catholic intrigues should become generally known remain a mystery, though it seems probable that his beloved sister Henrietta Anne has assured him of French backing.

The king has spun an elaborate web of intrigue in order to gain his ends. He signed a treaty with the Dutch against the French while he was also in contact with Louis through Henrietta (→ 30/6).

Insatiable Charles woos a new lover

Charles's new mistress, Nell Gwynn.

London, 1670
She calls him Charles the Third because, she says, he is the third Charley she has taken to her bed. Nell Gwynn graduated from serving beer in bawdy houses to selling oranges outside a Drury Lane theatre before taking to the stage five years ago, when she was 15. Her sauciness and high humour – and her shapely legs – have delighted the king, who is trying to cope with the demands of several other mistresses at the same time. Nell has moved from lodgings at the Cock and Pie tavern in Drury Lane to a house in Pall Mall. And although she has known Charles II for only a short time she is said to be carrying his child already (→ 8/5).

In an English garden: King Charles is presented with the first pineapple grown in England by Rose, the gardener at Dawney Court, Bucks.

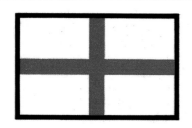

Charles II
1660–1685

Whitehall, 9 February 1671. Anne, the Duchess of York, gives birth to her eighth child, a daughter named Catherine (→ 31/3).

London, 31 March 1671. Anne Hyde, the Duchess of York and sister-in-law of King Charles, dies aged 34 (→ 5/12).

Newmarket, October 1671. Charles seduces Louise de Kéroüalle, one of his late sister Henrietta Anne's maids-of-honour (→ 29/7/72).

London, 5 December 1671. Catherine, the youngest daughter of James, the Duke of York, dies aged ten months.

London, 29 July 1672. Louise de Kéroüalle bears Charles a son, Charles Lennox (→ 18/8/73).

England, April 1673. After the Duke of York refuses to take the Anglican sacrament in public, rumours are rife that he is a Catholic convert (→ 6/1673).

Westminster, June 1673. The Duke of York is forced to resign as lord high admiral on the passing of the Test Act (→ 30/9).

London, 18 August 1673. King Charles creates Louise de Kéroüalle, his mistress, Duchess of Portsmouth (→ 1675).

England/Italy, 30 Sept 1673. James, the Duke of York, marries by proxy Mary of Modena, the only daughter of Alfonso IV, the Duke of Modena; aged 15, she is a devout Catholic (→ 21/11).

London, 10 January 1675. Mary of Modena gives birth to a daughter, Catherine Laura (→ 3/10).

London, 3 October 1675. Catherine dies aged nine months (→ 18/8/76).

London, 1675. Charles's mistress Louise de Kéroüalle, the Duchess

of Portsmouth, receives an annuity of £10,000 (→ 9/1677).

London, 1675. The beautiful Hortense Mancini, the Duchess of Mazarin, becomes the king's mistress (→ 1676).

London, 1675. Charles's palace at Whitehall undergoes a programme of renovations (→ 1676).

London, 18 August 1676. Mary of Modena gives birth to a second daughter, Isabella (→ 12/12/77).

London, September 1677. Good health returns to the Duchess of Portsmouth after a period of melancholy brought on by jealousy of Charles's attentions to the Duchess of Mazarin.

England, October 1677. In pursuit of improved Anglo-Dutch relations, Charles agrees to the marriage of Mary, the Duke of York's eldest daughter, to Prince William III of Orange (→ 4/11).

London, 12 December 1677. Charles, the Duke of Cambridge, the son of Mary of Modena and James, the Duke of York, who was born five weeks ago, dies (→ 2/3/81).

Scotland, 24 January 1678. King Charles's ministers order highland troops, who support the king's plan for a return to an episcopal church, to be deployed in the strongly Presbyterian areas in the south-west of the country (→ 3/3/79).

Low Countries, spring 1678. Princess Mary, the wife of William of Orange, suffers a miscarriage, giving rise to fears that she may not be able to bear children (→ 7/1679).

New England, 10 July 1678. The English crown claims New Hampshire as a colony.

London, March 1679. Charles sends away his brother James, the

Duke of York, who is rapidly becoming unpopular, before parliament reconvenes (→ 21/4).

Westminster, 21 April 1679. Charles expands his privy council and brings in some opponents to James, the Duke of York; the appointment of the Earl of Shaftesbury appeases the "Whig" party – which seeks to exclude James from the succession – but the crown and its parliamentary allies (the "Tories") still control the council (→ 30/4).

Westminster, 30 April 1679. King Charles assures the Commons that the powers given to any future Catholic monarch would be severely limited (→ 27/5).

Scotland, 29 June 1679. Following the crushing of the Covenanters' rebellion, Charles offers a third Indulgence to dissenting clergy in the hope of reducing tension in the country.

Paris, July 1679. Rumour has it that William of Orange is having an affair with Elizabeth Villiers, one of Mary's ladies-in-waiting.

London, 2 June 1680. Charles denies that he was ever married to Lucy Walter, the mother of his eldest son James, the Duke of Monmouth (→ 21/3/81).

Middlesex, June 1680. On his return from exile, parliament attempts to try James, the Duke of York, as a recusant (→ 11/1680).

London, 1680. George Louis, the son of Sophia, the Electress of Brunswick-Lüneburg, is considered as a possible suitor for the Duke of York's younger daughter Anne (→ 11/1682).

London, 2 March 1681. Isabella, the five-year-old daughter of Mary of Modena and James, the Duke of York, dies (→ 6/10/82).

Oxford, 21 March 1681. Parliament opens; the Whigs campaign publicly to exclude James, the Duke of York, from the succession in favour of James, the Duke of Monmouth, King Charles's illegitimate but Protestant son (→ 28/3).

Oxford, 28 March 1681. King Charles dissolves parliament; troops are standing by in case the Whigs protest, but they are not needed.→

London, 6 October 1682. Charlotte Maria, the two-month-old daughter of Mary of Modena and James, the Duke of York, dies.

Surrey, 1682. Lady Castlemaine, one of Charles's former mistresses, orders the destruction of Nonsuch palace, which the king gave to her.

London, 19 July 1683. Prince George of Denmark arrives to complete the arrangements for his marriage to Princess Anne, the younger daughter of James, the Duke of York, and niece of King Charles (→ 28/7).

London, autumn 1683. Charles forbids William of Orange to visit England in the light of the prince's support for the exiled Duke of Monmouth, Charles's illegitimate son (→ 1684).

London, 1683. Princess Anne employs Sarah Churchill, her attendant from her stepmother's house, as her lady of the bedchamber.

London, 12 May 1684. Princess Anne gives birth to a stillborn daughter (→ 2/6/85).

England, 6 February 1685. King Charles II, who had a stroke four days ago, dies aged 54; despite protests at the Catholic succession, his brother James, the Duke of York, is now king.→

Plot to steal the crown jewels is foiled

Thomas Blood is caught trying to steal the crown: a later illustration.

London, 18 June 1671
To the amazement of most of the establishment, the king has pardoned the leader of a gang that attempted to steal the crown jewels. Thomas Blood, a noted criminal who was already wanted for kidnapping at the time of his arrest, walked free today after a secret talk with Charles – who has even granted him a £500 a year pension.

Blood, a tall and rangy former Cromwellian soldier with a pock-marked face and beady eyes, has been involved in various plots in England and Ireland since the 1660s. The most notorious of these was the kidnapping of the courtly Duke of Ormonde at the behest of the Duke of Buckingham. Ormonde managed to break free, and the king put a reward of £1,000 on the heads of each of the gang. Blood could have expected to come to a gruesome end for such a crime; so why the spectacular reprieve?

Some believe that it was the king's secret admiration for Blood's daring; others are sure that Charles has engaged Blood to spy on the nonconformists. Mystery surrounds a book that was found on Blood containing the record of 60 alleged escapes from great danger. Whether it contains material potentially damaging to the king is not known; but Blood has become a firm favourite at Charles's court.

King suspends laws against dissenters

London, 1672
In an extraordinary religious volte-face, the king has suspended all penal laws against both Protestant dissenters and Catholics. Catholics will be allowed to celebrate Mass in private; dissenters' services will need permission. Many thought at first that this Declaration of Indulgence was temporary, to persuade the Catholic king of France to speed preparations for the coming war with the United Provinces, but Charles insists that it is permanent, and that the liberal and tolerant approach will produce a more stable country. The reality appears to be the king's need to cultivate a "special relationship" with Louis XIV – and to secure possible French subsidies (→ 5/1673).

Jailbirds not freed

London, May 1673
Despite the royal declaration which offered greater freedom to worship to both Catholics and Protestant dissenters, the prisons remain filled with men and women arrested and fined for such crimes as not attending church. Despite a recommendation that those held only for their principles should be pardoned and released, the bureaucracy is moving at a snail's pace, with clerks insisting on treating each case individually and demanding substantial fees from each person named in the pardon.

Popery fears raised by duke's wedding

London, 21 November 1673
The secret conversion to Catholicism of the king's younger brother and his marriage to the Catholic Mary of Modena are causing serious parliamentary storms. James has been a Catholic for over four years, but it was only last Easter that he publicly refused to take the Anglican sacrament; in June he resigned as lord high admiral.

MPs have passed a new Test Act which limits the power of future Catholic sovereigns and provides for the Protestant education of their children. It proposes that Catholics should not be allowed to sit in parliament. It is even being suggested that Charles should divorce his childless wife and remarry to provide a Protestant heir (→ 10/1677).

James's bride: Mary of Modena.

Brilliant Dutch naval campaigns run rings round English efforts

New York, August 1673
A series of Dutch naval victories has added a note of urgency to King Charles's efforts to ally with Catholic France against the United Provinces. Despite inferiority in numbers, Dutch commanders have wreaked havoc on the British and French fleets. Admiral Michael de Ruyter led a brilliant raid on the French fleet wintering in Brest. Victory at Texel has foiled a possible English invasion, and a daring cross-Atlantic dash by a Dutch fleet of 23 ships has captured Manhattan Island and Fort James from the English garrison (→ 10/1677).

A grand panorama of the battle at Texel by Willem van de Velde (d.1707).

Pressure breaks up king's inner circle

Westminster, 1673
Parliamentary opposition to the foreign policy of the king's five favourite ministers has brought their influence as a group to an end. The "Cabal", so called because of their secretive consultations with the king and after their initials (Clifford, Arlington, Buckingham, Ashley-Cooper and Lauderdale) had had the king's ear since the fall of Clarendon. Charles played on their internal differences to secure his own policy of religious toleration. But now they are no more. ▷

King backs colonisation of America

New World is arena for British traders

New England, 1676

The corrupt governor of Virginia, Sir William Berkeley, has been dismissed and recalled to England on the king's orders for his cruelty to rebels led by Nathaniel Bacon. The new governor, Colonel Jeffreys, has halted hundreds of executions ordered by Berkeley. Bacon and his men had rebelled against the government's failure to protect them adequately from Indian raids.

Occasional hiccups like this do not mar the progress of the steady colonisation of North America. King Charles is locked in deadly competition with the Dutch to secure control of these lucrative new lands, and with slaves fetching as much as £18 apiece in Virginia it is a prize well worth fighting for.

The king has given a huge tract of territory in America's north-east to the Duke of York and named it New York. The former New Amsterdam has been annexed and renamed New York City. The duke has rewarded two of his most devoted followers, Sir George Carteret and John, Lord Berkeley, with a huge tract of land west of the Hudson river. It has been renamed New Jersey after Carteret's birthplace in the English Channel.

New Hampshire was given a royal governor and independent status this year, and Boston saw the opening of its first coffee house. The colony of Carolina, founded in 1660, was created largely by Sir John Colleton, a Civil War royalist exile, to attract white farmers from the island of Barbados with their slaves. The new settlers will become freeholders within three years.

But the cost of the extended campaign against rival Dutch attempts to colonise the "New World" continues to drive the king into the arms of France, eager to give him aid to fight their common enemy. He is already suspected of pro-Catholic leanings, and the public Catholicism of his brother James, the Duke of York, has aroused fears that the royal family is encouraging Catholicism back into Britain by the back door (→10/7/78).

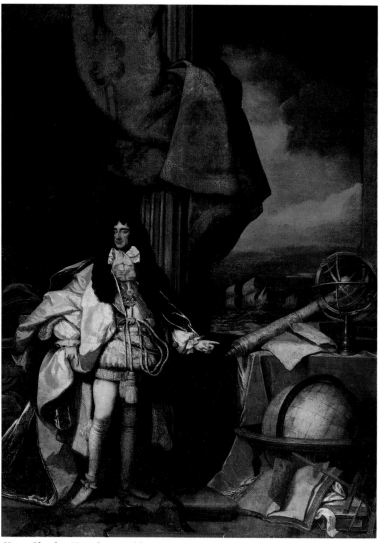

King Charles II with a world map, and trading ships in the background.

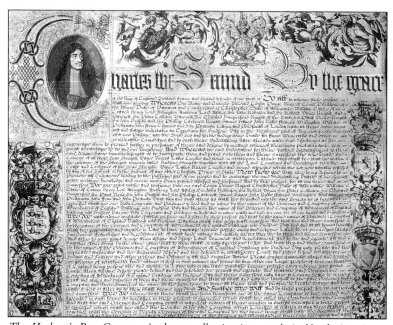

The Hudson's Bay Company's charter allowing it to trade in North America.

Charles finds new thrills with eager mistress from Italy

London, 1676

A ravishing Italian duchess has supplanted Louise, the Duchess of Portsmouth, as Charles's favourite mistress. Hortense Mancini is a 30-year-old divorcée whose bewitching eyes, jet-black hair and powerful personality are matched by a rare sexual expertise – gathered, it is said, from lovers of both sexes. A self-confident, handsome woman, she has captivated the middle-aged king with her unfettered gusto for life. Charles has installed her in St James's palace and crosses the park from Whitehall to visit her there every night.

Hortense: the king's new mistress.

Peter Lely portrays all the top people

London, 1676

Peter Lely, the royal portrait painter, is in the process of completing a nude picture of Nell Gwynn commissioned by her greatest admirer, the king of England. Lely first came to England from Westphalia in the 1640s and gained a reputation as a landscape artist before turning to the more lucrative role of portrait painter. Although Lely painted a striking portrait of Oliver Cromwell he remained in favour, and Charles has in fact conferred a £200 annual pension on him. The king frequently visits Lely's studio and regards the painter as a personal friend.

Charles builds a new London in right royal style

The new Royal Exchange building, in the heart of the City of London.

King Charles's Whitehall palace: undergoing general refurbishment.

Sir Christopher Wren, scientist and architect: he was knighted in 1673.

London, 1676

A new London is springing up from the ashes of the Great Fire which destroyed it ten years ago – and much of the credit must go to the king, who has given great impetus to the task of reconstruction. Back in 1666, Londoners shocked by the destruction were comforted by King Charles's promise that he would build a new city made of brick and stone on the smoking embers of the last one.

Charles was as good as his word and immediately set up a committee of councillors to agree rebuilding plans with the City fathers. To encourage swift development he issued a decree repealing the hearth tax on all new buildings. Moreover, he took a direct role in supervising the new plans. Parliament also assisted in the rebuilding, providing funds by a tax on coal in 1670.

Perhaps Charles's most inspired move was to put Christopher Wren, the Savilian professor of astronomy at Oxford, in charge of the reconstruction. Soon after the fire Wren had attracted the king's attention with a plan to replace London's mediaeval streets with a series of wide, straight avenues radiating from a series of piazzas. The plan was rejected, largely because of re-

'A new city of brick and stone is being built on the smoking embers of the old'

sistance from City landlords and lack of funds to compensate them, but Wren's aptitudes were noted, and he has held the office of surveyor-general of the king's works for the last seven years.

Wren's major task is to rebuild 52 of the 109 parish churches lost in the fire. Last year construction started on a new St Paul's cathedral to replace the burnt-out shell of the old one. Wren himself laid the foun-

dation stone, asking a workman to find a flat stone from the rubble of the old cathedral; it happened to be a gravestone inscribed *Resurgam* [I will rise again]. The design, the third that Wren has produced, has a breathtaking dome set over the crossing of transept and nave. Wren

is said to have wept with frustration after his first, most innovative design was debated, modified and finally dropped as a result of clerical and court interference.

The king's interest in architecture and town planning predates the Great Fire by many years. On accession, he started to make alterations to his palace at Whitehall, and in 1671 he built an opulent suite of apartments for his mistress,

Louise de Kéroüalle, the Duchess of Portsmouth. Charles also designed his own bedroom, installing black-and-white marble floors and statuary of eagles and cherubs.

Only lack of funds has prevented him from demolishing the ramshackle collection of buildings that makes up the palace complex and replacing it with a new, unified design. It has proved easier to improve his other palace at Greenwich, on a greenfield site on the Thames south-east of the City.

Nor has the royal residence at Windsor escaped the attentions of a king who seems positively to enjoy having the builders in. Work on renovating the castle continues apace, having started two years ago. Charles's architect here, Hugh May, has obliterated the old 14th-century floorplan in order to create a set of appropriately grand rooms, adorned by superb allegorical murals and ceiling paintings by Antonio Verrio.

King's niece is married to Prince William of Orange amid tears and funereal black

The bridegroom: Prince William.

The bride: Princess Mary.

London, 4 November 1677
One could hardly call it a joyous wedding – the couple were so ill-matched for a start. The bride, Mary of England, the king's niece, was 15, tall (5ft 11ins), attractive and elegant in her court dress; the groom, William of Orange, was 27, four inches shorter than his bride and dressed in funereal black. He looked glum throughout the proceedings; James, his father-in-law to be, looked equally solemn; the bride wept constantly.

The only merriment came from the king, especially when the newly-married couple were put to bed. Then Charles drew the curtains and shouted: "Now nephew, to your work! Hey! St George for England!"

The ceremony may have been a sad business – the bride's sister is suffering from smallpox and could

not attend – but London was celebrating in style tonight. The union of the *stadhouder* of Holland and the daughter of the heir to the English throne suggests the beginning of a break from French influence.

William has made no secret of the fact that he hopes that the marriage will bring England into his war with France. The heavy taxation required to fight the war is costing him popularity at home, and he needs to convince the Dutch that they must fight on with their new allies. Unfortunately for William, Charles Stuart has no intention of fighting.

Life in Charles's flippant and amoral court is unlikely to appeal to the staid and stuffy stadhouder. He has already announced his intention of taking his bride back to Holland, an idea that clearly does not attract Mary (→ 1678).

'Popish plot' is revealed

London, 21 October 1678
Parliament has been recalled for an emergency session, following the discovery four days ago of a badly bruised corpse on Primrose Hill, for the body is that of Sir Edmund Berry Godfrey, a magistrate who had taken evidence of a Catholic plot to kill King Charles and organise a French takeover of England. The country is in a frenzy, believing that the Catholics killed him.

Charles's attention was brought to the alleged plot last month when he met a crack-brained clergyman, Israel Tonge, who relayed a dreadful secret. The king, he said, was to be waylaid in St James's park, stabbed by Irish ruffians and Jesuits, then shot with silver bullets and poisoned by the king's physician.

Charles referred the matter to the privy council and went off to the races. Titus Oates, a triple-chinned, piggy-eyed ex-clergyman convicted of gross indecency, appeared before the council and outlined the alleged plot, details of which he had already laid before

The trouble-maker: Titus Oates.

Godfrey. On his evidence, the council ordered a nationwide search of Catholic homes for arms. Anti-Catholic hysteria spread, increasing when incriminating letters to Louis XIV from the Duke of York's secretary were discovered. Now Godfrey's death seems to confirm everyone's worst fears (→ 4/1679).

Charles makes secret deal with France

London, 17 May 1678
Mysterious negotiations between the kings of England and France are causing increasing concern and confusion in court and parliamentary circles. Charles is apparently pursuing two quite different lines of policy. On 17 May he negotiated a secret agreement with Louis XIV that promised disbandment of the English army, prorogation of parlia-

ment and neutrality in return for a substantial payment.

Charles seemed quite unaware at the time that King Louis was already bribing opposition members to oppose any royal measures that might produce a peace with the United Provinces. And all of this has been taking place after England signed an alliance with the Dutch *stadhouder* (→ 1681).

James to remain heir in spite of Whigs

London, Autumn 1678
Despite efforts by the Earl of Shaftesbury, leading the country party, or "Whigs" (as those who wish to exclude the Catholic Duke of York from the succession are nicknamed), James Stuart remains heir to the throne. However, the new Test Act passed this year means that no other Catholic can take a seat in Parliament.

It ends a dramatic series of events that began with the king arguing that the alleged "popish plot" [*see above*] should be left to the normal

process of law rather than inspire rushed legislation. The Commons preferred to accept the story of the plot told by Titus Oates and kept up pressure against the king's brother.

With anti-Catholic mania at fever pitch, and Shaftesbury able to call mobs onto the streets at short notice, Charles had to agree to the laws as long as they did not affect James's succession. Other Catholics are less fortunate than James. They are to be exiled from London and confined within five miles (8km) of their homes (→ 21/10).

THE MARRIAGE OF WILLIAM AND MARY				
James VI of Scots and I of England 1567–[1603]–1625		**William I** Prince of Orange		
		Frederick Henry Prince of Orange		
Charles I 1625–49				
Charles II 1660–85	**Mary** Princess Royal	= **William II** Prince of Orange	**James II** 1685–88	**Frederick** = **Louise** William **Henrietta** Elector of Brandenburg

Dates = reigns

Popish plot linked to king's brother

London, April 1679

As a reign of terror continues to grip England following allegations of a "popish plot", attention is focusing on the activities of the king's brother, James, the Duke of York, whose secret conversion to Catholicism became known six years ago. His former secretary, Edward Coleman, was executed for treason last December after admitting writing to Jesuits and French agents with wild and improbable schemes to help Catholics in England.

When Coleman told a Commons committee that his master had approved this correspondence, the Whig party, led by the highly vocal Lord Shaftesbury, began a sustained attack on the heir to the throne. William Sacheverell, regarded as one of the more moderate Whigs, has proposed that James – and all Catholics – should be excluded from the list of royal heirs. His more cynical colleagues see political capital in the present panic.

The terror continues. Rumours of French landings abound. Silk armour – guaranteed to ward off even silver bullets – is the latest fashion. Pistols designed for use by ladies are selling well. The prisons are filled with Catholics. But there are many, and the king is among them, who feel that the evidence offered by Titus Oates is nothing but make-believe (→ 21/4).

Rioters burn an effigy: a later view.

'Turncoat' archbishop killed in Scotland

Archbishop Sharp is roughly dragged from his carriage and murdered.

Fife, 3 March 1679

In a shocking act of political terrorism, James Sharp, the archbishop of St Andrews, has been brutally murdered by Covenanters – defenders of the Scottish Presbyterian tradition – who targeted him because of his collaboration with Charles II.

In 1661, when the king reintroduced the episcopacy to Scotland, he persuaded Sharp to become its head. As a leading minister, Sharp had been entrusted with presenting the Presbyterian case to both Cromwell and the young Charles. His present role in a government which suppresses dissident Covenanters made him to many a turncoat whose betrayal had to be punished. The 61-year-old cleric and his

daughter, Isabel, were travelling across Magus Moor when they noticed a gang of armed men closing in on them. Sharp ordered his driver to whip up the horses. The men gave chase, firing muskets; eventually one of them brought the carriage to a halt by slashing the postilion and the leading horse with a sword.

The archbishop, grazed by a bullet, was dragged out and stabbed in the side; then, as he pleaded for his life and for his daughter's safety, his attackers hacked him to death. Having split his skull open, the assassins – nine men in all – rifled his possessions, taking papers and armaments before fleeing to safety across the moor (→ 22/6).

Party labels reveal deep policy split

London, 1679

The problem of the succession to the throne has solidified political alliances into two distinct parties in the Commons. The Whigs, or exclusionists – led by Lord Shaftesbury, once a fervent royalist, then a Cromwellian, a politician skilled enough to survive the Restoration – are pledged to a Protestant succession. The Tories, the court party, are led by Thomas Osborne, Earl of Danby, and back the Duke of York. Their name has been applied as an insult: "tory" is a nickname for an Irish Catholic thief.

James recalled as Charles becomes ill

London, August 1679

With the king seriously ill and his brother James recalled by senior ministers, England may be on the brink of yet another outbreak of violence. Charles has angered Whigs like Lord Shaftesbury by his policy of proroguing parliament – he has done so quite legally five times since last October to prevent discussion on the exclusion issue and threatens to do it again. The Whigs, for their part, are organising petitions and printing a constant stream of pamphlets with James as their principal target (→ 28/1/80).

Commons block the Catholic succession

London, 27 May 1679

A newly-elected Whig parliament has taken a major step forward in its determination to make certain that no more Catholics will wear the crown of England, but the king has moved to ensure that the Duke of York remains his heir. Last week the Commons passed the Exclusion Bill to stop James becoming king; but, to ensure that the bill would not become an act, Charles today prorogued parliament and once again is threatening to dissolve it.

The king has acted against the advice of the privy council, which consists of both his friends and his enemies. The council was created to check the king's manoeuvring and in the hope that it would act as an umpire between Charles and parliament. "God's fish!" exclaimed the king to a close friend. "They have put a set of men around me, but they shall know nothing and keep this to yourself." Charles had promised to abide by the council's decisions, and Lord Shaftesbury, its president, is livid at yet another royal gambit to gain time.

One major act was passed by this parliament, however – and then only by accident. The Habeas Corpus Act, under which anyone holding a prisoner must produce him on the writ of a court, was only passed by the upper chamber because the tellers counted one very fat peer as ten votes and failed to rectify their figures (→ 8/1679).

Elias Ashmole, a distinguished antiquarian and astrologer, who published his "History of the Order of the Garter" in 1672.

Duke of Monmouth routs rebellion by Scots Covenanters

Glasgow, 22 June 1679

Royalist troops have smashed a group of desperate rebels who, encouraged by their murder of Archbishop Sharp [*see report on previous page*], decided to risk a full-scale confrontation with the government.

The royalist army, under the command of the king's illegitimate son James, the Duke of Monmouth, met the rebel Covenanters – who had sworn to fight interference from south of the border – at

The victorious Duke of Monmouth.

Bothwell Bridge, a few miles from here. Monmouth had 10,000 well-armed soldiers with him, compared with the ill-disciplined rebel army which had only one small cannon. The struggle around the bridge over the Clyde was short, and there were few casualties. However, in the resulting pursuit Monmouth's dragoons cut down as many as 400 rebels and took another 1,200 prisoner.

Today's victory is likely to bring to an end the latest period of unrest. Crown control over the south-west of Scotland has slipped badly, culminating in the murder of Sharp and the Rutherglen Declaration in which the rebels denounced the doctrine of royal supremacy, the king's imposition of the Episcopal Church and the abandonment of the Covenant which attempted to guarantee the future Presbyterianism of Scotland (→ 29/6).

Duke of York returns from long exile

King Charles II's brother, James.

Whitehall, 28 January 1680

King Charles today told the privy council that he is formally inviting his brother James, the Duke of York, back from exile in Scotland. In the aftermath of the popish plot and the general hysteria against Catholics, James was a focus for anti-Catholic hatred. At first he was sent to Brussels, where he spent his time in stag-hunting while the Commons passed a bill excluding him from the succession.

Then Charles fell seriously ill and in August last year looked likely to die. Suddenly it seemed possible that the Duke of Monmouth, the king's illegitimate son, who was captain-general of the forces, might

seize the crown on Charles's death. James came back to Windsor in disguise, wearing a black wig. He found the king recovering; the brothers embraced with tears of joy.

Feeling more able to control the Whig supporters of Monmouth, Charles stripped the duke of his command and ordered him to the Low Countries. But as bonfires celebrated the king's recovery he played safe by sending James back, too. However, the Duke of York was soon allowed to return to Scotland where he had become popular, establishing a royal court at Holyrood palace from which he began to introduce his own supporters into the Scottish Parliament (→ 6/1680).

Commons show preference for Monmouth instead of James

Westminster, November 1680

Parliament is sitting at last, after being repeatedly prorogued by the king since its election last year. The first action of the Commons was to pass another bill to exclude James, the king's Catholic brother, from succeeding him on the throne. Charles has already made it plain that he will refuse to assent to any such bill. He had written to several lords urging them to oppose it.

When the bill came to the House of Lords, Charles attended the entire debate, having his meals brought in a portable cabinet. He

greeted every speech with a show of smiles and nods of approbation or scowls of anger if they were in favour of excluding James. When his son, the Duke of Monmouth, who is the Commons' favourite choice to succeed him, spoke of his solicitude for his father, Charles commented loudly: "It is a kiss of Judas which he gives me." It was above all the king's presence and hostility which ensured that the bill was defeated by 63 votes to 30.

Monmouth returned from exile a year ago and is being favoured by the Commons because of his great

popularity in the west country, demonstrated on a tour there this summer. He has now changed his coat of arms in a way designed to show that he is a legitimate son of Charles. Rumours have been put about that a certain black box contains the marriage contract of Charles and Monmouth's mother, Lucy Walter. The king was goaded into issuing a statement denying that they were ever married. Meanwhile he has sent James back to Scotland, after the Whigs accused him before a grand jury of being a popish agent (→ 3/1681).

Oliver Plunkett executed in Irish purge

Ireland, March 1681

Oliver Plunkett, the Catholic primate of Ireland, has been executed for treason after being brought to London against the king's wishes to face trial in connection with an alleged "Irish plot" against the crown. The Earl of Shaftesbury claimed to have discovered this plot as part of his campaign against Catholics – particularly James, the Duke of York.

A committee of the privy council sent for "witnesses", and a group of ragged informers (nicknamed "the McShams") accused Plunkett of treason. Charles wanted him to be tried in Ireland, where he would have been acquitted, but the Whigs brought him to London (→ 21/3).

The Whigs' victim: Oliver Plunkett, the Catholic primate of Ireland.

Loyal and efficient minister has died

Tunbridge Wells, 20 August 1682

John Maitland, the Duke of Lauderdale and the king's longest-serving minister, has died. He had been in poor health since suffering a stroke two years ago. For most of the last 20 years Lauderdale has ruled Scotland with a grip that has infuriated his many defeated rivals. As a young man he was an enthusiastic Covenanter and helped to draft the Solemn League and Covenant [*see page 240*]. But he remained a royalist and in 1647 helped to negotiate the "Engagement" with the imprisoned Charles I. The restored king appointed him as Scottish secretary.

Parliament dissolved to stop Whigs

Charles seals pact with French king

Oxford, 28 March 1681

Charles II once again demonstrated his political finesse here today by dissolving parliament, just a week after he had opened it, at the very moment that the Commons were giving a first reading to a new bill to exclude his brother James from the succession. The king had summoned parliament to meet in the royalist stronghold of Oxford, away from the populist pressures of London, and at the opening session he had offered a compromise which he thought would satisfy all except his brother James. This was to establish a regency after his death so that, while James was king in name, William of Orange and his wife Mary, James's daughter, would rule as joint protectors.

But the Commons – dominated by a group of members now known as Whigs who champion parliamentary supremacy and toleration for dissenters – rejected this and proposed for the first time to name the Duke of Monmouth, Charles's bastard son, as his successor. Charles then attacked Presbyterians as "ten times worse than the pope". So today the king sprang his surprise on the Whigs. He was carried from his lodgings at Christ Church in a sedan chair, followed by another in which he had concealed his crown and state robes which he put on, as is obligatory for dissolving a parliament, in the geometry school where the Lords were meeting.

He then summoned the Commons from the convocation house. They found their king in full regalia, waiting to pronounce their dissolution in one sentence. Charles then had lunch and drove away to Windsor while the Commons fled the city in disarray (→ 6/1683).

Louis XIV, by H Rigaud (d.1743).

Whitehall, 1681

Just before meeting parliament at Oxford, Charles concluded a secret agreement with Louis XIV of France. The French king wanted to ensure that England would not support Spain against him despite Charles's pact to help defend the Spanish Netherlands. In return Louis offered money – two million *livres*, with more to follow, amounting to £385,000 over three years. The negotiations were so secret that nothing was written down. Charles made a verbal treaty with the French ambassador in the privacy of the queen's bedroom. He did not even sign receipts for the money.

A piece of Whig propaganda (1680) showing the terrible consequences of a Catholic succession after Charles's reign.

Poet adds his weight to royal argument

London, 1681

The appearance of a new long satirical poem by the poet laureate, John Dryden, is making the Whigs smart. *Absalom and Achitophel* is the title of the poem, but its real subjects are the king's enemies. Achitophel, whom no one doubts is the Earl of Shaftesbury, is cruelly described, while the Duke of Buckingham is mocked as "stiff in opinions, always in the wrong,/ everything by starts and nothing long/ ... statesman and buffoon". Dryden, who wrote both a glowing obituary of Cromwell and a panegyric on the return of Charles II, has served his royal patron well.

John Dryden, the poet laureate.

Anne in torrid affair, say court gossips

London, November 1682

Princess Anne, the younger daughter of James, the Duke of York, and the king's niece, is the centre of a court scandal. She is 17, and gossip is linking her name with that of Lord Mulgrave, who is 35 and a bachelor. One of the king's favourites, he is now banned from court.

John Mulgrave claims that he is innocent of anything more serious than "ogling" the princess, but what has damned him is the discovery of his letters to her. These suggest that a more intimate relationship had developed, and London gossip concludes that he has seduced her "to spoil her marrying anybody else" and has given him the nickname of "King John".

All this is acutely embarrassing for the princess, whose life has been harmlessly occupied in hunting, dancing, playing cards and attending the Anglican Church, of which she appears to be a most devout member. Now that Mulgrave has been packed off to Tangier there is a move to get her married as soon as possible. One of those most upset is her sister Mary, the Princess of Orange, who wrote to a friend: "It makes me mad she should be exposed to such reports and now what will not this insolent man say, being provoked?" (→ 19/7/83).

A restored court breathes renewed life into the arts

London, 1683

After the kill-joy years of the Commonwealth, the court of King Charles prizes wit above morality under a king who is ready to laugh at most things, including himself. The Earl of Rochester knew that he was safe to write:

We have a pritty witty king,
Whose word no man relies on;
Who never said a foolish thing
Nor ever did a wise one.

Charles's taste for the theatre began with the acting of Nell Gwynn, who retired from the stage at the age of 19 to join the king in the audience. The novelty of watching actresses, as opposed to actors dressed as women, has increased the popularity of the theatre. New playwrights have also helped; Dryden's neo-Shakespearean tragedies, such as *All For Love*, go down very well, as do Wycherley's comedies (*The Country Wife* and *The Plain Dealer*) exposing the hypocrisy of a society that revolves around sex and money. The king, a good talent-spotter, has put his money where his mouth is, appointing Henry Purcell as his court composer, Godfrey Kneller court painter and Grinling Gibbons "master sculptor".

A lady in a fine theatre costume.

'Rye House plot' to kill king uncovered

The trial of Lord William Russell, who was one of the Rye House plotters.

Hertfordshire, June 1683

Rye House in Hertfordshire stands on the road from London to Newmarket, along which King Charles travels on his frequent visits to go racing at Newmarket. On the day scheduled for his return this month a plot had been hatched to hold up his coach and kill both the king and his brother James.

The plotters were supporters of the Duke of Monmouth and included several Whigs, who hatched the plan at the Green Ribbon Club, the party's social headquarters in Chancery Lane, in London. The owner of Rye House, Richard Rumbold, was one of the instigators. Whig leaders such as Shaftesbury, Russell, Essex, Sidney and Hampden had been talking of a general insurrection since they had realised that the king was not going to call any more parliaments.

The attack on the king's coach and Life Guards never took place because his journey was prevented by accident, but the plot was betrayed to the government, causing popular opinion to turn violently against the Whigs. Most members of the Green Ribbon Club are under arrest; its president, Shaftesbury, had died in exile in the Low Countries earlier this year. Russell and Sidney are in the Tower, indicted for treason, and Essex has committed suicide. The Duke of Monmouth is expected to go into exile in the Low Countries (→ 1684).

Exiled Monmouth welcomed by Dutch

The Hague, 1684

Prince William of Orange has angered King Charles by extending a warm welcome to the exiled Duke of Monmouth who fled to the Low Countries after being convicted of involvement in last year's Rye House plot against the king. Monmouth, who is Charles's eldest illegitimate son, had not been deeply involved, but Charles and, more especially, his brother James, the Duke of York, are irritated by his reception at the Dutch court.

William, who is married to James's elder daughter, Mary, has taken Monmouth on hunting trips and even arranged for his guest to review English regiments stationed nearby. Monmouth has spent most of the summer as an honoured guest with the Dutch court, with William claiming that the English king was not really angry with his bastard son. Charles summoned the Dutch ambassador to complain, and James wrote letters to William and Mary protesting about Monmouth's treatment, but to no avail.

James's concern is easy enough to understand. The Whig group of MPs in parliament has promoted Monmouth as an alternative successor to Charles, instead of himself. And William himself occupies a key role as not only the champion of the rotestant cause in Europe but also the husband of Mary, who is next in line after James himself to the British throne (→ 11/6/85).

Anne, daughter of the Duke of York, marries Danish Protestant

St James's, 28 July, 1683

Princess Anne, the younger daughter of James, the Duke of York, was married this evening in the Chapel Royal of St James's palace, without ceremony or ostentation, at the king's command. The bridegroom, Prince George of Denmark, is 12 years older than the 18-year-old English princess, a man of few words and trained as a soldier. He is the brother of the Danish king.

He is above all a Protestant, which makes him doubly welcome to his wife and to the English. The marriage negotiations were kept secret from William of Orange – the husband of Mary, Anne's elder sister – who feels that his influence may be diminished by another Protestant prince in the British royal family. But Anne seems more concerned that her childhood friend, Sarah Churchill, to whom she is passionately attached, will approve of the marriage and that James will allow her to become a lady of the bedchamber.

Sarah Churchill's husband, Lord John Churchill, is a favourite of the Duke of York. Princess Anne wants desperately to come first in Sarah's affections after her husband, prizing her honesty and candour in a court riddled with insincere flattery (→ 12/5/84).

Groom: Prince George of Denmark.

Charles II, the king who restored monarchy, dies

In the end, king becomes a Catholic

Final act is to ensure mistress and bastards are looked after

Whitehall, 5 February 1685

This evening the dying King Charles was received into the Catholic Church in a private ceremony arranged by his brother James. The bedchamber was emptied of everyone except two reliable witnesses, and Father John Hudlestone, who ministered to Charles following his escape after the Battle of Worcester, was admitted in disguise. Seeing him, the king cried out: "You that saved my body is now come to save my soul." The priest, having given him absolution and extreme unction, departed by the back stairs, and the courtiers were re-admitted. Charles told them he had made his peace with God (→ 6/2).

James, the Duke of Monmouth.

Whitehall, 6 February 1685

The sufferings of King Charles ended at midday today, four days after he fell unconscious from a stroke. He was bled and blistered but bore it with humour, saying: "I am sorry, gentlemen, for being such an unconscionable time a-dying."

Last night he made his farewells to his many illegitimate offspring. His childless queen sent word begging forgiveness. "Alas, poor woman," he said. "She beg *my* pardon? I beg hers with all my heart." Five sons, the Dukes of Grafton, Southampton, Northumberland, St Albans and Richmond, knelt before him; Monmouth, the eldest of his bastard sons, was in exile. He asked his brother James to look after them – and Nell Gwynn (→ 10/2).

Charles, the Duke of Richmond.

Charismatic king of dramatic contrasts

Whitehall, 10 February 1685

Charles II, who died this week, will be mourned by his people "as for the loss of the best friend in the world", according to one commentator. "By him such blessings to his realm were given,/he seemed created for his people's good," runs one of the many memorial verses. Not all his citizens would endorse this eulogistic view. There was broadly peace after the turmoil of the Civil War, but Scottish Presbyterians, English dissenters and many Irish encountered a harsher side of the monarch than that now being portrayed by his champions.

He certainly had a charisma that set men to analysing his singular character. "He said to me once that he could not think God would make a man miserable for taking a little pleasure," says Bishop Burnet. Charles was accused of laziness and indulgence, yet not when it came to his pursuit of pleasure. He rose at five or six o'clock, breakfasting on whisky and water, and showed immense energy at his sports of riding, dancing, sailing, swimming, and especially his long solitary walks, which he took twice a day, timing them with his watch and raising his

A sophisticated court: King Charles relaxing with friends in the days before his death, by WP Frith (1819-1909).

hat to others. At Newmarket, his favourite outing, he enjoyed dining with the jockeys. And although he changed his mistresses frequently, he remained fond of them and looked after them, as he did his illegitimate children.

He took his kingship seriously, however. He is said to have touched 90,000 of his subjects for the "king's evil", and he often attended the privy council and the House of Lords. Yet he never went to the Scottish Parliament. Indeed, he never returned to Scotland after the Restoration, and he presided over a corrupt regime in Scotland which relied increasingly on military force and repression. This contrasts starkly with a scientific curiosity which, in the age of Newton, Boyle and Halley, led to his patronage for the Royal Society. It is not the only paradox; despite his undoubted charm he could be calculating and vindictive to those who thwarted his plans or desires.

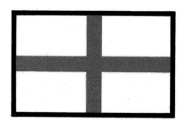

J a m e s   I I
1685–1688

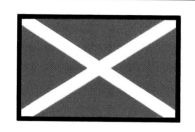

England, 6 February 1685. James, the Duke of York, a Catholic, accedes to the throne (→ 23/4).

Westminster, 23 April 1685. James II is crowned king of England.→

London, 2 June 1685. Princess Anne, the wife of George of Denmark and younger daughter of James, gives birth to a daughter, Mary (→ 12/5/86).

Lyme Regis, 11 June 1685. James, the Duke of Monmouth, the eldest illegitimate child of Charles II, lands, claiming the throne as the Protestant heir (→ 6/7).

Westminster, 20 November 1685. James closes parliament after informing his government that he wants the Test and Corporation Acts and all penal laws against the Catholics repealed (→ 7/1686).

Edinburgh, January 1686. Riots follow the reintroduction of the Catholic Mass by James (→ 6/1686).

Windsor Castle, 12 May 1686. Princess Anne gives birth to a second daughter, to be named Anne Sophia (→ 8/2/87).

Scotland, June 1686. The Scottish Parliament refuses to grant toleration to Catholics even when offered economic union with England (→ 1686).

London, 14 October 1686. James orders a national holiday to celebrate his birthday.

England, November 1686. In an attempt to ally with Protestant dissenters against the Church of England, James allows them to purchase dispensation from penal legislation (→ 4/4/87).

Low Countries, November 1686. William Penn, a leader of the Quakers, fails on a mission here to rally the support of Prince William

of Orange for his father-in-law, James II, in his efforts to repeal the penal laws and the Test Act against dissenters (→ 4/1688).

Low Countries, 1686. Work begins on a new palace for William of Orange at Het Loo.

Scotland, 1686. King James is delighted with the conversion to Roman Catholicism of three of his most important Scottish ministers: Lord Perth, the chancellor, and the secretaries Lords Melfort and Moray (→ 12/2/87).

Windsor Castle, 8 February 1687. Lady Mary, aged two, the elder daughter of Princess Anne and Prince George, dies of smallpox only six days after her one-year-old sister, Anne Sophia (→ 22/10).

Scotland, 12 February 1687. James issues a proclamation granting a measure of religious toleration to Quakers and Catholics in Scotland (→ 10/12/88).

Windsor, 22 October 1687. Anne has a miscarriage (→ 24/7/89).

London, November 1687. James sets up a commission to question local officials in order to establish their stances on the repeal of the penal laws; all those not in favour are to be replaced with Catholic officials (→ 1687).

London, 1687. Nell Gwynn, a mistress of the late King Charles II, dies.

Oxford, 1687. King James tries to convert Magdalen college into a Catholic seminary in an attack on Anglicanism in the universities (→ 27/4/88).

London, 29 January 1688. Following the surprise announcement that Queen Mary of Modena is pregnant, prayers are widely said for the safe birth of the baby (→ 10/6).

London, 27 April 1688. James becomes more unpopular when he issues his second Declaration of Indulgence; his first had suspended penal laws against Catholics and all dissenters (→ 4/5).

Low Countries, April 1688. Prince William of Orange informs Edward Russell, the Earl of Orford, of his intention of leading an invasion of England (→ 30/6).

England, 4 May 1688. King James orders that the recently-issued Declaration of Indulgence be read out in churches throughout the land (→ 30/6).

English Channel, 21 October 1688. William of Orange and his Dutch invasion fleet are forced to turn back due to bad weather (→ 5/11).

Torbay, 5 November 1688. Prince William lands to a tumultuous welcome (→ 9/11).

Exeter, 9 November 1688. William, with an army of 12,000 foot and 3,000 mounted soldiers, marches into the city.

Salisbury, 23 November 1688. On the king's orders to return to London, many members of the royalist forces, including John Churchill, defect to support William (→ 26/11).

London, 27 November 1688. James is advised by a council of peers to call a free parliament, issue a general pardon, ban all Catholics from office and send commissioners to meet William (→ 8/12).

Hungerford, 8 December 1688. A commission consisting of the Marquis of Halifax, Lord Godolphin and the Earl of Nottingham is received by Prince William (→ 17/12).

Gravesend, 9 December 1688. Queen Mary and her infant son, James, flee to France (→ 28/6/92).

Edinburgh, 10 December 1688. Royal government collapses as the chancellor, Perth, flees from the city where anti-Catholic riots have broken out.

London, 17 December 1688. James, after failing to escape earlier this month, returns to London and, on the advice and with the help of William, flees to Rochester to make his escape (→ 23/12).

Rochester, 23 December 1688. Despite attempts by the Tories and Catholics to persuade him to stay, King James flees into exile in France.→

The life and times of King James II

Name: James Stuart.
Birth: St James's palace, 14 October 1633.
Accession: 6 February 1685.
Coronation: 23 April 1685.
Predecessor: brother.
Hair: brown.
Eyes: blue.
Marriages: 1) Anne Hyde, 3 September 1660, London; 2) Mary of Modena, 21 November 1673, Dover.
Children: 14 legitimate, several illegitimate
Likes: women, sailing.
Greatest problem: being a Roman Catholic.
Greatest success: attaining the throne in spite of being Catholic.
Exiled: 11 December 1688.
Deposed: 28 January 1689.
Death: 6 September 1701.

Opposite: regally clad, the Catholic king, James II.

Sedition and rebellion greet Catholic King James

Devout new ruler seems set for conflict

Westminster, 23 April 1685

King James was today crowned king of England, succeeding his brother Charles – the second monarch named James in England and the seventh in Scotland. He is 51 and, more importantly, the first avowedly Catholic monarch since Mary Tudor. James is truly devout, and this conviction seems set to bring renewed conflict to these kingdoms – not least because he is persuaded of the divine right of kings, which caused a civil war in the reign of his father.

Relations between Charles II and parliament were never easy, but he did acquire a group of parliamentary supporters who have become known as Tories. They back the rights of hereditary succession and the royal prerogative. In order to retain Tory support, Charles remained a member of the Church of England until his death-bed conversion to Catholicism. James, however, was converted in the 1660s and shows few signs of recognising that England and Scotland are predominantly Protestant nations.

As a young man James served bravely in the French army; he was also naval commander in the Dutch wars. His heirs are his two daughters by his first wife, Anne Hyde: Mary, who is married to her cousin William of Orange, and Anne. Both are Protestants. The king married Mary of Modena 16 years ago; their children have died (→ 20/11).

A Catholic accession: the coronation of King James II and Queen Mary.

Duke of Monmouth defeated in the west

Sedgemoor, 6 July 1685

The Duke of Monmouth was defeated here last night. He had been joined by 4,000 anti-Catholics and former parliamentarians after landing with 82 men on 11 June, but he failed to raise the country and was faced by a royal army whose most active leader was John Churchill. Monmouth tried a night attack against the royalists, but his troops were blocked. The duke fled; his men were slaughtered.

Monmouth was Charles II's eldest illegitimate son. He was in the Low Countries when Charles died, and his supporters persuaded him that England would rise to him if he invaded. He promised justice, annual parliaments and no standing army. When that failed to rouse the country he proclaimed himself king, claiming that Charles II had secretly married his mother (→ 15/7).

Frantic combat at Sedgemoor.

Duke of Monmouth executed for treason

London, 15 July 1685

The Duke of Monmouth was beheaded for treason today. He had grovelled at the feet of his uncle, King James, begging for his life. He continued to beg for mercy in the Tower but refused to make his peace with the Church of England or to renounce his mistress, Henrietta Berkeley. On the scaffold he proclaimed that he died a Protestant. The headsman, Jack Ketch, botched the execution. It required half a dozen blows to kill the duke, and Ketch's assistants finished the work with knives.

Argyll captured as Scottish revolt flops

Glasgow, 1685

The Earl of Argyll's revolt has ended in utter failure. The earl, who is one of the most prominent Scottish Presbyterians and under the name *MacCalein Mor* is the hereditary chief of Clan Campbell, had been living in exile in the Low Countries. When King Charles died he set off to raise Scotland in revolt against King James while the Duke of Monmouth sailed for England. The earl landed in Campbell country and summoned his clan. About 1,500 men came in, but the navy seized the rebels' base, and the council of war which directed the operation insisted on invading the lowlands. The rebels were intercepted north of the Clyde, and their army disintegrated without a battle. Argyll tried to escape in disguise but was discovered and arrested. He will be executed in Edinburgh, where his father was executed 24 years ago (→ 11/5).

The Presbyterian Earl of Argyll tries to escape in disguise: a later engraving.

'Killing times' claim two more martyrs

Dumfries/Galloway, 11 May 1685
Two women were drowned at Wigtown today for refusing to accept the Episcopalian Church backed by King James II. They were tied to stakes on the beach at low tide, and the rising waters drowned them. The older, a woman in her 60s, died first. The other, a girl of 18, sang psalms and prayed loudly as the tide came in. She was twice released and asked to abjure her faith, and twice refused.

Scores have died in a series of outrages – the "killing times" – which began in 1681 and have been intensified by James and the Episcopalian party. Parliament in Edinburgh has passed laws against Presbyterians which the king and his agent, John Graham, enforce with great brutality (→ 1/1686).

William is waiting

The Hague, 1686
Prince William of Orange, the Protestant husband of the heir to the British throne, is being informed by supporters of the increasing tension in England and Scotland. William, the Dutch head of state, has a great reputation as a statesman and soldier. His wife, Mary, is James II's elder daughter, and unless the king has a son she is heir to the throne. William has thus become the Protestants' great hope (→ 11/1686).

The Duchess of Portsmouth, a mistress of the late Charles II.

England becomes more Catholic

King wants church to be more Roman

Westminster, 4 April 1687
The king has issued a declaration of indulgence suspending all the penal laws against dissenters and Catholics. For many months he has been issuing individual exemptions to dissenters, including William Penn, the Quaker, and has promoted many Catholic officers in the army. The new declaration makes the exemptions general.

The king wants an alliance with the dissenters against parliament and the Church of England, hoping that they will support his plans to eliminate the laws against Catholics. The Test and Corporation Acts provide that no dissenter or Catholic may serve the government in any capacity, be a magistrate or an army officer, or teach in the universities. The king hopes with the dissenters' help to elect a new parliament to repeal the acts.

The Church of England must now accept popery or renounce its loyalty to the crown. The king has dismissed his leading Anglican ministers the Earls of Rochester and Clarendon, who were brothers of his first wife, Anne Hyde. He has admitted Catholics to the privy council and has appointed several crypto-Catholics to church livings and bishoprics (→ 3/7).

King James does homage to the papal nuncio, Cardinal Adda: a later view.

King welcomes cardinal and breaks law

Windsor, 3 July 1687
The papal nuncio, Cardinal Adda, was formally received by the king here today in a ceremony of great splendour. The king intended to demonstrate again his fidelity to the pope. Last month the cardinal was consecrated archbishop in the queen's chapel at St James's palace in the most elaborate public Catholic service held in England since Queen Mary Tudor's time. It was flagrantly illegal. The king instructed the Duke of Somerset, known as "the proud duke", a lord of the king's bedchamber, to lead the procession. He refused, telling the king: "I am advised that I cannot obey your majesty without breaking the law."

The king expostulated: "Do you not know that I am above the law?" "Your majesty may be above the law," replied the duke, "but I am not." He was then dismissed from all his positions (→ 21/10).

Commission set up to gag anti-Catholics

Westminster, July 1686
The king has set up a court of high commission to rule the Church of England by decree, in flagrant violation of the law. The chief commissioner is Lord Jeffreys, the lord chancellor, notorious for his cruelty in the "bloody assize" after Monmouth's rebellion. Another key member is Father Edward Petre, the king's Jesuit adviser. Together with James they want to purge the church of anti-Catholics and replace them with Catholics and sympathisers. The commission's first act has been to suspend the bishop of London for refusing to discipline a rector for preaching an anti-Catholic sermon (→ 11/1686).

Edward Petre: a later view.

Angry king expels rebellious fellows

Oxford, 21 October 1687
The president and all 25 fellows of Magdalen college were dismissed today after a clash with the king. They had refused to elect James's nominee, a Catholic and technically unqualified, as college president, and last month they resisted a plea from the king to change their minds. "You have affronted me," he said angrily. "Know I am king and I will be obeyed." John Hough, the president, defiantly refused to hand over the keys but was today expelled. It is believed that the king now plans to turn the college into a Catholic seminary (→ 11/1687).

Catholic heir born to James and Mary; tension increases

Prince James: a Catholic heir.

London, 10 June 1688
The queen gave birth to a son at St James's palace today, and the king has ordered bonfires and celebrations to mark the event. The prince, James, will be christened in the Catholic faith, to the alarm of Protestants, some of whom are already suspicious about the birth.

Mary of Modena has had no surviving children since she married James in 1673; four died in infancy, and there have been at least as many miscarriages. Until today therefore the king's heirs were his daughters from his first marriage: Mary of Orange and her sister Anne, both staunch Protestants.

No representative of either Mary or Anne attended the birth, fuelling rumours that the baby is not the queen's and that he was smuggled into the palace in a warming-pan to guarantee a Catholic heir (→ 15/10).

Nobles urge William to lead invasion

Defiant bishops win support of public

London, 30 June 1688
A conspiracy is afoot to overthrow King James and bring over William and Mary of Orange. A group of Tory and Whig nobles today wrote to Prince William, urging him to bring an army to oust James and secure the Protestant succession. Prince William is the husband of Princess Mary, the king's eldest daughter who, until the birth of Prince James earlier this month, was the heir to the throne.

The birth of a Catholic prince has transformed the succession and, more than any other factor, prompted today's call to William and Mary to intervene. Protestant concern had also been heightened, however, by the arrest of seven bishops on charges of seditious libel for refusing the royal command that the clergy be ordered to read the king's Declaration of Indulgence from their pulpits. This sought to promote Catholicism by suspending the Test Act and other penal laws against Catholics and dissenters.

The church leaders, headed by William Sancroft, the archbishop of Canterbury, were briefly held in the Tower before coming to trial. They argued that the king did not have the legal right to nullify measures passed by parliament, and today a judge and jury found the bishops not guilty. The bishops were released to cheers from the London crowds. Bonfires lit to celebrate the court's decision were still burning when the rebellious nobles met in London tonight. Seven lords signed

The seven bishops whose arrest for libel has swung opinion against James.

the letter to be sent to William; although they sought to hide their identities by using numbers, it is believed that one of the plotters is the Earl of Shrewsbury. What they proposed was treason: they urged William to intervene before James could pack parliament and the forces with his Catholic supporters. An overwhelming majority of the country would support him, they claimed.

The king's pro-Catholic moves had long alarmed the Whigs within parliament; it is they who are most sceptical of the legitimacy of the recent royal birth. But by arresting the bishops James has now united the Church of England in opposition to his policies and fuelled discontent among the traditionally pro-royalist Tories in parliament.

Until now the Tories have argued that it was never lawful to resist a king, so long as the king was defender of the Church of England. But an increasing number of Tories are now ready to join the Whigs in attacking James, while most others seem certain to stay neutral if William heeds today's call to head a Protestant revolt (→ 30/9).

William of Orange proclaims better rule

London, 30 September 1688
Prince William has accepted the call to arms against King James. A "Declaration of Reasons" – a manifesto for a Protestant nation issued today – promises a free and legal parliament, with his armies guaranteeing public order and protecting honest citizens. Abjuring all thought of conquest, William denounces James's "illegal acts", in-cluding the case of the seven bishops, and the violation of *Magna Carta*. He says that the birth of the prince was a hoax. As a grandson of Charles I, and at the invitation of the lords spiritual and temporal, he will lead an army to England "for preserving of the Protestant religion and for restoring the lawes and liberties of England, Scotland and Ireland" (→ 21/10).

Pope is godfather to infant heir to throne

London, 15 October 1688
James Francis Edward, the Prince of Wales, was baptised today as a Roman Catholic. Pope Innocent XI has agreed to stand as godfather, although he disapproves of King James's policies which he fears may lead to a revolution ending the hopes for English Catholics. Even though James has belatedly awoken to the challenge posed by Prince William and his own daughter, Princess Mary, he went ahead with what many will see as a provocative christening. The Catholic Dowager Queen Catherine was also a godparent. Now the king intends to confront the sceptics who doubted the legitimacy of the prince's birth. No fewer than 40 witnesses to the birth are to be paraded to give their evidence in public (→ 9/12).

William and James join battle for the throne

Military chiefs rally to support William

Salisbury, 26 November 1688

The king has been deserted by several of his most senior officers, including Churchill, Kirke and Trelawny, who put down Monmouth's rebellion, the Duke of Grafton, Charles II's illegitimate son, and several others. He has therefore ordered a retreat and is returning immediately to London.

The king's armies had gathered here to confront Prince William of Orange, who landed at Torbay on 5 November with 12,000 infantry and 3,000 cavalry. The prince seized Exeter and marched east. He is now at Axminster, and his supporters have raised the north and west of England in his name.

The king has 25,000 men under arms, but they will not fight without leaders. He tried to inspect them at Warminster two days ago but was seized by a violent nosebleed and was confined to bed. John Churchill went over to Prince William last night, and the others followed today. The army's retreat from Salisbury was disorderly and hasty, and this evening Prince George of Denmark, Princess Anne's husband, and the Duke of Ormonde deserted.

Prince William sailed on 21 October but was driven back by a gale. He sailed again on 1 November. He intended to sail north, but a strong east wind, the "Protestant wind" promised in the song *Lillibulero*, kept the Royal Navy in the Thames and carried William to Devon. The west country rose to greet him. King James started to march west but turned back, fearing that London would rise behind him. Now he has discovered that the army has betrayed him (→27/11).

The invading army: William and his troops disembark from their ships.

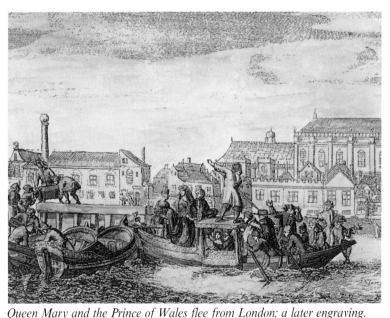

Queen Mary and the Prince of Wales flee from London: a later engraving.

James throws seal in Thames and flees

London, 23 December 1688

King James II has fled the country. The queen and Prince of Wales left two weeks ago. William of Orange entered London on 18 December and is now undisputed master of England, having overthrown James in six weeks.

James was deserted by his army, his court and the people of England. The only men who would fight for him were the Irish regiments sent over by Tyrconnel, and they were not enough. Princess Mary supports her husband in everything, and Princess Anne has joined the rebels.

The victorious Prince of Orange opened negotiations with the king on 8 December. William said that a parliament must be elected at once and the king must leave London. James feared that he would be murdered, like Edward II and Richard II before him, or even tried and executed like his own father. At three o'clock in the morning on 11 December he left London in disguise. As he crossed the Thames at Vauxhall he dropped the Great Seal into the river – the nearest he got to a formal abdication. When his flight became known, serious riots broke out in London as the mob sacked Catholic property and foreign embassies.

The king sailed from Faversham but was arrested by sailors who thought him a papist priest. He was brought ignominiously back to London on 16 December, in a state of collapse. By then William was at Windsor and ordered James out of London. James went to Rochester the next day and escaped to France today (→12/3/89).

Princess Anne backs Protestant cause

Westminster, 26 November 1688

Even the king's family has deserted him. Princess Anne, James's younger daughter, fled from Whitehall at dead of night with her best friend, Sarah Churchill, whose husband John has joined Prince William's cause. They escaped down the back stairs to be met by a hackney carriage driven by Lord Dorset and the bishop of London, Henry Compton, who is a former cavalry officer. Armed with pistols and a sabre, he led them to a hideaway in Epping Forest. The king is said to be shattered by the news (→27/11).

Peers ask William to take over throne

Westminster, 23 December 1688

The peers of the realm and the bishops, gathered in the House of Lords, have invited William of Orange to assume the government and to issue writs for the election of a new parliament. The prince has also summoned all surviving members of the parliaments of Charles II to meet in the House of Commons, and they will certainly come to the same conclusion. The prince has rejected a suggestion that he proclaim himself king by right of conquest. The new parliament will decide the issue (→28/1).

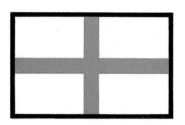

William and Mary
1689–1694

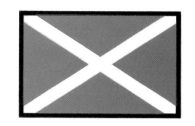

Westminster, 28 January 1689. Following James II's flight into exile last month, the Commons declare the throne of England vacant (→ 3/2).

London, 3 February 1689. William of Orange tells parliament that he is not prepared to rule as a regent or consort with Mary as queen regnant (→ 6/2).

Ireland, 12 March 1689. James II, now living at St Germain-en-Laye, arrives at Kinsale to reclaim his throne (→ 19/4).

Westminster, 11 April 1689. William of Orange and Mary are crowned as joint king and queen of England.→

Dundee, 13 April 1689. Viscount Dundee raises the standard of the exiled James II, signalling his intention to fight (→ 6/1689).

Londonderry, 19 April 1689. With the support of the Earl of Tyrconnel, James lays siege to the city (→ 4/5).

Dublin, 4 May 1689. James II is proclaimed king.

London, 11 May 1689. William and Mary take the Scottish coronation oath at Whitehall (→ 6/1689).

England/France, 13 May 1689. William, as king of England, declares war on France (→ 30/12).

Hampton Court, 24 July 1689. Princess Anne gives birth a son, William, the Duke of Gloucester (→ 7/1689).

London, July 1689. William reduces the income of Anne and Prince George of Denmark after a financial row (→ 14/10/90).

Europe, 30 December 1689. William joins Britain to the "Grand Alliance", thus linking it to the

Low Countries and the Holy Roman Empire in an attempt to prevent French domination of Europe (→ 26/7/90).

Highland, 1 May 1690. The remnant of the Jacobite army is defeated in battle at Cromdale, thereby securing Scotland for William (→ 7/6).

Scotland, 7 June 1690. The crown agrees to the establishment of Presbyterian government in the Church of Scotland (→ 1/7).

London, 14 October 1690. Anne gives birth to a premature daughter named Mary, who lives only two hours (→ 10/1691).

London, December 1690. Richard Graham, Viscount Preston, and Lord Clarendon, both loyal supporters of the exiled King James, are charged with treason on the discovery of their involvement in a secret plot to overthrow William and Mary (→ 19/1/91).

London, 19 January 1691. Viscount Preston is found guilty of treason and condemned to death.

London, October 1691. Anne and her friend Sarah Churchill begin corresponding under the pennames of "Mrs Morley" and "Mrs Freeman" (→ 1/1692).

London, January 1692. William dismisses John Churchill, the Earl of Marlborough and one of his leading generals, on suspicion of plotting with James II (→ 5/5/92).

London, January 1692. Anne infuriates William and Mary by refusing to remove Sarah Churchill from her staff as lady of the bedchamber after her husband, the Earl of Marlborough, is dismissed for plots against the king (→ 19/2).

London, 19 February 1692. With the rift between herself and the queen widening, Anne moves out of the "Cockpit", her apartments in Whitehall (→ 17/4).

Richmond, Surrey, 17 April 1692. Anne gives birth for the ninth time, to a son, George. He dies an hour before his baptism (→ 6/1692).

London, 5 May 1692. The Earl of Marlborough is arrested on suspicion of treason.

Paris, 28 June 1692. Mary of Modena, the exiled queen, gives birth to a daughter, Louisa Maria (→ 8/4/12).

London, June 1692. Princess Anne suffers a serious attack of rheumatism, which leaves her almost crippled (→ 23/3/93).

England, 1692. On hearing rumours of discontent in the navy, Queen Mary writes to assure the sailors that she is convinced of their loyalty and congratulates them on their triumph at La Hogue (→ 1693).

England, 1693. King William assumes full responsibility for all naval affairs.

Kensington, 20 December 1694. Mary falls seriously ill with smallpox (→ 28/12).

Westminster, 31 December 1694. King William breaks down before parliament, distraught with grief after the death of his wife, Queen Mary (→ 12/1694).

England, December 1694. King William gives his assent to the Triennial Bill, which lays down that parliament is to meet every three years and last no longer than three years.

England, 1694. The Bank of England is founded in an attempt to raise much-needed funds for the long-running war between England and France.

The life and times of William and Mary

Name: William Henry of Orange.
Birth: The Hague, 4 November 1650.
Accession: 13 February 1689 (jointly with Mary).
Coronation: 11 April 1689 (jointly with Mary).
Predecessor: father-in-law.
Hair: brown.
Eyes: brown.
Height: 5 feet 6 inches (168cm).
Marriage: Mary Stuart, 4 November 1677, London.
Children: none.
Likes: architecture, gardens.
Favourite home: Hampton Court.
Greatest problems: dislike of Britain and lack of popularity.
Greatest success: keeping James II, the ex-king, at bay.
Death: 8 March 1702.

Name: Mary Stuart.
Birth: St James's palace, 30 April 1662.
Accession: 13 February 1689 (jointly with William).
Coronation: 11 April 1689 (jointly with William).
Predecessor: father.
Hair: brown.
Eyes: grey.
Height: 5 feet 11 inches (180cm).
Marriage: William of Orange, 4 November 1677, London.
Children: none.
Likes: interior decorating, socialising.
Favourite home: Hampton Court.
Greatest problem: relationship with her sister, Anne.
Greatest success: attracting popular adulation.
Death: 28 December 1694.

Opposite: the joint rulers King William and Queen Mary.

Treaty of Limerick ends war in Ireland

A 20th-century picture of the stone in Limerick on which the treaty was signed.

Limerick, 3 October 1691
Fifteen months after the Battle of the Boyne, King James's headquarters here has fallen and with it the last hopes of the Jacobite cause (so called from *Jacobus*, the Latin for James) in Ireland. The town surrendered, and a treaty was signed to end the Irish war.

William's first attempt to take Limerick, where 14,000 Irish troops were based, failed last August after citizens hurled broken bottles and rocks at his troops as they breached the walls. Around 2,300 – a tenth of William's force – were killed or wounded. The next day rain turned the area into a quag-

mire, and William called off the siege. Limerick held out but became more and more isolated. Cork and Kinsale fell last autumn, and Athlone and Aughrim this summer. Limerick was besieged again, to little avail until a week ago when, frustrated because French reinforcements had not shown up, Jacobite chiefs agreed to talks.

The terms signed today allow the troops safe conduct to France and provide safeguards for Irish Catholics. King William is keen to see the war and the consequent bitterness over, but whether his pledges to the Catholics can be enforced is another matter.

Mass murder at Glenco

Highland, 13 February 1692
A brutal massacre of men, women and children took place this morning in the bleak setting of Glencoe, west of Loch Leven. Dozens of members of the Macdonald clan, including their chief, Alasdair MacIain, were butchered by soldiers of the Argyll regiment led by Robert Campbell of Glenlyon.

On 1 February Glenlyon, a sworn enemy of the Macdonalds, quartered 120 Campbells in Glencoe, ostensibly to collect taxes. They were welcomed by their Macdonald hosts, but treachery was afoot, for Glenlyon had orders to

kill every Macdonald under 70. A 5am today the murder began.

Some troops warned the vi lagers, many of whom escaped be ing shot, stabbed or clubbed t death. But MacIain was shot in th back and his wife left naked in th snow. Glenlyon shot nine victim himself, and some soldiers wen wild, smearing corpses with dun and killing a sick man and his five year-old son. Thirty-four men, tw women and two children died. Th savage, treacherous manner of thei deaths is sure to cause widesprea disgust and raise queries about wh ordered the killings [*see below*].

Did King William know of the killing?

London, late February 1692
It has emerged that the order which led to the massacre at Glencoe [*see above*] was signed by the king himself. But was William really responsible? The grounds for the killing were that the Macdonalds had not sworn loyalty to the crown by 1 January. But the chief, Alasdair MacIain, had arrived in Fort William the day before to be told he should be in Inveraray, where he eventually swore on 6 January.

Apparently Sir John Dalrymple, the under-secretary for Scotland,

who was in London, heard onl that MacIain had missed the dead line. On 16 January he gave a pil of papers to William for signature one said that it would be a "vindica tion of public justice to extirpat that set of thieves [the Macdonalds]"

Harsh words and possibly, to king whose English is imperfect ambiguous. Maybe he was busy an signed without reading the pape carefully. What is certain is tha William seems as shocked as any one by the way in which "his orders were carried out.

British navy scuppers James II's attempt to reclaim the throne

La Hogue, France, 19 May 1692
A bid by the exiled King James II to invade England and regain his throne has been thwarted by a brilliant British naval victory off La Hogue. James and the three-year-old Prince James Edward, the Prince of Wales-in-exile, are heading back to the Jacobite court in Paris following the defeat of the French fleet at the hands of Admiral William Russell.

The French ships were supplied and funded by King Louis XIV, who also provided a large French army under the command of one of his top generals, Marshal Bellefonds. By assenting to a French invasion James has probably lost much of his remaining support in his former kingdom, as well as handing Louis's enemies a morale-boosting victory (→ 1693).

A lost cause: James's followers are defeated in a sea battle at La Hogue.

William loses wig at height of battle

Landen, Flanders, July 1693
King Louis XIV of France has in flicted another humiliation on th allied armies of the Grand Alliance at Landen in the Low Countries King William III, the leader of th coalition forces, also suffered a per sonal humiliation when his wig wa shot off during the battle; anothe bullet passed through his Garte sash. The 50,000-strong allianc forces were outnumbered by French army of at least 80,00 soldiers.

Although the allies look upo Landen as a defeat, it was actuall more of a draw. The encounter ha been both financially and militaril costly to Louis, and it is unlikel that he has the strength to marc on Liège or Brussels (→ 27/4/96).

Anne's loyalty to Sarah Churchill brings wrath of Queen Mary down on her head

Mary dies of smallpox

Kensington, 28 December 1694
Just over a week ago Queen Mary began to complain of feeling ill. Two days later her doctors diagnosed smallpox, and this morning she died, leaving her desolate husband as sole ruler of the kingdom.

Mary was only 32, but she had been in poor health for some time and sensed that she should prepare for death. William was devastated by her illness – both his parents died of smallpox – and had a bed made up for him in Mary's room, where his constant crying upset the queen. Yesterday Mary, who said she felt little pain, took the sacra-

ment and said farewell to William, now beside himself with grief. She died at one o'clock this morning.

Mary will be remembered as a woman of great honesty, piety and selflessness. As joint monarch she happily left politics, government and military affairs to William, but she showed considerable judgement and diplomatic skills when she took the helm during his absences abroad. Lively and talkative, she excelled at ceremonial and social duties and was respected for her sensitive handling of church affairs. She was much loved and will be genuinely missed (→ 31/12).

Princess Anne and Sarah Churchill with Queen Mary: a later engraving.

London, 27 April 1693
A bitter row has broken out between Queen Mary and her sister, Princess Anne, over Anne's friendship with Sarah Churchill, the wife of the disgraced Earl of Marlborough. Soon after the earl's dismissal on suspicion of plotting against the king at the end of 1691, Anne appeared at court with Sarah, an outspoken woman who has long been her confidante. Mary saw Sarah's presence as an affront and ordered Anne to dismiss her and

leave Whitehall. Anne moved to Syon House in Middlesex, but she would not get rid of Sarah.

Enraged at this disobedience Mary wrote to Anne that she expected "to be complied with"; Anne replied that "never anybody was so used by a sister". The lively, voluble Mary has never really been close to the slow, taciturn Anne, but the affair has surprised courtiers with its bitterness. Certainly the breach shows no sign of being healed (→ 20/12).

Queen Mary lying in state after her tragic early death from smallpox.

A decorated vase bearing the arms of William and Mary.

Worn-out Anne loses her tenth child

London, 23 March 1693
After a week of pain, Princess Anne today suffered her fourth miscarriage. It was her tenth pregnancy and the ninth child she has lost. Only her three-year-old son, William, has survived longer than two years; the rest have miscarried, been stillborn or died in infancy. Even William's health is delicate. He suffers fits in which feverish convulsions seem at times to threaten his life. Plagued with gynaecological problems, desperate to have another healthy child and suffering from various ailments, Anne is becoming a depressive; she says that she will never find ease in this

world, and is looking forward to the eternal rest of the next one.

She has suffered from an eye disease since she was a child and was weakened by smallpox in 1687 during the epidemic that killed her two daughters Mary and Anne Sophia. She has recently started to suffer painful attacks of rheumatism, and her doctors fear that the excruciating swellings on her feet may be the start of gout. What amounts to a neurotic obsession with pregnancy and childbirth – fired by the desperate need to provide a healthy heir to the throne – does not help Anne to cope with her other physical ills (→ 27/4).

France and England hold secret talks

Paris, autumn 1693
Representatives of William and Mary and of King Louis XIV are holding secret talks aimed at ending the long and inconclusive European war which is proving both destructive and expensive to all sides.

Despite the success of Admiral Russell at the battle of La Hogue last year [*see opposite*], the members of the Grand Alliance are no closer to defeating Louis. After defeats on land King William faces great pressure to concentrate on the war at sea, while Louis has financial reasons for wanting peace.

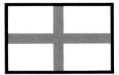

William III
1694–1702

William III reigns alone

King William by candlelight: a portrait by Godfried Schalken (d.1706).

London, January 1695. To the fury of Princess Anne, William gives land officially belonging to the exiled James II to his own former mistress, Elizabeth Villiers (→ 2/1695).

London, 5 March 1695. Queen Mary is buried at Whitehall.

London, April 1695. Princess Anne is diagnosed as having been suffering from an hysterical pregnancy ever since last autumn (→ 18/2/96).

Westminster, December 1695. William establishes a council of trade, avoiding demands for a council nominated by parliament (→ 1/1696).

Westminster, January 1696. William gives his assent to the Treason Trials Act (→ 27/4).

London, 18 February 1696. Princess Anne suffers her fifth miscarriage (→ 20/9).

Windsor, 24 July 1696. William, the Duke of Gloucester, Princess Anne's seven-year-old son, is made a knight of the Garter (→ 30/7/1700).

Windsor, 20 September 1696. Anne miscarries, losing two foetuses, one of seven months, the other of two (→ 25/3/97).

London, 25 March 1697. Anne has a miscarriage – the fourth child that she has lost in thirteen months (→ 25/1/1700).

Europe, October 1698. William and King Louis XIV of France sign a partition treaty to try to solve the Spanish succession question peacefully (→ 3/1700).

Scotland, 1699. Jacobites claim that the terrible famine which is killing thousands in the country is an act of God; they blame

William for usurping the throne from James.

London, 25 January 1700. Princess Anne loses a baby son in her twelfth miscarriage (→ 30/7).

Westminster, 11 April 1700. William prorogues parliament after it is suggested that he remove all foreigners from his court.

Spain, November 1700. King Charles II of Spain dies; as his will leaves the throne to Philip of Anjou, the crowns of France and Spain will not be united (→ 8/1701).

Westminster, February 1701. William supports the choice of Robert Harley as speaker of the Commons (→ 5/1704).

England, June 1701. The Earl of Marlborough, John Churchill, becomes army commander-in-chief (→ 21/8/04).

London, August 1701. William declares war on France to prevent its domination of Europe (→ 6/9).

France, 6 September 1701. Louis XIV of France recognises James Francis Edward as James III on the death of his father, the deposed James II.→

Westminster, 31 Dec 1701. Parliament votes unanimously in favour of war with France after Louis XIV's recognition of James Francis Edward as king of Great Britain.

London, 8 March 1702. William dies from complications which developed from an injury sustained two weeks ago when he fell from his horse; he is succeeded by his sister-in-law, Anne, aged 37.→

Kensington, autumn 1695
Overcome with grief at Queen Mary's death last December, King William has retreated into a morose routine here, broken by weekend hunting trips to Richmond and Windsor. Although he remains closely in touch with English politics – more than with Dutch ones – he is spending more and more of the day in prayer and contemplation; in the evening he relaxes in the company of Dutchmen, and is liable to drink too much.

When his wife died, the king's sense of loss was so acute that he broke down in parliament and was unable to reply to a speech of condolence. He appears to see his bereavement as a punishment for his sins, which he is determined to expiate. He rapidly broke off his long-standing affair with Betty Villiers, who is now expected to marry Lord George Hamilton.

Although not as active as he was (he is troubled by swelling of the legs), King William is still pursuing the war with France. After years starved of military success, the summer campaign, directed by the king, reached a glorious climax with the capture of Namur. King Louis XIV must be looking for peace.

At home, however, the tax burden continues to increase, and the Whigs are becoming fractious. New excises have been introduced on salt and alcohol, but, most significantly, a land tax now accounts for about a third of the money raised by taxation.

Repentant king makes Anne his heir

Westminster, February 1695

Still in a penitent and conciliatory mood after the queen's death, King William has recognised Princess Anne as his heir and given her St James's palace. Her son, the five-year-old William, later Duke of Gloucester, is the only surviving hope for a future Stuart succession.

The relationship between William and Anne remains frosty. According to the Earl of Dartmouth, "the king often said that if he had married her, he should have been the miserablest man upon earth". It may be Princess Anne's superior hereditary claim to the throne which lies behind the king's animosity towards her – although there is no viable opposition to his continued reign. When he goes campaigning abroad, he leaves in power a council of regency to which neither Princess Anne nor Prince George are admitted.

The princess's attempts to compliment the king on matters of state are simply not acknowledged. But most hurtful of all has been Wil-

Betty Villiers: granted Irish land.

liam's decision, without any reference to the princess, or any consideration of her legitimate claims, to grant James II's Irish estates to his own former mistress, Elizabeth Villiers. As for Anne's husband, Prince George of Denmark, the king has shown no inclination to repay him for the surrender of his mortgages in Holstein (→ 4/1695).

Rheumatic princess is heir to be queen

Windsor, 1695

Formal acknowledgement of Princess Anne as the new heir to the throne has not led to an outburst of public rejoicing. She and Prince George spend most of their time in the castle here, out of the public gaze, while her health appears to deteriorate steadily. There is a cruel rhyme which goes as follows:

King William thinks all,
Queen Mary talks all,
Prince George drinks all,
And Princess Anne eats all.

James II's daughter, who is 30, is an uninspiring heir to the throne, being tedious, plain and increasingly fat. Her recent phantom pregnancy did nothing for her public image or self-esteem. A condition which began in the autumn of 1694 and continued well into this year was expected to lead to a birth in May, but in April her physician told her that her pregnancy was "nothing but the vapours".

Rheumatism has left her unable to climb stairs or stand straight. There is also anxiety for the precarious health of her sole surviving child, William, the Duke of Glouc-

Princess Anne: heir to the throne.

ester. Anne married Prince George of Denmark in 1683, and was advised by Sarah Churchill and her husband, the Earl of Marlborough, to support the 1688 revolution against her father. Devout, kind-hearted and dutiful, Anne hangs on Sarah's every word (→ 4/1695).

Assassination plot by Jacobites foiled

Westminster, 27 April 1696

In the aftermath of a failed Jacobite plot to assassinate King William, parliament today passed the Act of Association, requiring all office-holders to take an oath that "his majesty is rightful and lawful king ... and to assist each other in the defence of his majesty and his government". To prevent further plots which might be instigated by the exiled James II and King Louis, unauthorised travel from France to England is now to be high treason.

This latest plot, hatched at the French court, involved Sir George Barclay, who had served under Dundee and acted as agent among the highland clans; he arrived in England earlier this year to raise troops on James's behalf and to link up with Sir John Fenwick, a prominent opponent of William of Orange. Barclay planned to seize and kill the king on 15 February at Turnham Green as he returned from Richmond. The plot was discovered and various conspirators were arrested, although Barclay escaped to France. Fenwick and the Duke of Berwick are still at large.

For the first time in the reign of William III, public opinion has swung decisively in his favour. Despite discontent in Scotland and financial problems, at the heart of government there is no appetite for James's return, and William, the aloof Dutchman, is seen as a just and stable king (→ 10/1698).

Young Dutchman is king's favourite

Westminster, 1696

The young soldier Arnout Joust van Keppel has been created Earl of Albemarle, confirming his status as King William's favourite. He was one of the king's pages when he broke his leg in a hunting accident in 1691; William was moved by his stoicism and has promoted him steadily, so that he now supplants in royal favour another Dutchman, William Bentinck, whom the king created Duke of Portland.

The rapid rise of the handsome Keppel as the king's personal assistant has prompted the envy of Portland and other courtiers, who have whispered that the relationship may be homosexual. There is no evidence for this; William has always preferred the company of his own countrymen.

The new earl, painted by Kneller.

'Civil list' will secure future royal funds

Westminster, 1698

Parliament has granted the king £700,000 a year for life. Known as the "civil list", this new arrangement underscores the relationship between crown and parliament by which the monarch has a degree of freedom to pursue foreign policy or other initiatives but is fundamentally dependent on parliament for his creditworthiness.

Charles I was the first king who was obliged to accept the principle of no taxation without the people's consent. After the Restoration the principle of parliamentary control over royal finances gradually became established as successive

kings sought to raise taxes to finance foreign adventures. King William's own need to secure funds for his war with France has made parliament effectively responsible for the maintenance of the armed forces and has ensured that it meets every year to grant money.

At the same time, the financial revolution whereby the national debt is covered by parliament, working through the Bank of England, means that even in peacetime MPs must be ready to sit to guarantee the monarch's creditworthiness. The result is that parliament has far greater influence over both the king's advisers and his policies.

William signs pact and perplexes MPs

Westminster, March 1700
Parliament remains bewildered by King William's foreign policy. He has just concluded the second of two partition treaties with King Louis of France. The first, in October 1698, was nullified by the death of a Bavarian claimant to the Spanish succession, leaving the Bourbons and Habsburgs vying for the Spanish succession. Louis wants to divide the Habsburgs, while William will accept a partition of Spanish-held lands if this limits French expansion. Parliament dislikes this independent diplomacy (→ 4/1700).

Commons urge king to sack advisers

Westminster, April 1700
Infuriated by King William's conclusion of two treaties on European partition without reference to parliament, the Lords and Commons have insisted that the king get rid of all his foreign advisers. They also demand that William revoke his grant of Irish estates confiscated from Jacobite rebels to the Duke of Portland and other Dutchmen. A Tory majority in parliament, opposed to war and suspicious of foreigners, is clearly determined to restrict the royal prerogative as much as possible (→ 11/4).

Scots turn against unpopular William

Scotland, May 1700
King William, already detested here after the massacre of Glencoe [*see page 286*], has attracted yet more odium, and the Scottish Parliament is now threatening to withhold funds from a king who prefers to leave Scottish affairs entirely in the hands of his ministers.

The Scots blame the failure of the Scottish attempt to establish a colony on the Darien isthmus on Panama, at a cost of some 1,200 lives, on the king. William refused to help the ailing colony when it was attacked by the Spaniards, because he did not want to jeopardise Anglo-Spanish relations at a delicate time.

Death of duke jeopardises succession

Princess Anne with William: who will succeed now that he, too, has died?

Unlucky Anne loses sole surviving child

Windsor, 30 July 1700
William, the Duke of Gloucester, the only survivor of Princess Anne's 18 pregnancies, died early this morning. Anne and Prince George were at his bedside. Six days ago the young duke danced at his 11th birthday party here, but he retired soon afterwards complaining of a chill and sore throat. Fever set in two days later; bleeding offered him temporary relief, but he then became delirious and his condition – thought to be either smallpox or scarlet fever – worsened.

Princess Anne doted on her sole surviving offspring. Although she may yet conceive again, this tragedy could be the conclusion of the saddest of all records of royal motherhood. Afflicted by gout, rheumatism and obesity, and worn out by her succession of miscarriages, Anne believes that she is being punished for betraying her father. Now, barring the conversion of the former King James's 12-year-old son, James, to Protestantism, the crown will go to the Hanoverians (→ 12/6/01).

Act of Settlement ensures crown remains in Protestant hands

Westminster, 12 June 1701
A parliament of unprecedented party strife, with recurrent spats between Lords and Commons, has produced the Act of Settlement and ensured that the crown will remain in Protestant hands, even at the cost of inviting a foreign royal family to take over the throne.

A granddaughter of James I, Sophia, the Electress of Hanover, has been declared the next heir after Anne and William. Catholics who might claim the throne by marriage to Stuart princesses are excluded. Although parliament is reconciling England to a foreign ruler, the act specifically provides that no war shall be undertaken "for the defence of dominions or territories not belonging to the crown of England, without consent of parliament". It also says that no successor to the crown shall leave Britain without

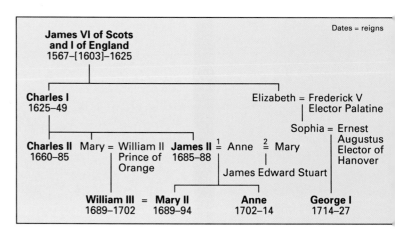

that consent – preventing any repetition of William's French campaigns.

The other hated feature of William's reign – his promotion of foreigners – is guarded against by barring from the privy council anyone born outside Britain. Yet parliament has made a *faux pas* which could have costly consequences. In claiming to speak for the Scots, the English parliament has stoked yet further the flames of rebellion north of the border. Many Scots are minded to reject the Hanoverian succession.

Deposed king and his successor are both dead

Prince James is proclaimed king by order of Louis XIV: a later view.

A romanticised view of King William's riding accident in Richmond park.

Stroke claims life of James II in France

St Germain, 6 September 1701
James II, the deposed king of England, died today, three weeks after suffering a stroke while he was hearing Mass. In a death-bed gesture, he commanded James, his 13-year-old son and heir, to die rather than abandon his Roman faith. Jacobitism, the movement to restore the Stuarts, may live on, but for now it seems a lost cause.

After his flight from England in 1688, during which he briefly enjoyed the protection of William of Orange's Dutch guards, James

made various abortive attempts to regain the throne. He fled to France again in 1690 after the Battle of the Boyne, watched his invasion fleet being destroyed at La Hogue in 1692 and made a third, half-hearted invasion attempt in 1696.

For the past few years James has devoted himself to penitence and piety, in between hunting trips. He never stopped planning for another invasion. A lady of the French court described him as "a brave and honest man, but the silliest I have ever seen in my life" (→ 31/12).

William dies after falling from his horse

Kensington, 8 March 1702
King William III died this morning, two weeks after a fall from his horse in Richmond park. He was 51 years old. The king's health had been failing for a year or more, with asthma and leg swellings, but his final decline was precipitated by his horse tripping over a molehill. His Jacobite opponents have started drinking toasts to the mole, "the little gentleman in the velvet coat"; nor is William of Orange much mourned in many corners of his kingdom. Nonetheless, William's

last parliament achieved an overwhelming consensus in favour of William's pursuit of war with the French, no small thanks to King Louis of France. Louis had had the temerity to pronounce the Jacobite Prince James heir to the English throne, thereby arousing William's ire and offending all Englishmen, who had no desire to subject their country to French overlordship. The king's last speech to parliament warned against the French and called for unity. His message was heeded (→ 10/4).

Anne feigns pregnancy to put off visitor

Windsor, October 1701
Princess Anne has sent word to King William that she is pregnant again and cannot therefore meet George Augustus, the grandson of the presumptive heiress after Anne to the throne, Electress Sophia of Hanover. George is now expected to call off his planned visit to London. The princess is not, in fact, expecting a child, but is simply trying to prevent the Hanoverian prince from coming. She suspects that King William is manoeuvring for George to supplant her as heir. Besides, the Jacobites have shown her the destabilising effect of having a rival dynasty at court (→ 11/3/02).

Prince George Augustus of Hanover.

The Dutch prince at the helm of England

England, 1702
When William of Orange accepted the throne of England and Scotland with Queen Mary in 1689, he warned that he would not be content to be his wife's "gentleman usher". He went on to steer the United Provinces and Britain with considerable skill through war with France. In England he has left a secure constitutional monarchy, a sound economy and a confident parliament. But in Scotland his reign has been disastrous; he showed no interest in the country, and the Glencoe massacre and the Darien affair made him the object of personal hatred. King William's broad-

mindedness was reflected in the Toleration Act of 1689 which guaranteed freedom of worship for nonconforming Protestants. He was able to disagree with the Commons without precipitating revolution or civil war. Parliament was left to decide major policy issues, and the courts were free from interference.

The king's chief concern was to maintain European stability, which for most of his reign meant war with France. His successes were few, but he kept his worst nightmares at bay. Victory at the Boyne kept Ireland safe from the French. Not being an Englishman, he never won the honour he deserved.

Anne
1702–1714

House of Stuart

Westminster, 11 March 1702. Queen Anne, in mourning – black for her father James II and purple for her brother-in-law William III – makes her first appearance before parliament (→ 30/3).

Westminster, 30 March 1702. Voted the same annual income as William, Queen Anne decides to give a seventh of it to the public service (→ 10/4).

Westminster, 10 April 1702. William's funeral takes place; Anne's husband Prince George of Denmark is chief mourner.

Kensington, 12 April 1702. Anne moves into Kensington palace and appoints her great friend Sarah Churchill as "groom of the stole", keeper of the privy purse and mistress of the robes (→ 1703).

Westminster, 23 April 1702. Anne is crowned queen of England, Scotland, Wales and Ireland.→

Europe, 4 May 1702. England and its allies, the United Provinces, and Austria, declare war on France and Spain (→ 7/1704).

Westminster, May 1704. The supporters of Sir Robert Harley, the speaker of the House of Commons who has also become the secretary of state, form a government (→ 19/1/08).

Spain, July 1704. The English, led by Sir George Rooke, seize Gibraltar (→ 14/10/05).

Westminster, 5 February 1705. The English Parliament passes the Aliens Act, forcing the Scots to agree to the Hanoverian succession or to negotiate a union of parliaments (→ 11/4).

Edinburgh, 11 April 1705. The Scottish government ignores the queen's pleas for clemency and executes four English sailors accused of piracy (→ 1/5/07).

Spain, 14 October 1705. The English navy, led by the Earl of Peterborough, takes Barcelona.

Lisbon, 31 December 1705. Catherine of Braganza, the widow of King Charles II, dies; on her return to Portugal in 1693 she acted as regent for her brother, King Pedro II (→ 23/5/06).

England, 1705. George Louis and George Augustus, respectively the son and grandson of Sophia, the Electress of Brunswick-Lüneburg and heir to Queen Anne, become naturalised British subjects.

Woodstock, Oxfordshire, 1705. John Vanbrugh begins work on Blenheim Palace, a new residence for the Duke of Marlborough; it is a gift from the queen for service to his country (→ 1719).

Low Countries, 23 May 1706. The Spanish Netherlands fall to the English when the French are defeated by troops under the Duke of Marlborough in battle at Ramillies (→ 10/12).

London, 12 June 1707. Abigail Hill secretly marries Samuel Masham, the leader of Lord Windsor's regiment in Ireland (→ 9/1707).

Hanover, 1706. Prince George Augustus of Hanover is promoted to the English peerage and invested as a knight of the Order of the Garter.

Westminster, 18 Dec 1707. Queen Anne agrees to annual finance bills and all-party government.

London, 19 January 1708. Sir Robert Harley, the secretary of state, loses support when his clerk is found guilty of treason – he has been selling official papers to the French (→ 24/1).

London, 24 January 1708. In an audience with the queen, Harley reveals his plans for forming a government which will exclude Lord Godolphin (→ 8/2).

Kensington, 8 February 1708. The Duke and Duchess of Marlborough and Lord Godolphin visit the queen and threaten their resignation if Harley is not dismissed (→ 11/2).

Westminster, 11 February 1708. Sir Robert Harley resigns (→ 15/4).

Scotland, March 1708. An attempted Jacobite invasion is driven off after the failure to land any troops.

England, 15 April 1708. The Whigs score an overwhelming victory in the general election (→ 5/4/10).

Kensington, 5 October 1708. Queen Anne is unable to attend the christening of Abigail Masham's first baby because her husband, Prince George, is seriously ill (→ 28/10).

London, 19 November 1711. Queen Anne cannot forgive the Duchess of Marlborough for her accusations, and the long correspondence between "Mrs Morley" and "Mrs Freeman" comes to a bitter end (→ 11/1712).

Paris, 8 April 1712. Mary of Modena, the widow of the exiled James II, is heartbroken at the death of her only daughter, Louisa Maria, aged 20, from smallpox; she will be buried at St Germain-en-Laye where the family has lived since 1689 (→ 4/1718).

Europe, November 1712. The Duke and Duchess of Marlborough leave the employment of Queen Anne and go into self-imposed exile on the continent (→ 1/8/14).

Europe, March 1713. The Treaty of Utrecht is signed by Britain and France, bringing an end to the War of Spanish Succession.

Kensington, December 1713. The queen falls seriously ill (→ 31/12).

Hanover, 8 June 1714. Sophia, the 84-year-old Electress of Brunswick-Lüneburg, who is the heir to the British throne, dies; her son George, aged 54, becomes heir in her place (→ 1/8).

Kensington, 30 July 1714. Anne falls into a coma (→ 1/8).

Kensington, 1 August 1714. Queen Anne dies at the age of 49; she has become so stout that her coffin is almost square.→

The life and times of Queen Anne

Name: Anne Stuart.
Birth: St James's palace, 6 February 1665.
Accession: 8 March 1702.
Coronation: 23 April 1702.
Predecessor: brother-in-law.
Hair: auburn.
Eyes: grey.
Marriage: Prince George of Denmark, 28 July 1683, London.

Children: six, of which one was stillborn and five died in childhood, plus 12 miscarriages.
Likes: hunting, racing and gambling.
Greatest problem: chronic ill-health brought on by smallpox and perpetual pregnancy.
Greatest success: union of England and Scotland.
Death: 1 August 1714.

Opposite: Queen Anne, holding orb and sceptre.

Ailing princess is queen of England

London, 23 April 1702
Queen Anne, the second daughter of King James II, was crowned today. A plain-looking and stout woman of 37, she is not regarded as being particularly clever and is certainly not in physical good health. Married to Prince George of Denmark in 1683, she has been pregnant annually ever since and has suffered six miscarriages and had twelve babies, none of whom have survived to see her crowned. Only two years ago her deeply-loved son William, the Duke of Gloucester, died at the age of eleven.

Her gynaecological problems have left her psychologically scarred, but as she ascended the throne today it was her physical infirmity that was more apparent. Prematurely aged, overweight, plagued with gout, rheumatism and circulatory diseases caused by her run of disastrous pregnancies, Queen Anne can walk only for short distances with the aid of a stick.

Given that the queen has had little training for the post of monarch – William III never allowed her to attend meetings – many wonder how she will cope with a political situation in which parliament has split into two distinct parties. The Tories and the Whigs are pushing for quite separate policies, but the queen's two main advisers, the Earl of Marlborough and Lord Godolphin, have so far stayed aloof from both (→ 1703).

Anne, the plain princess who is now queen, with her husband, George.

Furious Scots want to bar Hanoverians from taking throne

Edinburgh, August 1703
The Scottish Parliament has united against the idea of union with England, and this month it has voted a series of measures to try to protect Scottish sovereignty. The most serious of these, the Act of Security of the Kingdom, threatens to bar the Hanoverians – the heirs to the English throne – from the throne of Scotland, raising the spectre of war and the return of the Catholic Stuarts from exile.

Anti-English sentiment in Scotland is still running high following William III's insensitive and negligent Scottish policy. Five successive bad harvests had brought near-starvation to the country, compounded by the English war in Europe, which has disrupted Scottish trade, and a ban on Scottish trade with English colonies overseas. Union, never very feasible, looks increasingly unlikely. William first proposed it in 1699; desultory negotiations followed which were restarted under Queen Anne, only to fail this March (→ 5/2/05).

Queenly touch tries to cure 'king's evil'

London, 1703
Queen Anne has revived the ceremony of touching for scrofula, the "king's evil", a tubercular condition that enlarges the lymph glands and also affects the skin. For centuries it has been believed that it can be cured by the royal touch. This tradition originated with Edward the Confessor in 1058 and has been used by subsequent monarchs to emphasis the divine origins of their office.

The ceremony was discontinued by William III, who did not believe in it, but Anne has not only revived it but takes it seriously. She fasts for a day as a penance before going to the Banqueting House to meet groups of up to 300 sufferers, who are touched and presented with a small medal of "healing gold". Entry to these ceremonies are by ticket only; they are so popular that they are always over-subscribed.

Sarah's protégée becomes a new favourite of the queen

Sarah Churchill (r) playing cards with Lady Fitzharding.

Kensington Palace, 1703
The relationship between Queen Anne and Sarah, the wife of John Churchill (who was made Duke of Marlborough last year) has been so extraordinarily close that many marvel at it. Others, however, feel that it has corrupted Anne and given far too much power to Sarah's husband and his political allies. The two women have their own language in which they talk to each other, and they even have secret names for each other.

Sarah and the duke address the queen and Prince George as "Mr and Mrs Morley", while the queen refers to them as "Mr and Mrs Freeman". This degree of intimacy came about before the queen came to the throne, but since then the closeness between the two couples, and particularly between Sarah and "Mrs Morley", has begun to cool.

Ironically, this follows the introduction by Sarah of a young relative, Abigail Hill, into the queen's household as a lady of the bedchamber. The appointment reflected Sarah's influence at court, but as her friendship with the queen began to go sour, it was plain-faced Abigail who struck up a relationship with the queen which has become so close that there are now signs that Sarah is being displaced as the queen's favourite by her own protégée (→ 12/6/07).

George visits spa to aid lung trouble

Bath, October 1703
Prince George has been at Bath since the end of August and is now, after six weeks, preparing to return to London. He has been taking the waters in the hope of finding a cure for his increasingly serious respiratory problems. At Windsor in mid-August he suffered a prolonged and serious attack of asthma, and the royal doctors, stongly supported by Queen Anne, encouraged him to make the journey here.

The queen insisted on accompanying her husband here, along with Lord Godolphin, the Duchess of Marlborough and much of the court. It took three days to travel from Windsor, but their arrival in Bath was spectacular. Two hundred maidens carrying bows and arrows and dressed as Amazons were sent out from the city to welcome them. However, the stay has not done the prince much good. In the week before he was due to return to London he relapsed and had to be bled three times in as many days. His health remains in a poor state, to the distress of the queen, who is devoted to him (→ 5/10/08).

Queen's bounty set up to help poor clergy

Queen Anne kneels in prayer.

Parliament, 6 February 1704
The government has introduced a proposal into the House of Commons to ease the lot of poor clergy, some of whom are very poor indeed. Known as "Queen Anne's Bounty", the plan would allow the crown to surrender its traditional revenues derived from the church, at present amounting to between £16,000 and £17,000 a year. The money would be given to enable an income supplement to be paid to the most impoverished section of the priesthood.

Since the passage of the Toleration Act of 1689, which granted religious freedom to all non-Anglican Protestants, there has been a serious deterioration in church attendance, while disputes over tithes have multiplied. The situation has not been helped by the widespread evasion of the Test Act of 1673, which limited the holding of public office to those who took Communion in the Church of England. Evaders have got round the law by visiting their parish church once a year to take the Anglican sacrament and then reverting to their dissenting chapels.

All this has had a serious effect on the Church of England and allowed the Tories to run a "Church in Danger" campaign which has greatly annoyed the queen. She hopes with her bounty to redress the balance and to reassure any who doubt her ability to govern and care for the church, of which she is head, and its clergy.

Sick queen takes on her full share of the royal tasks

London, 1704
The huge expansion in government in recent decades means that Queen Anne can exercise nothing like the personal control that was possible for Queen Elizabeth. Nonetheless, she is still the only authority able to appoint ministers to office, so controlling the direction of policy. Ministers remain servants of the crown, and the queen has surprised many by revealing herself to be far more able and astute than they had suspected.

She has vested the conduct of government in three skilled politicians. John Churchill, the Duke of Marlborough and husband of the queen's confidante Sarah, holds supreme power as commander-in-chief and architect of war and diplomacy. He also controls domestic policy via his great friend Sidney, Baron Godolphin, whose post of lord treasurer makes him Anne's official principal minister. Godolphin's main task is to manage parliament to ensure the flow of funds for the war on the continent. Sir Robert Harley, the secretary of state, completes the triumvirate. His love of intrigue has earned him the nickname of "Robin the Trickster".

Marlborough annihilates French threat in battle at Blenheim

The plan of the battle at Blenheim is presented to Queen Anne: a later view.

London, 21 August 1704
John Churchill, the Duke of Marlborough, has won a stunning victory, hailed as another Crécy or Agincourt, over the united forces of France and Bavaria. At the village of Blenheim, on the river Danube in south central Germany, he has routed them so decisively that the threat from King Louis XIV of France is said to be ended.

News of his victory arrived in London today with Colonel Daniel Parke, who has ridden for eight days across Europe. He brought with him a message from the duke that was written in great haste in pencil on the back of his tavern bill. Addressed to the duchess, it says in part: "Give my duty to the queen and let her know her army has had a glorious victory." Colonel Parke has given the message to the queen and been rewarded with a purse of 1,000 guineas, twice the normal reward, plus a miniature portrait set with diamonds (→ 1705).

Marlborough: supreme power.

Marlborough faction is in the ascendant

Queen Anne is surrounded by ministers while, above, the sun is eclipsed.

London, 10 December 1706
Charles Spencer, the Earl of Sunderland and Whig son-in-law of the Duke of Marlborough, has joined the government, to the intense annoyance of the queen. Anne has hated him since he led parliamentary opposition to the granting of any income to Prince George, but he is now to take up the office of secretary of state for the south, a vital post in the foreign office. The queen has been forced to accept a minister against her choice, as party politics have become more important than the royal will.

The last year has seen triumphs in Europe following Marlborough's defeat of France at Ramillies, but at home government has become almost impossible. Power in parliament lies with a group of Whigs known as the *junto* [council], which refused to vote funds for Marlborough's wars unless one of them was accepted in the government.

Anne refused, wanting to remain above party strife and fearing that she would become the prisoner of parties. She was supported by Robert Harley, the secretary of state for the north, who belongs to neither party. The pressure on the queen became intense. Godolphin threatened to resign as lord treasurer, writing to her: "I cannot struggle against all the difficulties of your majesty's business and yourself at the same time." Sarah so persecuted her that she is losing the queen's friendship. Finally Marlborough added his voice. Faced with such relentless assaults Queen Anne finally gave way.

Secret marriage is new blow to Sarah

Kensington, September 1707
Relations between Queen Anne and her longtime confidante, Sarah Churchill, the Duchess of Marlborough, have never been worse. Earlier this month Sarah discovered that the queen had kept from her the marriage of a relative, Abigail Hill, a royal servant who has become a close companion to Anne. The duchess sees in this secrecy a sign of the increasing influence at court of Mrs Masham (as Abigail has become); as a supporter of the Whigs she is unhappy about Anne's favouring of Robert Harley, the Tory lord chancellor, and blames Abigail for both this policy and her own exclusion from court. In fact, the queen is simply tired of Sarah's domineering manner (→ 6/4/10).

Sarah upbraids Anne: a later view.

Jacobite Pretender calls off invasion

James Stuart: potential challenger.

Edinburgh, 14 March 1708
James Stuart, the only son of James II, has failed to land in Scotland and regain his family's kingdom. The queen, who was reported by the Duchess of Marlborough to have been close to panic, is much relieved. So are the Whigs.

The expedition was ill-fated from the start. In Le Havre the prince came down with measles, and departure was delayed for a week. He eventually set sail on 6 March in a gale; his convoy was shadowed by Admiral Byng's fleet. When he arrived at the Firth of Forth his supporters on shore failed to give the pre-arranged signal. The French commander, Admiral Forbin, refused to land, and James has returned to France without setting foot on British soil (→ 4/1714).

Commissioner describes miserable queen

Kensington, spring 1707
The queen's illness has become the dominant factor in her life, according to Sir John Clerk, one of the Scottish commissioners for the union with England. He found Anne a pitiful sight, as he recorded in his diary last year:

"Her majesty was labouring under a fit of the gout, and in extreme pain and agony," he writes. "Her faec, which was red and spotted, was rendered something frightful by her negligent dress, and the foot affected was tied up with a poultice and some nasty bandages ... What are you, poor mean-like mortal, thought I, who talks in the style of a sovereign?"

His more recent visit this year found her in much the same state, "surrounded with plasters ... and dirty-like rags". The queen has increasingly taken refuge in isolation, says Clerk: "I never saw any body attending her but some of her guards in the outer rooms." Her illness, and the distance of Kensington from London, mean that she does little socialising. Clerk says that she depends on her ministers and her few confidantes for everything, with her husband George a devoted but inactive consort.

Anne loses her husband, Prince George

Kensington, 28 October 1708
The queen is a widow. Prince George of Denmark died at 1.30pm today. Anne, who was nursing him personally, is desolate, and hugs and kisses the corpse. She had married George in 1683, and they were devoted to each other. Now stricken by gout, and saddened by the death of her husband coming after the loss of all her 18 children, she awaits her own death and the end of a royal line.

The indolent but good-natured Prince George, "who loves news, his bottle and the queen", as the journalist John Mackay put it, married Anne in 1683. He was more suited to family life than to the command of the Royal Navy which was given to him, and his stewardship marked a particularly inglorious era for the service. Anne constantly had to protect him from the fury of the Whig majority in parliament.

In September he was seized by a violent attack of asthma. As the country followed Marlborough's siege of Lille – the strongest fortress in Europe – which fell on 12 October, the prince declined, fighting for breath. Finally, with the queen protecting him as usual, the indolent man gave up.

Act of Union joins England and Scotland

EARLY DESIGNS
FOR THE UNION FLAG

The Duke of Queensberry formally presents the Act of Union to Queen Anne: a later 18th-century engraving.

London, 1 May 1707

A thanksgiving service, attended by Queen Anne and all the great officers of state, was held today at St Paul's to mark the creation of the United Kingdom of Great Britain. The act uniting the parliaments of England and Scotland, which received the royal assent on 6 March, is now in effect. To symbolise the historic occasion, the queen wore the combined Orders of the Garter and the Thistle and offered fervent prayers for the success of the union – the achievement of which has been her dearest wish. Londoners reacted enthusiastically to the celebration, but many Scots stayed away. There has been great opposition in Scotland to the union, including riots in Edinburgh, Glasgow and several other towns.

Last year the queen appointed 31 commissioners from each country to negotiate a union. They agreed terms of a treaty to be kept secret until it was presented to the Scottish and English Parliaments. It was proposed to unite the kingdoms under the name of Great Britain, with a common flag, great seal and coinage. Crucially, the treaty secured the Protestant succession,

specifying that the monarchy of Great Britain would descend to Princess Sophia, the Electress of Hanover, and her heirs.

The commissioners decided that the parliament of each country would be dissolved and a new body, known as the parliament of Great Britain, created. Scottish representation in the new parliament would consist of 16 peers and 45 MPs, compared with the English contingent of 190 peers and the 513 MPs from England and Wales. But it was agreed that Scotland would keep an independent church, legal

system and educational system. There would be economic union and free trade between the two countries, and arrangements were made for almost £400,000 to be paid to Scotland for the settlement of public and private debts and to subsidise industry.

When the draft terms became known in Scotland last October, huge public opposition was evident throughout the country, fuelled by the fear that Scotland would be swallowed up by England and left permanently at the mercy of the English majority at Westminster.

But, remarkably, the whole treaty was passed by the Scottish Parliament on 16 January after a few adjustments, notably the passing of separate acts to secure the religious independence of Scotland and England. Given the generally poor relations between the two countries, and recent notorious incidents such as the Glencoe massacre, there has been much speculation about the reason for Scottish acquiescence. The Scots seem to have been swayed by their common determination with the English to ensure a Hanoverian succession, a recognition of economic necessity and a combination of expert political management and the judicious use of bribes.

The Act of Union, first sought by James VI of Scotland and I of England when he united the crowns a century ago, was ratified by the English Parliament in March. Giving her assent, the queen declared: "I desire and expect from all my subjects of both nations that from henceforth they act with all possible respect and kindness to one another, that so it may appear to all the world they have hearts disposed to become one people. This will be a great pleasure to me."

Stepping-stones to merger of nations

24 March 1603: James VI of Scotland becomes James I of England, uniting the crowns.
1607: Both parliaments reject plans for constitutional union.
1660: Temporary union effected by Cromwell in 1654 fails to survive the Restoration.
21 April 1689: William and Mary crowned king and queen of England, and promise to become monarchs of Scotland, but

constitutions remain separate.
1701: English Act of Settlement ensures Hanoverian succession.
1703: Scottish Act of Security threatens to bar Hanoverians from Scottish throne.
22 July 1706: Commissioners agree terms of draft treaty.
16 January 1707: Scottish parliament ratifies Act of Union.
6 March 1707: Act of Union receives the royal assent.

$\triangleright$

Anne falls out with Sarah over Abigail

Kensington, 6 April 1710
A 30-year friendship was finally severed today in a tearful confrontation at Kensington palace between Queen Anne and Sarah Churchill, the Duchess of Marlborough. Sarah had been demanding an interview for days in order to "vindicate myself". She rejected Anne's suggestion that she write and threatened to visit the palace daily to secure an audience. For a woman who had once been the most powerful member of the royal circle, the need to resort to such threats shows how her influence has declined.

This afternoon the two women met when the duchess forced her way into the queen's closet. It ap-

Abigail Masham: the relative who supplanted a duchess at court.

pears that Sarah broke down in tears as she complained of a "thousand lies" spread about her, but the queen was unmoved. She repeatedly declared: "I shall make no answer to anything you say."

Great issues of state, quarrels over money and petty jealousies have all played a part in this rupture. Sarah and her Whig supporters have blamed the influence of Abigail Masham for Sarah's own decline. Mrs Masham was introduced into the royal household by Sarah, to whom she is related. Two years ago Sarah retaliated, accusing Anne of lesbianism with Abigail; she wrote of the queen having "no inclination for any but of one's own sex" and quoted a ballad ridiculing Abigail [*see right*]. Anne, as she showed today, was neither amused nor forgiving (→ 19/11/11).

Anne suspends parliament to halt Whigs

Anne is shown on a set of playing cards; now she has dissolved parliament.

Westminster, 5 April 1710
Enraged by parliament's attacks on Henry Sacheverell, whose Tory sermons were not to the Whig government's taste, the queen has prorogued the session just days after Sacheverell, on trial for his views, was suspended from preaching for three years. His mild punishment had been urged by the queen, and her growing dislike of the Whigs is underlined by today's intervention.

Two years of Whig government, which in turn followed three of a balanced Whig-Tory parliament, have seen the Queen become pro-Tory. This had been brought to a head by the Sacheverell affair but

stems from the popular anger at the intransigent refusal of the Whig government to contemplate peace with France. Unprecedented taxation, and "victories" like that at Malplaquet last year, where Marlborough sacrificed 10,000 men for a minor strategic advantage, have led to a general war-weariness in the country.

Anne's instincts have been backed up by support for the opposition within the country. It is likely that the government led by Marlborough and Godolphin may find its days numbered and its place taken by a Tory administration led by men like Robert Harley.

The 'lesbian' poem which angered Anne

The poem with the lesbian implications quoted by Sarah Churchill [*see left*] was probably written by her secretary, Arthur Maynwaring:

> *When as Queen Anne of great Renown*
> *Great Britain's Scepter sway'd,*
> *Besides the Church, she dearly lov'd*
> *A Dirty Chamber-Maid*
> *O! Abigail that was her Name,*
> *She stich'd and starched full well,*
> *But how she pierced this Royal Heart*
> *No Mortal Man can tell.*
> *However, for sweet Service done*
> *And Causes of great Weight,*
> *Her Royal mistress made her, Oh!*
> *A Minister of State.*
> *Her Secretary she was not*
> *Because she could not write*
> *But had the Conduct and the Care*
> *Of some dark Deeds at Night.*

Racing at Ascot is part of the season

Berkshire, 1712
Queen Anne, using money from the secret service fund, has established prizes of plate for races both at the well-established racing centre of Newmarket and at Ascot, near her favourite rural palace, Windsor. Unlike her predecessors, the queen displays negligible interest in either the visual arts, where her appreciation is hindered by her notoriously poor eyesight, or music.

She has always preferred to patronise outdoor activities – not only horse-racing, but gardening and hunting. The improvements to the gardens at Kensington and Hampton Court palaces bear witness to the former, and she has maintained her interest in hunting even now that she is an invalid, following the hounds in a specially-built light two-horse carriage. It is a far cry from her youth, when she used to ride every day, but those who see her career around the countryside in her carriage agree that she is no mean huntress.

Queen is struck by a serious illness

Windsor, 31 December 1713
The queen, for some time already an ill woman, has been struck down yet again today – and this time the attack appears worse than ever. She remained unconscious for several hours, terrifying the court which presumed her to be dead. Her doctors diagnosed a violent inflammatory fever, although not an ague. Her pulse has been irregular, and she has complained of leg pains.

Lady Masham (as Abigail became in 1711) has remained in constant attendance, and the Duchess of Somerset is expected, but Robert Harley, the Earl of Oxford, whom the queen has called for, has not come. Apparently he is not impressed by this latest illness, claiming that Anne suffers in much the same way every year. In addition he believes that any emergency dash to Windsor would merely panic the public, not to mention the City, and he has chosen instead to drive openly around London and set people's minds at rest (→ 4/1714).

Pretender is approached to take up the throne as succession crisis looms larger

Westminster, April 1714
With the queen's health showing little signs of improvement, government circles are filled with talk of a succession crisis. There is no heir, and all eyes are turned to the House of Hanover, poised to take over the English crown as laid down in the Act of Settlement [*see page 290*]. Anne may not like this Whig solution, but the only alternative is Anne's half-brother James Stuart, the Pretender living in exile in France, whose refusal to give up his Catholicism makes him anathema to the Protestant Whigs.

The leading Tory minister Henry St John, Viscount Bolingbroke, has told James that should he give up Rome, or even to pretend to do so, London would be his. James's secret agent in London, Abbé Gaultier, has echoed this, suggesting that James could pray as he wished so long as he appeared Protestant and made no changes in England's laws or freedoms.

The Pretender, however, has shown no appetite for deceit. He might give up his life for England, he has said, but "to my last breath, by the grace of God, I will maintain my religion". His case rests, but the succession crisis does not, and as the politicians wrangle the queen's health deteriorates (→ 20/10).

Parliament dissolved to save Bolingbroke

Westminster, 9 July 1714
Queen Anne, supported to the throne, prorogued parliament today as a storm blew up which threatened the positions of her current favourites Abigail Masham and Viscount Bolingbroke. The Whigs, led by the Earl of Wharton, are in uproar at revelations that the two may have received income meant for the crown from the South Sea Company. Meanwhile the rivalry between the two great Tories – Bolingbroke and Robert Harley, the Earl of Oxford – has reached fever pitch. Informed opinion has no doubt that one of the pair must fall. But which? The queen seems to favour the former (→ 27/7).

Bolingbroke: under fire.

Queen sacks Harley, the lord chancellor

Harley: relentlessly undermined.

London, 27 July 1714
Robert Harley, the Earl of Oxford, the lord chancellor, has lost his place, and a career that has lasted throughout Queen Anne's reign has ended. His rival Bolingbroke has schemed successfully, and Harley's own decline, and his alienation of the queen, led to today's dismissal.

Since 1710, when he became Tory leader, Harley's domination of politics has placed him at the heart of every controversy, and for the last two years his position has been relentlessly undermined, particularly by his inability to inspire real party loyalty.

Weary Queen Anne dies

The queen has died at Kensington.

Kensington Palace, 1 August 1714
The queen died today at 7.30am. She had not emerged from a coma into which she had fallen some hours before. One of her seven physicians, Dr Arbuthnot, said: "Sleep was never more welcome to a weary traveller than death was to her." For the last few days the cabinet has debated the succession controversy. Viscount Bolingbroke lobbied for James Stuart to succeed, but the pragmatic decision was made to support Elector George of Hanover. Parliament had ordained it, and to invite James Stuart would surely bring civil war back to the nation. Queen Anne's last major act was to confirm the appointment of Lord Shrewsbury as lord treasurer, a move that will strengthen the Whigs' hands considerably.

Anne's death pleases religious dissenters

London, 1 August 1714
In a display that sets religious ideology above national loyalty, a group of nonconformists and dissenters has offered prayers today thanking God for the queen's death. The group had gathered to pray for divine deliverance from what it believed was the onset of a new era of persecution. When its members heard of the queen's death, they burst into a psalm of thanksgiving.

Their rejoicing, which few have bothered to hide, stems from their belief that the hated Schism Act, hurried through parliament last June, will now never be implemented. The accession of the Protestant George, which is all but confirmed, should guarantee that.

The act, which was proposed by Bolingbroke, is in many ways a revival of the Clarendon Code (a series of measures passed under Charles II which attempted to suppress dissent). Its main provision is that dissenters may not educate any children – even their own.

A pair of chairs with an elegant line characteristic of a distinctive style in the decorative arts which flourished in Queen Anne's reign.

George I
1714–1727

**House
of
Hanover**

Westminster, 1 August 1714. Parliament proclaims the accession to the British throne of Prince George of Brunswick-Lüneburg, the Elector of Hanover, a second cousin of and the Protestant successor to Anne.→

Dover, 1 August 1714. The Duke of Marlborough, who began his return from exile on hearing of Queen Anne's illness, is welcomed back but arrives too late for a reconciliation with Anne (→ 6/8).

Hanover, 6 August 1714. King George signs his first official document as king; he reinstates the Duke of Marlborough as captain-general of the forces.

London, 20 September 1714. The king makes his state entry; with him are his son, George, and a mistress, Madame von der Schulenberg, nicknamed "the Maypole"; he divorced his wife, Sophia Dorothea of Celle, in 1694 for infidelity with Count Philip Christopher von Königsmarck, and she has been imprisoned in Ahlden castle ever since (→ 22/9).

Westminster, 22 September 1714. George invests his son, George Augustus, who became Duke of Cornwall and Rothesay on his father's accession, as Prince of Wales (→ 15/10).

London, 15 October 1714. The Princess of Wales, Caroline, and her daughters, Anne, Amelia and Caroline, join the Prince of Wales in London; the only son, Frederick Louis, aged seven, remains behind in Hanover, a sign of George's continued concern for his lands there (→ 20/11/16).

Westminster, 20 October 1714. Despite the outbreak of Jacobite riots backing James Edward Stuart, the son of James II and Catholic pretender to the throne, George is crowned king of Great Britain.→

Grampian, 6 September 1715. John Erskine, the Earl of Mar, a former secretary of state for Scotland, who fell from favour on the accession of George, joins the Jacobites, raising the Stuart standard at Braemar and proclaiming James Edward Stuart as James III (→ 14/9).

Perth, 14 September 1715. The town falls to the Jacobites (→ 9/11).

Preston, 9 November 1715. The Jacobites storm the town (→ 13/11).

Preston, 13 November 1715. The Jacobites are besieged (→ 14/11).

Stirling, 13 November 1715. The Jacobite rebellion fails; the Earl of Mar is unable to oust government troops under the leadership of John Campbell, the Duke of Argyll, from Sheriffmuir (→ 22/12).

Preston, 14 November 1715. The Jacobite force surrenders.

Grampian, 22 December 1715. James Edward Stuart, the Pretender, lands at Peterhead.→

Perth, 21 January 1716. The Pretender, who arrived at Scone early this month to be crowned as James III, flees when the Duke of Argyll marches on Perth (→ 4/2).

Montrose, 4 February 1716. James Stuart sets sail for France.→

London, June 1716. The rift between George and the Prince of Wales worsens as plans go ahead for George's visit to Hanover; the Prince of Wales is to be "Guardian of the Realm", not regent (→ 1717).

London, 20 November 1716. Caroline, the Princess of Wales, gives birth to her fifth child, a stillborn son (→ 2/11/17).

Europe, January 1717. Britain, France and the United Provinces form a triple alliance upholding the terms of the Treaty of Utrecht, signed in 1713 (→ 7/1718).

London, 2 November 1717. Caroline, the Princess of Wales, gives birth in St James's palace to her sixth child, a son named George William (→ 1717).

London, late 1717. After a family quarrel at the christening of George William, the Prince and Princess of Wales leave St James's palace and their children on the king's orders; they establish a rival court at Leicester House, in Leicester Square.→

London, 6 February 1718. Prince George William, aged only three months, dies of a heart defect (→ 15/4/21).

Paris, April 1718. Mary of Modena, the wife of the late James

VII and II and former queen, dies of cancer.

Sicily, July 1718. Philip V of Spain invades the island, thereby contravening the terms of the Treaty of Utrecht (→ 8/1718).

Europe, August 1718. A quadruple alliance of Britain, France, the United Provinces and the Holy Roman Empire is formed in an attempt to avoid the outbreak of a war with Spain (→ 28/12).

England/Spain, 28 Dec 1718. Britain declares war on Spain (→ 7/3/19).

Cadiz, Spain, 7 March 1719. Spanish troops, led by the Irish Duke of Ormonde, set sail for Britain intending to overthrow the Hanoverian regime, put James Stuart on the throne and prevent the blockade of Spanish ports by British ships (→ 10/6).

Spain, 28 March 1719. James Stuart arrives from Rome (→ 1/9).

London, 1719. George donates £1,000 to found a royal academy of music.

London, 1719. Madame von der Schulenberg, a mistress of the king, is made Duchess of Kendal.→

Hanover, 1719. King George visits his native land again.

London, April 1720. The king gives the royal assent to the South Sea Company Act (→ 1/3/21).

Westminster, June 1720. Robert Walpole, who resigned in 1717 on the dismissal of Charles, Viscount Townshend, returns to the government as paymaster-general to the forces (→ 14/4/21).

The life and times of King George I

Name: George Louis of Brunswick-Lüneburg.
Birth: 28 May 1660.
Accession: 1 August 1714.
Coronation: 20 October 1714.
Predecessor: second cousin.
Eyes: blue.
Marriage: Sophia Dorothea of Celle, 22 November 1682, Germany.
Divorce: December 1694.

Children: George Augustus and Sophia Dorothea.
Favourite home: Herrenhausen palace, Hanover.
Likes: music.
Dislikes: his wife.
Greatest problems: his son, the Jacobites.
Greatest success: protecting Hanoverian interests.
Death: 11 June 1727.

Opposite: detail from a portrait of King George I by Kneller.

British crown passes to Prince George of Hanover

Monarch can speak very little English

London, 1 August 1714

Cannon fired, drums rolled and trumpets blared as the herald proclaimed the news outside St James's palace at noon today: "The High and mighty Prince George Elector of Brunswick-Lüneburg is now ... become our only lawful and rightful liege lord, George, by the grace of God king of Great Britain, France and Ireland. God save the king."

And so George, not James III, has acceded to the throne. Tory grandees had contemplated declaring the Pretender king this morning, but their leader, Viscount Bolingbroke, realised that the tide had turned against them. The Whigs seized the initiative and will dominate the council of regency appointed today by George's representative, Baron Bothmer. The prospect of a Catholic king who could have brought dreadful intolerance and strife in his wake has receded.

Yet George Louis, aged 54, is hardly a comfortable choice himself. He is a man firmly rooted in Germany, who cannot speak very much English and prefers to converse in French. He appears to be more interested in what happens in Hanover than in Britain, and it is impossible to predict what role he will take in government.

Divorced from his wife Sophia Dorothea of Celle 20 years ago, after she had an affair with a Swedish count, King George is expected to bring with him his long-standing mistress Melusine von der Schulenberg – to whom, it is said, he is secretly married. Londoners wait with bated breath.

A large congregation looks raptly on as King George is ceremonially crowned.

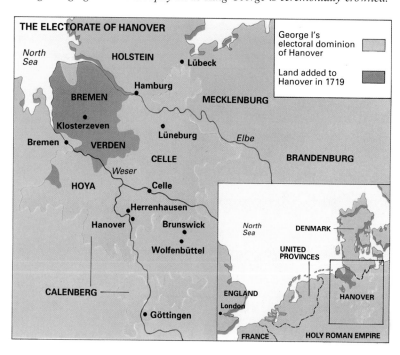

THE ELECTORATE OF HANOVER

	George I's electoral dominion of Hanover
	Land added to Hanover in 1719

North Sea · HOLSTEIN · Lübeck · Hamburg · BREMEN · MECKLENBURG · Klosterzeven · Lüneburg · Elbe · Bremen · VERDEN · CELLE · BRANDENBURG · Weser · HOYA · Celle · Herrenhausen · Hanover · Brunswick · Wolfenbüttel · CALENBERG · Göttingen

North Sea · DENMARK · UNITED PROVINCES · ENGLAND · London · HANOVER · FRANCE · HOLY ROMAN EMPIRE

King throws Tories out of high office

London, 1 October 1714

In his first executive act as king, George has appointed his ministers, and they are virtually all Whigs [*see story below left*]. His declaration that he would choose his ministers on merit alone and not on party allegiance seems to have fallen by the wayside. The Tories have paid the price for supporting James's rival claim to the throne by being excluded from office. They continue to hold a clear majority in parliament, although this is expected to disappear in the general election which must now be held.

While the king made all the decisions personally, he relied on two trusted friends for advice on the London political scene. Baron Bothmer is already well known as George's ambassador in London and knows exactly who supports the king most strongly. Jean de Robethon, a French Huguenot refugee, has come with King George from Hanover as his private secretary. The two advisers recommended for promotion only those men who supported the Hanoverian succession – hence the retention in the government of the Earl of Nottingham, one of the few Tories who throughout their careers have been consistently pro-Hanoverian.

In fact the king has proved more radical than Bothmer, who suggested that a core of pro-Hanoverian Tories should remain in office. Even the office of lord high treasurer, which enabled the Earls of Oxford and Bolingbroke to wield such enormous influence, is to be left vacant (→ 3/1715).

Halifax and Wharton lead government

London, September 1714

King George's new ministers are a very strong team of experienced and keen men. Lord Halifax, who created the Bank of England, is first lord of the treasury; the fiercely Whiggish Marquis of Wharton is lord privy seal. Interesting new appointments include that of James, Earl Stanhope, and Charles, Viscount Townshend, as secretaries of state at the foreign office. Stanhope, a witty and irascible former soldier, has an excellent grasp of foreign affairs. Townshend, who comes from an old Norfolk family, has a reputation for hard bargaining. Finally, Robert Walpole, the former war secretary, has returned as paymaster-general (→ 1/10/14).

Jacobite demos fail to mar coronation

Westminster, 20 October 1714

Just a month after arriving in England, George was crowned king at the abbey today. Swathed in crimson velvet and ermine, and sheltered by a canopy held by the barons of the Cinque Ports, Britain's first Hanoverian monarch had Queen Anne's crown – all 2.5lbs (1.1kg) of it – placed on his head by the archbishop of Canterbury. Demonstrations in favour of the Stuart Pretender, James, did not dent the dignity of the occasion. Nor did the presence of no fewer than three former mistresses of previous kings, although one remarked to the others: "Who would have thought we three whores would have met together here?"

Pretender lands, but rebellion flags

Whigs predominate in new parliament after poll triumph

London, March 1715

The Tory majority in the Commons has been overturned, and the new house, which started its session this month, has a Whig majority of 150. The landslide victory for King George's preferred party owes more than a little to the proclamation that he issued in January. Dissolving parliament and calling a general election, George demanded that electors return only those who "showed a firmness to the Protestant succession, when it was in danger". The Pretender, meanwhile, delivered a severe blow to Tory interests with a response which confirmed his Catholicism and failed to give any assurances that the Church of England would be protected.

The Whigs are now moving to prosecute leading Tories, including the Earl of Oxford and Henry St John, Viscount Bolingbroke, for treason. The main aim seems to be to satisfy their bloodlust by attacking former supporters of the Stuart cause (→ 12/1715).

Riot Act makes big gatherings illegal

England, December 1715

Disturbed by the Jacobite rising, and by sporadic outbursts of anti-Hanoverian sentiment, the Whigs have clamped down on public gatherings. The Riot Act makes it an offence for gatherings of 12 or more people to refuse to disperse when ordered to by a magistrate.

The statute follows attacks on dissenting chapels in the northwest and Midlands by rioters inspired by the Jacobite rising and Tory agitators. The dissenters are a special target because they are most closely associated with the Hanoverian cause. In Manchester this summer, a month of rioting had to be suppressed by three companies of dragoons. Law and order must be preserved, but some say that this draconian measure has been made necessary by King George's blind distrust of the Tories, fomented by Whig paranoia (→ 7/5/16).

The battle at Sheriffmuir, near Stirling: the Jacobites threw away a chance to crush the inferior Hanoverian forces.

Scotland, 22 December 1715

James Francis Edward Stuart, the Pretender, landed today at Peterhead to stake his claim to the throne. His arrival is the climax to a series of confrontations which have seen disturbances in England and a wholesale rebellion in Scotland, but he is about to learn that the rising on his behalf is already half dead.

James has garnered support with a promise to repeal the hated Act of Union, which effectively delivered the Scots into the hands of the English. He also promised to stop "corruption" in Westminster, another potent Scottish complaint. But the Jacobite rising (from *Jacobus*, the Latin for James) has less to do with any great love for him than with a hatred of King George and his total distrust of all except the Whigs who have secured such an iron grip on the nation. The Earl of Mar, the architect of the rebellion, is one of the many Tory grandees summarily thrown out of office to establish a Whig monopoly.

The rising started on 6 September when Lord Mar raised his standard at Braemar. He did not know that his main backer, Louis XIV, the king of France, had just died. Louis's successor is a five-year-old boy whose regent, the Duke of Orleans, is seeking a *rapprochement* with George. Fuelled by hatred of the Act of Union, English customs duties and other complaints, support for Mar snowballed. By mid-October most of Scotland had declared for the Pretender, who promised to right these wrongs.

The only problem with the rising has been Mar himself. After some initial successes, including the capture of Perth, he has shown a remarkable lack of military acumen or decisiveness. On 13 November, at Sheriffmuir, north of Stirling, the Hanoverian leader, John Campbell, the Duke of Argyll – "Red John of the Battles" – managed to hold Mar's superior force to a draw. The Jacobite leader had the chance to regroup and deliver a crushing blow to Argyll but opted for a strategic retreat instead. It was a disastrous error of judgement.

On the very day that Mar threw away his chance at Sheriffmuir, a second disaster came at Preston. A Jacobite army managed to occupy the town, only to allow itself to be surrounded by a force sent by Stanhope under General Wills, and then hoisted the white flag of surrender. The failure of the armies to link up or to gather any real support south of the border, together with King George's better organisation, will make things very difficult for the Pretender (→ 21/1/16).

The Jacobite leader, the Earl of Mar, raising the Pretender's standard.

Pretender flees Scotland

The Pretender's followers in miserable retreat: a later engraving.

Montrose, 4 February 1716

James Stuart, the son of James II and Catholic pretender to the throne, boarded a French ship here tonight and left Scotland when it became clear that his uprising was a disaster. He expressed his "deep regret" at having burnt several villages – he had introduced a scorched-earth policy, destroying houses, corn stocks and forage to deprive the Duke of Argyll's army of vital supplies and succour. The Earl of Mar – named "Bobbing John" for his constantly changing views – has joined the king on this voyage back into exile.

James, who was wounded by a British bullet at the Battle of Mal-

plaquet in 1709 when he fought with the French army, made his first moves for the crown two years ago when Queen Anne died. Plans for Jacobites to muster in the west of England were foiled by good intelligence, but Mar raised James's standard at Braemar in September and proclaimed the Pretender king before marching south with an army of 5,000. The campaign went well at first, with Perth falling to supporters of the Pretender.

In France, James was unaware of the rebellion until it was under way, but then promised massive French support – which would have been forthcoming but for the death of Louis XIV (→ 7/3/19).

Prince of Wales sets up rival court to his father's at Leicester House, in London

London, 1717

The blistering row between the king and the Prince of Wales came to a climax this autumn when George placed his son and daughter-in-law under close arrest in Kensington palace, refusing them access to their children and threatening to throw them into the Tower of London. The affair has reached such a state that the prince and princess, safely out of the king's reach, have established what is literally a second court at Leicester House in the west end of London.

The first hint of trouble came when the king returned from Hanover to find that his son had become increasingly popular. Com-

munication between father and son grew increasingly difficult.

In November Caroline gave birth to a son. The king called to offer congratulations; the prince ignored him. The king insisted on naming the Duke of Newcastle, the lord chamberlain, as godfather; the prince immediately rowed with Newcastle who, misunderstanding the prince's heavy German accent, thought he had been challenged to a duel and complained to the king.

Now the prince and princess are living in a two-storeyed house in a district noted for its brothels, footpads and duels, where they are attracting an ever-growing number of political visitors (→6/2/18).

Leicester House, the Prince of Wales's home in the west end of London.

Act lays down seven-year parliaments

Westminster, 7 May 1716

Fears that the next election – due in two years' time under the present triennial system – might trigger off a new Jacobite revolt led parliament to vote to extend itself for a further six years today. Under the Septennial Act, general elections will take place every seven years from now on.

The original system has not been exactly an unqualified success. The first year is usually spent in hearing election petitions and the last in preparing for a new election, leaving only a year in which legislation can be debated and passed and the country be adequately governed. Whig MPs and peers regard the

Septennial Act as a boon to their ambitions because it has put off an imminent general election in which the Tories were expected to do especially well.

Today's act met serious opposition from Tories in both houses. The principal arguments were that no parliament had the right to prolong its own life and that longer parliaments are bound to lead to corruption and the undermining of the Commons' independence. The act was nevertheless passed today in the House of Lords by 65 votes to 36 and in the lower house by 264 to 121. Twenty-four Tory peers have entered a formal protest against it (→9/6).

Walpole accuses Tories of 'Jacobitism'

Robert Walpole: a timely victory.

London, 9 June 1716

The king's leading minister, Robert Walpole, has won a significant victory over his arch-enemies, Henry St John, Lord Bolingbroke, and the Duke of Ormonde, both now exiled in France after their part in the Jacobite uprising. Walpole took great pleasure today in reading a Commons committee report which charges the two Tories with "Jacobitism" – support for the Stuart Pretender – and calls for their impeachment. The report is timely. The Tories are known to be exploiting serious disturbances throughout the country against both the Hanoverian crown and the Whig government (→9/4/17).

King loses patience in foreign policy clash

The Commons in session: King George has clashed with his leading ministers.

London, 9 April 1717
The long-running conflict between the king and several of his ministers came to a climax today when he dismissed Charles Townshend, his former secretary of state who was only recently appointed lord lieutenant of Ireland. Townshend's brother-in-law, Robert Walpole, has resigned in protest, as will other ministers.

It was the government's Baltic policy – heavily influenced by the king, who in turn is influenced by his Hanoverian advisers – that triggered the row. The king is worried about the possible accord between Russia, Sweden and Prussia and is urging haste in cementing the proposed alliance treaty with France. Townshend and Walpole argued that haste was a sign of weakness and that the French had not yet exiled the Pretender.

The king, in Hanover, became increasingly irritated with the two men and was easily persuaded that they were in league with the Prince of Wales. Walpole did not help matters by suggesting that if the king did not return soon to open parliament, the prince should be allowed to do so. The answer was a firm "no!" (→ 1719).

Handel plays 'Water Music' for the royals

On the river: a later view of the Thames by Westminster Bridge (c.1750).

London, 18 July 1717
It was not until 4.30am today that the king and the rest of the royal party arrived back at St James's after a day and a night of revelry on the river with music composed especially by George Frederick Handel. Handel's music, played by an orchestra on a barge adjoining the king's, so delighted George that he insisted on command performances before and after supper, even though each lasted for an hour.

The music was an expensive triumph for Baron von Kielmannsegge, the husband of George's half-sister Charlotte Sophia. He paid the musicians £150 for their efforts, while the countess made arrangements for a "splendid supper" in a Chelsea garden.

The countess was forced to flee her native Hanover in a post chaise, pursued by creditors; she joined her half-brother in the Low Countries while *en route* to London. She was once beautiful but now has a figure that – so unkind observers remark – borders on the obese. She sat close to the king throughout the performance.

Handel, a fellow German, has for a long time been a royal favourite and has even become something of a national institution. George patronised him from the moment that he arrived in London and has attended countless performances of *Rinaldo* and *Amadigi*. Unfortunately, the king is invariably accompanied to the opera by one or other of his ladies, whose noisy gossip tends to anger serious music lovers in the audience (→ 14/2/26).

In demand: the composer Handel.

George makes hasty pact with France

Hanover, 28 November 1716
Dangerously isolated in Europe, Britain signed a vital alliance here today with its old enemy France. A triple alliance – with another old antagonist, the United Provinces – is likely to follow. King George, on holiday here, had good reason for haste in forming this alliance: Russian troops have landed in Mecklenburg, where the Hanoverian king has interests, and there is the threat of yet another Jacobite attempt on the British throne, this time with Russian and Swedish backing. The alliance shrewdly takes account of France's good relations with the latter two countries.

The treaty with France guarantees the successions to the thrones of both countries and the exile of the Pretender to Italy (→ 1/1717).

Sermon to king attacks Church of England

London, 31 March 1717
Benjamin Hoadly, the bishop of Bangor, has started a furious row by a sermon that he gave today in the presence of the king. Preaching as usual on his knees owing to his severe physical handicaps, Bishop Hoadly argued that the church should abandon tests of orthodoxy intended to keep dissenters out of government office. Tory clergy have taken this as a direct attack on the Church of England's claim to doctrinal authority.

There is also a political angle. Hoadly is known to be a political activist for the Whigs, the party favoured by King George. The predominantly Tory lower clergy fear that bishops such as Hoadly are serving the state far more than the church.

The 'Elephant' and a 'Maypole' accompany king

London, 1719

The household that has come with "German George" is a motley crew consisting of his mistress, his 44-year-old half-sister and various Germans, few of whom speak English. Their saving grace, in the eyes of many, is that while they know little of the country or its people, they can be easily bribed to award offices, titles and favours.

Melusine von der Schulenberg, now the Duchess of Kendal, is 50 years old and has been the king's mistress for the last 27 years. A "very tall, lean, ill-favoured lady", she is said to take bribes from politicians who rely on her to persuade King George to do as they ask. She is not overly intelligent and is unpopular with the people, who call her "the Maypole"; but George remains loyal to her.

The vivacious Sophia Charlotte von Kielmannsegge is George's illegitimate half-sister. In contrast to the Duchess of Kendal she possesses an enormous figure, its contours unrestrained by the stays that ladies of fashion wear. She has been inelegantly dubbed "the Elephant" by Londoners. The king will make her Countess of Darlington but has refused to settle her German debts, which are so great that she had to flee Hanover in disguise.

Sophia von Kielmannsegge, the king's vivacious half-sister.

Marlborough completes Blenheim Palace

A 20th-century view of Marlborough's bold and magnificent Blenheim palace.

Blenheim Palace, Oxon, 1719

This year has seen the completion for the Duke of Marlborough of the great palace of Blenheim, built for him by a nation grateful for his continental victories that put paid to King Louis XIV's ambition to dominate all Europe. Intended to be a monument to Marlborough's achievements as much as a house, and named after his most famous battle, Blenheim Palace is splendid indeed.

Marlborough and his duchess, Sarah, were the particular favourites of the late Queen Anne, who elevated Marlborough, previously John Churchill, to his dukedom and arranged for the palace to be built for them from state funds. Queen Anne and the Marlboroughs were so close that they wrote to each other under pet names, but later they fell out and relations became extremely strained, leaving the duke to find tens of thousands of pounds to pay for the completion of the house.

Blenheim was planned by Sir John Vanbrugh, the leading architect of his day, but he too quarrelled with the duchess and left before it was finished. Nevertheless the house is a masterpiece and is one of the biggest country mansions in England, with magnificent decorations and apartments and acres of gardens (→ 16/6/22).

Pretender marries a Polish princess

Bologna, Italy, 1 September 1719

James Stuart – James III to his supporters but "the Pretender" to others – has married the 17-year-old Princess Maria Clementina Sobieska, a granddaughter of King John III of Poland. James, 14 years older than his bride, now lives in Rome where the pope still recognises him as Britain's rightful king. He has been defeated twice in his attempts to conquer England, and so wary are rulers of upsetting the increasingly powerful British that when the Holy Roman Emperor heard of the intended match Clementina was incarcerated in an Innsbruck convent, only to be freed later by James's agents (→ 31/12/20).

King loses key vote

Westminster, 1719

The Commons have voted down the Peerage Bill, intended by the first lord of the treasury, Lord Sunderland, and his colleague Lord Stanhope to clip the wings of the rival Whig Robert Walpole. The bill proposed that just 31 more peers should be created by the king, who backed the idea, and after that no more. This would have given Sunderland's ministry an inbuilt majority in the Lords, vital in case the Prince of Wales, with whom Walpole sides, creates peers loyal to him on becoming king (→ 24/4/20).

Spanish allies of Jacobite cause sent packing by royalist forces

Glenshiel, 10 June 1719

A small army of Jacobite highlanders, backed by about 300 Spanish troops, was utterly defeated today – James Stuart's 31st birthday – at Glenshiel by a loyal army that marched out from Inverness. The two armies were so small, with scarcely 1,200 on each side, and the fighting so short, that the clash can hardly be called a battle. The Spanish soldiers had landed in March, but a supporting fleet was sunk in a storm before it could leave Spain. Arguments between the Jacobite leaders meant that no decisions were made until the Inverness garrison was upon them, by which time it was too late.

The Jacobites are routed at Glenshiel by royalist troops: a later view.

Walpole Whigs try 'bribing' the king

London, 24 April 1720

Robert Walpole has performed a remarkable feat in bringing about at least a temporary reconciliation between King George and the Prince of Wales. So deep had the rift between them become that political opposition to the king's policies had gathered around the prince, opening the gulf still wider.

This had made problems for Walpole, an ally of the prince and opponent of the present Whig administration of Lord Stanhope. Walpole has been out of office for some time and has had little chance of regaining it while the king associates all political opposition with his deeply unloved son. Walpole's answer to this – and his solution for getting himself and his Whig supporters back into office – is to get the king and the prince to make peace, thus forcing Lord Stanhope to take him back into office.

In effect Walpole's plan is to bribe the king by promising to persuade parliament to pay off his civil list debts of £600,000 once a reconciliation takes place. As King George cares more for money than for his son, he received him at St James's palace today. The meeting was not a great success, and the king was heard berating the prince for his conduct. Yet from Walpole's point of view he and his followers are as good as back in office – and in the royal favour (→ 5/5).

King and Prince of Wales constantly row

In constant conflict: King George and the Prince and Princess of Wales.

London, 5 May 1720

The discord between the king and the Prince of Wales goes on unabated, despite attempts at reconciliation. Walpole managed to bring the two together briefly last month at St James's palace, but the meeting was not particularly successful. Since then they have barely spoken, and it has become increasingly clear that the only person to have achieved much by the meeting is Walpole, now back in office.

The hostility between the king and the prince has its roots in Hanover, where the prince's beloved mother has been imprisoned for 26 years on George's orders, although the couple have been divorced for all that time. More recently King George fell out with the prince when the king insisted that the Duke of Newcastle should be godfather to the prince's second son, George William.

A row blew up at the baptism when the prince was falsely accused of having challenged the duke to a duel. The king had his son arrested and held for some days until he was advised that this was illegal. He then banished him and the princess from the palace. Cruelly, he refused them permission to take their children with them. He has since taken over the children's education and allows their parents only one visit a week (→ 15/5).

Parliament agrees to settle civil list

Westminster, 15 May 1720

Robert Walpole has marked his return to royal favour by keeping the promise that he made to King George last month to relieve him of £600,000 worth of debts. Walpole had persuaded the king that he would get parliament to pay off these civil list debts once the king effected a reconciliation with his son, the Prince of Wales – who just happens to be Walpole's patron. The king kept his part of the bargain last month, and in a successful Commons vote tonight Walpole kept his. There is no one who can judge the mood of parliament – or the mood of its large number of solid country gentlemen – better than Walpole.

The king made the outcome of the vote more secure by offering to approve the creation by parliament of two large new insurance companies, with special privileges by which MPs would be able to buy lucrative shareholdings. George made his offer conditional on having his debts paid, and when one member began to question how the debts were incurred he was silenced by a vote of thanks to the king, seconded by Walpole. In fact Walpole is already involved with a big insurance company, and in a transaction that looks more like a bribe he stands to net £2,612 within a few days of parliament voting through the measure (→ 6/1720).

Birth of a son to exiled Pretender gives new hope to Jacobites

The Pretender's heir: Prince Charles Edward Stuart is baptised.

Rome, 31 December 1720

Fresh life has been breathed into the fading Jacobite cause with the birth of a son to the exiled James Stuart, the Pretender. It is said that at the moment of his birth a new star appeared in the heavens and a terrible storm fell upon Hanover, causing great damage and loss of property. These heavenly portents are likely to count for less in Great Britain than do the facts that the birth of Charles Edward Stuart was attended by several cardinals and that his christening linen has been consecrated by the pope. With the passage of time, the Catholic Stuart pretenders seem ever less attractive to a Protestant nation (→ 19/4/22).

The triumph of King George's family: a detail from a decorative ceiling at Greenwich hospital painted by J Thornhill (d.1734).

George I
1714–1727

House
of
Hanover

Greenwich, 9 February 1721. Edmund Halley is appointed as astronomer-royal.

Westminster, 1 March 1721. The Commons pass ten resolutions condemning the South Sea Company for gross breach of trust (→ 14/4).

Westminster, 14 April 1721. Robert Walpole is appointed as first lord of the treasury and chancellor of the exchequer in recognition for having salvaged the government's finances following the collapse of the South Sea Company (→ 1721).

London, 15 April 1721. Caroline, the Princess of Wales, gives birth at Leicester House to her seventh child, a son named William Augustus (→ 1721).

Spain, 12 June 1721. George writes to Philip V assuring him that he will consult parliament as soon as possible over resolving the question of Gibraltar (→ 1725).

Westminster, 1721. Robert Walpole decides not to accept a peerage when it is offered by the king because of his opposition to the 1719 Peerage Bill (→ 1/5/22).

London, 30 April 1722. Charles Spencer, the Earl of Sunderland, a great rival of Robert Walpole, dies of pleurisy during the election campaign (→ 1/5).

Westminster, 10 May 1722. King George, who called the general election in the hope of gaining a government more favourable to his policies, has been disappointed by the Whig triumph in it.

London, 1722. George makes his half-sister Sophia Charlotte von Kielmannsegge – nicknamed "the Elephant" because she is enormously fat – Baroness of Brentford and Countess of Darlington (→ 1724).

London, 1722. Caroline, the Princess of Wales, makes the surprise appointment of Dr Freind, a dedicated Jacobite, as physician to her daughters (→ 22/2/23).

London, 22 February 1723. The Princess of Wales gives birth to her eighth child, a daughter named Mary (→ 7/12/24).

London, 25 February 1723. Sir Christopher Wren, the architect responsible for the rebuilding of St Paul's cathedral, dies.

England, 29 June 1723. Francis Atterbury, the disgraced bishop of Rochester, is sentenced to exile after being tried for his involvement in the Jacobite plot uncovered last year; he claims, incorrectly, that Robert Walpole plans to bring back the Pretender, James Stuart, after George dies.

London, June 1723. George plans another trip back to his beloved Hanover; he will take with him two secretaries of state, Charles, Viscount Townshend, and John, Baron Carteret.→

England, 2 October 1723. The British block the trading activities of the Holy Roman Empire by passing a law against trade with the Ostend merchants (→ 10/10).

Prussia, 9 October 1723. King George suffers a fainting fit on the first day of his stay at Charlottenburg (→ 10/10).

Prussia, 10 October 1723. George and King Frederick William of Prussia, his son-in-law, sign the Treaty of Charlottenburg, confirming their alliance of 1719 and joining forces against Holy Roman Emperor Charles VI and his Ostend mercantile trading company (→ 1725).

London, 19 October 1723. Sir Godfrey Kneller, court painter to the last four English monarchs, dies (→ 1723).

Harwich, 1 August 1724. Anti-royalists mark the anniversary of George's accession to the throne with demonstrations.

London, 7 December 1724. The Princess of Wales, in giving birth to her ninth child, a daughter named Louisa, has suffered an umbilical rupture (→ 1727).

London, 1724. King George's half-sister, Sophia Charlotte von Kielmannsegge, the Countess of Darlington, dies.

Rome, 6 March 1725. The Pretender, James Stuart, and his wife, Maria Clementina, have their second child, a son named Henry, styled the Duke of York (→ 7/1727).

London, September 1725. George gives a full pardon to Henry St John, Viscount Bolingbroke, a leading Tory and Jacobite supporter; he returns from exile in France but is barred from resuming his seat in the House of Lords.

England, 1725. Britain signs the Treaty of Hanover with France and Prussia as they join forces against Spain and Austria (→ 7/1727).

Highland, 1725. An Englishman, General George Wade, is appointed commander of the army in the highlands. He begins a vigorous policy of road- and bridge-building.

Westminster, 1725. Robert Walpole revives the moribund Order of the Bath; he accepts a knighthood from King George and now styles himself "Sir Robert" (→ 1726).

Westminster, 14 February 1726. George gives the royal assent to the bill which naturalises George Frederick Handel, the German composer resident in England, as a British subject (→ 20/2).

Ahlden, Germany, 2 Nov 1726. Sophia Dorothea of Celle, the divorced wife of King George, dies, aged 60; she is to be buried with her parents at Celle.→

Westminster, 1726. Sir Robert Walpole is awarded the Star and Garter by the king, the first commoner for generations to receive the honour (→ 5/1727).

London, winter 1726/27. George takes a new mistress, Ann Brett, the daughter of the Countess of Macclesfield, and grants her an apartment in St James's palace.

Scotland, 1727. The Royal Bank of Scotland is established.

London, 11 February 1727. The *Daily Courant* reports that a feast at St James's palace for the City, hosted by King George, broke up amongst scenes of wild and drunken debauchery.

London, 20 March 1727. Sir Isaac Newton, the president of the Royal Society, which was chartered by Charles II, dies aged 86; he is to be buried in Westminster abbey.

Greenwich, 3 June 1727. George sets out for Hanover after ensuring that the Prince of Wales has no more power in his absence than at any other time (→ 8/6).

Low Countries, 8 June 1727. King George breaks his journey at Delden, where he dines very heavily on both strawberries and oranges (→ 11/6).

Osnabrück, 11 June 1727. George suffers a cerebral haemorrhage brought on by a serious stomach upset and dies at Osnabrück castle, aged 67; he is succeeded by his son, George Augustus, the Prince of Wales, aged 44.→

King sucked into 'South Sea bubble'

London, 1721

The collapsing South Sea financial bubble has claimed as its victims not only politicians but also the royal family. Now the prominent Whig politician Robert Walpole has been appointed chancellor of the exchequer and first lord of the treasury in a bid to restore confidence in the country's finances.

Lured by the chance of hefty profits, King George took £60,000 from the civil list funds to invest in the South Sea Company, which had been granted a monopoly of trade with Spanish South America. Within months the king was able to sell his £60,000 of stock for £106,400. Greedy for even bigger profits, he reinvested the money and persuaded his German mistresses to put their money into the company. Now the stock is practically worthless, and a Commons committee has reported that the company's books are full of fictitious entries and that ministers were bribed to do favours for the company.

The anticipated trade with South America never materialised, and the company's activities consisted of little more than trading in its own shares. Two years ago the company's directors offered to take over the national debt by issuing new shares at £1 for each £1 of the debt. Since the company's shares were then trading at very much

The "South Sea bubble" scandal, satirised by William Hogarth (d.1764).

more than £1, the directors acquired a large surplus of shares which they subsequently sold back to the public.

Politicians, courtiers and royal mistresses backed the scheme in return for £1,500,000 in bribes. The shares soared from 128 points to 1,000 in a matter of weeks. The company hoped to liquidate the national debt by persuading the public to exchange their government annuities for company stock. Many people fell for the promise of big capital gains, but then towards the end of last year the bubble burst

and the stock collapsed. Not everybody was taken in. Thomas Guy, by repute the meanest man in England, made a quick profit and used the money to found a hospital in his name. Walpole invested a modest £9,000, although he had originally criticised the national debt scheme. So far he has managed to distance himself from the scandal and has joined the government's efforts to sort out the mess.

For his efforts to protect the king and company directors he has earned the nickname of Skreen Master General (→19/4/22).

Walpole appointed 'prime minister' to the grateful George

Westminster, 1 May 1722

The sudden death from pleurisy of the king's senior minister, Charles Spencer, the Earl of Sunderland, has brought supreme power within the grasp of an ambitious and determined Whig politician, Robert Walpole. It is well-known that King George fears and dislikes him and that he made the appointment with reluctance, perceiving perhaps that Walpole will not be satisfied merely to don Sunderland's mantle but will establish himself as "prime minister".

Walpole has been an MP for more than 20 years, with a brief interregnum when he was accused of corruption and sent to the Tower; he later served as first lord of the treasury until the intrigues of the king's German advisers forced him to resign. He was brought back into the government one year ago to

Robert Walpole (left) in the house.

tackle the immense financial problems created by the "South Sea bubble" scandal.

Although widely criticised for the efforts to protect the king and the South Sea directors in the aftermath of the financial collapse, Walpole refused to give way, convinced that the stability of both the monarchy and the government were at risk. He sees the threat of a Stuart restoration as a real one, and the best defence against it is a strong Whig government with himself at the head. At the age of 46, Walpole is now being given the chance to show his mettle (→6/1723).

The Princess of Wales tries out new inoculations for smallpox

Lady Mary Wortley Montagu.

London, 1721

Caroline, the Princess of Wales, has horrified relatives and friends by subjecting two of her daughters to a new and largely untested treatment for the prevention of smallpox known as inoculation. The girls, Caroline and Amelia, have often been a cause of anxiety because of their colds, catarrh, bronchitis and swollen neck glands.

The recommendations of court physicians are not always to the princess's liking; she ignored a proposal to administer antimony to Amelia to induce vomiting, although she was willing for doctors to draw off blood from her, a practice supposed to remove impurities from the body. Now Lady Mary Wortley Montagu, the wife of the

British ambassador to the Ottoman Empire, has returned from Constantinople with what she claims is a successful serum used for inoculation against smallpox. The princess, to her family's consternation, has decided to have Caroline and Amelia inoculated.

Her great-aunt Liselotte said that she could never treat any children of her own in this way "even though it was for their own good ... my doctor doesn't think the remedy is safe". Liselotte prefers to hope that the disease will simply go away and not come back. But the princess has become an enthusiastic supporter of Lady Mary's serum treatment and seems to have overcome the misgivings of the Prince of Wales (→1722).

Plot to take over London discovered

London, 19 April 1722
The discovery of a Jacobite plot to seize power has caused near panic in London and brought about a run on the Bank of England. The plotters planned to go into action as soon as King George left for a visit to Hanover. The king's German mistress, Melusine von der Schulenberg, the Duchess of Kendal, claims to have received an anonymous warning of an attempt to assassinate the king and proclaim James Stuart, the 34-year-old son of James II, as James III. Arms are said to have been distributed to supporters who were to capture the Tower of London, the Royal Exchange and St James's palace.

At the centre of the plot is a high-churchman, Francis Atterbury, the bishop of Rochester, the man who had hoped to bring back the Stuarts when Queen Anne died. Although he was outmanoeuvred on this he went on to take the oath of allegiance to George. In reality he has always remained a firm Jacobite, a point demonstrated by his appearances in the House of Lords to deliver violent attacks on Robert Walpole's Whig government.

Some observers are sceptical about the seriousness of a Jacobite threat and accuse Walpole of ex-

A medal struck to mark the defeat of the Atterbury plot shows the conspirators (left) making their plans and (right, on the reverse) after their discovery.

ploiting public fear in order to consolidate his power base in the House of Commons. Certainly the recent events have enabled him to attack his political rivals, since the Jacobite supporters include not only Catholics but also some high-church and extreme Tory groups.

A little-known element in the Atterbury story is the fact that Walpole once tried to lure the bishop to join the Whigs' side by offering him the see of Winchester and a post for his son-in-law at the treasury. Atterbury rejected the proposition out of hand. It was apparently then that Walpole decided that Atterbury had to be cut down (→ 1/5).

Atterbury, the bishop of Rochester.

London, 1 May 1722
Public apprehensions over th threat of a Jacobite coup increase today when Robert Walpole gav orders for several thousand troop to be drafted into London and en camped in Hyde Park. The king ha agreed to postpone his visit to Han over, Catholics have been ordered to leave town, and the mail is be ing intercepted in the search fo evidence.

First reports of the plot reache Walpole through his spies on th continent, one of whom has pene trated the inner circle of the Pre tender, James Stuart. Walpole also has an arrangement with the post master-general in Brussels, wh passes on copies of correspondenc between Jacobite plotters.

Even so, Walpole has been un able to produce sufficient evidenc to convict Bishop Atterbury o Rochester of treason. Despite hi high-church views and his ope Jacobite sympathies, the bishop i admired for his courage. He ha been sent to the Tower, along wit the Duke of Norfolk and other sus pected noble plotters. When par liament meets Walpole intends t ask MPs to suspend the Habea Corpus Act and agree to a specia tax on Catholics (→ 17/5/23).

Marlborough dies, shortly after his hero's palace is completed

The Duke and Duchess of Marlborough, by Johann B Closterman (d.1713).

Windsor, 16 June 1722
John Churchill, one of the greatest soldiers that Britain has ever seen, has died just before his 72nd birthday. Ironically, his death comes only a short while after the completion of Blenheim Palace, the nation's reward to Churchill for his victory at Blenheim over Louis XIV in 1704. Churchill began his soldiering in the Guards and was a staunch supporter of William of Orange. His career received a considerable fillip when he was married to Sarah Jennings. Sarah was a close friend of Princess Anne, and her husband soon won the princess's good favour. As queen, Anne made Churchill both Duke of Marlborough and commander-in-chief of English troops on the continent fighting the French. A succession of stunning victories followed, most notably at Blenheim and Ramillies.

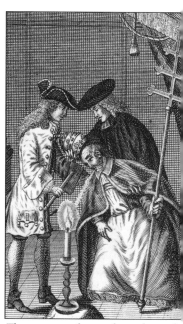

The propaganda war here shows the Antichrist supported by Jacobites.

'Puerile' Atterbury plotter is executed

The conspirator Christopher Layer.

Tyburn, London, 17 May 1723

A barrister of the Middle Temple, whose role in the so-called Atterbury plot to stage a Jacobite coup has been described as both "incompetent" and "puerile", was executed at Tyburn today. Christopher Layer planned to raise an armed band to seize the Tower of London and other key points. He was betrayed by one of his mistresses and brought to trial last November; he was the only one of all the conspirators to be sentenced to a traitor's death (→ 29/6).

Political tension running high at court

London, June 1723

Long-standing antagonisms among ministers have flared up anew following King George's departure from London for Hanover with two secretaries of state: Charles, Viscount Townshend, and John, Baron Carteret. Robert Walpole, the prime minister, has no anxieties about Townshend, who is his brother-in-law, but he profoundly mistrusts Carteret and is convinced that he is plotting to turn the king against him.

Walpole's handling of the "South Sea bubble" crisis and the Jacobite conspiracy has, in fact, substantially strengthened his political position, but he has never forgotten the betrayal six years ago when he and Townshend were brought down by supposedly trustworthy colleagues who had gained the king's ear. Now the threat comes from the overbearing and ambitious Carteret who has the advantage of being fluent in German, the king's language.

Walpole, desperate for some sign of the king's approval and ever ready to disparage Carteret, has complained to the king about the actions of William, Earl Cadogan, an old friend of Carteret. When the Duke of Marlborough died last year Cadogan, who had served on the duke's staff, expected to succeed him as commander-in-chief

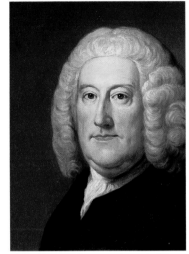

John, Baron Carteret, later in life.

and promptly began giving orders about troop dispositions.

In Hanover Townshend had to deliver to the king Walpole's angry letter denouncing Cadogan's presumption. George, who usually displays a prickly sensitivity about army matters, on this occasion expressed his confidence in Walpole's judgement. But then Carteret turned up with a stinging reply from Cadogan protesting at Walpole's behaviour. The king managed to smooth things over, and Townshend has written a reassuring letter to Walpole, but it is certain that we have not heard the last of this feud.

As health declines, an obese king falls prone to fainting

London, 1724

At court almost the only topic of conversation is the growing infirmity of the king. At the age of 54 George is obese, subject to crippling attacks of gout and given to fainting fits. He still attires himself in splendid clothes and surrounds himself with great ladies, German-born and struggling with their English; but he has lost the respect – if he ever had it – of the English aristocracy at court.

George himself has almost no English, preferring to speak in

George suffering a fit: a later view.

French, and has never attempted to hide his preference for his native Hanover, to the point where he seems to be losing interest in the government of Britain. His frequent absences from here and his ministers' lack of German have caused him to absent himself from cabinet meetings with increasing regularity over the years.

Nowadays his son George Augustus, the Prince of Wales, who used to interpret for him during meetings, gives the king a résumé of what was discussed. The king then signs what he agrees with and throws out what he does not. This is, of course, when father and son are on speaking terms; it is no secret that there is considerable ill-feeling between them. King George's ambitions, meanwhile, extend little beyond amusing his German cronies and using the military strength of England to protect his beloved Hanover.

Jervas succeeds Godfrey Kneller as official royal painter

St James's, London, 1723

The fashionable society portrait painter Charles Jervas has been appointed king's painter in succession to the German-born Gottfried von Kniller, who Anglicised his name to Godfrey Kneller after settling in London.

Jervas, a Dubliner who studied in Paris and Rome, is best known for his portraits of comely young women; he was chosen to paint the Duke of Marlborough's four daughters, Henrietta, Elizabeth, Anne and Mary. He has also painted his friend Alexander Pope and for several years lived with him in Cleveland Court, St James's.

Painter and poet were in the habit of spending mornings together in the studio, with Pope looking on as Jervas entertained his aristocratic sitters. These sessions at the easel

provided Pope with the inspiration for verses such as this:

She wears no colours (sign of Grace)
On any Part except her Face;
All white and black beside;
Dauntless her look, Gesture proud,
Her voice theatrically loud,
And masculine her Stride.

In the *Tatler* magazine, Jervas was described as "the last great painter Italy has sent us". Kneller, who had Jervas as a pupil for a time, has another view. He said that Jervas could never break the second commandment prohibiting graven images "because he could not make a figure that was like anything in heaven or in earth". On being told that Jervas had acquired a coach-and-four, Kneller said: "Ach, mein Gott, if his horses draw no better than he does, he will never get to his journey's end."

King George: by Godfrey Kneller.

King's interest in architecture leads to building of superb squares and churches

An elegant aspect: Hanover Square, a development in London's west end.

London, 1727
King George's reign has seen the virtual transformation – with the king's encouragement – of the face of London through the addition of many fine churches and houses and several spectacular new squares, some of which are still in the early stages of construction.

Notable among them is Hanover Square, laid out between 1717 and 1719 in the west end, south of the road to Oxford. Hanover Square acquired its name from the present royal family, as did its church (St George's) and the wide street (George Street) that leads up to it from the south. The German style of the grand houses built in the

square was adopted in honour of the king. In 1725 building began, in the same area, of Grosvenor Square, which belongs to the huge Grosvenor estate. Covering all of six acres, it will be London's largest residential square. Then last year Edward Harley, the Earl of Oxford, drew up plans with his architect, James Gibbs, for developing part of his estate known as Marylebone Fields, the centrepiece of which will be known as Cavendish Square.

Gibbs is also responsible for two of London's new churches – St Martin-in-the-Fields and St Mary-le-Strand – while Nicholas Hawksmoor, who studied under Sir Christopher Wren, has built six more, five of them in the east end and one in Bloomsbury.

Lord Burlington, meanwhile, has been developing his estate to the south of Hanover Square. Burlington returned from a visit to Italy in 1719 fired with huge enthusiasm for the work of the 16th-century Italian architect Andrea Palladio. Since then he has set about "Palladianising" his Burlington House in Piccadilly and the surrounding area to brilliant effect.

The popularity of Palladio is clear to see in many of the new buildings. It was stimulated in 1715 by the publication in Britain of Giacomo Leoni's new edition of Palladio's influential work *I quattro libri dell'architettura*, which is dedicated to King George.

St Mary-le-Strand, London.

Sophia Dorothea, king's former wife, dies

Celle, Germany, 2 November 1726
Sophia Dorothea, the former wife of King George, died today at the castle of Ahlden in her father's territory of Celle at the age of 60. She had been kept a virtual prisoner at Ahlden for over 30 years, since her questionable divorce in 1694.

Sophia Dorothea, in her youth an impetuous and attractive woman, married her cousin George Louis in 1682 and bore him two children, both of whom survive her. Seven years later, however, she began a romantic relationship with the dashing Count Philip von Königsmarck, provoking a scandal which proved her undoing.

One night in July 1694, with George away in Berlin, von Königsmarck was seen entering the palace in Hanover. He later vanished and is thought to have been murdered. A divorce was swiftly arranged after incriminating letters from her lover were found in Sophia Dorothea's rooms. Sophia Dorothea was

Sophia Dorothea of Celle.

confined in the castle of Ahlden, banned from ever remarrying and denied access to her children, George Augustus and Sophia Dorothea. She remained a prisoner there for the rest of her life.

George makes Handel a British subject

London, 20 February 1726
King George today signed a bill making the German-born composer George Frederick Handel a British subject. Handel – widely acclaimed as the greatest musician in Europe – has been in England for some 16 years and, until recently, has not given much thought to naturalisation. Like the king, Handel speaks poor English, but otherwise he has assimilated

English characteristics and has been thoroughly accepted by the people. With the declining reputation of the German court, however, Handel found his origins telling against him. When the Italian composer Giovanni Bononcini started to spread anti-German propaganda against him, Handel decided that it would be prudent to take the oath of allegiance to the British king (→ 1734).

Mary Tofts "giving birth to rabbits": in 1726 she caused a sensation by convincing the king's surgeon that she could breed rabbits in her womb.

Royal architect and playwright is dead

Vanbrugh: architect and writer.

England, 26 March 1726

The royal architect and playwright Sir John Vanbrugh has died of quinsy at the age of 62. The most spectacular monuments to his baroque genius are Blenheim Palace in Oxfordshire – commissioned by Queen Anne in 1705 as a reward for the Duke of Marlborough – and Castle Howard in Yorkshire. In 1705 Vanbrugh was knighted, and that same year he was appointed to one of the top heraldic positions, Clarencieux king-of-arms. Made comptroller of royal works in 1714, he remodelled Kensington palace for King George.

Vanbrugh also won huge acclaim as a dramatist, specialising in the comedy of manners; among his best-known works are *The Relapse* and *The Provok'd Wife*.

Exiled writer gives a royal dedication

London, May 1727

François Voltaire, the controversial writer and philosopher exiled from his native France last year, intends to dedicate to King George his epic poem on France's Henry IV, *La Henriade*. Voltaire's compliment may not be entirely unconnected with £200 paid to him this month by the king's prime minister, Sir Robert Walpole. The money is perhaps a tribute to Voltaire's literary gifts – or, possibly, a reward for information on Jacobites now living in France (→ 22/6).

Britain's first Hanoverian king dies

Hanover, 11 June 1727

Britain's first Hanoverian monarch died early this morning in his bed at Osnabrück. George, who was 67, had been king of Great Britain and Ireland since 1714. He is succeeded by his son George Augustus, who becomes George II; he also assumes his father's title of Elector of Hanover.

The late king's last journey to his beloved Hanover began a week ago, when he embarked on his yacht at Greenwich and sailed for the Low Countries, arriving on 9 June at the small Dutch town of Delden, where – having consumed a large amount of fruit for dinner – he spent the night. The next morning, only an hour's journey out of Delden, where he had breakfasted on just a cup of chocolate, he passed out after a bad attack of diarrhoea. He regained consciousness on being bled and insisted that the journey should continue, shouting "Osnabrück! Osnabrück!". He fainted again before his party reached its destination late yesterday evening; there the king recovered sufficiently to raise his hat in greeting before lapsing back into unconsciousness. All efforts to revive him were in vain, and he died at about half-past one this morning.

The Duchess of Kendal, who had accompanied the king only as far as Delden, was summoned when he was taken ill, but she reached Osnabrück too late – she is reported to have beaten her breast and torn her hair in grief.

George's son is told: a C19th view.

Public unmoved at the death of the king who shunned them

London, 11 June 1727

When George Louis acceded to the throne of Great Britain and Ireland on 1 August 1714 he was 54 and had been Elector of Hanover since 1698, playing an active role in the war against Louis XIV. His claim to the throne, secured by the 1701 Act of Settlement, was through his maternal grandmother, Elizabeth of Bohemia, the daughter of James VI of Scotland and I of England.

King George disliked England and, during his 13-year reign, he visited Hanover as often as possible, staying away for long periods. These frequent absences fuelled the British people's lack of enthusiasm for their king, whom they perceived as a dour, unglamorous old man. The king's poor command of English, his bitter public quarrels with his son, the Prince of Wales, and his preference for German company did not add to his popularity. He lived openly with his mistress, Madame von der Schulenberg, the Duchess of Kendal; meanwhile his former wife, Sophia Dorothea of Celle – divorced in 1694 – was kept imprisoned as punishment for her adultery.

Politically, George was supported by the Whigs and openly partial to them while he hated the Tories and Jacobites. But he was never seriously threatened by the Jacobite rebellion of 1715 and the attempts

A keen horseman: a fine portrait of King George by John Vanderbank.

of 1719 and 1722. He took a more active part in government than was commonly believed, although the real ruler of the country in the latter part of his reign was Sir Robert Walpole.

The king was a shrewd judge of foreign affairs, expert in European diplomacy, playing a part in the negotiations for the 1718 Quadruple Alliance. After the "South Sea bubble" disaster of 1721, which brought the country to the brink of anarchy, the rest of the reign was generally quiet, allowing the king more time to supervise the landscaping of Kensington gardens and listen to the music of Handel.

George II
1727–1760

House
of
Hanover

Richmond, Sy, 11 June 1727. George Augustus, the Prince of Wales, accedes to the throne (→ 15/6).

London, 15 June 1727. George is formally proclaimed king (→ 22/6).

Westminster, 27 June 1727. King George opens the first parliament of his reign (→ 7/1727).

France, July 1727. The French give full support to George II as king of England rather than to James Stuart, the Pretender.→

Westminster, 11 October 1727. George is crowned king of Great Britain and Ireland.→

Rome, January 1728. James Stuart returns after an unsuccessful visit to France seeking aid for an expedition to Britain (→ 18/1/35).

England, 17 May 1729. George sails for Hanover on his first visit since 1714.

England/Spain, 9 November 1729. The Treaty of Seville is signed; the Spanish renounce all claims to Gibraltar (→ 1731).

London, 15 May 1730. Much to the king's regret Charles, Viscount Townshend, resigns from the government.

London, June 1731. George makes his mistress Henrietta Howard, at present a lady of the bedchamber, "groom of the stole" (→ 11/1734).

London, 1731. Rumours abound of a Spanish attack on a British cargo ship in the Caribbean (→ 3/1738).

London, 1732. Speculation is rife after the christening of Cornwall Fitz-Frederick Vane, the illegitimate son of Anne Vane and, supposedly, the Prince of Wales; Lords Hervey and Harrington also claim paternity (→ 6/1734).

London, 12 April 1733. Effigies of Robert Walpole and Queen Caroline, his staunch supporter, are burnt following his introduction of the Excise Bill (→ 23/4).

London, November 1733. The dwarfish Prince William IV of Orange arrives to complete his marriage arrangements to Anne, the Princess Royal (→ 1734).

London, spring 1734. George Frederick Handel, the court composer, writes *Parnasso in Festa* for the wedding of Anne, the Princess Royal, to Prince William of Orange (→ 13/4/42).

London, June 1734. Frederick, the Prince of Wales, demands to know from his father the king why he has not yet arranged a suitable marriage for him (→ 1735).

London, November 1734. The recently-widowed Countess of Suffolk retires from court after 20 years as George's mistress (→ 1735).

Rome, 18 January 1735. Maria Clementina, the wife of the exiled Pretender James Stuart, dies of scurvy, aged 32.→

London, 1735. Frederick, the Prince of Wales, who is betrothed to Augusta, the youngest daughter of Frederick II of Saxe-Gotha, attempts to rid himself of Anne

Vane, his mistress; she refuses to leave England because of her affair with Lord Hervey (→ 25/4/36).

London, May 1736. George returns to Hanover and to Madame von Walmoden, his mistress (→ 1736).

Hanover, 1736. Madame von Walmoden gives birth to a boy, Louis, an illegitimate son of King George (→ 1738).

London, 1736. Augusta, the Princess of Wales, creates a stir when she refuses to partake of the Anglican sacrament, preferring to take Communion at a German Lutheran chapel (→ 3/8/37).

London, February 1737. George is operated on for piles.

London, 3 August 1737. George writes to his son, Frederick, expressing annoyance at his escapade of moving himself and his wife from the royal residence for the birth of the king's first grandchild, Augusta (→ 8/8).

London, 8 August 1737. Queen Caroline visits her new grandchild; the family feud worsens as her son does not speak to her, despite keeping up public appearances by kissing her hand (→ 12/8).

London, 29 August 1737. Frederick, the Prince of Wales,

announces at the christening of his first child that his daughter will be known as Lady, not Princess, Augusta (→ 10/9).

London, 11 September 1737. King George informs all foreign diplomats that any visits to his son, Frederick, the Prince of Wales, will arouse great annoyance on the king's part (→ 12/9).

London, 9 November 1737. Queen Caroline falls seriously ill from an umbilical rupture sustained during the birth of her last child (→ 11/11).

London, 11 November 1737. Despite the queen's illness, George still refuses to allow his son to visit his mother (→ 20/11).

London, 1737. Parliament repeals the Witchcraft Act, thereby abolishing witchcraft as a crime.

Westminster, March 1738. Anglo-Spanish relations worsen when Captain Jenkins, who was tortured and lost an ear, appears before parliament to relate the story of the attack on his ship by Spaniards in 1731 (→ 26/10/39).

London, 1738. George instals his mistress, Madame von Walmoden, in St James's palace (→ 1739).

London, 25 March 1739. Augusta, the Princess of Wales, gives birth to her third child, a son named Edward Augustus (→ 30/12/40).

England/Spain, 26 Oct 1739. Britain declares war on Spain over the freedom of British navigation in the Caribbean (→ 11/1739).

London, 1739. Madame von Walmoden is formally divorced from her husband, Gottlieb Adam von Walmoden (→ 23/4/40).

The life and times of King George II

Name: George Augustus.
Birth: 30 October 1683, Hanover.
Accession: 11 June 1727.
Coronation: 11 October 1727.
Predecessor: father.
Eyes: blue.
Marriage: Caroline of Brandenburg-Ansbach, 22 August 1705, Herrenhausen.
Children: four sons (one died in

first year), five daughters.
Favourite home: Hampton Court.
Likes: the army, opera.
Dislikes: his eldest son Frederick.
Greatest problems: The Jacobites; protecting Hanover.
Greatest success: leadership at the Battle of Dettingen.
Death: 25 October 1760.

Opposite: George II; detail from a portrait by Charles Jervas.

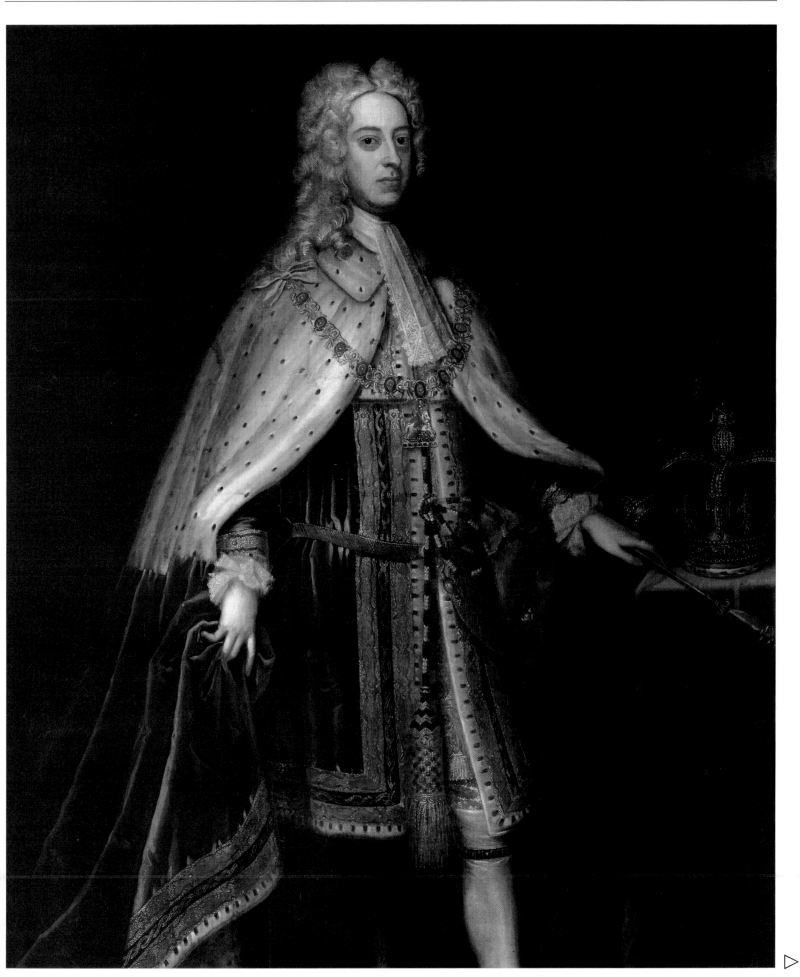

George II continues the Hanoverian dynasty

New monarch loves German homeland

Richmond Palace, 22 June 1727

When Sir Robert Walpole brought the unexpected news that he was now king, George Augustus was in bed after dinner with his wife. He has mistresses, usually for long-term relationships, like his ten-year affair with Mrs Henrietta Howard. He paces up and down waiting for nine o'clock to strike each evening, then goes to her apartments. He is highly methodical, ruled by the clock, but also by Caroline, the wife whom he clearly adores.

Now 43, George has the prominent eyes and belly of the Hanoverians and their peevishness, exploding with rage over trifles. His main interest is royal genealogy and military uniforms. He speaks English with a thick accent. "I hate bainting and boetry," he remarked in his thick German accent – but luckily not music, for he is Handel's patron. He thinks all things Hanoverian – music, horses, cooking or dress – are superior to anything English. "He looks on men and women as creatures he may kick or kiss for his diversion," says Lady Mary Wortley Montagu (→ 27/6).

The Duke of St Albans carries Queen Caroline's crown at the coronation.

George shakes off his father's shadow

Richmond Palace, June 1727

The new king, at 43, succeeds the father who so disliked him that he never allowed him to see his imprisoned mother. After a fierce quarrel George and his wife Caroline lived separately from the king for the last nine years of his reign, at Leicester House, courted by wits such as Lord Chesterfield, who said of the old king's German mistress: "She looks not more than 18 or 20 – 18 or 20 stone."

Their elder son, Frederick, is in Hanover, looking after family interests there. Their other son and five daughters are being brought up strictly over here. "You English are none of you well bred because you were not whipped when young!" George once said.

Late king's will is kept secret by son

London, June 1727

Word is spreading through the court that George II wishes his father's will to remain secret. In a recent meeting of the council the archbishop of Canterbury produced the document, only to have the king pocket it without a word of explanation.

Explanations are being hazarded all the same. One is that George I's will outlines proposals for separating Britain from Hanover in a way that would favour a rival German dynasty. It appears that George I intended that on the death of Frederick, his grandson, Britain should go to Frederick's elder son and Hanover to the younger son. Yet if Frederick dies without a son – at present he has none – Hanover should go to the German Duke of Wolfenbüttel.

No one is sure what George II's objection to the will is. It may be that he prefers Frederick to win Hanover himself while William, the king's younger and favourite son, gains Britain – a plan which was opposed by the late king since it was unfair to Frederick.

Magnificent formal coronation for king

London, 11 October 1727

George Augustus and his consort Caroline have today been solemnly crowned as the new king and queen of Britain. At noon a glittering procession of peers and churchmen moved along a route covered with blue cloth from Westminster Hall to the abbey, the king's maids strewing sweet herbs before them.

In the abbey the king took the coronation oath, whereupon trumpets sounded, all present cheered, and guns in Hyde Park and the Tower fired a salute. Everyone then returned to Westminster Hall for a banquet during which the king's champion rode into the hall in white armour on a white horse and demanded if anyone contested the king's title. No one did (→ 20/10).

King George, Queen Caroline and family shown taking their pleasure outdoors: engraved from a painting by William Hogarth (d.1762).

Queen Caroline is power behind throne

Cardinal gives political blessing to George and turns his back on Catholic Pretender

London, 1727

Caroline of Brandenburg-Ansbach married George of Hanover in 1705, long before anyone thought that they would one day rule England. In her forties she is still a good-looking woman, with a fine complexion and flaxen hair. Well aware of the king's infidelities (which he admits to her), she knows that it is she whom he really loves.

She is a popular figure, as was demonstrated when a drunk who insulted her in Leicester Fields was almost lynched by the crowd before he could be arrested. She is clever enough to have discussed philosophy with Leibnitz and enjoys theological debate. Her rapport with Walpole has ensured that he will continue to rule. It is said that if anything needs to be done, the first move is to persuade Walpole, who will persuade the queen, who will convince the king, who will then instruct Walpole to do it.

As George was bullied by his father so does he bully Caroline and his children but, in private, he is easily led by her. "As soon as ever the prince became king, the whole world began to find out that her will is the sole spring on which every movement in the court

Wielding power: Queen Caroline.

turns," says Lord Hervey. The wits put it:

> *You may strut dapper George but 'twill all be in vain,*
> *We know 'tis Queen Caroline, not you that reign.*
> *If you would have us fall down and adore you*
> *Lock up your fat spouse, as your dad did before you* (→ 12/4/33).

Paris, July 1727

Sir Robert Walpole's brother Horatio, the English ambassador in Paris, has seen King Louis XV's chief minister, Cardinal Fleury, and won an assurance that France will remain true to its British alliance under the new king. The Jacobites in exile in Paris are cock-a-hoop at the death of George I, but the cardinal assured Horatio that there will be no recognition of James Stuart, the Pretender, pro-claimed king in exile by Louis XIV in 1701.

The cardinal wrote a letter which Horatio Walpole took to London to present to the king, who promptly exploded at him for leaving his post without permission. He calmed down on reading the letter, which expressed Fleury's affection for England, George and Robert Wal-pole's administration.

Fleury also delighted George by agreeing with the suppression of his father's will. The cardinal knows that the Duke of Wolfenbüttel, named in the will as the inheritor of Hanover if George's son Frederick dies without an heir, has a copy of the will, as has the Holy Roman

French ally: Cardinal de Fleury.

Emperor, Charles VI. Fleury calls the plan "mischievous" and says it would be most embarrassing if the will were published. He advises George to wait and see what Wolfenbüttel does. Meanwhile he promises help to ensure that will remains secret and that neither the duke nor the emperor press home their claims (→ 1/1728).

Walpole scores triumph by securing generous civil list for king

Westminster, 27 June 1727

Parliament today voted an increase in the civil list for the new king, George II, after Sir Robert Walpole had argued that he needs to be more generously treated than his father because of his large family. The king was accordingly guaranteed £800,000 – a rise of £100,000 – and £100,000 more for the queen.

Walpole's success in getting the increase through the Commons, with only one dissenting vote, is an astute move in his own interest. When George succeeded, he intend-ed to appoint Sir Spencer Compton as chief minister in Walpole's place. Compton had only proposed £60,000 for the queen, who is a close friend of Walpole. Her influence with the king ensured his survival while his rivals cultivated the king's mistress, Walpole knew that Caroline's favour was what mattered. In his words, he "had the right sow by the ear" (→ 1732).

The House of Lords: parliament has voted more money for King George.

Court prepares to settle up accounts

London, 20 October 1727

The court of claims has met at Westminster to arrange payment for those who helped to organise the coronation. The lord great chamberlain, for one, has put in a claim for dressing the king on the morning of the great day as well as providing crimson velvet for his robe and his bedding for the night before. More modestly the lord of the manor of Worksop is claiming payment for supporting the king's right arm while he held the sceptre.

These and other successful claim-ants will receive gold, or honours such as knighthoods, for their ser-vices. Not all are so lucky. The clerk of the great wardrobe's claim for a cloth of gold held over the king while he was anointed is to be disallowed, although like others he may "take his course at law if he think fit".

King George pays off mistress's husband

The king's mistress, Henrietta Howard, by the court painter Charles Jervas.

London, 1728

King George has agreed to pay a yearly fee of £1,200 to Charles Howard, the husband of the royal mistress Henrietta, on condition that in future he gives her as little trouble in the capacity of husband as he had ever given her pleasure. The payments will continue until Howard succeeds his brother, the Earl of Suffolk.

Howard, who is described as "obstinate, drunken and brutal", has become a nuisance after con-doning the royal liaision for some 15 years. He obtained a warrant from the lord chief justice auth-orising him to seize his wife, who is a lady of the bedchamber to Queen Caroline, and at one point tried to drag her from the queen's carriage.

The irony of this situation is that the king is bored with Mrs Howard and she with him. He loves the queen but feels that it is his royal duty to keep a mistress, while the queen tolerates Henrietta because she sees no threat in her (→ 6/1731).

River view: a later (1749) engraving of Marble Hill House, the home of the king's mistress, Henrietta Howard, near Twickenham, in Middlesex.

King condemns foxhunting as a pursuit unworthy of serious-minded gentlemen

Windsor, 1728

The king is enjoying the stag-hunting at Windsor, where he is riding hard to hounds in the great park. With his children, led by the fear-less Princess Amelia who spends most of her time in the stables, he is out in all weathers, sometimes until nine in the evening. The king's mistress, Henrietta Howard, takes a rather jaundiced view of these pro-ceedings. In a letter to a friend she complains: "We hunt with great noise and violence, and have every day a considerable chance to have a neck broke."

King George's love of the hunt does not, however, extend to fox-hunting. A true German, he thinks the stag a noble beast, worthy of the attentions of gentlemen, but, much to the distress of his British sub-jects, he regards the fox as no true quarry for men of quality.

He expressed himself forcibly on this subject to the Duke of Grafton when the duke asked his permission to leave the court for a few days' fox-hunting. He should not, said the king, spend his time "torment-ing a poor fox, that was generally a much better beast than any of those that pursued him; for the fox hunts no other animal but for his sub-sistence, while those brutes who hunt him did it only for the plea-sure they took in hunting."

When the duke protested that he did it for his health, the king told him to walk instead, pointing to his corpulent figure and doubting whether any horse "can carry you within hearing, much less within sight of your hounds".

Hounds slaver at the kill – but King George has condemned fox-hunting.

New opera ridicules king's first minister

London, 30 January 1728

Court circles have been scandalised by a new and biting political satire called *The Beggar's Opera*. Written by John Gay and premièred at Cov-ent Garden last night, it flouts the conventions of Italian opera with its tales of romance among the aris-tocracy. In their place we have bal-lads among highwaymen and whores in Newgate prison.

What has upset those near to the king is the portrayal of the court as a den of thieves and of the king's first minister, Sir Robert Walpole, as a two-timing rogue called Peachum. Gay is an ardent Tory and thus keen to ridicule Whigs such as Walpole and those who sup-port him – even if one is the king.

Gay's denunciation of corruption in public life and at court might have amused King George while he was still a prince at loggerheads with his father, but now it is a rather different matter (→ 12/4/33).

Hanoverian royal heir arrives in England

Frederick, the Prince of Wales.

St James's Palace, December 1728
Frederick, the Prince of Wales, arrived at the palace today after a hazardous, freezing voyage from Hanover. It is a measure of how little his father, the king, thinks of him that he had to make the final part of his journey in an ordinary hackney carriage. The king was, in fact, reluctant to send for his son despite pressure from parliament and the people to see the man destined to rule them.

What finally forced the king's hand was the discovery of his son's plans to rush into marriage with Princess Wilhelmina of Prussia. Negotiations for this marriage had been started by George I, but Frederick's father cancelled them as

soon as he ascended the throne. "I do not think", he said, "that ingrafting my half-witted coxcomb upon a mad woman would improve the breed." The king now thinks that it is safer to have Frederick where he can keep an eye on him.

Frederick's dislike of his father is just as intense as and repeats the antagonism of that which existed between the king and his own father. In both cases the hatred has a common cause: the father's fear that the son would provide a focus for opposition politicians to undermine his rule. The king wants to make sure that Frederick does not have the financial resources to become influential in the world of politics. Whereas he himself received £100,000 from his father, George is allowing his son only £24,000.

What is unusual in Frederick's case is that his mother has disliked him from the moment that he was born. This and his unprepossessing appearance have given rise to rumours that Frederick is a changeling. This seems unlikely, but he certainly does not look as if he comes from the Hanoverian mould.

He was a sickly child, nourished on goat's milk which his mother thought would curb his sexual prowess. This appears not to be the case, for among his faults is a sad lack of discretion in his choice of mistresses. He seems a foolish but not an evil young man (→ 1732).

Princess Anne betrothed

The royal match: Princess Anne and Prince William have been betrothed.

London, 1733
Princess Anne, the eldest daughter of King George and Queen Caroline, has been betrothed to Prince William of Orange. The king's choice of the Dutch prince as a husband for the Princess Royal is regarded at court as somewhat bizarre because the couple are so ill-matched. Anne is large and plump, while William is small and deformed by a humpback. He also has breath which, according to the court wit Lord Hervey, is "more offensive than it is possible for those who have not been offended by it to imagine".

Yet, despite what seems an impossible basis for a happy marriage,

the young couple apparently adore one another. The prince has a sensitive face to compensate for his twisted body and has come to terms with his deformity, while the princess is a kind-hearted woman who told her father that she would marry him "if he were a baboon". The king, never noted for tact, replied: "Well then, there is baboon enough for you."

Perhaps the true measure of the prince's worth has been taken by the London crowd, which cheers him loudly whenever he appears. The cheers may, however, stem from his relationship to a previous Prince of Orange who deposed his father-in-law (→ 11/1733).

Downing Street house to be prime minister's official residence

London, 1732
King George has given the fine town house at 10 Downing Street to the government. He originally intended it as a personal gift to Sir Robert Walpole, his first lord of the treasury, but Sir Robert, now known more and more as the "prime minister", would only accept it as his official residence.

The earliest building known to have stood on the site was a brewhouse called the Axe. Sir George Downing, the MP for Carlisle, acquired it and in about 1680 built a cul-de-sac off Whitehall of plain brick terraced houses described as "fit for persons of honour and quality; each house having a pleasant prospect into St James's park with a terraced walk" (→ 12/4/33).

A 19th-century view of Downing St: the king has given No 10 to Walpole.

Region of Georgia wins royal charter

London, June 1732
Another colony has been added to Britain's possessions in North America. King George has granted a royal charter to an area to be called, appropriately, Georgia.

The new colony owes its existence to Colonel James Oglethorpe, a Tory philanthropist. His plan is to take debtors from London's prisons and offer them the chance of a new start in America. Under the royal charter a board of trustees is granted a tract of land south of Carolina for this purpose for 21 years. Apart from public subscriptions, which amount to £18,000, the king has himself donated £600 towards Oglethorpe's project.

King supports Walpole in excise crisis

London, 23 April 1733

The king has demonstrated his support for Sir Robert Walpole by dismissing members of the royal household who voted down Walpole's bill to tax imported wine and tobacco – the so-called excise crisis. Lords Chesterfield, Stair, Burlington and others, who opposed Walpole in George I's reign and had hoped to replace him under George II, have used the crisis as an excuse to discredit him. But Queen Caroline remained loyal to him.

When Lord Stair told her that his opposition was a matter of conscience she replied: "My lord, speak not to me of conscience. You make me feel faint." The king has followed Caroline's advice and has dismissed his former friends. Walpole wanted to establish bonded warehouses to store tobacco, and later wine and brandy, where the goods could be properly taxed; this would have reduced smuggling and increased government revenue. Yet William Pulteney, the leader of the opposition in the Commons, denounced "that monster, the excise, that plan of arbitrary power", and everyone who profited from the tobacco trade joined him.

Walpole could still carry the Commons but faced defeat in the House of Lords. There were threats of mob violence, and he admitted that he had lost, saying: "I will not be the minister to enforce taxes at the expense of blood." He withdrew the bill on 9 April and then demanded that the king dismiss the disloyal courtiers. Walpole's position is now stronger than ever.

Londoners rejoice at the news that the Excise Bill has been withdrawn.

Scurvy claims life of Pretender's princess

Rome, 18 January 1735

The fortunes of James Stuart, the Pretender, continue to go from bad to worse. Today he lost his wife, Maria Clementina Sobieska; only 32 years old, she had been suffering for a long while from scurvy. She leaves behind two sons, 14-year-old Charles Edward and nine-year-old Henry Benedict. Married since 1719, James and Maria Clementina were unhappy together. A young and vivacious girl, she found James, 14 years her senior, a dour and haughty man. She especially resented his attempts to garner Protestant support; her revenge was to leave her vast fortune to her beloved Catholic Church and not to James (→ 1/1766).

Anne, the Princess Royal, is married to dwarfish Prince William of Orange

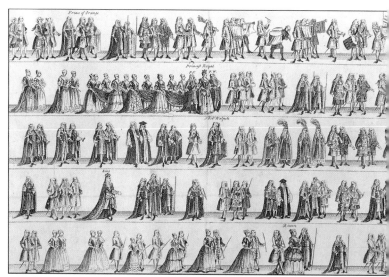

The formal procession for the marriage of Princess Anne to Prince William.

London, 1734

Princess Anne, the king's eldest daughter, has married Prince William of Orange, now fully recovered from the fever that he contracted after arriving in London last year. Although the king chose William as a safe political and religious partner for Anne he thinks, ironically, that she is marrying beneath herself. No one had heard of the prince, he says, until the Hanovers deigned to raise him from obscurity.

The king also shows complete insensitivity about poor William's humpback and planned to have him hidden behind a curtain when the couple were bedded so that the assembled courtiers might not see him. He was persuaded otherwise, and the groom appeared in a nightcap and brocaded gown, looking from behind as if he had no head and from in front as if he had no neck or legs. Queen Caroline was very greatly distressed and could barely stomach the sight of her daughter going to bed with "that monster". Anne, the Princess Royal, counts herself lucky to be married, however. This way she can escape from the boredom of family life and from the king's vanity, endlessly repeated military stories, boasts of sexual conquests and vile temper (→ 12/1/59).

A family group: Princess Anne with two sisters and the Prince of Wales.

George falls in love on trip to Hanover

Hanover, 1735

The king has fallen in love with Amelia Sophia von Walmoden, an attractive young woman whose husband has been bought off with a large sum of money from the royal purse. The position of royal mistress has been vacant since the king and Lady Suffolk parted last year. She had been his mistress for 20 years and had grown weary of George. The queen tried to persuade her to stay, fearing that her replacement might be less understanding, but the king protested to his wife: "Why will you not let me part with an old deaf woman of whom I am tired?"

The king has been in Hanover since the spring, and he regularly writes to the queen about the progress of his amatory adventures. Some of the letters are 40 to 50 pages long, written in French and full of detailed accounts of Madame von Walmoden's charms. He proposes to have her painted in the nude and to bring the portrait to Caroline so that she may the better appreciate her. He instructs the queen to show the letters to Sir Robert Walpole, whom he refers to as "the Fat", and to ask his advice about the best way of winning and holding the lady's affections.

Extraordinary as the letters are, what is even more remarkable is that the queen has allowed her court confidant, Lord Hervey, to know their contents. Through his gossiping tongue they have unfortunately become common knowledge at St James's (→ 5/1736).

Royal pleasures: George with his mistress Madame von Walmoden.

Prince of Wales marries German princess

The royal couple: Frederick, the Prince of Wales, with Princess Augusta.

London, 25 April 1736

Frederick, the Prince of Wales, was married today to Princess Augusta of Saxe-Gotha. She is 17, a big, gangling, simple girl who speaks not a word of English. Her mother reassured her, however, that since the House of Hanover had reigned in Britain for 20 years, everyone there must by now speak German.

The prince was born in Hanover in 1707 and was brought up there. George I kept his son from playing any part in Frederick's education. He came to England for the first time after his father became king in 1727, and his parents and sisters soon came to hate him.

Yet he was soon more popular than the king. The queen raged: "My God, popularity always makes me feel sick, but Fritz's popularity makes me vomit." She said of her son: "That wretch, that villain! I wish the ground would open this moment and sink the monster to the lowest hole in hell." His sister Caroline calls him "that nauseous beast", who "cares for nobody but his own nauseous self". The king considers him "the greatest villain that ever was born".

The prince is small, fair-haired, pop-eyed and fond of music and the arts. He is also mean-spirited and lecherous, like his father. He detests his parents quite as much as they do him and is always quarrelling with the king over his income. Now that he is the leader of the opposition to Walpole, the dispute between the king and the prince has become a matter of national concern (→ 1736).

Violent sea-storm endangers king's life

London, December 1736

The king has arrived in England after crossing from the continent in a gale which raised fears that he was drowned. The mob was delighted at the prospect; the queen and Walpole were deeply worried. Walpole lamented the prospect of "a poor, weak, irresolute, false, lying, dishonest, contemptible wretch, that nobody loves, that nobody believes, that nobody will trust" becoming king. He meant the Prince of Wales. The king had tried to sail from Helvoetsluys in the Low Countries in the teeth of the gale, telling Admiral Wager: "Let the weather be what it will, I am not afraid." Wager replied: "If you are not, I am." The king insisted "I positively order you to sail", and the yacht put to sea but was driven back.

Rumours reached London that the king was drowned, and the opposition leaders went to the Prince of Wales to congratulate him. With unusual wisdom he replied that he hoped his majesty safe and could not bear the thought of it otherwise.

Mutual dislike grows between king and people

London, 1735

After nearly ten years on the throne George is the most unpopular monarch since James II. His constant absences in Hanover are the subject of much mockery. An old horse was recently let loose in London, wearing a broken saddle and carrying a placard reading "Let nobody stop me – I am the king of Hanover's equipage going to fetch his majesty and his whore to England". The English ask why, if the king must take a whore, did he not take an English one and stay at home?

The king dislikes England as heartily as it dislikes him. Before his accession he used to boast that he had not a drop of blood that was not English, but now he denigrates English cooking, acting, riding, horses and the way that Englishmen come into a room and Englishwomen dress, and claims that the men talk of nothing but dull politics and the women of nothing but dull clothes. By contrast, everything in Hanover is sheer perfection.

The king prefers his absolute authority in Hanover to the constraints of a constitutional monarchy in Britain. "I am sick to death of all this foolish stuff," he exclaimed, "and wish with all my heart that the devil may take all your bishops, and the devil take your minister, and the devil take your parliament, and the devil take the whole island, provided I can get out of it and go to Hanover."

Fortunately, the king defers to the queen in everything, and she continues to support the prime minister, Sir Robert Walpole. The king is bored by politics, preferring the military life (he served with distinction under Marlborough at the Battle of Oudenarde in 1708) and, perhaps surprisingly, music. With luck posterity will remember him more for his patronage of Handel than for his quarrels with Prince Frederick or his bad temper.

Prince Frederick haggles with politicians in bid to increase his share of civil list

St James's, February 1737
Frederick, the Prince of Wales, has had a spectacular row with King George and Queen Caroline, who have described him as "the lowest, stinking coward in the world" after he rejected an offer from parliament of a £50,000-a-year settlement, plus a guaranteed tenancy for his wife, Augusta.

Opposition MPs were well disposed towards Frederick until this latest dispute. He and his friends had asked parliament for £100,000 a year and were confident of getting it. Sir Robert Walpole, the prime minister, feared for his own position, and was initially keen to accommodate the prince. But when the offer of a £50,000 settlement was rejected out of hand, Walpole began suggesting to MPs that the prince was really interested in taking the throne from his father.

The king, who has been acutely ill with piles, seems much better, while the prince's apparent greed has done his own standing no good at all. The opposition's motion to

Frederick: at odds with his parents.

double his allowance was defeated by 30 votes after the Tories abstained. Walpole is now urging the king to settle permanently for the prince's present temporary allowance of £50,000 (→ 3/8).

Queen Caroline becomes a grandmother

St James's, 12 August 1737
The queen has been to St James's to pay a second visit to her granddaughter, born here 12 days ago in the most bizarre circumstances. The Prince of Wales was seen to kneel and kiss his mother's hand, but public civilities cannot disguise the mutual contempt of the royal couple and their son.

The king and queen were very keen to witness the birth of their grandchild, and Augusta, the Princess of Wales, was at Hampton Court, on the king's orders, when she went into labour on 31 July. Frederick, who had managed to keep the pregnancy secret for eight of the nine months, was however determined that the birth would not take place under his parents' noses.

With the help of Dunoyer, the dancing master, he carried his wife downstairs to a waiting carriage, the princess's waters breaking as they drew up at St James's. While towels and napkins were quickly produced the prince had the lights extinguished so that people would not see. Augusta was put to bed between two tablecloths, and at a

Augusta, the Princess of Wales.

quarter to eleven that night she gave birth to "a little rat of a girl, about the bigness of a good large toothpick case".

It seems that the Prince of Wales organised this night-time flit, endangering his wife and child, purely to spite his parents, who are predictably furious (→ 29/8).

George and prince fail to make peace

London, 10 September 1737
Bitterness between the king and the Prince of Wales over the recent birth of Lady Augusta has erupted into a war of words between Hampton Court and St James's. On 3 August, shortly after the birth, King George wrote to his son at St James's to upbraid the prince, calling the secrecy surrounding the pregnancy "a deliberate indignity". The prince wrote back the same day to apologise but insisted that it was his wife's fault: she had begged to be taken to St James's where she could be taken better care of. The king was left even angrier after reading this attempt to shift the blame.

Smitten with contrition, Frederick begged in a letter of 20 August to throw himself at his father's feet at the forthcoming baptism. In a letter today King George dismissed this offer and once again attacked Frederick for his "extravagant and undutiful behaviour" (→ 11/9).

Prince and Princess of Wales move from St James's to Kew

Kew, 12 September 1737
The Prince and Princess of Wales have moved here in response to an edict from King George that anyone attending the prince's court will no longer be welcome at the king's. This family squabble has left a number of City magnates, independents and Tory MPs prepared to risk royal ostracism to pay court to the Prince of Wales at his new Thames-side home seven miles (11km) west of Whitehall.

When the young couple fled from Hampton Court last month to have their baby at St James's it was the final straw. To the king's mind it was an act of "premeditated defiance". His patience had already worn perilously thin over disagreement with the prince concerning his allowance from the civil list. A recent flurry of letters between father and son has now ended with Frederick receiving his marching orders. Handel has been forbidden to give a concert for the prince, who has had his guard removed as well as his royal furniture (→ 4/6/38).

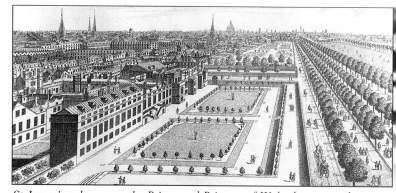

St James's palace: now the Prince and Princess of Wales have moved out.

The royal palace in Kew gardens, Surrey: a late-18th-century engraving.

Much-loved Queen Caroline dies

St James's, 20 November 1737
Britain is today mourning the most popular queen since Elizabeth. Queen Caroline has died, 11 days after falling ill with an infection from an umbilical rupture sustained during childbirth. Apart from the king, who is genuinely distraught at his loss, one of the chief mourners is the prime minister, Sir Robert Walpole, who enjoyed an understanding with Caroline that did much to ease relations between crown and parliament.

The queen, who was 44, fell ill with colic, stomach pains and vomiting on 9 November. Every kind of medicine was tried without effect; then Dr Ranby, a royal surgeon, bled the patient. Far from helping, the treatment made things worse. Two days later the king told Dr Ranby about the rupture, which the queen had been too ashamed to reveal. The swelling was immediately lanced, but the infection spread, and it soon became clear that the queen was going to die.

Deeply upset as he was, King George continued his bullying ways

In happier days: Queen Caroline at the garden entrance of St James's palace.

even as his wife lay on her death-bed, while she suffered with the fortitude for which she was renowned. Whenever she shifted about in bed he demanded how the devil she could expect to sleep if she did not stay still. On one occasion he likened her, as she lay there, eyes open and staring, to a calf that had just had its throat cut. The king forbade the disgraced Prince of

Wales to visit. In all her suffering Caroline was grateful for one thing: that she would "never see that monster again".

As popular throughout the realm as her husband is disliked, Queen Caroline was an important influence on him. Walpole once remarked: "She can make him propose the very thing which a week before he had rejected."

Prince inaugurates Vauxhall nightspot

Londoners take their pleasure in Vauxhall gardens: a later view, c.1752.

Vauxhall, 1738
The Vauxhall gardens in south London, opened this year by the Prince of Wales, have become the envy of Europe. Socialites from all over London come to dine here, meet the ladies of the town, and listen to the music of George Frederick Handel played by the finest orchestras in the country. The gar-

dens, owned by Jonathan Tyers, include a rotunda, named after the Prince of Wales, with decorations by Hogarth. Roubillac, the foremost sculptor of the day, is working on a statue of Handel to add further cachet to the place. Food and wine are only of the very highest quality; revellers of modest means bring their own (→ 2/1742).

Sickly son is born to Prince of Wales

London, 4 June 1738
George William Frederick, King George II's first grandson, was born at Norfolk House today. He is the second child and first son of Frederick, the Prince of Wales, and Augusta, the daughter of Duke Frederick of Saxe-Gotha. Born two months prematurely, the baby is sickly, and he has already been christened since there is no great confidence that he will survive.

Despite his frailty, the royal infant is a fillip for the House of Hanover. King George II, his paternal grandfather, was the second of his line to wear the crown of Great Britain. At the beginning of the century the family ruled the Duchy of Brunswick-Lüneburg in northern Germany. Known as Hanover after the main town, the duchy now rivals Prussia for prominence within the Holy Roman Empire. With a grip on the British throne, the Hanoverians are a new force in Europe (→ 25/3/39).

(→ 2/1742).

(→ 25/3/39).

King George grows impatient for foreign war

London, November 1739
This month has seen the start of King George's first shooting war with an attack by six ships under Admiral Vernon on the great Spanish-American base and treasure depot of Porto Bello. If this is to be the start of a full-scale war it will be one with the oddest of beginnings.

Members of the "Patriot" opposition, led by the Prince of Wales, stirred up trouble last year when they produced a sea-captain called Jenkins who claimed to have had an ear chopped off by a Spanish coastguard in 1731. To back up his claim Jenkins exhibited the severed organ to the House of Commons.

The stunt was well timed. Not only the king but public opinion had grown increasingly tired of the pacifist foreign policy of the prime minister, Walpole, over the last decade. People are itching for a war, and this could be the excuse that they need. The war's aims are less to do with seamen's ears, however, than with breaking the strong hold that Spain enjoys on Caribbean trade.

The present strife highlights important character differences between the king and Walpole. George is passionate about all things military. He is himself no stranger to combat, having fought with distinction at the Battle of Oudenarde in 1708. Walpole, however, is keenly aware of the political cost of war in the higher taxes it causes.

King George and Walpole have clashed before over foreign policy. In 1733 Holy Roman Emperor Charles VI wanted Britain's support in the War of the Polish Succession. The king wanted to fight, not least because the proposed alliance was against the old foe France. Walpole, however, stuck to his policy, and the war ended in 1735 without Britain having fought in it. In the present débâcle, by contrast, it is likely that the king will call the shots.

George II
1727–1760

House
of
Hanover

London, 23 April 1740. George makes his Hanoverian mistress, Madame von Walmoden, Countess of Yarmouth.

Berlin, 31 May 1740. King Frederick William of Prussia, who married Sophia Dorothea, the sister of George II, dies.

Cassel, Germany, 28 June 1740. Princess Mary, the youngest daughter but one of George II, marries Frederick II, the ruler of Hesse-Cassel.

London, 30 December 1740. Augusta, the Princess of Wales, gives birth to Elizabeth Caroline, her fourth child (→ 14/11/43).

London, April 1741. Frederick, the Prince of Wales, joins forces with the Duke of Argyll against Sir Robert Walpole (→ 26/6).

Britain, 26 June 1741. Walpole's majority is greatly reduced in parliamentary elections owing to support for the Prince of Wales and the Duke of Argyll (→ 2/2/42).

London, February 1742. The Prince of Wales attends the court of George II for the first time for many months.

Dublin, 13 April 1742. George Frederick Handel conducts the first performance of *Messiah* (→ 2/1743).

London, February 1743. The king attends the second performance of *Samson* by Handel at Covent Garden (→ 1743).

London, 14 November 1743. Augusta, the Princess of Wales, gives birth to William Henry, the Duke of Gloucester, her fifth child and third son (→ 27/10/45).

London, 1743. On the British victory at Dettingen in Germany, Handel composes the *Dettingen Te Deum* (→ 1/5/49).

London, 2 February 1744. Fears of a French invasion, led by Charles Edward Stuart, the son of James Stuart, to overthrow George, grow with the knowledge that Charles left Italy for France three weeks ago and that the French fleet has left port (→ 8/2).

Paris, 8 February 1744. Charles Stuart arrives from Italy (→ 24/2).

Kent, 24 February 1744. The French fleet is dispersed by a storm off Dungeness (→ 27/6).

Nantes, 27 June 1745. En route to England, Charles Stuart and his fleet are attacked by an English frigate and return to port (→ 5/7).

Nantes, 5 July 1745. Charles sets sail again with two ships and 700 men (→ 23/7).

Highland, 19 August 1745. Charles raises the royal standard at Glenfinnan (→ 4/9).

Perth, 4 September 1745. Charles enters the city; he proclaims his father James VIII of Scots and James III of England (→ 17/9).

London, 27 October 1745. Augusta, the Princess of Wales, gives birth to Henry Frederick, her sixth child (→ 8/3/49).

Carlisle, 9 November 1745. The Jacobite forces besiege the town (→ 15/11).

Derby, 6 December 1745. The main Jacobite army refuses Charles Stuart's plan to advance and begins its retreat from England (→ 30/12).

Carlisle, 30 December 1745. The Duke of Cumberland's army forces the town's Jacobite garrison to surrender (→ 16/4/46).

Westminster, 12 August 1746. Parliament bans highland dress for all but serving soldiers.

France, 18 October 1748. The Peace of Aix-la-Chapelle ends the War of the Austrian Succession; Britain returns Louisburg, the gateway to Canada, to the French, while France will retreat from the Low Countries (→ 1/5/49).

London, 8 March 1749. Augusta gives birth to Louisa Anne, her seventh child (→ 13/5/50).

London, 13 May 1750. Augusta gives birth to Frederick William, her eighth child (→ 11/7/51).

London, September 1750. To the horror of the city's small Jacobite contingent, Charles Stuart attends St Martin-in-the-Fields in disguise, abjuring Catholicism and becoming an Anglican (→ 29/10/53).

London, 11 July 1751. Augusta, the Princess of Wales, recently widowed, gives birth to a daughter, Caroline Matilda.

Denmark, 8 December 1751. Louisa, the youngest daughter of George II, dies, aged only 27.

Westminster, 1751. After the death of Frederick, the Prince of Wales, the Regency Act is passed; in the event of the king's death Augusta, the Princess Dowager of Wales, will be regent until her son is of age.

London, 1751. John Stuart, the Earl of Bute, a lord of the bedchamber to Frederick, is appointed as "groom of the stole" to George, the Prince of Wales (→ 4/6/55).

England, 3 September 1752. The Gregorian calendar is introduced to replace the Julian; the year will now begin on 1 January instead of 25 March, and 11 days will be lost, so today becomes 14 September.

Liège, 29 Oct 1753. A daughter, Charlotte, is born to Charles Stuart and his mistress Clementina Walkinshaw (→ 7/1760).

Hanover, 28 April 1755. George II begins negotiations for a reconciliation with Frederick the Great of Prussia (→ 16/1/56).

Britain/France, 8 July 1755. Anglo-French relations break down as the land dispute in North America continues (→ 25/11/58).

London, 16 January 1756. The Treaty of Westminster is signed by George and Frederick of Prussia to secure the neutrality of German states in the developing Anglo-French struggle (→ 17/5).

France/Britain, 17 May 1756. War breaks out on the continent (→ 9/1757).

London, 28 December 1757. George II's daughter Princess Caroline Elizabeth dies, aged 44.

North America, 25 Nov 1758. After losing Louisburg and Fort Frontenac to the British, the French are forced to evacuate Duquesne, which the British rename Fort Pitt (→ 10/1760).

London, November 1758. King George II, a believer in fresh air, is suffering from a severe cold, caught from travelling with his coach windows open.

The Hague, 12 January 1759. Anne, the Princess Royal and wife of William IV of Orange, dies, aged 50.

London, 4 September 1759. Princess Elizabeth Caroline dies at Kew palace, aged only 18.

Germany, 31 July 1760. The Marquis of Granby decisively defeats the French in battle at Warburg (→ 8/6/61).

London, 26 October 1760. George II dies, aged 76, of a ruptured coronary artery; his grandson, George, aged 22, succeeds him.→

Petition brings down prime minister

King adds pressure to end the war for Austrian succession

London, October 1741

Queen Maria Theresa, who inherited the Habsburg lands when her father, Holy Roman Emperor Charles VI, died last year, has bowed to British pressure to end the war that her succession has precipitated and that has imperilled King George's Hanover lands.

Although Charles died without a son as heir, the major European powers had agreed that Maria Theresa would succeed him. The title of emperor would go to her husband, the Duke of Tuscany. This agreement was challenged by Elector Charles of Bavaria, Philip V of Spain and Augustus III of Poland. When Frederick II of Prussia invaded Silesia, part of Maria Theresa's lands, war broke out, with France, Spain, Bavaria and Saxony supporting Frederick.

Maria Theresa appealed for help, but Walpole was reluctant to embroil Britain in another war. The king, however, saw dangers in a Franco-Prussian alliance. Money and men were supplied, but these failed to avert the French invasion of Westphalia which threatened Hanover. George has now done a deal with France to respect Hanover's neutrality, leaving Walpole to persuade Maria Theresa to cede Silesia to Prussia (→ 12/1742).

Princess Louisa weds Danish king

Denmark, 11 December 1743

Princess Louisa, aged 19, the youngest child of King George, was married today at Christiansborg to Frederick V, the 20-year-old king of Denmark and Norway. The couple had been married by proxy in Hanover at the end of October. Queen Louisa, as she now becomes, was born in December 1724 and is the ninth surviving child of the British king. She is a pretty and vivacious young woman, although not a particular favourite with her father. He seems to find little joy in family life, being close only to Prince William, the Duke of Cumberland (→ 8/12/51).

Walpole addresses his cabinet.

King acts swiftly to fill political vacuum

Westminster, 16 February 1742

King George has moved with speed and skill to fill the void left at the heart of his government by Sir Robert Walpole's resignation as prime minister earlier this month. He has cunningly brought into the administration enough opponents of Walpole to secure a parliamentary majority without rewarding the Tories or a large number of the opposition Whigs such as William Pitt, the MP for Old Sarum, whom he dislikes intensely.

Lord Wilmington – a man loyal to the king, yet a politician who has good links with opposition groups both Tory and Whig – is to be the first lord of the treasury (or prime minister). But the more significant appointment is that of John, Baron Carteret, as secretary of state. He and William Pulteney are leaders of a group sometimes called "New Whigs". Pulteney had the greater following in the Commons but had sworn that he would never accept office. So he has been awarded an earldom while Lord Carteret joins the government.

This alliance of old ministers and "New Whigs" leaves the Argyll camp, which includes many friends of Frederick, the Prince of Wales, still in opposition in parliament despite their success in overthrowing Walpole (newly ennobled as Earl of Orford) (→ 12/1742).

Westminster, 2 February 1742

Sir Robert Walpole today resigned after more than 20 successive years as the king's "prime minister". He was the first to be regarded as the principal minister of government in this way, although his formal title remained that of first lord of the treasury. He held that post (along with the chancellorship of the exchequer) from 1715 to 1717, returning as first lord in 1721 during the "South Sea bubble" crisis.

The immediate cause of Sir Robert's downfall was his defeat in parliament over a petition contesting an election at Chippenham, in Wiltshire. All general elections in recent years have been followed by petitions alleging sundry malpractices or seeking to overturn results. Until now Walpole had maintained control of the house, but his theoretical majority there of 21 was increasingly vulnerable to political attacks and absenteeism.

On 21 January Walpole's critics, who included the Prince of Wales, tried to set up a select committee to examine his conduct of the recent war, but seven days later the first vote over the Chippenham petition went against him. Walpole lost by just one vote, but it symbolised his loss of parliamentary support. On 31 January he told the king that he would resign. And today he told the Commons (→ 18/3/45).

Parliament to pay for Hanoverian troops

Foreign policy pays off: booty taken abroad is stored in the Tower of London.

Westminster, December 1742

Members of parliament have reluctantly approved the king's request that 16,000 of his Hanoverian troops should be paid for by Britain. Although he has got his way, George has been angered by hostile comments made by certain MPs, in particular William Pitt, who complained that Britain had been reduced to little more than a province of "despicable" Hanover.

The controversy stems from attempts to settle the ongoing War of the Austrian Succession. Interim peace agreements with France, Prussia and Russia had removed the threat to Hanover, but Maria Theresa, the Hungarian queen, protested that George's plans to reduce the size of the Hanoverian force would leave her empire vulnerable to attack.

Lord Carteret, the secretary of state, asked parliament to appease Maria Theresa by putting the Hanoverian troops on the English payroll, although many MPs had already grumbled about paying for what they saw as a German war. Pitt was scathing, accusing these troops of "marching to the place most distant from the enemy". Despite his scorn, the Commons voted by a majority of 67 to pay for the Hanoverian army (→ 27/6/43).

England launches war against France

King takes field in battle at Dettingen

Dettingen, Germany, 27 June 1743
The king of Britain has led his troops into battle as their commander-in-chief – and has shown himself to have all the qualities of a first-rate soldier. He won the battle against Marshal Noailles's French army, which came as a surprise to him, but failed to follow it up, which surprised nobody.

Although they are not formally at war, the dispute over the Austrian succession brought British, Hanoverian, Hessian and Austrian troops here, where, hemmed in by the river Main and a dense forest, the French army descended on them. The king was his army's main encumbrance, for although resolved to die like a common soldier he had no intention of living like one and brought with him a personal baggage train of 13 coaches, 35 wagons, 54 carts and 662 horses.

There was confusion when the French attacked, with most of the allied infantry and artillery caught in an enormous traffic jam in Dettingen's narrow streets, but the attack was uncoordinated. George rallied his troops and counter-attacked at their head: "Now, boys, for the honour of England; fire, and behave bravely and the French will soon run." Fortunately for his majesty, they did (→ 11/1743).

A royal warrior: King George on horseback at the Battle of Dettingen.

George returns in triumph to London

London, November 1743
King George has returned to London, welcomed by his subjects as a victorious hero. The fact that the victory was inconclusive and has brought no benefits to the allied cause has hardly been remarked on. The great London mob has not had such a chance to vent its anti-French spleen since Blenheim.

The scene was unforgettable. Pall Mall was lit up when the king came into St James's palace at about 5.30pm; all the churches in Westminster rang their bells. "It was incredible how well his reception was," said Horace Walpole, the son of the former prime minister. "You would have thought that it had not been a week after the victory at Dettingen. They almost carried him into the palace on their shoulders; and at night the town was illuminated and bonfired" (→ 1743).

British army loses Scots soldier who beat the Jacobites

Edinburgh, 4 October 1743
John Campbell, the second Duke of Argyll and a field marshal in the British Army, has died. One of the most powerful Whigs of his generation, he was an opponent of the king and a supporter of Frederick, the Prince of Wales. He secured the Hanoverian succession in 1714 by his timely arrival at the privy council when Queen Anne was dying, and he saved it in 1715 by his defeat of the Jacobites at the Battle of Sheriffmuir.

A soldier and a politician, he learnt his military tactics from John Churchill, the brilliant Duke of Marlborough. Argyll's father had supported the Glorious Revolution, but the son only agreed to the union

John, the Duke of Argyll.

'Broad Bottoms' come to power after ousting of royal favourite

John Carteret, Earl Granville.

London, 23 November 1744
John Carteret - now Earl Granville - has resigned the seals of the northern department, to the fury of the king. He has been replaced by Lord Harrington, an ally of the Whig leaders the Earl of Newcastle and his brother, Henry Pelham.

The change of ministry follows a virtual ultimatum by the Pelhams that if Carteret was not dismissed all the "Old Corps" would resign. The king was forced to accept it, which he did with much bad grace. "I was forced, I was threatened," he grumbled. Harrington and the Pelhams will form a new "broad-

bottomed" administration of Whigs and Tories. Virtually every major figure in the Whig opposition is in it, except young William Pitt who has made himself so obnoxious to the king that not even a Pelham would dare put his name forward.

Frederick, the Prince of Wales, the effective paymaster of the opposition until yesterday, is furious at this parliamentary compromise that leaves him out in the cold. "Remember, my lord," he warned Lord Harrington before the latter accepted office in the new ministry, "the king is sixty-one, and I am thirty-seven."

of England and Scotland in return for a major-generalship, the dukedom of Greenwich and considerable financial rewards. He proved loyal to the Union, however, and used his powers of patronage and corruption to control half of Scotland's constituencies and ensure that they returned Unionist candidates to parliament.

He was less loyal to King George II, and in the political quarrels between the king and his son he took the side of the Prince of Wales and the Leicester House set, throwing the whole weight of the Argyll political machine against Walpole in the 1741 election – and thus excluding himself from any chance of a seat in the government.

rench defeat hybrid 'pragmatic' army

Troops of the British alliance are routed in battle at Fontenoy.

Fontenoy, France, 11 May 1745
The "pragmatic army", a curious amalgam of British, Hanoverian, Hessian, Dutch and Austrian troops, assembled to secure Grand Duke Francis of Tuscany as Holy Roman Emperor, has been defeated. British diplomacy is in ruins. All of Flanders, including the British base at Ostend, now lies open to French attack.

The pragmatic army was commanded by the brave, painstaking yet unimaginative Duke of Cumberland, the king's son; the French by that master of war Marshal Saxe. In the event France hardly needed the marshal's genius. The 44,000-strong force threw itself at the 76,000-strong French army in a frontal assault against an impregnable position. The result, which only the 23-year-old duke was not able to foresee, was disastrous.

Everyone, including Saxe, recognises the bravery of the British infantry in continuing its hopeless assaults. Ironically, what finally broke it was a cavalry charge by Saxe's Irish Brigade, made up of Irish supporters of Prince Charles Edward Stuart, the son of the Pretender, James.

For Britain this is not only a major military defeat but an even more serious political setback. The charge of the Irish Brigade means that Fontenoy will not only be seen as a French victory but also as a Jacobite one (→ 18/10/48).

Rousing patriotic song composed to rally support for king against Jacobite rebels

London, autumn 1745
With the Jacobite armies of Prince Charles Edward Stuart marching through England [*see report overleaf*], people have taken up a new patriotic song to show their loyalty to King George and the Protestant succession. Called *God save our Noble King* or *God save the King*, it started life in London's west end theatres and was an instant success.

The song first came to public notice when it was sung in an arrangement by the composer Dr Thomas Arne at the Theatre Royal, Drury Lane, on 28 September, a week after the Jacobite victory at Prestonpans. The words were printed in the *Gentleman's Magazine* on 1 October, and another arrangement, by the eminent musician Dr Charles Burney, was sung at the Covent Garden theatre. A fourth verse has recently appeared to make the song more vehemently anti-Jacobite.

No one is sure who wrote the song's words, although the tune resembles a melody written over a century ago by a composer called, appropriately, John Bull. Neither lyrics nor music are of the highest quality, and in different times the song might soon have been forgotten. But with crown and government facing their most serious internal emergency this century, the bullish words and stately tread of *God save the King* have timed their arrival perfectly to fire the patriotic imagination.

1
God save great George our king
Long live our noble king
God save the king!
Send him victorious
Happy and glorious
Long to reign over us
God save the king!

2
O Lord our God arise
Scatter his enemies
And make them fall!
Confound their politics
Frustrate their knavish tricks
On thee our hopes we fix
O save us all!

3
Thy choicest gifts in store
On him be pleased to pour
Long may he reign!
May he defend our laws
And ever give us cause
To sing with heart and voice
God save the king!

Additional verse
Lord, grant that Marshal Wade
May by Thy mighty aid
Victory bring!
May he sedition hush
And like a torrent rush
Rebellious Scots to crush
God save the king!

Prince's army career hangs in the balance

Royal commander: Prince William.

Fontenoy, France, 11 May 1745
As Prince William, the Duke of Cumberland, surveys the heaps of redcoat dead lying on the battlefield, the question must be asked: is he really leadership material? He is personally courageous. After the Battle of Dettingen in 1743 Major Wolfe of the 12th Foot said: "He behaved as bravely as a man could do." In spite of his inexperience the duke has proved a good administrator and cares for his men's welfare. But he has also shown himself too sluggish and unimaginative to grasp the fleeting opportunities that bring victory (→ 13/7/65).

Walpole dies after transforming politics

The late great statesman: Walpole.

London, 18 March 1745
Britain's greatest parliamentarian and first prime minister, Sir Robert Walpole, the Earl of Orford, died today. He entered parliament in 1701, aged 25, and in 1708 became secretary-at-war. In 1712 he was sent to the Tower for corruption, but his fortunes were restored by George I and in 1715 he became chancellor of the exchequer and first lord of the treasury. He was ousted in 1717 but returned to power in 1721, sustaining his Whig majority for 21 years through a combination of artful political manoeuvring and wide-reaching patronage.

'Bonnie Prince Charlie' heads Jacobite offensive

Stuart Pretender is to bid for throne

Western Isles, 23 July 1745
Prince Charles Edward, the elder son of the Stuart Pretender, set foot in Scotland for the first time today when he landed on Eriskay in the Outer Hebrides. Disguised as a priest in case of capture, and with only a handful of advisers, the 24-year-old prince disembarked from his French ship, the *Du Teillay*, to be gruffly told by the local clan chief to go home. Charles was un-ruffled. Speaking with his curious Irish-Italian accent, the result of his Roman upbringing at the hands of Catholic tutors, his reply was simple: "I am come home, sir."

The prince has a tough task on his hands in this latest bid to restore the Stuarts. He assembled a size-able arsenal before sailing from France last month but lost most of it when one of his two French ships, the *Elisabeth*, was forced back by the Royal Navy. Neither his father nor the French have much confid-ence in his expedition, which owes a lot to Charles's own charisma and determination (→ 19/8).

Edinburgh falls to the Jacobite forces

Edinburgh, 17 September 1745
For the first time for over 60 years a Stuart prince resides in the royal palace of Holyroodhouse. Tonight Prince Charles Edward occupied all of the Scottish capital apart from the castle and declared his father King James VIII of Scotland.

Charles's success has surprised even his confident self. All key Scottish towns are now his, with only Dumbarton, Stirling and Edin-burgh castles holding out for King George. The English commander in Scotland, Sir John Cope, hastily scraped together a force and headed north at the first sign of rebellion. But he avoided the mountains for fear of ambush and arrived in Inver-ness as the Jacobites headed south undisturbed. Realising his blunder, Cope is now sailing for Dunbar with 2,500 men (→ 21/9).

A hero's welcome: "Bonnie Prince Charlie" rides into Edinburgh.

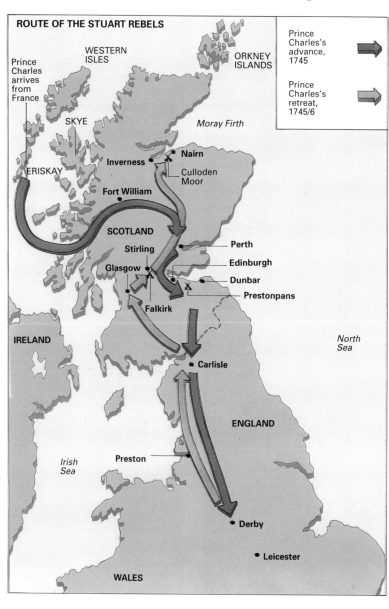

ROUTE OF THE STUART REBELS

Prince Charles's advance, 1745

Prince Charles's retreat, 1745/6

WESTERN ISLES

ORKNEY ISLANDS

Prince Charles arrives from France

SKYE

Moray Firth

ERISKAY

Inverness

Nairn

Culloden Moor

Fort William

SCOTLAND

Stirling

Perth

Glasgow

Edinburgh

Dunbar

Falkirk

Prestonpans

IRELAND

North Sea

Carlisle

ENGLAND

Irish Sea

Preston

Derby

Leicester

WALES

Highlanders crush the king's forces

Lothian, 21 September 1745
Prince Charles's Jacobite troops have dealt a humiliating blow to King George at Prestonpans, ten miles (16km) east of Edinburgh. In a battle lasting just ten minutes a well-armed but inexperienced army of 2,500 under General Sir John Cope was routed this morning by a similar number of ill-equipped high-landers.

Cope landed three days ago at Dunbar and set up camp beside a great marsh near Prestonpans. Cope thought that the Jacobites, ad-vancing from Edinburgh, would be unable to cross the marsh undetect-ed. But Charles was led through it last night by a local lad, and the whole army silently moved up to a position close to Cope's troops.

The battle began at first light. Cope's terrified recruits fired only once before the claymore-wielding highlanders charged and left 500 of them dead. The rest of Cope's men fled, leaving "Bonnie Prince Charlie" virtually supreme in Scotland (→ 9/11).

Jacobite soldiers march into England

Carlisle, 15 November 1745
Having defied the odds to win Scot-land for his father, the Pretender King James VIII, Prince Charles is advancing through England. To-day, a week after crossing the river Esk into Cumbria, the Jacobite army, now swollen to 5,000, has taken Carlisle after a short siege.

For five weeks after occupying Edinburgh the prince and his coun-cillors planned their next move. The Scottish Jacobites advised him to consolidate his rule in Scotland until England rebelled against King George or the French sent assist-ance. But the idealistic Charles, backed by his French and Irish ad-visers, wanted no delay before he went for the English throne. A bal-lot was taken, and Charles won by one vote. Thus began the riskiest stage of his great adventure (→ 6/12).

Rebels forced into retreat by King George's forces

The battle at Culloden: the highlanders are bloodily slaughtered (right).

"Bonnie Prince Charlie" escapes after the defeat at Culloden: a later view.

Jacobites routed in Culloden bloodbath

Highland, 16 April 1746

In just 40 minutes today all hope died that King James VIII and III might sit on the British throne. The road to today's showdown on Culloden Moor, south-east of Inverness, began when Prince Charles's army reached Derby on 5 December last year. Charles was ecstatic to have got as near as 127 miles (204km) from London, but his 5,000-strong army was overstretched and now faced some 30,000 government forces under the Duke of Cumberland, the 24-year-old, 20-stone son of King George II.

Charles's general, Lord George Murray, urged a retreat to Scotland to consolidate, and the prince's council agreed. Charles was furious and sulked all the way during Murray's skilful withdrawal; but more men joined him at Glasgow, and at Falkirk, on 17 January, he smashed a government force, already weakened by numerous desertions, under General Hawley. Charles headed for his power base, the highlands, and set up headquarters at Inverness.

But Charles's supply lines began to break down as the weather turned foul. Cumberland, in hot pursuit with 10,000 men, set up camp at Nairn on the Moray Firth. This morning he led 14,000 well-equipped troops and cavalry (including anti-Jacobite Scots) to face Charles's 3,000 cold, soaked and hungry men drawn up – against the advice of Murray, who had wanted a guerrilla war – on the flat, sodden Culloden Moor.

Such a battlefield denied the Jacobites their deadliest weapon: the terrifying downhill charge of claymore-wielding highlanders. When they did charge, Cumberland's musketeers tore them to shreds. In one afternoon the Stuart dream has turned into a nightmare. Nor has the bloodshed stopped. Cumberland ordered his men to take no prisoners; the wounded have been finished off where they lay and fugitives executed on the spot. There are also reports of government troops committing atrocities against civilians (→20/9).

'Bonnie Prince Charlie' takes his leave

"Bonnie Prince Charlie" (left, a later view) bids farewell to Flora MacDonald, the canny young woman who helped him to escape from Uist thoroughly disguised (right) as an Irish spinning-maid.

Pretender escapes disguised as a woman

Loch na Uamh, 20 September 1746

Prince Charles Edward Stuart's great adventure ended today where it began 14 months ago, west of Fort William on the shores of Moidart. In the five months since Culloden he has eluded capture in a string of escapades that have made him a folk hero among some highlanders. Others, however, are glad to see him go, regarding him as an arrogant fool who did not care how many people died for him.

The day after his defeat, with a price of £30,000 on his head, the prince decided to seek a passage back to France. With a few associates he headed down the Great Glen into Moidart, whence on 26 April he was rowed to Benbecula. At Stornoway he was turned away by locals fearful of government revenge, so his party went back south, dodging the Royal Navy, and on South Uist sympathisers put him up in secluded Coradale. Here he spent his time in shooting, fishing and bouts of heavy drinking.

But Cumberland was on his track, and on 28 June a local woman, Flora MacDonald, reluctantly helped to disguise the prince, by now suffering terribly from scurvy, as an Irish spinning-maid and accompanied him from Uist to Skye. Back on the mainland, more sympathisers led the prince from Morar northwards, hearing of a French ship in Loch Broom in Wester Ross. But word came that this ship had been captured, and the party turned south. From Achnacarry Charles was led south-east to the remote Ben Alder, while others went west to await news of a ship. A fortnight ago two French frigates, *L'Heureux* and *Le Prince de Conti*, put into Loch na Uamh; word was sent to the prince, who arrived after another gruelling trek.

Before boarding *L'Heureux* today he addressed comrades who had chosen to stay behind: "My lads, be in good spirits. It shall not be long before I shall be with you and shall endeavour to make up for all the loss you have suffered." With that he, and the Stuart cause, departed (→9/1750).

329

Prince establishes an 'opposition' party

Leicester House, February 1748
Disappointed with the failure of the Tories at last year's general election, Frederick, the Prince of Wales, has formed what amounts to an opposition party. He has issued a manifesto in the form of a letter to his son, George William Frederick, setting out a number of optimistic promises which he intends to fulfil only "when we shall have the misfortune to lose his majesty". King George is now 65, and in poor health; evidently the prince expects that this "misfortune" will befall Britain soon.

Although the manifesto promises of a modest civil list, lower taxes and a reduced national debt once the Prince of Wales is king may not fool anyone, hopes for his future patronage are high. His old ally George Bubb Doddington, lured to the king's faction by the job of treasurer to the navy, is now planning to rejoin Frederick for the promise of a peerage.

Other parts of the prince's programme call for military officers to be excluded from parliament and for gentlemen with £300 a year in land to be made justices of the peace. Frederick also uses the manifesto to criticise the war against France, making in effect a direct attack on his father (→ 20/3).

King sees royal fireworks end in disaster

London, 28 April 1749
A firework display in Green Park exploded out of control shortly after it began at 8.30pm yesterday. Ironically, the display, ordered by the king to celebrate the end of the War of the Austrian Succession, has left Green Park looking like a battlefield. A specially erected Temple of Peace is now a smoking ruin, three spectators are dead, and the temple's Italian architect has been arrested for brawling with the comptroller of his majesty's fireworks. King George was present, but he escaped unhurt when the conflagration started, putting paid to what should have been a grand occasion. The celebration was also marked by the king's favourite composer, Handel, who wrote a piece, the aptly-entitled *Music for the Royal Fireworks*.

A hundred musicians were to play in the rococo Temple of Peace, which also housed the 10,650 rockets that were to light up the night sky. Disaster struck when the rockets set fire to the temple. The night's entertainment had cost £90,000 – all quite literally gone up in smoke.

Despite the disastrous fire at the celebrations on 27 April to mark the Peace of Aix-la-Chapelle, a second firework display, sponsored by the Duke of Richmond, was held on the river Thames on 8 May (picture above).

Prince of Wales is dead

Frederick: the attending cherubs may represent the arts and sciences.

London, 20 March 1751
Muttering "I feel death!" Frederick, the Prince of Wales, breathed his last in his bedroom last night at the age of 44. His son, George William Frederick, not yet 13, becomes the heir to the kingdom. All those plotters who had gathered around the Prince of Wales in the Leicester House set have found their schemes made worthless overnight and their hopes dashed.

A chill which Frederick had contracted in his gardens in Kew had turned to pleurisy, but doctors hoped that he was recovering. Last night, however, an abdominal abscess burst, and the Prince of Wales died before help could reach him. The abscess had apparently been growing since the prince was struck with a tennis ball three years ago.

"Poor Fred" was blighted in his life by the bad feeling between his parents and himself. They made their lack of love quite clear and denied him any proper place in the government of Britain – unlike his younger brother, the "Butcher" general, Prince William, the Duke of Cumberland. Frederick chose instead to become the centre of opposition politics and thus a focus for a motley collection of ambitious and disappointed men.

This bitter family feud led on occasion to some bizarre events. When Frederick's wife Augusta went into labour with their first child the couple escaped by carriage from Hampton Court to St James's so that the birth would not take place under the in-laws' eager gaze. The king and queen for their part were enraged that the pregnancy had been kept secret for almost its entire course and feared that the real child would at birth be exchanged for another.

Although Frederick did not come to England until his early twenties and spoke with a strong German accent, he believed that the link with Hanover should be broken and was popular with the English people generally.

Opposition woos the new Prince of Wales

London, 4 June 1755
The young Prince of Wales, George William Frederick, reaches his legal majority today, just four years after the death of his father Frederick. The opposition to the king is already forming around him, in the best traditions of this quarrelsome royal family. He is 17 now and the heir to the throne; his grandfather is 73, so the frustration of Frederick's long and fruitless wait for kingship is unlikely to be repeated.

His mother Augusta's great friend and adviser, John Stuart, the Earl of Bute, has been appointed tutor to the prince. Bute is a shrewd man who has been rumoured to be Augusta's lover, but, despite what the scandal sheets say, this is not the case. What is true, however, is that Bute has long opposed the policies of the king's government. Now Augusta and he have convinced George that the king's ministers are plotting against him.

Bute has in fact done his best to ingrain a deep distrust of all poli-

Coming of age: the Prince of Wales.

ticians in the prince. Yet at the same time Bute and Augusta have no intention of letting their residence, Leicester House, lose any of its power to attract politicians opposed to the king – such as the formidable William Pitt, detested by the king but likely to become a major force in politics (→ 4/6/56).

John Stuart, the Earl of Bute.

William Pitt, the Whig MP.

King tries to isolate grandson from allies

London, 4 June 1756
Using the Prince of Wales's 18th birthday as an excuse, the king has tried to prise the boy away from the influence of his mother, Augusta, but has been rebuffed. Despite being offered new apartments at Kensington palace and St James's, plus an allowance of £40,000 a year, the young George has written to his grandfather to ask that he may continue to live with his mother. And with a nerve that is

close on effrontery, George has also asked the king for permission to make the Earl of Bute, already his tutor, his own first minister or "groom of the stole". Bute is well known as an opponent of the king. Weary of quarrelling, the 74-year-old king has agreed, on condition that his grandson is obedient to him. But that will do nothing to halt the growing opposition faction based on George's establishment at Leicester House (→ 20/6/58).

King weeps for shame over bungling of Hanoverian treaty by Prince William

Hanover, September 1757
Royal tears have greeted a shameful end to the campaign against France. King George can only blame himself, although he is doing his best to blame almost everyone else, for the humiliating terms agreed by the Duke of Cumberland at Klosterzeven this month following his comprehensive defeat by the French army at Hastenbeck on 16 July. However good a soldier "Butcher" William may be, he has not the experience to be a subtle and effective negotiator. At first the king took the defeat well, giving his

favourite son full powers to act in his interests, not as King George of England but as Elector of Hanover.

The aim was a separate peace which would preserve both the army and what was left of the Hanoverian possessions. The Convention of Klosterzeven, signed on 8 September, achieved neither. The German alliance was broken up, the army effectively immobilised, and Hanover occupied by the detested French. The king has never suffered such a disgrace and is accusing his son of what amounts to treason (→ 1/8/59).

Hogarth becomes official court painter

"The Polling", from a series by William Hogarth, the new court painter.

London, 6 June 1757
The greatness of William Hogarth has been recognised by his appointment at the age of 60 as official painter to the court of King George. Although better known to the wider public for his series of paintings and prints on moral themes – *The Rake's Progress*, *The Harlot's Progress* and, after a long gap, *Marriage à la Mode* – Hogarth's portraits also show a gritty realism, in contrast to the studied artificiality of most contemporary European artists with their monotonous concentration on religious themes.

The down-to-earth willingness to paint what he sees, whether in a

low tavern or in the face of a society lady, gives Hogarth's art its essential quality. He is openly scornful of "phizmongering", the making of flattering likenesses for rich patrons, and his interest in depicting common people as well as the great with equal honesty makes him both a uniquely personal and a quintessentially English artist.

William Hogarth was born in London in 1697, although his father came from Westmorland. Apprenticeship to a silver-plate engraver, whose daughter he secretly married, gave him an understanding of the techniques of printmaking as well as a strong formal sense of design.

British Museum to receive donation of books and manuscripts from the king

London, 1757

King George has made a handsome donation of 10,000 books and 1,800 manuscripts collected by the kings of England to the British Museum. Enormous as this contribution to the nation's cultural life is, it is only the latest in a series.

When the museum was founded four years ago Sir Hans Sloane, the famous physicist, sold to the government his library of 50,000 books and 3,500 manuscripts along with his collection of curiosities. Although the collection was estimated to have cost him £50,000 to build up, the selling price was only £20,000.

Also in 1753 the Earl of Oxford's widow sold off to the government for £10,000 her husband's library of over 7,500 volumes. In the same year Lord Pelham, the then chancellor of the exchequer, raised enough money to buy these collections as well as a place to put them – Montagu House in Bloomsbury. Sir Robert Cotton's vast library was then added to this nucleus of a national collection. King George's

Sir Hans Sloane, the physicist.

donation is thus in a long line of patronage of the arts. There is, however, a further bonus in the king's gift.

He has also stipulated that, in future, the British Museum will have the unique privilege of receiving a free copy of every volume entered at Stationers' Hall – in effect, a copy of every book published in Britain.

King awards Garter to insolent minister

Richard Grenville, Earl Temple.

London, September 1758

While Earl Temple, the lord privy seal, counts himself "the happiest man in the world", King George complains that he was "wheedled, forced and bullied" into the decision, but after a year of arm-twisting and royal displeasure

Temple has at last received the much-coveted Order of the Garter.

Temple has long been regarded by the king with loathing, but he ardently yearned for this order, one that is very much in the king's personal gift. A year ago, undaunted by "his majesty's displeasure", he duly applied to join the order. He was swiftly rebuffed. But Temple has powerful friends, notably his brother-in-law William Pitt, who said that he would resign if Temple were denied – and as the king's confidant Newcastle pointed out, no member of parliament "will set his face against Pitt".

The king resisted at first, believing that Pitt would not really resign. His bluff called, Pitt admitted that resignation was not his intent, promising instead to boycott the court. This threat did the trick and the king, much put upon, gave in. Now he talks of ministerial pressure and wishes out loud that he had stayed in Hanover. Lord Temple simply wears his Garter.

George to veto grandson's military career

Leicester House, 20 June 1758

The Prince of Wales has written to his grandfather the king offering his services as a soldier should the French invade south-east England. The 20-year-old prince thinks that such a move will encourage the people and be "a terror to the enemy". King George no doubt recalls a similar request made by his son Frederick, the prince's father, in 1745. He turned that one down and is likely to do the same with his grandson's, suspecting the motive to be ambition rather than patriotism. Instead of blood and glory in the field the prince can more reliably look forward to the usual tedious round of reviewing troops and visiting the fleet (→ 25/10/60).

A would-be soldier: the 20-year-old George, the Prince of Wales.

British defeat French in battle at Minden

A glorious victory: the British rout the French in battle at Minden.

Germany, 1 August 1759

British troops won an important victory today when, backed by Prince Ferdinand of Brunswick's Hanoverians, they routed a French force under Marshal de Contades at Minden, some 40 miles (64km) west of Hanover. The battle is yet another triumph in a year in which, according to Horace Walpole, the son of the late Sir Robert, "the church bells are worn threadbare with ringing for victories".

Like last year's expeditions to West Africa, where France's colonial settlements fell to British attack, and this year's in Canada,

where General Wolfe is making excellent headway, Minden is a further example of the far-reaching policies of William Pitt.

A year ago it seemed that the French and their allies were set to take over most of Germany. By August of this year, as French troops massed on its border, it seemed that Hanover was doomed. Luckily Prince Ferdinand rallied his forces; he also imported six regiments from Britain, which were eventually to bear the brunt of the fighting. When his 42,000 men met the 54,000 Frenchmen, they gloriously won the day (→ 31/7/60).

'Young Pretender' deserted by mistress

'aris, July 1760
'lementina Walkinshaw, who for ɩore than ten years has been the ɩistress of Charles Stuart, "the 'oung Pretender" (now 40 years ld), has finally left him. Taking ,ith her their seven-year-old aughter Charlotte, she has fled to 'aris and entered the convent of the 'isitation. Charles is furious but an do nothing. His mistress would ather die than return to him and ,ould sooner kill their child than ive her up to her father.

As might have been expected, 'lementina has tired of the life she ed with Charles. It had turned into a seemingly endless round of movement, debts and insecurity – not to mention the abuse and drunken beatings that Charles meted out to her. Jealous of the attentions of other men, Charles kept his wife a virtual prisoner.

Clementina's decision was, ironically, hastened by Charles's father, James. Believing that his son must make a good marriage to have a chance of claiming Britain's throne, he begged Clementina to leave, promising his financial support to her if she complied. With little alternative, she has done as James wished (→1770).

'ing revels in army's Canadian successes

,ondon, October 1760
'ing George can hardly contain his elight at the news of the fall of Montreal to British forces, which effectively brings to an end the war in 'anada against the French. The ord privy seal, Lord Temple, has ,ritten to William Pitt that "the lose of the king's reign is distinguished by lustre of every sort".

Only a few years ago it was the 'rench who were enjoying success n both Canada and India, but, hanks to the aggressive foreign olicy pursued since 1756 by Pitt, s secretary of state, Britain's forunes have revived. In 1757 Robert Clive regained Calcutta from the French, and in July 1758 Louisburg on Cape Breton Island fell to the British.

Last year Major-General James Wolfe became commander-in-chief of British forces in Canada, an appointment of which the king heartily approved. When told that Wolfe was said to be mad, George quipped: "I wish he would bite some of my other generals." Although Wolfe was killed in the fall of Quebec last September, victory has followed upon victory, culminating in the collapse of French power in Canada.

Westminster abbey, with a procession of knights of the Order of the Bath, by Canaletto (d.1798), a Venetian view-painter active in London 1746/56. King George bought a large collection of his work in 1758.

George II dies in closet

"The late good old king": a 19th-century portrait of King George.

Kensington Palace, 25 Oct 1760
The king is dead. King George II breathed his last just after 6am following a massive heart attack. Horace Walpole has called it an enviable death, "in the greatest period of the glory of his country and of his reign, in perfect tranquillity at home". Quite true, but it is perhaps unfortunate that the king was in fact seated on the lavatory when he suffered the attack.

Tributes yet more fulsome than Walpole's have poured in, and even Pitt, hardly a royal intimate, has declared: "The late good old king had something of humanity and, among other manly virtues, he possessed justice, truth and sincerity in an eminent degree."

Much of that is true, although some might say that the "manly virtues" were perhaps overdone when it came to his infidelities. But this reign may be as much remembered for the developments in the nation's government as for the character of the king himself. This has been a period in which "constitutional monarchy" has become firmly established. Kings have always reigned, but ever since the turmoil of the Civil War there has been a gradual movement away from allowing them to rule as well.

This process has accelerated under George II. During the ministries of Sir Robert Walpole, the first "prime minister", and Pelham, George still played an active part in government, sharing his powers with the Whigs, but as he grew older first Newcastle and then Pitt increased governmental power at his expense. By the time of his death he ruled in name only.

George was always thirsty for military glory and achieved something that few other monarchs attempt today: he actually led his forces in battle. At the same time, thanks especially to Pitt, he has seen a substantial expansion of Britain's power abroad.

George III
1760–1820

**House
of
Hanover**

Westminster, 25 October 1760. King George III accedes to the throne (→ 26/10).

London, 27 October 1760. John Stuart, the Earl of Bute, a favourite of Augusta, the Princess Dowager of Wales, and tutor to George, joins the cabinet (→ 4/3/62).

Westminster, 19 May 1761. In his first speech to parliament, George says: "I glory in the name of Briton."

London, 31 May 1761. George drops plans to marry Lady Sarah Lennox, a sister of the Earl of Richmond, after manoeuvres by her uncle, Henry Fox, which have angered the king (→ 8/7).

France, 8 June 1761. The British seize Belle Ile, off the French coast, as Anglo-French peace talks fail.

London, 8 July 1761. George announces to the privy council his plan to marry Charlotte, the daughter of Duke Charles of Mecklenburg-Strelitz (→ 9/9).

Europe, August 1761. Spain allies with France (→ 4/1/62).

Westminster, 22 Sept 1761. George is crowned king.→

Britain, 4 January 1762. Britain declares war on Spain (→ 5/10).

Caribbean, 16 February 1762. The British seize the French island of Martinique (→ 12/1762).

Westminster, 4 March 1762. The Earl of Bute, the prime minister, proposes to maintain an army in the American colonies, to be paid for by British taxpayers (→ 28/5).

Westminster, 28 May 1762. The Duke of Newcastle resigns as prime minister after a dispute on foreign policy with the Earl of Bute; Bute replaces him (→ 5/6).

London, 5 June 1762. The first edition of the *North Briton*, a satirical magazine edited by John Wilkes, the MP for Aylesbury, is published; the Earl of Bute, the prime minister, is savagely attacked in it (→ 20/1/64).

London, 12 August 1762. Queen Charlotte gives birth to George Augustus Frederick, the first son and heir of George III (→ 8/9).

Philippines, 5 October 1762. The British capture Spanish-held Manila (→ 12/10).

Caribbean, 12 October 1762. After a siege, the British seize Havana, the capital of Spanish-held Cuba (→ 12/1672).

Westminster, November 1762. In order to keep Bute in government, George is forced to make Henry Fox, the paymaster-general, leader of the Commons (→ 24/7/67).

Portugal, December 1762. With British help, the Portuguese succeed in repelling a Franco-Spanish invasion (→ 10/2/63).

London, 1762. Sir Charles Sheffield sells Buckingham House to the king for £28,000 (→ 1775).

Westminster, March 1763. The Earl of Bute, the prime minister, introduces a cider tax (→ 15/4).

London, 16 August 1763. Queen Charlotte gives birth to her second son, Frederick (→ 21/8/65).

London, 16 January 1764. Charles, the hereditary Prince of Brunswick, marries Augusta, the elder sister of King George III (→ 7/1765).

Westminster, 22 March 1765. Parliament passes the Stamp Act, imposing a duty on legal transactions in America in order to pay for colonial defence (→ 17/12).

London, 21 August 1765. Queen Charlotte gives birth to her third son, William Henry (→ 29/9/66).

London, 31 October 1765. Shortly after his promotion to prime minister, the Duke of Cumberland dies, aged 44.

Westminster, 17 Dec 1765. King George favours a repeal of the Stamp Act (→ 7/2/66).

Westminster, 26 Dec 1765. King George invests his eldest son, George, the Prince of Wales, as a knight of the Garter (→ 1766).

Westminster, August 1766. William Pitt, the newly created Earl of Chatham, favours a repeal of the Stamp Act (→ 30/5/67).

London, 6 September 1766. William Henry, the Duke of

Gloucester and younger brother of George III, secretly marries Maria, the widowed Countess Waldegrave and daughter of Sir Edward Walpole (→ 13/9/72).

London, 29 September 1766. Queen Charlotte gives birth to a daughter, Charlotte Augusta Matilda, the Princess Royal (→ 2/11/67).

Denmark, 8 November 1766. Caroline Matilda, George's youngest sister, aged 15, marries King Christian VII of Denmark and Norway (→ 6/4/72).

Westminster, June 1767. Charles Townshend, the chancellor of the exchequer, imposes duties on certain goods imported into America (→ 1/10/68).

London, 2 November 1767. Queen Charlotte gives birth to Edward, her fifth child (→ 8/11/68).

London, 10 May 1768. Rioters mob the opening of parliament in an attempt to free the radical MP, John Wilkes, who has been imprisoned for seditious and obscene libel (→ 3/2/69).

London, 13 May 1768. Louisa Anne, King George's younger sister, dies aged only 19.

Germany, 17 May 1768. Augusta, the Duchess of Brunswick and elder sister of King George, gives birth to a daughter, Caroline.

Westminster, October 1768. The Earl of Chatham resigns as leader of the government in the Lords, suffering from gout and nervous collapse (→ 11/5/78).

London, 8 November 1768. Queen Charlotte gives birth to Augusta Sophia, her sixth child (→ 22/5/70).

The life and times of King George III

Name: George William Frederick.
Birth: 24 May 1738.
Accession: 25 October 1760.
Coronation: 22 September 1761.
Predecessor: grandfather.
Marriage: Princess Charlotte of Mecklenburg-Strelitz, 8 September 1761, London.
Children: George, Frederick, William, Charlotte, Edward, Augusta, Elizabeth, Ernest, Augustus, Adolphus, Mary, Sophia, Alfred and Amelia.
Regency: 1811-20
Likes: religion, stability.
Dislikes: political parties.
Favourite home: Windsor.
Greatest problem: ill-health.
Famous saying: "I glory in the name of Briton."
Death: 29 January 1820.

Opposite: the young King George III in regal robes.

Third Hanoverian monarch accedes to the throne

George III becomes king at age of 22

London, 26 October 1760
An immature and impressionable young man has been proclaimed king of Great Britain and Ireland following the death yesterday of his grandfather, George II. The 22-year-old Prince of Wales, who also becomes Elector of Hanover, was riding across Kew Bridge when a messenger told him that he was king. Typically, he insisted that the news be kept secret until he had confided in the Earl of Bute, his beloved mentor.

George III is the first Hanoverian monarch to be born in England, and, in the Hanoverian tradition, he distrusts politicians – William Pitt in particular, whom he regards as a traitor. He comes to the throne at a time when Britain is developing a great empire and controls half the world's trade, but his main preoccupation, as expressed in a speech to ministers yesterday, is to secure "an honourable and lasting peace" in Europe.

George, whose own father died in 1751, is determined to produce an heir as soon as possible; his first task is to select a queen from among a considerable number of eager European princesses (→ 8/7/61).

King George's bride: Queen Charlotte, portrayed by John Zoffany.

Jewel tumbles from crown at coronation

Westminster, 22 September 1761
A unique glimpse of the king's sense of humility caused much admiring comment at his coronation in Westminster abbey today. When the moment came for George to take the sacrament, the king removed the crown, a rare precedent.

The coronation service was an unusual mixture of solemn simplicity and regal showmanship. Thousands paid premium prices – one house near Westminster Hall was rented for 1,000 guineas – to see the king and queen brought from St James's in sedan chairs.

The banquet was a spectacular affair, with the hall kept in darkness until the arrival of the queen. A great fanfare rang out and the hall was suddenly glittering brilliantly, transformed by a thousand lamps lit by the dangerous device of putting tapers to waxed strings, showering the guests with burning wax.

All went well, but there were occasional hiccups. Despite days of training, the lord high steward's horse advanced towards the king and queen rump-first to make obeisance, instead of backing out; and a large jewel fell from the crown. Some see this as a bad omen.

King bans French wine from palace

London, 18 December 1760
One of George III's first acts on becoming king has been to ban the drinking of French wine at St James's palace, the royal residence in London which became his home on the death of his grandfather.

The move was made as a gesture of hostility towards France, with which Britain has been at war for the past four years. It was reported in the *Monitor* newspaper this morning that, in addition to damaging the French export trade, the ban – which applies throughout the palace, including at the king's own table – is calculated to save the royal coffers more than £40,000 per year (→19/5/61).

Charlotte is new queen of Great Britain

London, 9 September 1761
Within 24 hours of her arrival in England, the somewhat plain yet sturdy Charlotte of Mecklenburg-Strelitz was tonight married to the king. Chosen by George after much debate about the relative merits of available German Protestant princesses, Charlotte had been travelling for two weeks. Ten days of the trip were spent at sea, giving her ample time to learn to play Thomas Arne's tune "God Save the King" on the harpsichord before her ship docked at Harwich.

Yesterday morning the princess journeyed by coach to London. The king – who, following a common royal practice, had never set eyes on his future wife before – greeted her at St James's palace. There was little time for Charlotte to rest; she had to try on her wedding dress and then meet her husband's mother and her new brothers-in-law, who were to escort her in the wedding procession. Ten unmarried daughters of dukes and earls carried her train to the altar.

It cannot have been an easy day for the bride. She has arrived in a strange country to marry a man whose language she does not speak and wear a wedding dress not of her own choice. Her stamina is remarkable, however. Before she and the king retired she gave a song recital, accompanying herself on the harpsichord. Even then the guests refused to leave until 3am, when Charlotte denied them entry to the bedchamber (→12/8/62).

The Chinese-style pagoda in the royal gardens at Kew – designed in 1761 for Queen Charlotte by the architect William Chambers.

George is delighted by Pitt resignation

London, 5 October 1761
A delighted King George accepted William Pitt's resignation today and rewarded his former chief minister with a £3,000 annual pension for him and his son and a peerage for his wife. The feud between the two men came to a head when peace talks with France broke down and Pitt learnt that France was negotiating an alliance with Spain. Pitt proposed that war should be declared on Spain; the cabinet was solidly against him. Pitt is popular with the British people who support the war – and the merchants who profit by it. Both the king and the Earl of Bute, his close adviser, are now facing increasing hostility (→ 31/7/66).

New heir baptised

London, 8 September 1762
The infant Prince of Wales, born on 12 August, was baptised today by Thomas Secker, the archbishop of Canterbury. He was named George Augustus Frederick, and his sponsors were the Dukes of Cumberland and Mecklenburg-Strelitz and the Princess Dowager of Wales. The prince was just a few hours old when his father presented him with £500. The king could afford the gift: on the same day the wealth taken from an unlucky Spanish galleon had passed St James's on its way to the bank (→ 16/8/63).

Earl of Bute, king's mentor, quits office

A mob of Londoners pursues King George's unpopular adviser, Lord Bute.

Westminster, 15 April 1763
The political career of John Stuart, the third Earl of Bute and the king's closest adviser, is over. Bute, a champion of the royal prerogative, became prime minister last May, but it was not a job for which he was well suited, and he presided over a faction-ridden and indecisive administration.

He was hated by the English people, who disliked both the fact that he was a Scotsman and his powerful influence over the king. His recent introduction of a cider tax provoked bitter opposition, and Bute resigned in fear of his political enemies and the public. He is succeeded as prime minister by George Grenville. At an early age the king formed a strong attachment to Bute, a close friend of his mother. George saw in the handsome, confident earl the kind of person he would like to be, and when his grandfather's death seemed imminent he clung hard to his mentor, seeking advice on every matter, including his love life.

George was in love with the 15-year-old daughter of the Duke of Richmond and sought Bute's counsel. "If I must lose my friend or my love, I will give up the latter, for I esteem your friendship above every earthly joy," he wrote. Bute advised against, recommending a German Protestant princess (→ 10/1804).

Peace treaty establishes Britain as leading colonial power

Paris, 10 February 1763
George III has emerged from the peace talks here as king of the most powerful country in the world. Under the Treaty of Paris – signed today with France and Spain, ending seven years of war – Britain has gained Canada, Nova Scotia and Cape Breton Island, as well as the right to navigate the Mississippi river. In the West Indies, Britain has gained Grenada, St Vincent, Dominica and Tobago, and, elsewhere, Florida, Senegal and Minorca. The British may have the territorial strengths, but the return of some conquests has been criticised by the opposition.

A firework display held in London's Green Park to celebrate the new treaty.

Satirical MP sent to Tower after libel

London, 20 January 1764
Forty-four issues of John Wilkes's *North Briton* newspaper were devoted to savage attacks on the king and his ministers ... and then came number 45. Published last April, after the signing of the Treaty of Paris, it claimed that a lie – referring to the treaty as "honourable to my crown and beneficial to my people" – had been inserted into the king's speech to parliament. Reflecting a popular view that Britain accepted humiliating terms, the paper accused Lord Bute, the former prime minister, of having bribed the Commons to ratify the treaty. Wilkes, the sardonic and lecherous

Citizens' rights are cut apart: an allegory on the John Wilkes affair.

MP for Aylesbury, went on to suggest that the king should not profane St Paul's cathedral by attending a thanksgiving service there.

Wilkes was arrested for seditious libel and taken to the Tower. A popular outcry followed, with "Wilkes and Liberty!" adopted as a slogan. He was freed in May on the grounds of privilege as an MP.

The king ordered that "that devil Wilkes" should be brought to book. Following the seizure of an allegedly obscene poem from the MP's private printing press, Wilkes – described by William Pitt as "a blasphemer of his God and a libeller of his king" – was today expelled from the Commons after the house voted that parliamentary privilege did not cover his case (→ 10/5/68). ▷

Josiah Wedgwood is to be queen's potter

Burslem, Staffs, 1765

The Staffordshire craftsman Josiah Wedgwood has been appointed potter to the queen. Wedgwood, who opened his own pottery in 1759, is known particularly for his recently introduced Queen's Ware, which is attracting admiration not only in Britain but also in both continental Europe and America. This exquisite pottery – noted for its delicate blue and white neo-classical design – was dedicated to Queen Charlotte because she is an ardent collector of ceramic ware.

Such is the demand for his work that Wedgwood has decided to standardise output by employing mechanised mass-production techniques. Among the processes he favours are slip-moulding, which speeds up the drying process, and "jigging", in which templates are used to shape the wet clay. He also uses transfers – another innovation – to paint the china.

A noted liberal and reformer, Wedgwood plans a "model village" for his employees. He believes that his success is due to scientific experiment and his refusal to accept traditional attitudes of the sort encouraged by King George.

Master potter: Josiah Wedgwood.

A fine Wedgwood trinket box.

Wolfgang Amadeus Mozart, the eight-year-old son of a famous violin teacher from Salzburg, visited London in 1764 with his sister Anna and amazed the king and queen by his musical genius. During a visit to Buckingham House, he played the organ and harpsichord and accompanied the queen in an aria.

King is laid low by a mystery disease

London, April 1765

King George appears to be on the road to recovery after an alarming bout of illness that has mystified his doctors. From mid-January he has suffered a series of attacks involving sharp pains in the chest and serious fits of coughing. The symptoms, which include hoarseness and a rapid pulse, are similar to those suffered by the king during another illness three years ago.

Although not bedridden, George has been unable to carry out all his duties over the past three months. He has been visited by ministers at Buckingham House; after one such visit, the prime minister, George Grenville, said that the king's "countenance and manner were a good deal estranged". The king himself has been worried enough by the episode to propose provisions for a regency in the event of his early death (→ 13/5).

Pretender dies in Rome

Rome, January 1766

James Stuart – the son of James II and pretender to the British throne – had lived here as a king in exile for 50 years, but his funeral was that of a reigning monarch. In crimson velvet robes, a golden crown on his head, a sceptre in one hand, an orb in the other, his body was laid on a bier of purple silk and taken to the church in which he had worshipped for so many years. Twenty cardinals followed his remains, which were placed under a canopy of lace and purple velvet topped by a massive gold crown. Below it was a banner emblazoned with the legend *Jacobus Tertius Magnae Britannia Rex* [James III, King of Great Britain]. After two Requiem Masses, his body was laid to rest in St Peter's, beside that of his wife, Clementina, who died more than 30 years ago.

James died on 1 January, aged 77, at the end of a life that had become increasingly lonely. His Italian hosts had had the greatest respect for the man who refused to sacrifice his Catholic faith for the British crown. Although he had begun to stoop, his bearing remained regal in his old age. His son Henry had been appointed vice chancellor of the Catholic Church and looked after the old man's affairs, but James's greatest wish was to see his elder son, Charles, before he died. Charles refused to visit his father until the pope recognised him as the true British heir and a true king on James's death.

Had he regained his father's throne, James Stuart would have reigned for 64 years – the longest reign in British history.

James Stuart: an exile for 50 years.

Politicians wrangle over Regency Bill

Westminster, 13 May 1765

Sceptics see the hand of the unpopular Earl of Bute in the Regency Bill which received its final reading today. The bill, prompted by the king's illness earlier this year, has caused an open rift between George and some of his ministers.

The king had at first insisted on having the power to name the regent without specifying who that person might be. Opponents of Bute – led by Grenville, the prime minister – suspected a device to give the regency to the king's mother, the Princess Dowager of Wales, a friend of Bute. But George seems to have wanted to avoid rows in his family and to stop his brother Edward, the Duke of York – of whom he disapproves – becoming regent. After much argument, the king agreed to name the queen as regent, and the princess dowager in the event of the queen's death.

George distressed by his sister's visit

London, July 1765

King George has been profoundly distressed at a visit to London by his elder sister, Augusta, and her husband, Charles, the hereditary Prince of Brunswick, who have courted the political opposition. The king's attitude is reminiscent of his reaction in January last year when the hereditary prince – an allied commander in the recent European war – arrived to marry Princess Augusta and won a more enthusiastic welcome from the London people than that which the king himself usually receives.

Charles is reputed to be temperamental and difficult to live with, but Augusta is defensive about her marriage. The 27-year-old princess maintains a regular correspondence with her brother the king in which she mentions her husband's kindness and emphasises how much she loves him.

Cumberland, king's uncle, is first royal duke to preside over British cabinet

Westminster, 13 July 1765
After finding himself at odds with such leading parliamentary figures as William Pitt, King George has taken the unprecedented step of asking a member of the royal family to form a new government. His uncle, the Duke of Cumberland, has roped in several of his Jockey Club friends: the Marquis of Rockingham takes over at the treasury, and another Newmarket friend, the Duke of Grafton, becomes secretary of state. Almost all the senior ministers are men who have never before held political office.

The king has acted against a background of escalating social and political problems, at home and in the American colonies. The English silk weavers have been rioting in protest at their conditions, and this year's harvest promises to be poor. The Stamp Act, imposing a tax on

William, the Duke of Cumberland.

legal documents to provide funds for the defence of the North American possessions, has caused resentment among the colonists, who say they will not pay (→ 31/10/65).

Indian chief ends rebellion in Canada

Fort Ontario, 24 July 1766
The Ottawa Indian chief, Pontiac, has abandoned his rebellion against British rule in the Great Lakes region. Three years ago Pontiac and members of other tribes in the Ohio valley planned to capture Fort Detroit by pretending to seek peace talks while actually entering the fort with weapons. The plot was betrayed by an Indian squaw, and Pontiac fled. He kept the fight going until today, when he signed a treaty of peace and friendship with the superintendent of Indian affairs, Sir William Johnson.

Pontiac, the Ottawa Indian chief.

King reveals humility in letter to his son

London, 1766
Prince George Augustus Frederick, the king's eldest son, is scarcely five years old, but George III is already concerned with the boy's moral and intellectual well-being and the duties of royalty. He has begun to write an apologia for his own conduct, to be used for the instruction of the prince. He says that when God "of his infinite goodness" calls him from this world he does not want sycophants to extol him beyond what he deserves. "I do not

pretend to any superior abilities," the king writes, "but will give place to no one in meaning to preserve the freedom, happiness and glory of my dominions, and all their inhabitants, and to fulfil the duty to my God and my neighbours in the most extended sense. That I have erred is undoubted, otherwise I should not be human, but I flatter myself all unprejudiced persons will be convinced that whenever I have failed it has been from the head not the heart" (→ 10/1769).

George backs plan to placate Americans

Westminster, 7 February 1766
The king has at last made up his mind; today he assured his prime minister, the Marquis of Rockingham, of royal approval for the repeal of the controversial Stamp Act, which has led to widespread disturbances in the North American colonies. The act, introduced in March last year, imposes a tax on legal documents, college diplomas, newspapers and many other items, including playing cards, which are taxed at one shilling [five pence] a pack. It was brought in with the intention of producing revenue for colonial defence.

When the Seven Years' War ended in 1763, Britain had decisively defeated the French in North America and was ruler of the seas. But the cost had been heavy, so King George and his ministers decided that it was reasonable to ask the colonists to help to pay for their security.

The Americans – who have long been accustomed to greater liberty than most Britons enjoy – protested that the British Parliament had no right to impose an internal tax on the colonies. The Stamp Act simply became unenforceable; the problem for the government was how to get rid of it without seeming to give in to the Americans. The answer has been provided by British merchants, who complained that the act was harming the country's export trade (→ 31/7).

A hated law: soldiers in New York defend paper taxed under the Stamp Act.

Pitt, Earl of Chatham, forms a government

William Pitt: now Lord Chatham.

Whitehall, 31 July 1766
William Pitt has accepted King George's invitation to head a new ministry "of the best of all parties", but he has ceased to be "the great commoner" and has gone to the Lords as the Earl of Chatham. For this he is being criticised by friends who remember that the House of Commons has been his power base since he was first elected over 30 years ago. Though in opposition in recent years, he has remained a formidable figure – a fact now acknowledged by the king's decision to send for him in a bid to end political squabbling (→ 8/1766).

Joshua Reynolds wins royal commission as first president of the Royal Academy

"Academicians of the Royal Academy", as seen later by John Sanders.

London, 1768

A Royal Academy "for the purpose of cultivating and improving the arts of painting, sculpture and architecture" has been formally created by the king, who has declared himself its "patron, protector and supporter". The king hoped that his favourite painter, the American Benjamin West, would be its first president, but West insisted that it should be Joshua Reynolds.

Reynolds, aged 45, is the top portrait painter of fashionable London and charges 200 guineas for a portrait. Oliver Goldsmith put the reason in verse: "A flattering painter who made it his care/To draw men as they ought to be, not as they are." Reynolds accepted the presidency on condition that he was commissioned to paint the king and queen. The king's main portrait painter is Allan Ramsay, a Scot, and he intends to make West "historical painter to the court". West's huge canvases, such as *The Death of General Wolfe*, have begun a vogue for dramatic "history painting".

The king also patronises John Zoffany, a German whom he has nominated to the new academy. Thomas Gainsborough, Reynolds's principal rival, is one of the 50 members. The academy's premises are at a print shop in Pall Mall, where the first exhibition will be held. But its art schools, the first in the country, will be set up in part of Somerset House, a royal palace.

A self-portrait by Reynolds, the first president of the academy.

The great actress Sarah Siddons, as portrayed by Reynolds.

Dr Johnson 'glows' at royal encounter

London, February 1767

Dr Samuel Johnson – who played a key role in the formation of the royal library at Buckingham House – has had a private audience with the king. Johnson, the author of the monumental *Dictionary of the English Language*, was allowed to visit the library after its completion in order to browse. When the king learnt of this he asked to be informed the next time that the great lexicographer paid a visit.

Led by a servant carrying a lighted candle, the king came into the library to find Johnson "in a profound study". Asked what he was writing at the present time, Johnson said that he had no work in hand, since he believed he had done his part as a writer. The king said that he would have agreed if Johnson had not been such a good writer; he went on to suggest that Johnson undertake a history of England.

Johnson reported that the royal encounter left him "glowing with satisfaction". He has good reason to be grateful to the king; five years ago George granted him a pension of £300 a year, thereby greatly improving the writer's financial circumstances. Initially Johnson had doubts about accepting, since in his dictionary he had defined "pensioner" in disparaging terms.

Denial of earldom by king angers Fox

Henry Fox: still Baron Holland.

Westminster, 24 July 1767

Henry Fox, Baron Holland, is a politician with a grievance. He has written to tell his son Charles that the king has refused to make him an earl. In 1763 Fox played a key role in persuading the Commons to accept the Treaty of Paris ending the Seven Years' War, but his reputation for corruption has damaged him with the king. Instead of being rewarded, he was sacked from the government, and the man whom he hated most, Pitt, was placed above him in the Lords as an earl. Never trust anyone, Fox told his son.

King loses patience with elusive Chatham

Westminster, 30 May 1767

King George has lost patience with William Pitt, the Earl of Chatham, the veteran politician whom he had called on to bring stability to his government. "No one", he wrote to Pitt, "has more cautiously avoided writing to you than myself during your late indisposition; but the moment is so extremely critical that I cannot possibly delay any longer."

The king has a personal dislike of Pitt, not least for his excessive flattery; every letter from him begins by Pitt "laying himself at his majesty's feet" and ends by expressing gratitude for the king's "exceeding condescension and transcendent goodness". But George has great respect for Pitt's political skills, and with the government in disarray amid a sea of pressing domestic and foreign issues he turned to him and promised him full backing.

Unfortunately, Pitt is a sick man, ravaged by gout and other ills. He retreated to Bath, too unwell to attend parliament. Members of his cabinet, lacking his firm leadership, have taken to quarrelling on the floor of the House of Commons. As a result of the king's letter, Pitt agreed to see the Duke of Grafton, the nominal prime minister, and give him authority to take what measures he judges to be necessary.

Grafton is trying to agree powerbroking deals with opposition politicians in a bid to win them over to the government. But the opposition is itself divided on policy and united only in the desire to bring down the ministry. Meanwhile, Pitt remains incommunicado (→ 10/1678).

Pseudonym masks attacks on crown

Westminster, 1767
A mysterious polemicist is provoking fury and consternation among cabinet ministers with a series of scandal-mongering and invective-laden letters in the *Public Advertiser*. Using the pen-name "Junius", the writer attacks the prime minister, the Duke of Grafton, who is alleged to prefer love-making and horse-racing to politics. Grafton, says Junius, lacks the wisdom of a great minister but displays "the ominous vibration of a pendulum".

Another letter says of King George: "While he plumes himself upon the security of his title to the crown, he should remember that, as it was acquired by one revolution, it may be lost by another." The government is roundly condemned for its incompetence, corruption and disregard of the law; the attacks show an intimate knowledge of behind-the-scenes intrigues.

William Pitt, the Earl of Chatham, is nominally head of the government, but he is a sick man, suffers from melancholia and remains for days in a darkened room. In his absence cabinet ministers quarrel and go their own ways without any settled policies. Speculation as to the identity of Junius has named such men as Edmund Burke, John Wilkes and Edward Gibbon, but the favourite is Sir Philip Francis, a clerk in the war office.

George blames fiery MP for social unrest

The controversial John Wilkes is called to account before the King's Bench.

Westminster, 3 February 1769
The rabble-rousing John Wilkes – who returned from exile in France last year and was re-elected to parliament as MP for Middlesex – was today expelled by his fellow MPs on the grounds that (in his absence) he had been declared an outlaw and found guilty of libel and blasphemy. When Wilkes first returned to England the government took no action against him, but soon after his election he was sentenced to 22 months' jail. Though King George has been careful to avoid giving the impression of intervening in the affair, his ministers were told last month that the king believed that the survival of the crown depended on Wilkes being thrown out of the Commons.

Apart from his delight in flouting authority, Wilkes has a gift for rousing Londoners disaffected with the government. After he was sentenced, a mob gathered outside his prison in St George's Fields, intent on carrying him in triumph to Westminster. Clashes with troops were followed by two days of rampaging through the city to cries of "Wilkes and Liberty!" Wilkes was first elected to parliament 12 years ago. For an attack on the king in his paper, the *North Briton*, he was accused of seditious libel; an obscene poem, *Essay on Woman*, caused more trouble (→ 8/10/74).

Young prince hosts a 'drawing room'

London, October 1769
The seven-year-old heir to the throne has been presented to the public at a "drawing room" which for the first time was formally held in his name. This is not the first time, however, that the Prince of Wales has been displayed in this way. Within a fortnight of his birth, he was put on show in his cradle at St James's palace. Visitors were invited to inspect him between one and three o'clock in the afternoon during the customary royal receptions known as "drawing rooms". The huge numbers of people who came were refreshed with cake and gruel as they waited their turn.

The prince is now used to being the focus of such public attention; he was only two and a half when he gave his first public audience, presenting a donation of £100 to representatives of a charity (→ 1773).

The prince: focus of public attention.

King's brother dies in Monaco aged 28

Monaco, 1767
The king's frivolous and fun-loving younger brother Edward, the Duke of York, who left for a continental tour last summer, has died in Monaco on his way to Italy, reportedly of a "putrid and irresistible fever". He was 28. "Thus," writes Horace Walpole, the author, "has ended his silly, good-humoured, troublesome career in a piteous manner." Edward, who was just one year younger than George III, earned his brother's mistrust by dabbling in opposition politics. That, perhaps, was the explanation for his trip abroad.

British regiments sent to Boston to put down tax disturbances

Townshend, the former chancellor, who imposed the taxes last year.

Boston, 1 October 1768
Men-of-war of the Royal Navy dropped anchor in Boston harbour yesterday evening, their guns covering the town, and today two regiments from Britain disembarked to join the two already arrived from Halifax, Nova Scotia. One American colonist, Paul Revere, who watched the soldiers come ashore, said that they "formed and marched with insolent pride, drums beating, fifes playing, and colors going, up King Street".

The colonists have been angered by taxes on lead, paper, paint, glass and tea, passed by Westminster last year at the instigation of Charles Townshend, the then chancellor of the exchequer, in spite of cabinet objections. Townshend died last autumn of "putrid fever".

Opposition to the taxes has been led by Boston after a fiery local lawyer, James Otis, persuaded a town meeting to call a boycott of all goods from Britain. Riots have broken out and the British commissioners responsible for collecting the taxes, fearful for their safety, appealed for protection. The 50-gun HMS *Romney* put into port. Other New England colonies have now joined in the campaign against the taxes. The colonists view the arrival of British troops as an enemy occupation and a threat to their liberties (→ 5/3/70).

George III
1760–1820

**House
of
Hanover**

Westminster, March 1770. The duties on glass, paper and paint imported into the American colonies are lifted, but the tax on tea remains. The duties were imposed in 1767 by Charles Townshend, the then chancellor of the exchequer (→ 10/1773).

Australia, April 1770. Captain James Cook, who discovered the islands of New Zealand last year, explores eastern Australia and names Botany Bay and New South Wales (→ 12/7/71).

London, 22 May 1770. Queen Charlotte gives birth to her seventh child, Elizabeth (→ 5/6/71).

South Atlantic, 1770. Tension rises as Spain expels British settlers from the Falkland Islands, where a British colony was established in 1765.

Rome, 1770. Charles Edward Stuart, the 49-year-old pretender to the British throne, who came to live at the Palazzo Muti after the death of his father James, the "Old Pretender", in 1766, is said to be leading a life of drunkenness and debauchery (→ 17/4/72).

London, 5 June 1771. Queen Charlotte gives birth to her eighth child, Ernest Augustus (→ 27/1/73).

London, 2 October 1771. Henry, the Duke of Cumberland and younger brother of George III, marries Ann, the widow of Christopher Horton and daughter of the Earl of Carhampton, an Irish politician (→ 1/11/71).

Richmond, 1 November 1771. George is furious on learning of his brother Henry's marriage to a commoner (→ 24/3/72).

India, 1771. Warren Hastings, a council member in Calcutta and Madras, is appointed British governor of Bengal.

London, 13 February 1772. The funeral of the Princess Dowager of Wales, Augusta, is mobbed by rioters.

Denmark, 6 April 1772. Caroline Matilda, the youngest sister of George III, is divorced from King Christian VII of Denmark and Norway after being disgraced for adultery (→ 5/1775).

Southampton, 13 July 1772. Captain James Cook sets out on his second voyage of exploration to the southern seas (→ 26/7/75).

London, 27 January 1773. Queen Charlotte gives birth to her ninth child, a sixth son, Augustus Frederick (→ 27/2/74).

London, October 1773. The Tea Act is passed to aid the finances of the East India Company; it allows the direct export of tea to North America (→ 16/12).

London, 24 February 1774. Queen Charlotte gives birth to her tenth child and seventh son, Adolphus Frederick (→ 25/4/76).

Westminster, 20 May 1774. Parliament passes the Coercive Act to punish the American colonies for their anti-British attitude (→ 2/6).

Westminster, 2 June 1774. The Quartering Act is revived; all colonies are to provide housing for British troops (→ 9/2/75).

Westminster, 29 Nov 1774. John Wilkes, the new lord mayor of London, is re-elected to parliament as MP for Middlesex.

Westminster, 9 February 1775. Parliament declares Massachusetts to be in a state of rebellion (→ 13/4).

London, 13 April 1775. Lord North extends to many other parts of the American colonies a New England act forbidding trade with any country other than Britain and Ireland (→ 19/4).

North America, 19 April 1775. Shots are fired on British troops as the colonists rebel against the strong measures enforced by Lord North's government (→ 1/5).

Montreal, 1 May 1775. A bust of George III is defaced by rampaging rioters (→ 12/6).

Massachusetts, 12 June 1775. General Gage, the commander-in-chief of British troops in America, imposes martial law on all colonial traitors; a free pardon is offered to those who swear allegiance to the crown (→ 23/8).

Britain, 23 August 1775. King George prepares for war, raising troops from his Hanoverian lands; he declares the American colonies to be in open rebellion against the crown (→ 3/1776).

Boston, March 1776. British troops, under the command of General Howe, withdraw (→ 4/7).

London, 25 April 1776. Queen Charlotte gives birth to her 11th child, Mary (→ 3/11/77).

Philadelphia, 4 July 1776. The American colonies jointly declare their independence of the British crown.→

North America, August 1776. General William Howe defeats the American forces in battle on Long Island (→ 9/1766).

North America, Sept 1776. General Washington, the commander-in-chief of the American forces, is forced to order a retreat from New York (→ 26/12).

North America, 26 Dec 1776. American forces defeat an army of Hessian auxiliaries fighting for Britain at Trenton (→ 7/7/77).

New York, 7 July 1777. American troops surrender Fort Ticonderoga, on Lake Champlain, to the British forces (→ 11/9).

North America, 11 Sept 1777. General Howe and the British defeat George Washington and seize Philadelphia (→ 17/10/77).

New England, 17 October 1777. British forces under General John Burgoyne surrender to Horatio Gates, the American general, at Saratoga (→ 6/1778).

London, 3 November 1777. Queen Charlotte gives birth to her 12th child, Sophia (→ 23/2/79).

Indian Ocean, 24 Dec 1777. Captain Cook discovers a group of islands which he names the Christmas Islands.

Westminster, 31 January 1778. Following the surrender of British forces at Saratoga last year, the prime minister, Lord North, tells King George of his desire to retire from government (→ 5/1778).

Europe, 17 June 1778. France declares war on Britain (→ 27/7).

North America, June 1778. British troops under General Clinton evacuate Philadelphia (→ 27/7).

London, 23 February 1779. Queen Charlotte gives birth to her 13th child, Octavius (→ 22/9/80).

London, summer 1779. George, the Prince of Wales, falls in love with Mary Hamilton, a lady at court who is six years his senior; he sends her a series of sentimental love letters (→ 3/12).

Gibraltar, 1779. William Henry, the third son of George III, aged 14, begins his naval career as an ordinary able-seaman, serving under Captain Robert Digby in the relief of Gibraltar (→ 24/8/81).

George puts faith in new prime minister

Lord North, the new prime minister.

Westminster, 28 January 1770
To the king's relief, 37-year-old Frederick, Lord North – chancellor for the past two years – has agreed to become prime minister. He succeeds the Duke of Grafton, who resigned over the Wilkes affair. In an age when good personal relations between crown and premier are paramount for effective government, George has so far been unlucky with his ministers – and political factionalism has been rife. North, a shrewd and cultivated man of immense charm, has known the king since boyhood and is thought to be the only minister able to command the confidence of both crown and Commons (→ 13/4/75).

British troops open fire on demonstrators

American troubles: British troops firing at demonstrators in Boston.

Boston, N America, 5 March 1770
The strained relations between King George and his American colonies took a turn for the worse today when five people were shot dead by British troops at the port of Boston. The incident, which is being described locally as a "massacre", occurred after a group of drunken Bostonians attacked soldiers guarding the customs house, causing them to open fire.

Troops were sent to Boston in 1768 to quell unrest caused by the Townshend Revenue Act of 1767, which imposed new customs duties on the American colonies. The act – which the new British prime minister, Lord North, is in the process of repealing – has led to an American campaign banning the importation of British goods.

There have been suggestions that the Boston massacre was deliberately provoked by the militant "Boston Sons of Liberty" in order to stir up popular feeling against the British presence (→ 3/1770).

King's power over ministers attacked

Burke, the author of the pamphlet.

England, April 1770
The king has come under implicit personal attack by Edmund Burke, the philosopher MP. Burke's pamphlet *Thoughts on the Causes of the Present Discontents*, published this month, defends the value of political parties as an obstacle to royal influence. Dissecting the Earl of Chatham's failed attempt to govern without a party, Burke condemns a system in which the success of a ministry depends on the crown's support. He argues that instability and political factionalism can only be avoided by party unity in both government and opposition.

King meets costs in duke's divorce case

London, November 1770
King George has been forced to find thousands of pounds to pay the damages and costs incurred by his brother Henry, the Duke of Cumberland, in a divorce case. Apart from the money – raised through an approach to the prime minister, Lord North – the king is worried about the impact that his 25-year-old brother's amorous exploits will have on the royal family's image.

Having embarked on a passionate affair with Lady Grosvenor earlier this year, Cumberland was accused by her husband of criminal conspiracy, found guilty and presented with a bill for £13,000. Not having the money himself, he applied to the king for help, promising repayment in 18 months.

George's first ten years bring him a baptism of fire

London, 25 October 1770
When George III acceded to the throne, ten years ago today, he was only 22 years old and had little experience of politics or world affairs. His first decade has been a baptism of fire.

At first George depended for advice and guidance on his idolised tutor, the Earl of Bute, whom he appointed prime minister in May 1762. But Bute proved weak and incompetent at the helm, lasting less than a year in office. Ever since then the king has been searching for a minister on whom he felt able wholly to rely. The ministries of Grenville, Rockingham, Chatham and Grafton brought crisis after crisis, intensified by the activities of John Wilkes. Although the king has often been accused of overreaching his powers, he has undoubtedly grown in political maturity, and the advent of Lord North promises a more settled future.

Among George's successes have been the 1763 Peace of Paris, ending seven years of war in Europe, and the achievement of a happy marriage with Queen Charlotte, by whom he already has seven children. However, troubles continue to fester at home, and dissent is mounting in the American colonies.

A fount of good things: George represented as a spring feeding a growth of artistic expression.

Princess Dowager, king's mother, dies

King George's mother, Augusta.

London, 8 February 1772

Augusta, the Princess Dowager of Wales, the king's mother, has died after a long illness, at the age of 52. Despite rumours that she wielded too much influence over her eldest son and criticism of her supposed interference in politics – she was a very close friend of Lord Bute – the princess was a pious and retiring woman, who lived in either London or Kew and desired no excessive involvement in her son's life. She grew more querulous and demanding as her illness worsened but remained resolute and brave to the end. The king and his family are expected to move into her White House at Kew (→ 13/2).

Kew to be a centre for botanical study

Kew, 1772

The gardens of the royal palace of Kew, known also as the White House, are to have a new role as the nation's centre of botanical research. Based on the collection of plants amassed by the late Frederick, the Prince of Wales, which was preserved and expanded by his widow, Augusta, the botanical gardens will be a place of both beauty and scientific study. The centre will be directed by Sir Joseph Banks, the leading scientist, among whose achievements has been his work with Captain James Cook during the explorer's voyage to the Pacific [*see report right*].

George wins veto on royal marriages

London, 24 March 1772

The Royal Marriages Act – largely written and wholly supported by King George – was passed by parliament today. With a few exceptions, it forbids any future royal marriages that have not been sanctioned by the monarch.

The act has become law within a few months of the king learning that his youngest surviving brother, Henry, the Duke of Cumberland, had married Ann Horton, a 27-year-old commoner – since when George has refused to have anything to do with them. The king explained his objection to such a marriage in a letter to another of his brothers, the Duke of Gloucester:

"In any country a prince marrying a subject is looked upon as dishonourable ... but here, where the crown is but too little respected, it must be big with the greatest mischiefs. Civil wars would by such measures be again coming in this country" (→ 13/9).

To the king's dismay, the Duke of Cumberland marries Ann Horton.

Captain James Cook claims Australia for the British crown

The king's territory: Captain Cook lands in Botany Bay, Australia.

Portsmouth, 12 July 1771

Captain James Cook returned to England today at the end of his expedition in search of the great southern continent, which began in 1768. The climax of the voyage came in the spring last year, when Cook claimed a distant land known as Australia for the British crown, naming Botany Bay, New South Wales and Port Jackson [*Sydney*]. Cook has also visited Tahiti and circumnavigated New Zealand.

While empire-builders such as Robert Clive have opened up the Indian subcontinent, that land is filled with political problems and international rivalries. Cook's hope is that Australia, an apparently virgin territory, will present no such difficulties (→ 13/7/72).

Exiled 'Bonnie Prince Charlie' finds a princess fit to be queen

Rome, 17 April 1772

Charles Stuart, otherwise known as Bonnie Prince Charlie, the 51-year-old pretender to the British throne, was married here today. His bride is Princess Louise of Stolberg-Geldern, a young aristo-crat in whose blood is mingled that of many of Europe's noblest families. The idea of marriage was fostered by the king of France, who promised Charles a pension of 40,000 crowns a year if he married a suitable woman. Charles's first choice was another Louise, the daughter of the Prince of Salm-Kyrburg; she was not enthusiastic. Instead he turned to this Louise, a sophisticated, self-possessed 19-year-old who is very happy to be a queen, even in name alone (→ 1774).

Duke tells king of his secret marriage

Windsor, 13 September 1772

Fully six years after the event took place, William Henry, the Duke of Gloucester, has finally informed his brother the king of his secret marriage to Maria, the dowager Lady Waldegrave, whom he had always promised not to marry. In a letter received by the king today the duke admitted that, since so many people were already aware of the marriage, the least he could do was formally explain the facts to his royal brother. The king is deeply hurt – not least because Gloucester sided with him against another ill-advised alliance, that of the Duke of Cumberland (→ 25/8/05).

Gloucester's secret bride: Maria.

Prince of Wales is at odds with father

Kew, 1773

The 11-year-old Prince of Wales, who could speak in formal company at the age of two, and who has been progressing in all branches of learning ever since, has become increasingly irked by his father's apparent refusal to acknowledge his growing maturity. Although the prince regularly fulfils duties which might tax an older person, the king seems determined to keep him a baby for ever. He is still dressed in baby clothes, albeit outsize ones, and is carefully sheltered from external influences. Despite the demands made on him, he remains tied to the nursery (→ 1779).

Censure of Clive supported by king

Westminster, 21 May 1773

Robert Clive, the 47-year-old architect of Britain's success in India, whose clever manipulations of the ruling princes have ensured that Britain rather than France has become the dominant political and commercial power in the subcontinent, has suffered a severe reversal of his fortunes: the passage of a motion of censure in the House of Commons – backed not just by the MPs but by King George himself.

The roots of the censure, in which Clive is condemned for promoting his own fortunes "to the dishonour and detriment of the state", lie both in Clive's own personality and in events that are ultimately beyond his control.

Clive's efforts to simplify the role of the East India Company, which runs Anglo-Indian trade, and to reduce the corruption that often underpins relations between the company's wealthy nabobs and the local princes are seen as hypocritical. Clive – who spent about 12 years in India, returning in 1767 – himself received substantial gifts.

More important is the effect of national politics on company profits. These have fallen, after years of boom, through the company's involvement in local princely wars. Clive, vilified by those who have lost money, has been made the scapegoat (→ 22/11/74).

Revolt threatens British rule in America

Boston colonists dump tea into the ocean in a well-orchestrated protest.

Boston, Mass., 16 December 1773

Hundreds of tea-chests were tossed overboard in Boston harbour today as furious American colonists brandishing axes, their faces disguised by coats of bronze paint, attacked three British ships that had brought a cargo of tea to the Massachusetts port. Some 90,000 pounds of tea were lost in the carefully-orchestrated raid, which followed a public protest meeting.

The "Boston Tea Party", as wags have called the incident, is the most dramatic protest so far against the loathed Tea Act passed by the parliament in London in October. The British government's intention was to give the East India Company a monopoly on tea imports to America and at the same time to under-cut the price of smuggled Dutch tea. Although the move made few headlines in Britain, it infuriated the colonists. The Tea Act was seen as a sinister plot – not simply an extension of the Townshend Revenue Act of 1767, which imposed the original duties on tea, but a means of extending government control over the colonies.

As part of the consequent agitation, tea merchants have been attacked and their merchandise boycotted. When three tea-carrying ships arrived at Boston late last month they were unable to unload. The "patriots" could not force them to leave, but the merchants dared not pay the duty owing. Now the stalemate is over, but the future looks grim (→ 20/5/74).

Royal architect publishes design manual

Architectural genius: Robert Adam.

London, 1773

The former royal architect Robert Adam, now in lucrative private practice, has published what promises to be an influential manual of architecture. In it Adam, who was in charge of the king's works from 1761 to 1769 (and was then succeeded by his brother James), has described his modifications to the popular Palladian style. To that rather severe tradition Adam has made variations both elegant and romantic. Drawing on a wide selection of Greek and Roman originals, he offers a style of interior decoration typified by his use of the oval, with lines of decoration in hard plaster, and for extra appeal painted panels in low relief.

Surveying the heights of fashion: a colourful caricature suggesting that a fashionable lady these days needs a brave man as her hairdresser if she wishes to appear adequately coiffured.

Stuart heir reported to have been born

Rome, 1774

Not only does Britain have a pretender to its throne – Charles Stuart – but, if rumour is to be believed, there is now a rival royal line. According to supporters of the Stuart cause, the Pretender's wife has given birth to a son.

The alleged birth has at least one eye-witness, although his account reads like some far-fetched melodrama. A young Scottish physician, Dr Beaton, was in Rome, visiting a church, when he was approached by a stranger who asked for his help in delivering a child. Bundled into a carriage, Beaton was driven to a *palazzo*, where he was blindfolded and led through a series of rooms into a great salon. Here the blindfold was removed and he found himself in a lavishly-furnished room, on one wall of which was a portrait of James Stuart, the "Old Pretender". Asking after the woman to whom he had been called, he was told that he was too late; the child had been born. He then met the new mother and a nurse, who was holding the baby. Another portrait, of Charles Stuart, made him sure that this was the child of the self-proclaimed Charles III.

Beaton claims that, a few days later, at Livorno, he saw the same nurse spiriting the baby onto a British ship. But, again, he appears to have been the only witness (→ 1783).

Royal critic is to be the new lord mayor

London, 8 October 1774

John Wilkes, the former radical politician, editor of the notorious *North Briton* and alleged author of the obscene *Essay on Woman*, has been elected to one of the nation's most conservative posts: lord mayor of London. The choice reflects London's prized independence. And while it is an ironic elevation for a man who for so long was the principal thorn in the side of king and parliament, it is also a tribute to his impact on contemporary politics. Wilkes has spearheaded agitation for a bill of rights and introduced into the cosy world of party rivalries a new force: militant public opinion (→ 29/11).

The new lord mayor: John Wilkes.

Clive of India dies by his own hand

Robert Clive: British ruler in India.

London, 22 November 1774

Robert Clive, once the embodiment of British rule in India, brought a tempestuous career to a halt today when he took his own life. He was a victim of depression and sickness, but above all of a broken heart – driven to suicide by a country that, rather than acknowledge his successes, preferred to condemn him for his alleged failings.

Clive gained many enemies by his campaign against corruption in India. In 1772 they had him investigated, and in May of the following year his behaviour was censured by parliament, which nevertheless paid tribute to his "great and meritorious services".

Buckingham House is transferred to the queen for life by an act of parliament

Buckingham House: here the Turkish ambassador pays a formal visit.

London, 1775

Buckingham House, built in 1702 for John Sheffield, the Duke of Buckingham, and bought in 1762 by King George for £28,000, has been given to the queen for life by act of parliament. In return she has handed over her residence Somerset House to the new Royal Academy of Arts. A superb building, it has a particularly fine staircase.

Buckingham House, now to be known as the Queen's House, was designed by William Winde and built on land known as the Mulberry Garden, once a walled garden planted with mulberry trees as part of James I's scheme to encourage silk production in England.

That scheme foundered, and the land became first a fashionable pleasure garden and then the site of Buckingham's new house – which, within weeks of its completion, was seen as "one of the great beauties of London", thanks not just to the building itself but also to its splendid view of St James's park (→ 1826).

Magnificent Royal Crescent built at Bath

Bath, 1775

The Royal Crescent, Bath's magnificent new terrace of palatial houses, has been completed. Designed by John Wood the Younger, its 30 houses, arranged in one "palace frontage" – a single design incorporating a number of residences – blend the formality of Palladian architecture with the needs of communal housing. Wood's father was one of the first town planners; he would work on the loose collection of different houses that made up a street or square, imposing on them a uniform design. Now his son has made his own modifications to this system, giving 30 householders a share in a superb new building and offering the city in which it stands a fine monument to architectural innovation.

A magnificent aspect: a 20th-century view of the Royal Crescent, Bath.

Americans attack George's 'tyranny'

George's sister, the queen of Denmark, dies in exile at 23

Celle, Germany, May 1775

The king's youngest sister, Queen Caroline Matilda of Denmark, has died in exile at the age of only 23. She had been arrested for her part in a political plot, and after a spell of imprisonment in Denmark she was banished to Celle, in her brother's Hanoverian kingdom, but forbidden to take her children.

Caroline was married at the age of 15 to a cousin, Christian VII of Denmark and Norway. He was a far from ideal husband, living a debauched life which left him diseased. Caroline bore him children but took a lover, the court physician Struensee. She also became involved in her lover's political schemes, and their collapse led in 1772 to her arrest and divorce.

The queen greatly missed her children and until her illness continued to intrigue for her restoration to the throne, seeking the help of George without success. The king sympathised with her distress and disapproved of Christian but wanted no part in any plot.

Cook claims new lands in the Pacific

Plymouth, 26 July 1775

James Cook has completed a second voyage of exploration in the southern seas to claim more lands for the crown of King George. In a voyage which began in 1772 Cook, the Yorkshire collier master who rose to be a master in the Royal Navy, has visited New Zealand and the smaller islands of Fiji and Tonga – each now adorned with the British flag.

The king's ministers are backing Cook's travels. In his first major voyage between 1768 and 1771 he became the first European to visit Australia. This time he headed further south to look for a new southern continent. He encountered instead the icefields of Antarctica, charting his experiences with characteristic attention to scientific detail. Next year he plans an attempt to sail round North America from the Pacific (→ 24/12/77).

The first days of independence: a statue of King George in New York is hauled down by a crowd of angry Americans.

New York, 10 July 1776

A gilt statue of King George was pulled down here today as American troops joined New Yorkers in celebrating the signing of their Declaration of Independence earlier this month. The statue on Bowling Green at the southern tip of Manhattan Island was an inevitable focus for American anger, given that Americans see the king as a "tyrant" [*see report below*]. Much of the Declaration of Independence signed in Philadelphia on 4 July consists of a detailed catalogue of his alleged crimes and failures.

But the rhetorical abuse and even the symbolic attack on the royal statue will matter less to the king and his ministers than the worsening situation they now face in what has become an open war of independence against the British crown.

The declaration asserts that the colonies now regard themselves as "free and independent states ... absolved from all allegiance to the British crown". And as independent states they vow to continue the fight for their freedom. After hostilities broke out last year, the British suffered reverses at Lexington and Concord and then a serious blow at Bunker Hill, in Massachusetts, where they lost a quarter of their force. This year has seen the Americans win Boston, while Britain is sending reinforcements from across the Atlantic (→ 8/1776).

A serious blow to British forces: the battle at Bunker Hill in June 1775.

America declares its independence

Philadelphia, 4 July 1776

The American Declaration of Independence, agreed here today, insists that "the history of the present king of Great Britain is a history of repeated injuries and usurpations, all having in direct object the establishment of an absolute tyranny over these states". The declaration proceeds to list an enormously long series of alleged undemocratic abuses by a man described as "totally unfit to be the ruler of a free people" (→ 10/7).

Tension mounts in Britain over war with America

King rejects a plea by premier to quit

Westminster, May 1778

Pessimistic about Britain's ability to fight the American war and depressed about his own ability to fulfil the duties of prime minister, Lord North has again asked the king's permission to resign. George has again refused, saying that to do so would be "at the hour of danger to desert me". The king has rejected several such requests in the past, but North has been particularly despondent in recent months, since the British surrender to the American rebels at Saratoga last October.

Although it seems cruel and unwise to leave a man in charge of the government who is sure that he cannot do the job, George can see no alternative. Despite his sense of inadequacy North is a commanding figure in the House of Commons, fighting off the attacks of Charles Fox and Edmund Burke and retaining the support of the independents.

The alternative would be for Fox to form a Whig ministry, which George fears would lead to British recognition of American independence. The king is confident that, despite reverses, Britain's position remains strong, and that the colonists are driven more by their grievances than by any passionate desire for self-rule. This seems to be the majority opinion in parliament and the country, and, despite his gloom, North has agreed not to resign until the king can settle on a satisfactory new administration (→21/6/79).

Lord North is shown as a false god on whose altar civil rights are sacrificed.

A disastrous surrender: the British general John Burgoyne submits at Saratoga.

France takes sides with rebel colonists

Ushant, France, 27 July 1778

British and French fleets have fought an indecisive engagement at Ushant, off the Brittany coast, as the dire consequences of "Gentleman Johnny" Burgoyne's surrender to the Americans at Saratoga last October have become clear. Realising that Britain might not win outright, the French formally entered the war on the side of the rebels last month. There are already French warships off the American coast, as well as in the Channel, and it is feared that Spain may follow suit.

Some people in Britain are coming to believe that the strain of holding on to the 13 states may be too much for an economy still paying the bills of the Seven Years' War, which ended in 1763. Command of the sea is vital but, with the king and Lord North determined to cut back on naval spending, the peace lobby grows stronger by the day.

Although the British still control New York City – Philadelphia was evacuated last month – the difficulties of providing reinforcements in the teeth of the French fleet may perhaps account for the poor morale in Britain's navy. The commander at today's battle, Sir Hugh Palliser, has quarrelled with his admiral, Keppel, over who was to blame for failure. However, as the war continues fitfully, peace envoys have been sent to try to find a settlement, short of independence, with the rebel congress (→12/5/80).

Royal children win financial settlement

Westminster, 1777

Parliament's vote of a civil-list settlement on the king's children may help the next generation of the ruling family to avoid the squabbles of the present. On George III's death, each of his sons is to receive £10,000 a year, and each daughter £6,000.

There is also an allowance for the children of his brother William, the Duke of Gloucester – the first sign of public reconciliation in the five years since the king found out about William's secret marriage to Maria Waldegrave. The discovery came soon after the Royal Marriages Act had forbidden any of the royal family to marry without the crown's consent.

The king's youngest surviving brother, Henry, the Duke of Cumberland – whose own happy marriage to Ann Horton, the daughter of an Irish politician, was also unapproved – is excluded from the family settlement since he has allied himself with the opposition.

Chatham collapses in House of Lords

Hayes, Middlesex, 11 May 1778

William Pitt, the first Earl of Chatham, died here today, a month after collapsing in the House of Lords as he spoke against negotiating with the Americans. He had sympathies with the rebels but became fervently warlike once it was clear that his old enemies the French would side with the colonists. Although there had been talk of bringing him back into government, he was already frail, and crippled by gout, when he rose to speak on 7 April. The effort was too much, and Britain's great war leader had to be carried out, his last speech unfinished.

A leading minister when George came to the throne, Chatham had been a key figure in political life for more than 40 years. Although they disagreed on many things, he and the king held the same view about American independence. Indeed, Chatham's last speech was an unequivocal condemnation of any "dismemberment of this ancient and most noble monarchy".

George exhorts cabinet to give stronger leadership, as American crisis intensifies

A perspective view of Gibraltar, which is now being besieged by the Spanish.

London, 21 June 1779

With confusion both in politics at home and in the prosecution of the war abroad, King George has taken the unprecedented step in his reign of summoning the cabinet to the Queen's House. His message is simple: Britain's problems stem as much from a failure of leadership as from any external threats and, if no one else is willing, then the king must drive the nation on.

Although his foes accuse him of trying to reconstruct a royal absolutism in the Stuart image, he has resolved to act within, and in defence of, "the beauty, excellence, and perfection of the British constitution". He has agreed to accept an enlargement of the ministry pro-vided that it will offer him "firmness and support" and an unanimous pledge to keep the empire intact. Charles Fox has indicated a willingness to join, but his price is the resignation of Lord North, while the Marquis of Rockingham and the Duke of Grafton have laid down terms that George has rejected as unwarranted "dictation".

The king said that he would sooner die "than suffer his dominions to be dismembered", and he is clearly trying to compensate for the lack of backbone and leadership shown by Lord North's government. But he also told ministers today that he has "never harboured a thought of injuring the constitution or abridging his people's liberties".

Courtly pleasures: among the guests at a splendid royal ball at Windsor is Georgiana, the extrovert Duchess of Devonshire (centre), a Whig supporter, who is thought to have caught the eye of the Prince of Wales.

Prince of Wales is captivated by actress

London, 3 December 1779

The Drury Lane theatre audience was entertained last night by the public spectacle of a prince falling in love with a shepherdess. The Prince of Wales was so openly entranced by the beauty of Mary Robinson – playing Perdita in a performance of Shakespeare's *The Winter's Tale* – that he stood and bowed to her as the curtain fell.

But while the "Florizel" in the romance is indeed the heir to the throne of England, "Perdita" has only the beauty of a princess, not the background. Mary Robinson was a protégée of David Garrick and made her début three year ago as Juliet. She is 21 to George's 17 and is to be seen parading in her carriage before every performance with a court of admirers. The prince has asked his friend Lord Malden to arrange an introduction.

Mary is the daughter of an American whaling captain and was born

Beautiful actress: Mary Robinson.

in Bristol. Garrick first offered her the part of Cordelia in his *King Lear*, but the start of her stage career was interrupted when she and her husband, Thomas Robinson, whom she married at 15, were jailed for debt along with their baby daughter (→ 12/1780).

The prince and Mrs Robinson represented as "Florizel" and "Perdita".

Two of royalty's favourite performers die

London, 2 February 1779

The death today of the composer William Boyce, Master of the King's Musick since 1757 and the principal organist of the Chapel Royal, has deprived the royal family of two favourite performers in quick succession. It follows the death less than a month ago of the great actor David Garrick, at the age of 61. Apart from their well-known devotion to music, both King George and Queen Charlotte are keen and regular theatre-goers and often saw Garrick on stage – he was the most versatile and magnetic of actors, equally at home in tragedy, comedy or farce.

George III
1760–1820

House of Hanover

London, 8 February 1780. Reformers led by Christopher Wyvill, a Yorkshire clergyman, petition parliament for economic and social reform.

North America, 12 May 1780. The town of Charleston and more than 5,000 Americans surrender to the British (→ 5/1780).

France, May 1780. Over 6,000 French troops will reinforce the American rebels against the British (→ 20/11).

London, 6 June 1780. As rioting continues, Newgate prison is destroyed and the inmates are freed (→ 8/6).

London, 8 June 1780. Lord George Gordon, the instigator of the recent riots, is arrested on a charge of treason (→ 9/6).

Windsor, 22 September 1780. Queen Charlotte gives birth to her 14th child, Alfred (→ 20/8/82).

Britain, 20 November 1780. Anglo-Dutch relations collapse and war breaks out on the discovery that the Dutch have been supplying French and Spanish arms to American rebels through Dutch Caribbean bases (→ 9/5/81).

North America, 9 May 1781. Pensacola, the last British base in western Florida, falls into Spanish hands (→ 24/8).

New York, 24 August 1781. The *Prince George* arrives in Sandy Hook; on board is Ordinary Seaman Prince William, the third son of George III (→ 5/9).

North America, 5 Sept 1781. British naval forces are defeated by the French in a battle in Chesapeake Bay (→ 19/10).

Virginia, 19 October 1781. General Charles Cornwallis, the British

commander in Virginia, surrenders to the American force under General George Washington at Yorktown (→ 25/11).

London, 21 January 1782. King George refuses to accept the independence of America (→ 27/2).

Mediterranean, 5 February 1782. The British garrison in Minorca surrenders to the Spanish.

Westminster, 27 February 1782. The Commons, despite the feelings of George, vote against continuing the war in America (→ 28/2).

Westminster, 28 Feb 1782. Lord North introduces a bill to make peace with the colonies (→ 20/3).

Westminster, 20 March 1782. After being defeated by a Commons vote over the American war at the end of last month, Lord North resigns as prime minister (→ 1/4).

Westminster, 27 March 1782. Charles Fox is appointed as secretary of state (→ 14/7).

Britain/France, 7 May 1782. Anglo-French talks begin following the French defeat in the West Indies (→ 20/1/83).

Windsor, 20 August 1782. Prince Alfred, aged almost two, the youngest son of King George and Queen Charlotte, dies (→ 3/5/83).

London, 1782. Prince William, the third son of the king, receives the Order of the Garter (→ 20/5/89).

Europe, 20 January 1783. Britain makes peace with Spain and France (→ 3/9).

Britain, 4 February 1783. Britain proclaims an end to hostilities in America (→ 3/9).

London, 3 May 1783. Prince Octavius, aged four, dies (→ 7/8/83).

Windsor, 7 August 1783. Queen Charlotte gives birth to her 15th child, Amelia (→ 26/10/93).

Sussex, September 1783. The Prince of Wales visits his uncle, the Duke of Cumberland, and samples the delights of the small fishing town of Brighton (→ 11/11).

Westminster, 11 November 1783. The Prince of Wales, who came of age last August, takes his seat in the House of Lords.

Rome, 1783. A formal separation is arranged for Charles Edward Stuart, the pretender to the British throne, and his wife, Louise, who left him three years ago after a drunken attack (→ 30/1/88).

Brighton, 13 July 1784. The Prince of Wales sends Louis Weltje, a member of his household, to find a house for him in the increasingly popular resort (→ 2/9).

London, 2 September 1784. George forbids the Prince of Wales to leave the country, suspecting that he intends to go to France in order to join Mrs Maria Fitzherbert, his latest love (→ 5/1/85).

London, 29 November 1784. Frederick, the second son of King George III, is made Duke of York and Albany (→ 19/11/91).

Hanover, 1784. Prince Edward, George III's fourth son, arrives at Lüneberg to begin his military training (→ 10/5/96).

London, 5 January 1785. The Prince of Wales amasses huge gambling debts, estimated at £150,000 (→ 15/12).

London, 31 October 1786. Princess Amelia, an aunt of George III, dies aged 75.

Westminster, 30 April 1787. Charles Fox assures the Commons

that the Prince of Wales is not married to the Catholic Mrs Maria Fitzherbert (→ 4/1787).

Brighton, 6 July 1787. The Prince of Wales returns to his new seaside home with his finances now in order (→ 1788).

Europe, 13 August 1788. The Triple Alliance is agreed between Britain, Prussia and the Batavian Republic, as a counterweight to the combined power of France, the Holy Roman Empire and Russia.

Windsor, 10 November 1788. George, who is suffering from a serious undiagnosed illness, has fallen into a coma (→ 30/11).

Kew, 3 December 1788. George is moved to Kew palace as rumours intensify about the strange illness afflicting the king (→ 15/1/89).

Kew, 15 January 1789. The king's condition is reported to be improving slowly (→ 23/4).

Westminster, February 1789. William Pitt, the prime minister, considers the outline of a bill which would make the Prince of Wales regent during the incapacity through illness of the king (→ 1789).

London, 20 May 1789. Prince William is made Duke of Clarence and St Andrews and Earl of Munster (→ 1790).

France, June 1789. Massive unrest results in an overthrow of the royal family. A national assembly is established (→ 14/7).

Dorset, June 1789. The king, the queen and their three eldest daughters travel to the seaside at Weymouth to promote the king's recovery (→ 9/1789).

Paris, 14 July 1789. The Bastille, the largest prison in Paris, is stormed by rebels (→ 21/6/91).

King sends in troops to curb riots

London, 9 June 1780

Some 500 people have been killed or injured, five jails sacked and scores of Catholic houses and chapels burnt down in a week of the worst riots that London has ever seen. Calm was finally restored today after King George took personal charge of the privy council and ordered troops to move in and quell the unrest. Impatient with the indecision of the civil authorities, the king told the council two days ago that, if need be, he himself would lead the guards into action.

The riots were instigated by Lord George Gordon, a 29-year-old Wiltshire MP and the head of an ardent Protestant organisation. On 2 June Gordon led a procession to parliament to protest against the 1778 Catholic Relief Act, which repealed some of the penal laws against Catholics and was alleged to have increased Catholic influence. Racing in and out of the House of Commons, one moment addressing MPs, the next haran-

Soldiers take control: the "Gordon riots" are finally brought to an end.

guing the "no popery" fanatics outside, Gordon created a frenzy of excitement. The crowd tore across London, looting and burning. The mayhem continued for five days, with magistrates paralysed by the

confusion. Then the king stepped in, saying: "The tumult must be got the better of ... examples must be made." The uproar swiftly subsided when soldiers emerged onto the streets and opened fire.

MPs condemn excessive powers of crown

London, 11 April 1780

Lord North has offered to resign following parliament's verdict that "The influence of the crown has increased, is increasing, and ought to be diminished". The motion was passed five days ago by 233 votes to 215. Urging his prime minister to stay in office, King George insisted that the censure was levelled not at

North but at himself. Indeed, the king's personality and behaviour have increasingly come under political scrutiny, as parliament agitates to end the war in America in the face of royal opposition. Ironically, however, the crown's influence on government is demonstrably less today than it was when the king came to the throne (→1/4/82).

The king rides in procession to parliament, where his power has been attacked.

Deep religious faith is key to king's life

London, December 1780

Frederick, the Duke of York, King George's second son, left England for Hanover this month to complete his military training. Before he set out his father gave him a bible, saying: "I trust you will every morning and evening read in this book, and I am convinced you will soon feel the comfort I do from that constant practice."

The king's strict observance of religious custom reflects an unshakeable trust in divine providence – one of the key influences in his life. Most mornings he attends a private chapel service, and takes Holy Communion 12 times a year.

The king is no religious bigot, however. Bound by his coronation oath to maintain the Church of England's privileges, he has shown no desire to persecute dissenters or Roman Catholics – or to make their situation any easier. He believes that, like the crown or parliament, the Church of England should be kept intact as part of the established constitution (→8/8/86).

Brief liaison lands Prince of Wales in 'shameful scrape'

London, December 1780

Determined to keep the Prince of Wales on a tight reign, the king has written to his eldest son explaining the behaviour expected of him now that he has reached the age of 18. The prince, whose birthday was on 12 August, has been given his own apartments at Windsor castle but has been told to obey certain rules about how he spends his time. "In the exalted station you are placed in," stresses the king, "every step is of consequence, and your future character will greatly depend in the world on the propriety of your conduct at the present period." The letter springs from George's grow-

The Prince of Wales: now aged 18.

ing exasperation with his son's irresponsibility. He is particularly angry at present about what he calls the prince's "shameful scrape" with the actress Mary Robinson.

Their brief liaison ended in fiasco earlier this year, with her demanding a generous financial settlement for the return of compromising correspondence. To his embarrassment, the king had to approach Lord North, the prime minister, for the money to pay off the blackmailing actress. While taking a firm line on the prince's profligacy and fondness for extravagant living, King George is keen to forge closer relations with his son and heir. "I wish more and more to have you as a friend," he writes, "and in that light to guide you, rather than with the authority of a parent" (→9/1783).

British troops surrender

Military disaster: Cornwallis surrenders to the Americans at Yorktown.

London, 25 November 1781
Three weeks ago King George III was in a resolute mood over the war in America, telling the prime minister, Lord North, that he had "the greatest confidence" in his armed forces. Little did he know that General Cornwallis, the British second-in-command, had already surrendered with most of his army to General George Washington at Yorktown in Virginia.

Reports of the humiliation on 19 October arrived in London today; Lord North is said to have taken the news "like a ball in the breast". Events in America seemed to be going in Britain's favour after the victories last year in Carolina. But although Generals Clinton and Cornwallis won battles they lacked

the resources to follow them up, and their supply and communication lines were constantly harassed by American guerrillas. Then, in September, Britain's control of the sea passed to the rebels' French allies after the Royal Navy's defeat at Chesapeake Bay. Cornwallis, besieged in Yorktown by Washington and the French on land and the French navy at sea, stood little chance.

As Cornwallis signed the surrender a band played, aptly, "The World Turned Upside Down". But despite the defeat and mounting calls at home for peace, the king detests the idea of American independence. Optimistically, he has told North that "a good end may yet be had to this war" (→ 21/1/82).

King forced to accept successor to North

Westminster, 1 April 1782
A reluctant George today handed the seals of office to a new prime minister, the Marquis of Rockingham, the leader of the opposition. The move follows the resignation of Lord North on 20 March.

After Yorktown North planned to scale down the American war, but in February the Commons passed an opposition motion to end offensive fighting in America; North only narrowly survived a vote of no confidence and decided that his time was up, advising the king not to oppose "the deliberate resolution of the House of Commons". George was "drove to the wall", as he said, but there was no viable alternative to Rockingham and his ally Fox, the arch-enemy of royal prerogative. George takes some

The Marquis of Rockingham.

comfort from the fact that Rockingham needs the support of Lord Shelburne, who is more sympathetic to the king and becomes number three in the new cabinet (→ 14/7).

Earl of Shelburne takes over as premier

Taking office: Lord Shelburne.

Westminster, 14 July 1782
Lord Shelburne met the king today to take office as prime minister, following the death from influenza of the Marquis of Rockingham on 1 July. Rockingham's government, split by old feuds and America, did not long outlive him. Fox said that American independence should be unconditional, while Shelburne said it should be part of a general peace; Shelburne won the day, and Fox, isolated, resigned. The king's new cabinet includes William Pitt, the brilliant 23-year-old son of the late Earl of Chatham (→ 2/4).

Irish call for end to Westminster's rule

Dublin, 16 February 1782
Henry Grattan, the leader of the Irish Parliament, today called for an end to Westminster's dominance of Irish affairs. The move comes as the climax of a movement for the legislative and judicial independence of Ireland, which has grown over the last five years. Grattan declared last year that only the king and the Irish – Protestant – Parliament could "enact laws to bind Ireland". With memories of America fresh in everyone's mind, the king and his government seem likely to come to some arrangement.

Royal Navy secures Caribbean position

West Indies, 12 April 1782
The Royal Navy has pulled off a spectacular victory over the French near The Saints, the small islands between Guadeloupe and Dominica. After an 11-hour battle, Admirals Rodney and Hood have captured the French naval commander, the Comte de Grasse, with seven ships and scattered the rest of his fleet. The victory has secured Britain's position in the Caribbean and weakened France's bargaining power in the talks to end the war with America and its allies, which are expected to begin soon (→ 7/5).

King appoints Herschel astronomer-royal

Windsor, 25 May 1782
King George's interest in science was boosted today when he received the astronomer William Herschel at Windsor castle. Herschel, born in 1738 in Hanover, came to England in 1757 with his equally brilliant sister and colleague Caroline. He caused a sensation last year by discovering a new planet, Uranus. The king means to make Herschel astronomer-royal; he will get a pension of £200 a year and a commission to build six telescopes for the king's new observatory at Windsor. One of them will, at 40 feet (12 metres) long, be the biggest in the world.

The 40-foot telescope at Windsor.

George embroiled in political crises

Charles James Fox: unfairly represented here as a repellent man.

Humiliated king contemplates abdication

Westminster, 2 April 1783
King George today accepted a new ministry headed by the most unlikely bedfellows imaginable: Charles James Fox, the most inveterate opponent of the king's power and policies, and Lord North, premier and unshakeable king's man for 12 years. The king is so crushed by what he sees as a massive political humiliation that he is on the verge of quitting England for Hanover.

It was on 14 February that Fox and North made their unlikely pact, united by their dislike of Lord Shelburne. George strove to find an alternative to this "infamous coali-

tion" but in the end had to face the fact that no one else could command a majority of the Commons. In the new cabinet the first lord of the treasury and formal prime minister is the Duke of Portland, with North as home secretary and Fox, the dominant personality and effective premier, at the foreign office.

In a draft letter to the Prince of Wales the king says that abdication is the "one step to take without the destruction of my principles and honour". Once again he feels that his interests have fallen victim to "parties", the factionalism which he hates in British politics (→ 19/12).

Firebrand MP despises crown influence

Westminster, 1783
According to Charles James Fox, "one grand evil" is the source of Britain's political woes: "the influence of the crown". The brilliant firebrand MP for Westminster was born in 1749, the son of Henry Fox,

the first Baron Holland. Loathed by the king for his "democratical" leanings, the affable Fox is a feared opponent whose relish for the hurly-burly of politics is matched only by his fondness for wine, women and the gaming table.

Fox and North are dismissed by king

Westminster, 19 December 1783
King George has pulled off a political coup and engineered the fall of the Fox-North coalition after less than nine months in office. Today the 24-year-old William Pitt took over as the king's first lord of the treasury and Britain's youngest ever prime minister.

Relations between the king and the Whig-led coalition were generally frosty. George was especially furious that Fox and Portland, previously eager to curb royal expenditure, proposed to vote £100,000 – twice his recommendation – to the Prince of Wales, with whom his relations have chilled recently.

The government's India Bill gave the king his chance to act. The bill proposed to reform the government of India by replacing the East India Company with appointed commissioners. George saw the bill as a move to increase the Whigs' power of patronage and undermine that of the crown. The bill passed the Commons last week, but before it went to the Lords the king lobbied waverers and had it put about that anyone voting for it "would be considered by him as his enemy". His tactic worked: the Lords rejected the bill two days ago. Once assured that Pitt would take over, George despatched a terse note to North asking him and Fox to send back their seals of office.

In power at 24: Pitt the Younger.

Canada and India to remain British in Versailles treaty

Versailles, 3 September 1783
The United States of America took its place among the world's free nations today when Britain and its former adversaries in the American war signed a peace treaty at Versailles, near Paris. A separate peace between Britain and the USA was signed in Paris at the same time.

Apart from the loss of the 13 former colonies Britain has not done too badly under the treaty, largely owing to naval successes last year. France gains Senegal and Tobago, and Spain gets Florida and Minorca, but Britain remains supreme in Canada, India and the West Indies, and retains Gibraltar.

King George has accepted American independence with a heavy heart, but refuses to blame himself, as he told Lord Shelburne last year. He added, with an uncharacteristic spitefulness, that "knavery seems to be so much the striking feature" of the Americans "that it may not in the end be an evil that they become alien to this kingdom" (→ 1/6/85).

Prince's new home to be Carlton House

London, 11 November 1783
Work has begun on refurbishing Carlton House in London's west end, the new home of the Prince of Wales, who turned 21 this year and took his seat in the House of Lords today. Built at the beginning of the century by Henry, Lord Carlton, the house was bought in 1732 by an earlier Prince of Wales, Frederick, the present king's father.

Since Frederick's widow, Augusta, died in 1772 the building has fallen into disrepair. The king has granted it to his son on condition that he undertakes "all repairs, taxes and keeping of the garden". The prince intends to refurbish the rather mediocre house in accordance with the extravagant tastes which have caused a rift between the pleasure-seeking prince and his sober, upright father. The refurbishment will include new wings, a colonnaded portico and a "Chinese" drawing-room (→ 3/1784).

▷

353

Prince of Wales hosts great banquet and ball for London society at Carlton House

London, March 1784

The Prince of Wales threw a magnificent, glittering ball this month to mark the end of the first stage of the refurbishment of Carlton House, his new home off Pall Mall in St James's. The conversion, by the architect Henry Holland, is turning the house into one of Europe's most opulent, and expensive, palaces, with its colonnaded hall, "Chinese" drawing room, planned "Gothick" conservatory, exquisite furniture and old-master paintings.

The prince's extravagance and wild living are a constant worry to his sober-minded father, and the two have barely been on speaking terms for months, especially since the prince became involved with members of the opposition like Fox and the playwright-MP Sheridan. He is vain, goes to church rarely, eats too much, spends too much and cultivates the company of actors, dandies and whores. Sometimes he drinks for days on end and has to take to his bed to recover.

But when he is not inebriated few can resist the amiable prince's warmth, charm, wit and mimicry – his impersonations of ageing German relatives cause particular mirth. And while he loves the bottle, he is also an intelligent and perceptive lover of the arts (→ 13/7).

A 19th-century view of Carlton House, showing the prince's refurbishments.

King's Indian lands beset by corruption

Westminster, July 1784

The prime minister, William Pitt, has introduced a bill to reform the government of India by the East India Company. The bill comes amid growing concern that King George's Indian domains are being mismanaged by a private trading company that is becoming increasingly corrupt and by its governor-general, Warren Hastings.

Pitt's India Bill will create a board of six privy councillors, appointed by the king, to oversee the company's affairs. Last year's India Bill – the defeat of which brought down the Fox-North ministry – was similar but proposed a government-appointed board. The king approved of that bill in principle but saw it, probably correctly, as a threat to his powers of patronage (→ 4/1785).

Political reforms opposed by George

Westminster, April 1785

The king has deftly thwarted a bid by his prime minister, Pitt, to bring in limited parliamentary reform. Pitt's idea was to take seats from 72 small or "decayed" boroughs – like Old Sarum in Wiltshire, deserted for centuries but still with two MPs – and give them to London and under-represented counties. Also, some new electors would have been created by giving the vote to certain types of landholders.

Limited though the bill was, it was too much for the king. But he was anxious not to cause another political crisis, so he did not openly oppose the measure but discreetly made his views plain. Pitt did not insist on the king's backing, so the bill's defeat – by 248 to 174 – entailed no rift between minister and monarch.

George wins big vote of popular support

The Duchess of Devonshire has her own way of winning votes for Fox.

Westminster, 18 May 1784

A new parliament assembled today following last month's general election which gave the prime minister, William Pitt, a Commons majority of more than a hundred and temporarily silenced Charles Fox and his supporters. The election is a triumph for King George, who has hailed the result as an end to the factionalism which has dominated British politics for two years and as a clear vote in favour of unified government under the crown.

Although the old parliament still had three of its full seven years to run, the king was keen to go to the polls almost as soon as Pitt was installed last December, to set the seal on his outmanoeuvring and dismissal of the Fox-North ministry. Pitt advised against it, because a snap election would have left little time to renew annual measures such as the Mutiny Act, due early in the spring. A delay was also needed to set in motion the elaborate system of patronage (and plain bribery) operated by governments to win the many Commons' seats in the control of a few individuals.

Opposition leaders made last-ditch attempts to defeat the government, but to no avail. People in and out of Westminster had clearly grown weary of shortlived ministries and constant political feuding; the king had won the day (→ 7/1784).

King receives first American ambassador

George meets the American envoy.

London, 1 June 1785

King George today faced an occasion that he had been putting off for two years: meeting the first ambassador to the Court of St James's from the United States of America. He was the more nervous as the envoy, John Adams, presented his credentials, but in the event Adams, who signed the Declaration of Independence, was conciliatory. The king was frank but gracious in return, telling Adams: "I was the last to consent to the separation; but the separation having been made and having become inevitable, I have always said, as I say now, that I would be the first to meet the friendship of the United States as an independent power."

Prince marries in secret

London, 15 December 1785

The Prince of Wales has secretly married Maria Fitzherbert, a Catholic widow six years his senior. In the presence of two witnesses, the ceremony was performed at Mrs Fitzherbert's house in Park Street, Mayfair, by John Burt, a young Anglican curate released from the Fleet prison after the prince had promised him £500 to expunge his debts. Although the prince's infatuation has been the subject of drawing-room gossip for several months, the prince wrote to Charles Fox only a few days ago to assure him that he would not embark on a marriage which would bar him from succeeding to the throne.

Mrs Fitzherbert is the convent-educated eldest daughter of Walter Smythe, a northern Catholic. The prince met her in Lady Anne Lindsay's box at the opera. Widowed for the second time in Nice, she had just returned to London, where her grace of manner won her admirers. The prince fell madly in love, but she refused to become his mistress.

Disconcerted by the prince's passion, Mrs Fitzherbert was only dissuaded from leaving the country when the prince stabbed himself. After agreeing to marry him she nonetheless spent a year on the continent, bombarded with royal love letters, until her return to England last month (→ 30/4/87).

The newly-weds: a satire on the prince's marriage to Mrs Fitzherbert.

George survives assassination attempt

An incident in St James's: Margaret Nicholson tries to stab King George.

Kew, 8 August 1786

The king and queen were rapturously received here today, six days after the failure of an assassination attempt. For the past few days people have been pouring into Windsor to pay their respects to King George, the first Hanoverian to have won the deep affection of his people. Today the local populace filled Kew Green, and the lame, old, blind and sick lined up in their Sunday best as the royal carriage passed. Several choruses of *God save the King* were followed by loud huzzas.

It was at St James's that the king was alighting from his horse for a reception when a woman, later identified as Margaret Nicholson, tried to stab him. As his guards and attendants seized her, the king cried: "The poor creature is mad! Do not hurt her! She has not hurt me!" Having reassured the crowds, the king went into the palace and received his guests.

King George, an upright, honest Briton who has never seen Hanover, has always been popular in the provinces, although he rarely travels far from the capital. Londoners had their reservations early in the reign – perhaps because they mistrusted George's mentor, the Scotsman Bute – but the capital has now taken the king to its heart. In recent decades, evangelicals from the upper and middle classes, and Methodists among the lower classes have guided a revolution in behaviour. A nation with a moral conscience wants a decent monarch like King George (→ 11/1787).

Debts force prince's move to Brighton

Brighton, April 1787

The Prince of Wales moved here temporarily last year with Mrs Fitzherbert, to a farmhouse on the east side of the fashionable Steine thoroughfare. The move was meant to cut the prince's spending – he has formidable debts – and to enable him to escape the austerity of the king's court. Work is now in hand to replace the farmhouse with a new royal residence, for more frequent habitation: a marine pavilion in Graeco-Roman style, topped by a domed rotunda. The

prince first visited Brighton in 1783 to stay with his uncle, the Duke of Cumberland. He likes walking, riding out with staghounds, swimming in the sea and attending horse-races. On a recent visit he pursued a pretty girl whom he saw on the beach, and word got round of the prince's roving eye. The North Street theatre and balls at the Castle Inn offer evening entertainment, but there is less opportunity for the prince to lose money gambling, as he often did in London (→ 5/1587).

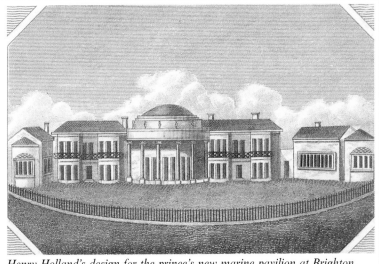

Henry Holland's design for the prince's new marine pavilion at Brighton.

Scandal mounts over prince's debts

London, May 1787
The Prince of Wales has been to see the king and queen to assure them of his intention not to incur any further debts. For the past few years the prince's extravagance has been the source of growing acrimony between father and son. It has also concerned parliament, which has agreed to grant him an additional £10,000 a year, to pay £161,000 towards his debts, and to put £60,000 towards the completion of Carlton House.

George Hotham, the prince's treasurer, discovered in October 1784 that he had commissioned work on Carlton House without any regard to cost and was in debt to his builder, upholsterer, jeweller and tailor. The maintenance of his stables alone was accounting for £31,000 a year, out of annual income from all sources of £50,000. It took Hotham another two years to work out the full scale of the prince's indebtedness. By the end of

The Prince of Wales (in brown) multiplies his problems at the gaming table.

last year the heir to the throne's debts amounted to £270,000, more than a quarter of the annual civil expenditure of the realm, and he was overspending at a rate of around £80,000 a year. The current financial settlement was reach-

ed after Charles James Fox told MPs at the end of last month that rumours of the prince's marriage to Maria Fitzherbert were untrue, insisting that he had the prince's "direct authority" for this declaration (→ 6/7).

Royal proclamation against vice and immorality published

London, November 1787
A movement to restore moral rectitude appears to be sweeping the nation, set off by a royal proclamation against vice and immorality. Persuaded of its necessity by John Moore, the archbishop of Canterbury, and other leading churchmen and politicians, King George – who is convinced that many of the troubles of his reign spring from

profligate behaviour – issued the proclamation on 1 June. Copies were sent to the sheriff of every county and to mayors, accompanied by letters from Lord Sydney, the home secretary, urging immediate and vigorous compliance with the king's wishes. The publication of the order led to a frenzy of activity among magistrates. The royal edict has been followed this

month by the foundation of a society dedicated to the reformation of manners. Known as the Proclamation Society, it is the brainchild of William Wilberforce, the MP for Yorkshire and a friend of William Pitt, the prime minister. As one of its campaigns to improve the nation's morals, the organisation aims to launch an attack on the pornography industry.

King supports new methods of farming

London, 1787
King George has contributed two letters to Arthur Young's *Annals of Agriculture* under the name of Ralph Robinson (one of his shepherds at Windsor). As part of his passion for agriculture, the king has been a keen reader of the *Annals* since they began publication three years ago, edited by the foremost exponent of the new farming methods. In his letters, the king praises husbandry that "unites the system of continued pasture with cultivation" (→ 1795).

Legendary Stuart figurehead dies in Rome, at age of 67

Rome, 30 January 1788
Charles Edward Stuart, known as the "Young Pretender", has died in the splendour of the Palazzo Muti, a sad, bloated man of 67. The man who once struck terror into the English as "Bonnie Prince Charlie", leader of the '45 rebellion, has done nothing for the past 42 years but live on memories and brandy. His death, on the anniversary of his great-grandfather Charles I's execution, brings down the curtain on the Stuart legend. Like a relic from another age Charles has held court here, cosseted by his daughter Charlotte, periodically revived, then depressed by thoughts of his ill-fated campaigns.

"Prince Charlie" earlier in life.

Prince of Wales is first past the post in the Epsom Derby

Racing at Epsom, where the Prince of Wales has this year won the Derby.

Epsom, 1788
The Prince of Wales's victory in the Derby this year has given a large boost to horse-racing as a national sport. There are rules and a code of conduct, which prevent racing from being simply a betting business. Both the Prince of Wales and the Duke of York maintain racing stables. The king enjoys watching the races at Epsom and Ascot, and has given a 100-guinea prize for horses hunted with his hounds. He does not go to Newmarket, where the stakes are high and the practices dubious. The queen dislikes the sport intensely (→ 1789).

King's alarming bouts of illness mystify his doctors

George seeks cure at Cheltenham spa

Cheltenham, July 1788

The king is taking the waters here after what he described to William Pitt, his prime minister, as "a pretty smart bilious attack". He has been seriously ill twice before, in 1762 and 1765, when he suffered violent chest pains. This time Sir George Baker, the king's doctor, prescribed rest at Kew, but when the illness persisted he recommended a visit to Cheltenham.

Bays Hill Lodge is a charming country house, and the king seems to be in much better spirits without the courtly routine and pressures of life in London. He takes the waters early, rides for several hours – contrary to the doctor's orders – and sits down to dinner at four. After dinner the king and queen and their daughters take a public stroll. The royal family went to Worcester for a performance of Handel's *Messiah* and are visiting several country houses in the vicinity (→ 10/11).

Keeper of asylum solicited for advice

Kew, December 1788

The king has been moved here from Windsor on account of another alarming bout of illness which appears to have unbalanced his mind. His usual doctors have failed to find a cure for his fits, and the Reverend Francis Willis, who runs a private asylum in Lincolnshire, has been called in. The king has been talking incessantly, complaining of mist before the eyes, and behaving irrationally – sometimes violently. On a recent outing in Windsor great park he was seen in deep conversation with an oak tree.

Willis is not a qualified doctor and is distrusted by others who have tended the king. But he alone has promised a cure, and he has the confidence of the queen, who has been sorely upset by her husband's change of character. The Prince of Wales has unofficially taken over the sovereign's role, summoning Pitt to Windsor (→ 3/12).

A humorous view of the king at Cheltenham, with his wife and daughters.

The king's dissolute sons shown bursting into their father's sick-room.

The service of thanksgiving for King George's recovery, at St Paul's.

Service celebrates the king's recovery

London, 23 April 1789

Amid great rejoicing, the king attended a service of thanksgiving at St Paul's today for his recovery. Public buildings were decorated, and people put candles and crowns in their windows; banners proclaimed "God save the King". The king and Pitt, his prime minister, were loudly cheered, whereas boos and hisses greeted Fox, other prominent Whigs and the Prince of Wales. The king's sons were said to have chewed biscuits rudely during the service (→ 6/1789).

George recuperates on Dorset coast

Weymouth, September 1789

Accompanied by the queen and three of his daughters, the king has spent the past three months here recuperating from his illness. The royal family stayed at a house lent to them by the Duke of Gloucester. On their way here they were acclaimed in every village, and when the king took his first sea dip a hidden band struck up *God save the King*. A frigate was moored in the bay for the family's use, and they made excursions to Plymouth and other towns (→ 11/3/01).

King's sons take out further loans

Westminster, 1789

Abortive attempts by Charles Fox and his fellow Whigs to make provisions for the Prince of Wales to assume the regency – should it become necessary – have brought renewed public criticisms of the prince's extravagance. When he and his brother, the Duke of York, were at Kew they angered the queen by removing items of jewellery and money, which she accused them of using to pay off debts. The brothers have now taken out new loans against repayment when the king dies (→ 11/1791).

George III
1760–1820

House
of
Hanover

London, 21 January 1790. George's coach is stoned by a madman while the king is travelling to the opening of parliament.

India, 5 May 1790. General George Harris seizes Seringapatam. With the fall of Bangalore to General Cornwallis in March, the British now control most of southern India.

Canada, May 1790. William, the Duke of Clarence, is summoned back to the navy from his retirement in Richmond to captain the *Valiant* (→ 12/1790).

London, 18 September 1790. The king's brother Prince Henry, the Duke of Cumberland, dies at the age of 44 (→ 9/1790).

London, December 1790. William, the Duke of Clarence, the king's third son, is appointed rear-admiral and his active naval career ends (→ 7/1793).

London, 2 March 1791. John Wesley, the minister who founded the Methodist movement, dies.

France, 21 June 1791. King Louis XVI and his family are arrested at Varennes, fleeing from the mob in Paris (→ 21/1/92).

Belfast, 14 October 1791. The Society of United Irishmen is founded by a Protestant, Theobald Wolfe Tone; its main aims are to achieve religious equality and reform (→ 1793).

Paris, 21 January 1972. Revolutionaries execute King Louis XVI (→ 13/12/92).

London, 18 February 1792. Sir Joshua Reynolds, the first president of the Royal Academy, dies.

West Indies, 14 April 1792. The British seize control of the island of Tobago.

Brighton, June 1792. The Prince of Wales appears more devoted than ever to his secret wife, Maria Fitzherbert (→ 1/1793).

France, 19 September 1792. Thomas Paine, who fled from England after the publication of his book *The Rights of Man*, which supported the French Revolution, arrives in France.

Westminster, 13 December 1792. Parliament votes to support William Pitt's preparations for war with France (→ 1/2/93).

London, January 1793. The Prince of Wales is appointed colonel commandant of the 10th Regiment of Light Dragoons (→ 24/8/94).

London, 26 October 1793. Queen Charlotte, despite her allowance from the civil list of £58,000, falls into debt (→ 5/1801).

Ireland, 1793. The Catholic Relief Act is passed, removing some of the restrictions on Roman Catholics in education, marriage and professional life.→

London, January 1794. The actress Dorothea Jordan gives birth to a son, George Fitzclarence, the illegitimate son of William, the Duke of Clarence (→ 4/1794).

London, April 1794. The Duke of Clarence is appointed vice-admiral in the Royal Navy (→ 1/1797).

Germany, 28 November 1794. Lord Malmesbury, the British envoy, arrives to begin discussions for a marriage between the Prince of Wales and Princess Caroline, the daughter of Duke Charles of Brunswick (→ 5/4/95).

Greenwich, 5 April 1795. Following Princess Caroline of Brunswick's arrival in England, she is met by the Countess of Jersey, a mistress of the Prince of Wales,

who has been chosen as Caroline's lady of the bedchamber by Queen Charlotte (→ 8/4).

Westminster, 30 May 1795. Parliament makes a contribution to the huge debts of the bankrupt Prince of Wales in view of his marriage (→ 7/1/96).

Westminster, November 1795. Following the attack on the king's coach last month, and in fear of pro-French Jacobite agitation, parliament extends the treason laws (→ 1/2/96).

London, 7 January 1796. Despite the marital problems of the Prince and Princess of Wales, the prince is overjoyed at the birth of his first child, a daughter to be called Charlotte (→ 24/5).

London, 1 February 1796. As rebellion continues in Europe anti-royal feelings spread to England; the king's carriage is stoned as he returns from the theatre.

France, 2 February 1796. Wolfe Tone, the leader of the United Irishmen, arrives in an attempt to secure French support for a planned Irish rebellion against British rule (→ 25/12).

Nova Scotia, 10 May 1796. Prince Edward, the king's fourth son, arrives in Halifax as commander of the garrison (→ 1802).

London, 24 May 1796. The *Times* newspaper carries a report on the separation of the Prince and Princess of Wales (→ 31/5).

Brighton, 1796/97. Aware of his present unpopularity the Prince of Wales spends much time away from London (→ 6/1799).

London, January 1797. George makes his son William, the Duke of Clarence, ranger of Bushy Park, near Hampton Court (→ 1811).

Portugal, 14 February 1797. A Royal Navy fleet, led by Admiral Sir John Jervis and Commodore Horatio Nelson, defeats a Spanish fleet off the coast of Cape St Vincent (→ 20/2).

Caribbean, 18 February 1797. The British seize control of Spanish-held Trinidad.

London, 20 February 1797. Commodore Horatio Nelson, a great friend of the Duke of Clarence, is knighted for his services to the nation (→ 19/12).

India, 18 April 1797. British rule here is threatened by the signing of a Franco-Indian alliance (→ 4/1797).

London, 18 May 1797. Charlotte, the Princess Royal, is married to Frederick, the hereditary prince of Württemberg.→

Spain, 15 November 1798. The British capture the island of Minorca.

Dublin, November 1798. Following the failure of the Irish rebellion and the capture of its leader, Wolfe Tone, he is brought to Dublin to stand trial.

Europe, 29 December 1798. A second military alliance is formed by Britain, Austria, Russia, Naples and Portugal against France.→

Canada, 1 February 1799. St John Island is officially named Prince Edward Island after Prince Edward, the king's fourth son.

London, 24 April 1799. Ernest, the king's fifth son, is made Duke of Cumberland (→ 31/5/10).

London, June 1799. Lady Jersey, a former mistress of the Prince of Wales, is moved from her residence next door to Carlton House in an attempt by the prince to avoid seeing her (→ 16/6/00).

Actress lures sailor prince from the sea

Richmond, Surrey, 1790

Prince William, the king's rakish third son, has retired from the sea to set up home with an Irish actress. Mrs Dorothea Jordan, who at 28 is three years older than the prince, already has children by two previous lovers. She is the darling of London's theatre-goers.

William is a bluff, good-natured man who learnt his manners in the navy. He went to sea – initially with a tutor, who tried in vain to teach him Latin – in 1779 at the age of 14. At times he clashed with authority, but he served his country solidly. By 1786 he was a captain in command in the Leeward Islands under Horatio Nelson, with whom he became fast friends.

The prince speaks his mind openly and sometimes in very plain English. King George was so horrified by his son's bad language and behaviour that he sent him to Hanover to pick up some social graces. For a long while William struggled to raise money to support his lifestyle. Last year he was created Duke of Clarence with an allowance of £12,000 a year (→ 5/1790).

Duke of York marries Prussian princess

Frederick, the Duke of York.

The diminutive princess: Frederica.

London, 19 November 1791

Prince Frederick, the Duke of York, arrived home to a warm welcome today with his new wife, Princess Frederica of Prussia. The royal couple, married in Berlin, are now to hold a second ceremony at the Queen's House here.

Frederick, the king's second son, is clearly delighted in his wife. His primary motive in getting married was to solve his financial problems, and for marrying Frederica, the eldest daughter of Frederick William II of Prussia, he is to receive an extra £18,000 a year. But he is also said to have grown very fond of his bride prior to the wedding and has told the Prince of Wales that he is "head over ears in love".

Frederica is short in stature and is not considered pretty, but her lively manners are winning her friends wherever she goes. The tiny shoes she wears are the source of keen public interest after the Prince of Wales commissioned six pairs to be ready for her arrival (→ 1795).

King's brother dies leaving large debts

London, September 1790

A royal scandal is brewing over the king's refusal to grant the Duchess of Cumberland, the widow of his brother Henry, a more substantial pension. Henry died on 18 September after a childless marriage, leaving huge debts, but King George will not give the duchess more than £4,000 a year. George was furious when his brother married Ann Horton in 1771, because he thought that no prince should wed a subject. Although she proved herself a devoted wife, the couple were never reconciled with the king. In refusing her more than a merely adequate pension, George wants to make it plain that Ann is not a member of the royal family.

The duke with his wife, Ann.

Threat of war with Russia is averted

London, 15 April 1791

Britain today backed down from an ultimatum to Empress Catherine of Russia demanding the return of Russian war gains in Turkey. The prime minister, Pitt, was initially keen to enforce the concessions, which are linked to a separate peace between the Holy Roman and Ottoman Empires, as a way of maintaining the European Triple Alliance against Russia, but has relented because of opposition at home. Relations with Russia are strained at best: Catherine and King George have deep contempt for each other. ▷

Prince of Wales linked to horse-racing scandal at Newmarket

The prince (in foreground) supervises the exercise of his horses, which have won 185 races since 1788.

Newmarket, November 1791

The Prince of Wales, outraged at insinuations that he was involved in plans to fix a race here last month, has said that he will have nothing more to do with Newmarket – where he has built up a large racing establishment. He has also declared support for his jockey, Sam Chiffney, who was at the centre of the scandal. Chiffney failed to win on the prince's mount Escape on 20 October but rode the same horse to an easy victory – at odds of five to one against – the next day. Many lost heavily on the second race, and charges were made that Chiffney had behaved dishonourably, and even that Escape had been deliberately winded to fix the odds for the next day. The Jockey Club enquiry proved nothing, but nevertheless the club steward, Sir Charles Bunbury, told the prince that if he allowed Chiffney to ride for him again no gentleman's horse would start in the same race (→ 31/5/92).

Lawrence appointed painter to the king

London, 1792

Thomas Lawrence has been made painter-in-ordinary to the king. Only 23 years old, he is the youngest painter to hold the rank. The son of a Bristol innkeeper, Lawrence was a child prodigy; he had his own studio at the age of 12 and entered the Royal Academy at 18. His portrait of Queen Charlotte, painted in 1789, won the admiration of the court, while his dramatic use of light and shade has been praised by the French painter Delacroix (→ 4/1815).

A portrait by Thomas Lawrence.

Prince makes his maiden speech in Lords

The Lords, who have now heard the views of the 29-year-old Prince of Wales.

London, 31 May 1792

The Prince of Wales spoke in the House of Lords today in support of the recent proclamation by the government suppressing seditious publications. There were no interruptions while the prince was speaking, though it was difficult to tell from the mood of the chamber whether this was the silence of respect or of cynicism.

Although he first took his seat nine years ago, the prince has never spoken before in the House of Lords. Indeed, he has shown no interest in the place until today. His friends say that this new concern with politics is sincere, and that he was severely shocked by events in France and wishes to reconcile himself with his father and with parliament.

Critics of the prince concede that he was shocked by the French revolution but suggest that his newfound enthusiasm is motivated more by self-interest than by national interest. The prince, they point out, is bankrupt, owing £370,000, and urgently needs funds to be voted by parliament to pay his debts off – this, they allege, accounts for his new interest in parliamentary affairs (→ 6/1792).

British government surprised by French declaration of war

London, 1 February 1793

The revolutionary government in France has today declared war on Britain. The move comes nine days after the execution of King Louis XVI, and it is accompanied by an appeal to British radicals to demonstrate their support.

For Britain the declaration comes as a surprise. Believing that the revolution across the Channel would eat up its own children, the prime minister, William Pitt, had cut the naval estimates 12 months ago, saying as he did so:

"There never was a time in the history of this country when from the situation in Europe we might more reasonably expect 15 years of peace than at the present moment."

George, fearing a new revolution, peers at a portrait of Cromwell.

But the momentum of the revolution in France – with the government declaring war on the Holy Roman Empire, massacring the aristocracy, annexing part of the Low Countries and violating a crucial 1648 treaty – made hostilities inevitable.

Pitt believes that the war will be short and manageable and will lead to a negotiable peace, but Edmund Burke, the former Whig radical, is less optimistic and is talking of a moral crusade that may well last for several years (→ 7/1793).

Haydn makes great impression on king

London, 18 February 1792

Musical London is buzzing with talk of Haydn's latest symphony, which today's *Times* called "sublime". Since he arrived here in January 1791, London has taken the Austrian composer to its heart, and none more so than the royal family. Last November he was a guest of the newly-wed Duke and Duchess of York. The Prince of Wales, who Haydn said played the cello "quite tolerably", was there and has commissioned a fine portrait of the composer. Even the king, who normally likes only Handel, has taken to Haydn. Haydn will repay the compliment by referring to *God save the King* in a new symphony.

A royal favourite: Joseph Haydn.

George sacks Pitt's ministerial rival

London, 15 June 1792

Lord Thurlow, the cabinet minister closest to the king, has resigned as lord chancellor. A few days ago the prime minister, William Pitt, and the foreign secretary, Lord Grenville, confronted the king and told him that he had to chose between them or Thurlow. The king had no choice; he dropped Lord Thurlow. The former lord chancellor, who entered parliament in 1765, has seen his relationship with Pitt turn sour. Now Pitt has succeeded in reinforcing his power as prime minister by establishing his right to choose his own cabinet (→ 13/12).

King's son upsets George by call for French peace talks

William, the Duke of Clarence.

London, July 1793
The king's son William, the Duke of Clarence, has embarrassed king, parliament and country by speaking in the House of Lords in favour of peace talks with France. One listener called his "idle and indiscreet abuse ... a matter of scandal and discomfort". William has never got on with his father, and his naïve nature was better fitted for the navy, in which he served for 11 years, than politics. This is his second indiscretion. Last April he spoke in favour of slavery. Westminster wits now say that William Pitt, the prime minister, would be only too happy if the honest duke could be sent to sea again (→ 1/1794).

Prince concedes to king on marriage

Weymouth, 24 August 1794
The Prince of Wales told his father today that he intends to marry – much to the relief of everyone interested in the Hanoverian succession. His wife will be Princess Caroline of Brunswick, the 26-year-old daughter of George's sister Augusta. Caroline, who is plain and unsophisticated, was thought the least likely candidate for the prince's hand. The British envoy in Berlin, Arthur Paget, believes the marriage is more likely to "ensure the misery of the Prince of Wales than promote his happiness".

The prince has made this move because a marriage would enable him to raise money from parliament to have his debts paid. The biggest obstacle was Maria Fitzherbert, the Catholic widow whom the prince secretly married in 1785. Cool relations between her and the prince have been worsened by the prince's new infatuation, with the

The prince's intended bride, Caroline (left), and Mrs Fitzherbert, whom he married secretly in 1785 and has now repudiated in order to marry Caroline.

Countess of Jersey. His legal obligations to Mrs Fitzherbert were removed by a recent ruling annulling his brother Augustus's secret marriage because it contravened

the Royal Marriages Act [*see report below left*]. Augustus's wife had a much better claim to be accepted as a royal bride than Mrs Fitzherbert would have had (→ 28/11).

King sees Irish Catholic emancipation as threat to constitution

Dublin, 1793
The Irish Parliament has passed an act enabling Catholics to vote as 40-shilling freeholders, bear arms and hold commissions up to the rank of colonel; they are still barred from sitting in parliament and holding high offices of state. The act is William Pitt's response to the wave of radicalism that has swept through Ireland since the French revolution, winning over Pres-

byterians in the north and Catholics in the south. The most militant of the radicals, Catholic and Protestant, have joined together in the Society of United Irishmen which openly endorses the aims of French republicans.

Pitt's reform and his promises of further reform aim to win the majority of the Irish over to the war effort and the policy of gradualism, and to isolate extreme republicans

of both churches. The strongest opposition to Pitt's reforms comes from King George himself, who believes that Catholic emancipation is contrary to the first principles of the constitution. He was brought up to believe that the House of Hanover was brought to Britain to preserve Protestant rule, treating as sacred his coronation oath to maintain the rights and privileges of the Church of England (→ 2/2/96).

King's law broken by duke's marriage

London, 5 December 1793
The king's son Augustus married Lady Augusta Murray today at St George's, Hanover Square. The bride is eight months pregnant. The couple, who met in Italy, had already married in Rome last April and see this second ceremony as putting their marriage beyond doubt. The king, who never gave his approval for the union and was not told that it was to take place, is furious and regards it as null and void according to the Royal Marriages Act of 1772 (→ 27/11/01).

George holds review of Royal Navy fleet stationed at Spithead

Howe kneels before King George.

Portsmouth, 30 January 1794
On a cold day, raked by a midwinter wind, King George reviewed his fleet off Spithead. The fleet's commander, Admiral Lord Howe – "undaunted as a rock and as silent", according to the commentator Horace Walpole – stood beside the king, naming the ships as they heaved past.

In spite of Pitt's economies, the Royal Navy is still the most powerful maritime force in the world and is unlikely to be challenged in its blockade of the French Atlantic coast. Last year, when France declared war, the navy had 28 ships-

of-the-line and 47 frigates. Now it has 85 ships-of-the-line. For the navy the problem is lack of men; it was only able to man the new ships with "the hottest press ever" at the end of last April, which emptied the Thames estuary and Port of London of seamen, who bitterly resent their fate.

There is no doubt of British supremacy at sea; even the French do not dispute it. Since the revolution, France has lost three-quarters of its officers to exile or the guillotine; the French navy has mutinied at Brest, and 52 French warships have been lost to British guns.

Heir to throne weds Caroline of Brunswick

A royal match: the Prince of Wales marries Princess Caroline of Brunswick.

London, 8 April 1795

The 32-year-old Prince of Wales married his 26-year-old cousin Princess Caroline of Brunswick today – with great difficulty. In spite of the optimism of his new mother-in-law, who wrote to him that "Caroline is so happy with your picture", the couple took a dislike to each other on their first meeting at the end of March. Only the hopes of getting his debts paid by parliament persuaded the prince to go through with the ceremony.

In some ways the couple bear a strong resemblance to each other; both are fat and dumpy, and both are reputed to be easily attracted to members of the opposite sex. Unluckily they find each other repulsive. Critics of the prince say that

they deserve each other. He has been virtually forced to marry both by parliament and by the king, who is desperate for an heir to secure the Hanoverian succession.

Caroline definitely lacks finesse. On the journey to England she had to be chaperoned by her mother to keep her away from good-looking officers, and her escort, Lord Malmesbury, had to bring up with her the delicate question of personal cleanliness. But her good qualities include honesty, openness and a complete lack of pretension, which have made her popular with the people. The prince, on the other hand, thanks to his extravagance and excesses, remains profoundly unpopular among virtually the entire nation (→ 30/5).

Three model farms created at Windsor

Windsor, 1795

King George, a passionate agriculturalist, has created three model farms at Windsor. The king took control of the land at Windsor five years ago, following the death of his brother Henry, the Duke of Cumberland, who was the ranger of Windsor forest. Hundreds of acres of parkland have been turned over to pasture or improved by draining, clearing and planting. Arthur Young, the famous advocate of the new agricultural methods, was

invited to tour the Windsor farms. The king – who took offence when Young found fault with his hogs – stressed the benefits of integrated farming, saying: "Cattle give manure, and manure corn."

Elsewhere, the king has turned over the Old Deer Park at Richmond to sheep, and in 1789 he brought to Kew the first merino sheep to be seen in Britain. He was praised by the botanist Sir Joseph Banks for his "truly patriotic plan" for improving British flocks.

King's coach attacked

London, 28 October 1795

The king was stoned by an angry populance as he was being driven to the House of Lords today. Cobbles, sods of earth and other even more earthy matter hit the royal coach, while the angry crowd chanted "Down with George!".

It is hardly the republican outburst that the government feared. There were no calls for the guillotine. Indeed, "Farmer George" [*see report below left*] is loved by his subjects. It is the Prince of Wales who is unpopular, and his unpopularity is rubbing off on the king.

The cause of the prince's unpopularity is his reckless and extravagant life-style. With taxes at an all-time high, to pay for the war with France, the nation was shocked to learn that the prince's debts amounted to £630,000, and angered at the increase in his income to £138,000 on his marriage, plus a bonus of £52,000 to cover the cost of the wedding and the completion of Carlton House (→ 11/1795).

Angry crowds attack the king's coach on its way to the House of Lords.

Duke of York becomes chief of the army

Soldier-prince: the Duke of York.

London, 1795

The king has made his second son, Frederick, the Duke of York, commander-in-chief of the army in Great Britain. The duke is not only the king's favourite son but also an experienced military officer.

Frederick spent seven years in Germany learning his profession, giving him a more thorough military education than any other officer in the British Army. In 1793 he took command of the British expedition sent to the Low Countries and proved to be competent in the field and caring of his men. The venture failed through no fault of his, but the failure tarnished his image and, on the advice of the cabinet, he was recalled last November. The Duke of York himself shrugs off the humiliation – which upset his father – and is already drawing up plans to reform the whole army (→ 1804).

Prince and Princess of Wales part after a year of marriage

London, 31 May 1796

The Prince of Wales today made a formal request to the king for a separation from his wife, Caroline, whom he married in April last year. The couple's decision to part has delighted the press and public, who detest the prince. The marriage has been a disaster from the start. When they met, the prince found Caroline large, clumsy and unwashed. He backed away from her, calling to his aide, Lord Malmesbury: "Harris, I am not well; pray get me a glass of brandy."

The prince was persuaded to abandon Mrs Fitzherbert, whom he had married secretly, by the promise that his debts would be paid if he married Caroline, the king's niece, and fathered an heir. Mrs Fitzherbert wrote: "I shall have the approbation of my own conscience and heart in knowing I have never said or done anything to hurt him."

On his wedding day the prince said to his brother: "William, tell Mrs Fitzherbert she is the only woman I shall ever love." He was drunk and had to be propped up by his best man; he spent his wedding night on the floor. By the time their daughter, Charlotte, was born on 7 January, the prince's dislike of Caroline had turned to hatred, and on 30 April he proposed a permanent separation.

Irish revolt against British rule fails

Dublin, 25 December 1796

A French fleet attempting to land in the west of Ireland has been dispersed by a gale and forced to sail for home. Thirty-five ships carrying 14,000 troops escaped the British naval blockade and reached Bantry Bay on 21 December. But the frigate bearing their general, Hoche, was delayed, and while the fleet waited for him a gale blew up, making the landing impossible. The French were responding to a call from Wolfe Tone, the founder of the Society of United Irishmen, for help in mounting a rebellion against British rule in Ireland (→ 8/9/98).

Brilliant caricaturist arrested as attacks on the behaviour of younger members of royal family become more outspoken

"Thoughts on Matrimony" – the prince reflects on his fate.

"Affability" – the king meets his subjects in a rural setting.

London, 1796

As public disillusionment with the behaviour of the younger members of the royal family continues to mount, the caricatures of James Gillray grow ever more cruel. In January this year, the artist and illustrator was arrested for selling his print *The Presentation*, a satirical view of the first meeting between the Prince of Wales and his newborn daughter, Charlotte.

Described by one magazine as "vile, most obscene", the picture shows the prince swaying drunkenly into the room, with his ubiquitous cronies Charles James Fox and Richard Brinsley Sheridan in grovelling attendance. The case against Gillray was later dropped – possibly after the intervention of the Tory politician George Canning, who is courting the caricaturist – and has done little to dampen his spirits. It is not the first time that Gillray has crossed swords with the royal family.

In common with much of the press – especially the recently launched *Times*, whose editor has twice been imprisoned for libelling the prince – Gillray delights in attacking the extravagance and loose-living of the Prince of Wales, famously satirised in *A Voluptuary under the Horrors of Digestion*. Among his other popular representations of the royal family is *Fash-ionable Contrasts*, produced shortly after the Duke of York's marriage to the diminuitive Princess Frederica of Prussia; gentler in tone, it plays on the well-known smallness of the duchess's feet and the rage in fashionable circles to wear imitations of her shoes.

As in *Affability*, King George himself is depicted more kindly, often in rural settings and in the company of country people. Such images recall his deep and abiding interest in agriculture, which has won him the nickname of "Farmer George". *Affability* reflects the king's apparently condescending attitude towards his subjects and his habit of using speech mannerisms such as "Hey? Hey?" and "What? What? What?" when trying to elicit a response.

The failure of the Prince of Wales's marriage to Caroline of Brunswick has provided a wealth of material for other satirists, among them Isaac Cruikshank, whose *Thoughts on Matrimony* shows the prince contemplating his mistresses. The prince gazes up at a portrait of the Countess of Jersey in her youth, while a oval miniature of the Princess of Wales dangles disregarded from his hand. On the walls are portraits of his other loves, including the actress Mary Robinson and the Catholic widow Maria Fitzherbert.

"Fashionable Contrasts": the Duke of York's marriage in 1791 was represented by placing the duchess's tiny shoes in a submissive position.

"A Voluptuary" – the prince recovers from an enormous meal.

Princess Royal marries German prince

Princess Charlotte: now she has married Prince Frederick of Württemberg.

London, 18 May 1797

Charlotte, the Princess Royal, was married today to a fat and plain German: Frederick, the hereditary Prince of Württemberg. Bonaparte, the French general, remarked of Frederick that God had created him to show how far the human skin could stretch without bursting. Now aged 31, Charlotte is grateful for even this portly personage.

For many years the princess has been urging her eldest brother, the Prince of Wales, to find her a husband, since the king showed no interest in the matter. The Prince of Prussia was too young, the Duke of Oldenburg too old, and the king would never hear of her marrying an English commoner. When the Prince of Württemberg turned up, Princess Charlotte was delighted. She will now live in Frankfurt – as long as the French and General Bonaparte do not extend their revolution into Germany.

King acquiesces in French peace talks

London, April 1797

William Pitt, the prime minister, has proposed asking France for peace talks because of the financial crisis, the naval mutinies and the difficulty of finding allies on the continent. The king has reluctantly agreed. The talks will not be easy. The war party in Paris, led by General Bonaparte, will insist on stiff terms: to retain France's conquests in Europe and to recover its losses in India and Canada. The king believes that an honourable peace may be unobtainable. "Though an Englishman is soon tired of war," he said, "he is not easily satisfied with peace" (→ 29/12/98).

Charlotte is first of six royal princesses to escape tedious life of Windsor 'nunnery'

Windsor, 18 May 1797

There are five princesses left at Windsor after the marriage of the Princess Royal [*see left*]. They lead a life of exquisite tedium and decorum, unlike their profligate brothers, and they call their home "the nunnery". The king and queen appear indifferent to the plight of their daughters, even though several are now of marriageable age. One wants to marry the Prince of Orleans, a penniless French exile and a Catholic. Some have fallen in love with unsuitable and elderly courtiers. None is allowed out to meet young men.

Their one pleasure in summer is to go "terracing" – walking up and down the castle's long terraces. Once a year the king takes the family to Weymouth, which is even more boring than Windsor. The king gets up at five, and so do the princesses. They walk to the bathing machines, take a dip in the sea,

Princess Augusta (born 8/11/68).

walk along the beach, attend the Assembly Rooms and every evening go to the playhouse. The king enjoys the worst sort of provincial play. Princess Mary writes that Weymouth is "more dull and stupid" than she can find words to express.

Princess Elizabeth (born 22/5/70).

Princess Mary (born 25/4/76).

Princess Sophia (born 3/11/77).

Princess Amelia (born 7/8/83).

Britain wins strategic advantage in French war

Irish volunteers prepare for battle before a statue of William III in Dublin.

Massed ranks: King George reviewing British troops in Hyde Park.

French are forced to surrender in Ireland

Dublin, 8 September 1798
The French army in Ireland has surrendered. It landed at Killala, in Co Mayo, on 22 August, too late to help the rebellion against British rule. General Humbert, with 900 Frenchmen and 1,000 rebels, marched boldly towards Dublin, and was cornered at Ballinamuck, in Co Longford. He resisted for a while and then surrendered.

The government tried to prevent the revolt: Grattan's party in the Irish parliament was defeated, Protestant dissidents in the north were suppressed, and plotters were arrested in Dublin, including Lord Edward Fitzgerald, who died resist-ing arrest. However, the rebels' agitation among the Catholic peasants stirred up a mass revolt. They captured Wexford, and the rebellion spread across the south. Protestants were murdered, and in return the Protestant militia and the regular army fought a ferocious war against the rebels.

The rebellion in the north was crushed near Belfast on 12 June. General Lake attacked the rebel encampment at Vinegar Hill, in Co Wexford, on 21 June, and destroyed it. The French thus came too late. The remnants of the rebellion will now be stamped out with great severity (→11/1798).

Important new alliance forged in Europe

London, 29 December 1798
Britain and Russia have signed a treaty aimed at France. In return for a subsidy, the czar will provide 45,000 men to fight alongside Prussia if that country can be induced to join the alliance. Russia is already allied with the Holy Roman Empire, so the makings of a new anti-French coalition are in place. The Ottoman Empire, Naples and Portugal are also in the alliance.

Lord Grenville, the foreign secretary, hopes that an Anglo-Russian attack on the Low Countries will provoke a general uprising there, and that an attack by the empire and Prussia on France can be arranged at the same time. The armies would all march on Paris and destroy the French republic.

All this was made possible by Admiral Nelson's victory at the Battle of the Nile in August. France's most brilliant general, Bonaparte, is isolated in Egypt, French ambitions in India, the Levant and Ireland have all been defeated, and Britain controls the Mediterranean. Grenville thinks that now is the time for a decisive push. However, the empire and Prussia are uncertain allies, and there are no signs that French energy and revolutionary enthusiasm are in any way diminished (→9/11/99).

King leads nation's thanks for victories

London, 19 December 1797
The king went to St Paul's today to give thanks for the naval victories at Cape St Vincent on 14 February and Camperdown in October. Admiral Jervis, with 15 ships of the line, defeated the Spanish fleet of 27 ships off Cape St Vincent, the southern tip of Portugal. His commodore, Horatio Nelson [see story right], captured two Spanish ships. The battle at Camperdown was equally important: the French ordered the Dutch to leave the Texel and attack the Royal Navy. They did so on 11 October and were soundly defeated (→1798).

Nelson heralded as brilliant naval leader

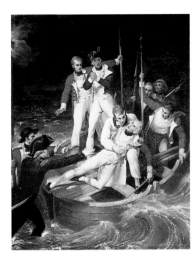

The courageous Admiral Nelson is wounded at Cape St Vincent.

London, 1798
Horatio Nelson is among the most admired of British admirals. He is also vain and moody, and has started a scandalous liaison with Lady Hamilton, a former dancer, now the wife of the envoy to Naples. Nelson is 40; he joined the navy at 12 and was a captain at 21. He lost an eye in a land attack on Corsica in 1794 and an arm at Santa Cruz last year. He acted with conspicuous courage at the Battle of Cape St Vincent. The Battle of the Nile this August was the most complete victory that Britain has ever won at sea. Nelson took or destroyed 13 of the 17 ships in the French fleet, with no British losses (→22/5/01).

Napoleon in power after military gains

Paris, 9 November 1799
General Napoleon Bonaparte has seized power in France a month after his return from Egypt. He is seen as the saviour of his country because, in 1796 and 1797, he conquered Italy and defeated Austria. French armies have been defeated during his absence, while he won victories over the Turks. Today is 18 Brumaire under the revolutionary calendar, and Bonaparte announced: "Citizens, the Revolution is completed." The directory is abolished; Bonaparte will be "first consul", and he will now deal with the coalition (→27/3/02).

George III
1760–1820

London, 16 June 1800. Mrs Maria Fitzherbert gives a huge breakfast party to announce publicly her reconciliation with the Prince of Wales (→ 6/1806).

London, 26 June 1800. James Hadfield, the man who attempted to kill the king earlier this year, is brought to trial.

London, August 1800. Princess Sophia, aged 22, George's fifth daughter, has given birth secretly to a son, Thomas; it is rumoured that the father is one of the royal equerries, Major-General Garth.

Europe, 16 December 1800. The League of Armed Neutrality is formed between Russia, Sweden, Denmark and Prussia, to resist the British right to search any ships that they choose.

Britain/Ireland, 1 January 1801. As the Act of Union with Ireland becomes law, George III is proclaimed king of Britain and Ireland, and his title of king of France is dropped.→

London, 14 April 1801. The Prince of Wales is allowed to visit his father, the king, following his recent illness (→ 7/12/03).

London, 22 May 1801. Britain's naval hero, Horatio Nelson, is created a viscount (→ 21/10/05).

London, May 1801. Queen Charlotte is badly shaken by the king's fits of mental instability this month (→ 9/1804).

London, 27 November 1801. George bestows on his sons Augustus and Adolphus the dukedoms of Sussex and Cambridge respectively (→ 1/6/18).

France, 27 March 1802. Britain signs the Treaty of Amiens to bring about peace with France, Spain and the Batavian Republic (→ 18/5/03).

London, 29 April 1802. George approves the formation of the Royal Marines (→ 17/5/02).

England, 7 December 1803. George is outraged by the publication in three national newspapers of letters from the Prince of Wales to his brother the Duke of Kent about the king's refusal to give the prince military promotion (→ 1804).

Caribbean, 1803. The British seize control of St Lucia, Tobago and Dutch Guyana.

Windsor, 1803. Queen Charlotte learns of and keeps secret the passionate affair of her youngest daughter, Princess Amelia, with Major-General the Honourable Charles Fitzroy, one of the king's equerries (→ 3/11/10).

Windsor, February 1804. King George suffers another attack of illness; his usual physicians are replaced by Dr Simons of St Luke's Hospital for Lunatics, who favours treating such illnesses with a strait-jacket (→ 24/8).

France, 12 May 1804. Napoleon Bonaparte is proclaimed emperor of France, and his crown becomes hereditary (→ 9/8/05).

Kew, 21 August 1804. George arranges a meeting with his eight-year-old granddaughter, Princess Charlotte, for whom he has a great fondness. To her husband's fury, the Princess of Wales is also present.

Dorset, 24 August 1804. Following his recent bout of illness, George and his household visit Weymouth to allow him to convalesce.→

London, September 1804. Queen Charlotte is beginning to suffer from the strain of looking after her husband; she refuses to see him alone and locks her bedroom door at night (→ 20/1/17).

London, 12 November 1804. George and the Prince of Wales meet and publicly appear to be reconciled.

London, 1804. The dispute between the Prince and Princess of Wales over the custody of Princess Charlotte is settled by George III taking over the guardianship of his granddaughter (→ 9/1806).

Scotland, 8 April 1805. Henry Dunbar, Viscount Melville, faces impeachment proceedings; he held a string of high offices in the government which made him the most powerful man in Scotland over the last 20 years.

London, July 1805. George is losing his eyesight; the king now has a cataract in one eye, and his sight has almost gone from the other (→ 19/9/07).

Europe, 9 August 1805. The Holy Roman Empire joins the Anglo-Russian alliance against Napoleon, signed in April, following his seizure of the Italian crown in May and Genoa in June (→ 21/10).

Spain, 21 October 1805. The British, led by Vice-Admiral Viscount Nelson, defeat the combined forces of Spain and France off Cape Trafalgar; Viscount Nelson is killed (→ 9/1/06).

Austria, December 1805. Napoleon Bonaparte defeats a Russo-Imperial army in a battle at Austerlitz (→ 15/1/06).

France, 15 January 1806. Britain declares war on Prussia after a Franco-Prussian treaty is signed in Paris.

Portsmouth, 1 February 1806. George renames the Naval Academy the Royal Naval College.

London, June 1806. Mrs Maria Fitzherbert is allowed to continue

to act as the guardian for the niece of Lord Hertford, Minnie Seymour (→ 18/12/09).

London, 13 September 1806. The Prince of Wales is greatly upset by the death of Charles Fox, the former minister and bitter opponent of King George.

London, 4 June 1807. The Princess of Wales is received at court for the first time since the findings were published of an investigation into allegations that she had had an illegitimate child (→ 1810).

Windsor, 8 January 1808. A deranged man who tries to secure an audience with king is discovered to have escaped from Bethnal Green madhouse and has to be restrained in a strait-jacket.

London, 26 January 1809. The Duke of York, the favourite son of George III, goes on trial after allegations made by Mrs Mary Anne Clarke, an ex-mistress, implicate him in a financial scandal (→ 23/2).

London, 6 April 1809. The City votes to award Colonel Wardle, who brought the Duke of York to court, the freedom of the city.

London, 18 December 1809. Mrs Maria Fitzherbert gives a final refusal to the Prince of Wales, who had attempted to rekindle their shattered relationship after his interlude with Lady Hertford.

Windsor, 3 November 1810. George suffers a recurrence of his mental illness, from which it is feared that he may not recover.→

Blackheath, London, 1810. Caroline, the Princess of Wales, moves back to Montague House after her mother, Augusta, the Duchess of Brunswick, a sister of George III, moves to a house in Hanover Square (→ 19/6/11).

Assassin shoots at king

The madman James Hadfield tries to kill King George at the theatre.

London, 15 May 1800

The king survived a dramatic public attempt on his life tonight. He was attending the première of Mozart's opera *Le nozze di Figaro* at the Drury Lane theatre when James Hadfield, a member of the audience, tried to shoot him. George remained unflustered, although the bullet came close enough to pierce one of the pillars in the royal box, and he slept as quietly as usual during the interval between performance and after-piece. This is the second such attack that he has suffered. He was equally unperturbed when a woman tried to stab him in August 1786 (→ 26/6).

Royal Institution created to boost science

London, 1800

A new body to promote the spread of technical and scientific knowledge has been set up as the Royal Institution of Great Britain. The institution, which has been funded by private subscriptions, is the brainchild of the American scientist Benjamin Thompson, Count Rumford, who has based it on a similar French body, the *Conservatoire des arts et metiers*, created in 1794. As well as promoting scientific knowledge, the Institution aims to encourage "the application of science to the common purposes of life".

Scientists discover new ways of harnessing wind power: a cartoon by Gillray.

Act of Union joins Britain and Ireland

London, 1 January 1801

Ireland and Britain have been brought together as the United Kingdom under the terms of the Act of Union, which comes into effect today. The separate parliament in Dublin has been dissolved, and 100 MPs and 32 peers will travel to Westminster to represent Ireland. The Church of Ireland is to be united with the Church of England.

Concessions made by the British government in 1782 established the independence of the Dublin parliament, but they were not a solution to Ireland's political problems, since this body excluded Catholics and remained under the influence of the London-appointed executive in Dublin castle. In the light of persistent Irish insurrection, union became increasingly attractive to the London government as a means of maintaining English domination.

William Pitt, the prime minister, engineered an impressive consensus. The Dublin parliament was persuaded to vote for its own dissolution by a mixture of bribes, in the form of peerages, jobs and cash, and diverse arguments which persuaded Protestants that union would make the Catholics a minority and Catholics that union would be protection against militant Protestants within Ireland. King George is very enthusiastic about the act, which he says is "one of the most useful measures that has been effected during my reign" (→ 2/1801).

James Gillray's satirical view of pro-Unionists in their true colours.

Pitt resigns after row with the king

London, February 1801

William Pitt has resigned after 18 years as prime minister in response to the king's insistent refusal to accept Catholic emancipation. Henry Addington, the speaker of the House of Commons, will form a new government. George is not intolerant, but he believes that emancipation goes against his coronation oath to uphold the rights and privileges of the Church of England. Pitt feels that the extension of Catholics' civil rights is a necessary part of the reform of Irish government begun in the Act of Union. Despite the row, the pair are parting on good terms (→ 10/5/04).

King recovers from troublesome illness

London, 11 March 1801

King George is safe today, having recovered from a recurrence of the debilitating illness that first struck him in 1788. For four weeks the country has followed the bulletins on his health, since he was taken ill on 13 February in the midst of the upheaval surrounding Pitt's resignation. The symptoms of the illness – hoarseness, nausea and an increasing mental confusion – were the same as in the first attack. The low point came on 2 March, when his physicians feared that he would die, but on that same day he began his recovery. He is keen to return soon to his public duties (→ 2/1804).

George supports resumption of war

King set to lead his forces into action

Westminster, 18 May 1803
The king gave his backing today to the cabinet's decision to renew the war with France. The Peace of Amiens has run for only just over a year, but already opinion has hardened against the terms to which Britain agreed before Napoleon Bonaparte was made "first consul" for life. It is thought better that Bonaparte is forced into war before his military recovery has advanced any further and while Britain's forces are mobilised. There is still a regular army of 130,000 men, of which 80,000 are in Britain, plus 50,000 militia. This is a far greater force than any which Bonaparte can muster.

The British ultimatum was for French withdrawal from the Batavian Republic and a lease of Malta, captured in 1800, for at least ten years. Under the Amiens treaty Britain gave the island back to the knights of Malta, but British forces continue to occupy the naval base.

If Bonaparte should invade, the king has declared that he will put himself at the head of his troops. If it is Kent which is attacked he will go to Dartford; if Essex, to Chelmsford. He has his camping equipment ready for action and gets angry if anyone suggests that the

A diminutive Napoleon Bonaparte confronts the mighty British king.

invasion may not be attempted. He has also made plans for the queen and their daughters to cross the Severn and take refuge in the bishop of Worcester's palace – "should the enemy approach too near to Windsor", he told the bishop.

Meanwhile he is busy inspecting the preparations to resist invasion – Martello towers, camps of the Volunteers, parades of Yeomanry – and talks scornfully of defying "the Corsican usurper". The raising of volunteers is expected to produce a civilian force of over 350,000 men. They are drilling in every town. There is to be a grand parade in Hyde Park at which the City of London Volunteers will be reviewed by King George and his seven sons on horseback, with the ladies of the royal family in carriages. He will also review another parade of the volunteers of Westminster. He is cheered by the crowds everywhere (→ 12/5/04).

Emmet's rebellion in Ireland against union is crushed

Dublin, 19 September 1803
Robert Emmet, whose attempt to seize Dublin castle and proclaim an Irish republic in July failed ignominiously, was tried and sentenced to death today. He made a speech from the dock that has electrified Irish patriots. "Let no man write my epitaph," he began. "When my country takes her place among the nations of the earth, then and not till then let my epitaph be written." He is to be executed tomorrow.

His words have had more influence than his deeds. Following the implementation of the Act of Union in 1801, Emmet appealed personally to Napoleon and Talleyrand to support the Irish nationalist cause. He returned to Ireland, spent £3,000 on muskets and pikes, and printed a proclamation of "the Irish Republic". He planned to attack the castle with 2,000 men, but, after his intentions became known to the authorities, only 80 men turned out on the night of 23 July. Emmet led them with drawn sword, but abandoned the assault when it degenerated into a street riot. It was then that Ireland's chief justice was piked to death in his coach.

Emmet went into hiding in the Wicklow hills, but was caught when he came out to meet his sweetheart, Sarah Curran.

Royal military college comes into being

The military college (modern view).

Great Marlow, 17 May 1802
The first 16 gentlemen cadets of a new royal military college assembled today in temporary quarters here in Buckinghamshire until an estate at Sandhurst in Berkshire, sold to the government by William Pitt, the former prime minister, is ready. The idea of officer training for boys of 13 to 15 was put forward by Colonel John le Marchant to replace the system of obtaining commissions by purchase; the rate at which current officers sell their commissions and retire on the proceeds varies from £800 for a lieutenant to £3,500 for a lieutenant–colonel. The plan is supported by the Duke of York (→ 1/2/06).

Duke of Kent is governor of Gibraltar

Gibraltar, 1802
Prince Edward, the Duke of Kent, the fourth son of King George, is well known to the citizens of Gibraltar, where his father has sent him as governor. In accordance with the king's policy of keeping his sons at arm's length, especially from their brother the Prince of Wales, Prince Edward was sent here as a colonel in 1790 when he was 23. He took pride in his regiment, but was bored by local society. He sent to Geneva, where he had previously lived, for a mistress, Mademoiselle Julie de St Laurent, and formed a band in order to indulge his love of music. Now his martinet rule is causing trouble in the garrison (→ 25/1/18).

Edward, the Duke of Kent.

George moves into Windsor castle

Bitter row erupts between Prince of Wales and brother

London, 1804

Furious that he has not been given high military rank during the current threat of a French invasion, the Prince of Wales has now quarrelled with his brother Frederick, the Duke of York, who is commander-in-chief of the army in Britain.

The row springs from a decision to withdraw the regiment of dragoons of which the prince is colonel from the front-line defences on the Sussex coast and send it inland. When the duke called at Carlton House to explain, the prince – who insists he will never speak to his brother again – refused to see him.

In December the prince published in the newspapers his letters to the king asking not to be left "a tame, idle, lifeless spectator of the mischief that threatens us". The king was livid (→ 12/11/04).

King spurns Bute

Hampshire, October 1804

King George has repudiated his relationship with the Earl of Bute, his former favourite, who died in 1792. Although he began his reign 40 years ago entirely under Bute's influence (and made him prime minister), the king has confided in the politician George Rose, with whom he is staying near the New Forest, that he had a low opinion of Bute's ability, and that Bute joined the cabinet against his wishes.

King George riding to hounds in Windsor great park; it was hunting that first kindled his love for the place.

Windsor, 2 November 1804

The royal family today moved into new apartments within Windsor castle. For the last 20 years George has spent more time at Windsor than at Kew, but until now he has stayed at Queen Anne's lodge in the grounds south of the castle. Queen Charlotte introduced him to Windsor, and at first he stayed there only when he had been hunting. But he grew to like the place, revelling in his role as country squire, walking in the park and meeting his subjects, watching cricket or kite-flying, visiting the Windsor shops or developing his model farms.

The new apartments are part of a substantial building programme at the castle over the last 20 years.

St George's chapel and the state apartments were restored before the architect James Wyatt converted buildings around the upper ward of the castle into the new royal apartments. The king is pleased enough with his sunless, north-facing room, but the queen prefers the cosier lodge that she has left behind.

Pitt is prime minister again after Addington's government falls

Westminster, 10 May 1804

William Pitt is prime minister again after the fall of Henry Addington, the king's friend and son of one of his doctors, who took office at the king's request when his friend Pitt resigned over Catholic emancipation in 1801. One of his services to the king was to suggest that he should use a hop pillow during his recent attack of dementia, which gave him his first night's sleep.

Pitt supported Addington for a time but refused to rejoin the government in any capacity other than prime minister. He has now returned to office on the understanding that he will abandon Catholic claims. In view of the resumption of war with France, and the fear of an invasion, Pitt intends to combine the most eminent men of all parties in his new ministry, including, perhaps, Charles James Fox.

Royal family heads for the seaside

Weymouth, 24 August 1804

The king and the royal household have arrived here on the Dorset coast for what has become an annual summer pilgrimage to the seaside. George first came here in 1789 to convalesce, having previously patronised Cheltenham spa. His regular visits to the coast have not only established Weymouth as a resort but also popularised the seaside generally.

At Weymouth he stays in a house facing the sands owned by his brother the Duke of Gloucester. From here he bathes in the sea almost every day. "A machine follows the royal one into the sea, filled with fiddlers who play *God save the King* as his majesty takes his plunge!" wrote the novelist Fanny Burney.

Weymouth is not the only town to enjoy royal patronage. Brighton is favoured by the Prince of Wales [*see overleaf*], Princess Amelia has been to Worthing, and Southend is the choice of the Princess of Wales.

Bathing machines in the sea at Weymouth, which has become a regular retreat for the royal family since their first visit to the resort in 1789.

Prince gives Brighton an eastern style

The Prince of Wales (centre) throws a party in the Yellow Room.

Brighton, East Sussex, 1806

An immense riding school and stables in the Indian style is rising behind the Prince of Wales's sea-front residence. He has decided to have the entire Marine Pavilion – built for him in 1787 by Henry Holland – remodelled in the Indian style. This was a typically last-minute change. Until last year it was to have been in the Chinese style, to match the interior where he has reproduced the Chinese Room from his London home, Carlton House, with a gallery of Chinese wallpapers, porcelain, bamboo and lacquered furniture and lifesize figures of Chinese fishermen in silk robes dangling lanterns from fishing rods.

The delays in starting work on the alterations are due to the prince's chronic inability to pay his bills to the local craftsmen, who are complaining loudly. But Brighton as a whole has much to thank him for. When he first came here in 1783 to take the sea cure it was a fishing port, originally Brighthelmstone, of a mere 3,500 people. It has more than doubled in size since the prince had the pavilion built as his summer residence.

The prince is at his most amiable and relaxed at Brighton. In the mornings he sits on the balcony of Mrs Fitzherbert's house on the Steine, or promenades, greeting friends such as George Brummell, known since Eton days as "Beau". Dinner at the pavilion is at six, after which Mrs Fitzherbert plays cards while the prince talks, sings or listens to his band. Under her influence he no longer gets drunk, though his friends do, particularly Richard Brinsley Sheridan, the playwright. The prince ("Prinny") is always "merry and full of his jokes", says Thomas Creevey. "He says he will never be as happy when he is king" (→ 12/1807).

George ("Beau") Brummell.

Richard Brinsley Sheridan.

George mourns death of brother

London, 25 August 1805

William, the Duke of Gloucester, the king's younger brother, died today and, despite their prolonged dispute over his wife, the king was genuinely upset. In 1766 William secretly married Maria, the beautiful widow of Earl Waldegrave. She was an illegitimate daughter of Horace Walpole's brother Edward and in George's eyes totally unsuitable, being a commoner and a Whig. He had forbidden the marriage, which was one of the sort of imprudences that the 1772 Royal Marriages Act was meant to prevent in future. George refused to acknowledge her, though he accepted and provided for her children.

Guards 'troop the colour' for birthday

Whitehall, 4 June 1806

The first sovereign's birthday parade on Horse Guards Parade today introduced a new ceremony o' "Trooping the Colour", performed by the king's three regiments o' Foot Guards. Since the restoration of Charles II every garrison town has held a daily guard-mounting parade, and when the sovereign is in residence this parade includes "trooping" the colour or battalion flag through the ranks, originally in order that every man should recognise it.

On his birthday the king gives a gratuity to his guard, which is chosen from all three regiments so that they can all share it.

King leads tribute to Nelson's triumphs

A magnificent occasion: Nelson's remains are buried in St Paul's cathedral.

London, 9 January 1806

Vice-Admiral Horatio Nelson was buried at St Paul's today with the utmost pomp, mourned by the entire nation with the king at its head. Last October he had led Britain to victory over the forces of France and Spain in a battle off Cape Trafalgar near Cadiz. The king has approved an earldom for his son and an annual pension of £5,000 for his heirs in perpetuity, although nothing has been given to his mistress, Emma, Lady Hamilton.

Viscount Nelson's flagship, HMS *Victory*, had been towed up the Thames to Greenwich, where Nelson's body lay in state in the Painted Hall of the seamen's hospital for three days, placed in a coffin made from the mainmast of the ship *L'Orient*. Thence it travelled in Nelson's barge from the *Victory*, pulled by his own crew, accompanied by a procession of boats draped in black, to lie at the Admiralty.

Today it was borne through London to St Paul's on a funeral car like a warship preceded by sailors from the *Victory* carrying the white ensign flown at Trafalgar, showing its shot-holes to the silent crowds.

'Delicate investigation' clears princess

London, September 1806
Commissioners who have been investigating charges that Caroline, the estranged wife of the Prince of Wales, had given birth to an illegitimate son have announced their "perfect conviction" that the accusation was unfounded.

There have been all manner of scandals and rumours about the princess and the way in which she conducts her household at Blackheath. The prince had chosen to ignore them, but the government set up the enquiry when Lady Douglas, a former friend of the princess, openly accused her of having the baby and of claiming: "I have a bedfellow whenever I like, nothing is more wholesome."

The commissioners, after hearing the evidence of Lady Douglas, the princess's servants and a number of gentlemen said to have enjoyed her favours, have concluded that William Austin, the boy living in her house, was the son of a poor family who was being brought up by the good-natured princess.

She has not, however, escaped with an unsullied reputation from

The Prince and Princess of Wales: the couple are now estranged.

this "delicate investigation". The evidence given of her indiscreet and vulgar behaviour has caused the king to order that she can no longer be received as an intimate of the royal family (→ 4/6/07).

King reunited with sister after 36 years

Blackheath, 19 Sept 1807
There was a poignant meeting here today between the king, now blind and crippled with disease, and his elder sister, Princess Augusta, the mother of the Princess of Wales, a near penniless widow following the death of her husband, the Duke of Brunswick, from wounds received fighting Napoleon at Auerstedt.

King George disapproved of the way the duke treated the princess,

and today was the first time that the royal brother and sister had met for 36 years, although they have kept up an affectionate correspondence. Following the duke's death and Napoleon's occupation of Brunswick, the princess was left with little except her husband's coin collection, so the king sent a frigate to bring her to England and gave her a house not far from where they used to play together (→ 3/11/10).

Racing at Ascot: a passion of the Prince of Wales, horse-racing is also enjoyed by both rich and poor, who are equally keen on having a flutter.

'Ministry of All the Talents' falls as king blocks new army positions for Catholics

London, March 1807
Lord Grenville's "Ministry of All the Talents" has been forced to resign on a constitutional matter raised by the king's adamant opposition to the emancipation of the Catholics. The affair started with Grenville and his cabinet proposing to allow Catholics the right to hold colonels' commissions in England as well as Ireland.

The king reacted violently, and Grenville withdrew the proposal, but at a meeting not attended by the anti-Catholic members the cabinet reserved its right to submit similar advice to the king in the future. He replied by demanding individual pledges that the members would never again tender such advice. They refused, arguing that no ministers could bind themselves as to what advice they might tender the king in the future, and resigned.

The ministry came into being a year ago after the death of Pitt, when Charles James Fox and Grenville agreed that they had to form a national government of the best men available. Its most notable achievement has been to abolish the slave trade.

Sailing to hell: the last voyage for the ghosts of Grenville and his ministers.

Lady Hertford is focus of princely passion

London, December 1807
The Prince of Wales has become infatuated with the Marchioness of Hertford who, although rich, handsome and statuesque, is a grandmother, nearing 50, and looks her age. She is driving him to distraction, for he wants her to live openly as his mistress and she refuses.

He is as lovesick as a boy for this matronly figure. He writes to her every day, is feverish and has lost his appetite. He has even switched his affection to Cheltenham from his beloved Brighton to be near Ragley, where Lady Hertford lives with her amiable husband. Mrs Fitzherbert, the prince's "official" mistress, who in the past has defeated many previous rivals, is said to be most concerned (→ 18/12/09).

The Marchioness of Hertford.

Duke of York resigns as army chief

Scandal rages over duke's ex-mistress

Westminster, 23 February 1809
The Duke of York resigned his post as commander-in-chief of the army today. This follows a parliamentary enquiry into allegations that his former mistress, a clever but extravagant actress, Mrs Mary Anne Clarke, had used her position to take money from people who wished to buy commissions, promotions and particular positions. She needed the money, she said, to augment the irregular allowances made to her by the duke.

The affair, which has horrified the nation with its revelations of a web of corruption in the highest circles in the land, was exposed by the radical MP for Okehampton, Colonel Gwylym Lloyd Wardle. In the House of Commons on 20 January he demanded an enquiry into rumours that Mrs Clarke had accepted money from officers, and that the duke not only knew of her activities and agreed her list of promotions but actually shared in the proceeds.

The colonel's accusations were swiftly taken up by other radical members of parliament, and the streets of London rang with witty songs: "You'll be treated with honours if you secrecy mark, sir,/For my master is noble and I am his Clarke, sir." Mrs Clarke, discarded by her royal lover two years ago, proved a vengeful witness at the

Mrs Clarke shown presenting the duke with a list of promotions to be effected.

enquiry, telling the gleeful members how she used to remind the duke of her transactions by pinning notes to their bed-curtains.

She also tried to involve General Sir Arthur Wellesley but, as he wrote to a friend: "I was happy to find that not a single man ... imagined that I knew anything about the matter." However, Wellesley thought that the duke "must have suspected" Mrs Clarke's practices.

Parliament voted by 278 votes to 196 that the duke was not guilty of corruption, but he was so compromised that his resignation became inevitable. The affair has damaged not only him but also the king and the government, and, especially, the Prince of Wales, who is thought to have deserted his brother in his hour of need (→ 6/4).

Mrs Clarke, the duke's ex-mistress.

Cabinet ministers quit after a duel which upset the king

Windsor, 30 September 1809
The king has reacted with disgust to a duel fought earlier this month between Lord Castlereagh, his war secretary, and George Canning, his foreign secretary, on Putney heath. The duel arose from Canning's intrigues to secure the dismissal of Castlereagh from the government. Canning was wounded in the thigh, and Castlereagh had a button shot off his lapel. The king has written a paper to the cabinet on the impropriety of the duel. Now both ministers have resigned from the government (→ 26/9).

Pistols at dawn: King George actively opposes the practice of duelling.

'Straightforward' Spencer Perceval to be prime minister

Westminster, 26 September 1809
Spencer Perceval, described by his friends as an "honest little fellow", is to be the next prime minister following the collapse of the present premier, the Duke of Portland, and the resignation of the embittered rivals Lord Castlereagh and George Canning [*see report below left*]. Perceval, the younger son of a peer, had been a successful lawyer before entering parliament as a Tory in 1796. He has won the king's support for his intention to build a government of national unity.

An unassuming figure but a skilful debater, Perceval has served as solicitor-general, attorney-general and, latterly, chancellor of the exchequer. He is somewhat colourless, but is an evangelical fanatically opposed to Catholic emancipation; otherwise he has a generous disposition and is regarded as straightforward at a time of much political chicanery (→ 29/1/11).

King's son linked to murder of valet

St James's Palace, 31 May 1810
Joseph Sellis, the valet of one of the king's sons, the Duke of Cumberland, was found dead this morning with his throat slashed by a razor. Rumours suggesting that the duke murdered his valet after being caught in bed with Sellis's wife are already rife. These rumours are being readily believed because of the duke's controversial behaviour and reactionary politics. It would seem, however, that he is innocent of these charges and was lucky to have escaped with his life from a murderous attack by Sellis.

According to another valet, Cornelius Neall, Sellis attacked the duke with a sabre as he slept. The duke woke up, grabbed the sabre – almost severing his thumb – and then ran into Neall's room with his assailant slashing at him so violently that only the thickness of his nightcap saved him. When Neall appeared, armed with a poker, Sellis fled to his room and cut his own throat (→ 29/8/15).

King devastated by daughter's death

Windsor, 3 November 1810

The king was confined in a strait-jacket by his doctors today following a series of violent outbursts interspersed with feverish restlessness and incessant rambling. His last vestiges of mental stability were destroyed yesterday by the death of his youngest and favourite child, Amelia, at the age of 27.

The princess contracted tuberculosis when she was 15 and had since suffered harsh treatments for other maladies. During her last illness the king spent much time with her, holding her hand and trying to make out her features with his failing sight. When she knew that she was dying, Amelia had a ring set with one of her jewels and a lock of her hair under a glass disc. It bears the inscription "Remember Me". The king broke down and wept when she put it on his finger. This personal tragedy comes on top of humiliating retreats by British armies in the Low Countries and Spain [*see report below*].

While agreeing that the king is at present incapable of government, his doctors believe that he will recover from his illness, as he has done from similar attacks in the past. But the king is an old man now, and ministers' thoughts are inevitably turning to the question of a regency (→ 29/1/11).

Overcome with grief: King George was appalled by Princess Amelia's death.

Wellington holds the line against French in Peninsular War

Lisbon, October 1810

The British commander General Viscount Wellington has withdrawn behind the secretly constructed fortifications at Torres Vedras and halted the French army outside Lisbon, much to the fury of Marshal Masséna, who had sworn to "drive the leopards into the sea". The move follows Wellington's advance last month at Bussaco, when he turned on the pursuing French and gave the British and their Portuguese allies an important victory.

Wellington was sent to protect Lisbon last year when France invaded Portugal, following Britain's defeat at Corunna and forced evacuation of Spain. He led British forces back into north-west Spain, securing victory at Talavera before retreating to Portugal (→ 8/5/11).

The British commander General Wellington leads his army into battle.

George's jubilee reflects changing face of Britain

Britain, 25 October 1810

As George III marks the golden jubilee of his reign – greeted today with elaborate celebrations throughout the country – he can look back on half a century of social and economic change that has revolutionised the face of Britain and reduced the power of the crown.

The population of England and Wales has grown from six and a half million in 1760 to over ten million today, and the total population of the United Kingdom (including Ireland) now stands at more than 18 million. This growth has prompted an increased demand for goods and services, fuelled by the needs of war, and industrial cities such as Manchester and Birmingham, Liverpool and Glasgow have developed.

The iron and cotton industries have been transformed, mainly through technological innovations by men such as Henry Cort, James Hargreaves and Richard Arkwright. The period has seen James Watt's invention of the steam engine and the development of the iron-smelting works at Coalbrookdale. Turnpike roads and canals have speeded up the pace of transport, and booming overseas trade has produced substantial capital for investment.

Although the hold of the old ruling classes is intact, a rich middle class is emerging; there has been a great expansion in informed public opinion, reflected in flourishing daily newspaper sales, and an increase in political participation.

Many factors have contributed to a diminution of royal power – particularly the growing importance of the office of prime minister. There has also been a steep decline in royal patronage, coupled with a deterioration in crown finances. The increasing volume and complexity of public business has made it impossible for a single individual to maintain total control.

George III
1760–1820

**House
of
Hanover**

Britain, 10 January 1811. The government is forced to accept paper money as currency as the economic crisis worsens.

Westminster, 29 January 1811. Spencer Perceval, the prime minister, discusses the provisions of the Regency Bill; Queen Charlotte will care for King George, while the Prince of Wales will accede as regent (→ 6/2).

Portugal, 8 May 1811. Troops led by General Viscount Wellington defeat the French forces at Fuentos d'Oñoro (→ 6/4/12).

London, 23 May 1811. George and the Prince Regent are reconciled after the prince's deft handling of the late Princess Amelia's will and his reinstatement of Frederick, the Duke of York, as commander-in-chief of the army (→ 7/1811).

London, 19 June 1811. The Prince Regent gives a huge celebration at Carlton House to mark his accession to the regency; his wife, Caroline, the Princess of Wales, and his daughter, Charlotte, are not invited (→ 11/1811).

Windsor, November 1811. Dr John Willis arrives to help his brother Robert treat the king; both are sons of the Reverend Francis Willis, who had treated the king when he was ill in 1788 (→ 2/1812).

London, November 1811. The Prince Regent has a badly sprained ankle, sustained while teaching his daughter, Charlotte, to dance the "highland fling" (→ 1812).

London, autumn 1811. The Duke of Clarence, keen to marry for money, separates from Mrs Dorothea Jordan, his mistress for twenty years and the mother of his ten children (→ 11/7/18).

London, February 1812. The regency of the Prince of Wales is made permanent following the king's failure to recover.

Spain, 6 April 1812. The Earl of Wellington, who seized Ciudad Rodrigo earlier this year, takes control of Badajoz (→ 6/1812).

Spain, June 1812. Forces under the Earl of Wellington reach Salamanca (→ 22/7).

Britain/America, June 1812. The United States of America declare war on Britain (→ 27/5/13).

Spain, 22 July 1812. The Earl of Wellington defeats the French at Salamanca (→ 27/6/13).

London, 1812. The Prince Regent forbids his wife, the Princess of Wales, to see their daughter, Charlotte, more than once a fortnight (→ 8/8/14).

North America, 27 May 1813. US troops capture the city of York [*Toronto*] from the British.

Europe, 27 June 1813. The Treaty of Reichenbach seals the Anglo-Russian-Prussian alliance against Napoleon (→ 10/1813).

Franco/Spanish border, Oct 1813. Forces under the Marquis of Wellington capture the town of Pamplona (→ 12/3/14).

France, 12 March 1814. On the abdication of Napoleon, the allies, led by the Marquis of Wellington, seize Bordeaux, leading to the restoration of the Bourbon monarchy in France (→ 30/3).

Elba, 30 March 1814. Napoleon is exiled to the island (→ 20/4).

Europe, 30 May 1814. The Treaty of Paris is signed; Britain restores all French colonies apart from Tobago, St Lucia and Mauritius; France agrees to a union with the Dutch Republic.

London, 12 July 1814. Princess Charlotte, after a row with her father, the Prince Regent, over her allegedly improper behaviour with Prince Augustus of Prussia, runs away from home (→ 25/12).

London, 25 December 1814. Princess Charlotte tells her father of her unchaperoned meetings with Captain Charles Hesse; the meetings took place at Kensington palace with the approval of her mother (→ 1/1816).

Europe, 20 November 1815. The Quadruple Alliance between Britain, Austria, Russia and Prussia is renewed.

Brighton, January 1816. Princess Charlotte is invited by her father to stay at the Marine Pavilion; Prince Leopold of Saxe-Coburg-Saalfeld is also invited (→ 2/5).

London, 2 May 1816. Princess Charlotte, aged 20, marries Leopold of Saxe-Coburg-Saalfeld, much to the delight of her father; the young couple will live at Claremont Park, near Esher, in Surrey (→ 5/11/17).

Paris, 5 July 1816. Mrs Jordan, the former mistress of William, the Duke of Clarence, who fled from England to avoid her creditors, dies destitute.

Esher, 5 November 1817. Princess Charlotte gives birth to a stillborn son (→ 6/11).

Westminster, November 1817. The succession is thrown into crisis by the death of Princess Charlotte; parliament proposes that the single royals marry.

Brussels, December 1817. Julie de St Laurent, for many years the mistress of the Duke of Kent, collapses on reading a report which recommends that the royal dukes should marry (→ 25/1/18).

Brussels, 25 January 1818. Princess Victoria of Leiningen, who has been courted by the Duke of Kent for two years, accepts his marriage proposal (→ 11/7).

London, 7 April 1818. Princess Elizabeth, the third daughter of George III, marries Frederick VI of Hesse-Homburg.

London, 1 June 1818. Adolphus, the Duke of Cambridge, marries Augusta, the daughter of Frederick, the ruler of Hesse-Cassel (→ 1829).

Kew, 11 July 1818. The Duke of Clarence and the Duke of Kent, King George's third and fourth sons, celebrate their marriages, both of which are to German princesses.

Britain, July 1818. The Duke and Duchess of Cumberland return to Germany; Queen Charlotte has refused to receive the new duchess, thinking her to be a most unsuitable wife for her son (→ 26/2/29).

Dover, 23 April 1819. The Duke of Kent and his pregnant wife arrive for the birth of their child (→ 24/5).

London, June 1819. The Prince Regent attends the christening of his niece and goddaughter, Alexandrina Victoria (→ 23/1/20).

Germany, 26 August 1819. A son, Albert, is born to the Duke and Duchess of Saxe-Coburg-Saalfeld; his parents plan that he should eventually marry his cousin, Princess Alexandrina Victoria.

Devon, 23 January 1820. Edward, the Duke of Kent, dies of pneumonia, aged 54; he leaves behind a legacy of debt (→ 7/10).

Windsor, 29 January 1820. George, who has suffered from blindness, madness and deafness for ten years, dies aged 82. →

Prince of Wales sworn in as regent

George hands over government to son

London, 6 February 1811

The Prince of Wales took the oaths of office as regent today and assumed charge of the government. The Regency Act, which parliament passed yesterday, states that the prince "shall have full power and authority, in the name and on behalf of HM, and under the style and title of Regent of the United Kingdom of Great Britain and Ireland, to exercise and administer the royal power". The act nonetheless limits the prince's powers in certain matters, such as creating peerages and granting offices.

Although the Prince of Wales has not been keen to take this step, something had to be done. Whatever his father is suffering from, he is clearly in no state to govern the country. Last November he had to be put into a strait-jacket after a particularly violent relapse into illness, and he has not yet shown signs of recovery.

The prince can at least comfort himself that the act is only to last one year. The best medical opinion is that the king should be better by next February. Because the measure is temporary, furthermore, the prince has told his Tory ministers that he will not be throwing them out of office in favour of his Whig friends. These same Whigs are hoping all the same that their patience will eventually be rewarded.

The Prince Regent, as he will be commonly known, is to look after the property of the crown as if the king were dead. The king's private property is meanwhile in the care of one Colonel Taylor. The colonel will draw £60,000 a year for the king's privy purse – money to pay for the royal library, George III's private property and his servants' allowances.

Medical care for the king will be one of the larger items in Colonel Taylor's accounts. With physicians and an apothecary in almost daily attendance, the bill will be huge. Unless King George makes the recovery that everyone expects, it is estimated that medical fees for the coming year will total several thou-

The Prince of Wales in Garter robes: now he has become regent.

A satirical view of Prince George's transformation into the country's ruler.

sands of pounds. Queen Charlotte and a small committee of privy councillors under the archbishop of Canterbury will take care of King George himself. He is in reasonably good health at present and is fully aware of the new act; the prime minister, Spencer Perceval, discussed it with him just a week ago. After an hour's conversation George said he was sure that everything was being done for the best – but he insisted that he will retain the title "king" (→ 23/5).

Fears for king's life mount after he has a startling relapse

Windsor, July 1811

The king has suffered a sudden and alarming relapse which has put his family and doctors in fear of his life. Since the onset of his latest bout of mental instability last year, George has had a series of attacks followed by periods of remission, but this latest manifestation of the illness has made him so violent that he has often needed restraint. The king's speech is incoherent and he is easily angered; apparently unaware of his condition, he refuses to eat and is unable to sleep, even with the help of laudanum.

Dr Robert Willis, who has treated the king in the past, has been put in overall charge of the patient's care. He favours a harsh regime, making frequent use of the strait-jacket – to the frustration of the other royal physicians, who believe that the king should lead as normal a life as possible (→ 11/1811).

Premier is slain; Liverpool in power

London, 8 June 1812

At about 5pm on 11 May John Bellingham, a commercial agent ruined by the war with France, went calmly up to the Tory prime minister, Spencer Perceval, in the lobby of the House of Commons and shot him dead. He also, metaphorically, finished off the government. The secretary for war, Lord Liverpool, took over from Perceval, but on 22 May the Tories resigned after a back-bench motion of no confidence.

After two weeks of frantic negotiations the Prince Regent has reappointed Lord Liverpool as prime minister. Buckling under the strain of the political horse-trading, the prince kept himself going on a dizzying mixture of alcohol and laudanum.

The prince's one-time Whig allies are furious at his desertion of them. Yet he has got what he wanted: a government determined to win the war but vague on thorny domestic issues such as political reform and poverty.

Editor imprisoned for libelling regent

The jailed author Leigh Hunt.

London, February 1813
Two brothers have been imprisoned for libelling the Prince Regent in an article published last year in a radical newspaper, the *Examiner*. John Hunt, the newspaper's editor, and his brother Leigh, the author of the offending words [*see below*], were each fined £500 and sentenced to two years in jail after a hearing at the court of the king's bench.

The sentences have been greeted by widespread protests in the world of the arts. A subscription fund is planned by a group including the poet Shelley. The Hunt brothers were charged before Lord Ellenborough and a special jury with "intention to traduce and vilify His Royal Highness the Prince of Wales, Regent of the United Kingdom". They were defended by Henry Brougham, a lawyer who used the trial to launch a spirited attack on the Prince Regent which was widely reported in the press, not least in a special issue of the *Examiner* which sold 10,000 copies within an hour of publication.

The words that upset the Prince Regent

London, February 1813
In response to a description of the regent in the *Morning Post* newspaper as an "Adonis of Loveliness", the *Examiner* remarked that he was in fact "a corpulent gentlemen of 50". It went on to call him "a violator of his word, a libertine over head and ears in debt and disgrace, a despiser of domestic ties, the companion of gamblers ... a man who has just closed half a century without one single claim on the gratitude of his country or the respect of posterity".

Prince puts out the flags to exploit the peace and hail the restored French king

A royal celebration: the Prince Regent at a military review, 1814.

London, 20 April 1814
The Prince Regent today escorted Louis XVIII through the streets of London to celebrate the restoration of the monarchy in France after 25 years of exile. The white flags of the Bourbon family were flying alongside the British flag as the two rather portly royals made their way in a state carriage drawn by eight white horses down Piccadilly towards Grillon's hotel in Albemarle Street where Louis will tonight spend his first night as head of state. The Royal Navy will escort Louis when he leaves for France in four days' time.

Napoleon was exiled to Elba on 30 March after troops led by the Marquis of Wellington had captured Bordeaux earlier in the month, but it was only today that the monarchy was formally restored. The Prince of Wales sent a message to Louis at Hartwell, near Aylesbury, in Buckinghamshire, where he has been living in exile. The Prince of Wales is determined to celebrate the triumphs of Wellington – a spectacular gala is planned – and the return of the French monarchy in style, bedecking Carlton House with white cockades, flags and illuminations.

The public response has so far been muted, however. Today's royal procession attracted few cheers from the people of London. The end of the European war is undoubtedly popular, but the Prince Regent's own unpopularity seems unaffected (→ 30/5).

Princess Charlotte breaks off engagement to Prince of Orange

London, 16 June 1814
Princess Charlotte, the only child of the Prince Regent, today broke off her engagement to William, the Prince of Orange. The Dutch prince, who had hoped to be prince consort to a future English queen, is disappointed. The Prince Regent is said to be furious. Relations between George and his 18-year-old daughter have been deteriorating all year; George had accused her of flirting with the Duke of Devonshire, Charlotte had refused to live abroad if she married William. The Dutch and English governments were both consulted, but the princess remained intractable (→ 12/7).

A new suitor for the princess? Charlotte dancing with the Duke of Devonshire.

King's doctors do not expect recovery

London, 2 April 1814
A pessimistic report about the king's condition was given by his doctors to the queen's council today. "We do not expect the king's recovery," they said, "but it is not impossible." George is said be living in a world of his own, no longer asking about his family, although the queen continues to visit him regularly. His senility is worse, but he is more tranquil than a few years ago, spending hours playing the harpsichord (often talking to himself) but not needing the restraint of a strait-jacket (→ 20/1/17).

Princess of Wales leaves England

Celebrations held for centenary of House of Hanover

Worthing, Sussex, 8 August 1814

The Princess of Wales has left England. After 19 years of increasingly acrimonious marriage Princess Caroline has abandoned the Prince Regent and is returning to her childhood home in the Duchy of Brunswick in northern Germany. She is now sailing to Hamburg on the frigate *Jason*.

Relations between Caroline and her husband have never been good, and they have not lived under the same roof for 18 years. The prince had sought to ignore her, not only preferring other women in private but also seeking to deny her any public role. Caroline was barred from seeing visiting dignitaries and was recently refused a seat at a thanksgiving service in St Paul's. The worsening feud had also kept Caroline apart from her only child, Princess Charlotte.

She was not unpopular with the people. "Where's your wife?" they sometimes hissed as the prince's carriage passed. But many of her friends felt unable to maintain their friendship in the face of the prince's hostility. Those friends who stayed loyal urged her to protect her rights as the potential future queen by staying in the country, but she now seems to have been goaded by her treatment into flight abroad. The prince will be pleased (→ 1819).

Caroline, the Princess of Wales: now she has left her husband's country.

London, 1 August 1814

One hundred years of Hanoverian kings were celebrated today by an elaborate gala in the parks of London. The Prince Regent personally orchestrated the festivities, which featured exotic buildings, a hot-air balloon and a mock naval battle on the Serpentine. The day ended with a firework display above the battlements of a Gothic castle specially erected in Green Park.

It has been a summer of festivities in the capital. First there was the restoration of the French monarchy; then there was a huge fête at Carlton House to honour the Duke of Wellington. But today's celebrations were the largest and most spectacular. Pagodas, towers and brightly-coloured bridges sprang up in the royal parks; lamps and lanterns looped through trees; arcades, refreshment booths and roundabouts turned Hyde Park into popular pleasure grounds.

And despite gloomy foreboding in the *Times* (and one early downpour) the crowds came in great numbers and good humour. They even cheered when the pagoda in St James's park burst into flames, killing one person, believing that the fire was part of the spectacle.

New novel set against Jacobite rebellion

An illustration from "Waverley".

Edinburgh, 1814

An anonymous novel, *Waverley, or 'Tis Sixty Years Since*, has had an instantaneous success with the reading public here. It is set during the Jacobite rebellion of "Bonnie Prince Charlie" in 1745. The hero, Edward Waverley, is a young English officer who falls in love with Flora, the daughter of a Highland chieftain, and joins the Jacobites. They are defeated, but he is saved from being executed by an English officer whose life he has saved.

The book is a romantic blend of history, Scottish folklore and humour and vivid descriptive writing. Some see in it a resemblance to the romantic poetry of Sir Walter Scott, the Edinburgh lawyer and clerk of session, who wrote *The Lay of the Last Minstrel*.

A cartoon by Richard Dighton satirising the extravagant appearance of the socialites commonly known as "dandies". The fashion has reached new heights during the Prince of Wales's regency – tight waistcoats, high collars and ornamental hairstyles such as these are often seen in London society. It is a style favoured by the prince himself, who is never averse to cutting a dash in public. He has maintained a close friendship with George ("Beau") Brummell, perhaps the most famous dandy of them all.

Prince Regent wins renown for role as lavish and discerning patron of the arts

London, 1815

The Prince Regent spares no effort (or expense) in his lavish patronage of painters, sculptors, musicians, architects and authors. Carlton House is full of old masters, chosen with a discerning eye, and artists from Reynolds to Lawrence (who was knighted this year) have received commissions. Sculptors whom the prince has fostered include the great Italian Antonio Canova, and he supported Lord Elgin's removal to Britain of the Parthenon's marble friezes.

The prince loves music and is a perceptive critic. He became a patron of Haydn, who praised his cello-playing, when the composer visited England in the 1790s. He is also a keen reader and enjoys the novels of Jane Austen, whom he invited to Carlton House this year. She means to dedicate her next novel, *Emma*, to him.

The regent's greatest expenses have been on buildings, such as the dazzling Pavilion at Brighton, currently undergoing alterations by the architect John Nash, who is also involved in the plan for a new street to link Carlton House with Regent's Park [*see page 380*]. The prince has also encouraged eminent scientists, such as William Herschel, astronomer-royal since 1782, Humphry Davy, the inventor of the miners' safety lamp, and William Congreve, the inventor of the ballistic missile known as the Congreve Rocket.

Theseus and the Minotaur, by the Italian sculptor Antonio Canova.

Safety lamps for miners, invented by the scientist Humphry Davy.

A detail from the Parthenon marbles, brought to Britain by Lord Elgin.

Regent hears news of Napoleon's defeat

London, 18 June 1815

The news of Napoleon's defeat at Waterloo was brought to the Prince Regent tonight while he was at a party given by the well-known hostess Mrs Boehm at her house in St James's Square. The party was going well, and the regent's presence had set the seal upon it, when the dusty and still bloodstained figure of Major Henry Percy suddenly appeared, having ridden directly from the battlefield.

Announcing victory, Major Percy went down on one knee before the regent and laid at his feet the captured eagles of the French.

Then the prince asked the ladies to leave the room while Lord Liverpool read out the dispatch which Percy had brought him. When it was finished he turned to Percy and said: "I congratulate you" – and then promoted him to colonel.

All were delighted with the news, save Mrs Boehm, who felt that it had quite ruined her party. Later, when he had had time to reflect upon events, the Prince Regent grew sombre. "It is a glorious victory and we must rejoice at it," he said. "But the loss of life has been fearful." And the tears rolled down his cheeks (→ 20/11).

Duke of Cumberland weds German cousin

London, 29 August 1815

The marriage of the Duke of Cumberland to his cousin, Frederica of Mecklenburg-Strelitz, was solemnised at Carlton House today according to the rites of the Anglican Church. The Prince Regent was at the ceremony, but the queen and her daughters pointedly stayed away. Queen Charlotte is the bride's aunt, but Princess Frederica's chequered history has made her unsuitable in the queen's eyes to marry her youngest son.

The queen's disapproval is not altogether without justification. The princess has already been married twice, once to Prince Frederick of Prussia and then, while she was engaged to the Duke of Cambridge, hurriedly to Prince Frederick of Solms-Braunfels, by whom she had discovered herself to be pregnant. Parliament shares the queen's sentiments. It is customary to increase

The Duke of Cumberland.

the allowance of a member of the royal family upon marriage, but parliament has refused to raise the duke's allowance from £18,000 to £24,000 a year (→ 7/1818).

Court painter knighted by Prince Regent

London, April 1815

The court painter Thomas Lawrence has been knighted by the Prince Regent for his magnificent work in painting the allied sovereigns, ministers and generals who contributed to Napoleon's fall. The idea came from the regent himself, who commissioned Lawrence to do the work, even though Lawrence was in France when the summons from the regent came.

He had been studying the works of art that Napoleon had looted from throughout Europe and gathered together in the Louvre. He was recalled to London where he began painting the collection that so pleased the Prince Regent. So delighted was the prince that, when he knighted him, he told Lawrence that "he was proud to confer a mark of his favour on one who had raised the character of British art in the estimation of all Europe". Even the severest critics of both Lawrence and the prince agree that the work is magnificent.

Princess Mary marries Duke of Gloucester

Queen's House, 23 July 1816
The marriage of the Duke of Gloucester to Princess Mary took place here today, to the surprise and, as it turned out, the discomfort of many of the wedding guests. The duke is not the most handsome man in the world. Indeed, he has been described as "large and stout, with weak helpless legs, prominent meaningless eyes and without being actually ugly, a very unpleasant face with an animal expression".

While she does not love the duke, Princess Mary is one of the few people to be genuinely fond of him. As she is his favourite sister, the regent gave his permission and personally helped to negotiate the marriage contract.

The marriage ceremony was a disaster. The room was far too small and became excessively crowded and hot. Seats were so badly arranged that few people could see what was happening, with the result that the congregation became

Princess Mary with her husband.

increasingly restless and noisy. The bride looked as if she was about to faint, her sisters and ladies could not stop crying, and the regent, who gave her away, also burst into tears.

Regent loses only child

Claremont, 6 November 1817
Princess Charlotte, the only daughter of the Prince Regent and heir to the British throne, died suddenly here today after a 50-hour labour. Her child, an abnormally large boy, was born dead, but there had been no suggestion that there was anything wrong with the princess.

At midnight the princess began to complain of feeling cold and of a singing in her head. The doctors were hastily summond and recommended brandy, but Princess Charlotte failed to respond and, with a gentle sigh, died. The Prince Regent had arrived at Carlton House at between three and four in the morning and being assured his daughter was well had gone to bed. Roused by the Duke of York and Lord Bathurst to be told that the princess was dead, he collapsed into the arms of the duke. The loss of the heir is not only a tragedy for the family but also a crisis for the country as it leaves the long-term succession uncertain (→ 11/1817).

The funeral ceremony for Charlotte, the Prince Regent's only child.

Playwright Sheridan dies in great poverty

London, 7 July 1816
The playwright Richard Brinsley Sheridan died today in great poverty. Despite being a friend of the Prince Regent and having successful careers both as a playwright and as a member of parliament, Sheridan did not invest wisely. He became so indebted that he was once described as "the man who extend-ed England's credit". Sheridan did not think this particularly funny, but the regent, who was present, begged him not to take offence. Despite successes with *The Rivals*, *The School for Scandal* and *The Critic*, Sheridan lost most of his wealth when the Drury Lane theatre, which he partly owned, burnt down. His wife squandered the rest.

Stone is hurled at the Prince Regent

Westminster, 28 January 1817
Amid a background of mounting unrest a stone was hurled at the Prince Regent's carriage today as he made his way to parliament. No harm was done, but the incident underlines the disorder that has been growing since the end of the Napoleonic wars. Bad harvests and a drastic reduction in demand for British goods have come at a time when tens of thousands of soldiers and sailors are returning from the war to look for work in a country without jobs. Agitation for revolutionary change is sure to grow as hunger increases.

Queen Charlotte: royal splendour.

King fails to recognise the queen during her visits to Windsor

Windsor, 20 January 1817
The king's mental illness has not improved as had been hoped, and he remains here at Windsor in what can only be described as a sorry state. He is blind and senile, and, while every effort is made to ensure his comfort, he is often left alone all day with servants who are in effect his keepers. If he becomes violent he is restrained in a strait-jacket, but most of the time he does nothing except talk incessantly and spend hours playing his harpsicord.

Queen Charlotte visits him from time to time, and although he does not recognise her she is able to write to reassure the other members of the royal family that "the dear king is very comfortable in every sense". However, the king's medical treatment and its expense is being questioned, and the queen's council has openly asked Dr Robert Willis: "Do you think that by throwing buckets of water upon your patient's head he can be cured?"

Apart from Robert and John Willis, the king has three other doctors, each of whom attends two days a week and is paid 30 guineas a visit. Medical expenses are now over £30,000 a year, prompting the prime minister, Lord Liverpool, to ask if it is necessary to spend so much "merely to have a physician shake his head and say the king is no better" (→ 29/1/20).

Regent's vision has monumental legacy

Brighton and London, 1820

The Prince Regent's grand architectural schemes are the most striking monuments to both his imagination and his extravagance. Foremost among them is his Royal Pavilion at Brighton, an exuberant explosion of mock Orientalism. It has recently been remodelled by John Nash, who is also responsible for the new Regent's Street in London whose majestic classical sweep links Regent's Park with Pall Mall. The prince has sponsored a more prosaic new thoroughfare in the Regent's Canal, which opened this year, linking the Grand Union Canal near Paddington to the docks.

A coloured print of the splendid Royal Pavilion at Brighton, which has been utterly remodelled for the Prince Regent by the architect John Nash.

The Regent's Canal: the east entrance to the Islington tunnel. Building took eight years and required 12 locks, 40 bridges and two tunnels.

Regent's Street in central London, built by John Nash in 1818 to link the Prince's Carlton House in Pall Mall with Regent's Park to the north.

Queen Charlotte dies at Kew, aged 74

Kew, Surrey, 17 November 1818

Queen Charlotte died here today aged 74. Her health had been failing for some time, and this autumn she had moved to Kew to be cared for by two of her daughters, Princesses Augusta and Mary. The queen had asked to be moved to Windsor to be with the king, but because of her condition this was impossible. She had been married to George for 57 years; it had been an arranged marriage, but they came genuinely to love each other, and she nursed George with compassion long after his illness meant that he no longer recognised her.

Princess Augusta tried to prepare both the Prince Regent and her mother for Charlotte's approaching end. She wrote to the prince from Kew to warn him that the doctors had told her that their mother was "very ill", and she also broke the news to the queen. On hearing this Charlotte murmured "So!" and laying her head on her pillow began to weep endlessly.

She had suffered a great deal of physical pain, and the thought that she was dying seemed to distress her very greatly, but after a while she grew calmer and was able to discuss her will. Yesterday the will was brought for her to sign, and it came not a moment too soon because her condition was already critical. The doctors were alarmed enough to send for the Prince Regent, who drove post-haste down to Kew. He arrived in time to see his mother before the end and was sitting on her bed, holding her hand, when she died.

Four royal weddings celebrated in a year

England, 1818

There have been four royal weddings this year, prompted by the death last year of the Prince Regent's only child, Princess Charlotte, after giving birth to a stillborn boy. This created a crisis because there was then no one to succeed the regent: every marriageable member of the royal family who might produce an heir was asked to marry at once.

There were four unmarried dukes, all living more or less happily with mistresses of long standing. The Duke of Sussex refused to leave his mistress, Lady Cecilia Underwood, but the other three, the Dukes of Clarence, Cambridge and Kent, were prepared to answer the nation's call. So was their sister, the 47-year-old Princess Elizabeth, who used the opportunity to marry the despised Frederick, the hereditary ruler of Hesse-Homburg, a man described as looking like "a vulgar German corporal".

Of the dukes, Adolphus of Cambridge married first, to Princess Augusta of Hesse-Cassel. Then, in a double ceremony held at Kew on 11 July, William of Clarence married Princess Adelaide of Saxe-Meiningen, while Edward of Kent married the business-like Princess Victoria of Saxe-Coburg, the 31-year-old widow of the Prince of Leiningen.

Victoria, the new Duchess of Kent.

Edward, the Duke of Kent, aged 50.

Duchess gives birth to Princess Victoria

Princess Victoria during her infancy dressed in an elaborate bonnet.

Kensington Palace, 24 May 1819

At 4.15am today a daughter was born to Princess Victoria, the wife of the Duke of Kent. The child is described as being strong and is expected to be called Victoria after her mother. Both mother and baby appear well. The princess had promised her husband a son, but the duke was once told by a gypsy fortune teller in Malta that he would one day father a great queen.

He reflects philosophically that "the decrees of Providence are at all times wisest and best". On a more practical level, the new princess's family is far from well off. The duke had been living in his wife's castle in Germany but was determined that the birth would be in England. Lacking the money to get here, he loaded his heavily pregnant wife, their belongings and the only qualified woman doctor in Germany into his coach and, to save the expense of a coachman, drove them himself across Europe, arriving at Dover on 23 April.

It seems certain that the little princess will grow up with a strong German background. Her mother speaks so little English that her official speeches are rendered into phonetics for her: "Ei regrett biing aes yiett so littl conversant in thie Inglish lenguetsh" (→ 6/1819).

'Topless' princess under fire in Europe

London, 1819

After her separation from the Prince Regent, the behaviour of Caroline, the Princess of Wales, has attracted much criticism in Europe. A large, fat, elderly woman possessed of an enormous bust, she is said to surround herself with handsome young men and wear little-girl frocks, and she allegedly likes to dance topless at balls and parties. On visiting Jerusalem, Caroline – who will be queen if or when the prince becomes king – had herself led, Christ-like, into the city on an ass and founded the Order of St Caroline, of which she made her Italian lover Bartolomeo Pergami grand master (→ 11/2/20).

A satirical view of the immodest appearance of the Princess of Wales.

George dies at Windsor

Windsor, 29 January 1820

King George III died this evening at Windsor castle. He was 82 years old and had been king for 60 years [*see below*], although his mental instability had rendered him incapable of ruling since 1811. Despite his great age and long illness, his end came suddenly, and he died at precisely 8.38pm in a small, sparsely furnished room.

After the death of Queen Charlotte in 1818, responsibility for the king's welfare had been taken over by the Duke of York, who was warned by the doctors that "without any apparent illness, his majesty appears to be declining fast". By January he spent most of his day in bed; he had suffered a rupture and could take only liquid food, but when the Duke of York saw him on 10 January he still appeared reasonably well. Ten days later it was a different story. The duke wrote to his brother, the Prince Regent, on 20 January: "Alas, upon going into the room yesterday, I never was more shocked than in perceiving the melancholy alteration which has taken place in him during the ten days that I have not seen him. The degree of weakness and languor in his looks and the emaciation of his face struck me more than I can describe."

By 27 January the king was unable to rise from his bed. He could no longer speak and had to be fed with a spoon. After his death the duke wrote to his brother that "the only immediate consolation under such a calamity is the almost conviction that his last moments were free from bodily suffering and mental distress".

A 60-year reign draws to a close: King George's sombre funeral procession.

Long reign has seen momentous changes

Britain, 1820

The 60-year reign of George III has seen vast social and political upheaval and a number of momentous international developments, the most far-reaching of which were the loss of the American colonies and Napoleon's defeat. The power and influence of the monarchy are much reduced from what they were when he came to the throne.

He inherited the crown from his grandfather, George II, in October 1760, at a time when the country was enjoying a peak of prosperity. It took him some time to establish himself, and the strain of trying to do so may have precipitated the first signs of the illnesses that be-devilled him until the end of his life. In 1788 he suffered a mental illness which left him seriously deranged for four months.

The French Revolution brought increasing danger, and in the 1790s the king was the target of assassination attempts. The last ten years of his active reign were dominated by the Napoleonic wars and the threat of invasion. This, coupled with the his youngest daughter's death, triggered the final attack of his illness in 1811, from which he never recovered. His keen interest in agricultural science and his creation of model farms at Windsor earned him the nickname "Farmer George" – of which he was intensely proud.

George IV
1820–1830

**House
of
Hanover**

London, 30 January 1820. The Prince Regent accedes to the throne as George IV (→ 31/1).

Windsor, 7 February 1820. Edward, the Duke of Kent, a brother of George IV, is buried in St George's chapel (→ 12/2).

London, 11 February 1820. The king begins divorce proceedings against his estranged wife, Queen Caroline (→ 17/8).

London, 12 February 1820. The newly-widowed Duchess of Kent and baby Victoria arrive; they are dependent on the charity of Prince Leopold, the brother the duchess and former husband of the late Princess Charlotte (→ 5/1825).

London, 15 February 1820. The funeral of George III takes place. George IV does not attend because of an attack of pleurisy; on the advice of his doctor he is convalescing in Brighton, where Mary Mitford is keeping him company.

Surrey, 6 August 1820. Frederica, the Duchess of York, aged 43 and childless, dies of water on the lung.

London, 17 August 1820. The inquiry into Queen Caroline's conduct opens; it will determine whether or not George is able to divorce her (→ 29/11).

Britain, August 1820. Women protest at the king's shoddy treatment of his wife.

London, 10 December 1820. The Duchess of Clarence gives birth to a daughter, Elizabeth Georgiana Adelaide, the heiress to the duke and therefore second in line for the throne (→ 4/3/21).

Britain, January 1821. Queen Caroline accepts £50,000 and a house as part of her settlement after the public enquiry (→ 7/1821).

London, 4 March 1821. Elizabeth, the 12-week-old daughter of the Duke of Clarence, dies, and Princess Victoria is again heiress to the throne.

London, July 1821. Queen Caroline demands to be crowned alongside George (→ 19/7).

Westminster, 19 July 1821. George is crowned king in a long and splendid ceremony.→

London, 25 July 1821 The dowager Countess of Jersey, one of the king's former mistresses, dies.

London, 14 August 1821. A week after Queen Caroline's death her crimson coffin, with the inscription "Caroline of Brunswick, the injured Queen of England" begins its voyage to Brunswick.

Britain, 24 September 1821. Days after his return from Ireland, George plans to visit Hanover, calling at the site of the Battle of Waterloo on the way.

London, 23 April 1822. The Duchess of Clarence gives birth to stillborn boy twins.

London, 12 August 1822. The suicide of Robert Castlereagh, the Marquis of Londonderry, George's foreign secretary, causes political chaos (→ 9/9).

Brighton, 19 August 1822. The elaborate renovation of the Marine Pavilion commissioned by George is finally finished (→ 12/1823).

Westminster, 9 September 1822. George sets aside his reservations and appoints George Canning, a former favourite of Queen Caroline and one of Castlereagh's rivals, as foreign secretary (→ 4/1823).

London, April 1823. The existence of a "cottage clique", led by the king and the Duke of Wellington, meeting in the Windsor lodge and allegedly intent on obstructing the policies of George Canning, the foreign secretary, causes increasing concern (→ 7/1823).

Windsor, autumn 1823. George plans to renovate the castle buildings (→ 12/1842).

London, December 1823. George pays off the debts of his brother, the Duke of York (→ 15/4/25).

Westminster, February 1825. George pleads gout and loss of his false teeth as an excuse not to read the king's speech recognising the independence of Buenos Aires, Mexico and Colombia (→ 2/2/26).

London, May 1825. Princess Victoria is granted an allowance of £6,000 to live in the style of the heiress to the throne (→ 8/1826).

Windsor, 2 February 1826. George, suffering from gout, is unable to open parliament for the second time (→ 1827).

Windsor, summer 1826. George Canning is in royal favour; he accepts an invitation to visit George at the royal lodge (→ 10/4/27).

Windsor, August 1826. George is visited by his seven-year-old niece, Princess Victoria (→ 18/2/28).

London, 4 January 1827. Carlton House is demolished for renovation.

London, 20 January 1827. Against medical advice, George attends the funeral of his brother Frederick.→

London, February 1827. Lord Liverpool, the prime minister, suffers a stroke (→ 10/4/27).

London, April 1827. William, the Duke of Clarence, is appointed as lord high admiral after Lord Melville resigns (→ 10/1827).

Ludwigsburg, 6 October 1828. Charlotte, the Princess Royal, the wife of King Frederick of Württemberg, dies aged 72.

London, 1829. George puts pressure on his brother Adolphus, the Duke of Cambridge, who is viceroy of Hanover, to live in England (→ 8/7/50).

London, 12 January 1830. The Duchess of Clarence has annoyed her sister-in-law, the Duchess of Kent, by writing to warn her about allowing her husband's executor, John Conroy, to become too influential in her affairs.→

Windsor, 26 June 1830. George dies after a series of strokes at the age of 67.→

The life and times of King George IV

Name: George Augustus Frederick.
Birth: 12 August 1762.
Regency: began 6 February 1811.
Accession: 29 January 1820.
Coronation: 19 July 1821.
Hair: grey.
Eyes: blue.
Marriage: Caroline of Brunswick, 8 April 1795.
Child: Charlotte (died 1819).

Favourite homes: Windsor castle and the Royal Pavilion, Brighton.
Likes: eating, drinking, women and gambling.
Dislikes: his wife.
Greatest problems: debt and unpopularity.
Greatest success: patronage of the arts.
Death: 26 June 1830.

Opposite: King George IV, in formal clothes but a relaxed pose.

At long last, the Prince Regent becomes George IV

Dissolute king is disliked by the people

Regent becomes king: George IV.

London, 31 January 1820
George IV was proclaimed king at noon today in the forecourt of Carlton House. He is 57 years old and has been regent for the past nine years; he took the regency oaths in February 1811, after his father's mental illness had made him incapable of ruling.

In his many years at the forefront of public life – during which he has been an extravagant patron of the arts – the new king has not endeared himself to the British people. From an early age he acquired a reputation for dissolute living and self-indulgence which made him the butt of popular ridicule. In part, the rebellious behaviour of his youth seems to have been a reaction against the strict upbringing insisted on by his father.

The Prince of Wales was only 17 when his affair with an actress – the first of many for the prince – became the talk of London. Three years later, the heir to the throne secretly married a Catholic widow, Maria Fitzherbert. Meanwhile, his debts soared, and at one stage he had to shut up his London residence, Carlton House, and move to Brighton, starting a long association with the town. In 1795, having broken his ties with Mrs Fitzherbert, the prince married Princess Caroline of Brunswick – whereupon parliament paid his debts. The marriage was a disaster; the couple soon separated and their only child, Charlotte, died in 1817. Caroline – seen by the British people as a victim of her husband's maltreatment – left England for the continent in 1814; one of the king's great fears is that she may now return to claim her rights.

Politically, the prince has been close to the Whigs – with Fox, Burke and Sheridan numbered among his friends – but as regent he has, like his father, governed with the aid of the Tories (→ 11/2).

Public inquiry clears Caroline's reputation

Queen Caroline looks on as her future is debated in the House of Lords.

London, 29 November 1820
Queen Caroline drove in state to St Paul's today to give thanks for her deliverance from her enemies. Thousands cheered her on her way, although the cathedral itself was half empty. The service came after three weeks in which the queen – who is generally thought to have been abysmally treated by her husband – has enjoyed an astonishing show of popularity across the land.

The celebrations began after the Lords withdrew a bill that would have deprived Caroline of the title of queen and dissolved her marriage to King George IV. When news of the bill's failure became public, there were bonfires and fireworks, dances and processions in many provincial cities, as well as widespread rejoicing in London, which was "illuminated" for three nights. The bill had been hurriedly introduced in the House of Lords in June following the princess's return from the continent, where she had been for six years, to assert her rights as queen after her husband's accession.

Debate on the bill, which lasted for 11 weeks, took the form of a public inquiry, every stage of which was eagerly followed by the British people. It focused on Caroline's alleged adultery with Bartolomeo Pergami, the former soldier who had been appointed chamberlain in the queen's household during her exile. Eventually, the Lords found themselves unable to reach a clear decision about the queen's guilt or otherwise, giving the bill a third reading by such a slim majority that it had to be withdrawn – to the consternation of the king, who has long been trying to rid himself of his troublesome wife (→ 1/1821).

Conspirators of Cato Street are arrested

The conspirators are arrested.

London, 23 February 1820
Within a month of becoming king, George IV has faced a major crisis. A gang plotting to kill the entire cabinet has been apprehended in the nick of time. Led by Arthur Thistlewood, an estate agent turned revolutionary, the gang had planned to murder the ministers this evening as they dined at a house in Grosvenor Square. Told about the plot by an informer, the government today had the conspirators arrested in a loft in Cato Street, off the Edgware Road. Praising Lord Sidmouth's calm handling of the operation, a relieved king described the home secretary as "the Duke of Wellington on home service".

A public celebration: Queen Caroline riding in state to St Paul's.

Queen denied entrance to coronation

Maltreated queen dies, to the king's undoubted relief

With glittering ceremony: George IV, in splendid velvet robes, is crowned in a five-hour service in Westminster abbey.

London, 7 August 1821
The woman who had bedevilled the king's life for 26 years died today at a house in Hammersmith, west of London, aged 53. Queen Caroline's death comes within three weeks of the coronation from which she was excluded; she fell ill at the theatre that same evening and was said to be suffering from an "acute inflammation of the bowels" from which she never recovered.

Caroline of Brunswick married the then Prince of Wales in April 1795 a few days after their first meeting. They disliked one another instantly and within a year – after the birth of their only child, Charlotte – had decided to live apart. Caroline moved to Blackheath,

Caroline: a maltreated queen.

Westminster, 19 July 1821
Shortly before half-past ten this morning, a glittering procession set off from Westminster Hall for the abbey to celebrate the coronation of King George IV. Preceded by massed ranks of bishops, peers, privy councillors in white and blue satin Elizabethan dress, and other dignitaries of church and state, the king walked under a canopy of cloth-of-gold wearing a 27-foot-long train of crimson velvet embroidered with golden stars. The long brown curls of his wig were topped by a hat decorated with ostrich feathers, making him look, in the words of one onlooker, "like some gorgeous bird of the east".

The abbey service lasted for five hours, during which the king, burdened by his heavy robes, at times looked on the point of collapse. He was seen nodding and winking at his friend Lady Conyngham before the archbishop of York gave a sermon on a king's duty to preserve his people from "the contagion of vice". After the crowning ceremony, the congregation in the abbey waved their hats and shouted "God bless the king!". Then, while the people enjoyed fireworks in Hyde Park and church bells pealed across the country, the king sat down with 300 guests to a spectacular banquet at Westminster Hall.

The coronation – perhaps the most magnificent ever seen in this country – cost parliament almost a quarter of a million pounds. The only sour note was struck by Queen Caroline, who returned from the continent last month. Outraged by her exclusion, she made several unsuccessful attempts to gain admittance to the abbey, but was finally persuaded to give up (→ 7/8).

where she helped poor people. She was denied any part in the upbringing of Charlotte (who died in 1817), and her husband's ill-treatment of her evoked great public sympathy.

In 1806 allegations that she had had an illegitimate child led to a "delicate investigation" which exonerated her. Since 1814 she has been travelling in Europe, where allegations of sexual misbehaviour culminated in last year's failed attempt in parliament to deprive her of the title of queen. Before she died, the queen asked to be buried in Germany in a coffin engraved with the inscription "Caroline of Brunswick, the injured Queen of England" (→ 14/8).

George's state visit to Ireland has a romantic ulterior motive

London, 16 September 1821
King George returned to Carlton House today after a hugely successful visit to Ireland which ended with a long and perilous homeward voyage in his yacht, the *Royal George*. He had been preparing to set out for Ireland when he heard news of the queen's death [*see report right*]. The king loved the welcome that he received in Ireland where, for once, religious differences were put aside to celebrate the new monarch's first state visit. In Dublin he enjoyed a ceaseless round of processions, banquets and receptions. After one feast, at Trinity college, he apparently "glowed with pleasure" at the singing of *Rule, Britannia*.

But he derived most joy from a stay at Slane castle, the home of Marquis Conyngham, north of Dublin. Elizabeth, the marchioness, a rich and ample woman of 52, has replaced the Marchioness of Hertford in the king's affections. Their relations are said to be flirtatious and playful; they spend their time holding hands, whispering and kissing. To many, such behaviour by a portly, ageing king seems more absurd than scandalous (→ 24/9).

King George dons the kilt and wins over the Scots during two-week royal tour

A satire on the king's Scottish trip shows George (left) wearing a kilt.

Lothian, 29 August 1822

George IV's visit to Scotland, which ended today, has put a question mark against many Scots' idea of the king as a fat, ageing lecher. He has won them over with his enthusiasm for Gaelic customs, even putting on a kilt for a levée at Holyrood House, although regal modesty obliged him to wear flesh-coloured tights on his legs.

The admiration is mutual. "Good God! What a fine sight!" George exclaimed a week ago as he looked down from the battlements of Edinburgh castle at the thousands of citizens who had turned out to see him despite the pouring rain. "I had no conception there was such a scene in the world ... the people are as beautiful and extraordinary as the scene." Sir Walter Scott, a writer whom the king admires, deserves the credit for the smooth running of the tour, although he had only a month to prepare for the arrival of "our fat friend", as he once referred to George. He has organised literally everything from the Holyrood levée and an Edinburgh pageant to details of court dress – and, of course, a command performance of a play based on his own *Rob Roy*.

One particular success was a reception at Holyrood at which 456 ladies were presented to the king in the course of an hour and a quarter – one every ten seconds. The only hitch, meanwhile, happened at a peers' ball in the Assembly Rooms when one of the Celtic chiefs bowed so low that his pistols dropped onto the king's big toe.

George retires to Brighton as health fails

East Sussex, 1823

King George is rapidly acquiring a reputation as a recluse. He is rarely seen in the capital, preferring to spend time at his seaside hideaway, the Brighton Pavilion. But not even the pavilion keeps him happy, and his attention is turning more and more to Windsor where he spent two months over the autumn, assessing the castle as a residence.

George comes to London only to open and prorogue parliament, and he strives to keep out of the public gaze as he becomes increasingly sensitive about his appearance, much altered through ill-health. Crippling rheumatic pain in the joints makes him hobble, while dropsy has bloated his already stout figure. In May of this year the Duke of Wellington felt that George had barely eight months' life left in him.

Brighton has proved a great disappointment to the king, and he began to lose interest in the ornate pavilion almost as soon as it was completed last year. The town's recent growth has put an end to the seclusion that George longs for. Furthermore, the pavilion's exposed position makes him fret about would-be assassins.

To make matters worse the king's mistress, Marchioness Conyngham, does not like Brighton society, not least because she fears that she is the butt of many a wit's barbed remarks. This may well be so: most people at court regard her as little more than an overweight gold-digger (→ 2/1825).

Orientalism by the sea: the king's fabulous Royal Pavilion at Brighton

King George III's library: his son has given the collection to the nation.

King's library given to growing museum

London, January 1823

Arrangements are under way to bring George III's vast library of 65,000 books to its new home: the British Museum in Bloomsbury. The museum's trustees were delighted with the news that their intense lobbying of the present king had paid off. They faced competition, it is rumoured, from Czar Alexander of Russia who wanted to buy the collection. New space has to be found to house the King's Library, as it will be known. The museum was opened 70 years ago and has grown enormously since then, not least thanks to generous contributions from the House of Hanover. Parliament has promised money to build an extension for King George IV's gift.

Although the Dukes of York and Clarence are furious with their brother for giving away their father's property, the king sees the gift as both a tribute to George III and a way of "advancing the literature of the country" (→ 12/1823).

King resents new limits on his power

London, July 1823
At a Carlton House ball this month the French *chargé d'affaires*, the Viscount de Marcellus, was treated to the spectacle of the king shouting abuse at one of his ministers. The hapless victim was George Canning, the new foreign secretary, appointed after Lord Castlereagh's suicide last August.

Canning later explained to de Marcellus that "ministers have to endure without answering back the epigrams by which a king seeks to avenge himself for his impotence". He was referring to the principle established by his recent appointment in the teeth of royal opposition – that politicians, not kings, have the last word in deciding government posts. George had bitterly opposed Canning's appointment

Canning: abused by King George.

but was overruled by Lord Liverpool. Several cabinet members on the liberal wing had threatened to resign if Canning were not accepted, which would have meant the collapse of the government.

George despises Canning, partly for having supported Queen Caroline but more because he stands for a liberalism that goes against the king's every instinct. While George prefers a conservative, monarchical Europe, Canning's foreign policy favours national interests above those of the crown. But the king has to accept that his powers have their limit and accept Canning's appointment – the "greatest sacrifice" that he has ever made (→ 25/1/25).

King shows appetite for music and books

John Liston: operatic star.

Rossini: favourite of King George.

London, December 1823
The plump figure of Gioacchino Rossini may not cut much of a dash among the dandies at court, but the composer of *The Barber of Seville* is more than welcome there. Rossini is visiting England and has been presented to the king, ever eager to be seen as a patron of the arts. George is particularly keen on opera, admiring stars such as John Liston at Covent Garden.

Courtiers present at the meeting between King George and Rossini were left indignant at the Italian's easy familiarity. Lady Granville, for one, noted how the "fat and lazy" Rossini sat himself down next to the king without a by-your-leave. King George was, however, unperturbed and insisted on accompanying his guest on the piano.

The king played his best, although not well enough to stop

Rossini wishing that he could keep time rather better than he did. George did get a compliment of sorts from the maestro, none the less. Rossini, perhaps more taken with the king's charm than with his playing, declared that "there are few in your royal highness's position who could play so well".

The king has an equal passion for literature. He was, for example, characteristically generous when he helped to found the Royal Society of Literature three years ago.

George originally promised 1,000 guineas towards its foundation plus 100 guineas each year thereafter as a grant. But Thomas Burgess, the bishop of St David's and the person who suggested that the king be patron of the new society, misunderstood. He thought that the 1,000 guineas was the annual grant. King George did not bother to correct him.

Duke dishes Catholic emancipation move

Westminster, 15 April 1825
A fiery speech by the king's brother Frederick, the Duke of York, has killed off the latest attempt to free Britain's Catholics – the Catholic Relief Bill, which had successfully passed its third reading in the House of Commons.

The duke did not mince his words. Removing bars on Catholics from joining the civil service or the universities, he said, means breaking the coronation oath in which King George had sworn to defend the Protestant faith. So how could he sign a bill making concessions to

the Catholics? Today's setback is not entirely unexpected. In April 1821 the Lords threw out the Roman Catholic Disability Removal Bill after it also had been passed by the Commons.

Since the king agrees with Frederick, the outlook for Catholics seems gloomy. But the lord chancellor, the Earl of Eldon, has suggested an interesting way to get round these difficulties. Given that the king cannot sign a bill freeing the Catholics (because of the oath), he could perhaps sign one allowing his successor to do so (→ 20/1/27).

American policy is bone of contention

London, 25 January 1825
The king is up in arms with his detested foreign secretary, George Canning, over his policy towards newly-independent states in South America. Lord Liverpool's government formally recognised the independence of Buenos Aires, Mexico and Colombia on 31 December last year, much to Canning's satisfaction and the king's displeasure. Now George has asked Liverpool for a draft of the king's speech ten days before the opening of parliament to think out his own ideas on this matter.

The king thinks that Britain is promoting revolution by recognising states that have used it to depose their monarch – in this case, the Spanish king. Britain, he argues, is condoning the American

Lord Liverpool: the prime minister.

War of Independence and the French Revolution, encouraging "the evil and discontented" in every land. But Canning is unrepentant. He recognises the plain fact that there are big profits to be had from trade with these emergent states. He also knows that James Monroe, the US president, will not tolerate any intervention in South America.

Although King George has recruited a clique of European ambassadors and others to support him, in the long run the cabinet is bound to get its way, as it did over Canning's appointment. As for the king's speech, it is possible that George will try to make some excuse not to make it (→ 1826). ▷

Nash's new look for Buckingham House

The old Buckingham House built in 1702, before the builders moved in ...

London, 1826

The brick façade of Buckingham House, as lived in by George III, has disappeared under a grandiloquent redesign by George IV's favourite architect, John Nash. The new frontage in Bath stone sweeps out towards the Mall in two wings, making three sides of a hollow square. In the centre of the forecourt between the wings stands a marble arch, modelled on the arch of Constantine at Rome, and along the garden front, with its semicircular bow, Nash has placed the State Dining Room, the Blue and White Drawing Rooms, the Music Room and the Picture Gallery.

The king, who lived at the other end of the Mall in Carlton House when he was Prince Regent, told Nash: "If the public wish to have a palace, I will have it at Buckingham House. There are early associations which endear the spot

to me." Nash had been at work since 1813 on a grand town-planning exercise to link Carlton House with the newly-laid-out Regent's Park, whose classical terraces in stucco leading up to the Regent's Canal have just been completed. Between the two he has laid out from north to south a new street, Regent Street, from All Souls' church at the top end to Carlton House, closing the vista below Piccadilly Circus. The new plan for the projected Buckingham Palace means that Carlton House will no longer be needed; it is to be pulled down.

Nevertheless, Regent Street and its connected buildings, such as the park terraces and the Quadrant with its colonnades curling into Piccadilly Circus, have given a completely new look to London, which has been transformed since Waterloo in accordance with the ambitions of George IV (→ 11/1834).

... and a cartoonist's vision of John Nash ("the architect wot builds the arches") standing in the courtyard of the proposed Buckingham Palace.

Duke of York is dead

Windsor, 20 January 1827

Disregarding the advice given by his physicians, the king turned out at Windsor today for the funeral of his brother Frederick, the Duke of York. It has been a bitterly cold day, with the royal party and cabinet ministers shivering in the dank and gloomy atmosphere. The Duke of Wellington is already going down with a bad cold.

Frederick, who was 64, was carried off by dropsy, probably caused by kidney disease. He was 26 when he took Princess Frederica of Prussia as his bride. It was a dismal marriage; rather than go to bed, she would lie fully dressed on a couch while a lady-in-waiting read to her; she had no children, but kept upwards of 40 dogs. For the 25 years of their marriage the duke was brazenly unfaithful. In 1809 he

was even forced to resign as army commander-in-chief after a parliamentary committee found evidence that one of his mistresses had been selling army promotions and commissions. The prime mover in bringing the scandal to light was the duke's brother, the Duke of Kent, who considered that he should be C-in-C himself. But York easily outmanoeuvred Kent and regained his command.

At today's funeral King George was said to be "most grievously affected" and to feel that each detonation of the 21-gun salute was "like a nail driven into his heart". The new heir presumptive is the king's younger brother, William, the Duke of Clarence. During the ceremony he was overheard asking another mourner how many head of game he had killed.

The king's brother Frederick, the Duke of York, at work in his Garter robes.

King gives oriental look to English lake

Virginia Water, Surrey, 1826

The king, it is said, is obsessed with building. At Virginia Water near Windsor a Chinese temple stands on an island in the middle of an artificial lake; now George IV is having a string of Moorish and Chinese pavilions built along the shore of the lake. On most summer afternoons he is to be found there fishing with his mistress March-

ioness Conyngham, the wife of the lord steward of the household. At five o'clock they dine in a hut and afterwards play cards until supper, which lasts into the early hours. The Duke of Wellington, a frequent guest, finds this routine boring and Lady Conyngham vulgar. But she is a woman to be reckoned with; the king says he is "more in love with her beauty than ever".

Hard-drinking king crippled by gout

Windsor, 1827

On his good days King George still eats heartily and usually gets through two or three bottles of claret before leaving the table. On other days, though, he complains of his gout and other infirmities. The Duke of Wellington, a regular visitor at the royal lodge, has little sympathy for the 65-year-old king.

There is nothing the matter with the king, Wellington says, "except what is caused by the effects of strong liquors taken too frequently and in too large quantities. He drinks spirits morning, noon and night." After one particular heavy drinking bout, the king greatly vexed Wellington by being "very drunk, very blackguard, very much

out of temper, and a very great bore". The hard-drinking king has long been using laudanum to calm the "irritation" caused by alcohol. The royal physicians cannot agree on the likely consequences of the habit. One says that the laudanum will drive him mad; the other argues that the spirits will drive him mad if the laudanum is not given.

On one of his more sober days recently, George was visited by Victoria, the seven-year-old daughter of his late brother Edward, the Duke of Kent. He pulled her onto his knee for her to kiss him. Though disgusted by his greasy make-up, she hid her feelings and told him that her favourite piece of music was *God save the King* (→ 18/2/28).

King George: a heavy drinker.

Canning takes over from Liverpool as new prime minister

Westminster, 10 April 1827

Two months after Lord Liverpool, the prime minister, had to resign after being paralysed by a stroke, the king has at last reconciled himself to accepting his old foe, George Canning, as prime minister. He dislikes Canning for defending Queen Caroline during the quarrels that followed the breakdown of the royal marriage. Canning has also upset the king by appointing the Duke of Clarence, George's brother and heir presumptive, as head of the Royal Navy. But though Canning has many enemies he is the only choice for prime minister.

William, lord high admiral, backs Royal Navy's Turkish foray

London, October 1827

William, the Duke of Clarence and lord high admiral, has praised Admiral Sir Edward Codrington, commanding the British fleet in the eastern Mediterranean, for defeating the Ottoman fleet at Navarino Bay, in Greece. "I believe the Turk never before felt the British eloquence of our guns," the duke has written. "A splendid victory. I admire your perfect conduct on the day of battle."

The duke has asked his brother, the king, to reward Codrington with the Grand Cross of the Order of the Bath. Others are less enthusi-

astic. At the admiralty, senior officers say that Codrington went far beyond his instructions, which ordered him to liaise with the French and Russian fleets and simply to keep an eye on the Turco-Egyptian fleet in order to prevent a massacre of the Greeks, who are fighting to gain independence from the rule of the Ottoman empire.

Clarence has been a controversial figure since his appointment earlier this year. He was meant to be a figurehead to give the government the appearance of royal support, but he sees his job as giving him executive authority (→ 14/8/28).

Hero at sea: Admiral Codrington.

Potter to the royal household is dead

Stoke-on-Trent, 16 July 1827

The craftsman whose porcelain is of unrivalled transparency and beauty died today after serving as potter to royalty for more than 20 years. Josiah Spode learned his trade in his father's workshop in Stoke-on-Trent and in 1800, when he was 46, he began to use bone as well as feldspar in his paste. The resulting bone china is as fine as anything produced by the famous Sèvres works in France. Spode decorated his pottery with the much-admired "willow pattern".

A cartoon satirising King George's love affair with Lady Conyngham.

Adoring king showers mistress with gems

Brighton, 1828

When George IV fell in love with the banker's daughter Elizabeth, Marchioness Conyngham, he went on a strict diet and lost some 30 pounds in order to make himself more attractive. Not that the lady is any mere slip of a girl; she is a buxom woman in her fifties with four children. A popular ballad going the rounds in London says that the king will never need pillows to lie on so long as he has Lady Conyngham as his mistress.

Her husband, Henry, the first marquis, has done well out of

the liaison. He is a privy councillor and lord steward of the royal household. In London the Conynghams live in style in one of the king's houses, their servants, horses and carriages provided by the king.

When the royal party stays at the Royal Pavilion, in Brighton, it is Lady Conyngham who gives the orders. The two lovers dote on each other; he, eager to please, panders to her taste for jewellery by showering her with lavish gems, including a magnificent sapphire that used to belong to the Stuarts.

Clarence quits as admiral after series of clashes with the king and politicians

Whitehall, 14 August 1828
William, the Duke of Clarence, attended his last meeting of the navy council today and announced his resignation as lord high admiral. The move came after months of bitter clashes over the duke's powers, during which he found himself opposed by his own brother, the king, and the prime minister, the Duke of Wellington.

The struggle between William and the council came to a head when William appointed a commission of naval officers to inquire into the poor standard of naval gunnery and to make recommendations. The council, headed by Admiral Sir George Cockburn, protested that the duke had exceeded his powers. William appealed to Wellington to dismiss Cockburn; Wellington in his turn appealed to the king to reason with his brother. George IV told William: "You are in error from beginning to the end. You must give way."

William stormed off and went out to sea for several days, telling nobody the purpose of his journey or where he was going. When at length he came ashore at Plymouth he found another letter from the king: "Can the lord high admiral suppose that the laws are to be infringed ... without notice or remonstrance by the responsible

Clarence in full naval dress.

advisers of the crown? I am well aware that I am drawing fast to the close of my life; it may be the will of the Almighty that a month, a week, a day may call the lord high admiral to be my successor. I love my brother William, I always have done so to my heart's core [but] the lord high admiral shall strictly obey the laws enacted by parliament ... or I desire immediately to receive his resignation." William knew that he had to go (→ 26/2/29).

Victoria is bridesmaid at royal wedding

The royal bride: Princess Feodora.

Kensington Palace, 18 Feb 1828
The king was to have given away Feodora, the daughter of the Duchess of Kent by her first marriage, at her wedding to a German prince today. But George IV, crippled by gout and rheumatism and suffering from bouts of fever, was unable to leave Windsor for London. However, his eight-year-old niece, Princess Victoria, who is Feodora's half-sister, attended as bridesmaid.

Victoria is named after her mother, Victoria of Leiningen, who married Edward, the Duke of Kent, in 1818 in a ceremony arranged when it became apparent that the king and his brothers were failing to produce possible heirs. Their child is second in line to the throne, after the Duke of Clarence (→ 11/3/30).

Dukes are at loggerheads over Catholics

Westminster, 26 February 1829
Two royal dukes clashed today in the House of Lords over one of the most controversial questions of the day. William, the Duke of Clarence and heir to the throne, supports the Catholic Emancipation Bill now before parliament; his brother, Ernest, the Duke of Cumberland, fanatically opposes it.

The bar on Catholics holding public office has been debated for several years, but political leaders did nothing until the Duke of Wellington, as prime minister, decided to act and brought the king round to his point of view. This brought Cumberland rushing back to London from Berlin, where he was living with a twice-widowed German princess, to try to persuade the king to change his mind. In the Lords' debate Clarence spoke of his "pleasure and satisfaction" in supporting the bill and denounced his brother's

Ernest, the Duke of Cumberland.

opposition. Cumberland objected to being called "factious and ... I have forgotten the other epithet". "Infamous," his brother interjected helpfully (→ 26/6/30).

George's hand is forced over Catholic bill

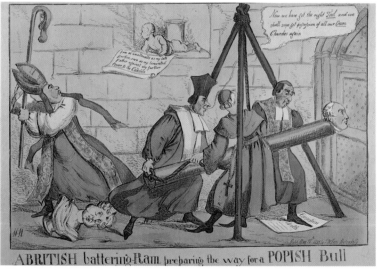
Battering down the door: a satirical cartoon of Catholic emancipation.

Windsor, 10 April 1829
The king has at last resigned himself to the fact that he must accept the Duke of Wellington's Catholic Emancipation Bill, which removes the barriers to Catholics holding public office. For months the duke has been going to Windsor to press George IV to accept the bill; on numerous occasions he believed that he had been successful, only to find that the fanatically anti-Catholic Duke of Cumberland had harangued his brother into resisting

the bill again. Matters came to a head when the king told Wellington that he would have to resign as prime minister if he persisted with the bill. The duke handed in his resignation and left.

Then the king's household advisers went to work on a weary and ailing king. He finally conceded that the opponents of emancipation were not strong enough to form a government and so he would have to give his assent to the bill and thus keep Wellington.

Victoria learns that she could be queen

King dies after illness

Growing up into a queen: a portrait of Princess Victoria as a young girl.

Windsor, 26 June 1830

At 1.45 this morning, after a brief sleep in his chair, George IV awoke and drank a little clove tea. He slept again for an hour, and then, so his physician, Sir Wathen Waller, reported: "He had instantly a purgative motion." The king said: "I do not think all is right."

He complained of feeling faint and ordered the windows to be opened. He tried unsuccessfully to drink some sal volatile and, grasping Waller's hand, looked him in the face and cried: "My dear boy! This is death!" After a few short breaths he passed away as the clock was striking at a quarter past three.

His death comes after a long and painful illness. He experienced severe pains in his bladder, for which he took large doses of laudanum. He had alarming spasms of breathlessness when not only his face but even his finger ends would turn black. His eyesight was so bad that he could scarcely see papers presented to him for signature.

Still, he retained his appetite almost to the end. The Duke of Wellington recently watched him eat a breakfast of two pigeons and three beefsteaks, washed down with a bottle of Moselle, a glass of champagne, two glasses of port and a glass of brandy (→ 15/7).

The king is dead: the body of King George IV lying in state.

Kensington Palace, 11 March 1830

Today is a day that the ten-year-old Princess Victoria will never forget. When she opened her book on the kings and queens of England to begin her history lesson, she found that her governess, Baroness Louise Lehzen, had placed a genealogical table between the pages.

"I have never seen this before," she said. "No, Princess," Lehzen said. "It was not thought necessary that you should." As Victoria studied the list of heirs to the throne, she saw that they were either elderly or already dead. Two childless uncles remain: the ailing 67-year-old George IV, and William, the Duke of Clarence, who is 64. "I am nearer the throne than I thought," the princess exclaimed. Realising the gravity of what she had learnt, she tearfully promised Lehzen: "I will be good" (→ 3/9).

Duchess makes plans for future regency

Extravagant king without political power

Kensington Palace, January 1830

The Duchess of Kent and her alleged paramour, Sir John Conroy, the comptroller of her household, are trying to manipulate the duchess's young daughter, Princess Victoria, to gain wealth and power for themselves. Conroy's plan is to isolate Victoria and make her entirely dependent on her mother, who will be regent if the throne becomes vacant before the princess is 18 years old. In order to keep her away from her royal uncles, he is claiming that some of Victoria's relatives are plotting to poison the child. Victoria dislikes Conroy. She has witnessed "some familiarity" between him and her mother (→ 3/9).

Amorous: the Duchess of Kent.

London, 1830

For most of his adult life, as Prince of Wales, regent and ultimately king, George IV was short of money. George's extravagance was legendary. Music, painting, sculpture and the theatre benefited, yet this won him few tributes. The Royal Pavilion at Brighton, Regent's Park and Buckingham House are legacies of his energetic activity, but are seen by many as expensive indulgences at a time when the nation was plunged into the hardships that followed the Napoleonic wars.

The king's temperament and reputation inevitably weakened his position in his relations with his ministers. He had neither the firmness nor the determination that had enabled his father in the early years of his reign to gain the upper hand for the monarchy over the ministers.

Time and again George IV was obliged to give way. He tried to appoint Marquis Conyngham, the husband of his mistress, as lord chamberlain, but was refused by Lord Liverpool, the prime minister. He was overruled when he objected to recognising the South American states that had rebelled against Spain; he expressed his pique by refusing to read the king's speech, saying he had lost his false teeth. His reign has seen the balance of power moving steadily in favour of ministers and parliament.

William IV
1830–1837

London, 26 June 1830. William, the Duke of Clarence, accedes to the throne, aged 64 (→ 21/8).

London, June 1830. The Duke of Wellington holds a ball in honour of William's accession.

Westminster, 6 July 1830. Parliament debates the regency question; the Duke of Wellington and Lord Grey both refuse to allow the Duchess of Kent to be created Dowager Princess of Wales (→ 11/1830).

Windsor, 15 July 1830. The funeral of George IV takes place.

Belgium, July 1830. Prince Leopold of Saxe-Coburg-Gotha, the brother of the Duchess of Kent and widower of the late Princess Charlotte, is asked to become king of the Belgians (→ 29/9/35).

Westminster, 16 November 1830. King William asks Lord Grey to form a Whig government (→ 23/11).

Westminster, 23 November 1830. Minutes after the old Tory ministers hand in their seals, the new Whig administration arrives to receive them (→ 30/1/31).

London, November 1830. The Duchess of Kent is to be regent should Princess Victoria, her daughter and the heir to William IV, accede to the throne before coming of age (→ 1831).

Westminster, 30 January 1831. Lord Grey puts forward his plans for parliamentary reform (→ 22/4).

London, January 1831. Rumours spread about Queen Adelaide and her alleged lover, Earl Howe.→

London, spring 1831. As the rift between the Duchess of Kent and William grows wider, the duchess refuses to allow Victoria to attend royal functions (→ 14/10).

Westminster, 22 April 1831. William dissolves parliament to save the Reform Bill from being destroyed in its committee stage.→

Westminster, May 1831. The Whigs triumph in the general election (→ 4/6/32).

London, May 1831. After a bitter row, William creates George Fitzclarence, his eldest illegitimate son, Earl of Munster (→ 12/1832).

Westminster, February 1832. Earl Spencer, a Whig and a former cabinet minister, proposes a radical bill to reform the Irish church.

London, August 1832. Prince Augustus, the Duke of Sussex, infuriates William by siding with the ultra-radicals in the struggle for parliamentary reform (→ 21/4/43).

London, December 1832. George Fitzclarence, the Earl of Munster, becomes constable of the Round Tower (→ 6/1837).

Wales/Midlands, 1832. John Conroy, the Duchess of Kent's adviser in the absence of her brother, King Leopold, and suspected of being her lover, arranges for Victoria to make a series of royal processions (→ 9/11).

London, January 1833. Victoria is enchanted by a small King Charles spaniel named Dash, given to her mother by John Conroy (→ 14/5).

London, 14 May 1833. Victoria celebrates her 14th birthday with a ball at St James's palace (→ 1834).

Britain/Hanover, 1833. The king clashes with Lord Palmerston, the foreign secretary, over his response to Austrian opposition to liberalisation within German states such as Hanover, of which William is also king.

London, November 1834. William is livid when his offer of Buckingham House as a replacement for the Houses of Parliament, destroyed by fire last month, is refused.→

London, November 1834. The Duke of Cumberland, annoyed with William, spreads rumours that the king is mad (→ 28/6/43).

London, 1834. Victoria finds another father-figure, in the absence of her uncle King Leopold, in his brother, Prince Ferdinand of Saxe-Coburg-Kohary (→ 30/7/35).

London, 30 July 1835. Victoria's confirmation is marred by the on-going feud between the Duchess of Kent and King William (→ 21/8/36).

Westminster, summer 1835. William and his ministers clash over the future of Canada; William is strongly against anything which involves self-government.→

Ramsgate, 29 September 1835. King Leopold of the Belgians and his new wife, Louise of Orléans, go on holiday with Victoria and her mother; a sisterly bond is instantly formed between Victoria and her young aunt (→ 3/1838).

Ramsgate, October 1835. Victoria's dislike of John Conroy is made clear when she stubbornly resists his attempt to force her, while still weak from an attack of typhoid, to agree to appoint him as her private secretary on her accession to the throne (→ 21/8/36).

London, 10 June 1836. Victoria is lonely after her German cousins, Albert and Ernest, return home.→

London, June 1836. William's health is deteriorating rapidly. He suffers badly from arthritis in his hands, asthma and liver complaints.

London, 10 April 1837. William's favourite illegitimate daughter, Sophia, Lady de L'Isle, dies in childbirth.

Windsor, 17 May 1837. William collapses on his return from a horse tournament (→ 20/5).

London, 24 May 1837. Victoria comes of age; William increases the rift existing between mother and daughter when he offers Victoria an independent household.→

Westminster, 27 May 1837. William attends the privy council in a wheelchair (→ 20/6).

London, 20 June 1837. William dies in his sleep, aged 71.→

The life and times of King William IV

Name: William Henry of Hanover.
Birth: 21 August 1765.
Accession: 26 June 1830.
Coronation: 8 September 1831.
Predecessor: brother.
Hair: grey.
Eyes: blue.
Marriage: Princess Adelaide of Saxe-Meiningen, 11 July 1818.
Children: Four; two stillborn

and two died in infancy, plus ten illegitimate children by Mrs Dorothea Jordan.
Favourite home: Windsor.
Likes: entertaining.
Dislikes: formality.
Greatest problem: electoral reform.
Greatest success: rescuing the monarchy from disrepute.
Death: 20 June 1837.

Opposite: King William IV, as portrayed by Sir David Wilkie.

William IV is a more sober prospect than brother

A cheerful man with the common touch

Surrey, 26 June 1830

At six o'clock this morning, William, the Duke of Clarence, was woken at his house near Hampton Court to be told that he was king of England. His brother, George IV, was dead at last. William is said to have shaken his informers by the hand and gone straight back to bed, joking that he had always wanted to sleep with a queen. A few hours later, refreshed, he rode to Windsor – a token piece of black mourning crêpe in his white hat – smiling broadly and waving cheerfully to passers-by. He did not mourn his brother for long, if at all.

The king, aged 64, became heir to the throne only three years ago when the Duke of York, George III's second son, died. Many fear that this bluff former sailor will not be up to the task, particularly now when political and constitutional reform are in the air. Nor can he provide the stability of a male heir. The children of his marriage to Adelaide of Saxe-Meiningen, 27 years his junior, have all died, although he has ten illegitimate children, surnamed Fitzclarence, by the actress Dorothea Jordan, his mistress for 21 years.

William's cheerful manner and unaffected style are a pleasing contrast to his brother's heavy drinking, incessant womanising and childish behaviour, and this has already helped to make him popular with the public. He is a very public man, who enjoys going for walks and chatting to fellow strollers.

Low-key coronation marks start of reign

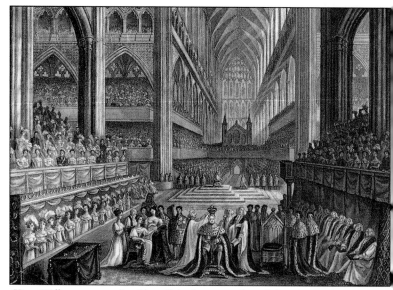

King William crowned: a big affair, but more frugal than its predecessors.

London, 3 September 1831

They are already calling it the "half-crownation", so hard has the king stamped on extravagance at today's coronation in Westminster abbey. King William is very much aware of public hostility to royal ostentation after the excesses of his elder brother. Today's coronation was a relatively frugal affair, costing little more than £30,000: George IV's cost £240,000.

The traditional banquet in Westminster Hall was dispensed with; so, too, was the usual hire of a crown for the queen. The pages' blue frock coats, white breeches and stockings were paid for by their parents, and the grandest carriage at the ceremony belonged to a foreign ambassador. Nonetheless, everything passed off well, although the king was "very infirm in his walk and looked oppress'd with the immense weight of his robes and crown". In honour of the coronation, the Mall, leading to the rebuilt Buckingham House (now in reality a palace), was opened to the public for the first time.

King William at his leisure: a stylish portrait of the new monarch.

William gives birthday banquet for poor

Windsor, 21 August 1830

The king celebrated his birthday today with a banquet for the poor people of this royal borough. Three thousand places were laid for the open-air feast of boiled and roast beef, veal, ham and plum pudding, and the king sat at the centre table clearly enjoying every moment. William is proving to be very much a "people's king". At both Windsor and Brighton he makes a point of talking to strangers, even though a recent "walkabout" in London ended in chaos when an Irish whore covered him in kisses. In Brighton he scans lists of hotel guests in the hope of finding old shipmates whom he entertains lavishly at the Royal Pavilion (→ 3/9).

Victoria is kept away from the crowning

Princess Victoria with her mother.

London, 3 September 1830

Ten-year-old Victoria, the heiress to the throne, watched in tears from the window of Marlborough House as her uncle's coronation procession drove past. Her mother, the Duchess of Kent, had refused to allow her to attend the ceremony after the king had insisted that she should follow his brothers in the procession instead of coming directly behind him as heiress presumptive. It is the latest chapter in the quarrel between the king, who would like to involve Victoria in court life, and the duchess, who is anxious to make sure Victoria that needs her to act as regent should the king die soon (→ 11/1830).

'Reform Billy' backs new election

Commons clean-up plan leads to clash

London, 22 April 1831

The king has stepped in to save the Reform Bill from oblivion, despite his personal lack of enthusiasm for the proposals. Today he rushed over to the House of Lords, where the Tories were attempting to force through a resolution against dissolution, jammed his crown onto his head and declared parliament dissolved immediately. The bill aims to widen the franchise and redistribute seats to reflect changes in society [*see panel overleaf*]. The king had told Lord Grey, the prime minister, of his fears that the reforms would provoke a clash between the Whig-controlled Commons and the Tory Lords, but loyally backed his ministers' proposals.

After the bill passed its first reading by one vote, a wrecking amendment was carried in the committee stage two days ago. The Whigs made it an issue of confidence and threatened to resign unless parliament was dissolved, forcing an election which would boost their majority in the Commons. The king, angered by Tory moves to restrict his power of dissolution, today backed dissolution as the "lesser of two evils", unwittingly winning popular acclaim and the nickname of "Reform Billy" (→ 5/1831).

King William prorogues parliament and saves the Reform Bill from oblivion.

"Reform Bill? Can that mean me?" asks the king in this contemporary cartoon.

Courtier friend of the queen ousted by prime minister

London, October 1831

Earl Howe, the lord chamberlain, has been forced to resign after voicing his opposition to the Reform Bill too often and too publicly. His dismissal has embroiled the royal court in even greater controversy because of his close friendship with Queen Adelaide. Howe is said to be like a "boy in love with this frightful spotted majesty". The queen was even said to be pregnant by him at one stage, but there seems to be no foundation in the rumours of an affair between Howe and the 39-year-old queen, whose attachment to him is platonic, if indiscreet.

It was Howe's political machinations, inappropriate to his position, that brought about his downfall. A hardline Tory, like the queen, he infuriated the king by signing two addresses opposing the Reform Bill. It was not until this month that matters came to a head when the London *Standard* published a letter strongly attacking the government thought to have been written by Howe. Lord Grey, the prime minister, demanded, and got, Howe's resignation.

Queen Adelaide is angry both with Grey and with her husband for giving in to him. Indeed, so furious is Adelaide that there is talk of her uniting opponents of reform in a "queen's party" (→ 4/6/32).

William designs a new look for his clean-shaven servicemen

Windsor, August 1830

In true Hanoverian tradition, King William is obsessed with uniforms and the appearance of his soldiers and sailors. His old service, the navy, was the first to undergo a royal redesign. William had been king for only a few days when he decreed that naval officers' cuffs should be changed from white to scarlet. Soon afterwards he created a simplified design for the Hussars and designed a new uniform for the master and brethren of Trinity House.

William's latest decree bans moustaches for all the cavalry except the Life Guards, Horse Guards and Hussars, and orders hair to be cut short back and sides by noncommissioned officers and men. At least one noted dandy, Jack Spalding, has resigned his commission rather than lose the splendid growth on his upper lip.

Ministers are happy with the king's interest in uniforms because it keeps him occupied, allowing them to govern without royal interference. His other pastime – speech-making – is proving less popular. William upset Anglo-French relations by referring to the king of France as "an infamous scoundrel". The Duke of Wellington gave the king, who has admitted being drunk, a strong reprimand.

One of the army uniforms designed by William: the Eighth Hussars.

German ladies are sacked by duchess

Kensington, December 1830

The campaign by Sir John Conroy and the Duchess of Kent to control Princess Victoria continues, regardless of the cost to the happiness of the young heir to the throne. This autumn Baroness Spaeth, for 25 years a lady-in-waiting to the duchess, was dismissed for criticising both the duchess's intimate relationship with Conroy and the régime whereby Victoria is cut off from her uncle, the king. From now on the Kents' household is to be manned by English ladies: Victoria fears that her governess, Baroness Lehzen, could be next to go (→ 1832).

King forced to give way on peerages

Reform Bill passed after long struggle

Westminster, 7 June 1832

A royal commissioner today gave the revived Reform Bill the royal assent because King William was unwilling to do so himself. William had been unenthusiastic about the reforms but agreed with the Whigs that concessions must be made now to prevent revolution later. An increased majority for the Whigs in elections last year showed the popularity of reform, and last October's riots, which exploded when the Tory-dominated Lords threw out the bill, drove the point home.

Lord Grey, the prime minister, asked the king to create enough Whig peers to get the bill through the Lords. When William refused – saying that he would never ennoble commoners – the cabinet resigned, and mass protest again gripped the country. Thousands signed petitions demanding reform. The king, blamed for blocking reform, was hissed in his carriage.

When the Duke of Wellington failed to form a Tory government, William had to ask Lord Grey to return. Grey would only return to office if the king promised to create more peers if necessary, and William was forced to agree. In the event the Lords caved in rather than suffer an influx of Whigs.

Under the king's benevolent gaze, the enemies of reform are put to flight.

How the Reform Act will transform the political face of Britain

London, 4 June 1832

The Reform Act passed by parliament today is being hailed as a great democratic triumph, but it will do little more than give the vote to the middle classes. The electorate in England, Scotland and Ireland has been expanded from about 478,000 to 814,000, out of a total population of about 13.9 million.

The first effect of the act is to abolish 56 corrupt "rotten" and "pocket" boroughs – depopulated constituencies, the parliamentary seats of which are in the gift of patrons. Old Sarum, for example, a ruined castle near

Salisbury, returned two MPs for a population of zero. Thirty other boroughs have been deprived of one member each.

The seats are to be redistributed to give representation to new industrial towns like Birmingham, Manchester and Leeds – half a million people without a single MP. London and the shires will have a fairer distribution of MPs as well.

Finally, the right to vote has been put on a new footing, ending the worst abuses, although it is still limited to property-owning gentry. Women remain firmly excluded (→ 7/6).

The Reform Bill is voted through.

Victoria is shocked by her first visit to the 'black country'

Kensington, 9 November 1832

Thirteen years of a sheltered upbringing came to a sudden halt for Princess Victoria when she came face to face with the less attractive side of the industrial revolution in Wales and the Midlands. The heir to the throne has just returned home from touring the country on a trip designed by her mother, the Duchess of Kent, to raise her public profile. The king is annoyed by the duchess's attempts to attract the grandiose honours fit only for crowned monarchs.

Victoria was horrified by what she saw in one coal district. "The houses are all black," she wrote. "The country continues black, engines flaming ... smoking and burning coal heaps, intermingled with wretched huts and carts and little ragged children" (→ 30/7/35).

William defies his foreign secretary

London, autumn 1833

An open clash between the king and his foreign secretary over Britain's European policies may have serious constitutional consequences for the country. Turmoil in the German states of Hesse, Baden and Bavaria had led to the introduction of democratic constitutions. The reactionary Habsburg foreign minister, Count von Metternich, countered with a series of illiberal laws including press censorship.

Lord Palmerston, who had welcomed the move to democracy, has now attacked Metternich in an outspoken dispatch. But William, who is also king of Hanover, and the Hanoverian government supported Metternich. When Palmerston declared that the constitutional states were "the natural allies" of Britain, the king was furious and insisted on amending the dispatch.

This autumn, despite Palmerston's objections, the king's viceroy in Hanover, accepted an invitation from Metternich to a conference of German states in Vienna at which the Hanoverians backed Austria on every issue (→ 11/1834).

Parliament passes two important bills on Ireland, despite opposition from king

Divided house: MPs crowd to an important debate in the House of Commons.

London, November 1833
Fears of a new split between Commons and Lords have persuaded the king, much against his will, to give his assent to two controversial bills involving Ireland and the Irish clergy. The prime minister, Lord Grey, had made it clear to King William that he would ask for the creation of new peers should the Tories in the Lords reject the bills.

William objected to the first of these measures – the Irish Coercion Bill – because it was too soft, even though it suspends *habeas corpus* and introduces martial law. The king wanted any attempt to repeal the union with Britain to be de-

clared high treason with harsh penalties. The Irish Church Bill also came in for royal disfavour because William felt that it went too far in meeting Catholic demands. The king accepted that some reform was necessary, given that well under a million of the eight million Irish population were Protestants, leaving the Catholic majority to support 1,385 benefices, 22 bishops and archbishops plus an annual revenue of £750,000, raised mostly from tithes. In the end William backed the reform, but he made public his strongly-held conviction that he might be betraying some of his most loyal subjects.

King's only extravagance: entertainment

London, November 1834
Although the king has a passion for entertaining – 36,000 bottles of wine were drunk in St James's alone this year – a rigid economy drive is under way in the royal palaces. The king's French chefs have been sent back to France, the royal yachts cut down from five to two, his German band has been dismissed and the royal stud cut by half.

Despite this, some 2,000 people are still entertained each week.

William is keeping well within his income, however – a sure indication of the excesses of George IV. For the first time in many years, royalty is popular. "This is not a new reign, it is a new dynasty," said the Duke of Wellington, who rarely has anything good to say about the sailor king.

Palace of Westminster destroyed by fire

London, November 1834
The Houses of Parliament have been reduced to ruins by a huge fire which swept through the conglomeration of buildings known as the Palace of Westminster. The night sky blazed orange and red, drawing a large crowd of onlookers who cheered as the roofs to the House of Lords and the House of Commons fell in. Three regiments of the king's Household Division and a group of cavalry were powerless to help to save the situation.

The fire started when two weary workmen – burning wooden tallies whose use had been discontinued by the exchequer – overstocked a

stove before going home. The flames raced through the old buildings. Because London has no unified fire brigade, several private operators, as well as the king's guards, tried to defend the buildings. They succeeded in saving Westminster Hall by taking fire engines inside and shooting water up at the hammer-beam roof.

In the face of the tragedy, plans are already being made to rebuild the palace. Many see it as an opportunity to create a new and splendid home for parliament. The *Times* has called for the "erection of a noble parliamentary edifice worthy of a great nation" (→ 10/1841).

Crowds gather to watch as the blazing Houses of Parliament crumble.

King is snubbed after offering his palace

A cartoon satirising King William's alleged desire to run the country.

London, November 1834
King William could hardly hide his pleasure as he stood in the burnt-out shell of Westminster palace. He saw it as an ideal opportunity to offload Buckingham House, now a palace itself after the rebuilding commissioned by George IV. The king does not like the palace at the end of the Mall, seeing it as a symbol of his brother's pomposity and extravagance. He tried to foist the building onto the army before proclaiming it as "the finest in Europe" for a new parliament. The prime minister, Lord Melbourne, regards it as unsuitable, and some politicians suspect the king's motives, fearing that he wants greater power. William is miffed – and saddled with an unwanted palace (→ 2/1/41).

King learns lesson: stay out of politics

Westminster, 8 April 1835

King William suffered a serious political setback today when Sir Robert Peel resigned as prime minister. William's attempt to bring about a Tory government has failed after a series of spectacular parliamentary defeats, bringing a long saga of royal interference in politics to an undignified end.

The crisis started last November, when Lord Melbourne resigned. The Whig government, which was badly split over its Irish policy, had finally crumbled when Melbourne tried to appoint the radical Lord John Russell to the cabinet. The king used this as a pretext for dismissing Melbourne and the Whigs, whose radical tendency he had long

A fine caricature of Robert Peel.

distrusted, and asked the Tory leader Robert Peel to take office. The Whigs were outraged, and Lord Brougham, the lord chancellor, protested by sending his great seal of office back to the king wrapped in torn newspaper.

Peel, accepting the king's invitation, called an election in January. But he failed to win an overall majority, and a coalition in the Commons between Whigs and radicals defeated him six times in six weeks. Now he has fallen, and the king is learning that he no longer has the constitutional right to make or unmake governments: the Whigs will return to power (→ 10/5/39).

German cousins please Princess Victoria

Albert: a reflective intelligence.

Kensington, 10 June 1836

The king's niece, Princess Victoria, is feeling rather sad tonight, for Albert and Ernest of Saxe-Coburg-Gotha, her German cousins, have left after a visit which she enjoyed very much. She is particularly taken with 16-year-old Albert.

She found him very handsome indeed. "The charm of his countenance is his expression, which is most delightful," the princess noted in her diary. And while both are intelligent, she warms more to Albert as being the more reflective of the two. The visit was timed to

Victoria: pining for her cousin.

coincide with Victoria's 17th birthday on 24 May. Albert, used to a simple, quiet life, found the socialising too much; as he whirled Victoria, now fully recovered from typhoid [*see story below*], around the dance floor at her birthday ball he nearly fainted and had to go and lock himself into his room.

While his heartier cousins laughed, Victoria was concerned for his health and seems likely to miss him. This morning, as he sat playing the piano, she came and stood beside him. He looked up to see her eyes brimming with tears (→ 3/1838).

William warns over Canadian reforms

London, summer 1835

King William has outraged his ministers by haranguing the Earl of Gosforth, the governor-elect of British North America, about the possible liberalisation of the government of Canada. "Mind what you are about in Canada," he spluttered, "the cabinet is not my cabinet; they had better take care or by God, I will have them impeached ... Does your lordship understand me? Canada must not be lost to this country." The royal outburst follows days after the cabinet formally rebuked the king for shouting at Sir Charles Grey – commissioned to inquire into the problems of the reform-minded colony – that since Canada had "been obtained by the sword" it deserved neither liberal nor conciliatory treatment.

King and duchess fall out at dinner

Windsor, 21 August 1836

The simmering row between King William and his sister-in-law, Victoria, the Duchess of Kent, blew up spectacularly tonight when the king publicly insulted her. The duchess and her paramour Sir John Conroy have taken every opportunity to slight the king, desperate to seize power for themselves as regents of the heir, the duchess's daughter Victoria – an unwilling pawn in an ever more bitter argument.

The duchess has turned Victoria's tours into royal progresses, taking honours and salutes which should go to the king. The duchess's deliberate snubbing of Queen Adelaide on her birthday, combined with her annexing to herself the king's suite of 17 rooms at Kensington palace, were the last straw.

At tonight's banquet to celebrate the queen's birthday, William delivered his riposte: "I trust in God that my life may be spared for nine months longer, after which period ... no regency would take place. I should then have the satisfaction of leaving the royal authority to the personal exercise of [Victoria] and not in the hands of a person now near me, who is surrounded by evil advisers" (→ 20/5/37).

Strict governess is Victoria's best friend

Ramsgate, 10 November 1835

Princess Victoria is at last starting to recover from typhoid, the disease which laid her low for most of last month. Her appetite is returning and, although she is still painfully thin and weak, her diet of plain soups and boiled meat should help her to make a speedy recovery.

She is being nursed back to health by Baroness Louise Lehzen, the formidable, caraway-seed-chewing governess who has brought her up from the age of five. The daughter of a Lutheran pastor, Lehzen has educated the princess with a mixture of strict discipline and kind devotion which has earned her both the love and the respect of her pupil. Fiercely loyal, Lehzen has fought for Victoria's best interests, protecting her against some of her mother's wilder schemes to advance her as queen bar only the

Lehzen: sketched by Victoria.

crowning. Aware that her charge would, one day, be queen, Lehzen used to read her tales from history while she had her hair brushed. Now the baroness is Victoria's most trusted friend at court (→ 16/1/42).

Princess celebrates birthday solemnly

Kensington, 24 May 1837

"Today is my 18th birthday!" wrote Princess Victoria in her journal tonight. "How old! and yet how far am I from being what I should be." It is a typically grave response from the heir to the throne, who has grown up to be a solemn young lady, short of stature, with a round face. A white and gold banner bearing her name has been hoisted above Kensington palace, and the king has thrown a ball in her honour. He is celebrating the fact that the Duchess of Kent, whom he detests, will now never achieve her ambition of being regent (→ 20/6).

Sir John Conroy: would-be regent.

Princess forced to reject king's cash

London, 20 May 1837

The Duchess of Kent has forced her daughter, Princess Victoria, to sign a letter to King William refusing his proposal to give the princess her own income, which would have removed her from her mother's control. The king offered £10,000 a year, a privy purse managed by the duchess's old foe, Sir Benjamin Stephenson, and the right to appoint her own ladies-in-waiting. Sir John Conroy, the duchess's friend, drafted a letter in which Victoria demanded that he should be regent, and made her sign. The king was not taken in. "Victoria has not written that letter," he said (→ 24/5).

William IV dies after brief illness

Windsor, 20 June 1837

At 12 minutes past two this morning, King William IV breathed his last. He was 71. He had been seriously ill with asthma for a month and had been expected to die for the last two days; today's news will come as no surprise to those close to him in recent weeks.

His decline started in April, shortly after his daughter, Sophia, died in childbirth. His distress at the loss of a much-loved daughter is said to have weakened his will to survive. His vulnerability to asthma returned, and he had a serious attack which deprived him of sleep for several weeks.

In the middle of last month he suffered from a series of fainting fits and lost his appetite. He was confined to his rooms, where Queen Adelaide – not in the best of health herself – did her best to look after him. Public alarm about the king's welfare was allayed until 6 June, when he failed to appear at Ascot. Last Sunday, as the nation prayed for the king's recovery, the archbishop of Canterbury gave him the sacrament. But William lasted a few more days more before he finally expired, propped up in a heavy leather chair.

He died safe in the knowledge that his heir and niece, Princess Victoria, is old enough to assume power in her own right, preventing his sister-in-law, the Duchess of

He steered the monarchy through difficult waters: now King William is dead.

Kent, and her confidant Sir John Conroy from assuming power as regents. He wanted to pass the monarchy to someone fit to hold it, for when he ascended the throne the crown had been deeply damaged by

the two Georges who had preceded him. William steered the monarchy safely through the dangerous straits of reform and towards a consensus with another powerful breed of rulers: politicians (→ 8/7).

King dies without any reconciliation with his disinherited family

George Fitzclarence, the king's son.

London, June 1837

The king has died without the hoped-for reconciliation with his eldest illegitimate son, George Fitzclarence, the Earl of Munster. Although the king wrote to Munster in April begging him to visit, the earl refused "until justice had been done him". Munster's three surviving brothers, Frederick, Adolphus and Augustus, share his grudge.

They are among the ten children of the king and Dorothea Jordan, an actress who was William's mistress from 1790 to 1810. The quarrel broke out after William's accession, when the dukedoms and pensions which they expected from their father failed to materialise. Their illegitimacy made it difficult

for the king to provide them with the incomes that they needed. "As natural children," they complained, "[we] feel too acutely that in the eyes of the law we are devoid of many rights and advantages."

Treading carefully, William did create George an earl and his three brothers – one, Henry, had died in 1817 – marquises, but they were never satisfied and continued to harass him until his death. William gained more from his daughters, Sophia, Mary, Elizabeth, Augusta and Amelia, who married into the aristocracy. Their lively personalities have graced the court, and their children, whom William adored, were allowed the run of Windsor castle (→ 12/1837).

Victoria
1837–1901

House of Hanover

London, 20 June 1837. Victoria, aged 18, accedes to the throne; one of her first actions is to dismiss Sir John Conroy (→ 21/6).

Hanover, 20 June 1837. Prince Ernest Augustus, the Duke of Cumberland, becomes king of Hanover on the death of his brother William as under Hanoverian rule a woman is not allowed to reign.

London, 21 June 1837. Alexandrina Victoria is proclaimed queen; she orders the name Alexandrina to be removed from all her official papers and from now on will be called Victoria.→

London, 9 November 1837. Rumours are spreading about an increasing rift between Victoria and her mother, the Duchess of Kent, after the queen attended a dinner in her honour at the Guildhall alone this evening (→ 1/1838).

Germany, March 1838. Victoria's uncle, King Leopold of the Belgians, questions her cousin and his nephew, Prince Albert of Saxe-Coburg-Gotha, a student in Bonn, as to his views on marrying the queen (→ 1/1839).

Kensington, 25 April 1838. Lady Flora Hastings, described by Victoria as "that odious woman" returns as a lady-in-waiting to the household of the Duchess of Kent, the queen's mother (→ 24/3/39).

Italy, January 1839. Prince Albert of Saxe-Coburg-Gotha begins a grand tour of Europe (→ 7/1839).

London, 27 May 1839. Victoria hosts a state ball as part of her entertainments for Grand Duke Alexander of Russia.

Ascot, June 1839. Victoria is denounced by Tory women as "Mrs Melbourne" after gossip about her relationship with the Whig prime minister (→ 4/7).

London, 4 July 1839. Victoria is racked with guilt on the death of Lady Flora Hastings, whom she had wrongly believed to be pregnant; she has died of an inflamed liver.

London, July 1839. Victoria writes to her uncle, King Leopold, saying that her relationship with her cousin, Prince Albert, must be platonic (→ 10/10).

London, 10 Oct 1839. Prince Albert and his brother, Ernest, arrive in London (→ 23/11).

London, 10 February 1840. Victoria marries Albert today.→

Windsor, 21 March 1840. Queen Victoria discovers that she is pregnant (→ 21/11).

London, 30 May 1840. Albert is attempting to heal the rift between Victoria and her mother, the Duchess of Kent, who recently took up residence at Ingestre House opposite Kensington palace.

London, 10 July 1840. Edward Oxford, who tried to kill Victoria, is found to be insane and committed to an asylum (→ 3/7/42).

Westminster, July 1840. Prince Albert is appointed to be prince regent if Victoria should die in childbirth (→ 21/11).

London, 21 November 1840. Albert has access to government boxes and represents Victoria at the privy council (→ 10/1841).

London, 28 December 1840. Victoria and her ministers, Lord Melbourne and Lord Palmerston, discuss the possibility of a Coburg cousin marrying Queen Isabella of Spain (→ 8/9/45).

London, 2 January 1841. The royal court moves from Windsor castle to Buckingham Palace (as the former Buckingham House is now known) (→ 8/1846).

London, 19 January 1841. Princess Victoria - "Vicky" - is given the title of Princess Royal (→ 9/1841).

Westminster, 18 May 1841. The Melbourne government is defeated by 36 votes (→ 3/9).

London, September 1841. The Princess Royal – nicknamed "Pussy" by Victoria – is not in good health (→ 1849).

London, October 1841. Prince Albert is appointed as chairman of a royal commission on the arts; his first task is to oversee the decoration of the rebuilt Houses of Parliament (→ 25/12).

London, 4 December 1841. Prince Albert Edward, aged less than one month, is invested as Prince of Wales (→ 25/1/42).

London, 16 January 1842. Victoria and Albert argue over Baroness Louise Lehzen, the queen's former governess, who is now in charge of the royal nursery; Albert wants her to be dismissed (→ 30/9).

Windsor, 25 January 1842. Prince Albert Edward is christened despite government opposition to the choice of foreigners to be his godparents (→ 4/1849).

Windsor, December 1842. Albert sets a room aside in the castle in which to house the royal art collection (→ 1846).

Kensington, 21 April 1843. Augustus Frederick, the Duke of Sussex and uncle of the queen, dies aged 70.

London, 25 April 1843. Victoria gives birth to her third child, a second daughter, named Alice Maud Mary (→ 6/8/44).

Ascot, 14 June 1843. Victoria and Albert miss the horse-racing, showing their general disapproval and snubbing the king of Hanover.

London, 18 June 1843. Albert inspects the new royal yacht at the West India Docks (→ 2/9).

Germany, 28 March 1844. Albert travels to Germany to sort out his late father's affairs (→ 11/4).

London, 3 May 1844. Victoria and Albert attend a private viewing of the Royal Academy paintings at Charing Cross.

Windsor, 6 August 1844. Victoria gives birth to her second son, Alfred Ernest Albert.→

The life and times of Queen Victoria

Name: Alexandrina Victoria of Hanover.
Birth: 24 May 1819.
Accession: 20 June 1837.
Coronation: 28 June 1838.
Hair: light brown.
Eyes: blue.
Height: five feet.
Marriage: Albert Augustus Charles Emmanuel of Saxe-Coburg-Gotha, 10 February 1840.

Children: nine.
Favourite homes: Balmoral, Windsor castle.
Likes: family life.
Dislikes: dictatorial politicians.
Greatest problems: relationship with her eldest son; deep grief for Albert.
Greatest success: building an empire.
Death: 22 January 1901.

Opposite: Queen Victoria on the throne, by Sir George Hayter.

Victoria becomes queen

London, 20 June 1837

The archbishop of Canterbury and the lord chamberlain, Marquis Conyngham, arrived at Kensington palace at five this morning to tell Princess Victoria that the king was dead and she was now queen. The Duchess of Kent, who always shares a room with her daughter, woke her to tell her that the two dignitaries were waiting. Victoria put on a dressing gown and went to see them alone. She is 18 years old.

Lord Conyngham knelt before her to say that William IV had died at Windsor. She later wrote in her diary: "Since it has pleased Providence to place me in this station, I shall do my utmost to fulfil my duty towards my country."

She wrote to her uncle Leopold, the King of the Belgians, and summoned Lord Melbourne. She received him alone and told him that she wished him to remain prime minister. At half-past eleven the whole council, led by the Duke of

Victoria is told that she is queen.

Wellington, gathered in the red saloon to do homage to the new queen. She entered the room alone, in a simple black gown, with extraordinary dignity. Afterwards, she told her mother that in future she would sleep alone (→9/11).

Young queen depends on her 'Lord M'

London, January 1838

Lord Melbourne has achieved a total ascendancy over young Queen Victoria. He is not merely her prime minister; he is private secretary, confidant and father-figure. He treats her with deference and love, advises her on everything and also tells her naughty stories about her wicked uncles. The queen has never met anyone like Melbourne before. She calls him "Lord M" and defers to him in everything.

Lord Melbourne is a Whig, a conservative whom the accidents of politics have made heir of the agitation for the 1832 Reform Act. He is opposed to change of any sort, believing that it only makes things worse. The queen is a Whig largely because she thinks that her father, the eccentric Duke of Kent, was one. Lord Melbourne has surrounded her with Whig gentlemen and ladies. As she never meets Tories on terms of intimacy, she tends to dislike them all, even the Duke of Wellington.

Melbourne is seeking to educate the young queen in her duties, explaining, for instance, that Uncle Leopold (the Belgian king) must not be allowed to interfere in British foreign policy. In some ways a throwback to the 18th century, he takes a sceptical attitude to political questions. The queen accepts his advice, even though she seems to be much more dogmatic than he and far more obstinate (→28/6).

Victoria in government: the queen's first meeting with ministers in council.

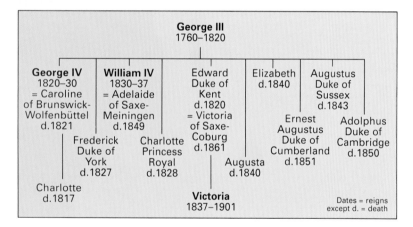

	George III 1760–1820				
George IV 1820–30 = Caroline of Brunswick-Wolfenbüttel d.1821	William IV 1830–37 = Adelaide of Saxe-Meiningen d.1849	Edward Duke of Kent d.1820 = Victoria of Saxe-Coburg d.1861	Elizabeth d.1840	Augustus Duke of Sussex d.1843	
	Frederick Duke of York d.1827	Charlotte Princess Royal d.1828		Ernest Augustus Duke of Cumberland d.1851	Adolphus Duke of Cambridge d.1850
Charlotte d.1817		Augusta d.1840			
		Victoria 1837–1901		Dates = reigns except d. = death	

King William buried with great ceremony

Windsor, 8 July 1837

King William IV was buried in St George's chapel, at Windsor, today, next to his brothers and his father. The ceremony was long, a mixture of pomp and irreverence. Few outside his family appear to mourn the king. Some courtiers chatted and joked while the dean of Windsor conducted the service, which he did badly. Only the soldiers and pallbearers kept up an air of appropriate solemnity.

William was, a typical Hanoverian – overweight, irritable, but also kind to his friends and an ex-

cellent husband to his two wives – one unofficial, one official – a kind father to his children and an affectionate brother to his many spinster sisters. Although he was bigoted, stupid and reactionary, his judgement was not always defective and he did not block the 1832 reforms.

He detested the Duchess of Kent, yet her daughter, Princess Victoria, was very fond of him, despite his unkindness to "Dear Mama". He was intensely English, despite his German mother and his German wife. Cartoonists loved to depict his pineapple-shaped head.

Civil list will keep William's sons in jobs

Westminster, December 1837

Parliament has agreed not only the terms of a new civil list for the new reign but also to keep the late king's sons employed in their present appointments. William had ten children, the Fitzclarences, with Mrs Dorothea Jordan, the celebrated Irish actress.

The eldest, the Earl of Munster, is a distinguished general who fought with Wellington in Spain and served in India during the Mahratta wars, from which he returned overland and wrote of his travels. He is a fellow of the Royal Society and a founder of the Royal Geographical Society. Of his three surviving brothers, one is also a

general, and another captains the royal yacht. They have five sisters who married into the nobility.

The queen's civil list stemmed from a tactful agreement between Lord Melbourne, the prime minister, and Sir Robert Peel, the leader of the opposition. She will receive £370,000 a year, in addition to the £54,000 that she receives from the duchies of Lancaster and Cornwall. The queen has been well schooled in frugality and intends to devote £50,000 in the first year to paying off her father's debts. The annuity for her mother, the Duchess of Kent, is to be increased by £8,000 a year, to £30,000, a sum the duchess still considers small.

Victoria's coronation is proudest day of her life

Westminster, 28 June 1838
Queen Victoria was crowned today in a long and splendid ceremony. She said that it was the proudest day of her life. It began with cannons in the park and ended with fireworks as millions of people crowded the streets in celebration.

Victoria rode to Westminster abbey in an open carriage in the first coronation procession since that of George III. The abbey, bedecked with crimson and gold, was packed with princes, dukes and nobility, adding yet further colour through their robes and coronets. A new crown of state, lighter than the traditional St Edward's crown, had been made from historic jewels because of fears that the five-hour rituals would pose too great a burden on the diminutive young queen.

Occasionally the lack of rehearsal became apparent. The archbishop often lost his place, and he jammed the coronation ring onto the wrong finger of the queen's hand so that he hurt her badly – and had great trouble getting it off again later. The archbishop also thought that he was meant to give her the orb, but he could not find it; in fact, he had already given it to her. Yet nothing could dim the unforgettable climax when, with the queen seated on St Edward's chair and the sun blazing through the high windows, the archbishop crowned Victoria queen. The trumpets blared, the bells pealed, the peers and peeresses all put on their coronets together, and the whole congregation shouted: "God save the queen!"

A proud moment: the young Victoria is crowned queen in a splendid ceremony in Westminster abbey; detail from an anonymous painting of the coronation.

Miserable, irritable queen puts on weight

London, 28 June 1838
A year ago Queen Victoria wrote that it was "the pleasantest summer I ever passed in my life and I shall never forget this first summer of my reign". She is now 19 and has found that being queen is not always entirely pleasant. She has put on weight, is estranged from her mother and is even occasionally irritable with her beloved prime minister, Lord Melbourne.

Although she enjoys the formalities and rituals of court – and woe betide anyone who neglects any of them – she is finding life rather dull. Lord Melbourne and Uncle Leopold, the Belgian king, think that she should get married. She is very popular, however. The country remains delighted with the contrast between the fresh, young, personable queen and the sequence of mad, dissipated and embarrassingly stupid kings who preceded her.

Britain is on the threshold of immense social change, and the monarchy is changing for the better along with it. The only problem is that the queen appears too partisan, too firmly Whig, for a constitutional monarch (→ 9/1838).

Baron sacked to rid court of 'foreigners'

London, September 1838
Baron von Stockmar has returned to Coburg. There were thought to be too many foreigners around the queen, and Stockmar was the most important. He has been confidential adviser to King Leopold of the Belgians, the new queen's uncle, for 20 years. Stockmar was Leopold's doctor when the latter married the late Princess Charlotte, the Prince Regent's daughter. His advice helped Leopold to his crown, and he is the private adviser of the Coburg family. He will now take Prince Albert of Saxe-Coburg-Gotha on a tour of Italy and will advise the family on the wisdom of marrying Albert to the queen. If that happens, Stockmar could return more powerful than ever.

He has pointed out to Leopold that the queen's husband "ought to have not merely great ability, but a *right* ambition and great force of will. To pursue for a lifetime a political career so arduous demands more than energy and inclination – it demands also that earnest frame of mind which is ready of its own accord to sacrifice mere pleasure to real usefulness."

Melbourne returns after queen vetoes plan for Tory ladies of the bedchamber

London, 10 May 1839

Lord Melbourne has resumed office as prime minister despite his defeat in parliament. This follows the refusal of the queen to allow the Tory leader, Sir Robert Peel, to appoint new ladies of the bedchamber in the royal household in order to weaken Whig influence at court. Peel then declined to form a government.

Lord Melbourne had lost the support of the Commons but not of the queen. When he told her that he must resign, she wrote: "All my happiness gone! That happy peaceful life destroyed, that dearest kind Lord Melbourne no more my minister!" She was further distressed when Peel demanded changes in her attendants; they are all married to prominent Whigs, and Peel thought that some at least should be Tories. He and the Duke of Wellington explained their position to the queen, but she refused to agree. She wrote to Melbourne: "The queen ... will not submit to such trickery. Keep yourself in readiness for you may soon be wanted" (→ 6/1839).

A political see-saw: the queen decides between Wellington (l) and Melbourne.

Court pregnancy scandal ensnares queen

London, 24 March 1839

A scandal over the rumoured pregnancy of a lady-in-waiting to the queen's mother was brought into the open today when a letter from the woman at the centre of the affair – Lady Flora Hastings – to an uncle was reprinted in a newspaper. Victoria had been convinced by her German confidante, Baroness Lehzen, that Lady Flora was pregnant and refused to see her at court. She also told Lord Melbourne, the prime minister, of the "pregnancy". Now doctors have said that Flora's swollen stomach has been caused by a tumour. The queen has apologised, but she is still widely blamed for maligning Flora, while Melbourne is criticised for condoning the banishment (→ 10/5).

Flora Hastings: in a court scandal.

Victoria is to marry her German cousin

A royal courtship: Victoria plays the piano for her listening cousin, Albert.

London, 23 November 1839

The queen is to marry her cousin, Prince Albert of Saxe-Coburg-Gotha. He arrived at Windsor on 10 October, and she wrote that "it was with some emotion that I beheld Albert – who is beautiful". The courtship went fast, and on 15 October the queen told him that it would make her "too happy" if he would consent to marry her. She made the formal announcement to the privy council today.

They are both 20, and their families have planned the marriage for years. They had unhappy childhoods – she because of her father's death and her mother's eccentricity, he because his mother deserted her family when he was four. Lord Melbourne, the prime minister, doubted the wisdom of a foreign match, but there are no appropriate British suitors. The queen must produce an heir; her uncle, the Duke of Cumberland, is heir presumptive, and few consider him suitable.

Victoria liked Albert when they first met two years ago, writing that he had "every quality that could be desired to make me perfectly happy". Later, she thought that she would prefer to stay single for a few years, but the doubts were swept away when she met him again: she has fallen in love (→ 10/2/40).

Sighs of relief greet Conroy resignation

London, June 1839

Sir John Conroy has resigned from the Duchess of Kent's household. He has long been a controversial figure, a bustling Irishman who became the duchess's "confidential adviser" after serving initially as the Duke of Kent's equerry. He was, with Lady Flora Hastings, one of the duchess's attendants, a principal cause of the perpetual disputes between the queen and her mother as they sought to influence Victoria. The queen detests him and suspects that he and the duchess are lovers. His departure should eventually improve relations between the two. At her accession the queen gave him a baronetcy and a pension of £3,000 a year but refused to admit him to her presence. Lord Melbourne and the Duke of Wellington have now persuaded him to retire (→ 1848).

Business stops (briefly) for royal wedding

London, 10 February 1840
Queen Victoria and Prince Albert were married at St James's palace today and left for a two-day honeymoon at Windsor. The queen wrote when he suggested a longer one: "You forget, my dearest love, that I am the sovereign and that business can stop and wait for nothing."

The prince arrived two days ago, groggy from a violent crossing. The queen was ecstatically happy and ran down to watch his arrival through a window. The worries of the past three months were swept away: parliament had voted Albert only £30,000 a year (the consort of Queen Anne got £50,000); her uncles and her mother had argued over precedence and with Albert over his household; Lord Melbourne had insisted that the Duke of Wellington, whom the queen dislikes, must attend the wedding.

Despite these problems the ceremony went well, and afterwards the queen kissed Queen Adelaide but only shook hands with her mother. There was a grand wedding break-

The royal couple make their vows.

fast at Buckingham Palace before the newlyweds went off to Windsor. When they reached their apartments, the queen collapsed on a sofa with a headache. However, she noted: "Ill or not, I never, never spent such an evening!!! Really how can I ever be thankful enough to have such a husband" (→ 21/3).

Albert settles down, but has little to do

The artist prince: Albert (l) has introduced a love of the fine arts at court.

London, 24 May 1840
Prince Albert has still to find a role for himself. The queen does not consult him on political matters, leaving all that to Lord Melbourne. He is not even involved in domestic arrangements, which are still controlled by Baroness Lehzen.

Melbourne and Baron von Stockmar, who has returned to London as the prince's closest adviser, are trying to persuade the queen to give

him something to do. Stockmar believes that Lehzen is the main culprit and that she is advising the queen to exclude the prince. Albert himself complains that he is "the husband, not the master of the house". He hopes to change` this, using the queen's love and his own intellectual gifts. He has already introduced her to a love of nature and music and is imposing a new decorum on the court (→ 7/1840).

Shots fired at the queen

London, 10 June 1840
A man tried to shoot the queen today, firing two pistols at her as she drove up Constitution Hill in a low open carriage with Prince Albert. The prince flung his arms around her and she saw "a little man on the footpath with his arms folded over his breast, a pistol in each hand". He aimed his second gun at the queen and, as she ducked, he was seized by a passer-by, a Mr Millais, who was assisted by his young son, an art student.

The crowd shouted "Kill him! Kill him!", and the ladies and gentlemen riding in the park formed a guard of honour around the royal carriage as it returned to Buckingham Palace. The assailant is a youth of 18 called Edward Oxford. Lord Melbourne says that he has been infected with French revolutionary enthusiasm, but it seems more probable that he is simpleminded.

The incident has provoked great demonstrations of loyalty to the queen. The fact that she is pregnant adds to her popularity and the sympathy her subjects feel for her. The courage and poise she showed during the attack are also much admired. She insisted on continuing her drive, taking no further notice of the event (→ 10/7).

Edward Oxford fires at the queen as she passes in an open carriage.

Remarriage incurs royal disapproval

London, 1840
The queen is upset with the foreign secretary, Lord Palmerston. He was once a favourite, a Whig like Lord Melbourne, but now he has married the widowed Lady Cowper, Melbourne's sister, and the queen disapproves of second marriages. Moreover, he does not show the deference which she feels she deserves and which her prime minister, Lord Melbourne, provides in such abundance. Palmerston is often high-handed and neglects to show dispatches to the queen before they are sent (→ 19/12/45).

Daughter born to Victoria and Albert

Windsor, 21 November 1840
The queen gave birth to a princess here today, three weeks prematurely. A moment after the birth, the large gathering in the next room heard the doctor inform her: "Oh Madam, it is a princess" and the queen's composed reply: "Never mind, the next will be a prince." Prince Albert, who was with Victoria during her labour, was named regent by parliament if she were to die in childbirth, like her cousin Charlotte. It would have been his first British title, though happily now hypothetical (→ 19/1/41).

Victoria upset by advent of Peel ministry

Surrey, 3 September 1841
The queen today bade a sad farewell to Lord Melbourne as prime minister and acquiesced in the appointment of Sir Robert Peel as his successor. It is nearly two months since Peel won an overwhelming majority in a general election and two years since his first commission to form a government foundered on an acrimonious argument with Victoria in the "bedchamber crisis".

Victoria still has no great affection for her new prime minister, a more austere figure than the fatherly Melbourne. But this time relations have been smoothed by secret talks between Peel and George Anson, Prince Albert's private secretary. These talks began earlier in May, by which time it had become obvious that Melbourne's Whig administration was nearing the end of its life. Albert thought that it would be a disaster for the monarchy if the queen's antipathy for Peel were seen to thwart the will of the Commons.

By the time that Melbourne had lost a Commons' vote of no confidence in June, Anson and Peel had thrashed out a formula designed to avoid a repetition of the bedchamber crisis. Peel agreed not to demand resignations from the royal household publicly, while the queen would voluntarily announce three key resignations. Following the Tories' sweeping election gains Victoria accepted this compromise, and in the leafy surrounds of Claremont near Esher, in Surrey, the queen – now seven months pregnant – has summoned a council to appoint her new ministers (→ 1842).

The young queen riding out with the fatherly Lord Melbourne (right).

Albert brings 'Christmas tree' to England

London, 25 December 1841
Prince Albert has introduced a Christmas tradition from his native Germany to the palace this year. It is a fir tree which has been chopped down and brought inside the palace where it stands waiting to be covered with candles and other decorations. The prince calls it his "Christmas tree".

Although this German idea of a decorated tree is not entirely new – the queen's grandmother, Queen Charlotte, had noted the custom – the royal couple's adoption of this tradition is likely to be emulated by others in the court circle and possibly beyond. The "Christmas tree" has certainly added even more sparkle to the delight of Victoria and Albert, who this year have two young children to whom they can give presents. The queen, now fully recovered from the birth of the Prince of Wales, is in a particularly joyful mood, saying it is "like a dream". And Albert has written to his own father saying that his children were "full of happy wonder" on Christmas Eve.

Albert Edward, a son and heir, is born

The new prince, Albert, is baptised as Queen Victoria looks on nervously.

London, 9 November 1841
For the first time in English history a reigning queen today gave birth to a son and heir. Albert Edward was born at 12 minutes to 11 o'clock this morning. The labour, like the pregnancy before it, had not been easy, but Victoria was comforted throughout by Prince Albert and is said to be delighted with her "fine large boy" with dark-blue eyes.

Sir Robert Peel, the prime minister, the Duke of Wellington and the queen's mother, the Duchess of Kent, were also present for the birth in Buckingham Palace. On leaving the palace Wellington met Lord Hill, a former military colleague, and boomed: "All over – a fine boy, very fine boy, almost as red as you are, Hill!"

A more measured announcement came from Sir James Clark, the queen's personal physician, who released a bulletin saying that "her majesty and the infant prince are going on well". The labour had been difficult, however, after several false alarms. Victoria had also been worried by an illness suffered by her first child, the Princess Royal, or "Pussy" as she calls her. But all that is now forgotten in the joy of a male heir, and it is intended that he will soon be given the title of Prince of Wales (→ 4/12).

A queen's best friends: Victoria has loved dogs since adopting Dash in 1833. Here Dash (left) is with Hector and Nero, plus an oriental parrot.

Queen has a ball to help poor weavers

Victoria and Albert enjoy a polka.

London, 12 May 1842

The queen and Prince Albert tonight staged a magnificent costume ball at Buckingham Palace to raise funds for unemployed silk weavers in the Spitalfields area of London. The royal couple went to the ball – as Queen Philippa and King Edward III – just ten days after a petition signed by more three million people had been presented to parliament demanding universal suffrage and improvements in poor law. The queen has no sympathy for the militant Chartist movement, but she is increasingly concerned about social conditions. Sir Robert Peel, the prime minister, has advised her to live simply in order to avoid arousing public hostility.

Victoria is the target of a second attack

London, 3 July 1842

For the second time this year shots have been fired at the queen, but again Victoria has escaped injury. Today's attack comes just two days after the first would-be assassin, John Francis, was reprieved from the gallows for his attack on 30 May – a reprieve that some people at court feared would encourage further attempts on the queen's life.

The second assailant is allegedly a youth named John William Bean. He fired a pistol at the queen, but later examination showed that there was as much tobacco and paper in the pistol as gunpowder. Bean's age is not known, but he was described as no more than four feet tall and somewhat deformed, with a "pitiable" expression. No injury was caused, yet the fact that the pistol was fired shows the vulnerability of the queen.

The attack on the queen on 30 May occurred in the Mall when she was riding in a carriage with Prince Albert. It later emerged that on the previous day they had seen what Albert described as a "swarthy, ill-looking rascal" pointing a pistol at them from the crowd. On that occasion the gun misfired.

Without telling anyone in the royal household about it, the couple rode out again the next day. The queen said that she could not bear being "shut up for days" and so went out, expecting an attack. A man later identified as John Francis fired from five paces; luckily, the gun was unloaded (→ 19/5/49).

The first attack: John Francis fires at Queen Victoria in the Mall.

Albert changes the royal household

Lady Lyttelton, later in life.

London, 30 September 1842

Baroness Louise Lehzen today left the court, for a life of retirement in Germany. The queen's former governess and confidante has been outmanoeuvred by Prince Albert, who is now indisputably master of the royal household. She had been with Victoria since 1819, but her departure had become a key element in Albert's drive to make the royal household more efficient. Albert – with Victoria's support – was especially determined to control the education of their children, and in April they appointed a new governess, Lady Lyttelton. And so today, loyal to the end, Lehzen left without seeing the queen "to spare her a scene".

New colonies extend Victoria's empire

London, 1843

The queen has gained another territory this year. Natal, in South Africa, has been proclaimed a British colony, and the rival Dutch settlers have retired. Whether or not the declaration of sovereignty will end the "Kaffir Wars" seems doubtful, but the annexation of Natal marks yet another stage in the development of a British empire. New Zealand was annexed three years ago, and the separate provinces of Canada are being combined into a new united colony. The Canadian developments follow a report by Lord Durham which suggested that the new colony be given virtual self-government in domestic affairs while remaining loyal to the British crown for foreign policy. Durham believed that this would bind colonies closer to Britain and weaken moves for independence. For Britain, too, it could mean changes. Colonies would offer global political power as well as economic strength. But in the short term it is the fighting in places like South Africa and Afghanistan which commands most attention.

Peel backs free trade in budget proposals

Peel reading to the queen.

London, 1842

Sir Robert Peel, his government now tolerated by a queen more preoccupied by family duties, has begun moves to balance the budget by simultaneously introducing a tax on incomes and scrapping duties on a wide range of goods. Duties are to be cut or abolished on no fewer than 769 of the 1,042 types of goods under measures introduced this year. The cuts will concentrate on raw materials, as Sir Robert hopes that the lower duties will boost consumption at home and free trade overseas. No changes have been made to the politically-sensitive sugar and corn (→ 8/1845).

Queen's uncle bids to upstage Albert

London, 28 June 1843
Prince Albert was at the centre of some undignified scenes today at the wedding of one of the queen's cousins, Princess Augusta of Cambridge, to the Grand Duke of Mecklenburg-Strelitz. The trouble began when the Duke of Cumberland, Victoria's uncle and king of Hanover since her accession, attempted to take precedence over Albert. Albert only prevented him from doing so by physically shouldering him out of the way down the altar steps. Cumberland tried again in the registry but was thwarted by the queen herself, who handed the pen straight to Albert.

The queen's uncles and aunts in the old royal family have never accepted that they should take second place to Albert. The Duke of Cambridge, for example, called him a "young foreign upstart", and his wife refused to stand to toast him. Only Queen Adelaide, William IV's widow, has been conspicuously kind to Albert and the queen.

Victoria breaks mould by visiting France

Victoria and Albert arriving at King Louis Philippe's palace at Eu.

France, 2 September 1843
Queen Victoria today became the first ruling English sovereign to be greeted on French soil by the king of France since Henry VIII met Francis I on the Field of Cloth of Gold in 1520. Accompanied by Prince Albert she arrived off Le Tréport late this afternoon aboard the new royal yacht *Victoria and Albert*, to be met by the 70-year-old King Louis Philippe at the start of her first state visit. She will stay at the royal residence at nearby Eu. There are links between the two royal families – the French king's eldest daughter is married to King Leopold of the Belgians, Victoria's uncle – but politicians are nervous of Louis Philippe's pursuit of links with Spain. However, it is also hoped that the visit will heal the strain in Anglo-French relations caused by conflicts over Egypt.

Chartist stronghold welcomes royalty

Birmingham, 20 November 1843
Prince Albert was given a rousing welcome today when, against the advice of government ministers, he paid a short visit to Birmingham. The city is a stronghold of Chartism, the radical but non-violent movement formed in the late 1830s to agitate for greater political reform in the wake of the 1832 Reform Act. It is named after its manifesto, the People's Charter, which calls among other things for the vote for all men, voting by secret ballot, constituencies of equal size and salaries for MPs.

Birmingham's Chartist mayor, described by the prime minister, Robert Peel, as "of extreme political views", welcomed the prince. Peel counselled against the visit, fearing republican demonstrations or worse, but Albert was determined to see one of Britain's industrial heartlands for himself. His informal manner and obvious interest in industry and social conditions have won him many hearts.

Albert and Wellington try to stop duelling

London, 1843
Duelling to satisfy the honour of army officers could become a thing of the past owing to the intervention of Prince Albert. The death this year of one Colonel Fawcett prompted Albert to consult the Duke of Wellington on what he called an "unChristian and barbarous custom". It was wrong, he said, that officers who were insulted had to face humiliation or break the law by killing an opponent. The duke agreed, and a proclamation has been issued that officers can simply "apologise or offer redress for wrong or insult committed" and keep their honour (→ 1/5/50).

A gentleman's honour: Prince Albert hopes that there will now be fewer duels.

Albert's father, Duke Ernest, has died

Germany, 11 April 1844
Prince Albert is heading home to England after a fortnight which he has spent in the land of his birth at the invitation of his elder brother, Duke Ernest II of Saxe-Coburg-Gotha. Invitation is a mild word, for Ernest had virtually begged Albert to come and help sort out the tangled mess left behind by their father, Duke Ernest I, who died on 29 January.

Albert arrived in Coburg, the ducal capital, on 28 March to a welcome as enthusiastic as the official mourning for his father would allow. After a tearful reunion with his family he set about trying to sort out the hopeless muddle that was the late duke's chief legacy. For although Albert is a model of uprightness, keeping a careful eye on his finances and devoted to his wife and family, the same could not be said of his father.

Ernest ran up huge debts and in his last years constantly badgered Albert for money, shamelessly exploiting his son's elevated position and using his name for credit;

Duke Ernest as a younger man.

when Albert baulked, he threatened to mortgage his duchy to the Russians. His attempts to gain the title "Royal Highness" from the queen to boost his prestige embarrassed Albert and the government, and he made little effort to hide his extra marital affairs.

Czar arrives to exploit Anglo-French rift

Windsor, 1 June 1844

The court was abuzz today for the arrival of an unexpected visitor: Czar Nicholas of Russia. Rooms in the best suite at Windsor were hastily prepared for the man who rules from Poland to the Pacific.

The reason for the czar's visit at short notice is unclear, but Prince Albert shrewdly suspects it is to exploit the strain in Anglo-French relations caused by an anti-British naval tract published last month by the Prince of Joinville, a son of King Louis Philippe. The queen and prince were especially dismayed by the affair because Joinville had been their guest last year when they visited his father at Eu. The czar will no doubt probe into what went on during that visit.

Nicholas, a charming but pig-headed reactionary, is unlikely to prosper in any attempt to split the two major powers who are keeping

Visiting: Czar Nicholas of Russia.

an eye on his own ambitions in the Balkans. Largely owing to the moderating influence of Prince Albert, both the queen and Lord Aberdeen, the foreign secretary, are doing their best to play down the Joinville affair.

Queen finds 'paradise' on Isle of Wight

Isle of Wight, 10 October 1844

The royal family have arrived for their first holiday at Osborne, a moderately sized house and estate belonging to Lady Isabella Blachford on the Isle of Wight. The queen and prince were first attracted to the island when they passed it in the royal yacht on their way to visit King Louis Philippe last year; with the help of the prime minister,

Sir Robert Peel, they began to look for an estate and chose Osborne.

The couple have rented Osborne for a week and are delighted; Albert calls it "a second paradise". They are so taken with it that they are thinking of buying it as a seaside alternative to the Brighton Pavilion. Albert especially craves somewhere where he and the queen can be genuinely alone (→ 23/6/45).

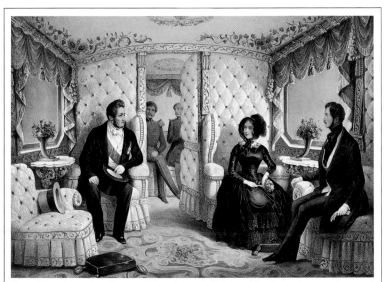

Travelling in style: Queen Victoria and Prince Albert in the comfort and seclusion of the saloon car of the royal train, playing host to King Louis Philippe of France. Victoria has liked trains since her first ride, in 1842.

Victoria's family grows and grows with the arrival of babies 'Affie' and Alice

Windsor, 6 August 1844

Queen Victoria's expanding brood gained a new member today with the birth, at Windsor castle, of a new prince. He will be christened Alfred Ernest Albert and is likely to be created Duke of Edinburgh. Alfred ("Affie") is the fourth child and second son to be born to the queen and Prince Albert. Their third child and second daughter, Princess Alice Maud Mary, was born on 25 April last year, nearly a year and a half after the new heir to the throne, Prince Albert Edward

("Bertie"). The reason for that gap – Bertie was born almost exactly a year after Victoria ("Pussy"), the Princess Royal, suggesting that a pattern of one child a year appeared to be emerging – was probably the queen's need for a long period of recuperation.

She suffered serious postnatal depression after Bertie's birth, which was not helped by a dispute with Albert over the governess, Baroness Lehzen, which resulted in Lehzen's forced retirement from the royal household (→ 25/5/46).

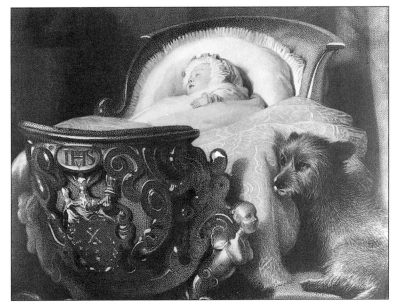

Guarded by a friend: the queen's second daughter, Alice, fast asleep.

Crowds cheer opening of Royal Exchange

London, 29 October 1844

The queen was in the financial heart of the British empire yesterday to open the new Royal Exchange in the City of London. It was a splendid royal occasion, with huge cheering crowds – greater, the queen believed, than at her coronation six years ago – lining the royal route to the city. Today's papers have given the occasion enthusiastic coverage, which marks another step in the renewed popularity of the monarchy. Victoria is delighted at reports which she finds "most kind and gratifying", as she has written to her uncle, King Leopold of the Belgians. She attributes her success to the good example of her "happy domestic life".

Victoria at the Royal Exchange.

Victoria
1837–1901

House of Hanover

Britain, August 1845. Victoria is able to travel abroad freely without appointing a regent to govern in her absence as Sir Robert Peel, her prime minister, is in complete control of her affairs (→ 6/12).

Germany, autumn 1845. Victoria visits Rosenau in Coburg, the birthplace of her beloved husband, Albert.

London, 25 May 1846. Victoria gives birth to a fifth child, Helena Augusta Victoria (→ 1/1847).

London, 19 July 1846. Lord Palmerston, acting on his own initiative, sends a list of marriage candidates to be considered by the 16-year-old Queen Isabella of Spain; this infuriates Louis Philippe of France (→ 9/1846).

London, August 1846. Parliament gives £26,000 for improvements to Buckingham Palace (→ 1858).

London, September 1846. Victoria receives Princess Augusta, the wife of Prince William of Prussia, on a state visit.

Windsor, 1846. Albert makes internal and external improvements at the castle (→ 1858).

Isle of Wight, 30 July 1847. Victoria goes sea-bathing for the first time with the aid of a bathing machine.

Scotland, 1847. Victoria and Albert purchase the lease of Balmoral castle, near Ballater, when the existing tenant, Sir Robert Gordon, dies (→ 8/9/48).

London, 10 April 1848. The Chartist movement holds a protest march from Kennington to Westminster.

Kensington, 27 May 1848. Princess Sophia, a daughter of George III and Victoria's aunt, dies aged 70.

London, 24 November 1848. Lord Melbourne, the former prime minister and a close friend of Victoria and Albert, dies.→

Windsor, Dec 1848. Professional actors appear for the first time in the royal Christmas theatricals.

London, 1848. The Society of Arts, of which Prince Albert is the president, receives its first royal charter (→ 12/6/49).

London, 1848. Sir John Conroy, a former comptroller of accounts and adviser of the Duchess of Kent, is questioned by solicitors as to the whereabouts of money belonging to Victoria's aunt Augusta Sophia, who died in 1842 (→ 1850).

London, 1848. Following changes in the Theatres Act of 1843 Victoria gives royal patronage to the acting profession.

London, April 1849. Henry Birch, an Eton schoolmaster, is selected as tutor to Albert – "Bertie" – the Prince of Wales (→ 31/1/52).

London, April 1849. Queen Victoria gives Bertie, the eight-year-old Prince of Wales, an independent suite of rooms in Buckingham Palace (→ 31/1/52).

Paris, 12 June 1849. With the success of the Paris Exhibition, members of the Royal Society of Arts urge Albert to open a similar exhibition in London (→ 1/1850).

Balmoral, 11 September 1849. Victoria praises the Highland servants who have looked after her family during their holiday; among those given a special thanks is a young man named John Brown who works as a "ghillie" or huntsman's guide (→ 9/1852).

London, 8 October 1849. George Anson, Prince Albert's private secretary, dies aged only 37.

London, 1849. Bertie, the Prince of Wales, and his sister, Vicky, the Princess Royal, make their first public appearance with their father, Prince Albert, at the opening of the new Coal Exchange (→ 1/5/51).

Windsor, January 1850. Albert presides over the inaugural meeting of the commissioners of the exhibition of British goods proposed for 1851 (→ 21/3).

London, 1 May 1850. Victoria gives birth to her third son, Arthur William Patrick Albert; born on the 81st birthday of the Duke of Wellington, he is named Arthur in honour of him.→

London, 2 July 1850. The death of Sir Robert Peel after a serious riding accident distresses Victoria.

London, 8 July 1850. Prince Adolphus, the Duke of Cambridge and uncle of Victoria, dies aged 76.

London, 15 August 1850. Lord Palmerston, the foreign secretary, visits Prince Albert, feigning a state of high emotion. Close to tears, he apologises for having failed to consult the queen in his conduct of foreign policy, and promises to reform in future. He is forgiven.

Belgium, 11 October 1850. Victoria is deeply distressed on hearing of the death of Queen Louise of the Belgians, the wife of Leopold, her favourite uncle; a close bond had developed between Victoria and Leopold's youthful queen on their first meeting (→ 1851).

London, 1850. Sir George Couper, the new comptroller to the Duchess of Kent, Victoria's mother, looks into her accounts and finds what he says is complete chaos left by his predecessor Sir John Conroy (→ 1/3/54).

Britain, 30 March 1851. Victoria and her family take part in a

national census of the British population for the first time (→ 1/5).

London, 1 May 1851. Vicky, the Princess Royal, aged ten, meets and becomes an ardent admirer of Prince Frederick William of Prussia, aged 22 (→ 29/9/55).

Isle of Wight, summer 1851. Princess Charlotte of Belgium, the 11-year-old daughter of Victoria's late and much-loved Aunt Louise, joins the royal family for a holiday at Osborne.

London, 2 November 1851. Albert organises the foundation of a museum at South Kensington to commemorate the success of the Great Exhibition.

Germany, 18 November 1851. Ernest, the Duke of Cumberland and king of Hanover, dies; he was an uncle to the queen but had become unpopular, and he is not greatly mourned.

London, April 1852. Victoria invites Benjamin Disraeli, the new chancellor of the exchequer, and his wife to dinner (→ 7/1867).

England, 30 August 1852. Victoria is left £250,000 in the will of an eccentric miser, John Camden Neild (→ 9/1852).

Balmoral, September 1852. Victoria, using the money left to her by John Camden Neild, purchases the castle and estate of 17,400 acres (7,045 hectares) at Balmoral from the trustees of the Earl of Fife (→ 28/9/53).

London, 14 September 1852. The Duke of Wellington, a state hero for his victory over Napoleon at Waterloo in 1815, dies at the age of 83 (→ 18/11).

London, 1852. Victoria opens the newly-renovated Houses of Parliament.

Victoria embroiled in political crisis as Peel falls

Tory party is split by corn law reform

Westminster, 6 December 1845

Sir Robert Peel announced today that he was resigning as prime minister. The queen is dismayed, having overcome her initial hostility now to trust and rely utterly on Sir Robert. The Tory Party has been split, however, by Peel's proposals for the reform of the corn laws.

He had seen the corn laws, which controlled imports of foreign wheat, as a barrier to free trade. However, the agricultural interests within the Tory Party saw the corn laws as the means to keep prices of their own wheat at high levels. With the Anti-Corn Law League formed in 1839 campaigning for their abolition, Peel was moving cautiously in that direction, but this year's poor wheat harvest allied to the failure of the Irish potato crop persuaded him to back outright abolition. The cabinet, led by Lord Stanley and the Duke of Wellington, disagreed.

Divisions over Ireland have also exacerbated Peel's problems. The government incurred Protestant protests by increasing its grant to Maynooth, a college for Catholic clergy in Ireland. The queen and her husband, Prince Albert, have backed Peel over both Ireland and free trade (→ 19/12).

Queen Victoria and the Duchess of Kent in a carriage at Windsor, attended by Albert, Sir Robert Peel and others.

Queen's dislike of Palmerston helps to block new government

Westminster, 19 December 1845

The queen's dismay at Sir Robert Peel's resignation 13 days ago turned to elation today with the news that Lord John Russell has been unable to form a Whig government. Peel will now soldier on as prime minister, but the issue which prompted his resignation – his plan to reform the corn laws – remains explosively divisive for the Tories. Benjamin Disraeli, one of the Tory supporters of protection, commented that Russell had returned the poisoned cup to Peel.

A crucial factor in Russell's failure to form a new government seems to have been the queen's opposition to Lord Palmerston's return as foreign secretary. Under Lord Melbourne's leadership, Victoria was protected from Palmerston for much of the time, but she found his manner overbearing and deplored his "rude, rough" dispatches. Her reservations were shared by Lord Grey, and his refusal to work alongside Palmerston gave Russell the pretext for declining office. Peel now sees himself as the only man who can govern and a man motivated by national rather than party interest (→ 26/6/46).

Insatiable prince adds new energy to arts

Isle of Wight, 23 June 1845

Prince Albert embarked on his latest grand scheme today when the foundation stone was laid for building work which will transform Osborne House, the new royal residence on the Isle of Wight. Albert plans to turn the house, which he and the queen bought in the spring for £26,000, into a grand Italian villa of his own design.

The prince has an insatiable interest in architecture and other branches of the arts. He is a shrewd connoisseur of painting, sculpture and music, reorganising and adding to the royal collections and patronising such great musicians as Mendelssohn; he is also a good amateur artist and a fine organist. Albert's talent and expertise were recognised in 1841 when he headed a royal commission into the fine arts in Britain in general and the decoration of the new Palace of Westminster in particular.

He is equally interested in the application of technological advances to art and design, and in June 1843 he succeeded the late Duke of Sussex as president of the Society of Arts, founded in 1754 to promote innovation in "Arts, Manufacture and Commerce". Albert's energy and now considerable prestige have seen a revitalisation of the society, which had run into financial difficulties (→ 9/1846).

French visit ends in royal marriage deal

Victoria with King Louis Philippe.

Château d'Eu, 8 September 1845

England and France have come to terms over the potentially divisive matter of the marriage of Queen Isabella of Spain. A cordial meeting took place here involving Queen Victoria and her foreign secretary, Lord Aberdeen, and King Louis Philippe and his foreign minister, Guizot. Britain has promised not to press the suit of the queen's cousin, Prince Leopold of Saxe-Coburg-Kohary, and to let the 15-year-old Isabella marry a Spaniard. In return, Louis will only allow a marriage between his son the Duke of Montpensier and Isabella's younger sister Louisa when the queen has bred an heir (→ 19/7/46).

Victoria learns to keep her distance as prime ministers and governments change

Westminster, 26 June 1846
Sir Robert Peel's government fell today, defeated on a measure for Irish coercion, at the same time as the House of Lords was passing the repeal of the corn laws. The reform of these laws had split the Tory Party, with 231 protectionist MPs voting against Peel. The queen is upset to lose Sir Robert again, but she is becoming inured to political change and, with the encouragement of Albert, learning that a constitutional monarch must keep her distance.

She was once so close to Lord Melbourne that it caused gossip and made her hostile to Peel. Despite her affection for Melbourne, a conservative Whig, she now dislikes the Whigs for what she sees as their ambition; however, she is resolved to work as best she can with her new prime minister, Lord John Russell. He is very much a party man and the queen calls him "little", in spirit as well as stature.

The queen's attitude to politics is also tempered by the birth three weeks ago of her fifth child. "When one is so happy and blessed in one's home life as I am, politics – provided my country is safe – must take only a second place," she said.

A stylish character sketch of Lord John Russell, the new prime minister.

Queen is furious at disloyalty of French

Windsor, September 1846
The queen is outraged that the Duke of Montpensier, the son of King Louis Philippe of France, has married Princess Louisa of Spain, in clear contravention of the Anglo-French agreement reached last year. A letter from Palmerston seems to have set events in motion. The new foreign secretary wrote to Madrid on 19 July, mentioning Prince Leopold of Saxe-Coburg-Kohary as a possible husband for Queen Isabella of Spain. Louis immediately assumed bad faith on England's part and endorsed his son's marriage. Anglo-French relations have now chilled (→ 3/1848).

Victoria is upset by Irish potato famine

Ireland, 1847
The plight of the Irish people, ravaged by famine after the failure of the potato crop, has touched the queen, who is resolved to visit the country as soon as possible. Terrible tales have reached England of deprivation, greedy landlords stealing the people's corn, and such poverty that the dead are buried without coffins. Victoria is not impressed by calls for days of fasting; she does not believe that the famine is the result of sinfulness. But the murder of landlords and other acts of savagery prompted her to observe: "Really, they are a terrible people" (→ 7/8/49).

Osborne rebuilt as magnificent residence

Osborne House: Italian style.

Isle of Wight, September 1846
The royal family has moved into the newly-completed Pavilion Wing of Osborne House here. In a touching ceremony on their first evening Prince Albert called for God's blessing on their residence by reciting part of an old Lutheran hymn. Work is continuing under Prince Albert's direction on the redesign and reconstruction of the modest house and estate which he and Queen Victoria first visited two years ago and later bought. He is working closely with Thomas Cubitt, the successful London architect and developer.

The main pavilion has been planned as part of a grand composition amid a landscaped estate. The prince has based his design on that of Italian villas which he has admired on his travels; his plans for Osborne are being compared with the work of the architect James Barry who since 1834 has been rebuilding Trentham Hall in Staffordshire as an Italian *palazzo*.

Victoria calls Osborne her "little paradise". Throughout the decorative scheme indoors, the initials "V" and "A" recur to celebrate her union with Albert. It is beautifully situated, and from its flat-roof promenade the royal family and guests can enjoy a breathtaking view of the Solent. Above all, it is a place of privacy.

Royal couple keep children on tight lead

Windsor, January 1847
The queen and Prince Albert have drawn up a memorandum laying down the form and content of their children's education. The atmosphere in the royal palaces is warm and often informal, and on Sundays Prince Albert loves to play with the children. But both parents have a strong sense of duty and want to ensure that their offspring maintain their high standards.

The princes and princesses – who number five at the moment – are to be divided into classes. Until the age of six most will stay in the charge of their governess, Lady Lyttelton, learning French, English, German and religious instruction. The Princess Royal, now six, will move next month into class two, under a Miss Hildyard and the Prince of Wales, although still five, will join her. All problems or punishments are referred to the queen. The children kneel beside their beds every evening to say their prayers.

Naturally, the greatest care is taken over "Bertie", as the Prince of Wales and heir to the throne is known. The queen does not seem to

A happy Christmas: but the young royals live under a strict regime.

want a close relationship with him but rather insists that he work hard. Soon he will move into class three, to be taught entirely by men. In the past year or so Bertie has become ever more wilful, preferring sport to study. He is also developing a stammer. The Princess Royal is a model student, though she has a fierce temper (→ 18/3/48).

Victoria shaken by year of revolution

French king finds shelter with queen

Isle of Wight, March 1848

King Louis Philippe, the deposed king of France, has landed safely here and been accepted under the queen's protection. Her house at Claremont in Surrey has been put at his disposal, and Palmerston has provided the destitute French royal family with £1,000 from secret service funds under the guise of a gift from "a well-wisher".

The fall of the French monarchy has been just one element in a wave of revolutions which appears to be sweeping Europe, much to the concern of Victoria. In Italy, the states have expelled their Austrian rulers; in Vienna, riots have ousted the chancellor, Metternich; and rebellions in Budapest and Berlin have wrested reforms from Habsburg and Prussian monarchs. Chartists are now planning protests in England [see story right].

The French king's escape was masterminded with great panache by the British consul at Le Havre, George Featherstonehaugh. He had the king and queen brought separately to the port where they boarded the British steam packet *Express*. Louis, with his whiskers shaved off, and disguised by a cap and glasses, carried a British passport in the name of William Smith. If challenged he was to say that he was the consul's uncle (→ 8/4).

Victoria the guardian angel: giving asylum to Europe's fleeing monarchs.

Nervous royal family leaves the capital

London, 8 April 1848

The queen, Prince Albert and their children, including the three-week-old Princess Louise, left for their home at Osborne on the Isle of Wight today on the advice of their ministers who fear that a huge demonstration of Chartists planned for two days' time could bring revolution to the capital.

The discontent of the London poor, focused by the demands of the Chartists, and the growing threat of rebellion in Ireland in this year of revolution has roused fears that the queen might suffer the same indignities as the French king, Louis Philippe, at the hands of the mob. The fear is very real at the palace. Prince Albert has written to a friend: "The organisation of these people is incredible. They have secret signals and correspond by means of carrier pigeons."

Stern measures have been taken in the capital. The Duke of Wellington is in command. Yeomanry regiments have been called up and guns positioned to command the Thames bridges. Peers have brought their gamekeepers from the country to defend their town houses.

A seaside resort showing the horse-drawn bathing machines first used by Victoria in July 1847; bathers enter the water directly from the machines.

New children swell large royal family

Buckingham Palace, 18 March 1848

The royal family increased again today when the queen gave birth to her sixth child, a daughter who joins three sisters, Victoria, Alice and Helena and two brothers, Albert, always known as "Bertie", and Alfred ("Affie"). The new princess is to be called Louise after Prince Albert's mother. Her birth follows swiftly on that of Helena in May two years ago and is proof of not only the queen's fecundity but also the importance of family life to the royal couple (→ 1/5/50).

Balmoral enchants new royal tenants

Aberdeen, 8 September 1848

The queen and Prince Albert have begun a family holiday at an estate which they have leased called Balmoral. Avid readers of Sir Walter Scott, they became enchanted by Scotland five years ago when they stayed with Lord Breadalbane at Taymouth castle. "Scotland has made a most favourable impression on us both," wrote the prince. "The country is full of beauty, perfect for sport and the air is remarkably light and pure." The royal couple are immersing themselves in Scottish traditions and have become fascinated by the clan tartans which were proscribed by the queen's forebears after the defeat of "Bonnie Prince Charlie's" Jacobite rebels at Culloden in 1745 (→ 11/9/49).

Prince Albert Edward in tartan.

'Lord M', mentor to the queen, is dead

London, 24 November 1848

The queen has been saddened today by the death of Lord Melbourne who was prime minister when she ascended the throne as a young, inexperienced woman. He treated her rather like a favourite daughter and guided her in everything from politics to the theatre. In his later years "Lord M", as the queen used to call him, became a rather solitary, crusty figure, so her genuine affection for her old mentor became tinged with pity. Lord Melbourne was 69.

▷

Foreign policies of Lord Palmerston make the queen furious, not to say bilious

London, January 1849

The queen is furious with Lord Palmerston, her foreign secretary, following the revelation in the *Times* that he has secretly allowed a private British contractor to draw arms from the royal ordnance for the Sicilians who are in revolt against the tyrant King Ferdinand, known as "Bomba" from his practice of bombarding insurgent cities. The queen, grumbling "I have to bear it all", insists that Britain will have to apologise to Ferdinand.

"Pam" has angered the queen and her husband further by sending a fleet to the Dardanelles to protect Turkey which was being bullied by Russia and Austria into surrendering Hungarian insurgents who had taken refuge with the Turks. The differences between the queen and Palmerston are now so great that they are virtually irreconcilable.

The foreign secretary persists in acting impulsively and without consultation. He has offended foreign powers and his colleagues as well as the queen by his support for the

Lord Palmerston: out of favour.

revolutionary movements which have swept Europe this year. When called to task by the queen, "Pam" is contrite but then carries on precisely as before. Victoria complains that when she has to read one of his dispatches before dinner it makes her bilious (→ 25/6/50).

Another assailant singles out the queen

Onlookers desperately try to stop William Hamilton firing at the queen.

London, 19 May 1849

The queen was attacked today by a deranged Irishman, William Hamilton, who fired a pistol at her as she was driven down Constitution Hill on her way to Buckingham Palace after her official birthday celebrations. Fortunately the pistol was not loaded, for Hamilton fired at point-blank range and could hardly have missed his royal target. Apparently he had conceived the idea of frightening the queen with a fake gun made out of the spout of a tea-kettle, but as this did not work he borrowed his landlady's pistol. He certainly succeeded in frightening the queen, for she did not know the gun was unloaded. This is the fourth attack on her (→ 27/7/50).

Victoria's visit to Ireland is great success

Ireland, 7 August 1849

Queen Victoria disembarked at Cove, in Co Cork, at the start of her state visit three days ago and renamed the little port "Queenstown" to mark the occasion. Later she knighted the mayor of Cork and toured the city in an open landau, to the delight of the crowd.

The royal party then sailed for Kingstown, but rough weather and seasickness forced them to shelter in Waterford for the night before going on to Dublin yesterday, where a crowded diary of engagements awaited the queen. She and Prince Albert inspected the Book of Kells in Trinity college, visited the royal hospital in Kilmainham, and went on to a grand levée at Dublin castle with 4,000 guests.

She then attended a concert in the vice-regal lodge and this morning she inspected a military review in Phoenix Park. Her final visit was to the Duke of Leinster who gave the queen a tour of his estate in a jaunting-car. Despite reports of kidnap plots and planned insurrections, the visit has proved popular with the people, after years of famine and despair. Even the previously hostile *Freeman's Journal* has been approving of the queen's "frank and confiding manner" (→ 12/5/53).

Well-wishers bid the queen and Albert farewell on their way to Ireland.

Queen grieves over death of Adelaide

Middlesex, 2 December 1849

Queen Adelaide, King William IV's widow, died today at Bentley Priory, in Middlesex. A kind, tolerant woman who coped admirably with the eccentricities of her unpredictable husband, she became Queen Dowager on his death, the first to hold that title since Charles II's widow, Catherine of Braganza.

Queen Victoria adored her aunt and is distraught at her death. With her own attempts at motherhood ending in miscarriages and tragically early deaths, Adelaide lavished her love on the young Victoria and, surprisingly, on her husband's children by his mistress, Mrs Jordan. She was 57.

Victoria gives birth to seventh child

Buckingham Palace, 1 May 1850

The queen gave birth to her third son today. By a happy chance it is the Duke of Wellington's 81st birthday, and the new prince is to be named Arthur after him. The duke will be his godfather. The queen and Prince Albert are delighted that this new arrival, their seventh child, is a boy. However, the queen, who thinks new-born babies ugly, is not at all pleased about her constant pregnancies. When told how fine it is to give life to an immortal soul she replied: "I think much more of our being like a cow or dog at such moments when our poor nature becomes so very animal and unecstatic" (→ 7/4/53).

'Great exhibition' launched by Albert at Mansion House

London, 21 March 1850

Prince Albert met with thunderous applause tonight as he formally launched plans for the greatest exhibition the world has ever seen, to be held in London next year. In a speech at the Mansion House, in the City, Albert was enthusiastically received when he spoke of how the event would celebrate "the achievements of modern invention".

The idea of a "great exhibition" of British products had been brewing in his mind for a while before it was floated in public last year at a meeting of the Royal Society of Arts, of which he is president. To his surprise the idea was welcomed, and he won an instant lieutenant in Henry Cole, a 40-year-old former civil servant with a name for prodigious energy and determination to get his way. Albert assembled a distinguished "think tank" to develop the project, and the idea of a British exhibition soon grew into an international one.

Cole was sent to the continent to publicise the project, with tremendous success. Albert has opened a fund to finance the exhibition. Provided that the fund attracts donors, London should next year play host to one of the greatest spectacles of modern times (→ 1/5/51).

Palmerston clashes with royal couple

A cartoon showing Palmerston as a mischievous boy set to stir up conflict.

Gunship diplomacy wins public support

Westminster, 25 June 1850

Lord Palmerston – or "Pam", as he is affectionately known – has had a triumph in the House of Commons with a stirring speech in defence of his conduct of foreign policy. Palmerston sent the British fleet to blockade the Greek port of Piraeus to support a British subject, Don Pacifico, whose Athens house had been burnt down in a mob attack. When the Greek government refused his claim for compensation, "Pam" sent in the gunships. As a result Russia and France, as joint guarantors of Greek independence, are threatening war.

Palmerston told parliament: "As the Roman in the days of old held himself free from indignity when he could say *Civis Romanus sum* [I am a Roman citizen] so also a British subject, in whatever land he may be, shall feel confident that the watchful eye and strong arm of England will protect him ... " The queen and Prince Albert, however, are not impressed (→ 12/8).

Prince backs move to dismiss 'Pam'

Buckingham Palace, 12 August 1850

The queen and Prince Albert are determined to get rid of Lord Palmerston, despite the popular acclaim that he won after the Don Pacifico affair [*see left*]. In an extraordinary interview with the prime minister, Lord John Russell, the prince dragged up an old charge against the foreign secretary: that he had attempted a brutal sexual attack on one of the queen's ladies at Windsor castle.

The royal quarrel with "Pam" runs deep. He is accused of sending the queen copies of his dispatches too late for her to take any action and of ignoring the amendments she makes. Today the prince has sent Russell a letter from the queen, drafted by Baron von Stockmar, their unofficial but influential adviser, which argues that the queen has an undoubted constitutional right to dismiss a minister who "commits an act of dishonesty towards the crown". Russell is appalled. He fears that the government will fall if Palmerston is sacked. "Pam" has asked for an interview with the prince. If all goes according to form he will promise to reform and be forgiven (→ 15/8).

Street attacker gives queen a black eye

Bystanders restrain Robert Pate after he slashed at the queen with his stick.

London, 27 July 1850

Queen Victoria was attacked and hit in the face today by a man wielding a stick. She suffered a black eye, facial bruises and a headache, but she was otherwise unharmed. The deep brim of her bonnet probably saved her from worse injuries, and she was well enough to go to the opera this evening. The attack came in Piccadilly as she visited her uncle Adolphus at Cambridge Park. As she was driving in an open carriage with her children, but without an escort, people surged forward and she was struck. The assailant was held by the crowd and turned out to be a deranged retired lieutenant of the Tenth Hussars named Robert Pate, the son of a former high sheriff of Cambridge.

Prince Albert's model lodging-house for workers, erected in Hyde Park as part of the planned displays for next year's "great exhibition".

Victoria and Albert open Britain's Great Exhibition

London, 1 May 1851

The springtime drizzle gave way to brilliant May sunshine this morning as the queen and Prince Albert drove in regal splendour to open the Great Exhibition in London's Hyde Park. The royal party set out from Buckingham Palace at half-past eleven in nine state carriages and proceeded through vast crowds – "as far as the eye could reach", the queen said – to the "Crystal Palace", the stupendous glass and steel hall erected for the exhibition of industry and art of all nations.

The edifice sparkled like some massive version of the fabulous Koh-i-Noor diamond which was adorning the queen's coiffure. A glorious blaze of fanfares filled the air as Victoria, in pink watered silk, and Albert, in field marshal's uniform, entered the magnificent nave of this breathtaking cathedral of light with their eldest children, Vicky and Bertie, at their sides. The party processed to the dais at the centre of the building, near a beautiful crystal fountain, and at a word from Albert the Marquis of Breadalbane boomed: "Her majesty commands me to declare the exhibition opened!" A deafening cheer went up from the thousands who packed the hall and continued as the queen and prince walked the length of the colourfully festooned building.

Victoria and Albert were deeply moved by their reception and hid their emotion only with difficulty. Above all this was Albert's day, a spectacular reward for years of toil on behalf of his queen and adopted nation; there can be no doubt now that Britain has taken the "foreign upstart" to its heart (→ 2/11).

Make way for the queen: Victoria and Albert at the opening of the exhibition.

Displays show British imperial power

London, May 1851

The great "Exhibition of the Works of Industry of All Nations", to use its official title, is a monument to Prince Albert's belief that humanity can be improved by fostering scientific and technological advances. In particular, though, it celebrates the international supremacy which the industrial revolution has given Britain in commerce and manufacturing: nearly 7,500 of the 14,000 exhibitors are from Britain and its empire. The 100,000 items on display range from an Irish crofter's cottage to a North American Indian's wigwam, from paintings to working printing-presses.

Most spectacular of all is the great exhibition hall itself, the stunning "Crystal Palace" designed by Joseph Paxton and built from 300,000 panes of glass on a cast-iron skeleton. It is the very essence of Albert's vision for the Great Exhibition, which he said should "combine engineering, utility and beauty in one staggering whole".

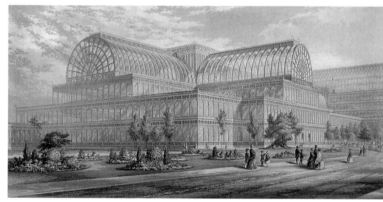

The cathedral of light: a later view of the exhibition's "Crystal Palace".

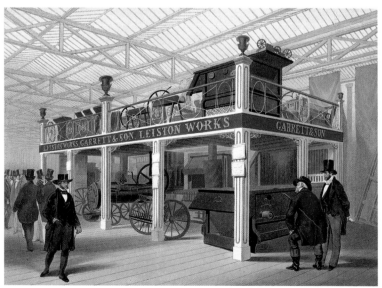

How does it work? Exhibition visitors examine the latest inventions.

A chaotic scene as crowds fill London's streets on the way to the exhibition.

Palmerston forced out of office over Louis Napoleon

Westminster, 19 December 1851
Lord Palmerston, the foreign secretary, has finally been forced out of office over his handling of Louis Napoleon's coup in France. His departure has been brewing for a long time, with both the queen and Prince Albert irritated beyond measure by Palmerston's insubordination and looking for an excuse to get rid of him.

Louis Napoleon, the nephew of the great Napoleon, was elected president of France, but on 2 December he carried out a brilliantly successful coup and declared himself emperor. The queen likened it to a takeover by Oliver Cromwell and ordered that the government should take no action either to help or to hinder him but must remain "entirely passive".

Palmerston was rather pleased to see a strong hand in control of France and was unwise enough to assure the French ambassador of his cordial support for the new emperor. Most of his cabinet colleagues secretly agreed, but "Pam" was on bad terms not only with the royal family but also with the prime minister. Remaking British policy without consulting anyone lost him the confidence of the prime minister, and thus he was forced to resign (→ 24/12/52).

Albert organises national hero's funeral

A splendid ceremony: the funeral procession for the Duke of Wellington.

London, 18 November 1852
The funeral of the Duke of Wellington, which took place today, was organised by Prince Albert, who supervised every detail down to designing the "Iron Duke's" funeral car and coffin – both of which, as befitted the victor of Waterloo, were truly enormous. The funeral car was made of bronze and was 21 feet long. On top of it rode the coffin which, to avoid being dwarfed by the magnificent vehicle, was made six feet six inches long, although the duke was only five feet nine inches tall. The prince and Queen Victoria watched the cortège from the newly-built balcony of Buckingham Palace, where the queen was seen to be weeping unrestrainedly.

The duke had been her most respected and closest adviser, and she had never yet had to face a crisis without his help and guidance. She will miss him badly. When the procession had passed by, the royal party cut across to St James's to watch it go past again. The queen was particularly moved by the sight of the duke's charger following behind the funeral coaches with his master's boots reversed in the stirrups as a symbol of death.

Albert lectures the new prime minister

Osborne, February 1852
Prince Albert and Queen Victoria have ticked off the new prime minister, Lord Derby, who has a reputation for being more interested in horse-racing than in politics. His plan to allot the best ministerial jobs to "the dandies and roués of London and the turf", as the prince calls them, is going too far. Alarmed that such men are likely to embroil the queen and the court in scandal, the prince insists on a new morality in court appointments. From now on these plum positions must never go to men on the verge of bankruptcy or whose moral characters will not stand up to scrutiny. This rules out most of Derby's friends (→ 24/12).

Derby government falls after defeat

Edward Stanley, the Earl of Derby.

London, 24 December 1852
A new government has at last been put together under the leadership of Lord Aberdeen, following the collapse of Lord Derby's premiership on 17 December when he was defeated by 19 votes. To strengthen his government, Lord Derby had suggested bringing in Lord Palmerston as leader of the House of Lords, a suggestion that the queen dismissed immediately. The queen's suggestion that Gladstone might take over was vetoed by Derby, who replied that Gladstone was "quite unfit for it" (→ 19/12/53).

New tutor is engaged as concern grows for Bertie's education

The Prince of Wales: slow at lessons.

Windsor, 31 January 1852
A new tutor has been engaged for the Prince of Wales, who has not been making great progress. The new tutor is Frederick Gibbs, but whether he will be able to do much with his new charge remains to be seen. While not stupid, Bertie does not appear to prosper under a regime of lessons for five hours a day, six days a week.

Worse, from the queen and Prince Albert's point of view, young Bertie was most attached to his previous tutor Henry Birch, a young, good-looking teacher. Birch treated his young charge with great kindness and did what he could to keep the hours of lessons to levels that the prince could cope with. Rewards for good work often took the shape of rambles and walks in the afternoons, which Birch felt were better for him than extra maths.

However, such progress as the Prince of Wales has made is not judged to be satisfactory, and the discussion of "what to do with Bertie" has been going on for some time. After consulting Lord Granville on the subject of education and phrenology, Prince Albert has had the bumps on Bertie's head submitted to professional study, but this has done no good. Loath to punish her son for his slow progress, the queen has decided on a new tutor, but Bertie is sullen at losing his friend and dislikes Gibbs (→ 3/1855).

V i c t o r i a
1837–1901

London, 7 April 1853. Queen Victoria gives birth to her eighth child, a son named Leopold George Duncan Albert (→ 9/5).

Windsor, 5 July 1853. It is discovered that young Prince Leopold, a thin and sickly child, suffers from haemophilia, a rare disease in which the blood fails to clot (→ 2/8/59).

Ireland, 29 August 1853. Victoria arrives on a state visit (→ 26/8/60).

London, 23 November 1853. Victoria returns to London on hearing of the Ottoman declaration of war on Russia and the worsening situation in the Black Sea (→ 30/11).

Black Sea, 30 November 1853. The Ottoman fleet is sunk at Sinope by the Russian navy (→ 19/12).

Windsor, 24 December 1853. Victoria realizes that her new parliament, led by George Gordon, the Earl of Aberdeen, will not succeed without Lord Palmerston, who resigned earlier this month because of his unpopular pro-war ideas (→ 1/1854).

Britain, 28 February 1854. The British ally with France and declare war on Russia in support of the Ottoman Empire (→ 28/3).

Russia, 28 March 1854. War breaks out in the Crimea (→ 30/11).

France, September 1854. Albert, now cleared of accusations of pro-Russian loyalties, accepts Napoleon III's invitation to visit his camp at St Omer (→ 4/1855).

London, February 1855. Albert falls ill with a serious chill.

Windsor, April 1855. In an attempt to ease the strain of Anglo-French relations, Victoria and Albert entertain the emperor and empress of France (→ 31/8).

Balmoral, 10 September 1855. While enjoying a holiday with her family and guests, Victoria learns of the fall of Sebastopol. →

Balmoral, 29 September 1855. Prince Frederick William of Prussia declares his love for 14-year-old Victoria, the Princess Royal, but the queen will not let her eldest daughter marry until she has had her 17th birthday (→ 1/1856).

Windsor, 1855. Victoria and her daughters help the war effort by knitting scarves and socks.

London, 1855. Victoria visits war casualties in hospitals and dispenses medals.

London, spring 1856. Prince Frederick William of Prussia accompanies Vicky, the Princess Royal, to the waxworks of Madame Tussaud's exhibition (→ 20/3).

Windsor, 20 March 1856. Vicky, the Princess Royal, is confirmed in the Church of England (→ 9/5).

London, 9 May 1856. A ball is held to celebrate the coming-out of Vicky, the Princess Royal, who is now 15 (→ 5/1857).

London, June 1856. Prince Alfred, aged 11, is given his own tutor, Lieutenant John Cowell, in an attempt to separate him from what his parents see as the rebellious influence of his elder brother, the Prince of Wales (→ 4/1857).

Balmoral, 21 September 1856. Victoria meets the celebrated nursing heroine of the Crimean war, Florence Nightingale (→ 5/10).

Balmoral, 5 October 1856. Victoria, totally fascinated by Miss Nightingale, asks her to dinner.

Germany, 17 November 1856. Prince Charles of Leiningen, the only son of the Duchess of Kent by her first marriage and half-brother of Victoria, dies.

Windsor, 9 March 1857. Victoria is asked to choose the federal capital city of Canada.

London, 30 April 1857. Mary, the Duchess of Gloucester, the sole surviving child of George III, dies aged 81.

Switzerland, April 1857. Prince Alfred, the second son of Victoria and Albert, spends some time in Geneva improving his French, under the supervision of his tutor, Lieutenant John Cowell, before making a visit to relations at Coburg, in Germany (→ 8/1858).

London, May 1857. Victoria, upset already by the thought of her favourite daughter getting married, is further alarmed by the Prussians' wish for Vicky and Frederick to be married in Berlin (→ 6/1857).

Windsor, June 1857. Prince Frederick William of Prussia's engagement to Vicky, the Princess Royal, is announced officially when he arrives in England for the christening of Victoria's youngest child, Princess Beatrice (→ 25/1/58).

Isle of Wight, August 1857. At the request of parliament, Queen Victoria and Prince Albert entertain Emperor Napoleon III and Empress Eugénie of France at Osborne House (→ 1870).

Europe, 1857. After a successful walking tour of the Lake District, the Prince of Wales makes a tour of Europe (→ 1/4/58).

Gravesend, 2 February 1858. After their marriage last month, Prince Frederick William of Prussia and Vicky, the Princess Royal, depart for Prussia (→ 4/1858).

Windsor, 1 April 1858. The Prince of Wales is confirmed (→ 10/11).

Windsor, summer 1858. After consulting a nutritionist, Dr Clark, Victoria orders a new diet for the Prince of Wales in the hope that it will improve his temperament and his intellect (→ 10/11).

Windsor, 10 November 1858. Colonel Robert Bruce is appointed as the new governor to the Prince of Wales (→ 1/1859).

Surrey, November 1858. The Prince of Wales, aged 17, gets his first taste of independence when he moves into White Lodge in Richmond Park (→ 1/1859).

Berlin, November 1858. The Prince of Wales visits his sister, Vicky, for three weeks (→ 1/1859).

London, 27 January 1859. Victoria becomes a grandmother on the birth of Prince William, the first son and heir of Prince Frederick William of Prussia and Vicky, the Princess Royal. →

Rome, January 1859. At the queen's request, the Prince of Wales dines with the poet Robert Browning (→ 10/1859).

London, May 1859. Victoria's mother, the Duchess of Kent, suffers an attack of erysipelas, an acute infectious disease that affects the skin (→ 16/3/61).

Europe, 12 July 1859. The Peace of Villafranca is signed between Austria-Hungary and France, bringing peace to Europe.

London, 2 August 1859. Victoria writes to her uncle, King Leopold of the Belgians, expressing her fears for young Prince Leopold. Because of his haemophilia, she fears that he will never be able to live an active life (→ 11/1872).

Opposite: Victoria, Albert and the children, a family portrait (detail).

Queen pioneers anaesthesia in childbirth

Before chloroform: the queen recovers from the birth of the Princess Royal.

Windsor, April 1853
The decision of the queen to use chloroform during the birth of Prince Leopold, on 7 April, has done a great deal to popularise what has hitherto been a controversial form of medication. As is often the way with innovations, many arguments have been used against it, not the least being that the great pain of childbirth enabled women to love their children all the more.

The use of chloroform in childbirth was pioneered in Edinburgh where the first woman to try it, a doctor's wife, was so entranced by the experience that she christened her new daughter Anaesthesia. The queen can hardly be expected to go

so far, but, not being short of mother-love and knowing full well the suffering of giving birth, she welcomed the arrival at Windsor of the famous anaesthetist Dr John Snow.

Dr Snow relieved her by the simple method of dripping half a teaspoon of chloroform onto a handkerchief, which he then rolled into a cone and placed over her mouth and nose, dripping more chloroform onto it as necessary.

The resulting numbness was such that, while the queen at no time lost consciousness, her pain was greatly reduced, and she has made a better recovery than from any previous labour (→9/5).

Albert begs queen to share problems

Buckingham Palace, 9 May 1853
The agonies caused by the failure of the baby Prince Leopold to thrive have precipitated an emotional crisis in the royal household. This has shown itself in a series of highly-charged rows between Queen Victoria and Prince Albert. When Albert made a mistake while sorting through some prints one evening this week, Victoria went into hysterics for an hour, followed by 24 hours of sullen silence. Today the prince has written a long letter to his wife, begging her not to bottle things up but to share her troubles with him (→5/7).

At odds: Victoria and Albert.

'Pam' intervenes in crisis over Crimea

London, 19 December 1853
With the news today of the sinking of the Ottoman fleet by the Russsans it appears that Lord Palmerston's intervention in the Turkish crisis, by resigning as foreign secretary, is about to pay off. His resignation was really a signal to the country that he was prepared to lead it to war against Russia, something that the peopls greatly favour but which is being blocked by the prime minister, Lord Aberdeen, and the queen.

Palmerston ("Pam", as he is known) and the British ambassador in Constantinople, Lord Stratford de Redcliffe, want to bring Britain into the war in order to check the Russian advance on the Bosphorus with its strategic access to the Mediterranean. Redcliffe has sent so many letters supporting the Turkish (or Ottoman) cause that it is said that his autobiography will have to be called "1,001 Notes".

Far more dangerously, and without informing the queen, Palmerston sent the British fleet into the Black Sea, where it is bound to encounter Russian warships. Today's news that the Russians have sunk the Ottoman fleet at Sinope has further inflamed anti-Russian feeling. It now seems certain that the government will ask "Pam" back, in which case he will surely steer Britain into war against Russia in the Crimean peninsula (→24/12).

Balmoral castle becomes the family's favourite autumn retreat

Balmoral, 28 September 1853
Autumn in Scotland has become a regular holiday for the royal family since they bought the estate at Balmoral. Set on the banks of the river Dee, near the town of Ballater, it is an ideal spot with abundant game to hunt. The original house is now too small for the growing family, and so Prince Albert is having a new mansion built, a hundred yards to the north-west of the old one. The royal couple relax here with their children and go on expeditions into the hills on foot or by pony-trap. One of Queen Victoria's favourite pastimes is to be rowed around the nearby Loch Muick by Prince Albert (→15/10/67).

The royal family's autumn retreat: Balmoral castle, in Scotland.

Dublin exhibition is opened by Victoria

Dublin, 12 May 1853
The queen has come to Dublin specially to open the Exhibition of Art-Industry, which is intended to promote the industry and arts of Ireland. Possibly because of the devastation caused by the potato famine of 1848, there is a good deal more art than industry on display. Most of the Irish industrial products take the form of already famous textiles, cabinets from Dublin and damasks from Belfast, but what catches the eye of visitors – including the queen – are the magnificent reproductions of early Celtic jewellery (→29/8).

Albert comes under fire

A danger to himself: "Punch" warns Albert to steer clear of foreign affairs.

London, January 1854
Press attacks on Prince Albert have reached a peak as tension over the Russian attack on Turkey continues to grip the country. The prince is widely suspected of plotting the downfall of Lord Palmerston, of being pro-Russian and of planning through his large network of German relatives to keep Britain out of the coming war and so away from the expected spoils. So wild has speculation become that one newspaper actually reports that "lovely Albert" has been arrested. The queen suspects that Lord Palmerston is behind many of these attacks, and it is true that Palmerston does nothing to deny or control them (→ 10/2).

Queen wants Albert to be Prince Consort

London, 10 February 1854
The queen's 14th wedding anniversary today has put her in the mood to do something about Albert's anomalous position. There has been tremendous criticism of the stance that she and Albert have taken towards the war with Russia. Things became so bad last month that crowds gathered at the Tower of London on a rumour that the queen and prince were to be arrested and brought through Traitors' Gate.

Eventually the queen had to appeal to parliament to put matters straight and was rewarded by a string of flattering speeches about Albert. The root of the discontent is that her husband attends meetings with ministers, and acts as her private secretary and chief adviser, yet has no right to do so. He is also German, which does not help.

A queen's husband with no right to rule in his own name is a novel situation in modern Britain, but the experts are clear that Albert has no business under the British constitu-

Aberdeen: urges queen to wait.

tion to interfere in government, as he does daily. To correct this the queen has asked the prime minister, Lord Aberdeen, how her husband could be made Prince Consort and be recognised as her rightful adviser. "Easy," replied Aberdeen, "but not just now" (→ 9/1854).

Queen knits socks for soldiers in Crimea

London, 30 November 1854
Queen Victoria today made known her intention to give a medal to all servicemen who have fought in the bloody battles of the Crimean war, believing that "nothing will gratify and encourage our noble troops more". The medal is to have the word "Crimea" on it and the names of the British Army's great victories at Alma and Inkerman.

Britain made its formal declaration of war against Russia, in support of the Turks of the Ottoman Empire and in alliance with France, on 28 February this year. British policy has long been to safeguard the territorial integrity of Turkey, which has been threatened by Russian expansion into the Balkans and the Mediterranean. The Turks declared war in October last year after a series of Russian encroachments into their territory. In January this year the Royal Navy sailed into the Black Sea to confine the Russian fleet to its base at Sebastopol, whence it had sailed to destroy the Ottoman navy in a single blow.

Battle was joined on 20 September at the river Alma, when the British captured the Russian positions and forced them to retreat but then lost the initiative and their chance to capture Sebastopol. In the last few months Russian attacks on Balaclava and Inkerman have been beaten off, but the army is now facing a bleak winter.

The queen is taking a keen personal interest in the campaign. She feels deeply for her troops, and spends much of her spare time knitting socks and mittens for them and writing letters of condolence to the families of the dead (→ 10/9/55).

Tending the wounded: a view of a hospital ward in the Crimea.

Conroy, scandalous adventurer, is dead

London, 1 March 1854
News has come of the death of Sir John Conroy, whom the queen hated more than anyone else on earth. Conroy was adviser to her mother, the Duchess of Kent, and so dominated her that even Queen Victoria believed that they were lovers. Conroy was self-important and dishonest and had ambitions to rule the country by making the duchess regent. He kept Victoria away from her uncle, King William IV, and when she was seriously ill with typhoid he tried to force her to sign a document making him her private secretary. When Conroy finally left the duchess's employ he had kept no accounts for nine years – and £60,000 was missing.

Conroy: Victoria's arch-enemy.

Russell government falls; 'Pam' is back

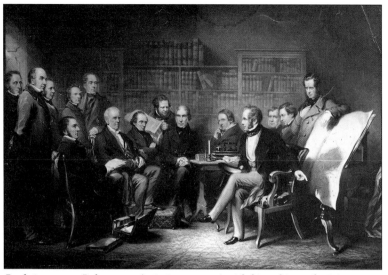

Back in power: Palmerston (pointing at map) with his cabinet of ministers.

London, 5 February 1855
Lord Palmerston, the home secretary, has kissed the queen's hands and become prime minister. For a week the country had been without an effective government; the queen asked Palmerston to form a government after exploring every alternative. Few hands have been held out so unwillingly to be kissed.

On 30 January Lord Aberdeen's coalition government resigned, unable to withstand the Commons' vote of censure on its conduct of the war in the Crimea. The end had been bitter, hastened by the resignation of Lord John Russell, who was both foreign secretary and leader of the house, on 24 January. The queen first asked Lord Derby,

the Tory leader, to form a government. "It must be Palmerston," he replied, "the whole country wants him." None the less Derby tried to persuade "Pam" to accept the leadership of the house, but without success.

The queen then asked the veteran Whig leader, Lord Lansdowne. He refused on the grounds of age and health. She next travelled from Windsor to London in a blizzard and asked Russell to head a government, but so bitter are his former colleagues at his resignation that he could find none to serve under him. Reluctantly the queen reconciled herself to "Pam". Her "eternal government hunting errand", as she put it, is over (→ 2/1858).

Frustrated by Bertie's progress, Albert draws up scheme to improve education

London, March 1855
Bertie, Prince Albert Edward, that most difficult eldest son of Queen Victoria and Prince Albert, is causing his parents grave concern. This evening, when the queen and Prince Albert escaped into the Buckingham Palace gardens, they spoke to each other of their worries: about his laziness, his stupidity, and his refusal to learn.

If he had knuckled down as his parents had constantly urged him, they argued, he would have become a scholar. But the young prince shows no regard for the values of the severe Mr Gibbs, his tutor. His grammar is eccentric to say the least. He shows no appreciation whatsoever of classical studies and is only interested in the more frivolous disciplines of modern history and contemporary politics.

Prince Albert's plan is to bribe Bertie – to promise him a commission in the Brigade of Guards if he passes a general examination under Mr Gibb's disciplined direction. The queen has agreed. Something must be done about the boy. He has become too close to his younger brother, Prince Alfred, and must be separated from him if he is to learn. The problem now is whether the young prince is capable of passing a general examination (→ 9/1856).

The royal academy: a satire on the Prince of Wales's difficult education.

Victoria is charmed by Emperor Napoleon during visit to Paris

Paris, 31 August 1855
Queen Victoria has been mesmerised by the French emperor, Napoleon III. "I should not fear saying anything to him. I felt – I do not know how to express it – safe with him," Victoria confided in her journal during the state visit to Paris just completed. She expressed amazement to her foreign secretary, Lord Clarendon, that Napoleon remembered every frock that she wore. The government is relieved at the success of the visit, the first since Louis Napoleon was proclaimed emperor in 1852. Clarendon said later: "She has never before been on such a social footing with anybody" (→ 8/1857).

Victoria and Albert are honoured by a formal procession through Paris.

Fall of Sebastopol sets queen dancing

Balmoral, 10 September 1855
On hearing today of the fall of Sebastopol, the Russian stronghold in the Crimea, Victoria ordered the great bonfire standing ready on Craig Gowan to be lit. The royal family danced around it with abandon – "a veritable witches' dance supported by whisky", said Prince Albert. All the queen's profound patriotism has come to the surface in this war. She is intensely proud of her army, but no one has yet told her that it was the French, not the British, who stormed the city, and that the British attack on the Redan actually failed (→ 29/1/56).

Press leaks news of Vicky's engagement

London, January 1856

Victoria, the Princess Royal, is to marry Crown Prince Frederick of Prussia. The news was broken by the *Times*, which dismissed the prince's family as "a paltry German dynasty". Bismarck, the Prussian chief minister, equally dismissive, describes the Coburgs as "the stud-farm of Europe", and the Prussians are insisting that the marriage takes place in Berlin. In Paris Emperor Napoleon is personally offended.

The queen is furious at the leak and at the Prussian haughtiness. "I resent bitterly the conduct of the Prussian court and government, and do not like the idea now, of *our child* going to Berlin, more or less the *enemy's den*," she wrote.

The princess herself, who is only 15 years old, has little to say on the matter except to concur with the wishes of Prince Albert, whom she worships. "What she learns from ... her dear father, makes a deeper impression than all the rest," her mother wrote.

The queen has thrust her eldest child speedily into womanhood and writes with relief of her "growing visibly". The princess is no longer permitted childhood irresponsibilities and is only allowed to dance with princes. The queen is pleased by the Princess Royal's progress, and keeps her qualms about Vicky's readiness for marriage to herself,

Princess Victoria: set to marry.

consoling herself with her daughter's growing maturity. She noted in her diary that Vicky had gone through a critical time without "even the slightest indisposition".

In spite of their youth (Prince Frederick is only 12 years Vicky's senior) – or possibly because of it – they will be admirably suited in one way at least. According to her mother, the Princess Royal has "liberal English" opinions. Frederick is also known for his political liberalism, which makes him a rarity amongst Prussian princes and is disturbing to conservative counsels in Britain and Prussia (→ 20/3).

Victoria Cross new reward for courage

London, 29 January 1856

The queen has introduced a new award, the Victoria Cross, in admiration of the courage of the ordinary British soldiers in the Crimea. Inscribed simply "For Valour", it will be open to all ranks of the army and navy, will only be awarded for exceptional deeds of heroism performed in the face of the enemy, and will carry a pension of £10 a year (→ 30/3).

For valour: the Victoria Cross.

Prince walks round Dorset – incognito

Dorset, September 1856

The Prince of Wales has abandoned his walking tour of Dorset. The prince was travelling with his tutor Mr Gibbs and one of the queen's grooms-in-waiting, the redoubtable Colonel Cavendish. But when the editor of the *Bridport News* informed its readers that "his royal highness is making a tour of the provinces incognito" and had recently stayed at the Bull Hotel, the party was so pestered by sightseers that it has returned to Osborne House on the Isle of Wight.

The walking tour had been the prince's idea, taken up by Mr Gibbs, who saw no academic hope in the boy and supported the proposal as a desperate measure to interest him in his subjects. For the young prince, only 14 years old, it is a disappointment. Cut off from his family, without friends, and kept under the stern gazes of Mr Gibbs, Colonel Bruce and Major Teesdale at White Lodge, where cards, billiards and the slightest lightheartedness are forbidden, he is not a happy boy.

One of the major causes for his unhappiness is his inability to win any approval for what he does from his parents. True, they write to him, but it is only to offer that most cruel of gifts – good advice (→ 1857).

Crimea peace deal dismays the queen

London, 30 March 1856

News of the end of hostilities in the Crimea has not been welcomed in Buckingham Palace. "I own that peace rather sticks in my throat, and so it does in that of the *whole* nation," she wrote. She had sensed the mood of the country rightly. This morning the heralds who proclaimed the Peace of Paris at Temple Bar were hissed.

The lack of a clear-cut victory by British arms to compensate for the terrible suffering of the ordinary soldier disturbs Victoria. The "unpatriotic" dispatches from the front line by William Russell published in the *Times* anger her. The army, she believes, has been cheated of its rightful glory.

Victoria welcomes the exhausted troops back from the Crimea

Victoria greets an invalid soldier just returned from the Crimean war.

Aldershot, 30 July 1856

Wearing her scarlet tunic, and seated on her horse Alma, the queen reviewed "the largest force of Britishers assembled in England since the Battle of Worcester" – as she enthusiastically calls the returned Crimea veterans who marched past her today. The queen, despairs Charles Greville, the clerk to the privy council, "has a military mania on her".

The war and the most "unsatisfactory" peace brought on the mania. She has met hundreds of returning soldiers, "some strikingly handsome", who have given her "a real idea" of what it was like out there. But the meetings have not been without sorrow, and the sight of the blind and the limbless has moved her to pity.

Beatrice, queen's ninth child, is born

Princess Beatrice with her nurse.

London, 14 April 1857
The queen has given birth to a daughter to be called Beatrice. The birth was arduous, but it has taken the queen out of her depression at the prospective departure through marriage of her eldest daughter, Vicky. She wrote later that she had felt stronger than before: "I was amply rewarded and forgot all that I had gone through when I heard dearest Albert say – It is a fine child, and a girl." (→ 1875).

Albert becomes Prince Consort to Victoria

London, 26 June 1857
Prince Albert was appointed Prince Consort yesterday. The queen made the appointment herself by letters patent after the lord chancellor discovered that parliament did not have the power to confer the title itself.

This morning's *Times* is cynical and disrespectful about the elevation. What does it matter, its editorial asks, if Prince Albert be given precedence immediately after King Leopold of the Belgians on his next visit to the continent? It was the question of precedence that had prompted the queen to act, but it had nothing to do with Leopold. The old Hanoverian royal family, which had so objected to giving Albert a title in 1840, are now all dead. The young Saxe-Coburg royal family are growing up. What would Vicky's status *vis-à-vis* her father be if she became queen of Prussia? How would the Prince of Wales cope with being treated as a more senior prince than his father?

The queen also believes that Prince Albert's work entitles him to the consortship. He was relentlessly energetic in making a success of the Great Exhibition in 1851, and in encouraging science and establish-

Albert: now the Prince Consort.

ing museums such as the Museum of Manufactures which moved last year from Marlborough House to a new site in South Kensington.

Parliament is less convinced of the prince's worth, and after negotiating the marriage settlement of the Princess Royal, the prime minister, Lord Palmerston, was glad that he did not have to bring Albert's status before the Commons.

Queen wants India given to the crown

London, 23 November 1857
Queen Victoria is so shocked by the news of atrocities and counter-atrocities coming out of India that she has noted in her diary a universal feeling "that India should belong to me".

For six months India has been torn by mutiny and rebellion. First the queen's heart went out to the victims of the rebels, the fair-skinned Christian women who suffered fates worse than death. Then, as British forces reasserted themselves, she became shocked at the army's own excesses – the blowing of rebels from the mouths of cannons and the bayoneting of prisoners. For weeks she had been urging Palmerston to ensure that there would be no vindictiveness.

Disappointed in the East India Company for precipitating the rebellion through its greed and misrule, and despairing at the complacency of her government at home, she is convinced that only benevolent despotism, with Victoria as the most benevolent of all despots, can reconcile India to British rule – and to the gentle imposition of civilising Christian values (→ 2/1858).

First photocall for the royal family

Isle of Wight, 26 May 1857
The royal family have been captured in a photograph, taken on the terrace of Osborne House. Though they have frequently sat for portrait paintings, and the queen was photographed with the Prince of Wales and his two eldest sisters in a pony-trap three months ago, this is the first time that the entire family has been formally photographed. The photograph reveals more about the queen, her husband and children than would a gallery of royal portraits. Victoria, tiny, with Beatrice in her arms, is almost lost among her offspring. Prince Albert, towering above wife and children, appears semi-detached. Prince Alfred is the only one who stares, with curiosity, at the camera lens.

Left to right: Prince Alfred, Prince Albert, Princess Helena, Princess Alice, Prince Arthur, Queen Victoria and Beatrice, Vicky, the Princess Royal, Princess Louise, Prince Leopold and Albert Edward, the Prince of Wales.

Queen's eldest daughter is married

Prussian prince for the Princess Royal

Windsor, 25 January 1858
Princess Victoria, the queen's eldest and favourite daughter, was today married to Crown Prince Frederick William of Prussia. Delighted crowds gathered outside Buckingham Palace to cheer the young couple as they left, after helping to eat a "splendid wedding cake", for a brief honeymoon at Windsor.

So magnificent an occasion has brought half of Europe's royal houses to London, led by a positive army of Frederick's family and reinforced by Britain's own nobility, all mixed together at a mammoth state banquet and, a few days later, at a ball for 1,000 guests.

As the excitement rose to its climax, Victoria remained calm, although Prince Albert was "quite torn to pieces". The groom arrived two days ago; yesterday – "poor dear Vicky's last unmarried day", as the queen put it – was spent as a family. The Princess Royal "clung to her truly adored father with indescribable tenderness", while the queen went to her room and cried. Today, watching her daughter as a married woman, the brave face was restored, betraying only calm and unsullied joy (→ 2/2).

An emotional parting: Victoria and Albert look on as Vicky is married.

Lonely queen misses her beloved Vicky

Windsor, April 1858
"The idea of not seeing you for so long seems unbearable. Everything I do or see makes me think of you ...," thus the queen has written to her daughter Vicky, now Princess Frederick William of Prussia. Monarch she may be, but there is no doubt that her majesty's maternal feelings are as strong as those of any mother, proud to see her daughter married but equally sad not see her in the family home.

Indeed, the queen writes to her absent daughter almost daily, offering details of family life and peppering her with demands for similar tales of life in the Prussian court. At the same time having a married daughter, who is thus a married woman just as she is, is providing Victoria with something that she has lacked: a confidante who can by turns be questioned, advised, scolded and even asked for advice.

However, the queen remains a mother first, and her daughter is only 17. Her letters are filled with suggestions, most particularly on the delights and duties of marriage. "Let it be your study and your object to make your husband's life and his home a peaceful and a happy one," she advised (→ 27/1/59).

Palmerston cabinet is toppled; Derby is back in power

Westminster, February 1858
Lord Palmerston, prime minister since 1855 and, as such, the architect of Britain's Crimean campaign, has been defeated in the Commons and has resigned. The new government will be led by Lord Derby.

This abrupt change of prime minister has not pleased the queen. It is true that she has often been angered by Lord Palmerston, especially over his ostentatious sang-froid in the face of what she, like the public who elected his government, saw as real national disasters. Yet she has been obliged to respect "Pam's" patriotism which, like her own, is marked by an unashamed devotion to all things British.

Lord Derby, on the other hand, has few redeeming characteristics. Indeed, his attitude to India, for which part of her empire the queen cherishes a special affection, seems cold. She may well oppose any excessive reforms there (→ 5/1858).

African lake named after the queen

East Africa, 1858
A British explorer in East Africa has discovered a huge inland lake which he has named in honour of Queen Victoria. John Hanning Speke declares that in Lake Victoria he has discovered what he was looking for – the source of the river Nile.

Speke was travelling with a fellow explorer, Richard Burton, on a trip sponsored by the Royal Geographical Society. Their brief was to explore the equatorial lakes of Africa and seek out the headwaters of the river. However, at Lake Tanganyika Burton fell ill, and Speke went on alone.

In the wake of the discovery the two men, veterans of a hazardous trip four years ago to nearby Somaliland, have fallen out quite seriously. Burton is not convinced that the lake is the source of the river and has publicly challenged Speke's claim. The solution to the controversy will have to wait until the pair return to Britain.

Albert builds model dairy as part of improvements at Frogmore

Windsor Great Park, 1858
Prince Albert has built a remarkable dairy to complement the other farm buildings which now adorn the garden at Frogmore House. He directed the sculptor John Thomas in creating the elaborate, tiled room, which is equipped with solid marble tables and decorated with an Italianate frieze and fine medallion heads of the royal children.

The prince, who is greatly interested in architecture and design, has been making improvements to the castle, grounds and associated buildings at Windsor since the early 1840s. In this he has been encouraged by the queen, who has said of his untiring work here: "It is a nice feeling that it will be something of our creation."

A Windsor idyll: calm reigns at the beautifully-situated Frogmore House.

Queen deplores bureaucratic rule in India

Windsor, May 1858
Just as the queen had feared, her government, led by Lord Derby, has taken a radical step in its proclamation of a new constitution for India. The Conservatives have, almost literally, torn up the plans on which she and Lord Palmerston had agreed and replaced them with a new scheme.

In essence, where before India was to come under the direct control of the crown, now it is to be governed by a council. Far from taking a personal role in the government of the *Raj*, the queen is to be, as she puts it, "a mere signing machine". Her loathing of what she sees as a bloodless, barely human organisation is intensified by the new plans for selecting Indian civil servants not by appointment but by competitive examination. While critics may claim that the queen is

simply annoyed at such diminution of her personal power, her objections go deeper. As a girl she saw India as place of romance, of the exotic; now she sees her own servants subjecting it to a faceless bureaucracy and ignoring the humanity of its millions of people.

Like her more astute advisers, Victoria realised that last year's mutiny of the Indian Army stemmed from a wholesale rejection of the ruling East India Company and its disregard for tradition. After the mutiny that system had to be changed, and she believed that there was a "universal feeling that India should belong to me".

Palmerston agreed and planned accordingly, placing India under crown rule administered through a council, but with his fall those plans were abandoned. The council alone will have real power (→2/6/59).

A base for Britain's trade in the Orient: East India House in London.

Builders leave Buckingham Palace much grander than before

London, 1858
Queen Victoria at last has a satisfactory London base after a campaign of improvements to Buckingham Palace lasting for more than a decade. In its original form the building was too small either to house the royal family in comfort or to entertain important guests in style. The alterations, funded by a £150,000 parliamentary grant and the proceeds from the sale of Brighton Pavilion, began in 1847 with the construction of a new east wing, under Edward Blore. From 1851, James Pennethorne oversaw the creation of a splendid ballroom.

An impressive aspect: Buckingham Palace, as seen from St James's park.

Alfred is posted to the Mediterranean

Midshipman "Affie": sailor prince.

Gosport, August 1858
Fourteen-year-old Prince Alfred, better known within the royal family as "Affie", has joined the Royal Navy. The move was confirmed today when he sat and passed, with great distinction, his entrance examination. He has been posted to his first ship, HMS *Euryalus*, part of the Mediterranean fleet. Affie's interest in the navy is by no means recent. So keen has he shown himself that two years ago he was given a special tutor, Lieutenant John Cowell, who began training him for the exams. It is largely due to Cowell that the prince performed so well today (→23/10/62).

Bertie receives the Order of the Garter

Windsor, November 1858
The Prince of Wales – "Bertie", as he is known to his loving, if concerned, parents – gained a new honour today: membership of the Order of the Garter, a distinction that dates back to King Edward III and is bestowed only at the sovereign's express command. For a young man who has always delighted in such things, doting since childhood on the splendours of uniforms and similar finery, the order will be especially welcome, although some hope that the award will also alter his character.

The prince, a loving and indeed lovable young man, remains a problem for his parents. Unlike his brother Alfred, whose heart is set on a sailor's life [*see left*], Bertie has shown no such purpose. Apparently incapable of learning, devoid of any positive aims, and prone to petulant outbursts that at best can be put down to adolescence, the heir to the throne has yet to demonstrate the sort of personality that will fit him for the role that he is to take in the life of the nation.

Prince has difficult audience with pope

Rome, January 1859
The Prince of Wales, visiting Rome to study the fine arts, has paid a visit to the pope, Pius IX. But the meeting, like the visit of which it was a part, proved a disaster. His daily round carefully censored by Colonel Bruce, his governor, Bertie has been forced to reject society's keen advances, seeing only ruins, which he bitterly rejects as "mouldering stones".

The papal audience was to be one human exception, and, with Bruce at his shoulder, the prince made small talk. Then the pope opened a new topic, his restoration of the Catholic hierarchy in Britain. This subject, which has been heavily criticised at home, outraged the colonel. Flouting the usual rule, whereby the pope ends his audiences, Bruce ended the interview and abruptly removed his charge. Such heavy-handedness is likely to take months to repair (→10/1859).

Vicky gives queen her first grandchild

Berlin, 27 January 1859

Queen Victoria is a grandmother. Her first grandchild, Prince William of Prussia, was born today to her daughter Vicky. Unfortunately it was not an easy event – the labour was protracted and the birth itself terribly painful. Indeed, the doctors feared for the lives of both the tiny prince, whose left arm was dislocated during the breech birth, and his young mother. The queen, who has been a constant source of advice throughout the pregnancy some people have even suggested that her constant letters have increased, rather than allayed, her daughter's natural apprehension is overjoyed but regrets that her "precious darling" has suffered so very much (→ 9/1864).

Prince of Wales enjoys life as a student

Bertie as an undergraduate.

Oxford, October 1859

Despite his mother's efforts to keep his life supervised by her representative, General Bruce, who acts as the prince's "governor", Bertie, the Prince of Wales, is managing to enjoy life at the university here.

The queen does not like the town and sees the university as a necessary evil, its sole function being to provide "a place for study". But if Oxford is a home of lost causes, then it is her majesty's cause that has been lost this time. Her son, undaunted by Victoria's stern restrictions, is finding Oxford a place of many charms. He talks university slang, accepts all the invitations that Bruce wishes him to turn down and has attracted a group of friends whose main pleasure – in which the prince takes due part – is in riotous living (→ 10/7/60).

Tennyson gives a poetic comment on reign's events

Alfred Tennyson: poet laureate.

London, 1859

The publication of *The Idylls of the King* this year is being hailed as the crowning achievement of the poet who succeeded Wordsworth as poet laureate in 1850. The *Idylls* take further the current fashion for Arthurian legend, which Alfred Tennyson helped to create with his earlier *Morte d'Arthur* and *The Lady of Shalott*.

The queen is one of his greatest admirers, and when she appointed him laureate he wrote *Revered, beloved*, part of which visualises future generations saying of her:

> *"Her court was pure, her life serene,*
> *God gave her peace, her land reposed;*
> *A thousand claims to reverence closed*
> *In her as Mother, Wife and Queen."*

Victoria particularly admires the poet's poignant elegies entitled *In Memoriam* (1850). Tennyson's duties as laureate have enabled him to write memorable poems on events such as the *Ode on the death of the Duke of Wellington* and *The Charge of the Light Brigade* at Balaclava.

Scottish servant is new court favourite

Victoria, Albert and John Brown.

Balmoral, September 1859

The queen has a new favourite, and he is no ordinary courtier but a simple employee on the royal estate here. John Brown, a Scottish *ghillie* [huntsman's guide] described by Victoria as "really the perfection of a servant", seems to be fulfilling the queen's every need. Indeed, there is no one quite like him in the royal entourage. Apart from what she calls his "handiness", no other intimate, let alone a servant, would be permitted – as he is – to enter her rooms without knocking, still less to call her "Woman" (→ 12/1864).

Palmerston set for new rows with Albert

Westminster, 2 June 1859

Lord Palmerston, whose last premiership ended in parliamentary defeat 14 months ago, has returned to power following the resignation of Lord Derby. It is not a event that is likely to please the court. In the first place the queen dislikes his dependence on the radicals and his rejection of the old Whig policies. Secondly, Albert, whose many Coburg relations make him staunchly pro-Austria, deplores Palmerston's foreign policy, which prefers Italy to the Habsburgs.

While Palmerston backs the plans of France's Napoleon III to free Italy from Austrian occupation, the prince is utterly opposed to them. The Habsburg empire may have a dreadful record, but Albert still hates the idea of any policies that might weaken or, worse still, destroy it (→ 12/7).

Lord Palmerston's power base: an interior view of the House of Commons.

V i c t o r i a
1837–1901

Toronto, 27 June 1860. The Queen Victoria Plate race is run for the first time at Carlton race-track.

Plymouth, 10 July 1860. The 18-year-old Prince of Wales sets sail for Canada, where he is to act as Victoria's representative during a royal tour (→ 12/10).

Killarney, 26 August 1860. Victoria and Albert visit Ireland.

Coburg, 1 October 1860. Prince Albert is involved in a coach accident which leaves him lacking in stamina (→ 2/12).

Oxford, November 1860. The Prince of Wales returns to the university (→ 12/1860).

Windsor, 2 December 1860. Albert, suffering from exhaustion, is confined to bed (→ 15/11/61).

Britain/Denmark, December 1860. Victoria negotiates for a marriage alliance between her son, the Prince of Wales, aged 19, and Princess Alexandra, the eldest daughter of Prince Christian, the heir to the Danish throne (→ 24/9/61).

Canada, 1860. Charles Sabatire composes *Cantata in Honour of the Prince of Wales* to commemorate his Canadian trip.

Cambridge, 18 January 1861. The Prince of Wales begins his studies at Trinity college (→ 26/8).

London, 16 March 1861. Victoria is shattered by the death of her mother, the Duchess of Kent.→

Dublin, 26 August 1861. The Prince of Wales joins the Grenadier Guards at the Curragh military camp (→ 24/9).

South Germany, 24 Sept 1861. The Prince of Wales meets Princess Alexandra of Denmark for the first time at Speyer (→ 16/11).

Cambridge, 25 November 1861. Suffering from a chill, the Prince Consort visits the Prince of Wales to discuss the scandal involving Nellie Clifden (→ 14/12).

Windsor, 14 December 1861. Prince Albert dies of typhoid fever; the queen, who is distraught, blames the Prince of Wales for his death (→ 15/12).

Isle of Wight, 19 December 1861. Victoria, beside herself with grief at the loss of Albert, removes to Osborne House with the Prince Consort's brother, Ernest, for company (→ 20/12).

Windsor, 23 December 1861. Albert is buried; at the funeral the Prince of Wales represents Victoria, whose grief prevents her from making a public appearance.→

Norfolk, 1861. The Prince of Wales purchases the Sandringham estate as his country home (→ 1864).

Windsor, 14 June 1862. The Prince of Wales's relations with Victoria improve after the success of his recent Middle East tour.→

Isle of Wight, 1 July 1862. Still in mourning for Albert, Victoria attends the sombre wedding of her daughter, Alice, to Prince Louis of Hesse and the Rhine (→ 5/4/63).

Germany, 8 September 1862. The Prince of Wales proposes to Princess Alexandra of Denmark (→ 7/3/63).

Athens, 23 October 1862. Victoria's second son, Prince Alfred, is offered the vacant Greek throne; Victoria declines the offer, respecting her late husband's wish that Alfred should eventually succeed his uncle, Duke Ernest of Saxe-Coburg (→ 24/5/66).

London, December 1862. The Prince of Wales purchases

Marlborough House, formerly occupied by the Queen Dowager, Adelaide, William IV's widow and the prince's great-aunt (→ 5/1863).

London, 7 March 1863. Huge crowds welcome Princess Alexandra, who is to marry the Prince of Wales (→ 10/3).

Germany, April 1863. After the Prussian invasion of Danish-owned land in Schleswig-Holstein, Prussia and Denmark sign an armistice (→ 31/12).

London, May 1863. The Prince and Princess of Wales move into Marlborough House.→

Denmark, November 1863. Alexandra's father, Prince Christian, succeeds to the throne as King Christian IX (→ 8/1/64).

London, 8 January 1864. The Princess of Wales gives birth, two months prematurely, to Albert, the first son and heir of the Prince of Wales (→ 14/1).

Denmark, 7 September 1864. The Prince and Princess of Wales arrive at Elsinore; it is their first visit to Alexandra's native land since their marriage (→ 3/6/65).

Germany, September 1864. The Prince and Princess of Wales meet Crown Prince Frederick William of Prussia and his wife, Vicky, the elder sister of the Prince of Wales; it is an awkward meeting due to Prusso-Danish hostilities over Schleswig-Holstein (→ 11/1864).

Denmark, November 1864. Anti-Prussian feelings grow in Britain after the recent Prussian invasion of Denmark.

London, April 1865. Lord Palmerston, the prime minister, draws Victoria's attention to the gambling habits of the Prince of Wales (→ 25/10).

Dublin, 9 May 1865. The Prince of Wales opens the International Exhibition.

Windsor, 7 July 1865. Prince George, the second son of the Prince and Princess of Wales, is christened (→ 20/2/67).

Edinburgh, 24 May 1866. Prince Alfred is created Duke of Edinburgh, the first English prince to bear a Scottish title (→ 28/11/67).

Kew, 12 June 1866. Princess Mary Adelaide of Cambridge, a cousin of Victoria, marries Prince Francis of Teck (→ 26/5/67).

London, 20 February 1867. The Princess of Wales gives birth to her third child, Louise.→

London, 20 May 1867. Victoria lays the foundation stone of the Royal Albert Hall (→ 15/10).

Kensington, 26 May 1867. Princess Mary Adelaide of Teck gives birth to her first child, Victoria Mary ("May") (→ 31/12/85).

Balmoral, 15 October 1867. Victoria unveils a statue of Albert (→ 7/6/69).

London, February 1868. Benjamin Disraeli replaces Lord Derby as prime minister (→ 17/11).

Dublin, April 1868. The Prince and Princess of Wales arrive for a short visit (→ 24/4).

London, 6 July 1868. The Princess of Wales gives birth to her fourth child, Victoria (→ 7/4/71).

Britain, 17 November 1868. Despite the disapproval of the queen, the Prince of Wales and his family leave on a visit to Europe.

Montreal, 10 August 1869. Prince Arthur arrives to complete his army training (→ 20/5/72).

Princess Alice is to wed German prince

Windsor, November 1860

In a carefully-contrived moment of solitude, Prince Louis of Hesse and the Rhine has proposed to the queen's second daughter, the 17-year-old Princess Alice. The two were left alone by the fire after dinner in order to give the German prince, aged 23, the opportunity to ask Alice to marry him. Victoria likes Louis, whom she finds unaffected and quickwitted. What is more, he will not have to spend as much time in Germany as does Vicky's husband Fritz (→ 1/7/62).

Princess Alice: now she is engaged.

Victoria's mother is dead after illness

The late Duchess of Kent.

Frogmore, 16 March 1861

The queen's mother, the Duchess of Kent, died this morning, aged 74. She had been ill with an abscess on her arm for some time. Although she had made life very difficult for the young Princess Victoria by trying to drive a wedge between her and her brother-in-law, the king, she matured into a much-loved and kind-hearted old lady, and Victoria is distraught at the loss of her mother. Above all, she regrets their quarrels in the past, blaming them on the duchess's companion and adviser Sir John Conroy.

Prince and actress in seedy sex scandal

Windsor, 16 November 1861

News that the Prince of Wales has lost his virginity in a session of debauchery at the Curragh army camp, near Dublin, has reduced his father to furious tears. All the careful tutoring and chaperonage to instil the virtues of purity and chastity have been undone by a local actress called Nellie Clifden, well-known as a woman of easy virtue.

The prince, who has just turned 20, had been given permission by his parents to go to the Curragh for ten weeks this summer in spite of warnings from his mentor, General Bruce, that army life was beset by "temptations and unprofitable companionship". Amazed by the prince's unworldliness, his fellow officers decided to broaden his horizons. Nellie – said to be so regularly entertained by the men of the Curragh that she knew her way around the camp in the dark – was smuggled into the prince's tent one night; it was the start of a light-hearted fling.

The affair soon became the subject of scandalised gossip which has just reached the ears of Prince Albert. Today he penned an anguished letter to his son, now studying at Cambridge. Nellie is already being nicknamed "the Princess of Wales", says Albert, and will no doubt have a child which she will

Growing up: the Prince of Wales.

say is Bertie's, and drag him through the courts where he will have to give "before a greedy multitude disgusting details of your profligacy ... Oh horrible prospect ..!"

Albert's annoyance and pain are not just the results of his strict moral views and horror of the sins of the flesh. He is also anxious that the monarchy should preserve the highest standards of behaviour and propriety for the sake of its own survival in an age of republicanism and revolutions (→ 25/11).

Prince of Wales enjoys a trip to Canada and the United States

New York, 12 October 1860

A grand ball has tonight provided a catastrophic climax to the Prince of Wales's triumphant tour of North America. Under the pressure of 5,000 people, all desperate for a glimpse of the prince, the floor of the Academy of Music gave way with a loud bang. The prince was unruffled, unlike several guests who had fallen through the floor; hurried repairs were undertaken, in the course of which a workman was nailed in under the boards.

The prince has won much admiration on his tour, which included a long stay in Canada where he opened Montreal's Victoria Bridge, laid the foundation stone of the parliament building in Ottawa and saw the French rope-dancer Charles Blondin walk a tightrope across the Niagara Falls (→ 11/1860).

A more successful evening: a grand ball in Boston, on the prince's tour.

Typhoid claims life of Portugal's king

Windsor, November 1861

Victoria and Albert are stunned by the news that typhoid has claimed the lives of Albert's cousins Prince Ferdinand and King Pedro of Portugal within days of each other. Albert was particularly close to the 25-year-old king, who looked to him as a wise uncle. Albert, in turn, doted on Pedro, who seemed to him to have all the qualities which he thinks that his own son, Bertie, lacks. Albert, inclined by nature to depression, is in danger of sinking into a deep melancholy. The revelation of Bertie's affair with Nellie Clifden has put him in a quite abnormal frame of mind. The queen has written: "We did not need this fresh loss in this sad year, this sad winter ... " (→ 16/11).

Albert dies, and the queen goes into mourning

Prince Albert's funeral hearse approaching St George's chapel, Windsor.

Albert as the head of the family: with Victoria and the children, in 1859.

Nation's grief expressed at sombre funeral

Windsor, 23 December 1861
Prince Albert was buried today, nine days after his death, at the age of 42, had plunged the queen and the nation into mourning. Soldiers of the Grenadier Guards lined the route as the hearse was drawn from the castle to St George's chapel where the coffin was lowered into the royal vault. The distraught queen, who withdrew to Osborne four days ago, was represented at the funeral by the Prince of Wales.

Albert became ill last month, but he continued to work on state papers and agonised over the scandal surrounding the Prince of Wales's affair in Ireland. Even when typhoid was suspected the doctors told the queen that there was no cause for alarm. But as the fever worsened an enfeebled Albert became more fatalistic, and on 11 December bulletins were issued for the first time, confirming the seriousness of his condition. His family were called, and five of his children were in the Blue Room at the castle, with the queen, when the prince died at 10.50pm on 14 December. "He was my life," Victoria said – and now he had gone.

Great patron of arts, crafts and industry

London, 15 December 1861
Prince Albert has been acclaimed upon his death as "the pillar of our state". The words are those of the *Times*, and they reflect not only the nation's shock at his death but also the influence of the prince during his marriage to the queen.

The Great Exhibition of 1851 epitomised Prince Albert's diverse interests – and it would never have taken place without his drive and vision. Yet this celebration of Britain's place at the forefront of the industrial revolution was also inspired by the prince's social concerns. He had long been distressed by the housing and working conditions of poor families and hoped that poverty would be eased if industry could prosper.

Science, education, the arts and the army were other areas of passionate interest. He also reorganised the royal household and played a key role as, in effect, the queen's principal private secretary at the very heart of government. He helped to confirm the role of constitutional monarchy by persuading Victoria that the queen should be above party politics (→ 19/12).

Victoria to handle affairs of state alone

Isle of Wight, 20 December 1861
The queen arrived here at Osborne yesterday accompanied by the sympathy of the nation tempered with some anxiety as to the future. Albert had been not only her beloved husband but also the centre of her working life as a constitutional monarch. Her grief is unmistakeable, but so apparently is her determination to continue as Albert would have wanted. "I will do my duty," said Victoria on the day after Albert died, and her composure has impressed ministers and other royal advisers. It seems that she will reign alone. If so, she has greater experience than most contemporary politicians; although she is only 42, she has reigned for 24 years (→ 23/12).

Prince Albert: the last portrait.

Duty becomes the royal watchword

Queen Victoria: a wife mourns.

London, 15 December 1861
The shops of London are draped in black today as the city mourns the death of Prince Albert. The people remember him as a great patron of the arts, craft and industry as well as a devoted husband. Yet beyond these public achievements Albert also brought a new perception of values to the British royal family. After the excesses of the Hanoverians, Albert instilled duty as the watchword of Victoria's reign. Publicly this meant that he worked hard and encouraged a sense of social responsibility to others. Privately, fidelity to the family was paramount, which was why the Prince of Wales – as heir to the throne – caused so much parental dismay.

Prince of Wales becomes the centre of attention

Queen blocks move to involve Bertie

Windsor, 14 June 1862

The Prince of Wales was reunited with the queen today following his return from a five-month tour of the Middle East and European cities. The trip had been planned by the late Prince Consort as part of the education of his eldest son, and Victoria has been pleased by reports of how Bertie, as she calls him, conducted himself. British diplomats in Constantinople noted the prince's tactful handling of the sultan, while his meeting with the Austrian emperor in Vienna was also deemed a success by his advisers. "There's more to him than I thought," said Canon Arthur Stanley, a clergyman who accompanied the prince.

Despite the achievements of his tour, however, the queen has no plans to give the prince, who will be 21 later this year, a greater role in public life. Such a move has been floated in influential quarters, including the *Times* newspaper, as a way of filling the vacuum created by the death of Prince Albert and the queen's own protracted mourning. But Victoria still regards her son as immature and remains bitter about his affair with the Irish actress Nellie Clifden. She once said that it was the news of Bertie's "fall" which had caused Albert's fatal illness.

When Lord Palmerston, the prime minister, suggested that the Prince of Wales might succeed his father as master of Trinity House, the lighthouse authority, the queen at once rejected the idea, making clear her opposition to Bertie's taking over any function previously performed by Albert (→ 8/9).

A royal match: Edward and Princess Alexandra on their wedding day.

Marlborough House in London, home for the Prince and Princess of Wales.

Prince marries into Danish royal family

Windsor, 10 March 1863

The Prince of Wales was married today to Princess Alexandra, the strikingly attractive 18-year-old eldest daughter of Prince Christian of Denmark. They first met in Germany in September 1861, with Bertie's elder sister, Vicky, acting as matchmaker. No fewer than seven European princesses had been considered as potential brides for the heir to the British throne. Alexandra had made a favourable first impression upon Bertie, but her more important conquest was Victoria herself, who was charmed during a private visit to King Leopold last year. Even so, delicate political talks continued, as the queen does not want to be drawn into the dispute between Denmark and Prussia over the future of Schleswig-Holstein (→ 5/1863).

Parties planned at Marlborough House

London, May 1863

The Prince and Princess of Wales are making their London home in Marlborough House. It was named after the duke for whom it was built by Wren, but it has been a royal residence since 1817. The house has been refurbished for the prince, who particularly likes the large ballroom and the extensive lawns. Lavish garden parties and balls are planned as the prince turns the house into the centre of society life. It also has a "smoking room", kept hidden when the queen visited by a hastily-chalked sign: "lavatory under repair" (→ 11/1863).

Princess Alice gives birth to a daughter

Windsor, 5 April 1863

The queen today gained a grandchild who is to be named after her. The baby Princess Victoria was born to Princess Alice, the queen's third child, who last year married Prince Louis of Hesse and the Rhine. The couple were married in private on 1 July last year in the dining room of Osborne House, which was converted into a temporary chapel for the ceremony. The queen, dressed in funereal black, sat near the altar in an armchair, screened from sight by her sons, Bertie and Affie (→ 5/1873).

Royal family torn over Prussian invasion

London, 31 December 1863

The royal family is split over the Prussian threat to seize Schleswig-Holstein from Denmark. On one side is Vicky, the eldest daughter of the queen, married to Crown Prince Frederick of Prussia. On the other is Bertie, the eldest son of the queen, married to the eldest daughter of the Danish king. Alexandra's father succeeded to the throne last month as Christian IX and now faces the prospect of a Prussian invasion. The Prince of Wales backs the Danish cause, but the queen is pro-Prussian (→ 9/1864).

Son and heir born to the Prince of Wales

London, 14 January 1864
Insisting that her newborn grandson should be christened Albert Victor, the queen today informed his father, the Prince of Wales, of her wish that he should be known as Albert Edward when he became king, and that all his descendants should bear the names of Albert or Victoria until the end of time.

The Princess of Wales gave birth to her first child six days ago at Frogmore. He was two months premature and weighed only three and three-quarter pounds. The princess had been watching her husband play ice-hockey at Virginia Water and went into labour soon after returning home for tea. No preparations had been made, and a local doctor arrived at a gallop not long before the birth at ten minutes to nine; as there were no clothes for him, the baby was wrapped in cotton wool.

The premature delivery of the prince has been attributed to his

Mother, father and the new prince.

mother's distress at developments in Denmark, where her father, King Christian IX, is involved in a bitter territorial dispute with Prussia over the duchy of Schleswig-Holstein (→ 8/1864).

Bertie causes a storm by meeting Italian republican leader Garibaldi in London

London, 1864
Victoria has been so incensed by a private meeting between the Italian patriot Giuseppe Garibaldi and the Prince of Wales – even though it was arranged on neutral ground at the Duke of Sutherland's London residence, Stafford House – that she has forbidden Bertie to take any "step of the slightest political importance" without her agreement from now on.

Bertie had earlier infuriated his mother by backing Denmark rather than Prussia in the Schleswig-Holstein dispute. Now, in her eyes, he has proved to be a liability once again, entertaining a guerrilla leader and revolutionary. The prince has defended himself, however, calling Garibaldi the driving force behind the unification of Italy, a noble patriot who was quite "uncharlatanlike". Public opinion is behind him on this issue, as it was

Guiseppe Garibaldi, later in life.

over opposing Prussia. Garibaldi has, furthermore, been warmly welcomed by establishment figures such as Lord Palmerston, the archbishop of Canterbury and the provost and fellows of Eton.

Distrustful queen stops prince reading official state papers

London, August 1864
The recent war between Prussia and Denmark has left its mark on Britain's royal household. The Prince of Wales is being forced to pay a price for openly supporting his father-in-law, King Christian of Denmark – whose small army proved no match for the Prussians.

Victoria has forbidden him to read any government dispatches. He is, in effect, to share none of his mother's power as sovereign. Ironically, Victoria insisted only two years ago that Bertie should be compelled to read dispatches for an hour every day. The queen is outraged by her son's sympathy for

Denmark and disgust with the Prussians, whom she regards as compatriots of her beloved Albert. It is as if Bertie were attacking his own family, she says. She has, not surprisingly, warned him to avoid any inflammatory remarks during his forthcoming trip to Copenhagen to meet King Christian (→ 7/9).

Queen rumoured to have held seances

London, December 1864
A report has appeared this year in the *Spiritualist* magazine that Queen Victoria is trying to make contact with the spirit of her late husband, Prince Albert. The unsigned article alleges that Albert, aware that his days were numbered, made a point of showing the queen how she could communicate with him after death.

A more extraordinary allegation is that Victoria has been persuaded to hold seances under the guidance of a teenage medium called Robert James Lee, after the boy claimed last year that he had received a message from the Prince Consort. Few people at court, however, give these stories any credence.

It is true that the queen refers to Albert's opinions as though he were still alive and says that she feels him watching over her. But this is not unusual for someone who is in mourning as deep as Victoria's. If anything, the rumours about royal seances testify to the current vogue for spiritualism. Certainly no one has yet come forward to corroborate them.

Waleses move into country home at Sandringham in Norfolk

Norfolk, 1864
The Prince and Princess of Wales have moved into a property near King's Lynn which the prince bought three years ago for £221,000. It is the Sandringham estate, consisting of a rather neglected country house, a number of farms and 8,000 acres of land. This new acquisition is in addition to their comfortable London residence, Marlborough House, recently refurbished at considerable expense.

At Sandringham Bertie plans to indulge his passion for shooting; the land is especially suited to raising gamebirds. He also intends to enlarge the house and make the farms models of agricultural management (→ 12/1870).

A 20th-century view of Sandringham house, the Prince of Wales's new home.

Palace appoints its first press officer

London, 1864

Greatly shocked by foreign press reports that she had secretly married her Scottish manservant John Brown while secluded at Balmoral, Queen Victoria has decided to intervene to control public comment about the royal family. She has appointed Septimus Beard, the 37-year-old grandson of the original court newsman, Joseph Doane, to be the first full-time salaried royal press secretary.

Created by George III in 1806 to suppress certain press stories regarding his alleged madness, this previously part-time post remained always in the hands of the Doane family. The new appointee will be required to attend on the queen every afternoon and evening while she is in London. He will also be expected to deliver bulletins personally to the editors of the nine daily newspapers.

Healthy second son born to Alexandra

London, 3 June 1865

The Prince of Wales is celebrating the birth of a second son, only 18 months after the birth of his first. The baby, who is to be christened George Frederick Ernest Albert, already looks healthier than his elder brother, Albert Victor; "Eddy", as everyone except the queen calls the child, is proving to be a slow developer (→ 7/7).

The Princess of Wales with Prince George and his brother, "Eddy".

Scottish servant is to stay at Osborne

John Brown: new to the island.

Isle of Wight, 4 February 1865

Victoria has decided that John Brown, the royal ghillie brought down from Balmoral in December, should remain permanently at Osborne. Brown was invited to the Isle of Wight at the suggestion of the queen's physician, Dr Jenner, who wanted her to keep up her riding and thought that she should have a familiar groom in attendance. Brown, 39 this year, is handsome and intelligent. He shows great concern for the queen's well-being and has a rough and direct manner which she finds attractive.

Victoria today insisted that from now on Brown will be known as "the queen's highland servant". He will take orders from her alone and attend on her both indoors and outdoors; his tasks will include cleaning her boots and skirts (→ 1867).

Leopold, king of the Belgians, dies

Belgium, 10 December 1865

Leopold of the Belgians, Victoria's much-loved uncle, died today at the age of 75. The king was a father-figure and mentor to Victoria in her youth, warned her against her mother's favourite, Sir John Conroy, and promoted her marriage to Albert. She often corresponded with him and continued to rely on his advice; only recently he urged her to abandon her seclusion. Leopold's death puts Victoria at the head of the Saxe-Coburg dynasty.

Queen shaken by death of Palmerston

London, 25 October 1865

Queen Victoria today admitted how deeply she feels the loss of Lord Palmerston, who died on 18 October. Victoria did not always get on with Palmerston – she once told King Leopold of the Belgians that she "*never* liked him" – but today she praised his courage, practicality and other "great qualities".

Lord Palmerston was twice prime minister and three times foreign secretary. He clashed with the royal family over many aspects of foreign policy, including the Don Pacifico affair, the Crimean crisis and his attitude towards the Habsburgs. He was particularly criticised for remaking British policy without consulting anyone.

A great loss: Lord Palmerston.

Prince of Wales leads riotous social life

The Prince and Princess of Wales attending a meet in Norfolk.

London, 1865

To some he is merely a *bon viveur*, but to others he has the makings of a dissolute. Bertie, the Prince of Wales, is courting scandal, much to his mother's anxiety – especially when she hears of his gambling debts. Earlier this year Lord Palmerston told Victoria about the prince's delight in playing whist for high stakes. Victoria at first refused to believe it, and when at last she did found the thought so shocking that it kept her awake at night.

The queen's eldest daughter, Vicky, the Princess Royal, has been no less astonished at tales of her brother's visits to music halls, pleasure gardens and the Midnight Club – about which she knows nothing but suspects it to be a place unlikely to foster moral improvement. For his part Bertie appears happy to be labelled a bohemian.

The Prince and Princess of Wales also enjoy the pastimes more often associated with royalty. January is spent in sport at Sandringham, while in March Bertie amuses himself in Paris – without his wife. The London "season" begins in the summer with the Waleses back at Marlborough House. Racing at Goodwood and yachting at Cowes are followed by a stay in a German spa. Christmas is celebrated at Sandringham, after the autumn grouse shoots at Balmoral (→ 30/4/69).

Clad in black, queen opens parliament

Westminster, 6 February 1866
Dressed all in black and shrouded in a long black veil, Victoria opened parliament today for the first time since Prince Albert's death. An arduous ordeal for the queen, who likened the occasion to an execution, it was undertaken through fear that, unless she came out of her four-year seclusion – highly unpopular with the public – her children's usual annuities might be denied. The queen refused to travel to parliament in the state coach or to wear her crown. She insisted that the lord chancellor read her speech, while she sat still and expressionless, maintaining steely self-control throughout, with Prince Albert's empty chair beside her.

Queen Victoria opens parliament.

Prussian aggression divides royals again

Prague, 23 August 1866
A treaty signed here today ends seven weeks of war in Europe that have again caused bitter divisions within the British royal family. By the treaty Otto von Bismarck, the chief minister of Prussia, has attained his aim of securing Prussian supremacy over the German states.

In June, Bismarck – intent on breaking Austrian dominance of the German confederation – provoked hostilities by occupying the duchy of Schleswig-Holstein, under Austrian administrative control since 1864. After several minor battles, the Prussians routed the Austrians at Königgrätz in eastern Bohemia on 3 July.

As one of the commanding officers, Prince Frederick of Prussia – the husband of Victoria's daughter Vicky – played a key role in the Königgrätz triumph. But Vicky's sister Alice, the wife of Prince Louis of Hesse and the Rhine, supported the Austrian cause – as did King George of Hanover and Duke Ernest of Coburg, both cousins of the queen. Victoria's attempt to mediate was then denounced by Bismarck (→ 20/1/69).

Two weddings bind Britain to Europe

Windsor, 5 July 1866
Princess Helena (known as Lenchen), Victoria's third daughter, today married Prince Christian of Schleswig-Holstein at Windsor. The queen promoted this marriage with a man who would agree to live in England – Christian's territory has been appropriated by Austria and Prussia – but it was bitterly opposed by the Prince and Princess of Wales and Helena's sister, Alice. It comes within a month of the marriage of Princess Mary Adelaide of Cambridge, Victoria's cousin, to Prince Francis of Teck, a member of the German royal house of Württemberg (→ 1872).

Victoria backs widening of franchise after Liberal government falls on reform issue

Westminster, 17 August 1867
Seen as the personal triumph of Benjamin Disraeli, the Conservative leader in the House of Commons, the new Reform Act became law today. A great advance on the act of 1832, the new measure almost doubles the previous electorate. Despite opposition from both sides of the house, suffrage has been extended to one million extra people, mainly from the urban working classes. There has also been a redistribution of seats, with 45 boroughs of fewer than 10,000 inhabitants losing one member of parliament, and consequent gains to other boroughs and counties. However, a large proportion of the population, including agricultural workers and women, remains without the vote.

Disraeli became chancellor of the exchequer again last year after the defeat of the Liberals' own measure for limited reform had caused the fall of their government. He turned down Queen Victoria's offer to mediate between the political parties in the reform debate. Increasingly intolerant of aristocratic frivolity, the queen backed an extension of the parliamentary franchise but feared a ministerial crisis over the issue and wanted it resolved on a non-party basis. Disraeli, however – keen to turn the matter to his party's advantage – insisted

Disraeli: rejecting the queen's offer.

that a reform bill must be carried by a Conservative government.

Although she failed to keep the issue separate from party politics, Victoria is pleased with the new measure. She envisages a redistribution of power in Britain at the expense of the aristocracy, whose corrupt self-indulgence has been the undoing of her eldest son, the Prince of Wales. "The lower classes are becoming so well-informed – are so intelligent and earn their bread and riches so deservedly," the queen has written, "that they cannot and ought not to be kept back – to be abused by the wretched ignorant highborn beings who live only to kill time" (→ 2/1868).

Queen assents to act creating confederation of Canadian states

Representatives of the Canadian colonies meet in London to discuss union.

Quebec City, 21 June 1867
It was announced here today in the name of Queen Victoria that from 1 July the Dominion of Canada will officially exist as North America's newest country. The queen gave her assent in March to the British North America Act, which creates a confederation of the British colonies of Upper and Lower Canada, New Brunswick and Nova Scotia. It is the climax of years of struggle and negotiation by colonial politicians with each other and the mother country. Key issues such as the system of self-government are ill-defined, and many colonists oppose the confederation. The Prince Edward Island and Newfoundland governments have refused to join.

Alix gives birth to her first daughter

London, 20 February 1867

The Princess of Wales gave birth to a daughter today at Marlborough House. The baby girl, who will be named Louise Victoria, is a sister for Albert Victor ("Eddy"), now three, and George, who was born in June 1865. She is Queen Victoria's sixth granddaughter.

The birth of Louise was an especially challenging experience for the princess, who five days ago, after complaining of serious pains and a chill, was diagnosed as suffering from rheumatic fever. In the circumstances, when the princess went into labour, her doctors thought it too dangerous to administer chloroform.

Alix's ordeal was not mitigated by the absence of her husband, who has made himself scarce since the onset of her illness. On the day that his wife's symptoms first appeared, the Prince of Wales decided to attend the Windsor races, and although he was kept informed of her condition it took three telegrams to induce him to return to Marlborough House. Since then – courting public disapproval – the prince has repeatedly stayed away from home until the early hours of the morning. The princess, who has apparently come to terms with her husband's infidelity, nevertheless finds this blatant neglect particularly hard to bear (→ 6/7/68).

Queen nicknamed 'Mrs Brown' by gossips

Pictured together: Queen Victoria and her "highland servant", John Brown.

Isle of Wight, 1867

Speculation is increasing about the nature of the relationship between Victoria and her former highland ghillie, John Brown. The rugged, handsome 41-year-old Scot was in the queen's service at Balmoral for many years, accompanying her and Prince Albert on all their excursions. Three years after Albert's death he was brought down to Osborne and swiftly promoted to the post of "the queen's highland servant".

Since then the queen has been almost inseparable from Brown, who combines the roles of secretary, servant and confidant. He always accompanies her when she

drives out in her carriage and has several times saved her from assassination attempts. He ensures that the queen's practical needs and comforts are attended to, and addresses her in blunt speech.

There is no doubt that Victoria – now aged 48, and referred to by gossips as "Mrs Brown" – is devoted to this reliable, direct man, on whom she depends as much for support and companionship as for the service he provides. But Brown's high-handed manner, and the fact that the queen will not hear a word against him, have made him unpopular in the royal household and with other members of the royal family (→ 29/3/83).

Australians put out the flags for Alfred

Melbourne, 28 November 1867

Australians have put out the bunting and opened the champagne to welcome Prince Alfred, the Duke of Edinburgh, as he makes his progress through the colonies. Alfred, recently promoted to navy captain, arrived in Adelaide last month in HMS *Galatea*, on the latest stage of an unprecedented royal cruise that has already taken in Gibraltar, South America and Tristan da Cunha. At every stop in Australia the prince has been greeted by lavish entertainments and expressions of affection (→ 12/3/68).

Alfred, the Duke of Edinburgh.

In memory of a prince and husband. Queen Victoria (left), in inclement Scottish weather, inaugurates a statue of Prince Albert on the royal family's estate at Balmoral, and (right) lays the foundation stone for the Royal Albert Hall in Kensington, near the site of the 1851 Great Exhibition in London.

Prince is made a knight of St Patrick

Crowds press close to see the Prince and Princess of Wales in Dublin.

Dublin, 24 April 1868
The Prince and Princess of Wales returned to England today after a nine-day visit to Dublin which has generated intense enthusiasm and vindicated the belief of the prime minister, Benjamin Disraeli, that a royal presence would allay discontent in Ireland. The highlight of the trip came on 18 April, when the prince was installed as a knight of St Patrick in the Protestant cathedral. The royal couple carried out a crowded programme of balls, reviews and race meetings, and the prince unveiled a statue of Edmund Burke outside Trinity college. The viceroy, Lord Abercorn, is said to be delighted by the prince's reception, and the lovely weather made the visit even more enjoyable.

Gas illuminations were lit each night as thousands thronged streets adorned with bunting. The interior of the Royal College of Surgeons was redecorated for a ceremony at which the prince conferred an honour on its president. The visit was somewhat marred, however, by the activities of gangs of hooligans who, taking advantage of people being out on the streets, carried out systematic robberies of shops and houses.

Terrorist attempts to kill Alfred in Sydney

Sydney, 12 March 1868
"Good God! I am shot; my back is broken," Prince Alfred cried as he slumped to the ground after being shot while attending a fund-raising fête at Middle Harbour today. But the bullet, fired at close range by a man later described as a "deranged Fenian", narrowly missed its mark, wounding the 23-year-old prince slightly in the side. The attacker aimed his pistol at the prince and cried "stand back" as he fired again, but the pistol malfunctioned and he was overwhelmed by other guests. The would-be assassin, Henry James O'Farrell, was rescued from the furious crowd by police and British sailors – a rope had been thrown over a tree amid cries of "Hang him! Lynch him!". O'Farrell was recently an inmate of a mental hospital (→ 5/1871).

Alfred goes hunting on his tour.

Victoria's account of life in the highlands is immediate runaway publishing success

Britain, 1868
A new book on Scotland appeared in the nation's bookshops this year and was an instant runaway best-seller. Called *Leaves from the Journal of Our Life in the Highlands*, the book sold 20,000 copies at once and won critical acclaim for its author: Queen Victoria. The book is drawn from her own prolific journals and was originally meant as a gift for her friends and family, until she was persuaded how popular it would be. It portrays her life at Balmoral with Prince Albert, stressing simplicity and marital bliss, and the text is illustrated by her own sketches. Benjamin Disraeli, the prime minister, told the queen that her book had "a freshness and fragrance ... like the heather amid which it was written". Other critics praise its simple, direct style, while some find it all a little precious. None, however, has gone quite so far as the Prince of Wales, who privately referred to his mother's book as "twaddle".

Where it all happened: the queen and Princess Louise at Balmoral.

Royal prose: the queen as a reporter

In her book Queen Victoria describes a Highland Games which were held at Balmoral:
"The morning dawned brightly. Suddenly a very high wind arose which alarmed us, but yet it looked bright, and we hoped the wind would keep off the rain; but after breakfast, while watching the preparations, showers began and from half-past eleven a fearful down-pour ... and this lasted till half-past twelve. I was in despair; but at length it began to clear ... At two o'clock we were all ready. Albert and the boys were in their kilts, and I and the girls in royal Stewart skirts and shawls over black velvet bodies ... The games began about three o'clock: 1. Throwing the Hammer. 2. Tossing the Caber. 3. Putting the Stone. We gave prizes to the three best in each of the games.

"We walked along the terrace to the large marquee, talking to the people, to where the men were "putting the stone". After this returned to the upper terrace, to see the race, a pretty wild sight; but the men looked very cold, with nothing but their shirts and kilts on; they ran beautifully. They wrapped plaids round themselves, and then came to receive the prizes from me."

Liberals defeat Disraeli

London, 17 November 1868
The queen is set to appoint a new prime minister today following the defeat of Disraeli in the general election by the Liberals under their new leader, William Gladstone.

Born in Liverpool of Scots descent, the new premier has been an MP since 1833. He took office as a Tory in 1835, but became a Peelite and finally a Liberal in 1859. His relations with the queen have been good if formal (he cannot flatter like Disraeli), and she admires his intelligence and virtue. But some of his ideas worry her, in particular his plan to disestablish the Anglican Church of Ireland, of which she is head. It has long been seen as a symbol of English injustice towards Irish Catholics (→ 22/7/69).

A mischievous cartoon imagines Gladstone "sent for" by the queen.

Prince of Wales linked to adultery case

London, 30 April 1869
The Prince of Wales has been dragged into a sensational divorce case involving the deranged mother of a blind baby and a jealous husband who is the Conservative MP for South Warwickshire. Today the MP, Sir Charles Mordaunt, served his wife, Harriet, with divorce papers on the grounds of her adultery with two of the prince's friends, Lord Cole and Sir Frederick Johnstone. Bertie, who had written Lady Mordaunt a number of letters and visited her occasionally, has been subpoenaed to appear as a witness in the trial.

The prince has known Lady Mordaunt since she was a child, and her family, the Moncrieffes, are neighbours of the queen at Balmoral. She married Sir Charles in 1866 when she was 18, and last year she had a son, who was born prematurely and blind. "Charlie, you are not the father of that child," she told her husband tearfully. "Lord Cole is the father of it and I am the cause of its blindness." She said she had been "very wicked" with many men, including Cole, Johnstone and the Prince of Wales, "often and in open day". Enraged, Sir Charles broke into his wife's desk, where he found a diary and several letters, some from the prince. The case is not clear-cut, however. Harriet had a difficult pregnancy and was mentally ill after the birth; despite this Sir Charles believed her deranged confession. He has vowed never to see her again, and despite her condition he has gone ahead with divorce proceedings (→ 28/2/70).

Prince meets Bismarck on German trip

Bismarck: Prussia's chief minister.

Berlin, 20 January 1869
The Prince of Wales today ended a five-day visit to the Prussian capital during which he met Otto von Bismarck, the chief minister of King William of Prussia, as well as his own brother-in-law and sister, the crown prince and princess. The prince's trip was a great success, despite the fact that he finds the Prussian court too stiff and dull for his Francophile tastes, acquired during his times at the colourful and pleasure-seeking court of Napoleon III's second empire.

Nonetheless, the prince's charming manner and unfailing courtesy successfully belie his unease regarding Prussia in general. Ever since the Prussian invasion of his wife Alexandra's native Denmark, in 1864, he has been suspicious of Bismarck's intentions (→ 6/8/70).

Queen hides feelings to push Irish bill

Westminster, 22 July 1869
Against her own inclination, the queen has agreed the passage of a bill to disestablish the Church of Ireland, the Irish counterpart to the Church of England, of which she is head. Victoria opposed disestablishment in principle not only because she saw it as a blow to the Protestant cause but also because she thought it might stir up extreme Protestant agitation. However, Gladstone's measure removes one source of anti-British feeling among Ireland's overwhelmingly Catholic people. The bill easily passed the Commons with a Liberal majority of 112, but the Lords, with their permanent Conservative majority, seemed set on a collision course with the lower house.

At this point the queen decided that her duty not to undermine her government came before her own feelings and let it be known that she did not want a constitutional clash between the two houses. The peers gave way, and the Conservatives have suffered their first defeat in the House of Lords for 20 years.

Bertie and the queen grow closer together

Alexandra and her daughter Louise.

Osborne, 1869
Time is beginning to heal the rift between Victoria and the Prince of Wales. When he accompanied her to Aldershot this year she wrote: "I am sure no heir apparent ever was so nice and unpretending as dear Bertie is." But she still worries about the company he keeps and does not trust his discretion enough to let him undertake any but ceremonial state duties. Although she is very fond of Bertie's children, her feelings fluctuate towards Alexandra, of whom she once wrote – referring to the princess's Danish origins – that she was "not worth the price we paid for her – in having such a family connection".

Come out, your majesty, urges Gladstone

London, 7 June 1869
Victoria's continued seclusion and ill-health following the death of Prince Albert are causing increasing concern to her ministers who are worried about the damage they are doing to the image of the monarchy. The prime minister, William Gladstone, today decided that the time had come to launch a clandestine campaign on behalf of the government to try to bring her out of isolation. Gladstone has resolved to do three things: find out the "simple truth" about the queen's mental and physical health (some ministers privately accuse her of malingering); rid the queen of the wilfulness which he says lies at the heart of many "female complaints"; and try to entice the queen from her virtual exile at Osborne (→ 8/4/71).

Victoria
1837–1901

Britain, 15 July 1870. Britain declares its neutrality in the Franco-Prussian war. The royal family's loyalties are divided: the queen is pro-Prussia; the Princess of Wales is anti-Prussia, while her husband is ambivalent, believing the French to be in the wrong in this case (→ 6/8).

Balmoral, 21 August 1870. Victoria will not allow the Prince of Wales to negotiate for peace in the Franco-Prussian war (→ 9/1870).

Britain, September 1870. The queen sends a message urging her son-in-law Frederick William, the Crown Prince of Prussia, to seek peace in the war.→

Isle of Wight, October 1870. The engagement is announced of the queen's fourth daughter, Princess Louise, to John Campbell, the Marquis of Lorne, the heir of the Duke of Argyll (→ 21/3/71).

Norfolk, December 1870. The estate at Sandringham undergoes massive renovation (→ 29/11/71).

Windsor, 21 March 1871. The wedding of Princess Louise and Lord Lorne takes place amid an outcry about the cost to the nation of the civil list.→

Norfolk, 7 April 1871. Prince John Charles Albert, who was born yesterday to the Prince and Princess of Wales, dies.

Frankfurt, 10 May 1871. France and Prussia sign a peace treaty.

London, May 1871. Prince Alfred, the Duke of Edinburgh, expresses his wish to marry Marie, the Grand Duchess of Russia, the daughter of Czar Alexander II (→ 11/7/73).

Balmoral, 6 September 1871. Victoria, who has retreated to her highland home, is suffering from gout (→ 18/9).

London, 18 September 1871. The *Times* publishes an apology to Victoria for its attacks on the royal family (→ 30/9).

Balmoral, 30 September 1871. Victoria, despite her illness, gives an audience to William Gladstone, the prime minister (→ 6/11).

Norfolk, 29 November 1871. Victoria sees the Sandringham estate for the first time when visiting the Prince of Wales, who is ill with typhoid (→ 13/12).

Germany, March 1872. Victoria travels to Potsdam for the christening of Margaret, the sixth child born to Vicky, the Crown Princess of Prussia (→ 27/3/79).

Liverpool, 20 May 1872. Prince Arthur opens Sefton Park (→ 1873).

Oxford, November 1872. Victoria's youngest son, Prince Leopold, is granted an honorary degree from Christ Church college (→ 5/1878).

London, 1872. Princess Helena, the third daughter of Victoria, founds the School of Needlework in a house in Sloane Street.

Kent, 9 January 1873. The exiled emperor, Napoleon III, dies at his home in Chislehurst.→

Britain, 12 March 1873. Victoria again refuses to give the Prince of Wales any official responsibility.

Jugenheim, 11 July 1873. Prince Alfred, the Duke of Edinburgh, announces his engagement to Grand Duchess Marie of Russia, the only daughter of Czar Alexander II (→ 23/1/74).

Aldershot, 1873. Prince Arthur is promoted to brigadier-major (→ 5/1874).

Westminster, 10 February 1874. Disraeli, who during his five years

out of office has kept in contact with Victoria, returns to power at the election as the Conservative prime minister (→ 8/1874).

London, March 1874. Prince Alfred, the Duke of Edinburgh, and his wife, Marie, take up residence in Clarence House (→ 15/10).

London, May 1874. Victoria gives Prince Arthur the dukedom of Connaught and Strathearn and the earldom of Sussex (→ 3/1878).

London, 21 July 1874. The Prince of Wales hosts a huge costume ball at Marlborough House; he is dressed as Charles I (→ 1/10).

London, 15 October 1874. Marie, the Duchess of Edinburgh, gives birth to her first son, Alfred.

Bombay, 8 November 1875. The Prince of Wales arrives to begin a tour of India (→ 13/3/76).

London, 1875. Princess Beatrice, the youngest daughter of Victoria, is confirmed (→ 1/6/79).

Britain, 1875. Victoria authorises the publication of the *Life of the Prince Consort*, Volume I, by Theodore Martin.

Britain, May 1876. The Prince of Wales returns from a successful Indian tour.

Russia, April 1877. Russia, much to Victoria's horror, declares war on the Ottoman Empire (→ 25/4).

Mediterranean, April 1877. Prince Alfred, the Duke of Edinburgh, in command of HMS *Sultan,* is ordered to protect the lives of any British in Turkey.

Newmarket, July 1877. The Prince of Wales introduces his own racing colours of purple, gold and scarlet, much to the disapproval of his mother.

Prussia, March 1878. Against the queen's wishes, Prince Arthur, the Duke of Connaught, proposes to Princess Louise, the third daughter of Prince Frederick Charles of Prussia (→ 13/3/79).

Rome, March 1878. The signing of the Treaty of San Stefano ends the war between Russia and the Ottoman Empire but confirms European fears of huge Russian gains.

Prussia, 12 May 1878. Victoria becomes a great-grandmother when her granddaughter Charlotte, the Duchess of Saxe-Meiningen and the daughter of Vicky, the Crown Princess of Prussia, gives birth to Princess Feodora.

Paris, May 1878. The Prince of Wales opens the Paris Exhibition as president of the British section.

London, May 1878. Victoria is furious when her youngest son, Prince Leopold, refuses to accompany her to Balmoral, preferring to visit Paris (→ 5/1881).

London, 8 December 1878. Victoria learns that her daughter Alice, the Grand Duchess of Hesse, has diphtheria (→ 14/12).

Windsor, 20 January 1879. Louis, the Grand Duke of Hesse, and his children arrive for a two-month stay (→ 1/4/80).

Prussia, 27 March 1879. Vicky, the Crown Princess, is devastated by the death of her youngest son, Waldemar, Victoria's favourite grandson, from diphtheria.

South Africa, 1 June 1879. Prince Louis Napoleon, the son of the late Napoleon III and an officer in the British army, is killed fighting the Zulus; he is said to have been a possible husband for Beatrice, Victoria's youngest and only unmarried daughter (→ 31/12/84).

Scandal and political unrest pose crisis for royalty

Prince of Wales is witness in sex case

London, 28 February 1870
For the first time since the reign of Henry IV, a Prince of Wales has been forced to account for himself in a court of law. Subpoenaed to appear as a witness in the Mordaunt divorce case [*see page 437*], Bertie was asked during a seven-minute appearance in court whether there had ever been "improper familiarity or criminal act" between him and the 21-year-old Lady Mordaunt. The prince replied firmly and without hesitation: "There has not." He was not cross-examined, and, in the event, Sir Charles Mordaunt's divorce petition failed on the grounds that his wife was disabled by insanity from being a party to the suit.

The Prince of Wales was implicated in the case by several letters he had written to Lady Mordaunt, whom he has known since childhood. The letters were discovered by Sir Charles Mordaunt after his wife, in a deranged state, told him that she had committed adultery, naming the prince as one of her lovers. To the surprise of the public, the letters – which found their way into the newspapers before the trial began – proved to be harmless notes such as might have been written to anyone.

The prince was not on trial, but he has been found guilty by the public and by the press, which has alluded to "unbridled sensuality". Since Bertie appeared in court a week ago, he and Alexandra have been hissed while driving about the streets of London (→ 1871).

At ease together: the Prince and Princess of Wales, on holiday at Cowes.

Keeping one eye on nearby scraps: Britain and the Franco-Prussian war.

Radicals attack the 'useless' royals

London, 1870
The defeat of Napoleon III by the Germans and the proclamation of a French republic have let loose a wave of republican sentiment in England. Sir Charles Dilke, the radical Liberal MP, Charles Bradlaugh, the atheist campaigner, and George Odger, the radical trade union leader, have been calling for a "Republic of England". Dilke ridicules the monarchy as a useless waste of money. During a republican meeting in Trafalgar Square, the *Marseillaise* was sung and red caps were thrown in the air. Republican clubs are multiplying.

The queen has been greatly distressed by Dilke's disloyalty. She had admired his father, who helped the Prince Consort with the Great Exhibition; on one occasion she had met Sir Charles as a small boy and stroked his head. Remarking on his republicanism, she now says that she "supposed she had stroked it the wrong way".

Republicanism was given a boost when the novelist William Makepeace Thackeray delivered a series of sneering attacks on Victoria's Hanoverian ancestors in his public lectures on "The Four Georges". So deeply did the queen resent these that when Thackeray died in 1863 she refused to allow him to be buried in Poets' Corner in the abbey.

Now Bradlaugh, calling himself "Iconoclast", has published a calumnious pamphlet in which he compares the Prince of Wales to his rakish ancestor who became George IV (→ 18/9/71).

Franco-Prussian war splits royal family

Isle of Wight, 6 August 1870
Just before dinner at Osborne this evening the queen received news of a crushing victory over the French by her son-in-law Crown Prince Frederick of Prussia. Victoria was relieved that the Prussians were not being beaten, as she had feared, but she felt sorry for "the poor French always to be driven away". The war, precipitated by moves to place a junior member of the Prussian royal family on the Spanish throne, has divided the British royal family. The queen, though firmly supporting her government's neutrality, is rolling bandages for the Prussian wounded. The Prince of Wales is widely believed to support the French, while his wife, according to the queen, is a "very violent" anti-Prussian (→ 21/8).

Republicans throw out the French king

London, September 1870
Utter disaster has overwhelmed the French. Louis Napoleon, who set himself up as Emperor Napoleon III a few years ago, has been taken prisoner by the Prussians, and the road to Paris lies open to the enemy. Empress Eugénie and the Prince Imperial have fled to England. From Paris the news is of a bloodless revolution and a proclamation deposing Napoleon and setting up a republic as Prussian armies encircle the French capital in preparation for a siege. Deeply distressed by this succession of calamities, Victoria wrote to Prussia's King William appealing for peace; the only result has been a riposte from Bismarck, the chief minister of Prussia, about "petticoat" interference (→ 10/5/71).

Victoria opens hall in memory of Albert

A memorial to her husband: Victoria opens the Royal Albert Hall.

Kensington, 8 April 1871
Increasingly, the queen is emerging from the seclusion into which she retreated with her grief after the death of the Prince Consort nearly ten years ago. Today she opened the magnificent Royal Albert Hall, a £200,000 tribute to her late husband, who had first suggested a centre devoted to the arts and sciences.

Gazing upon the building today, Victoria said that it was as solid as the British constitution. Six million bricks have gone into its walls, and the double-domed roof is support-ed by a 400-ton iron frame. The hall has 11,000 gas burners, and above the gallery are 1,400 gallons of water in 15 tanks, as a fire pre-caution. There is seating for 7,000.

This year the queen agreed to take part in the opening of parlia-ment, having refused last year. She is also opening St Thomas's hos-pital, across the Thames from the Houses of Parliament. The prime minister, William Gladstone, has congratulated her on making the monarchy "visible and palpable to the people".

Princess Louise is married to Liberal MP

The royal couple's wedding cake.

Windsor, 21 March 1871
In an imposing ceremony at St George's chapel today, Princess Louise, Queen Victoria's fourth daughter, married the Liberal MP for Argyllshire. He is John Camp-bell, the 24-year-old Marquis of Lorne, the heir to the Duke of Argyll. The 23-year-old bride was given away by her mother, who had supported Louise's opposition to a Prussian match promoted by her eldest sister, Vicky.

Lorne enjoys reading and walk-ing in the highlands and has much in common with the artistic Louise, who was set on a marriage which would enable her to stay in Britain. She threatened to enter a nunnery if her plans to marry Lorne were thwarted (→9/1875).

Prince faces blackmail

Pregnant mistress demands payments

London, 1871
The Prince of Wales has received a string of letters from a widow with whom he had a four-year relation-ship, and also from a woman friend of hers. The letters speak of "the crisis" and of "certain events" im-pending which were revealed to the prince during the summer. The widow is Lady Susan Vane Tem-pest, whose alcoholic and insane husband died leaving her penniless. Now her friend, Mrs Harriet What-man, has told the prince: "With-out any funds to meet the necessary expenses and to buy the discretion of servants, it is impossible to keep this sad secret."

Lady Susan told the prince that she had done her best to obey his orders, but it was now "too late and too dangerous". He was made to un-derstand that unless he paid up "£150 at the least" the reputation of "all parties" would be put in jeopardy.

The prince handed the problem to Francis Knollys, the comptrol-ler of his household. Lady Susan was discreetly moved to a cottage in Ramsgate. That was by no means the end of the matter. Soon she was back in London and writing to Knollys that she felt very unwell: "I am too sorry to be obliged again to have recourse to the kindness of one who has already been generous to me, but the expenses of two houses and the extra servants have been very great ..."

'Delicate' letters to whore put on sale

Sandringham, 9 November 1871
The sordid attempt to blackmail the Prince of Wales began with a letter from Florence, written by a Pirro Benini, saying that following the death of his sister, Giulia Baruc-ci, a number of letters to her from his royal highness had come into his possession. The prince could have these letters returned on pay-ment of £1,500; otherwise they could fall into the wrong hands.

Giulia Barucci was passionate, immensely rich, devoutly religious – and one of the most dazzlingly beautiful courtesans of France's second empire. She called herself the "greatest whore in the world", and her clients included a string of princes and dukes.

Here was another problem for Francis Knollys; "that scoundrel Benini" must be dealt with. One suggestion was that a robbery should be staged, which "might be managed in a country like Italy". But the letters were being held in Paris. Knollys discussed the possi-bility of a blackmail charge against Benini, but the prince would have none of that. In the end it came down to one question: How much?

A confidential agent of the prince inspected the letters, noted that they were "of a delicate nature" and, when Benini asked for £400, offered £40. A telegram to Sand-ringham today reports that the let-ters have been acquired for the "not too terrible" sum of £240.

The fast-living prince: here with a group of shooting cronies at Windsor.

Prince rejects plans for job in Ireland

Dublin, 1 August 1871

The Prince of Wales arrived in Dublin today to open the Royal Agricultural Exhibition and was greeted by cheering crowds. Behind his visit, however, there is considerable political tension as a result of a new plan by William Gladstone.

The prime minister, at odds with the queen over the performance of her ceremonial duties, is pursuing a scheme whereby the Prince of Wales would undertake royal duties in Ireland, spending his winters here and learning the art of constitutional sovereignty. Under this proposal the office of viceroy, or lord lieutenant of Ireland, would "disappear", and its functions would be taken over by the prince.

Not only is the queen unhappy with Gladstone's intentions to give the royal family a greater political role, but the Prince of Wales himself is also opposed to the plan, preferring to remain close to his other interests in London.

Victoria retreats to Balmoral sanctuary

Balmoral, 17 August 1871

The queen, seriously ill with a sore throat and a painfully swollen arm, today travelled to Balmoral despite appeals from William Gladstone that she should remain at Osborne, on the Isle of Wight, until after parliament had debated a radical motion attacking the annuity for Prince Arthur. Though the prime minister doubts whether she is really ill – he talks of "the woes of fancy" – the queen has a sting on her right elbow which has turned septic, and her throat has swollen so badly that she is fearful of choking. She says that she has never felt so ill since she had typhoid some 35 years ago.

There is worry among politicians and Victoria's own family that the queen gives too little thought to the dangers threatening the monarchy. She, on the other hand, complains of overwork, writing that, unless she receives more support from her ministers, "[I] cannot go on and must give [my] heavy burden up to younger hands" (→6/9).

Anti-monarchist tide dismays queen

Radical MP: Sir Charles Dilke.

Balmoral, 6 November 1871

For the first time for many weeks the queen was well enough to attend Sunday service yesterday, with her faithful ghillie, John Brown, helping her up the steps of the kirk. Today, though, she has been deeply distressed by a violent denunciation of her alleged "dereliction of duty" delivered by the radical MP Sir Charles Dilke at a meeting in Newcastle.

In his speech, which was received with storms of applause, Dilke denounced "the political corruption that hangs about the monarchy" and called for Victoria to be deposed and a republic established. He extolled "the republican virtues" which he claimed had been demonstrated by "history and experience". The queen is said to have been so upset by Dilke's outpour-ings that she wept when she read the reports. Sir Charles, though, is only the best known of the anti-monarchist agitators.

A copy of a pamphlet which was sent to Balmoral accused the queen of "hoarding" £200,000 out of the millions which she is supposed to have received from the civil list annuity and various inheritances. The purported author is named as "Solomon Temple, Builder"; he is in fact George Otto Trevelyan, a Liberal member of parliament.

The attacks have been taken up in the press. The *Bee Hive*, which represents trade unions and co-operatives, says that "the gee-gaws of the court" should be cut down, and the Catholic *Universe* says mockingly that the queen does not appear in public because she cannot afford a new bonnet (→ 29/11).

Nation rallies round sick Prince of Wales

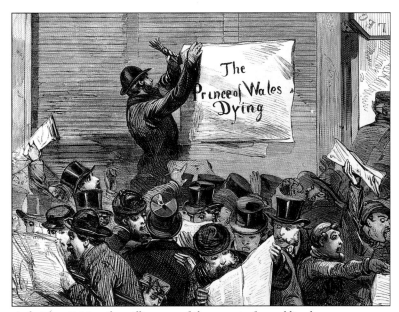

A sketch satirising the willingness of the press to fan public alarm.

Sandringham, 14 December 1871

Yesterday, on the eve of the tenth anniversary of the Prince Consort's death, the queen sat by the bed of the Prince of Wales fearful that this day of morbid remembrance would be marked by her eldest son's passing. For the past month the prince, stricken with typhoid, has been delirious, gasping for breath and seized by severe spasms. Bellringers at St Paul's have been standing by to toll the prince's death. Yesterday evening, though, he took a turn for the better; after sleeping peacefully he awoke and, smiling, kissed his mother's hand.

The prince's illness has produced a tremendous upsurge of royalist sentiment among the public. Letters and telegrams have been pouring into Sandringham. The anti-monarchist tirades of Sir Charles Dilke, the radical MP, are being drowned by stormy renderings of *God save the Queen* (→26/12).

Queen thanks her people for support

Sandringham, 26 December 1871

As the Prince of Wales begins to recover from his severe attack of typhoid, the queen has expressed her heartfelt gratitude for the concern shown by her people. "The feeling shown by the whole nation is quite marvellous and most touching and striking," she says; it shows how the people are "really sound and truly loyal" at heart.

The prince is being nursed by his sister, Princess Alice. Her care and dedication are being widely praised by press and public, but some of those in attendance at Sandringham are less enthusiastic. Lady Macclesfield, a lady-in-waiting to the Princess of Wales, finds Alice domineering, meddling, jealous and mischief-making. Even so, she has done more than anyone else to see her brother through his worst days.

The queen has today written a letter of thanks to her people for their sympathy. The prime minister, William Gladstone, believes that a more demonstrative effort should be made, and he is trying to persuade her to take part in a public thanksgiving service in St Paul's. But Victoria has had little liking for ceremonial events since her husband's death (→27/2/72).

▷

441

Thanksgiving service for prince's recovery

London, 27 February 1872
There were more than a few surprised comments on the queen's appearance when she entered St Paul's cathedral today for the thanksgiving service for the recovery of the Prince of Wales from a severe bout of typhoid. Victoria herself went down last autumn with gout, a festering sore on her right elbow and crippling rheumatism; ing is still not fully recovered, havtwo lost two stones in weight. At first opposing the prime minister's proposal for a service as a distasteful "public religious display", she finally consented and requested an open carriage.

This morning, at Buckingham Palace, the queen took the prince by the arm and led him downstairs to the state landau. The Princess of Wales sat next to the queen, and the prince sat opposite with his eldest son. As the carriage drew away in the sunshine, an upstairs window opened and the exiled Emperor Napoleon appeared on the balcony with Empress Eugénie to watch the procession leave.

The streets to St Paul's were thronged with cheering crowds. The service, however, the queen found depressing. The prayers and anthems were too long, and she thought the cathedral dreary. Back at the palace, the prince collapsed exhausted on a sofa, but the queen went out onto the balcony to wave to the cheering crowds – all fears of republican agitation having faded into oblivion (→ 7/1782).

The service in St Paul's to give thanks for the Prince of Wales's recovery.

Victoria vetoes planned role for Bertie

London, July 1872
The queen has coldly rejected the suggestion by the prime minister, William Gladstone, that the Prince of Wales should be found useful employment in Ireland. The prime minister's idea was that the prince should spend four or five months of the year engaged in administrative duties in Dublin. "The nature of his duties," argued Gladstone, "would afford an admirable opportunity for giving the prince the advantage of a political training which, from no fault of his own, he can have hardly be said hitherto to have enjoyed."

The queen, speaking for her son, now a man of 30 with five children,

has replied that Ireland was "in no fit state to be experimented upon". It is, she said, the least loyal of her dominions; it would mean exile for the prince and do his health much harm. He was, moreover, not of a sufficiently strong character to resist pressures making him favour one political party or the other.

Victoria has, therefore, stopped another attempt to train the Prince of Wales to take over the throne. Some see dangers in this for the monarchy because, during the queen's extended mourning for her husband, her governments have learnt to control the country without her (→ 12/3/73).

Gunman attacks queen

Horrified Londoners look on as the Irishman O'Connor attacks the queen.

London, 29 February 1872
A young Irishman, Arthur O'Connor, pointed an unloaded pistol at the queen today as her open landau drew up at the garden entrance to Buckingham Palace after a drive through Regent's Park and Hyde Park. He intended to frighten the queen into releasing some Fenian prisoners.

Victoria threw herself across her lady-in-waiting, Jane Churchill, crying "Save me". Prince Arthur tried to jump over the carriage at the attacker, but John Brown, the queen's redoubtable Scottish servant, who had descended to lower the landau step, was nearer and pinioned O'Connor, knocking the pistol out of his hand. The queen, who

afterwards confessed that "I was trembling very much and a sort of shiver ran through me", is to reward Brown with a gold medal and a £25 annuity. Prince Arthur is to get a gold pin, which the Prince of Wales thinks is rather ungenerous, and O'Connor, who shows every sign of being weak-minded, is to be put on trial.

When the Princess of Wales arrived to congratulate the queen on her escape she said that she was relieved she had not been in the carriage and that it was no pleasure being a queen – a sentiment to which the queen replied that she "most readily agreed". This is the sixth attack on Queen Victoria in 35 years on the throne (→ 2/3/82).

French emperor dies in lonely Kent exile

Lying in state: Napoleon III.

Chislehurst, Kent, 9 January 1873
Napoleon III, the former emperor of France and nephew of the great Bonaparte, died in exile at Camden Place here today after a long and painful illness. He was 64. Previously exiled in Switzerland and banished to the United States, Louis Napoleon Bonaparte was accepted as emperor in 1852 and ruled until he was deposed in the turmoil following the Franco-Prussian war – which saw his defeat by the Prussians at Sedan in September 1870. He and Empress Eugénie and the Prince Imperial sought refuge in England, where they have lived ever since.

Victoria's grandson killed in tragic fall

Darmstadt, May 1873
Princess Alice's three-year-old son, Frederick, known as Frittie, has died in a most appalling tragedy at the family home here. Early today, while Prince Louis was away inspecting his army, Frittie and his elder brother, Ernest, went into their mother's bedroom to wish her good morning. They began to play, running in and out of the bedroom and leaning out of the windows.

The princess got up to follow Ernest, leaving Frittie in her room. He continued the game, leaning out of the bow window to play "peep-bo" with his brother, who was looking out of the window of the drawing-room opposite. Suddenly Frittie slipped and tumbled out of the window to crash onto the stone terrace 20 feet (six metres) below.

He died this evening without regaining consciousness. There was in fact no chance of his recovering even if he had survived the initial injuries, for he suffered from haemophilia, the inheritable bleeding disease transmitted only to males. He had almost bled to death on at least one occasion. By a quirk of fate Ernest is untouched by the disease. Princess Alice is inconsolable, while Ernest, consumed with guilt, asks: "Why can't we all die together? I don't want to die alone, like Frittie" (→ 8/12/78).

Queen finds shah of Persia 'improvable'

London, 1873
The queen has kept her promise to Gladstone and has received the barbaric Nasr ed Din, the shah of Persia, who is travelling Europe with an exotic entourage including at least three wives. The queen, who wore the Koh-in-noor diamond to outdazzle his display of gems, finds him "dignified and improvable".

The Prince of Wales, who bears the burden of entertaining him in London because of the queen's refusal to come to Buckingham Palace, has a different impression. He tells stories of disgusting behaviour, and of the shah's remark after a visit to the Duke of Sutherland's home: "Too grand for a subject. You'll have to have his head off when you come to the throne."

Nasr ed Din, the shah of Persia.

Alfred marries into Russian royal clan

A cartoon of Prince Alfred.

St Petersburg, 23 January 1874
Victoria's son Alfred, the Duke of Edinburgh, and Grand Duchess Marie, the daughter of Czar Alexander of Russia, were married here today in a magnificent double ceremony – the first Greek Orthodox and the second Church of England. The queen is not pleased at her beloved "Affie's" marriage to a Romanov. She thinks that they are false and arrogant, with "Asiatic ideas of their rank". This is the only wedding of one of her children that she has not attended (→ 3/1874).

Victoria delighted by return of Disraeli

Isle of Wight, August 1874
Prime minister again following a Conservative election victory, Benjamin Disraeli visited Osborne this month to see Victoria, whom he calls "the faery". He has set out to charm her, and there is no doubt that he is succeeding. "Gladstone," he says, "treats the queen like a public department; I treat her like a woman." He admits that he is a flatterer, saying: "When you come to royalty, you should lay it on with a trowel." One bond between queen and premier is that both mourn a dead love (Disraeli's wife died two years ago). Victoria also approves of his policies, especially his commitment to her empire (→ 25/11/75).

Disraeli: prime minister again.

Queen acts to halt creeping Catholicism

Westminster, May 1874
The queen, working behind the scenes, has pushed the Public Worship Bill through parliament in order to stamp out the papist practices which she fears are undermining the Church of England. She hopes that now there will be no more "bowings and scrapings" or, above all, "confession". Victoria's determination to sustain Protestant orthodoxy stems from the pope's declaration of infallibility four years ago. When the German chancellor, Bismarck, retaliated by introducing anti-Catholic measures, she set out to show that she, too, could defend the faith. The passage of the bill against Gladstone's opposition has given her much pleasure.

Royal visit charms radical Birmingham

Birmingham, 3 November 1874
The much-anticipated encounter between the Prince of Wales and Joseph Chamberlain, the radical mayor of Birmingham, took place here today. The prince, apprehensive about his meeting with a man who makes no secret of his republican views, and Chamberlain, who some said would refuse to shake the prince's hand, could not have been more pleasant to each other, and the visit has been a great success.

The "Birmingham Lion", formally dressed in a frock coat and top hat, was the epitome of dignity. At lunch in the town hall he proposed a toast to the prince and princess, telling the assembled citizens: "Here in England the throne is recognised and respected as the symbol of all constituted authority and settled government." It seems that the radical lion has been tamed by royal charm.

What the queen is eating: the menu for dinner, 9 March 1874.

Prince of Wales makes tour of India

Poverty shocks but hunting pleases

Bombay, 13 March 1876
The Prince of Wales left Bombay today on board HMS *Serapis* at the end of his long visit to India, undertaken in the face of fierce opposition from Queen Victoria. For the first three months the tour was an exhausting succession of *durbars* [court receptions], investitures and other ceremonies, so much so that the queen complained that "Bertie's progresses lose a little interest and are very wearing, as there is such a constant repetition of elephants, trappings, jewels, illuminations and fireworks".

The prince also grew bored with the ceremonial life, although his tedium was relieved by the beautiful girls provided to entertain him. He enjoyed his tour more when the ceremonies finished and he was able to hunt upcountry with his friends, "a fast set", travelling by elephant and camping out.

The prince has, however, shown much interest in the state of the country. The poverty of the people appals him, and he has been greatly angered by the arrogance shown to the Indians by British officials. Like the queen he is strongly opposed to racial prejudice, and he has written to his mother deploring the "brutality and contempt" with which the Indians are treated. Despite her initial misgivings, the queen is delighted with his conduct (→ 5/1876).

A royal reception: the prince is lavishly welcomed during his Indian tour.

A different kind of mount: the Prince of Wales goes hunting in India.

In full regalia: Edward is now a grand master of the Masons.

Royal duties put a strain on cashflow

London, January 1875
The Prince of Wales starts the year no doubt hoping that, in twelve months' time, his finances will not be in their present unhealthy state. For a long time now he has been asking for an increase since, in order to fulfil the duties ignored by his mother in her self-imposed seclusion, he is left some £20,000 out of pocket each year. Only last October the *Times* urged the queen to increase the prince's allowance, but so far she has not obliged.

Princess tells tale of woe to mother

Inveraray Castle, September 1875
The queen is visiting her daughter Princess Louise here at the family home of the princess's husband, the Marquis of Lorne. It is an idyllic place, but the princess is miserable and pours out complaints: her rooms are not good enough, she receives insufficient respect, she cannot dine alone as she wishes, her husband is dull and the company tedious. The queen, who has virtually taken over the household, listens sympathetically (→ 5/10/78).

Victoria shows her aproval by giving Disraeli an earldom

Buckingham Palace, 11 August 1876
The queen has shown her appreciation of and affection for Disraeli by creating him Earl of Beaconsfield. Although he remains prime minister he has withdrawn from the turmoil of the House of Commons to the more restful atmosphere of the Lords, something that he was reluctant to do while Gladstone still posed a threat in the lower house.

The matriarchal queen, who terrifies her family, and her prime minister, a dandy of Jewish origins, are unlikely friends, but they have always held the warmest regard for each other. Both set out to charm and flatter, as if they are playing a game by well-known rules. Disraeli is gallant to the queen and she is coquettish with him, yet there is a sound practicality to their relationship. He attends to her empire with an almost mystical devotion, while she makes her support for him and his policies quite plain to the world.

The earldom marks the summit of a glittering political career which cannot be very far from its end, for Disraeli is 72. Beaconsfield, as he must now be called, is the son of the literary critic Isaac D'Israeli who converted to Christianity and had Benjamin baptised; he has applied his brilliant, enigmatic mind to writing novels, building a "Tory democracy" at home and making Britain a great imperial power – an aim to which the queen gives her wholehearted approval (→ 7/1678).

Queen backs a plan to buy Suez shares

London, 25 November 1875
Disraeli, in a whirl of diplomatic and financial activity, has bought a controlling interest in the Suez Canal Company from the bankrupt *Khedive* Ismail of Egypt. Urged on by Queen Victoria, he told the French government that Britain would not tolerate France adding to its shares, persuaded a hesitant cabinet to borrow £4 million from Lord Rothschild to pay for the shares and secure Britain's lifeline to India (→ 11/8/76).

Prince dragged into aristocratic scandal

Arrogant: Randolph Churchill.

London, 12 July 1876
Lord Randolph Churchill has apologised to the Prince of Wales today following an aristocratic scandal which began during the prince's visit to India. Lady Aylesford, the wife of Lord "Sporting Joe" Ayles-

ford, one of the touring party, wrote to him from England to confess her adultery and her intention of running away with Churchill's brother, the Marquis of Blandford.

Aylesford made preparations to return, threatening to call out Blandford and divorce his wife. Desperate to help his brother, Churchill wrote to the prince asking him to intervene with Aylesford; the prince replied stiffly that as a man of honour he could not presume to do so. But the prince is partly to blame, as he pressured Aylesford into joining the Indian tour, thereby giving Blandford the chance to seduce Lady Aylesford.

Churchill then tried blackmail, threatening to reveal letters that the prince had written to Lady Aylesford some years previously and boasting: "I have the crown of England in my pocket." He has now been made to confess that he was mistaken, but it is a reluctant apology (→ 11/3/83).

Bulgarian massacre dismays Victoria

Windsor, 30 September 1876
Queen Victoria has been appalled at recent reports of the slaughter of Bulgarian Christians by bands of Turkish cut-throats known as *Bashi-Bazouks*. At first the Earl of Beaconsfield cynically dismissed the killings as just "Bulgarian atrocities", but the appearance of a brilliant pamphlet by Gladstone,

The Bulgarian Horrors and the Question of the East, has caused such public outcry that the government is being forced to take notice. Outraged as she is, the queen still ignores Beaconsfield's failure to take any action over the massacres, preferring to concentrate on suspected Russian involvement with the Bashi-Bazouks.

Stylish prince sets new fashion trends

Bertie: the fashionable royal.

London, October 1876
The Prince of Wales, denied a role in his country's government, has instead become its arbiter of fashion. He is fiercely critical of the slightest impropriety in dress. One unfortunate peer caught wearing the wrong hat at Epsom was fixed with a cold stare and asked: "Have you come ratting?"

The prince has also been responsible for a number of innovations: the Homburg hat, the Norfolk coat, the dinner jacket and the practice of leaving the bottom button of the waistcoat undone. The undone button is, however, more a matter of necessity than of fashion as the royal girth expands (→ 7/1877).

Albert's memory is a feast for souvenir hunters as Victoria creates new cult

Remembering the prince: the Albert Memorial in Kensington Gardens.

London, 1876
The capital has a new monument: the Albert Memorial. Situated in Kensington Gardens, it took its designer, Sir George Gilbert Scott, 12 years to complete, at a cost of £120,000. It is by far the most sumptuous of the many memorials raised throughout Britain by Victoria to Albert.

Sir George has created a sort of shrine to Albert, whose 14-foot (4.5-metre)-high bronze statue stands in contemplation under a Gothic canopy. The memorial is 175 feet high and lavishly ornamented with life- or near-life-size figures, the whole work executed in marble, granite, bronze, onyx, jasper and crystal. To some, it is a fitting tribute to the prince; to others, it is a vulgar confection.

Albert's bust on a porcelain jug.

Albert has also been commemorated on everyday articles such as jugs and teasets. They are part of a virtual cult of Albert, initiated by the queen, who has only recently come out of mourning. The printed page serves the cult further. Last year Sir Theodore Martin published his *Life of the Prince Consort*, authorised by Victoria. Sir Theodore claims to be objective, but his lavish praise of Albert will only add to the saintly aura surrounding his memory.

A tazza, or shallow wine cup, to commemorate Prince Albert.

Queen Victoria is empress of India

Bond with eastern empire cemented

Windsor, 1 January 1877
At a banquet held this evening at Windsor, Queen Victoria was toasted for the first time as "Empress of India", the title that she has coveted for some four years. After a suitably fulsome speech in praise of his elevated sovereign, Benjamin Disraeli, the Earl of Beaconsfield, proposed the toast to "Your Imperial Majesty!". The new empress graciously responded, to the astonishment of everyone present, by getting to her feet and appearing to curtsey to him.

The queen had been toying with a royal titles bill since the transfer of India to the crown in 1858, but it was only in 1871, when King William of Prussia became emperor of Germany, that she was spurred into action. William's elevation means that the queen's eldest daughter Vicky, who is married to William's heir, Crown Prince Frederick, will one day be an empress, thus outranking her mother. Even worse, Frederick can now claim that he is heir to an empire while Victoria's Prince of Wales will inherit a mere kingdom.

Victoria has been further put out by Czar Alexander II of Russia, who has recently insisted that his daughter, Grand Duchess Marie – who is the wife of Victoria's second son, Prince Alfred – should be called "Her Imperial [not simply Royal] Highness". The queen resents her Russian daughter-in-law claiming a higher title than her own daughters hold.

Lord Beaconsfield agreed to steer the Royal Titles Bill through parliament, but from sound political reasons rather than a desire to satisfy the queen. Making Victoria "Empress of India" is good foreign policy: it tells Czar Alexander, whose own empire is seeking to expand in Asia, that the British mean to hang on to what they have got. Although the bill did not get an easy ride through the Commons it was passed on 1 May last year. Now Victoria can proudly sign herself VR&I – *Victoria Regina et Imperatrix*, Queen and Empress.

"Victoria Regina et Imperatrix": Queen Victoria is now empress of India.

Lavish celebrations in India celebrate Victoria becoming empress.

Victoria develops a distaste for Russia

Windsor, 25 April 1877
Russia's recent declaration of war on the Ottoman Empire has appalled Queen Victoria. "The queen," she wrote to Lord Beaconsfield today, "wishes no general war – God knows! for no one abhors it more than she does; but we cannot allow the Russians to occupy Constantinople." She firmly believes that this would allow Russia to threaten Britain's land and sea routes to India. While Lord Beaconsfield, to placate the queen, is content to talk of war without declaring it, Victoria's blood is up. She wants firm action against the detested Russians for threatening her empire (→ 3/1878).

Prince brings down wrath of the queen

Constantinople, Turkey, 1878
Prince Alfred, the Duke of Edinburgh, has received a furious letter from the queen after allowing a Russian officer on board his ship. Russia and Britain have been on the brink of war since the Ottoman surrender; the prince's ship HMS *Sultan* was in port when one of his officers, Prince Louis of Battenberg, met his brother Alexander, an aide-de-camp to the Russian commander-in-chief, and asked him aboard. The British ambassador feared that peace negotiations might be compromised and cabled London. The queen has deplored Alfred's "imprudence and want of discretion".

Prince flaunts his Prussian sympathy

Berlin, 1878
Prince William, the son of the Princess Royal and Frederick, the heir to the Prussian throne, has become quite aggressively anti-English. "Why does Willy always sign himself "William Prince of Prussia"?" Queen Victoria asked her daughter. The boy is so influenced by his proud Prussian grandparents, and by Bismarck, that he is said once to have refused help for a nosebleed so that he could shed every drop of his English blood (→ 2/1880).

Eddy and George train for life at sea

Princes Albert Victor and George.

Dartmouth, 30 September 1877
Prince Albert Victor ("Eddy") and Prince George, the two eldest sons of the heir to the throne, have started their training on board the *Britannia*, anchored here in the river Dart. The *Britannia* is a relic from Nelson's era; the princes' sole privilege aboard her is to sling their hammocks in a private cabin.

While Prince George was always destined for the navy, his backward elder brother was sent to join him because he seems to benefit from George's influence. The queen had favoured sending the elder boy to Wellington College but was dissuaded by the Rev John Dalton, the princes' resident tutor (→ 30/9/80).

Victoria dances to celebrate peace treaty

Isle of Wight, July 1878
Queen Victoria is delighted at the conclusion of the congress which has been held in Berlin, ending the Russo-Turkish war. The queen had been in anguish over Russian attempts to crush Turkey and capture Constantinople, thereby threatening British routes to India. Although extremely keen for war, she was so pleased that her ministers had at last forced the Russians to the negotiating table that she held an impromptu dance at Osborne House, at which she waltzed for the first time for 18 years. She wrote afterwards: "Arthur dances like his beloved father. The band played admirably."

Lord Beaconsfield has cleverly depicted the settlement as a surrender of the Russian emperor to the British empress. The German chancellor Bismarck murmured in quiet admiration: "The old Jew, that's the man!" The queen regret-

Victoria receives Beaconsfield.

ted that the Russians had been allowed to retain the Caucasus, but no one doubts that they would have had more if her ill and ageing prime minister had not driven the hardest bargain possible.

Royal son-in-law wins top Canadian post

Ottawa, 5 October 1878
The Marquis of Lorne was today officially proclaimed the next governor-general of Canada. He will bring a touch of royalty to the country: he is married to Princess Louise, the fourth daughter of Queen Victoria, who was at first reluctant to allow "poor dear Loosy" to move so far away. Lorne is a Liberal MP who has sat in the House of Commons as the member for Argyllshire since 1868. His appointment is one of Lord Beaconsfield's few political acts to be applauded – not, in this case, unexpectedly – by his Liberal rival Gladstone. Yet the Conservatives now have control in Canada, which should please the queen (→ 2/1880).

Prince of Wales attracted to the charms of a 'Jersey Lily'

The prince's wife, Alexandra...

London, May 1877
The Prince of Wales is being linked romantically with the 23-year-old daughter of the Dean of Jersey, Lillie Langtry. Born Emilie Charlotte Le Breton in the Channel Islands, Mrs Langtry has been nicknamed "the Jersey Lily" because of her outstanding beauty. The prince was introduced to her this month at the house of a friend, the Arctic explorer Sir Allen Young. Although she is married, her husband, Edward, has made no complaint about the growing romance between his wife and the prince. As the Princess of Wales is also disinclined to protest about her husband's habitual infidelity, the risk of a scandal is small.

...and his new love, Lillie Langtry.

Queen's daughter dies of diphtheria

Darmstadt, 14 December 1878
Princess Alice, Queen Victoria's second daughter, died today after catching diphtheria from Ernest, her only surviving son. The queen received the news in the Blue Room where she and Alice mourned the death of the Prince Consort 17 years ago. Princess Alice was a frail woman whose health had been unsteady for several years. Her baby daughter May died of diphtheria on 16 November, and soon afterwards Ernest was gravely sick with it. In giving a comforting kiss to her son, who has survived, she may have sealed her own fate (→ 20/1/79).

Royal wedding lifts gloom of mourning

Windsor, 13 March 1879
Court mourning for Princess Alice [*see story above*] was suspended today for the wedding of Prince Arthur to Louise, the daughter of Prince Frederick of Prussia. The queen wore a long white veil and court train for the first time since becoming a widow. The only hitch in the day's festivities was the bride's father. Nicknamed the "Red Prince" because of his scarlet tunic, he was rude to everyone and complained that the couple's home in Surrey is too small (→ 28/7/82).

Critical Gladstone annoys the queen

Dalkeith, 26 November 1879
Gladstone is enraging the queen with his campaigns against the government. Today he fulminated against Britain's treatment of the natives of Afghanistan. "Remember the rights of the savage," he told an audience here. Gladstone's deep indignation is building up a passion for peace and against imperialism. He has denounced the queen's title "Empress of India" as nothing but "theatrical bombast and folly" and the latest British annexations as "false phantoms of glory". He is calling for a prime minister and a chancellor who believe in hard work and thrift (→ 8/3/80).

V i c t o r i a
1837–1901

Canada, February 1880. Princess Louise and her husband, the Marquis of Lorne, are involved in a sleigh accident; the princess suffers severe concussion and loses an ear (→ 10/9/81).

Berlin, February 1880. Prince William of Prussia announces his engagement to Princess Augusta, the daughter of Duke Frederick of Schleswig-Holstein, deposed by Prussia in 1864 (→ 28/2/81).

Westminster, 8 March 1880. Lord Beaconsfield, with Victoria's support, dissolves parliament, confident of a Tory majority in the general election (→ 23/4).

Germany, 1 April 1880. Victoria visits Baden-Baden to attend the confirmation of her grand-daughters, Princesses Victoria and Ella of Hesse, the daughters of the late Princess Alice.

Britain, 1880. Victoria criticises the Prince of Wales for failing to have his sons, Albert Victor ("Eddy") and George, taught any foreign languages (→ 17/5/81).

Canada, 1880. The Royal Canadian Academy of Arts is founded by the Marquis of Lorne and his wife, Princess Louise (→ 9/1884).

St Petersburg, 13 March 1881. Czar Alexander II is assassinated (→ 31/3).

London, May 1881. Victoria gives her youngest son, Prince Leopold, the dukedom of Albany (→ 27/4/82).

Canada, 10 September 1881. The Marquis of Lorne, the governor-general of Canada, attends a Blackfoot Indian conference and hears their grievances (→ 9/1884).

Dublin, 13 October 1881. Charles Stewart Parnell, the Irish MP for Meath and Cork, is jailed for inciting violence against landlords.

London, 31 December 1881. Lillie Langtry, the mistress of the Prince of Wales, makes her stage début at the Haymarket theatre.

London, 10 March 1882. Roderick MacLean, who last week tried to assassinate Victoria, is committed for trial.

London, 12 December 1882. Victoria opens the new City of London School on the Victoria Embankment.

Lausanne, 31 December 1882. Princes "Eddy" and George, the sons of the Prince of Wales, begin a crash course to learn French and German.

London, 25 February 1883. Princess Helen of Waldeck-Pyrmont, the wife of Prince Leopold, gives birth to their first child, a daughter, Alice.

Windsor, 17 March 1883. Victoria is injured falling downstairs and is unable to walk.

Darmstadt, Germany, April 1884. Members of the royal family converge on the palace for the wedding of Princess Victoria of Hesse, the eldest daughter of Princess Alice, to her first cousin, Prince Louis of Battenberg, an officer in the Royal Navy.→

Germany, April 1884. Victoria forces her son-in-law Louis, the Grand Duke of Hesse, the widower of Princess Alice, to annul his recent secret marriage to the Russian Alexandrina Kalomine, which has upset the family (→ 30/4).

Newcastle upon Tyne, 21 Aug 1884. The Prince and Princess of Wales receive a warm welcome.

London, December 1884. Princess Beatrice, the youngest daughter of Victoria, announces her engagement to Prince Henry of

Battenberg; Victoria approves of the marriage after her initial dislike of Henry (→ 23/7/85).

Windsor, 25 February 1885. Victoria takes command at the birth of Princess Alice, her great-granddaughter and the first child of the recently-married Princess Victoria of Battenberg.

Surrey, 31 December 1885. Prince Francis and Princess Mary Adelaide of Teck return to England to live at Richmond.

Britain, December 1885. The Prince of Wales is given unofficial access to papers on foreign affairs by Lord Rosebery, the foreign secretary (→ 6/1886).

London, 23 November 1886. Princess Beatrice of Battenberg gives birth to her first child, a son, Alexander (→ 24/10/87).

Windsor, 8 December 1886. Victoria receives the recently-deposed Prince Alexander of Battenberg, known as Sandro, the elder brother of Prince Henry.

Berlin, May 1887. At the request of her daughter, Vicky, the Crown Princess of Prussia, and German doctors, Victoria sends a specialist, Dr Morell Mackenzie, to examine Crown Prince Frederick William, her son-in-law, for cancer of the throat (→ 9/1887).

Australia, 22 June 1887. Adelaide celebrates Victoria's golden jubilee and the jubilee of the colony of Australia (→ 19/7).

Balmoral, 24 October 1887. Princess Beatrice of Battenberg gives birth to a daughter, Victoria Eugénie, the first royal baby to be born in Scotland since the birth of Charles I in 1600.

Berlin, February 1888. Crown Prince Frederick William of

Prussia undergoes surgery on his throat (→ 9/3).

Berlin, 9 March 1888. The German emperor, William, dies; he is succeeded by his son, Crown Prince Frederick William of Prussia, who becomes Frederick III (→ 10/3).

Windsor, 16 March 1888. Victoria holds a memorial service for the emperor of Germany; she is thrilled by her daughter, Vicky, becoming empress (→ 25/4).

Berlin, 18 June 1888. The Prince and Princess of Wales attend the funeral of their brother-in-law, Emperor Frederick III, who died three days ago; his son, William, succeeds (→ 9/1888).

Vienna, September 1888. The Prince of Wales is snubbed by his nephew, Kaiser (Emperor) William II, who insists on the prince's departure from Vienna before his own visit begins (→ 19/11).

London, 19 November 1888. A grief-stricken Vicky, the dowager empress, arrives to visit her mother and escape the anti-British feelings in Germany.→

Germany, February 1889. Vicky, the dowager empress, returns to Berlin (→ 9/1898).

Isle of Wight, August 1889. Victoria invites her grandson, Kaiser William, to Osborne for the Cowes week of yacht races (→ 8/8).

Athens, 27 October 1889. Princess Sophie, the third daughter of Vicky, the dowager empress of Germany, marries Constantine, the Crown Prince of the Hellenes.

London, 1889. Rumours are rife of homosexual antics in a Cleveland Street brothel involving Prince "Eddy" and Sir Arthur Somerset, the superintendent of the royal stable (→ 24/5/90).

Reluctantly, the queen recalls Gladstone

Westminster, 23 April 1880
After repeated abdication threats and attempts to find an alternative, the queen has invited Gladstone to form a government. Their meeting this evening was brief and tense, but polite; she spent most of the time urging him to do nothing that would undermine the foreign policy of his predecessor, Lord Beaconsfield. Since Gladstone has been tirelessly campaigning for a reversal of Beaconsfield's imperialism, the request seems absurd, but Gladstone evidently chose not to argue.

Queen Victoria was in Germany at the beginning of the month when she received news that Beaconsfield's six-year-old majority had evaporated. He blamed consecutive bad harvests, while she simply could not understand what she saw as the folly of parliament. The slaughter of Lord Chelmsford's army by the Zulus at Isandhlwana had certainly given more force to Gladstone's anti-war campaign, but she swore to abdicate rather than deal with "that half-mad firebrand who would soon ruin everything and be a dictator".

On her return to England, the queen remained resolute against Gladstone, and Ponsonby, her private secretary, feared that she would force the issue. Gladstone himself had told Ponsonby that no

Inspecting the new "cabinet".

minister who forced the queen to abdicate would ever survive. The only possible alternatives were the Liberals Hartington and Granville. Lord Beaconsfield advised the queen to send for Hartington, which she did.

Hartington outlined the problem: it would be impossible to form a Liberal government without Gladstone, and he would join it only if he could be its leader – in other words, prime minister. Granville had nothing more to offer, and as a constitutional crisis threatened, the Prince of Wales advised the queen to relent. Finally, at 6.30 this evening, she did (→ 2/1881).

Princes Eddy and George get ready for two-year voyage to the southern seas

Spithead, 30 September 1880
Prince Albert Victor, known as Eddy, and Prince George, the two surviving sons of the Prince of Wales, have set sail for Australia at the beginning of a tour that will last two years and take them virtually around the world. Preparations began last September with a voyage to the West Indies, from which they returned in May. The decision to send them off in the 4,000-ton *Bacchante*, taken after much family wrangling, was made primarily to encourage the development of Eddy, the elder brother, who remains backward and listless.

The Prince of Wales and the princes' tutor, the Rev John Dalton, were the chief enthusiasts for the plan, but the queen was not keen. The cabinet also doubted the wisdom of entrusting the two heirs to the throne, after the Prince of Wales, to the mercies of the deep in the same ship. Even Dalton then began to doubt the *Bacchante*'s seaworthiness. After testing the vessel in a storm, the captain, Lord Charles Scott, pronounced her safe. The dithering continued for some while after that, but eventually the queen decided to back the scheme.

Although nearly three years in all afloat is a daunting prospect,

The princes return from a voyage.

there will be long periods of shore leave. There are some comforts, too: Eddy and George share a cabin and have Charles Fuller, a Sandringham footman, as their personal attendant; they will be excused boat duty during storms. The officers have also been carefully vetted by Dalton. Lord Charles Scott is a son of the Duke of Buccleuch; the commander, George Hill, is a kinsman of Viscount Hill, who succeeded Wellington as commander–in–chief of the army (→ 30/12/80).

Prince enjoys table talk with a Liberal

London, 13 March 1880
The Prince of Wales and the Liberal politician Sir Charles Dilke met last night at Lord Fife's house for dinner. They got on extremely well, as Dilke gladly admitted. "The prince laid himself out to be pleasant," he said, "and talked to me ... chiefly about French politics and the Greek question." Dilke no doubt enjoyed the talk: he hopes to be appointed to the foreign office in Gladstone's new government.

It was the prince who requested the meeting; he has made a point of getting to know various Liberals and radicals. In fact Sir Charles and the prince have much in common, both being keen imperialists in favour of détente with France and reform of the armed forces.

Bertie finds friends on fringe of society

London, 14 January 1881
The Prince of Wales's presence today at the financier Leopold de Rothschild's wedding in a synagogue is typical of his desire to make friends with those on the fringe of fashionable society. To the distaste of his wife's family, he favours the company of actors, Americans, Jews and self-made men. The prince believes in opening up society and is fascinated by the new rich.

Critics say that there is something un-English about the prince's fascination with such people as the Rothschilds, who owe their social standing to wealth alone. But the prince thinks that placing breeding above success – of which money is a measure – stifles the vitality and sparkle that he has found in more egalitarian France and America.

Rothschild: the prince's friend.

Queen loses battle to alter her speech

Osborne, February 1881
The queen has sought the advice of her old ally, Lord Beaconsfield, after a furious row with her ministers over her speech at the opening of parliament. The speech, which Lord Hartington failed to show her in advance, announced the evacuation of British forces from Kandahar in Afghanistan, where they have been attempting to block Russian expansion towards India. The queen had refused to approve the evacuation, but her ministers would not submit the speech without the controversial paragraph. Eventually she agreed to express her disapproval in a memorandum to Gladstone.

Sir William Harcourt, the home secretary, then outraged the queen by stating that "the speech of the sovereign is only the speech of the ministers". If that was so, she asked Beaconsfield, why ask her to read the speech? Harcourt's remark, he replied, was unconstitutional – "a piece of parliamentary gossip". This eccentric judgement may have comforted the queen, but it does not alter the essential principle of ministerial responsibility (→ 19/4).

Lillie Langtry, an actress and a mistress of the Prince of Wales, here playing in Goldsmith's "She Stoops to Conquer".

Prince attends assassinated czar's burial

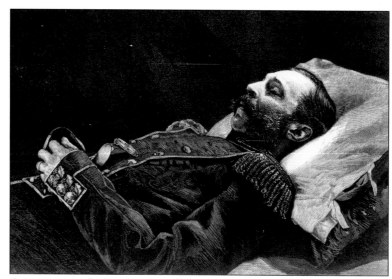

Lying in state: the Russian Czar Alexander II who was killed by a bomb.

St Petersburg, 31 March 1881
The funeral of Czar Alexander II, killed by an assassin's bomb, has passed off peacefully despite fears for the safety of mourners, who included the Prince and Princess of Wales and the Prussian heir. Russia is teeming with revolutionary groups, and there were rumours of mines beneath the church.

The prince came at the request of his brother Alfred, whose wife Marie is the late czar's daughter. Despite Queen Victoria's misgivings, her ministers felt that the royal couple's presence at the funeral would help relations between the two imperial powers. Although he introduced reforms which included the emancipation of serfs in 1861, Alexander II was an autocratic ruler who relied on a secret police force. He brutally crushed a revolt in Poland, and it was a Polish student who threw the bomb that killed him. It landed as the czar was standing beside his carriage asking questions after an initial bomb had missed its target.

Colonel Wellesley, the British military attaché here, says that "the minimum of political liberty" in Russia – press censorship and secret police – coexists with "the maximum of social freedom" – restaurants staying open until 1am.

Queen's grandson married in Prussia

Prussia, 28 February 1881
Prince William, a grandson of Queen Victoria and of the German emperor, has confirmed his Germanic leanings by marrying the somewhat cumbersomely named Princess Augusta Victoria of Schleswig-Holstein-Sonderburg-Augustenburg. The Prince of Wales attended the wedding, but his warmth and generosity have been met with nothing but rudeness from his nephew William, who is becoming increasingly estranged from Fritz and Vicky, his worried parents. Prince William's behaviour stems from his belief that his Uncle Bertie is a corrupting influence on his parents (→9/1887).

Disraeli's death is a blow to Victoria

Westminster, 19 April 1881
Benjamin Disraeli, the Earl of Beaconsfield, former prime minister and one of the great statesmen of the century, died at 4.30am today, aged 76. He had been ill for some time, and when a tearful John Brown came to see Queen Victoria at Windsor she knew the worst. After the death of Albert, Disraeli became the queen's greatest friend and counsellor, and she will miss him terribly. Not only was he the one politician to have enjoyed her absolute confidence but also, by flattering and cajoling her, he drew her out of her prolonged mourning into an active role as head of state, to be a popular monarch again.

Princes survive the perils of sea gales

Western Australia, 17 May 1881
Princes Eddy and George, the two sons of the Prince of Wales, have arrived here in Albany on board the *Bacchante*, in which they have spent nearly two years since leaving England in September 1879. They have survived gales and the monotony of a ship's diet, while the Rev John Dalton, their tutor, has been doing his best to fill their spare time with teaching.

The *Bacchante*, which left Britain last September, was damaged in a severe gale between South Africa and Australia, drifting out of control for three days until makeshift repairs could be made. Prince

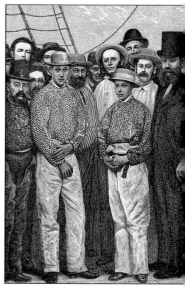

Eddy and George in Australia.

George made a particular impression upon his shipmates, being calm and resourceful under pressure. Yet he was deeply upset when a seaman fell to his death from the foretopsail yard.

While the *Bacchante* was in the West Indies last year, a British newspaper ran a story that both young princes had been tattooed on the nose while ashore in Barbados. Dalton had to write to an anxious Prince of Wales to assure him that this was not true. On their shore leave there were opportunities for bathing and cricket, riding and dancing, picnics and inland expeditions. Dalton also tried to fit in as much sightseeing as possible, but he seems to have been unable to enthuse his two charges (→31/12/82).

Shot fired at queen on leaving station

MacLean tries to murder Victoria.

Windsor, 2 March 1882

The queen has survived a seventh attempt on her life. Roderick Mac-Lean, well-educated but impoverished and mentally disturbed, fired a single shot at her carriage as it left Windsor station for the castle this evening. He missed. Two Eton boys wielding umbrellas then set upon the luckless MacLean. The queen was unperturbed and calmly took tea with Princess Beatrice when she reached the castle. Like the former Empress Eugénie of France, she regards assassination attempts as inevitable hazards. "It is worth being shot at," the queen said, "to see how much one is loved" (→ 10/3).

Egyptian sea attack pleases the queen

Windsor, 28 July 1882

Tonight, as the queen bade farewell to her son Prince Arthur, the Duke of Connaught, she experienced the feelings of a mother sending her son to war. "When I read that my darling, precious Arthur, was really to go, I quite broke down. It seemed like a dreadful dream," she wrote a week ago. "Still, I would not have him shirk his duty."

The growing crisis in Egypt, where the nationalist Arabi Pasha is leading a revolt against British heavy-handedness and the corruption of the ruler, *Khedive* Tawfiq, is making armed intervention by Britain inevitable. Prince Arthur now commands the First Guards Brigade, which has been assigned to the expeditionary force now being assembled.

This evening Victoria dined with her son and his wife, Louise, for the last time before his departure. Trying to remain cheerful, they spoke of the preparations for war and the equipment Arthur would be taking with him: one horse, serge field dress, breeches, boots and a white solar topee. His mother is giving him a canteen and field glasses. It is all very different from the Battle of Dettingen in 1743, when George II went to war with a personal baggage train of 102 coaches, waggons and carts (→ 13/9).

Prince shines in battle

Leader of men: Prince Arthur with the troops in battle at Tel-el-Kebir.

Balmoral, 13 September 1882

Prince Arthur, the Duke of Connaught, the queen's youngest son but one, is alive. This evening his mother received a telegram from Egypt, where the prince has been fighting with Sir Garnet Wolseley's expeditionary force: "A great victory, Duke safe and well." The queen rejoices, and tonight a bonfire blazes from Craig Gowan, as it did when Sebastopol fell 27 years ago.

The celebrations are for victory in battle at Tel-el-Kebir, where British troops have today defeated Arabi Pasha, the leader of a revolt against the British-backed *Khedive* Tawfiq. By all accounts Prince Arthur greatly distinguished himself in the fighting.

Ever since she first heard of Arabi Pasha's rebellion Victoria had been convinced that military action was necessary to keep the *Khedive* in power, thus protecting British access through the Suez canal and beyond it to India. She was witheringly critical of both Gladstone and France for hesitating to use force. "Egypt is vital to us," she said. The queen is convinced that Arabi should be hanged, and she is shocked by Liberals such as Wilfrid Scawen Blunt who regard him as a patriot (→ 1892).

Prince Leopold marries Dutch princess

Windsor, 27 April 1882

The queen's fourth son, the haemophiliac and accident-prone Prince Leopold, married Princess Helen of Waldeck-Pyrmont, the sister of Queen Emma of the Netherlands, at Windsor castle this morning. The queen is relieved. "Though the idea of his marrying makes me anxious," she wrote on Leopold's birthday three weeks ago, "still, as he has found a girl, so charming, ready to accept and love him, in spite of his ailments, I hope he may be happy."

What the queen likes about her new daughter-in-law, which distinguishes her from the rest of Victoria's family, is that the young Princess Helen appears totally unafraid of her (→ 25/2/83).

Leopold's bride: Princess Helen.

Epping Forest is opened to public

London, 6 May 1882

Queen Victoria formally opened Epping Forest this afternoon – just two months after the attempt on her life at Windsor. The 5,600 acres (2,240 hectares) of unenclosed land north-east of the capital were purchased by the City of London to prevent them from being built on and have been presented to the poor of east London as a public recreation ground in perpetuity. Vast crowds lined the three miles (4.8km) from the station to High Beach, where the queen and the lord mayor gave short speeches. "Nothing but loyal expressions and kind faces did I hear and see," said Victoria. "It was most gratifying."

Queen shocked by Irish assassination

London, 6 May 1882

Within hours of her triumphal opening of Epping Forest, the queen received a telegram telling her that Lord Frederick Cavendish, the chief secretary for Ireland, had been seriously wounded and his under-secretary, Frederick Burke, killed in Phoenix Park, Dublin. The assassins were Fenians (Irish nationalists), who ambushed the two men and stabbed them relentlessly. The queen is deeply distressed and – unfairly – blames the prime minister, William Gladstone, whose policy on Ireland she so abhors, for the killing. Gladstone himself is in deep sorrow: Cavendish is the husband of his favourite niece.

Queen stunned by death of 'best friend'

Windsor, 29 March 1883
The queen was devastated today by the death of her faithful servant John Brown. The news was broken to her in her dressing room by her son, Prince Leopold. "It is the loss not only of a servant, but of a real friend," she wrote in her journal.

Ten days ago at Easter Victoria had developed rheumatism following a fall on her knee on the stairs at Windsor. Brown had carried her from the sofa to her little pony-chair. But he caught a chill checking the castle grounds for Fenians, developed erysipelas, an acute feverish skin infection, and died. The queen has not suffered such a shock since the death of her husband, Prince Albert, 22 years ago.

Brown had served the queen for 34 years as royal ghillie, groom and confidant. When her family, embarrassed at rumours about their closeness, accused him of drunkenness and arrogance she was quick to

John Brown: in close attendance.

defend him, tolerating in him informal behaviour that would have been insufferable from any other subject. "He became my best and truest friend," the queen told a Scottish minister, adding: "As I was his" (→ 29/3/84).

Prince of Wales ends feud with Churchills

London, 11 March 1883
The Prince of Wales and the Tory rebel, Lord Randolph Churchill, have dined together, ending their long-standing feud. In 1876, while the prince was touring India, his friend Lord Aylesford heard that his wife had eloped with Churchill's rakish brother, the Marquis of Blandford. The row escalated when Churchill sought to persuade the

prince to discourage a divorce by threatening to call him as a witness and reveal letters written by him to Lady Aylesford. He even showed some of the letters to the Princess of Wales. The prince was furious: his challenge to a duel was declined, as was the Marlborough family's apology. Churchill was ostracised at court, with the prince refusing to be seen in his company until today.

Royal colours give style to the railways

Windsor, 1883
The gold and brown lines of the royal carriage are becoming a familiar sight on the Great Western Railway. The queen uses it regularly for travelling up to London. Victoria made her first train journey in 1842, taking a liking to the new form of transport. At that time each railway company had a different gauge, so each built her its own carriage. A standard gauge will soon make it possible for one royal train to go anywhere, but her favourite is still the Great Western carriage: it has a central saloon, compartments for the queen and her court, and her own lavatory, discreetly concealed inside a sofa.

The queen's private railway saloon.

Queen backs plea to recall Gordon

Balmoral, 22 December 1883
The British government has horrified the queen by planning to abandon the Sudan rather than make war on the rebel leader known as the *Mahdi*. Her reaction was instantaneous: "Send for Gordon!"

Mohamad Ahmed ibn Addullah emerged out of the western desert last year, fulfilling ancient Moslem prophesies. He was given the name of Mahdi, meaning the "expected one", and his armies have since destroyed every Egyptian force sent against them and are now besieging Khartoum, the Sudanese capital.

Sudan has been an area of Anglo-Egyptian influence, and the queen sees General Charles Gordon as the man to restore this. A veteran of the Crimea and an evangelical Christian, he resigned the governor-generalship of the Sudan in 1880; a hero of the queen, he is also highly regarded by both the Liberal anti-slavery lobby and the Conservative imperialist lobby.

Gladstone, the prime minister, is not keen on military involvement, and Sir Evelyn Baring, the agent-general of the Sudan, claims that it would be disastrous to employ a Christian zealot to stop a Moslem movement. But the pressure for sending Gordon is mounting. It would be cheaper than sending an army; it would satisfy the British public; and it would lessen the royal pressure on Gladstone (→ 5/2/85).

Remarkable device comes to Balmoral

Balmoral, 1883
A telephone was installed here this year so that all the queen's major residences – Buckingham Palace, Osborne House, Windsor and Balmoral – now have the invention patented by Alexander Graham Bell in 1876. Victoria first used a telephone in 1878, when Bell demonstrated the apparatus to her at Osborne House, and she listened to Miss Kate Fields singing *Kathleen Mavourneen* down the line. Bell then presented her with two ivory-handled telephones. Most royal household business, however, is still done in writing.

New naval posting for tattooed prince

Portsmouth, 1883
The Prince of Wales's son, Prince George, has been posted to the corvette HMS *Canada* on the North America and West Indies station. After three years as a midshipman on HMS *Bacchante* with his elder brother, Albert Victor ("Eddy") and their tutor, the Rev John Dalton, he will now pursue his naval career alone.

George's intellectual progress was slow as a child, but he was neat, orderly and always punctual, and a constant source of encouragement to his more sickly brother. At

Prince George: a new naval post.

12 years old he was sent with his brother to the *Britannia*, a cadet training ship, and his two years there were a success.

From the *Britannia* the two grandsons of the queen were posted to the *Bacchante*. They served on three voyages with her, the last taking them to the Indian and Pacific oceans. It was an exciting experience for George. The ship encountered a gale in the Indian Ocean that nearly sank her; in Australia he caught a kangaroo; and in Tokyo he had his arms tattooed with dragons and acquired a new habit – smoking (→ 1890).

Prince of Wales speaks out for poor

London, 22 February 1884
The Prince of Wales today made his first speech in the House of Lords. "The condition of the poor, or rather of their dwellings, was perfectly disgraceful," he said.

Alleviating the sufferings of the poor has given the prince something to do which he can take pride in. Some weeks ago William Gladstone, the prime minister, suggested that he sit on Sir Charles Dilke's all-party royal commission investigating the housing conditions of the working class. Surprisingly, the queen did not object. She herself is shocked by the state of the poor, and relieved that her son has found

time from his frivolity for some Christian works. The prince is taking his work seriously, visiting some of London's worst slums in Holborn and St Pancras, disguised in a "slouch" hat. He was shocked by the sight of half-naked children huddling in rags for protection against the mid-winter winds.

Bertie's enthusiasm has shown another quality in a man whom many dismiss for being concerned solely with pleasure – honesty. There is no hypocrisy in him. As he admitted in his speech today, the Duchy of Cornwall (part of the royal estate) is one of London's worst landlords (→ 5/1885).

Edward delivers his maiden speech.

Queen postpones a planned memoir of a 'faithful friend'

Windsor, 29 March 1884
The queen will not be publishing her planned memoir of John Brown, to the relief of her family. Sir Henry Ponsonby and Randall Davidson, the dean of Windsor, have persuaded her to "delay" publication. Last month she published *More Leaves from a Journal of Our Life in the Highlands*, with a dedication to "my loyal Highlanders and especially to the memory of my devoted personal attendant and faithful friend John Brown". In the USA a satire was published called *John Brown's Legs; or, Leaves from a Journal in the Lowlands*, with such entries as: "Louise has just been here and is fearfully dejected. Brown had comforted her, as he has done me many a time."

Then she announced that she had been writing a memoir of Brown, to show him as "a great deal more" than just a servant. She showed it to Ponsonby. He was horrified, not least because it contained details of their spiritualist seances together.

On 6 March she showed it to the dean. He was forthright: "I should be deceiving your majesty were I not to admit that there are, especially among the humbler classes, some who do not shew themselves worthy of these confidences." The queen, furious, refused to speak to him – but she has taken his advice. There will be no book.

Princess Louise separates from husband

Ottawa, Canada, September 1884
Victoria's sixth child, Princess Louise, is separating from her husband, the Marquis of Lorne, the governor-general of Canada. Initially their life in Canada was a success. They showed themselves suitably "democratic", encouraged the arts and made an epic tour of the west, travelling by horse and wagon. But a sleigh accident four years ago, in which Louise suffered severe concussion and a torn ear, seemed to change her. She went for a lengthy convalescence in Europe which provoked criticism in Canada while increasing her disenchantment with her husband whom she has long found boring.

Louise: at odds with her husband.

Queen helps avert constitutional rift

London, 17 November 1884
The queen has brought the Liberal and Cnservative leaders, William Gladstone and Lord Salisbury, together to avert a constitutional crisis. The cause was Gladstone's Reform Bill, which if passed would sweep hundreds of Liberals into Westminster. The Conservatives would only support it complemented by a bill to redistribute seats. Gladstone refused and the Lords threw out his bill, provoking calls for their abolition. Now the Reform Bill will return to them at the same time as a Redistribution Bill is put to the Commons (→ 5/2/85).

Royal wedding masks grief for Leopold

Darmstadt, 30 April 1884
In barely a month the royal family has experienced a death, a wedding, a scandal and a possible engagement. Members of the family are gathered here in Germany for the wedding today of Victoria, the eldest daughter of the late Princess Alice, to a cousin, Prince Louis of Battenberg. Louis, a serving officer in the Royal Navy, has greatly impressed Queen Victoria.

For the queen the wedding is a chance to set aside her grief over the death of Prince Leopold, her eighth child, who died last month in Cannes. Leopold, who suffered from haemophilia, had slipped on

the staircase of his hotel and died of a brain haemorrhage. Ironically, he had been sent to Cannes for his health – to escape the English winter. His widow, Princess Helen, is expecting her second child – she had a daughter, Alice, last year – in the summer. Helen is much respected by Victoria.

Meanwhile, at Darmstadt, the queen's daughter Beatrice is talking of an engagement to a brother of Prince Louis, Henry, a 25-year-old army officer known as "Liko". However Queen Victoria has been scandalised by the secret wedding of Grand Duke Louis of Hesse to a Polish divorcée (→ 25/2/85).

A keen sportsman: the Prince of Wales playing tennis with friends in September 1883 at a new club at Baden-Baden, in Germany.

Mustard pies add spice to weekend fun for a prince

Sandringham, 1885

If you happen to be invited to a spend a weekend with the Waleses at Sandringham, be prepared for some right royal fun – even if the joke is on you. The Prince of Wales is an inveterate practical joker – a recent ploy was putting a live lobster in a guest's bed, while at Christmas he served mince pies stuffed with mustard. Sandringham is noted among its guests for practical jokes and royal merriment; if you are not caught out by one of Bertie's apple-pie beds, be careful as you climb the stairs – you might get knocked over by the Princess of Wales using a silver tray as a toboggan.

The prince is a gracious host, but the emphasis at the East Anglian estate is on informality. The bishop of Peterborough reports that he arrived at the house to find family and guests at tea in the entrance hall. "I had to walk in all seedy and dishevelled from my day's journey and sit down by the Princess of Wales while the prince feasted on poached eggs and preserved ginger," he wrote. The guests that weekend included a Rothschild, Disraeli and an Italian duchess.

This year Henry Broadhurst, a radical MP who sits with the prince on the Royal Commission on the Housing of the Working Classes, was invited to Sandringham to study cottages provided fr the estate workers. "I can honestly say that I was never entertained more to my liking," he wrote later. "His royal highness personally conducted me to my rooms, made a careful examination to see all was all right and stoked the fire for me." (Broadhurst had no evening dress, however, and so dined in his room each night.)

The prince has established a breeding stud at Sandringham, but his real passion is for shooting. He has spent thousands of pounds to ensure huge "bags" at the end of each day.

Victoria clashes again with Gladstone

In memory of General Gordon: his death has had serious consequences.

Queen voices anger over Gordon's death

Isle of Wight, 5 February 1885

A figure dressed entirely in black today appeared to announce, in a voice of deepest gloom: "Gordon is dead!" Queen Victoria was not content simply to mourn at the news received today of General Charles Gordon's death on 26 January after being besieged in Khartoum for 315 days. She is determined to lay the blame for Gordon's death at the door of her prime minister, Gladstone, and his government.

The queen believes that Gladstone failed to act quickly enough in sending reinforcements – relief troops finally arrived just two days after Gordon had been speared to death. And she made no attempt to disguise her anger, breaking all protocol to send uncoded telegrams to Gladstone and his ministers: "These news from Khartoum are frightful and to think that all this might have been prevented and many precious lives saved by earlier action is too frightful."

Victoria sees Khartoum as national humiliation; Gladstone, affronted by the public rebuke and unpopular in the country, is contemplating resignation (→ 24/6).

'Grand Old Man' to resign as premier

Windsor, 24 June 1885

The queen refused to shake hands with Mr Gladstone today when he came to present his ministerial seals of office following his government's resignation earlier this month. When the "grand old man" humbly begged to kiss his queen's hand, however, Victoria offered her fingers accordingly.

Gladstone's Liberal coalition, already reeling from public criticism over Gordon's death in the Sudan, began to break up in May with the resignations of two radical leaders, Charles Dilke and Joseph Chamberlain, over the government's policy for Irish home rule. It was finally defeated by 12 votes on 8 June. Gladstone telegraphed his resignation to the queen the next day, but Lord Salisbury did not take over formally as prime minister until today to head a minority government.

The queen has not disguised her anger at Britain's defeat in the Sudan and the death of General Gordon – and she saw Gladstone as the villain. But Victoria was in no hurry to accept his resignation. "As a lady nearer 70 than 60 ... she is quite unable to rush about as a younger person and a man could do," she wrote of herself (→ 8/6/86).

Boos and black flags mar visit of Prince of Wales to Ireland

Locals inspect the Prince of Wales at Killarney on his tour of Ireland.

Ireland, April 1885

The Prince and Princess of Wales have spent three weeks touring Ireland. Their reception in Dublin, Belfast and Londonderry was enthusiastic, but quite a different response awaited them in Cork where they were booed continuously by crowds waving black flags and even pelted with onions. The prince's equerry reported the prince, although shocked, as showing calmness in front of the crowd. The prince had been reluctant to visit Ireland, but he was persuaded to go by Gladstone, the prime minister, who felt that it would be a good way to test the temper of the Irish nation (→ 5/1885).

Prince loses a new battle of the boxes

London, May 1885

The queen has won the latest round in what has become known as "the battle of the boxes" – Victoria's refusal to allow the Prince of Wales access to cabinet secrets. Gladstone hoped that the dignified way in which the prince had carried out the difficult tour of Ireland last month might have softened the queen's opposition to Bertie seeing government papers. In fact, he asked to do no more than supply openly what Disraeli had passed to the prince surreptitiously. But the queen was adamant: there could be no communication between the prime minister and the prince. Gladstone has bowed to her wishes, but thinks it is "injudicious" that the prince is still excluded from government affairs (→ 12/1885).

Exhibitions are opened with royal pomp

Liverpool, 12 May 1886

Wrapped in waterproofs and holding an umbrella against the driving rain, Queen Victoria drove through gaily decorated streets here today to open the International Exhibition of Navigation and Commerce. "The crowds were enormous, and every shop window was full of people," she wrote in her journal later. "In spite of the weather, the whole thing was a great success ... the wonderful loyalty and enthusiasm displayed most touching ... we got home at seven, quite bewildered and my head aching from the incessant perfect roar of cheering."

Six days ago the queen opened the Indian and Colonial Exhibition at South Kensington. Anxious that the queen should sustain the image of an expanding empire, the foreign secereraty, Lord Rosebery, asked her to invest the occasion with all

Victoria at the Liverpool show.

conceivable pomp. "With all the pomp you like," said the queen, "as long as I don't have to wear a low dress." The queen also refused to wear her crown out of doors.

Home rule rejected to queen's relief

London, 8 June 1886

Sixteen days of impassioned debate in the House of Commons on Irish home rule ended today with the defection of 93 Liberals, ensuring the defeat of the Home Rule Bill by 30 votes. It now seems certain that Gladstone will resign as prime minister for the second time in a year. The queen is pleased, even though the bill included the role of the crown among subjects reserved for the Westminster parliament. "Cannot help feeling relieved," she wrote in her journal. Irish policy had brought down Gladstone's second administration a year ago, but Lord Salisbury's minority government had lasted only seven months before falling over agricultural policy. Now he seems set to try again (→ 9/1886).

Lord Rosebery covertly briefs the prince

London, June 1886

Risking the queen's wrath, Lord Rosebery, the foreign secretary, is secretly briefing the Prince of Wales on the affairs of state. It is now known that Benjamin Disraeli, the Earl of Beaconsfield, covertly kept the prince informed. Victoria refused to believe Gladstone's claim that Disraeli had acted behind her back when last year she rejected the prime minister's plea to pass cabinet papers openly [*see report above*]. "Communications to the prince should be under the immediate control of the sovereign," she says. But now Gladstone is to exercise a "judicious indiscretion" via Rosebery (→ 30/9/90).

Lord Rosebery: briefing the prince.

Queen warns against 'Russian villainy'

Windsor, September 1886

The telegraph wires have been humming between this royal borough and Westminster all week with furious messages from Victoria to her ministers after the arrest of her "dear Sandro" – Prince Alexander of Bulgaria – during a Russian-inspired invasion of that country. The queen, a skilled practitioner of the telegraphic art, has told Lord Salisbury that she blames "Russian fiends". Moreover she sees the invasion as "the stepping stone to Constantinople" and has talked of "sickening treachery" ... "Russian villainy" ... "a slap in *our* face" and "Russia must not triumph".

The latest news is that Sandro has escaped after returning to Sofia, where he was nearly murdered in the cathedral (→ 8/12).

Victoria's youngest child, Beatrice, weds

Isle of Wight, 23 July 1885

The royal family broke with tradition when Princess Beatrice, Victoria's youngest daughter, was married in the little country church of Whippingham here to Prince Henry of Battenberg. Victoria was surprised when Beatrice – whom many had thought doomed to spinsterhood and a career as her mother's secretary – said that she was in love. The idea of another German marriage – Henry's brother, Louis, married one of Victoria's grandchildren last year – was criticised in the country, and the queen revealed "her most violent dislike" of her "precious baby marrying at all". But when Henry said that he would live in England and not deprive the queen of her daughter's services, Victoria was mollified. "I never felt more deeply than I did on this occasion though full of confidence," she wrote of the wedding (→ 23/11/86).

A card inviting the bearer to attend the laying of the memorial stone of Tower Bridge, London, by the Prince of Wales on 2 June 1886.

Vicky's husband is suffering from cancer

San Remo, Italy, September 1887
Crown Prince Frederick (Fritz) of Prussia, the son of the German *kaiser* [emperor] and Queen Victoria's son-in-law, has left Berlin for the warmer climes of Italy with his wife, Vicky. There is now little doubt that he has cancer of the throat, a diagnosis confirmed by five specialists. Vicky's anguish has not been eased by a stormy visit by their elder son, William, demanding to know the facts about his father's health and clearly eager to succeed him. Desperate that Fritz should have peace, Vicky refused permission for William to see Fritz, but he has ensured that the villa here is under siege by hostile German reporters (→ 2/1888).

Fritz: he is now in very poor health.

Abdul Karim is new favourite of queen

Balmoral, August 1887
The queen has been delighted this summer by the arrival of two young Indian servants. One in particular has attracted her attention: Abdul Karim. He is 24, a *munshi* [clerk] from Agra, with ambitions to improve his station from his present duties of waiting at table. Victoria, impressed by his studiousness since he arrived at Balmoral on 23 June, engaged an English tutor who was astonished to find that his pupil was a servant. The queen is now learning some Hindustani (→ 1890).

Victoria takes up a soft line on divorce

Windsor, 1887
In a surprising departure from the strict rules laid down by her late husband, Queen Victoria has insisted that "poor ladies" – innocent parties in divorce cases – should be allowed to share her jubilee and attend her drawing room parties. The queen has even asked that innocent foreign divorcées might be excluded from the ban. Lord Salisbury, the prime minister, has advised against the move – "on account of the risk of admitting American women of light character".

Monarchs and people cheer as the British empire celebrates queen's golden jubilee

Britain and Empire, 19 July 1887
The queen arrived at Osborne on the Isle of Wight today after a month of celebrations that would have taxed even the youngest monarch, let alone one aged 68. Britain and the empire [*see opposite*] have been celebrating her golden jubilee – the 50-year reign of this tiny woman who chose not to appear in front of her people in her crown and robes and golden state coach, preferring instead a simple black dress, white bonnet and open landau.

Never has a monarch been so revered and fêted with such sincerity. The country has forgiven and forgotten the dreary years when Victoria was a remote and unseen widow. Thousands lined the route from the palace to Westminster abbey to cheer the queen – only a small minority of Irish dissidents hurled abuse – holding up placards reading "Fifty runs not out!" and "Good sovereign – no change required". The abbey echoed to the sound of music by Handel as the queen made her way slowly up the centre aisle with the aid of a walking stick to listen to the *Te Deum* composed by her late husband.

Fifty kings, queens, princes and princesses attended Victoria's celebration lunch at the palace before Victoria – "exhausted and ready to faint" – retired to read hundreds of telegrams from all parts of the world. One gave her special delight. It read: "Empress of Hindoostan, Head of all Kings and Rulers, and King of all Kings, who is one in a hundred, is Her Majesty

Fifty years of dignity and majesty: a jubilee portrait of Queen Victoria.

Queen Victoria." (Another from India announced the opening in Sind of the Queen Victoria Jubilee Burial and Burning Ground.)

Bonfires burnt throughout Britain, fireworks blazed, and 30,000 children were given buns, milk and jubilee mugs in Hyde Park as the queen, more animated than any could remember, rode past. In Australia, too, there was a public holiday with fireworks, parades, souvenir medals, church bells and children's parties. Canadians also celebrated in style, decorating houses and businesses with flags, streamers and red-white-and-blue bunting. There have been jubilee sports contests, special church services and military displays. In Quebec, even French societies have joined huge parades.

A family occasion: the christening, on 23 November 1887, of Princess Victoria Eugénie Julia Enid, the daughter of Queen Victoria's youngest child, Beatrice, and Prince Henry of Battenberg (by RT Pritchett).

Colman's Mustard joins in to celebrate the 50 years of Victoria's reign.

From Hindustan to Hartlepool, Victoria is praised

Buying flags for the street parties.

Royal fever: a calendar from the magazine "The Queen" of December 1887.

Australians toasting the queen.

Fighting for a view: huge crowds attend the jubilee procession in London.

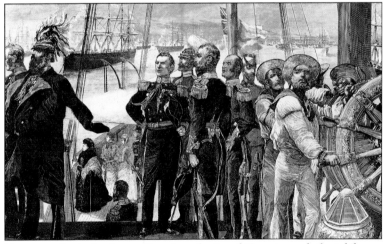

The queen (in the background) reviews the Royal Navy to mark the jubilee.

India celebrates: the queen's statue and triumphal arch in Bombay.

The jubilee drawing room: Victoria plays host to a celebration.

457

Arts and crafts give style to era of 'Victoriana'

The later years of Victoria's reign have seen a great flowering of the arts, basking in an era of unprecedented stability and confidence. Prince Albert, an enthusiastic amateur architect and designer, was an influential royal patron of the arts; since his death Britons have continued to produce magnificent buildings and beautiful if often sentimental paintings. Meanwhile the techniques of mass-production and the opening of great municipal art galleries have made the visual arts more accessible than ever before. Technology has both inspired and facilitated artistic endeavour. Improvements in transport and education have helped people to go out and find inspiration; sketching and painting, arts and crafts, are more popular than ever. Even the stations from which travellers depart, and the bridges over which their trains pass, are graceful marriages of architecture and engineering, brute iron girders made to soar like cathedrals. And it all has an eclectic aura, deriving its forms equally from classical Greece, mediaeval Europe, Renaissance Italy and the English rustic tradition, which can only be called "Victoriana".

A contrast in contemporary styles. On the left, a plain Minton vase in Parian ware with passion flowers in relief (1854). On the right, a brightly-coloured French-style Coalbrookdale vase encrusted with figures and gilt (c.1840).

A selection of objects by William Morris and William de Morgan, exponents of the Arts and Crafts movement which became important in the 1890s.

Victorian clutter: framed photographs, "busy" fabrics and decoration, heavy, dark furniture, brass and mirrors in a late-19th-century lady's bedroom.

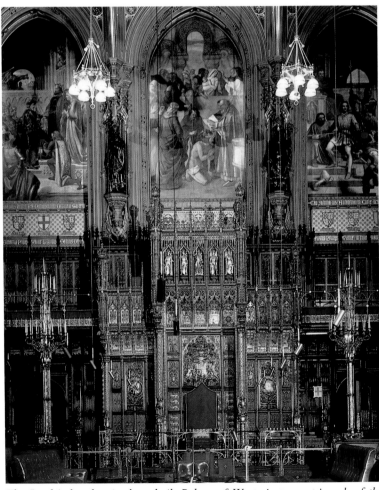

The Lords' chamber in the rebuilt Palace of Westminster, a triumph of the Gothic revival, with magnificent interiors designed by Augustus Pugin.

"Derby Day" by William Powell Frith, the artist whose narrative and historical pictures are enormously popular.

Queen Victoria enjoys sentimental animal pictures like this "Dignity and Impudence" by Landseer.

John Ruskin, the artist and foremost critic of the day, by Sir John Millais.

A portrait of Victoria's son Prince Leopold, by Sir Edwin Landseer.

Typical ornament: a Staffordshire cottage with an unusual turret.

A portrait of Prince Albert inset in a chair by Eyles of Bath (1851).

A Victorian Gothic cupboard and secretaire by William Burges, an architect whose study of mediaeval art influenced his designs for buildings, furniture, jewellery and silver.

The Victorian passion for ornament and detail is clear in this silver teaset in the French style by Hunt & Roskell, designed by Aristide Barre (1875).

Victorian kitsch: a mass-produced Christmas card, c. 1880. Pull out the top of the tree to reveal all the presents; pull the string at the bottom and they disappear back into the tree. ▷

459

Relations with Germany test patience of queen

Victoria impresses 'iron chancellor'

Berlin, 25 April 1888
The two most powerful rulers in Europe, Queen Victoria and Otto von Bismarck, came face to face today at what many believed would be an explosive meeting. British ministers argued against it, Bismarck was apprehensive; yet they parted with mutual respect. She found the German chancellor "amiable and gentle". Bismarck said: "That was a woman! One could do business with her."

Until today, relations had been difficult. The "iron chancellor" had opposed the proposed marriage of the queen's granddaughter, Victoria, to the Crown Prince of Bulgaria as he feared that this would endanger the friendship between Germany and Russia which he saw as vital to his foreign policy. Now, however, the match seems unlikely.

The queen came to Berlin to comfort her daughter Vicky whose husband, Frederick (Fritz), is close to death from cancer of the throat only weeks after succeeding to the title of German *kaiser* [emperor]. Victoria was warned that she would face angry anti-British demonstrations in Berlin. In fact, the queen was cheered whenever she appeared in public (→ 18/6).

Victoria in Berlin: she is escorted from her train by Crown Prince William.

The late German emperor, Frederick, with his wife, Victoria, and family.

Frederick dies and Vicky is maltreated

Windsor, 19 November 1888
The dowager Empress Frederick, the queen's eldest daughter and the widow of the late German emperor, today arrived at Windsor after several weeks at the centre of a vicious hate campaign by German newspapers. The queen has also been incensed by what she sees as an insult delivered by her grandson, William, the new *kaiser* [emperor]. He had declined to meet his uncle, the Prince of Wales, at the Austrian court in September.

The queen is inclined to believe those in her court who blame Bismarck for these assaults on her family's dignity. She has asked her prime minister, Lord Salisbury, to complain to the German chancellor, but Salisbury feels it wiser that she should take no notice. The campaign against Vicky, the dowager empress, follows a controversy between Dr Morell Mackenzie, the Scottish specialist who treated the late emperor, and his German doctors. Mackenzie has been accused of diagnosing the emperor's cancer too late, and the German doctors are complaining that the empress had distrusted their opinions – even though they asked her to call in the Scottish doctor (→ 2/1889).

Bertie and Alix celebrate silver wedding

Marlborough House, 10 March 1888
The Prince and Princess of Wales celebrated their silver wedding with a family dinner here tonight. With the court in mourning for Emperor William, there was no public celebration. The queen was the guest of honour – but it was Alix who stole the show. The princess decorated her hair with orange blossom in the midst of which she placed a real orange – "no bud, but the ripened fruit," she described it.

Alix's bridesmaids presented her with a silver casket. One of them said: "We all looked old ladies, but the princess was as fresh and young as she did on her wedding day."; the queen agreed that her daughter-in-law looked ... "more like a bride just married than the silver one of 25 years". Victoria was inevitably sad at being reminded of her beloved Albert.

It was a happy occasion, owing much to Alix's obvious tolerence of her husband's often public philandering with Lillie Langtry and Lady Brooke among others. The princess has devoted much of her time to family life, and Bertie – her "beloved hubby" in her own words – defers to her in domestic matters. Most people accept that Bertie is truly devoted to Alix, that he "loves her the best". Victoria's sympathies are with the princess. "Her lot is no easy one," she wrote. "But she is very fond of Bertie, though not blind" (→ 16/3).

Prince is awarded state income for life

London, 1889
A carefully staged public relations campaign has succeeded in getting the Prince of Wales an additional parliamentary grant of £36,000 a year towards the upkeep of his family. The first shots in the campaign came in an article in the *Times* entitled "The Prince of Wales's Affairs".

The article had argued that the prince is "saddled" with the cost of performing ceremonial duties for the queen during her "persistent seclusion". This drain on his resources had not been anticipated when his original allowance was agreed in 1863. Through her equerry, Sir Henry Ponsonby, the queen strongly denied the allega-tion. The prince is said to be £100,000 in debt, saved from bankruptcy only by the Rothschild family. This story was vehemently denied by the *Daily Telegraph* at the queen's behest.

Some radical MPs argued that the queen was clearly "salting away" about £200,000 a year during the years of her widowhood, while others questioned the prince's notorious gambling habits. It was not until this year that the prince wrote to the prime minister, Lord Salisbury, asking for help. A select committee was set up, and with the active support of Gladstone, the leader of the opposition, the Commons backed a capital sum of £60,000 and the new annual grant.

Irving puts on show fit for the queen

Henry Irving: an honoured actor.

Sandringham, 26 April 1889
The queen broke with precedent tonight and invited actors to dine with her after performing scenes from *The Merchant of Venice*. Henry Irving and Ellen Terry would normally have been expected to eat with the servants, but Victoria is particularly keen on theatricals and next year plans to produce *Little Toddlekins* with members of the court. At Windsor recently the queen was seen to be in fits of laughter at an item by George Grossmith entitled *How Ladies of the Future will Make Love*.

Brash young kaiser gets mixed reception

Cowes, 8 August 1889
A fierce enmity is developing between the Prince of Wales and his nephew William, the 30-year-old German *kaiser*. The prince cannot bear William's bombastic manner and calls him "the boss of Cowes". He says: "The regatta used to be my favourite relaxation; but since the emperor has been in command here, it's nothing but a nuisance. Most likely I shan't come at all next year." The kaiser has made great play of the fact that he is *emperor* of Germany whereas Bertie – he sneers – is a mere *prince*.

He had snubbed the prince in Austria last year, and his compulsive desire to win at Cowes this year has made matters worse. The queen's grandson is extremely vain: he is flamboyant, insensitive, blustering and bullying. Victoria has not forgiven him for strutting on the world's stage at a time when he should be mourning his late father; nor for his treatment of his mother, Vicky, who was virtually held a prisoner by William's soldiers in Charlottenburg castle on the day of her husband's death.

The youthful kaiser has sought to mollify the queen this week by appearing as a charming and grateful guest. He responded to the honorary military ranks bestowed on him by not only making her an honorary colonel of a German regiment but also renaming it after her. In the eyes of William, this is no token

Kaiser William: a later picture.

gesture. His maiden proclamation – made on the day of the late emperor's funeral – startled the rest of the world by its militant tone. William ignored the German people and aimed his address at the army: "We were born for each other and will cleave indissolubly to each other whether it be the will of God to send us calm or storm."

William's relationship with his mother has never been easy. Vicky, who is well-informed on international affairs, has often reproached her son for his imperialistic views. He, on the other hand, has accused her of conspiring with Victoria and trying "to make Anglophiles of her children" ($\rightarrow$ 1/1896).

Victoria discovers a new zest for travel

North Wales, September 1889
Despite her age – she is 70 this year – Victoria is showing remarkable energy and is enjoying travelling more than ever before. Earlier this year she enjoyed the spring sunshine in Biarritz and crossed the Spanish border to visit the queen regent – thus becoming the first British sovereign to set food on Spanish soil.

After a gruelling visit by her grandson, Kaiser William [*see left*], most people assumed that Victoria would hasten to the remoteness of Balmoral. Instead, the queen chose to spend four days in a house near Lake Bala in Wales lent to her by Sir Theodore Martin. A Welsh choir sang to her, and she thanked them in a few words of Welsh. The Welsh gave her such a warm welcome that she determined that her son, the Prince of Wales, should visit the principality again. His wife Alexandra has never visited Wales.

The queen is clearly enjoying life after her years of seclusion and has told her courtiers that she is praying that she may have a lot more of it. Her empire continues to prosper – she recently invited Cecil Rhodes to dine at Windsor and was much impressed by his ideas on colonisation. She is at ease with her government; 50 years as sovereign have given her a political awareness to match any that of minister.

Princess Louise marries new Duke of Fife

The royal wedding breakfast.

London, 27 July 1889
Princess Louise, the Prince and Princess of Wales's eldest daughter, was married today in the private chapel of Buckingham Palace. Her groom is the Duke of Fife, elevated from the earldom of Fife for the wedding. The duke is 18 years older than the 22-year-old bride and a close friend of the prince. As Lord Macduff, heir to the earldom, he sat in the House of Commons as a Liberal MP, but he is now more preoccupied by his landowning and business interests. The new duke is one of prince's friends of whom the queen approves, and so she bowed, albeit reluctantly, to the prince's request that his son-in-law be created a duke.

Prince Albert ("Eddy"), the eldest son of the Prince of Wales, opening the new Alexandra docks in Belfast on 22 May 1889. The prince is also due to lay the foundations for the Albert Bridge here in the city.

Victoria
1837–1901

House
of
Hanover

Sandringham, 30 November 1891. Prince George, who was recently promoted to naval captain, is seriously ill with typhoid (→ 5/1892).

Sandringham, 31 December 1891. A new wing is added to the house after fire damage earlier this year.

Sandringham, 14 January 1892. Prince Albert ("Eddy") has died of pneumonia at the age of 27.→

Germany, 14 March 1892. Louis, the Grand Duke of Hesse and the widower of Princess Alice, Victoria's second daughter, dies.

France, 30 April 1892. Victoria suggests Princess Mary ("May") of Teck, who was engaged to the late Prince Albert, as a possible wife for his brother, George (→ 6/1892).

London, May 1892. Prince George, heir to the Prince of Wales after the death of his brother, Albert, is created Duke of York (→ 30/6).

Westminster, 30 June 1892. George, the Duke of York, makes his first appearance in the House of Lords.

Britain, June 1892. The Duke of York is disappointed by the engagement of his cousin Marie, Prince Alfred's daughter, to Ferdinand, the heir to the Romanian throne (→ 6/7/93).

Westminster, June 1892. Parliament is dissolved pending a general election (→ 8/1892).

Westminster, August 1892. Lord Rosebery is persuaded by the Prince of Wales and Victoria to be foreign secretary in Gladstone's fourth administration.→

Devenport, 3 June 1893. Prince Alfred, the Duke of Edinburgh, is promoted to admiral of the fleet prior to becoming the reigning Duke of Coburg (→ 10/2/99).

Mediterranean, June 1893. Britain suffers a great naval loss when *HMS Victoria* sinks; Victoria is infuriated by Gladstone's refusal to replace the ship.

London, 31 July 1893. The Duke of York receives 1,500 new stamps for his collection as a wedding present.

Westminster, September 1893. Parliament rejects the Home Rule Bill (→ 28/2/94).

Leeds, 1893. Victoria gives the borough a royal charter so that it can be called "city".

London, 28 February 1894. Gladstone writes to the Prince of Wales to inform him of his decision to retire as prime minister (→ 3/3).

Windsor, 3 March 1894. Victoria invites Gladstone and his wife to join her for dinner (→ 4/3).

Norfolk, 4 March 1894. The Duke of York hosts his first dinner party in York Cottage, his new home on the Sandringham estate.

Germany, 19 April 1894. Victoria attends the wedding of her granddaughter, Princess Victoria Melita of Coburg, the second daughter of Prince Alfred, the Duke of Coburg, to Ernest, the Grand Duke of Hesse, the son of the queen's daughter Alice (→ 20/4).

Germany, 20 April 1894. Queen Victoria is surprised when her granddaughter, Princess Alix of Hesse, announces her engagement to Nicholas, the *czarevich* [crown prince] of Russia (→ 10/1894).

Manchester, May 1894. Victoria opens the new ship canal.

London, 30 June 1894. The Prince of Wales opens Tower Bridge.

Russia, October 1894. Princess Alix becomes Empress of Russia

when her husband, Nicholas, succeeds his father, Alexander III, as czar (→ 30/9/96).

Britain, December 1895. Henry of Battenberg, the husband of Princess Beatrice, joins the Ashanti expedition to Africa (→ 1/1896).

Britain/Denmark, 1895. Princess Maud, the youngest daughter of the Prince of Wales, announces her engagement to her cousin, Prince Charles of Denmark (→ 22/7/96).

Balmoral, June 1896. Victoria presents the small church of Crathie, dedicated to the royal family, with a three-panelled stained-glass window in commemoration of her mother, the Duchess of Kent, her daughter, Alice, the Grand Duchess of Hesse and Alice's husband, Louis.

London, 21 July 1896. A statue of Victoria is unveiled on the Victoria Embankment by her cousin, George, the Duke of Cambridge.

London, 22 July 1896. Princess Maud, the youngest daughter of the Prince and Princess of Wales, marries Prince Charles of Denmark (→ 18/11/1905).

Balmoral, 30 September 1896. The Prince of Wales, who is still forbidden any official function, is excluded by Victoria from talks with Czar Nicholas (→ 3/10).

London, 30 June 1897. The first typewritten letter is sent from the queen's offices.

Belfast, 9 September 1897. George and May, the Duke and Duchess of York, return from a successful Irish tour (→ 9/5/1901).

London, February 1898. The Prince of Wales makes the acquaintance this month of Mrs Alice Keppel and Miss Agnes Keyser (→ 23/4).

Kew, 21 May 1898. The palace gardens are opened to the public.

Germany, September 1898. Vicky, the dowager empress, seriously injures her back in a riding accident (→ 28/2/1901).

Britain, 31 December 1898. The Prince of Wales fractures his kneecap falling downstairs.

Coburg, 10 February 1899. Alfred, the Duke of Coburg, is distraught at the suicide of his only son; "Young Alfred" shot himself after his mother refused to allow him to marry a commoner (→ 30/7/1900).

Portsmouth, 19 November 1899. Kaiser William and his family visit Victoria (→ 15/1/1901).

Hampshire, 31 December 1899. The Prince of Wales has his first drive in a car.

London, 1899. Victoria lays the foundation stone for the Victoria and Albert Museum.

Southampton, 3 January 1900. The new royal yacht capsizes.

Epsom, 30 May 1900. The Prince of Wales's horse, Diamond Jubilee, wins the Derby (→ 26/5/09).

Isle of Wight, 15 January 1901. Victoria, now resident at Osborne House, orders her ambassador in Berlin to decline an honour from Kaiser William (→ 23/8).

Osborne House, 17 Jan 1901. Victoria has suffered a mild stroke; her children start to gather (→ 22/1).

Osborne House, 22 Jan 1901. Victoria dies after a 63-year reign; she is succeeded by the Prince of Wales, aged 59.→

Opposite: Victoria in reflective mood; a lantern slide of c.1897.

Queen gives a new title to the grandson whom gossips say is the prince of folly

London, 24 May 1890
The queen has decided to make her grandson Albert Victor, the son of the Prince of Wales and known to everyone as "Eddy", the Duke of Clarence and Avondale. This is perhaps an unfortunate choice of title for a young man already burdened with an unenviable reputation for folly and vice, as the only Duke of Clarence prominent in the public memory is the villain immortalised by Shakespeare for being drowned in a butt of Malmsey wine.

The problem with Eddy is that he is the kind of slow child who can be born into any family. Personally likeable, he is dyslexic, partially deaf, lacking in initiative and quite incapable of acting on his own behalf. He attended the naval college at Dartmouth as a boy but made little progress, and when he arrived at Cambridge university he could hardly read. After Cambridge he joined the army but proved incapable of either giving or carrying out even basic orders.

Eddy just wants to be left alone to enjoy himself, but because he is so easily led he has become a favourite target of gossip, with whispers linking him with every vice and folly. Among the more ridiculous are those accusing him of being Jack the Ripper, despite the

"Eddy": Prince Albert Victor.

fact that at the times of the killings he is known to have been elsewhere.

His slow wit notwithstanding, women seem to find him irresistible. The actress Sarah Bernhardt claimed that he was the father of her son, and after a number of reckless affairs his father has been forced to consider sending him on a long colonial tour. However, his success with women did not stop his name being linked to a scandal surrounding a homosexual brothel in London, despite there no evidence against him (→ 3/12/91).

Denied a useful role, Bertie enjoys leisure

London, 30 September 1890
As his mother will still not allow him to take any part in running the country, not even letting him see state papers officially, the Prince of Wales continues to throw himself into a life of leisure. Queen Victoria complains constantly that Bertie lives too fast a life and overdoes the going out and getting around, but she will do nothing to divert him by way of giving him reponsibility.

So many events does the prince attend that he has attracted the attention of the statistician Arnold White, who has shown that this year the prince has attended 28 race meetings, 30 theatrical performances, 43 dinner parties, banquets, balls and garden parties, but only 45 official ceremonies and 11 sittings of the House of Lords.

It is a daunting list; but as the prince's friends have been quick to point out, the idea that he has actually been enjoying himself at all these functions is quite erroneous. At many of them he is bored to death and has only attended out of duty. The fact that he managed to look happy at all is a great credit to him, they say (→ 6/1891).

A prince's diversions: Bertie bowling in the alley at Sandringham.

Abdul Karim, the queen's 'munshi', arouses jealousy at court

Balmoral, 1890
The queen's favourite Indian servant, Abdul Karim, is causing considerable alarm not only in the court but also in the government. Last year he was elevated from Victoria's servant to her *munshi*, or clerk. This already involves more than merely writing or blotting her letters; at the age of 26 he is being shown and consulted about state papers. There is concern that he is passing information to disreputable acquaintances in India, and he is certainly pressing the queen hard to make him a grant of land in Agra. The munshi claims that his father is a doctor, but there are doubts about this and his origins remain obscure. What is clear is that he is closer to Victoria than any employee since John Brown (→ 12/1894).

Queen Victoria works at her papers with her Indian servant in attendance.

Prince George is a captain of gunboat

Plymouth, 1890
Prince George has been given a commission as captain of the first-class gunboat HMS *Thrush*, after distinguishing himself in the rescue of a sister ship whose engines had failed. Arriving on board the prince found nothing in his cabin but an enormous sackful of official papers and correspondence. Never one to stand on ceremony and disliking administration, he dealt with it in his own way. He told friends: "I fished out the ship's log and one or two other things. All the rest I threw overboard. I knew it would take the admiralty three months to discover the loss and I didn't expect the *Thrush* to have a long commission" (→ 30/11/91).

Prince of Wales hit by fresh scandals

Bertie has been linked to a scandal involving an illegal game of baccarat.

Gambling prince is questioned in court

London, 9 June 1891

The Prince of Wales has found himself in the witness box again, this time to give evidence in what has become known as the "baccarat trial". An action for slander was brought by Lt-Col Sir William Gordon-Cumming, a friend of the prince for 20 years, who had been accused of cheating at cards while playing with the prince and others on two nights last September.

The moral indignation generated by this tale of scandal in high places has been added to by the fact that baccarat is illegal and the disclosure that the prince is so fond of the game that he carries his own betting counters, marked with his crest on one side and amounts of five shillings to ten pounds on the other.

The case arose after two evenings at Tranby Croft, a mansion near Hull owned by Arthur Wilson, a successful shipping magnate. Sir William was accused by five of the houseparty of cheating. He utterly denied it and asked to see the prince, but faced with social ruin he signed a paper, counter-signed by the prince and all present, agreeing never to play cards again in return for silence. But a secret known to so many was bound leaked out, and when it became common gossip Sir William issued a writ for slander against his five original accusers, with the prince to be a witness. The solicitor-general, Sir Edward

Clarke, was retained by Sir William, which led the Prince of Wales to think that he would not be asked "disagreeable questions". He could not have been more wrong.

The prince had not himself seen or accused anyone of cheating, but Sir Edward suggested that Sir William had "sacrificed himself to protect a tottering throne" and was being victimised to save the honour of a prince who habitually indulges in illegal gambling. The prince's agony ended today with the jury rejecting Sir William's case; he is ruined and the prince badly tarnished by what the queen called this "fearful trial".

Sir William Gordon-Cumming gives evidence in the baccarat court case.

Marital row ends in 'blackmail' charge

London, 24 December 1891

The Prince of Wales has found himself drawn into a another social scandal. This time it began with a short, but volatile, affair between two of his friends, Lord Charles Beresford and Frances, Lady Brooke. Beresford then became reconciled with his wife, prompting Lady Brooke to write a furious letter to her former lover. He was away from home and had authorised his wife to open his post. Lady Brooke, regretting her intemperate letter, sought help from the Prince of Wales with whom she had by then become a great favourite.

Lady Charles: "blameless wife".

When the prince failed to get the letter destroyed, he barred Lady Charles from court functions. She complained that the prince had taken sides against a "blameless wife", and Beresford threatened to reveal to the press details of the prince's private life. He also wrote to Lord Salisbury, the prime minister, who was reluctantly drawn into talks with Beresford, the prince and the queen to try to avert publicity. Today a deal was done: the prince is still furious over what he sees as "blackmail", but he apologised to Beresford, saying that it was never his intention "to wound the feelings" of Lady Charles.

Danish prince loses an eye after being shot by royal duke

Sandringham, 1892

Prince Christian of Schleswig-Holstein has recovered well after being accidentally shot in the eye by the Duke of Connaught while out shooting pheasant. Shooting has become popular among the royal family, thanks largely to the Duke of York, who has become one of the best shots in the country and is always eager to shoot over his own land, or accept an invitation to shoot over anyone else's.

Unfortunately, not all members of the royal family share his skill, as the Duke of Connaught has amply demonstrated by potting Prince Christian, whose eye had to be removed under choroform. The prince is now amassing a collection of glass eyes for use on various occasions, his favourite being a bloodshot one to wear when he has a cold. In retrospect, it is clear that he is lucky to be alive (→ 6/10/1911).

Duke of Clarence to wed Princess May

Luton Hoo, 3 December 1891

The Duke of Clarence, the eldest son of the Prince of Wales, has become engaged to Princess Mary ("May") of Teck, the daughter of the queen's first cousin Princess Mary Adelaide, the sister of the Duke of Cambridge. The match has been in the offing for some time, and the 27-year-old duke finally proposed today.

The news will come as a relief to the queen and other members of the royal family, who have been concerned about some of the scrapes that "Eddy", as he is generally known, has become involved in, not least his unfortunate habit of selecting completely unsuitable women as prospective marriage partners.

Last year he became secretly engaged to the Catholic Princess Hélène, the daughter of the Orleanist claimant to the throne of France, but her father refused her permission to change her religion. Princess May has no such drawbacks and has been approved by the queen (→ 14/1/92).

At last, queen lets prince see papers

London, 1892

At long last the queen has decided to allow the Prince of Wales access to state papers. This is something that he has been asking for over many years but which has always been officially denied to him. The queen has finally accepted that, at the age of 50, it is difficult for him to prepare himself for the throne if he is denied the opportunity to know what a monarch is supposed to do.

Although he has occasionally received edited reports of cabinet meetings from the queen, these have arrived only irregularly and not at all when the queen does not wish it. But now the foreign secretary, Lord Rosebery, has sent him a golden key. It is the same key that was made for his father Prince Albert, the Prince Consort, to open the dispatch boxes which he received from the foreign office.

The prime minister, Mr Gladstone, has thought for some time that Queen Victoria ought to abdicate and the Prince of Wales take her place, but he has never dared to tell her so. Not that it would make much difference who suggested it, as the queen has no intention of going; but from now on Bertie will at least be abreast of government thinking (→ 23/4/98).

Concerned prince heads commission

London, 1893

The Prince of Wales has been working hard on a royal commission into the plight of the aged poor, set up to examine the problems of those who become destitute in old age. The commission is controversial because the issue is between those who want pensions to be provided by the state, either with or without contributions from individuals, and those who think people should make their own arrangements. The commission has some radical members, but all of them have been impressed by the prince's hard work, his devotion to the task, his grasp of a complicated subject and his ability to ask searching questions (→ 3/1895).

Prince's eldest child dies of pneumonia

The late Prince Eddy on the bed in which he died at Sandringham.

Sandringham, 14 January 1892

The Duke of Clarence, the eldest child of the Prince of Wales, has died suddenly of pneumonia. His death is a terrible family tragedy, coming as it does so unexpectedly and only weeks after he had announced his engagement to Princess May of Teck.

The couple were due to marry on 17 February, and his fiancée had come to Sandringham to be with him when he celebrated his 28th birthday last week. There was an influenza epidemic raging just after Christmas, and Princess Victoria was among those who had already been ill. "Eddy", as the duke was generally known, felt unwell and took to his bed, but on his birthday, 8 January, he managed to come downstairs to receive his presents. He quickly returned to bed, the fever quickly turned to pneumonia, and the doctors abandoned hope. Today – the same day of the month as the Prince Consort died – the duke passed away (→ 5/1892).

Duke weds his late brother's fiancée

St James's Palace, 6 July 1893

Princess Mary ("May") of Teck married Prince George, the Duke of York, here today. The princess had been engaged to his brother "Eddy", the Duke of Clarence, who died of pneumonia at Sandringham last year. After an uncertain beginning their courtship blossomed, and the duke proposed on 3 May this year. The bride wore a white silk dress with a train of silver and white brocade, while the Duke of York wore his naval captain's uniform (→ 26/6/94).

The bride: Princess Mary of Teck.

Queen blocks royal critic from a cabinet post on moral grounds

Labouchère: banned by the queen.

Windsor, August 1892

For the third time in 12 years the queen has had to swallow her personal dislike and send for William Ewart Gladstone to form a government. It will be the Liberal leader's fourth administration. But while the queen cannot avoid sending for Gladstone, she has blocked his plan to include her old enemy Henry Labouchère in the government. Labouchère is a radical MP and the owner of a newspaper called *Truth*, which is disliked in court circles for its constant attacks on royalty.

The queen has told Gladstone that she will refuse to have Labouchère in the government except on two conditions. The first is that he severs all connections with *Truth*, and the second that he occupies a non-cabinet post where she does not have to meet him. The court knows that Labouchère makes so much money from *Truth* that he can scarcely afford to leave it, but the queen has made the second stipulation on moral grounds; Labouchère had lived with his wife before marriage, and Victoria said that she could not be received at court.

The queen's action has raised the delicate constitutional issue of how far her powers run. In particular, does the sovereign have the right to stop a prime minister appointing anyone he wishes to have to his government, once she has appointed him prime minister? It appears that she probably does have the right, but rather than put the issue to the test Gladstone has decided not to bring Labouchère into his government after all (→ 9/1893).

Court officials question munshi's status

Windsor, December 1894

A battle has developed in the court around the queen's Indian servant Abdul Karim. He had begun royal service in 1887 waiting at tables; two years later he was promoted to be a clerk with the title *munshi*; now Victoria has made him her Indian secretary with an office, clerks and the enhanced title of *hafiz*. All photographs of him waiting at table are to be destroyed. His elevation has aroused jealousy among other court officials, who have obtained evidence from India that he has low social origins. They say that his father is not a doctor, as claimed, but the queen does not believe this (→ 1897).

Abdul Karim waiting on the queen.

Gladstone quits, to the relief of queen

Windsor, 4 March 1894

To the queen's great relief William Gladstone has resigned, but the resignation came so suddenly that she did not at first realise what was happening. He left her presence without being asked for advice on his successor or being offered a word of thanks. Only when she read his formal letter did she reply with a reference to his "arduous labours". Her letter said that she would not offer him a peerage, as she knew he would not accept one. He has been prime minister four times and is 84 (→ 28/5/98).

Princely pleasures: the Prince of Wales, still largely denied a fulfilling public role by his mother, keeps himself busy in other ways. Here he is seen enjoying the bracing sea air on the royal yacht.

Crisis as Rosebery challenges Lords

Westminster, 1894

After watching bill after bill of his Liberal Party pass through the House of Commons only to be sabotaged by the House of Lords, the prime minister, Lord Rosebery, has alarmed the queen by questioning the future of the Lords. The Conservatives have a built-in majority in the upper house, and the prime minister has warned the queen that he will have to propose measures either to abolish their lordships' house or to reform it so radically that its right of veto will be taken away for ever.

Labour MP attacks new royal prince

Westminster, July 1894

Keir Hardie, the first Independent Labour Party MP, has caused a storm in the House of Commons. During a motion to congratulate Queen Victoria on the birth of her first great-grandson [*see right*] a direct heir to the throne, he told the house: "From his childhood onward this boy will be surrounded by sycophants and flatterers by the score and will be taught to believe himself as of a superior creation." He went on to warn of royal mistresses of the future and prophesied: "The country will be called upon to pay the bill."

The birth of a son to the Duke of York makes three direct heirs to the throne

Four generations of royalty: Victoria, Bertie, George and the new prince.

London, 26 June 1894

The birth today of a son to the Duke and Duchess of York has brought about an event never before known in British history. The child is Queen Victoria's first great-grandchild, and his birth means that there are now three heirs apparent in direct line to the throne, plus an already reigning monarch in Queen Victoria. During the last three centuries the next occupant of the throne has often not been known for long periods of a reign, or only become obvious towards the end of a reign thanks to a series of births and deaths, as happened to Victoria herself.

The succession has often been so uncertain that when the Prince of Wales was born at Buckingham Palace on 9 November 1841 he was the first heir apparent to be born for 101 years. His eldest son Prince Albert ("Eddy"), the Duke of Clarence, was the next in line, but he died at Sandringham on 14 January 1892, and now his younger brother George, the Duke of York, stands in line for the throne.

The birth today of a son to the duke means that there are now three kings in waiting, and the succession is clear for the next three reigns for the first time. It also serves to underline the enormous spread of Queen Victoria's family, not just throughout Britain, but throughout Europe. The queen's children and grandchildren are now heirs to, consorts of, or actually sitting on, almost every throne in Europe, and the royal family is now truly international (→ 14/12/95).

Queen asks Tories to form government

London, 22 June 1895
Lord Rosebery and his Liberal government have resigned, and the queen has sent for Lord Salisbury and the Conservatives to return to power. The government was defeated in the House of Commons, ostensibly over the question of the supply of cordite to the army but in fact because the Liberal Party is split on fundamental questions. These divisions make the Tories favourites to win the general election to be held next month.

The queen is not displeased. She remains a staunch Conservative, although she does not feel for Lord Salisbury the same affection that she felt for Disraeli, and she greatly preferred Lord Rosebery to Gladstone. She believed that Rosebery was a moderating influence on Gladstone, whom she suspected of the worst radicalism.

Lord Rosebery's brief government was not a success, however. Gladstone retired in March 1894 after defeats in cabinet over the power of the Lords and naval expenditure. The queen had chosen Rosebery as Gladstone's successor, disregarding the claims of Sir William Harcourt, the Liberal leader

A caricature of Lord Rosebery.

in the House of Commons. But the Rosebery government was fatally crippled by the inability of the prime minister in the upper house to cooperate with Harcourt in the lower. The administration was therefore weak and divided.

The Tories, on the other hand, are united and confident, with a clear political programme, and in Lord Salisbury they have a hugely experienced leader who was prime minister between 1886 and 1892.

Queen holidays on the French Riviera

Cannes, France, 1895
The queen now spends part of every spring in the south of France. She has stayed in Grasse, the scent capital in the Alps, and at Hyères near Toulon; this year she is in Cannes. She travels under the transparent incognito of Countess of Balmoral, but the president of France and local dignitaries all pay their respects, and when she arrived here the whole town turned out to cheer and four regiments of troops were required to manage the crowd.

Victoria has her own royal train for use on the continent and travels with a full complement of maids, footmen, equerries, ladies-in-waiting, daughters and even some of her favourite furniture. Her presence on the Riviera has lured other royalty here, including the emperor of Austria-Hungary, the dowager czarina of Russia and many of the queen's own family.

Prince sits on fence in pension dispute

London, March 1895
The Prince of Wales has declined to take sides in an argument over state pensions for old people which has split a royal commission of which he has been an active member. The prince accepted Gladstone's invitation to join the commission into the problems of the aged poor in December 1892. He attended 35 of the 48 meetings held by the commission, and one of its radical members said: "When his turn came, he asked very good questions; he really had a very considerable grasp of the subjects he dealt with."

The commission was divided between those who recommended a system of state old age pensions and those who wished to continue the present private system. The prince was eager to ease suffering but was worried by "socialist" solutions. He therefore said that he had to maintain political neutrality.

Ministers reject duke as army supremo

London, 21 November 1895
The Duke of Cambridge has been ejected from his position as commander-in-chief of the army. His successor will be General Lord Wolseley. The queen had hoped that her son, the Duke of Connaught, might win the post, but the former prime minister, Lord Rosebery, and the war secretary, Henry Campbell-Bannerman, insisted on Wolseley; the new prime minister, Lord Salisbury, confirmed his predecessor's decision, and today an order in council proclaimed Wolseley as the principal military adviser.

The Duke of Cambridge is the queen's cousin; his father was George III's youngest son. He has been commander-in-chief for 39 years, is exceedingly conservative, and has opposed all reforms in the army. When Gladstone formed his fourth ministry in 1892 and appointed Campbell-Bannerman, conflict was inevitable. The duke opposed the abolition of the purchase of commissions, but the government insisted on the reform.

Lord Wolseley distinguished himself in the Crimea and the Indian Mutiny, and has commanded during the Ashanti wars and in the conquest of Egypt. His new posts as C-in-C and supreme military adviser show his prowess on the Whitehall front, but they may pose clashes of interest in the future.

Prince Albert is second son for the Yorks

The young princes: the baby Albert, with his elder brother David.

Sandringham, 14 December 1895
The Duchess of York has given birth to a second son, Albert Frederick Arthur George. It is the anniversary of the Prince Consort's death, and the queen, the child's great-grandmother, wrote: "This terrible anniversary returned for the 34th time. When I went to my dressing-room I found telegrams saying that dear May had been safely delivered of a son at three this morning. Georgie's first feeling was of regret that this dear child should be born on such a sad day.

I have a feeling it may be a blessing for the dear little boy, and may be looked upon as a gift from God!"

The prince is fourth in line to the throne after his elder brother, Edward, known as David, who is 18 months old. The queen wanted the first son to be christened Albert, so that eventually he might reign as Albert II (she expects that the Prince of Wales will be Albert I). The Yorks insisted on Edward, however, after the late Duke of Clarence. Christening their second son Albert may mollify Victoria.

Kaiser angers the queen

Windsor, January 1896
The royal family, like the public, are deeply incensed by Kaiser William, the queen's grandson. His telegram to President Kruger of the Transvaal, congratulating him on the defeat of a raid on Johannesburg led by a British administrator, Dr Jameson, is seen as a deliberate snub to Britain. The Jameson raiders were captured or killed by the Boers earlier this month.

The *kaiser* [emperor] professes affection for Britain, which he visits each year, but is now accused of hypocrisy. The Prince of Wales, who dislikes his nephew, wanted the queen to reprove him sternly. Victoria, more diplomatic, said that "it would not do to snub" the kaiser, but wrote to him: "As your grandmother to whom you have always shown so much affection, I feel I cannot refrain from express-

The defeated Jameson raiders.

ing my deep regret at the telegram you sent President Kruger. It is considered very unfriendly towards this country and has, I am grieved to say, made a very painful impression here" (→ 19/11/99).

African wars claim life of Prince Henry

Windsor, January 1896
Terrible news has reached the queen. Her son-in-law, Prince Henry of Battenberg, has died of fever in the Ashanti wars. He had served the queen as aide-de-camp during the ten years since his marriage to her youngest daughter, Beatrice. He volunteered for the expedition, in which the Ashanti kingdom behind the Gold Coast has been annexed, partly because he

was bored with court life. There he caught malaria and died. One of his brothers is the former prince of Bulgaria; another, Louis, is a British naval officer and married to one of Victoria's granddaughters. Beatrice has been the queen's closest companion for many years. The queen wrote: "A terrible blow has fallen on us all, especially on my poor darling Beatrice. What will become of my poor child?"

Victoria's long reign breaks all records

London, 23 September 1896
Queen Victoria has been on the throne longer than any of the monarchs of England or Scotland before her. Today she passed the record set by her grandfather, George III, who reigned for 59 years and 96 days. The next longest in England was Edward III – over 50 years – with James VI ruling Scotland for over 57 years, 22 of which also saw him king of England.

Furthermore, George III in his dotage was blind, mentally ill and incapable of governing. The queen, who is 77, is at the height of her popularity in Britain and throughout her empire. She has received congratulations from all over the country but has asked that no celebration be held until her diamond jubilee next year (→ 22/7/97).

The Royal Victorian Order.

Czar rebuffs queen's political overtures

Balmoral, 3 October, 1896
Czar Nicholas II and Czarina Alexandra have left Scotland after their first visit to Britain. The arrival of the Russians was marked by bonfires on surrounding hills and the ringing of church bells. Politically the visit failed to achieve its goals, but it did cement family ties. The czarina is the queen's granddaughter, and she proudly showed her jewels to Victoria. They were "all her own property", she said. The czar's daughter, Olga, played with David, as Prince

Edward, the two-year-old son of the Duke of York, is now known. However, Nicholas was less enthusiastic than his British relatives about being dragged up mountains by the Duke of York, looking for stags.

The queen tried personal diplomacy with the czar, discussing Afghanistan and the future of the Ottoman Empire. She also asked Nicholas to use his influence in France to lessen anti-British feeling there, but nevertheless he remained noncommittal (→ 4/6/1908).

Prince of Wales scores his first Derby victory in 'sport of kings'

Epsom, Surrey, 3 June 1896
The Prince of Wales won the Derby with Persimmon today, and everyone at the track threw their hats in the air, even policemen who threw their helmets and gentlemen who threw their grey toppers. Everybody, except the queen and the strict nonconformists who disapprove of any sport associated with gambling, is delighted. The prince has long been one of Britain's leading horse-breeders and most enthusiastic racegoers, but until today he had never won any of racing's classics. He currently has 13 horses in training and maintains his sporting image by racing yachts and shooting (→ 30/5/1900).

A memorable victory: the Prince of Wales with Persimmon after the race.

Courtiers grumble about the munshi

Windsor, 1897
Senior court officials have protested at the queen's proposal to take Abdul Karim, her Indian *munshi*, and his friend, Rafiuddin Ahmed, with her to Nice. Some refuse to sit down with the Indians, calling Karim a fraud and Ahmed a spy. Victoria has replied angrily that her courtiers are racist and insolent, but she has agreed to leave Ahmed behind. Abdul Karim has replaced the late John Brown as her confidential servant, and she has suggested that Ahmed be employed as a diplomat. So far, the government has resisted.

Wave of popular affection marks diamond jubilee

Sixty glorious years: Queen Victoria arriving at St Paul's cathedral as part of the celebrations to mark the diamond jubilee of her reign.

London, 22 June 1897

The sun blazed upon London today as the queen celebrated her diamond jubilee. It was a magnificent pageant extolling the empire in all its diversity as well as the queen-empress herself. The procession took her past St Paul's cathedral, where a short service of thanksgiving was held, across London Bridge and through the working-class districts south of the Thames. Her poorer subjects there welcomed her with even greater enthusiasm than did the people who crowded Westminster and the City of London.

This was a British celebration: there were none of the emperors, kings and princes who came to London for the golden jubilee. There were only Victoria's children and a great gathering of representatives of every corner of the empire, where there were celebrations to rival those of the "mother country" with pageants, parades, church services, fireworks and children's parties. There have even been jubilee price cuts in Canada for many goods. The idea of celebrating the empire was suggested by Joseph Chamberlain, the colonial secretary.

Eleven colonial prime ministers are attending the jubilee and will hold a conference on imperial matters. In the procession were princes from India, headhunters from Borneo, troopers from Australia and trappers from Canada. Before leaving the palace, the queen sent a telegram across the empire: "From my heart I thank my beloved people. May God bless them!"

The empire has greatly expanded during the reign and is now at its zenith. The British people have become cheerfully imperialistic. The United States and Germany may challenge British industrial supremacy, but the empire is the greatest in history and a source of unabashed national pride. The queen is the symbol of nation and empire, loved and revered by all her multitude of subjects. Abroad, she is seen as Britannia personified, the grandmother of Europe. She has given her name to an age not just in Britain but in America and Europe too.

The long, dark years of Victoria's seclusion in Windsor, in miserable widowhood, made her deeply unpopular. Since then she has blossomed in public affection. Today she wrote: "A never to be forgotten day. No one ever, I believe, has met with such an ovation as was given me, passing through those six miles of streets. The crowds were quite indescribable, and their enthusiasm truly marvellous and deeply touching. The cheering was quite deafening, and every face seemed to be filled with real joy." William Gladstone, who met her in Nice this spring and was permitted to shake her hand for the first time, considers that this would be the moment for her to abdicate. She has no intention of doing anything of the sort. Perhaps he feels that now that he has retired, so should she. He is the last survivor of political figures of previous reigns and can himself measure the immense changes that have marked the Victorian age.

There are now electricity, motor cars, machine guns and socialism; railways and steamships girdle the earth; the sources of the Nile and the Niger have been discovered; both Germany and Italy are now united; France has endured three revolutions; the United States have reached the Pacific; Africa has been partitioned, and all India has been brought under British control. The world has seen more changes during this reign than in any other.

In Britain, the queen has provided stability through 60 revolutionary years. Above all, the monarchy – which was unsettled and unpopular when she ascended the throne – is now, thanks to her, a national institution.

'There have been more changes in the Victorian reign than in any in history'

Victoria is hailed as mother of far-flung empire

Above: the royal family at the diamond jubilee with a key shown left. 1: Duke of Fife. 2: Prince Christian of Schleswig-Holstein. 3: Princess Helena of Schleswig-Holstein. 4: Duchess of Connaught. 5: Princess Margaret of Connaught. 6: Duke of Connaught. 7: Princess Victoria of Wales. 8: Duchess of York. 9: Duke of York. 10: Empress Frederick. 11: Marquis of Lorne. 12: Princess Louise, Marchioness of Lorne. 13: Prince of Wales. 14: Maud, Princess of Denmark. 15: Prince Charles of Denmark. 16: Duchess of Coburg. 17: Duke of Coburg. 18: Duchess of Albany. 19: Prince Christian Victor of Schleswig-Holstein. 20: Lady Maud Duff. 21: Duchess of Fife. 22: Lady Alexandra Duff. 23: Princess Patricia of Connaught. 24: Prince Arthur of Connaught. 25: Princess of Wales. 26: Prince Edward of York. 27: Queen Victoria. 28: Prince Leopold. 29: Prince Alexander. 30: Princess Beatrice. 31: Prince Maurice. 32: Princess Victoria Eugénie: 33: Duke of Albany. 34: Princess Alice of Albany. 35: Princess Christian Victor of Schleswig-Holstein.

A grand parade to honour the queen: part of the jubilee celebrations.

An adored queen: a later view of Victoria making a public appearance.

471

Prince of Wales takes charge of privy council, but keeps his eye for the ladies

London, 23 April 1898
At the age of 56, when many of his European relations have already been ruling their own kingdoms for decades, Edward, the Prince of Wales, has finally been given a fleeting glimpse of real responsibility. He presided at a ten-minute meeting of the privy council called urgently to-day to sign a British declaration of neutrality in the Spanish-American war.

Yet it seems unlikely that at this late stage this crumb from her majesty's table is likely to alter the habits of a man who has become used to rather richer fare. It is many years since Bertie has had to bend his knee, other than formally, to his mother's wishes. Court life may demand certain standards, but the prince has carved out a very different world in which he, not the queen, is ruler.

He remains at the heart of society life, whether it be in London, Ascot or the fashionable watering-places of Europe. He is a frequent visitor to France, speaking the language fluently and relishing the country's culture. He is also, as society has long known, a prince with an eye for the ladies. There have been many over the years whom the Princess of Wales has learnt to tolerate.

Liaisons with Lady Brooke (later the Countess of Warwick)

The prince with French friends.

and the actress Lillie Langtry have faded, with Mrs Alice Keppel, whose husband George is Lord Albemarle's heir, being the current favourite. At 29 Mrs Keppel is half his highness's age, but she has the wisdom and subtlety, not to mention the charm and beauty, of the most accomplished of women.

The prince met Alice Keppel in February this year – the same month that he met Miss Agnes Keyser, a formidable woman of 47 who used her inherited fortune to found a nursing home for officers which she runs as matron. She has begun to form a close, but platonic, friendship with the prince, offering companionship and understanding.

Frances Maynard, Lady Brooke (left) and Mrs Alice Keppel (right): past and present intimate acquaintances of the fast-living Prince of Wales.

Queen lays down rules for funeral

Windsor, January 1898
Seventy-nine on her next birthday, and ever-mindful of the possibility of her death, the queen has drawn up precise instructions for what is to happen at her funeral. These have been sent to the royal undertakers with the express instruction that everything be carried out to the letter. There is to be minimal pomp, no dead march and a complete absence of mourning black. The queen's decision follows the death of her cousin, the Duchess of Teck, who it appears left neither will nor directions for her funeral. This shocked Victoria, as did the news that the body had not been embalmed properly (→ 12/1900).

Gladstone, old foe of Victoria, is dead

Westminster, 28 May 1898
William Ewart Gladstone, four times Britain's Liberal prime minister, was buried in Westminster abbey today, close to his illustrious predecessors Peel and Disraeli. The Prince of Wales and the Duke of York were among the pallbearers. The queen, for all that she sent Mrs Gladstone a charming telegram of sympathy, is furious with her son – who also kissed the widow's hand – for paying homage to a mere subject. Victoria and Gladstone were often political foes. "The harm he did cannot easily be undone," she wrote, although she admitted he was "a good and very religious man".

African wars inspire patriotic fervour

Windsor, 16 December 1899
The queen has been dismayed by a wave of defeats for British forces this week in the war against Boer irregulars in South Africa. In what the newspapers are calling a "black week" three generals have been defeated with the loss of 2,000 men.

Victoria's anguish was intensified when her weakening eyesight caused her to read one telegram as an announcement of victory. Her emotions on hearing the truth were thus all the more painful. Yet she is nothing if not resolute. "Please understand that there is no one depressed in this house," she told one cabinet minister. "We are not interested in the possibilities of defeat; they do not exist."

War broke out in South Africa two months ago when the Boers attacked Cape Colony. The Boers want to rid themselves of English influence in the Transvaal and the Orange Free State, where they are most numerous. Britain has sent reinforcements from India to fight 50,000 Boer irregulars, who have used their numerical superiority to put Britain on the defensive. British forces are being besieged in Ladysmith, Kimberley and Mafeking.

The war was preceded by splits among politicians over whether negotiations could solve the dispute, but since the fighting began the country has been plunged into a fit of unashamed patriotism. The

Victoria is told the latest war news.

queen shares the imperialistic fervour; while no warmonger, she appreciates just how vital is her role as the nation's figurehead.

For the first few weeks, in common with her subjects, her majesty was busy wishing Godspeed to her soldiers, and "with quite a lump in my throat I thought of how these fine men might not return". She has attempted to use her influence by urging Lord Salisbury, the prime minister, to prevent war taxation from falling most heavily on working people, and has been busy reviewing troops and directing a huge volume of voluntary work.

Assassin fires at prince

A Belgian anarchist fires at the Prince of Wales in Brussels railway station.

Brussels, 4 April 1900

The Prince of Wales escaped an assassin's bullet today when a young Belgian anarchist, a 15-year-old youth called Jean-Baptiste Sipido, apparently inflamed by his support for the Boers, fired several shots into the royal carriage as it left the station in Brussels.

Ironically, the prince was only in Belgium because, fearing an attack were he to visit Biarritz, his usual spring resort, he had decided to holiday in Denmark, his wife's native land. His journey through Brussels was merely part of the trip north. Both the prince and princess displayed exemplary courage. The assassin, who had jumped onto the footboard of the carriage, fired through the open window. One shot hit the seat between the royal couple. None of the royal party flinched, although the princess's lapdog shivered with fright.

The prince described his attacker as a poor madman and remarked that it was fortunate that anarchists were such poor shots – after all, it seems difficult to miss at so short a range. He blames Boer propaganda for the attack.

Victoria shocked by death of third child

Germany, 30 July 1900

Prince Alfred, the Duke of Coburg, died at Rosenau in Germany tonight in his sleep, a victim of cancer of the throat. His death comes only five months after his estranged son shot himself, a tragedy that surely accelerated the decline of his own health. The duke, who was 55, was Queen Victoria's fourth child.

His death means that the queen, now 81, has lost three of her children and three sons-in-law. As she has written in her journal: "It has come as such an awful shock. I pray to God to help me to be patient and have trust in Him." The news has been made even worse by its suddenness. Prince Alfred's illness was diagnosed nearly two months ago, but it was thought best to spare his ageing mother the truth. Now the shock is all the greater, and the queen is all the more desolate.

Victoria in Dublin

Dublin, 4 April 1900

Queen Victoria has arrived in the capital to begin a three-week visit. Strict security is to be observed at all times, with police cyclists in constant attendance. Despite her age, the queen's busy schedule will include visits to hospitals, schools, convents and factories, and she will review 52,000 children in Phoenix Park. Evening engagements include dinner with Cardinal Logue and other clerics (→ 12/1900).

Weakening queen succumbs to illness

Osborne, December 1900

The queen, whose health has been showing increasing signs of strain over the last year, now appears to be seriously ill. A woman whose apparent refusal to acknowledge the effect of any sickness has only embellished her image as the very cornerstone of the empire she rules is at last weakening.

Not that this should come as any great surprise. In the first place the queen is 81 and simply cannot hope to maintain the same active life that she once did. In the second, this last year has seen disasters, both private and public. The death of her son Alfred last July was brutally sudden, and, for all her public courage, the continuing tale of reverses and defeats in South Africa has seriously distressed her.

Signs of persistent weakness began more than a year ago. Her summer holiday was ruined by feelings of tiredness and indigestion that simply would not go away. So bad had her eyesight become that last Christmas, more than 20 years after they were first prescribed, she consented to wear her glasses in public.

Now, 12 months on, there is no denying that Victoria is a permanent invalid. She goes to bed, quite exhausted and then fails to sleep, despite draughts of chloral and Benger's food. When she does sleep, it is nearly morning, and she lies in a drugged doze until noon. Her sight, meanwhile, has become even worse (→ 17/1/01).

Buckingham Palace is damaged by fire

London, 7 March 1900

Buckingham Palace, a royal residence since the old Buckingham House was purchased by George III, was hit by fire today. Part of the roof was damaged by the blaze, although the main structure was not affected. Despite the fact that the new palace was not finished until 1847, ten years after she came to the throne, Queen Victoria is fond of her London house. "I have been so happy there," she wrote in 1843, on the eve of setting out for Scotland (→ 16/5/11).

Prince scoops the major races on the flat and over the fences

The Prince of Wales's horse Ambush II winning the Grand National.

Marlborough House, 1900

The "sport of kings" lived up to its name this year when, to his great delight, the Prince of Wales finally achieved a lifelong ambition: he is the country's most successful racehorse owner this season. His horse, the suitably-named Diamond Jubilee, has won five major races including three of the "classics" – the 2,000 Guineas, the Derby and the St Leger. Just for good measure another of the prince's horses, Ambush II, won this year's Grand National steeplechase. It is an unprecedented achievement, for prince or commoner.

Victoria dies and remarkable era comes to an end

A nation mourns: the queen's funeral procession leaving Osborne House.

Victoria's body is brought up the Solent from the Isle of Wight.

Isle of Wight, 22 January 1901
At four o'clock this afternoon the first bulletin was read out at the gates of Osborne House: "The queen is slowly sinking." At 6.40 the messenger loomed again through to the darkness to the anxious, waiting crowd, and said: "Her majesty the queen breathed her last at 6.30pm, surrounded by her children and grandchildren." And a pack of pressmen yelling "Queen dead!" raced to be first to the telephones.

The 81-year-old queen had been suffering from insomnia and loss of appetite since October, and by the beginning of this year she was starting to feel the strain. "Another year begun and I am feeling so weak and unwell that I enter upon it sadly," she wrote in her journal; a fortnight later she was too weak to make any more entries. By now her problem was not lack of sleep but inability to stay awake.

On 17 January she had a minor stroke; her sons were alerted and rushed to her bedside. All her daughters except Vicky (who is too ill to travel) were already there, and as soon as Kaiser William heard the news in Berlin he headed for Osborne House, heedless of the Duke of Connaught's hints that he might not be entirely welcome. In the event, the dying queen thought that he was his father, Fritz, and his dignified sorrow earned the respect of his relatives so that he took his place with them for the final 150 minutes of the queen's life.

Victoria died in the bosom of her family, surrounded by her children and grandchildren. Her last conscious act was to hold out her arms to the Prince of Wales and whisper his name, "Bertie", at which the prince burst into tears and had to leave the room to recover his composure. The deeply religious tenor of her life persisted to the end, with Randall Davidson, the bishop of Winchester, leading prayers and hymn-singing. As she faded away, the children started to call out their names – Louise, Arthur, Helena, Beatrice, Bertie; but at the end their voices fell silent as an expression of calm came over her face. At last, 40 years after losing him, she was to join her beloved Albert.

And so the era to which Victoria gave her name has come to an end. She graced the throne for nearly 64 years of great change, queen for so long that it is hard to imagine what life will be like without her (→ 3/2).

Politicians prepare to mourn the queen

London, 22 January 1901
As the news of Queen Victoria's death reaches the corridors of Westminster, via the newfangled telephone, there can be few who would gainsay the evaluation of Otto von Bismarck, the German chancellor: "That was a woman!" While her constitutional power was diminished by a series of reform bills, her personal influence remained strong until the very end. Gladstone remarked in 1883 that the queen was "enough to kill any man", while Lord Salisbury is preparing a speech in which he will note her amazing ability to know what the people of Britain wanted (→ 23/1).

Londoners learn the tragic news.

Dominions lament the passing of a queen whom they never saw

Britain and Empire, 23 Jan 1901
Black-bordered newspapers today carry the details of Queen Victoria's passing not only in Britain but also around the globe as the news reaches the furthest-flung parts of the world's largest empire. At home sombre citizens queued to buy special editions of newspapers which chronicle the reign of the only monarch whom almost anyone can remember. Since 1837, when she became queen, the British Empire had changed out of recognition [*see opposite*], so it was fitting that the dominions and colonies should reflect the sense of loss.

In Australia, all public meetings, sporting and social events have been cancelled until after the funeral. A forest of flags fly at half-mast, windows are shuttered, black crêpe drapes many buildings, businesses are closed, guns have fired tributes and church bells have tolled to summon people to special services. There is already talk of a national monument to the late queen, to be erected in Melbourne.

Canada, too, mirrors the gloom. In Ottawa the cabinet officially conveyed the nation's "universal sorrow", and everywhere buildings are draped in black and all public and commercial business has shut down. In nine cities, 101-gun salutes were fired, and everywhere church bells have tolled the sad tidings. The queen is dead, they say; but long live the king!

Nation turned into an empire is her great legacy

Colonial links and family ties abound

The World, 22 January 1901

Victoria's unprecedented influence on the world stage means that her death will have wider reverberations than that of any other monarch. For not only have her subjects created an wealthy trading empire that spans every continent, but her children have married into no fewer than eight of Europe's royal families. The result is that the death of the "mother of Empire" and "grandmother of Europe" is truly a world event.

She has ruled over an era of tremendous change. When she came to the throne in 1837, she travelled by coach on ill-constructed roads; fifty years later, her golden jubilee tours were undertaken by train. Photography, moving pictures, electric light, the motor car and the telephone have transformed people's view of the world.

Her longevity means that she has outlived two entire generations of politicians, from Melbourne and Peel to Disraeli and Gladstone. Her ministers have noted the insight into foreign affairs which her family connections have given her. Vicky is mother to Kaiser William and mother-in-law to Constantine of the Hellenes; Bertie's daughter Maud has married Charles of Denmark; Alice married into the German nobility to produce a daughter, Alix, whose husband is the czar of Russia. Prussia, Schleswig-Holstein, Battenberg, Waldeck and Teck are among the aristocratic German families with whom Saxe-Coburgs are interrelated.

In Victoria's reign, Britain consolidated and enlarged the empire on whose creation it had already embarked. She ended up as empress of India as well as queen of Britain, with dominions in Canada and Australia and colonies in eastern, western and southern Africa, South America and numerous islands scattered around the world. Thanks to photography, her face is well-known in all these countries. She has transformed the crown from a parochial monarchy into a symbol of international stability.

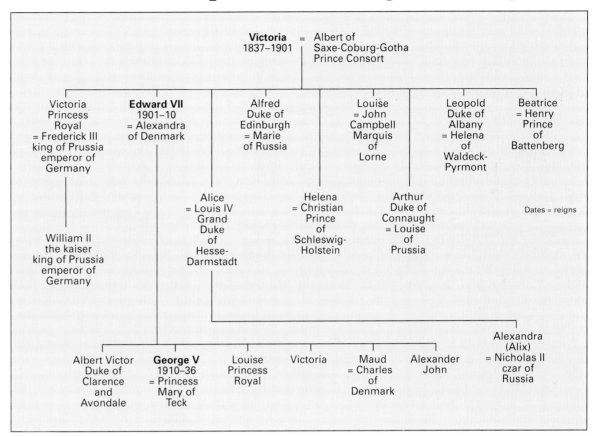

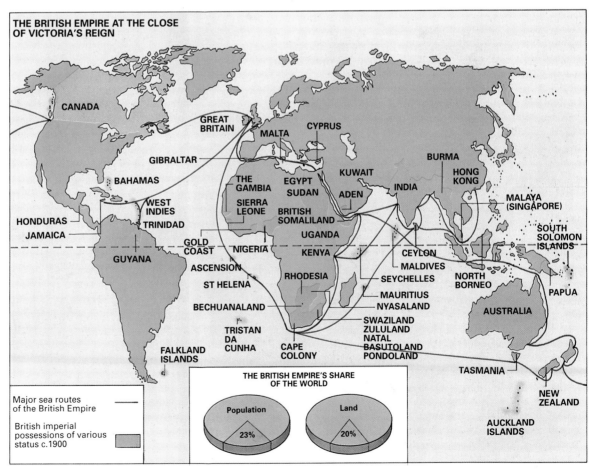

THE BRITISH EMPIRE AT THE CLOSE OF VICTORIA'S REIGN

Major sea routes of the British Empire

British imperial possessions of various status c.1900

THE BRITISH EMPIRE'S SHARE OF THE WORLD

Population 23%

Land 20%

Edward VII
1901–1910

England, 22 January 1901. Albert Edward, the Prince of Wales, accedes to the throne, aged 59.→

Canada, 3 February 1901. Memorial services are held across the country for Victoria (→4/2).

Berlin, 28 February 1901. Edward visits his elder sister, Vicky, the dowager empress, who has been ill for some time with cancer (→5/8).

Berlin, 5 August 1901. Vicky, the dowager empress, dies (→23/8).

Germany, 13 September 1901. Edward travels to Potsdam, near Berlin, for the funeral of Vicky, the dowager empress.

Ontario, 21 September 1901. The Duke and Duchess of York open the Queen Alexandra Bridge in Ottawa (→9/11).

London, 9 November 1901. The Duke of York becomes Prince of Wales.

Britain/Japan, 30 January 1902. The Anglo-Japanese treaty is signed.

Windsor, January 1902. The Prince of Wales engages Henry Hansell as a tutor for his sons, David and Albert (→2/1904).

London, 24 June 1902. Edward's coronation is delayed when he undergoes emergency surgery for appendicitis (→7/7).

Westminster, 9 August 1902. Edward VII is crowned as king.→

London, 8 November 1902. Kaiser William begins an eight-day visit in an attempt to improve Anglo-German relations (→3/1905).

Lisbon, 2 April 1903. Edward is rowed ashore for his royal visit; he has planned this European trip in complete secrecy (→29/4).

Paris, 4 May 1903. King Edward leaves after playing a key role in improving Anglo-French relations during his visit (→8/4/04).

Isle of Wight, 4 July 1903. Edward, despite disagreement with his sisters, makes Osborne House, the favourite residence of Victoria, part of the royal naval college.

Vienna, August 1903. King Edward and Queen Alexandra visit Emperor Franz Josef of Austria-Hungary (→29/4/04).

Windsor, December 1903. King Edward hosts the first state ball to be held in the castle for over 60 years (→31/12).

London, February 1904. George, the Prince of Wales, forces his second son, Albert, to wear leg splints in an effort to combat his knock-knees (→31/12/07).

Vienna, 29 April 1904. Edward is made an honorary field marshal of the Austro-Hungarian army.

London, March 1905. The Prince and Princess of Wales are forbidden to attend a German royal wedding because of Edward's row with his nephew, the *kaiser* (→1/1906).

Paris, 30 April 1905. Edward gives his support to the French president, Emile Loubet, backing the French

claims in Morocco against the German ones.

India, 20 August 1905. Lord Curzon resigns as governor-general (→9/11).

Bombay, India, 9 November 1905. The Prince and Princess of Wales arrive to begin their first tour of India (→19/3/06).

Norway, 18 November 1905. Edward's son-in-law, Prince Charles of Denmark, accepts the crown of Norway, taking the name of Haakon VII, after the abdication of King Oscar II.

Westminster, 4 December 1905. King Edward accepts the resignation of Arthur Balfour as prime minister (→7/2/06).

London, January 1906. Edward writes to Kaiser William, his nephew, in an attempt to reconcile their differences (→15/8).

London, 17 January 1907. The king and queen donate £1,000 for the Jamaican earthquake victims.

Windsor, 28 February 1907. Edward, suffering from severe bronchitis, talks of abdicating.

Malta, 13 April 1907. King Edward and Queen Alexandra arrive on a state visit.

Glasgow, 30 May 1907. Edward's new turbine yacht, the *Alexandra*, is launched.

Wimbledon, 24 June 1907. The Prince of Wales becomes president of the All England Lawn Tennis and Croquet Club.

Oxford, 15 November 1907. The *kaiser* is awarded an honorary degree (→8/1908).

Sandringham, 31 December 1907. The Prince of Wales takes his sons David and Albert on their first day's shooting (→15/1/09).

London, 14 May 1908. The Prince of Wales opens the Franco-British exhibition.

London, 11 June 1908. The Prince and Princess of Wales join 1,000 children from the east end on a trip to Epping Forest.

Amsterdam, 5 August 1908. The Cullinan diamond is cut to make a necklace for Alexandra; the four largest stones will join the regalia of the crown in the Tower of London.

Germany, August 1908. Edward meets the *kaiser* at Friedrichshof to discuss the naval arms race (→2/11).

Isle of Wight, 2 August 1909. Great pomp and ceremony greet Czar Nicholas II of Russia, the husband of Edward's niece Alix, on his arrival at the yachting centre of Cowes for a state visit (→1/8/14).

London, 4 May 1910. Reports reveal that Edward, who returned recently from a holiday in Biarritz, is seriously ill (→6/5).

London, 6 May 1910. Edward dies; his son, George, the Prince of Wales, succeeds him.→

The life and times of King Edward VII

Name: Albert Edward.
Birth: 9 November 1841.
Accession: 22 January 1901.
Coronation: 9 August 1902.
Predecessor: mother.
Height: Five feet six inches.
Marriage: Princess Alexandra of Denmark, 10 March 1863.
Children: Albert, George [later George V] Louise, Victoria, Maud, Alexander.

Favourite home: Sandringham.
Likes: society, foreign travel, horse-racing, food, cars, women.
Dislikes: loneliness, breaches of etiquette, racial prejudice.
Greatest problem: Germany.
Greatest success: consolidating the *Entente Cordiale*.
Famous saying: "Thank God, he's gone" (of Kaiser William).
Death: 6 May 1910.

Opposite: King Edward VII in 1907, by Sir Arthur Stockdale Cope.

Edward takes monarchy into new era

King will bring the crown up to date

London, 23 January 1901
This morning's *Times* editorial expresses the hopes and doubts of many people today, the first day of the reign of King Edward VII. The king, it says, has been led astray by "temptation in its most seductive forms ... we shall not pretend that there is nothing in his long career which those who respect and admire him would wish otherwise". In public life, however, he has "never failed in his duty to the throne and the nation", and this gives promise for the future.

Similar thoughts were perhaps going through the minds of members of the privy council at St James's palace this afternoon as Frederick Temple, the archbishop of Canterbury, administered the oath of sovereignty. His majesty then announced that he wished to be known as Edward VII – not Albert I as his mother had hoped. At last, at the age of 59, he was making a clean break from all the years of her domination.

The king's friends say that his warmth, strength of character and

The crowd presses close to hear King Edward's accession proclaimed.

charm will stand him in good stead. He is well-travelled, fluent in many languages and knows Europe's rulers, many of whom are related to him, well; indeed, ministers will have to be careful not to talk down to him. Edward is sure to make his views felt, although he knows that policy must be left strictly to the politicians.

In many ways, King Edward's task is to reinvent the monarchy.

Victoria's style of leadership was beginning to seem out of date. Edward's sense of fun contrasts with the gloom that settled on Victoria's court after Albert's death, and, if his soirées and house-parties of the past are any guide, the court will be much more glamorous from now on. He will certainly make more public appearances than his mother – and clad in colours other than black (→ 14/2).

Duke of York goes down under as new dominion is created

Melbourne, 9 May 1901
George, the Duke of York, today opened the first parliament of the newly-born nation of Australia. It was the climax of the duke and duchess's tour of the former colony, which became a dominion on 1 January this year. George read out a message from King Edward, who said: "My thoughts are with you on today's important ceremony. Most fervently do I wish Australia prosperity and happiness."

The Yorks set off for Australia in March on board the chartered steamship *Ophir*. Since they arrived, they have been kept busy by the long round of receiving addresses, shaking hands, laying foundation stones, opening institutions, awarding medals, attending receptions and reviewing troops.

King Edward and Queen Alexandra were reluctant to be separated from their only surviving son for so long, and so early in their reign. The cabinet, however, insisted that he should go. The monarchy is the bond that unites the empire, they explained; the task of the king is to work to strengthen that bond (→ 21/9).

The fast-living prince who is a relaxed family man at home

London, 22 January 1901
The new king may have a reputation for fast living, gambling and womanising, but at home he is an indulgent and relaxed father and a kind, loving husband. His family is unusually close and affectionate, largely as a result of his determination not to impose the same harsh discipline on his children as his father had on him. The king and queen have four children: George, the Duke of York (aged 36), Louise (34), Victoria (32) and Maud (31); their eldest son, Albert Victor, the Duke of Clarence, died of typhoid eight years ago, and another lived for only 24 hours in 1871. Edward is particularly close to George: "We ... are more like brothers than father and son," he wrote a few years ago. He enjoys spoiling his children, while leaving their upbringing to Queen Alix (→ 23/1).

A happy family: the king at Balmoral with the Duke of York's four children.

First parliament is opened by Edward

Westminster, 14 February 1901
Crowds lined the sunny but frosty streets of London this morning to see the new king and queen drive from Buckingham Palace for their first state opening of parliament. Victoria had not opened parliament in person since 1886, and Edward has seized his chance to show the public how different he is from his reclusive mother by insisting on the maximum pageantry possible. The magnificent gold state coach, mothballed since Albert's death 40 years ago, was brought out again, and the king and queen wore magnificent robes of velvet and ermine. Edward ordered the peers of the realm to arrive in their finest robes and smartest carriages as well. The result was a splendid spectacle of the new, very public monarchy (→ 28/2).

White funeral sees Victoria back at Albert's side

Windsor, 4 February 1901

The queen who had spent so much of her life in black was buried in white today. She had planned her own funeral – "to see me placed next to my dearly loved husband in the mausoleum" – to the smallest detail.

She had expressly forbidden any undertakers to be involved, so it was her grandson, the *kaiser*, who measured her tiny frame for the coffin and her sons, King Edward and Arthur, the Duke of Connaught, who placed her inside it. Dressed in white, her wedding veil covering her face, sprinkled with spring flowers and clutching her silver crucifix, the late queen lay in state at Osborne House for ten days.

On 1 February the coffin, draped in white and gold, arrived at Victoria station by special train. London, decorated in purple and white as she had wished, watched silently as eight cream-coloured horses wearing purple wreaths drew a gun-carriage bearing her remains through the streets to Paddington station, and then by rail again to Windsor.

There, a guard of sailors had to pull the gun-carriage after one of the horses shied and destroyed the harness. The long procession

Victoria's funeral cortège in Cowes.

King Edward and Kaiser William riding in the funeral procession.

wound its way up to St George's chapel as the Royal Artillery gave an 81-gun salute – one for each year of her life. A short service was held before her coffin was taken to rest in the Albert memorial chapel. For two nights the Grenadiers and the First Life Guards kept vigil over the tiny coffin, surmounted by the crown jewels. Finally, there came Victoria's last journey to the mausoleum that she had built for Albert in 1862. Her family saw her take her place at Albert's side, fulfilling the wish she had had inscribed over the door: "Farewell most beloved. Here at length I shall rest with thee, with thee in Christ I shall rise again." As the royal family left, snow started to fall. She had wanted a white funeral. Her command was truly fulfilled.

King safe as yacht is wrecked at sea

Isle of Wight, 22 May 1901

King Edward had a narrow escape from death or serious injury this afternoon when a squall damaged the racing yacht *Shamrock II*. The king was on board as a guest of Sir Thomas Lipton, the grocery magnate, who is making a challenge for the America's Cup. A vicious gust of wind caught *Shamrock II* as she performed speed trials, snapping the mast and bringing down the rigging and sails. Sir Thomas's other yacht, *Shamrock I*, last year's challenger for the cup, lost her topsail as she rushed to the rescue, but another ship sent a dinghy which transferred the royal party to the steam yacht *Erin*. Luckily, no one was hurt; but had the rescue not been prompt, Edward's reign could have been over.

Parliament backs a big rise in civil list

Westminster, 25 June 1901

Parliament today passed a bill raising the civil list – the sum granted to the king by the nation – by £85,000, to £470,000 a year. The opposition of radical MPs such as Henry Labouchère and Keir Hardie failed to make much of a dent in the Commons' vote of confidence in the new king, for the bill was carried by 370 votes to 60.

Edward's allowance as Prince of Wales having lapsed, and Victoria having left her fortune to her younger children, he was left with a mere £60,000 a year income from the Duchy of Lancaster. Coming after years of financial embarrassment, mainly because Victoria had denied him any of her money, today's grant is a great relief; the king has resolved to spend it wisely.

Royal diplomacy follows Vicky's funeral

Prussia, 23 August 1901

King Edward and his nephew, Kaiser William, met today at Wilhelmshöhe, near Homburg, for long-awaited talks to try to resolve the tension between their two countries. Their meeting came just ten days after the funeral of the *kaiser*'s mother, Edward's sister, the dowager Empress Frederick, or Vicky, as she was known in Britain.

The kaiser's aggressive insistence that Britain join the Triple Alliance of Germany, Austria-Hungary and Italy only reinforced the arguments against joining it. He spoke of "perfidious Albion" and demanded that the king prove his friendship. But the British cabinet is determined not to alienate France or Russia – the members of the opposing Dual Alliance. Today's talks achieved nothing, and Anglo-German relations remain strained (→8/11/02).

Bloated Edward: a Berlin view.

Edward crowned in glittering ritual

King lays on lavish spread for the poor

London, 7 July 1902

Nearly 500,000 poor people at 700 venues all over the capital toasted the health of King Edward last night as they tucked into a great feast laid on for them to celebrate his forthcoming coronation. The king wanted to visit many of the parties himself, but he is still laid up after an operation for appendicitis on 24 June. Instead, the Prince and Princess of Wales spent a busy evening touring the celebrations, managing to show up at over 20 parties in London's east end.

The festivities have cost the royal purse an estimated £30,000, with brewers being prominent among people who contributed to the cost.

A proud day: Edward and Alexandra enjoy the coronation procession.

Grateful Londoners toast the king.

Thousands of volunteers (including the learned counsels of the Inns of Court) were also recruited to prepare and serve the food, and two entertainers on average were booked for each banquet to make sure that things went with a swing.

The king's illness caused great anxiety and meant postponing the coronation, which was due to have taken place on 26 June, and all the eminent foreign guests who had begun to arrive in London had to pack up and go home again. Happily he seems to be recovering well, and the coronation looks set to take place some time next month (→ 9/8).

Slimmed-down sovereign is full of pomp

Westminster, 9 August 1902

Just seven weeks after lying at death's door with appendicitis, King Edward VII was crowned today amid all the splendour and majesty of the ancient coronation ritual. It was a slimmed-down sovereign – two stones lighter from the diet he was put on by his doctors – who set out from Buckingham Palace at eleven o'clock this morning with Queen Alexandra in the golden state coach for the first coronation for 64 years. Half an hour later he entered the abbey to fanfares and was greeted with cries of *"Vivat Rex Eduardus! Vivat Rex Eduardus! Vivat! Vivat! Vivat!"*.

Despite his recent illness the king looked remarkably well, although the ceremony was slightly shorten-ed to spare him too much effort. In the event the glittering congregation (which included two of the king's lady friends, Mrs Keppel and Sarah Bernhardt) was more worried about the frail, 80-year-old archbishop of Canterbury, Frederick Temple, who is nearly blind and had to conduct the ceremony using special cards.

He stumbled over his words several times and nearly dropped the crown as he carried it from the altar. In straining to lift the crown onto the king's head he held it the wrong way round, until he was put right by a discreet royal hand. He knelt and paid homage to the king – but then could not get up without the help of his monarch and three nearby bishops (→ 1/1/03).

A commemorative coloured tin to mark King Edward VII's coronation.

New Order of Merit is inaugurated on Edward's initiative

London, 23 June 1902

King Edward VII has created a new honour to reward, as the official announcement puts it, "in a special manner officers of the Navy and Army, and civilians distinguished in Arts, Sciences, and Literature". Called the "Order of Merit" (abbreviated to OM), the honour is inspired by the order *Pour le Mérite* [For Merit] set up by King Frederick the Great of Prussia and reflects the king's preference to give awards for outstanding national – rather than political – service. Among the first group of recipients are three of the commanders in the South African war, Lords Kitchener, Wolseley and Roberts, along with the scientists Lords Lister and Kelvin.

King protests over shah's knighthood

A royal guest: the shah of Persia.

Portsmouth, 31 August 1902

A visit to England by the shah of Persia this month has sparked off a row over the foreign office's promise that the shah would receive the Order of the Garter. King Edward refused to give a Christian award to a Moslem, and he only gave in when the prime minister said that Britain would be dishonoured if it was seen to break a promise, and that it was necessary to woo the shah from dependence on Russia.

Edward proclaimed emperor of India

Delhi, 1 January 1903

The Indian people officially have a new sovereign today following the proclamation of King Edward as the first emperor of India in succession to his mother, for whom the title of queen-empress was created by Disraeli in 1876. The viceroy, Lord Curzon, rode with his wife, the vicereine, in ornate splendour at the head of a glittering elephant-borne procession to the great plains near the capital, Delhi, where the grand *durbar*, as the ceremony was called, took place.

Once arrived, the viceregal pair mounted a splendid gold and white dais for the proclamation. At Lord Curzon's signal a blaze of trumpets sounded and a single horseman approached the dais to declare the enthronement of the British *Raj's* new king-emperor. The viceroy then read out a message to the people of India from Edward himself, who has taken a keen interest in Indian affairs ever since he visited the subcontinent as Prince of Wales in 1875/6. Much of his sprawling domain is currently in the grip of famine, and his message included a pledge to remit interest on British loans to affected states.

After the viceroy's speech the *Nizam* of Hyderabad, in blue frock coat and yellow turban, led a succession of 100 *maharajahs, nawabs* and other splendidly titled and attired native princes to present personal messages to their new supreme overlord (→ 20/8/05).

King meets pope on diplomatic rounds

The king on his travels: Edward is greeted at the Gare d'Orsay in Paris.

Rome, 29 April 1903

King Edward has become the first English king to visit the city of Rome since King Æthelwulf of Wessex, the father of Alfred the Great, went there over 1,000 years ago. Today he also became the first supreme head of the Church of England to meet the pope when he had a private audience with the 93-year-old Leo XIII at the Vatican.

The decision to meet the pope was entirely the king's own. The prime minister, Arthur Balfour, advised against it for fear of stirring up Protestant bigotry in Britain, and the king received a whole pile of critical letters from Protestant societies. But he refused to be swayed. As Prince of Wales he had met Pope Pius IX three times, and to snub the Vatican now would needlessly offend his Catholic subjects

and pander to what he called "narrow-minded people". The pope praised the king's tolerance of Catholics in the British Empire.

The interview came as part of Edward's current triumphant state visit to Portugal, Italy and France. Like meeting the pope, the whole tour was his own idea; he planned it himself, down to the last official handshake, and has ignored the misgivings of his ministers. In particular they are worried by his plan to visit France, his next stop, where there is some anti-British feeling left over from the Boer War. Again, the king will have none of it. He adores Paris and has always been popular there, and France's President Loubet has promised a cordial welcome. Edward's ability to win hearts seems certain, once again, to confound his critics (→ 4/5).

Edward leads royal return to Ireland

Ireland, 1 August 1903

King Edward and Queen Alexandra have today completed a highly successful nine-day royal visit during which they were cheered by huge crowds wherever they went. Dublin corporation had refused, by 40 votes to 37, to offer the king an address of welcome, but, happily, 82 loyal addresses were presented by other bodies and received enthusiastically by the king.

Edward's time in Dublin was packed with engagements. He held a levée, visited Trinity and Maynooth colleges, attended race meetings, and held a court at Dublin castle and a military review in Phoenix Park. To mark the occasion, Lord Iveagh gave the king £50,000 to be distributed among Dublin hospitals. The royal couple then left the capital for the country. They drove through Connemara and then to Kenmare, where they visited Lord Lansdowne, before moving on to Cork.

Before leaving the country, the king issued an address of thanks to the Irish people. He assured them that "his expectations had been exceeded" and that "for a country so attractive and people so gifted we cherish the warmest regard." His visit was timed to coincide with the third reading of the Irish Land Purchase Bill, and the news that it had been carried by a substantial majority is regarded as a happy omen for better relations between the two countries (→ 10/7/07).

Edward lets light into the Victorian court

Windsor, 31 December 1903

The accession of King Edward VII has breathed fresh air into the staid and dreary life of the late Victorian court. He has introduced evening courts, and this year he held the first state ball at Windsor castle for 60 years, dazzling occasions very different from the dull drawing rooms of the late queen.

Nowhere does the new regime hold sway more than at Buckingham Palace, which the king decided to make his main residence rather than Victoria's be-

loved Osborne, which he has given to the navy as a college and convalescent home. Victoria rarely lived at Buckingham Palace in her later years, and it had become almost a sepulchral monument to Prince Albert. Last year, under the king's supervision, the old-fashioned furnishings were carted off to Windsor, and the palace was extensively redecorated and refurnished in brighter styles. The refit also included a boost to the palace's notoriously small number of bathrooms and toilets.

Edward and Alexandra hold their first court at Buckingham Palace.

Triumph for King Edward the diplomat as 'Entente Cordiale' is signed with France

An end to quarrelling: a postcard published to celebrate the "Entente Cordiale".

London, 8 April 1904
King Edward is being hailed as a peacemaker following the signing this morning of a momentous pact which aims to sink centuries of rivalry and mutual mistrust between Britain and France. The *Entente Cordiale* ["Cordial Understanding"] follows months of patient diplomacy in the wake of the king's successful visit to Paris last year. The king had arrived in Paris to mutterings of "*Vivent les Boers!*", but left to shouts of "*Vive le Roi!*"

and "*Vive l'Angleterre!*". He lost no opportunity to praise France, and declared that "there are no two countries whose mutual prosperity is more dependent on each other".

The fruit of his visit is today's entente. Among other issues, it irons out a 200-year-old quarrel over fishing rights and recognises both France's interest in Morocco and Britain's in Egypt. The king's nephew, Kaiser William, with his own claims in Morocco, is following events with interest (→ 30/4/05).

King's love affair with all things French

King Edward with friends in Paris.

Paris, 8 April 1904
The politicians may have planned and settled today's Anglo-French accord in detail, but there is no doubt that King Edward himself broke the diplomatic ice after years of at best cool relations. The -*Entente Cordiale* – he invented the phrase as long ago as 1870 – crowns the king's lifelong love of France, which dates back half a century to when, as a boy, he was captivated by the glamorous court of Emperor Napoleon III.

The king, who speaks perfect French, began then a lifetime's habit of visiting France whenever he could, and Paris society grew used to the presence of the *Prince de Galles*. As well as Paris, resorts such as Cannes and Biarritz are favourite haunts, and when he is at home his French chef ensures that the enormous royal appetite for Gallic cuisine remains satisfied.

Queen Alexandra launches jobless fund

London, 20 November 1905
Following a speech last week by Arthur Balfour, the Conservative prime minister, in which he pleaded for assistance to be given to the deserving poor, a new fund for the unemployed was opened today by Queen Alexandra. In an announcement made at Buckingham Palace through the treasurer of her household, Earl de Grey, the queen appeals to "charitably disposed people in the empire" for help in "alleviating the suffering of the poor starving unemployed this winter". She has opened the fund with a personal donation of £2,000.

Although further details of how the fund will operate have not yet been made clear, the queen's spokesman today suggested that for the time being the best place for the public to send donations was the palace. The creation of the fund is a further demonstration of the deeply pious queen's active involvement

Helping the poor: Alexandra at a church sale in London's east end.

in charitable work and has been widely welcomed. In particular she has recently become interested in two religious organisations working for the poor, the Salvation Army and the Church Army.

Admiral Fisher is king's new naval aide

London, 31 December 1904
King Edward is putting his weight behind sweeping reforms of the Royal Navy following the appointment this year of the brilliant Admiral John "Jackie" Fisher as first sea lord and Edward's chief naval aide-de-camp. The tough, peppery and single-minded admiral can expect stiff opposition to his radical proposals from what he calls the "fossils and ineffectives" who run the navy. But he will find a solid

ally in the king, who is greatly impressed with his abilities and ideas.

Fisher sees Germany as the chief threat to Britain. To counter it, he believes that the navy must move some of its ships from the Mediterranean to form a new "Home Fleet". This fleet will be spearheaded by a new class of superbattleship, equipped with more numerous and more powerful guns, which will render every other ship obsolete overnight (→ 31/10/07).

Glamis Castle, in Tayside, which was inherited by Claude George Bowes-Lyon along with the earldom of Strathmore in 1904.

Prince of Wales in India

Bombay, 19 March 1906

The Prince and Princess of Wales ended their highly successful visit to India today, exactly five months after leaving England. Since the royal couple landed here in November they have covered almost 10,000 miles (16,000km), taking in places as far apart as Karachi, Delhi, Madras and Rangoon as well as the capital, Calcutta.

They were greeted at Bombay by the outgoing viceroy, the brilliant but haughty Lord Curzon, who had resigned in a row over the running of the Indian Army with its commander, Lord Kitchener. Curzon marred the start of the tour by not leaving time for his viceregal train to be thoroughly prepared for his guests, and by deliberately snubbing his successor, the Earl of Minto, who arrived shortly after the royal couple. The prince went out of his way to be courteous to the new viceroy, insisting that Lord Minto, as his father's representative, should take precedence.

Everywhere they went, in fact, George and May struck those whom they met by their shrewdness and lack of prejudice. George was unimpressed by the snobbery shown to Indians, whose leaders were regarded, he believed, "like schoolboys".

Fast cars become part of royal lifestyle

King Edward, a keen motorist, pictured in the latest model of car.

London, 1906

King Edward takes after his father, Prince Albert, in his fascination with new inventions, and none has taken his fancy more than the motor car. He made his first trip in a car in 1899, in a Daimler belonging to one of the first aristocratic fanatics, Lord Montagu of Beaulieu, and this year was thrilled when the car taking him to Brighton touched 60 miles per hour (96kph).

Before Edward came to the throne motoring was still regarded as a reckless pastime, and Queen Victoria made no secret of her disapproval of her eldest son's interest. She forbade the master of the horse to allow "those horrible machines" in her stables, and she denounced automobiles as "very shaky and disagreeable conveyances" which "smell exceedingly nasty".

Since Edward's accession, however, motoring has almost become respectable as a result of royal patronage of such events as the automobile exhibitions of 1903 and this year. The king's own cars now include a Renault and a Mercedes-Benz, readily distinguishable by their deep red colour and lack of number plates. For all his interest, though, it is unlikely that the king could even tell you what fuel the cars run on. He leaves such technical matters to his driver, Charles Stamper, the "king's motor mechanic", who looks after the royal cars.

King and kaiser seal German friendship

A family meeting: Edward with his nephew Kaiser William of Germany.

Germany, 15 August 1906

King Edward today paid a cordial visit to his nephew, Kaiser William. The royal party arrived at Frankfurt this morning and was taken by train to Kronberg, where the king was met with open arms and a kiss on both cheeks by an ebullient *kaiser*. The steel-helmeted German sovereign was dressed in the resplendent uniform of one of his recently-created regiments, but the tone of the visit was nonetheless informal, with King Edward and his party wearing civilian clothes. After lunch both monarchs travelled by motor car to the nearby spa town of Homburg.

Throughout the day the king steered clear of the controversies which have marred Anglo-German ties in the last 18 months, and his imperial host also seemed anxious to be conciliatory. Relations suffered a severe strain in March 1905 when the kaiser caused a storm by landing at Tangier in French Morocco to express his support for the local sultan's grievances against France. Britain felt bound under the *Entente Cordiale* to back the French, and for a while there was even talk of war. The king stopped the Prince of Wales going to Germany, and the kaiser likewise ordered his son not to visit Windsor.

The Tangier dispute was resolved in France's favour at an international conference at Algeciras on 6 April, and Edward has taken the lead in patching things up with his tempestuous nephew (→13/11/07).

King Edward faces up to a 'radical wave'

Westminster, 7 February 1906

The Liberal government of Sir Henry Campbell-Bannerman has won a landslide general election victory which gives the Liberals 400 seats to 157 for the Unionists (Conservatives), 83 Irish Nationalists and 30 for the new Labour Party. The election was fought on the issue of whether to keep free trade (the Liberal view) or bring back import tariffs to foster trade with the empire (the Conservative view). The Liberals said that new import tariffs would mean dearer food. The king is suspicious of the populist zeal of some Liberals and has called the election result a "radical wave". But he has also gone out of his way to cultivate Sir Henry, and he regards it as his royal duty to act as a conciliator between the new Commons and the Conservative-controlled Lords (→8/4/08).

Life on the ocean wave for Prince Edward

Osborne, May 1907
Prince Edward, the eldest son of the Prince of Wales, has entered the naval college established here at Queen Victoria's favourite home. He will be 13 next month, and so far he has been educated by a private tutor noted for humourlessness rather than intellectual qualities.

The Prince of Wales himself went to naval college; he excelled there, but he was not then expected to be heir to the throne (his elder brother subsequently died). It is something of a mystery why he should send his son, who is in the direct line of succession, to a school that will prepare him for a career he will never follow while completely neglecting subjects such as history, languages and constitutional theory which will be essential to a future king. The prince also intends to send his second son, Albert, there.

The king was subjected to a rigorous education by Prince Albert and, like Queen Victoria, he is tri-

Prince Edward: a naval education.

lingual. The Prince of Wales, however, barely understands German and is quite lost in French; he knows little of history or constitutional theory, although his private secretary, Sir Arthur Bigge, is trying to correct this (→ 31/12).

Irish visit spoilt by theft of royal jewels

Ireland, 10 July 1907
King Edward has arrived in Dublin to visit the International Exhibition, but what should have been a festive occasion has been marred by a dramatic controversy. While attending Leopardstown Races, the king was informed by the viceroy, Lord Aberdeen, of the theft of the crown jewels of the Order of St Patrick from Dublin castle. Although

the jewels had been stolen a month earlier, their loss was only discovered yesterday. It is believed that the robbery could only have been initiated by someone highly placed within the castle. The king is extremely angry and has insisted that Sir Arthur Vicars, the Ulster king-of-arms, who is responsible for the safe custody of the jewels, be suspended during a public inquiry.

Edward and Alexandra in court at the Old Bailey, which the king opened in February 1907.

Army reform plan wins royal support

London, 31 October 1907
The king has thrown himself wholeheartedly into the battle for army reform, giving every support to the proposals of Richard Haldane, the secretary for war, to form a territorial army. The Liberals are continuing the programme begun by the Conservatives and also continue to support Admiral Fisher's proposals for naval reform. The king plays a key role in both matters.

Haldane's policy is to give priority to the Royal Navy to defend the kingdom, but also to prepare an expeditionary force that could be sent to the continent in an emergency. He proposes to reorganise the Militia, the Yeomanry and the Volunteers into a semi-professional territorial army (TA) which could be expanded rapidly in the event of war. The king has summoned the lords lieutenant of England, Scotland and Wales to Buckingham Palace to urge them to support the proposed county associations that will be the nucleus of the TA.

Fisher has aroused intense opposition by his policies of scrapping obsolete warships and replacing them with large battleships known as "Dreadnoughts" and of concentrating the navy in the North Sea to face Germany. He has forced many senior officers to retire, and would never have survived the opposition without the king's constant support. Now the king is offering the same support to Haldane.

Kaiser arrives to a rapturous welcome

The king with Kaiser William (r).

London, 13 November 1907
Kaiser William has been received with all the splendour that the court can muster at Windsor castle. His relations with the king, who is his uncle, have always been strained, and his policy of challenging the Royal Navy by building battleships has provoked much animosity. So has his style of personal diplomacy: Britain has not forgotten his interventions in the Boer War and the Morocco crisis of 1905. But the king is doing his best to smooth things over. The *kaiser* arrived at Portsmouth two days ago, with a large naval escort, and proceeded to Windsor for a huge banquet in his honour last night (→ 15/11).

Incognito king plunges into diplomatic waters at summer spa

Marienbad, 5 September 1907
The king has once again spent the summer at his favourite spa in Bohemia. Here he mixes business with pleasure: today he met the Russian foreign minister, having met the French prime minister, Georges Clemenceau, on 31 August. The meeting with Baron Islovsky follows the signing six days ago of the Anglo-Russian convention and symbolises the completion of the Triple *Entente* between Britain, France and Russia.

The king describes himself as the Duke of Lancaster, to avoid an excess of protocol, but he is often visited by the Austro-Hungarian

emperor, the *kaiser* and other royalty, as well as by diplomats. The British prime minister, Sir Henry Campbell-Bannerman, is another regular visitor to Marienbad. The king's invitation to the French premier will have been much appreciated in Paris, where the *Entente Cordiale* is still in its infancy.

The king is an inveterate traveller, even more so than Queen Victoria. He regularly visits Biarritz in the spring and has been here every summer since 1903. He drinks the waters but declines to moderate his usual hearty appetite. He also enjoys the company of the many divorced or single ladies here.

Edward lunches with Georges Clemenceau at Marienbad.

New PM treks to France to see king

Asquith (r), with Lloyd George.

Biarritz, France, 8 April 1908
Herbert Asquith was received by the king here this morning and kissed hands on his appointment as prime minister. He succeeds Sir Henry Campbell-Bannerman, who is very ill and resigned a week ago. The king, as usual, is vacationing here because of his health. He suffers from bronchitis, and his doctors insist that he must be out of England during the cold weather. However, the fact that Asquith had to go to south-western France to become prime minister has caused criticism at home (→ 31/12/09).

Edward is first king to visit Russia

Reval, Russia, 9 June 1908
The king arrived here today in the royal yacht *Victoria and Albert* for a state visit to Czar Nicholas II. The visit marks the new *entente* between the two countries. Britain, France and Russia are now clearly associated (but not allied) against Germany, Austria and Italy.

Last September the British and Russian governments signed a convention settling various differences over Afghanistan, Persia and Tibet. There has been much enmity since the Crimean War, and the czar's regime is still deeply unpopular in Britain, but the government, like the king, believes that it needs

Russian support against the *kaiser*. The king is accompanied by General French and Admiral Fisher, which adds a military note to the visit. When the yacht passed through the Kiel canal she was met by the whole German navy, which performed manoeuvres to impress the British party – which duly noted the number and efficiency of German battleships.

The czarina is the king's niece and the czar is Queen Alexandra's nephew, so this is also a family gathering. Reval, also known as Tallinn, is in festive mood and has given the king and queen a rousing welcome (→ 2/8/09).

Edward on a Russian battleship.

Kaiser's belligerent interview upsets Edward – and Germany

London, 2 November 1908
The king is once again astonished at and enraged with his nephew Kaiser William. The *kaiser* has given an interview to the *Daily Telegraph* in which, while insisting that he harbours only the warmest feelings for Britain, he reveals that during the Boer War he discussed ways to "humiliate England to the dust" with France and Russia.

The interview has also annoyed the Germans by a claim that during the war he sent his grandmother, Queen Victoria, a plan of campaign that Lord Roberts then adopted.

This has infuriated the German people who were vehemently on the Boers' side. They think the kaiser's attitude akin to treachery.

"You English are mad, mad as March hares," he said. "What has come over you that you are so completely given over to suspicion quite unworthy of a great nation?" In fact the kaiser's behaviour for years past has given Britain every cause for concern. He is eccentric, vain and prone to wild swings of mood; he suffers from an inferiority complex because of his withered arm, is jealous of his uncle, King Edward,

whose charm and good-humour make him so popular a man in Europe, and yet is convinced that he is the greatest statesman of his day.

Unfortunately, Bismarck, who built the German empire, neglected to bring its ruler firmly under constitutional control. The kaiser wields a great deal of direct power in Germany, especially in military matters: it is William who has been the driving force behind the naval arms race. He wants a bigger navy than his Uncle Bertie, whatever the consequences for the peace of Europe (→ 28/2/09).

King is shocked by Portuguese killings

London, 31 March 1908
King Edward has urged ministers to send warships to Portugal in the wake of the assassination last month of King Carlos and the Portuguese Crown Prince. Edward was profoundly shocked by the killings and feared that a revolution would sweep the new king, the 19-year-old King Manuel, off the throne. The British king wrote: "We ought to have ships ready at a moment's notice ... [although] we have no desire to interfere in their normal internal affairs, unless they become of an alarming nature!" Ministers have urged caution, fearing that intervention might jeopardise both lives and British interests.

King and queen make royal occasion of the London Olympics

London, 30 July 1908
Queen Alexandra today presented a gold cup to the Italian runner Dorando Pietri, who won the hearts of Britain – but lost the winner's medal – when he collapsed near the finishing line of the marathon in the first Olympic Games to be held in Britain. He was helped to his feet and disqualified, but today won his royal consolation prize. A new stadium was built at White City in west London to stage the games, alongside a Franco-British exhibition which has also drawn large crowds. The exhibition was opened by the Prince of Wales in a downpour last May and includes exhibits of British industrial goods, an Irish village, French cuisine and colonial produce.

Dorando Pietri is presented with his prize by Queen Alexandra.

Derby win for turf-loving King Edward

"The sport of kings": King Edward has had a hat trick of Derby wins.

Epsom, Surrey, 26 May 1909
The king won the Derby here today with Minoru; it was his third victory in English racing's premier classic. Once again, people cheered and threw their hats in the air. He first won the race when he was still Prince of Wales, in 1896, with Persimmon. His second victory came in 1900, with Diamond Jubilee.

Queen Victoria, who deeply disapproved of horse-racing and gambling of all sorts, was seriously displeased on each occasion. In 1908, after Persimmon died, the king presented the skeleton to the Natural History Museum. The late queen and Prince Albert would not have been amused. The king is the most ardent royal patron of the turf since Charles II. He established his own stud in the 1880s, under the management of Lord Marcus

Beresford, and he has become strikingly successful. In 1900 he won £29,586 – more than any other British owner. In that year he won not only the Derby but also the Grand National, with Ambush II. He attends the major race meetings and counts other owners among his closest friends.

Thanks partly to his patronage, the "sport of kings" is now more popular than ever in Britain, and the king's popularity has risen with it. Betting on horses is a game that anyone can play, unlike shooting or yachting, and people feel, metaphorically speaking, that they are rubbing shoulders with the king when they place a bet. The popularity of today's win was also due to the number of punters who bet on the horse and who were cheering their own winnings.

King caught in crisis as Commons clash with Lords over the 'people's budget'

London, 31 December 1909
The general election campaign will resume in the New Year, as the deepest constitutional crisis since 1832 continues. The Liberal government is locked in combat with the Lords, with the king reluctantly caught in the middle of an increasingly bitter battle over who governs Britain.

Ever since the Liberals won their landslide election victory in 1906, much of their welfare legislation has been rejected by the Lords, amongst whom the Conservatives have a huge majority. The growing Labour Party has joined the Liberals in condemning what is seen as an hereditary chamber blocking the will of the elected chamber. David Lloyd George, the chancellor of the exchequer, says that the upper house is not "the watchdog of the constitution" but the poodle of Arthur Balfour, the Tory leader.

The simmering row has been brought to a head by what has become known as the "people's budget" introduced last April by Lloyd George. This proposed increasing income tax by 2d, introducing a supertax of 6d on annual incomes over £5,000, and taxing "unearned income" more severely than "earned income". A development tax of 1/2d in the pound was proposed on land. The Tories denounced this budget as "socialist" and defeated it in the House of

Lloyd George: a radical budget.

Lords. The Lords have never before rejected a money bill, and Asquith dissolved parliament on 15 December to fight an election on the question "Shall peers or people rule?".

The king is much distressed at these events. He urged the Tories to accept the budget because he fears even more the proposal mooted by Herbert Asquith, the prime minister, to end or limit the Lords' power to defeat legislation, perhaps by asking the king to create pro-Liberal peers. Edward believes that this is an attack on the hereditary system, and therefore on the monarchy (→15/11/10).

Second son of the Prince of Wales enrols at naval college

Osborne, IoW, 15 January 1909
Prince Albert, the second son of the Prince of Wales, has joined his elder brother at the naval college. Prince Edward, or David as he is known in the royal family, is now in his final term at Osborne before leaving to join the naval college at Dartmouth. He has not enjoyed either the severe discipline or the concentration on mathematics, navigation, engineering and knots. But he has weathered the bullying and gained in self-confidence. His father has asked him to "look after Albert all you can". Albert is 13, small for his age and with a stutter; he will not find life here any easier than his brother did (→31/12/10).

Edward (seated, third from left) and Albert (on ground, centre) at Osborne.

Visit to kaiser fails to end naval race

Berlin, 28 February 1909
The king's visit to Berlin this month has concluded without any improvement in relations between the two countries. Edward is feeling his age; he was seized with a attack of bronchitis here, and the queen feared that he might not be able to go on. Despite this, he made speeches in perfect German, visited parliament and attended the opera and several state dinners. He raised German naval spending with Kaiser William, who would not modify his policies. They parted, as usual, with public affection and concealed amimosity (→15/5/11).

King who shed playboy image dies of bronchitis

London, 6 May 1910

The whole country is in mourning at the sudden death of the king. He was beloved by all his subjects, who loved the man for his charm, friendliness and humanity as well as revering the monarch. The event was so sudden that Queen Alexandra had barely time to return from Corfu, where she was visiting her sister, the queen of the Hellenes. The prime minister is still abroad.

The king was 68 and had suffered from bronchitis for many years, but only his family and closest friends knew how ill he was. The first medical bulletin was issued yesterday evening, saying that the king's "condition causes some anxiety".

The king was in Biarritz, as usual, in March. He stopped in Paris on the way south and caught a chill at the theatre. The sea air appeared to restore him, and when he returned to London on 27 April he went straight to Covent Garden to hear Tetrazzini in *Rigoletto*. He returned to the opera on Friday to hear *Siegfried*. He spent the following weekend at Sandringham, much of it outdoors, despite the rain, and returned to town on 2 May with a chill, but he refused to curtail his usual activities.

He was obviously seriously ill, seized with severe fits of coughing. "I shall work to the end," he said. "Of what use is it to be alive if one cannot work?" The queen had been told that he was ill and returned early from Corfu with her daughter Victoria. When they reached Dover yesterday, the princess was handed a letter from the Prince of Wales warning her of the seriousness of the situation.

Queen Alexandra found the king hunched in a chair, battling for breath. He had a cylinder of oxygen next to him. He was much worse this morning, but insisted on dressing in a frock coat to receive his old friend Sir Ernest Cassel. The archbishop of Canterbury was brought to see him, and the queen, in a gesture of extraordinary magnanimity, summoned Mrs Keppel so that the king might bid farewell to his last mistress. Late this afternoon, he was told that his horse Witch of Air had won the 4.15 at Kempton Park. "Yes, I have heard of it," he replied. "I am very glad." Those were his last words (→ 20/5).

The king's last holiday: Edward taking the sea air in Biarritz, only weeks before his death from a severe chill.

The king's death is made public.

Domestic strife overshadowed final years

London, 6 May 1910

The king was more preoccupied by foreign policy than affairs at home, but in the closing months of his relatively brief reign domestic strife had begun to overshadow the menace of German militarism in Europe. Edward had come to terms with the election of a Liberal government, even though many of its proposals were inimical to his own instincts. But the clash over Lloyd George's "people's budget" was involving the king more directly in domestic politics than ever before. Despite his own extravagant lifestyle Edward was not without sympathy for the plight of the poor. He had made it one of his interests as Prince of Wales, but it was essentially a paternalistic concern, and he had no time for radicals, be they socialists or suffragettes. As a constitutional monarch, however, he was being forced to back the government in its clash with the Lords – a dilemma which he has bequeathed to his son.

Royal diplomacy led the way in Europe

London, 6 May 1910

King Edward VII reigned at a time when the British Empire was more powerful than ever before, covering one-fifth of the globe, with more than 400 million people, according to a survey in 1905. Appropriately, therefore, it was overseas interests which attracted most of Edward's attention after he became king.

It was a 1903 visit by Edward to France (a country which he had loved since his first visit in the 1850s) which paved the way for the *Entente Cordiale* signed in the following year between France and Britain. He also became the first reigning British monarch to visit Russia, and regularly met the rulers of other European countries. It helped that so many were related to him, of course, although this did not diminish his concern over the militarism of his nephew, Kaiser William, in Germany. He therefore coupled his interest in diplomacy with close encouragement for military expansion at home.

G e o r g e V
1910–1936

**House
of
Windsor**

London, 6 May 1910. George, the Prince of Wales, accedes to the throne; his wife May is to be known as Queen Mary (→ 7/5).

London, 7 May 1910. Prince Edward becomes Duke of Cornwall and heir to the throne (→ 13/7/11).

South London, 12 May 1911. The king and queen open the Festival of the Empire at the Crystal Palace.

London, 15 May 1911. George and his cousin, the *kaiser*, reconcile their differences.

London, 16 May 1911. King George unveils the Queen Victoria memorial outside Buckingham Palace (→ 23/10/12).

London, 30 June 1911. King George hosts a coronation fête for over 100,000 people at the Crystal Palace (→ 31/12).

Balmoral, 1 September 1911. Prince Albert bags his first partridge (→ 11/5/12).

Britain, September 1911. The Prince of Wales embarks on three months' naval training in the *Hindustan* (→ 31/10/12).

Quebec, 6 October 1911. The Duke of Connaught, an uncle of King George, is appointed as governor-general of Canada.

London, 1911. The press is full of excited speculation after the visit of Princess Victoria Louise, the daughter of the *kaiser*, concerning a possible romance with the Prince of Wales.

Weymouth, Dorset, 11 May 1912. George reviews the fleet and, with Prince Albert, takes part in a submarine dive (→ 31/1/13).

Britain, 31 January 1913. Prince Albert joins HMS *Cumberland* for the final part of his naval training.

Oxford, February 1913. The Prince of Wales dines with Walter Monckton, the president of the Oxford University Debating Society (→ 15/11/36).

Greece, 20 March 1913. King George of the Hellenes, the brother of the dowager Queen Alexandra and thus George V's uncle, who was assassinated two days ago, is succeeded by his eldest son, the Duke of Sparta, who takes the throne as King Constantine.

Greece, 14 December 1913. Prince Albert celebrates his 18th birthday with a cigarette; he is now officially allowed to smoke.→

London, 7 May 1914. George opens the King Edward VII Gallery of the British Musuem.

London, 22 May 1914. Police arrest 57 suffragettes when they attempt to storm Buckingham Palace with their "Votes for Women" petition.

Spithead, 17 July 1914. George reviews the fleet, including the ship in which Albert is based (→ 19/9).

Berlin, 1 August 1914. The *kaiser* declares war on his cousin-in-law, Czar Nicholas II (→ 4/8).

Britain, 4 August 1914. Under the 1839 Treaty of London, which guarantees Belgian neutrality and

protects the French coasts, Britain declares war on Germany (→ 3/9).

London, 3 September 1914. The queen starts a "work for women" fund (→ 31/12).

Aberdeen, 19 September 1914. Edward, the Prince of Wales, visits his brother, Prince Albert, who is recovering in hospital from appendicitis (→ 26/8/16).

France, 16 November 1914. The Prince of Wales becomes aide-de-camp to General Sir John French, who is commanding the British Expeditionary Force (→ 26/11).

France, 4 December 1914. George meets King Albert of the Belgians when he reviews front-line troops.

France, February 1915. Edward, the Prince of Wales, is given permission by King George to visit the trenches (→ 5/1915).

Windsor, April 1915. The Prince of Wales meets and plays golf with Lady Sybil Cadogan (→ 5/1/16).

France, May 1915. The Prince of Wales joins the 1st Army Corps, commanded by Sir Charles Monro.

London, 5 January 1916. Rumours concerning the Prince of Wales's romance with Lady Sybil Cadogan are rife (→ 6/1917).

London, 27 June 1916. George announces that the Military Medal may be awarded to women.

London, July 1916. Queen Mary opens two hospitals for women in Clapham and Chelsea.

Britain, 14 December 1916. Prince Albert receives the Order of the Garter (→ 11/1918).

Russia, 16 March 1917. Czar Nicholas II, a first cousin of George, abdicates after months of turmoil (→ 25/7/18).

Britain, 2 May 1917. The king urges Britons to eat less bread.

London, June 1917. Lady Sybil Cadogan announces her engagement to Edward Stanley, an old university friend of the Prince of Wales.

France, 17 July 1917. Edward, the Prince of Wales, is very enthusiastic about flying after making his first flight (→ 12/1927).

London, March 1918. The Prince of Wales meets Mrs Freda Dudley Ward in an air raid (→ 1920).

London, 25 July 1918. George attends a memorial service for the czar and his family, all massacred earlier this month.→

London, March 1919. The Duke of Connaught initiates the Prince of Wales into the Household Brigade Lodge of the Freemasons (→ 2/12).

London, July 1919. The Prince of Wales moves to York House.

London, 2 December 1919. Prince Albert follows his elder brother in becoming a member of the Freemasons (→ 5/6/20).

The life and times of King George V

Name: George Frederick Ernest Albert.
Birth: 3 June 1865.
Predecessor: father.
Accession: 6 May 1910.
Coronation: 22 June 1911.
Height: five feet six inches.
Marriage: Princess May of Teck, 6 July 1893.
Children: David (later Edward VIII), Albert (George VI),

Mary, Henry, George and John.
Favourite home: Sandringham.
Likes: shooting, sailing, stamps.
Dislikes: abroad, colour bar.
Greatest problem: divisions within Britain and Ireland.
Greatest success: helping to unify the country.
Famous saying: "Bugger Bognor" (about the Sussex resort).
Death: 20 January 1936.

Opposite: King George V, in full naval uniform.

Shooting stamp collector is new king

London, 7 May 1910
This is one day when his royal highness has no time to spare for his favourite pastime – browsing through his stamp collection, which is said to be the most complete in existence. The day began early when he was told that his father had died just before midnight and so he was now King George V. Told that the royal standard was at half-mast over Buckingham Palace, he gave orders for the flag to be raised to full-mast over Marlborough House, his own residence.

The new king spent the morning attending a meeting of the privy council. Herbert Asquith, the prime minister, is on a visit to Europe, so the first minister to meet the king was David Lloyd George, the chancellor of the exchequer, whose "people's budget" has provoked a clash with the Lords.

Among the king's cherished possessions is a set of 12-bore hammer guns. He enjoys tramping the Norfolk coverts matching his skill against the pheasants. Invariably well-groomed, with a neatly trimmed beard dabbed with lavender water, he slips his manicured hands into gloves for shooting. George is acutely self-conscious about a physical defect which he is unable to hide: his knock-knees (→ 20/5).

King George with a family group.

Nation mourns much-loved King Edward

Windsor, 20 May 1910
In a coffin made from one of the oaks in Windsor great park, King Edward VII was laid to rest today in the family vault at St George's chapel. While the nation mourned the loss of a much-loved monarch, the solemnity of the ceremony was marred by a succession of petty squabbles and muddles.

The Duke of Norfolk, as Earl Marshal, had responsibility for organising the funeral, but his programme was riddled with mistakes and had to be rewritten by clerks. Then Marie Feodorovna, the dowager empress of Russia and sister of Edward's widow, Alexandra, insisted that the widow had precedence over the wife of the new king – the custom at St Petersburg but not at the court of St James's. Still, she had her way, and Queen Mary had to move to the rear.

The French foreign minister, Stephen Jean Marie Pichon, was furious when the Orleanist princes were given precedence over him. He also complained that his coachman was dressed in black, while the coachmen of the royal carriages wore scarlet liveries. One foreign envoy asked if the king would receive him and his compatriots first, since they had an engagement in Manchester. "I will receive them last," King George said. Eight kings and an emperor, Kaiser William of Germany, attended the funeral, along with 50 dukes, princes and princesses; the bill for feeding them totalled £4,644.

Journalist is jailed for libelling king

London, 1 February 1911
A scurrilous article accusing the king of committing bigamy has led to a 12-month jail sentence for Edward Mylius, an obscure republican who publishes an English-language paper in Paris. He claimed that the king had secretly married the daughter of a British admiral in Malta before he became the husband of Princess May of Teck in 1893. Mylius sent copies of the paper to all British MPs. He was arrested, bail was fixed at a prohibitive £20,000, and he was brought before the lord chief justice and a jury today. Evidence showed that the king had not been in Malta on the relevant dates.

Bertie last in class

Osborne, IoW, 31 December 1910
After two years as a cadet at the naval college at Osborne on the Isle of Wight, Prince Albert (Bertie) has emerged from his final examinations in 68th place out of 68. In the words of his tutor, the 15-year-old prince has "gone a mucker". His fellow cadets gave him a hard time, on one occasion leaving him trussed up in a hammock. Because he is small and rather delicate he was nicknamed Sardine. His stammer often caused him to remain silent when he was asked a question in class (→ 1/9/11).

George's secretary at centre of row as Lords' crisis grows

London, 15 November 1910
The king's two private secretaries are at odds over the advice that they should proffer the sovereign in handling the constitutional crisis provoked by the Lords' rejection of the "people's budget" introduced by David Lloyd George, the chancellor of the exchequer.

Lord Knollys, whose family have been in royal service since Queen Elizabeth's reign, believes that George should agree to the demand of Herbert Asquith, the prime minister, that, if the Lords remain ob-

Asquith: confronting the Lords.

durate, several hundred Liberal-voting peers should be created to overwhelm the resistance. The other secretary, Sir Arthur Bigge, is equally certain that Asquith should be resisted; to give in, says Bigge, would be to surrender to socialists and Irish home rulers, whose MPs are keeping Asquith in power.

There is a suspicion that Knollys is not being entirely frank with the king. He has drafted a letter to be sent to Sandringham in which he urges the king to support Asquith's Parliament Bill to limit the powers of the Lords. He is also enclosing a note from the Liberal chief whip, who says that "a spirit of unrest pervades the working classes" and the Liberals must be seen to be unflinching in confronting the crisis; otherwise, "extreme forces" could gain control. It is believed that the sentiments in this letter are in fact those of Knollys (→ 10/8/11).

The king's charger and his terrier, Caesar, following Edward's coffin.

George crowned in sumptuous pageantry

Prince of Wales is invested at Caernarfon in first ceremony for over three centuries

King George's coronation procession returns to Buckingham Palace.

Westminster Abbey, 22 June 1911
In a ceremony enriched by a thousand years of history, George V was today anointed with consecrated oil and crowned king of Great Britain and Ireland, the dominions beyond the seas and emperor of India. Queen Mary was pale and strained; the king nearly broke down when his eldest son, Prince Edward, knelt to offer his allegiance. In the abbey were premiers and cabinet ministers from the far corners of the empire and Indian princes resplendent in jewelled turbans. The royal diary touches on the eventful day in words appropriate for the sailor-king: "Overcast and cloudy, with some showers and a strongish cool breeze" (→30/6).

Special decorations in Bond Street.

In royal robes: Edward is invested as Prince of Wales at Caernarfon.

Caernarfon, 13 July 1911
The 17-year-old Prince of Wales was today formally presented to the Welsh people in an elaborate ceremony held in the castle built by Edward I in the 13th century. The climax came when the prince cried out: "*Diolch fy nghalon i Hen wlad nhadua* [Thanks from the bottom of my heart to the old land of my fathers]" – a phrase taught to him by David Lloyd George, the Welsh chancellor of the exchequer.

After Winston Churchill, the home secretary, had announced the prince's many titles, his father, King George, placed a coronet on the young man's head, a gold rod in his hand as a symbol of authority, and a gold ring of responsibility on his middle finger. The prince was then led onto the battlements to be presented to the Welsh people.

These elaborate rituals, seemingly of ancient origin, had in fact been hastily devised for the occasion. It is about 300 years since an investiture for a Prince of Wales was held,

and none had ever taken place in Caernarfon before today's ceremony. The castle has been refurbished, and gold from the hills of Merioneth was used for the prince's regalia. A costume of white satin breeches and purple velvet tunic, fashioned for the occasion, was not to the young prince's liking. "What will my navy friends say if they see me in this preposterous rig?" he protested, before giving in to his mother's frantic appeals.

When the idea for the investiture was first mooted it was enthusiastically backed by Lloyd George, who saw it as a chance to boost Welsh pride and also make political capital. After the ceremony, he told the prince that he had won the admiration of the Welsh people.

As Prince of Wales, Edward (or David as the family call him) now has access to the revenues of the Duchy of Cornwall, which owns property in London and estates in the west country, altogether worth £90,000 a year (→9/1911).

Bill to curb Lords is passed, ending crisis

Westminster, 10 August 1911
After two days of heated and repetitious speeches the Parliament Bill to curb the powers of the Lords was tonight accepted by a voting majority of peers. At the last moment the archbishop of Canterbury rallied the bench of bishops in support of the bill, and a handful of Unionists, mostly Liberals who had deserted to the Conservatives over Irish home rule, joined in to give the Asquith government a majority of 17 – 131 to 114. To balance the enhanced powers of MPs the life of the elected Commons is being re-

duced from seven years to five. The debate opened yesterday in a stifling atmosphere, with outdoor temperatures touching 100 degrees Fahrenheit. The upper house was under threat that the king would agree to the creation of up to 250 new peers to join the Liberals and overwhelm the opposition; 300 Tories promised to abstain, but another 100 said that they would resist to the last. The voting figures were telephoned to Buckingham Palace, but the equerry on duty failed to pass them on to the king, who heard them by chance (→13/2/13).

Royal family goes on tour at home and abroad

India's king-emperor: George and Queen Mary enthroned in Delhi.

Grand imperial splendour of Delhi durbar

Delhi, 31 December 1911
Wearing a £60,000 crown created specially for the occasion, King George V was presented to the Indian people as their king-emperor in a magnificent *durbar* in Delhi this month. Clad in the richest vestments and guarded by a colourful array of troops, the king-emperor and the queen-empress sat enthroned beneath a golden dome to receive the tributes of India's most powerful princes.

The king had visited India in 1905 and was determined to attend his enthronement as emperor. The cabinet had agreed reluctantly and insisted that the ceremonial splendour of the durbar be used for George to announce two important decisions: the transfer of the Indian capital from Calcutta to Delhi, and the annulment of the partition of Bengal, which had caused so much trouble since it was introduced by the then viceroy, Lord Curzon.

The durbar on 12 December was characterised by great luxury, but the king was delighted to leave afterwards for a hunting trip in Nepal. He is one of the best shots in England, and his 12-bore Purdey guns accounted for no fewer than 39 tigers, 18 rhinos and four bears.

Royal safari: King George mounted on an elephant during his Indian trip.

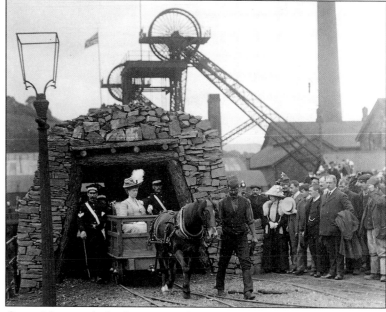

Queen Mary overlooks the grime on her visit to this South Wales colliery.

King and queen tour industrial centres

Bristol, 31 July 1912
Against a background of widespread industrial unrest, the king has completed a week-long tour of South Wales and Bristol during which he has visited docks, collieries, and iron and steel works. In Cardiff he laid the foundation stone for the National Museum of Wales.

Last month King George and Queen Mary visited Yorkshire, and more visits are planned to industrial and commercial centres in the provinces. These journeys represent a significant departure from tradition since they offer for the first time an opportunity for ordinary people to see the royal family. Admittedly, the contacts are minimal. At Lewis Merthyr colliery, the 60 or more miners on parade were all bemedalled ex-soldiers. At another pit, a few men and a redhaired boy of 13 were brought to the surface. The queen asked for a photograph of the boy.

Some of the places visited have been the focus of unrest. Last month nine striking miners died in clashes with soldiers at Llanelli, and only days before the royal tour began the dock strike which had paralysed Bristol and other ports was called off. The king gave £1,000 to a fund to relieve distress among striking miners' families.

New look planned for Buckingham Palace

London, 23 October 1912
After moving into Buckingham Palace two years ago, Queen Mary said that it was "not so *gemütlich* [cosy]" as Marlborough House, where she had lived as Princess of Wales. For a year after Edward's death, court mourning kept dust-sheets over the furniture; but now Queen Mary is beginning to give the palace apartments a new look. The king has given the queen a free hand to redecorate and refurnish the palace, and she is seeking a less ostentatious style without, as she puts it, "this surfeit of gold plate and orchids". The building itself was redesigned for Edward VII by the architect Sir Aston Webb – the most recent of several changes to the original building put up for the Duke of Buckingham. It was later bought by George III and remodelled by Nash for George IV. The present George is unimpressed, regarding the palace as an official place of work rather than a home and disliking its grandiose style.

Informal prince embraces Oxford style

The prince as undergraduate: Edward at Oxford, driving his first car.

Oxford, 31 October 1912
The Prince of Wales has enthusiastically embraced the Oxford fashion for informal clothes, and he is regularly to be seen in wide flannel trousers and sports coat, plusfours, or – the latest thing – trousers with turn-ups. In other ways, the 18-year-old prince, arriving at Magdalen college in the company of several minders, including Major the Hon William Cadogan, has found little to his liking.

David, as Prince Edward is generally known, is somewhat shy and, not knowing any of the other undergraduates, will stand in a room looking around and fingering his tie. When the king told his son that he was sending him to Oxford to study languages, history and political economy, an unhappy prince said that he had no interest in learning, a point well made in his letters, which have him writing "colision", "dammaged" and "explaned".

The king's will prevailed, and the prince now finds himself settled in his own suite of rooms, with Sheraton furniture provided by his mother. He will not be required to take exams (→ 2/1913).

Top courtier sacked in 'deception' row

London, 13 February 1913
The king's longest-serving private secretary, the 76-year-old Lord Knollys, has resigned under royal pressure. Though the court circular expresses "gratitude" for more than 50 years of devoted service, the formalities mask a mistrust of Knollys that goes back to the constitutional crisis of 1910.

At that time, Asquith's Liberal government was pressing the king to agree to create several hundred peers to outvote the opposition (Conservative) majority in the Lords. George was reluctant. Knollys then told him that if Asquith should be dismissed or forced to resign, the opposition leader in the House of Commons, Arthur Balfour, would refuse to form an alternative government. The king felt obliged to submit to Asquith.

Months later, though the crisis had passed, the king was still unhappy at having given in, and he asked Knollys to ask Balfour if he would have formed a government. Again, Knollys said that Balfour would not. Balfour later complained bitterly that Knollys had misled him by not telling him that the king was under pressure to give a secret undertaking about the mass creation of peers. Had he known that, Balfour said, he would certainly have formed a government.

King hosts talks on future of Ireland

London, 21 July 1914
In the shadow of imminent war in Europe, British politicians find themselves locked in bitter conflict over home rule for Ireland, with threats of mutiny should the army be called on to put down an uprising by the Protestant Ulster Volunteers. Now, at last, the seemingly complacent prime minister, Herbert Asquith, has agreed to the king's urgent appeals for a meeting of all parties – British and Irish – to be held at Buckingham Palace.

Asquith believed that he had solved the home rule problem with the Parliament Act, which curbs the Lords' powers to block bills passed by the Commons. As the Home Rule Bill is about to become law, a long-smouldering issue has brought Ireland to the brink of civil war. Protestant Ulster firmly rejects rule by a Dublin government, a stand backed by the Conservative opposition at Westminster.

Having first refused to exclude Ulster from home rule, Asquith has tacitly accepted it. But as the party leaders gather in Buckingham Palace, another stumbling block has appeared. Ulster claims the border county of Tyrone because of its Protestant community; Dublin claims Tyrone because Catholics live there. The conference seems doomed to failure (→ 7/12/16).

Midshipman Albert lights up his birthday

Royal midshipman: Prince Albert.

Salamis Bay, 14 December 1913
After two months on manoeuvres in the Mediterranean, the 19,250-ton battleship HMS *Collingwood* has arrived at Salamis Bay, in Greece, with Prince Albert in the crew as a midshipman. Today the prince celebrated his 18th birthday by smoking his first cigarette.

The voyage has marked the official start of a career chosen for him by his father, George V, the "sailor-king". Albert, however, suffers from sea-sickness, and he once told his mother that he wished he could have gone to Oxford with his brother David. Like other midshipmen, Albert is known as a "snotty" because the three buttons on his sleeve are to prevent him from wiping his nose on it (→ 17/7/14).

The 1913 Derby disrupted: the suffragette Emily Davison was fatally injured when she threw herself under King George's horse, Anmer.

War erupts: king and family lead the war effort

London, 31 December 1914
The royal family is leading the nation's war effort by example as well as by position. King George V has carried out the first of a planned series of visits to his troops in the field. He finds it difficult to radiate warmth, but as he moves among the soldiers of the British Expeditionary Force his concern for them and his no nonsense approach have won their respect as well as their unquestioning loyalty.

What they like about him is that he is so obviously a decent man. At the beginning of the war he treated the Austro-Hungarian ambassador, Albert Mensdorff, with the utmost courtesy, inviting him to tea at Buckingham Palace to express his hope that war could be averted between their two nations. In another telling incident he rebuked his son, Prince Henry, for wanting to see German prisoners in their camp. "How would you like it," he wrote, "if you were a prisoner, for people to come and stare at you as if you were a wild beast?"

At the same time, he has never swerved in his abhorrence of the behaviour of his cousin, the *kaiser*, and the German methods of waging war. He refuses, however, to countenance retaliation, believing that at the end of the war Britons will be able to stand before the world knowing that they had conducted the war as far as possible with humanity and like gentlemen.

His sense of duty has led him to inflict a regime on Buckingham Palace far more severe than that of many of his subjects. He has given away most of his civilian clothes, has abandoned dining out and the theatre, and has turned his private gardens over to growing potatoes.

The queen is playing a full part in the war work, inspecting canteens and organising comforts for the troops as well as ensuring that austerity rules at the palace. They also share the anxieties of other parents [*see below*]: one son is with the Grenadiers in France and another is in the navy (→6/1915).

King George on the Belgian front.

German links force prince to resign

London, 29 October 1914
The rising tide of hatred against all things German has brought about the resignation of Admiral Prince Louis of Battenberg as Britain's first sea lord. It is true that Prince Louis, a member of the Hesse family, was born a German and still retains a thick German accent, but he became a British citizen when he was 14 and has devoted his life to the Royal Navy. He is married to a granddaughter of Queen Victoria and is utterly loyal. He mobilised the fleet with speed and efficiency, so that when war broke out it was ready for action; but he has been so vilified for being German that he must go. He is said to be heartbroken (→13/5/15).

Arms factory visits

London, 1915
King George has been following a punishing programme ever since the war started, visiting not only the troops in the field but also the workers in the arms factories and shipyards who are providing them with the means to fight the war. He does not enjoy the visits to the clamorous factories, for he is shy, yet somehow an affinity appears to grow between him and the workers, who now include a growing number of women doing men's jobs.

Royal brothers plead to join the front line

Royal soldier: the Prince of Wales in his new army uniform in London.

London, 26 November 1914
The Prince of Wales, to his great relief and delight, joined the army in France ten days ago. He has been attached to the staff of Sir John French, the commander-in-chief of the British Expeditionary Force.

It is not what the prince wanted, which was to serve as a regimental officer with his friends in the Grenadier Guards, but at least he is within sound of cannon fire, and he feels that having got to France he will soon be able to make his way to the front line. He was humiliated when he was refused permission to fight with the Grenadiers. "What does it matter if I am killed?" he asked Lord Kitchener, the secretary of state for war "I have four brothers." Kitchener would have none of it. "What if you were not killed but taken prisoner?" he asked.

His equally frustrated brother, Prince Albert, a midshipman in the Royal Navy who has been kept away from active service by ill health, has today been appointed to join the war staff at the admiralty. Keenly aware that he might be thought a slacker, he sees it as the first step of his return to his ship, HMS *Collingwood* (→2/1915).

Kaiser stripped of Order of the Garter

London, 13 May 1915
King George has stripped Kaiser William of all his British honours including the Order of the Garter and ordered the removal of his Garter banner from St George's chapel at Windsor. The king had been reluctant to do this, not out of any lingering family feeling for his cousin but because he believes that the exchanges of honours are part of history. He maintained this belief despite public resentment but capitulated after being rebuked by his mother, who wrote: "It is but right and proper for you to have down those hateful German banners in our sacred church ..." (→26/5/17).

Just a year ago: king and kaiser.

Royal homes to be alcohol-free zones

London, June 1915

A visit to dine at the palace is no longer quite the feast that it was before the war. Luxury at table has been replaced by an austere regime by which the king sets an example of self-sacrifice to his country. One equerry, requesting a boiled egg at breakfast, was accused of being a "slave to his insides". Padlocks have also gone on the royal cellars.

In March the king decided, albeit reluctantly, that no more alcohol would be served in the royal residences until the end of the war. His decision follows a plea by the minister of munitions, David Lloyd George, to set an example to the nation. Lloyd George is alarmed by the effects of heavy drinking among the well-paid armament workers. The king's private secretary, Lord Stamfordham, wrote to the minister: "If it be deemed advisable, his majesty will be prepared to set an example by giving up all alcoholic liquor himself and throughout his household, so that no difference shall be made so far as he is concerned between the treatment of rich and poor."

Privately, George confesses: "It is a great bore." And, alas, his self-denial seems unlikely to have the effect which Lloyd George sought. His courtiers, forced to drink ginger beer, are furious, while there is no evidence that the liquor consumption of the workers has been diminished by royal abstinence.

King injured in fall from horse in France

King George on horseback: now he has been injured in a fall.

France, 28 October 1915

The king was seriously injured today when he was thrown from his horse while inspecting a detachment of the Royal Flying Corps (RFC) near the village of Hesdigneul. He is in great pain, and it is feared that he may have cracked some ribs and fractured his pelvis. He is to be X-rayed to see how much damage has been done; he will then be evacuated by hospital train among his wounded soldiers.

The accident happened when he left his motor car and mounted a chestnut mare trained to stay calm while bands played and guns fired. Unfortunately, it had not been trained to withstand the cheers of the RFC. One of the officers present when these rang out watched in horror as she "reared up like a rocket and came over backwards", falling on top of the king.

The Prince of Wales rushed to his father's side fearing that he had been killed, and he was, in fact, only saved from death by the soft ground. The king, in agony, was picked up and driven to the château where he had spent the previous night, and was put to bed in an understandably foul temper.

When General Haig, fearing that the Germans might bomb the château, suggested that he should be moved, George replied: "You can tell him from me to go to hell and stay there. I don't intend to move for any bombs." Typical of his kindness, however, is his inquiry after the health of the mare.

Albert sees action, but falls ill again

Windsor Castle, 26 August 1916

Prince Albert's recurring stomach problems were at last diagnosed today as being caused by a duodenal ulcer. It is feared that he will no longer be able to continue with his naval career, which has been interrupted throughout the war by bouts of ill health. The one highlight, of which "Bertie" is very proud, is that he took part in the Battle of Jutland on 31 May, even though he was in the sick-bay as his ship, HMS *Collingwood*, sailed with the Grand Fleet to give battle to the German High Seas Fleet.

According to the log kept by the prince, the *Collingwood* sank two light cruisers and set a big battle cruiser on fire before it disappeared into the mist. The *Collingwood* suffered no damage despite being straddled by several salvoes. She was also missed by torpedoes which passed ahead and astern.

During the action the prince's post was in A turret, and he tells how he was sitting on top of the turret during a lull "when a German ship started firing at us, and one salvo straddled us. We at once returned the fire. I was distinctly startled and jumped down the hole in the top of the turret like a shot rabbit!" He was delighted to have been in action and proved himself against the whisperers who doubt his courage. His new bout of sickness will be a great disappointment to him (→ 14/12).

Wartime paperwork: King George feels that he will not be helped by the arrival of a dynamic radical prime minister, David Lloyd George.

Lloyd George brings new style for king

Westminster, 7 December 1916

David Lloyd George became prime minister today, and the king is displeased at the manner in which the fiery Welshman ousted Herbert Asquith. The king regards Lloyd George as a blackmailer and fears that the loss of Asquith "will cause a panic in the City and in America and do harm to the Allies. It is a great blow to me and will I fear buck up the Germans."

There is no doubt that the new prime minister intends to revolutionise the conduct of the war. He accuses Asquith of being ineffectual and is certain he can win it with a war council of three, led by himself. Among his first targets is Sir Douglas Haig, the C-in-C in France, and here he faces a clash with the king, who has promised Haig his support "through thick and thin".

Another area where a clash seems inevitable is in the prime minister's constitutional duty to consult the king. Asquith was punctilious in this respect. Lloyd George, however, is quite capable of delaying news of a decision until it is too late for the king to have any influence.

Royal family leads Britain's victory celebrations

Prince returns from service in the army

France, 11 November 1918
The war is over, and the Prince of Wales will return to London something of a hero in the eyes of the world after his four years in the army. Not in his own eyes, however, for he has not been allowed to serve in the front line where so many of his friends have died. He has been awarded the Military Cross and a number of foreign decorations, but he has to be forced to wear them because he does not think that he deserves them.

He has had his share of narrow escapes, however, and nobody can question his courage. His driver was killed by shrapnel during one visit to the front, and two soldiers detailed to guard him were heard to grumble: "It's all very well for him, but if he gets killed, we'll get the blame." He has gone about the duties assigned to him as a staff officer in an efficient fashion, getting about on an old green bicycle. He was a particular success with troops from Australia and New Zealand in the Middle East.

Royal family hides its German origins

Buckingham Palace, 26 May 1917
The king, pre-eminently an English country gentleman, has decided to cut his family's last connections with its German origins. It now becomes the House of Windsor instead of Saxe-Coburg-Gotha, and members of the royal family have been asked to give up all their "German degrees, styles, dignities, titles, honours and appellations".

This step, thought long overdue by many, has been forced on the king by anti-German agitation in this year of defeats abroad and hardship at home. There are ugly rumours about the king's loyalty, and he is mindful of the fate of his cousins Czar Nicholas and Czarina Alexandra, who have lost their thrones partly because the Russians believe that "the German woman" is a traitor (→ 25/7/18).

The royals at war: the Prince of Wales with his father in France.

King mobbed by cheering London crowds

London, 15 November 1918
The king and queen were mobbed by cheering crowds as they drove in an open carriage through Hyde Park to celebrate Victory Day with their people and servicemen from all over the world. The royal couple provide a focal point for the joy and relief of the people for the victorious end of a war during which 750,000 Britons were killed plus 200,000 men from the empire.

Crowds have gathered outside Buckingham Palace every night since the armistice was signed four days ago, waiting until the king and queen walk onto the balcony to wave to the celebrating throng and receive their cheers. There is an intimacy about the elation, a sense that "we have all been through this together", that would not have been possible at the start of the war. Then the king was a rather remote figure; today he is a member of the family. Nowhere is this felt more strongly than among the wounded. The king's gruff sympathy has won the affection of men who could easily be embittered.

King mourns czar, after blocking exile

London, 25 July 1918
The king and queen attended a memorial service for the murdered czar of Russia today. The king's devotion to his cousin is well known, but there is more than a hint of hypocrisy about his grief. Last year Lloyd George proposed to agree to the Russian provisional government's request and grant the czar's family asylum; the king at first agreed, but changed his mind. Afraid of stirring up revolutionary forces at home, he abandoned "dear Nicky" to his fate (→ 6/2/28).

King plays host to American president

London, 31 December 1918
The state visit of the United States president, Woodrow Wilson, has not been a great success with the king. In the first place, David Lloyd George, the prime minister, did not consult George over the arrangements for the visit, which interfered with the king's eagerly-anticipated shooting holiday at Sandringham. The prime minister would not listen to the king's protests, replying coldly that he had put his objections to the war cabinet, which had "overruled the king".

So the king grudgingly gave up his holiday, received the president at Buckingham Palace and held a state banquet in his honour. It was an embarrassing occasion. The moralistic Wilson made an ungracious reply when his health was drunk, completely ignoring the part played by the British Empire in the war and succeeding in enraging both king and prime minister.

President Wilson, "an odious man", according to the king, is on his way to the peace conference at Versailles. He is a cold, aloof and often arrogant professor; his mind is filled with plans for his League of Nations, and he has no sympathy with the British Empire or its rulers. It would perhaps have been better if Lloyd George had allowed the king to shoot his partridges.

Albert tastes action as a flying captain

In uniform: Albert with his parents.

Autigny, France, November 1918
Prince Albert fulfilled his longing to see action in the front line with just weeks to go before the war ended. Bertie, as the family call him, arrived here last month to join General Trenchard's Independent Air Force as a staff officer with the rank of captain in the newly-formed Royal Air Force. The prince had to give up his career at sea because of ill-health soon after Jutland, but an operation cured him; despite the king's dislike of aeroplanes, Bertie won George's permission to transfer to the Royal Naval Air Service (→ 18/11/19).

Prince John, king's epileptic youngest son, has died at 13

Prince John: he has died after a fit.

Sandringham, January 1919

Prince John, the 13-year-old youngest son of the king and queen, has died. He suffered from severe epilepsy and he was rarely seen in public, living, happily enough, in seclusion here. His family was very fond of him, and the Prince of Wales used to wheel him around the estate in his specially made push-cart. It had been apparent for some time that he would not live long, but his death has deeply affected the royal family.

Queen Mary has written to a friend: "For him it is a great release ... I cannot say how grateful we feel to God for having taken him in such a peaceful way."

Student princes to study at Cambridge

Cambridge, 18 November 1919

Prince Albert and his younger brother, Prince Henry, have come up to Cambridge to spend a year at Trinity. It is hard to see what benefit Prince Henry will gain from the university, as he is profoundly non-intellectual. Prince Albert's case is different. He is interested in constitutional history, and the university could provide this shy stutterer with the opportunity to mature and escape from the shadow cast by the more worldly and gregarious Prince of Wales (→ 2/12).

Prince makes his first British tours

London, 31 July 1919

The Prince of Wales, who spent most of the war abroad, is undertaking a series of tours around provincial Britain. Wherever he goes he is met with such enthusiasm that the king is beginning to grumble about a loss of royal dignity. The prince has a natural empathy with the ex-servicemen, some of whom recall him going about his duties in France on a bicycle.

Despite the politicians' promises, they have not come home to "a land fit for heroes", and they look to the young man who knows what they suffered to ease their lot. In his speeches he constantly refers to "the welfare of our ex-servicemen and the improvement of housing conditions, both of which I have very much at heart".

His first tour last month was to the mining areas of South Wales, where he saw for himself the misery of the miners' slums. He was also taken down a coal mine in the Rhondda Valley, and there he saw, chalked on the coal-face 1,000 feet (305m) underground, a message

Popular with the ex-servicemen: the Prince of Wales visiting a mine.

saying "Welcome to our soldier prince. Long may he live." He took a piece of chalk and added: "Thank you. Edward, Prince."

He received a similar warm welcome in the west of England, but he will soon face a much sterner test of his popularity when he visits the "Red" Clyde, the most revolutionary area in Britain, where the radicals of Glasgow are suspected of communist sympathies which would sweep away the prince and his family for ever. The prince will pit his charm and sympathy against this revolutionary fervour (→ 31/10).

Canada falls to the charm of the prince: next stop America

Canada, 31 October 1919

The Prince of Wales is feeling the strain of his triumphant tour of Canada. His right hand is so bruised by thousands of hearty handshakes that he is having to use his left. He is surrounded by enthusiastic crowds wherever he goes, attends lunches, dinners and receptions, and makes speech after speech, pointing out that he is a Canadian as well as an Englishman.

The king, not too pleased at the hurly-burly surrounding his son, has written to him: "I warned you what it would be like, these people think one is made of stone and that one can go on for ever; you ought to have put your foot down at the beginning and refused to do so much." The prince has written back to his parents that it really is not his fault if the crowds go mad.

He has, in fact, succeeded in the most difficult circumstances, winning over the French-Canadians in Montreal with an elegant speech in French in which he pointed out that the union of the two races

The Prince of Wales signing a visitor's book on his Canadian tour.

The prince was made "Chief Morning Star" by Stony Creek Indians.

"was, and will always remain, an example of the highest political wisdom". Wherever he goes, he sees men he met during the war.

His travelling in this vast country has been prodigious, and he has fallen in love with the open spaces, telling the people of Calgary: "I am

rapidly becoming a westerner." He is among friends here, but he expects soon to have a more testing time because he has been invited by President Wilson to extend his tour to the United States. New York is already preparing a ticker-tape welcome for him (→ 18/8/20).

G e o r g e V
1910–1936

**House
of
Windsor**

London, 17 March 1920. Dowager Queen Alexandra unveils a monument by the National Gallery to Edith Cavell, the nurse who was shot as a spy by the Germans in 1915.

London, 5 June 1920. Prince Albert is created Duke of York (→ 8/7).

London, 9 June 1920. George opens the Imperial War Museum at the Crystal Palace.

Edinburgh, 15 July 1920. Lady Elizabeth Bowes-Lyon, the fourth daughter of the 14th Earl of Strathmore, is presented to the king and queen (→ 10/1920).

London, October 1920. The Bowes-Lyons move into 17 Bruton Street (→ 8/1921).

London, 1920. Captain Alan "Tommy" Lascelles, a Grenadier Guards officer, joins the staff of the Prince of Wales as assistant private secretary (→ 12/1928).

Britain, 1 April 1921. The Prince of Wales, with his love of riding, takes part in and wins the Welsh Guards Challenge Cup.

Corfu, 10 June 1921. Alice, the daughter of Louis Mountbatten (formerly of Battenberg), now the Marquis of Milford Haven, and his wife, formerly Princess Victoria of Hesse, and thus a great-granddaughter of Victoria, gives birth to Philip, the son of Prince Andrew of Greece (→ 5/12/22).

Britain, 4 August 1921. The Marquis of Milford Haven is promoted to admiral of the fleet by George in recognition of his magnificent service to the Royal Navy.

Scotland, August 1921. Reports in the press link the Prince of Wales and Lady Elizabeth Bowes-Lyon (→ 5/1/23).

Kent, August 1921. The Duke of York sets up a boys' summer camp on Romney Marsh (→ 8/1929).

Britain, 1921. Major Edward "Fruity" Metcalfe, a captain in the Indian cavalry, who met the Prince of Wales on his Indian tour, joins his staff.

Britain, 1921. George is infuriated by Lytton Strachey's ireverent biography of Victoria.

Westminster, 28 February 1922. Princess Mary, the only daughter of George and Mary, marries Henry, Viscount Lascelles, the eldest son of the Earl of Harewood (→ 7/2/23).

Britain, 30 April 1922. Lord Louis Mountbatten, the son of the late Marquis of Milford Haven, announces his engagement to Edwina Ashley (→ 18/7).

Yugoslavia, 8 June 1922. The Duke of York represents the king at the wedding of Princess Marie of Romania, the daughter of Queen Marie and a great-granddaughter of Queen Victoria, to King Alexander of Serbia.

Paris, 5 Dec 1922. Prince Andrew of Greece and his family, exiled by a coup, are offered a home here by the British government (→ 9/1930).

Britain, 5 January 1923. The press reveals that Lady Elizabeth Bowes-Lyon is to be married, amid rumours that it will be to the Prince of Wales (→ 16/1).

London, 16 January 1923. The Duke of York announces his engagement to Elizabeth Bowes-Lyon (→ 26/4).

London, 7 February 1923. Princess Mary, Viscountess Lascelles, gives birth to a son, George (→ 1/1/32).

Richmond, Surrey, 7 June 1923. The Duke and Duchess of York

move into White Lodge in Richmond park (→ 30/6).

London, 7 June 1923. George grants a royal charter to the Federation of British Industries.

Hendon, 30 June 1923. The Duchess of York takes part in her first royal engagement when she accompanies her husband to an RAF pageant (→ 21/7/24).

London, 4 May 1924. Sir Edward Elgar becomes Master of the King's Musick.

London, 29 June 1924. The Prince of Wales is quoted by the press as having said he will look for a wife.

Paris, 7 July 1924. The Prince of Wales unveils a memorial to British war dead in Notre Dame.

London, 2 August 1924. The Prince of Wales attends a boy scouts' jamboree at Wembley.

Hampshire, October 1924. The Prince of Wales is bruised after a fall in the Aldershot point-to-point.

London, 1 December 1924. The Duke and Duchess of York set off on their safari of Africa (→ 31/12).

Sandringham, 1925. George moves into the large house after the death of his mother, Alexandra, the dowager queen (→ 12/1927).

Mediterranean, December 1925. George, on the advice of his doctors, takes a cruise.

London, 21 April 1926. Elizabeth, the first child of the Duke and Duchess of York, is born. →

London, 11 Feb 1927. Princess Elizabeth, who is staying with her grandparents at Buckingham Palace while her parents are away, cuts her first tooth (→ 27/6).

Cardiff, 21 April 1927. King George opens the National Museum of Wales.

Britain, December 1927. King George agrees to the Prince of Wales using a small aeroplane for touring (→ 10/1929).

United States, 6 February 1928. A woman claiming to be Anastasia, the youngest daughter of the murdered Russian czar, Nicholas II, arrives in New York.

Britain, 13 November 1928. The dowager Czarina Marie of Russia, the sister of the late Queen Alexandra, dies.

East Africa, 27 November 1928. The Prince of Wales, on tour in Tanganyika, refuses to believe the telegram which tells him of his father's serious illness (→ 12/1928).

London, 1928. Prince Henry, the third son of King George, is created Duke of Gloucester (→ 6/11/35).

London, 1928. The Prince of Wales becomes a patron of the National Council for Social Services.

London, August 1929. The Prince of Wales intervenes in the undesirable friendship of his youngest brother, Prince George, and an American woman, Kiki Preston (→ 28/8/34).

London, summer 1929. Edward, the Prince of Wales, is said to be infatuated with Thelma, Lady Furness (→ 10/1/31).

England, October 1929. The Prince of Wales purchases his own plane and plans to have a course of flying lessons.

Windsor, 1929. The Prince of Wales is given permission by his father to use Fort Belvedere, on the edge of Windsor great park, as his weekend retreat (→ 31/12).

Prince of Wales makes Australian tour

The Prince of Wales ready, in his overalls, to go down an Australian goldmine.

Sydney, 18 August 1920

A vast crowd lined Circular Quay and Sydney Harbour vantage-points today to give a resounding send off to Edward, the Prince of Wales, after his six-month tour of Australia and New Zealand. The tour has been characterised by the prince's informality and easy manner with ordinary Australians.

He has toured factories, gone down mines, visited war veterans and schools, and – on horseback – hunted kangaroos with the same enthusiasm that he has shown at parliamentary functions and all the balls and dinners in his honour. The only serious mishap on the tour was when his train was derailed in Western Australia. The train was stopped 170 miles (272 kilometres) south of Perth by a bullock on the line. As it was picking up speed it was derailed, and the royal cars tumbled over a five-foot embankment. The Prince of Wales was found amid the wreckage, calmly smoking a cigar. "Hurt?" he said. "Bless your heart, no; and I'm glad to say the whisky flask is not broken either."

The prince has visited all the Australian states and the main cities of New Zealand on the tour, in which he thanked both countries for their part in the Great War.

Edward is presented to a group of young Maori women in New Zealand.

Royal princes succumb to the charms of two lively yet contrasting commoners

London, 1920

The Prince of Wales and the Duke of York do not have much in common, but both have this year found themselves in love. The prince left for his latest overseas tour in tears at the prospect of separation from Mrs Freda Dudley Ward, while "Bertie" is smitten by the charms of Lady Elizabeth Bowes-Lyon.

Freda Dudley Ward first met the prince in the spring of 1918, when she and her escort sheltered from an air raid in a Belgravia doorway. Invited into the house, she entranced the prince who danced with her for the rest of the evening. He saw her the next day and has tried to do so every other day since. She is an attractive, intelligent woman of the same age as the prince. It is clear that he is quite besotted with her, moping when parted for tours. The king is less pleased: Freda is a commoner, with the further disadvantages of having a husband (a Liberal MP) and two daughters.

Lady Elizabeth Bowes-Lyon would be altogether more suitable. She was born in 1900, the ninth child of the Earl of Strathmore, and brought up largely in the family's imposing Glamis castle. She met Prince Albert at a Mayfair ball on 10 June this year shortly after he was made Duke of York. Three months later the duke visited her at Glamis, and by the year's end the queen was telling friends that he was in love. But the lively Elizabeth has many other admirers.

Mrs Freda Dudley Ward.

Lady Elizabeth Bowes-Lyon.

Duke of York wins RAF tennis prize

London, 8 July 1920

Prince Albert, the Duke of York, has won the RAF tennis doubles championship. His partner was Louis Greig, the comptroller of the duke's household. The duke is a keen tennis-player and frequently plays before breakfast. In addition to partnering Greig, he likes playing with the South African "Lizzie" Lezard. The RAF is unlikely to resent his triumph. He has strong links with it and trained as a cadet at Cranwell before serving as a staff officer in 1918 (→ 30/6/26).

Oxford gives Mary an honorary degree

Oxford, 11 March 1921

The university here today awarded Queen Mary an honorary degree, in recognition of her war work for women and children. It is also a recognition of her popularity, for though she can be so formidable that – says one MP, "Chips" Channon – talking to her is "like talking to a cathedral", she can also be charming and informal. She is frequently to be seen nosing around antique shops, and she thinks nothing of telling the mighty what to do with the prefix: "Be an angel ...".

▷

King George opens Belfast parliament

Belfast, 22 June 1921

Despite appeals urging him not to risk his life, King George today insisted on performing the opening ceremony of the new Northern Ireland parliament, held in the city hall. "I could not have allowed myself to give to Ireland by deputy alone my earnest prayers and good wishes in the new era," he said. Calling for an end to strife, regardless of race or creed, the king added: "I appeal to all Irishmen to pause, to stretch out the hand of forbearance and conciliation, to forgive and forget."

The king and queen received a tumultous welcome, with many streets bedecked in red, white and blue. Yet none of the 12 opposition MPs – six Sinn Fein and six nationalists, out of 52 – were present at the opening, and only, ten days earlier, seven people had died in Belfast riots (→ 16/11/32).

Royal staff sacked

London, 31 October 1922

The royal household is feeling the effect of the post-war world. Twenty-two servants of the royal mews were made redundant today. Inflation and the cost of repairs held over during the war have contributed to a deficit of £45,000 on this year's civil list, but the redundancies have been softened by generous pensions and gratuities.

Emperor's heir is cheered by Indians

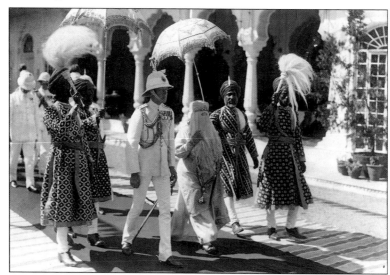
The Prince of Wales in India: here with Her Majesty the Begum of Bhopal.

Edward wearing a kimono in Japan, on his extensive tour of the east.

Karachi, 17 March 1922

The Prince of Wales left India today on the battleship *Renown* after a triumphal four-month tour. In spite of fears by officialdom that nationalist agitation would wreck the visit, he was greeted warmly by innumerable Indians wherever the police allowed him to meet them.

The visit of the king-emperor's heir almost did not take place. The prince's ill-health, together with threats by both the Hindu Congress Party and the Moslem League to boycott the visit, fuelled speculation that it would be cancelled. After all, it was only a year since British troops had opened fire on demonstrators at Amritsar. But to cancel the visit, the viceroy Lord

Reading argued, would be seen as a victory for the nationalists. In the event, from the time that the prince landed at Bombay last November, the fears of serious political disturbances were groundless.

Thousands welcomed him, and when he called on the police – ever-anxious for his security – not to hold the crowds back, they cheered him. In Poona, where he dedicated a memorial for Indians killed in the Great War, crowds threw coins in his path.

The prince travelled all over India, visiting Lucknow, Nepal, Burma, Calcutta, even the Khyber pass, his royal train followed by a second one carrying 25 polo ponies for matches against Indian princes.

Only at Allahabad, where the much-respected Pandit Motilal Nehru (the father of the Congress politician Jawaharlal Nehru) was arrested by over-zealous police, in Moslem Peshawar on the north-west frontier, and at Aligarh university were there any serious nationalist demonstrations. Most Indians saw no conflict between their welcome to the prince and their nationalist aspirations.

The exhausted prince is now heading for Hong Kong and then to Japan before finally returning home. He had wanted to visit China, but this was vetoed by the foreign office. Now he cannot wait to get home and be reunited with Freda Dudley Ward.

Honouring a heroine: King George and Queen Mary at the memorial to Edith Cavell, the British nurse shot by the Germans in October 1915.

Prince is 'best man' at cousin's wedding

Westminster, 18 July 1922

The Prince of Wales was best man, and the king and queen were among 1,400 guests, when Lord Louis Mountbatten today married Edwina Ashley. Mountbatten is a cousin of the prince – his mother was a granddaughter of Queen Victoria, who attended his christening in 1900 – and took leave from the Royal Navy to accompany him on his tours of Australia, New Zealand and India. The bride, one year younger than Lord Louis, is the daughter of a Conservative MP and heiress to the fortune left by Sir Ernest Cassel, a close financial adviser to Edward VII (→ 15/8/47).

Royal bridegroom: Mountbatten.

Shy duke weds Scottish commoner

Lady Elizabeth on her wedding day.

The happy couple departing from Buckingham Palace for their honeymoon.

London, 27 April 1923
Albert, the Duke of York, the second son of George V, married Lady Elizabeth Bowes-Lyon, the ninth child of the 14th Earl of Strathmore, yesterday. The marriage is a break with precedent in two ways: it was held in Westminster abbey (previous royal marriages had taken place in the relative privacy of the Chapel Royal at Windsor), and a king's son was marrying a commoner.

The bride played her role perfectly. As she came into the abbey a mistiming in the ceremony meant that she had to hold both a handbag and a bouquet of roses and heather in the same hand. Without a second's hesitation she gracefully left her father's side and dropped the bouquet onto the tomb of the Unknown Warrior, then returned to her place.

The duke first met her as a shy and awkward five-year-old at a children's Christmas party in 1905. They met again at a ball in May 1920. "The more I see of her the more I like her," he wrote to his mother, Queen Mary. Elizabeth refused his first proposals, wary of the public life that she would be forced to lead, of his moodiness and nervousness (that came out in a twitch and a stammer), and of his liking for whisky. The king's son did not accept failure and persevered. Under the combined weight of her mother and her future mother-in-law she accepted. She has always had a very strong sense of duty.

Over a million people watched the procession, but the feeling amongst them was that they were watching a second-best. As the *Times* puts it this morning: "There is but one wedding to which [the public] look forward with still deeper interest – the wedding which will give a wife to the heir to the throne" (→7/6).

Lady Elizabeth is a bride whom a prince wouldn't ask twice

Elizabeth: engagement portrait.

London, 26 April 1923
Lady Elizabeth Bowes-Lyon may be the first commoner to marry a second-in-line to the throne since James II married Anne Hyde, but she is hardly common. She was brought up in Glamis castle in Macbeth country, favours conservative clothes and conservative views, and does not mix with the "fast set" around the Prince of Wales. She can be naive, as when she gave an interview and was asked if she had refused the prince three times. But she is capable of using her *naïveté* to charming effect: "Do you think I am the sort of person Bertie would have asked twice?" (→27/4).

The bride as a baby, aged two.

King plays crucial role in choice of the prime minister

London, 22 May 1923
The king has been at the heart of a constitutional crisis which has gripped Britain since the resignation two days ago for health reasons of Andrew Bonar Law, the prime minister. Bonar Law declined to offer George any advice about his successor, leaving the king to weigh the competing claims of Lord Curzon, the foreign secretary, and Stanley Baldwin, the chancellor of the exchequer.

The more experienced Curzon was the favourite, and Baldwin expressed his willingness to serve under his rival. Yet the king was uneasy about appointing a prime minister from the Lords. This view was supported by Arthur Balfour, a former Conservative premier, and by close advisers to Bonar Law. Over the Whitsun weekend, with the king in Aldershot, his private secretary Lord Stamfordham took soundings. Lord Salisbury backed Curzon, but to no avail; tonight the king told Curzon that he was asking Baldwin to form a government. Curzon was shattered. "There are circumstances in which it is very undesirable that a peer should be prime minister and in my view this is such a case," King George told him (→22/1/24).

King George makes royal visit to Italy

Rome, May 1923
King George has this month made one of his rare state visits overseas. He had hoped that his trip to Rome would help to improve Anglo-Italian relations, but the government would not countenance any talk of colonial concessions. This left the king with a ceremonial role which did little to enhance his low view of foreigners; he took a particular dislike to Benito Mussolini. Last year's visit to Belgium was no better. George was assigned to one end of the palace at Laeken and Mary to the other. He refuses to go to the Netherlands. "Amsterdam, Rotterdam, and all the other dams! Damned if I'll do it." ▷

King endorses first Labour premier

London, 22 January 1924

King George today became the first British monarch to ask a leader of a socialist party to form a government. Ramsay MacDonald is to be Britain's first Labour prime minister, following the defeat of the Tory government last night. It will be a minority government, relying on Liberal support, but the king had no doubt about the historic nature of MacDonald's appointment. "I wonder what dear Grandmama [Queen Victoria] would have thought of a Labour government," he wrote in his diary. MacDonald also recorded his view of the day: "I fear the king is apprehensive. It would be a miracle if he were not."

George has indeed muttered strong words in private about the socialists, but in public he is the neutral constitutional monarch. He had wanted Baldwin to face parliament rather than resign after the Tories lost seats at last month's general election. But he had expected Baldwin to lose yesterday's vote of no confidence and told one adviser that "it was essential that the socialists' rights under the constitution should in no way be impaired".

He is even willing to countenance his new ministers attending court functions without the traditional uniform, which includes cocked hat and knee-breeches (→ 12/5/26).

George opens Empire Show at Wembley

All aboard! Queen Mary has a go on the model railway at the Empire Show.

Wembley, 23 April 1924

The king opened the British Empire Exhibition here today by sending a telegram via Canada, New Zealand, Australia, South Africa, India, Aden, Egypt and Gibraltar. The electric message took one minute 20 seconds to arrive back in London. Microphones hidden on the royal dais enabled King George's voice to be heard clearly for the first time by the millions of his people who now own the new wireless sets. A coal mine with real pit ponies, replicas of Niagara Falls and a Maori village, and a butter effigy of the Prince of Wales are among the exhibits on the 220-acre (88ha) site, but the most popular is Queen Mary's Dolls' House, designed by the architect Sir Edwin Lutyens.

The Georgian-style house is seven feet eight inches (230cm) high, is furnished with Queen Anne and Chippendale replicas and miniature watercolours by prominent artists, and has working sash windows, doors and locks (→ 10/5/25).

Yorks make a tour of Northern Ireland

Belfast, 21 July 1924

The Duke and Duchess of York today had honorary degrees conferred on them before unveiling a war memorial at Queen's university here. In his address the dean of the law faculty lauded the duke's dedication to public service, while the duchess demonstrated an instant rapport with the crowds. In bright sunshine, the Yorks went on to lay the foundation stone of an art gallery at Stranmillis and receive the freedom of Belfast. They will spend a week in the province (→ 1/12).

The Duke and Duchess in Belfast.

The "sailor-king" at the helm: George V adroitly steering the royal yacht "Britannia", with his look-out busy beside him.

Duke and Duchess of York take a safari holiday in Africa

The Yorks, well protected against the sun, visiting the Makwar dam in Kenya.

Kenya, 31 December 1924

The Duke and Duchess of York are on safari here, sleeping under canvas, riding mules through the bush and shooting all manner of wild game. The young couple are fit and hardy, and both are competent shots. They are revelling in a few weeks free from official duties.

After a rough Mediterranean crossing, the P&O liner *Mulbera* took the Duke and Duchess via the Suez canal to Aden, then round the Horn of Africa to Mombasa, where they were welcomed by Sir Robert Coryndon, the governor of Kenya, and 5,000 dancing African tribespeople. The governor's train took them to Nairobi through a landscape filled with zebra, ostrich, hartebeeste and wildebeeste.

Queen Alexandra dies

Mourners line the way as Queen Alexandra's funeral procession goes by.

Sandringham, 20 November 1925
Queen Alexandra, the Danish-born widow of Edward VII, died today after a heart attack. She was 80, very deaf, and increasingly eccentric. Often dressed in her favourite parma violet, her face invisible beneath a heavy fishnet veil and her hair beneath a wig, she was a slim, elegant figure at polo matches and garden parties. Her death signals the end of the Edwardian era.

The Duke of York and the Prince of Wales arrived too late to take their leave of their much-loved grandmother, but Princess Victoria, her only unmarried daughter, kept her company to the end. Alex-

andra was a constant wife to the Prince of Wales during Queen Victoria's reign, when he had several affairs, and a good queen when he became Edward VII. It was by his wish that she stayed at Sandringham after his death.

But no one will mourn the death of Queen Alexandra more than the king, her devoted son, who used to see her every day when she was at Marlborough House and would never miss a birthday or anniversary. When she became slightly senile, he would send the tactful Viscount Esher to reclaim the family heirlooms which she was wont to give away to friends.

Nervous duke faces broadcast ordeal

Wembley, 10 May 1925
The Duke of York today opened the second year of the British Empire Exhibition at Wembley, but only just; he was afflicted by the lifelong stammer which has always made public speeches something of an ordeal. Today's ceremony posed an even greater challenge, as his words were to be broadcast on the wireless to an expectant nation. The duke had practised for days, but still there were agonising moments when the words struggled to come out. Afterwards, a relieved duke thought that it had gone better than expected. King George was simply thankful that it was not a complete disaster (→19/10/26).

George backs pact, but fears 'Il Duce'

London, 16 October 1925
The king has welcomed the agreement reached today at Locarno in Switzerland under which Germany has finally accepted the post-war frontiers set out in the Treaty of Versailles. George has watched the turbulence in Europe since 1918 with mounting concern. The emergence of Mussolini ("*Il Duce*" – the leader) in Italy was a cause of particular dismay. He could not be trusted, the king told the foreign office in one memorandum: "He very much resembles a mad dog which must bite somebody." However, Italy as well as Germany is a signatory of today's Locarno Pact pledging European security.

Prince faces criticism for his behaviour on recent royal tour of South America

Edward: a good ambassador?

London, 17 October 1925
Striking a note of reproof rare in the contemporary British press, today's *Spectator* magazine criticises the Prince of Wales for neglect of duty during his recent visit to South America. The censure arose from an incident

in Argentina when he failed to keep an appointment at a school. The building had been specially decorated, and the children had learnt English songs for the occasion. Two ministers were there to greet the prince, and, when he did not appear at the agreed hour, one went to his house – to be told without explanation that the engagement had been cancelled.

The prince returned home yesterday from his latest arduous voyage; he has now visited 45 countries and travelled some 150,000 miles (240,000km). The tours have enhanced his glamour: the world's most eligible bachelor and a dashing sportsman (too dashing, thinks his father, about his point-to-point races). In fact, the risks of racing and hunting offer the prince respite from the physical and mental exhaustion of touring.

But these pressures have been worsened by the after-effects of too many late-night parties. The *Spectator* suggests that Edward should avoid inviting a link to be made between his pursuit of fun and blunders such as that in Argentina (→30/8/27).

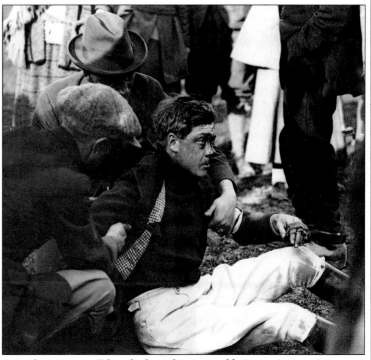

Princely pressures: Edward after taking a tumble in a point-to-point.

Princess Elizabeth is born to the Yorks

Proud parents: the Yorks look fondly at their first-born child, Elizabeth.

Westminster, 21 April 1926

To the delight of a crowd of people who braved the rain to keep watch outside 17 Bruton Street, the Duke and Duchess of York celebrated the birth early this morning of their first child, Princess Elizabeth, third in line to the throne. The baby was delivered by Caesarean section. The king and queen, alerted within half an hour of the birth, arrived this afternoon from Windsor.

The Duke of York is absolutely delighted at the birth of his daughter, whom he wants to call Elizabeth Alexandra Mary, after her mother, grandmother and great-grandmother. It was a difficult birth, the operation performed here at the home of the duchess's parents, close to the major London hospitals, in case of an emergency. The king and queen are thrilled with their new grandchild and have approved the suggested names. The press is welcoming, but is preoccupied with the possibility of a general strike (→ 11/2/27).

The Yorks with the Chief Druid after initiation at the Welsh Eisteddfod.

King urges caution in general strike

London, 12 May 1926

The general strike ended today, with the king heaving a sigh of relief over its peaceful outcome after nine days during which he urged the government to adopt a more conciliatory tone towards the strikers. George criticised some of the more vitriolic rhetoric in the *British Gazette*, an emergency newspaper edited for the government by Winston Churchill, as "unfortunate". Then, at a meeting of the privy council on 9 May, he urged the government to reconsider a proposal banning banks from paying out money to trade unions.

The king told the home secretary and the attorney-general that such a move would be unwise and, citing the friendly spirit exemplified by football matches between strikers and the police, said that it could incite lawlessness such as looting. Cabinet moderates agreed, but today it became academic: the TUC called off the strike, leaving the miners to battle on alone.

This is not the first time that George has shown sympathy for working people. In 1912 he donated money to strikers' families, and he wanted a plea for unity in the king's speech earlier this year. And last month, when one mine-owner condemned miners as "revolutionaries", the king angrily retorted: "Try living on their wages before you judge them" (→ 24/8/31).

Duke seeks advice to cure stammer

London, 19 October 1926

The Duke of York today had his first appointment in the Harley Street consulting rooms of Lionel Logue, an Australian speech therapist, in a wholehearted effort to cure his stammer. As the duke and duchess prepare for a tour of Australia that will include several speeches, it has become essential for Bertie to master the impediment that made his last major speech, at the closing of the British Empire Exhibition last year, an embarrassment shared with millions of wireless listeners. Logue is confident of making progress.

Duke makes poor Wimbledon début

Wimbledon, 30 June 1926

The Duke of York's passion for tennis undid him here today when he and his partner Louis Greig were trounced in the first round of the gentlemen's doubles by the veterans A W Gore and Herbert Roper Barrett, aged 58 and 52 respectively. In this jubilee year of the All England Lawn Tennis Club, the organisers were delighted with the royal entry and wanted the match played on the centre court. The duke wanted an outside court, so court two was chosen as a compromise. It was a

The Duke of York: trounced.

one-sided match, won 6-1, 6-3, 6-2 by Gore – a three-times winner of the gentlemen's singles – and Roper Barrett.

Tennis is one of the Duke of York's chief passions. He and Greig had won the RAF doubles championship in 1920, and when he lived at White Lodge in Richmond park he often played before breakfast on the lodge's well-kept courts. The duke also enjoys inviting professionals to play – the US champion Bill Tilden played him at Buckingham Palace – but today nerves got the better of him, and he confessed to the referee afterwards that he felt he had been outclassed. At one point, when the left-handed duke had mishit several shots, a wag in the crowd suggested: "Try the other hand, Sir."

King George's sons take off on world travels

The Yorks at the opening of the new parliament building in Canberra.

The Prince of Wales (r) and Prince George (second left) with Baldwin (centre).

The Yorks make wide tour of Australia

Portsmouth, 27 June 1927
The Duke and Duchess of York arrived home today after their first major imperial tour. The king and queen were at Victoria station to greet them before their joyful reunion with Princess Elizabeth, whose first birthday occurred whilst they were in Australia.

The tour had also taken in the West Indies, the Pacific and New Zealand as well as Australia where, on 9 May, the duke had opened the new parliament building at Canberra. The duke was not the only person to have been nervous about this tour. The Australian prime minister, Stanley Bruce, was disappointed that the Prince of Wales was not coming and fearful of the duke's stuttering. But the treatment by his new speech therapist, Lionel Logue, had worked wonders; in Melbourne as well as in Canberra the duke addressed crowds several thousand strong without a stutter. The duchess, too, was a hit with the crowds everywhere she went, with her outgoing personality a contrast to the shyer duke.

Prince attends Canadian jubilee parties

Toronto, 30 August 1927
The Prince of Wales and his younger brother Prince George are winding up their month-long, cross-country visit in celebration of Canada's diamond jubilee. The British prime minister, Stanley Baldwin, also attended the jubilee celebrations.

The princes began their triumphal tour in Quebec, where Edward charmed English and French Canadians alike by replying to addresses in both English and French and referring to himself as a Canadian.

In Ottawa, Edward accepted an appointment as a privy council member and unveiled an altar in parliament's peace tower commemorating the war dead. At Niagara Falls he opened the Canada-US Peace Bridge and met the Six-Nation Indians' Council. His speech there was broadcast to the United States. The prince also took time to dance and cruise with Valerie Jones, a Canadian beauty. Later, on a Calgary ranch which he has bought, he relaxed with the shyer, quieter Prince George.

King and queen settle into the 'big house'

Norfolk, December 1927
Christmas at Sandringham House has become a joyful occasion for the royal family and their staff. When King George's mother died two years ago, he and Queen Mary moved out of York Cottage, in the Sandringham grounds, which had been theirs for 33 years. Now, after initially missing the cosiness of their former home, they are putting their own mark on the "big house" – not only in décor but also in style of country living.

The Yuletide rituals begin on Christmas Eve with the distribution of beef to the estate workers: joints from five bullocks are laid out on tables decorated with holly in the coach-house. On Christmas morning, the walk through the park to the church is followed by the exchange of presents in the ballroom. At dinner, surrounded by bowls of roses and scarlet crackers, all except the king wear paper hats.

The way of life is relaxed, but the shooting season requires women to wear day clothes for breakfast, tweeds for lunch, Ascot dresses for tea, and full regalia in the evening. Breakfast is less formal, if only because of the hazards posed by the king's parrot, Charlotte.

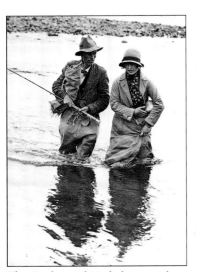

The Duchess of York learning how to fish for trout in New Zealand.

Home again: rain greets the Yorks on their return to England.

Emergency operation saves the life of the king

George unconscious as illness worsens

London, 12 December 1928
The king today underwent an emergency lifesaving operation at Buckingham Palace. George has been unwell since November, and doctors had diagnosed first bronchitis and then septicaemia (blood poisoning). They then feared that his illness was weakening his heart.

The privy council set up a council of state which would exercise the sovereign's functions while George was unwell. The Prince of Wales was told to return from his tour of East Africa; he was initially sceptical (and unwilling to let the summons interfere with a romance), but he arrived yesterday.

By then George was feverish, and by today he had slipped into unconsciousness. X-ray photographs had failed to identify the source of an infection which was now affecting all the blood. Lord Dawson, the most senior of the 11 doctors in attendance, decided that it was time for desperate remedies. He took a syringe and, plunging it into the king's chest, drew off 16 ounces of fluid from a lung. Later a surgeon, Hugh Rigby, removed a rib which had obscured an abscess and drained off the rest of the fluid (→ 5/1929).

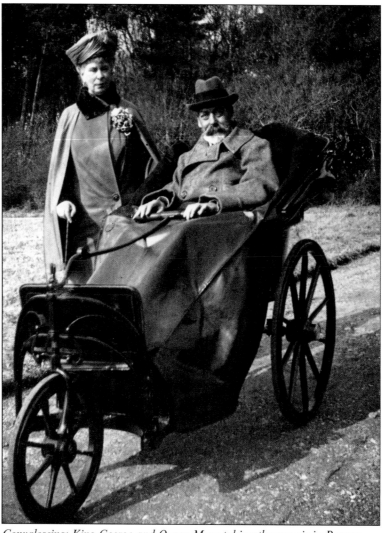
Convalescing: King George and Queen Mary taking the sea air in Bognor.

Sussex sea air aids the king's recovery

Bognor, West Sussex, May 1929
King George today ended three months of convalescence following the illness which nearly cost him his life towards the end of last year. He had rejected suggestions that he might recover abroad – "I was told in rather strong language that nothing of the sort would take place," wrote his secretary later – and moved into a house called Craigwell, near Bognor in Sussex, owned by Sir Arthur du Cros.

He was greatly cheered up during his stay at Craigwell by the arrival in March of his only granddaughter, Princess Elizabeth. She sat on his lap and, as he recovered, accompanied him on walks along the seafront. It is said that at one point the archbishop of Canterbury arrived to encounter the king on all fours, playing horses with the young princess. George now calls her "Lilibet", after the way she tries to pronounce her own name.

She was undoubtedly a tonic, and both king and town have cause for celebration: George has been told that he can resume smoking, and Bognor can add the word "*Regis* [royal]" to its name in recognition of its three months in royal history.

Prince's top aide to resign his position

London, December 1928
A close adviser to the Prince of Wales, Alan "Tommy" Lascelles, has resigned after nine years in his service. "I am thoroughly and permanently out of sympathy with him," Lascelles has said. It is understood that Lascelles, the prince's assistant private secretary, has lost patience with what he sees as the conflict between the prince's public duties and private life. The two men have just returned from a tour of East Africa cut short by the king's illness. Lascelles has said that the prince at first refused to believe a call from the prime minister that he should return to his father's bedside (→ 10/1935).

Duke of York backs camping to help break down social barriers

Dissolving class barriers: the Duke of York with campers on Romney Marsh.

Romney Marsh, August 1929
One of the phenomena of the 1920s has been the annual camp for boys sponsored by the Duke of York. Each year since 1921 some 200 boys from private schools and 200 working-class boys nominated by the Industrial Welfare Society have spent part of August on holiday together, trying to break down social barriers by playing games and making up their own entertainment. The duke backed the idea from the outset, despite some misgivings within the palace, and has spent one day each summer at the camp. One Eton schoolboy wrote that it undermined class hatred by showing that people from offices, factories or coal-mines could still be "good fellows" (→ 8/1938).

Princess 'Lilibet' is darling of press

A new star: Princess Lilibet.

London, 29 April 1929

The world's press has discovered a new star: Princess Elizabeth today made the cover of the US magazine *Time* in the week of her third birthday. "Lilibet", as the princess is now widely known, is setting fashions for other children, and she was inundated with presents this week. Crowds call out for her when her parents, the Duke and Duchess of York, travel. And she impresses VIPs, too. "She is a character," wrote Winston Churchill from Balmoral last year. "She has an air of authority and reflectiveness astonishing in an infant" (→ 5/1929).

Top church post for duke ends long rift

Edinburgh, 21 May 1929

The Duke of York today opened the general assembly of the Church of Scotland in a ceremony which reunited the church after a rift between two opposing wings which had lasted for nearly 90 years. It was also the first time for more than two centuries that a member of the royal family had acted as lord high commissioner, the ancient officer of the sovereign's representative within the church. With Edinburgh celebrating the 600th anniversary of the granting of its charter by Robert the Bruce, the city had only one complaint: the duke and his Scottish-born wife had left Princess Elizabeth at home.

Prince of Wales leaves his stamp on the 'roaring twenties'

London, 31 December 1929

As the 1920s draw to a close, the Prince of Wales, now aged 35, has been an influential figure in the fashions and images of the "roaring twenties".

During his first overseas tour, to Canada and the United States in 1919, the prince was received with wild enthusiasm. A similar reception met him the following year in New Zealand and Australia, and in India which he visited in 1921-22. Since then he has made numerous tours, both in Britain and throughout the empire, covering hundreds of thousands of miles and captivating the crowds with his charm.

However, forced to fulfil a rigorous programme of engagements, the prince himself has grown progressively more disenchanted with his job, confiding in one of his staff in 1927 that he was "heartily and genuinely fed up". Above all he regrets the invasion of his privacy. He would prefer to spend more time in the pursuit of pleasure – he enjoys vigorous sports, and has a seemingly insatiable appetite for nightlife. His glamour and fashion sense have drawn admiration, but his gambling, drinking and associations with women have sometimes attracted less favourable comment.

A keen sportsman: dressed in plus-fours for a game of golf.

On his travels: passing through a floral archway in Durban, S Africa.

Visiting the people: the prince is popular and talks freely and easily wherever he goes; here he is in the mining districts of Durham.

Visiting the Handley Page aircraft works at Cricklewood.

G e o r g e V
1910–1936

**House
of
Windsor**

London, 8 July 1930. King George opens India House in the Aldwych and makes an appeal for peace in India (→ 10/1931).

London, 1 September 1930. The Prince of Wales is promoted to vice-admiral, lieutenant-general and air marshal.

St Andrews, 24 September 1930. The Duke of York takes over from his brother, the Prince of Wales, as captain of the Royal and Ancient Golf Club.

London, September 1930. Prince Philip of Greece, a grandson of the late Marquis of Milford Haven, is enrolled at Cheam preparatory school (→ 9/1934).

London, 3 October 1930. The christening of Princess Margaret Rose, the second daughter of the Duke and Duchess of York, takes place at Buckingham Palace.→

Leicestershire, 10 January 1931. The Prince of Wales meets a Mr and Mrs Ernest Simpson, an American couple, at a weekend party in Melton Mowbray hosted by his close friend Thelma, Lady Furness (→ 1/1932).

London, 21 April 1931. King Alfonso XIII of Spain, who abdicated a week ago, arrives with his family in exile.

Westminster, 16 November 1931. The Prince of Wales gives his total support to the government's "Buy British" campaign.

London, 1 January 1932. The title of Princess Royal is conferred on Mary, the only daughter of King George, after the death last January of her aunt, Princess Louise, the eldest daughter of King Edward VII (→ 28/3/65).

London, January 1932. The Simpsons host their first formal dinner party for the Prince of Wales (→ 30/1).

Windsor, 30 January 1932. Thelma, Lady Furness, invites the Simpsons to join the Prince of Wales at his weekend home, Fort Belvedere (→ 3/1933).

Scotland, spring 1932. Marion Crawford – nicknamed "Crawfie" – joins the York household as governess (→ 1933).

Windsor, 21 April 1932. The people of Wales give Princess Elizabeth a 15-foot (4.5-metre)-high model of a Welsh cottage as her sixth birthday present (→ 1933).

London, 19 July 1932. King George opens Lambeth Bridge.

London, 28 February 1933. George watches his first moving picture – a Walt Disney cartoon and a version of J B Priestley's *The Good Companions.*

Southampton, March 1933. The Simpsons sail for New York; a *bon voyage* message signed "Edward P" is in their cabin (→ 5/7).

London, 12 June 1933. King George opens the world economic conference.

London, November 1933. The Prince of Wales surprises Count Albert Mensdorff, a former Austrian ambassador to London, with his strong pro-German sympathies (→ 6/1935).

Windsor, 1933. A new addition to the York household is Rozavel Golden Eagle, known by all as "Dookie"; he is a corgi, a Welsh breed of dog.

Southampton, January 1934. Thelma, Lady Furness, sets sail for New York, telling Wallis Simpson to entertain the Prince of Wales in her absence (→ 6/1934).

London, June 1934. Freda Dudley Ward, a close friend of the Prince of Wales, is told that he will not accept any calls from her.→

Britain, 28 August 1934. Prince George, the youngest son of King George, announces his engagement to Princess Marina, the youngest daughter of Prince Nicholas of Greece and Denmark and Grand Duchess Helen Vladimirovna of Russia (→ 12/10).

Biarritz, France, 31 August 1934. Wallis Simpson, without her husband Ernest, accompanies the Prince of Wales and his party cruising on board the yacht *Rosaura* (→ 11/1934).

Germany, September 1934. Prince Philip of Greece, who has been living with his sister Theodora and her husband Berthold, the ruler of Baden, is to leave the Salem school which he has attended for the last year; originally founded by Kurt Hahn, it has become a pro-Nazi establishment.

London, 12 October 1934. Prince George, aged 31, is created Duke of Kent (→ 29/11).

Scotland, autumn 1934. Prince Philip of Greece, having returned to live with his uncle, George, the Marquis of Milford Haven, begins at a new school in Grampian, Gordonstoun House; it is run by the founder of the Salem school, Kurt Hahn (→ 18/4/39).

London, November 1934. George is furious when the Prince of Wales presents the Simpsons at a pre-wedding celebration for the Duke of Kent and Princess Marina at Buckingham Palace (→ 2/1935).

Westminster, 29 November 1934. The wedding of Prince George, the Duke of Kent, and Princess Marina of Greece and Denmark takes place in the abbey (→ 9/10/35).

Austria, February 1935. Mrs Wallis Simpson accompanies the Prince of Wales on a ski-ing holiday in Kitzbühel (→ 14/5).

London, 14 May 1935. Despite disapproval from the king, the Prince of Wales invites Mr and Mrs Simpson to the state ball; he causes a stir when he chooses Wallis as his dancing partner (→ 7/1935).

London, June 1935. The press criticises the Prince of Wales when, speaking at a British Legion rally, he makes a proposal "to stretch forth the hand of friendship to Germany" (→ 1/1936).

London, July 1935. Admiral Sir Lionel Halsey, the head of the household staff of the Prince of Wales, confides to the king that Mrs Simpson receives an annual income of around £6,000 from the prince (→ 10/1935).

London, 9 October 1935. The Duchess of Kent gives birth to her first son, Prince Edward George Nicholas Paul Patrick (→ 25/8/42).

London, October 1935. Captain Alan "Tommy" Lascelles, the former assistant secretary to the Prince of Wales, returns from a five-year posting as secretary to Lord Bessborough, the governor-general of Canada, and becomes King George's assistant private secretary.

Buckinghamshire, 3 Dec 1935. King George's sister, Princess Victoria, dies aged 67.

London, early January 1936. Despite public disapproval, the Prince of Wales expresses a desire to attend the German Olympic Games (→ 8/1936).

Sandringham, 20 January 1936. King George dies aged 70; his son, Edward, the Prince of Wales, will succeed him.→

Princess Margaret Rose is christened

London, 3 October 1930
A select party at Buckingham Palace looked on today as the archbishop of Canterbury christened Princess Margaret Rose, the second daughter of the Duke and Duchess of York. Margaret, Princess Elizabeth's sister, was born on 21 August in Tayside, in Scotland. In the six weeks since her birth there has been some controversy in the royal family over her name.

The duchess wanted to call her daughter Ann Margaret, because, she said: "I think that Ann of York sounds pretty, and Elizabeth and Ann go so well together." But King George made it plain that he did not approve of Ann as a name, and the Yorks were forced to compromise with Margaret Rose.

The baby was born at 9.22pm on 21 August, in the middle of a violent summer thunderstorm, in the romantic setting of Glamis castle, reputedly Britain's oldest inhabited house. The following morning, pipers led the celebrations in the streets of Glamis, and a large crowd climbed nearby Hunter's Hill to light a great beacon.

Glamis holds many happy memories of childhood holidays for the duchess, and it was her particular wish to have her second baby here. The king granted her special permission for the royal birth to occur in Scotland. The duchess was a fortnight later than forecast

A second daughter: Margaret Rose.

giving birth, which caused some discomfort for two men – the home secretary, J R Clynes, and Harry Boyd, the ceremonial secretary at the home office. The law requires that the home secretary be present at a royal birth, a tradition begun after rumours in 1688 that a baby was smuggled into the royal bedchamber in a warming-pan. And so on 5 August the two men moved north to Airlie castle, some eight miles (13km) from Glamis.

For 15 days they waited in a state of some tension. On 21 August they reached Glamis for the birth with just 20 minutes to spare and only after a hair-raising, high-speed drive through the thunderstorm.

King George takes lead role in negotiating new government to tackle economic crisis

London, 24 August 1931
There have been five crucial meetings at Buckingham Palace in the last 24 hours. Three times King George has persuaded the Labour prime minister, Ramsay MacDonald, not to resign in the face of the current economic crisis. This morning MacDonald heads a new all-party national government which will take "whatever steps may be deemed necessary" to restore confidence in the pound.

MacDonald's cabinet was unable to agree on a package of tax increases and cuts in unemployment benefit proposed to tackle an economic crisis which has brought Britain to the brink of bankruptcy. MacDonald first went to the palace to resign yesterday, but the king told him that he was the only person to carry the country through. George then summoned Sir Herbert Samuel, representing the Liberals, and the Conservative leader, Stanley Baldwin; they backed the plan for a national government.

Last night, after failing to win cabinet support for his economic proposals, MacDonald told his colleagues "I'm off to the palace to throw in my hand." A second time George asked him to reconsider, and this morning MacDonald, Baldwin and Samuel agreed to form a national government, after the

MacDonald: denied three times.

king had for a third time turned the prime minister's resignation aside.

Most of MacDonald's Labour colleagues have refused to join the coalition and consider him a traitor. But the king is in good spirits. His private secretary Sir Clive Wigram, a keen cricketer, says that the king "played one of his best innings ... he was not out at the end and had hardly turned a hair" (→ 29/9).

Princes leave for South American tour

England, 16 January 1931
The Prince of Wales left today for an extensive tour of South America. The purpose of his visit is to boost trade between Britain and the South American continent, and the highlight will be in Argentina where he is due to open the British Empire Trade Exhibition at Buenos Aires. Before leaving, he told Queen Mary: "I hope I may be able to help our industries a little. That is my only desire, and if I can get some enjoyment out of it, so much the better."

Edward is accompanied on the voyage by his younger brother, Prince George. The pair are planning to brush up their Spanish on the long journey out. Their first destination is Peru.

Prince George with the Brazilian president, Sr Getulio Vargas, during an official visit with George's elder brother, the Prince of Wales.

Economic crisis forces royal pay cuts

London, 29 September 1931
King George returned to London today from Balmoral for further meetings with ministers in the new national government who are now divided amongst themselves about the terms on which they will fight a general election next month. The king wrote to the Duke of York: "I mean to do everything and anything in my power to prevent the old ship running on the rocks."

The national government was formed very much at the king's behest, and he has been determined that he (and his family) will set a royal example at a time of crisis when taxes have been increased, the pound has been devalued and pay cut for millions of people. He therefore announced on 7 September

that he would take a £50,000 cut in the annual civil list allocation for as long as the current crisis lasts.

This "pay cut" will force a few changes in the royal family's lifestyle. The king has decided that he will have to give up shooting in Windsor great park to save money and is urging similar economies upon other members of the family [*see report overleaf*]. The Prince of Wales has already agreed to give up £10,000 a year from the revenues of the Duchy of Cornwall.

The national government has been buttressed by loans from New York bankers, but it has also been buffeted by strikes, demonstrations and even a mutiny by naval ratings at Invergordon. The "sailor-king" was outraged (→7/11).

New Windsor home for the Yorks

Windsor, 18 September 1931

The Duke and Duchess of York visited their new country house, Royal Lodge in Windsor great park, for the first time today. It is a present from the king who has become more and more concerned about the rundown state of the lodge, which was used as a love-nest by King George IV.

The duke and duchess are clearly delighted with their gift – despite the fact that much of the original house was demolished by William IV and his queen, Adelaide, after parliament criticised royal excesses. The Yorks are restoring the house to its original proportions, adding two wings and new bedrooms for themselves, the duke's a simple affair designed like a ship's cabin. The duke has become a passionate gardener, specialising in rhodo-dendrons, and plans the biggest display of these plants to be found anywhere in Britain.

The Yorks will continue to use 145 Piccadilly near Hyde Park Corner as their London home. Royal Lodge will be their country retreat, just as Fort Belvedere across Windsor great park over-looking Virginia Water has offered the Prince of Wales a secluded home away from public gaze for the last two years (→ 7/11).

Louise, the Princess Royal, who died on 4 January 1931, here with her husband. Princess Mary, as the eldest daughter of the ruling monarch, is likely to receive the courtesy title of Princess Royal.

King meets Gandhi at empire conference

London, October 1931

Dressed in his familiar homespun loincloth, Mahatma Gandhi pad-ded barefoot through the carpeted corridors of Buckingham Palace to take tea with the king-emperor – who wore a frock coat for the meeting. The king had been reluctant to come face to face with the man whose non-violent defiance of Brit-ain has twice landed him in prison.

"What!" roared the king. "Have this rebel fakir in the palace after he has been behind all these attacks on my loyal officers?" The king relent-ed, however, after talks with his ministers, who had invited Gandhi to London for a round-table con-ference on the future of India.

Gandhi has demanded indepen-dence for his nation, and he out-lined his policy to the man who wears the Star of India in his crown. Gandhi told the king that he and his followers would accept citizenship in a commonwealth –

Gandhi hears some sartorial advice.

but not in the British Empire. The king warned him: "Remember, Mr Gandhi, I won't have any attacks on my empire." Gandhi said: "I must not be drawn into a political argument in Your Majesty's palace after receiving Your Majesty's hos-pitality" (→ 11/12).

George confronts changing face of empire

Westminster, 11 December 1931

The changing nature of the British Empire has been brought into sharp focus for the king over recent weeks. Two months ago he welcom-ed Mahatma Gandhi, the leader of India's nationalist movement, to Buckingham Palace; today the Statute of Westminster became law, formally confining the crown's role to a symbolic one within the dom-inions of a free commonwealth.

George is proud of his position as the head of the world's greatest 20th-century empire, but it is India in which he maintains the closest personal interest, particularly as the dominions have gained the self-governing freedom which was con-firmed today. George, the king-emperor of India, has twice visited the country and reads avidly the fortnightly letters from his vice-roys. And, for all his distaste for the nationalist movement, George has strongly condemned the colour bar as practised by many British offi-cials in India (→ 30/4/32).

Irish ban oath of loyalty to the king

Dublin, 30 April 1932

The Irish Free State took what ap-pears to be a final step in its separa-tion from Great Britain today when MPs in the *Dail* backed the move by the recently-elected *Fianna Fail* party, led by Eamon de Valera, to abolish the oath of allegiance to the British crown in the Irish constitu-tion. The government has opted for a republican policy and will also withhold land annuities amounting to more than £5 million owing to British landlords.

Economy-conscious duke sells horses

Ascot, Berks, 7 November 1931

Prince Albert, the Duke of York, fought back tears as he watched his string of hunters auctioned off at the Ascot bloodstock sales. Such is the economic climate which forced the sale that the duke received just over £900 for horses which would have fetched far more in normal times. "It has come as a great shock to me that with the economy ... my hunting should have been one of the things I must do without," he wrote to the master of the Pytchley, Ron-ald Tree. "And I must sell my horses too. The parting with them will be terrible."

The king had volunteered to take a £50,000 cut from the civil list to to show that the royal family is playing its full part in the nation's economic recovery. The Duke of York was also expected to take a reduction in his own £25,000 allowance, and he decided that the horses had to go. The king is giving up his beloved shooting in Windsor great park in the same selfless spirit, while the Prince of Wales has also sold his horses in addition to giving up £10,000 a year from his estates [*see previous page*].

The prince – who was in a French nightclub when the king telephoned demanding that he join the national economy drive – is now playing an active role in the government's "Buy British" cam-paign. Tonight he made a wireless broadcast from the BBC's Birming-ham studio, and he will shortly visit Paris to boost exports (→ 16/11).

Young princess begins to earn her spurs

Princess Elizabeth enjoying a ride on a shaggy Shetland pony.

Windsor, 1932

Princess Elizabeth, who has been taking riding lessons since she was three, is becoming an accomplished young horsewoman. She began rid-ing lessons last year, having been given her first pony as a Christmas present in 1929 when she was only three. She and her father are now to be seen regularly riding out in the great park at weekends, "Lilibet", impeccable in her equestrian habit, showing natural ability. Her love of horses is also shown in the number of toy horses which she rides around her home (→ 17/2/37).

George makes Christmas broadcast

Sandringham, 25 December 1932
Using a text written for him by Rudyard Kipling, King George broadcast Christmas greetings to his nation and the empire today. The king sat at a table in a make-shift "studio" under the stairs in a room once used by his father's secretary. A thick cloth covered the table to deaden the sound of rustling paper – this was the king's first "informal" broadcast, and he was very nervous – but the microphone used was not gold-plated as reported in some newspapers.

"I speak now from my home and from my heart to you all," said the king. "... to men and women so cut off by the snows, the desert, or the sea, that only voices out of the air can reach them."

The king's first broadcast was made in 1924, when up to ten million people heard him open the British Empire exhibition at

Speaking from the heart to his people: King George making a broadcast.

Wembley. Public interest was so great that halls were filled in Manchester, Leeds and Glasgow, and a government inquiry in Cambridge suspended its sitting to hear the king. Despite constant blandishments since 1923 by John Reith, the general manager of the BBC, the king has been reluctant to make an "intimate" broadcast until now.

Prince opens Belfast's Stormont building

Belfast, 16 November 1932
The Prince of Wales today opened the impressive new Northern Ireland parliament buildings at Stormont, on an elevated site on the outskirts of east Belfast. The neo-classical building was described by a Unionist as "the outward and visible proof of the permanence of our institutions ... that for all time we are bound indissolubly to the British crown". Nationalist MPs, who had virtually deserted the provincial parliament since the abolition of proportional representation in 1929, boycotted the celebrations. It was the first visit of the Prince of Wales to Northern Ireland; later he played a drum offered by an enthusiastic Orangeman.

At home in 1933: Elizabeth, Margaret and a favourite doll in the splendid model cottage given to Elizabeth on her sixth birthday last year.

'Crawfie' appointed as royal governess

Windsor, 1933
From the moment that she arrived at Royal Lodge, 22-year-old Marion Crawford knew that horses were going to play a major part in her life. The new governess arrived to find one of her charges driving an imaginary team of horses around her bedroom. Princess Elizabeth was using the cord from her dressing-gown for reins tied to the knobs on her brass bedstead.

"How do you do," she said to the Scots girl. "Why have you no hair ?" "Crawfie" – as she was to become very rapidly – took off her hat to reveal an Eton crop. Satisfied, the princess drove on. Princess Margaret met the governess on the following morning.

The princess delights in harnessing Crawfie with red reins and leading her governess around the gardens of either their London home at 145 Piccadilly, near Hyde Park Corner, or Royal Lodge at Windsor. "If ever I am queen," she told Crawfie, "I shall make a law that there must be no riding on Sundays. Horses should have a rest, too, and I shan't let anyone dock their ponies' tails" (→11/1950).

Friendship blooms between the prince and the Simpsons

London, 5 July 1933
The Prince of Wales last night attended a formal dinner party at the Bryanston Square flat of Mr and Mrs Ernest Simpson for the first time. Mrs Simpson celebrated Independence Day by serving an American menu with a red, white and blue colour scheme.

Among the guests were the American diplomat Benjamin Thaw and his wife, and the prince's close friend Thelma, Lady Furness, who first introduced him to the Simpsons in 1931. The Prince of Wales's friendship with Ernest and

Wallis Simpson: a later portrait.

Wallis Simpson has blossomed since their first visit to Fort Belvedere in January last year. They have spent several further weekends at the Fort, they have dined at York House, the prince's official London residence, and last month the prince threw a party at Quaglino's restaurant for Mrs Simpson's 37th birthday.

When they sailed to New York last March aboard the *Mauretania*, Ernest and Wallis became the talk of the ship after a *bon voyage* message was delivered to their stateroom signed "Edward P." The Simpsons sometimes dine out with the prince, and Wallis has been seen dancing with him at the Embassy club; but she has written jokingly to her aunt, Bessie Merryman, that "Thelma is still the Princess of Wales" (→1/1934).

Prince of Wales now only has eyes for Mrs Simpson

London, June 1934

The Prince of Wales has severed contact with Freda Dudley Ward, his closest friend and adviser for most of the past 16 years. On telephoning York House recently, Mrs Dudley Ward – who had been preoccupied for several months by the illness of her elder daughter – was shocked to be told by the switchboard operator: "I have orders not to put you through."

This comes just a month after the prince had dropped Thelma, Lady Furness, another important woman in his life, who often acted as hostess at Fort Belvedere.

Before Thelma set off on a visit to America in January, she asked her friend Wallis Simpson – whom she had introduced to the Prince of Wales in 1930 – to take care of the prince while she was away, saying: "See he does not get into any mischief." On her return, Thelma discovered that the prince's intimacy with Mrs Simpson had developed to such an extent that Wallis had usurped her position. Greeted coolly by the prince at the fort, Thelma at once packed and left.

The prince, it seems, now has eyes only for Wallis, whom he sees whenever he can, often with her husband, Ernest (→ 31/8).

Passers-by seem more than a little puzzled by these large-scale preparations for the wedding of Prince George, the newly-created Duke of Kent, to Princess Marina of Greece and Denmark.

Britons acclaim King George's jubilee

The royal family entering St Paul's for the thanksgiving service to mark the king's jubilee, by Frank Salisbury (b.1874).

The king drives through London's east end on 25 May to mark the jubilee.

Happiness all round: one of the many street parties to celebrate the jubilee.

London, 6 May 1935

For days now, the nation's mothers have been ordering hams for several million sandwiches, baking the cakes, setting the jellies and blancmanges and praying for good weather for today – the day of the king's silver jubilee. Almost every street in the country, it seems, is having its own party with a feast for children by day and a "knees-up" in the evening for parents. Church bells ring out and beacons blaze on every height tonight, and the whole country is echoing with the crackle of fireworks. Rarely has there been such a widespread display of affection for a monarch in Britain.

It is 25 years since George succeeded his father, Edward VII, as king, and even after 25 years on the throne he and the queen appeared dazed and surprised by the warmth of the welcome as they drove to St Paul's cathedral today. The king was suitably regal in the scarlet uniform of a field marshal, his medals glittering in the spring sunshine. Queen Mary was just as magnificent in a white dress and her inevitable necklace of five rows of pearls and other jewels. Her equally familiar toque was white, with white feathers. Much attention was paid to the king's granddaughter princesses. Elizabeth followed the service carefully; her sister Margaret fidgeted.

A huge crowd gathered outside Buckingham Palace tonight to sing *For He's a Jolly Good Fellow*. The king is genuinely surprised at the extent of the warmth. "But I am just an ordinary fellow," he said to the archbishop, who replied: "Yes, Sir, that's just it."

Prince of Wales and Mrs Simpson seek some privacy on a European holiday

London, October 1935
The Prince of Wales and Wallis Simpson are back in London after a summer spent cruising the Mediterranean and revisiting Budapest and Vienna. This is the third holiday they have spent together, and there is no longer any doubt that they are devoted to one another – although most of the British public remains unaware of the romance.

In August last year the prince invited Mrs Simpson and her husband, Ernest, to join him on holiday at Biarritz, on the south-west coast of France, where he had taken a house. By this time the Simpsons had become an almost permanent part of the prince's life. They paid frequent visits to Fort Belvedere – where Wallis had assumed Thelma Furness's role of hostess and annoyed the servants by taking a keen interest in the running of the household. In London, too, the Simpsons were often seen in the prince's company, and Wallis's intimate treatment of him in public surprised and shocked his friends.

Ernest Simpson was prevented by business commitments in New York from joining the prince's party in France, so Wallis was chaperoned on the holiday by her American aunt, Bessie Merryman. There were other guests at the house in Biarritz, but Wallis and the prince were seen dining alone

Edward and Wallis: holidaying.

together at local restaurants. From Biarritz, the party boarded the *Rosaura*, a yacht belonging to the Conservative politician Lord Moyne, and sailed down to Gibraltar for a Mediterranean cruise.

Last February the couple took another holiday together, this time at Kitzbühel in Austria – Ernest Simpson had again refused the invitation on the grounds of business in New York. At the end of a fortnight's skiing the party moved on to Vienna and Budapest before returning to London (→ 21/1/36).

King George V is dead

Sandringham, 20 January 1936
At five minutes to midnight tonight King George V died. He was 70 and had done his duty to the very end, meeting three cabinet ministers at 12.15pm to approve the formation of a council of state to act on his behalf during his illness. He signed his initials, and the ministers left in tears. A few hours later it was announced that "the king's life is moving peacefully towards its close".

Lord Dawson, the chief royal physician, had arrived at Sandringham three days ago when Queen Mary had also sent a note to the Prince of Wales at Fort Belvedere: "I think you ought to know that Papa is not very well." The chain-smoking monarch was bedridden with bronchial catarrh, and there were signs of cardiac weakness. It is possible that Dawson used drugs to ease the king's pain and perhaps precipitate the moment of death.

George's sons and daughter were

Lighting up: the king's downfall?

at his bedside when he died, his once powerful voice reduced to no more than a whisper. After he died, Queen Mary stooped to kiss the hand of the Prince of Wales in homage to the new king (→ 21/1).

King helped monarchy to survive changes

London, 21 January 1936
Perhaps the greatest achievement of King George V is that the monarchy itself has survived, unlike many in a Europe which was ripped apart by the Great War. George has played an unostentatious part in a tidal wave of social change. A private man, best known for his love of the sea, shooting and stamp collecting, he rarely had any instinctive sympathy for the causes of reform (except in his dislike of racism in India). Yet his sense of duty led him to back the primacy of the Commons over the Lords, to accept a Labour government, to urge moderation during the general strike and to seek national unity during the economic crisis in 1931. When he died he had two great fears: the suitability of his eldest son for the crown, and the rise of the Nazis in Germany (→ 28/1).

Henry, the Duke of Gloucester, marries

Prince Henry with his bride, Lady Alice Montagu-Douglas-Scott.

London, 6 November 1935
After the marriage of his third son, Prince Henry, the Duke of Gloucester, to Lady Alice Montagu-Douglas-Scott, a daughter of the Duke of Buccleuch, the king wrote in his diary tonight: "Now all the children are married except David." Because of the death of the bride's father the wedding took place in the chapel in Buckingham Palace, although the two princesses, Elizabeth and Margaret, still wore the bridesmaids' dresses designed by Norman Hartnell.

The duke, whose sole ambition, it seems, is to command his own regiment, has recently toured Australia and New Zealand on behalf of his ailing father (→ 11/1938).

A family group: King George V out riding with three of his sons.

**Edward VIII
1936**

**House
of
Windsor**

Sandringham, 20 January. Edward, the Prince of Wales, accedes to the throne (→ 21/1).

London, 21 January. Edward takes the accession oath in Mrs Simpson's presence (→ 22/1).

London, 22 Jan. Edward, as king, is left nothing in George V's will; his brother Albert gets a pay rise as heir presumptive and is promoted in the services.→

Britain, 1 March. Edward broadcasts as king (→ 16/5).

London, 28 May. Edward's coronation will be on 12 May 1937.

London, July. Ernest Simpson moves into his club as divorce proceedings begin (→ 23/9).

Yugoslavia, 10 August. Edward cruises on the *Nahlin* with Wallis Simpson (→ 14/9).

United States, 23 September. The press speculates on Edward's relationship with the US-born Wallis Simpson.→

London, 20 October. Stanley Baldwin, the prime minister, meets King Edward to discuss his relationship with Mrs Simpson (→ 27/10).

Ipswich, 27 Oct. Mrs Simpson wins a decree nisi (→ 31/10).

London, 31 October. Edward installs Wallis in a Regent's Park house (→ 13/11).

London, 13 November. Edward sacks Alexander Hardinge, his private secretary, for sending him a letter reminding him of his royal duties (→ 15/11).

London, 15 November. Walter Monckton, an Oxford friend and lawyer, becomes Edward's private secretary (→ 16/11).

London, 27 November. Baldwin puts the idea of a morganatic marriage to the cabinet.

Bradford, 1 Dec. Bishop Blunt criticises the king (→ 3/12).

Windsor, 7 December. Edward discusses his abdication with his heir, the Duke of York (→ 8/12).

Windsor, 10 December. A financial settlement is arranged for the abdication; Edward will become Duke of Windsor.→

Windsor, 11 December. Edward broadcasts on his abdication.→

Windsor, 11 December. Albert, the Duke of York, becomes King George VI (→ 12/12).

The life and times of King Edward VIII

Name: Edward (called David – one of seven names – by family).
Birth: 12 May 1894.
Accession: 21 January 1936.
Coronation: none – abdicated on 10 December 1936 and became Duke of Windsor.
Predecessor: father.
Height: five feet six inches.
Marriage: Mrs Wallis Warfield (previously Simpson), 3 June 1937.

Children: none.
Favourite home: Ft Belvedere.
Likes: sport, society.
Dislikes: bureaucracy.
Greatest problem: desire to marry a divorced woman.
Greatest successes: early tours; support for unemployed people.
Famous saying: "Something must be done."
Death: 28 May 1972.

Edward is new king

London, 22 January

Edward VIII was proclaimed king today at St James's palace and at three other places in London. The ceremony followed the 41-year-old king's first public appearance yesterday, at the accession privy council, when he addressed more than one hundred councillors in the banqueting hall of St James's. Edward promised to uphold constitutional government and to work for the happiness and welfare of his subjects, relying on "the loyalty and affection of my peoples throughout the empire".

The king had arranged for a number of his friends, including Wallis Simpson, to watch today's ceremony at St James's from a room in the palace. As it was about to start, he broke with precedent and moved over to the window to watch his own proclamation – and was photographed there talking to Mrs Simpson.

Edward's relationship with Mrs Simpson – who is still married to her second husband, Ernest – has been a cause of increasing concern to his family and close friends, though no one appears to have tackled him directly on the subject. The British public remains ignorant of the affair, but top politicians, including Stanley Baldwin, the prime minister, are fearful of its consequences. Before his death, King George V is said to have confided to Baldwin his belief that: "After I am dead the boy will ruin himself in 12 months" (→ 28/1).

Mourners pay tribute to King George V

The royal mourners: following the gun carriage at King George's funeral.

Windsor, 28 January

George V's funeral service at St George's chapel today was delayed for an hour by the late arrival of the coffin, which had been held up by crowds blocking the way from Windsor station. The mourners included the prime minister, Stanley Baldwin, two former premiers and five foreign monarchs. The new king sprinkled symbolic earth from a silver bowl into the royal vault.

This ended a week of ritual to mark the death of the old king. The coffin was first placed in the church at Sandringham before being taken to the local station by gun carriage and transported by train to London. There a royal standard was draped over it and the imperial crown secured to its lid, but during the procession to Westminster Hall the Maltese cross fell off the top of the crown. During the four days that the coffin lay in state, nearly a million people filed past it (→ 1/3).

Opposite: the new king, Edward VIII, was an honoured soldier.

Concern grows over the cavalier attitude of 'bored' monarch to his official duties

A monarch's official duties: King Edward broadcasting to his people.

London, 31 July 1936

The king has been criticised for neglect of duty at a presentation of débutantes at Buckingham Palace. In consequence of the period of court mourning following the death of George V some 600 débutantes were awaiting presentation, and it was decided to hold two garden parties this month to clear the backlog. At the first of these events, Edward, who had been photographed looking bored, retired indoors during a shower and never re-emerged, giving orders that the presentations should be taken as made. Although the king conducts himself with dignity on most formal occasions, there are times when he fails to hide feelings of tedium and is clearly unwilling to conform to the behaviour expected of him.

He rarely attends church, for example. He has been censured by his staff for unpunctuality and lack of consideration. His cavalier attitude towards urgent state papers – which are sometimes left unread for days on end – has given rise to security concerns. Observers believe that he may be too preoccupied by his relationship with Wallis Simpson to give matters of state the attention that they deserve (→ 10/8).

Guests are presented to King Edward at a reception in the palace garden.

King Edward attacked at army parade

London, 16 May 1936

Edward won the admiration of on-lookers today for his calm reaction to an apparent attempt on his life. The king had presented colours to three battalions of Guards in Hyde Park and was riding back towards Constitution Hill when a man in the crowd pulled a gun. In a struggle with police, the gun was thrown under the feet of the king's horse. Believing the object to be a bomb, the king braced himself for an explosion; when none came, he rode on without flinching. The gunman was later identified as George McMahon, an Irish journalist with a grudge against the home secretary.

Police drag the assailant away.

Edward said to back pro-German policy

London, August 1936

Joachim von Ribbentrop was this month made German ambassador to London, and there is speculation that Adolf Hitler, the German *führer*, made the appointment in the belief that Ribbentrop – who last year negotiated an Anglo-German naval treaty – enjoys a special relationship with the king and Mrs Simpson. While there is little evidence to support Hitler's view, there is no doubt about King Edward's pro-German sympathies.

The king, who wishes to avoid a war at all costs, believes that communism presents the greatest threat to the peace and stability of Europe. He makes no secret of his opposition to much of the foreign policy of his government, or of his admiration for Hitler's National Socialist Party – and its position as a bulwark against communism. Despite Hitler's remilitarisation of the Rhineland last March, he favours conciliating Germany.

Edward has made a number of pro-German statements that have caused embarrassment to Britain. Last year, as Prince of Wales, he incurred his father's anger by suggesting that representatives of the British Legion should visit Germany so that the ex-servicemen could "stretch forth the hand of friendship"; he was ordered never again to speak on controversial matters without consulting the government (→ 10/1937).

George's favourite yacht is scuttled

English Channel, 10 July 1936

Six months after George V's death, the royal yacht *Britannia* was this morning towed into the Channel south of the Isle of Wight and sunk. *Britannia* was built in 1892 for the future Edward VII, who launched her on her first racing career; re-rigged by King George, she began a second racing career after the war – winning in all some 350 prizes. A keen sailor, George sometimes took the helm himself, and only last year he commented: "As long as I live, I will never own any other yacht than *Britannia*."

A royal namesake: the "Queen Mary", a giant Cunard ocean liner, preparing to leave Southampton for her trials.

Royal romance blossoms as cruise fans gossip

King and Wallis sail into headlines

Windsor, 14 September

The king returned home today after a summer holiday which has shown the world (but not Britain) how close is his relationship with Wallis Simpson. Edward made no effort to disguise his affection for the twice-married American lady who accompanied him. The openness of the holiday – spent mostly on a chartered yacht, the *Nahlin* – has fuelled fears at court that the king wants to marry Mrs Simpson, despite the constitutional problems that this would cause for a monarch who heads the Anglican Church.

From the moment that the king and Wallis boarded the *Nahlin* at the Yugoslavian port of Sibenik on 10 August the cruise attracted extensive publicity – outside the

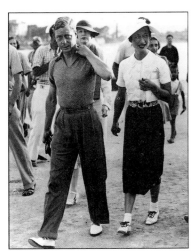

Edward and Wallis in Yugoslavia.

British press. American reporters followed the couple around the Mediterranean to Greece and Turkey. Crowds cheered members of the royal party when they stepped ashore, with shouts of the local equivalents of *"Vive l'amour!"*.

After so much tension at home the enthusiasm lifted the mood of melancholy which dogged the king, who made no pretence of masking his closeness to Mrs Simpson. They were frequently photographed together – swimming, sightseeing, and once with Wallis tenderly resting a hand on his arm as the king looked on full of affection (→ 23/9).

An intimate moment: Edward and Mrs Simpson snapped during the cruise.

Divorce fans speculation over marriage

Balmoral, 23 September

Wallis Simpson arrived here today as speculation in the newspapers of her native country continued about the possibility of the king becoming the third husband of the 40-year-old American. An article in today's *New York Woman* proffers the view that if Ernest Simpson, Wallis's current but estranged husband, wanted a divorce he could not sue a British king on the grounds of adultery. In fact, it seems more likely that it will be Mrs Simpson who takes the initiative in seeking a divorce. Her English-born husband moved out of their home in July, and Mrs Simpson has consulted lawyers about her next moves; it is thought that she will seek a divorce on the grounds of her husband's adultery (→ 1/10).

King puts mistress before royal duties

Aberdeen, 23 September

The king has shocked his court advisers by turning up in this city to meet Mrs Simpson on the very day that he had declined to open a new hospital building because of "court mourning" for George V. The hospital was opened in his absence by the Duke and Duchess of York.

Edward had been invited some months ago to open the new Aberdeen infirmary formally. He gave the official court mourning for his father as a reason for declining, even though he had attended Ascot races and enjoyed a lengthy Mediterranean cruise. Disappointment at his decision (and puzzlement at why his brother was somehow exempt from mourning) escalated into criticism when the king was seen in Aberdeen on the very day that he had declined a public duty.

The king had driven 60 miles (96km) to meet Wallis Simpson and other guests at the railway station to take them to Balmoral [*see report left*]. Wearing driving goggles he was photographed by the local newspaper, which published a picture of the king in Aberdeen alongside one of his brother deputising for him at the infirmary.

The woman from Baltimore who has entranced the British king

In the United States and Europe the divorce of Wallis Simpson was big news (above); in Britain the press barons had agreed to keep it quiet.

Ipswich, 1 October

Wallis Simpson will seek a divorce here later this month on the grounds of her husband's adultery with a lady of the unlikely name of Buttercup Kennedy. It will be the second divorce for the woman from Baltimore whose charm and vitality have entranced a British king.

She was born Bessiewallis Warfield on 19 June 1896 but dropped the disliked "Bessie" as she grew older. Her father died when she was a baby, leaving Wallis to be brought up by wealthy relatives. At 20 she met and married Earl Winfield Spencer, a lieutenant in the US Navy. He was attractive but prone to alcoholism, and in December 1927 Wallis won her petition for divorce. The following year she married Ernest Simpson, the son of an English father and American mother. They had met in New York, but she moved to London after they married. Two years later she met the Prince of Wales.

It was another of the prince's close female friends, Thelma, Lady Furness, who introduced them. At first their meetings were infrequent, but by 1933 the prince was dining at the Simpsons' flat and giving a party for Wallis at a nightclub. The next year Lady Furness went to America for three months, asking Wallis to look after the prince. By the summer of 1934 it was clear that the American newcomer had supplanted not only Lady Furness but also Freda Dudley Ward as the prince's favourite (→ 27/10).

King's love affair plunges monarchy into a crisis

London, 16 November

The king today told his family and his prime minister the news that they had dreaded to hear: he intends to marry Wallis Simpson when her divorce becomes absolute next year. He has said that he would rather abdicate as king than be denied the possibility of marrying the woman he loves. Stanley Baldwin, the prime minister, told Edward that the king's decision was "very grave" because he did not think that the country or commonwealth would accept the king's marriage to a woman who had been married and divorced twice before.

As Baldwin returned to Downing Street, the king left to dine with his mother, Queen Mary, and the Princess Royal, his sister. The queen was shocked and angered by her son's apparent determination to abdicate if necessary. She urged him put his duty to the country first and refused his request that she receive Mrs Simpson. Edward now plans to see his brothers, including the man who would become king if he does abdicate – the Duke of

Publicly, royal duties continue: the king at a farm in South Wales.

York. The illusion that the king did not contemplate marriage to Wallis Simpson began to be eroded last month when she filed for her second divorce. An agreement with Lord Beaverbrook had maintained press silence at home [*see below*], but Baldwin became increasingly alarmed by foreign coverage. He saw the king on 20 October at Fort Belvedere to urge him to try to put off the divorce, but Edward said that this was the lady's own business. Although the king had made it clear how much Wallis Simpson meant to him, Baldwin left hoping that the discussion would persuade Edward that marriage would be unacceptable to public opinion. However, he decided to brief other party leaders about the potential crisis.

The divorce nisi was granted on 27 October at Ipswich (prompting headlines in America such as "King's Moll Reno'd in Wolsey's Home Town"), but any hopes harboured by the king that the storm was over were soon dashed. Three days ago he received a letter from Alexander Hardinge, his private secretary, warning him that the press silence would not last and that the government could fall over his relationship with Mrs Simpson. Hardinge urged the king to send Mrs Simpson abroad "without further delay". Edward angrily rejected the advice, dismissing Hardinge and calling in an old friend, Walter Monckton, to be his new adviser. Over the weekend the king decided to take the initiative: the summons went out which brought Baldwin to the palace this evening (→ 19/11).

Press baron agrees newspaper silence

London, 16 October

Lord Beaverbrook, the Canadian-born proprietor of the *Daily Express*, today met the king to hear a plea to curb press coverage of the court case due later this month for the divorce of Wallis Simpson. Edward had taken the unusual step of telephoning Beaverbrook earlier this week to request a meeting. He told the newspaper proprietor that he wanted only a brief mention of the divorce; otherwise, he argued, Mrs Simpson would gain notoriety in seeking to end an unsuccessful marriage simply because she was known to be a friend of the king. Beaverbrook was convinced and has agreed to talk to other newspaper proprietors. It is thought that they will agree to maintain the silence which has kept the British public ignorant of the king's attachment to Mrs Simpson. Editors in the United States and the rest of Europe show no such restraint, however (→ 20/10).

Edward pledges action on unemployment

South Wales, 19 November

The king today completed a tour of depressed areas of South Wales which left him shocked by the scale of unemployment. "Something must be done to find them work," he told an official at one point. Edward was cheered throughout an arduous two-day visit which clearly left him profoundly moved, particularly at Dowlais where hundreds of men stood amid the debris of a derelict industrial site to greet the king with an old Welsh hymn. Forgetting his own troubles, he spoke directly to men who had been out of work for years. Short of food, with no money to clothe their families and no chance of jobs, they brought out the best in the king. At Pontypool today he told a crowd: "You may be sure that all I can do for you I will." Later, at Blaenavon, in Gwent, he returned to this theme: "Something will be done about unemployment" (→ 27/11).

The supporting players in the royal drama

The key protagonists in the drama over Mrs Simpson: from left to right, Stanley Baldwin, the prime minister; Major Alexander Hardinge, the king's private secretary; Walter Monckton, the lawyer friend called in by Edward to be his adviser; and Lord Beaverbrook, the Canadian newspaper baron.

Empire asked for views on marriage

London, 27 November

Leaders of the dominions are to be asked their views about the constitutional crisis caused by the king's desire to marry Wallis Simpson. There are three possible choices, the British cabinet was told today by Stanley Baldwin, the prime minister.

First, that the king marries Mrs Simpson and she becomes queen.

Second, that the king marries Mrs Simpson, but she should not become queen – the proposal for a so-called "morganatic" marriage which Edward now favours.

Third, that the king abdicates in favour of the Duke of York.

The morganatic proposal would give Mrs Simpson a title such as "duchess" and leave any children without rights of succession. It would require legislation in parliament, and Baldwin is doubtful that this would be passed. The dominions have been told to reply by 2 December (→ 3/12).

Abdication: the final days of King Edward VIII

The storm breaks: Mrs Simpson flees

London, 3 December
The people of Britain today know what the rest of the world has long known: the press silence over Mrs Simpson has ended, and the lady herself tonight fled to France to avoid the attentions of reporters. A sermon by the bishop of Bradford, commenting on the king's need to show more awareness of his Christian duty, was the unlikely trigger for the publicity. It was picked up yesterday by the *Yorkshire Post*, and today the nationals joined the fray. The reporting has dismayed the king, who had thought that his popularity with the people would counter official disapproval (→ 7/12).

News shocks MPs

Cannes, France, 7 December
Wallis Simpson today said that she was willing to "withdraw from a situation both unhappy and untenable", but the statement – issued from a French house besieged by reporters – seems unlikely to deflect the king from his determination to abdicate. Despite attempts by supporters such as Winston Churchill and Lord Beaverbrook to rally the country behind him, the cabinet, parliament and the dominions are against any form of marriage with Mrs Simpson. "Our cock won't fight," said Beaverbrook.

York is called in

Windsor, 8 December
The Duke of York today met the king's legal adviser, Walter Monckton, to discuss the plans now being made by the king and the government for Edward to abdicate later this week. The duke saw his brother last night after days of unreturned telephone calls and unanswered requests for a meeting. Shortly before 7pm the king summoned the duke to Fort Belvedere to be told formally that he is to be the new king. They then joined the prime minister and others for dinner (→ 10/12).

"God bless you all": Edward broadcasts the news of his abdication.

Members of the public calling on the prime minister to let Edward stay king.

The man who would not be king: Edward is now plain "Duke of Windsor."

Edward signs the abdication papers

Windsor, 10 December
The king this morning signed the "instrument of abdication" by which he declared his "irrevocable determination to renounce the throne for myself and my descendants". This act, unprecedented in more than 1,000 years of British royalty, was witnessed by Edward's brothers, including the Duke of York who is to be his successor. The news was later given to sombre members of the Commons by Stanley Baldwin, the prime minister, who for the first time gave details of his lengthy and anguished discussions with the king over the last two months (→ 11/12).

Edward speaks out

Windsor, 11 December
Seated alone in Windsor castle, the now former king spoke on the wireless tonight. He pledged allegiance to the new king who, he said, had the "matchless blessing" of a happy family. "I have for 25 years tried to serve," he said, "But you must believe me when I tell you that I have found it impossible to carry the heavy burden of responsibility and to discharge my duties as king as I would wish to do without the help and support of the woman I love ... God bless you all. God save the king" (→ 12/12).

Edward sails away

Portsmouth, Hants, 12 December
The king who was never crowned slipped quietly from his former kingdom in the early hours of this morning. The Duke of Windsor, as Edward is now to be known, left England aboard a warship, HMS *Fury*, after saying goodbye to his family at Windsor. He had gone to see them at Royal Lodge after his poignant farewell broadcast. It was after midnight when he left, bowing to the new king before heading for Portsmouth to begin his journey to France for a reunion with Wallis Simpson, and exile (→ 1/1937).

George VI
1936–1952

**House
of
Windsor**

London, 12 December 1936. George VI, who accedes to the throne on the abdication of his brother, the Duke of Windsor, takes his oath of accession at St James's (→ 25/12).

London, 25 December 1936. The Duchess of Kent gives birth to her second child, Princess Alexandra.

Vienna, January 1937. The Duke of Windsor, who is a guest at Schloss Enzesfeld, the home of Baron Eugène de Rothschild, is joined by his friend, Major Edward "Fruity" Metcalfe (→ 11/4).

London, 16 March 1937. George meets Winston Churchill and David Lloyd George to discuss the civil list allowance (→ 28/4).

London, 11 April 1937. George writes to the Duke of Windsor to explain why the family will not be at his wedding (→ 28/4).

Windsor, 23 April 1937. George unveils a memorial to George V.

London, 28 April 1937. The civil list excludes the Duke of Windsor; he receives an income from family sources (→ 3/5).

London, 3 May 1937. Wallis Simpson's divorce decree becomes absolute (→ 8/5).

London, 6 May 1937. George hosts a pre-coronation ball (→ 12/5).

France, 8 May 1937. Wallis Simpson changes her name by deed poll to Wallis Warfield, her maiden name (→ 28/5).

Westminster, 12 May 1937. George VI is crowned king.→

London, 28 May 1937. George issues "Letters Patent" which exclude Wallis Warfield from the title HRH should she marry the Duke of Windsor (→ 3/6).

Paris, 3 October 1937. The Duke of Windsor issues a statement about his forthcoming visit to Germany.

London, 1 February 1938. The queen visits a community housing project for the poor.

London, 23 June 1938. The Countess of Strathmore, the mother of Queen Elizabeth, dies.

London, July 1938. Dowager Queen Mary refuses to accept Wallis, the Duchess of Windsor, as her daughter-in-law (→ 11/1938).

Southwold, Suffolk, August 1938. George visits a boys' summer camp this month (→ 5/8/39).

Germany, 30 September 1938. The signing of the Munich Agreement averts the immediate threat of war.

Paris, November 1938. The Duke and Duchess of Gloucester are the first royals to meet the Windsors since the abdication (→ 30/9/39).

Devon, 18 April 1939. Prince Philip of Greece enters the royal naval college at Dartmouth (→ 22/7).

Windsor, 21 April 1939. Princess Elizabeth celebrates her 13th birthday (→ 22/7).

Dartmouth, Devon, 22 July 1939. Princess Elizabeth meets Prince Philip of Greece during a family holiday (→ 1/1/40).

Balmoral, 5 August 1939. The Duke of York summer camp opens.

France, 30 September 1939. The Windsors return to France after a brief visit to England; the duke takes up an army position, with no royal status, under the command of Major-General Sir Richard Howard Vyse (→ 10/6/40).

United States, December 1939. Queen Elizabeth is voted "woman of the year" by the American press after the royal visit.

Britain, 1 January 1940. Prince Philip of Greece joins the Royal Navy (→ 10/1942).

Windsor, 30 April 1940. The princesses and "Crawfie" move to Windsor castle (→ 18/7).

France, 10 June 1940. Italy declares war on France; the Windsors join the refugees heading south to Spain (→ 23/6).

Lisbon, 23 June 1940. The Windsors arrive; their war role is still unclear (→ 1/8).

London, 18 July 1940. George strongly opposes the evacuation of his daughters to Canada for the duration of the war (→ 13/10).

Britain, 23 September 1940. King George institutes the George Cross, to be awarded for conspicuous civilian courage (→ 15/4/42).

Windsor, 25 December 1940. Princesses Elizabeth and Margaret produce their first pantomime.

Bahamas, 1941. The Duke of Windsor, as governor of the island, sets up an economic advisory committee (→ 31/8/42).

Malta, 15 April 1942. The island is awarded the George Cross for bravery (→ 20/6/43).

Windsor, 21 April 1942. Princess Elizabeth celebrates her 16th birthday and is eager to register for war service (→ 25/4).

Britain, June 1942. Princess Elizabeth, who has a passion for horses, meets the champion jockey, Gordon Richards.

London, 4 July 1942. The Duchess of Kent gives birth to her third child, Prince Michael.

Scotland, 31 August 1942. Dowager Queen Mary is reconciled with her son the Duke of Windsor after the death of a younger son, George, the Duke of Kent (→ 8/12).

Britain, 8 December 1942. King George repeats his determination not to give the Duchess of Windsor the title of HRH (→ 6/1943).

United States, June 1943. The Duke of Windsor turns down the post offered to him of governor of Bermuda (→ 1944).

Windsor, November 1943. Cecil Beaton, the royal photographer, takes the official pictures for Elizabeth's 18th birthday (→ 23/12).

The life and times of King George VI

Name: Albert Frederick Arthur George.
Birth: 14 December 1895.
Accession: 11 December 1936.
Coronation: 12 May 1937.
Predecessor: brother.
Height: five feet eight inches.
Marriage: Lady Elizabeth Bowes-Lyon, 16 April 1923.
Children: two – Elizabeth, Margaret.

Favourite home: Royal Lodge.
Likes: shooting, tennis.
Dislikes: public speaking.
Greatest problem: relations with former king, Edward VIII.
Greatest success: unifying role during Second World War.
Famous saying: "If the new year brings continued struggle, we shall remain undaunted."
Death: 6 February 1952.

Opposite: King George VI in his splendid coronation robes.

George takes his father's name as new king

Norfolk, 25 December 1936
George VI is spending his first Christmas as king at his father's beloved Sandringham. More than 6,000 well-wishers turned out to cheer the royal family as they arrived at nearby Wolferton church for the morning service. Amidst all his anxieties over his new status, George must be greatly comforted by such a show of affection.

Some men are born kings; some achieve kingship; and others, such as George, have kingship thrust upon them. At 41, a shy man with an embarrassing stammer, he now faces a stern test of character: to remove the blemish on the family honour left by Edward. Christened Albert Frederick Arthur George, he chose to be George VI in order to emphasise continuity with the values of his father's reign.

The decency of Bertie, as he was known, is not in doubt; yet all kinds of doubts as to his ability to do the job of constitutional monarch are being raised in the newspapers, the Stock Exchange and a country at large which hardly knows him. In particular people wonder if George is up to the coronation ceremony itself. There are rumours that the service will be cut short. Even if he manages this hurdle, will George be up to the strain of official duties week in, week out? Then there is Edward.

The two brothers parted on 11 December with dignity, but it will be hard for the former king to accept his reduced status in exile.

The new king had promised Edward a royal title, as His Royal Highness the Duke of Windsor, before he left the country. But there are all the makings of a bitter struggle over the duke's demands for similar status for Mrs Simpson if, as she surely will, she becomes his wife next year. The king, fully supported by his wife and mother, is determined to resist this demand. Money is another source of potential fraternal strife.

Not all is gloom, however. The new king never expected to succeed, but he was closer to his father than any of his brothers were and shares the same sense of public duty. His personal manner is engaging, and what he lacks in physical strength he makes up for in determination. His father once said of him that he "has more guts than the rest of them put together".

George also possesses what Edward called in his abdication broadcast "one matchless blessing ... a happy home with his wife and children". Queen Elizabeth is a robust and tireless woman. Her devotion to the king is beyond question, and she can handle public duties with as much skill as Edward once showed (→17/2/37).

Receiving the acclaim of the king's people: the royal family on the balcony of Buckingham Palace on the day of King George VI's coronation.

Elizabeth, the new heir, moves house

London, 17 February 1937
The new heir to the throne moved into Buckingham Palace today from the family home just up the road at 145 Piccadilly. Princess Elizabeth, at the age of ten, has had her life transformed by her uncle's abdication as dramatically as those of her parents have been. It seems unlikely that her parents will have another child who, if it were a boy, would supplant her claim to the throne. So far her change of status has not produced any alteration to the daily routine of lessons with her governess, "Crawfie". The young princess (known as "Lilibet" within the family) and her sister Margaret are pleased by one benefit of today's change of address: their new garden is much larger (→30/4/40).

Enthroned in majesty: George's coronation in Westminster abbey.

Queen Mary gives moral support to shy king on his coronation

London, 12 May 1937
On a day originally chosen for the coronation of King Edward VIII, the nation today celebrated the crowning of his brother as King George VI. The ceremony in Westminster abbey was attended by Queen Mary, the widow of the late King George V. It is the first time that a dowager queen has attended the coronation of a successor; Mary's presence is seen as a sign of support to her shy second son, who succeeded to the crown amid the scandal of Edward's abdication last December. Certainly the public seemed in a mood to forget the troubles of the past, turning out in huge numbers to cheer the royal couple as they rode in their golden coach and later as, accompanied by the two young princesses, they came out on the palace balcony.

An eager crowd using periscopes to see the coronation procession.

Edward marries Wallis

France, 3 June 1937

The Duke of Windsor has finally married the woman for whom he gave up the crown. At the Château de Candé near Tours today Wallis Warfield (she had changed her surname by deed poll last month) became the Duchess of Windsor. She will not be known as "Her Royal Highness", however. Months of negotiations had failed to sway the king who, in letters patent issued on 28 May, ruled out a royal title. "This is a nice wedding present," said the duke, already bitter over financial haggling. But at least they were married by Anglican rites: a clergyman from Darlington conducted the service (→ 3/10).

Edward and Wallis: newly-weds.

Windsors meet Hitler during German visit

Herr Hitler welcomes the Windsors.

Germany, October 1937

The Duke of Windsor has both angered his brother, King George, and dismayed his friends by visiting Germany. Ostensibly there to study "housing and working conditions", he and the duchess were fêted by the Nazi leaders and cheered by large crowds. The high spot of his tour – at least for the German propagandists – was a meeting with Adolf Hitler at Berchtesgaden, the *führer's* mountain retreat in southern Germany. The Germans see the duke's visit as evidence of his alleged sympathy with their regime and apparently hope that he will one day return to the throne (→ 28/2/38).

Duke of Windsor's finances are settled

London, 28 February 1938

Edward, the Duke of Windsor, has struck a deal with his brother, King George. After some 14 months of wrangling Edward has been granted an annual income for life of £21,000. Nearly half will come from the estates of Sandringham and Balmoral, with the rest a voluntary allowance from the king. There are strings attached: Edward forfeits the allowance if he returns to Britain (at present he is in Austria) without the government's permission.

Today's settlement goes back to a furious row at Windsor on 11 December 1936, the day of the abdication, when Edward demanded from his brother a secure financial future – and a royal title. Eventually they agreed on £25,000 for life, together with the title of HRH the Duke of Windsor.

Six months later George changed his mind, believing that his brother had enough money with which to support himself. In a bitter exchange of letters Edward threatened to release details of the king's own fortune if his income were stopped. The reduced sum agreed today is therefore a tactful compromise by both men (→ 7/1938).

King opens Glasgow empire exhibition

Strathclyde, 3 May 1938

The king and queen were treated to a rapturous welcome in Glasgow early today as they arrived to open the empire exhibition in Bellahouston Park. Part of the morning was taken up at the "Fitter Britain" stand in the United Kingdom pavilion, with its eye-catching displays such as a stream of ping-pong balls to illustrate the circulation of the blood. The royal couple's circulations were no doubt given a boost when they went up the Empire Tower in a lift that moves at 500 feet (150 metres) a minute.

There was a particularly warm welcome for Queen Elizabeth, who received Scotland's highest order of chivalry, the badge of the Order of the Thistle, presented by the exhibition's president, Lord Elgin. In the afternoon the king and queen visited a typical highland village, An Clachan, complete with thatched cottages and wool-spinners imported from Barra. The five-hour

The king at the Empire Show.

visit ended with a tour of the new North Hillingdon trading estate, where 1,400 men are turning farmland into an industrial estate. The royal couple finally left Glasgow this evening for a quiet overnight stop at Drumclog, on the moors south of the city.

Queen delights Parisians on royal visit

Versailles, France, 21 July 1938

The king and queen have breathed fresh life into the *Entente Cordiale* between Britain and France with a spectacularly successful state visit to Paris – the first overseas visit of their reign. Today, as the French president toasted the royal couple at Versailles, the links between the two nations seem closer than ever. Thousands of people had poured into the French capital to join

Parisians in welcoming George and Elizabeth when they arrived two days ago. The streets and buildings were garlanded with flags and other decorations. It was a particular triumph for the queen. The visit had been delayed last month by the death of her mother, but her wardrobe – designed by Norman Hartnell in the alternative mourning colour of white – delighted fashion-conscious Paris.

An actor-prince: Philip of Greece, standing second from left, who is a cousin of the Duchess of Kent, taking the part of one of the Three Wise Men in a nativity play put on by pupils of Gordonstoun School, Scotland.

King and queen triumph in Canada and the United States on long royal tour

London, 23 June 1939

It could have been coronation day all over again, as 50,000 people in front of Buckingham Palace last night sang *God save the King* to celebrate the return of the king and queen after a six-week tour of North America.

The tour took George and Elizabeth 10,000 miles (16,000km) to be seen by some 15 million people, during which they became the first reigning British monarchs to set foot in North America. They knew that the ex-king had been much loved in Canada, but the warm welcome – even among the French-speaking population – melted any initial apprehensions. In Toronto they met the famous Dionne quintuplets, and the queen in particular earned plaudits for her easy grace and charm on public occasions.

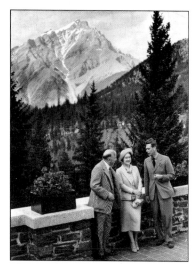
The royal couple in Canada.

The United States were next to fall under the royal spell, with huge crowds cheering their appearances. On 8 June the king and queen were greeted in Washington by President Roosevelt, with whom they struck up an immediate rapport. The king revelled in this chance to meet a world leader. After visiting the World's Fair in New York, the royal pair stayed at the US president's home in upstate New York where the two men discussed politics late into the night (→ 12/1939).

The queen with Mrs Roosevelt.

The royal family visiting Dartmouth naval college on 22 July 1939 with Lord Louis Mountbatten, when Princess Elizabeth (front row, far end) was impressed by Mountbatten's nephew, Philip (second from right).

George visits the troops

France, 7 December 1939

A royal tour of inspection is under way on the Western Front as King George, who arrived here three days ago, is being shown round British and French defences. The tour, which will last another two days, has taken the king 100 miles (160km) around the front. He has already met men who have exchanged fire with the enemy, on night patrols or in the air.

The king has been shown the defences which are being constructed along the border with Belgium, plugging the gap between the fortifications of the "Maginot Line" and the Channel coast. The French appreciate the king's decision to come over and have awarded him their Maginot medal. Today, while inspecting French lines, he was met by President Albert Lebrun and General Maurice Gamelin, the Allied commander-in-chief.

The general took King George on one of the trains which ferry men and ammunition to various parts of the defences. They arrived at an observation post from which the king could see German positions only three miles away. He was also shown the Order of the Day: "Be vigilant, keep cool and fire low – to the last round and the last man and a bit more." The king has talked to some of the British soldiers paraded in his honour and seems impressed by their efficiency – and their spirit (→ 25/12).

Mucking in: King George consults with army chiefs in the front line.

Women's role vital in war, says queen

London, 11 November 1939

Queen Elizabeth broadcast this evening to the women of the British Empire. In an Armistice Day message relayed from Buckingham Palace, she recalled that in past conflicts women could do little more than encourage their men at the front. But all that has changed: now "we no less than men have real and vital work to do". Sympathising with women whose families have been split up by the war, the queen nevertheless reminded her listeners of their "proud privilege of serving our country in her hour of need".

King makes stirring Christmas speech

Sandringham, 25 December 1939

King George has used his Christmas radio broadcast to rally the nation to the war effort. Dressed in the uniform of admiral of the fleet and speaking live, the king warned listeners that our enemies want to suppress "all that we hold dear". The Allied cause, he said, was no less than the survival of "Christian civilization". Speaking with slow, deliberate assurance, he went on: "A New Year is at hand. We cannot tell what it will bring. If it brings peace, how thankful we shall be. If it brings continued struggle, we shall remain undaunted."

Royal family rallies a nation and empire at war

The royal couple inspecting the bomb damage done to Buckingham Palace.

The king and queen join London children in an underground air-raid shelter.

German bomber hits Buckingham Palace

London, September 1940
King George and Queen Elizabeth narrowly escaped death this month when a lone German bomber flew up the Mall and dropped six bombs on Buckingham Palace. Two bombs that fell in the quadrangle exploded 80 yards (72 metres) from the room in which the king and queen were sitting, destroying the royal chapel. It was the second time that the palace had been hit since the *Luftwaffe* first turned its fire-power on British cities on 7 Sep-

tember. Both the king and queen remain adamant that they will stay in London. Indeed, they appeared to relish the attacks.

They toured blitzed areas of the capital after the palace had been hit, and the queen said: "I am glad we have been bombed. It makes me feel I can look the east end in the face." As the royal couple walked amid the debris after one night's bombing, a man whose house had been hit called out: "You're a good king, Sir" (→16/11).

King and queen visit bomb-struck cities

Coventry, 16 November 1940
Unable to enter the city by train – such was the devastation wrought by the *Luftwaffe* two days ago – King George was today driven into the ruins of Coventry. The bombing by 449 German planes has left near-ly 600 people dead, over 850 injured and 60,000 buildings damaged. The shocked survivors at least drew some comfort from today's visit, part of the king's campaign to keep up morale by going to Britain's bomb-damaged cities. The wel-

come is warm because people know that the king and queen share the risks by staying in London, which has now been bombed nightly for more than two months.

But the "Blitz" is by no means confined to London, as this week's attack on Coventry shows. Liver-pool, Bristol, Birmingham and Glasgow have been among the tar-gets since the war began. As for the risk to himself, the king has bluntly commented: "What's the point of worrying?" (→12/1943).

Windsors to make home in Bahamas

Lisbon, 1 August 1940
The British government heaved a sigh of relief today when the Duke of Windsor finally sailed from here to take up his new post as governor of the Bahamas. The foreign office wants the duke beyond the reach of German sympathisers who have been urging him to return to Spain. There have been talks of plots to kidnap the duke, who met Hitler and other Nazi leaders in 1937 – encouraging some Germans to see him as a potential champion of peace. This hope was fuelled by sev-eral delays to the duke's departure to the Bahamas (→1941).

Princess Elizabeth broadcasts on the BBC's 'Children's Hour'

Margaret looks on as her sister, Princess Elizabeth, makes the broadcast.

London, 13 October 1940
"We know, every one of us, that in the end all will be well". With these cheering words the 14-year-old Princess Elizabeth addressed boys and girls in Britain and around the Commonwealth tuning in to the BBC's *Children's Hour*, hosted as usual by "Uncle Mac" (Derek McCulloch). After the young prin-cess, expertly coached by her mother, had passed on her words of encouragement, she further sur-prised listeners by announcing that her sister Margaret was at her side. Speaking in public for the first time, ten-year-old Margaret confidently joined in on cue: "Goodnight and good luck to you all" (→25/12).

Princess joins war service register

Windsor, 25 April 1942

Four days after her sixteenth birthday, Princess Elizabeth today registered for war service at the local labour exchange. All women aged 16 or over are required to register by law, although it is unlikely that they will be called up immediately. The king and queen refused to send their daughters to Canada. "The children won't leave without me, I won't leave without the king, and the king will never leave," said the queen. Now the princess wants to start war work and is eager to volunteer for nursing duties. George disapproves, however; he thinks that she is too young.

Princess Elizabeth: signing up.

Exiled royals find wartime sanctuary

London, 1942

Britain has become a temporary home for royal families forced to flee from Europe. Queen Wilhelmina of the Netherlands was the first to arrive, following a 5am telephone call to King George pleading for help. He sent a warship to rescue the queen, and she is now living in Sussex. King Haakon of Norway, whose late queen was a sister of George V, lives in London, calling at Buckingham Palace weekly to collect his post. King George of the Hellenes and King Peter of Yugoslavia were later arrivals, regularly dining at the palace to which they bring their ration books.

Duke of Kent is killed in flying tragedy

The wreckage of the flying boat after the crash in which the duke died.

Scotland, 25 August 1942

Flying at 700 feet in dense mist, the Sunderland flying boat hit the top of a hill in the middle of remote Scottish countryside near Berriedale. Spinning round, it came down the side of the hill on its back before exploding into flames. One of the 15 men on board was Prince George, the Duke of Kent; an air commodore in the RAF, he was on his way to inspect installations in Iceland. He was killed instantly.

The king was told of his brother's death by telephone during dinner at Balmoral this evening. He is deeply upset, especially as the duke had recently settled down to family life after a long career in the Royal Navy. He leaves a widow, Princess Marina of Greece and Denmark, whom he married in 1934, and three children: Edward, Alexandra and little Michael, who was christened just three weeks ago (→ 31/8).

The christening, three weeks ago.

Philip's 'alertness' praised by captain

HMS Wallace, October 1942

After being involved in heavy fighting in the Mediterranean and in the defence of Crete, Prince Philip of Greece has returned to home waters and been promoted to first lieutenant and second in command of the destroyer HMS *Wallace*. An ageing and unglamourous vessel, the *Wallace* is employed in the dangerous task of escorting convoys.

When war loomed in 1939 Prince Philip was at Dartmouth naval college where, as Cadet Philip of Greece, he won the "king's dirk", the prize for best cadet, and passed his final examinations with distinction. But his attempts to join the Royal Navy were frustrated by the facts that he was not a British citizen and that Greece was neutral. It was not until 1 January 1940 that his uncle Lord Louis Mountbatten, by now a Royal Navy captain himself, managed to pull the right strings.

After the Axis countries attacked Greece, Philip was transferred to the battleship HMS *Valiant* for an attack on the Italian fleet in the Battle of Cape Matapan in March 1941. Philip manned a searchlight under heavy fire, and his captain later reported that Philip's alertness helped the *Valiant* to sink two cruisers in five minutes. His role was mentioned in dispatches and prepared the way for further promotion (→ 23/12/43).

Windsor great park is ploughed as the royals 'dig for victory'

The royal family energetically inspecting the harvest at Sandringham.

Windsor, autumn 1942

The royal estates have answered the government's call to boost food production at home. Around 1,500 acres (600 hectares) of Windsor great park have been ploughed up and turned over to cereal crops. King George VI may not rejoice in the nickname of "Farmer George" that so delighted George III, but he is determined to set an example to other British landowners. Before the war Britain relied heavily on imported food; this has been cut dramatically by the U-boat blockade mounted by the Germans. "Dig for Victory" has become the government's battlecry, with downland put to the plough and city parks converted to allotments.

Royal family shares burdens of a nation at war

Economy drives are ordered at palace

London, autumn 1942
Eleanor Roosevelt, the wife of the US president, has gained a first-hand experience this autumn of the stringent wartime regime introduced by the king and queen at Buckingham Palace and other royal residences. The welcome may have been warm, but the temperature, she reported, was extremely chilly. No central heating is used and there are no fires in the bedrooms, each of which is lit by a solitary bulb and often heated by only a single bar of an electric fire. And when bathing, Mrs Roosevelt would have found a line painted at five inches as a reminder not to waste water.

The king and queen have been determined to show that they share the problems of their people. They live themselves on the rations allotted to the people (one egg per fortnight, for instance), and even for distinguished guests the food is simple, albeit served on plates of gold or silver. Food shortages have persuaded the king to plough up part of Windsor great park [*see opposite*], while the princesses have been collecting tinfoil and the queen has unearthed furniture from storerooms for people whose houses have been damaged by bombs.

Mobbed by the men: King George visiting troops in North Africa.

King visits Malta and the troops in Africa

Malta, 20 June 1943
At considerable personal risk – for the enemy is just 60 miles (96km) to the north in Sicily – the king has spent today visiting this island that stood up to a Nazi siege for 14 months. Last year he awarded the island the George Cross – the honour which he himself created for civilian valour. George sailed into Valetta harbour this morning in HMS *Aurora* to the cheers of a massive crowd before touring the island by car. Tonight he sails back to Tripoli.

The king's day trip comes in the middle of his stay in Algiers, where in a punishing schedule during the midsummer heat he is reviewing the allied armies in North Africa preparing to land in Italy. He has met the top military men, including Admiral Cunningham, General Eisenhower and General Montgomery, the hero of El Alamein, whom he knighted last week (→11/10/44).

Cosy lunches bring king and PM closer

London, December 1943
Nearly every Tuesday since September 1940, King George and Winston Churchill have lunched together at Buckingham Palace. No servants are present; the men help themselves to food from a buffet on a side table before sitting down to talk in complete privacy. Although the king had resisted Churchill's appointment as prime minister, he has come to admire and respect him enormously.

Churchill flatters George by telling him everything, including his future plans – at times, before he has mentioned them to his cabinet or generals. A warm friendship has blossomed. The king has also worked hard to improve relations with the United States. He was disappointed at one stage by the failure of President Roosevelt to reply to a personal letter of thanks for his support. But a visit to London by Mrs Roosevelt has helped to restore friendly relations, and the king has frequently met senior US envoys and generals such as Eisenhower. He has even welcomed the Soviet foreign minister, Vyacheslav Molotov, the emissary of a regime which murdered his cousins but is now also an ally (→26/7/45).

Princesses stage Christmas pantomime for the family at Windsor

Windsor, 23 December 1943
For the fourth year running the princesses have staged a Christmas pantomime for their family and the staff of the royal household. The tradition started with a nativity play called *The Christmas Child*. This year's *Aladdin*, featuring Elizabeth in the title role and Margaret as Roxana, was the usual mixture of song, dance and corny jokes ending in a spectacular finale. Elizabeth tap-danced, sang and led the slapstick humour with extra sparkle. Marion Crawford, her governess, wonders whether her special verve might have something to do with the presence, in the front row, of a dashing young naval officer: Philip of Greece (→21/4/44).

Elizabeth and Margaret: centre stage after their production of "Aladdin".

Queen gives boost to factory workers

Windsor, December 1943
The "Blitz" of Britain's cities may be over, at least for the time being, but Queen Elizabeth has remained a prominent figure on the home front this year. She has toured factories to encourage the drive for increased production, inspected allotments which have sprung up on bomb sites and comforted the wounded recovering in hospitals. The queen makes a particular point of emphasising the role of women in the war, saying that whether women were in the armed forces, in factories or bringing up their families, their role was "more important than ever".

George VI
1936–1952

House
of
Windsor

London, 16 February 1944. Group-Captain Peter Townsend, a 30-year-old war hero, joins the royal family on a three-month appointment as equerry – royal attendant – to the king (→ 2/1945).

Italy, 18 June 1944. George Lascelles, the son of Mary, the Princess Royal, and the Earl of Harewood, is taken prisoner and imprisoned in Colditz.

Sussex, 26 October 1944. Princess Beatrice, the youngest daughter of Queen Victoria, dies aged 87 at Balcombe Park.

United States, 1944. The Duchess of Windsor undergoes an operation for stomach cancer (→ 3/5/45).

Canberra, 30 January 1945. Henry, the Duke of Gloucester, the younger brother of George VI, is Australia's first governor-general from the royal family (→ 24/5/51).

Surrey, February 1945. Princess Elizabeth, shortly before her 19th birthday, enrols in an ATS (Auxiliary Territorial Services) course in vehicle maintenance at Camberley (→ 3/1945).

Windsor, February 1945. As a mark of affection George is a godfather to Hugo George, the second son of his equerry, Group-Captain Peter Townsend, and his wife Rosemary (→ 9/1948).

Bahamas, 3 May 1945. The Duke of Windsor resigns as governor after five years; the Windsors head for Miami on an extended holiday, unsure as to where their next home or job will be (→ 10/1945).

London, 13 May 1945. The royal family attend a thanksgiving service, held in St Paul's, to commemorate VE Day (→ 7/6).

Westminster, 26 July 1945. Winston Churchill resigns as prime minister after an election defeat; he is replaced by Clement Attlee.

Plymouth, 2 August 1945. George meets the US president, Harry S Truman, on board *HMS Renown*.

London, October 1945. George meets his brother, the Duke of Windsor, to discuss his future and where he will live (→ 24/4/46).

Southern France, 24 April 1946. The Windsors rent a house at La Cröe, outside Cannes (→ 8/1946).

Balmoral, August 1946. Prince Philip of Greece is a guest of the family (→ 9/1946).

Windsor, August 1946. The Duke of Windsor is to be allowed to erect a mausoleum in the grounds of Fort Belvedere, his old country home, for himself and Wallis (→ 2/1947).

London, early September 1946. An official statement from Buckingham Palace denies the rumours of an engagement between Prince Philip of Greece and Princess Elizabeth (→ 18/3/47).

Portsmouth, 31 January 1947. The royal family set sail for South Africa (→ 21/2).

South Africa, 21 February 1947. George opens parliament in Cape Town (→ 21/4).

Britain, 18 March 1947. Prince Philip of Greece becomes a naturalised Briton, taking the surname of Mountbatten (→ 26/5).

London, 26 May 1947. Mary, the dowager queen, celebrates her 80th birthday by giving a luncheon party at Buckingham Palace; Philip Mountbatten is one of those who attend (→ 6/1947).

London, 11 June 1947. Princess Elizabeth is made a freeman of the City.

Windsor, June 1947. Philip dances all evening with Princess Elizabeth at the Royal Ascot Ball (→ 10/7).

London, 20 November 1947. Philip, aged 26, who joined the Anglican Church last month, marries Princess Elizabeth, aged 21; he is made a knight of the Garter, Baron of Greenwich, Earl of Merioneth and Duke of Edinburgh and receives the title "Prince".→

London, January 1948. George suffers from severe cramps in the legs (→ 30/4).

Paris, May 1948. Princess Elizabeth, pregnant with her first child, makes her first official trip abroad with Prince Philip (→ 14/11).

Netherlands, September 1948. Princess Margaret, accompanied by Group-Captain Peter Townsend, represents her father, who is ill, at the coronation ceremony of Queen Juliana (→ 5/1951).

London, 14 November 1948. Elizabeth gives birth to a son, Charles Philip Arthur George.→

London, 23 November 1948. George cancels his Australian tour due to his bad health (→ 12/3/49).

London, March 1949. George is recovering from an operation to improve his poor circulation.

London, 9 June 1949. Elizabeth represents her father and leads the trooping of the colour (→ 7/1949).

London, July 1949. Princess Elizabeth, Prince Philip and baby Charles move into their new home Clarence House (→ 12/1949).

London, 15 August 1950. Elizabeth gives birth to her second child, a daughter, Anne.→

Malta, 15 August 1950. Prince Philip is promoted to lieutenant-commander and takes his first command, the *Magpie* (→ 7/7/51).

London, November 1950. The royal family are shocked by the memoirs of Marion Crawford, the former royal governess (→ 12/1950).

Scotland, 11 April 1951. The ceremonial Stone of Scone, which was stolen last December, is found at Arbroath after a 107-day hunt.

Balmoral, mid-May 1951. The king, queen and Princess Margaret spend a week in the highlands; Group-Captain Townsend is in attendance (→ 12/12/52).

United States, 22 May 1951. *Life* magazine publishes the first in a series of articles written by the Duke of Windsor (→ 16/2/52).

London, 7 June 1951. Princess Elizabeth represents her father at the trooping of the colour (→ 7/7).

London, 23 September 1951. George undergoes surgery to remove a lung in an attempt to arrest his cancer (→ 14/11).

London, 14 November 1951. George attends his grandson Charles's third birthday party at Buckingham Palace (→ 30/1/52).

London, 1951. Group-Captain Peter Townsend separates from his wife, Rosemary, and is awarded a decree nisi (→ 12/12/52).

London, 30 January 1952. George and his family see *South Pacific* at Drury Lane (→ 31/1).

London, 31 January 1952. George waves goodbye to Elizabeth and Philip as they set off on their tour of Africa (→ 6/2).

Sandringham, 6 February 1952. George, aged 56, dies in his sleep; his daughter, Princess Elizabeth, aged 25, succeeds him.→

Princess grows up in shadow of war

King George defies fears to visit the troops in Europe

Windsor, 21 April 1944

Princess Elizabeth today celebrated her 18th birthday with a family luncheon party at Windsor. Her presents included pearls, a horse and a new role as counsellor of state [*see report below*]. She has grown up in the shadow of war which has exacerbated the private nature of a royal education that has relied overwhelmingly on her governess, Marion Crawford.

Academic skills were deemed to take second place to what her mother once called "all the distinctively feminine graces". Cultural outings around London were organised for the princess and her sister. The unexpected abdication of her uncle changed the career expectations of Princess Elizabeth overnight, however. Henry Marten, the vice-provost of Eton, was enlisted to add some constitutional history to the syllabus for the new heir to the throne.

At 18 the princess has emerged into womanhood from a cloistered childhood with no experience of life outside the royal circle. She speaks

A family portrait (complete with corgis) taken this year by Cecil Beaton.

French and is knowledgeable about history. She is intelligent without being intellectual, a fine horsewoman and imbued with a strong sense of public duty. She wanted to become a nurse at 16, saying: "I ought to do as other girls of my age do." Her father thwarted her then, but she is a determined individual, as the king is now discovering as he urges caution in her professed love for Prince Philip (→ 7/1944).

Netherlands, 11 October 1944

Four months after his visit to the Normandy beaches, just ten days after the first D-Day landings, King George is back in Europe, this time on an extended stay with Field Marshal Montgomery at his 21st Army Group HQ at Eindhoven.

Despite attempts to block the trip on the grounds of safety – less than two weeks ago Allied forces failed to break German lines at Arnhem, to the north – the king was determined to return to the continent. He expects to meet again key allied leaders, such as General Dwight Eisenhower, but will spend most of the visit with Montgomery, who has given his personal guarantee of the royal safety in the area

King George with Eisenhower.

around Eindhoven. So far, the visit has been an unqualified success. Montgomery has called his royal visitor "great fun", and as something of a spartan – he neither drinks nor smokes – he is pleased to find that the king demands no special treatment.

Indeed, "Monty" refuses to change his own regime and will be off to bed at 9.30 as ever, leaving his junior officers to entertain the monarch with news of the day's events. This, too, has been a success, and as one palace intimate has noted: "I can recall no occasion when HM was in better form or enjoyed himself more" (→ 8/5/45).

Elizabeth emerges from cloistered childhood to take public role

Windsor, July 1944

Princess Elizabeth is beginning to play a greater role in public life. She became a counsellor of state on her 18th birthday in April, and this month, with the king visiting the forces in Italy, she has signed her first acts of parliament (and a reprieve for a murderer). She has also made her first public speech – on behalf of the National Society for the Prevention of Cruelty to Children. Visits to factories, civil defence posts and airbases are planned, but the princess remains eager to do more for the war effort.

She had registered for war service at the age of 16, but the king had thwarted her hopes of acting as a volunteer nurse. He did not wish to expose his heir to undue danger. Only slowly did he loosen the controls over the lives of his daughters at Windsor. The Regency Act was passed last year, enabling the princess to act as a counsellor at 18 instead of 21 (and to be queen without a regent if her father died before she was 21). This was to help to pre-

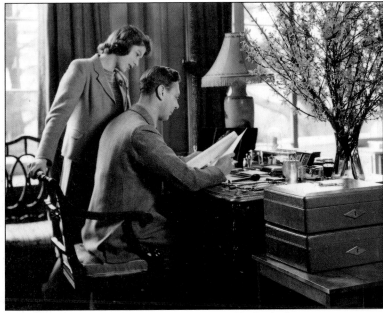

Learning the trade: the king shows a 15-year-old Elizabeth some papers.

pare Elizabeth for her future role, but her sense of duty chafes at the restrictions. Ironically, the new campaign by the Germans' V1, or "doodlebug", flying bombs has en-

sured that Windsor cannot guarantee safety. One flew over Windsor great park recently, causing Elizabeth and her sister Margaret to dive into a trench (→ 2/1945).

King and queen lead Britain's victory celebrations

Welcoming peace: the royal family and Mr Churchill on the palace balcony.

Rapturously received: the king and queen in the Candle Gardens, Guernsey.

Princesses join crowds to salute the king

London, 8 May 1945
Buckingham Palace was tonight the focal point of an all-day (and all-night) party as Britain celebrated victory in the war in Europe. Eight times the king and queen appeared on the balcony to acknowledge the cheers of the crowd. Alongside them was the prime minister, Winston Churchill, and – for part of evening – the two young princesses. But at one point Elizabeth and Margaret slipped from the palace, escorted by young officers, to mingle unnoticed in the crowd.

"We want the king," the crowd had chanted. And when they saw him, they sang *For He's a Jolly Good Fellow*. King George and his family had not fled the bombing, they had suffered the loss of a relative, they had shared the deprivations of war. And now, although the war with Japan continues, they share the triumph. The king said: "We give thanks for a great deliverance" (→ 13/5).

George visits liberated Channel Islands

Channel Islands, 7 June 1945
The crowds were out in force today on Guernsey and Jersey to greet King George and Queen Elizabeth when they arrived to visit the newly-liberated islands. A 21-gun salute boomed out as the royal couple landed, and thousands of islanders lined the streets to cheer and wave festoons of red, white and blue bunting as their procession made its way to one of the island parliaments, the States of Jersey. The Channel Islands were the only part of the British Isles to suffer Nazi occupation, which began after the fall of France in June 1940. There had been a number of commando raids there, but liberation did not come until the very end of the war in Europe.

In the meantime the islands were subjected to the same regime as the rest of Europe, with all its attendant horrors. Now that is over, as as the king put it today: "After long suffering, I hope the island will regain its former glory."

Second Subaltern Elizabeth Windsor becomes one of the girls

Camberley, Surrey, March 1945
Princess Elizabeth, the king's eldest daughter and heir to his throne, has taken on a new identity: No 230873 2nd Subaltern Elizabeth Windsor of the Auxiliary Transport Service. Attached to the No 1 Mechanical Training Centre here, the 18-year-old princess is making her own contribution to the war effort, something she has wanted to do for a very long time. She is now being trained by the ATS to drive a heavy goods vehicle through rush-hour traffic and to service it when necessary. She may still sleep at Windsor, rather than in barracks, but otherwise the princess is just one of the girls (→ 4/1945).

King George's brother, Henry, the Duke of Gloucester, who has become Australia's first royal governor-general this year.

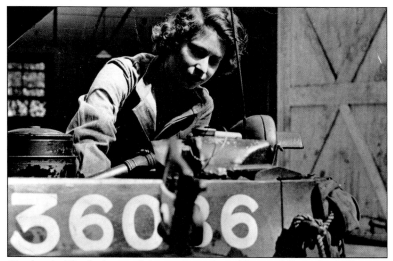

Hard at it: Elizabeth examining a piece of machinery while in the ATS.

Duke agrees to sell controversial life story to the press

Paris, February 1947

The Duke of Windsor has signed a contract with Henry Luce, the American owner of *Time* and *Life* magazines, to write a series of articles on his life. So far the deal is confined to his early life, with three or four articles covering the years up to the begining of the First World War in 1914. However, the idea of a full-blown autobiography has been canvassed for the future. The prospect of the former king rekindling the controversy which surrounded his abdication 11 years ago will alarm court circles.

Publishers would certainly pay hefty sums for his version of what the popular press called the "love story of the century". But money is not the only incentive: the duke also wants to give his side of the story and is piqued at being denied an official role after the war as a roving ambassador for Britain in the United States (→3/1951).

King loses his title as emperor of India

Windsor, 15 August 1947

From today, the king-emperor is no more. The title of *Imperator*, first bestowed on Queen Victoria 70 years ago in recognition of Britain's imperial rule over India, may no longer be used by the monarch. He now must sign official documents as "GR" and not "GRI".

Following the passage a month ago of the India Independence Act, under which the old *Raj* will be divided into two self-governing dominions, the role of emperor is over. The king played no active part in the transfer of power, although he asked Lord Mountbatten, who has been India's last viceroy, to do what he can "to see fair play for the princes", whose loyalty to the crown has remained constant ever since the Indian Mutiny.

This has been done. The 565 Indian princes are to work within the new state for their defence, foreign policy and communications, but will keep all other rights and administer their own incomes.

Princess Elizabeth engaged to marry

Elizabeth and Philip: engaged.

Buckingham Palace, 10 July 1947

The king today announced the engagement of "The Princess Elizabeth to Lieutenant Philip Mountbatten RN", adding that he had "gladly given his consent". The couple have been unofficially engaged for some time, and the official announcement had been scheduled for 15 July, but like many secrets this one leaked out early.

During the waiting period a number of Philip's difficulties were overcome. Becoming a British citizen was a simple matter of filling in form "S", brought in for foreign nationals who fought for the United Kingdom. The Greek royal family gave him permission to change his churchmanship from Greek Orthodox to Church of England, and he acquired a surname. As a member of the Greek royal family he did not have one, but he adopted "Mountbatten" on the suggestion of his uncle, Lord Mountbatten. However, he has no hidden wealth, and the financial problems of a man who is about to marry a princess but who has only £6.10s in the bank and a Royal Navy lieutenant's pay of £11 a week are not hard to imagine.

Unable to buy an engagement ring he approached his mother, Princess Andrew of Greece, who agreed to break down a tiara to make a ring and a bracelet for Elizabeth. She gave the job to the London jeweller, Philip Antrobus, but two days ago, when she went to pick up the ring, someone tipped off the newspapers, and the announcement was hurried forward (→ 20/11).

Elizabeth dedicates her life to the people of the Commonwealth

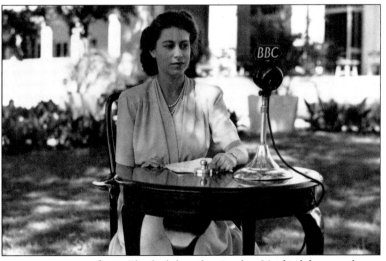

A princess comes of age: Elizabeth broadcasting her 21st birthday speech.

Queen Elizabeth, Margaret and Peter Townsend in South Africa.

Cape Town, 21 April 1947

Princess Elizabeth celebrated her 21st birthday today, not, as she might normally have expected to do, in England, but in South Africa – the first heir to the throne to celebrate such an occasion in the Commonwealth. Indeed, the princess has made it clear that this is far more than just another birthday, and that her own feelings for the Commonwealth nations whose head she is expected to become are more than simply ceremonial.

In a speech broadcast over South African radio, Elizabeth acknowledged that her coming of age was also a moment of self-dedication. "It is very simple. I declare before you that my whole life, whether it be short or long, shall be devoted to your service, and the service of our great Imperial Commonwealth to which we all belong. But I shall not have the strength to carry out this resolution unless you join in it with me, as I now invite you to do. I know that your support will be unfailingly given."

The princess's speech is undoubtedly one of the highlights of a very successful tour, although the king has been worried by the public impact of his family's journey at home. While he and his family enjoy the South African sunshine, his own country has suffered one of the worst winters ever, a chill that is only intensified by continuing wartime shortages, record unemployment and a policy, however necessary, of all-round austerity.

Still, as the royal equerry Peter Townsend, one of ten courtiers in attendance, has noted, the trip has delighted the South Africans, both black and white, even if the queen did attack a supposed assailant with her parasol. She feared violence, although the poor man only wanted to give "Lilibet" a present (→11/6).

Princess Elizabeth marries Philip Mountbatten

The bride arrives with her father.

London, 20 November 1947

Princess Elizabeth, the heir to the British throne, was married today in a ceremony which brought some glitter and cheer to the austerity of post-war Britain. Her husband was listed as Lieutenant Philip Mountbatten in the order of service, but he was given the title of Prince Philip, Duke of Edinburgh, by the king earlier today.

The princess, who is 21, wore an ivory satin dress designed by Norman Hartnell which was embroidered with flowers and encrusted with pearls and crystals. Her tulle veil hung from a circlet of diamonds. Like other brides, she had been granted an extra allotment of clothing coupons for her wedding day; unlike her British contemporaries, she was able to use material given to her by her family and sent as gifts from all over the world. With the country in the grip of austerity, ministers had recommended a low-key wedding, but for millions it was a long overdue chance to enjoy themselves. The streets were packed with cheering crowds; many slept out to secure a good view of the princess as she rode with her father in the Irish state coach to the service in Westminster abbey.

Some 2,500 guests awaited the princess at the abbey, where the service was as simple, as the archbishop of Canterbury put it, as for "any cottager who might be married in some small country church in the Dales this afternoon". Just so: but these newly-weds also had an appearance on the palace balcony and a royal train to begin their honeymoon at Broadlands, the Hampshire home of Philip's uncle, Lord Mountbatten (→ 5/1948).

The royal couple on their big day.

A Greek prince who 'looks like a Viking'

London, 20 November 1947

Although a prince of Greece, Prince Philip has a complex ancestry which owes more to northern Europe than to the south. His family has its origins in Schleswig-Holstein, from where the Danish royal family produced the first modern king of Greece in 1863. Tall, blond and, as a youth, thin, Philip comes close to the stereotype of a Dane, being described at school as looking "like a Viking". Yet the title "Philip of Greece" has stayed with him through years of living variously in France, Germany and Britain after his family were forced to flee Greece in 1922 – with the future consort of a British princess departing in an improvised cot made from orange boxes. Most of his education was in Britain, and he has since had an impressive career in the Royal Navy, passing exams in style and being mentioned in dispatches during the war.

How the royal wedding partners met

London, 20 November 1947

Princess Elizabeth and Prince Philip first met as early as 1934, when she was only eight, at the wedding of Philip's cousin Princess Marina to the Duke of Kent, but the first meeting which they both remember was at Dartmouth naval college in 1939 when Philip was a 18-year-old cadet. Elizabeth was only 13, but he apparently made such an impression that she never forgot him. By 1941 Philip, then on active service with the Royal Navy, was writing weekly to Elizabeth, and his uncle, Louis Mountbatten, was pulling strings behind the scenes to make sure that whenever possible Philip and Elizabeth were brought together. By 1944 things had progressed far enough for both Mountbatten and Philip's cousin King George of the Hellenes to speak to her father. The king replied that while he liked Philip he considered his daughter too young.

Greeting all their well-wishers: Princess Elizabeth and Prince Philip, flanked by the king and queen and, extreme right, the dowager Queen Mary.

Margaret prepares for society life as she comes of age

Margaret: dancing a samba.

London, 21 August 1948
Princess Margaret celebrated her 18th birthday today. Young, attractive and musically gifted, she is anxious to go out into society. The two royal sisters have led sheltered lives, spending most of the war years at Windsor castle where they were almost completely cut off from the rest of the world. But now the marriage of Elizabeth has started to underline the differences between them and focus public attention on the younger princess.

Margaret denies that there are many, saying: "Everyone seems determined to make out that we are totally different. Whatever is true of my sister, the opposite must be true of me." But in fact she has always been seen as the more vivacious, with a talent for mimicry and a more outgoing personality than her sister who, from the age of ten, was expected to become queen. When they were children and Elizabeth interfered on a shopping trip, Margaret told her: "You look after your empire and leave me to do my shopping!" (→ 9/1948).

A son, Charles, is born

London, 14 November 1948
At 9.14 this evening Princess Elizabeth gave birth to a son. The child, who will be known as Prince Charles, was delivered with the help of forceps by the gynaecologist Sir William Gilliatt in part of the nursery at Buckingham Palace which had been converted into a delivery room. The baby weighed seven pounds six ounces. It is the first royal birth since the 17th century that has gone ahead without witnesses and a government minister being present. This practice was started to insure against the substitution of royal children, when babies were suspected of being smuggled into bedchambers in warming-pans; the king changed the rules shortly before the birth.

The Duke of Edinburgh was also absent; he was playing squash as he waited for news. When the king's secretary told him that a son had been born, the duke bounded up the stairs three at a time, only to find

Mother and son aged one month.

his wife still unconscious from an anaesthetic. It was an hour before she awoke and he could present her with a bouquet of roses and carnations. Queen Mary was an early visitor, eager to see her first great-grandchild (→ 7/1949).

King and queen celebrate silver wedding

A photograph released to mark the king and queen's silver wedding.

London, 30 April 1948
King George and Queen Elizabeth have celebrated their silver wedding anniversary in style. Thousands jammed the streets as they drove to a thanksgiving service at St Paul's cathedral. There the archbishop of Canterbury told them: "The nation and the empire bless

God that He has set such a family at the seat of our royalty." Afterwards the royal couple undertook a 22-mile (35-km) drive through London, and the day ended with both making wireless broadcasts. It is rare for either to broadcast, and it is the first time that they have done so together (→ 23/11).

Fears are growing for king's health

Buckingham Palace, 12 March 1949
The deteriorating health of the king has been a cause of concern for some time, and today an operation has been performed to try to restore the circulation in his right leg. The king has been a lifelong smoker and the result is arteriosclerosis, a thickening of the arteries, which in his case means there is a danger of blood clots in his leg which could lead to gangrene and amputation.

The king is only 54, but cigarettes have already undermined his health and he is seriously ill. Smoking has been the curse of the Windsor family and has played a major role in the deaths of both his father, George V, and his grandfather, Edward VII. Now George VI is paying the price of his habit in the form of a right lumbar sympathectomy operation, which has cut the nerve that operates the constriction and expansion of the leg arteries in heat and cold.

Without this nerve the blood vessels of his leg will be permanently wide open, with the advantage that this will allow maximum circulation. However, with no way of restricting the blood supply the leg is likely to feel hot on a warm day. As he went in to the operation the king said: "I am not in the least worried." But his family is, and Queen Mary said sadly: "He is so ill, poor boy, so ill." The operation appears to have been a success, and he is now recovering (→ 24/5/51).

Elizabeth is now a naval officer's wife

Malta, December 1949
Bored with life ashore, Prince Philip has badgered the king into allowing him to return to the Royal Navy. Appointed first lieutenant aboard the destroyer HMS *Chequers*, he is stationed at Malta, where Princess Elizabeth has flown to join him, leaving their new son Charles behind. For the first time the princess is left to walk around unattended and drive her own car, and she has even been seen holding hands with her husband at the local cinema. For the moment she is just another navy wife (→ 15/8/50).

Scottish royal stone stolen from abbey

London, 25 December 1950
The Stone of Scone, the historic Stone of Destiny, has been stolen from under the Coronation Chair in Westminster abbey. The kings of Scotland were traditionally crowned on the stone before it was captured by the English in 1296, and it is said that if anyone but the rightful king is crowned upon it the stone will cry out in protest. The 458-pound (207-kg) stone was brought to England by Edward I, after which it has always been used at coronations. Detectives are seeking a man and woman, thought to be Scottish Nationalists, who were seen near the abbey (→11/4/51).

The gap where the stone should be.

'Crawfie' accused of betraying royals

London, December 1950
Marion Crawford, the former governess to Princess Elizabeth and her sister Margaret, has outraged the royal family by publishing her memoirs, entitled *The Little Princesses*. The book is seen as a gross betrayal, and "Crawfie", as she was known to the princesses, has been cut off immediately from all contact with the palace and the two sisters whom she helped to bring up and to whom she dedicated half her working life.

Miss Crawford, who married in 1947, was apparently disappointed by the lack of an honour as much as by her retirement pension. With her husband unemployed, she accepted a publisher's offer of £3,000 for a book (→11/2/88).

Elizabeth gives birth to a daughter, Anne

Four generations: Mary, Queen Elizabeth, Princess Elizabeth and Anne.

Clarence House, 15 August 1950
At 11.50am today Princess Elizabeth gave birth to a baby girl. Since the birth of their son, Charles, the royal couple have taken up residence at Clarence House, and the new princess, who will be known as Anne, is the first child to be born there since it was refurbished by John Nash in 1825. The birth was immediately communicated to the crowd outside, and royal salutes were fired in Hyde Park and at the Tower of London. Queen Elizabeth was determined to be near her daughter, and so, despite her husband's illness, she has not accompanied him to Scotland.

Instead, she waited near her daughter's bedroom, and, as it is not the custom for royal fathers to be at the birth, the Duke of Edinburgh waited with her. Among the many honours offered to the new baby is instant membership of the Automobile Association, which made her its one millionth member at less than an hour old.

'A King's Story' is popular success for duke, but not at court

In stylish exile: the Duke and Duchess of Windsor at a villa in Biarritz.

King George opens Festival of Britain

London, 3 May 1951
Today, on the centenary of the opening of the Great Exhibition in 1851 by Queen Victoria, a new "Festival of Britain" was opened by King George. The government-sponsored event is seen as "the people giving themselves a pat on the back" and is part of the long haul back from the agony of the war and the austerity of the post-war years. The exhibition has been built on bomb sites along the south bank of the Thames, near Waterloo station, and its purpose is to point to a brighter future. Crowds have flocked to the exhibition, but the architecture did not impress Queen Mary. "Really extraordinary and very ugly," was her verdict (→24/5).

King is ill again

Westminster Abbey, 24 May 1951
Everyone has remarked on how ill the king looked today while investing his brother, the Duke of Gloucester, as Great Master of the Order of the Bath in King Henry VII's chapel. He appeared to have 'flu, but later examination and X-rays show a small shadow on his left lung that doctors say is "catarrhal inflamation" (→23/9).

Paris, March 1951
The Duke of Windsor, the former King Edward VIII, has published his memoirs, *A King's Story*, including sections on his love for the divorcée Mrs Simpson and his abdication. There has been a considerable amount of opposition to his writing them at all, but having read them most observers believe that the duke has produced a reasonable, if carefully worded, version of events. However, the royal family – already smarting over the Crawford memoirs [*see left*] – will never be reconciled to his having published anything, and when a speech to a publishers' lunch was cancelled the duke immediately suspected a palace plot. He can take consolation in the book's success, with 80,000 copies being sold in the United Kingdom in the first month (→22/5).

King George dies after long illness

Princess Elizabeth and Prince Philip are a hit in Canada

Canada, 17 November 1951
Princess Elizabeth has ended her 48-day Canadian tour with an emotional "not goodbye, but *au revoir*". With tall, blond Prince Philip, the graceful, vibrant princess travelled 18,000 miles (28,800km), visited each province and waved to millions who jammed the streets to glimpse the royal pair. In French-speaking Montreal they enjoyed a Canadian victory over the New York Rangers; out west, they huddled for warmth under Hudson's Bay blankets at a special stampede. They also met the famed Dionne quintuplets and learned to square dance (→ 30/1/52).

Cowboy style: Elizabeth and Philip.

Philip takes leave of the Royal Navy

Malta, 7 July 1951
Less than a year after achieving his ambition of commanding a ship of his own, the Duke of Edinburgh has left the Royal Navy on indefinite leave. He had been promoted to lieutenant-commander last August and given command of the frigate HMS *Magpie* of the Mediterranean fleet. But with the king's illness becoming progressively more serious, Princess Elizabeth needs to take on more state duties – a regency has been mooted – and she wants her husband to be by her side (→ 17/11).

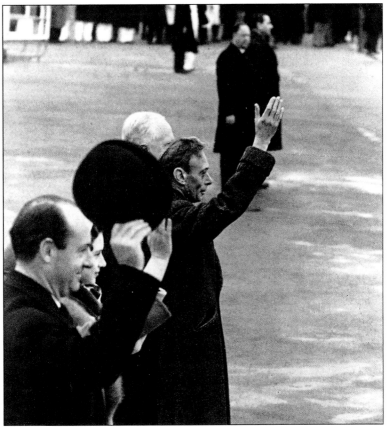
The last time he saw Princess Elizabeth: George waves her off on her tour.

The unexpected king who rallied a nation

London, 6 February 1952
Nobody ever expected Prince Albert, the second son of George V, to become king, least of all the prince himself. His childhood was undistinguished, his naval career blighted by illness, and his early public appearances were dogged by a persistent stammer. He had little experience of public life when his brother abdicated in 1936. Yet his innate sense of duty and simple decency struck a chord with the nation, never more so than during the war when he and his wife stayed in London to share the risks of his people. Buckingham Palace, itself hit by bombs, was the focus of national celebration on VE Day.

In wartime the king had established a close relationship with Winston Churchill, lunching alone with him most weeks. Peace was followed by a Labour prime minister in Clement Attlee. George lost his role as emperor of India, but he was scrupulous in observing his role as a constitutional monarch as

The king with his grandson Charles on the boy's third birthday.

he presided over the creation of a welfare state and a free commonwealth with which he had little sympathy. By doing so he bequeathes a monarchy far more respected than that which he inherited.

Sandringham, 6 February 1952
His Majesty King George VI died in his sleep during the night. He had been at Sandringham for a short holiday to recover from an operation last autumn to remove his right lung. His doctors had then diagnosed that he had lung cancer – he was a heavy smoker – but the king had not been told and thought that the lung was removed because of a bronchial blockage.

He had been out shooting yesterday, protected by a specially designed electrically-heated waistcoat, and after dinner had been entertained by Princess Margaret playing the piano. After listening to the wireless news, to keep up with the tour of Africa by Princess Elizabeth and the Duke of Edinburgh, he retired to bed.

At about 11pm he was sitting in bed reading when a servant brought him some cocoa. At about midnight a watchman noticed the king go to his window and close it for the night. At some time between midnight and 7.30am the king suffered a heart attack and died in his sleep. He was just 56 (→ 11/2).

New queen is told the news on safari

Treetops, Kenya, 6 February 1952
The news of her father's death, and the fact that she is now queen, was broken to Elizabeth by her husband. The royal couple had been enjoying a stay at this remote lodge, built in the branches of a giant wild fig tree in the Kenyan bush, when a local reporter informed one of the party's aides, Major Martin Charteris, of a Reuter news agency flash that the king was dead.

It took Charteris and a senior aide, Commander Michael Parker, an hour to confirm the news, after which Parker went to the window of the Queen's room and urgently beckoned to the Duke of Edinburgh to come out. He then broke the news to him, and the duke took it on himself to break it as gently as he was able to his wife. Asked at a hurriedly called press conference how Elizabeth had taken the news, Major Charteris replied: "Bravely, like a queen" (→ 7/2).

Elizabeth II
1952–

Kenya, 6 February 1952. Princess Elizabeth accedes to the throne, aged 25 (→ 7/2).

London, 7 February 1952. Elizabeth arrives at London's Heathrow airport to be met by the prime minister for the first time as Queen (→ 8/2).

London, 11 February 1952. The body of George VI arrives from Sandringham (→ 16/2).

London, 16 February 1952. The Duke of Windsor attends the funeral of George VI; he is not accompanied by the duchess.

London, 5 May 1952. Elizabeth and Prince Philip move into Buckingham Palace to allow the renovation of Clarence House to begin; the Queen Mother and Princess Margaret will live there.

Paris, October 1952. The city offers the Windsors a house in Neuilly (→ 23/6/64).

London, 4 November 1952. Elizabeth opens her first parliament.

London, 8 December 1952. Elizabeth agrees to her coronation being televised (→ 2/6/53).

London, 12 December 1952. The Queen Mother employs the recently-divorced Group-Captain Peter Townsend, who was an equerry to her late husband, George VI, as comptroller to her household (→ 2/1953).

Sandringham, February 1953. The friendship between Group-Captain Peter Townsend and Princess Margaret grows closer (→ 14/6).

Westminster, 2 June 1953. Elizabeth is crowned Queen.→

Belfast, 30 June 1953. Elizabeth begins a three-day tour of

Northern Ireland; Group-Captain Peter Townsend is in attendance, in an attempt to hush the press reports of his romance with Princess Margaret (→ 3/7).

London, 30 June 1953. The Queen Mother and Princess Margaret leave together to make a tour of Rhodesia (→ 6/1954).

London, 3 July 1953. Group-Captain Peter Townsend is transferred to Brussels to take up the position of air attaché to the British embassy (→ 6/1954).

Westminster, 11 November 1953. Parliament approves the Regency Bill, which will allow Prince Philip to become regent if necessary.

Sydney, 3 February 1954. Queen Elizabeth becomes the first reigning monarch to visit Australia (→ 1/4).

London, 15 April 1954. The Queen and Philip return to a tumultuous welcome after their successful Commonwealth tour.

London, June/July 1954. Peter Townsend makes a secret trip from Brussels to England in order to visit Princess Margaret and to see his two sons (→ 21/8/55).

Westminster, 30 November 1954. Winston Churchill celebrates his 80th birthday, which coincides

with the state opening of parliament (→ 5/4/55).

London, 1 February 1955. Princess Margaret goes to the Caribbean in order to convalesce after a bout of influenza (→ 26/2).

Balmoral, 21 August 1955. Princess Margaret, on her 25th birthday, asks the Queen for permission to marry Townsend, in accordance with the Royal Marriages Act of 1772. A member of the royal family under 25 must obtain the sovereign's consent to marry; over 25 the sovereign still has the power to delay a marriage (→ 12/10).

London, September 1955. Princess Anne begins lessons with Prince Charles's Scottish governess, Miss Peebles (→ 5/1958).

London, 12 October 1955. Peter Townsend arrives from Brussels to see if the Queen will allow him to marry Princess Margaret (→ 31/10).

London, 21 October 1955. The Queen unveils a statue to her father, George VI.

London, 31 October 1955. Princess Margaret announces her decision not to marry Peter Townsend.→

Nigeria, 29 January 1956. The Queen and Prince Philip receive a warm welcome in Africa (→ 15/2).

Heathrow, 15 October 1956. Prince Philip sets off on his first solo tour; he will open the Olympic Games in Melbourne before travelling on to Antarctica (→ 16/2/57).

Portugal, 16 February 1957. The Queen and Prince Philip are reunited in Lisbon before beginning their official state visit (→ 22/2).

Ghana, 6 March 1957. Marina, the Duchess of Kent, represents the Queen at the ceremony of independence.

Westminster, 30 November 1957. The Queen opens parliament and announces the creation of life peerages for both sexes.

Trinidad, 22 April 1958. Princess Margaret opens the parliament of the new British West Indies Federation.

London, May 1958. Princess Anne has her tonsils and adenoids removed at Great Ormond Street hospital (→ 7/1959).

London, July 1958. The Queen undergoes surgery on her sinuses.

London, 1958. Peter Townsend, returning from abroad, visits Princess Margaret in conditions of great secrecy (→ 31/12).

Canada, 26 June 1959. The Queen inaugurates the St Lawrence Seaway while on her tour of Canada (→ 27/7).

Britain, 19 November 1959. The government will reintroduce £10 notes and put the Queen's head on notes for the first time.

Brussels, 1959. Peter Townsend marries Marie Luce Jamagne, a 20-year-old heiress (→ 26/2/60).

The life and times of Queen Elizabeth II

Name: Elizabeth Alexandra Mary.
Birth: 21 April 1926.
Accession: 6 February 1952.
Coronation: 2 June 1953.
Predecessor: father.
Height: five feet four inches.
Hair: dark brown.
Eyes: blue.
Marriage: Philip Mountbatten, 20 November 1947.

Children: Charles, Anne, Andrew and Edward.
Favourite homes: Windsor, Sandringham, Balmoral.
Likes: horses, corgis, rural life.
Dislikes: invasions of privacy.
Greatest problem: changing attitudes to divorce within the royal family and church.
Greatest success: symbolising unity of the Commonwealth.

Opposite: Queen Elizabeth II; a portrait by Denis Fildes.

Vivat Regina! A new Elizabethan age has begun

London, 8 February 1952
For several days the weather has reflected the gloom of a nation in mourning, with sleet pelting down from dark grey skies. But the sun suddenly shone today as if welcoming the proclamation of Elizabeth II, "by the grace of God Queen of this Realm and of all Her other Realms and Territories, Head of the Commonwealth, Defender of the Faith".

The new Queen arrived back from her curtailed visit to Kenya yesterday afternoon. This petite young woman – she is 25 years old – looked even tinier than usual as, clad in mourning black and alone, she descended the steps of the BOAC plane at Heathrow airport. Winston Churchill, her prime minis-ter, and Clement Attlee, the leader of her majesty's opposition, waited to greet her beside her uncle, the Duke of Gloucester. But she did not allow them to kiss her hand: the privilege of being the first to do so was reserved for her grand-mother, Queen Mary.

Her official life started this morning, when the accession council met at St James's palace. Barely containing her emotion, she told the assembled elder statesmen that she would continue her father's work. "I pray that God will help me to discharge worthily the heavy task that has been laid upon me so early in my life," she added. Then the guns started booming out across Hyde Park, and heralds throughout the land declared her accession as the youngest monarch to succeed to the throne since 1837, when the 18-year-old Princess Victoria be-came queen.

Elizabeth was not expecting to be queen so soon; indeed, until the king started to suffer from arterio-sclerosis four years ago, she had hoped to live her own life well into the 1960s or even the 70s. But she is meeting the unexpected, and the sudden loss of her father, with tre-mendous dignity and calm – qual-ities that have impressed all who know her. She will need them, and all the support Philip can give, to deal with the heavy responsibilities that were laid on her young shoul-ders today. And they start with the lying-in-state and funeral of the late king.

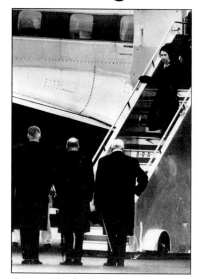
Queen Elizabeth in mourning, after her flight back from Kenya.

The nation bids a fond farewell to a man not born to be king

Windsor, 16 February 1952
To the beating of muffled drums, the coffin of King George VI was lowered into the sarcophagus in St George's chapel. Queen Elizabeth, deathly white behind her black veil, threw a handful of red earth onto the coffin, the final gesture of fare-well to a much-loved father. Then the lord chamberlain snapped his staff of office in two and tossed it into the open grave. No act could have symbolised the end of an era more clearly. Meanwhile the nation observed two minutes of silence, breathless moments in which memories of the past mingled with hopes for the future symbolised by the new Queen and her family.

A royal thank you

London, 18 February 1952
Queen Elizabeth the Queen Mother, as she has elected to be called to avoid confusion with her daughter, today thanked the world for its sympathy in her bereave-ment. "I want you to know how your concern for me has upheld me in my sorrow," she wrote. "I com-mend to you our dear daughter. Give her your loyalty and devo-tion: in the great and lonely station to which she has been called she will need your protection and your love" (→17/11/54).

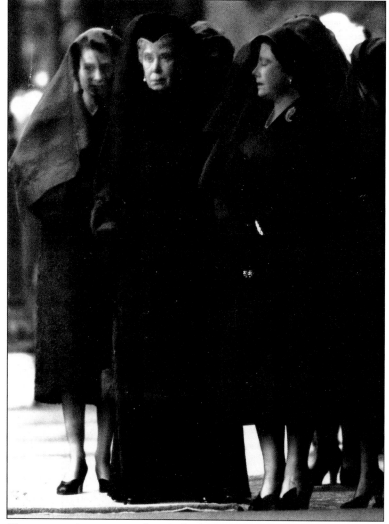
Three queens in mourning: (l to r) Elizabeth, Mary and the Queen Mother.

'House of Windsor' confirmed by order

London, 9 April 1952
To the fury of both Philip and his uncle, Earl Mountbatten, the Queen today signed an order in council declaring that "she and her children shall be styled and known as the House of Windsor". Philip exclaimed bitterly: "An amoeba ... I'm just a bloody amoeba!"

Two months ago, Uncle Louis crowed that the House of Mount-batten – Philip's name – had supplanted the House of Windsor. Queen Mary was livid. Her hus-band, she said, had founded the House of Windsor for all time. Now his will has been done (→8/2/60).

Queen Mary dies

London, 24 March 1953
Queen Mary, aged 85, died today at Marlborough House. She had been a queen since 1910, when her hus-band, George V, acceded to the throne. She married George after his elder brother Eddy, to whom she was engaged, died. She has seen six rulers, from Victoria to Eliz-abeth. The abdication of her eldest son was the greatest blow to a woman with a profound sense of duty and dignity. "She looked like a queen, and she acted like a queen," said Churchill.

Thousands defy the rain to cheer the coronation

London, 2 June 1953

The vast crowds who ignored the rain and camped out last night along the coronation route were rewarded this morning with over two hours of pageantry as guests and VIPs made their way to Westminster abbey. The lord mayor of London led the procession, followed by coaches bearing visiting heads of state, representatives of all the Queen's dominions, the Commonwealth prime ministers and members of the royal family.

Finally, at just after half-past ten, Elizabeth and Philip rolled out of the gates of Buckingham Palace in the magnificent, ornate gold state coach, guarded by "Beefeaters". The Queen was the last to arrive at the abbey, a splendid sight in a diamond diadem and crimson velvet robes trimmed with ermine and bordered with gold lace. These rich robes and jewels she took off until she stood divested of all her finery, wearing a simple linen overdress for the central act of the ceremony.

The archbishop of Canterbury, Dr Geoffrey Fisher, anointed the Queen with holy oil made to a formula devised by Charles I, and declared her dedication "as kings, priests and prophets were anointed". Then she was dressed in golden robes and was seated on King Edward's chair, above the Stone of Scone, to be given the symbols of her authority: the orb (a reminder that her worldly power is subject to that of Christ), the sceptre (symbol

The Queen enthroned: the bishops pay homage to her majesty during the coronation service in Westminster abbey.

of justice), the rod of mercy and the royal ring of sapphire and rubies. Finally, in absolute silence, the archbishop held St Edward's crown high in the air, then lowered it slowly onto her head.

The shout rang out: "God Save the Queen", trumpets blared, bells rang, and at Hyde Park and the Tower the guns fired with great booms of joy. Philip led the peers of the realm in doing homage to his wife, who sat enthroned, bearing the heavy crown and equally heavy responsibilities with a humble and solemn calm.

For the first time, television had given millions of people across the world a ringside seat at the ceremony. Letting the cameras into the abbey was, perhaps, a recognition of the greatest challenge Queen Elizabeth II will face: making the ancient traditions of the British monarchy relevant in the modern world of rapid political, social and technological change.

An aerial view of the procession.

Elizabeth and Prince Charles particularly enjoy the RAF coronation fly-past.

Booking the best seat for the parade. ▷

Margaret in divorcé romance rumours

London, 14 June 1953
The rumours started less than two weeks ago at her sister's coronation. At the end of the service, Princess Margaret went up to a tall, handsome RAF officer, spoke for a few moments and affectionately, intimately, brushed a loose thread off the breast-pocket of his sky-blue uniform. Cameras clicked, and the next day American newspapers carried the story of Margaret's affair with a divorcé: Group-Captain Peter Townsend.

The British press stayed silent until today, when the *People* newspaper ran a front-page splash revealing all the speculation printed by its foreign counterparts. It vehemently denies the rumours, adding that it is "unthinkable that a royal princess ... should even contemplate marriage with a man who has been through the divorce courts". But that is precisely what

Princess Margaret *is* contemplating. Shortly before the coronation, she presented the Queen with the first major dilemma of her reign by asking permission to marry this dashing hero of the Battle of Britain [*see page 542*], one of her father's equerries and now comptroller of her mother's household.

Townsend is a much-respected and well-liked household servant. The Queen, knowing the depth and sincerity of her sister's love, was sympathetic, but Townsend, who is 38, was divorced only last December (on the grounds of his wife's adultery). Permission could not be given; the Queen wanted to avoid scandal in the coronation year. Wait until after the coronation, she said, and we will see. Subject to certain conditions, Margaret will be able to marry without the Queen's permission in three years' time when she will be 25 (→30/6).

Queen goes on tour to meet her people

Elizabeth and Philip in Edinburgh.

Britain, summer 1953
The Queen is spending this summer making coronation tours to meet her people. Northern Ireland was today's destination, with Scotland also on the royal schedule. Among the court officials who accompanied the Queen to Belfast was Peter Townsend, but he is to have a new posting to the British embassy in Brussels – away from the court and Princess Margaret.

Queen Mother is a hit on solo tours

Ottawa, 17 November 1954
Queen Elizabeth the Queen Mother has left for home five cold, raw days after she arrived here. "I'm sad to be leaving," she said. Earlier she had described Canada as a magnificent adventure in human brotherhood: "In her unity and diversity she is an example for all men," she said. The Queen Mother is showing that widowhood has neither dimmed her rapport with crowds nor ended her role as a member of the royal family. She visited Rhodesia last year and has now returned to North America where she had such a success with the late King George VI in 1939.

In Canada she paused often on her formal tours to chat with children and was always happy to oblige the photographers – even the one who shouted out: "Look this way, Queen!" – with her famous smile. Her visit here followed an 18-day one to the United States. In New York she saw a Broadway show and joined in the celebrations of the bicentennial of Columbia university. In Washington she met President and Mrs Eisenhower before touring Maryland and Virginia (→3/1958).

Queen makes royal history by being first ruler to tour Australia and New Zealand

On tour: the royal couple during their successful visit to Australia.

Australia, 1 April 1954
The high emotions that have followed the royal couple through Australia and New Zealand were evident in the farewell given by the Australians as the liner *Gothic* left Fremantle today. It is just over three months since the people of Auckland gave a rapturous greeting to the first reigning monarch to visit the Antipodes.

"I want to show that the crown is not merely an abstract symbol of our unity, but a personal and living bond between you and me," said the Queen in a Christmas Day broadcast from New Zealand, the first to be delivered from outside

Britain. The elation of New Zealand was matched a few weeks later when the Queen and Prince Philip arrived at a sunlit Sydney harbour to begin a tour that has taken them to many parts of Australia.

It has been the reaction of the crowds that has made the tour so memorable. The Maori dances at Rotarua, the 102,000 children at the Melbourne cricket ground, the people of north Queensland who crossed flooded rivers by horseback to see her, the streets of towns and cities jammed with cheering, flag-waving people – these are memories that the royal couple will hold for years to come (→15/4).

Elizabeth at a banquet in Canberra.

The royal liner is welcomed home.

Margaret inspires a calypso tribute

Jamaica, 26 February 1955

Princess Margaret today sailed away from the West Indies in the royal yacht, the *Britannia*, at the end of an official visit to some of Britain's most beautiful colonies. Among other things, the stunning 24-year-old princess has inspired several calypsos like this one:

Lovin' sister of Queen Lilibet,
Is the Princess Margaret!
She ain't married, she ain't tall,
Like to dance, like to sing,
Like to try anything!
If she be a boy
She be king!

The press did not share this complimentary view. While Britons languished in the wintry fog, it complained, Margaret was visiting several islands blessed with abundant sunshine at the taxpayers' expense. Despite press sniping at home, the princess did have a schedule which regularly included six hours of official engagements each day, often in wilting heat. The crowds were certainly enthusiastic, as was the white expatriate community wintering in the West Indies. The playwright and actor Noël Coward says that the visit to Jamaica was a "very great success", although he regrets what he has been told was the protocol that prevented Margaret from dancing with any black men (→ 21/8).

Churchill steps down with a royal toast

Elizabeth leaving Sir Winston's farewell dinner at 10 Downing Street.

Buckingham Palace, 5 April 1955

Sir Winston Churchill, Queen Elizabeth's first prime minister, emerged from her study this afternoon, his eyes moist with emotion. He had just had his last audience with the Queen, at which he had tendered his resignation. It is the end of a remarkable partnership.

Churchill, now 80, was at first doubtful that a queen in her twenties would be able to cope with the responsibilities of the job. He soon realised that she was wise beyond her years, but her youth brought out his most protective and chivalrous instincts. He had first met her as a child of barely two at Balmoral; now he has a large photograph of her next to his bed at his home, Chartwell. The Queen, for her part, was nervous in the presence of the national hero and Nobel prize-winner who had fought in the Boer War and led his country to victory in the Second World War.

All fears were dispelled as soon as they started to work together, when they found they had an immediate rapport. Last night the Queen attended Sir Winston's farewell dinner party at Downing Street – the first time that a reigning monarch had ever visited the prime minister's residence. Greatly moved, she broke with tradition and proposed the health of her very special prime minister (→ 25/1/65).

Annigoni's majestic portrait pulls crowd

London, 14 August 1955

The Royal Academy has a suitably royal hit on its hands this summer. A portrait of the Queen by the Italian artist Pietro Annigoni has proved so popular that attendance records at the academy's summer exhibition have been broken. The Queen is shown wearing the dark-blue cloak of the Order of the Garter against a spring landscape. "I had to try to get into the portrait the feeling of being close to the people, yet very much alone," says the artist.

Majestic: the Annigoni portrait.

Royal family help out at 'sale of work'

Anne and Charles inspect the goods.

Balmoral, 20 August 1955

A sale of work was held today at Crathie church, near Balmoral, today which drew more customers than usual. The attraction which lured an estimated 3,000 people was not the goods on sale but the people helping out behind the trestle tables. Queen Elizabeth the Queen Mother had organised the sale, and she had roped in her family to work on the various stalls. The Queen, Prince Philip, Princess Margaret and the Queen Mother herself helped on stalls, while Prince Charles and Princess Anne just enjoyed themselves. Behind the good works, however, there is worry over Margaret; she is 25 tomorrow and will be free to marry without her sister's approval.

Brother and sister at their books: a portrait of Prince Charles and Princess Anne by the society photographer Antony Armstrong-Jones, who was commissioned by the royal family to make an intimate series of studies of the childhood of the prince, now heir to the throne, and the princess.

Margaret puts 'duty' first and spurns Townsend

London, 31 October 1955
After two weeks of soul-searching and intense press speculation, Princess Margaret tonight declared that she would put duty before love and not marry Peter Townsend, a former Battle of Britain hero and an equerry to her late father. At the age of 25 the princess could now marry Townsend, a divorced man, without the permission of the Queen, although she would have to wait a year; she would also lose payments from the civil list and her place as third in line to the throne.

But tonight Princess Margaret said: "I have been aware that, subject to my renouncing my rights of succession, it might be possible for me to contract a civil marriage. But mindful of the church's teaching that Christian marriage is indissoluble, and conscious of my duty to the Commonwealth, I have resolved to put these considerations before others. I have reached this decision entirely alone, and in doing so I have been strengthened by the unfailing support and devotion of Group-Captain Townsend." Her romance with Townsend be-

came public two years ago. He then left the royal household to work as air attaché at the British embassy in Brussels. On 13 October he returned to meet Margaret to decide their future. They found that they were still very much in love. The Queen had left Margaret in no doubt as to her opinion: she would never approve of a member of the royal family marrying a divorced person unless the church and parliament gave their permission.

Nevertheless, both Margaret and Peter remained determined to marry; even dinner with the archbishop of Canterbury failed to change the princess's mind. But last week the Queen relayed the advice of the prime minister, Anthony Eden: she would have to marry abroad and stay there, at least for a few years. Church, state and family were against Townsend. Margaret pulled back from the brink over which her uncle, the Duke of Windsor, had hurtled in 1936. He had given up the throne for the woman he loved, but Margaret has given up the man she loves rather than face exile and ostracism (→ 1958).

The agony of decision: Margaret just two weeks before the announcement.

The dashing divorced pilot whose love was shot down in flames

East Sussex, 31 October 1955
The newsmen who had tracked down Group-Captain Peter Townsend to a friend's house in Uckfield were told by the butler: "He is not in a position to make a statement ... he is very distressed." And that is not surprising. Townsend might be a hero of the Battle of Britain, but he is sensitive, gentle and even poetic – characteristics which so attracted Margaret to him.

Peter Wooldridge Townsend, DSO, DFC and bar, joined the royal household in 1944 as one of George VI's equerries. The king was recruiting men who had shown bravery in war, and Townsend – leader of over 500 combat missions, shot down twice – had certainly done that. His impact on the 14-year-old Princess Margaret was immediate; he was not like the pampered, shallow aristocratic youths she was accustomed to meeting.

Indeed he was 29, married and a father. But his marriage to Rosemary Pawle, a brigadier's daughter,

Townsend and Margaret in South Africa in 1947, when they fell in love.

started to creak under the dual pressures of his devotion to the king and her social ambitions, which he did not share. In December 1952 he obtained a divorce on the grounds of her adultery with a man whom

she has since married. As Townsend has been a trusted friend of all the royal family, it was with reluctance that the Queen intervened in the second divorce scandal to rock the royal family in 20 years (→ 1958).

The social 'set' of Princess Margaret

London, 31 October 1955
In these difficult times, Princess Margaret has been leaning on her friends more than ever. She and Townsend have stayed in and dined at their homes for the last two weeks, in order to avoid the commotion that going out would have caused. But she has seen more of her mature, married friends, steering clear of what the press calls "the Margaret set" – the fast-living, well-heeled youngsters who cut a swathe through high society.

At the centre of this lively social group is Margaret herself, elegantly smoking a cigarette in a long holder, wearing a dress that emphasises her hour-glass figure while keeping it well covered: she is a princess, after all. Her escorts are men like Johnny Dalkeith (the heir of the Duke of Buccleuch), the artistic Simon Phipps, Billy Wallace and the horse-loving Henry, Lord Porchester.

African colonies are on royal itinerary

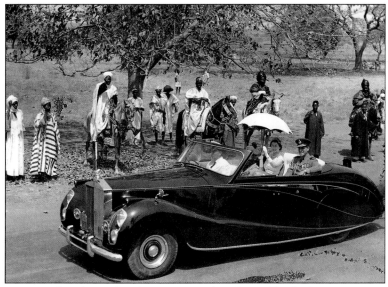

Nigerians line the road to the airport to salute Queen Elizabeth.

Nigeria, 15 February 1956
The Queen and Prince Philip are resting in Lagos at the end of an immensely successful official visit to Nigeria, the largest of Britain's remaining colonies. The visit is intended to demonstrate a commitment to establishing closer links with black Africa.

The royal couple arrived on 28 January to a tumultuous welcome. The following day, when they attended morning service in the capital's cathedral church of Christ, enthusiastic crowds had to be restrained by police. Wooden posts and steel barriers were snap-

ped and bent by the surging masses. A curious but moving point in the visit took place a week ago when the royal party stopped at a leper colony on the Oji river.

While local drums beat out the message "Our mother is coming!" Queen Elizabeth and Prince Philip were taken to see those suffering from this much-feared disease. The Queen and the prince both decided to adopt a leper child financially, to the delight of the colony's super-viser. He said that the visit "will do more to conquer man's fear and hate of the disease than any other single act I can think of".

Soviet leaders pay visit to the Queen

Windsor, 23 April 1956
Two rather unusual guests dropped in for tea at Windsor castle this afternoon: the Soviet leader Nikita Khrushchev and his prime minister Nikolai Bulganin. The two men are here on an eight-day visit to discuss, amongst other things, the prospects for European security.

Although, of course, no reporters were present, one might guess that the Queen felt somewhat unenthusiastic about her visitors. Mr Khrushchev disowned the Stalinist past in a momentous speech in Moscow last month, but the Queen may still regard him as the political heir of those who killed the Russian royal family – relatives of her own family – during the revolution.

So far the meetings between the Russians and the British government have not been particularly fruitful. The diplomatic temperature was raised when a Labour politician, George Brown, got into a row with Khrushchev at a dinner party. The Russian leader said afterwards that if he was British he would vote Conservative.

The best that can be said about the visit is that both sides have agreed to differ. Khrushchev has put it this way: "You do not like communism. We do not like capitalism. There is only one way out – peaceful coexistence."

The palace to host new lunch parties

London, 31 May 1956
Newspaper editors, bishops and businessmen will soon be among those rubbing elbows over lunch at Buckingham Palace. The Queen has decided that an informal lunch with some half dozen guests is a good way to get a view of things beyond the royal railings. Although some of the likely candidates hardly qualify as men on the Clapham omnibus, these midday gatherings show Queen Elizabeth's keen interest in everyday affairs.

Suez plan revealed

Hampshire, 29 October 1956
Earl Mountbatten today gave the Queen details of the government's preparations for war over Suez. Mountbatten, as first sea lord, has been a leading internal critic of the policy adopted by Anthony Eden's government. He used the royal visit to his Broadlands home, near Romsey, to brief the Queen. It is understood that she was surprised by what Mountbatten told her. However, government sources insist that there has been no disagreement between the Queen and her prime minister. Elizabeth signed a proclamation calling up army reserves back in July – in a box at the Goodwood races.

Queen Mother's horse takes a tumble within yards of the post

Liverpool, 24 March 1956
The entire royal family, gathered here for this afternoon's Grand National, shared the Queen Mother's disappointment as she watched her horse, Devon Loch, sprawl over the turf just 50 yards (45.5m) from the finish. Hopes had been high that Devon Loch would be the first royal horse to win the National for half a century. Ridden by an experienced jockey, Dick Francis, Devon Loch was six lengths in front of the field when he fell. The race was won by ESB, whose jockey could hardly have believed his luck. The Queen Mother went down to the enclosure afterwards to comfort Francis. She herself maintained a stoical attitude: "That's racing" (→31/12/58).

Devon Loch and the top jockey Dick Francis tumble out of the race.

New award scheme announced by duke

London, 31 December 1956
Prince Philip has announced the launch of a new scheme designed to encourage young people to take up sports and other outdoor activities. The Duke of Edinburgh's Award Scheme was outlined in a statement issued today from Buckingham Palace. Through training in a number of outdoor pursuits it is meant to be "an introduction to leisure-time activities, a challenge to the individual to personal achievement and as a guide to those ... concerned about the development of our future citizens". There will be different levels of achievement, to be marked by bronze, silver and gold awards (→20/12/65).

Queen in dilemma after Eden resigns

London, 10 January 1957

Harold Macmillan is the surprise choice to be Britain's new prime minister after two days in which Queen Elizabeth has faced the greatest political crisis of her reign. Anthony Eden saw the Queen at Sandringham two days ago to tell her that his doctors had advised him to step down as premier. Elizabeth, at the age of 30, had to choose a new leader for a country and party still split over the aborted intervention at Suez last year.

Two candidates soon emerged: "Rab" Butler, who had deputised for the ailing Eden, and Harold Macmillan, the chancellor of the exchequer. Butler seemed to be the favourite, but the Conservative Party had no mechanism for electing a leader. Instead, the cabinet asked two peers to take soundings within the government. Most ministers backed Macmillan, and this was also the verdict of MPs, according to the chief whip, Edward Heath; Butler was thought to have been too lukewarm over Suez.

One of the peers, Lord Salisbury, went to see the Queen this morning. The Queen also called in Sir Winston Churchill. The consensus was clear – and more widely based than it may seem to the public – and Macmillan saw the Queen at 2pm (→ 18/10/63).

New title for prince spikes rift rumours

London, 22 February 1957

Prince Philip was today named as a prince of the United Kingdom for the first time. Until today he was a prince of Greece by birth and a royal duke of Britain by marriage; now, 100 years after Queen Victoria gave the same honour to Albert, he is honoured for services to the Commonwealth and to the Queen. The award comes one day after the couple returned from Portugal where they were reunited after four months apart which have fuelled rumours of a rift in their marriage.

American newspapers have been speculating about marital problems for some time, seizing upon Philip's prolonged royal tour as evidence of estrangement. News that the wife of one of Philip's aides was seeking a divorce heightened speculation to such an extent that Sir Michael Adeane, the queen's private secretary, was forced to issue a statement. "It is quite untrue that there is any rift between the Queen and the Duke of Edinburgh," he said.

Philip has spent the last four months visiting several Commonwealth countries and also Antarctica, where he pursued his interests in wildlife and conservation. The Queen sees his new royal title as a reward for service to the Commonwealth and, perhaps, a riposte to the rumour-mongers.

Royal new boy starts at boarding-school

Out walking: at Hill House school.

Taking a step up: at Cheam.

Hampshire, 23 September 1957

Amongst the shining morning faces at Cheam preparatory school today was one with a shy and nervous look: that of the eight-year-old Prince Charles. He arrived here for the new term after an overnight journey, accompanied by his parents, from Balmoral. He has good reason to look tense: he is the first royal heir to be educated outside the palace. Although school is not an entirely novel experience for him – he was enrolled at Hill House in Knightsbridge last January – at Cheam he will be a boarder, away from the family for a whole term.

The school, which moved to its present site at Headley from Cheam village in 1934, is fee-paying, the Queen and Prince Philip having resisted calls from some Labour MPs to have Charles sent to a state school. Tradition also played a part in the choice of this particular school: Charles's father was a pupil at Cheam nearly 30 years ago.

Everything has been done to ease acceptance of the royal new boy. The joint headmasters, Mark Wheeler and Peter Beck, assured parents by letter that he would be treated just like anyone else. They even let journalists tour the school before today's arrival, pleading to be left alone from now on. It is probably a vain hope; all eyes – of staff and pupils as well as the press – are now on Charles (→ 26/7/58).

Take that! Lord Altrincham suffers for his attack on the Queen.

A day out at the Badminton horse trials: from left, the Queen Mother, Princess Margaret, Queen Elizabeth and Mary, the Princess Royal.

Literary peer attacks 'priggish' Queen

London, 31 August 1957

A furore has erupted over this month's edition of the *National and English Review*. Lord Altrincham, its editor and owner, has lashed out at both the Queen and her advisers. Elizabeth, he writes, comes over as "a priggish schoolgirl, captain of the hockey team", apparently "unable to string even a few sentences together without a written text". Altrincham, a young peer who still considers himself a monarchist, dismisses the royal entourage as "tweedy" and "a tight little enclave of English ladies and gentlemen". Fleet Street has pounced on these remarks, delighting in the aristocratic cries of outrage. "Altrincham should be shot," said the Earl of Strathmore (→ 19/10).

Queen scores a triumph in America

Opening parliament in Ottawa.

The royal couple with President and Mrs Eisenhower in Washington.

Washington, 18 October 1957

The United States has extended an ecstatic welcome to the Queen and Prince Philip as they near the end of their first tour of North America since the coronation. Thousands lined the streets of the American capital tonight to glimpse the royal couple as they returned from the White House after a state banquet with President Eisenhower and his wife. Senior Republicans, it is claimed, were almost scrambling over each other to get an invitation to the banquet.

The Queen now heads for New York to address the United Nations general assembly for the first time on 21 October. The Queen arrived here after visiting Jamestown in Virginia to commemorate the 350th anniversary of the founding of the first permanent English settlement in the New World. In a speech at Williamsburg, the old colonial capital, she pointed out that "there is a county in Virginia named after every English king and queen from Elizabeth I to George III".

Today's success in Washington was foreshadowed by the enthusiasm of crowds in Canada, where the Queen and Prince Philip arrived on 12 October. Two days later Queen Elizabeth opened parliament in Ottawa, becoming the first monarch to do so in person – normally the governor-general performs this duty. Clearly Elizabeth wants to stress that she is as much Queen of Canada as of Britain.

Media coverage of the tour has been intense, with some 3,000 journalists and photographers officially accredited. The press secretary, Commander Richard Colville, sees his job as keeping the press at bay. He is doing it well. The *Washington Post*, thwarted of easy access, laments: "As far as we can tell, she is human." The *Chicago Daily News*, however, must have got closer: it has pronounced Elizabeth "a doll, a living doll" (→ 19/10).

Christmas broadcast is seen on television for the first time

London, 25 December 1957

In line with her desire to anchor the monarchy firmly in the modern world, Queen Elizabeth gave her Christmas speech to the nation this afternoon live on television. Although it must have been a nerve-racking experience, the Queen's voice kept steady throughout. Queen Elizabeth decided earlier this year that all her Christmas talks should be on television as well as radio. A BBC announcer was filmed in July addressing the camera from different angles. From these poses the Queen chose the one she used today, the most demanding of all: direct-to-camera.

Speaking directly to her people: Elizabeth making the Christmas broadcast.

Muggeridge decries 'soap opera' lives of the royal family

New York, 19 October 1957

Malcolm Muggeridge, the editor of the humorous magazine *Punch*, has described the royal family as "soap opera ... a sort of substitute or ersatz religion" in an article in today's *Saturday Evening Post*. It is sure to provoke a storm of protest both here in America, where the Queen and Prince Philip are on a visit, and in Britain.

The same article appeared last year in a left-wing weekly, the *New Statesman*, where it attracted little attention. But after last August's criticisms of the Queen by Lord Altrincham [*see story opposite*], Muggeridge's remarks are bound to be seized upon. Fleet Street is likely to concentrate on the negative side, although Muggeridge has a lot of good things to say about Queen Elizabeth herself. He calls her "charming" and argues that, far from deserving abolition, the monarchy acts as an impartial and elegant symbol of Britain.

Debs curtsey out of the royal calendar

Edinburgh, 3 July 1958

Miss Fiona Macrae today became the last débutante to curtsey before the Queen. Today's presentation at Holyrood palace brings to an end the tradition of the ruling classes parading their daughters in front of the reigning monarch. The final presentation of debs at Buckingham Palace took place in March.

Prince Philip was among those who urged an end to the practice, arguing that it goes against the modern image he feels the monarchy needs. It also had a whiff of corruption. The girls needed to be brought forward by women who were themselves once presented. It seems that some of these ladies had been approaching the fathers of prospective debs and offering their services – for a fee. The Queen is said to have been initially reluctant to break with the tradition, but agreed as she is sensitive to charges of the monarchy's social élitism. For the debs, the royal party is over.

Queen Mother welcomed home from tour

Schoolchildren make a farewell tableau as the Queen Mother leaves Perth.

Hugging a koala bear in Brisbane.

London, March 1958
A welcome-home banquet was held this evening in the Guildhall for the Queen Mother, who has just returned from a gruelling world tour. Since January she has been to Canada, Honolulu, Fiji, New Zealand, Australia and Tasmania. Enthusiastic crowds met the Queen Mother wherever she went – even in Launceston, Tasmania, where gale-force winds swept hats off the ladies waiting for a royal introduction. Informality marked the tour: in Canberra the Queen Mother walked freely amongst the well-wishers who had gathered in the federal capital (→ 4/1959).

Schoolboy Charles is now Prince of Wales

Cardiff, 26 July 1958
The Commonwealth Games, which opened here on 18 July, today came to an end in a somewhat unusual manner. Queen Elizabeth was due to perform the closing ceremony in Cardiff Arms Park but was unable to because of having to undergo an operation on her sinuses. Instead the Duke of Edinburgh played a tape-recorded message from her to the 36,000-strong crowd.

In her message Queen Elizabeth said that the Games, together with the Festival of Wales, "have made this a memorable year for the principality". Then, to everyone's astonishment, she continued: "I have decided to mark it further by an act which will, I hope, give as much pleasure to all Welshmen as it does to me. I intend to create my son Charles Prince of Wales today."

The roar of Welsh approval in Cardiff was echoed – at reduced volume – by a small crowd of Charles's school-friends, who were watching the event on television with him in the headmaster's study at Cheam.

Yet despite the cheering the nine-year-old prince was acutely embarrassed. Ever since he arrived at the school last September there has been a conscious effort to treat Charles like any of the other boys. Today's announcement goes to show how very different he is.

Charles also immediately becomes Earl of Chester and a KG – a Knight Companion of the Most Noble Order of the Garter. But he will not be officially invested with his Welsh honour or his knighthood until, in the Queen's words, "he is grown up" (→ 23/1/61).

Townsend and the princess meet in secret

London, 31 December 1958
Peter Townsend and Princess Margaret have finally parted. Clandestine meetings between them went on for some time after their marriage plans were called off, but they came to an end this year.

During the summer Townsend, now resident in Brussels, made a last visit to Clarence House where he and the princess took tea under the watchful eye of the Queen Mother. On Townsend's arrival the princess reportedly broke free from her mother's restraining hand and embraced him in full view of the assembled servants. Tea lasted for half an hour, after which Townsend took silent leave of a tearful Princess Margaret.

Since this farewell the princess has been kept busy with a heavy and official social calendar. A well-known society photographer, Antony Armstrong-Jones, is among the people whom she sees frequently. He was commissioned to take photographs of Prince Charles and Princess Anne a few years ago (→ 1959).

Royal runners win two racing classics

Epsom, 7 June 1958
Queen Elizabeth has had a much better season of horse-racing than seemed likely at the beginning of the year. In February one of her favourite horses, Winston, fell and had to be destroyed. But in the 2,000 Guineas at Newmarket last month another of the Queen's horses, Doutelle, came in first, while today she scored her second victory in one of racing's classics: in a photo-finish at Epsom the royal filly Carrozza won the Oaks, with the Queen jumping for joy in the royal enclosure.

New phone system has royal connection

Bristol, 5 December 1958
A new dial-it-yourself telephone system has today been inaugurated by the Queen. She made a direct call from Bristol to Edinburgh, where the lord provost of the city was waiting to pick up the 'phone. After she had made her own call, Queen Elizabeth flipped a switch to link some 18,000 Bristol subscribers to the new service. The system is called STD, or "Subscriber Trunk Dialling". It has not been installed throughout the country yet, but eventually everyone will be able to make long-distance calls without having to go through the operator.

Making the first cheap trunk call.

Philip gets irked by the press in India

India, spring 1959
Prince Philip has banned pressmen covering his present tour of India and Pakistan from coming aboard the royal yacht *Britannia* or any of the jets he is using on the tour. He has, it seems, no patience with journalists. Surrounded by them in Delhi, where he met the prime minister, Pandit Nehru, the prince angrily inquired who "these damned people" were. And when a photographer slipped off a flagpole at a horse show in Lahore the prince muttered that he hoped "to God he breaks his bloody neck".

Queen Mother pays visit to the pope

The royal party leaving the Vatican.

Rome, April 1959
The Queen Mother and Princess Margaret, on an official tour here, have been received by Pope John. A royal audience with the head of the Catholic Church has caused some controversy at home, and a statement has been issued stressing that such a "courtesy ... does not imply or reflect any views as to [their] political or religious opinions". The Queen Mother has also unveiled memorials here to Scottish soldiers and a statue of the English poet Lord Byron. She reacted graciously when confronted by a demonstrator shouting for "bread and work".

Princess Anne joins the Royal Brownies

The princess in her Brownie uniform.

Pregnant Queen Elizabeth tours Canada

Toronto, 27 July 1959
The Queen's gruelling 45-day tour of Canada has ended with a melo-dramatic flourish as police today arrested six men sneaking across a field to spy on the royal couple, who are resting at Batterwood Farm, the home of the governor-general, Vincent Massey, at Port Hope near Toronto. The tour – which included a brief flying visit to the United States – has been particularly demanding for the Queen because, unknown to the public, she is pregnant. An announcement that Elizabeth is expecting her third child is planned to be made after she returns home next week.

The royal tour has been marked by a national reluctance to splurge on lavish personal gifts. Instead, the federal government created a million-dollar Queen Elizabeth II Fund for Research in Children's Diseases. Ontario offered a $500,000 scholarship in her name. Other provinces established similar funds. One of the highlights of the cross-Canada tour was the dedication by the Queen of the newly-opened St Lawrence Seaway. The royal yacht *Britannia* entered the seaway to the roar of a 21-gun salute and rocket fire. The US president, Dwight D Eisenhower, and the Canadian prime minister, John Diefenbaker, were also present.

Elizabeth and Prince Philip presided at many ceremonies. On the Plains of Abraham, the Queen presented new colours to the Royal 22nd Regiment, the Van Doos. On Dominion Day she spoke of "the strength which comes from unity". Renamed "Respected by All, Mother of all People", she became an Indian princess of the Salish nation in Nanaimo. The royal couple also attended a performance of Shakespeare's *As You Like It* at the theatre in Stratford, Ontario.

The Queen and Prince Philip were greeted by enthusiastic crowds throughout their tour of Canada, even though a new national anthem, *O Canada*, replaced *God Save the Queen* at the governor-general's inauguration.

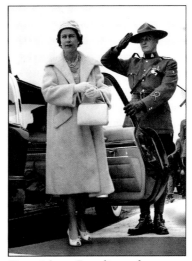

Eyes right: a Canadian welcome.

Alexandra joins in Australian party

Brisbane, 19 August 1959
"If history had been kinder I would have spent my childhood here in Australia," Princess Alexandra told the crowd as she opened the Brisbane Centenary Show today. The princess, in Australia for the Queensland centenary celebrations, was referring to the wartime death of her father, the Duke of Kent, who was to have become the country's governor-general. Princess Alexandra's six-week tour will also take her through towns and cities in New South Wales and Victoria. Her beauty and her easy manner have already won the admiration of the crowds that have flocked to see her (→ 24/4/63).

London, July 1959
Princess Anne has become a member of a strict new royal organisation – the Buckingham Palace Brownie Pack. The princess, who is almost nine, has had a sheltered schooling so far under the stern eye of her governess, Miss Catherine Peebles. Now her social life will be transformed by the formation of the "B'hams". Margaret, the princess's aunt, takes a sympathetic interest in Anne, perhaps because she remembers what it is like playing second fiddle to the heir to the throne. She has been instrumental in setting up the pack, in which Anne will mix with girls from Holy Trinity church in Knightsbridge and the daughters of members of the royal household staff (→ 7/1961).

Hartnell becomes synonymous with royal fashions

Hartnell at work on his designs.

London, 31 December 1959
As the 1950s end, 58-year-old Norman Hartnell – whose name is now synonymous with royal dressmaking – can look back on more than two decades as the top court couturier. When King George VI and Queen Elizabeth were crowned in 1937, he was called upon to glamorise the new queen's wardrobe. He argued that light colours helped royalty stand out from the crowd, and he advised the queen on the correct image to present to her people during the war. The younger generation of royals has also fallen under the Hartnell spell; among numerous triumphs, he designed the present Queen's wedding and coronation dresses.

Classic lines: the wedding dress.

Elizabeth II
1952–

Hampshire, 13 January 1960. Princess Anne, aged nine, is bridesmaid at the wedding of her cousin, Lady Pamela Mountbatten, to David Hicks at Romsey abbey.

London, 26 February 1960. The engagement of Princess Margaret to Antony Armstrong-Jones, the society photographer and son of Ronald Armstrong-Jones QC and the Countess of Rosse, is announced (→ 6/5).

London, 22 March 1960. The bombed chapel at Buckingham Palace is to be rebuilt as an art gallery (→ 25/7/62).

Westminster, 6 May 1960. Princess Margaret marries Antony Armstrong-Jones.→

Southern Rhodesia, 17 May 1960. The Queen Mother inaugurates the Kariba dam (→ 12/6/62).

Britain, 21 October 1960. The Queen launches Britain's first nuclear submarine.

India, 23 January 1961. The Queen and Prince Philip go tiger-hunting.

London, 23 January 1961. The palace announces that 12-year-old Prince Charles, a pupil at Cheam preparatory school, will attend Gordonstoun public school next term (→ 11/5/62).

Glasgow, 30 June 1961. The Queen visits the Gorbals, a slum area of Glasgow.

London, July 1961. Anne joins the newly-formed palace girl guides, enrolling in the "Kingfisher" patrol (→ 6/1962).

London, 3 October 1961. The Queen creates Antony Armstrong-Jones Earl of Snowdon (→ 3/11).

London, 3 November 1961. Princess Margaret gives birth to a

son, David Albert Charles, Viscount Linley (→ 1/5/64).

Britain, 1961. Prince Philip becomes president of the World Wildlife Fund.

London, 26 June 1962. Katharine Worsley, the Duchess of Kent, gives birth to a son, George Philip Nicholas (→ 28/4/64).

Sussex, June 1962. Anne goes camping with the girl guides.

London, 11 February 1963. The Queen cancels Princess Margaret's state visit to France as a snub to General de Gaulle after his veto of Britain's entry into the European Economic Community.

Westminster, 17 June 1963. Harold Macmillan, the prime minister, faces criticism over John Profumo, the secretary of state for war, and Profumo's alleged romance with Christine Keeler, a former showgirl linked with the Soviet naval attaché, Eugène Ivanov (→ 7/1963).

London, July 1963. The Queen writes to John Profumo, thanking him for his work as minister for war, after his recent resignation from the government (→ 17/11/71).

Washington, 25 November 1963. Prince Philip represents the Queen at the funeral of John Kennedy, the murdered US president.

London, 3 February 1964. The Queen Mother's Australian tour is postponed due to her operation for appendicitis (→ 4/1966).

London, 29 February 1964. Princess Alexandra gives birth to her first child, a son, James Robert Bruce (→ 31/7/66).

London, 28 April 1964. The Duchess of Kent gives birth to her second child, Helen Marina Lucy Windsor (→ 25/5/70).

London, 1 May 1964. Princess Margaret gives birth to her second child, a daughter, Lady Sarah Frances Elizabeth.

United States, 23 June 1964. The Duke of Windsor, recovering from heart surgery, receives a 70th birthday telegram from his niece, Queen Elizabeth (→ 3/1965).

Westminster, 25 January 1965. The Queen mourns the death of Winston Churchill, the former prime minister.

London, 12 March 1965. The Duke of Windsor is recovering from a third eye operation.

London, mid-March 1965. The Queen visits the Duke of Windsor and meets the duchess for the first time since the abdication (→ 7/6/67).

Leeds, 28 March 1965. Mary, the Princess Royal, the Countess of Harewood and Queen Elizabeth's aunt, dies aged 67.→

London, June 1965. The pop group The Beatles receive an MBE from the Queen.

London, 20 December 1965. Charles wins the Duke of Edinburgh's silver award (→ 23/12).

Australasia, May 1966. Charles visits Papau New Guinea and tours Australia during his school holidays (→ 1/1967).

London, 31 July 1966. Princess Alexandra gives birth to her second child, a daughter, Marina Victoria Alexandra (→ 15/12/89).

Scotland, January 1967. Prince Charles is made head boy at Gordonstoun (→ 8/10).

Cambridge, 8 October 1967. Prince Charles begins his studies at Trinity college, reading archaeology and anthropology (→ 17/6/68).

Westminster, 31 October 1967. Anne attends her first state occasion, the opening of parliament.

London, 17 April 1968. Anne passes her driving test at the first attempt.

London, 17 June 1968. The Queen invests Charles as a knight of the Garter (→ 11/6/69).

London, 25 July 1968. Anne attends her first royal garden party at Buckingham Palace.

France, August 1968. The Queen agrees to continue the Duke of Windsor's annual payment, after his death, to the duchess; the amount will drop from £10,000 to £5,000 (→ 8/1970).

Britain, 25 December 1968. The Queen calls for racial tolerance in her Christmas broadcast.

London, autumn 1968. Princess Anne meets Lieutenant Mark Phillips when she accompanies the Queen Mother to a celebration for the Olympic equestrian team's gold medal (→ 4/1969).

Britain, 14 January 1969. Prince Charles makes his first solo flight in an aeroplane (→ 10/10/70).

Cardiff, 11 June 1969. Prince Charles, the colonel-in-chief of the Royal Regiment of Wales, takes part in a ceremony in which he receives the freedom of the Welsh capital (→ 30/6).

Chester, 30 June 1969. A hoax bomb, found under a railway bridge, delays the Queen on her journey to Caernarfon for the investiture of Charles as Prince of Wales (→ 1/7).

Caernarfon, 1 July 1969. Charles is invested, in a splendid ceremony here, as Prince of Wales.→

Elizabeth gives birth to a son, Andrew

London, 19 February 1960

The nation is rejoicing tonight at the birth of a second son to Queen Elizabeth and Prince Philip. The baby boy is almost ten years younger than his sister Anne and over 11 years younger than Charles. The parents are planning to christen him Andrew, after Philip's father.

The new arrival caused great excitement in the family. It was already a big day for Prince Charles, for he was unexpectedly called on to star as the ambitious Shakespearean Duke of Gloucester in a play at his school, Cheam. He was understudy for the role in a compilation of Shakespeare plays called *The Last Baron*, and stepped into the breach when the first-choice actor fell ill. But for all his stage nerves, the prince was clearly delighted when he was told about Andrew's birth.

His sister Anne was so excited this morning that her strict governess, Miss Peebles, gave her a day off her lessons. She has missed Charles since he left for Cheam, and although two girls, Caroline Hamilton and Susan Babington-Smith, have been brought in to join her at her lessons, she seems to have grown a little lonely. She is thrilled to have a younger brother.

Antony Armstrong-Jones, the photographer commissioned to portray the older royal children last year, is on hand to take photographs of the new prince (→ 26/2).

Princess Margaret weds

The princess leaves the palace.

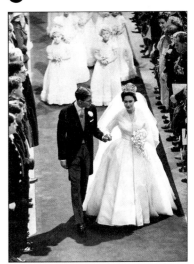

The happy couple in the abbey.

London, 6 May 1960

Princess Margaret was married to the society photographer Antony Armstrong-Jones in a breathtaking ceremony in Westminster abbey today. Television viewers around the world joined more than 2,000 guests to watch as the couple were married by the archbishop of Canterbury.

It was a fairy-tale wedding. Margaret rode to the abbey in a glass carriage through a perfect morning of May sunshine. A packed crowd cheered as the bride passed down the Mall beneath a 60-foot (18m) arch of pink and white roses and crimson banners bearing the initials "M" and "A". For the ceremony she wore an exquisite silk dress designed by Norman Hartnell; her niece Princess Anne was one of her eight bridesmaids. Afterwards, crowds lined the route to Buckingham Palace and then on to the Tower where the couple boarded the royal yacht *Britannia*, especially refitted for their honeymoon in the Caribbean.

Margaret's glorious wedding is all the more welcome because of her tragic involvement with the former royal equerry Group-Captain Peter Townsend. It is four and a half years since she announced her decision not to marry Townsend, because he was divorced. Last year he remarried.

Her new choice of husband, however, caused concern in some quarters. Besides being a commoner, Antony is from a rather "fast" London set. There was a scandal when his best man was found to have been convicted as a homosexual, and he was replaced. But the bridegroom is very popular with Margaret's close family and is said to share a sense of humour with the Queen (→ 3/10/61).

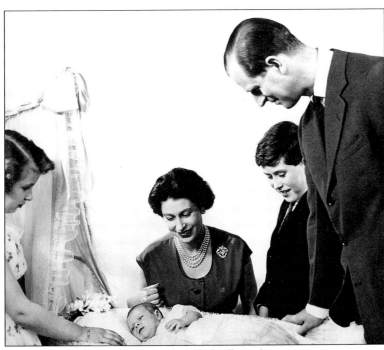

Centre of attention: the royal family look fondly at the new prince.

Queen gives the royal family a new name

London, 8 February 1960

Queen Elizabeth has changed the royal family's surname. Today she declared her "will and pleasure" that in future her descendants will be called Mountbatten-Windsor. She and her own children will continue to be the House of Windsor. The change is intended to be used by those members of the family who are not entitled to be known as His or Her Royal Highness and therefore have greater need of a surname. A statement from the palace said: "The Queen has always wanted, without changing the name of the royal house established by her grandfather, to associate the name of her husband with her own and his descendants." Yet Mountbatten is not the name of either Philip's father or mother: it is the name first taken by the Battenbergs of his mother's family in 1917 and chosen by the Greek prince when he was naturalised as a British subject prior to his engagement to the young Princess Elizabeth in 1947.

South African voters reject the Queen

Cape Town, 6 October 1960

White South Africans decided yesterday by a huge majority of more than 74,000 to abolish the monarchy in their country. But black South Africans were denied a vote.

The country's future has been widely debated this year. At the Commonwealth prime ministers' conference, hosted by Queen Elizabeth at Windsor in May, there was considerable tension over the continuing South African *apartheid* system of racial segregation. The referendum itself was first announced by Dr Verwoerd, the South African prime minister, on 20 January. Britain's Harold Macmillan visited the following month and spoke of a "wind of change" blowing through Africa. He asked for "a breathing space" before the poll, but the South African government was keen to press on. The outcome will greatly sadden the Queen, who is particularly fond of the country where she celebrated her 21st birthday.

Yorkshire cheers a rare royal wedding

York, 8 June 1961

Three queens today attended the first royal wedding to take place in York for more than 600 years. The Duke of Kent, a cousin of the queen, was marrying Katharine Worsley, a member of a leading local family whose Yorkshire pride could be seen in the white roses which bedecked the minster.

There were 2,000 guests in the minster, including the Queen, the Queen Mother and Queen Victoria Eugénie of Spain. The 28-year-old bride, wearing a veiled diadem over her blonde hair, promised to "obey" her husband, even though the word did not appear in the printed service. The couple requested it, said the dean of York later. Miss Worsley wore a dress of silk gauze containing some 273 yards (242.8m) of silk. The couple left the minster under an archway of swords formed by the Scots Greys, the duke's regiment (→ 26/6/62).

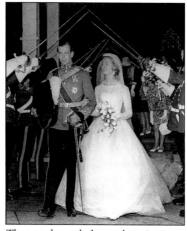

The royal couple leave the minster.

Queen defies bomb risks in Ghana

Accra, 10 November 1961

The Queen has braved the risk of bomb attacks and defied the doubts of ministers by visiting Ghana, the first of Britain's former black colonies in Africa to win independence. She arrived yesterday to a tumultuous welcome, driving from the airport in an open car along a road lit only by torches after an electrical failure had hit Ghana's capital.

The Queen, accompanied by the Duke of Edinburgh, had arrived at night after being delayed by five hours because of fog in London. But a bomb blast five days earlier had made it doubtful that the visit would take place at all. The bomb damaged a statue of Ghana's president, Kwame Nkrumah, and as opposition politicians were rounded up fears were expressed in London that the country might be on the brink of revolution.

But the Queen was determined to visit Ghana; only a formal veto from the cabinet would stop her. The prime minister, Harold Macmillan, feared that cancellation would push Ghana out of the Commonwealth and into the arms of the Soviet Union. The Queen agreed. "If I were to cancel now," she said, "Nkrumah might invite Khrushchev, and they wouldn't like that, would they?"

Yesterday's ecstatic welcome has so far vindicated that decision – and the Queen's own courage. At a banquet President Nkrumah said tonight that whatever changes might be wrought in Africa by the "wind of change", the personal regard of Ghanaians for herself and the duke would be unaffected.

Ghana's president Kwame Nkrumah asks Queen Elizabeth for a dance.

Greetings: Queen Elizabeth meets an African chief at Kumasi in Ghana.

Prince Philip's stern views on British industry cause a furore

London, October 1961

Prince Philip has found himself making headlines again this month, after an outspoken speech to leading British industrialists at a London meeting of the Industrial Co-Partnership Association. It was not his views of British industry's need to change with the times that caused the consternation, nor even the propriety of the queen's husband speaking publicly about industrial problems. What elevated the speech onto the front pages was the prince's choice of language. "I think it is about time," he said, "that we pulled our fingers out."

The popular press has since had a field day with the outspoken Duke of Edinburgh and his "get your finger out" message which the newspapers asserted was addressed to bosses and workers alike. Some politicians have said that the duke should not get involved in matters best left to parliament; others have welcomed the royal intervention in the national debate about the need for Britain to adapt more speedily to industrial and economic change.

Like Victoria's Prince Consort a century before him, Prince Philip has long paid attention to industrial matters, being particularly keen to encourage scientific and technical developments but, again like Prince Albert, emphasising the social responsibilities of industrialists, as in the conference he sponsored on this theme in 1956. Unlike Prince Albert, however, he tends to express his views bluntly (→ 1962).

Queen Mother's wheelchair launch

Newcastle upon Tyne, 1961

The Queen Mother delighted the crowds by arriving in a wheelchair to launch the liner *Northern Star*, despite breaking a bone in her foot in a fall at an Ascot houseparty at Royal Lodge in Windsor. She had refused to cancel her appointments, and shipworkers cheered as she arrived on a specially-lowered platform at the Vickers-Armstrong works on Tyneside.

Cold showers await Charles at new school

New boy: Prince Charles is greeted on his first day at Gordonstoun.

Elgin, 11 May 1962

Prince Charles arrived at his new school today to face a tough, even spartan, regime that puts as much emphasis on physical education as academic attainment. The Queen had favoured Eton for Charles, but Prince Philip strongly urged his own school – Gordonstoun, a few miles from Elgin in Scotland and many more miles from the prying enquiries of Fleet Street.

The prince will be living in a block called Windmill Lodge, along with 59 of the school's 400 pupils. He will be woken each day at 7am for the first of the day's two cold showers and a morning run. The school (motto: "There is more in you") aims to develop public service by involving pupils in work as coastguards, in fire-fighting or in mountain rescues. Cross-country trips are designed to stretch boys to their limits. Whether or not this life will suit the shy prince as much as it did his more extrovert father in the 1930s is uncertain (→ 18/6/63).

Efficiency experts tackle the palace

London, 1962

Alongside the Groom of the Robes, the Clerk of the Closet, the Gold Sticks, the Bargemaster, the Ladies of the Bedchamber (and not forgetting the Extra Ladies of the Bedchamber and the mere Women of the Bedchamber), a new species has been seen in Buckingham Palace this year. It is the Business Efficiency Expert – called in by Prince Philip, the Duke of Edinburgh, to run a slide-rule over the ways in which the royal household is organised.

The duke has spent the ten years since the Queen's accession trying to modernise what he saw as an old-fashioned organisation still steeped in traditions which went back to the reign of Victoria. He has tried to make the palace more efficient, whether by using modern office and domestic household equipment or by simply installing more internal telephones (to cut down on servants taking messages by hand). Traditional customs have also been subjected to scrutiny, often upsetting senior staff.

Now, as if to practise what he has preached to British industry – "pull your finger out" was his controversial advice last year – he has recruited outside experts to offer advice on how the palace should be organised and managed (→ 9/11/69).

Queen Mother gets bingo-style cheers

Ottawa, 12 June 1962

Wherever she goes on her ten-day Canadian tour, the Queen Mother is as unassuming as she is regal. Her evening at the home of the prime minister, John Diefenbaker, was typical. She was greeted by Happy, the prime minister's golden labrador, and then enjoyed a very simple Canadian dinner.

At McGill university in Montreal, as she presented new colours to the Black Watch (Royal Highland) Regiment before a crowd of 18,000, the Queen Mother, the regiment's colonel-in-chief, casually handed her white handbag to a brigadier to carry. Later, Elizabeth recalled the Black Watch's role in the conquest of Quebec. "The virtues of courage, hardihood and honour crossed the sea from Scotland and made new history in helping to build this great country," she said. But at City Hall she spoke in graceful French as the mayor welcomed her to his largely francophone city. In Ottawa, the mayor, Charlotte Whitton, raved that Ottawans had greeted their royal visitor with an enthusiasm normally reserved for "football and hockey, or the excitement of our monster bingos".

The Queen Mother travelled to Canada on a scheduled commercial airline – which was another royal first (→ 3/2/64).

Royal collection is opened to public

London, 25 July 1962

Long queues today marked the opening of the Queen's Gallery at Buckingham Palace. It is the first time that any part of the palace has been open to the general public, although members of the public paying their two shillings and sixpence (12.5p) were greeted by a notice saying that "no other part of the inside of the palace will be seen". The gallery has been created out of the ruins of the private chapel which had been damaged in the bomb raids on the palace in 1940. The first exhibition is called "Treasures of the Royal Collection", and another is planned for next year on "Royal Children".

Prince stays cool to open the games

Perth, 22 November 1962

Prince Philip looked comfortable in his summer naval uniform, but the official opening of the Commonwealth Games today was marked by the pile-up of heat casualties in the scorching weather. The temperature in the centre of the arena was 105F (40C) as the prince declared the games open.

The prince arrived in the Australian capital of Canberra two days ago. He took the opportunity, when opening the Australian Academy of Science, to make a plea for the detailed recording of Australia's rich heritage of plants and animals, as a step towards saving them from extinction.

The Queen Mother shakes hands with Maurice Chevalier, the French singer, after the 1961 Royal Variety Show. Next in line is the British singer Shirley Bassey, and behind her the American comedian Jack Benny.

Menzies goes over the top for Queen

Canberra, 12 March 1963

Nothing can stir the newly-created knight of the Thistle, Sir Robert Menzies, to greater heights of florid oratory than a royal visit. The Australian prime minister was in full flight when the Queen arrived in Canberra last month for the capital's jubilee, but somehow his words brought a strained silence from his audience and a glow of embarrassment from the Queen.

In his Anglophile fervour the great man had overgushed. He told the Queen: "I ask you to remember that in this country every man, woman and child who even sees you as a passing glimpse will re-

The Queen and Robert Menzies.

member it with joy. In the words of the 17th-century poet: "I did but see her passing by. But yet I love her till I die"."

The moment – as the Queen announced that she had conferred the Most Noble Order of the Thistle on the prime minister – was duly noted by journalists who are running a private book on the greatest "grovel" of the current tour of Australia and New Zealand.

The jubilee celebrations today were marked by a gathering of 8,000 people on the Parliament House lawns. The Queen described Canberra, once known as the "bush capital", as a flourishing city growing daily in national and international stature. She visited the Australian War Memorial and watched a spectacular display of fireworks tonight on Capital Hill.

Princess Alexandra weds a city banker

An unforgettable moment: the bride and bridegroom after the ceremony.

Westminster, 24 April 1963

Princess Alexandra, a 26-year-old cousin of the Queen, was married in Westminster abbey today in a ceremony attended by 2,000 people and watched by an estimated 200 million on television. The bridegroom was Angus Ogilvy, the second son of the Earl of Airlie.

"We want to thank everyone for being so kind," said the princess as she held hands with her husband before boarding a plane of the Queen's Flight last night to fly to Scotland for their honeymoon. Princess Anne was the chief brides-

maid, as she had been for the wedding of Princess Margaret. With the help of four other bridesmaids and two pages she helped to steer Alexandra's long train as the bride made her way to the chapel of St Edward behind the altar, where the Queen and members of the two families were waiting.

The streets of London were lined by cheering crowds as Alexandra and her husband, a 34-year-old businessman, made their way to a reception at St James's palace in a glass coach, escorted by troopers of the Household Cavalry (→ 29/2/64).

Public protests at royal's Nazi links

London, 11 July 1963

Angry crowds gathered outside Buckingham Palace tonight to protest at the visit of King Paul and Queen Frederika of the Hellenes. Prince Philip is related to them both, but it is his cousin, the Greek queen, who attracts most of the anger; a former member of the Hitler Youth movement, she is also condemned by the demonstrators for supporting the arrest of left-wingers in Greece. Despite heavy security, shouts of "*Sieg heil*" and boos greeted the royal party when they visited a theatre last night, startling Queen Elizabeth. Ninety-four people were arrested tonight.

A controversial visitor: Frederika.

Under-age Prince Charles orders cherry brandy in a Scottish bar

Prince Charles: growing up fast.

Scotland, 18 June 1963

Buckingham Palace last night admitted that Prince Charles had bought a cherry brandy in a hotel bar in the Outer Hebrides. At 14, the prince is below the legal age for buying a drink in a bar and now faces disciplinary action by his school's headmaster, Robert Chew.

Charles and four other pupils from Gordonstoun – a school which emphasises outdoor pursuits – were on an expedition in the school yacht *Pinta*. When they arrived at Stornoway, on the Isle of Lewis, the boys waited in the appropriately-named Crown Hotel while their accompanying master (and the prince's detective) made arrangements for the evening. To

avoid the stares of locals through the hotel windows, Charles went into the bar – and ordered a cherry brandy. Whether or not he knew the Scottish licensing laws is unclear; but he certainly did not know that a young free-lance journalist was also in the bar.

As the story broke (even challenging the current Profumo affair for headlines) the palace made matters worse by changing its version of events in Stornoway, at first denying it, but then admitting that it was true. The luckless detective seems set to lose his job, and the errant prince to lose a recent school promotion which gave him greater freedom of choice in outdoor (if not indoor) activities (→ 20/12/65).

Queen embroiled in Tory succession crisis

London, 18 October 1963
The Earl of Home was today named as Britain's new prime minister after the Queen found herself embroiled in a Conservative Party leadership crisis for the second time in her reign. At least two ministers, Iain Macleod and Enoch Powell, are saying that they will refuse to serve under Home in protest against what they see as a "magic circle" within the Tory Party.

Harold Macmillan plunged his party into disarray last week by saying that illness would force him to quit as prime minister. This morning the Queen visited the ailing "Supermac" in hospital. He gave her a lengthy memorandum, claiming that Home was the candidate most likely to command support. The front-runners at a turbulent Tory conference in Blackpool last week had been "Rab" Butler, Lord

The Queen leaves the PM's hospital.

Hailsham and Reginald Maudling. Lord Home is the outsider with the fewest enemies. The Queen took Macmillan's advice, leaving Home to form a government and renounce his peerage to fight for a seat in the House of Commons (→ 4/3/74).

Quebec is a city under siege as police protect Queen from French separatists

Quebec City, 10 October 1964
Fears that French-Canadian separatist demonstrators might endanger Queen Elizabeth on the Quebec leg of her Canadian tour have led officials to introduce unprecedented security arrangements. Quebec has been rocked lately by bomb attacks by separatists seeking independence from the English-speaking majority in Canada. The separatist leader Pierre Bourgault insists that demonstrations would be against the federal capital, not against the Queen as a person, but the authorities were taking no chances. The police presence was so heavy when the Queen arrived today that crowds were small as the royal couple drove through the silent streets which were ringed by police (→ 2/7/67).

Separatists protest at the royal visit.

Anne packs her bags for boarding school

Anne: meeting her new teachers.

Kent, 20 September 1963
At the age of 13 Princess Anne today began her first day at school when she was among the new girls enrolling at Benenden, in Kent. Until now she has been educated privately in Buckingham Palace. Anne's first-day nerves – she had been sick on the journey – were probably not helped by the sight of the entire school of 300 pupils and 40 staff lined up to greet her, despite protestations that she would be treated normally. The princess will share a dormitory with three other girls. The Queen has asked the headmistress, Elizabeth Clarke, to treat Anne like any other girl. The detective in the grounds will be the only difference (→ 31/10/67).

Elizabeth heads a vintage year for births

London, 1964
This has been a vintage year for royal births, headed in the spring by the queen's fourth child. Edward Antony Richard Louis was born on 10 March when the queen was almost 38. The pregnancy and labour went well, although she was subsequently reported to be tired and took a break from her engagements.

Princess Margaret and Lord Snowdon had their second child, Lady Sarah Armstrong-Jones, on 1 May. The sound of a new baby crying has also been heard this year in the nurseries of the Duke and Duchess of Kent, who had their second child, Lady Helen Windsor, and of Princess Alexandra and Angus Ogilvy – their first child, James. There was another royal birth, but not one that has been celebrated publicly. The Earl of Harewood, the Queen's cousin, had a son, Mark, by Patricia Tuckwell, an Australian musician.

Queen's telegram cheers the ailing duke

Paris, 23 June 1964
The Duke of Windsor was cheered today to receive a telegram from the Queen to celebrate his 70th birthday. He saw this as further evidence of his niece's desire to heal the bitterness within the royal family caused by his abdication. The Queen Mother is less enthusiastic, but the Queen has none the less encouraged younger members of the royal family, such as the Duke and Duchess of Kent and Princess Alexandra, to visit the Duke and Duchess of Windsor when they are in Paris where the Windsors now live.

Such signs of a thaw in the chilly attitude of the royal family towards him and Wallis have gone some way to offset the duke's concern at his own poor health. He underwent open-heart surgery in the United States this year and is also experiencing eye trouble (→ 3/1965).

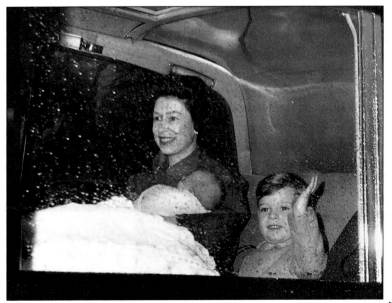
Andrew waves as the Queen takes baby Prince Edward to Windsor.

Princess Royal, the sister of George V, dies at age of 67

Leeds, 28 March 1965

The Princess Royal died today after collapsing while walking in the grounds of her home, Harewood House, near Leeds. She was 67. Mary, the Countess of Harewood, was the only daughter of King George V and Queen Mary. She worked as a nurse during the First World War and remained close to her mother for the rest of her life. The title of Princess Royal, which is reserved for the eldest daughter of monarchs, was conferred on her in 1932, ten years after her marriage to Viscount Lascelles, who became the sixth Earl of Harewood. Their sons were childhood companions of the Queen. Her husband died in 1947, and the title passed to their elder son, George (→ 12/6/87).

Mary, the late Princess Royal.

Controversy over Margaret's US trip

London, 20 November 1965

Princess Margaret returned to Britain this week from a tour of the United States bedevilled by charges of extravagance and by her own ill-health. Exhaustion caused her to cancel several appointments during a tour which included both New York and Los Angeles, where she danced with Fred Astaire while Lord Snowdon partnered Shirley Maclaine at a glittering Hollywood party. Three planes were used on the trip, prompting questions to be asked in the House of Commons.

Queen makes historic German tour

West Berlin, 27 May 1965

The Queen came face to face today with the most potent symbol of a divided Europe: the Berlin Wall erected by East German authorities to stop their people fleeing to the West. It was the most dramatic moment of the Queen's historic 11-day and ten-city tour of West Germany, the first German tour by a British monarch for 52 years.

Since that last visit, two world wars have pitched Germany against Britain, and diplomats from both country were nervous about how the visit would go. In addition to the standard advice given to foreigners who might meet the Queen on how to curtsey, German crowds were told not to shout "*Sieg Heil!*" but to call out her name. Anything with remotely Nazi connotations was omitted from the itinerary.

Both Elizabeth and Philip have strong family connections with Germany. In Hanover, the Queen was showed a letter from leading Englishmen to George, the Elector of Hanover: "Queen Anne's dying.

Surveying a divided city: Elizabeth and Philip are driven through West Berlin.

Come quick, certain persons want a Jacobite heir and not you." The present-day successor to George I is estimated to have some 400 German relatives. She met some privately, but the real triumph was more public. Vast crowds gathered to cheer her in every city, including today as she toured West Berlin, accompanied by the city's mayor, Willy Brandt, and the West German chancellor, Ludwig Erhard.

Ethiopia plays host to Queen Elizabeth for the first time

Addis Ababa, 1 February 1965

The Queen and Prince Philip today began their first-ever state visit to Ethiopia. Crowds estimated at more than 200,000 cheered and chanted on the four-mile (6.4km) drive from the airport to the palace of Emperor Haile Selassie. On several occasions the enthusiasm was so great that people spilt over the barriers to halt the glass and gold coach carrying the two monarchs. Girls in white muslin dresses showered the coach with white petals in the greatest welcome which Ethiopians had ever extended to a visiting head of state. The royal couple, who will spend eight days in the country, were the guests of honour tonight at a state banquet. The Ethiopian emperor recalled his own days in exile in Britain after Italian forces had defeated his country in the war of 1935-36. "We were received with a warmth which nourished and strengthened our will," he said.

Philip's Rhodesia speech starts public row

London, July 1965

Prince Philip has landed himself in trouble this month by his forthright comments on the Rhodesian crisis. Speaking to students at Edinburgh university about Commonwealth relations, he discarded his prepared text in which he had said that he would not comment on Rhodesia, currently the focus of conflict because of the independence plans of its minority white population.

"I recognise the impressions of many Africans about Rhodesia," said Philip. "But I think it is better to spin out the solution of these difficulties with patience, and with a bit of luck get a better result than risk a bloodbath by forcing a pace."

Labour MPs tabled a motion saying that constitutional monarchy required that "royalty should not give expression to contentious political opinions". A Kenyan minister joined the criticism, as did newspapers at home. Cecil King, the proprietor of the *Daily Mirror*, told Harold Wilson, the British prime minister, that the paper's attack was to "fire a shot across the bows" of the prince to deter him from voicing in public controversial views expressed in private about the reunification of Germany.

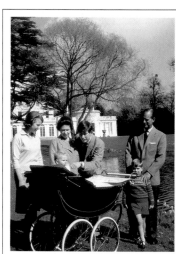

A happy family around the pram of the young Prince Edward.

Palace summit plans career of prince

College and service life await Charles

London, 23 December 1965

A highly select dinner party was assembled at the palace last night to discuss the future of the heir to the throne. The guests of the Queen and Prince Philip included the prime minister, the archbishop of Canterbury, the chairman of the university vice-chancellors, and the recently retired chief of the defence staff. The only significant absentee was the subject of the discussion.

Prince Charles has indicated his desire to go to university and so, over soft drinks and beer after the dinner (with a brandy for Harold Wilson, the prime minister), the merits of various establishments were canvassed. Wilson suggested a "redbrick" university, but he was keen to hear from Earl Mountbatten, Charles's great-uncle, who retired as defence chief earlier this year. Mountbatten had no doubts.

"Trinity college, like his grandfather," he said. "Dartmouth, like his father and grandfather, and then to sea, with a command of his own." The discussion went on into the early hours, but the Mountbatten prescription was broadly accepted. Unlike his grandfather, however, Charles will live in Trinity college, Cambridge, as a normal undergraduate and will also take his degree (→ 2/2/66).

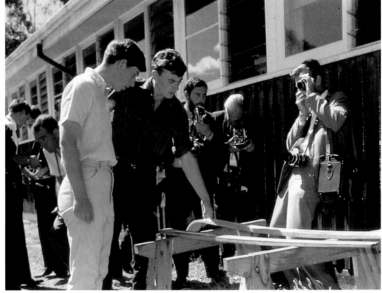
Learning a thing or two down under: Prince Charles at Timbertop school.

Prince joins an Australian bush school

Victoria, 2 February 1966

Prince Charles went to sleep last night with the smell of gum trees in his nostrils at his new school at Timbertop, in the bush country 200 miles (320km) north of Melbourne. The prince arrived in Australia only two days ago and just had time to catch up on his sleep, dine with the governor-general, Lord Casey, and tour Canberra before being whisked to Timbertop.

The 17-year-old prince first met fellow student Stuart McGregor, who has been chosen to be his companion for his first month at the school, which is an outpost of Geelong Grammar School. The time at Timbertop was planned before last December's summit on Charles's future as a way to broaden his education and introduce him to Australia. The prince will live in a hut as prefect-supervisor of 14 younger boys. His quarters are austere, with a bathroom, shower and small kitchen. Tomorrow he will rise for roll call at 7.25am. Long hikes and camping in the bush are part of the curriculum (→ 5/1966).

Royal car is hit by a block of concrete

Belfast, 4 July 1966

The Queen and Prince Philip today escaped injury when a block of concrete was dropped from an office block onto the royal car on the first day of their two-day visit to Northern Ireland. The incident occurred in Belfast city centre two minutes after a beer bottle had been thrown at the procession. The car did not halt, but its bonnet was dented. "It's a strong car," said the Queen later. Two people were arrested, and Harold Wilson, the prime minister, faces questions in parliament about the safety of the Queen in the province. The incident has cast a shadow over what had begun as a highly successful visit, with enthusiastic, flag-waving crowds lining the streets.

Royal homes on TV

Windsor, 25 December 1966

Six royal palaces were featured in a television documentary shown tonight which had been filmed by a joint BBC/ITV team. It was the first time that television cameras had been allowed into the private apartments of the royal palaces, and it reflects a new attitude within the royal family to the media in general and to television in particular. Sir Kenneth Clark, a former keeper of the royal art collection, was the guide in the hour-long inside view of the palaces (→ 1/7/69).

Queen Mother hooks New Zealand trip

The Queen Mother receives a gift.

New Zealand, April 1966

Thirty-nine years after her first visit to these islands, the Queen Mother showed her enduring affection for New Zealand by returning this month for a trip which was as much holiday as official visit. She had begun this latest tour in Australia last month (where she visited Prince Charles) and had spent Easter in Fiji. Arriving in New Zealand she spent as much time as possible pursuing her life-long passion for fishing. But two days in her waders on North Island produced only one small trout. "It would have been better to get one out of the deep freeze," she said.

The Queen and Prince Philip with a young survivor of the tragedy at Aberfan in Wales: a coal tip "avalanche" killed more than 130 people.

Duchess of Windsor meets two queens

The Windsors look on as Elizabeth unveils a plaque to the late Queen Mary.

London, 7 June 1967
The Queen and the Queen Mother today met the Duke and Duchess of Windsor in public for the first time since the abdication crisis of 1936. Elizabeth had invited the duke to attend the unveiling of a memorial plaque at Marlborough House to the memory of his mother and her grandmother, Queen Mary.

It was a tense occasion. The Queen Mother, in particular, has remained bitter about the duchess; it was the duke's love for Wallis Simpson that catapulted the Queen

Mother into Buckingham Palace with King George VI. The duchess did not curtsey, but bowed to the Queen and accepted the Queen Mother's hand; the Queen and the duke exchanged a formal kiss.

The duke was delighted by the decision of his niece, the Queen, to invite the duchess to accompany him to London. He remains bitter about the refusal to give his wife the title of "Her Royal Highness", but welcomes today's ceremony as a significant step towards ending the worst of the family feud (→8/1968).

Queen celebrates Canada's century

Ottawa, 2 July 1967
It was long past midnight before Queen Elizabeth and Prince Philip got to bed last night, after an exhilarating, exhausting day celebrating Canada's centennial here in the nation's capital.

The royals opened the festivities at a Parliament Hill children's party. Elizabeth sliced through iced fruitcake, Philip laughed delightedly as 1,000 coloured ballons rose into the air, and 35,000 people, mostly children, snatched up 40,000 cupcakes, ice-cream and drinks. Next came the "Royal Hullabaloo" at Lansdowne Park: 20,000 cheered, and 400 teenagers demonstrated their physical fitness with sit-ups and other exercises.

The Queen also made a national broadcast that reflected her concern at French-Canadian alienation. "Since Champlain founded his habitation at Quebec ... this air has been sweetened with the French tongue and the French culture and sharpened with French intelligence and French resources," she said.

Late at night, the royals watched spectacular centennial fireworks until a carillon pealed *O Canada* and *God Save the Queen*. Then they headed back to Government House to rest for tomorrow's visit to Montreal's Expo 67.

Harewood, Queen's cousin, divorces

Yorkshire, July 1967
With the Queen's consent, her first cousin, the Earl of Harewood – currently 18th in line to the throne – has divorced his wife of 18 years and remarried. Harewood's new wife is Patricia Tuckwell, his ex-secretary, by whom he has a three-year-old son. As governor of the Church of England, the Queen could not condone divorce, so the cabinet devised a way to make the granting of her consent – required under the Royal Marriages Act – a formality. Public views on divorce have liberalised since 1955, when Princess Margaret had to abandon plans to marry Peter Townsend and memories were fresher of the 1936 abdication crisis (→6/1978).

Court censor axed

London, 1968
The lord chamberlain's role as theatre censor, which was instituted under Elizabeth I to protect the monarch against abuse from the stage, has been abolished. Lord Cobbold, the present lord chamberlain – the chief official in the royal household – argued that censorship was out of date and that it was inappropriate for a monarch to be the arbiter of taste.

Nation is enthralled by TV's behind-the-scenes view of royals

Britain, 1 July 1969
The royal family has entered a new era following the television screening last night of the joint BBC/ITV documentary *Royal Family*, on the eve of the Prince of Wales's investiture. The film, seen by some 23 million viewers, gave the British people an unprecedented glimpse of the private life of the royal family. Shot over the course of a year, the scenes included a barbecue picnic at Balmoral, the feeding of the royal corgis and the decorating of the royal Christmas tree. The documentary was the brainchild of William Heseltine, the Queen's assistant press secretary, who persuaded the Queen to overcome her instinctive reluctance to such exposure in the interests of an invaluable public relations exercise.

What the viewers saw: Prince Edward (r) with fellow-pupils in the nursery.

Royals are 'in the red', claims Philip

United States, 9 November 1969
Prince Philip said today that the royal family was in danger of going "into the red" and might have to leave Buckingham Palace next year. In an interview with American television, the prince claimed that the problem stemmed from the fact that the Queen's allowance of £475,000 a year was "based on costs of 18 years ago". He argued that there was no question of "bad housekeeping" but that the practice of fixing the monarch's allowance at the start of a reign needs to be reviewed, particularly as the Queen's reign looks like being a long one. "We sold off a small yacht, and I may have to give up polo," he said (→2/12/71).

A new generation emerges in the royal family

Anne scores first win at horse trials

Riding high: Princess Anne is in training for the Windsor horse trials.

Windsor, April 1969

Princess Anne, riding the Queen's horse Royal Ocean, has emerged the victor in her first attempt at serious three-day eventing. The 18-year-old princess triumphed in the novice class at the Windsor horse trials after several months of intensive training for this most demanding of equestrian sports, with three different tests of riding over three days. The princess went into training last year with the distinguished riding instructor Alison Oliver, who agreed to take her on only after she was sure of Anne's ability and potential as a three-day eventer.

Anne – who rides three horses, Purple Star, Doublet and Royal Ocean – has since had her stamina and determination put to the test by a gruelling regime, which she has to combine with her official duties. The next goal for the princess is the Badminton horse trials (→9/1971).

The young royals attend first state event

Prince Charles and Princess Anne are present for the first time at the state opening of parliament by their mother, Queen Elizabeth, on 31 October 1967.

Charles is invested as Prince of Wales

Caernarfon, 1 July 1969

To the relief of the royal family, the organisers of the magnificent ceremony and a worldwide television audience of 200 million, the investiture of the Prince of Wales at Caernarfon castle today passed off without violent incident. It was here in 1282, that King Edward I – having killed the Welsh prince Llywelyn ap Gruffudd – declared his own son the first English Prince of Wales. Today, following his great-uncle, the future King Edward VIII, who was invested here in 1911, the 21st Prince of Wales took the oath of allegiance to his Queen, pledging "faith and truth I will bear unto you to live and die against all manner of folks".

Opposition to the investiture from Welsh nationalists has been fierce. Extremists have mounted 15 bomb attacks on government and military buildings in Wales, and only this morning two men were killed while trying to plant a bomb. The 21-year-old prince won himself a lot of supporters, however, by a speech in Welsh at Aberystwyth three weeks ago, which pleased many but also gave rise to a satirical song, *Carlo* (→10/1969).

An eager crowd cheers the prince.

Actor prince takes refuge in a dustbin

Cambridge, October 1969

As he approaches his 21st birthday, the Prince of Wales is back in Cambridge for his last year at Trinity college before finals. After a year of archaeology and anthropology, the prince, keen to study the British constitution, changed to a history course – against the advice of his mentor, R A Butler, the former Tory politician, now master of Trinity. Frequently diverted from his studies by official duties, the prince spent last term learning Welsh at Aberystwyth university in preparation for his investiture.

As at school, the prince finds his position an obstacle to close friendships, but he enjoys taking part in undergraduate revues; the sight of him on stage in a dustbin in a show called *Revulution* this year sparked worldwide interest (→23/6/70).

The prince in a dustbin: Charles taking part in a student revue with friends at Trinity college.

E l i z a b e t h I I
1952–

**House
of
Windsor**

London, 1 January 1970. Anne is made president of the Save the Children Fund.→

Westminster, 11 February 1970. The Prince of Wales takes his seat in the House of Lords (→ 13/6/74).

London, 19 February 1970. The Prince of Wales is to join the Royal Navy, it is announced (→ 10/1971).

Cambridge, 23 June 1970. The Prince of Wales, at Trinity, is awarded a 2:2, the first heir to the throne to gain a degree.

Coventry, 30 June 1970. The Queen, after the success of her New Zealand "walkabout", mingles with the crowd in the city.

London, July 1970. Anne is recovering after surgery to remove an ovarian cyst.

London, 25 July 1970. The Duchess of Kent gives birth to her third child, Nicholas Charles Edward Jonathan.

Windsor, August 1970. The Queen gives permission for the Duke and Duchess of Windsor to be buried at Frogmore (→ 3/10).

Paris, 3 October 1970. The Prince of Wales, after a shoot in the Bois de Boulogne, meets the Duke of Windsor (→ 1/5/72).

Westminster, 27 May 1971. The Queen's request for a pay rise meets fierce opposition from left-wing MPs (→ 26/2/75).

Cambridgeshire, Sept 1971. Anne, aged 21, wins the European Three-Day Event Championship at Burghley House (→ 12/1971).

Dartmouth, October 1971. The Prince of Wales, as an acting sub-lieutenant, begins a six-week course at the royal naval college here (→ 11/1971).

London, 17 November 1971. The Queen meets John Profumo, the former secretary of state for war, for the first time since the 1963 scandal, at the opening of a residential home in the east end. He is involved in charity work.

Gibraltar, November 1971. The Prince of Wales joins HMS *Norfolk* as a sub-lieutenant.

Britain, November 1971. Anne, with her love of horses, becomes patron of the Riding for the Disabled Association (→ 23/4/85).

Paris, 21 May 1972. The Queen visits the Duke of Windsor who is dying of throat cancer (→ 28/5).

Paris, 28 May 1972. The Duke of Windsor dies (→ 5/6).

Windsor, 5 June 1972. The funeral takes place of the Duke of Windsor; the duchess has been a guest at Buckingham Palace since her arrival in England three days ago.→

London, 8 July 1972. Prince Richard of Gloucester marries Birgitte Eva van Deurs, the daughter of Asger Preben Wissing Henriksen (→ 28/8).

Yugoslavia, 17 October 1972. The Queen arrives for the first state visit to a communist country by a British monarch (→ 28/8/73).

Bridgend, Glamorgan, 1972. The Prince of Wales opens the new Sony factory, a result of his visit to the Japanese Expo in 1970.

Ethiopia, February 1973. Anne makes her first trip to Africa as president of the Save the Children Fund (→ 15/11/82).

London, 2 March 1973. Anne denies rumours of a romance with Lieutenant Mark Phillips of the Queen's Dragoon Guards (→ 29/5).

London, 29 May 1973. The palace announces the engagement of Princess Anne, aged 23, to Lt Mark Phillips, aged 25 (→ 14/11).

Bahamas, July 1973. The Prince of Wales attends independence day celebrations.

USSR, 28 August 1973. Princess Anne is the first member of the royal family to visit Russia since the murder of Czar Nicholas II and his family.

London, 22 May 1974. Ian Ball, the man who tried to kidnap Princess Anne in London in March, is found guilty and detained under the Mental Health Act for an unlimited time.

Windsor, May 1974. Doublet, the much-loved champion horse of Princess Anne, is put down after breaking a leg.

Scotland, September 1974. Prince Andrew begins school at Gordonstoun (→ 4/1/77).

London, 24 October 1974. The Duchess of Gloucester gives birth to her first child, a son, Alexander Patrick George Richard, the Earl of Ulster (→ 19/11/77).

Somerset, December 1974. The Prince of Wales joins the royal naval air station at Yeovilton for a helicopter course (→ 11/1976).

Birmingham, 2 February 1976. The Queen opens the £45 million National Exhibition Centre.

Britain, 28 February 1976. The *News of the World* publishes a story about Princess Margaret's holiday with Roddy Llewellyn, aged 27, on the island of Mustique (→ 19/3).

Montreal, July 1976. Princess Anne becomes the first member of the royal family to compete in the Olympic Games (→ 31/7).

Gloucestershire, 29 Sept 1976. Anne and Mark move into Gatcombe Park, a gift from the Queen.

Britain, November 1976. The Prince of Wales leaves the navy.→

London, 15 November 1977. Princess Anne gives birth to her first child, a son, Peter Mark Andrew Phillips (→ 5/11/80).

London, 19 November 1977. The Duchess of Gloucester gives birth to a second child, Davina Elizabeth Alice Benedikte (→ 1/3/80).

Northamptonshire, 30 Nov 1977. The Prince of Wales meets Lady Diana Spencer, aged 16, the youngest daughter of Earl Spencer, at a shoot at Althorp (→ 3/1/79).

Mustique, 25 February 1978. Rumours of Princess Margaret's romance with Roderic ("Roddy") Llewellyn are rife (→ 10/5).

Britain, April 1978. Captain Mark Phillips resigns from the army.

Britain, 20 November 1978. The palace announces that Prince Andrew will follow his brother in joining the Royal Navy (→ 17/9/82).

Sandringham, 31 January 1979. Lady Diana Spencer and members of her family join the royal shooting party (→ 8/1979).

London, 6 April 1979. Princess Michael of Kent gives birth to a son, Frederick Michael George David Louis (→ 23/4/81).

Cowes, August 1979. Lady Diana Spencer joins the royal family holidaying on their yacht, the *Britannia* (→ 9/1980).

Britain, 5 September 1979. The funeral takes place of Earl Mountbatten of Burma, murdered by the IRA on 27 August.→

Queen goes 'walkabout'

Close to the people: Elizabeth on an informal "walk-about" in New Zealand.

Australia, 3 May 1970

During her tour of New Zealand and Australia, which ended today, Queen Elizabeth has initiated a new royal ritual – the "walkabout". Instead of merely driving past the crowds who flocked to see her, the Queen made a habit of walking informally among them, stopping at frequent intervals to exchange a few words of conversation with individuals or accept small gifts.

Soon after the Queen arrived in New Zealand in late March there was a bomb threat in Dunedin, where she was due to hear a concert. She nevertheless attended the concert, but thereafter the elaborate arrangements to ensure her safety were made even more stringent. When the Queen insisted on going about on foot, she brushed aside security fears, joking that there was no point in walkabouts if she could only talk to those protecting her.

Although the walkabouts proved tiring for the Queen and forced her to maintain a smile for long periods, they were hugely popular with the crowds, generating a great deal of respect and warmth from people who were thrilled to come face to face with the British monarch and hear the sound of her voice (→ 30/6).

The graduate prince: Charles at the Commonwealth Secretariat on the day it is announced that he has gained his honours degree in history.

President Nixon is impressed by prince during Charles and Anne's American visit

Washington, July 1970

Following a tour of Canada with their parents, the Prince of Wales and Princess Anne have spent three days in Washington as the guests of President Richard Nixon.

While the president was impressed by the dignity and perception of the prince, the American press has been critical of Anne's gaucheness. The princess caused offence to her hosts by commenting that the bald eagle was "rather a bad choice" as the American national symbol. Her impatience was remarked on, and the *New York Times* said that her behaviour did not live up to what Americans expected from a princess. The prince was praised for his "outgoing nature, dashing charm, intelligent interest", but the *New York Sunday News* countered: "Good ole Charley Windsor ... is really as common as a new shoe."

Although irritated by attempts to pair him off with the president's

Anne jokes with well-wishers.

daughter Tricia, the prince had a triumphant private meeting with Nixon in the Oval Office during which he won the president's admiration for his mature grasp of world affairs. Their talk lasted eight times longer than planned.

Charles has début as a solo tourist

Japan, April 1970

Following a tour of Australia and New Zealand with his parents, the Prince of Wales this month made his first solo official visit abroad – to Japan, where he proved a keen champion of the Welsh economy. At Expo 70, in Tokyo, the prince met the president of the Sony electronics group. On hearing of Sony's plans to expand its manufacturing into western Europe, the prince suggested that the company consider Wales as a possible location for a new plant (→ 1972).

Anne to head 'Save the Children Fund'

London, 1 January 1970

Princess Anne today formally accepted the presidency of the Save the Children Fund. She is the sixth president of the charity in its 70-year history and the second woman to hold the job; the late Countess Mountbatten of Burma, her great-aunt, was president during the 1950s. It is the first such position that the 19-year-old princess has assumed; she took part in her first public engagement last year, standing in for her father at a St David's day parade (→ 2/1973).

Prince takes to sky on RAF flying course

Oxfordshire, 10 October 1970

The Prince of Wales today made his first flight, in a twin-engined Beagle Basset aircraft specially provided for him by the RAF. The prince received his preliminary flying badge last August and was judged proficient to graduate to a more sophisticated aircraft than the Chipmunk in which he learnt to fly. He began flying lessons during his first year at Cambridge, and in 1968 a special training unit was set up for him at RAF Benson near Oxford. After less than 15 hours' instruction, he made his first solo flight in January 1969: "The moment I was in the air it was absolutely marvellous ... Fortunately I landed first time. I had visions of myself going round and round until eventually the fuel ran out" (→ 20/8/71).

▷

Charles is awarded his wings by RAF

The flyer-prince in RAF uniform.

Lincolnshire, 20 August 1971
At RAF Cranwell today Prince Philip looked on proudly as his eldest son was awarded his flying wings by Air Chief Marshal Sir Denis Spotswood. The Prince of Wales, who took up flying in 1968, has spent the past five months on a jet conversion course at Cranwell, where he won glowing reports from his instructors. He was judged to have a natural aptitude for flying, and it was remarked that he would make "an excellent fighter pilot at supersonic speeds" (→ 12/1974).

Silence greets the Japanese emperor

London, 8 October 1971
Emperor Hirohito of Japan arrived in London today on his first state visit to Britain since before the Second World War. As he drove to Buckingham Palace, large crowds lined the route but remained curiously silent as he passed. In a speech the Queen told the 70-year-old emperor: "We cannot pretend that the past did not exist. We cannot pretend that relations between our two peoples have always been peaceful and friendly."

Some British veterans who were Japanese prisoners of war have called for a boycott of Japanese goods in protest at the emperor's visit (→ 29/1/89).

MPs approve move to boost royal pay

Westminster, 2 December 1971
Agreeing the first increase in the civil list since Elizabeth's accession in 1952, parliament has voted to double the Queen's allowance from £475,000 to £980,000. This follows a study of royal finances by an all-party Commons committee set up last year by the then prime minister, Harold Wilson. Most of the extra money will go to pay the salaries of the Queen's 375 full-time and 100 part-time staff.

The debate about the civil list began two years ago, after Prince Philip said on American television that the royal family was under such financial pressure that it might "go into the red". He was heavily criticised in Britain for talking about poverty when his wife was the richest woman in the world, and Richard Crossman, the then leader of the House of Commons, wrote an article in the *New Statesman* magazine about "The Royal Tax Avoiders". In the ensuing furore the royal finances were probed in greater detail than ever before, with views about private wealth and public duties starkly polarised. Some loyal citizens were so concerned that they sent donations to the palace (→ 26/2/75).

Duke of Windsor dies

Windsor, 5 June 1972
The funeral service of the Duke of Windsor, who died in Paris on 28 May at the age of 77, took place at St George's chapel this morning. Among the mourners were most of the royal family, the prime minister and representatives of the church and the armed forces, as well as the Duchess of Windsor, who arrived from Paris three days ago. In accordance with the duke's wishes, his body was buried in a private ceremony at Frogmore, near the garden where he played as a boy.

Since his abdication in 1936 to marry Wallis Simpson, the former Edward VIII had lived most of his life in France, apart from a wartime tour of duty as governor of the Bahamas. A fortnight ago he was visited at his Paris home by Queen Elizabeth, Prince Philip and the Prince of Wales. Although he was very ill from throat cancer, the duke insisted on leaving his bed for the occasion and rose to bow to his niece when she entered. Eight days later he was dead.

Flown back to England, the duke's body lay in state for two days at St George's chapel, while 60,000 mourners filed past. The duchess arrived on the second day, visited her husband's coffin and

Fighting back tears: the Duchess of Windsor at her husband's funeral.

stayed with the Queen at Buckingham Palace. At the funeral service, the 75-year-old widow sat with the Queen and heard the proclamation of her husband's numerous titles, past and present, including "King Edward VIII of Great Britain, Ireland and the British Dominions beyond the Seas, Emperor of India". This evening, frail and alone, she left Heathrow, not even pausing on the aircraft steps for a last look at the land that her husband gave up for her (→ 24/4/86).

Princess Anne scoops two awards as sportswoman of the year

With grace and elegance: Princess Anne, the Sportswoman of the Year.

London, December 1971
Princess Anne has been voted BBC Television Sports Personality of the Year. The award follows the accolade last month of being voted Sportswoman of the Year by the national press. The two awards round off a marvellous year for the 21-year-old princess, during which she won the European three-day-eventing championships.

The princess achieved her first success of the year in April when she came fifth in the gruelling Badminton horse trials. She was then selected to ride in the European championships at Burghley in September. Despite an operation for an ovarian cyst, she was fit for the competition, securing first prize after a fine clear round on Doublet in the show-jumping to fulfil an ambition to achieve success on merit alone (→ 2/3/73).

Queen's cousin dies in a flying accident

Wolverhampton, 28 August 1972
Prince William of Gloucester was killed today when the plane he was flying in an air race crashed and exploded in flames after taking off from a Wolverhampton airfield. A keen pilot since Cambridge days, the 30-year-old prince was ninth in line to the throne. He was the elder son of the Duke of Gloucester, the queen's uncle. His 45-year-old co-pilot, Vyrell Mitchell, the only other occupant of the prince's Piper Cherokee Arrow 200, also died in the crash. As a consequence of the tragedy, the Queen has cancelled her planned visit to the Munich Olympics and ordered family mourning until the funeral (→ 10/6/74).

Stirling boos Queen

Stirling, 12 October 1972
The Queen reacted calmly today when she was greeted by a crowd of Stirling university students chanting "Out with the monarchy!". She stopped to ask individual students the nature of their complaint, and learnt of their anger that so much money had been spent on her visit when students were suffering financial hardship. Her sympathetic approach so impressed the students that 930 later signed a letter apologising for their behaviour.

Queen celebrates her silver wedding

London, 20 November 1972
Queen Elizabeth and Prince Philip today celebrated their silver wedding. The occasion was marked by a relatively simple service of thanksgiving at Westminster abbey, followed by an informal walk among the crowds by the royal couple. Afterwards, at a luncheon at the Guildhall, the Queen said that today, of all days, she felt justified in beginning her speech with the words which have so often been used to parody her: "My husband and I". She went on to say: "If I am asked today what I think about family life after 25 years of marriage, I can answer with simplicity and conviction. I am for it."

Glittering abbey wedding for Anne

The royal bride and groom bow to the Queen before leaving the abbey.

London, 14 November 1973
Under the fascinated gaze of more than 500 million television viewers around the world, Princess Anne – who had wanted a quiet wedding – married Captain Mark Phillips today in a glittering ceremony at Westminster abbey.

Well before Princess Anne left Buckingham Palace at 11.12am, Captain Phillips and his best man, Captain Eric Grounds, had arrived to join the 1,800 guests at the abbey. The 23-year-old princess rode with her father, the Duke of Edinburgh, in a glass coach along a route lined by some half a million people – thousands of whom had camped on the streets overnight – all straining to get a first glimpse of the royal wedding dress, whose design had been kept a closely guarded secret. When she emerged at the abbey, Princess Anne looked stunning in a white silk gown embroidered in pearls with a high neckline and Tudor-style puffed sleeves.

Attended by her brother Prince Edward and her cousin Lady Sarah Armstrong-Jones, both aged nine, Anne walked down the aisle with her father to join 25-year-old Mark, resplendent in a scarlet and gold uniform with blue velvet collar and trousers. During the service, the bride and groom smiled repeatedly at one another. At the princess's insistence, the television cameras were not allowed to film the moment when Mark placed the wedding ring on her finger.

Back at Buckingham Palace, the princess and her husband appeared with the rest of the royal family on the balcony to greet the ecstatic crowds before retiring inside for a sumptuous wedding breakfast. The couple then left the palace for the first night of their honeymoon at Thatched House Lodge in Richmond park. Tomorrow they fly to Barbados where they will join the royal yacht *Britannia*.

The "wedding of the decade" has given an enormous boost to the British television and tourist industries, and every conceivable souvenir stamped with a likeness of the couple has sold in its hundreds of thousands (→ 24/1/74).

Mark becomes one of the family after weeks of official denials

More than just good friends.

London, 14 November 1973
Captain Mark Phillips of the Queen's Dragoon Guards today became a member of the Queen's own family. He married Princess Anne [*see story above*] just nine months after the princess had said: "We are not engaged and there is no prospect of an engagement."

That denial came in February after a similar statement from the palace in January had failed to stem a mounting tide of rumour. The media were not best pleased therefore when, on 29 May, the palace announced the engagement. Until then, the public fiction was that the army lieutenant (as then was) and the Queen's only daughter only had horses in common. It is indeed true that horses brought the couple together. Mark, a handsome 25-year-old, comes from an army family; he went to Marlborough college and Sandhurst before joining the Guards in 1969.

His relaxed attitude masks great stamina and determination, as shown by his notable equestrian achievements. He met the princess in 1968 at a party to celebrate Britain's gold medal for eventing at the Mexico Olympics – Mark was a reserve member of the winning team. By 1971, when Mark won the Badminton horse trials and Anne became European champion, they were often seen together. Mark proposed at April's Badminton horse trials, but Buckingham Palace continued to issue denials of a planned engagement.

561

Royal prerogative becomes issue as Heath seeks pact

London, 4 March 1974
At 7.19pm today Harold Wilson arrived at Buckingham Palace to begin his second spell as prime minister. His appointment follows a weekend of intrigue which highlighted the royal prerogative of choosing a prime minister when no party has a clear majority in the Commons.

Last week Heath's Conservative Party won 296 seats in the general election against 301 for Labour, 14 Liberals and 24 from other parties. Heath, as the incumbent, sought a deal with the Liberals which would command a majority of the Commons. The Queen accepted that he had a right to do so, but royal advisers were uneasy about the prospect of Heath seeking to resign and be reappointed as head of a new coalition government. Should the Queen endorse this without first giving the largest party a chance to form a government?

In the event the Tories and Liberals were unable to work out a deal, and it is Wilson who now returns to Downing Street. He was prime minister for six years from 1964, the first one of the Queen's reign not to come from the old upper class, but they appear to have got on well. Wilson speaks highly of the mastery of detail in her daily flow of government papers.

Harold Wilson: back in power.

Mark gets his first taste of royal duty in New Zealand

Christchurch, 24 January 1974
Just two months after his marriage to Princess Anne, Captain Mark Phillips has been initiated into the tough world of royal duties. Mark was with his wife and in-laws today for the opening of the Commonwealth Games at Christchurch in New Zealand, which the Queen and Prince Philip are visiting as part of their current tour of Australasia and Commonwealth islands in the Pacific.

Although the New Zealand trip is Mark's first big engagement – he is one of the Queen's official aides-de-camp – he had a foretaste of his new life as a member of the royal family after his honeymoon cruise with Anne aboard the royal yacht *Britannia* last month. The couple's busy schedule took in Jamaica, Antigua and Montserrat, together with Ecuador and Colombia. They also flew to Canada en route to New Zealand for a three-day stay which included the first royal visit for some time to the separatist hotbed of Quebec.

For Mark, the whole experience – chatting to hundreds of strangers in a single day and having to show interest in all he sees – has made him realise quite how much stamina and professionalism go into being royalty on show (→ 20/3).

Queen's uncle, Duke of Gloucester, dies

London, 10 June 1974
The royal family is in mourning today following the death of the Queen's uncle, Prince Henry, the Duke of Gloucester. The 74-year-old prince was a younger brother of King Edward VIII and King George VI and the last survivor of King George V's six children.

"Prince Harry" was born at Sandringham in 1900 and pursued a career in the army. He became the first royal governor-general of Australia in 1945, but on the whole the modest duke preferred to avoid what he called "princing about". He is succeeded by his younger son, Prince Richard of Gloucester; his elder son, Prince William, died in an air crash in 1972.

Prince Henry, Duke of Gloucester.

Shots fired at princess

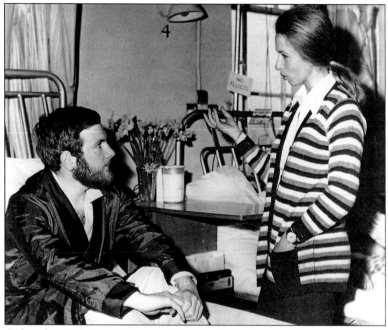

Safe in hospital: Anne with one of the men injured in the kidnap attempt.

London, 20 March 1974
Princess Anne and Captain Mark Phillips are recovering tonight after a terrifying kidnap attempt just yards from Buckingham Palace in which four people were shot. The ordeal began just after 7.30pm, when a Ford Escort screeched to a halt in front of the royal limousine as it approached the palace.

A man, Ian Ball, sprang out of the Escort and fired at Anne's car, before attempting to drag her from her seat. Mark, however, held onto his wife, whose dress was ripped, and slammed the door shut again. The princess's detective, Inspector Beaton, was shot in his bid to tackle Ball, as were her chauffeur, a constable and a reporter who was first on the scene. As help arrived Ball fled into St James's park, but was brought down by another officer. Miraculously, no one died, and neither Anne nor Mark, nor Anne's lady-in-waiting, also in the car, was injured. The whole incident lasted about ten minutes (→ 22/5).

Charles makes his Lords début speech

London, 13 June 1974
Prince Charles left Buckingham Palace for the Palace of Westminster today to make the first speech in the House of Lords by a Prince of Wales this century. It is four years since he took his seat in the upper house. Custom demands that royals do not speak on controversial or partisan political topics, so the prince's maiden speech was on the subject of creating a "ministry of leisure". He called for more government spending to help people to make better use of their leisure and thereby "remove the dead hand of boredom and frustration from mankind".

Labour MPs oppose royal 'pay' increase

London, 26 February 1975
The House of Commons has voted a large increase in royal finances despite the opposition of 90 Labour MPs. The prime minister, Harold Wilson, asked the Commons three weeks ago to vote a big rise in the annual civil list of £500,000 on top of the £980,000 agreed after a Commons' inquiry into the royal finances in 1971. By then the civil list of £475,000 – in force since 1952 – was clearly inadequate.

Opponents of the increase claim that the Queen is getting a massive "pay rise". This is not strictly true; the civil list covers the expenses of the Queen herself, those of her family who carry out public duties, and their staff. A further £5 million (£500,000 more than in 1971) comes from government departments to pay for specific costs like the Queen's Flight, covered by the ministry of defence. The privy purse – the Queen's private income – comes not from the taxpayer but, since 1971, only from the monarch's private holdings such as the Duchy of Lancaster (→ 24/2/88).

Anne and Mark set horsey tour style

Adelaide, 6 May 1975
Princess Anne and Captain Mark Philips have spent a lot of time around horses and in the outback during their tour of South Australia, Western Australia and the Northern Territory. Princess Anne officially opened the International Equestrian Expo, and the couple have watched a rodeo in the Adelaide Hills and a "horsey" film called *Bite the Bullet*. They have visited Alice Springs and the iron ore mines of Western Australia and have seen the new Darwin rising after Cyclone Tracey. Their tour has been somewhat dogged by hot weather and cars and planes which keep breaking down.

Charles composes a song for monarchy

Canada, 27 April 1975
The Prince of Wales today delighted guests at a dinner in the village of Resolute Bay, 600 miles (960km) inside the Arctic Circle, with a song he composed. Newsmen and 200 villagers, including many non-English-speaking native people, applauded wildly when Charles sang:
"So where, may I ask.
Is the monarchy going
When princes and pressmen,
Are on the same Boeing?"
On this part of his Canadian tour, Charles has snowballed, dogsledded and eaten raw scal liver. He also donned diving gear, plunged through an ice hole and swam for 20 minutes in the Arctic waters.

Queen's man in Australia sacks the prime minister and starts constitutional furore

The sacked Labor leader Gough Whitlam outside the Australian parliament.

Canberra, 11 November 1975
The Queen was plunged into the greatest constitutional crisis of her reign in Australia today when Sir John Kerr, the governor-general, sacked the Labor prime minister, Gough Whitlam. Sir John has appointed Malcolm Fraser, the Liberal leader, to form an interim government before an election.

Crowds took to the streets in the federal capital, Canberra, and other cities to protest against the governor-general exercising his power, as the monarch's representative in Australia, to change a government against the prime minister's wishes. Sir John's move follows weeks of tension over the refusal of the Liberals in the Senate, the upper house, to pass the Labor government's budget. By convention the Senate does not reject budgets, but Fraser thought the deadlock would force Whitlam to call an election. Whitlam, equally determined, thought Fraser would back down. What nobody anticipated was that Sir John would intervene and present the crown with a constitutional crisis.

'Sunnyboy' is Queen Mum's 300th win

Ascot, 10 April 1975
The Queen Mother's horse Sunnyboy galloped passed the winning post at Ascot today to a great roar from the spectators. Its royal owner was unable to contain her delight at the win, her 300th in a long and distinguished career as a patron of National Hunt racing.

The Queen Mother has been a keen follower and breeder of racehorses for about 30 years, although she could never manage to arouse the same enthusiasm for the "sport of kings" in her husband, George VI. From the beginning her first love has been steeplechasing, unlike her daughter, the Queen, who after a brief flirtation with what she calls the "winter game" in 1949 turned her whole attention to the more glamorous world of flat-racing.

From early on it was the Queen Mother's ambition to win the greatest of all steeplechases, the Grand National. She came within 50 yards of doing so in 1956 when her horse, Devon Loch stumbled within yards of victory [*see page 543*]. "That's racing," the Queen Mother told the horse's distraught jockey Dick Francis (now a thriller writer).

Undaunted by this setback, she has maintained her interest, often turning up to watch her horses at their dawn gallops. She takes a close interest in planning where and when her horses will compete and is also active in promoting the welfare of National Hunt jockeys. ▷

Arise Sir Garfield: the Queen knights the West Indian cricketing hero Gary Sobers before a huge crowd in Barbados on 19 February 1975.

Margaret and Snowdon to separate

London, 19 March 1976

Weeks of gossip and years of speculation came to an end today when Buckingham Palace announced that Princess Margaret and the Earl of Snowdon are to separate. They have been married for 15 years.

Rumours that all was not well with the marriage began to circulate as far back as the late 1960s, when it became clear that Margaret and her husband were seeing less of each other. In recent months the rumours have become a torrent of gossip in the popular papers, culminating in a *News of the World* splash three weeks ago on Margaret's friendship with 27-year-old Roderic "Roddy" Llewellyn.

In fact, strains in the marriage showed themselves soon after Margaret and Antony Armstrong-Jones – he was made Earl of Snowdon in 1961 – were married in 1960. They were obviously madly in love, but Margaret's passion seemed to border on an intense possessiveness that made Snowdon feel at times stifled. He, a gregarious and talented society photographer, wanted a life of his own and disliked the routine side of duties as a princess's husband. Tensions grew, erupting occasionally in fierce rows, not all of them in private.

The Queen has shown much sensitivity during the split. As monarch and head of the Church of England, she may have to give consent to a divorce under the Royal Marriages Act of 1772. This would probably have been unthinkable so close to the throne in previous reigns, but there is a precedent in the divorce of her cousin, the Earl of Harewood, in 1967 (→ 25/2/78).

Margaret: putting on a brave face.

New country home for Anne and Mark

Gloucestershire, 1976

Princess Anne and Mark Phillips now have a house of their own. With the Queen's help, the couple are paying £450,000 for Gatcombe Park, a country house in 530 acres (212ha) near Minchinhampton in Gloucestershire which was once home to the statesman "Rab" Butler. The house, which will be in Anne's name, needs a lot of patching up. But it is ideal for their horses and only an hour and a half from London and the palace, from where the princess runs her official duties. As a "housewarming" present the Queen has bought the 600-acre estate next door to help Mark set up as a country farmer (→ 29/9).

Charles quits navy

London, November 1976

Prince Charles has left the Royal Navy in style, sailing the minehunter HMS *Bronington* into the Pool of London this month before retiring from the senior service at the age of 28. He had commanded the *Bronington* since February. Charles has spent six years in the services, with a stint in the RAF before joining the Royal Navy.

Princess competes for Britain in Olympics

Making a splash: a determined Princess Anne riding hard in the Olympics.

Montreal, 31 July 1976

Princess Anne and Captain Mark Phillips are heading home with the rest of Britain's equestrian team after failing to win any medals in this year's Olympic Games, which ended today. They were selected for the games after their successes last year – Anne, for example, won a silver medal in the European Championships. They insisted on living as far as possible like their Olympic team-mates, flying economy class and queueing at the buffet. In the event Mark was dropped to the reserve and did not ride, while Anne turned in a disappointing, if determined, performance in the three-day event.

On the first day she came 26th in the dressage and on the second, in the cross-country, she fell and was badly concussed – knocked unconscious, according to doctors – in front of the Queen. But she finished the course and put in a creditable performance next day in the show-jumping, coming fourth.

Young people first in line to benefit from Prince's Trust

London, 31 December 1976

Four years ago a man rang George Pratt, London's second highest probation officer, and said that his employer had seen Pratt on television talking about helping young offenders and wanted to know if he could be of any use. The man happened to be the Prince of Wales's private secretary, and that call sparked the creation of the incentive schemes which this year officially became known as the Prince's Trust. The trust aims to give a start to disadvantaged young people, such as offenders and the jobless. It already has seven regional committees which expect to grant around £35,000 this year to some 250 projects (→ 9/1985).

Andrew is sent to college in Canada

Toronto, 4 January 1977

Prince Andrew, on his way to attend the private Lakefield College School in Ontario, turned the tables here today at the first press conference which he has ever held by asking journalists more questions than he answered. The friendly and grinning Andrew – 17 next month – confided that he hopes to study dramatics because he enjoys pretending to be someone else. The prince, on a one-year exchange programme, will live simply and share a small furnished room with one of the other 250 students (→ 20/11/78).

Andrew with a friend in Canada.

Cheers ring out for the Queen's silver jubilee year

The superb Jubilee Day procession.

Giving heartfelt thanks: the commemorative service in St Paul's cathedral.

Greeting jubilee well-wishers.

London, 31 December 1977

As her silver jubilee year draws to a close, the Queen can look back on 12 months which have witnessed the most extraordinary outpouring of affection and goodwill towards her from the millions of people of whom she is Queen. Celebrations began on 6 February, the anniversary of the day in 1952 on which her father, King George VI, died and she became the first British monarch to succeed while up a tree.

On 10 February she set out on the first of two triumphal jubilee year tours of her several kingdoms. The first port of call was Fiji, which gave its head of state a huge welcome. Similar explosions of loyalty and warmth greeted the Queen of New Zealand and the Queen of Papua New Guinea; even Australia, where republicanism is a hot issue, joined in the jubilation.

At the end of March it was back home for the first of 7,000 miles (11,200km) of travelling to many parts of Britain, and as Jubilee Day – 7 June – approached, the letters and cards offering congratulations poured into Buckingham Palace. Over 100,000 arrived in the jubilee year, including 3,500 on one day at the height of the festivities.

On the night before Jubilee Day the Queen lit a bonfire at Windsor to start a chain that eventually stretched from Land's End to the Shetlands, and the next day, a public holiday by royal decree, she celebrated 25 years on the throne with a solemn and splendid thanksgiving service in St Paul's cathedral. Her people, in cities, towns and villages the length and breadth of the kingdom, marked the occasion with colourful street parties in a carnival atmosphere not felt since 1945.

The royal tours then resumed with visits to the east end of London and the troops in Germany. One climax of these tours was on 10 August, when the Queen arrived on her first visit to Northern Ireland since the current troubles began, in defiance of IRA threats and bomb attacks. She was anxious to show, as she had said in a speech to both houses of parliament on 4 May, that she was "Queen of the *whole* United Kingdom". In October it was abroad again, this time to Canada, where the Queen showed local sensitivity by opening the Canadian parliament in English and French. The last stops on the 56,000-mile (89,600km) jubilee year itinerary were in the West Indies, where the Bahamas and Barbados gave her a warm Caribbean welcome.

The celebrations were not quite over. On 15 November a telephone call from Princess Anne made the Queen ten minutes late for an investiture at the palace. But no one minded: she was a grandmother.

Fun for all: one of many joyful street parties to celebrate the Queen's reign.

Elizabeth happily talking to children in Ottawa during her Canadian tour.

565

Princess Margaret petitions for divorce

London, 10 May 1978
Princess Margaret and the Earl of Snowdon are to be divorced. The couple, who were married in 1960, have lived apart for the last two years. They have two children, Viscount Linley, aged 16, and Lady Sarah Armstrong-Jones, aged 14; it has been agreed that the princess will have custody of them.

Margaret is currently being treated in hospital for gastro-enteritis, and tonight the earl said that he hoped that she "will get the support and encouragement she needs when she comes out of hospital and goes back to public duties". It is unlikely that either the princess or Lord Snowdon will appear in court; the case will be heard in the high court's family division as an undefended petition. Two years of separation are now sufficient grounds for divorce.

Since the couple separated in 1976 Lord Snowdon has increased his work as a photographer, while the princess has attracted criticism because of her friendship with

Roddy: Princess Margaret's friend.

"Roddy" Llewellyn, a 29-year-old landscape gardener 18 years her junior. However, it was said tonight that she has no plans to remarry and intends to resume royal duties when her health allows (→7/1/85).

Pope's ban frustrates Prince Michael's plans for a wedding in a Catholic church

Vienna, 30 June 1978
Prince Michael of Kent today became the first close member of the royal family to marry outside the British Isles since the Duke of Windsor married Wallis Simpson in 1937. His bride was a Czech-born divorcée, Baroness Marie-Christine von Reibnitz, aged 33.

She is a Roman Catholic and the couple had wanted a more elaborate wedding, but their plans were thrown awry this month when the pope denied them a dispensation to marry in a Catholic church. This is required when one of the partners has a different faith. The pope declined the request for a dispensation because Prince Michael, aged 36 and a cousin of the Queen, intends to bring up any children as members of the Anglican Church.

Although the previous marriage of Princess Michael, as she will now be known, was not an obstacle to the Catholic Church, it prevented the marriage from taking place in

Prince Michael: no church wedding.

an Anglican church. As a member of the royal family Prince Michael was also unable to marry in a register office within Britain, forcing the couple to wed in a civil ceremony at Vienna town hall today (→6/4/79).

Divorce poses dilemmas for royal family

London, June 1978
The divorce of Princess Margaret and the marriage of Prince Michael this month have highlighted the problem of divorce within the royal family. The Queen, as "defender of the faith", has a pivotal, if symbolic, role in the Church of England. The law has become liberal, but the church still bars the remarriage of divorced people in church. Under the 1772 Royal Marriages Act, members of the family in the line of succession are required to seek the monarch's permission to marry, although after they are 25 objections can be overcome by waiting a year and giving up some rights.

Canadian government protects royal role

Ottawa, 15 October 1978
The Canadian government will reform the constitution even without the provinces' consent, but will not alter the role of the monarchy in Canada, says Marc Lalonde, the federal-provincial relations minister. His comment follows a Canadian Bar Association special committee report recommending that the Queen be replaced by a Canadian head of state appointed by the Canadian House of Commons. A recent justice department legal opinion backs Ottawa's right to change parts of the constitution unilaterally, including those covering the monarchy and Senate (→17/4/82).

The prince is seized in the surf.

Serious prince gains action man image

London, 14 November 1978
The Prince of Wales is 30 today. He is still, despite the best endeavours of the matchmakers in the popular press, the "world's most eligible bachelor". The image of the playboy prince does not do justice to the serious graduate interested in music and painting. Yet, while he searches to find a role in public life (as well as a wife), the public image is fostered by pictures of the "royal action man".

His schooldays at Gordonstoun may not have been the happiest of his life, but they do seem to have left Charles with a burning desire to compete in physical activity. Without reaching the heights of his sister, he is a good horseman, enjoying polo in particular, and he has also taken part in cross-country steeplechases. He flies planes, parachutes, skis, and goes windsurfing (much to the delight of Australian beachgirls and photographers alike). There are also the more traditional pursuits of a country gentleman – shooting and fishing – during family holidays at both Balmoral and Sandringham (→30/12/80).

Charles: weary after a long ride.

Commonwealth conference ends in row

Zambia, 5 August 1979
The danger of a rift in the Commonwealth over the future of Rhodesia appears to have been averted today after a conference in Lusaka where the Queen exercised a significant backstage role.

Rhodesia – or Zimbabwe, as the black nationalists call Britain's last remaining African colony – has been subjected to increasing violence ever since the minority white population, led by Ian Smith, made a unilateral declaration of independence in 1965. In April this year Bishop Abel Muzorewa became its first black prime minister, but the settlement excluded the two nationalist groups led by Joshua Nkomo and Robert Mugabe. Until today it seemed that Margaret Thatcher, attending her first Commonwealth conference, backed independence for a Muzorewa-led government. Other Commonwealth countries said that Nkomo and Mugabe must be given voices if there were to be any lasting peace.

Away from the formal sessions of the conference in Lusaka, the Queen took an active role. It is said that Mrs Thatcher had irritated the Queen by wondering whether the security risks meant she should stay at home. However, strong personal contacts and a lifelong commitment to the Commonwealth made the Queen determined to attend at a time of crisis. In the event, Mrs Thatcher endorsed a new proposal for a conference in London for all parties to devise a new constitution, with elections to be supervised by Commonwealth observers.

Not seeing eye to eye: the Queen and Mrs Thatcher at the conference.

Queen's art adviser named as Soviet spy

Westminster, 21 November 1979
Sir Anthony Blunt, the Queen's principal art adviser, was named in the House of Commons today as a Russian spy. Margaret Thatcher, the prime minister, gave details in a lengthy written answer which revealed that Blunt had confessed after being granted immunity from prosecution as long ago as April 1964. It is not clear whether or not the Queen knew of this confession, but tonight the palace announced that Blunt, who is aged 72, is to lose not only his position as keeper of the Queen's pictures but also his knighthood. The prime minister surprised MPs by giving so many details about the shadowy world of espionage.

It appears that Blunt had been a talent spotter for Soviet intelligence in pre-war Cambridge, and had then betrayed military secrets to the Russians during the early years of the war before Hitler attacked the Soviet Union in 1941. Blunt is now thought to have been the "fourth man" in the spy web which involved Burgess, Maclean and Philby – all of whom later defected to Russia.

IRA kills Mountbatten

In mourning: the royal family attending the funeral of Lord Mountbatten.

Ireland, 27 August 1979
Shortly after 11.30am today an IRA bomb blasted a 29-foot fishing boat out of the water at Mullaghmore, Co Sligo, killing three people. One of them was Earl Mountbatten of Burma, the 79-year-old cousin of the Queen whose career had reached the highest levels of the forces and diplomacy [*see below*]. Also killed were his 14-year-old grandson and a local youth.

Mountbatten had spent most Augusts at his house, Classiebawn castle near the quiet fishing port of Mullaghmore, for 30 years. Today, as was often the case, was to have been a day for some fishing. But as his boat *Shadow V* cleared the harbour wall, she was ripped apart by what the IRA later said was a 50-pound (22.5kg) bomb. Mountbatten died instantly. Fragments of the boat and the family party's personal belongings were found floating on the water when the bodies were recovered. Three people, including the earl's daughter and son-in-law, are tonight said to be in a critical condition in hospital.

As tributes poured in from all over the world, the Queen was "deeply shocked" by the outrage which came on a day when the IRA also killed 15 soldiers in a blast at Warrenpoint, Co Down (→5/9).

Mountbatten: war and peacetime hero

Mountbatten in 1955: first sea lord.

Hampshire, 5 September 1979
Earl Mountbatten of Burma, killed last month by an IRA bomb, was buried today at his Broadlands home. He called himself the "shop steward" of the royal family: a great-grandchild of Victoria (who attended his christening in 1900), aide to Edward VIII on royal tours, cousin of the Queen, uncle to Prince Philip (and, as much as anyone, matchmaker of that marriage) and mentor to Prince Charles. He had reached the top in the Royal Navy: supreme allied commander in Asia during the war, first sea lord and chief of the defence staff. He was also India's last viceroy, preparing it for independence.

Elizabeth II
1952–

**House
of
Windsor**

London, 1 March 1980. The Duchess of Gloucester gives birth to her third child, Rose Victoria Birgitte Louise.

Zimbabwe, 18 April 1980. The Prince of Wales represents the Queen at the independence celebrations of Britain's last African colony.

Netherlands, 30 April 1980. The Prince of Wales represents the royal family at the accession ceremony of Queen Beatrix.

London, 15 July 1980. The Queen Mother attends a special service in St Paul's to celebrate her 80th birthday on 4 August (→ 17/2/81).

London, September 1980. The press speculates about a relationship between the Prince of Wales and Lady Diana Spencer, a 19-year-old nursery teacher.→

Rome, 17 October 1980. The Queen pays her first state visit to the Vatican and has a meeting with the pope (→ 28/5/82).

Britain, 5 November 1980. The news of Princess Anne's second pregnancy is leaked (→ 15/5/81).

London, 12 November 1980. The Queen opens the general synod, praising the Church of England's new Alternative Service Book.

London, December 1980. Frances Shand Kydd, the mother of Lady Diana Spencer, complains of the constant press harassment of her daughter (→ 2/1/81).

Sandringham, 2 January 1981. Much to the distress of the Queen, the press invades her estate on rumours of the engagement of the Prince of Wales to Lady Diana Spencer (→ 5/2).

London, January 1981. Princess Alice, the Countess of Athlone, the

eldest surviving grandchild of Queen Victoria, dies aged 97. She was the only daughter of Prince Leopold (1853-1884)], the Duke of Albany, a younger brother of King Edward VII, and his wife Princess Helen (1861-1922).

London, 5 February 1981. The Prince of Wales proposes to Lady Diana Spencer at Buckingham Palace (→ 24/2).

London, 17 February 1981. Princess Anne is appointed chancellor of London university on the resignation of her grandmother, the Queen Mother, who, at 80, felt it was time to retire (→ 10/1981).

London, 23 April 1981. Princess Michael of Kent gives birth to her second child, Gabriella Marina Alexandra Ophelia (→ 17/4/85).

London, 15 May 1981. Princess Anne gives birth to her second child, a daughter, Zara Anne Elizabeth Phillips (→ 6/6).

London, 11 June 1981. The Queen opens the National Westminster Tower, Europe's tallest building.

London, 14 September 1981. Marcus Sergeant, the 17-year-old youth, who fired blank shots at the Queen during the trooping of the colour parade earlier this year, is found guilty and jailed for five years.

Egypt, 12 October 1981. The Prince of Wales attends the funeral of President Sadat, who was assassinated on 6 October.

London, October 1981. Princess Anne is installed as chancellor of London university; she refuses to accept an honorary degree.

Britain, 28 February 1982. The *Sun* newspaper publishes pictures of the Princess of Wales, who is pregnant, in a bikini on holiday (→ 28/6).

London, 3 March 1982. The Queen opens a long-awaited arts complex in the Barbican area of the City. It has taken 11 years to build and cost £154 million.

Ottawa, Canada, 17 April 1982. The Queen signs an act transferring sovereignty of the 1867 Canadian constitution from Britain to Canada.→

Windsor, 8 June 1982. The Queen goes riding in the home park with the American president, Ronald Reagan (→ 1/3/83).

London, 28 June 1982. The Prince and Princess of Wales announce the name of their son, born on 21 June: William Arthur Philip Louis.→

Southampton, 11 July 1982. The Prince of Wales welcomes the liner *Canberra,* which is bringing back servicemen from the conflict in the Falklands (→ 17/9).

London, 19 July 1982. The Queen's bodyguard, Commander Michael Trestrail, resigns after admitting to a homosexual affair.

The Solent, 11 October 1982. The wreck of the *Mary Rose,* King Henry VIII's flagship, is raised from the seabed mud where she has lain since she sank in 1545.

West Indies, 12 October 1982. Prince Andrew has to cut short a holiday with his actress friend Koo Stark because of excessive media attention (→ 22/2/83).

London, January 1983. Princess Anne is appointed patron of the Royal Tournament.

California, 1 March 1983. The Queen and Prince Philip visit President Reagan on his ranch.

Britain, 30 June 1983. Princess Anne is appointed colonel-in-chief of the Royal Scots Regiment.

Delhi, 24 November 1983. The Queen presents the insignia of the Order of Merit to Mother Teresa of Calcutta, who has devoted her life to caring for the poor of India.

Britain, 14 April 1983. Princess Anne, with her sporting interest, becomes president of the British Olympic Association (→ 20/2/89).

London, 15 September 1984. The Princess of Wales gives birth to her second son, Henry Charles Albert David.→

Netherlands, 30 September 1984. The Prince of Wales, as colonel-in-chief of the Parachute Regiment, attends a service for the 40th anniversary of the Battle of Arnhem.

United States, 7 October 1984. The Queen visits a horse stud farm in Lexington, Kentucky, during her trip to the United States.

Windsor, 21 December 1984. Prince Henry Charles Albert David is christened in St George's chapel.

Britain, September 1985. Princess Anne becomes patron of the Lady Jockeys' Association of Great Britain.

Britain, September 1985. The Prince of Wales is appointed president of the "Business in the Community" programme, an organisation designed to encourage business development within British cities (→ 12/1985).

Tanzania, 18 November 1985. Princess Anne arrives at Dar-es-Salaam to begin a month-long tour of Tanzania, Mozambique, Zambia and the Sudan as part of the famine relief campaign (→ 1988).

Britain, 1985. The Princess of Wales is appointed colonel-in-chief of the Royal Hampshire Regiment.

Prince Charles is linked to new romance

Lady Diana with two of her pupils.

Cowes, August 1980

Prince Charles has a new love in his life. She is Lady Diana Spencer, the youngest daughter of John, Earl Spencer, the owner of Althorp in Northamptonshire and a former equerry to George VI. Lady Diana, aged 19, was the prince's guest for the traditional visit by the royal yacht *Britannia* to the sailing regatta at Cowes on the Isle of Wight. The pretty kindergarten assistant, who shares a flat in central London with three other girls, was seen earlier this summer watching the prince play polo at Midhurst in Sussex. Until now "royal watchers" have assumed she was just another in the long list of girls dated by the prince. However, an invitation to Balmoral this autumn is a further sign of royal approval. The prince, now 31, has said that 30 is a good age to marry.

Lucia Santa Cruz, the daughter of the then Chilean ambassador, was a friend of the prince at Cambridge, but the 1970s saw a host of aristocratic and showbiz girlfriends for the "world's most eligible bachelor". The *Daily Express* trumpeted his engagement to Princess Marie-Astrid of Luxembourg, but it was not to be. His last love was Anna Wallace, but he has also been linked with Amanda Knatchbull (Lord Mountbatten's granddaughter), Lady Jane Wellesley, Davina Sheffield, Sabrina Guinness, the film actress Susan George and Diana's elder sister, Lady Sarah Spencer (→ 12/1980).

Queen kept waiting on Moroccan visit

Morocco, 30 October 1980

The Queen is at the centre of an angry diplomatic incident today, at the end of her North African tour. On her three-day visit to Morocco she has repeatedly been kept waiting by King Hassan, who insisted on making last-minute changes to the tour schedule.

First, he played golf rather than joining her for a welcoming lunch, then he dismissed two of her senior ladies-in-waiting when he arrived at the guest palace. When she had been kept waiting for 30 minutes in her car before a state banquet, her private secretary Sir Philip Moore told reporters confidentially: "The Queen has never been so angry."

The erratic ruler left the Queen sweltering in the desert prior to a picnic lunch and then arrived an hour late for dinner on the royal yacht. Even so, several big contracts for British firms did get the go-ahead from the desert ruler.

Charles writes book for young children

London, December 1980

Prince Charles has demonstrated another facet of his talents this month with the publication of a children's book. The prince, better known for his "action man" image, wrote the illustrated book, *The Old Man of Lochnagar*, to amuse his brothers, Andrew and Edward, some years ago during their annual summer cruise on the *Britannia*. It has now been published to raise money for a Covent Garden appeal and is certain to be a bestseller.

The story centres around a grumpy old man who leaves his cave in the Scottish hills in search of adventure. Prince Charles has an affection for Lochnagar, which overlooks the Balmoral estate, and has often hunted stag around its craggy outcrops. Ironically, the last royal to write a bestseller was Queen Victoria, whose diaries centred on her days in the Scottish Highlands around Balmoral.

The world's most eligible bachelor: some women in the life of the Prince of Wales

September 1972: a young Prince Charles with his first girlfriend, Lucia Santa Cruz, whom he met while at Trinity college, Cambridge.

Davina Sheffield: a friend of Charles in the mid-1970s.

Lady Jane Wellesley, a close friend for several years.

Princess Marie-Astrid: reported as engaged to Charles in 1977.

Lady Sarah Spencer: she shared Charles's love of outdoor sports.

Charles is engaged to 'Shy Di', at 19 a woman destined one day to be queen

Youth shoots at Queen

The prince and his fiancée: Charles and "Shy Di" after the announcement.

London, 24 February 1981
Months of speculation about the latest love in the life of Prince Charles were ended today when Buckingham Palace announced his engagement to 19-year-old Lady Diana Spencer. The 15-second statement, issued on behalf of the Queen by her press secretary Michael Shea, said simply: "It is with the greatest pleasure that the Queen and the Duke of Edinburgh announce the betrothal of their beloved son, the Prince of Wales, to the Lady Diana Spencer, daughter of the Earl Spencer and the Honourable Mrs Shand Kydd."

Lady Diana, who has earned the title "Shy Di" because of her habit of dropping her head whilst being photographed, is a popular choice with the public because of her innocent charm and sense of humour. However, she comes from the aristocratic top drawer, tracing her roots to Henry VII and Charles II. At the interviews following the engagement, Lady Diana displayed her £28,500 sapphire and diamond ring while Prince Charles dismissed the 12-year age gap, saying: "I just feel you're as young as you think you are. Diana will certainly help keep me young. I think I shall be exhausted." When asked if they were in love, Lady Diana replied instantly: "Of course" while the prince was more circumspect. "Whatever "in love" means," he said. Lady Diana, who now has two armed Scotland Yard bodyguards, has left her bachelor flat in Earl's Court, initially for Buckingham Palace, to ensure her security – and privacy (→ 30/7).

Stepping out: Charles and Diana in September, after their wedding.

London, 14 June 1981
The Queen had a narrow escape from injury yesterday when a youth fired six blank shots at her during the traditional Trooping of the Colour parade. She struggled to control her horse, Burmese, as the shots – two spaced, the rest bunched – rang out from the ranks of spectators lining the Mall.

As Prince Philip and Prince Charles rode up to protect the Queen, Marcus Sergeant, an unemployed 17-year-old, was grabbed by police and soldiers. With shouts of "hang the bastard" clearly audible, the Queen, dressed in the uniform of the Welsh Guards, calmly continued with the review of the troops on Horseguards Parade. The only casualty was her Order of the Garter insignia which was jolted from her tunic as Burmese reared up. However it was quickly recovered, and the Queen was able to wear it for the traditional balcony appearance with other members of the royal family, who included Lady Diana Spencer for the first time.

While the Queen was uninjured she was certainly shaken by her ordeal and told her family later that she had been aware of the black revolver coming up in the crowd long before the shots were fired. When she was not hit, she feared for the safety of her husband, son and the escort who were riding behind her. "I didn't know what was happening," she said (→ 14/9).

Police race to grab the young man who fired six blank shots at the queen.

Anne and Mark opt for unroyal 'Zara'

London, 6 June 1981
Princess Anne and Captain Mark Phillips have taken "royal watchers" by surprise with the choice of names for their baby daughter. The Queen's second grandchild will be called Zara Anne Elizabeth. Like her brother Peter, Zara, who was born on 15 May, will not be given a royal title. "She is not royal, the Queen just happens to be their grandmother," says Anne.

Snow strands the Queen in Cotswolds

Old Sodbury, 13 December 1981
The Queen took refuge in a village pub for seven hours today after her car was stranded in waist-high snow drifts. She arrived at the two-star *Cross Hands Hotel* at Old Sodbury, near Bristol, wearing gumboots and a headscarf. "I could hardly believe it," said the manager, Roberto Cadel. The Queen was returning to Windsor after visiting Princess Anne's home.

Charles marries Lady Diana in fairy-tale wedding

A shy commoner becomes a princess

London, 30 July 1981

A commoner turned into a princess at 11.15am yesterday when Lady Diana Spencer married the Prince of Wales at St Paul's cathedral. The service, which was watched by 750 million TV viewers around the world, was attended by virtually every crowned head of Europe and many world leaders.

The new princess's best-kept secret – her wedding dress – was revealed for the first time as she stepped from the Glass Coach after making the 20-minute journey from Clarence House. Designed by David and Elizabeth Emanuel, the cream silk gown had a huge 25-foot (7.6-metre)-long train. Dr Robert Runcie, the archbishop of Canterbury, who officiated at the ceremony, later described the occasion as a "fairy-tale". As she made her vows the princess muddled the order of her husband's names, calling him "Philip Charles Arthur George". The day ended with celebrations at Buckingham Palace before the couple left for their honeymoon at Broadlands (→9/12).

Prince Charles steals a kiss: the royal couple on the balcony of Buckingham Palace after the wedding ceremony.

Queen asks press for more privacy

London, 9 December 1981

The Queen yesterday summoned Fleet Street editors to Buckingham Palace to discuss persistent press harassment of the royal family, especially the Princess of Wales. The meeting, the first for 25 years, was called because of growing concern about the strain on the princess, who is expecting her first child next year and has recently moved into her new home of Highgrove, in Gloucestershire. The royal press secretary, Michael Shea, told editors that it would be a pity if her future attitude towards the press were conditioned by the behaviour of maverick members of the media. The editors, who agreed to review their policy, later discussed press and palace relations with the Queen (→28/2/82).

A fairy-tale wedding: the bride and groom greet the crowds from the state landau as they are driven from St Paul's back to Buckingham Palace.

At the altar: the royal couple take their vows before the archbishop.

Intruder shocks Queen

London, 9 July 1982

A top-level Scotland Yard investigation was under way tonight after an intruder broke into Buckingham Palace and spent ten minutes in the Queen's bedroom while she vainly tried to raise the alarm. An unemployed north London labourer, Michael Fagan, climbed in through an unlocked window, evading police patrols and electronic security devices as he made his way along the picture gallery, through the throne room and finally into the Queen's private quarters.

He awakened the Queen, who telephoned the police lodge twice to call for help. It was only when her footman, Paul Whybrew, returned from walking her corgis that Fagan was held. Incredibly, this is the second that time Fagan has entered the palace. He broke in last month just hours before the US president, Ronald Reagan, arrived on the pal-

Palace intruder: Michael Fagan.

ace lawns. Fagan has only been charged with the first offence. The home secretary, William Whitelaw, has ordered Scotland Yard to make a full inquiry into royal security.

Queen proclaims end to old colonial ties

Ottawa, 17 April 1982

With a ceremonial flourish, Queen Elizabeth ended 18 months of bitter national debate as she today proclaimed Canada's new constitution. For the prime minister, Pierre Trudeau, this vindicated a long struggle to strengthen the federal government and end Britain's anachronistic right to approve amendments to the Canadian constitution. But Quebec's René Lévesque, the only provincial premier who refused to sign the accord, claimed that Canada has abandoned Quebec and, in doing so, dealt confederation a critical blow. The Anglo-French tension within the nation thus seems unresolved (→ 1/7/90).

Pope makes first visit to the Queen

London, 28 May 1982

Pope John Paul II, on the first visit by a pope to Britain for 450 years, arrived at Buckingham Palace today to meet the Queen. He spent 35 minutes alone with her. The Queen, who is the supreme governor of the Church of England, did not wear black, as she did in Rome in 1980, but wore long white gloves as a gesture of formality. "I will pray for your son in the Falklands," the pope said, before giving her a bas-relief of Christ on the cross. The warmth of the meeting underlines the desire of the individuals heading the two churches to improve inter-church relations (→ 29/4/85).

Andrew returns as Falklands war hero

Portsmouth, 16 September 1982

With a red rose clenched between his teeth, Prince Andrew arrived home a Falklands hero today. The Queen, Prince Philip and Princess Anne sailed from Portsmouth for an emotional reunion on board his ship, HMS *Invincible,* where he had served as the pilot of a Sea King helicopter during the conflict.

As soon as the aircraft carrier docked he bounded down the gangway to be met by an outburst of cheering from the crowds. Later the royal sub-lieutenant, now 22, revealed that his most dangerous role during the war was using his helicopter to act as a decoy for deadly Exocet missiles fired by Argentinian jets at British Task Force ships. He was airborne when the *Atlantic Conveyor* supply ship was hit by an enemy missile and helped rescue sailors from the sea. "It was horrific and terrible and something I will never forget," he said. "It was probably my most frightening moment of the war."

Before he sailed in April the prince faced political pressure to stay at home as it was feared he would be the enemy's number one target. So it proved – the Argentinian press regularly announced that Andrew's ship had been sunk. However, the prince was determined to be treated like any other member of his helicopter squadron and obey orders to sail to the South Atlantic (→ 12/10).

The hero returns: Prince Andrew with a red rose, back from the Falklands.

A prince is born: Diana has her first child

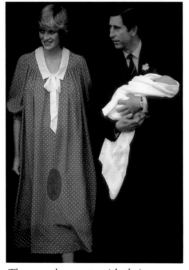

The proud parents with their son.

London, 28 June 1982

The Prince and Princess of Wales today finally chose the names for their baby son – the first child to be born to a Prince and Princess of Wales since 1905. He will be called William Arthur Philip Louis and is second in line of succession to the throne. Prince William was born at St Mary's hospital, Paddington, at 9.03pm on 21 June. He weighed in at 7lb 10oz (3.5kg) and had, according to the proud father, "a wisp of fair hair, sort of blondish, and blue eyes". Diana followed modern royal tradition by having her child outside Buckingham Palace, but the gynaecologist George Pinker, who delivered Princess Anne's children, led the medical team (→ 1/1983).

Charity work gives princess new image

London, 15 November 1982

Princess Anne returned home from a gruelling six-nation tour of Africa and the Middle East today – and for once left Fleet Street speechless in admiration. The Queen's only daughter, once dubbed "Princess Sourpuss" and the "Naff off royal" after clashes with the media, has seen a remarkable transformation in her image through her role as president of the Save the Children Fund. During the 14,000-mile (22,400-km) tour she saw starving children in refugee camps in Somalia, braved war-torn Beirut and visited primitive hospitals in Swaziland (→ 23/9/85).

Palace to sue over 'Queen Koo' saga

London, 22 February 1983
The Queen today took the unprecedented step of slapping a legal injunction on a former Buckingham Palace servant for revealing royal secrets. Her decision, made after consulting senior courtiers and her solicitors, follows revelations in the tabloid newspaper the *Sun* about life at Buckingham Palace. Under the headline "Queen Koo's Romps at the Palace", Kiernan Kenny, aged 20, the former palace stores officer, told of the alleged behaviour of Prince Andrew and his girlfriend, the former soft porn actress Koo Stark.

While there is little love lost between the *Sun* and the palace, senior courtiers made it clear today that the unusual action was taken because Kenny, like other royal servants, had signed an undertaking of confidence as a condition of his employment at the palace. By speaking to a newspaper he had breached his legal contract. It means that the next newspaper instalment, promoted as "Barefoot Diana buttered my toast", has been legally stopped by the Queen.

However, the move is seen by royal insiders as the palace's revenge for the *Sun*'s decision to take pictures of the pregnant Diana romping in her bikini on a Caribbean beach. A palace aide called their publication "in the worst possible taste" (→ 3/11/88).

Diana is a hit on her first overseas tour

Auckland, 27 April 1983
The Princess of Wales flew home today at the end of a triumphant first overseas tour. Her disarming smile and charming manner certainly won the hearts of the people of Australia and New Zealand. She arrived with Prince Charles in Alice Springs a nervous royal novice, but six weeks and 45,000 miles (72,000km) later the princess has proved herself to be a royal veteran.

More than one million people have turned out to greet the royal couple on their marathon journey. They warmed to Diana's decision to bring baby William along rather than leave him behind at Kensington Palace. Besides their son, the royal couple also brought their own hairdresser, bodyguards, dressers, valets, secretaries and butler. But most attention has been focused on Diana's stunning wardrobe, which weighed an estimated three tons. Her style has helped to revive the

Charles and Diana in Auckland.

British fashion industry while the royal couple's popularity has considerably subdued republican sentiments which have been growing Down Under (→ 15/9/84).

Slimming rumours 'appalling' says palace

London, January 1983
Buckingham Palace has dismissed as "appalling" rumours that the Princess of Wales is suffering from the "slimmers' disease" anorexia nervosa. The stories, in several tabloid newspapers, quote family friends as expressing their concern for Diana's health. Since the birth of Prince William she has drastically lost weight, and "royal watch-

ers" have noted that her sister Sarah once had the illness, going from 112 to 82 pounds (51-37kg). The latest round of rumours only serves to highlight the intense pressure placed upon the princess, now 21, since she arrived on the royal scene. Media stories have accused her of being a "shopaholic" and blamed her for a staff exodus from Kensington Palace (→ 28/4).

Edward follows in brother's footsteps

Cambridge, October 1983
Prince Edward followed in his eldest brother's footsteps this month when he started at Cambridge university. Like Prince Charles he will read anthropology and archaeology, but he admits that he is not academic and already shows interest in the local student theatre and rugby team. He has his own room at Jesus college and, while he is happy to get around Cambridge on a push-bike like other students, he is followed everywhere by an armed bodyguard. Edward, who was head boy of Gordonstoun school, is committed to joining the Royal Marines when his course ends (→ 6/1/87).

Surgeons operate on Queen Mother

London, 22 November 1982
The Queen Mother was rushed to hospital for an emergency operation last night when a fish-bone lodged in her throat. The drama happened when the Queen Mother, who is 82, was hosting a dinner party for friends at Royal Lodge, Windsor. As she ate a trout, she was suddenly convulsed by a fit of choking, gasping for breath and unable to swallow. She was taken to King Edward VII Hospital for Officers in London for an urgent operation to remove the obstruction.

Enjoying a close relationship: the Queen and US President Ronald Reagan (left) taking a peaceful early morning ride in Windsor great park in June 1982, while (right) her majesty makes a deadpan joke which has the president in stitches during a royal visit to California in March 1983.

Charles slams plan for gallery wing

Hampton Court, 30 May 1984
Prince Charles launched a stinging attack on modern architects and architecture tonight. In the most outspoken and heartfelt speech of his royal career, the prince singled out the proposed extension to the National Gallery for special scorn. He described the design, by Peter Ahrends, as "a kind of vast municipal fire station ... like a monstrous carbuncle on the face of a much-loved and elegant friend".

Ironically the prince's speech, at Hampton Court palace, was given for the 150th anniversary dinner of the Royal Institute of British Architects. Members of his audience listened in stunned silence as the prince made an impassioned assault on their profession. He told them: "A large number of us have developed a feeling that architects tend to design houses for the approval of fellow architects and critics – not for the tenants."

The prince, who wrote the speech after discussions with community architects, urged planners to involve local communities at the planning stage and listen to their ideas. He added that architects did not have a monopoly on taste, style and planning. The speech has caused a rumpus. His remarks were condemned by Peter Ahrends as offensive, reactionary and ill-considered (→ 1/12/87).

Princess is shocked by Nazi revelations

London, 17 April 1985
A shocked Princess Michael of Kent spoke today of her deep shame at learning that her father was in Hitler's feared Nazi SS. The princess, in her first interview about revelations of her father's past, said that the news came as "a very great blow because I had always hero worshipped him". She pointed out that her father, Baron Günther von Reibnitz, only held an honorary position of ranger within the fascist organisation and had no involvement with concentration camps. The scandal is the latest controversy associated with the Czech-born princess, whom the press has nicknamed "Princess Pushy."

A family portrait of the Kents.

Anne appeals for immediate famine aid

Anne: crusading against famine.

Inverness, 23 September 1985
Princess Anne today urged famine relief agencies to be better organised and focus aid where it is needed. The princess, who has earned international respect for her work for the Save the Children Fund, told a conference of 60 Third World countries that planning was the key to overcoming famine. She said: "Drought and famine are not new in Africa. Their effect can be moderated with sensible and basic precautions and planning by everybody." Her speech comes two months after the Live Aid concert [*see photograph opposite*] which was organised by the Irish rock star Bob Geldof to help Africa's starving millions (→ 18/11).

Charles and Diana give first TV interview

London, 21 October 1985
The Prince and Princess of Wales held 20 million TV viewers enthralled last night in their first interview since their engagement. During the 45-minute chat at Kensington palace they told the interviewer Sir Alastair Burnet about their marriage and family life. Diana admitted that she saw her role as that of wife, mother and "supporter" to her husband and confessed that she missed her children terribly when she was on tours. The royal couple also used the prime-time show to dispel a number of rumours. Charles was eager to point out that he did not try to contact Lord Mountbatten with a ouija board, while the princess denied that she was a fashion-conscious "shopaholic" or felt any rivalry with Princess Anne.

The couple, who allowed the cameras to follow them at Highgrove and at Kensington palace, were persuaded to appear on TV by the Queen Mother, who feels that television puts over a positive view of the royal family. The Queen is now cooperating in a film about the Commonwealth (→ 22/9/86).

Andrew sprays paint on US press corps

Los Angeles, 21 April 1984
Prince Andrew flew home from California yesterday to face a royal row over his disastrous first official visit to America. His five-day tour, described by one US commentator as "the most unpleasant royal visit since they burnt the White House in 1812", went badly wrong when he sprayed a group of American photographers with white paint. The incident happened when he took a spray gun from a painter during a visit to the black ghetto of Watts in Los Angeles and aimed it at the cameramen. He belatedly apologised, claiming it was an accident. Diplomats monitoring the visit believe the incident has harmed the royal family's US image.

Ill-advised: Prince Andrew's prank.

Second son born to Princess of Wales

London, 15 September 1984
The Princess of Wales gave birth to her second son, Prince Henry Charles Albert David, today at St Mary's hospital in Paddington. The baby prince, who was born at 4.20pm and weighed a healthy 6lb 14oz (3kg), will be known as Prince Harry and is third in line to the throne. Charles, who was present at his second son's birth, told well-wishers as he left: "We've nearly got a full polo team now." His wife's pregnancy has been difficult. She suffered badly from morning sickness and then developed a craving for bacon-and-tomato sandwiches (→ 21/12).

Margaret has tests on suspect lung

London, 7 January 1985
Princess Margaret is recovering tonight after a cancer scare operation. She was given a clean bill of health after part of her left lung was removed for tests. The operation, conducted at the Brompton hospital in west London, was performed by a team of surgeons including the Queen's physician, Dr John Batten. Her close friend, the publisher Norman Lonsdale, said: "I hope this will convince her to give up smoking." Margaret has a history of bronchitis and lung ailments, and the last four kings, one of them her father, George VI, ultimately died of smoking-related diseases.

William is eager pupil as he starts school

London, 24 September 1985
Prince William was so eager to start his first morning at nursery school today that his mother, the Princess of Wales, had to drag him back so that he could wave to the waiting army of photographers. Once that chore was over the prince, aged three, dashed down the stairs to his new classroom.

The £200-a-term school in Chepstow Villas is just five minutes drive away from Kensington palace; Diana chose it herself after drawing up a shortlist and interviewing the principals. The headmistress, Jane Mynor, was waiting to greet the prince when he arrived punctually with his parents.

She then introduced him to 12 other members of Cygnet class as simply "William". Later the princess was asked whether her son had enjoyed his first day at school. "Yes indeed," she said, "he is very grown up." William is the first heir to the throne to mix with ordinary children at such a tender age. Prince Charles was the first heir to the throne to be educated at a school, but he began in traditional mode with lessons at Buckingham Palace from a governess until he was eight years old. He spent two terms at a Knightsbridge prep school as a day boy before going to his father's old schools, first at Cheam and then Gordonstoun (→ 21/10).

Royal hairdresser sells his memoirs

London, 4 February 1985
The Princess of Wales was angry and upset last night after her former hairdresser betrayed her trust. Kevin Shanley sold his story about life with the princess to a Sunday newspaper for £30,000. While Tory MPs described him as a "rat", his partner Richard Dalton resigned from the salon. Dalton has taken over the job of royal crimper and felt he could no longer work with the man who "cut and told". Shanley was not covered by agreements of confidentiality (→ 31/7/90).

Queen stops prince from meeting pope

Vatican, 29 April 1985
The Prince and Princess of Wales were at the centre of a religious row today after a private Mass with the pope was cancelled. Vatican sources insisted that the Queen, acting as head of the Church of England, ordered the ban for fear of provoking a Protestant backlash in Britain. If the Mass, due to be held in the Vatican, had gone ahead it would have been the first time a future British king had attended Mass since Henry VIII split with Rome in the 16th century.

Diana sparkles on her Australian visit

Having a ball: Charles and Diana.

Melbourne, 1 November 1985
The Princess of Wales caused a sensation last night when she wore a £2 million emerald and diamond choker as an Indian-squaw-style headband. Party guests at a banquet in Melbourne burst into spontaneous applause in appreciation of Diana's sense of style. However, the real credit for the imaginative use of Queen Mary's heirloom jewels goes to her hairdresser, Richard Dalton. During the visit Australians have seen changes in Diana. Her initial tour nerves have been replaced by the confidence and exuberance of a young woman now clearly enjoying the limelight.

Charles fears a 'divided Britain'

London, December 1985
The Prince of Wales has been at the centre of political controversy this year after private remarks he made about the future of Britain became public. His friend, the community architect Rod Hackney, revealed in October that the prince does not wish to rule over a "divided Britain". These remarks were seized on by the Labour Party as a direct attack on Margaret Thatcher's style of government.

The prince had discussed his fears during dinner on board the royal train after a day when he and Hackney had toured Duchy of Cornwall estates. Hackney later told reporters: "He is very worried that when he becomes king there will be "no-go" areas in the inner cities and that the racial minorities will be alienated from the rest of the country. He does not want to become king in an atmosphere like that." Palace officials sought to put a gloss on the words by stressing that he "is doing everything possible to find a solution to the problem". However, political sources said that the prime minister, who first heard the reports while she was in Washington, angrily telephoned the prince to seek an explanation. The row adds fuel to the claim, officially denied, that the royal family are at odds with Mrs Thatcher's government (→ 3/1988).

Anne's ride raises thousands for disabled

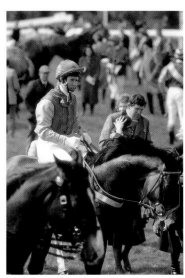

Charity rider: Anne after the race.

Epsom, 23 April 1985
Princess Anne turned royal jockey today when she was one of the riders in a charity race over the historic Derby course at Epsom. The princess, who had trained four times a week to prepare for the mile-and-a-half race, came a creditable fourth on Against the Grain. After the race she said: "I was immediately concious that I wasn't going fast enough when I came out of the stalls." However her efforts raised more than £30,000 for the Riding for the Disabled charity of which she is president. The princess, who was a member of the British Olympic Equestrian team in 1976, now plans to train for races on the flat as well as steeplechases.

July 13. Helping to feed the world: Diana and Charles in the royal box at Wembley Stadium with the singer Bob Geldof, who set up today's huge Live Aid concert to raise funds for the victims of famine in Africa.

Elizabeth II
1952–

Australia, 2 March 1986. The Queen signs the Australia Bill in Canberra, formally severing the nation's last constitutional links with Britain.

London, 19 March 1986. Prince Andrew announces his engagement to Sarah Ferguson, aged 27, the daughter of Major Ronald Ferguson, the manager of the Prince of Wales's polo team, and his first wife, Susan (now Mrs Hector Barrantes) (→ 23/7).

Windsor, 29 April 1986. The Duchess of Windsor, who died four days ago, is buried at Frogmore alongside her husband, the Duke of Windsor (→ 3/4/87).

Japan, mid-May 1986. The Prince and Princess of Wales pay an official visit.

London, 25 May 1986. The Prince and Princess of Wales meet the torchbearer in the charity "Race Against Time" before he sets off as part of Bob Geldof's latest idea to raise money for famine relief.

Westminster, 23 July 1986. Prince Andrew marries Sarah Ferguson and is created Duke of York.→

China, 12 October 1986. The Queen and Prince Philip arrive in Beijing on the first visit to China by a British monarch (→ 14/10).

China, 14 October 1986. The Queen and Prince Philip walk along the Great Wall (→ 18/10).

Britain, 27 November 1986. A report claims that King George V's doctor possibly relieved his final hours of suffering with cocaine and morphine.

Middle East, November 1986. The Prince and Princess of Wales begin their first visit to the Gulf States; they will visit Oman, Qatar, Bahrain and Saudi Arabia.

Gloucestershire, February 1987. Prince Edward, who left the Royal Marines last month, takes refuge with his sister, Anne, while he decides on his future (→ 15/6).

Belgium, 7 March 1987. The Prince of Wales meets the survivors of the Zeebrugge ferry disaster, which happened yesterday.

London, 3 April 1987. The Duchess of Windsor's lavish jewel collection is sold at auction for charity and raises £31,380,197.

Britain, 5 April 1987. It is revealed that two of the Queen Mother's female cousins have been in a mental home since 1941.

London, 13 June 1987. Princess Anne finally gives in to family pressure and accepts the title of Princess Royal which has been vacant since the death of Princess Mary in 1965.→

Britain, 24 February 1988. According to a survey the Queen is the richest person in the world, with a personal fortune of £3,340 million (→ 29/1/90).

Thailand, February 1988. The Prince and Princess of Wales visit Bangkok to celebrate the King of Thailand's 60th birthday.

London, 22 March 1988. The Prince of Wales urges the government to take drastic action against pollution.

United States, March 1988. The Prince of Wales attends a "Remaking Cities" conference in Pittsburgh.

Switzerland, 27 June 1988. A Swiss examining magistrate blames the Prince of Wales and his skiing party for causing the avalanche in which Major Hugh Lindsay, a royal equerry and personal friend of the prince, was killed last March.

Denmark, 2 August 1988. As patron of the Renaissance Theatre Trust, the Prince of Wales attends a performance of *Hamlet* at Helsingor, Shakespeare's Elsinore.

London, 8 August 1988. The Duchess of York – nicknamed "Fergie" in the popular press – gives birth to her first child, Beatrice Elizabeth Mary (→ 18/10).

Florence, 28 October 1988. Pietro Annigoni, the artist who rose to international fame with his two portraits of the Queen, dies aged 78.

London, 3 November 1988. Koo Stark, the actress friend of Prince Andrew, wins damages of £300,000 in a libel case against the *Sunday People*; it alleged that she had an affair with the prince after her marriage to Timothy Jeffries (→ 16/11).

London, 16 November 1988 The *Sun* newspaper agrees to pay £100,000 to charity after publishing one of the Queen's private photographs without her permission earlier this year.→

London, 20 December 1988. Princess Beatrice, the first child of the Duke and Duchess of York, is baptised (→ 23/3/90).

Gloucestershire, 21 Dec 1988. The Princess Royal arranges a surprise belated 40th birthday party for her husband, Mark Phillips, at their home, Gatcombe Park (→ 9/4/89).

London, 24 December 1988. The Queen alters her Christmas Day broadcast to include a message of sympathy for those involved in the recent tragedies in Armenia, Clapham and Lockerbie (→ 4/1/89).

London, 1988. The Princess Royal accepts the anonymous gift of a greyhound, in the name of the Save the Children Fund; all his winnings will go to the charity.

Britain, 29 January 1989. Prince Philip is severely criticised by many former British soldiers and prisoners of war of the Japanese for his decision to attend the funeral next month of Emperor Hirohito of Japan.

London, 20 February 1989. Princess Anne, the Princess Royal, launches a fund-raising campaign for the British Olympic Association, which hopes to raise money for Manchester to host the 1996 Olympic Games.

Northumberland, 13 April 1989. The Princess of Wales is involved in a minor security scare today during a royal walkabout when a 57-year-old man in the crowd lunges forward to greet her.

London, 23 March 1990. The Duchess of York gives birth to her second daughter, Princess Eugénie Victoria.→

Gloucestershire, 28 June 1990. The Prince of Wales breaks his arm in an awkward fall from his pony while playing in a polo match near Cirencester (→ 29/6).

London, 28 June 1990. The Queen Mother's 90th birthday celebrations begin a few days early when the evening rush-hour traffic is brought to a standstill when 16,000 people attended her official parade down Horse Guards Parade and the Mall (→ 1/8).

London, 4 August 1990. The Queen Mother celebrates her 90th birthday amid great pomp and ceremony.

Gloucestershire, 22 October 1990. Princess Anne is caught speeding at Stow-on-the-Wold and is banned from driving.

Opposite: Popular as ever – the Queen on her 60th birthday.

Angry Maoris hurl eggs at the Queen

Saddened: after the incident.

Auckland, 23 February 1986
The Queen was today pelted with eggs thrown by pro-Maori protesters. She was visibly shaken as one egg spattered on her thigh and ran down her pink coat. A second egg shattered against the windscreen of her open vehicle. Prince Philip, who was with her in the "Queenmobile", helped her wipe off the mess during a driveabout among 42,000 schoolchildren at Ellerslie racecourse, Auckland. Two white-coated women, who had been posing as officials, ran a gauntlet of abuse from the angry crowd as they were arrested.

Duchess of Windsor dies in Paris at 90

Paris, 24 April 1986
The Duchess of Windsor died peacefully at her home outside Paris today. Now the woman who shook the House of Windsor to its foundations will have her dearest wish granted – to lie beside her husband, the Duke of Windsor, in the royal burial grounds at Windsor castle. For the American divorcée who was never accepted by the royal family in life has joined their ranks in death.

In the end the duchess, who had been bedridden for years, was a sad and lonely figure, the days when she dazzled high society long gone. She was the woman whom Edward VIII loved so much that he gave up his kingdom and went into exile. While the Queen Mother is said to blame his abdication for the premature death of George VI, she will bury this feud when she attends the duchess's funeral (→ 29/4).

Royal yacht rescue

Aden, 21 January 1986
The royal yacht *Britannia* today sailed to the rescue of refugees fleeing from fighting in war-torn Aden. Launches from the Queen's yacht repeatedly braved bullets to pick up hundreds of civilians waiting in the water or on the beaches. So far 1,082 evacuees from 50 nations, including 22 Britons, have been rescued by the 5,700-ton yacht. The foreign secretary, Sir Geoffrey Howe, led tributes by the Commons to the *Britannia's* role.

Prince Charles admits talking to plants

London, 22 September 1986
Prince Charles gave millions of TV viewers a personal tour of his gardens at Highgrove last night – and admitted that he talked to his plants. During the documentary Charles and Diana were seen on tour in Australia, Japan and America and playing with their children at Highgrove. A TV camera crew filmed their working and off-duty lives for a year to make the hour-long documentary.

The prince, who had ultimate editorial control, decided to go ahead with the controversial gardening sequence against the advice of royal courtiers, who fear he will be ridiculed. However, he did censor a scene showing his family swimming in the Highgrove pool. As he walked round his garden the prince admitted that his plants were like his own children. He says: "I go round and I examine them very carefully and occasionally talk to them, which I think is very important – they do respond in a funny way. If they die I feel deeply saddened" (→ 29/10/88).

Prince Andrew marries Sarah Ferguson

Andrew and Sarah, with family, on the palace balcony after the wedding.

London, 23 July 1986
It was the perfect end to a fairy-tale romance as 800 million TV viewers saw Prince Andrew marry Sarah Ferguson in Westminster abbey today. Watching from the wings was the Princess of Wales, who first brought the Queen's second son and the daughter of Prince Charles's polo manager together over lunch at Windsor castle during Ascot week. Even the Queen played her part, creating the bridegroom Duke of York, Earl of Inverness and Baron Killyeagh just 90 minutes before the wedding service.

However, as tradition decrees, it was the bride's day. She chose outfits for the pageboys and bridesmaids which reflected Andrew's naval career as well as her own ancestry, while her wedding dress, designed by Lindka Cierach, had an intertwined "S" and "A" design.

During the service the new duchess remained relaxed. When she first saw Andrew she said: "I've forgotten to pack my toothbrush." After the obligatory kiss on the balcony of Buckingham Palace they left for a honeymoon cruise on the royal yacht *Britannia* (→ 8/8/88).

Diana faints after opening Canadian Expo

Diana earlier on her Canadian tour.

Vancouver, 7 May 1986
The Princess of Wales dramatically fainted today after she and Prince Charles opened the Expo exhibition in Vancouver. The princess was overcome as she toured the California exhibition at the huge site. Officials accompanying Diana on her Canadian tour quickly pointed out that she was not pregnant, simply overcome by the stuffy atmosphere. However, the incident has again focused attention on her pencil-slim shape and her apparent lack of appetite. One royal insider claims that Diana has fainted five times already this year. Harold Brooks Baker, the managing director of *Burke's Peerage*, the "bible" of the aristocracy, said: "Everyone has been very worried. She eats less than a bird and the plain fact is she is under-nourished."

Philip upsets Chinese on first royal visit

Beijing, 18 October 1986
The Duke of Edinburgh put his foot in it today during the Queen's historic first visit to China by a British monarch with a remark about "slitty eyes". Prince Philip, notorious for his public gaffes, told students he found the capital Bejing [Peking] "ghastly", and he joked with one student: "If you stay here much longer you will go back with slitty eyes."

While Buckingham Palace officials were quick to play down his remarks the British press dubbed him the "Great Wally of China" for comments which could jeopardise future trading and diplomatic relations. However, his press secretary insisted that no insult to

the Chinese was intended. The royal press secretary, Michael Shea, said: "Jocular comments have been taken totally out of context." Philip made his howlers as he and the Queen chatted to a group of Edinburgh students learning Chinese in the city of Xiam.

As the row raged the prince sipped jasmine tea in a Taoist temple on the outskirts of Lunming and said ruefully: "I've got to do something right some time." When asked if he thought his remarks were tactless he replied: "No, I thought that the Edinburgh students were a little tactless." However, the prince is no stranger to controversy. He says: "You can't go on forever producing bromides and platitudes."

The royal couple in China: now Philip's tactless joke has upset their hosts.

Edward leaves Marines

Edward: quitting the Marines.

London, 6 January 1987
Prince Edward resigned from the Royal Marines today after just four months' training with the élite fighting force. Prince Philip, who is the Marines' honorary captain-general, is said to be furious with his 22-year-old son for failing to win the Commandos' coveted Green Beret. Today their commanding officer, Commandant-General Sir Michael Wilkins, spent two hours at Buckingham Palace trying to change Edward's mind. He was due to report back to his base at Lympstone, Devon, after the Christmas break, but officials said he had 'flu. Edward had been earmarked for the Marines before he went to Cambridge, but university life gave him new interests, notably in the theatre (→ 2/1987).

Anne granted title of Princess Royal

London, 13 June 1987
Princess Anne was today given the title of Princess Royal. This courtesy title – reserved for the eldest daughter of the monarch – has remained unused since the death of Princess Mary in 1965. The Queen has been keen to confer the title as her personal gift for Anne's tireless work for children at home and abroad. Anne will be only the seventh Princess Royal.

Charles and Diana put on united front

Charles and Diana: at odds?

West Berlin, 1 November 1987
The Prince and Princess of Wales were a couple united in the divided city of Berlin today. Amid rumours that their six-year marriage is in trouble, they put on a display of togetherness for the world. As the princess was mobbed by the crowd, Charles asked: "Are you all right darling?" He even changed a speech to make gallant remarks about his glamorous wife. Their public show of affection has defused stories that the couple are living separate lives, which started when Charles spent 33 days at Balmoral with friends, including an old flame, Lady "Kanga" Tryon, while Diana was in London (→ 18/10/88).

Young royals take part in 'It's a Knockout' television show

Staffordshire, 15 June 1987
Prince Edward dramatically stormed out of a press conference tonight at the end of a day's filming for a controversial TV game show. The prince, who resigned from the Royal Marines earlier this year, organised the royal version of "It's a Knockout", which was staged at Alton Towers theme park today. Princess Anne, the Duke and Duchess of York and a host of celebrities were involved in the games, which were based on a mediaeval theme. But Edward was hurt by the media's response when he asked about the show's success – and walked out amid accusations that the show trivialised the royals.

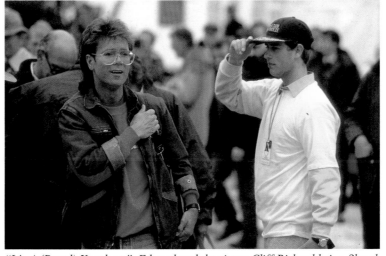
"It's A (Royal) Knockout": Edward and the singer Cliff Richard being filmed.

Royals young and old flock to celebrate the great bicentenary party in Australia

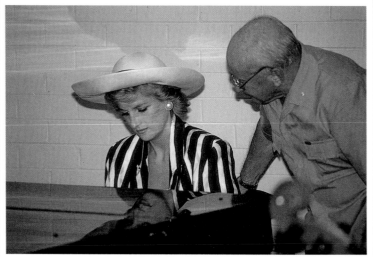

Diana tries her hand at the piano during a visit to a music school.

Canberra, 9 May 1988

The glitter of the young royals and the grace of the older ones has been as much a part of Australia's bicentenary year as the spectacles, the speeches, the protests and the parades.

It began in earnest on 26 January, with the celebration of the arrival of the First Fleet. A crowd of around 1.5 million crammed every vantage-point around Sydney harbour, and the Prince and Princess of Wales were at the very centre of the spectacle – watching the parade of tall ships, the air force fly-past and the fireworks display that transformed Sydney harbour bridge into a gigantic Roman candle. Charles told the crowd: "As history goes, 200 years is barely a heartbeat, yet look around you and see what has happened in that time – a whole new free country, Australia!"

In the ensuing days watching the young royals became as much an obsession as the bicentenary events themselves. Diana's hats, gowns and jewels, her every smile and blush and tiniest utterance were feasted on by the press. A great coup came in Melbourne, where Prince Charles tried his hand at the 'cello when visiting a music school. He was content with a few gentle strokes, but the Princess of Wales upstaged her husband by going to the piano and

launching into a Rachmaninov concerto for about 30 seconds. The performance earned her an impromptu kiss on the cheek from Professor Henri Touzeau. Meanwhile, the Duchess of York made it clear in London that her pregnancy will not stop her visit to Australia, due in October [*see story opposite*].

The Queen and Prince Philip arrived via Perth for today's great occasion, the opening of the new Parliament House in the capital, Canberra. The Queen unlocked its front door and later described the vast building on Capital Hill, overlooking the city, as a symbol of Australian unity and democracy.

On walkabout: the Queen and Prince Philip in Melbourne.

Charles escapes death in Swiss avalanche

Switzerland, 11 March 1988

Prince Charles escaped death by inches today when an avalanche engulfed his skiing party. The Queen's former equerry Major Hugh Lindsay was killed, and Charles's friend Patti Palmer-Tomkinson was critically injured, in the accident. The tragedy happened as the prince's party, including a Swiss guide, Bruno Sprecher, but not Diana, skied down the notorious off-piste black run known as the "wang" or "wall" at Klosters, Switzerland. They were overcome by a "whirling maelstrom" of snow which hurtled past the prince. The accident has renewed demands for the heir, who has come close to serious injury at polo, to give up dangerous sports (→ 27/6).

The royal couple come sadly home.

Charles's 'Luftwaffe' speech irks planners

London, 1 December 1987

Prince Charles took aim at planners again today, linking their work to the destruction wrought on Britain by Hitler's *Luftwaffe*. In a trenchant speech at the Mansion House he particularly focused on rebuilding around St Paul's cathedral and plans to redevelop the neighbouring Paternoster Square. He said that St Paul's was "without doubt one of the architectural wonders of the world" and went on to attack planning since the war, which he said had "wrecked the London skyline and desecrated the dome of St Paul's". Then he told his audi-

ence of City planners: "You have to give this much to the Luftwaffe – when they knocked down our buildings, it didn't replace them with anything more offensive than rubble. We did that."

But angry architects hit back at his speech accusing them of building "a stunted imitation of Manhattan". One of them, Tony Clegg, said: "We don't need a Hitler to help us deal with our mistakes." However, it is clear that the speech will cause planners to rethink their proposals for Paternoster Square – as they did over the National Gallery extension (→ 29/10/88).

Anne provokes row by Aids comments

London, 27 January 1988

The Princess Royal was plunged into controversy last night after making a hard-hitting speech about Aids. The outspoken princess outraged homosexual groups by describing the killer disease as a "classic own goal" scored by the human race on itself. She told doctors from 150 countries at a World Aids Summit in London that the Aids epidemic was a "self-inflicted wound" that only served to remind man of his fallibility. Her remarks were immediately condemned by Aids workers.

'Crawfie', the royal governess, is dead

Aberdeen, 10 February 1988

The Queen's former governess, Marion Crawford, died at her home in Aberdeen today, aged 78. "Crawfie", as she was called by the royal family, was governess to the future Queen and Princess Margaret for 15 years. When she left royal service she was given a cottage at Kensington palace, but fell from grace when she wrote about her time in royal employment. Whilst her books and articles were highly complimentary towards the royal family, they could not forgive what they saw as a betrayal of trust.

Fergie under fire for leaving her baby at home while she enjoys tour of Australia

Sydney, 18 October 1988
The Duchess of York has been sharply criticised for leaving her first baby, Beatrice, behind in Britain while she is in Australia on an official tour. The TV personality and children's rights campaigner Esther Rantzen has joined the chorus of complaint over the decision. Headlines such as "Worlds Apart", "Disaster Down Under" and "This is a baby, Fergie" have emphasised widespread public disapproval of the duchess.

Baby Beatrice, who was born on 8 August this year, is being cared for at home by the royal couple's nanny Alison Wardley. Prince Andrew, who is taking the salute at the naval review in Sydney harbour to celebrate Australia's bicentenary, has staunchly defended his wife. "If the critics bothered to think about it for one second, Beatrice is much better off where things are stable," he said.

Prince Andrew with baby Beatrice.

The duchess herself outlined the practical problems. She told guests at a reception: "I was worried that if I brought Beatrice along, with all the changes in climate she would catch cold or worse. Then I would have been worrying about Beatrice and not concentrating on my job – and that's important." But the duchess, who was rebuked for leading a jet-set lifestyle during pregnancy, knows that the fuss marks a significant change in her image with the British media (→ 20/12).

Sarah, without baby, in Australia.

Charles launches TV attack on architects

London, 29 October 1988
Prince Charles took his crusade for a better Britain into millions of homes last night with a passionate television appeal for a new age of architecture. The prince, who wrote and appeared in the BBC documentary *A Vision of Britain,* spent nine months travelling around the country to prepare his blueprint.

He launched a scathing attack on modern architects and planners who have created "Godforsaken" cities where nature has been driven out. At the same time he called for a new planning code as he damned skyscrapers and soulless tower blocks which "look like machines". He told viewers: "I have been fascinated to discover just how many people seem appalled by what we have done to so many of our towns and cities since the last war." He singled out Birmingham and London for particular attack. Birmingham central library looked "like a place where books are incinerated, not kept" while the new British Library looked like "an academy for the secret police."

However the prince, who is 40 next month, praised a Dorchester hospital, a housing association scheme in Skipton and a docks development in Cardiff. He called for a style of architecture that respected nature and urged planners to use natural materials for building. Architects were begged to appreciate that man is more than a "mechanical object" (→ 3/9/89).

Household aerosols banned by Charles

London, 22 February 1988
A green revolution inspired by Prince Charles is transforming the life of his family and staff. He announced today that he has banned the use of aerosols in his homes – including his wife's hairspray. He wants others to follow his lead to cut down on aerosols which contain the harmful chemicals which help to destroy the earth's ozone layer. The prince has also ordered staff to use recycled paper and has had vehicles converted to run on unleaded petrol (→ 22/3).

'Sun' found guilty of copyright breach

London, 16 November 1988
The Queen won a £100,000 high court victory today over the copyright of a royal photograph. The *Sun* newspaper, which published the private family picture of the Queen, the Queen Mother, the Duchess of York and baby Princess Beatrice, agreed to pay the cash to charity. The newspaper bought the photograph for £1,000, and Scotland Yard is considering theft charges against the woman who sold the photo. It was due to be made into a royal Christmas card.

Dutiful Diana extols virtues of family life

Diana poses with her two sons.

London, 18 October 1988
The Princess of Wales, in the first major speech of her royal career, today spoke about the dangers facing the family in modern society. Diana, who wrote the five-minute speech herself, spoke with feeling about children's needs within the family. She was launching a new look for the children's charity Barnardo's at a time when her sister-in-law is being criticised for neglecting her baby [*see above*]. Diana said that pressures on mothers were enormous but "we have to find a securer way of helping our children, to prepare them to face life as stable and confident adults".

Egging her horse on: the Queen at the Derby, held at Epsom on 1 June.

Anne and Mark decide to separate

'Sun' embroiled in private letters row

London, 9 April 1989
Scotland Yard tonight launched a top-level investigation to find the thief who stole four letters sent to the Princess Royal by the Queen's equerry, Commander Timothy Laurence. The letters, said to be "tender and affectionate", were handed to a journalist at the offices of the *Sun* newspaper by an un-identified man. Newspaper execu-tives examined the letters before passing them on to the police. The theft has renewed speculation that the 15-year marriage of the prin-cess and Captain Mark Phillips may soon end in divorce.

Detectives investigating the embarrassing theft are preparing a photofit picture of the culprit and will fingerprint Buckingham Palace staff. Laurence, who has been inter-viewed by detectives, is said to be "furious and humiliated" that his secret friendship with the princess has been exposed. Friends say that the dashing naval officer is "be-sotted" with the princess and has had secret meetings with her at a house in the country. Last night Buckingham Palace emphasised that Commander Laurence would continue in his post (→ 31/8).

Royal blunder over Lockerbie attacked

Lockerbie, 4 January 1989
Political and civic leaders angrily attacked the Queen and the rest of the royal family for failing to attend today's memorial service in the small Scottish town of Lockerbie for the 270 victims of Britain's worst air crash. Instead they sent local dignitaries to represent them while they carried on with their Christmas holidays or private busi-ness. It was left to the prime minis-ter, Margaret Thatcher, to lead the mourners. One Conservative MP, Terry Dicks, said: "It wouldn't hurt the royal family to grieve with the people they were meant to lead." Another added: "The royal family got it wrong this time."

Princess Anne with Timothy Laurence, in the grey hat, at Royal Ascot.

Palace announces end of royal marriage

London, 31 August 1989
In the end they gave up the pre-tence. The Princess Royal and Captain Mark Phillips officially announced their formal separation yesterday. Buckingham Palace said that the couple had no plans for divorce and that Captain Phillips would continue to manage their Gatcombe Park estate in Glouces-tershire and live on the farm.

The Queen has reluctantly en-dorsed the decision and will have to agree to any divorce settlement.

Mark's father, Major Peter Phil-lips, confirmed that the decision to split was forced upon his son by the princess who wanted to end a pho-ney marriage and lead her own life. Her friendship with the Queen's former equerry, Commander Tim Laurence, may have hastened the end. The princess, currently visit-ing Puerto Rico for an Olympic conference, seemed happy and re-laxed in spite of the press attention, while Captain Phillips stayed be-hind closed doors at home.

Queen is invited to visit the Soviet Union

The Queen with Mr Gorbachev.

Windsor, 7 April 1989
The Queen today accepted a formal invitation to visit the USSR. The offer came from President Gorba-chev during a lunch at Windsor castle. While no date has been fixed for when the Queen will set foot in Red Square, the visit will heal the 72-year-old wounds of the Russian Revolution which led to Czar Nicholas – a cousin of the Queen's grandfather, George V – and his family being brutally executed. From the start the Queen and the Gorbachevs got on famously, the Soviet president joking "It's a big house, isn't it?" as the Queen showed him round Windsor castle. Despite earlier doubts the invita-tion is now supported by the prime minister, Mrs Thatcher (→ 24/5/90).

Prince spells out a 'Vision of Britain'

London, 3 September 1989
The Prince of Wales made his most devastating attack yesterday on the "arrogance" of fashionable British architects. He described some of the nation's modern buildings as "deformed Frankenstein monsters" and outlined his ten ground rules for beautiful architecture. His abuse of post-war architects and their buildings is contained in his book *A Vision of Britain* which he wrote following his TV document-ary on the issue last year.

The prince, who has now found-ed his own school of design, out-lined the reforms needed to restore a sense of beauty, community and belonging to Britain's towns and cities. His planning code incorpor-ates ideas on scale, proportion, and careful use of natural materials.

New royal portrait starts controversy

The Queen Mother's new portrait.

London, 4 August 1989
A controversial new portrait of the Queen Mother was unveiled at the National Gallery today, her 89th birthday, to a disappointed public. In a radical departure from the tra-ditional chocolate box image of the Queen Mother, the artist Alison Watt depicts a woman who drew comments such as "frumpy" and "miserable" in newspapers. Ms Watt, who is 23, defended her work as "an honest portrait".

Marina's pregnancy causes family rift

Marina with Paul, her boyfriend.

London, 15 December 1989
Princess Alexandra's rebellious daughter, Marina Ogilvy, has made the first move to try to patch up a bitter public row with her family. She devastated her parents when she announced that she was pregnant by her photographer boyfriend Paul Mowatt and had no plans to marry him. She then told a newspaper that her mother wanted her to have an abortion rather than the baby. Marina, aged 23, accused her parents of being more concerned about their image than their own daughter. Now she and her boyfriend have decided to marry before the baby is born. Her parents have issued a statement saying that they love Marina and would welcome her home.

Second child born to Duchess of York

London, 23 March 1990
The Duchess of York gave birth to her second child, a girl, tonight. Mother and baby were both said to be doing well after the caesarean delivery at 7.58pm. Doctors pointed out that a breech birth is classed as an emergency. The baby, who has not been named, is sixth in line to the throne. Prince Andrew, who was present during the four-hour labour, said: "The baby is lovely." The Queen was said to be "delighted" with her sixth grandchild.

Palace bans royal servant's memoirs

London, 31 July 1990
The Queen yesterday won a worldwide ban on the publication of a book by a former royal household official containing behind-the-scenes revelations, in intimate detail, about the royal family. In the book, *Courting Disaster*, the ex-clerk Malcolm Barker makes disclosures which the Queen's solicitors say breach an undertaking of confidentiality signed when he joined the staff in 1980, and attacks what he calls "blatant censorship".

Lord Linley wins 'lager lout' damages

Viscount Linley after the hearing.

London, 29 March 1990
The Queen's nephew, Viscount Linley, made royal history today after winning a high court action for libel. Princess Margaret's son was awarded £5,000 in civil damages and £30,000 in punitive damages against the *Today* newspaper over allegations that he had poured lager over customers at a pub in Chelsea. It is the first time that a member of the royal family has brought an action for libel against a newspaper and appears to signify a tough new royal policy against the tabloid media. "Royal watchers" believe that the viscount would not have started the case without the Queen's approval.

Sarah finds the elegant Diana a tough act to follow in the royal fashion stakes

The young Diana: simplicity was the keynote of this 1982 outfit.

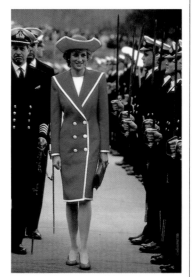

A more confident, sophisticated princess at Dartmouth in 1989.

London, 1990
The Princess of Wales eclipsed every other member of the royal family during the 1980s. It was she whose photograph on the cover was said to sell more magazines than any other, she who matured gracefully from shy teenager to caring mother, she who developed a flair for fashion which seemed flawless. Beside this paragon her sister-in-law has had a difficult time.

Sarah, the Duchess of York (or "Fergie", as she is popularly known), has been criticised for her holidays, her new ranch-style home near Windsor, her attitude to her family, her brashness and, most cruelly, her sense of fashion. Some memorable disasters were all the worse because of Diana's elegance and élan.

The duchess lacks Diana's sleek figure as well as her taste. But she is now far slimmer than she was in her early years of marriage – more sophisticated, too, and more content in family life. The Princess of Wales has also matured – even more so. "Shy Di" has acquired a flair for public relations which perhaps only the Queen Mother can rival.

The duchess in Los Angeles: a show-stopping shawl in 1988.

A slimmer and more elegant Sarah in Bristol, June 1990.

Royals see new faces of communism

Charles and Diana travel to Hungary

Budapest, 7 May 1990
The Prince and Princess of Wales arrived in Budapest today just months after Hungary ended 40 years of communist rule. Their arrival, the first by members of the royal family since the war, was clearly an emotional moment. As the national anthems were played, the acting president's wife, Zsuzsa Goncz, dabbed her eyes and then held Diana's hand as they walked along the guard of honour. During the four-day visit Charles wants to promote British goods (→ 24/5).

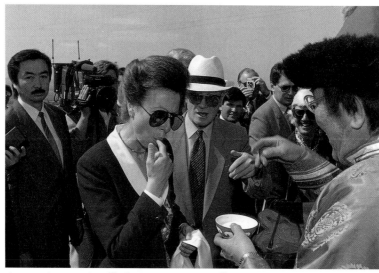

Anne trying goat's milk during a visit to a village in eastern Siberia.

Diana with a Hungarian admirer.

Anne makes historic visit to Soviet Union

Moscow, 24 May 1990
With a smile and a simple handshake, the Princess Royal and the Soviet president, Mikhail Gorbachev, yesterday healed a 72-year-old royal rift with the Soviet Union. The historic gesture showed that the royal family had forgiven the country for the murder of Czar Nicholas II, who was related to the British royals, in 1918. President Gorbachev greeted his royal guest in time-honoured English fashion by talking about the weather.

The princess has visited the Soviet Union before, but as a sportswoman in her years as a world-class equestrian competitor. Her current 17-day tour is strictly royal and is widely seen as a prelude to a visit by the Queen. President Gorbachev invited the Queen to visit the Soviet Union when he was a guest at Windsor castle in April of last year. At one stage it was suggested that the prime minister, Margaret Thatcher, was opposed to such a trip, but any objections that may have existed have now been withdrawn.

Anne will be visiting many areas of the Soviet Union, including a peasant village in Siberia and farms near Kiev.

Charles breaks his arm in an awkward fall from polo pony

Cirencester, 29 June 1990
Prince Charles was urged to give up playing dangerous sports after breaking his right arm in a polo accident yesterday. He was rushed to hospital after taking a tumble during a polo cup game whilst playing for Windsor Park on Lord Bathurst's Gloucestershire estate. However, Harold Brooks Baker of *Burke's Peerage* said that the sport was too dangerous for someone of his position. The prince, who loves the game, has suffered a number of injuries during his 25-year sporting career. He bears the scars of many falls on the polo field.

Charles with his arm in a sling.

Queen, richest woman in world, called on to pay income tax

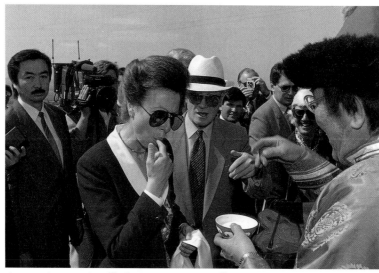

Elizabeth: glittering jewels.

London, 29 January 1990
The Queen's personal fortune came under renewed scrutiny today after it was revealed that she and the rest of the royal family will save £60,000 when the controversial new poll tax is introduced. As the Queen, who has been described as the world's wealthiest woman, is exempt from personal taxation, she will pay nothing under the community charge (as the poll tax is officially called) – although she did pay rates on her private estates. The other royals will save because the charge is on people not property. Now three out of four people want the Queen to pay the community charge and income tax, according to an opinion poll published today in the *Sunday Times*. The poll reflects growing unease with the monarch's untaxed personal fortune, estimated at between £1.2 and £6.8 billion.

The Queen and the Prince of Wales are legally exempt from paying tax, although Prince Charles makes a voluntary contribution of 25 per cent of his income to the Consolidated Fund, the equivalent of a state kitty. However, with pressure growing among MPs for the Queen to pay income tax, palace officials are quick to point out that the Queen is custodian of many palaces and priceless collections.

"She does not own Buckingham Palace or the royal paintings," said a courtier. "Many of her possessions are inalienable, passing down through the generations." Her fortune comprises untaxed stocks and shares, jewellery, family *objets d'art*, and the estates at Balmoral and Sandringham.

The nation cheers a special birthday

London, 1 August 1990

The Queen Mother renewed her friendship with the east end of London today – 50 years after it began. Half a century ago, she gave comfort to thousands of cockneys as she stepped through the rubble of the Blitz with her husband, King George VI. As the nation prepared to celebrated her 90th birthday on 4 August she returned and said: "It's good to be back."

Members of the same families welcomed her as she toured the streets, pausing at the places she recalled from the days of war. Old ladies in the crowd at South Hallsville school, Canning Town, remembered the night of 10 September 1940, when the school suffered a direct hit, killing 76 people sheltering from the bombing. Within hours Elizabeth was there, consoling orphans and comforting widows.

They recalled her words when Buckingham Palace was hit: "I am glad we've been bombed. It makes me feel I can look the east end in the face." She looked them in the face again yesterday – most of

Celebration: Queen Elizabeth the Queen Mother on her 90th birthday.

them from a generation that only knows the Queen Mother as a cosy figure wearing improbable platform shoes and clouds of chiffon. After all the nostalgia of touring the east end, the Queen Mother joined her family on the royal yacht *Britannia*, moored in the Pool of London. She invited every close member of the royal (except Marina Ogilvy and her husband Paul Mowatt) to dinner. Later, as she watched a firework display for her birthday, she no doubt recalled the nights when the capital's skyline was lit up in anger, not in celebration (→4/8).

Queen speaks out for Canadian unity

Ottawa, 1 July 1990

Queen Elizabeth disdained royal platitudes for an urgent Canada Day message to Canadians, now bitterly debating their nation's future. "It is my fondest wish for this Canada Day that Canadians come together and remain together, rather than dwelling on the differences which might further divide them," she declared as 70,000 people waved flags on Parliament Hill.

The Queen, in a striking green and white floral dress, spoke one week after the failure of the Meech Lake constitutional accord granting Quebec "distinct society" status. "I am glad to be here at this sensitive time," she said. "There is in Canada a constant search for fairness, a receptiveness to honourable accommodation, enabling the two principal language communities to flourish within the Canadian family. Those values are needed now more than ever."

Charles inspects British forces in the Gulf

Boosting morale: Prince Charles visiting British troops in Saudi Arabia.

The Gulf, 22 December 1990

Prince Charles arrived in Saudi Arabia today to inspect British troops ranged against Saddam Hussein's army in occupied Kuwait. However, the Princess of Wales, who suggested the morale-boosting visit, was banned from flying out to the Gulf with her husband by the defence secretary, Tom King. He considered it too dangerous. Instead, she has gone over to Germany to see the wives and families of tank crews serving in the allied forces now mustered against Iraq in the desert.

The current line of succession to Britain's throne

31 December 1990

What have King Harald V of Norway, Mrs Paul Mowatt of Kingston and the Earl of Macduff in common with the Prince of Wales? They are all in line of succession to the British throne.

Births and deaths mean that the list of those in succession is rarely constant for more than a few months. Anne the Princess Royal, was for many years second only to her brother Charles; but she has been overtaken, first by her younger brothers and then by her nephews. Sexual equality has no place as yet in the line of succession to the British throne.

The press office at Buckingham Palace does not bother to keep an up-to-date list beyond those named below. After them, it is a genealogist's delight. For the record: Mrs Paul Mowatt (formerly Marina Ogilvy) is at number 26 as the year ends, with the Earl of Macduff and King Harald of Norway between numbers 40 and 50. A somewhat less theoretical top 25 in the line of succession as of today are:

1. The Prince of Wales.
2. Prince William of Wales.
3. Prince Henry of Wales.
4. The Duke of York.
5. Princess Beatrice.
6. Princess Eugénie.
7. Prince Edward.
8. Princess Anne, the Princess Royal.
9. Peter Phillips.
10. Zara Phillips.
11. Princess Margaret.
12. Viscount Linley.
13. Lady Sarah Armstrong-Jones.
14. The Duke of Gloucester.
15. The Earl of Ulster.
16. Lady Davina Windsor.
17. Lady Rose Windsor.
18. The Duke of Kent.
19. Baron Downpatrick.
20. Lord Nicholas Windsor.
21. Lady Helen Windsor.
22. Lord Frederick Windsor.
23. Lady Gabriella Windsor.
24. Princess Alexandra.
25. James Ogilvy.

The royal 'firm' goes about its business in 1991

It has been called the oldest family firm in the country, perhaps the world. In 1991, as these pages show, it went about its business as usual, undeterred by newspaper speculation about the marriage of the Prince and Princess of Wales (the tabloid obsession) or the Queen's exemption from income tax (the upmarket media favourite).

In 1990 the hardest worker, according to details published in the *Times*, was Princess Anne, the Princess Royal, who undertook 449 official engagements in the United Kingdom and 319 abroad. The runner-up was the Queen, with 476 engagements at home and 94 over-seas. Prince Philip had a similar total (554), although more were overseas. The Queen Mother, at 90, had 118 engagements at home – more than she had ten years previously. Totals for other immediate members of the family were:
* Prince of Wales - 389.
* Princess of Wales - 323.
* Duke of York - 29.
* Duchess of York - 108.
* Prince Edward - 219.
The Yorks' totals were low because of the duke's naval commitments and the duchess's pregnancy. The royals are also patrons of many organisations – in the Queen's case, no fewer than 752.

Always in the public eye: Queen Elizabeth and the Queen Mother, at the Derby horse-race in June, being filmed for a BBC documentary.

A royal holiday: the Princess of Wales explaining the wonders of skiing to her sons William and Harry while on holiday in April at Lech, in Austria.

The Prince of Wales with President Havel on a visit to Czechoslovakia.

The Duchess of Kent at a memorial service for King Olav of Norway.

The Princess Royal opening a school on Rodrigues, off Mauritius.

Princess Alexandra arriving – in some style - for a state dinner.

A theatrical prince: Edward, who is keenly involved in the theatre, presenting the BBC "Radio Times" Drama Awards in London.

A popular princess: Diana bringing happiness to a day-care centre.

With authority: the Queen pictured beside the US president, George Bush, as she makes a speech during her state visit to the United States.

A family man: the Duke of York with his young daughter, Beatrice.

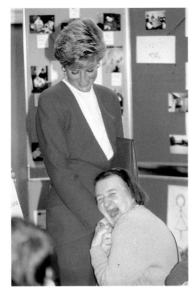

The Queen Mother inspecting the Women's Royal Army Corps.

The Duke of Gloucester, president of the Steam Locomotive Trust.

Princess Margaret opening a new holiday camp for girl guides.

Princess Michael of Kent (left) at this year's Ideal Home Exhibition.

Prince Philip, the Duke of Edinburgh, marks his 70th birthday.

A light-hearted moment: the Duchess of York sharing a joke with policemen of the Special Escort Group, who have been assigned to guard her.

Starting young: Prince William in Cardiff - on his first "job".

APPENDIX

A-Z gazetteer of palaces and royal residences

Balmoral: holiday home in Scotland

"Every year my heart becomes more fixed in this dear paradise and so much more so now that all has become my dearest Albert's own creation, own work, own building, own laying out ... his great taste and the impress of his dear hand have been stamped everywhere."
This entry in Queen Victoria's (1837-1901) diary sums up a royal love affair with a castle in a remote Scottish glen which continued long after the marriage of Victoria to her prince consort was ended by his sudden death from typhoid in 1861.

Victoria and Albert had loved Scotland since their first holidays at Taymouth and Blair Atholl early in the 1840s, and determined to buy Balmoral, then a manor house, on the upper Dee in Grampian. It was, wrote the queen, "a pretty little castle in the old Scotch style", and it came into royal hands in 1852 with 17,400 acres (7,045ha) of estate lands for 300,000 guineas – most of the money coming from a bequest to Victoria from an admirer, John Camden Neild.

Albert, an inveterate developer, immediately set about building a castle on the site. The house had been remodelled as recently as 1833 and stood on the site of a hunting lodge of King Robert II (1371-90). None the less, Prince Albert was determined to create an entirely new Balmoral. The old house was demolished and, some 100 yards away, Albert created a fairy-tale castle in the true Scots baronial tradition, with towers and turrets in grey Invergelder granite.

The new castle had 180 windows, and the prince consort ensured his beloved Victoria's comfort with 67 fireplaces and 14 water-closets. William Smith was responsible for the new building, while James Giles landscaped the gardens. By September 1855 the castle was ready for its royal owners.

Victoria was ecstatic, and so were the many royal children who

Unconventional guards: cattle keep a close eye on visitors to the royal holiday home of Balmoral, in Grampian.

could roam freely in the forest and glens away from the stuffiness of other royal palaces. Victoria and Albert established really warm relationships with the Highlanders – "cheerful ... happy and merry people", she wrote. The royal family arrived at Balmoral every autumn for the shoot to the sound of bagpipes and a genuine welcome from the locals.

Despite his German birth and up-bringing, Albert's enthusiasm for Scotland and all things Caledonian was boundless. It was he who helped to make the tartan fashionable, creating in the process a "Balmoral" of black, red and lavender on a grey background. The "Balmoral" and other tartans were displayed everywhere in the huge building.

Queen Victoria continued to visit the house for four months of every year after Albert's death in 1861. She had a granite memorial to him

raised on the spot where he had shot his last stag, and she continued to visit estate workers, taking a special interest in their families and conditions.

Victoria's love for this huge rambling house was based on her love for its designer. The present royal family also have a special love for Balmoral – although theirs, like that of Victoria's children, is based on the freedom that it offers them in a blissfully informal setting. Millions watched the Duke of Edinburgh serving up barbecued meat to the rest of the family in the first of the "informal" documentaries to be made about the royals; even so, not every aspect of a Balmoral holiday can be so easy-going, especially when the Book Trust prepares its hefty list of recommended reading and packs crates of books for the Queen – whether she reads them or not is another matter. If Balmoral is secluded, **Birkhall**, a small

house with a sloping roof of blue slates sheltered by a wooded hillside that Victoria bought for her eldest son Albert Edward (the future Edward VII) in 1852, is even more so.

Birkhall was built in 1715 with a bow-fronted wing added in the 1950s by the Queen Mother. It is a house that is much loved by the Queen and her family. It is now the Queen Mother's personal home on the Balmoral estate, having been given to her and her husband (George VI, 1936-52) after their marriage. It was here that Elizabeth and Margaret spent "magic moments" as children, playing in the terraced gardens which slope down to the river Muick. In one wooded corner is the Wendy House presented by the *Aberdeen Press* newspaper in 1935. The Queen spent part of her honeymoon at Birkhall; so did both the Duchess of Kent and Princess Alexandra.

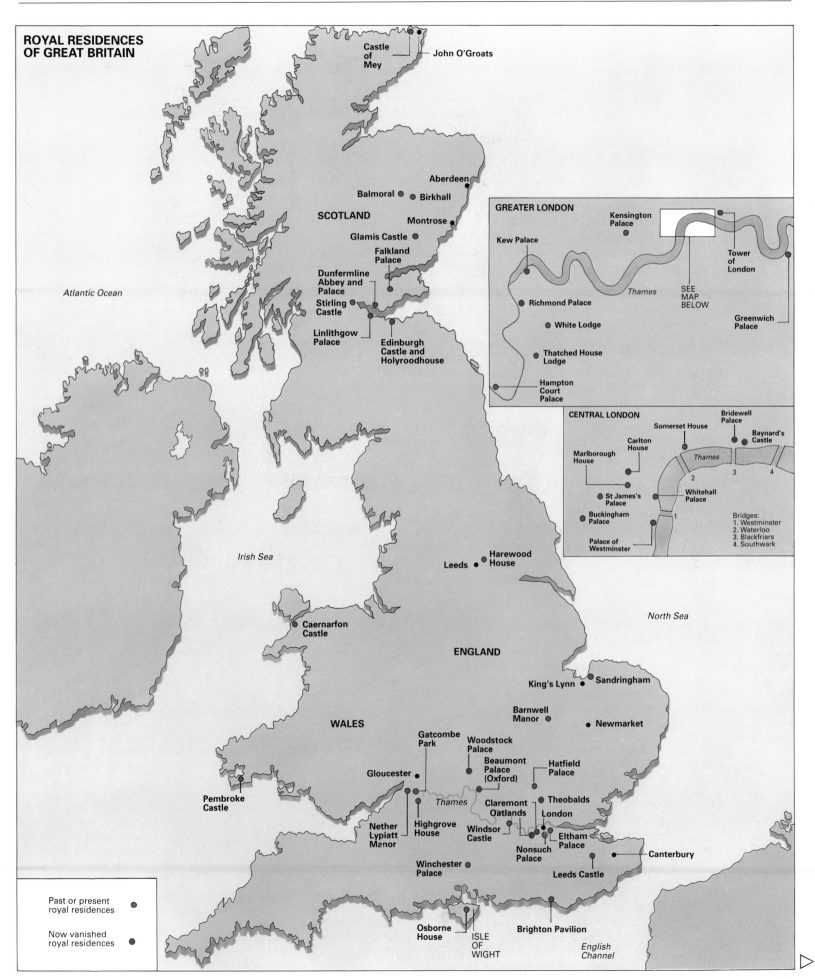

ROYAL RESIDENCES OF GREAT BRITAIN

SCOTLAND

Castle of Mey
John O'Groats

Aberdeen
Balmoral Birkhall
Montrose
Glamis Castle
Falkland Palace
Dunfermline Abbey and Palace
Stirling Castle
Linlithgow Palace
Edinburgh Castle and Holyroodhouse

Atlantic Ocean

Irish Sea

Leeds Harewood House

Caernarfon Castle

ENGLAND

North Sea

King's Lynn Sandringham

Barnwell Manor Newmarket

WALES

Gatcombe Park Woodstock Palace
Gloucester Beaumont Palace (Oxford) Hatfield Palace
Pembroke Castle Claremont Theobalds
Nether Lypiatt Manor Oatlands London
Highgrove House Windsor Castle Eltham Palace
Thames Nonsuch Palace
Winchester Palace Leeds Castle Canterbury

Osborne House ISLE OF WIGHT Brighton Pavilion

English Channel

GREATER LONDON

Kensington Palace
Kew Palace
Tower of London
Thames SEE MAP BELOW
Richmond Palace
White Lodge
Greenwich Palace
Thatched House Lodge
Hampton Court Palace

CENTRAL LONDON

Somerset House Bridewell Palace
Carlton House Baynard's Castle
Marlborough House *Thames*
St James's Palace Whitehall Palace
Buckingham Palace
Palace of Westminster

Bridges:
1. Westminster
2. Waterloo
3. Blackfriars
4. Southwark

Past or present royal residences

Now vanished royal residences

589

Barnwell Manor: a house with a castle

Barnwell Manor in Northamptonshire is the home of the Duke and Duchess of Gloucester and one of the least-known royal residences in Great Britain. This distinctive manor house, built in grey stone, is probably the most attractive of all the royal homes, however. Prince Henry, the Duke of Gloucester, a brother of George VI (1936-52), bought the house and the adjoining 13th-century castle in 1938, two years after he had married Lady Alice Montagu-Douglas-Scott.

Her father, the seventh Duke of Buccleuch, had sold the property 26 years earlier. The house had belonged to the Montagu family and, through marriage, to the Dukes of Buccleuch since the 16th century. Sir Edward Montagu, the son of Henry VIII's (1509-47) chief justice, built the house in the grounds of the castle in 1540. The land previously belonged to the le Moyne family, the last of whom, known as "Black Berengarius", bricked his brother into the castle walls, for reasons best known to himself and the hapless brother.

Six farms make up the 2,500 acres (1,012ha) of the estate; two were run by Prince William, the duke's heir, until his death in a flying accident in 1972. Barnwell is open to the public twice yearly.

Baynard's Castle: a lost London fortress

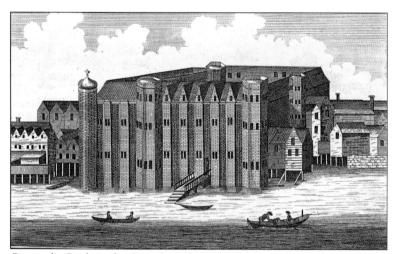

Baynard's Castle in the City of London, as redeveloped by Henry VII.

Nothing remains of Baynard's Castle today except the name of a street and of a public house on the corner of St Andrew's Hill and Queen Victoria Street in the City of London. Customers are no doubt unaware that they are quaffing their pints on the very spot that Richard III (1483-85) accepted the crown and rode to Westminster, as Shakespeare records in *Richard III*.

The original building, named after its first custodian, Ralph Baignard, was built in the 11th century by William the Conqueror (1066-87) at the same time as the Tower, to subdue the rebellious population of London. Destroyed by King John (1199-1216) in 1212, the castle was later rebuilt near the river, off the Upper Thames Street of today. In c.1500, Henry VII (1485-1509) redeveloped the castle more as a house than a fort, with the main gateway opening onto Upper Thames Street. Baynard's was then a square building surrounding a courtyard with an octagonal tower in its centre.

Three new wings were built around the site of a former garden in c.1550, five other buildings being replaced with a new north wing. Towers were built, together with a private watergate and landing stage – discovered during excavations in the mid-1970s. Queen Elizabeth I (1558-1603) was a frequent guest at the castle, held in her reign by the Earls of Pembroke.

Charles II (1660-85) was the last monarch to visit Baynard's. A few days after he dined there in 1666, the castle was burnt down in the Great Fire. The remains were demolished in the early 19th century.

Beaumont Palace: a birthplace of kings

Only a few bits of architectural flotsam remain of Beaumont Palace in Oxford. Part of a 12th-century arch, for example, survives in a back garden near the original site (now Beaumont Street). The friary on Boar's Hill, Oxford, also preserves some pieces of what was originally called the King's Houses, built by Henry I (1100-35) towards the end of his reign. Beaumont was often visited by Henry's grandson, Henry II (1154-89), on his way to Woodstock; it was also the birthplace of Henry's great-grandsons, Richard I (1189-99) and John (1199-1216).

By around 1250 the palace had grown to a considerable size. It contained, in addition to the royal apartments, stables, storerooms, two chapels (with quarters for the chaplains), kitchens and a great chamber. It passed out of royal ownership in 1275, and by c.1300 much of its fabric was already being carried off for other buildings.

Beaumont Palace: the ruins.

What was left became a Carmelite friary in 1318. At the beginning of the 18th century parts of the palace were used in the construction of Gloucester Hall (now Worcester College, University of Oxford), although this building was itself demolished in 1806.

Bridewell Palace: the gateway survives

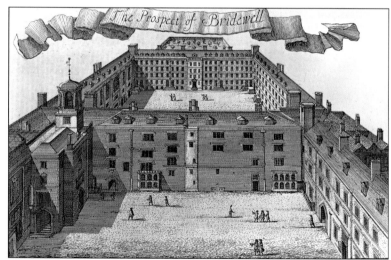

Bridewell Palace: built by Henry VIII as a royal stronghold in London.

After two great fires in 1512 destroyed much of both the Palace of Westminster and the Tower of London, Henry VIII (1509-47) was desperate for a new palace. He chose a plot of land between the present Fleet Street and the Thames, given to him by Cardinal Wolsey, as the site for Bridewell Palace. It was built at a cost of £39,000 and completed in c.1525. Its features included an 80-foot-long great hall and a grand staircase designed for state occasions. Two hexagonal towers overlooked the Thames.

Edward VI (1547-53) turned the castle into a "low-security" prison and hospital, as famous in its day as other London jails such as Newgate and the Fleet. Part of the palace was destroyed in the Great Fire of 1666. Although both the great hall and the court room were later restored, little now remains except the reconstructed gateway at 14 New Bridge Street.

Brighton Pavilion: a witty monument to regency extravagance

It was not until the middle of the 18th century that it became fashionable to board a coach in London and head south to the quaint fishing village of Brighton (Brighthelmstone) in Sussex. There, the quack-like "Doctor Brighton" supervised expensive duckings in the English Channel, or even prescribed drinking the sea water as a cure for all ills. Growing numbers of wealthy Londoners flocked to the seaside, but less and less for the cure than for the increasingly racy social scene – and it was not long before George, the Prince of Wales and later Prince Regent, arrived to join in the fun and games in 1783.

Soon after he rented a "superior farmhouse" near the sea front where he lived with Maria Fitzherbert, a widow whom he had fallen in love with and married in 1785 in great secrecy, since she was a commoner and, worse still, a Catholic. (His wedding ring to her is on display at the Pavilion.) In 1787 the farmhouse was converted into a Palladian-style villa by Henry Holland, who had redesigned Carlton House for the prince. At that time the prince was obsessed with all things Chinese, and he demanded that the house be decorated with dragons and other oriental motifs. As this work was being carried out, George developed a fascination with the opulence of the Indian Moghuls. In 1815 he commissioned the remarkable young architect John Nash to create a building that combined both styles. That building – today's Pavilion – was completed in 1820 after six years' work, at a cost of £155,000.

Nash took his inspiration from a book in the prince's library of Indian scenes painted by Thomas Daniell. He transformed the exterior into a representation of a Moghul's palace: a huge bulbous dome was built over the central salon, with smaller onion domes flanking it. Even the kitchens have an oriental touch, with their cast-iron and copper columns in the shape of palm trees.

Public opinion was, however, incensed by such extravagance: the early 19th century was a time of great economic hardship for much of the population. The Pavilion is a masterpiece of Regency "fun" architecture, its fantastic interior

An oriental aspect: a floodlit view of the Brighton Pavilion by night.

admired by visitors from all over the world.

The great banqueting-room is the most exciting of the state apartments, with its 45-foot (13.5-m)-high domed ceiling, giant chandelier – actually a "gasolier", so noisy in its time that William IV (1830-37), fearing that it might crash down on luckless diners, had it removed – and decorations of some of the fiercest dragons ever to snarl down on the guests of royalty. Although dinners in the Pavilion were always reputed to be highly agreeable occasions, many guests complained of headaches and sore throats from the patent stoves and newly-invented gas lighting. Soon after the Pavilion was completed, "Prinny" (as he was known) lost interest in it. In order to preserve

the secrecy of her marriage to the prince, Mrs Fitzherbert never lived in it, but was often entertained there by William IV, the ex-sailor, who loved it. Queen Victoria (1837-1901) disliked the design and found the people of Brighton "very indiscreet and troublesome". She even threatened to raze it to the ground before she and Albert moved to the seclusion of Osborne.

Much of the interior was dismantled in the 1840s, but the corporation of Brighton bought the Pavilion in 1849. In recent decades especially, restoration programmes have been undertaken with enormous care to return the Pavilion to its original splendour. The Prince Regent was criticised in his day for his extravagance, but there is no greater monument to regency wit.

An exotic interior: snakes adorn the walls in the Pavilion's Music Room.

Buckingham Palace – headquarters of the 'family firm'

Strange as it may seem, it was not until the beginning of the present century that Buckingham Palace really came into its own as Britain's principal royal residence. Queen Victoria (1837-1901) chose to spend most of her long widowhood at Balmoral or Osborne, and, apart from a spell of occupation by the Shah of Persia in 1873, the great house at the end of the Mall was little used until the more outgoing Edward VII (1901-10) came to the throne. Only then did the palace become the scene of glittering receptions, court balls and royal garden parties.

Crowds form daily outside the palace for the changing of the guard, but it is only the occupants (and the holders of cherished invitations to royal garden parties) who are fortunate enough to see it for what it really is – an elegant country house set in 40 acres (16ha) of parkland in the centre of London. Indeed, many Londoners who pass the palace daily would scarcely recognise the building from its western aspect.

The palace is built on a site where James I (1603-25) planted 30,000 mulberry trees in the hope that his silkworms would eat the black mulberries and start a new silk industry. The scheme failed – silkworms thrive only on white mulberries. The site was instead turned into a pleasure park. At least one of James's mulberry trees survives in a corner of the royal gardens.

Fire destroyed two houses built on the site before the Duke of Buckingham had Buckingham House built to designs by William Talman and a Dutch architect, William Winde, in 1702. The house stayed in the Buckingham family until 1762, when George III (1760-1820) bought it as a retreat from the rigid, formal round of ceremonial at St James's Palace. It was renamed "the Queen's House", and to it George – a noted collector of books – added a huge library. George IV (1820-30) spent nearly £600,000 completely rebuilding the palace to a design by John Nash. By 1855 it was beginning to take the shape that we recognise ▷

Fit for a Queen: Buckingham Palace has been remodelled several times.

The opulent interior of the white drawing-room overlooking the garden.

continued from previous page

as Buckingham Palace. Nash built a three-sided courtyard, open to the Mall and entered through a grand arch. He also added a dome, criticised for resembling, according to different observers, an inverted bucket or egg-cup. Considered too expensive, Nash was dismissed in 1830, and work continued under Edmund Blore. The offending dome was removed and, in 1847, an eastern wing built to enclose the courtyard. This forms the block facing the Mall today. Nash's arch was removed in 1851 to its present eponymous site – Marble Arch, on the old Tyburn execution ground. Nash's nephew, Sir James Penne-thorne, completed the palace, ad-ding the ballroom and state supper-room in 1851-55. The last major alterations were commissioned by George V (1910-36) and Queen Mary, who improved the eastern façade of the palace with Portland stone.

The main entrance to the palace in the centre of the forecourt now takes the visitor through to a quadrangle and a fine hall with great Carrara marble columns and elegant, although simple, décor in white and gold. At the far end of the hall the grand staircase divides into three flights, the centre flight leading to the east gallery, the state supper-room and the ballroom, the other flights converging at the entrance to the guard-room, which leads in turn to the green drawing room. Beyond lies the throne room itself, with its fine ceiling and sculp-tures by artists such as Bernasconi. A secret door leads from the royal closet to the white drawing-room, which overlooks the garden and lake, after which the fortunate visitor will find the music-room. Next come the blue drawing-room (once the ballroom) and the state dining-room, with its paintings by Lawrence and Gainsborough. After that there is the ballroom itself, now used mostly for investitures and state banquets.

One surprising feature of the palace lies in the north wing – where Prince Philip has his offices. The Chinese dining-room is made up from parts removed from the Brighton Pavilion when Queen Victoria began to dismantle it in the 1840s. The palace contains one of the best art collections in the world, with works by artists such as van Dyck, Hals, Cuyp and Rembrandt housed in the 155-foot (46.5-m)-long picture gallery, part of which was built on the site of the chapel bombed in the Second World War. In order to share her priceless col-lection with the public, the Queen opened a new "Queen's Gallery" in 1962. The public can also visit the royal mews where the great coaches – including the rococo State Coach first used for opening par-liament in 1762 and now used for coronations – are on display.

The throne room: a grand sweep.

A formal setting: royal portraits adorn the walls of the state dining-room.

The centre room and the balcony.

Caernarfon Castle: the Welsh stronghold

The outstanding royal event of 1969 was the investiture of Prince Charles as Prince of Wales at Caernarfon Castle. His great-uncle, later to be Edward VIII (1936), was similarly invested here in 1911, and Queen Victoria (1837-1901) came to this castle to present her son, Albert Edward, to the people of the principality.

The precedent for such a ceremony may have been in 1301 when Edward I (1272-1307) formally declared his son, later Edward II (1307-27), to be Prince of Wales (although his investiture took place at Nefyn, further down the coast). Edward II – who is said to have been born in a small room in the biggest tower in Caernarfon Castle – came to a horrific end at the hands of his wife and her lover 26 years later, and it was many years before the tradition was revived.

Founded in 1283, Caernarfon is the finest of the four greatest castles that Edward I built to subdue the Welsh after his conquest of their country. (The others – Harlech, Beaumaris and Conwy – demand attention for both their settings and their defensive capacity.) With its seven-foot (2.1-m)-thick walls and massive towers, Caernarfon follows the shape of the long rock upon which is built. Two towers dominate the sole entrance, the King's Gate, over which there is a statue of Edward II.

Caernarfon is situated on the Menai Strait, on what was once a peninsula between two rivers. Nine towers are the principal feature of this remarkable construction; the tallest is the Eagle Tower at the western – Menai Strait – end, clearly designed for a last-ditch defence in the event of the castle being overrun. This actually happened in 1294 when a Welsh rebel prince, Madog ap Llywelyn, broke into the castle with his compatriots and caused mayhem until guards managed to drive them off. The Eagle Tower with its three hexagonal turrets was named for the three eagles, one on each turret, which were added in 1317. Only one of them now survives.

It is a tribute to the castle's designer, James of St George, the master of the king's work in Wales, that it withstood three lengthy sieges by Cromwell's armies during the Civil War. After the Restoration, Charles II (1660-85) ordered the castle to be demolished, but, fortunately, no such action was taken.

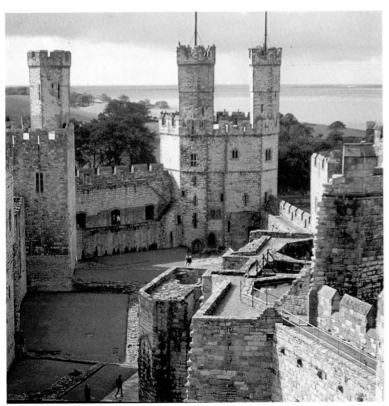

The interior of Caernarfon Castle, looking west towards the Menai Strait.

Carlton House: the regent's lavish home

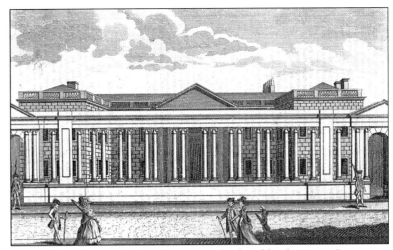

A splendid residence: Carlton House, as redeveloped by the Prince Regent.

The Prince Regent was given to extravagance, but never more so than when he commissioned Henry Holland to redesign his residence in Pall Mall, Carlton House (built in 1709 for a Yorkshire MP, Henry Boyle, later Baron Carleton [*sic*]). Before work was completed in 1791, "Prinny" had run up bills totalling nearly £225,000. It required a parliamentary committee of inquiry to bail the prince out and pay his debts – and only then on the condition that he agree to marry his cousin, Princess Caroline of Brunswick. Carlton House stood to the east of St James's Palace, on a site now occupied by Carlton House Terrace. The taste was impeccable, the cost outrageous.

When the regent became King George IV (1820-30), he decided against having a house in a street and, preferring Buckingham Palace, had Carlton House demolished in 1827. Various fixtures and fittings were removed to other sites. The elegant portico columns, for example, now support the portico of the National Gallery.

Castle of Mey: royal outpost in the north

The Castle of Mey: the Queen Mother's Scottish residence, in Highland.

Soon after the death of King George VI (1936-52), his grieving widow, Queen Elizabeth, was staying with friends in the very north of Scotland when she heard that Barrogill Castle in Caithness, six miles (9.5km) from John O'Groats and overlooking the Pentland Firth and the Orkneys, was for sale. The ancient building was desperately in need of major renovations, and it was three years before the Queen Mother could move in. When she did, Barrogill then reverted to its ▷

continued from previous page
old name, the Castle of Mey. Much of the furniture in the renovated castle was chosen by the Queen Mother herself. The castle's gardens, despite their northerly location and surrounding bleak moorland, are among the most beautiful in Britain. The castle was the seat of the Earls of Caithness, who were the Earls of Orkney until James II of Scots (1437-60) made them exchange the earldom of their island – which was at that time a Norwegian dependency – for that of Caithness. At first Mey was a fortified house, but in c.1560 the fourth earl, George Sinclair, turned it into a true castle. It remained in the Sinclair family, from which the Queen Mother is herself descended, until 1890, when it was bequeathed to an old schoolfriend of John Sinclair, the 14th Earl of Caithness.

Claremont: classical Palladian design in an English garden

A fine manor house in Surrey that is now a girls' boarding school, Claremont has a sad history. An heir to the throne died here, as did Clive of India. In 1769 Clive bought the estate, once owned by Sir John Vanbrugh, who had built himself a crenellated house in a superbly landscaped park. Clive demolished the house and commissioned Lancelot "Capability" Brown to build anew. The result was a classical design with outstanding gardens (now owned by the National Trust and open to the public). The hall is the finest room, with its red columns and oval ceiling.

Clive took a fatal overdose of opium here in 1774, following an enquiry into charges of corruption made against him. In 1816 the Prince Regent, the future George IV (1820-30), gave Claremont to his only child, Charlotte, as a

Set in parkland: a view of Claremont at the time of Princess Charlotte.

wedding gift; tragically, she died in childbirth here in November 1817. In 1866 the manor was bought by Queen Victoria (1837-1901), who often came here. She gave it to her youngest son, Leopold, the Duke of Albany, in 1881. His widow, Helen of Waldeck-Pyrmont, was the last royal resident of Claremont; she died in 1922.

Dunfermline Abbey and Palace: cradle and grave of kings

It was the Anglo-Saxon queen of a Scottish monarch who created royal and religious connotations with Dunfermline. Here was the favourite church of Margaret, the granddaughter of Edmund II of England (1016) and wife of Malcolm III of Scots (1058-93). Both Malcolm and Margaret were buried in the church, and their son, David I (1124-53), founded a Benedictine abbey on the site. English influence was strong: the masons were drawn from northern England, and the abbot appointed by David was from Canterbury.

Although little of the original abbey remains, most of the nave with its heavy round arches survives as an outstanding example of Scottish romanesque. Rebuilding was undertaken after Edward I (1272-1307) and Richard II of England (1377-99) both ransacked the abbey. The east end and the central tower are modern; none the less, the abbey church is in essence

Dunfermline Abbey: the original Benedictine foundation was in c.1150.

one of the most attractive mediaeval buildings in Scotland.

The abbey ceased to exist as a worshipping community after the Reformation. James VI (1567-1625), however, created a palace based around the old abbey guesthouse. A much favoured royal residence, it was the birthplace of Charles I (1625-49) in 1600.

Edinburgh Castle: imposing fortress above the capital

If there is one true symbol of Scotland's long fight for independence it must be the great castle on the rock overlooking the heart of the city of Edinburgh. It also symbolises the union of England and Scotland, for it was here that Mary Queen of Scots (1542-67) gave birth to her son James, who later became the first king of Great Britain. "This is the son who, I hope, shall first unite the two kingdoms," she said as she presented him to her people.

Although nothing of the earliest fortifications remains, Malcolm III (1058-93) built the first castle on the rock. His queen, Margaret, died here on hearing the news of his death in battle. She had wished to be buried at her beloved Dunfermline Abbey [*see left*], but before her body could be moved there the castle was blockaded by her husband's warlike brother, Donald, who was laying claim to the throne. The only exit was down the steep and dangerous west face of the rock, but her sons chose to take the risk with their mother's coffin. As they did so an allegedly miraculous mist came down, giving them cover from their enemies.

During decades of strife between the Scots and their southern neighbours (and rivals), the castle often changed hands. In 1313 a small unit of Robert Bruce's (1306-29) army took it from an occupying English army by scaling the west face, following a route known only to one of their colleagues (who had used it to court a serving-girl in secret). A victorious Robert stripped the castle of much of its defences, leaving only the tiny chapel of St Margaret untouched. A few years later Edward II of England (1307-27) was consequently frustrated in his need for a defensible castle when he sacked the city of Edinburgh; he was eventually forced to retreat.

It was in the reign of Robert Bruce's son, David II (1329-71), that the next great phase of work on the castle was initiated. King David entrusted it to Robert, the son of his half-sister Marjorie. Robert, the future Robert II (1371-90), had

Dominating the skyline: the magnificent Edinburgh Castle by night.

studied French methods of fortification and was responsible for the building of "David's Tower" on the northern side of the castle. It was here that David died in 1371, the last of the Bruce line of kings. The great tower named after him is nearly 60 feet (18m) high and is protected by three doors and a pit. Robert had built well, for the castle was now completely impregnable, staying securely in Scottish hands until the Act of Union between the two nations in 1707.

Edinburgh Castle continued in the meantime to play its role in Scottish history. It was, for example, from here that the seven-year-old James II of Scots (1437-60) went to his coronation in 1437, only to become a pawn in the hands of warring Scots lords who wanted to rule through him. The goriest episode in the castle's history took place in 1440 when the boy Earl of Douglas and his brother were beheaded in the great banqueting hall – which is still used for state occasions and banquets – after a mock trial, with the young king watching.

It was James II who brought "Mons Meg", reputedly the biggest cannon ever built, to the castle. Some believe that the cannon was built in Flanders – hence its name – although others think that it was built in Galloway by a blacksmith and his seven sons. It was meant for defence, but became an essential part of the Edinburgh scene when it boomed out for great royal occasions, such as the marriage of Mary Queen of Scots to the *Dauphin* of France in April 1558.

By the 16th century, however, Edinburgh Castle was rarely used by the monarch, even though Edinburgh was now the capital. Nearby Holyroodhouse was the preferred residence. In 1603 the Scots James VI (1567-1625) became James I of England as well; the king of both realms moved south to London. Apart from a visit by Charles II (1660-85), the castle was ignored by royalty until George IV's (1820-30) hugely successful tour of Scotland in 1822.

Edinburgh Castle reverted to its original role of fortress, becoming an armoury, a barracks, a prison, an administrative centre and a site for tournaments. The last time that a shot was fired in anger was during Charles Edward Stuart's unsuccessful attempt to capture it in the Jacobite rising of 1745. In the 19th century restoration work on the great hall and portcullis gate was begun. Since then the castle has regained much of its former glory, symbolised by the Scottish regalia, on view in the crown room.

Crowning the hill: Edinburgh Castle has an almost unassailable position.

Eltham Palace: splendour in the suburbs

Eltham, in south-east London, is such a suburban sprawl these days that it seems almost impossible to equate it with regal splendour, and yet Eltham Palace was once the favourite home of the kings of England, and the great hall, built by Edward IV (1461-83) c.1475, still exists and is open to the public.

Eltham Palace began life as a fortified manor house. Anthony Bek, the bishop of Durham, acquired it in 1295, eventually handing it over to the future Edward II (1307-27) when still Prince of Wales. Once king, Edward in turn gave it to his queen, Isabella of France.

Various Plantagenet monarchs added to the building, in particular Henry VI (1422-61, 1470-71), who demanded a rebuilt palace in which to welcome his wife, Margaret of Anjou. Henry VIII (1509-47) built a fine chapel and a tunnel under the moat, but preferred to spend more time at Greenwich Palace. His faithful aide and adviser, Cardinal Wolsey, laid down household ordinances at Eltham. Scullions, for instance, were forbidden to "go about or in such vileness as they now do, nor lie in the nights and days in the kitchens or stand by the fireside".

Royalty lost interest in Eltham – although Elizabeth I (1558-1603) came there to hunt. Charles I (1625-49) was upset to find the building in great disrepair, with the splendid great hall turned into a barn. Restoration began in the 19th century, and before long the hall was being used as a drill hall and venue for flower shows and fêtes. Nearly demolished by bombs in the Second World War, it was repaired in the 1950s. The palace is now leased by the University of London.

The rural palace at Eltham: a sketch by a 19th-century artist.

Falkland Palace: home of Scottish kings

In 1958 the Queen marked the 500th anniversary of the granting of a royal charter to the burgh of Falkland in Fife, a beautiful and unspoiled town under the Lomond Hills. In doing so she became the first monarch since Charles II (1660-85) to visit a royal palace which has largely escaped the public notice. Falkland Palace is still the property of the Queen and has been lovingly restored and maintained by its keepers, the descendants of the third Marquis of Bute, as well as the National Trust for Scotland and the local authority. The origins of the palace are obscure, but it was probably first built as a castle in the 12th century by the Earls of Fife, the Macduffs.

They were the principal earls of the ancient kingdom of Alba (Scotland) and had the great privilege of sitting the king on the coronation stone. James II (1437-60) had enlarged the castle (known as a palace after the granting of a royal charter in 1458), but it was to be his great-grandson, James V (1513-42), who, in the 1530s, then made it what

continued from previous page
it is today: Scotland's first building in the Renaissance style. James imported French craftsmen to produce work to the taste of his (successive) French queens, Madeleine of France and Mary of Guise. These craftsmen produced what has been described as the finest *château* in Scotland, whose architecture is similar to that of Nonsuch. Of especial merit are the king's bedchamber and the chapel royal. A curious distinction is that it also contains Scotland's oldest (real) tennis court, built in 1539.

Falkland Palace, Fife: developed into a splendid residence by James V.

Gatcombe Park: a horse-rider's dream

Gatcombe Park, Gloucestershire: home to Anne, the Princess Royal.

No one was surprised when, in 1976, the Queen bought Gatcombe Park in Gloucestershire from the former Conservative minister, Lord "Rab" Butler, for her daughter, Princess Anne, and Anne's husband, Captain Mark Phillips. Not only was this fine two-storeyed manor house set in the very heart of Beaufort Hunt country; it also contained the kind of stables and grounds which were eminently suitable for two Olympic-class riders. Gatcombe was built in the late 18th century by a wealthy sheep-farmer, Edward Shephard, and remodelled by George Basevi, a brilliant pupil of the classic revivalist architect Sir John Soane. Little has been altered since 1829, when the conservatory was added – a considerable factor in the house's charm.

Glamis Castle: bristling with battlements

Glamis Castle: the romantic setting for the birth of Princess Margaret.

Glamis Castle, the home of the Bowes-Lyon family, the Earls of Strathmore, stands some 30 miles (48km) south-west of Montrose, in Tayside. It was the Queen Mother's childhood home, and in 1930 she gave birth here to Princess Margaret – the first birth in the immediate royal family in Scotland since 1602.

Bristling with towers and battlements, the castle is on lands granted to the Lyon family in 1376 by Robert II (1371-90). The oldest part of the castle – the crypt and part of the central tower – dated from about a century later, however. When Mary Queen of Scots (1542-67) visited Glamis it already had its distinctive L-shaped keep. The banqueting hall, the most impressive room in the castle, was built in the early 17th century. The baronial-style east wing, reminiscent of Balmoral, was added in 1891. The present owner of Glamis is the 17th Earl of Strathmore, the Queen Mother's nephew.

Greenwich Palace: rich in Tudor history

River prospect: Henry VIII's palace at Greenwich (from an early drawing).

Although it has not been a royal residence since the middle of the last century – when it became the Royal Naval College – the former Greenwich Palace is rich in history. It was here that Henry VIII (1509-47) married Catherine of Aragon. It was the birthplace of their daughter Mary and the scene of her betrothal to the king of France's son. Henry first saw Anne Boleyn here, and it was from Greenwich that he and his second bride set out to be married in a raucous procession of 50 boats led by a giant dragon breathing smoke and fireworks.

Ironically, Anne Boleyn was to set out on the melancholy journey to the Tower and her beheading from Greenwich. It was later the location for Henry's marriage to Anne of Cleves in 1540. Queen Elizabeth I (1558-1603), who was born at Greenwich, also reinstated the Royal Maundy here.

The first palace on the site was built by Humphrey, the Duke of Gloucester, the brother of Henry V (1413-22), and elaborated throughout the 15th century. The Tudor palace was demolished in the late 17th century. The jewel of today's Greenwich is the Queen's House, built during the reign of James I (1603-25), which now houses the National Maritime Museum. The house was designed by Inigo Jones in 1616 for Anne of Denmark, King James's wife, and, with its gilt and fine sculptures, is one of the most interesting royal homes in Britain. The brick-built house with Portland stone facings was incorporated into a grand design by Sir Christopher Wren and Sir John Vanbrugh. The latter had been imprisoned in the Bastille by Louis XIV on a spying charge and later built what is known as Vanbrugh Castle at Greenwich.

The Queen's House is in Greenwich Park, with the buildings of the old Royal Observatory whose staff moved from the capital some years ago, when pollution clouded the London night sky.

The Queen's House at Greenwich, built by Inigo Jones in the C17th.

Hampton Court Palace: a gift from a cardinal to a monarch

In 1514 the most powerful man in the country – apart from King Henry VIII (1509-47) himself – was Thomas Wolsey, the Lord Chancellor and Archbishop of York. It was entirely natural that the corpulent cardinal should seek a home suited to his stature. He leased a site on the banks of the Thames at Hampton from the Knights Hospitallers of St John of Jerusalem, and built one of the finest palaces in the country – Hampton Court.

It took five years for 2,500 workmen to build Hampton Court, and for the next ten years, Wolsey entertained sumptuously at the great house which, it is said, had 1,000 rooms for guests alone. Henry was a regular guest at Wolsey's lavish parties, but as time went by he became increasingly resentful of his principal adviser's extravagance.

Wolsey shrewdly made a gift of the property to his monarch, but he fell rapidly from grace when he failed to secure papal approval for the king's divorce from his first wife, Catherine of Aragon. Arrested for treason, Wolsey was lucky to die peacefully of natural causes at Leicester on the way to face his accusers in London.

Henry immediately set about stamping his personality on the palace and did his utmost to remove every trace of its former owner. He added the great hall, a magnificent creation with a remarkable timber roof decorated in Renaissance style. The chapel royal has an equally striking ceiling which truly demonstrates the Tudor craftsmen's skills.

Little evidence remains that the cardinal ever lived here – although the sheer scale of his closet and chamber is a sure indication of the grandeur with which he loved to surround himself. The athletic Henry has left a remarkable legacy in the royal tennis court, the oldest in England, and one of the few courts left in Britain where "real" tennis is played. Henry also amused himself with bowling alleys, a tiltyard and archery butts.

The intertwined initials H and A – Henry and Anne (Boleyn) – replaced Wolsey's carved cardinal's hats on the gates and doorways. The initials can still be seen on the doorways (as they can at St James's Palace). Anne was executed in 1536

Hampton Court: the towering palace was begun by Cardinal Wolsey in 1514.

and it was Jane Seymour who provided Henry with his longed-for male heir (later Edward VI, 1547-53) at Hampton Court – only to die 12 days after giving birth. It was Catherine Howard, Henry's fifth wife, who was said to have screamed her pleas to Henry at the door of the chapel in Hampton Court before she was taken off for her trial and eventual beheading in 1542. Catherine's ghost is said still to scream down the long corridors of the palace – which is possibly why it lost royal favour.

More than half a million people visit Hampton Court each year – with another one-and-a-half million going to see just the gardens and the parks. History is all around them. Mary I (1553-58) spent her honeymoon here, where she also later suffered her tragic phantom pregnancy. Her half-sister, Elizabeth I (1558-1603), was a prisoner at Hampton Court, as was Charles I (1625-49), who escaped to the Isle of Wight from here.

William III (1689-1702) and Mary II (1689-94) disliked the old building but admired its situation, and they invited Sir Christopher Wren to build a new palace. Wren proposed a building along the lines of Versailles, with a mile-long approach across the park. He demolished much of the existing building, but then the money ran out. Nonetheless, Wren had built two sets of royal apartments – William and Mary were each sovereigns in their own right – with separate staircases leading to each. It is perhaps the combination of Tudor splendour and Wren's classicism that makes Hampton Court such a popular attraction. The interior of the palace is rich in

This part of the east front at Hampton Court was added in the 17th century.

A balanced design: the grand façade of Harewood House, Yorkshire.

Harewood House: Italian art and English furniture in Yorkshire

Few royal homes reflect the characters of their owners more than Harewood House in Yorkshire. It is a traditional stately home near Leeds, built of local yellow stone and set in magnificent parkland landscaped by Inigo Jones – the home of the Earl and Countess of Harewood, who represent the intellectual, classical-music-loving end of the royal family. Lord Harewood divides his time between looking after the house and running the English National Opera Company in London.

Robert Adam designed the interior, completing the work in 1772. He created a superb setting for the Harewood collection of Chinese and Sèvres porcelain. The family became part of the royal family when the sixth earl – the father of the present earl – married the only daughter of George V (1910-36). Princess Mary, the Princess Royal, a trained nurse who had the house commissioned as a hospital during the Second World War. The family has now built up one of the finest collections of Italian art in Britain, with works by Titian, Veronese, Bellini and Tintoretto. There are family portraits by Lawrence, Romney, Gainsborough and Reynolds, together with a portrait of Princess Mary, who died in 1965, by Sir Oswald Birley. A valuable furniture collection includes some of Chippendale's best pieces.

Hampton Court: the chapel royal.

continued from previous page
craftsmanship, much of it flamboyant. Work never stops on this great building. Air-conditioning has been added to ensure that the earliest paintings, especially those on wood panels, are displayed in a carefully controlled environment. One rare attraction is the king's guard-room with its display of 3,000 weapons laid out by the gunsmith of William III (1689-1702).

It was George III (1760-1820) who first granted "grace and favour" apartments, usually to widows of distinguished crown servants. In the reign of Victoria (1837-1901) nearly 1,000 rooms here were turned into 45 apartments. The practice ended in 1972, although there are still a few residents. Nowadays the larger rooms are used by craft organisations with royal connections, such as the Embroiderers' Guild and the Textile Conservation Centre.

Hatfield House: the palace where the Elizabethan age began

On 17 November 1558, a deputation led by the Earls of Pembroke and Arundel rode from London to Hatfield House in Hertfordshire. There, at her Greek studies under an oak tree in the park, they found Princess Elizabeth, the daughter of Henry VIII (1509-47) and Anne Boleyn. They broke the news to her that Queen Mary (1553-58), her half-sister, was dead and that, she, Elizabeth, was queen. Elizabeth fell to her knees in amazement.

Henry VIII coveted this great palace, developed in 1496 by John Morton, the bishop of Ely, in much the same way that he was to covet Hampton Court, and manipulated the deeds of the property into his possession by guile and threat.

Only the great hall, a staggeringly beautiful piece of Tudor architecture, remains of the original palace. Much was demolished by the Cecil family, to whom James I (1603-25) gave Hatfield in exchange for the Cecils' Theobalds, also in Hertfordshire [see page 606]. The 230-foot-long hall with its open timber roof has been described as "the foremost monument of mediaeval domestic architecture in Hertfordshire".

The magnificent south front at Hatfield House was once the entrance.

Hampton Court: an interior view.

A garden view: the east side of the 15th-century Tudor palace at Hatfield.

Highgrove House: a Cotswolds retreat

Home to the Prince of Wales: Highgrove House, in Gloucestershire.

Considering that it is the country home of our future king and queen, Highgrove, near Tetbury in Gloucestershire, is the least pretentious of royal homes. The Prince and Princess of Wales love this traditional late-18th-century English country house in the Cotswolds.

In 1980 Prince Charles bought the property from Maurice Macmillan, a minister under Edward Heath and the son of the former prime minister Harold Macmillan, the Earl of Stockton. It was advertised as "a distinguished Georgian house with spacious ... accommodation, comprising four reception rooms, domestic quarters, nine bedrooms, six bathrooms, nursery wing, and full central heating".

Prince Charles is a keen gardener, and the walled and wild-flower gardens at Highgrove are his special pride.

Holyroodhouse: official home in Scotland

An austere grandeur: Holyroodhouse, the Queen's official Scottish residence.

Holyroodhouse in Edinburgh, a vast and austere building that serves as the official residence of the Queen during her annual visits to Scotland, is perhaps best known for a horrific murder that took place there in 1566. Mary Queen of Scots (1542-67), newly married to Lord Darnley, was dining with her Italian secretary, David Riccio, when intruders burst into the tiny cabinet room. Riccio was dragged into the queen's outer chamber and stabbed to death, allegedly at Darnley's behest. Darnley himself was murdered a year later, and his murderer, the Earl of Bothwell, became Mary's third husband.

Little remains of the original building, an abbey founded in 1128 by David I (1124-53), which was enlarged by James IV (1488-1513), only to be badly damaged by the armies of Henry VII of England (1485-1509). Charles Edward Stuart, the Young Pretender, held court at Holyroodhouse for a few weeks, and the rotund George IV (1820-30) wore a kilt – with flesh-coloured tights – here, causing much delight and hilarity.

Queen Victoria (1837-1901) celebrated her love affair with Scotland by opening the palace to the public. The main entrance takes visitors into the west arcade of the inner court; the floor above contained the suites for Charles II (1660-85) and his queen, Catherine of Braganza, who never actually visited the palace. The west drawing-room has a particularly fine moulded ceiling dating back to c.1670. The old guard hall is now a dining-room and has served in the past as a throne room. The privy chamber is especially attractive, with its wood decorations, and was used by Victoria as a sitting-room. The present royal family's private apartments are on the second floor.

Permanent exhibitions of Flemish and French tapestries and armour attract thousands of tourists annually, as does the scene of Riccio's murder – although few would believe that so great a drama could take place in so small a room.

Kensington Palace: 300 years of royalty

Kensington Palace: the 17th-century south front, built by Christopher Wren.

Kensington Palace came into its own as a royal residence in the early 18th century. When he first saw the house in Kensington Gardens, George I (1714-27), a German who never liked England, was reminded of his own Herrenhausen palace in Hanover and ordered much of the place to be rebuilt. It had been a royal residence since 1689, when William III (1689-1702) bought it.

Commissioned by William to extend the house, Sir Christopher Wren built four pavilions and an impressive clock-tower. William Kent's decorations in the three new state rooms, now open to the public, are exquisite, as is his painting for the king's staircase, with its *trompe l'oeil* effects of George I and his courtiers gazing down from balconies. It is one of the great artistic attractions of London.

George II (1727-60) was robbed of his watch and other items in the gardens; much later, he was to end his days here. Other royal residents have included Mary II (1689-94), who, like her husband William III (1689-1702), died at the palace; Queen Victoria (1837-1901), who was born and grew up here. Queen Mary, who married George V (1910-36), was born here as May of Teck. Current residents include Prince and Princess Michael of Kent, Princess Margaret and the Prince and Princess of Wales.

▷

Kew Palace: royal houses whose gardens bring the countryside to the capital

The Dutch House: the only surviving royal building in Kew Gardens.

Between his terrible bouts of mental illness, George III (1760-1820) – "Farmer George" – loved gardens in general and the great gardens at Kew in particular. Together with his wife, Queen Charlotte, he was never happier than during the years spent at the **Dutch House** at Kew, which counts as a palace despite its comparatively small size.

This four-storeyed brick house was built in 1631 by a Dutch merchant (hence the name) and became the home of the lord mayor of London before it was leased by George and later bought by him in 1781. The Dutch House is the only royal building to survive in Kew Gardens. It is filled with souvenirs of "Farmer George" and his family, including tapestries by Charlotte and George's prayer book, in which he scratched out "our most religious and gracious King" and substituted "a most miserable sinner".

Although a palace, the Dutch House is really no more than a modest manor house, with a main entrance that opens onto a long passageway. The king's dining-room is 31 feet by 21 feet (9.3m x 6.3m), with a single Tudor rose in the centre of the ceiling. Several of George's 15 children – described by the Duke of Wellington as "the damnedest millstones about the necks of any government that can be imagined" – were born at the adjacent **White House** at Kew [*see below*], and the Dutch House was allotted to the Prince of Wales from the age of nine.

When he was 17 years old, the prince fell in love with an actress, Mary (Perdita) Robinson, who was playing in *The Winter's Tale* at Drury Lane. Despite his parents' stern views on morality, the future George IV (1820-30) arranged for his love to be smuggled into the house, and sent her love-letters signed "Florizel". Perdita became the prince's mistress and was given a bond worth £20,000, to be redeemed when George came of age.

Queen Charlotte died at Kew in 1818, content in the knowledge that, before she died, two of her errant sons (the Dukes of Kent and Clarence) had discarded their mistresses to make "respectable" marriages at the Dutch House. Their father, blind and senile, died two years later at Windsor, and the Dutch House was then closed up – apart from an occasional visit from the cleaners – for nearly 80 years, until Queen Victoria (1837-1901) decided to open it on the occasion of her diamond jubilee in 1897.

During George III's early attacks of "madness" he was confined to the **White House**, a little way from the Dutch House. It was rebuilt by William Kent, whose ceiling in the tapestry-hung drawing-room was said to be as notable as the one he designed for Kensington Palace. The gallery was particularly striking with its blue and gilt wainscoting. Kent was, however, saddened by the damage caused by the family playing ball-games in the drawing-room.

Little remains of the White House except for the famous pagoda built by Sir William Chambers in 1760 and the equally famous gardens begun by George III's mother, Augusta. In 1802 the house in which George had often been strait-jacketed was demolished to make room for the most grandiose scheme of his reign – a vast, gothic **New Palace** overlooking the Thames. Designed by James Wyatt, it turned out to be a hideous white elephant, an "extraordinary exercise in late Georgian baronial", as the guidebook described it at the time. Another commentator likened it to the Bastille, observing that the foundations were in a bog close to the Thames, and that the principal object within view was "the dirty town of Brentford".

The guide gives some indication of how the palace looked. The central keep was apparently four storeys high, and the courtyard building three storeys. The guide's author wrote: "It is obvious that the building, if completed, would have been highly inconvenient and uncomfortable."

By the time that £100,000 had been spent on the palace, George was seriously ill. His wife refused to live there. George IV hated it and had it demolished with explosives in 1827. The staircase, however, survives in Buckingham Palace, and one window was used in building a garden shed at Kew.

The New Palace at Kew, built by George III: it was destroyed after his death.

The White House at Kew: it was demolished to make way for the New Palace.

Leeds Castle: a moated fortress fit for kings and conferences

The romantic setting of Leeds Castle, in Kent: it was turned from a fort into a palace by King Henry VIII.

The superb Leeds Castle near Maidstone in Kent became a royal possession as repayment of a debt by William of Leyburn, its owner, to Edward I (1272-1307) in 1278. Even before that, King Stephen (1135-54) captured it from Robert, the Earl of Gloucester, and rebuilt the original Norman enclosed earthworks in stone.

Edward I carried out further work, including the provision of an outer stone wall with flanking towers. His most significant improvement was the creation of water defences by damming the river Len. The castle is on two islands, with the keep on the smaller.

According to romantic legend, it was at Leeds Castle that the widow of Henry V (1413-22), Catherine de Valois, fell in love with her clerk to the wardrobe, Owen Twdwr; from them the Tudor dynasty was de-scended. The great-grandson of Catherine and Owen, Henry VIII (1509-47), was a frequent visitor here. It was he who turned it from a fortress into a palace. Leeds was bought in 1926 by Lady Baillie, who did major renovation work and set up a trust to maintain it for the nation. It has since been used for international conferences and was a convalescent home in the Second World War.

Marlborough House: hosting dukes, mistresses and officialdom

Like so many of the great buildings of London, this elegant red-brick house in the Mall was built by Sir Christopher Wren, in this case for the victorious Duke of Marlborough in 1705. During its tenure by Edward VII (1901-10) when he was Prince of Wales it was renowned for the racy "Marlborough House set" that so upset Victoria (1837-1901). The socialite beauty and actress Lillie Langtry was a frequent guest, and large sums of money are said to have changed hands at the prince's card table.

The principal feature of the house is the Ramillies staircase, with its wrought-iron balustrade and black marble steps, decorated with scenes from the Battle of Ramillies (1706), one of the Duke of Marlborough's greatest victories over the French. The vast painting of the battle is by Louis Laguerre,

Stately elegance: Marlborough House in London, built by Christopher Wren.

a Frenchman who settled in England and completed pictures depicting most of the duke's battles – Blenheim and Malplaquet among them – for Marlborough House. After the death of George V (1910-36) it was the home of Queen Mary until her own death in 1953. She collected many of the *objets d'art* which are another of its features. It now houses the Commonwealth Secretariat and Conference Centre.

Linlithgow Palace: ruined masterpiece

Linlithgow Palace, which is between Edinburgh and Stirling, has been called "the fairest royal house in Scotland". Few would doubt it as they walk through the ruins of this granite masterpiece. Linlithgow was the birthplace of Mary Queen of Scots (1542-67), and it was from here that she was journeying when abducted by the Earl of Bothwell, whom she later married.

In later centuries the house of five Stuart kings, the original timber manor house built by David I (1124-53) of Scots was fortified by Edward I (1272-1307) of England. His architect was James of St George, who also built Edward's great Welsh castles. In 1313, a Scots force smuggled itself into the castle in a haywain and killed the

Linlithgow Palace, near Edinburgh.

English garrison. The house was demolished, to be rebuilt first by David II (1329-71), and then by James I (1406-37), who left the palace much as we see it today. Charles I (1625-49) was the last monarch to sleep in the palace, which was badly damaged by fire in 1746. Restoration was not begun until the 19th century.

Tradition has it that Margaret, the wife of James IV (1488-1513), waited in a room in the north-west tower for her husband to return from Flodden Field, unaware that he lay slain, along with thousands of his men. The chamber is still known as Queen Margaret's Bower. ▷

Nether Lypiatt Manor: 'golden triangle'

With the Prince and Princess of Wales at Highgrove and the Princess Royal at Gatcombe Park, the manor house in the village of Nether Lypiatt, near Stroud in Gloucestershire, makes up the third point of the so-called "Golden Triangle". It became a royal residence when purchased a few years ago by Prince and Princess Michael of Kent.

It is, by royal standards, a small house, the main block being only 46 feet square. Set high on a hill overlooking the village, the manor was built in the first decade of the 18th century by Judge Coxe, a local MP and clerk of the patent office in London. By the beginning of this century it had long been out of the Coxe family and needed urgent repairs. These were first carried out by the then owner, and continued by Princess Michael, a professional interior decorator. The manor is faced in blocks of top-quality Cotswold stone. All the original main rooms inside survive, as does the wainscoting. A new wing was added in 1923.

Nonsuch Palace: the lost 'pearl of realm'

A 16th-century view of Henry VIII's magnificent Nonsuch Palace in Surrey.

There was never a royal palace quite like it – hence the name, "none such". It was the greatest architectural triumph of Henry VIII (1509-47), his "pearl of the realm" – and yet hardly a trace of Nonsuch Palace remains today. One of the most exciting buildings ever to grace the Surrey countryside, it disappeared after a feud between landowners.

Intent on a palace to outshine the French *château* of Chambord, Henry demolished a priory and an entire village near Ewell to create the setting. Over 500 workmen, including craftsmen from France and Italy, were hired to build a palace consisting of two courtyards, each vying with the other for splendour. The inner court of Nonsuch contained the royal apartments and was built of white stone, decorated in gold and dominated by two towers five storeys high. The walls were alive with plaster statues depicting the arts and the virtues, classical gods and heroes.

Henry died before Nonsuch was completed. Charles II (1660-85) gave it to his mistress, Lady Castlemaine, in 1670. In the course of a long-running dispute with the park-keeper, the Earl of Berkely, first the banqueting house and then the inner court were demolished. By 1702 the once glorious palace was no more than a ruin.

Nonsuch design on an inlaid chest.

Oatlands: a hunting-lodge turned palace

Oatlands: favoured as a hunting base by Henry VIII and Elizabeth I.

Oatlands, a magnificent stately pile that once stood south of the river Thames at Weybridge, began life as a hunting-lodge. Henry VIII (1509-47) used to hunt in Oatlands Park and enlarged the lodge there for his then queen, Anne of Cleves. Visitors passed through the outer to the middle court, where the royal apartments, chapel and great hall were to be found. Beyond, in the inner court, lay the gardens.

Elizabeth I (1558-1603) also enjoyed hunting at Oatlands, and James I (1603-25) built a silkworm house here, possibly as part of his attempt to establish an English silk industry. Oatlands was demolished between 1650 and 1652, but in 1794 the architect Henry Holland was commissioned to rebuild it by Frederick, the ("Grand Old") Duke of York. Holland created a grand country house with views over the North Downs. In 1824 the duke sold the property to Edward Hughes Ball-Hughes. Nicknamed "Golden Ball" on account of his riches, Ball-Hughes carried out radical rebuilding on Oatlands. The present structure is now an hotel, with only the gate piers from Holland's work surviving unmolested.

Osborne House: Victoria's island retreat

Home to the nine royal children: the nursery at Osborne House.

In December 1861, just five days after Prince Albert's death, Queen Victoria (1837-1901) travelled to the Isle of Wight and the house in which she and her consort had been happiest. Victoria ordered that every one of her husband's possessions was to be kept exactly as he had left it. Her command was obeyed, and is obeyed to this day in the queen's suite at Osborne. Like Balmoral, Osborne was to acquire a special attraction for Victoria and Albert. It was their own choice as an escape from the formality of Buckingham Palace and Windsor, and, again like Balmoral, it was Albert's creation. Victoria had bought it in 1844 together with 1,000 acres (400ha) of land, but it soon became clear that the house would have to grow as her family itself grew.

The house was built in two sections: one, a pavilion for the family, the other for the household and servants. The architect Thomas Cubitt compared the Solent, which Osborne overlooks, to the Bay of Naples, hence the two Italianate *campanile* towers, the taller of them 107 feet (32.1m) high. Tiles and statues in the courtyard help to complete the Latin feel. Queen Victoria died at Osborne in January 1901. She lay in state there before being taken to the Frogmore mausoleum to join her deeply-mourned husband.

Neither Edward VII (1901-10) nor his son George V (1910-36) particularly liked Osborne – Edward preferred to sleep on board the royal yacht during Cowes week – and it was given to the nation. The main block became a military convalescent home, while the Royal Naval College stood in the grounds until 1921. In 1954 Elizabeth II opened Victoria's private apartments to the public.

A strong position: Pembroke Castle retains a forbidding aspect.

Italianate style: the splendid terrace and courtyard at Osborne House.

Pembroke Castle: subjugating the Welsh

Pembroke Castle in south-western Wales became important from the late 11th century onwards as a key English garrison in the occupation and final subjugation of Wales. It also served as a staging-post for armies moving west to occupy Ireland. By the 12th century, the earldom of Pembroke had been raised to a county palatine – which meant that the holder was the most powerful man in Wales.

Earl Roger of Montgomery built the first castle at Pembroke in around 1090. Although made of just stakes and turf, it was the only Norman castle in Wales to withstand attacks by the local Welsh. Between around 1190 and 1220 William Marshal, the Earl of Pembroke and the greatest nobleman and statesman of his day, built most of the castle as it now stands on a promontory of the river Pembroke, itself a natural defensive point.

It was improved by William de Valence, the half-brother of Henry III (1216-72), but it became neglected and had to be ransomed during Owain Glyndwr's uprising in the early 15th century. On a more peaceful note, Pembroke was the birthplace in 1457 of Henry Twdwr, the future Henry VII (1485-1509). The castle is "egg-shaped", its apex cut off to form an inner ward containing the huge round keep, 82 feet (25m) high and with walls 16 feet (5m) thick, that dominates the rest.

Part of the castle's charm is its proximity to the attractive town of Pembroke itself. Sadly, Cromwell's army destroyed much of the walls near the gatehouse, as well as the fronts of all the towers, to ensure that they were never used again. Pembroke Castle is still, however, a major tourist attraction, and much of it has been preserved in good condition – including the mediaeval graffiti in the Monkton Tower.

Richmond Palace: a showpiece for Tudors

It was the ambition of Henry VII (1485-1509) to build a palace that demonstrated to the world the wealth and power of the Tudor dynasty. He chose the site of the recently burnt-down Sheen Palace [*see overleaf*], a former royal residence, to create Richmond Palace.

Henry could not have chosen a better site. This one faced the Thames to the north and was set in gently rolling farmland. Richmond became much more than a palace, however. By the time that it was completed, in 1501, Henry had created a small self-supporting town with farms, hunting grounds, orchards and gardens. Sadly, no plans of Richmond Palace have survived, but contemporary descriptions refer to a great courtyard and a large ornamental fountain with "lions and red dragons and other goodly beasts".

The great hall, which measured 100 feet by 40 (30m by 12m), was notable for its timber roof decorated with carvings and hung with pendants. A giant brick fireplace was situated in the centre of the hall; the smoke rose up to be emitted through a domed turret in the roof. Pictures of warrior-kings decorated the walls, with the place

Tudor style: the east view of King Henry VII's superb palace at Richmond.

continued from previous page
of honour being occupied by a depiction of King Henry himself. The most spectacular feature of the palace was the so-called Canted Tower, 120 steps high, offering a spectacular view towards the distant hills of Surrey.

The royal library at Richmond was Henry's particular joy, with its priceless collection of manuscripts and books on which he lavished hundreds of pounds. It is thought that most of these were later taken to Whitehall Palace and, sadly, destroyed there in the fire of 1698.

Henry VIII (1509-47) often came to Richmond Palace to hunt. Catherine of Aragon gave birth to their first son here, but the poor child died aged only seven weeks.

Henry's daughter, Elizabeth I (1558-1603), also died here. Over succeeding centuries the palace fell into neglect, only Richmond Lodge surviving. All that remains now of the Tudor palace is the gatehouse and part of a courtyard.

The first building on the site was **Sheen Palace**, originally a manor house, occasionally used by Edward II (1307-27) and greatly extended by his successor, Edward III (1327-77), who ended his days there. Richard II (1377-99) carried out further improvements, but following the death of his queen, Anne of Bohemia, he ordered the manor's demolition. Henry V (1413-22) rebuilt what was left, but a fire in 1497 so gutted this building that Henry VII started afresh.

Sandringham: Edward VII established it as a favourite royal retreat.

The river view: Henry VII's Richmond Palace as seen from the Thames.

Sandringham: an estate fit for shooting

"I have always been so happy here, and I love the place," wrote George VI (1936-52) to his mother, Queen Mary. Like his grandfather, Edward VII (1901-10), and his father, George V (1910-36), the present Queen's father had a special attachment to this huge red-brick house set among woods in the flat and windy Norfolk countryside. The affection continues today, with the royal family spending their New Year holidays at the house.

All three kings had a passion for shooting, and Sandringham, which Edward VII made into one of the best shoots in England, provided excellent sport, with annual bags of 30,000 head of pheasants and partridges. Both George V and George VI died at Sandringham, the latter after a happy day spent shooting hares on "keepers' day" with local tenants, gamekeepers and friends.

It was Edward VII's wayward nature, when Prince of Wales, that brought Sandringham into the royal domain. His father, Prince Albert, wanted his son to spend more time in rural pursuits and less with his favoured courtesans. Edward was equally anxious to get away from his mother's censorious looks and saw both the path to freedom from parents and the prospect of good shooting when he was introduced to Sandringham. Edward persuaded Victoria and Albert to buy the house and 8,000 acres (3,200ha) of surrounding land in 1861 for £221,000.

The original house, then called Sandringham Hall, had been built in 1771 by Squire Cornish Henley on the site of an Elizabethan house. A three-storeyed porch and conservatory were added in the mid-19th century by the then owner, Charles Spencer Cowper, a stepson of Lord Palmerston. It was Palmerston who helped to negotiate the sale to the Prince of Wales.

When Edward moved in with his Danish bride, Alexandra, in 1863, he was delighted that his young wife shared his love for the countryside and was prepared to put up with the bracing Norfolk air. He should not have been surprised, though: the flat landscape must have reminded the princess of her native Denmark. He enlarged the house, adding lodges for the servants. Space remained tight, however, and in 1865 Edward decided that the only thing to do was raze everything to the ground and start from scratch. Only the conservatory survived, to be turned into a billiards room.

In 1867 Edward commissioned the architect A J Humbert to design the new building. Humbert had worked for the prince before, at Sandringham and Osborne; he had also done some work on the royal mausoleum at Frogmore. Construction was completed by the time of Edward's 29th birthday on 9 November 1870, and a celebration dinner was held, on the prince's orders, for the workmen.

The new Sandringham did not garner the kind of praise lavished on other royal residences. It is, to be candid, an indifferent example of mid-Victorian architecture, more homely than regal. Its owner was happy with it, however. Edward was especially fond of the gas illuminations at Sandringham – from a plant he had installed – and equally proud of the water-closets and even a primitive shower.

Edward had planned to celebrate his 50th birthday, in 1891, at Sandringham. Fires were lit in the guest-rooms, but one started a chimney fire that resulted in 14 rooms being gutted. The party went ahead, however, under tarpaulins and corrugated-iron sheeting. The Sandringham estate includes six villages and part of the royal stud, as well as the royal pigeon lofts (the Queen is a keen pigeon fancier). Other royal houses on the estate are described on the opposite page.

Anmer Hall, at Sandringham: now home to the Duke and Duchess of Kent.

York Cottage, when it was home to the Prince of Wales (later George V).

York Cottage is among the smaller royal residences on the Sandringham estate and was originally called Bachelor's Cottage. This building was erected by Edward VII, when Prince of Wales, before he had the main block demolished. The name changed when the cottage was given to George, the Duke of York, later also Prince of Wales. Despite having a large family, George stayed on at York Cottage even after he became George V. His mother, Queen Alexandra, remained in the "Big House", as Edward VII had particularly requested that she should. York Cottage is an unremarkable building, resembling three or four suburban houses with pointed gables and mock-Tudor beams.

Anmer Hall is a two-storeyed, late-Georgian house on the estate. Built by a local family which owned it until the turn of the century, since 1973 it has been the home of the Duke and Duchess of Kent. Set in ten acres of parkland, the house boasts an eleven-bay frontage.

Somerset House: from queens to taxmen

Somerset House, in London, from an early 18th-century engraving.

Somerset House is named after Edward Seymour, the Duke of Somerset, whose sister was Jane Seymour, the third wife of Henry VIII (1509-47). Edward was lord protector of the realm, charged with the care of the boy king Edward VI (1547-53). Needing a home to match his status, he built himself Somerset Place [sic] – as England's first Renaissance palace – on the banks of the Thames, just south of the Strand. A three-storeyed gatehouse led through to a quadrangle and the great hall, beyond which lay ornamental gardens and the river.

After Somerset was beheaded in 1552, his house became a crown possession. Mary I (1553-58) gave it to the young Princess Elizabeth, who rarely used it after she became queen in 1558. James I (1603-25) gave the house to his wife, Anne of Denmark, and she commissioned Inigo Jones to design private apartments for herself. Charles I (1625-49) gave Denmark House, as it was now called, to his wife, Henrietta Maria. She commissioned Jones, who lived here, to build a chapel (1630-35). Work continued after the Restoration (1660), but the last royal occupant – Catherine of Braganza, the widow of Charles II (1660-85) – left the renamed Somerset House in 1692.

Royal interest in the site waned, and in 1775 the old palace was demolished. Today's building, the first big block purpose-built for government offices, was begun in 1776. Once the home of the general register office of births, marriages and deaths (1836-1973), it now houses the Courtauld Institute galleries, the Probate Registry and the Board of Inland Revenue.

Stirling Castle: fortress and royal palace

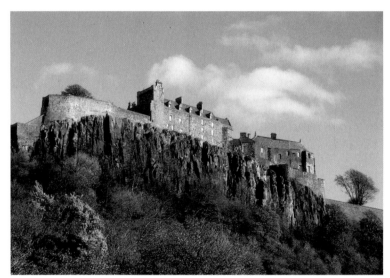

A forbidding position: Stirling Castle perches on top of a rugged crag.

Despite its apparently invulnerable position on a 250-foot (75-m)-high crag overlooking the Forth, Stirling Castle changed hands more than any other fortress during the centuries of war between England and Scotland. The first exchange occurred in 1174, when Henry II of England (1154-89) got it in return for releasing William I of Scots (1165-1214). It was still being fought over in 1746, when Charles Edward Stuart, the Young Pretender, unsuccessfully tried to capture it.

The first royal castle stood here in the early 11th century. What visitors see today, however, dates mainly from the 16th century, when a major rebuilding programme was undertaken. The defences were improved by James IV (1488-1513), and the Renaissance-style royal apartments were added by James V (1513-42). Despite its warlike reputation, Stirling is also distinguished for the exotic and, some might say, erotic Renaissance figures that grace the castle within the walls, which the Victorian architect Robert Billings described as "obscene" and "abominations".

Perhaps the greatest occasion in the castle's history was the 1542 coronation of Mary Queen of Scots (1542-67), in the chapel. Her son, James VI of Scotland and I of England (1567-1625), also spent time at Stirling, where his son and then heir, Henry, who became Prince of Wales, was born in 1594.

Restoration work on the castle has been going on for some years in an attempt to reverse the damage – some would say vandalism – caused in the 18th century when Stirling became a barracks, a status it retained until 1964.

St James's Palace: court of ambassadors

Entrance way: the 16th-century gatehouse at St James's Palace in London.

Little remains of the original palace built by Henry VIII (1509-47) on the site of the Convent of St James the Less, a 14th-century foundation. The initials of Henry and Anne Boleyn are still to be seen, however, on the gateway looking up St James's Street in the west end of London. It was here that Henry's elder daughter, Mary I (1553-58), ended her days.

Today's palace is a gaunt, brick-built building to which foreign ambassadors are brought in horse-drawn carriages to be accredited to the "Court of St James's". It consists mostly of grace-and-favour apartments and administrative offices, such as that of the lord chamberlain, the former theatrical censor. Despite its mundane role in the present royal scheme of things, it has a rich history. It was from here that Elizabeth I (1558-1603) rode out to inspect her troops at Tilbury. Charles I (1625-49) spent his last night at St James's before walking out across the park to Whitehall and his execution. The Act of Union between England and Scotland was signed here in 1707; and in 1840 Victoria (1837-1901) married Albert in the chapel.

Much of the abdication drama of 1936 was played out at **York House** on the north side of ambassadors' court at St James's. It was the London home of the Prince of Wales before he was proclaimed King Edward VIII here in 1936. **Clarence House**, an outbuilding of the palace in the 17th century but elaborated by John Nash in 1825, is the London home of the Queen Mother and contains a fine collection of chiefly English paintings.

A graceful design: Clarence House, the Queen Mother's London residence.

Thatched House Lodge: home in the park

Thatched House Lodge, Richmond Park: now home to Princess Alexandra.

It is an estate agent's dream: an elegant London country house set in beautiful Richmond Park and less than ten minutes from the nearest station. Thatched House Lodge, the home of Princess Alexandra and Sir Angus Ogilvy, is the only privately-owned house in the royal park. Although the park is the weekend playground of thousands of Londoners, the Ogilvys enjoy complete privacy on the property, which is set in three acres of grounds, fenced off against the Richmond Park deer.

Originally one of two lodges provided for the park rangers, Thatched House Lodge – the name derives from the thatched gazebo in the grounds – was built in the 1720s by Sir Robert Walpole, Britain's first prime minister.

Theobalds: favourite home of Stuart king

Theobald's Palace in Hertfordshire: a favourite haunt of King James I.

Although he once nearly drowned at Theobalds, James I of England (1603-25) formed a strong attachment to this now-vanished palace near Cheshunt in Hertfordshire, and exchanged it for Hatfield House [*see page 598*] with the Cecil family. The Cecils had owned Theobalds since 1564, when it was a moated manor house, and rebuilt it over the following few years. Elizabeth I (1558-1603) was a frequent visitor, and to please his royal guest William Cecil spent vast sums to turn Theobalds into one of the finest houses in England. Two noted features of the house were an 84-foot (25.2-m)-square courtyard with a black and white fountain, and the hall, paved with Purbeck stone, its arched roof a mass of fine carvings. Elizabeth delighted in picnics in the garden around the ornamental lake with its marble statues of twelve Roman emperors.

Very little remains of "Tibbalds", as it is correctly pronounced. Most of it was pulled down at the request of parliament in c.1650, although a few rooms survived to become part of the so-called Old Palace, built on the site in 1768. One stairway was removed to Herstmonceux Castle in Sussex.

The Tower of London: seat of power and punishment for over 900 years of royalty

"In truth there is no sadder spot on the earth ... thither hath been carried, through successive ages, by the rude hands of gaolers, without one mourner following, the bleeding relics of men who had been the captains of armies, the leaders of parties, the oracles of senates and the ornaments of courts."

So wrote Thomas Babington Macaulay, the 19th-century historian, about the fortress overlooking the Thames in the very heart of Britain's capital. The history of the Tower of London is besmeared with death, torture and cruel imprisonment – although sometimes it is hard for the visitor to believe this when, on a fine summer's day, the White Tower gleams almost benignly over the Thames.

William the Conqueror (1066-87) began building the Tower almost as soon as his invading army captured London, with the specific aim of subduing the city's population. William and his son William II (1087-1100) built the 90-foot (27-m)-high White Tower – its architect was Gundulf, the bishop of Rochester – and Henry III (1216-72) converted the whole building into a fortress with 13 bastion towers. By 1307 the Tower of London was one of the largest fortresses in the world, and it remains one of the most important works of mediaeval architecture to survive in Britain. Henry III also began a menagerie at the Tower. (In the 19th century the menagerie, apart from the royal ravens, transferred to Regent's Park to become part of the new London Zoo.) Edward I (1272-1307) completed the entire complex much as it exists today, including the moat.

The Tower's history as a royal residence is, naturally, a long one. King Stephen (1135-54) held court in the Tower during the civil strife of his reign. Living quarters were improved by Henry II (1154-89): he had both his rooms and those of his queen, Eleanor of Aquitaine, decorated with paintings. But Edward III (1327-77) preferred to use the Tower as a jail, over which he set his son, Edward, the Prince of Wales, as jailer. Richard II (1377-99) chose to hold court here. The Tower was less and less used as

a royal residence from c.1500. Charles I (1625-49)) was the last monarch to hold court here, and his son, Charles II (1660-85), was the last to follow the ancient tradition of beginning his coronation procession from the Tower. James II (1685-88), his successor, declined to do so because he considered it an unnecessary expense. The domestic apartments were finally demolished in the reign of William III (1689-1702) and Mary II (1689-94).

The building was for a time a symbol of repression. Anne Boleyn was confined in the Bell Tower before being led through Traitors' Gate to the place of execution. The Bloody Tower housed Sir Walter Raleigh for years until he, too, was beheaded. Graffiti that may still be read express the dread and sadness of some lesser-known prisoners. The Beauchamp Tower contains lines by one such, Sir Philip Howard: "The more suffering for Christ in this world, the more glory with Christ in the next."

The Tower of London has had many distinguished prisoners – some for but a short time before laying their necks on the executioner's block. Others, like the "Princes in the Tower", Edward V (1483) and Richard, the Duke of York, died mysteriously here. Henry VI (1422-61 and 1470-71) was another unwilling guest, emerging briefly to rule the country for a year from 1470 before returning here to die of "displeasure and melancholy" – although many believe that he, too, was murdered.

It was during the reign of Henry VIII (1509-47) that heads rolled freely on Tower Hill. Anne Boleyn [*see above*], Catherine Howard and Thomas More were executed here; so, in later reigns, were Lady Jane Grey, James, the Duke of Monmouth, and in 1747 the Jacobite rebel, Lord Lovat, who earned the dubious distinction of being the last man to be beheaded in Britain. The last prisoner of any notoriety was Rudolf Hess, Hitler's deputy, who was housed in the White Tower for a spell after his mysterious flight to Scotland during the Second World War.

The tiny chapel of St Peter ad Vincula also bears testament to the

The White Tower: begun in the 11th century by William the Conqueror.

terrors of the Tower. It was built on the site of a former chapel, and it is here that many of the executioners' victims are buried. In contrasting mood the crown jewels are housed nearby in the Waterloo barracks, where countless visitors line up to see them. The jewels vie as an attraction with the outstanding collection of armoury, including Henry VIII's suit of silvered armour.

Many of those visiting the Tower take the opportunity of watching

the archaic, yet fascinating, Ceremony of the Keys carried out by the Yeomen Warders in their colourful "Beefeater" uniforms. At ten o'clock each night the chief warder is escorted to lock the various towers, using the password "The Queen's Keys!". The ceremony – which has been carried out for the past seven centuries – ends with the cry "God preserve Queen Elizabeth!" to which the whole guard replies "Amen!"

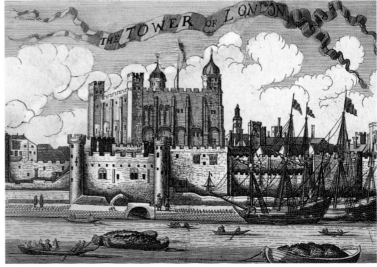

The Tower of London seen from the south bank of the Thames at the end of the 17th century, when the domestic apartments were demolished.

The Palace of Westminster: royal workplace for commoners

The Palace of Westminster has long since ceased to be a royal residence, but it is rich in history. The first palace was built by Edward the Confessor (1042-66) next to the Thames and east of Westminster Abbey, also built by Edward.

On a site alongside Edward's palace William II – Rufus – (1087-1100) built the great hall of what was then known as "the new Palace of Westminster". The building was greatly neglected by King Stephen (1135-54), and it was his successor, Henry II (1154-89), who created a new hall called "the white hall" to the south of the great hall, with a new chapel of St Stephen adjoining.

At this early period, when parliament met the Commons would go to the (now demolished) refectory or the chapter-house of the abbey. The king held sole sway in the palace proper, his judges – in effect, the court – meeting in the great hall. In later years the Lords met in the queen's chamber, which became known as the parliament chamber. This formed part of an extension to the palace and was the building that Guy Fawkes tried to blow up in 1605. In 1801 the Lords transferred to the white hall (then called the court of requests) in the old Norman palace.

Henry III (1216-72) rebuilt Westminster Abbey, giving it substantially the form it has today, and added to the palace the painted chamber, one of the most astonishing achievements of its time. The chamber was 80 feet (24m) long, 26

Westminster: home to parliament, but still the property of Queen Elizabeth.

feet (7.8m) wide and over 30 feet (9m) in height. Its paintings recorded biblical scenes and also the life of Edward the Confessor, whom Henry greatly revered. The decorations were later whitewashed over – only to be rediscovered in 1819 and finally destroyed in the great fire of Westminster in 1834.

Edward I (1272-1307) was born in the palace in 1239 and enlarged Henry II's chapel of St Stephen. The "crypt" of today's palace is in fact the lower storey of the enlarged chapel. Richard II (1377-99) then remodelled Rufus's great hall, adding the spectacular hammerbeam roof with its angels carved from massive pieces of Sussex oak.

Two disastrous fires have hit the palace, the first in the reign of Henry VIII (1509-47), who did not like it, preferring Greenwich. Luckily the great hall and painted chamber were untouched. The second fire in 1834 also spared the great hall, but most of the original "new palace" was destroyed, including the painted chamber. What could be restored was St Stephen's chapel – now St Stephen's hall – where the Commons had met since 1547. Rebuilding began to a design by Charles Barry in 1837. Although Lords and Commons had already moved in, it took Barry and that master of gothic architecture, A W Pugin, till 1857 to complete the work. Bombed in 1941, the Palace of Westminster arose once more from the ashes in 1948-50, to designs by Sir Giles Gilbert Scott.

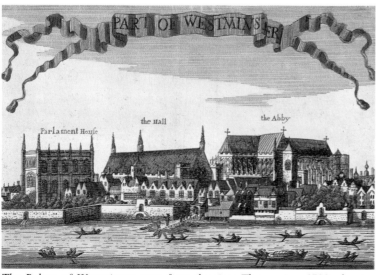

The Palace of Westminster seen from the river Thames in c.1700, showing the parliament house, the great hall, the abbey and surrounding houses.

The Jewel Tower, part of the 14th-century palace at Westminster.

Whitehall Palace: destroyed by fire

When it came to property, Henry VIII (1509-47) was the most covetous of kings. He admired Hampton Court, with which his obsequious lord chancellor, Cardinal Thomas Wolsey, was persuaded to part, even though it broke his heart to do so. The king also admired Whitehall Palace – or York Place, as it was then known – just up the road from Westminster and, once again, it was the king's craven lord chancellor who parted readily with another fine home of his in 1529. By that time, however, Wolsey was in disgrace, and Henry wasted no time in moving in.

Henry added new features to Whitehall, including a gallery from Esher, Surrey, also once owned by Wolsey, which he had taken down and brought to London in pieces. Two fine gates were built on the road that ran through the palace, the first of them, the Holbein gate – so called because it was mistakenly believed that Holbein had designed it himself – was built in three storeys of stone and flint, with two great turrets. The second gate also had domed turrets.

Henry also built an enclosed tennis court, bowling alley and cockpit on the site of the present St James's Park. Sadly, however, the king was growing old and fat by this time and had no time to indulge personally in such athletic activities.

One visitor who came to the palace in 1531 wrote of "ceilings being marvellously wrought in stone and gold and the wainscot of carved wood representing a thousand beautiful figures". It was indeed a spectacular building – fit for a king both to live in and die in. Henry did die there, with Archbishop Cranmer at his bedside.

Whitehall remained popular. Queen Elizabeth I (1558-1603) held great receptions there and added a banqueting hall – to receive the Duke of Alençon (later of Anjou), who came to propose to her. He arrived in 1581, but made himself generally unpopular by spending most of his visit trying to arrange loans. The banqueting hall was later demolished and rebuilt. In 1608 Ben Jonson wrote a masque to celebrate the reopening, but

The riverside palace at Whitehall in the early 17th century.

White Lodge: history in a royal park

It was September 1805, five weeks before the Battle of Trafalgar. The distinguished dinner guest was Horatio Nelson, who traced on the table part of his plan to divide the enemy's fleet. That table now boasts a bronze plaque and is a treasured possession of the descendants of Lord Sidmouth, a future prime minister and the host at that dinner in White Lodge.

The lodge, built by George II (1727-60) for his daughter Amelia, is one of three historic houses in Richmond Park (the others are Thatched House Lodge and Pembroke Lodge). It was given to Sidmouth by George III (1760-1820). In 1858 the Prince of Wales, later Edward VII (1901-10), was "banished" to White Lodge by Victoria (1837-1901) and Albert, anxious that the 16-year-old prince should associate "only with those who are good and pure". The hedonistic Edward said later that he had been bored to death here.

Later White Lodge was the family home of Princess May of Teck, who became Queen Mary, the wife of George V (1910-36), and it was here that she gave birth to the future Edward VIII (1936). The lodge was also the first married home of the Duke and Duchess of York, later George VI (1936-52) and Queen Elizabeth. It is now home to the Royal Ballet School.

in 1619 the building was accidentally burnt to the ground. Not long after the fire Inigo Jones was commissioned to create a new banqueting hall; the completed building remains to this day as one of the most exciting Renaissance buildings in Europe. The palace gates were later removed to clear a traffic bottleneck; some parts of them can now be seen at Hampton Court.

Charles I (1625-49) had a special affection for Whitehall and had a cabinet room built where much of his art collection was kept. Ironically it was here that he was brought after his trial; his last few hours were spent at prayer in the royal bedchamber before he donned an extra shirt – to stop him shivering from the cold and so appearing nervous – to face the crowd and his executioner on the scaffold in the street outside.

Charles had converted Henry VIII's cockpit into a theatre; it is another irony that one person who used it after his death was Oliver Cromwell, who entertained members of the House of Commons there with "voice and instruments".

Following Charles's execution, Cromwell moved into Whitehall Palace, where he died in 1658. Charles II (1660-85) reopened the theatre and built a tennis court, a laboratory and a library.

One night during the great frost of 1698, in the reign of William III (1689-1702), a Dutch woman left some clothes hanging up to dry too close to a charcoal brazier. The clothes caught fire, and within half an hour the palace was ablaze. By morning, the vast, rambling building – "... two thousand rooms badly arranged and no doors ..." – was almost uninhabitable. At least the banqueting hall (now the Banqueting House) survived with little damage, but a fine new building by Wren which had replaced the privy gallery was burnt out, and fireplaces by Grinling Gibbons and ceilings by Antonio Verrio were destroyed at a time when insurance was no more than a theory.

The site of Whitehall Palace was leased in plots for private building. Several great houses were to appear on it, among them Montagu, Pelham and Gwydyr Houses (all but the last are now demolished). There is one remnant left, however, of Henry VIII's palace: his 70-foot (21-metre)-long brick-vaulted wine cellar, in the basement of the modern Ministry of Defence.

The splendid White Lodge in Richmond Park: the birthplace of Edward VIII.

Winchester Palace: heart of old England

The bustling Hampshire county town of Winchester was once the capital of the powerful Anglo-Saxon kingdom of Wessex. Winchester was also an ecclesiastical centre from the middle of the seventh century, and it was used as the headquarters of the royal treasury for many centuries.

By the tenth century, a royal palace lay west of the old minster; it was not until the reign of Henry II (1154-89) that administrative power was shifted from Winchester to Westminster. By this time the old palace had become inadequate, and a new one was built north-west of the cathedral. Henry III (1216-72), who was born in the new palace, built the great hall that still stands. Much of the palace was destroyed by fire in 1302.

Part of Jones's banqueting hall.

The great hall, built by Henry III.

Windsor Castle: a royal favourite for 900 years

A controlling position: Windsor Castle commands a view of the Thames.

A stately prospect: the castle looks out over beautiful gardens.

William the Conqueror (1066-87) wasted no time in fortifying England with castles. It was natural that in particular he should wish to build a major castle to defend the approach to London and control the Thames valley. He chose a hillside overlooking the Thames, and Windsor Castle began life as a *motte* or earth mound and two open areas (baileys) enclosed by stakes.

Many such fortifications appeared as William's grip on England tightened. Windsor was an especial favourite with the king, however, and the castle flourished. The Conqueror's son, William II (Rufus) (1087-1100), celebrated Easter here in 1097 with English and Norman nobles. His brother, Henry I (1100-35), built a chapel and suitable accommodation before marrying his second queen at Windsor. Henry II (1154-89) improved the fortifications, erecting the first stage of Windsor's familiar round tower on the motte and replacing the wooden defences with stone.

King John (1199-1216) was besieged in the castle after signing *Magna Carta* at nearby Runnymede; his son, Henry III (1216-72), finished the encircling stone wall and added the semicircular towers that make Windsor a unique building. Edward III (1327-77),

who was born here, continued the work. It was also here that Edward created the Order of the Garter. The original garter slipped from a lady guest at a dance. Edward, picking it up and putting it on his own leg, said: "*Honi soit qui mal y pense*" – "evil be to him who evil thinks."

Every 24 June, knights of the Garter in blue velvet robes process with the Queen to the superb gothic St George's chapel within the castle walls. This remarkable perpendicular building was begun by Edward IV (1461-70 and 1471-83) and completed by Henry VIII (1509-47). Edward and Henry are among

the 14 monarchs buried here. Oliver Cromwell captured the building after the Battle of Edgehill (1642), and for the rest of the Civil War it became a prison as well as the parliamentary headquarters. In 1648 Charles I (1625-49) was held here before his trial, and following his execution, in London, his body was brought back to St George's chapel in a snowstorm.

Charles II (1660-85) returned to the throne determined to bestow on the much-damaged castle even greater splendour than before. It was he who created the three-mile (5km) Long Walk from the castle's south entrance towards the Great

A 19th-century picture of the splendid Chapel Royal at Windsor Castle.

A gold interior: the richly-decorated reception room at the castle.

Park. The cold and gloom of the castle's interior was a matter of dismay to several monarchs, including Elizabeth I (1558-1603). Anne (1702-14) chose to live outside the walls, a tradition which has continued for members of the royal family to this century [*see below*].

Under George IV (1820-30) Windsor became the complete castle that we know today. His architect, Jeffry Wyatville, created a gothic mood with new crenellations and windows. Inside he doubled the size of St George's hall, built the grand corridor and created the Waterloo chamber, regarded as a great architectural wonder.

Royal Lodge

When Prince Regent, George had wanted a house close to both London and Windsor, yet free from the stuffiness of the castle. He settled on the red-brick Queen Anne house, then known as the "lower lodge". John Nash redesigned the building, renamed Royal Lodge – or, ironically, the King's Cottage. In the 1930s it became a home of the Duke and Duchess of York (later George VI (1936-52) and Queen Elizabeth) and their daughters, Elizabeth (II) and Margaret.

Frogmore

Frogmore House, near Windsor Castle, served as a retreat for Charlotte, the wife of George III (1760-1820), but is best known for the mausoleum built by Queen Victoria (1837-1901) for Albert and herself. Victoria spent many happy hours here, often working outside in a tent with an Indian servant in attendance. Her mother, the Duchess of Kent, was the first royal to be buried in the mausoleum designed by Albert. Edward, the Duke of Windsor, was buried here in 1972, and his duchess, Wallis, is buried beside him.

Fort Belvedere

The present royal family probably wept few tears when the pseudo-gothic Fort Belvedere near Windsor Castle passed out of their hands a few years ago. It was the scene of much anguish during the abdication crisis of 1936, when it was the favourite retreat of Edward VIII (1936). It has little architectural merit: an 18th-century gazebo built for William, the Duke of Cumberland, with its tall tower added by Wyatville.

Dominating the landscape: Windsor Castle and its superb parklands.

A quieter royal base at Windsor: Royal Lodge and the private garden.

The round tower at the castle.

The mausoleum at Frogmore.

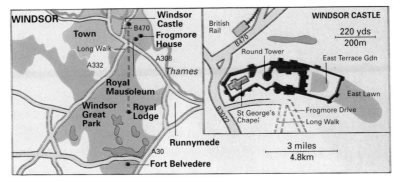

Woodstock Palace: demolished glory

Blenheim Palace, built for John Churchill, the Duke of Marlborough – a gift from Queen Anne (1702-14) for his victory at Blenheim in 1704 – is one of the most visited tourist attractions in Britain. Yet few visitors realise that this was also the site of a royal palace long before Vanbrugh designed the present great house.

Best known for the romance played out here between Henry II (1154-89) and his mistress Rosamund Clifford, Woodstock had been a haunt of kings since the 11th century. Henry I (1100-35) enclosed his palace grounds with seven miles of walls; fascinated by the exotic, he had a zoo here, with

The remains of Henry II's palace at Woodstock as they stood in 1714.

lions, leopards, camels and even a porcupine. The palace of Henry III (1216-72), large as it was – with numerous chambers and five chapels – was enlarged still further by Henry VII (1485-1509).

Woodstock suffered badly when it was besieged in 1646 at the height of the Civil War. Soon afterwards much of the palace was demolished, the only remnant being the gatehouse where Mary I (1553-58) had imprisoned her younger sister Elizabeth in 1554. Although a new house was created in the 1660s by the park ranger, Lord Lovelace, this and all else that remained was razed to the ground in 1718. By that time the Duke of Marlborough owned the manor and park; he was persuaded that the view from his magnificent new house was spoilt by Woodstock's ruins.

General Index

This index is a guide to all the "royals" mentioned in this book, plus the people, places, events and topics with which they were concerned and associated. It should be read in conjunction with the cross-referencing system (explained on page 4). In the case of the acquisition and/or changing of names and/or titles, the form used is normally the best known; this is also usually the latest form, with cross-referencing within the index from the other form(s). Thus, all entries about an individual appear in one place only. Two exceptions to this rule are the Duke and Duchess of Windsor, who also appear, respectively, under "Edward VIII, king of the United Kingdom" and "Simpson, Wallis Warfield". Knighthoods and baronetcies are not used. Page numbers in Roman type refer to main reports; those in italics refer to entries in the chronology summaries.

Photo Credit Index

Jacket

1: C.M. Dixon – 2: Hulton Deutsch Collection – 3: STB/Still Moving Picture Company – 4: Rex Features – 5 and 6: Topham Picture Library – 7: Bridgeman Art Library – 8: Camera Press – 9: Bridgeman Art Library – 10: Syndication International – 11: Peter Newark's Pictures – 12: Michael Holford – 13: Topham Picture Library – 14: Edinburgh Photographic Library – 15, 16, 17: Topham Picture Library – 18: Popperfoto – 19: Timothy Woodcock – 20: Photographers International – 21: Topham Picture Library – 22: reproduced by permission of the controller of HMSO, crown copyright reserved – 23: Tim Graham Picture Library – 24: Robert Estall – 25: Photographers International – 26: Fine Art Photographic Library – 27: Bridgeman Art Library – 28: Robert Opie

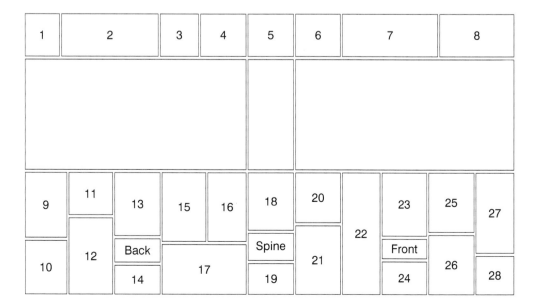

The position of the pictures is indicated by two letters: B: bottom, T: top, M: middle, L: left, R: right, X: middle left, Y: middle right, FP: full page

Photo Credit Index

623